PEOPLE OF THE EARTH

PEOPLE OF THE EARTH
An Introduction to World Prehistory

FOURTEENTH EDITION

Brian M. Fagan

Emeritus, University of California, Santa Barbara

and

Nadia Durrani

Routledge
Taylor & Francis Group

LONDON AND NEW YORK

First published 2014, 2010, 2007 by Pearson Education, Inc.

Published 2016 by Routledge
2 Park Square, Milton Park, Abingdon, Oxon OX14 4RN
711 Third Avenue, New York, NY, 10017, USA

Routledge is an imprint of the Taylor & Francis Group, an informa business

ISBN: 9780205966554 (pbk)

Cover Designer: Bruce Kanselaar

Library of Congress Cataloging-in-Publication Data
Fagan, Brian M.
   People of the earth : an introduction to world prehistory / Brian M. Fagan and Nadia Durrani. —Fourteenth Edition.
      pages cm Includes bibliographical references and index.
   ISBN-13: 978-0-205-96655-4
   ISBN-10: 0-205-96655-1
   1. Prehistoric peoples. 2. Civilization, Ancient. I. Durrani, Nadia. II. Title.
   GN740.F33 2013
   569.9—dc23
   2013019027

To

All the dozens of archaeologists and students who have read and used this book in its various editions and sent me their comments and criticisms. This is the only way we can thank them all and expose them for what they are: honest and unmerciful critics. We are deeply grateful.

And, as usual, to Brian's cats, who disapprove of authors in general and of his writing efforts in particular. Their contribution was to tread on his computer keyboard—with muddy paws, of course. Thanks also to Matthew, and to Nadia's baby Jacob—who joins Brian's cats in muddy paws and disapproval.

Brief Contents

Contents

Preface

Golden pharaohs, lost cities, grinning human skeletons—archaeology is the stuff of romance and legend. Many people still think of archaeologists as adventurers and treasure hunters, like Indiana Jones of Hollywood movie fame seeking the elusive Crystal Skull. This enduring image goes back to the late nineteenth century, when archaeologists like Heinrich Schliemann of Troy fame could still find lost civilizations and excavate three royal palaces in a week. Today, no archaeologists behave like Indiana Jones. They are scientists, not adventurers, as comfortable in an air-conditioned laboratory as they are on a remote excavation.

The development of scientific archaeology from its Victorian beginnings ranked among the greatest triumphs of twentieth-century science. Archaeology has changed our perceptions of ourselves in profound ways, giving us a better understanding of our biological and cultural diversity. Welcome to the fascinating world of archaeology!

New to This Edition

- Nadia Durrani has joined Brian Fagan as coauthor for this and future editions. She brings a wealth of practical experience in Yemen and other places, as well as a background in archaeological journalism and journal editing.
- Chapter 1 introduces world prehistory and presents new insights on the human past, including the latest theoretical advances.
- Chapters 2–6 have been completely reorganized and rewritten. They reflect new thinking and recent discoveries that alter our perceptions of the archaic world and human origins.
- Chapter 4 now covers the origins of anatomically modern humans, *Homo sapiens,* previously summarized in Chapter 3.
- Chapter 6 presents the latest evidence on the first settlement of the Americas. New sites and innovative hypotheses enliven the long debates on the subject.
- Chapter 7 includes new information on changes in hunter-gatherer societies at the end of the Ice Age, especially in Southwest Asia.
- Chapter 9 has been completely rewritten and updated to include the exciting discoveries of recent years that are changing our ideas on early farming in Southwest Asia profoundly, including climate change.
- Chapters 11–13 have been updated with new information and recent discoveries.
- Chapter 14 has been updated to include the latest theories on the origins of states and civilizations.
- Chapters 15–20 now reflect the latest discoveries on such topics as Stonehenge and the Shang civilization.
- Chapters 21 and 22 on Native American civilizations have been revised throughout to keep up with a new torrent of finds and fresh perceptions.
- Science and Site boxes throughout the text cover key concepts like radiocarbon dating and present important new discoveries (and some older well-known ones) in more detail. Many are newly written for this edition. Examples include the spectacular Grotte de Chauvet cave paintings in France and the Lords of Sipán from coastal Peru, one of the most important archaeological discoveries of the twentieth century.
- There are major changes in the illustrations throughout the book.

This fourteenth edition of *People of the Earth* comes at a time when new discoveries and archaeological methodologies are deeply affecting our understanding of the human past. This edition continues a nearly 40-year tradition of clear, jargon-free writing for the beginning student, the incorporation of the latest scholarship, and an accessible (five-part) organization of the story of world prehistory. This is a straightforward narrative, written by two authors (not the work of multiple scholars), which gives the book a coherence often lacking in edited volumes. The basic objective is a simple one: to provide an interesting journey through the 7-million-year-old landscape of the human past. At the same time, the book attempts to achieve geographic balance, giving equal time to both well-trodden and less well-known parts of the world. Any world prehistory that does otherwise is presenting a skewed picture of the human past. *People of the Earth* is an adventure in archaeology. We hope you enjoy your sojourn in its pages.

Writing a straightforward narrative of human prehistory is a mammoth task, especially at a time when a torrent of new literature about archaeological discoveries around the world is revolutionizing our knowledge of the remote past. We are well beyond the point where only two authors can possibly hope to keep up with every new find and intellectual development in world archaeology, but we have done our best, while trying to keep the narrative as simple and uncluttered as possible, without undue emphasis on individual sites or human societies.

This narrative of world prehistory is divided into five parts. Part I (Chapters 2 and 3) discusses human beginnings—what is sometimes called "archaic world," the human past from the earliest times up to the appearance of *Homo sapiens*, ourselves. Here we cover important new fossil discoveries of recent years and such fascinating sites as Boxgrove in southern England. We also continue to take account of new theoretical advances in cognitive, or "post-processual," archaeology, especially of the emerging synthesis of evolutionary psychology and archaeology. Part II (Chapters 4 to 7) discusses what we call the "Great Diaspora," the spread of anatomically modern humans throughout the world during and immediately after the late Ice Age. We go from Southwest Asia to South and East Asia, also Southeast Asia, tracing some of the earliest forays of modern humans, culminating in the settlement of Australia and the southwestern Pacific islands, before retuning to tropical Africa Then we follow moderns as they colonize Europe and Eurasia, and ultimately the Americas, a logical order preferred by many users. Part II includes coverage of the new AMS radiocarbon chronology for first settlement, made possible by extended calibration curves. "After the Ice," which follows, leads into the chapters on the first farmers.

Part III describes the origins of food production, with Chapter 8 devoted to the theoretical background and the following five chapters discussing the earliest farming in different areas of the world. New discussions in this edition include the increasing impact of refined AMS chronologies, genetic fingerprinting of potentially domesticable animals and plants, and a fresh generation of research into the origins of rice cultivation. Important new perceptions of the Mississippian and other, more complex farming societies in eastern North America also receive extended treatment.

Parts IV and V cover the early civilizations of the Old World and the Americas, with Chapter 14 describing the major theories of the origins and collapse of states. The ferment of theorizing has diminished somewhat in recent years as fieldworkers wrestle to document their theories with new data from the field. At the same time, a new emphasis on ideology and the archaeology of the intangible is throwing fresh light on preindustrial civilization. There is expanded coverage of the origins of Egyptian civilization, as well as of South and Southeast Asian states. Maya archaeology has been revolutionized in recent years by the decipherment of ancient glyphs and by our new understandings of the turbulent political history of Maya states. We take account of some of these advances here, but, alas, do not have space for extended coverage.

As always, the book is designed for easy accessibility and effective learning. *People of the Earth* is free of distracting features that draw the reader away from the main narrative. High-interest chapter-opening vignettes, which describe a moment of discovery or reconstruct life in the past, grab the student's interest from the outset. Chronological tables at the beginning of each chapter, as well as chapter summaries at the end of each chapter, also add to the effectiveness of the book as a learning tool.

Other pedagogical features include the following:

- Special timeline columns at the opening of each part of the book. By means of varied color, each timeline tells at a glance which period the part covers, as well as which periods have already been covered and are yet to be covered in the text.
- Expanded picture captions that augment the visual information.
- Double-page spreads that provide up-to-date overviews of major themes and developments in human prehistory.

Support for Instructors and Students

Please visit the companion website at www.routledge.com/9780205966554

A Note on the World Wide Web

The World Wide Web is an important medium of communication for archaeologists. Some of the more important sites offer links to other useful locations, as listed below. First off, we recommend you visit the virtual library for archaeology worldwide at ArchNet: http://archnet.asu.edu. This site is both geographically and subject matter based, covering everything from the archaeology of Australia to method and theory and site tours. There are also listings of academic departments, museums, and other archaeological organizations, even of journals. ArchNet is an extraordinary resource; it does not claim to be comprehensive but, nonetheless, covers a huge range of topics. The European equivalent is ARGE, the Archaeological Resource Guide for Europe: http://www.let.rug.nl/arge/. This site also lists areas and subjects, and is multilingual. Both ArchNet and ARGE have links to virtually any subfield of archaeology you are looking for.

Many departments of anthropology and archaeology and dozens of excavations and sites have Web sites, which you can access through ArchNet. For example, for information on archaeology in Southwest Asia and the eastern Mediterranean, go to http://www.argonet.co.uk/.

When seeking out information, it is worth remembering that the official Web sites of projects, museums, and universities are typically excellent sources of data, whereas those authored by interested members of the public, and indeed nonspecialist journalists, should be read with caution. Happy surfing!

Acknowledgments

This fourteenth edition has benefited greatly from the willing comments of many colleagues—alas, too many to name individually. We would like to thank the following archaeologists for their reviews: Christina L. Blanch, Ball State University; Stephen Brighton, University of Maryland; Steve Corbett, Johnson County Community College; Shanna M. Cox, University of Wyoming; Ricardo J. Elia, Boston University; and Barbara Hornum, Drexel University.

We appreciate their frank comments. We also want to thank the many instructors and users who have contacted me to correct errors, provide references, or make other useful suggestions—including the anonymous correspondent who sent BF a photocopy of p. 61 of the tenth edition, with a line marked against a paragraph and the word *wrong*. Nitpicking is one thing, and goes with the territory. But anonymous letters—forget it! He is still trying to figure out how he sinned!

Lastly, our thanks to our much beloved editor, Nancy Roberts; to our project manager, Nicole Conforti; and to the editorial and production staff at Pearson and in India. Without them, this revision would never have been completed. As always, we would be most grateful for criticisms, comments, or details of new work, sent to us at brian@brianfagan.com.

Brian Fagan
Nadia Durrani

Authors' Note

Conventions for Dates and Measurements

The following conventions are used for dates in this book:

B.P.	Years before present. In general, years before 40,000 B.P. are given in years before present, whereas dates after 12,000 B.P. are invariably expressed as B.C./A.D., unless the context is obvious.
mya	Million years ago.
kya	Thousand years ago.
B.C./A.D.	To avoid confusion, I use the common B.C./A.D. Another common convention is B.C.E./C.E. (Before the Common Era/Common Era), which is not used in this book.
"Present"	By scientific convention, "present" is A.D. 1950.

For clarity, all radiocarbon and potassium-argon dates are quoted here without their statistical errors. However, readers should be aware that such calculations exist for every chronometric date in this book.

All measurements are given in metric, with miles, yards, feet, and inch equivalents, as this is now common scientific convention.

Calibration of Radiocarbon Dates

The calibration of radiocarbon dates has now reached a high degree of refinement, as scientists develop ever more accurate time scales for the past 15,000 years, using tree-ring, coral, and ice-core data. It should be stressed that these calibrations are provisional, statistically based, and subject to modification, especially before 7000 B.C.

About the Authors

Brian Fagan is one of the world's leading writers in the field of archaeology and an internationally recognized authority on world prehistory. He studied archaeology and anthropology at Pembroke College, Cambridge University, and then spent seven years in sub-Saharan Africa working in museums and in monuments conservation and excavating early farming sites in Zambia and East Africa. He was one of the pioneers of multidisciplinary African history in the 1960s. Now Professor Emeritus, from 1967 to 2003 he was Professor of Anthropology at the University of California, Santa Barbara.

Professor Fagan has written seven best-selling textbooks: *Ancient Lives: An Introduction to Archaeology and Prehistory; In the Beginning; Archaeology: A Brief Introduction; World Prehistory; Ancient Civilizations* (with Chris Scarre), *A Brief History of Archaeology;* and this volume, which are used around the world. His general books include *The Rape of the Nile*, a classic history of Egyptology; *The Adventure of Archaeology; Ancient North America; The Little Ice Age; The Long Summer; Chaco Canyon; Fish on Friday; The Great Warming,* and *Elixir: A History of Humankind and Water.* He was also General Editor of the *Oxford Companion to Archaeology.* In addition, he has published several scholarly monographs on African archaeology and numerous specialized articles in national and international journals. He was the recipient of the Society for American Archaeology's first Public Education Award for his indefatigable efforts on behalf of archaeology and education.

Brian Fagan's other interests include bicycling, sailing, kayaking, and good food. He lives in Santa Barbara with his wife and daughter, three cats (who supervise his writing), and last but not least, a minimum of seven rabbits.

Nadia Durrani is an archaeologist and writer. For much of the past decade she was the editor of Britain's best-selling archaeology magazine, *Current World Archaeology,* becoming a contributing editor after the arrival of her son in 2010. She has authored and edited many hundreds of articles on archaeology from every corner of the globe, contributed to dozens of books, and written two: *The Tihamah Coastal Plain of South-West Arabia;* and *In Search of the Zeppelin War: the archaeology of the First Blitz* (with Neil Faulkner).

Throughout her career she has travelled widely in a professional capacity—from Peru to Pakistan—to report on the latest archaeological discoveries; worked as a specialist lecturer on archaeological tours to countries including Yemen and Jordan; and contributed to a range of television documentaries.

Her specialist area is Arabian archaeology and, following a degree in archaeology and anthropology from Cambridge University, she took a PhD in South West Arabian archaeology from University College, London (2001). Other research interests include the archaeology of the First World War and she is a founding member of the Great War Archaeology Group. She was made a fellow of the Society of Antiquaries in 2008. Nadia lives in London with her husband, Matthew, and son Jacob 'Caractacus' Hillier.

Introducing World Prehistory

The two men paused in front of the doorway that bore the seals of the long-dead pharaoh. They had waited six long years, from 1917 to 1922, for this moment. Silently, Howard Carter pried a hole through the ancient plaster. Hot air rushed out of the small cavity and massaged his face. Carter shone a flashlight through the hole and peered into the tomb. Gold objects swam in front of his eyes, and he was struck dumb with amazement.

Lord Carnarvon moved impatiently behind him as Carter remained silent.

"What do you see?" he asked, hoarse with excitement.

"Wonderful things," whispered Carter as he stepped back from the doorway.

They soon broke down the door. In a daze of wonderment, Carter and Carnarvon wandered through the antechamber of Tutankhamun's tomb. They fingered golden funerary beds, admired beautifully inlaid chests, and examined the pharaoh's chariots stacked against the wall. Gold was everywhere—on wooden statues, inlaid on thrones and boxes, in jewelry, even on children's stools (Reeves, 1990). Soon Tutankhamun was known as the golden pharaoh, and archaeology as the domain of buried treasure and royal sepulchers (Figure 1.1).

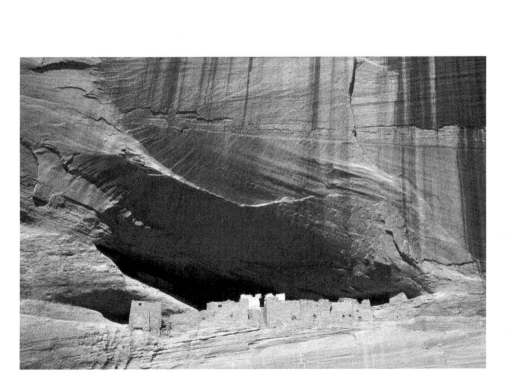

The White House, Canyon de Chelly, Arizona, c. A.D. 1200.

FIGURE 1.1 Howard Carter works on the pharaoh Tutankhamun's sarcophagus, 1922. Photography by Egyptian Expedition, The Metropolitan Museum of Art.

Gold, silver, lost civilizations, unsolved mysteries, grinning skeletons—all are part of the romantic world of archaeology in most people's minds. Archaeologists seem like adventurers, digging into pyramids and finding long-forgotten inscriptions in remote places. Like Indiana Jones of movie fame, we seem to be students of sunken continents and great migrations, experts on epic journeys and powerful civilizations. A century ago, many archaeologists were indeed adventurers. Even as late as the 1870s, you could go out digging in Southwest Asia and find a long-lost civilization. German businessman turned archaeologist Heinrich Schliemann was convinced that Homer's Troy had actually existed. Armed with a copy of the *Iliad*, he went to Turkey and cut great trenches into the ancient mounds at Hissarlik in northwest Turkey. Schliemann found the remains of nine cities stratified one atop the other and announced that the seventh was Homer's Troy (Traill, 1995). His discoveries caused an international sensation. So did Frenchman Emil de Sarzec when he unearthed Sumer in desolate southern Mesopotamia, a civilization that soon turned out to be one of the earliest in the world and the society where the Flood legend in Genesis probably originated (Fagan, 2007) (Figure 1.2).

Today, however, the excitement of the detective story has replaced the fascination of great adventure. Fictional detectives take a handful of clues and solve apparently insoluble murders. Archaeologists take a multitude of small and apparently trivial archaeological finds and use them to answer basic questions about past human behavior.

The twentieth century saw archaeology turn from a casual treasure hunt into a complex and demanding science (Fagan, 1985, 2005b). There have been dramatic discoveries by the dozens: Tutankhamun's tomb in 1922; the royal cemetery at Ur in Iraq in 1928; the spectacular early human fossils discovered by the Leakey family in East Africa during the last quarter of the century; and the magnificent royal burials in China and Peru in the 1980s and 1990s. Although these finds have stirred the popular imagination, archaeologists have been engaged in a less conspicuous but just as fascinating adventure of discovery—through over 2.6 million years of the human past.

People of the Earth takes you on a journey through these 2.6 million years, from the origins of the first humans through the evolution of modern humanity—ourselves—to the last 5,000 years, when literate civilizations appeared on earth. This is a book about the prehistory of humankind.

Archaeology and Prehistory

Contrary to popular belief, archaeologists do not study dinosaurs, for ancient fossil animals are the scholarly province of paleontologists. Archaeologists are anthropologists. **Anthropology** is the biological and cultural study of all humanity, ancient and modern. Anthropologists are concerned with living societies, whereas archaeologists study the human cultures and societies of the past. (No attempt is made to describe the basic principles, methods, and theoretical approaches of archaeology in this book. For information, the reader should consult one of the following widely available college texts: Fagan and Durrani, 2012; Renfrew and Bahn, 2008; Sharer and Ashmore, 2009; Thomas and Kelly, 2009.)

A British archaeologist once described archaeology as "the science of rubbish," a somewhat apt description, for archaeologists do indeed

FIGURE 1.2 The famous "Flood Tablet" from the Assyrian king Assurbanipal's library at Nineveh. The tablet, found by epigrapher George Smith in 1873, records the story of a flood that bears a remarkable resemblance to the one described in Genesis. This was a copy of a much earlier Sumerian legend, which dates from long before the writing down of the Old Testament. (Copyright The British Museum.)

FIGURE 1.3   Excavated prehistoric houses at Skara Brae, Orkney Islands, Scotland, occupied c. 3000 B.C.

spend much of their time delving into the garbage heaps and **middens** of long-vanished human societies. **Archaeology** is the study of past human behavior based on surviving material finds. These material remains come in many forms: as crude or finely made stone artifacts tens of thousands, even millions, of years old; as durable pot fragments from clay vessels used by early farmers; as house foundations; as seeds and broken food bones; in the form of cave paintings; and, when preservation conditions permit, as wooden artifacts, textiles, or human corpses. All these finds constitute the **archaeological record**, the archives of the past, which can be made up of surviving finds resulting from ancient human behavior. Reconstructing this behavior from such fragmentary records requires great scientific skill, insight, and creativity. Imagine trying to reconstruct twentieth-century life from a handful of artifacts, including two broken plates, a spark plug, a computer keyboard, three cow bones, and an aluminum beer can tab, and you will realize the challenge facing students of the remote past (Figure 1.3).

We use the word *remote* deliberately though some archaeologists deal with sites from the last (and even this) century, most of the archaeological research described in this book deals with biological and cultural developments thousands of years back in the past, with long-vanished environments and societies that lived on earth when it was very different. Few people realize just how much the world has changed during the past 2 million years, and especially during the past 780,000 years, when the constant climatic fluctuations of the Ice Age have kept global climate in a state of transition from extreme cold to warmer conditions (see Chapters 2 to 4). Only 15,000 years ago, the world was in the grip of a major glacial episode that covered much of northern Europe and North America with vast ice sheets, lowered sea levels everywhere by about 91 m (300 feet), and resulted in open, treeless plains from western France to Siberia. England was part of the European continent; Siberia was joined to Alaska; and Borneo was part of mainland Southeast Asia. The human inhabitants of this late Ice Age world lived on a planet unimaginably different from our own, which makes it doubly hard for us to reconstruct and explain their societies.

For the past 5,000 years, humans have used writing as a means of recording business transactions, making inventories of commodities, and measuring the passage of time (Robinson, 1995). From these simple records developed far more sophisticated writings: primordial epics and poems; king lists; histories and literature itself; written archives preserved on clay tablets and papyrus reed documents or as inscriptions on stone and eventually on parchment and paper. Such archives are the realm of historians, scholars who study the written records of the past.

History is very different from archaeology. Although eclectic in their interests, historians work with documents, which are sometimes chronicles of individual deeds, of great kings and lords anxious to trumpet their triumphs or justify their doings. They also study more prosaic archives: the records of royal palaces and governments, the day-to-day transactions of officialdom, to gain wider perspectives on every aspect of society from religious beliefs to food supplies, trade, and social interactions.

In contrast, archaeology is, most of the time, entirely anonymous. Its chronologies are not the years, even hours and minutes, found in history books but are much larger chunks of time, rarely shorter than a half century or a generation. The archaeologist's past is usually without written records to fill in vital gaps. Even when documents are available to amplify historical records on, say, the Egypt of Pharaoh Rameses II or the rituals celebrated by a Maya lord, archaeology brings a unique quality to the past. Only a few people in ancient societies were literate, so the scope of written records is immediately limited. But archaeologists study artifacts and food remains, a dispassionate record of all ancient human behavior, whether that of a monarch or an anonymous sea captain and his crew wrecked on the cliffs of southern Turkey. By excavating the humble dwellings of common folk or the middens of imposing palaces, also studying burials and human remains, among other finds, archaeologists add new dimensions to the study of even societies that are well documented with written records of all kinds (see the Site box on page 5).

Archaeologists make a clear distinction between two major types of archaeology:

- **Text-aided archaeology** is archaeology practiced with the aid of historical documents. Many of the civilizations described in Parts IV and V of this book involve specialist archaeologists, such as Assyriologists, Egyptologists, or Mayanists, who have at least some expertise in ancient scripts. Text-aided archaeology is confined to societies that have flourished during the past 5,000 years and sometimes provides fascinating insights into the people of the past. At the Roman frontier settlement at Vindolanda by Hadrian's Wall in northern England, slivers of bark paper dating to A.D. 95 to 105 have preserved intimate details of life on the wall. We learn that only 265 men, including 1 centurion, were at Vindolanda itself and "fit and well." The rest were serving elsewhere. Store inventories reveal allocations to soldiers and punishments. Occasionally, the correspondence takes a more personal note. "Why have you not written back to me for such a long time about our parents?" laments a soldier named Chrautius to an old messmate in distant London. "I have sent you . . . woolen socks . . . two pairs of sandals and two pairs of underpants," writes a friend of a Vindolanda officer, who was thankful for the gift. There are even fragments of school tablets, one a copy of a passage from Virgil's *Aeneid*, with the notation in another hand: "sloppy work" (Birley, 2009).
- **Prehistoric archaeology** is the archaeology of ancient societies that were nonliterate. The term *période anti-historique* was coined by French archaeologist Paul Tournal in 1833 for the period of human history extending back before the time of written documents (Grayson, 1983). In time, this phrase shrank to **prehistory**, and it now encompasses the enormous span of human cultural evolution that extends back at least 2.6 million years.

People of the Earth is about both prehistoric and text-aided archaeology. We draw on archaeology, geological evidence, linguistic and biological data, oral traditions, historical records, and many other sources of information about 2.6 million years of the human past, sometimes called **world prehistory**. Some people, notably Native Americans, object to the word *prehistoric*. They feel it implies racial inferiority and also expresses the belief that people without written documents have no worthwhile history. These objections are part of a wider debate about the ownership of the past and about archaeology's role in modern society (see the section "Who Needs the Past?" in this chapter).

Prehistory and *prehistoric* are convenient, and long-established, scientific terms without any pejorative implications. Although it is true that a century ago many scholars classified human societies in racist terms, those days are long gone. Modern archaeologists study both literate and nonliterate societies and how they changed without making any value judgments as to their superiority or inferiority to the archaeologists' own society. Their concern is the broad sweep of the human past, for scientific archaeology is a unique way of studying culture change in human societies over enormously long periods of time. From about 3000 B.C., written records and oral histories provide useful perspectives on the past. But in most areas of the world, these sources have but a limited chronological span. And earlier than that, the past is a blank, featureless landscape that can be filled in only by archaeological research.

The Beginnings of World Prehistory

Until the mid-nineteenth century, most Westerners believed that the Old Testament recorded the study of human origins. God created the world and humanity in six days and rested on the seventh. Under Christian dogma of the day, the stories of Adam and Eve, and of Noah's Ark, were the literal historical truth. The seventeenth-century Irish Archbishop James Ussher went even further and used the genealogies in the Bible to calculate the date of the creation—the night preceding October 23, 4004 B.C. His calculations allowed about 6,000 years for all of human history.

New geological, anthropological, and archaeological discoveries soon began to cast doubt on biblical chronologies. Geological observations presented evidence of gradual change over long periods of time through natural processes such as flooding and erosion, what became known as the doctrine of **uniformitarianism**. The bones of long-extinct animals such as the ancestors of the elephant and the hippopotamus came from European river gravels, some from the same strata as carefully

SiTE > The Amesbury Archer <

Archaeologists rarely discover individuals, but, when they do, thanks to twenty-first-century medical science and high technology, they can learn much about an individual's life. By the time the study is completed, archaeologists know more about the person's medical history than the person himself did. Witness the discovery of a Bronze Age archer burial in southern England 4,500 years ago.

The so-called Amesbury Archer was buried in about 2470 B.C., 4.8 km (3 miles) from Stonehenge in southern England (Figure 1.4). Aged 35 to 45 when he died, he lay on his left side with bent legs and his head facing north. He had

FIGURE 1.4   Artist's reconstruction of the Amesbury archer, c. 2470 B.C.

suffered from an abscess in his jaw and had had a serious accident a few years before his death that ripped off his left kneecap. As a result, he walked with a straight foot, which swung out to his left. He also suffered from a bone infection that caused him constant pain. His collar and shoulder bones were also relatively small and gracile, with no signs of the uneven alignment of the arm muscles that would have resulted from the frequent use of a bow. Osteologically, if he ever was an archer, then that was no longer his main role. Who was he then? His strong pronator muscle attachments may suggest that he was engaged in the fabrication of items that required strong wrist control and forceful movement. Some of the artifacts recovered from his grave, such as a copper knife that lay partially under his torso, hint that he was (perhaps among other things) a metalworker. Metalworking had only just appeared in Britain and his knowledge must have made people regard him as something of a magical alchemist.

Another grave lay close by, dug at the same time as the archer's, containing the skeleton of a man between 25 and 30 years old. Modern archaeological science, some of it unimaginable even a generation ago, tells us much more about the two men. For example, a detailed study of their bones found the same unusual bone structure in the foot—a heel bone with a joint with one of the upper tarsal bones in the foot itself. This strongly suggests that they were relatives.

Oxygen isotope analysis of the Amesbury Archer's teeth provided a startling clue as to his homeland. The oxygen isotope ratio of the water one drinks depends on the source of the water, the distance from the coast, and the altitude, latitude, and local temperature of the rainfall. Drinking water in warmer climates has more heavy isotopes than that from colder environments. Thus, the scientist can compare the isotope ratios of ancient teeth with those from modern drinking water samples and find out where the people lived. The oxygen isotope record of the Amesbury archer's teeth showed that he had spent his youth in a colder climate than that of southern Britain, in the Swiss Alps. In contrast, the younger man in the second grave had a lighter oxygen isotope ratio in his wisdom teeth, as if he spent his late teens in central England or northeast Scotland.

The archer is proof that people traveled long distances at this early time, far more than was hitherto suspected. We should not be surprised at this, for trade routes crisscrossed Europe at the time, carrying both exotic objects and commodities such as gold ornaments and shiny Baltic amber and foodstuffs and all kinds of artifacts. His metalworking skills may account for his wide travels and probably explain why he lived and died close to an important ritual center like Stonehenge.

chipped stone axes of obvious human manufacture. If one accepted these observations, then humans were on earth long before 4004 B.C. Two major scientific developments now produced critical evidence for the antiquity of humankind. The first was the publication of Charles Darwin's theory of evolution and natural selection in his *On the Origin of Species* in 1859. The second was definitive proof of the contemporaneity of humans and extinct animals, documented conclusively by finds in gravels of the Somme River in northern France in the same year, three years after the discovery of the beetle-browed Neanderthal skull in Germany, the first archaic-looking human ancestor. By the late nineteenth century, the antiquity of humankind was widely accepted, creating a framework for human existence that extended back tens of thousands of years into an unknown past. All archaeological research is ultimately based on this framework.

For generations, archaeology was largely a phenomenon of European and North American scholarship (Bahn, 1996). The first archaeologists were amateurs, often men and women with private means. Even 50 years ago, the community of professional archaeologists throughout the world was no more than a few thousand people, many of them trained in Europe or the United States. The spread of archaeological research into other parts of the world began in the 1920s and 1930s, as Belgian, British, and French colonial governments established museums and research institutes in their colonies. Sub-Saharan Africa saw much archaeological research between the 1930s and 1950s, conducted by a handful of prehistoric archaeologists like Louis and Mary Leakey and J. Desmond Clark. In the Americas, the Carnegie Institution of Washington, D.C., was active in Maya archaeology for many years; and other academic institutions, like Harvard University, organized expeditions to Southeast Asia, China, the Andes, and other archaeologically little-known regions. But right up to the late 1950s, most archaeology was decidedly provincial, focusing on relatively few areas of the world.

World prehistory developed as a result of two major changes in archaeology. The first was the development of **radiocarbon (¹⁴C) dating** by University of Chicago physicists Willard Libby and J. R. Arnold in 1949. For the first time, archaeologists had at their disposal a dating method of potential global application that enabled them not only to date sites in all corners of the world but also to compare the chronology of, say, the first agriculture in Southwest Asia with that in the Americas (see the box "Radiocarbon Dating" in Chapter 3). Until then, no one could make easy, direct chronological comparisons between widely separated regions, nor was there a way of measuring the rate of culture change through time. Within 15 years of Libby and Arnold's remarkable discovery, radiocarbon dates from hundreds of sites allowed the construction of the first reliable global chronologies (see Science box on page 7).

The second change resulted from an explosion in the number of professional archaeologists during the 1950s and 1960s. This rapid expansion resulted from increased funding for higher education after World War II and from the establishment of many more archaeological organizations outside the narrow confines of Europe and North America.

For years, Cambridge University had trained archaeologists and anthropologists, many of whom went into the British colonial service. From the late 1950s, Cambridge actively encouraged its archaeological graduates to emigrate to tropical Africa, Australia, the Pacific, and other archaeologically little-known parts of the world. These researchers took with them a new, multidisciplinary approach to archaeology, one that stressed environmental change and the importance of explaining as well as describing the past. Since the 1960s, **cultural resource management (CRM)** has assumed increasing importance in many countries, especially Canada and the United States, with a resulting explosion in the number of archaeologists. Archaeological activity has expanded greatly in many other nations too. In 1959, for example, there were just nine professional archaeologists in the whole of sub-Saharan Africa. In 2011, there were about 100 in South Africa alone.

In 1961, the Cambridge archaeologist Grahame Clark published his classic *World Prehistory* (third edition published in 1977), the first global synthesis of archaeology, which took full account of radiocarbon chronology and archaeological research. This groundbreaking volume became a modern classic and helped turn archaeology intellectually from a somewhat provincial discipline into the global enterprise it is today. All subsequent attempts to synthesize world prehistory, of which *People of the Earth* is one, have built on Grahame Clark's pioneering work.

Today, archaeological expeditions are at work in every corner of the world and in every environment imaginable: in the remote wilds of Siberia, in tropical rain forests along the Amazon River in South America, on Easter Island in the Pacific, in the depths of the arid Sahara, and under the world's oceans (Figure 1.5). The heaviest concentrations of research are still in Europe, Southwest Asia, and North America, but knowledge is accumulating rapidly in areas like Africa and Asia, from which the most spectacular discoveries of the twenty-first century will come.

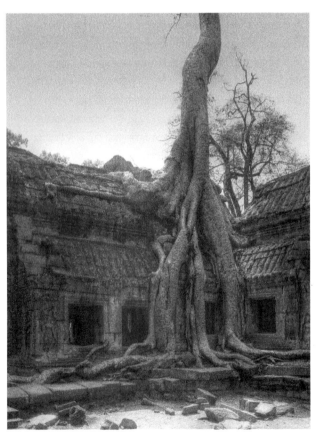

FIGURE 1.5 The overgrown ruins of Ta Prohm, Cambodia, built by the Khmer ruler Jayavarman VII in about A.D. 1186 dedicated to the ruler's mother. The most spectacular archaeological discoveries of the twenty-first century will most likely come from outside Europe, Southwest Asia, and North America, where the heaviest concentration of research has been carried out.

Science   Dating the Past

How do archaeologists date the past? Prehistoric chronologies cover long periods of time—millennia or centuries in most cases. Some idea of the scale of prehistoric time can be gained by piling up 100 quarters. If the whole pile represents the entire time that humans and their culture have been on earth, the length of time covered by historical records would be considerably less than the thickness of one quarter.

Archaeologists are constantly experimenting with new methods of dating the past (Fagan and Durrani, 2012; Renfrew and Bahn, 2008). However, four major chronological methods date the 2.6 million years of the human past (Table 1.1):

1. *Historical records* (present day to c. 3000 B.C.). Historical records can be used to date the past only as far back as the beginnings of writing and written records, which first appeared in Southwest Asia at about 3000 B.C. and much later in many other parts of the world.
2. *Dendrochronology (tree-ring dating)* (present day to 8000 B.C.). The annual growth rings of long-lived trees such as sequoias, bristlecone pines, and European oaks, whose wood was used for beams, posts, and other purposes by ancient people can be used to date sites in some areas such as the southwestern United States, the Mediterranean, and western Europe. Originally used on southwestern pueblos, **dendrochronology**, or tree-ring dating,

using sequences of growth rings, is also used to calibrate radiocarbon dates and is a useful source of information on ancient climatic change.
3. *Radiocarbon dating* (c. A.D. 1500 to 40,000 years ago). Radiocarbon dating is based on the measurement of the decay rates of carbon-14 atoms in organic samples like charcoal, shell, wood, hair, and other materials. When combined with accelerator mass spectrometry, it can produce dates from tiny samples, which are then calibrated, if possible, against tree-ring dates to provide a date in calendar years. Radiocarbon chronologies date most of prehistory after about 40,000 years ago, well after modern humans appeared in Africa for the first time (see the box "Radiocarbon Dating" in Chapter 3).
4. *Potassium-argon dating* (250,000 years ago to the origins of life). **Potassium-argon dating** is a chronological method, used to date early prehistory, which measures the decay rate of potassium-40 atoms in volcanic rocks (see the box "Potassium-Argon Dating" in Chapter 2). This method is an excellent way of dating East African hominid fossils, many of which are found in volcanic levels.

Other dating methods include obsidian hydration, paleomagnetic dating, thermoluminescence, and uranium-thorium dating. However, none of these methods is of universal application.

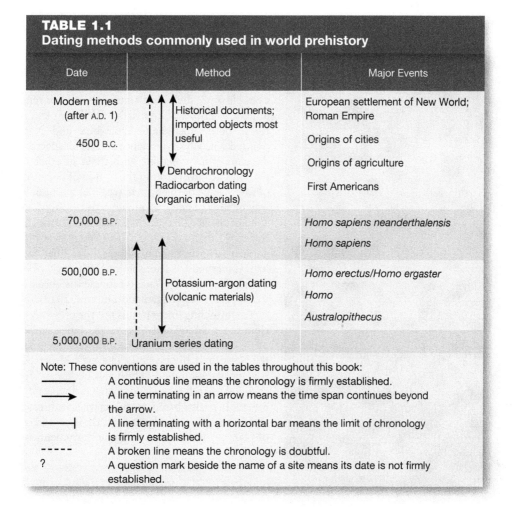

TABLE 1.1
Dating methods commonly used in world prehistory

Date	Method	Major Events
Modern times (after A.D. 1)	Historical documents; imported objects most useful	European settlement of New World; Roman Empire
4500 B.C.		Origins of cities
		Origins of agriculture
	Dendrochronology Radiocarbon dating (organic materials)	First Americans
70,000 B.P.		*Homo sapiens neanderthalensis*
		Homo sapiens
500,000 B.P.	Potassium-argon dating (volcanic materials)	*Homo erectus/Homo ergaster*
		Homo
		Australopithecus
5,000,000 B.P.	Uranium series dating	

Note: These conventions are used in the tables throughout this book:
——— A continuous line means the chronology is firmly established.
———▶ A line terminating in an arrow means the time span continues beyond the arrow.
———⊢ A line terminating with a horizontal bar means the limit of chronology is firmly established.
- - - - - A broken line means the chronology is doubtful.
? A question mark beside the name of a site means its date is not firmly established.

Who Needs the Past?

"There is not yet one person, one animal, bird, fish, crab, tree, rock, hollow, canyon, meadow, forest. Only the sky alone is there; the face of the earth is not clear. Only the sea alone is pooled under all the sky; there is nothing whatsoever gathered together. . . . Whatever is that might be is simply not there: only the pooled water, only the calm sea, kept at rest under the sky" (Tedlock, 1996, p. 64).

The Maya *Popol Vuh*, a book of counsel sometimes called the Maya Bible, tells the story of the creation and recounts the deeds of gods and kings in a brilliant celebration of the Quiché Maya past. The impact of its creation myth is as powerful as that in the book of Genesis. All societies have an interest in the past. It is always around them, haunting, mystifying, tantalizing, sometimes offering potential lessons for the present and future. The past is important because social life unfolds through time, embedded within a framework of cultural expectations and values. In the high Arctic, Inuit preserve their traditional attitudes, skills, and coping mechanisms in one of the harshest environments on earth. They do this by incorporating the lessons of the past into the present (Anawak, 1994). In many societies, the ancestors are the guardians of the land, which symbolizes present, past, and future (Figure 1.6). Westerners have an intense scientific interest in the past, partly born of curiosity but also out of a need for historical identity. There are many reasons to attempt to preserve an accurate record of the past, and no people, least of all archaeologists, should assume that they are uniquely privileged in their interest in the remains of that past (Layton, 1994).

We may all share an interest in the past, but we think of it, and use it, in different ways, just as we have different perspectives on time.

Cyclical and Linear Time

Archaeologists tend to claim that only they are qualified to reconstruct the early human past. Although it is true that archaeology is the only method Western science has of studying culture change through time, that fact does not give archaeologists unique authority over the past. In many societies, the past is a valued cultural commodity in ways that are fundamentally different from those of the archaeologist. The transmission of knowledge about the past lies in the hands of respected elders, who take pains to preserve the accuracy of oral traditions. Such traditions are of vital importance and are carefully controlled, for they define and preserve a group's identity from one generation to the next. The past is vested not in science but in household, community, kin groups, and territory. Among the Yolngu Aborigines of Australia's Northern Territory, for example, only the oldest clan members are repositories for the most important historical knowledge (Williams and Mununggurr, 1994).

As both Australian Aborigines and Native Americans have pointed out, Western science and its perspectives on the past are fundamentally incompatible with those of other societies. This incompatibility revolves around the notion of linear time. Westerners think of the passage of the human past along a straight, if branching, highway of time. The great nineteenth-century German statesman Otto von Bismarck called this the "stream of time" upon which all human societies ride for a while. The analogy is apt if you think of time in a linear fashion, as archaeologists do. They use a variety of chronological methods to date the long millennia of human prehistory (see Science box on page 7) and provide the chronological framework for world prehistory (Fagan and Durrani, 2012).

An unfolding linear past is not the only way of conceptualizing ancient times. Many non-Western societies, ancient and modern, think of time as a cyclical phenomenon, or sometimes as a combination of the linear and the cyclical. The cyclical perspective stems from the passage of seasons and of heavenly bodies and from the close relationships between foragers and village farmers and their natural environments. It is also based on the eternal verities of human life: fertility and birth, life, growth, and death. The endlessly repeating seasons of planting and harvest, of game movements or salmon runs, and of

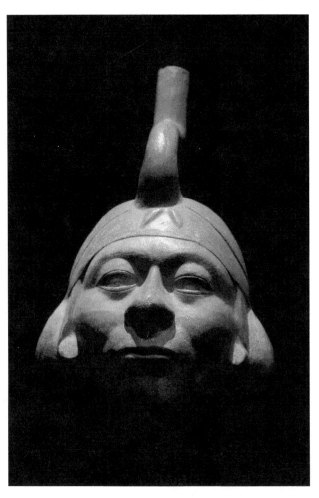

FIGURE 1.6　A Moche stirrup jar in the form of a portrait from the north coast of Peru, mid-first millennium A.D. The symbolism of these vessels is unknown, but the sculpture may depict a revered ancestor.

FIGURE 1.7 Art as history. A brass plaque from Benin City, West Africa, showing a heavily armed *oba* (king) with his attendants. These artifacts, which served as important history records of royal reigns and genealogy, were stored in the royal palace.

ripening wild foods have governed human existence in deeply significant ways. The ancient Maya developed an elaborate cyclical calendar of interlocking secular and religious cycles to measure the passage of the seasons and to regulate religious ceremonies (see Chapter 21).

But we should not assume that societies with a cyclical view of time did not have linear chronologies as well. The celebrated Maya "Long Count" was a linear sacred calendar that formed an integral part of the close relationship between Maya rulers and the cosmos. The ancient Egyptians developed a linear chronology for administrative purposes. But, in general, societies develop linear chronologies only when they need them. For example, Western societies use linear time to regulate times of prayer, to control the working day, and to schedule airline flights. It is hard to generalize, but societies with centralized political systems tend to use the reigns of chiefs or kings as signposts along a linear time scale. For instance, the history of the rulers of the state of Benin in West Africa shows a significant shift in the interpretation of time. Before the fourteenth century A.D., Benin history is essentially mythological, with inaccurate chronology and a variable number of kings. But with the founding of the Yoruba dynasty, the deeds and reigns of every *oba* (king) are remembered in detail with chronological accuracy right down to modern times (Ben-Amos, 1980) (Figure 1.7).

Robert Layton (1994) points out that many non-Western societies do not perceive themselves as living in a changeless world. They make a fundamental distinction between the recent past, which lies within living memory, and the more remote past, which came before it. For instance, the Australian Aborigine groups living in northeast Queensland distinguish among *kuma*, the span of events witnessed by living people; *anthantnama*, a long time ago; and *yilamu*, the period of the creation. Furthermore, the existence of culture change in the past has also been accepted by many societies, among them the Hindus, whose traditions of history speak of early people who lived without domesticated animals and plants, and the Hazda hunter-gatherers of East Africa, who speak of their homeland's first inhabitants as being giants without fire or tools. These paradigms of the past take many forms, with mythic creators of culture, usually primordial ancestors, deities, or animals, establishing contemporary social customs and the familiar landscape, or with a more remote, discontinuous heroic era like that of the Greeks, which allowed writers like the playwright Aeschylus to evaluate contemporary behavior (Sparkes, 1994).

Written Records, Oral Traditions, and Archaeology

Most human societies of the past were nonliterate, which meant that they transmitted knowledge and history by word of mouth. Written records are the most comprehensive source of information about the past, but they usually follow a strictly linear chronology. They also served as educational tools. Apart from anything else, written documents were useful as cues for people to memorize standardized historical, ritual, or mythical information.

The Aztec oral histories, partially set down after the Spanish Conquest of the fifteenth century A.D., are an excellent example of history transmitted by word of mouth. These oral histories (**oral tradition**) were recited according to a well-defined narrative plot that focused on charismatic figures in Aztec history; key events, like the dedication of the sun god Huitzilopochtli's temple in the Aztec capital in 1487; and the histories of favored groups. In these, as in other oral histories, there were formulas and themes that formed the central ingredients of a story that varied considerably from one speaker to the next, even if the essential content was the same. Many oral histories are mixtures of factual data and parables that communicate moral and political values. But to those who hear them, they are publicly sanctioned history, performed before and subject to the critical evaluation of an audience who may have heard the same stories before (Townsend, 2009).

Both written records and oral histories are subject to all kinds of bias. Neither can claim to be totally objective, any more than archaeology is. The problem for the archaeologist is to correlate data from excavations with that from oral traditions and to establish critically what is factual history and what is myth or moral exhortation. Oral traditions are hard to use, as their antiquity is very difficult to establish. In some cases—Australia, for example—there are instances where oral histories and archaeology coincide in general terms. For example, the traditions speak of the arrival of the first people from overseas, of the flooding of coastal areas after the Ice Age, and of the hunting of giant marsupials (pouched animals like the kangaroo). So Australia's past can be said to come from two sources: archaeological data and oral traditions. In some instances, the archaeologists and the indigenous people have shared interests and come together to identify sacred and historic places, often to ensure that they are preserved. However, the two groups may differ greatly on the significance of a particular location, such as a place where archaeologists find no buildings or artifacts, yet which the local people consider sacred.

But all too often the archaeologist and a local community have different interests in the past. To the archaeologist, the past is scientific data to be studied with all the rigor of modern science. To local people, the past is often highly personalized and the property of the ancestors. Such accounts are valid alternative versions of history that deserve respect and understanding, for they play a vital role in the creation and reaffirmation of cultural identity. And they raise a fundamental question that lies behind many Native Americans' objections to archaeological research: What do archaeologists, usually outsiders, have to offer to a cultural group that already has a valid version of its history? Why should they be permitted to dig up the burials of the ancestors or other settlements and sacred places under the guise of studying what is, to the people, a known history? It is a question that archaeologists have barely begun to address (Layton, 1994).

Archaeologists are not alone in considering the past of value, nor are they immune to the politics that sometimes surrounds the interpretation of aspects of the past. Many Westerners may consider "world prehistory" written from archaeological and many other sources the most reliable account of the human past. But we should never forget that alternative, and often compelling, accounts of ancient times exist that play an important role in helping minority groups and others to maintain their traditional heritage as it existed before the arrival of Westerners. *People of the Earth* offers an account of over 2.6 million years of human history based on the latest scientific archaeological research, but it does so with a profound respect for the cultures and histories of others with different historical perspectives. At the core of our story is the concept of culture.

Studying Culture and Culture Change

As anthropologists, archaeologists study human cultures and how they have changed through time.

Culture is a concept developed by anthropologists to describe the distinctive adaptive system used by human beings. Culture can be called a society's traditional systems of belief and behavior, as understood by individuals and the members of social groups and as manifested in individual or collective behavior. It is also part of our way of adapting to our environment. Humans are the only animals to manufacture tools for this purpose (for an extended discussion, see Fagan and Durrani, 2012; Sharer and Ashmore, 2009). Thus tools and dwellings are also part of our culture.

Ordinarily, when animals die, their experience dies with them. However, human beings use the symbolic system of language to transmit their ideas and their culture, their feelings and experiences, from one generation to the next (Figure 1.8). This is why language as communication is so important in many societies. Culture is learned by intentional teaching as well as by trial and error and simple imitation. People can share ideas, which in turn become behavior patterns that are repeated again and again—witness the long-lived stone hand ax, a multipurpose tool that remained in use for more than 1 million years of early prehistory (see Chapter 4). All archaeological research is based on the principle that culture is an ongoing phenomenon that changes gradually over time, although change can be abrupt as well.

Culture is nongenetic and provides a much quicker way than biological adaptation to share ideas that enable people to cope with their environment. It is the adaptiveness of culture that allows archaeologists to assume that artifacts found in archaeological sites are patterned adaptations to the environment. Many archaeologists think of cultures as ever-adjusting cultural systems adapting to changing natural environments and other stimuli.

A **cultural system** is a complex system comprising a set of interacting variables—tools, burial customs, ways of getting food, religious beliefs, social organization, and so on—that function to maintain a community in a state of equilibrium with its environment. When one element in the system changes—say, hunting practices as the result of a prolonged drought—then reacting adjustments will occur in many other elements. It follows that no cultural system is ever static. It is always changing, and these processes of culture change are a primary focus of archaeological research.

Cultural process refers to the processes by which human societies changed in the past. Culture changes take place through time, most changes, but by no means all, being gradual and cumulative. Inventions and design improvements result in dozens of minor alterations in the ways people live. Generally, cultural evolution was gradual in prehistoric times, although there are cases of sudden change, such as the Roman conquest of Gaul in the first century B.C. Dramatic cultural modification can also result from the spread from neighboring areas of a new idea or invention, such as the plow or maize agriculture.

FIGURE 1.8 Two !Kung San hunters from southern Africa's Kalahari Desert. Like all humans, they benefit from cultural knowledge and experience transmitted from one generation to the next.

The cumulative effects of long-term culture change are easily seen. A comparison of the simple flaked stone tools of the earliest humans and the sophisticated contents of the Egyptian pharaoh Tutankhamun's tomb will help one to understand the power of cumulative change over thousands of years.

Primary Cultural Processes

The term **process** is used in archaeology to refer to mechanisms by which cultures change. Archaeologists generally agree on three primary cultural processes that figured importantly in world prehistory:

- **Invention** involves creating a new idea and transforming it—in archaeological contexts—into an artifact or other tangible innovation that has survived. Other people will adopt inventions if they are useful; if sufficiently important, they spread rapidly. The microchip, for example, is in almost universal use because it is an effective advance in electronic technology. Most inventions in prehistory were the result of prolonged experimentation, a logical extension of the use and refinement of an existing technology, or a response to changes in the surrounding environment.

- **Diffusion** is the label for those processes by which new ideas or cultural traits spread from one person to another or from one group to another, often over long distances. These ideas are socially transmitted from individual to individual and ultimately from group to group, but the physical movement of many people is not involved. A classic modern example of diffusion is tobacco smoking, a favorite pleasure of North American Indians that was adopted by Elizabethan colonists in the sixteenth century. Within a few generations, tens of thousands of Europeans were smoking pipes and enjoying the narcotic effect of American tobacco.

- **Migration** involves the movement of people and is based on a deliberate decision to enter new areas and leave old ones. The classic instance of migration in prehistory is that of the Polynesians; they settled the remote islands of the Pacific in consequence of deliberate explorations of the open ocean by their skilled navigators (Finney, 1994).

Theoretical Approaches: Culture as Adaptation

Archaeological theory provides the guiding principles that allow us to make sense of the human past, so some brief discussion of the subject is essential here (for detailed analyses of contemporary theory, see M. Johnson, 2010; Trigger, 2006).

World prehistory is the story of an emerging and increasingly complex human biological and cultural diversity that unfolded over millions of years. We have made giant steps in describing the archaeological record in many parts of the world, but attempts to explain such major developments as the spread of modern humans, the origins of food production, or civilization are still at an early stage

(Trigger, 2006). The very diversity and local nature of most ancient human society make it well-nigh impossible to develop comprehensive, all-embracing theoretical frameworks for world prehistory; indeed, it is rash to attempt it. Nor does a single approach like, for example, the popular notion of culture as adaptation provide sufficient theoretical background. Several perspectives, taken together or used separately, provide significant insights, so a diversity of theoretical approaches is valuable.

Climatic Change

In recent years, we have begun to understand the enormous impact of short- and long-term climatic shifts as agents for culture change. The long cycles of cold and warm associated with the Ice Age occur on a millennial scale and have long-term effects on human existence (see descriptions in Chapters 3 and 4). For example, the existence of a low-lying land bridge between Siberia and Alaska during much of the late Ice Age may have allowed humans to make their way from Asia into the Americas before 15,000 years ago, but the actual formation of the shelf that linked the two continents would have taken many centuries and human generations (see Chapter 5). Short-term climatic changes, such as the floods or droughts caused by El Niño episodes or the volcanic eruptions that dump ash into the atmosphere, are another matter. Memories of catastrophic famines and other results associated with such events would have endured for generations, for they had immediate impact on hundreds, if not thousands, of people.

We look back at the past through shadowed mirrors, which become less blurred as we approach recent times. Our knowledge of Ice Age climatic change is necessarily on a grand scale, for, until recently, even ice cores did not attain the year-by-year resolution that is needed to track short-term shifts. Yet, such sudden changes are the most important of all to human populations, who have to adjust constantly to unusual weather conditions—droughts and floods, extreme heat and cold. It is only now that we are beginning to understand their profound impact on ancient societies. As research into these and other centuries-long events has intensified, so more scholars have paid increasing attention to violent, year-long episodes such as monsoon failures, volcanic eruptions, and, most important of all, El Niños (Fagan, 2004a, 2009a).

Identifying ancient short-term climatic change requires extremely precise and sophisticated environmental and climatic evidence, much of it obtained from ice cores, **pollen analysis**, and tree rings. Ice cores, in particular, are revolutionizing our knowledge of ancient climatic shifts, for they are now achieving a resolution of five years or less, which readily allows one to study drought cycles and major El Niño events of the past. From the archaeologist's point of view, El Niños are of compelling interest, for they had drastic effects on many early civilizations living in normally dry environments but where flooding, in hours, may have wiped out years of irrigation agriculture. Humanity was not so vulnerable to El Niños until people settled in permanent villages, then cities, and the realities of farming and growing population densities made it harder for them to move away from drought or flood. A classic example of such vulnerability comes from the north coast of Peru. Droughts and strong El Niños had a catastrophic effect on the Moche civilization of the first millennium A.D. (see Chapter 22).

It is very easy to attribute major cultural developments like the origins of food production or the collapse of a civilization to climatic change alone. But such straightforward environmental determinism is long outdated by realizations that climate was but one factor that came into play.

Culture as Adaptation

Most archaeologists believe that human cultures are best interpreted as adaptations to the subsistence and ecological requirements of a locality. This is the **culture as adaptation approach**, which places considerable emphasis on cultural systems and ecology. Under this approach, culture is the result of human beings' unique ability to infuse events and objects with meaning that can be appreciated, decoded, and understood (Gamble, 1999). This means that culture is participated in as well as shared by human beings. However, this process of participation and sharing differs greatly from place to place and from time to time, resulting in variations in prehistoric material culture—the data for studying prehistory. The widely used culture as adaptation approach employs a complex, multidimensional model to investigate the significance of patterning and variation in archaeological finds (Binford, 2001a).

Under the culture as adaptation approach, human behavior, both today and in the remote past, is an adaptation not to a single site but to environmental regions. Thus, to understand individual sites and artifact patternings, archaeologists have to study regions, as we do in this book. And they usually do so within a framework of evolutionary theory and cultural ecology.

Cultural Evolution and Cultural Ecology

Charles Darwin's theory of biological and natural selection has influenced theories of culture change since the mid-nineteenth century. Today, the archaeologist studies human culture change over long periods of time within a sophisticated framework of cultural evolutionary theory that has developed over more than a 100 years.

Following a theory of **unilinear cultural evolution**, early Victorian social scientists believed human societies evolved in a simple, linear fashion, slowly ascending an evolutionary ladder of human progress toward that ultimate pinnacle, industrial civilization. Under this rubric, humanity passed from a state of barbarism (hunting and foraging) through a stage of savagery (subsistence farming) to civilization. Such unilinear frameworks are not only too simplistic but also smack of assumptions of racial superiority and notions of universal human progress.

Multilinear cultural evolution is now widely accepted as a very general framework for studying the cultural evolution of human societies. Unlike early unilinear theories, multilinear evolution assumes that each human society pursues its own evolutionary course, determined by the long-term success of its adaptation, via technology and social institutions, to its natural environment (Steward, 1970).

Cultural ecology, the total way in which human populations adapt to and transform their environments, is at the core of multilinear evolutionary theory. Some societies achieve a broad measure of equilibrium with their environment, in which adaptive changes consist of little more than some refinements in technology and the fine-tuning of organizational structures. Other societies become involved in cycles of growth that are triggered by environmental change or from within society. If these changes involve either greater food supplies or population growth, accelerated culture change may result from the need to feed more people or the deployment of an enlarged food surplus. Continued growth may place additional strains on the society, triggering technological changes, adjustments in social organization, or alterations in the belief system that provides the society's integrative force.

Multilinear cultural evolution combines the notion of cultural systems and cultural ecology into a closely knit, highly flexible way of studying and explaining cultural processes. Under this approach, there is no one primary agent of cultural evolution but, rather, a series of important variables, all with complex interrelationships. When we seek to explain the major and minor developments of prehistory, we must consider the ways in which change took place, the processes and mechanisms of change (cultural evolution, experimentation), and the socioeconomic stresses (population pressure, game scarcity, and so on) that triggered those mechanisms.

Multilinear Evolution: Prestate and State-Organized Societies

The sophisticated concept of multilinear evolution has led to the (often controversial) classification of human societies into two broad groups that do not necessarily evolve into one another: prestate and state-organized societies (Service, 1962). We use these general groupings in these pages purely for convenience.

Prestate societies are societies on a small scale, based on the community, band, or village. They vary greatly in their degree of political integration and are sometimes divided into three loosely defined categories (Figure 1.9):

- **Bands** are associations of families of no more than 25 to 100 people. Knit together by close social ties, bands were the dominant form of social organization for most hunter-gatherers from the earliest times up to the origins of food production.
- **Tribes** are clusters of bands that are linked by **clans**. A clan is a group of people linked by common ancestral ties that serve as connections between widely scattered communities. Clans are important because they are a form of social linkage that gives people a sense of common identity with a wider world than their own immediate family and relatives.
- **Chiefdoms** are still kin-based but more hierarchical, with power concentrated in the hands of kin leaders. These leaders are usually individuals with unusual ritual, political, or entrepreneurial skills. Chiefdoms tend to have higher population densities (generally between 5,000 and 20,000 people) and display clear signs of social ranking. Often there is local specialization in craft products. Frequently, surpluses of food and craft products are paid to the chief, who redistributes them to his followers. Most chiefdoms have permanent ritual and ceremonial centers, which act as the central focus of the chiefdom, where the chief and his or her retainers live. Chiefdoms vary greatly in elaboration (A. Johnson and Earle, 2000). The chiefdom is not necessarily a precursor of a state, although some were (see Chapter 14), but another form of more complex society, bound by different environmental and social constraints (Yoffee, 2005).

State-organized societies (civilizations) operate on a large scale with centralized political and social organization, class stratification, and intensive agriculture. They have complex political structures and many permanent government institutions, and they are based on notions of social inequality. Such societies are ruled by a tiny group of elites, who hold monopolies over strategic resources and use coercion to enforce their authority. State-organized societies of the past were first ruled by priest-bureaucrats, then gradually came under the rule of secular kings, who sometimes became despotic monarchs, often with alleged divine powers. This type of social organization was typical of the early literate civilizations and was the forerunner of the classical civilizations of Greece and Rome.

		Prestate		
	Band	Tribe	Chiefdom	State-Organized Societies
Total Numbers	Less than 100	Up to a few thousand	5,000 – 20,000+	Generally 20,000+
Social Organization	Egalitarian Informal leadership	Segmentary society Pan-tribal associations Raids by small groups	Kinship-based ranking under hereditary leader High-ranking warriors	Class-based hierarchy under king or emperor Armies
Economic Organization	Mobile hunter-gatherers	Settled farmers Pastoralist herders	Central accumulation and redistribution Some craft specialization	Centralized bureaucracy Tribute-based Taxation Laws
Settlement Pattern	Temporary camps	Permanent villages	Fortified centers Ritual centers	Urban: cities, towns Frontier defenses Roads
Religious Organization	Shamans	Religious elders Calendrical rituals	Hereditary chief with religious duties	Priestly class Pantheistic or monotheistic religion
Architecture	Temporary shelters *Paleolithic skin tents, Ukraine*	Permanent huts Burial mounds Shrines *Neolithic shrine Çatalhöyük, Turkey*	Large–scale monuments *Stonehenge, England — final form*	Palaces, temples, and other public buildings Pyramids at Giza *Castillo Chichén Itzá, Mexico*
Archaeological Examples	All Paleolithic societies, including Paleo- Indians	All early farmers (Neolithic/Archaic)	Many early metalworking and Formative societies Mississippian, USA Smaller African kingdoms	All ancient civilizations, e.g., in Mesoamerica, Peru, Near East, Southwest Asia, India and China, Greece and Rome
Modern Examples	Eskimos !Kung San Australian Aborigines	Pueblos, Southwest USA New Guinea Highlanders Nuer and Dinka in East Africa	Northwest Coast Indians, USA 18th-century Polynesian chiefdoms in Tonga, Tahiti, Hawaii	All modern states

FIGURE 1.9 General categories of ancient human societies. (Modified from Renfrew and Bahn, 2008.)

We describe the prestate societies of prehistory in Chapters 2 to 13, and state-organized societies in Chapters 14 to 22.

Theoretical Approaches: Evolutionary Ecology and Hunter-Gatherers

Inevitably, biological evolution has had an important influence on contemporary thinking about prehistory, especially hunter-gatherer societies. Humans are animals, and, as such, are subject to the same evolutionary mechanisms such as natural selection. This assumption, which has generated sharp controversy, forms the basis of an important approach to explaining culture change, known loosely as evolutionary ecology.

Evolutionary ecology is based on the proposition that variation in the behavior of individual organisms is shaped by natural selection (Broughton and O'Connell, 1999). Thus, it identifies a single goal, the maximization of potential reproductive success, toward which all behavior is directed and in terms of which it can be predicted. Evolutionary ecology does not require rational choice on the part of its subjects, nor does it deny the existence of intentional behavior. All it assumes is that natural selection has designed organisms (including people) to behave in ways that tend to enhance fitness. In other words, the process of selection will tend to favor the best strategy among various alternatives available at the time. Evolutionary ecology has the advantage of being comprehensive, so that it can generate predictions about any aspect of fitness-related behavior. At the same time, it allows integration and provides a basis for predicting linkages between variation in one aspect of behavior and that in others. Above all, evolutionary ecology's predictions are testable.

Most evolutionary ecology in archaeology has been applied to settlement and subsistence, using optimal foraging models. **Optimal foraging strategy** argues that the most efficient **foraging** strategies adopted by human groups are those that produce the greatest return in energy relative to time and effort expended. From the archaeological perspective, optimal foraging theory assumes that, under certain, well-defined circumstances, human decisions are made to maximize the net rate of energy gain. These decisions can revolve around diet or breadth of diet, where to forage, the amount of time spent on different activities, or settlement location or group size. The hunter-gatherer would logically not choose to pass over a higher-ranked resource, like abundantly available pecan nuts, to exploit one with fewer benefits—there is no benefit in doing so. Therein lies the nub of optimal foraging theory: the implication that the hunter-gatherer uses higher-ranked resources when available.

This is fine in a world where everything is infinitely abundant. In practice, resources vary greatly in distribution and abundance and, thus, in the time needed to search for them. A new twist to optimal foraging theory now enters the picture. When a hunter in the Midwest's Illinois River valley hunted, say, a deer, a highly valued prey, he might have encountered a rabbit warren on the way, rabbits being the second or third highest-ranked food resource on his mental list. He stops and takes six rabbits, and forgets about deer, deciding on a new course of action based on anticipated energy consumption and immediate food needs at the time he encountered the warren. In this case, exploitation of the food resource is independent of its abundance, what optimal foraging theorists call a **contingency model**. Such models are important, for they imply a basic reality that repeats itself again and again in human prehistory: As food resources decline in abundance, the time required to search for them increases, and the breadth of the hunter-gatherer diet widens to compensate for this reality. Conversely, as resources become more abundant, selectivity increases.

A **prey model** has also come into wide use; it assumes that foragers will try and maximize the net rate of energy capture. The model predicts that foragers will exploit the highest-ranked prey should they encounter it, whereas lower-ranked items move in and out of the diet as rates of foraging return rise and fall within an area. In North America, acorns are a classic example of a resource that was extremely expensive to process relative to their caloric return, yet they assumed increasing importance to ancient foragers over the millennia and especially in late pre-Columbian times (Basgall, 1987). This suggests that overall foraging return rates declined after the Ice Age as populations rose and food resources became harder to find, reflected by an increase in acorn exploitation. In many areas such as the Midwest and parts of California, smaller terrestrial animals and acorns assumed ever-greater importance through time, as they also did in Southwest Asia immediately after the Ice Age. It is probably no coincidence that the technology used for processing such foods as acorns and small animals became more sophisticated as time went on, reflecting a far greater energy expenditure on such activities in environments where high-yielding prey were rare.

Theoretical Approaches: People as Agents of Change

The first known Egyptian ruler, Narmer, is at best a shadowy figure, but there seems little doubt that he lived in about 3100 B.C. This little-known king must have been a remarkably able man, for he unified a patchwork of competing chiefdoms along the Nile River into a single civilization that endured for nearly 3,000 years. Narmer lived at a time of political unrest, warfare, and intense rivalry, where different chiefdoms rose to prominence in the hands of able leaders, then vanished into obscurity after their deaths. This process of what is sometimes called "chiefly cycling" went on for centuries before Narmer rose to power and embarked on the military and diplomatic campaigns that joined narrow, valley-bound Upper Egypt with the flat delta country of Lower Egypt to form the "Two Lands." Narmer and his successors wore regalia that symbolized the unification of Egypt, the creation of order out of chaos. Unification was surrounded with powerful myth and religious symbolism and was a foundation of Egyptian life (see Chapter 16). Even if the process of forging a single state took many generations, one can easily imagine the powerful effect of having a single, exceptionally able general and statesman who conquered his neighbors, then created a well-organized state from his new domains. To some degree, the processes of culture change that led to ancient Egyptian civilization came from long-term adaptations to changing conditions. But they also resulted from the deeds of exceptionally able leaders, among them Narmer.

People are agents of culture change, even if most of them remain anonymous, unseen figures in the obscurity of a preliterate past. We just happen to know something of Narmer because he appears on Egyptian king lists. Many of the most recent theoretical approaches to world prehistory are now taking account of humans as agents (Flannery, 1999).

External and Internal Constraints

Three-dimensional laser scanning, radiocarbon dating, pollen analysis, statistical methods—the list of scientific innovations in archaeology over the past half century is almost unending. The culture as adaptation approach to world prehistory developed out of an increasingly "scientific" perspective on the past during the 1960s and 1970s. It has focused on explanations of culture change and on the relationships between people and their environments to the point where many archaeologists complained that this perspective is more concerned with the processes of culture change than with the people behind the changes. They pointed out that all human societies are made up of individuals—men and women, children and adults, members of families and entire communities, and their neighbors near and far. They spend their lives interacting with one another: agreeing, disagreeing, negotiating, quarreling, and living in peace. From these interactions stem cultural traditions that provide guidance for coping with the environment. The same traditions can be a powerful conservative force that inhibits change or one that encourages innovation in times of stress.

Ecological and other external constraints can be culturally mediated, but they operate independently of human actions, so they are susceptible to being understood in terms of evolutionary theory and other such generalizations. Cultural traditions are far more idiosyncratic and haphazard. Therefore, it is difficult to impose evolutionary order on human history, for despite external constraints, much culture change is contingent on ever-changing circumstances and cultural traditions, on ideologies and changing political realities, which may even depend on the whims of individuals. This led to a new generation of archaeological theory, loosely called **post-processual archaeology**, which placed a much greater focus on individual and group behavior, the cultural biases that archaeologists use in interpreting their data, and on the intangibles of human behavior, such as social organization, religious beliefs, and worldviews.

Post-processual archaeology is complex, contradictory, and often highly abstract. But it has been enormously valuable in drawing attention to the critical importance of individual and group human behavior in such major developments as the origins of food production and state formation, what is often called agency. As Ian Hodder (1999) has pointed out, processual and post-processual archaeology complement each other. Processual archaeology is concerned with external constraints such as environmental change, whereas post-processual archaeology concentrates on internal constraints such as social and political change, religious beliefs, and individual and group behavior (for constraints, see Trigger, 1991). These internal constraints include ethnic diversity, gender roles, knowledge, beliefs, values, and other culturally conditioned habits, all of them different in every culture.

In recent years, we have seen an explosion of interest in individuals, individual histories, and the ways in which individual variation and cultural innovation interacts with the wider population. Factionalism in, say, ancient Egyptian royal courts, changing gender roles, and so on are becoming major factors in our efforts to explain such issues as the emergence of social complexity and state-organized societies. We can talk as much as we wish about cultures, phases, and other such arbitrary classifications, but such groupings steer us away from simple human actions like building a fire, shaping a bone awl, or carving a figurine. Yet some of them are shared by cultures flourishing thousands of miles apart. For instance, two widely separated cultures may develop bronze metallurgy, which is based on a common body of technological know-how, but the cultural context of that knowledge may be radically different, as it was, say, in the Shang civilization of China (see Chapter 18) and the Moche culture in coastal Peru (see Chapter 22). Some symbols, like associations between rulers and the sun or the common practice of elevating chiefs or kings on a dais, have developed in many places. That does not mean, of course, that they are connected.

It would be foolish to describe one overarching theoretical approach that embraces all the internal constraints that have affected ancient human societies. Neither processual nor post-processual archaeology can explain every aspect of our past. The future lies in integrating different theoretical approaches, including findings from other academic disciplines, among them biological anthropology, psychology, and neuroscience. All such efforts will stem from extremely comprehensive sets of data from the intensive investigation of sites, cultures, and entire regions, a task that will occupy generations of archaeologists to come (Trigger, 2006). In this book, we summarize some of the progress made toward this goal and describe some of the factors that shaped our past.

Interactions

In the final analysis, it is people who share culture, and groups and individuals who make decisions about daily life: Men interact with women, children with adults; a kin group quarrels within itself, pitting small faction against small faction; ethnic groups compete for access to wealth or political power; or foreigners have their own enclave within a vast city. Such dealings between individuals, between individuals and groups, and between groups are the forces that constrain or encourage culture change. By its very nature, the archaeological record tends to be impersonal, its artifacts and food remains chronicling the dealings of blurred groups rather than individuals, or even categories of people—say, women at a given moment in time.

Only rarely can the archaeologist go beyond artifacts and food remains to study the roles of groups or individuals, the work they undertook, and the subtle ways in which they influenced the course of events. The great city of Teotihuacán on the edge of the Valley of Mexico housed tightly packed communities of foreigners from the Valley of Oaxaca and lowland Vera Cruz, identified by distinctive pottery and architecture quite unlike that of the Teotihuacános. At the early farming village of Abu Hureyra in Syria, dating to 7000 B.C., biological anthropologist Theya Molleson (1994) observed malformations of the toes, knees, and lower vertebrae in the skeletons of all the adult women, a condition due, almost certainly, to hours of grinding grain. Male skeletons did not display the same impairments. Molleson's discovery is some of the earliest evidence in human history for a division of labor between men and women. Such research requires very complete field data and fine-grained laboratory and recovery methods.

Gender: Men and Women

Archaeologists have long studied people and households, but only recently have they turned their attention to the complex issue of gender and gender relations, a promising avenue of new research. Gender is not the same as sex, which refers to the biological male or female. Sex is biologically determined (at its most common male or female). Gender is the socially and culturally constructed behavior associated with one's sex. Gender roles and relations acquire meaning in culturally and historically meaningful ways. This means that gender is a vital part of human social relations and a central issue in the study of ancient human societies.

The expression of gender varies, and has always varied, from society to society and through time. Some archaeologists, such as Margaret Conkey and Joan Gero (1991), write of "engendering archaeology," an attempt to reclaim men and women in nonsexist ways in the past. This goes much farther than merely demonstrating that pots were made by women and stone projectile points by men, or trying to identify women's activities in the archaeological record. The archaeology of gender deals with the ideology of gender, with roles and gender relations—the ways in which gender intersects with all aspects of human social life. How are roles and social relationships constructed? What contributions did men and women make to ancient societies? But, ask the latest wave of gender archaeologists, is it even possible to differentiate men's and women's roles in the past? Is our search for people's sex or gender obscuring other, potentially more important ways that people may have distinguished themselves? And how many of our own cultural biases and expectations, of what it means to be "male" or "female," do we put on the archaeological record in any such attempt? Thus, many further question the notion of a simple men/women dualism—instead acknowledging that there are—and presumably always have been—many more genders, and indeed sexes ("hermaphrodites," and all those along the chromosomal spectrum, who are not biologically male or female) (Joyce, 2008). In this way, gender studies make us truly examine our "cultural baggage"—and our assumptions about how people organized themselves. An engendered archaeology uses a wide diversity of archaeological methods and approaches to find out how gender might "work" in ancient societies, to unravel its cultural meanings.

To "engender the past" means to focus not only on major material achievements such as metallurgy or pot making or ancient environments but also on interpersonal relations and the social dynamics of everyday activity. These are the activities that take up most of people's daily lives—hunting, gardening, preparing meals, building houses, and so on. But gender also impacts on trade, craft specialization, state formation, religion, and ritual—to mention only a few major human activities.

Gender research in archaeology is concerned with people as individuals and their contributions to society. Elizabeth Brumfiel (1991) has studied Aztec women, who were expert weavers; indeed, weaving was a fundamental skill for an Aztec noblewoman. However, she points out that to characterize them merely as weavers ignores the vital links between weaving, child rearing, and cooking (to mention only a few of women's tasks) and the wider society in which the women lived. For instance, the population of the Valley of Mexico rose tenfold during the four centuries before the conquest, a striking testimony to the success of the Aztec household economy. Women wove textiles and the capes that were the badges of social status in Aztec society. Their woven products were vital to the enormous tribute system on which Aztec civilization depended. Cotton mantles even served as a form of currency. Cloth was a primary way of organizing the ebb and flow of goods and services that sustained the state.

Brumfiel shows that the Aztec household and the roles of women were much more varied than those attributed to them by early Spanish observers. Furthermore, the skills of cooking and weaving were important political tools, ways of maintaining social and political control. Thus, she argues, the idealization of these skills in both Aztec folklore and schooling developed because women were makers of both valuable goods and of people. It was they who assured the continuity of Aztec kin groups.

What, then, is an "engendered past"? Scientific reporting tends to obliterate the actors whose deeds created the past. An engendered archaeology ventures into new territory, using innovative approaches to present the multiple voices of the past in order to report both data and stories of the past. Such research requires exceptionally complete data and meticulously excavated sites.

Trade and Exchange

Exchange systems were part of human life long before the Sumerians and ancient Egyptians. Shells from the Black Sea appear in late Ice Age hunting encampments deep in Ukraine from at least 18,000 years ago. The Paleo-Indians of the Great Plains exchanged fine-grained toolmaking stone over long distances as early as 11000 B.C. Few human societies are completely self-sufficient, for they depend on others for resources outside their own territories. And, as the need for raw materials or for prestigious ornaments increased, so did the tentacles of exchange and trade between neighbors near and far. This trade often had powerful political or symbolic overtones, conducted under the guise of formal gift-giving or as part of complex exchange rituals.

People make trade connections and set up the exchange systems that handle trade goods when they need to acquire goods and services that are not available to them within their own local area. The movement of goods need not be over any great distance, and it can operate internally, within a society, or externally, across cultural boundaries—within interaction spheres. Both exchange and trade always involve two elements: the goods and commodities being exchanged and the people doing the exchanging. Thus, any form of trading activity implies both procurement and handling of tools and raw materials as well as some form of social system that provides the people-to-people relationships within which the trade flourishes. Not only raw materials and finished objects but also ideas and information passed along trade routes.

Conventionally, exchange and trade are recognized in the archaeological record by the discovery of objects exotic to the material culture or economy of the host society. For instance, glass was never manufactured in sub-Saharan Africa, yet imported glass beads are widespread in archaeological sites of the first millennium A.D. Until recently, such objects were recognized almost entirely on the basis of style and design—the appearance of distinctive pottery forms far from their known points of origin, and so on. Sometimes exotics such as gold, amber, turquoise, or marine shells, commodities whose general area of origin was known, provided evidence of long-distance exchanges. Between 3000 B.C. and the Christian Era, Late Archaic and Woodland peoples in the North American Southeast used native copper from outcrops near Lake Superior and conch shells from the Gulf Coast, both commodities of known origin (see Figure 5.12).

In the early days of archaeology, such exotica were deemed sufficient to identify trade, what were loosely called "influences" or even "invasions." The assumptions made about the nature of human interactions were very limited and never precise. Today, however, studies of prehistoric exchange are far more sophisticated, owing to two major developments. The first is a new focus throughout archaeology on cultural process and on regional studies. The second is the development of a wide range of scientific techniques that are capable of describing the composition of certain types of raw material and even of identifying their sources with great precision. As we shall see in Chapter 9, fine-grained obsidian, a volcanic rock used for toolmaking and ornaments, has distinctive trace elements that have allowed archaeologists to identify at least nine zones of obsidian exchange in the eastern Mediterranean region alone.

The Uluburun ship, wrecked off southern Turkey in the fourteenth century B.C., is a fine example of the importance of trade and exchange in the ancient world. Its cargo came from at least nine different areas (see Chapter 19). The study of prehistoric trade is a vital source of information on social organization and the ways in which societies became more complex. Trade itself developed a great complexity, in both goods traded and in the interactions of people involved. Such contacts ranged from simple interactions between individuals to exchanges by professional traders, such as the Aztec *pochteca* (merchants), who sometimes acted as spies.

Ideologies and Beliefs

Nothing informs one more about an ancient society than its worldview and religious beliefs. Unfortunately, the intangible ideologies and beliefs of ancient times are extremely difficult to reconstruct from material remains such as artifacts, art, and architecture. We can only guess at the beliefs and motivations behind late Ice Age cave art (see Chapter 4) or the celebrated plastered human portraits from the early farming settlement at Jericho, Jordan (see Chapter 9). But the study of ancient ideology and beliefs offers great potential when written records such as Egyptian documents or Maya glyphs can be combined with excavations (Figure 1.10). Intensive research combining deciphered hieroglyphs and archaeology is throwing new light on ancient Maya religious beliefs (summary in Coe, 2005) (see Chapter 21), on what are often called "ideologies of domination."

FIGURE 1.10   Harvesting and stomping grapes on a nobleman's estate—a mural from the Tomb of the scribe Menna, Thebes, Egypt, c. 1419–1380 B.C. Scenes such as this are an important amplification of the archaeological data from excavations and surveys.

Elites have used many tactics to exercise power over others, everything from gentle persuasion to divine kingship, precedent, economic monopolies, and naked force. The ancient Maya lords built great ceremonial centers with towering pyramids and vast plazas that were symbolic models of the sacred landscape—the Maya universe. Their pyramids were sacred mountains, the sites of sacred openings that were the threshold to the spiritual world of the ancestors. It was here that the ruler went into a shamanistic trance, communicating with the gods and ancestors in lavish public ceremonies. Everything validated the complex relationship between the living and the dead, and between the ruler and the commoner, displayed in lavish, pointed metaphors that confirmed the divine power of the supreme lords. Linda Schele and David Freidel wrote: "The Maya believed in a past which always returned . . . in endless cycles repeating patterns already set into the fabric of time and space. Our challenge . . . is to interpret this history, recorded in their words, images, and ruins, in a manner comprehensible to the modern mind, yet true to the Mayas' perception of themselves" (1988, p. 18).

Studying ancient beliefs, the intangibles of the past, can be likened to studying a series of pictures without the captions. Herein lies one of the great frustrations of archaeology. In looking at a giant bull from the 15,000-year-old frieze painted by Stone Age artists on the walls of Lascaux Cave in southwestern France (see Figure 4.10) or tracing the intricate engraving on a freshwater shell from the Mississippian culture of the southeastern United States (see Chapter 13), we can admire the artistry behind the image, but we can only rarely discern the complex beliefs and motives behind these magnificent achievements. We cannot speak to the ancients; we can only seek to understand some of the brilliant, and often frustrating, complexity of their diverse societies.

The most powerful new explanations of major developments in human prehistory will undoubtedly come from a combination of both processual and post-processual approaches, such as those being used with success with Mississippian chiefdoms in North America, with Maya civilization, and in Southeast Asia.

World prehistory is, in the final analysis, the study of unfolding human diversity in the context of four major developments: the origins and early evolution of Archaic humans, the emergence and spread of anatomically modern humans (ourselves after about 150,000 years ago), the beginnings of agriculture and animal domestication (food production), and the appearance of literate civilization. Steven Mithen (1996) has likened the long millennia of human existence to an archaeological play with several acts that reaches a climax with the appearance of farming a mere 10,000 years ago. In ten short millennia, humanity has moved from a simple village existence into a world of automobiles, aircraft, vast industrial cities, and an emerging global computerized society. *People of the Earth* presents most of this play, ending with the Spanish Conquest of Mexico and Peru, the climactic encounter between Westerners and the last of the preindustrial civilizations in the early sixteenth century A.D.

The actors are in the wings, the curtain is about to rise, and the inexorable stream of time is already flowing. Let the play commence!

Summary

- Archaeology is the study of the cultural evolution of human-kind, using the material remains of past human behavior. These material remains make up the archaeological record, the archives of the human past.

- Whereas historians study written records, archaeologists deal with an anonymous past. Archaeology is unique among the sciences in its ability to study culture change over long periods of time.

- Text-aided archaeology combines the evidence of archaeology with documentary sources, whereas prehistoric archaeology is the study of prehistory, the period of the human past before written records.

- The study of world prehistory, which developed in the 1950s, is the study of prehistory from a global perspective using archaeology and other sources.

- All human societies are interested in the past, but they think of it in different terms and use it for different purposes. Archaeologists, Westerners generally, conceive of time in a linear way, whereas many non-Western groups measure time by the cycles of the seasons and the movements of heavenly bodies. They use linear time only when it is of use to them.

- Archaeology is not the only way of approaching history, for many societies have oral histories, alternative perspectives on the past that are of vital importance in preserving traditional culture and values.

- Theoretical approaches to human prehistory abound, but they can be divided, in general terms, into processual and post-processual approaches.

- The processual (culture as adaptation) approach uses multi-linear cultural evolution and cultural ecology to provide a viable general framework for studying world prehistory, based on the assumption that human societies evolved in many diverse ways. Archaeologists conventionally make a distinction between prestate and state-organized societies as part of this framework.

- Evolutionary ecology makes use of the mechanism of natural selection and optimal foraging strategy to interpret hunter-gatherer societies in terms of energy costs and risk management.

- In recent years, archaeologists have distinguished between external constraints on culture change, such as environmental factors, and internal constraints, created by the actions of individuals and groups.

- A new generation of research is focusing on ideologies, human interactions, gender relations, and other topics, combining processual and post-processual approaches to study both types of constraints and their influences on the past.

Key Terms

anthropology (2)
archaeological record (3)
archaeology (3)
bands (13)
chiefdoms (13)
clans (13)
contingency model (15)
cultural ecology (13)
cultural process (10)
cultural resource management (CRM) (6)
cultural system (10)
culture (10)
culture as adaptation approach (12)

dendrochronology (7)
diffusion (11)
elites (19)
evolutionary ecology (14)
exchange systems (18)
foraging (15)
history (3)
invention (11)
midden (3)
migration (11)
multilinear cultural evolution (13)
optimal foraging strategy (15)
oral tradition (9)
pollen analysis (12)

post-processual archaeology (16)
potassium-argon dating (7)
prehistoric archaeology (4)
prehistory (4)
prestate societies (13)
prey model (15)
process (11)
radiocarbon (^{14}C) dating (6)
state-organized societies (civilizations) (13)
text-aided archaeology (4)
tribes (13)
uniformitarianism (4)
unilinear cultural evolution (13)
world prehistory (4)

Further Reading

Fagan, Brian M. 2005. *A Brief History of Archaeology*. Upper Saddle River, NJ: Prentice Hall.

Johnson, Matthew. 2010. *Archaeological Theory*, 2nd ed. New York: Willey/Blackwell.

Trigger, Bruce G. 2006. *A History of Archaeological Thought*, 2nd ed. Cambridge, MA: Cambridge University Press.

BEGINNINGS

7 MILLION TO 150,000 YEARS AGO

Six million years is a vast span of time. In order to begin to comprehend it, to grasp its salient pattern of events, it helps to think of those events as constituting a play, a drama of our past. A very special play, for no one wrote the script: 6 million years of improvisation. Our ancestors are the actors, their tools are the props and the incessant changes of environment through which they lived the changes of scenery. But as a play do not think of it as a "whodunit," in which action and ending are all. For we already know the ending—we are living it. The . . . Stone Age actors all died out leaving just one single survivor, Homo sapiens.

Steven Mithen, *Prehistory of the Mind* (1996)

Part I comprises two chapters. Chapter 2 describes the earliest stages of human evolution and the emergence of the first toolmaking hominins in tropical Africa some 2.6 million years ago. Chapter 3 begins with the appearance of *Homo erectus*, an archaic but true human, and traces the spread of these people throughout the Old World. The chapter ends with the Old World. The chapter ends with the Neanderthals and their relatives who flourished over a wide area of Europe, Eurasia, and the Near East 150,000 years ago.

Beginnings Timeline

Period already covered

Period covered in Part I

Partial coverage

| 5 mya | 2.5 mya | 1 mya | 150,000 B.P. | 10000 B.C. | A.D. 1 | A.D. 1500 |

FIG. 2.2

FIG. 3.1a

2 Human Origins

7 MILLION TO 1.9 MILLION YEARS AGO

It was a blazing hot day at Olduvai Gorge, East Africa, in 1959. Back in camp, Louis Leakey lay in his tent, suffering from a bout of influenza. Meanwhile, Mary Leakey, sheltered by a beach umbrella, was excavating the small scatter of broken bones and crude artifacts deep in the gorge. For hours she brushed and pried away dry soil. Suddenly, she unearthed part of an upper jaw with teeth so humanlike that she took a closer look. Moments later, she jumped into her Land Rover and sped up the track to camp. "Louis, Louis!" she cried, as she burst into their tent, "I've found Dear Boy at last." Louis leapt out of bed, his flu forgotten. Together, they excavated the fragmentary remains of a magnificent robust hominin skull. The Leakeys named it *Zinjanthropus boisei*[1] ("African human of Boise"), a Mr. Boise being one of their benefactors. With this dramatic discovery, they changed the study of human evolution from a part-time science into an international detective story (Figure 2.1).

Artist's reconstruction of *Australopithecus afarensis* walking on soft volcanic ash at Laetoli, Tanzania, c. 3.6 million years ago.

---

[1]Now known as *Australopithecus boisei*.

24

Not that the search for human origins began with the Leakeys. As long ago as 1863, the great Victorian naturalist Thomas Huxley called it the "question of questions," the nature of the exact relationship between humans and their closest living relatives such as the chimpanzee and the gorilla. Ever since his day, scientists have been locked in controversy as they trace the complex evolutionary history of humanity back to its very beginnings (Table 2.1).

The Great Ice Age

The story of humanity begins deep in geologic time, during the later part of the Cenozoic era—the Age of Mammals (Table 2.2). For most of geologic time, the world's climate was warmer and more homogeneous than it is today. During the Oligocene epoch, some 35 million years ago (mya), the first signs of glacial cooling appeared with the formation of a belt of pack ice around Antarctica (Maslin, 2009a). World temperatures dropped considerably between 14 and 11 mya. As temperatures lowered, glaciers formed on high ground in high latitudes. About 3.2 mya, large ice sheets formed on the northern continents, locking up enough water to lower world sea levels by about 40 m (130 feet). Then, about 2.5 mya, glaciation intensified still more and the earth entered its present period of a constantly fluctuating climate. These changes culminated during the **Pleistocene** epoch, the most recent interval of earth history, which began about 1.6 mya. This epoch is sometimes called the age of humanity, for it was during this time that human beings first populated most of the globe (see Table 2.3). The major climate and environmental changes that took place during the Pleistocene were the backdrop for some of the most important stages in human evolution.

The Pleistocene epoch had constant fluctuations between warm and intensely cold global climates (Maslin, 2009b). For long stretches of time, the northern parts of Europe and North America were mantled with great ice sheets, the last retreating only some 15,000 years ago. There have been at least nine of these glacial periods during the last 780,000 years, which is why the Pleistocene is sometimes called the Great Ice Age. Interglacials, with climates as warm as or warmer than that of today, were rare, and the constant changes repeatedly displaced plants and animals from their original habitats (O'Regan, 2009). During colder cycles, plants and animals usually fared better at lower altitudes and in warmer latitudes. Populations of animals spread slowly toward more hospitable areas, mixing with populations that already lived there and creating new communities with new combinations of organisms. This repeated mixing surely affected the direction of evolution in

FIGURE 2.1 Louis and Mary Leakey examining fragments of *Zinjanthropus* (*Australopithecus*) *boisei* soon after its discovery.

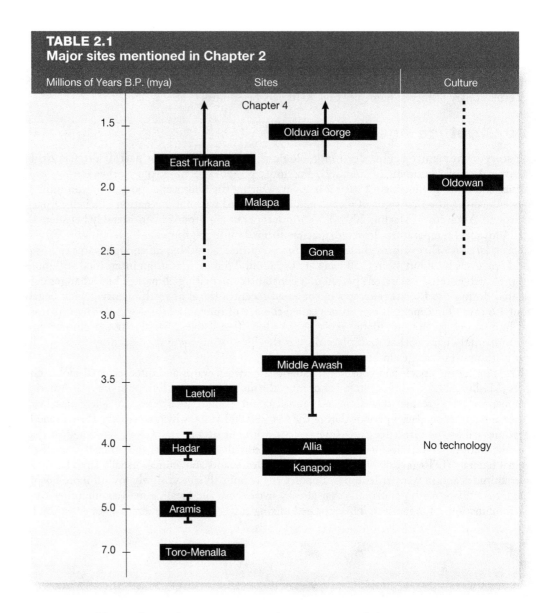

**TABLE 2.1
Major sites mentioned in Chapter 2**

Millions of Years B.P. (mya)	Sites	Culture

many ways. No one knows how many mammal species emerged during the Pleistocene, although paleontologist Björn Kurtén once estimated that no fewer than 113 of the mammal species now living in Europe and adjacent Asia have appeared during the past 3 million years.

Deep-sea cores lifted from the depths of the world's oceans and glacial ice cores from the Antarctic and Greenland ice sheets have revealed a complex picture of Pleistocene climate. These cores have shown that climatic fluctuations between warm and cold were relatively minor until about 800,000 years ago. Since then, periods of intense cold have recurred about every 100,000 years, with minor oscillations about 20,000 and 40,000 years apart (Petit et al., 1999). Many scientists believe that these changes are triggered by long-term astronomical changes, especially in the earth's orbit around the sun (MacDougall, 2004), which affect the seasonal and north–south variations of solar radiation received by the earth.

The earliest chapter of human evolution unfolded during a period of relatively minor climatic change—indeed, before the Pleistocene truly began. Between 4 and 2 mya, the world climate was somewhat warmer and more stable than it was in later times, and the African savanna, the probable homeland of humankind, contained many species of mammals, large and small, including a great variety of the order of primates, of which we humans are a part. (Details of later Pleistocene climatic change are discussed in Chapters 3, 4, and 5; see also Table 2.3.)

The Origins of the Human Line

All of us are members of the order **Primates**, which includes most tree-living placental mammals (Stringer and Andrews, 2011). There are two suborders: **anthropoids** (apes, humans, and monkeys) and **prosimians** (lemurs, tarsiers, and other "premonkeys"). The research of more

TABLE 2.2
Geological epochs from more than 60 million years ago

The curve demonstrates relative temperature changes on earth since the late Miocene.
Notice that the general trend is toward cooler temperatures with more frequent fluctuations.
(Pleistocene temperatures are shown in Table 2.3.)

Millions of Years B.P.	Geological Epochs	Global Temperatures ←— Lower Higher —→	Developments
2	Holocene		Human evolution
3	Pleistocene		Hominoid radiation
	Pliocene		
10			Many new mammal species
	Miocene		
20			
	Oligocene		
30	Eocene		Expansion of mammals
40			
50			
60			
	Paleocene		

CENOZOIC ERA

than a century has shown that the many similarities in behavior and physical characteristics between the **hominins** (primates of the family **Hominidae**, which includes modern humans, earlier human subspecies, and their direct ancestors) and the **ponginae** (our closest living primate relatives) can be explained by identical characteristics that each group inherited millions of years ago from a common ancestor (C. Chapman, 2004). (For an overview of human development covered in Parts II and III, see Table 2.4.)

The questions are: When did humankind separate from the nonhuman primates, and how do we define the genus *Homo*? N. ?

Aegyptopithecus

During the Oligocene, some 35 to 30 mya, large bands of small fruit-eating primates, known to paleontologists as *Aegyptopithecus zeuxis*, trooped through the lush, wet forests of the Nile Valley. Elwyn Simons (1992) has found their jawbones and skulls near the Faiyum Depression west of the Nile. These creatures were no larger than a fox and weighed no more than 4 to 4.5 kg (9 to 10 pounds). Their brains were small, but the visual cortex was well developed, good eyesight being a characteristic of primates. The bones bear some resemblance to those of later primates in East Africa dating to the Miocene epoch, which lasted from 23.5 to 5.2 mya. It was in Africa that apes and humans diverged from the monkeys, but no one knows when this divergence took place (Figure 2.2).

Seventeen mya the world looked very different from what it is today. New mountain ranges like the Alps formed, and the climate became cooler as atmospheric and oceanic circulation patterns changed. Continental drift linked Africa and Arabia with Europe and Asia. Hitherto, they had

TABLE 2.3
Geological events, climatic changes, and chronology during the Pleistocene (highly simplified), with approximate dates

Temperature Lower → Higher	Date (B.C.)	Epochs	Glaciations/Interglacial in Europe	Developments in Prehistory
		Holocene	Holocene	Origins of states
	10000			First food production
	18000		Weichsel Glaciation	First settlement of Americas
				Cro-Magnons in Europe
	40000			First settlement of Australia
				Radiation of modern humans
	118000		Eemian	Origins of *Homo sapiens*
	128000		Saale Glaciation	
		PLEISTOCENE		Archaic *Homo sapiens*
Uncertain climatic detail	500000		Uncertain climatic detail	
				Homo heidelbergensis
	780000			
	1.6 million			
		Pliocene		*Homo erectus*
				Homo habilis
				Australopithecus

been separated by sea. As a result, previously separated animal species came into contact via the new land bridges, which led them into new habitats.

Miocene Primates

During the initial stages of their evolution, apes were apparently restricted to the African continent. The oldest known African apes date to about 23 mya. Hominoids were almost entirely restricted to Africa, where they are known from Ethiopia to Namibia in the far southwest. At the time, Africa was covered by huge expanses of forest and moist woodland, where dozens of genera of monkeys and apes flourished. They are often called **dental apes, hominoids** with apelike teeth but with monkeylike bodies. These apes were small bodied compared with modern apes and walked on the soles of their feet instead of on their knuckles. Such apes were abundant and diverse in East Africa, ranging in size from small forms weighing as little as 3 kg (7 pounds) to species that were about as heavy as a modern-day female gorilla (Benefit and McCrossin, 1995). The best known is *Proconsul*, which lived about 20 to 18 mya, but a 20.6 mya ape, *Morotopithecus bishopi*, from Moroto in Uganda, unlike *Proconsul*, possessed the anatomy that one associates with brachiating—swinging from branch to branch, a behavior typical of modern apes (MacLatchy et al., 2000).

Around 14 mya, Africa's climate became much drier, a time when molecular evidence shows that African great apes and the human line diverged from Asian great apes. One Middle Miocene hominoid, *Kenyapithecus*, practiced a simple form of knuckle walking (see Figure 2.3) and was the first to descend to the ground. Between 15 and 12 mya, hard fruit- and grass seed-eating species like *Kenyapithecus*, apes with large molars, flourished throughout eastern Africa.

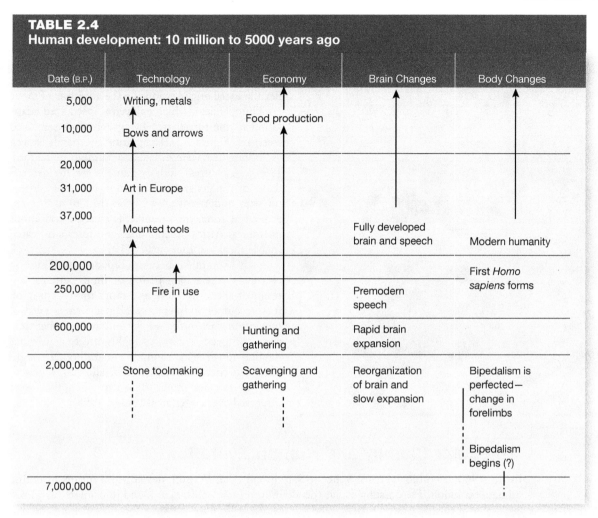

TABLE 2.4
Human development: 10 million to 5000 years ago

Date (B.P.)	Technology	Economy	Brain Changes	Body Changes
5,000	Writing, metals	Food production		
10,000	Bows and arrows			
20,000				
31,000	Art in Europe			
37,000				
	Mounted tools		Fully developed brain and speech	Modern humanity
200,000				First *Homo sapiens* forms
250,000	Fire in use		Premodern speech	
600,000		Hunting and gathering	Rapid brain expansion	
2,000,000	Stone toolmaking	Scavenging and gathering	Reorganization of brain and slow expansion	Bipedalism is perfected— change in forelimbs
				Bipedalism begins (?)
7,000,000				

These Miocene hominoids (Hominoidia) appear not to have been members of the modern ape and human branch of the evolutionary tree. *Kenyapithecus* walked on four feet and was semiterrestrial. These characteristics suggest that a transition from life in the trees to life on the ground had begun long before open savanna spread throughout eastern Africa in later times. Unfortunately, the almost complete lack of fossils between 11 and 5 mya means that we have no transitional forms between the quadrupedal *Kenyapithecus* and bipedal humans and knuckle-walking apes like gorillas and chimpanzees. A lower jawbone and 11 teeth of a 10 mya ape have recently been found on the east side of Kenya's Rift Valley, belonging to a new species: *Nakalipithecus nakayamai*, perhaps a close relative of the common ancestor of gorillas, chimpanzees, and humans.

The basic anatomical pattern of the large hominoids appeared in the Middle Miocene, 18 to 12 mya. One lineage of these hominoids has survived in modified form as the modern orang (Pilbeam, 1986). A second radiation began in the Late Miocene, between 8 and 5 mya. This radiation eventually produced four lineages, at least one of which, human beings, has been modified considerably. These evolutionary patterns have resulted from changing climates and habitats— from warmer, less seasonal, more forested environments to colder, more seasonal, and less forested conditions. Such changes have occurred throughout the past 25 million years, but there were major, pulselike shifts between 17 and 14 mya and again between 8 and 5 mya. These reflected changes in the configuration of continents, mountain systems, and Antarctic ice (Foley, 1995). The likelihood is that the critical evolutionary radiation that produced the hominin line occurred in Africa.

In the absence of key fossils, we can only speculate about the nature of the apelike animals that formed the hominoid segment during these millennia (Benefit and McCrossin, 1995). David Pilbeam (1986) has used existing fossils and evolutionary theory, as well as molecular biology, to guess—he can do no more—that these animals were mostly tree living, with long arms and legs and a broad chest. They would have used all four limbs in the trees, occasionally scrambling on the ground and even standing on their rear limbs at times. There was a marked difference in size between males and females, females perhaps weighing around 20 kg (44 pounds), males about double. At least one of the Late Miocene hominoid lineages led to the gorilla, a much larger, more terrestrial form.

FIGURE 2.2 Reconstruction of *Aegyptopithecus*, a primate with the skeleton of an arboreal quadruped.

Pilbeam goes on to speculate that a later hominoid lineage divided into western and eastern parts in Africa at least 5 mya. The western segment, the "protochimpanzees," remained dependent on fruit and other tree foods, scattered resources that required a flexible social organization. To the ancestors of modern chimpanzees, which enjoyed a specialized adaptation to the forest, tree-living behaviors remained essential (Figure 2.3). Long arms and hands as well as grasping feet were still vital for climbing (Stanford, 1998). In contrast, today's humans are the descendants of the generalized common hominoid ancestor who underwent an adaptive shift to a different ecological zone, the savanna, as climatic conditions in tropical Africa became drier and forests retreated (deMenocal and Bloemendal, 1995).

Early hominins became **bipedal** (walking on two feet) over a long period of time, perhaps as a result of spending more and more time feeding on food resources on the ground. Bipedalism is a way of moving that is configured for endurance rather than power or speed. Walking is highly effective for wide-ranging foraging or running a marathon. It might have had social advantages too, allowing males to monitor females more efficiently when they were dispersed over larger areas (Foley, 1995).

Molecular Biology and Human Evolution

In the 1960s, two biochemists, Vincent Sarich and Alan Wilson, developed a means of dating primate evolution. They assumed that the albumin protein substances found in primate blood had evolved at a constant rate (Sarich, 1983). Thus, the difference between the albumins of any pair of primates could be used to calculate the time that had elapsed since they had separated. Sarich and Wilson showed that the albumins of apes and humans are more similar than those of monkeys and humans. Thus, they argued, apes and humans have a more recent common ancestry. They estimated that chimpanzees and humans last shared a common ancestor about 5 to 6 mya.

A generation of research since then had refined the molecular clock using changes in beta globulin genes, whose rate of change appears to be different among some primate lineages. This phylogeny, developed by Morris Goodman (1999), dates the split between monkeys and apes to 25 mya and the split between the greater and lesser apes to about 17 mya. Gorillas split from the chimpanzee-human branch about 8 mya and the human line and chimpanzees about 7 to 8 million years before present (R. D. Wilkinson et al. 2010) (Figure 2.4). This molecular chronology places all known hominins to dates after the split off from chimpanzees.

The new studies confirm that African apes and humans are similar, orangs roughly twice as distant, and gibbons a bit more dissimilar than orangs. Chimpanzees share more than 99 percent of their genetic material with humans, even though it is packaged in their chromosomes in a different way. The precise relationships between any genetic differences and the geologic timescale are still uncertain and are the subject of much discussion (Cavalli-Sforza and Cavalli-Sforza, 1995).

We are unlikely to achieve a greater understanding of very early human evolution unless we discover hominoid fossils dating to between 10 and 5 mya. These 5 million years were a period of major environmental change. As recently as 5.5 mya, the Mediterranean basin dried up when it became separated from the Atlantic. This development must have had major effects on the climate and ecology of Africa, as well as on the evolution of many species. That such an evolution took place seems certain. During this critical period, many mammal species, as well as specialized tree-dwellers and other primates, inhabited the African savanna with its residual forests and extensive grassland plains (Vrba et al., 1995). Both the chimpanzee and the gorilla evolved in the forests, surviving from earlier times. On savanna plains, other primates were flourishing in small bands, probably walking upright and conceivably making tools. No fossil remains of these creatures have been found, so

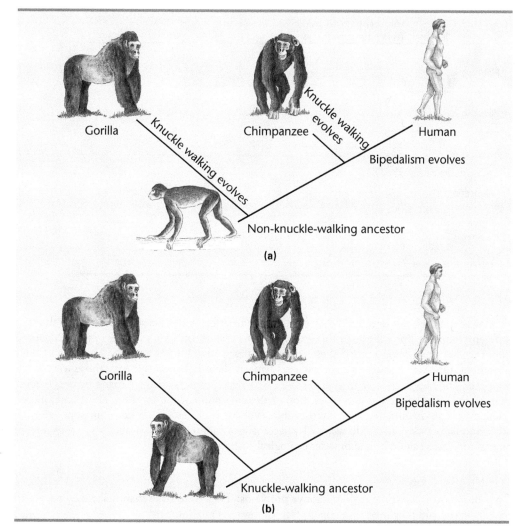

FIGURE 2.3 Bipedalism and four-footed posture. Two major theories account for the evolution of bipedalism. (a) If the last common ancestor of chimpanzees, gorillas, and humans was not a knuckle walker (the body's center of gravity lies in the middle of the area bounded by legs and arms), then knuckle walking would have evolved independently in both chimpanzees and gorillas. Under this theory, the ancestral locomotion for humans was not knuckle walking. (b) If the last common ancestor for chimpanzees, gorillas, and humans was a knuckle walker, then the ancestral condition for humans is knuckle walking. Humans are bipedal, where the body's center of gravity is displaced much less, and thus walking is much more efficient.

we do not know when primates first achieved the bipedal posture that is the outstanding hominin physical feature. We can, however, provide models of some of the ecological problems our earliest ancestors encountered.

The Ecological Problems Faced by Early Hominins

The evolutionary process is based on selection and other processes (Foley, 1984a, 1987a, 1995). For example, one can consider the emergence of the first humans in terms of adaptive evolutionary change. Organisms are mostly in balance with their environment. Mutations are the original source of variation in a population. They occur constantly and consistently, providing a reservoir of new variation. It is this variation, always present in a population that occasionally provides significant advantages to some individuals, especially during ecological transitions. Thus, a minority of the members of a population may increase their numbers through time because they have a selective advantage. As far as the behavioral evolution of the hominins is concerned, this process gives a model of terrestrial primates living in the increasingly dry environments of tropical Africa. In one hominin group, mutations led to adaptive shifts over several million years: bipedalism, toolmaking, meat eating, and so on. These shifts put the group at an advantage over other terrestrial primates.

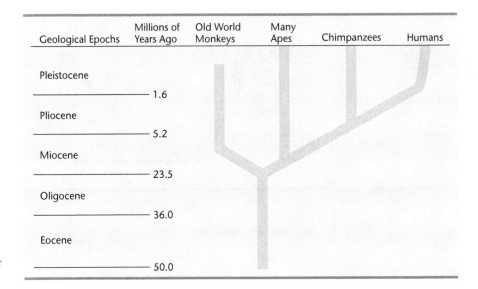

FIGURE 2.4 A much-simplified version of how Old World monkeys, apes, and humans evolved. For later human evolution, see Figure 2.10.

New adaptations are selected if they solve problems effectively. The selective agent is the organism's environmental problems. In this scenario, the characteristics of a hunter-gatherer adaptation would persist among hominins if these characteristics were solutions to problems faced in the environment. One viewpoint sees a species' problems as the other species it eats, those with which it competes, and those that eat it. In other words, an evolutionary advance made by one species in an ecosystem can be seen as a deterioration of the environment for another. Thus, environmental problems are not inanimate forces but dynamic, evolving processes. Early hominin populations, like other animal populations, underwent adaptive changes through natural selection to solve environmental problems caused by the broader ecological community.

Adaptive Problems

Early hominins faced three major adaptive problems: They were large mammals; they were terrestrial primates; and they lived in an open, tropical savanna environment.

Being Large Mammals Human beings are large relative to most warm-blooded animals. Hominins have become larger through their evolutionary history, a change that has led to additional food requirements because of higher metabolic rates. Thus, every individual has to range efficiently over a larger area to obtain food. Population densities must fall because the **carrying capacity** of any territory is finite. An increase in dietary breadth results. Hunter-gatherers use a wider range of foods, many of lower quality, than do some smaller nonhuman primates, often because these people are living close to the carrying capacity of the land.

Larger mammals are more mobile than their smaller relatives. They cover more ground, so they can subsist off resources that are unevenly distributed not only in space but also at different seasons. Mobility allows larger-bodied animals to incorporate unpredictable, often seasonal, resources in their diets. Larger mammals can also tolerate extremes of heat and cold, a capacity that may have contributed to the expansion of humans out of tropical latitudes later in prehistory. Humans have sweat glands and are heavily dependent on water supplies. These glands are a direct adjunct to bipedalism, for they enhance endurance for long-distance foraging. Efficient sweating aided early hominins because both large and small animals are at a disadvantage if attacked at high noon (Tattersall, 1996).

These and several other factors, such as increased longevity and brain enlargement, created adaptive problems for emerging humans. These problems resulted in a variety of solutions: wider territorial ranges, the need to schedule food gathering, broadening of the diet, a high degree of mobility, and much greater behavioral flexibility. This flexibility included enhanced intelligence and learning capacity, parental care, and new levels of social interaction (R. Potts, 1996).

Being Terrestrial Primates An upright posture and a bipedal gait are the most characteristic hominin physical features. Upright posture is vital because it frees the hands for other actions, like toolmaking. **Knuckle walking**—used, for instance, by chimpanzees—is a specialized way of walking in which the backs of the fingers are placed on the ground and act as main weight-bearing surfaces (Goodall, 1986). Human arms are too short for us to be comfortable with this posture, used by football linemen and runners at the starting block. However, this posture is highly adaptive in forest environments, where apes jump into trees and need the power of a fast, short sprint. In contrast, bipedalism favors endurance and the covering of long distances, important considerations on the open savanna. Bipedalism was a critical antecedent of both hunting and gathering and toolmaking (Aiello and Dean, 1990) (see Figure 2.3).

The fall in temperatures during the Late Miocene resulted in increasingly open environments in tropical latitudes. With this reduction in forested environments there probably came a trend toward terrestrially adapted species. The main constraint on arboreal primates is body size. Thus, to be part of the general trend toward larger body size among mammals, such primates would have to be at least partially terrestrial in their habits. Some 40 or more extinct and living primates, including the hominins, have adapted to a terrestrial existence. This secondary adaptation among tree-living forms may have occurred some time after 10 mya; expressed in the simplest terms, primates "came down from the trees" (Foley, 1995; Tattersall, 1996). The apes that stayed in the forest barely changed; they are the ancestors of today's chimpanzees. Those that ventured into newly formed habitats of dry grassland took the first step toward becoming human.

Coming down from the trees created three immediate problems: Locomotion difficulties arise for animals with limbs that are adapted for moving through forests and thus are less efficient for moving on the ground. All terrestrial primates underwent some modification of their way of getting about—in the case of hominins, a shift to bipedalism. We know that this selection was a powerful one. It was in existence over 4.5 mya.

Shelter becomes an acute problem in open country, where predators abound. Arboreal primates have special sleeping areas and are safe in the trees. Those adapted to living in open country return to trees at night or use cliff faces or caves, even if they have to disperse. Large hominins, which were safer from predators, made ground nests, where they slept and also sought shade on hot days—"home bases." Exactly what form these home bases took is a matter of constant scientific debate.

Competition for food was another pressing problem for primates that required high-quality plant food, abundant in the forests. Such foods were dispersed widely in open country. There were two possible solutions: to specialize in a small spectrum of plant foods and become an effective competitor, or to maintain a broad dietary niche and expand the range of foods consumed. It is striking that such a broad-based niche is characteristic of later hunter-gatherers in tropical environments. And as part of human evolution, hominins expanded their food range to include meat. Bipedal posture is also valuable for feeding off edible fruit from the ground.

Living in a Savanna Environment Although there are hints that the earliest hominins evolved in environments more wooded than the dry grasslands of East Africa today, the increase in drier grasslands and woodland presented another set of challenging problems. Water supplies are certain to be restricted in distribution and by season, a critical environmental reality for hominins, who need regular access to water. The distributions of water and of hominin populations are closely connected. Further, plant foods in a savanna are of lower quality, and early hominins had to compete for them with other animals.

Most plant species were seasonal and of low productivity, so a great deal of time would have been expended in searching for them. A whole range of species would have been needed to ensure year-round food supplies. Most plant species that do occur in the savanna are grasses, which are largely unsuitable for primates but not for a diverse population of herbivores. This secondary biomass of animals could have been a valuable walking food source if the hominins found a way of tapping it. But there were competitors—a great diversity of predators—that would also have eaten an occasional hominin if the opportunity arose.

The long-term solutions to living in the savanna centered on an adaptation that involved exploiting a broad but patchy subsistence base. The lifeway was highly mobile, the range dependent on restricted water supplies. Meat became a larger part of the diet as a way of coping with long periods of plant scarcity. Among mammal species, these characteristics are associated with a trend toward larger brain size (Fleagle, 1988). The earliest hominins lived at relatively low population densities. Their home ranges were larger than those of equivalent-sized mammals and primates; and they were highly mobile and omnivorous. This very general description coincides, in general terms, with that of human subsistence throughout most of prehistory.

If the ecological model is on track in assuming that this lifeway evolved in response to selective pressures in the open savanna more than 2 mya, were the hominins of 2 mya true hunters and gatherers? Or were they far more apelike in behavior than their successors? Before exploring this question, we must examine the fossil evidence (see Dating the Past box).

Dating the Past Potassium-Argon Dating

The world's first archaeological sites are so ancient that they lie far beyond the chronological range of radiocarbon dating (see Chapter 1). We are fortunate that a radioactive counting technique known as potassium-argon dating allows the dating of volcanic rocks between 2 billion and 100,000 years old. Many of the earliest hominin sites are in volcanically active areas. Human tools are found in direct association with cooled lava fragments or ash from contemporary eruptions, allowing the dating of the East Turkana locations: Olduvai Gorge and other famous early sites.

This well-established dating method is based on potassium (K), an abundant element in the earth's crust present in nearly every mineral. Potassium in its natural form contains only a small proportion of radioactive potassium-40 (^{40}K) atoms. For every 100 ^{40}K atoms that decay, 11 percent become argon-40, an inert gas that can easily escape from its material by diffusion when lava and other igneous rocks are formed. As volcanic rock forms by crystallization, the argon-40 concentration drops to almost nothing, but the process of ^{40}K decay continues. Thus, it is possible, using a spectrometer, to measure the concentration of argon-40 that has accumulated since the volcanic rock formed.

Potassium-argon dates come from many igneous minerals, among them biotite and muscovite. The rocks are crusted, concentrated, and treated with hydrofluoric acid to remove atmospheric argon from the sample. The various gases are then removed, and the argon gas is isolated and subjected to mass spectrographic analysis. The age of the sample is then calculated by use of the argon-40 and potassium-40 content and a standard formula. The resulting dates have large standard deviations—for early human sites, on the order of a quarter million years.

Recent advances in potassium-argon dating involve computerized laser fusion, a variant of the method that uses a laser beam to analyze irradiated grains of volcanic ash that give off a gas that is purified; this gas's constituent argon atoms are then measured in a spectrometer. The new method—somewhat akin to accelerator mass spectrometry (AMS) radiocarbon dating (see the box "Accelerator Mass Spectrometry (AMS) Radiocarbon Dating" in Chapter 8)— uses crystals of volcanic materials from layers associated with hominin fossils to produce much more accurate dates, like recent readings of about 3.18 million years for Lucy, *Australopithecus afarensis*. Computerized laser fusion has also produced controversial dates for the first human settlement of Southeast Asia of about 1.8 mya (see Chapter 3).

Potassium-argon dating has provided the first relatively reliable method of establishing the chronology of the earliest stages of human evolution and for the first human cultures on earth. Other methods used for early sites include paleomagnetism and fission-track dating.

Fossil Evidence: 7 to 4.0 mya

After 7 mya, molecular biology tells us, the last common ancestral hominoid stock split into two main lineages: the ancestors of chimpanzees and the ancestors of humans (see Figure 2.4). The details of this split remain a mystery, largely because fossil beds dating to this critical period are very rare in Africa.

A generation ago, people conceived of early human evolution as a simple ladder. Such simple schemes have now given way to highly tentative studies of early human evolution completed by reconstructing precise evolutionary relationships from fossil specimens, a process fraught with difficulty when bone fragments are the raw materials. It is a matter of fine and careful judgment, the weighing of anatomical details, the analysis of different characteristics, and the assessment of chronology and **stratigraphy** (Foley, 1995). The extremely thin fossil record between 7 and 1 mya, representing less than 1,500 individuals, compounds the problem. Most of these are single teeth found in fossil-rich South African caves. Very few are skull or jaw fragments, the most valuable of all fossil finds.

During this long period, our ancestors went through dramatic transformations, visible only through an incomplete paleontological lens. We know that many hominin forms flourished in tropical Africa during this period. Which of them, however, were direct human ancestors? We can only achieve an understanding of human evolution by getting to know as many species as we can, and this task has hardly begun. The summary of fossil hominins that follows is certain to be outdated within a few years. (For a guide through the many taxonomic labels and a basic chronology, see Table 2.5.)

Toumaï: *Sahelanthropus tchadensis*

Toro-Menalla
? 6–7 mya

The Toro-Menalla region of the Djurab Desert in Chad, Central Africa, is a brutal place for paleoanthropological research. Nevertheless, working there, French scholars Michel Brunet, Patrick Vignaud, and their colleagues have found a chimpanzee-sized skull of a hominin dated (albeit very loosely) to between 6 and 7 million years old (Brunet et al., 2002). The cranium is confusing. From the back, the skull looks like that of a chimpanzee. From the front, the facial structure and tooth layout look like those of a hominin of about 1.75 mya, an Australopithecine (for a discussion

TABLE 2.5
Five tentative groups of East and South African hominins, much simplified for this book

Variables	Aramis/Allia Group	Hadar/Laetoli Group	Gracile Group	Robust Group	Homo Group
Brain size	Comparable to that of a chimpanzee	Comparable to that of a chimpanzee	450–550 cc	500–550 cc	650–775 cc
Teeth	Small back teeth; large front teeth	Small back teeth; large front teeth	Large front and back teeth	Very large back teeth; relatively small front teeth	Variable; generally smaller than those of robust and gracile forms
Limbs	Bipedal; long arms	Bipedal; arms slightly longer than those of *Homo sapiens*		Some elements of limb bones differ from those of modern humans	Bipedal, but lower limbs still partially adapted to arboreal life
Species and sites	*Ardipithecus ramidus* *Australopithecus anamensis* East Africa: Allia Bay, Kanapoi, Aramis	*Australopithecus afarensis* East Africa: Hadar and Laetoli	*Australopithecus sediba* *Australopithecus africanus* South Africa: Taung, Sterkfontein, Makapansgat East Africa: Omo? East Turkana	*Australopithecus robustus* South Africa: Swarkrans, Kromdraai *Australopithecus boisei* East Africa: Olduvai, East Turkana, Omo *Australopithecus aethiopicus* East Turkana	*Homo* East Africa: Olduvai and East Turkana South Africa: Sterkfontein
Dates	East Africa: c. 5 million to c. 4 million B.P.	East Africa: c. 4 million to c. 3 million B.P.	East Africa: c. 3 million to c. 1.5 million B.P. South Africa: no reliable dates	East Africa: c. 2.6 million to c. 1 million B.P. South Africa: no reliable dates	East Africa: c. 2 million to c. 1.5 million B.P.

of *Australopithecus*, see below). The point at the base of the skull where the neck muscles attach suggests that this creature walked upright. Brunet and his team have named this remarkable fossil *Sahelanthropus tchadensis* ("hominin of the Sahel, of Chad").

Sahelanthropus tchadensis

Sahelanthropus tchadensis confirms what many people have long believed. Hominin evolution was much more complicated than was suspected a generation ago. In all probability, a wide variety of apes, some with larger brains, flourished in tropical Africa between 8 and 5 mya, of which the Chad find is but one. At this early stage in research, paleoanthropologists are uncertain whether *S. tchadensis*, usually called Toumaï, "hope of life," is a hominin or an ape. Nor is it clear whether these creatures walked upright, despite three-dimensional computer reconstructions of the distorted skull (Zollikofer et al., 2005). Many believe Toumaï may be a very early hominin, perhaps even an ancestor of *Ardipithecus ramidus*, hominins known from Ethiopia after 5 mya (see the following). It is also possible that the date when the ancestors of humans split off from apes may have to be pushed back somewhat earlier. The finders of Toumaï readily admit that they still have not dated their find accurately, so this remarkable discovery may prove to be of somewhat different antiquity in the future. Whatever the ultimate status of Toumaï, the new find shows that very early human evolution took many routes, and was not a matter of simple linear development.

Many paleoanthropologists believe that East Africa was the main crucible of early human evolution, largely because this is the area that has yielded the greatest number of primordial hominins. (For an excellent summary of the fossil record, see T. D. White, 2002.) Five to 4 mya, the now desertic regions of Ethiopia and northern Kenya were open savanna grassland, and woodland, teeming with herds of antelope and other mammals that were hunted by both predators and our remote hominin ancestors. And it is here that some of the earliest known hominins have been found, among them *Orrorin tugenensis*, a still little known hominin, which lived about 6 mya, about the time when humans and apes split from one another. Its relationships to later forms remain unknown.

Orrorin tugenensis
? 6 mya

Ardipithecus ramidus

Aramis
4.5 mya
Ardipithecus ramidus

This hominin was found in a 4.4-million-year-old layer at Aramis in the arid Awash region of Ethiopia (Figure 2.5). Paleoanthropologist Tim White and his colleagues named their find *Ardipithecus ramidus* to distinguish it from later, and different, australopithecines. Over ten years of research pieced together the fragmentary remains (T. White et al., 2009). *Ardipithecus ramidus* was a small creature, with a much smaller brain than hominins that was about 20 percent the size of that of a modern human. It stood upright and had thin-enameled teeth and a skull closer to those of apes, with a prognathous face. The teeth are unspecialized and suggest that this hominin ate soft fruit and other plant foods. At the same time, the upper canines are less well developed than those of chimpanzees, perhaps hinting at less aggression than is commonplace among chimpanzees. *Ardipithecus* stood upright, with feet better adapted for walking than those of the chimpanzee, but probably moved around on four limbs while in the trees. At least nine more *Ardipithecus* individuals have recently come from As Duma in northern Ethiopia, dated to between 4.5 and 4.3 mya (Semaw et al., 2005). Even earlier individuals, dating to 5.7 to 5.8 mya, came to light in 2004; they have more apelike dentition and are classified as *Ardipithecus kadabba*. Kadabba has been called a possible ancestor to *Ardipithecus ramidus* and is considered a separate species (Haile-Selassie and WoldeGarbiel, 2009).

As Duma
4.5 to 1.3 mya

Ardipithecus ramidus apparently lived in more wooded terrain than many of its successors and must lie close to the first hominins to diverge from the African apes. The relationship between this hominin and chimpanzees is still unclear, for both lines evolved in divergent ways after splitting off from a still-unknown common ancestor. This is, perhaps, the basic grade from which later hominins such as *Australopithecus* evolved, but the precise relationship between *Ardipithecus* and later human ancestors remains still unclear.

The First Australopithecines: c. 4 to 3 mya

After hundreds of thousands of years, *Ardipithecus* in its various, as yet largely unknown, forms evolved into or gave way to the Australopithecines. The term *Australopithecus*, meaning "Southern Ape-person" was coined by anatomist Raymond Dart as the result of the discovery of an unusual hominin skull at Taung, South Africa, in 1924 (Dart, 1925). The term now covers a

FIGURE 2.5 Tentative reconstruction of *Ardipithecus ramidus*.

wide diversity of different hominids known collectively as Australopithecines, which we must now briefly describe in chronological order. (From here on we use *A* to designate *Australopithecus, when referring to different Australopithecines*. Likewise, H. refers to *Homo* [below].)

Australopithecus anamensis

A. anamensis (*anam* is "lake" in Turkana) is the name given to the complete upper and lower hominin jaws, some teeth, and limb fragments of almost 80 individuals from Allia Bay and Kanapoi on Lake Turkana, Kenya. These fossil finds date to about 4.2 to 3.9 mya (M. G. Leakey et al., 1995). The jaws display parallel sides, like those of apes, in contrast to human mandibles, which are wider in the back. The earholes are smaller and also more apelike. *A. anamensis* is a mosaic of apelike and humanlike anatomy, for the limbs are far more human looking. The hind limbs are thick enough to support the extra weight of walking on two feet. Measurements of the hind limb suggest the hominin weighed between 47 and 55 kg (104 and 121 pounds).

Allia Bay
4.10 mya
Australopithecus anamensis

A. anamensis was notably primitive anatomically, with less mobile hands than the later *A. afarensis*, but was fully bipedal. However, this hominin had short legs and was not as efficient a walker as modern humans.

Australopithecus afarensis

A. afarensis is best known from the Hadar region of Ethiopia and from the Laetoli site in Tanzania (Johanson and Edey, 1981). When Maurice Taieb and Donald Johanson discovered a remarkably complete skeleton of a small primate at Hadar, on the Awash River, they named it "Lucy." Lucy was only 1.0 to 1.2 m (3.5 to 4.0 feet) tall and 19 to 21 years old. Nearby, they found the remains of at least 13 males, females, and children. Lucy herself (or perhaps more rightly himself, as some currently argue) has recently been dated to 3.18 mya by means of a variant of potassium-argon dating that uses computerized argon laser fusion. Subsequently, other finds have filled in the incomplete portrait of *A. afarensis*. *A. afarensis* skull and arm bones from several other males have come from another Awash location about 1.5 km (1 mile) upstream; they date to about 3 mya, some 200,000 years later than Lucy (Kimball et al., 1994) (Figure 2.6). These finds hint that all the thousands of *A. afarensis* fragments found over the past 20 years are from a single australopithecine species, although some authorities challenge this assumption.

Hadar
3.5 to 3.0 mya

A. afarensis displays considerable variation in size. Some individuals stood 1.5 m (5 feet) tall and probably weighed approximately 68 kg (150 pounds), a far cry from the small, slender Lucy. These creatures, however, were powerful, heavily muscled individuals, thought to be as strong as chimpanzees. *A. afarensis* was an anatomical mosaic, bipedal from the waist down, arboreal in the upper part of the body. All were fully bipedal, with the robust, curved arms associated with tree climbers. In 2011, a 3.2 mya foot bone found near the original Lucy discovery shows that *afarensis* had arches in its feet, which added to nimble walking abilities. Their movement on two feet was probably very similar to that of modern humans (Ward et al., 2011). They had humanlike hands, except that their fingers were slightly more curved. The Hadar hominins had brains approximating the size of chimpanzee brains, ape-shaped heads, and forward-thrusting jaws. There is no evidence that they made tools, but the finds confirm the expansion of the brain beyond the level found in our nearest living relatives, the African apes. Their bipedalism implies that later hominins were preadapted (had evolved sufficiently) to utilize their hands for toolmaking. However, *A. afarensis* probably spent a considerable amount of time in trees, living as it did in wooded environments.

Australopithecus afarensis

Originally, experts thought *A. afarensis* was confined to East Africa. However, French paleontologist Michel Brunet has discovered a 3.0-million- to 3.5-million-year-old fossilized hominin jaw with seven teeth at Koto Toro in Chad, in the southern reaches of the Sahara. The Koto Toro hominin teeth bear a strong resemblance to those of *A. afarensis*. The Chad hominin flourished in a savanna–woodland environment, much wetter than the arid landscape of today (Brunet et al., 1995).

Koto Toro
3.5 to 3.0 mya

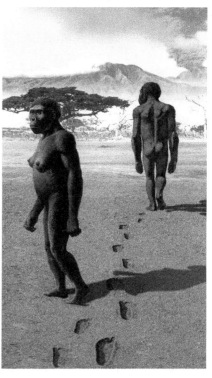

Koto Toro is the first australopithecine find west of East Africa's Rift Valley and debunks a long-held theory that the great valley formed a barrier separating ape populations and causing those in more open country to move from the trees onto the ground. The evolutionary picture was much more complex than that—witness the

FIGURE 2.6 Male and female *Australopithecus afarensis*.

discovery of a complete australopithecine skeleton that may also be *A. afarensis* at Sterkfontein in South Africa.

Many scientists consider *A. afarensis* a primitive form of the australopithecines, which displayed considerable anatomical variation yet was hardy enough to adapt to harsh, changing savanna environments and survive for nearly a million years.

Laetoli: Footprints of *A. afarensis*

Laetoli
3.75 to 3.59 mya

Dramatic confirmation of *A. afarensis* bipedalism comes from fossil-bearing beds at Laetoli in northern Tanzania, excavated by Mary Leakey and potassium-argon-dated to 3.75 to 3.59 mya. They have yielded not only the bones of extinct animals but also the incomplete jaws and teeth of at least 13 hominins, classified as *A. afarensis*. The footprints came from the buried bed of a seasonal river, where thin layers of fine volcanic ash once formed a pathway for animals traveling to water holes. The hardened surface of the ash, dated to more than 3.59 mya, bore the footprints of elephants, rhinoceroses, giraffes, a saber-toothed tiger, and many species of antelope. Mary Leakey also identified trails of prints of two hominins (Figure 2.7). "The tracks," she wrote, "indicate a rolling and probably slow-moving gait, with the hips swiveling at each step, as opposed to the free-striding gait of modern man" (M. D. Leakey and Harris, 1990: 74). The two hominin trails lay about 25 cm (10 inches) apart and probably had been laid down at different times. The feet display well-defined arches and distinctive heel and toe prints made by upright-walking individuals about 1.4 m (4 feet 7 inches) and 1.49 m (4 feet 11 inches) tall.

Australopithecus africanus
3 mya

Without question, however, there were several as yet largely unknown hominin forms that flourished in eastern Africa before 3 mya, perhaps the most widespread being *A. afarensis*.

Robust australopithecines
3 to 1 mya

Fossil Evidence: 3 to 2.5 mya

About 3 mya, at least half a dozen members of the genus *Australopithecus* flourished in tropical Africa, hominins who walked on two feet and navigated the open savanna with ease. What triggered this abrupt change is still unknown, but recently a gene called HAR (human accelerated region) has been discovered, which occurs in humans and in all kinds of animals from chimpanzees to chickens. Only two of its 118 chemical "letters" changed from 310 mya, when chickens and chimpanzees split from one another. However, 18 letters changed rapidly after humans split from chimpanzees. This high rate of change is a sign of a gene whose evolution keeps conferring advantages on those who carry it, perhaps starting with *Australopithecus*.

Somewhere around 3 mya, the descendants of *afarensis* split into lines. At this point, the evolutionary plot really thickens. One line comprised the more gracile *Australopithecus africanus*, first identified by Raymond Dart in 1924 and known entirely from South Africa, far from the putative East African cradle of humankind (Dart, 1925). The second line held at least three species of robustly built australopithecines, somewhat later than *africanus*, which became extinct about 1 mya. There are probably other, still undescribed lines. With this diversification, we emerge into a more complex chapter in human evolution, marked by geographic and biological diversification and many competing theories.

Gracile Australopithecines: *Australopithecus africanus*

A. africanus was a gracile, highly mobile hominin, marked in fossil form by small, almost delicate skulls and prognathous (jutting-out) faces (Figure 2.8, back). Found only in South Africa, *africanus* is an evolutionary mystery, for no one has yet found this form in East Africa, where *A. afarensis* flourished, even if it ultimately evolved from this widely distributed ancestor. It could be an evolutionary experiment that went nowhere, or even have been among the first of a doomed line of robust hominins.

Robust Australopithecines: *A. aethiopicus, A. boisei,* and *A. robustus*

The robust australopithecines, known by several taxonomic labels such as *Paranthropus robustus* or *Australopithecus robustus*, lived between 3 million and 1 mya. Found in both eastern and southern Africa, they are

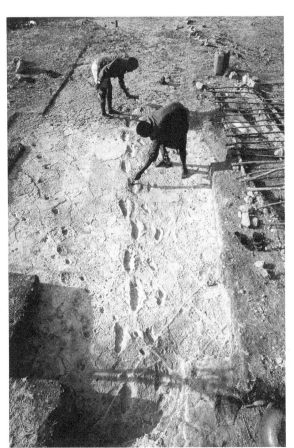

FIGURE 2.7 Hominin footprints from Laetoli, Tanzania.

remarkable for their heavy build (Figure 2.8, front). These hominins had small brains and large teeth that were specialized for chewing coarse, fibrous plant foods (McCollum, 1999). As a group, these squat, heavily built hominins were very diverse.

The shapes of the brains of *A. africanus* and *A. robustus* provide clues as to their organization. *A. robustus* has a teardrop-shaped brain, whereas *A. africanus* is more squared off, with a swooping shape on the bottom. This configuration probably means that *africanus* had a better developed area 10, which is the area of the brain that plays a major role in decision making, taking the initiative, and advance planning. This may be why *A. africanus* evolved whereas the robust australopithecines came to a dead end.

Australopithecus garhi

Two seemingly distinct branches of Australopithecines, yet a large-toothed, small-brained hominin with an apelike face defies classification within either the gracile or robust australopithecine lines. Working the arid washes of Ethiopia's Awash Desert, a team of 40 researchers from 13 countries unearthed teeth and skull fragments from yet another hominin form, dating to about 2.5 mya (Asfaw et al., 1999; de Heinzelin et al., 1999). The hominin, named *Australopithecus garhi* (*garhi* means "surprise" in the local dialect), stood about 1.46 m (4 feet 10 inches) tall and had protruding features, not unlike those of a chimpanzee. The lower molars are three times the size of those of modern humans, the canines almost as large. *A. garhi*'s brain was only a third the size of that of a modern human. The legs are long and humanlike, while the arms are long and more like an ape's. The hominin was an efficient scavenger. Bones of antelope and other large animals found only a few feet away display cut marks from stone tools, the earliest known instance of hominin butchery of animals. Unfortunately, no stone tools were found close to the fossil remains, but surface finds of crude stone flakes and cobbles have come from a nearby lake-bed level dating to about 2.5 mya. That this hominin was eating meat suggests that a switch to an at least partially high-energy, high-fat meat diet was under way. This, in turn, may have led to an increase in brain size among some hominins, which occurred only a few hundred thousand years later.

With its apparent toolmaking and meat-eating propensities, *A. garhi* could conceivably be the exclusive ancestor of the *Homo* family tree and technically the first human. No one, least of all Tim White, arguably the leading human paleontologist in the world, is prepared to make such a claim on so little fossil evidence. What we do know is that a far from robust australopithecine derived from *A. afarensis* survived until at least 2.5 mya. But whether this form participated in a rapid evolutionary transition or a series of transitions into an early form of *Homo* remains a mystery (Asfaw et al., 1999). We do know that major changes to the hominin skull and face occurred after 2.5 mya, many of them as a direct consequence of brain enlargement. New behavior patterns connected with obtaining more meat and marrow by using stone tools may have played a highly important role during what may have been a short, and highly critical, period of human evolution.

Genetics may also have advanced the brain's chemistry. A gene named PDYN began accumulating changes about 7 mya, soon after the first direct human ancestor appeared. This gene regulates the production of a molecule called prodynorphin, which has been likened to the brain's soup stock. Depending on what other ingredients are added, it can change into neurochemicals that underlie such qualities as behavior, memory, or perception. It is genomes that tell us what was involved in making language possible and in making human brains what they are today. Other factors are also involved, among them the combinations of genes active in the brain cortex, where higher thinking occurs in chimpanzees and humans. In people, the genes that influence how fast electrical signals jump from neuron to neuron are very active—those that affect how fast the brain processes information, those that enhance connections between cells and thus learning and memory, and those that promote brain growth. This pattern of brain activity appears to have emerged with *Australopithecus*.

FIGURE 2.8 Hominin skulls compared. In the back, a gracile *Australopithecus africanus*; in front, the massive cranium of *Australopithecus robustus*.

Australopithecus garhi
2.5 mya

Early *Homo*: 2.5 to 2.0 mya

Sometime around 2 to 1.8 mya, early forms of the genus *Homo* appeared, marked by larger brains, generally smaller jaws and teeth, and other features that seem to foreshadow modern human crania. (For details, see Aiello and Anton, 2011.) Perhaps they were descendants of a hominin somewhat

FIGURE 2.9 A tentative reconstruction of Skull 1470 from East Turkana, Kenya. This early *Homo* cranium is remarkable for its large capacity and rounded back.

Homo habilis
2.0 mya

like *A. garhi*—no fossils yet document such a relationship. These hominins had longer legs, shorter arms, and more dexterous hands with a larger, opposed thumb. Body size tended to increase; **sexual dimorphism** became less marked. These changes coincided in general terms with the first appearance of stone tools. At least three forms of early *Homo* may have flourished at the time, probably more—*Homo habilis*, *Homo rudolfensis*, and *Homo ergaster*, the latter sometimes considered to be a form of *Homo erectus* (see Chapter 3).

Homo habilis

Louis and Mary Leakey were the first to identify the first hominin that was classified as early *Homo*—at Olduvai Gorge in 1960. They named their fragmentary discovery *H. habilis*, "Handy Person," a label that commemorated the assumed toolmaking abilities of these hominins. Then Richard Leakey found the famous Skull 1470 in East Turkana, a large-brained, round-headed cranium that confirmed the existence of *H. habilis* in no uncertain terms (Lewin, 1987) (Figure 2.9).

If you had encountered *H. habilis* 2 mya, you would have seen little to distinguish the new hominin from *Australopithecus*. Both were of similar height and weight, about 1.3 m (4 feet 3 inches) tall and about 40 kg (88 pounds). Both were bipedal, but *H. habilis* would have looked less apelike around the face and skull. The head was higher and rounder, the face less protruding, the jaw smaller. Some of the most significant anatomical differences involved the more even and less specialized teeth. The molars were narrower, the premolars smaller, and the incisors larger and more spadelike, as if they were used for slicing. However, microscopic wear studies of the teeth have shown that both *Australopithecus* and *H. habilis* were predominantly fruit eaters, so there does not seem to have been a major shift in diet between the two (Tobias, 1991). *H. habilis* had a larger brain, with a larger cranial capacity between 600 and 700+ cc, in contrast with that of australopithecines, which ranged between 400 and 500 cc.

Thigh and limb bones from Koobi Fora and from Olduvai confirm that *H. habilis* walked upright. The hand bones are somewhat more curved and robust than those of modern humans. Theirs was a powerful grasping hand, more like that of chimpanzees and gorillas than that of humans, a hand ideal for climbing trees. An opposable thumb allowed both powerful gripping and the precise manipulation of fine objects. With the latter capacity, *H. habilis* could have made complex tools. There was probably considerable difference in size between males and females.

The skeletal anatomy of *H. habilis* gives a mosaic picture of both primitive and more advanced features, of a hominin that both walked bipedally and retained the generalized hominoid ability to climb trees. A telling clue comes from one Olduvai specimen's upper arm bones, which, like Lucy's, are within 95 percent of the length of the thighbone. The chimpanzee has upper arm and upper leg bones of almost equal length, whereas modern human upper arms are only 70 percent of the length of the upper leg bones. Almost certainly *H. habilis* spent a great deal of time climbing trees, an adaptation that would make them much less human in their behavior, and presumably in their social structure, than had been assumed even a few years ago.

H. habilis, like many taxonomic labels, accommodates what may actually be two or more early human species. The resulting proliferation of hominin names reflects a concern with documenting an anatomical variation that far exceeded possible differences between males and females. For example, *H. habilis* may have lived alongside another East African form, *H. rudolfensis* (see Table 2.5). For clarity, we retain the generic term *H. habilis* here, but we stress that it disguises considerable morphological variation, especially after 2 mya, when new human forms were evolving in Africa and perhaps in Asia, too (see Site box).

A Burst of Rapid Change?

Our scientific predecessors thought of evolution as a gradual and progressive mechanism. The early East African fossils suggest a very different scenario, coinciding with that of the current view of evolution as punctuated equilibrium—long periods of relative stability punctuated with bursts of rapid

SiTE > Malapa, South Africa: The Mystery of *Australopithecus sediba* <

Was *Homo habilis* the primordial human, as has been assumed for more than a generation? Linear views of human evolution are no longer the vogue, partly because of new theoretical perspectives, but also the number of hominin fossils has proliferated in recent years. The notion of a "missing link," so fashionable with the scientists of a century ago has long been discredited. Such a creature will never come to light, for the processes that led to humanity were far more complicated than that. A new debate over the transition from Australopithecines to the first humans has erupted with the discovery of *Australopithecus sediba* in South Africa.

Gauteng Province in northern South Africa has long been famous for its gracile and robust Australopithecine fossils, notably from Sterkfontein cave. In 2008, two partial Australopithecine skeletons came from Malapa cave, dated by paleomagnetic and uranium-lead (U-Pb) dating to around 1.95 mya—to the time when *H. habilis* flourished in East Africa (Berger et al., 2010). And human evolution entered a period of intense change, leading to the emergence of *H. erectus*, the archaic human described in Chapter 3. The two individuals displayed such a distinctive mosaic of features that the discoverers identified them as a new species of Australopithecine: *Australopithecus sediba*. (*Sediba* means "well-spring" in the local Sotho language.) The discoverers, paleoanthropologist Lee Berger and geologist Paul Dirks, speculated that the hominids were swept into a deep natural pit, having been attracted there by the scent of water. Subsequently, the bones of another adult and an 18-month-old infant have come from the same pit.

A. sediba is so far best known from a young male, not yet fully grown. But we know that he had long arms and stood about 4 feet 3 inches (1.3 m) tall, typical of other Australopithecines. His brain capacity was a mere 420 cc less than the smallest known *Homo* brain of 520 cc. Most likely, *A. sediba* evolved from gracile *Australopithecus africanus*, well known from the same area (Figure 2.10). There are important differences between the two. *A. sediba* has smaller teeth, less pronounced cheekbones, and a more prominent nose. There are changes in the hip bones that seem to point in the direction of *Homo* as do the longer limbs.

Is, then, *A. sediba* a more advanced form of his ancestor *africanus*, the ancestor of the earliest humans? Or should he be designated as *Homo*, like

H. habilis? One school of thought, led by Berger, believes that *sediba* is the direct ancestor of *Homo*. Others, like Tim White of *Ardipiothecus* fame, point out that the current studies are based on a juvenile individual. The seemingly more *Homo*-like traits could be the result of normal variation between Australopithecines, younger individuals looking more like *Homo* than adults.

The debate continues, but it should be pointed out that the Malapa finds are younger than *Homo*-like fossils found elsewhere in Africa that date to as early as 2.3 mya. Thus, the Malapa specimens themselves cannot be direct human ancestors. Berger counters by arguing that they are late surviving members of the species that arose earlier. Most likely, *A. sediba* is just that, a late surviving Australopithecine, which throws little or no fresh light on the origins of the genus *Homo*. But the Malapa finds are important, for they add a new dimension to the complex processes of human evolution that unfolded around 2 mya. Recent research has shown that they ate a diet characteristic of more wooded environments, somewhat akin to that of chimpanzees.

FIGURE 2.10 *Australopithecus sediba*

change caused by new, selective pressures resulting from altered conditions, perhaps environmental change or alterations in the organism itself.

Such a burst of rapid change could have taken hold during the brief 500,000 years that separate *A. garhi* from *H. habilis*. Whoever was the first toolmaker, the development of stone tool technology gave its inventors a major advantage over other hominin species. Stone hammers and flakes let them exploit predator kills and shift, at least in part, to an energy-rich, high-fat diet, which could lead to all manner of evolutionary consequences. Brain size increased from about 450 cc in *A. afarensis* to 1000 cc in the much more advanced *H. erectus* (see Chapter 3). There were further modifications in hips and limbs for bipedal locomotion and a reduction in sexual dimorphism. The primitive body form and sexual dimorphism characteristic of earlier hominins finally vanished completely only with the emergence of *H. erectus*. But what caused this change of evolutionary pace remains a mystery. Some authorities suspect that climate change, especially cooler temperatures, played a role (Vrba et al., 1995).

Who Was the First Human?

A generation ago, human evolution was thought of as a ladder through time, with an apelike ancestor at the base and modern humans at the top. As for humans, they first appeared when toolmaking began. This was the reasoning that caused the great controversies of the 1960s as to who was the earliest toolmaker. Was it *Australopithecus* or some closely related hominin form, like the hopefully named *H. habilis*? As the pace of discovery accelerated, it soon became apparent that several hominin forms were around at the time when toolmaking began, making identification of the first "human" an even more challenging task.

In recent years, four criteria have been generally used to assign a fossil to the genus *Homo:* .

- An absolute brain size of 600 cc.
- The possession of language, identified from casts of the brain patterns on the inside of the braincase.
- The possession of a modern, humanlike precision grip and an opposable thumb.
- The ability to manufacture stone tools.

As Bernard Wood and Mark Collard (1999) have pointed out, there are serious problems with all of these criteria. Absolute brain capacity is of dubious biological importance. We now know that evidence of language cannot be inferred from a braincase. Furthermore, we still do not know much about the range of precision grips found among early hominins. Stone tools are an inconclusive criterion to use, simply because 2.6 mya both early *Homo* and robust australopithecines flourished in the same area where the earliest artifacts are found.

Hominin evolution involves a greater level of species diversity than was previously thought (Foley, 1995, but see T. D. White, 2003). Human evolution can be seen as one or more **adaptive radiations** rather than a simple, one-way evolution of successive species. This view stems from cladistics, an analytic system for reconstructing evolutionary relationships, first proposed in the 1950s. Classical evolutionary analysis is based on morphological similarities between organisms. So is cladistics, but with a difference: Cladistic analysis concentrates not only on features that identify common ancestry but also on those that are derived independently and are unique to specific lineages. Inevitably, cladistics tends to emphasize diversity over homogeneity.

A cladistic definition considers the human genus a group of species that are more closely related to one another than to species assigned to another genus. This interpretation insists that the human genus is **monophyletic,** that is, with all its members ultimately descended from a common ancestor. Wood and Collard define the human genus "as a species, or monophylum, whose members occupy a single adaptive zone" (1999: 66). Using this definition, they carried out a cladistic analysis of all the known fossil *Homo* species and devised a cladogram that separates all the australopithecine forms, *H. habilis*, into one genus and later humans, starting with *H. erectus*, into another (Figure 2.11). Their intricate statistical analysis suggests that enough is known of body size and shape, locomotion, development, and relative size of chewing apparatus to divide fossil hominin adaptive strategies into two broad groups:

- The australopithecines and *Homo habilis* (also *H. rudolfensis*) belong in a group of hominins with a relatively low body mass, a body shape better suited to a relatively closed environment, and a postcranial skeleton that combines terrestrial bipedalism with expert climbing. The teeth and jaws of these hominins are well adapted to chewing and biting a varied and mechanically demanding diet. *Australopithecus* teeth and upper leg bone studies show that the rate of development (and dependence) of young hominins in this group was closer to that of modern African apes. The tooth development of

FIGURE 2.11 A provisional interpretation of the evolutionary relationships between known hominin forms after 6 million years.

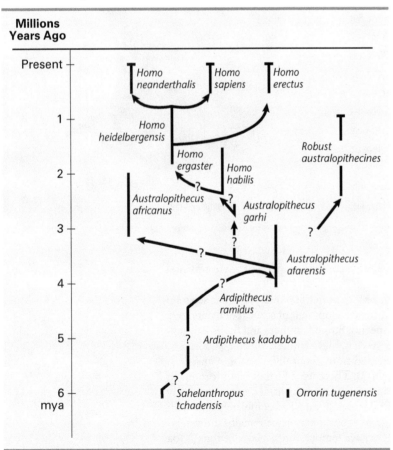

H. habilis and *H. rudolfensis* also appears to have been closer to that of African apes, as if their development period was also shorter than that of modern humans.

- *H. erectus* and contemporary and later human forms belong in a second group, marked by a larger body mass; a modern, humanlike physique that was adaptive in more open terrain; and a postcranial skeleton consistent with terrestrial bipedalism. The ability to move around in trees was very limited; teeth and jaws had similar mechanical properties to those of modern humans. Development rates were the same as our own.

This definition of *Homo* makes a clear distinction between the hominins of earlier than 1.9 mya and *H. erectus* and its successors who evolved after that date. It implies that a behavioral and evolutionary chasm separates true humans from the many other hominins who flourished in Africa before 2 mya. What caused this adaptive shift in human evolution is unknown. Did it correspond with significant climatic and environmental change, with equivalent evolutionary changes in other large mammal groups, or with specific changes in hominin culture? The answers will have to come from a new generation of research.

Hominin evolution can be thought of as a series of adaptive radiations that unfolded over at least 5 million years. The first radiation was of bipedal apes, which lived, for the most part, in the drier parts of Africa. Two later radiations gave rise to what is still called early *Homo* and the robust australopithecines, each with its own adaptive theme. In the case of early *Homo*, expanded brain size played a key role, while the robust australopithecines developed specialized teeth. Although the latter varied greatly in morphological terms, later humans radiated not so much morphologically as ecologically, spreading from Africa and creating distinct geographic populations (Figure 2.12).

This flowering of hominin types is exactly what evolution is about: "an endless production of novel ways of doing things, exploring alternatives, trying out new strategies as conditions themselves shift and change all driven by natural selection" (Foley, 1995: 103). Hominins were no different from other mammals, which began as a slim stem and radiated into distinct branches. We still do not know much about the relationships between such branches.

Archaeological Evidence for Early Human Behavior

Studying early hominin behavior is complicated both by poor preservation conditions and by the vast time chasm that separates us from our remotest ancestors. In general terms, four lines of evidence offer opportunities for testing hypotheses about early hominin behavior:

1. **Scatters of artifacts.** Scatters of artifacts and food remains form the archaeological record for hominin activities, perhaps at predator kills, home bases, or meat caches.
2. **Manufactured artifacts.** Because of preservation conditions, manufactured artifacts are mainly objects made of stone. The transport of the raw materials used to make these tools is also an important consideration.
3. **Surviving food remains.** Finds of food remains, almost entirely fragmentary animal bones, reveal valuable information about our remote forebears, but inevitably the dietary information is skewed because plant remains rarely, if ever, survive.
4. **Isotopic analyses.** There is a close relationship between diet and bone/tooth chemistry. Stable carbon isotopes (^{13}C and ^{12}C) can give an idea of the relative importance of tropical grasses as opposed to shrub and tree foods in the diet of herbivores like antelope and, indirectly, in the diets of the carnivores that prey on them. For instance, *A. robustus* had a diet rich in trees and shrubs, unlike modern African apes, who rely heavily on tropical grasses. Research into bone chemistry is in its infancy, but has the potential to answer fundamental questions about the diet of early *Homo*, which may still have been based very largely on plant foods, especially tubers.

Evidence for "Central Places"?

Later hunter-gatherers made habitual use of *central places*, sites where they returned to sleep, fabricate tools, cook food, and engage in a wide variety of social activities. Did hominins have similar central places?

The only archaeological evidence comes from East Turkana and Olduvai Gorge (see Site box), where a number of concentrations of bones and stone tools dating to around 2 mya and later have been excavated and studied with meticulous care. No such concentrations have been found with the earlier Laetoli or Hadar hominins.

FIGURE 2.12 Early Human Evolution to 2 mya

The earliest hominins appeared in tropical Africa by 7 million years ago, known from the somewhat controversial skull of *Sahelanthropus tchadensis*. *Ardipthecus kadabba* and *Ardipithecus ramidus* are the earliest known bipedal hominids. *Australopithecus afarensis* probably evolved from *Ardipithecus* in eastern Africa and was widespread there by 3.5 mya. *A. robustus* and *A. boisei*, evolved massive jaws, molar teeth, and cranial anatomy optimized for hard chewing. They may have consumed hard-to-open foods during hungry periods. *Homo habilis*, the first relatively well-known hominin on the human line, flourished after 2 mya and was probably the first toolmaker.

The relationship of *Sahelanthropus tchadensis*, the earliest known hominin, to *Ardipithecus* is the subject of debate. Some authorities consider it an early form of *Ardipithecus*.

The Ascent of Humanity

Human evolution unfolded not linearly, but with numerous branches and a trend toward larger brain size and greater stature, from the australopithecines and early *Homo* to modern *Homo sapiens*.

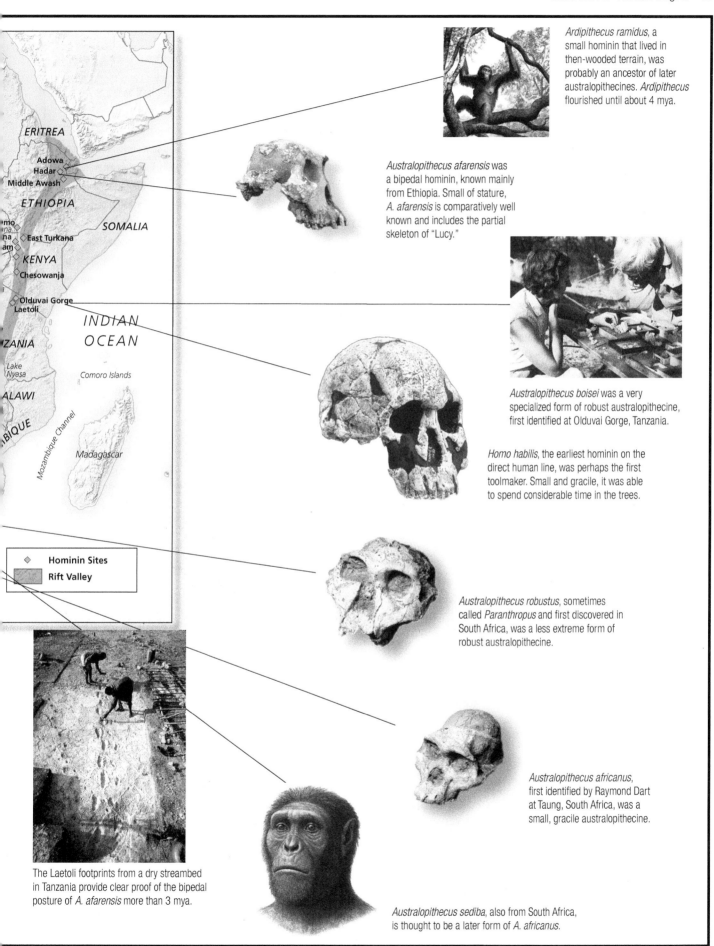

Ardipithecus ramidus, a small hominin that lived in then-wooded terrain, was probably an ancestor of later australopithecines. *Ardipithecus* flourished until about 4 mya.

Australopithecus afarensis was a bipedal hominin, known mainly from Ethiopia. Small of stature, *A. afarensis* is comparatively well known and includes the partial skeleton of "Lucy."

Australopithecus boisei was a very specialized form of robust australopithecine, first identified at Olduvai Gorge, Tanzania.

Homo habilis, the earliest hominin on the direct human line, was perhaps the first toolmaker. Small and gracile, it was able to spend considerable time in the trees.

Australopithecus robustus, sometimes called *Paranthropus* and first discovered in South Africa, was a less extreme form of robust australopithecine.

Australopithecus africanus, first identified by Raymond Dart at Taung, South Africa, was a small, gracile australopithecine.

The Laetoli footprints from a dry streambed in Tanzania provide clear proof of the bipedal posture of *A. afarensis* more than 3 mya.

Australopithecus sediba, also from South Africa, is thought to be a later form of *A. africanus*.

ERITREA

Adowa
Hadar
Middle Awash

ETHIOPIA

SOMALIA

mo
na
am
East Turkana

KENYA

Chesowanja

Olduvai Gorge
Laetoli

INDIAN
OCEAN

ZANIA

Lake
Nyasa

Comoro Islands

ALAWI

BIQUE

Mozambique Channel

Madagascar

◇ Hominin Sites
▨ Rift Valley

SiTE > Olduvai Gorge, Tanzania, East Africa <

Olduvai Gorge is a vast gash in the game-rich Serengeti Plains of northern Tanzania, formed by an earthquake more than 100,000 years ago and called a miniature Grand Canyon by many visitors (Figure 2.13). The earth movement exposed a long series of ancient lake beds, extending back as far as 2 mya, stratified in the walls of the gorge. Geologists have identified four major series of lake beds, labeled Bed I (at the base) to Bed IV, which formed in a semiarid environment much like that of today. Olduvai was discovered by German butterfly hunter Wilhelm Kattwinkel before World War I and was investigated by paleontologist Hans Reck in 1913 and thereafter. Reck found numerous fossil animal bones, including a long-extinct elephant that he named after himself. Today, more than 150 species of extinct animals ranging in size from elephants to birds and rodents are known from Olduvai.

The gorge will always be associated with Louis and Mary Leakey, who realized the great potential of Olduvai for documenting early human evolution. Louis Leakey first found stone axes in the gorge in 1931. Between 1935 and 1959, the Leakeys surveyed and excavated numerous sites and published an important monograph on the Olduvai stone tools (L. S. B. Leakey, 1951), in which they traced the evolution of stone artifacts from a simple technology based on lava lumps, which they named the Oldowan, to progressively more complex and better-made hand axes and flake tools (the Acheulian). Then, in 1959, they discovered *Zinjanthropus boisei* and changed the chronicle of human evolution forever. Subsequently, large-scale excavations by the Leakeys unearthed other hominin fossils, including *Homo habilis*, whom they considered the first toolmaker. Don Johanson of Lucy fame has also worked in the gorge and has recovered more *H. habilis* fragments.

The most important Olduvai hominin fossils come from Beds I and II. Bed I lies on a volcanic bedrock, known as a *tuff*, which has been potassium-argon dated to about 2 mya, an excellent baseline for the lake bed sequence above. The beds themselves were close to the shore of an extensive, shallow lake that expanded and contracted from one season to the next. The waters covered places where hominins had paused to process and eat animal parts they had scavenged from nearby predator kills, preserving both stone tool fragments and broken animal bones, as well as the occasional hominin fossil in situ.

Excavating these land surfaces requires great patience and skill. Once a location is identified, the investigators sift the ground surrounding the original find through fine screens, looking for significant fossils. Then they excavate into the lake bed to establish the stratigraphic relationship of the ancient land surface to the surrounding lake bed layers before exposing the scatter of artifacts and bones in the horizontal plane. This process is slow moving and calls for meticulous excavation and recording, with each fragment, even those as small as snake fangs, being exposed in place, then its precise location recorded, before removal. The end product after months of work is a precise three-dimensional plan of the artifact and bone scatter, so that the relationships between stone fragments and other finds, including (hopefully) hominin fossils, are established with the greatest possible precision.

The pioneer excavation methods used by the Leakeys at Olduvai have been adopted and refined in both the Lake Turkana and Hadar regions, where archaeologists work alongside human paleontologists, geologists, geomorphologists, and other specialists in a multidisciplinary investigation of the earliest human behavior (see Figure 2.13).

FIGURE 2.13　Olduvai Gorge, Tanzania.

For years, Louis Leakey and other pioneer paleoanthropologists believed that these scatters were "living floors," places where our ancestors slept, made tools, and butchered game. These were home bases, they argued, on the assumption that the hominins who created the artifact concentrations were hunters and gatherers behaving like primitive versions of contemporary hunting bands.

Recent thinking on the subject regards such assumptions as dangerous. First, the archaeological record is very ancient, so ancient that the only way one can hope to interpret it is with a thorough knowledge of the geologic and other processes that have affected the bone and tool scatter since its makers abandoned it. Second, we now know much more about contemporary hunters and nonhuman primates, enough to undermine confidence that direct analogies with such populations have any validity when we are dealing with 2-million-year-old hominin behavior. Third, a whole new generation of research involving controlled experimentation, edge-wear studies (microscopic examination of tool-working surfaces), and other sophisticated approaches has thrown doubt on the notion that *H. habilis* (or any other hominin of the day) was a hunter at all.

If the earliest artifact scatters are not central places, what behavior do they represent? Some of the earliest manufactured tools in the world come from Gona, Ethiopia (c. 2.6 mya) (Semaw et al., 1997). Others, often in association with animal bones, come from the Koobi Fora area of East Turkana and from west of the lake (Isaac and Harris, 1978; Roche et al., 1999). Several localities have been excavated, among them a dry streambed where a group of hominins apparently found the carcass of a hippopotamus about 1.8 mya. They gathered around and removed bones and meat from the dead animal with small stone flakes. The deposits in which the stones and flaked debris were found are so fine-grained that they contain natural pebbles no larger than a pea. Thus, every lump of rock at the site was carried in by the hominins to make tools nearby the carcass. Some of the cores came from nearly 14 km (9 miles) away, presumably so the people could strike off sharp flakes to butcher the carcass. This site provides clear evidence of toolmaking, raw material transport, and butchering. We simply do not know whether the hominins themselves killed the hippopotamus. The site may represent a place where they paused briefly to scavenge meat from a predator kill or an animal that had died of natural causes. (Archaeologists identify the uses of sites by their artifact content and other finds, for example, traces of brush shelters that suggest a site was a central place or a settlement. Judging from the finds, this location was certainly not a central place.)

Site FxJj50, also at Koobi Fora, is in an ancient watercourse, a place where the hominins could find shade from the blazing sun, located close to water and abundant supplies of stone for toolmaking (Figure 2.14) (Bunn, 1994). The site consists of a cluster of stone artifacts: choppers, crude scrapers, battered cobbles, and sharp-edged flakes. Approximately 2,100 bones representing at least 20 vertebrates, mainly antelope, are associated with the tools, some of them bearing carnivore chewing marks. There are clear signs that the bones were smashed and cut by hominins, for reconstructed fragments show signs of hammer blows and fine linear grooves that can have resulted only from cutting bone with stoneworking edges. The excavators noted the lack of articular ends of bones, a characteristic of bone accumulations resulting from carnivore kills. Perhaps the hominins simply chased away lions and other predators, then moved in on a fresh kill; we cannot be sure.

Another site consists of a scatter of stone tools and broken animal bones, these from several antelope and larger mammals. The scatter lies on the surface of a dry streambed where water could still be easily obtained by digging in the sand. The banks of the watercourse were probably shaded by dense stands of trees that provided both shelter and plant foods. Perhaps the people who left the tools and bones climbed into these trees at night. The site was so sheltered that even minuscule stone chips were still in place, unaffected by the strong winds that sweep over the area; the leaves, too, left impressions in the deposits. The nearest source of toolmaking stone is 3.2 km (2 miles) from the site, so the inhabitants must have carried in their tools and, in all probability, portions of the several animals whose bones accumulated at the site. This type of behavior—the carrying in of food to a fixed location—is fundamentally different from that of the nonhuman primates.

Much of our present knowledge about the lifeways of the earliest hominins comes from Olduvai Gorge, where Mary Leakey plotted and recorded sites in Bed I at the base of the gorge (M. D. Leakey, 1971). The *Zinjanthropus* floor at Olduvai was found to be 115 sq m (1,239 sq feet), consisting of more than 4,000 artifacts and bones. Many artifacts and bones were concentrated in an area some 4.5 m (15 feet) across. A pile of shattered bones and rocks lay a short distance away, the bones perhaps piled in heaps as the marrow was extracted. A bare, arc-shaped area between these bone heaps and the pile of more complete fragments remains unexplained. Leakey wondered whether it was the site of a crude windbreak of branches, because the area lies in the path of today's prevailing winds.

Later researchers have approached the Olduvai locations from several angles (Bunn and Kroll, 1986; R. Potts, 1984). Careful examination of the bones

Gona
2.6 mya

Koobi Fora
1.8 mya

Olduvai Gorge
1.75 mya

FIGURE 2.14 The forbidding, arid landscape of East Turkana, which was somewhat better watered 2.5 mya.

has revealed that many of them had lain on the surface for considerable periods of time, perhaps as long as four to six, even ten, years, to judge from weathering patterns on modern East African bones. The bones of many different animals are found in the assemblages, and the remains of carcasses are from a very ecologically diverse set of animals. Limb bones predominate on the "floors," as if these isolated bones were repeatedly carried to the site. Furthermore, the stone tools found on the Olduvai surfaces were all imported from raw material sources some distance away.

What is one to make of this pattern of meat and marrow-rich bones concentrated in a small area with stone tools? The percentage of carnivore bones is somewhat higher than the natural environment would suggest, about 3 percent in the Olduvai assemblages, as opposed to 1 percent in the local environment today (in one case, the figure was as high as 21 percent). Was there, then, intense ecological competition for game between hominins and other carnivores? It seems possible that the presence of carnivores restricted the activities of hominins at Olduvai. They may have grabbed meaty bones from carnivore kills, then taken them to a place where they had a collection of stone tools. There they could have hastily cut off meat and extracted marrow before abandoning the fresh bones to the carnivores hovering nearby. The Olduvai sites may not have been safe from carnivores, and without fire or domesticated dogs, early *Homo* probably had to rely on opportunistic foraging. As we have already noted, many of the Olduvai bones bear both carnivore teeth marks and stone tool cuts, perhaps a reflection of competition for game. It is also worth noting that one hominin bone found at Olduvai had been gnawed by carnivores.

Whatever their actual purpose, we can be sure that the Olduvai bone and artifact accumulation sites were places that were used only on a very transitory basis, perhaps favored locations used on several occasions. Were they locations to which hominins returned to sleep, feed their dependents, and carry out other activities, or were they merely used occasionally for breaking up bones and eating meat? We know that the hominins transported toolmaking stone and portions of animal carcasses from one place to another. We cannot be certain that they actually lived at the places where these objects were abandoned, in the way that later hunter-gatherers did. Several experts believe that the accumulations were useful caches of stone artifacts to which bones and other food resources were taken for processing (R. Potts, 1984). Perhaps these caches lay near water supplies or predictable food resources. Perhaps, too, they were maintained throughout a group's range, so the hominins did not have to carry meat or stone very far. However, a consistent pattern of caches spread throughout a territory requires a level of forethought, planning, and memory that may have been beyond the intellectual capacities of the Olduvai hominins.

All archaeology currently tells us is that the early Olduvai sites were places to which stone and food resources were carried. These may have been the remote predecessors of hunter-gatherer central places, which were to come into being in later times, conceivably with the regular use of fire for heat and protection.

Hunting and Scavenging

Were these hominins full-fledged hunter-gatherers, or did they scavenge predator kills for meat? Or both? Therein lie some of the fundamental controversies of paleoanthropology. **Taphonomy, microwear studies**, and other highly sophisticated approaches to the archaeological record of 2 mya have shown again and again the sheer folly of basing theories about early hominin behavior on crude analogies with modern hunting societies. Just for a start, the hominins belonged to a quite different species. Furthermore, no living apes display their behaviors. Nor, indeed, did all early hominins, some of whom never accumulated bones.

Diverse carnivore and **ungulate** communities had developed in eastern and southern Africa by 4 mya, with a wide diversity of hominins as part of the mammalian community. Some scientists believe that new ways of adapting to a heterogeneous environment like that of the East African savanna developed opportunistically. Under some ecological conditions, they argue, an opportunistic shift in the use of a food source such as meat could have led to a breakthrough in human behavior that had long-term significance. With a wide diversity of predators in the savanna, hominins consuming meat would have to have competed successfully with carnivores to obtain it. This competitive ability was selected because meat eating became vital to survival and reproductive success, and the dangers of competing with carnivores were more than outweighed by the advantages of more available food supplies and increased reproductive success because of better nutrition and easily transportable meat for social feeding. At present, it is difficult to choose between these very general ecological models.

There is mounting evidence that early hominins like the Australopithecines were more often prey than predators (Hart and Sussman, 2008). For generations, paleoanthropologists believed that the human ability at hunting and to vanquish competitors was the key to our ancestor's evolutionary success. However, Hart and Sussman argue that prey species like humans did not owe their survival to hunting or scavenging skills, but to their wits and social skills to survive. Being hunted brought evolutionary pressures on our ancestors to cooperate and live in small groups—their most powerful evolutionary legacy.

Genetics and paleoneurology provide supporting evidence. A hormone called oxytocin, which induces labor and lactation in women, also operates in both male and female brains. There it promotes trust between people who are interacting and cooperative behavior that allows groups to live together for the common good. By comparing the chimpanzee genome with that of humans, researchers infer that oxytocin existed in the common ancestor of both. But it has changed over the past 7 million years, perhaps affecting how strongly the brain responds to it and how much is produced. The change might have occurred when hominins first settled into social systems that involved enduring bonds between men and women, perhaps some 1.7 mya.

In the final analysis, however, the evidence for hunting or scavenging comes down to bones. The Olduvai sites contain bones of smaller animals for the most part, species that were less powerful than hominins. Rather than scavenging, hunters may have run down their quarry and thrown it to the ground before killing it. This is more of an apelike form of behavior, although apes have been observed scavenging meat from predator kills. Some microscopic evidence from very early archaeological sites at Olduvai Gorge suggests that scavenging may have been much more important than hunting. Pat Shipman (1984) and others have examined dozens of broken animal bones from Olduvai, peering at minute but distinctive cut marks resulting from such activities as butchery, disarticulation of carcasses, and skin removal. They made high-fidelity replicas of bone marks and then examined them under a scanning electron microscope, comparing the results with those obtained from a 2,300-year-old agricultural settlement in Kenya, where the inhabitants were actively engaged in disarticulation, butchery, and other activities. They found that 90 percent of the 2,300-year-old bones showed cut marks resulting from the disjointing of carcasses, but only 45 percent of those from Olduvai showed the same marks. This was also true of butchery marks, those made when removing meat from bones. In contrast, about 75 percent of both the Olduvai and the 2,300-year-old bones show the characteristic marks left by skin and tendon removal, which are especially visible on the lower limb bones since they had little meat on them.

Both disarticulation and butchery were, surprisingly, uncommon at Olduvai, so it seems doubtful that the hominins were butchering and disjointing large animals and carrying them back to base. They seem to have obtained meat without cutting up very many carcasses. It is possible that they scavenged it from predator kills. A tantalizing clue came from 13 Olduvai bones on which both carnivore and human-made markings were present. In eight instances, the human marks overlay carnivore tooth marks, as if the humans had scavenged the bones from carcasses that had already been killed by lions or other predators (see R. Potts, 1984).

The diversity of animals, including nonmigratory species, represented in the Olduvai bone accumulations is striking. Richard Potts (1984) believes that it represents the variety of animals found in a resident rather than a migratory ungulate population, where only a few species are represented. He argues that the hominins depended at least partially on resident animals in a situation in which the generalization about large carnivores being hunters and scavengers might apply. Thus, the Olduvai hominins were hunting resident mammals as well as competing with other carnivores in scavenging activity.

By studying body part frequencies in Olduvai accumulations, Potts (1984) has shown that carnivore bone assemblages contain a high proportion of forelimbs, the body part usually removed first from a carcass by a scavenger. In accumulations where hominin activity took place, higher forelimbs are also common, but hind limbs are relatively abundant as well, as if the hominins were obtaining meat both early and later in the sequence of carcass disarticulation.

What do these new archaeological findings mean in behavioral terms? Robert Blumenschine has spent long field seasons studying animal predators on the game-rich Serengeti Plain of northern Tanzania (Blumenschine and Cavallo, 1992). This semiarid grassland environment, intersected by occasional watercourses lined by trees, is the closest we can come to the open landscape exploited by our remotest ancestors. The Serengeti abounds in game animals of all kinds, and in predators that hunt them. It is an environment of plenty, yet of danger, where bipedal hominins would compete with lions and hyenas and were potential prey themselves. The treeless savanna offered little refuge to hominins armed not with sharp teeth and claws but with sticks and stones. Yet they acquired game meat successfully, either by being expert hunters or by opportunistic scavenging. Blumenschine observed dozens of predator kills and examined the surviving carcasses and shattered bones, comparing them to those from Olduvai and other hominin sites. At the same time, he identified two distinctive scavenging opportunities where hominins would have been at an advantage over their competitors.

The first lay in streamside woodlands, places where lions kill close to water in the dry season, feeding on a carcass under a canopy of trees and hidden from roaming vultures high above. In many cases, Blumenschine found that a day would elapse before even hyenas would find the abandoned kill, ample time for observant hominins to move in for their share. It is here, too, that leopards hide small antelope kills in trees, high above the ground. Two mya saber-toothed tigers may have killed much larger animals in similar riparian (riverside) environments. During the dry months, large animals sometimes starved to death or died of disease near streams, another potentially important source of fresh meat.

Blumenschine believes that scavenging would have been most important in the dry season, when plant foods were in shortest supply. During these months, the best food-getting strategy was to scavenge from kills by many predators near permanent water supplies. The rainy season found the same predators ranging over the open plains, killing in places where hyenas and vultures would make quick work of the remaining carcass—far away from the trees that were so vital to puny hominins. But our ancestors then relied more heavily on plant foods, which came into season at different times. Thus, scavenging and foraging went hand in hand, each complementing the other at different times of the year.

The Blumenschine scavenging theory assumes that hominins were subject to the same pressures as other animals and on a rapidly growing body of scientific data from many sources. He notes that scavenging was not easy for slow-moving animals like hominins. Careful observation was all-important—of the purposeful early morning flights of vultures toward new kills, of the telltale antelope fur tufts at the foot of a tree where a leopard had stashed its kill, of the triumphant laughs of a feeding hyena at a fresh kill. Blumenschine theorizes that early hominins made "mental maps" of their territories, which enabled them to predict where carcasses might be found and where clumps of fruit ripened in different months.

In recent years, the scavenging hypothesis has come under fire from a new generation of taphonomists, who argue that what was once considered to be tooth marks made by carnivores are, in fact, biochemical marks caused by fungi and bacteria from the roots of plants that grew in the deposits in which they were buried. This new data suggest that most hominin sites of this period are palimpsests of bones and that humans had little to do with their accumulation. Thus the evidence for scavenging is suspect (Dominguez-Rodrigo et al., 2007). The debate continues, as does fieldwork.

A generation ago, archaeologist Glynn Isaac (1984) argued that *opportunism*—a restless process, like mutation and natural selection—is a hallmark of humankind. The normal pressures of ecological competition were able to transform the versatile behavior of ancestral primates into the new and distinctive early hominin pattern. The change required feedback between cultural subsystems, such as hunting and sharing food. Weapons and tools made possible new ways of getting and processing foods, even with entirely new forms of diet: not only plant foods but meat as well. Foraging provided stability, making the savanna an ideal and vacant ecological niche for hominins, who lived on scavenging, hunting, and foraging combined. The microwear patterns on the tooth surfaces of *Australopithecus* and *H. habilis* show that both creatures flourished on a diet very similar to that of chimpanzees. But *H. habilis* had a much larger brain, a development that was probably associated with an increase in economic and social complexity and perhaps in food sharing as well.

Maybe our earliest ancestors shared food, dividing the labor of scavenging and foraging and of processing food between males and females. Such social cooperation and advanced planning were necessary, especially because the stone used for flakes and hammers was often found in one place, with animal carcasses far away. To bring the two together required planning and social cooperation to the point where some groups carried stone as far as 10 km (6 miles) from its source. And scavenging may have begun as a way of supplementing plant foraging as global cooling brought more open environments to tropical Africa. Thus, *Australopithecus* and *H. habilis*, with their flaked-stone tool kits, took not only marrow but also fresh meat, using sharp-edged stones as the equivalent of hyena teeth.

Plant Foraging and "Grandmothering"

Beyond some microscopic wear traces from plant tissues on early stone artifacts, there is as yet no archaeological evidence that plant foods were consumed by early hominins, because this kind of data does not preserve well (Sept, 1994). Yet, a scanning electron microscope focused on tooth microwear has shown that some Lower Pleistocene hominins had diets very similar to those of modern nonhuman primates (Walker, 1981). But *H. habilis* limb bones reveal an unexpected inconsistency, for their anatomy was far more arboreal than that of a terrestrial bipedal primate of 2 mya. Such adept tree climbers are certain to have relied on fruit and other plant foods, perhaps enjoying a diet closer to that of modern apes than to that of hunter-gatherers.

A new generation of research is causing some rethinking of the long-held assumption that the earliest humans transported meat and bones from animals of all sizes back to sites for processing.

More fieldwork among modern tropical foragers has shown that hunting, with its irregular success, although sometimes productive, is not a reliable strategy for feeding a family.

The old hunting arguments assumed that men hunted and women gathered plant foods, behavior typical of hunter-gatherers, but not found among the great apes. This behavior pattern, it was argued, developed as a result of a long-term trend toward a cooler, drier climate 2 mya that reduced the availability of plant foods while favoring the spread of game-rich savannas. Under this argument, males added large animals to the diet, a potentially sharable resource. Females paired with the hunters, which gave them access to the new food and enabled them to reduce their foraging activities. The nuclear family, sexual division of labor, and provisioning by the father came into being; female fertility and the survival of offspring increased; and long dependence on parents by children, larger brain size, increased learning, and much greater behavioral flexibility resulted. The new hominins were successful in evolutionary terms because they possessed a great ability to cope with environmental diversity and could range over much larger territories.

Today, we know a great deal more about both nonhuman primates and hunter-gatherer life. For instance, male primates such as chimpanzees hunt frequently and share the meat with others, but without any use of central places. Fieldwork among modern tropical hunter-gatherers shows that men do indeed hunt larger game, but the supply of such prey is unpredictable and certainly insufficient for effective feeding of entire families and bands. It often serves social ends as much as it does dietary needs.

If hunting meets other ends, what, then, was the role of plant gathering? Current opinion holds that early hominins scavenged meat from predator kills, but, even if the scavenging was aggressive, the meat supply can never have been sufficient to satisfy the daily nutritional requirements not only of adults but also of the young. Not even modern-day hunters using bows and arrows and other weaponry far more sophisticated than that of our remote ancestors can acquire sufficient meat for daily nutrition. Nor is there solid archaeological evidence that the scavengers transported meat to central places, rather, consuming it close to where they scavenged meat and bones. As James O'Connell and his colleagues point out (1999), these observations transform many long-held assumptions about the behavior of early hominids—the notion that there was division of labor between males (hunting) and females (plant gathering), and the theory that there were nuclear families this early in human history. The archaeological evidence upon which the traditional hunting theories are based is relatively accessible and tangible, even if it is open to diverse interpretations. But such a narrow approach ignores much larger ecological and evolutionary questions.

O'Connell and his colleagues have developed a "grandmother hypothesis," based on ecological theory and field observations of modern-day tropical hunter-gatherers, specifically the Hadza people of Tanzania in East Africa (Hawkes et al., 1989). Anthropologist Kristin Hawkes observed that everyone except the very old and very young is an active, productive forager. Very often, women in their 60s and 70s are more efficient foragers than their younger female kin of reproductive age. By the age of 5, Hadza children can supply as much as half their daily nutritional requirements by their own efforts. Both mothers and grandmothers deliberately target easy-to-acquire foods such as fruit during the rainy season, which children can also take in large numbers. Sometimes, in a form of team foraging, the women even bypass items that will give a higher return but are unexploitable by the young—to the point that the foraging opportunities for children largely determine adult female strategies, especially during the rainy season. Then, when foods easily exploited by the young are unavailable, the adults provision them with other foods—in the case of the Hadza the woody rootstock, a plant that favors deep, stony soils and requires considerable upper body strength and endurance to acquire, as well as the use of fire to process into food. Children under 8 years ignore woody rootstock, but adults can acquire as much as 2000 kcal/hour from this plant all seasons of the year. Hawkes learned an important lesson from this: The Hadza can live in habitats that would be precluded if their young had to forage for themselves, as is the case with nonhuman primates.

Another factor comes into play as well. When a mother bears a child and is nursing, her foraging time declines. Now the grandmother steps in and takes up the slack, feeding the weaned children of her kin. The O'Connell team remark that childbearing careers are of similar length in apes and humans, but humans survive far longer after menopause. Weaned children depend on food from adults; ancestral human grandmothers would have had a chance to affect their fitness in ways other apes could not. The result: a selection against rapid aging, lower adult mortality rates, and longer adult life spans.

There are other effects, too. Instead of a reduced fecundity that accompanies aging, the assistance of grandmothers would pay off in higher fertility, allowing mothers to have babies more frequently. Not only do humans have longer life spans than our nonhuman relatives, our ancestors began to mature later and to produce offspring at a higher rate.

Imagine an ancestral hominid group, with a life history and foraging patterns similar to those of modern-day chimpanzees. The members reached maturity at about 10 to 12 years, with only moderate fecundity. Life expectancy was at most about 50 years, while juveniles for the most part foraged for themselves, albeit with some (probably relatively insignificant) assistance from mothers and older siblings. Imagine, then, a scenario where food supplies accessible to the same juveniles became scarcer, perhaps because of more arid conditions. The groups might adjust their foraging ranges, even abandoning some areas. Alternatively, they could invest more in provisioning, that is, acquiring food resources that had been ignored before because they were inaccessible to the young. Such resources would have to be predictable, constantly available, and in sufficient quantity to feed not only the collector but others over long periods of time. Without such qualities, the new supplies would be of limited use to growing young.

As provisioning became a routine practice, so the role of older females, still active but no longer fertile, could have become more important, as they helped in feeding the young. The result: closer spaced births and a higher survival rate for immature members of the group. At the same time, the new role for older females would decrease adult mortality rates by selecting against senescence. After some time, the delayed mortality, a longer period of growth, larger adult body size, and later age of maturity would result. There would not have been extended fertility, but the conservation of a similar fertile span to that of apes and an extended postmenopausal longevity.

Such hypothetical ancestral hominin populations would have enjoyed reduced juvenile mortality because of provisioning, which removed the pressures of competition for food among the young. If this occurred in areas with abundant food resources, larger foraging groups may have come into being, a situation where grandmothers and other older kin would stay close to daughters and grandchildren so they could support them. In turn, the result would be the exploitation of much larger foraging territories, where members of the band were not restrained by the foraging capabilities of the young. Inevitably, such exploitation would have led to more efficient ways of foraging, including new technologies such as stone tools. We return to the implications of the grandmother theory in Chapter 3.

Toolmaking

Other animals, such as chimpanzees, use tools (Figure 2.15), but human beings manufacture tools regularly and habitually and with much more complexity (Boesch and Tomasello, 1998).

We have gone much farther in the toolmaking direction than other primates. One reason is that our brains allow us to plan our actions much more in advance. Prehistoric tools, in all their simplicity and sometimes extraordinary complexity, provide a record of ancient decision-making processes. By analyzing the ways in which prehistoric stone artifacts—the most enduring of all technologies—were made, we can gain insights into the mind processes of the people who created them.

All studies of stone artifacts are based on the assumption that a sequence of removing flakes ultimately produced a finished artifact, whether simple or complex, to be used for a specific purpose. Many details of the world's earliest stone technology are debated, but there is no doubt that it was the work of individuals with an impressive knowledge of the properties of stone (Figure 2.16). They knew how to select the right rock, could visualize in three dimensions how to put it to use and flake it, had mastered the routine steps needed to create a tool, and were capable of passing this knowledge on to others.

The Oldowan Industry

Everyone had always assumed that the earliest stone technology would be very simple (Schick and Toth, 2001). When the Leakeys found crudely chipped stones in the long-buried lake beds at Olduvai Gorge, the artifacts were indeed nothing much to look at. (The Leakeys called their early tool assemblages *Oldowan*, after the gorge where they were first identified.) Most were broken cobbles and flakes, flakes being in the majority. Some Oldowan tools were so

FIGURE 2.15 Chimpanzee using a stick as a tool to fish for insects. Chimpanzees also use objects for play, and display and carry them in their hands. Sometimes, they improve their sticks slightly with their teeth. They use leaves for cleaning the body and sipping water. Chimpanzees have inherited behavior patterns far closer to our own than to those of any monkey.

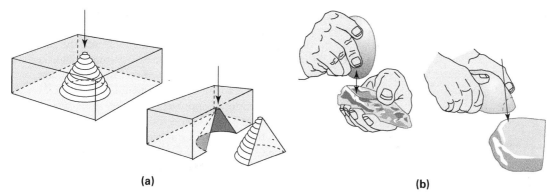

(a)   **(b)**

FIGURE 2.16 Early stone technology. The principles of fracturing stone were fully understood by early stoneworkers, who used them to make simple but very effective artifacts. Certain types of flinty rock will fracture in a distinctive way, as illustrated in (a). Early stoneworkers used a heavy hammerstone to remove edge flakes, or they struck lumps of rock against anvils to produce the same effect, as shown in (b). Oldowan tools were frequently made by removing a few flakes from lava lumps to form jagged working edges. Such flakes have been shown by experiment to be remarkably effective for dismembering and butchering game animals. Perhaps it is small wonder that this simple stone technology was so long lasting. (a) When a blow is struck on flinty rock, a cone of percussion is formed by shock waves rippling through the stone (left). A flake is formed (right) when the block (or core) is hit at the edge, and the stone fractures along the edge of the ripple. (b) Using a hammerstone (left) and an anvil (right).

crude that only an expert could tell them from a naturally fractured rock, and experts often disagree. All the Oldowan choppers and flakes strike one as extremely practical implements; many are so individual in design that they seem haphazard artifacts, not standardized in the way later Stone Age tools were. Classifying them is very difficult, for they do not fall into distinct types. The tools cannot be described as primitive because many display a sophisticated understanding of stone's potential uses in toolmaking. We now know that the Olduvai hominins were adept stone toolmakers, using angular flakes and lumps of lava to make weapons, scrapers, and cutting tools. The tools themselves were probably used to cut meat and perhaps wood. Most likely, the hominins made extensive use of simple and untrimmed flakes for many purposes.

Oldowan industries occur at several sites in East Africa dating to between about 2.6 and 1.5 mya. They are not just confined to Eastern Africa and have also come to light in the Democratic Republic of the Congo, in South Africa, and as far north as Morocco, where they date to around 1.8 mya. There appears to be relatively little variability among tool kits, and the artifacts show certain common technological features. All of them were made from cobbles, often struck from lumps, with edges flaked from both sides (Figure 2.17). Some of these cores may have served as crude choppers, for the tool kit consisted of both heavy- and light-duty tool forms, some modified into crude scrapers. This seems like a very simple technology, but the artifacts show a skilled appreciation of basic stone-flaking techniques and flaking sequences that were envisaged in the mind's eye.

For years, archaeologists have thought of the Oldowan as a static technological stage without any perceptible change. As more sites are discovered and analytic techniques are refined, though, the Oldowan appears in a different light—as a simple, highly effective technology that grew more complex over time, with the appearance of crude bifacial working in which cores were flaked on both sides (Figure 2.18).

Mary Leakey (1971) studied the Oldowan choppers and flakes from the early hominin levels at Olduvai and divided the artifacts into different morphological forms. Her classification remained unchallenged until Nicholas Toth and a new generation of scholars approached early stone technology from a more holistic perspective (Toth and Schick, 2006). The objective of their studies has been to learn as much as possible about early hominin behavior

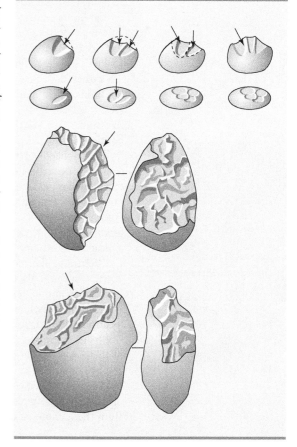

FIGURE 2.17 Oldowan technology. Many cobbles at Koobi Fora and Olduvai Gorge were used as cores to produce sharp-edged flakes. The technology was simple in the extreme. First, sharp blows were struck near the natural edge of a pebble to remove flakes. The pebble was then turned over, and more blows were struck on the ridges formed by the scars of the earlier flakes. A core with a jagged edge, perhaps used as a chopper, resulted. Many cores were "mined" for as many flakes as possible before being discarded. The figure shows Oldowan cores from Olduvai Gorge. Arrows show flake edges. Front and side views (two-fifths actual size).

FIGURE 2.18 A modern hand grasps an Oldowan chopper.

from the stone artifacts left behind. Such research is founded on every aspect of technology, from raw material acquisition through artifact manufacture and use, to the discarding and incorporation of the tools into the geological record. As part of his work, Toth became an expert stone toolmaker and carried out edge-wear and taphonomic studies on sites in East Turkana.

Toth emerged from his work with a very different view of the Oldowan. He points out that conventional approaches to the stone artifacts are based on the idea that the makers had specific artifact forms in mind. His experiments replicated thousands of Oldowan cores and flakes and led him to argue that much of the variety in Oldowan artifacts was, in fact, the result of flake production. Many of the choppers from Olduvai and Koobi Fora are actually "waste," cores discarded when as many flakes as possible had been removed from them. Toth also observes that the size of the available raw material can profoundly affect the size and variety of choppers and flakes at an Oldowan site (Toth and Schick, 2006).

Toth's experiments with replicated tools revealed that sharp-edged flakes are far more effective for butchering animal carcasses, especially for slitting skin. Flakes, then, were of much greater importance than hitherto suspected; but this does not mean that all choppers were just waste. Some may have served as wood-chopping and adzing tools or for breaking open bones for their marrow. Microwear studies of the few Oldowan flakes made of fine-grained materials have hinted at three possible uses: butchering and cutting meat, sawing and scraping wood, and cutting soft plant matter.

The Lokalalei sites on the west shore of Lake Turkana date to around 2.34 mya and have yielded lava cobbles, which hominins knapped to make sharp-edged flakes (Roche et al., 1999). By retrofitting flakes to cobbles, Roche and his colleagues have demonstrated that the hominins exercised a high degree of control over the force and direction of the blows to the stone. They believe that the toolmakers had a good understanding of their raw material and argue that clues as to toolmaking abilities can come from biomechanical studies of finger and hand bones.

What are the implications of these researches for our knowledge of early hominin cognitive skills? Nicholas Toth believes the early hominins had a good sense of the mechanics of stone tool manufacture and of the geometry of core manipulation. They were able to find the correct acute angle needed to remove flakes by percussion. Not even modern beginners have this ability; it takes several hours of intensive practice to acquire the skill. Although chimpanzees use sticks and crack nuts with unflaked stones, they rarely carry their "artifacts" more than a few yards. In contrast, the Koobi Fora and Olduvai hominins carried flakes and cores over considerable distances, up to 13 km (8 miles). This behavior represents a simple form of **curation**, retaining tools for future use rather than just utilizing convenient stones as chimpanzees do. Toth hypothesizes that the hominins tested materials in streambeds and other locations, transported the best pieces to activity areas, and sometimes dropped them there, carrying the rest off with them. He also points out that they must have relied heavily on other raw materials like wood and bone, and that stone artifacts do not necessarily give an accurate picture of early hominin cognitive abilities.

The archaeologists' traditional view of the Oldowan considers it a "protohuman culture," its simple stone artifacts being a first step on the long evolutionary trail to modern humanity. Perhaps this view has been colored by analogies with modern hunter-gatherers and by overoptimistic interpretations claiming that early hominins aimed and threw stone missiles, shared food, and so on. Another viewpoint argues that the Oldowan hominins were at an apelike grade of behavior, on the grounds that all the conceptual abilities and perceptions needed to manufacture Oldowan tools also appear in ape-manufactured tools like termite-fishing tools and sleeping platforms (Wynn, 1991). Furthermore, like the Oldowan hominins, chimpanzees also scavenge and hunt for game, chasing down small animals, carrying meat over considerable distances, and using "extractive technology" to break open animal bones and nuts.

Chimpanzees, like early hominins, use the same places again and again, pounding nuts at the same locations and carrying food to their favorite eating sites. Western African chimpanzees use stone "tools" to crack open hard-shell nuts and obtain more than 3,000 calories a day from them. Some of these nuts are very hard-shelled indeed, especially those of the panda tree. A single chimpanzee cracks as many as 100 nuts a day, forming heaps of discarded shells around immovable stone anvils. Females tend to crack more nuts than males, using a technique employing stone hammers weighing up to 15 kg (33 pounds) that can take as many as seven years for a young chimpanzee to master. Both the hammerstones and anvils display a characteristic pitting resulting from the pounding.

Julio Mercader and his colleagues (2002) followed the same methods used to excavate early hominin sites to investigate such a location in the Taï National Park in Ivory Coast, West Africa. The site lies near a stream in dense rain forest, away from human habitation. Six hardwood anvils lay around a single panda tree, which died in 1996, and are known from observation of the chimpanzees to have been in use since at least 1975. The excavators recovered 39,600 grams (about 21 pounds) of nutshell and 4,500 grams (9.8 pounds) of fractured stone. There was no question that the fractured stone resulted from chimpanzee activity, but the fragments bore no resemblance to early hominin tools, which are much more sophisticated. The stone fragments included some flakes derived from manufacturing hammerstones. The clusters of broken stone were about the same size as that of some early human occurrences.

This unusual excavation shows that chimpanzees leave a material record of nut cracking behind them. They transported stone to their processing place from some distance, gathered nuts, and shaped hammerstones. The patterns of this activity resemble those of early hominins but certainly do not represent formal toolmaking like that of early humans. But the excavation has important implications for paleoanthropology. Maybe it will be possible to trace such distinctive activities on early nonhuman primate sites occupied as early as the Miocene. And perhaps, too, one day we will be able to show that the stone byproducts of nut cracking became the sharp-edged choppers and cutting tools used by the first humans—the Oldowan culture. At the moment, however, the origins of human technology remain a mystery.

Even if the specifics vary in some instances and the natural environments are different, the behavioral pattern of Oldowan hominins was generally similar to that of apes. There are, however, two behavioral differences between apes and early hominins. First, hominins were at an advantage in that they were bipedal, a posture that is far more efficient than walking on four limbs. Second, the Oldowan humans were adapted to savanna living, where they had to organize and cover far larger territories in open country than their primate relatives in the forest. In the long term, this requirement may have resulted in new concepts of space and spatial organization, concepts that were definitely reflected in more complex stone tool forms after a million years ago (Mithen, 1996).

Early hominins, with their larger brains, probably would not have adapted or behaved the same way as modern apes. We can be certain that there were significant differences between nonhuman primates and hominins 2.5 mya, but these differences may not be reflected in stone artifacts. Without question, our ancestors became more and more dependent on technology. The opportunistic nature of primeval stone technology contrasts sharply with the better designed, much more standardized stone artifacts of later humans.

The Mind of the Earliest Humans

By 2 mya, there were probably several species of early *Homo*, but for convenience' sake, we can group them under a single species, *H. habilis*. Although many stone tools may have been manufactured by *Australopithecus*, who may also have fractured animal bones, we are safe in assuming that most early archaeological sites and their associated artifacts were the work of early *Homo*. What, then, were the specialized cognitive processes involved in the technical intelligence found in these earliest humans, as opposed to much earlier, nontoolmaking hominins (Mithen, 1996)?

Some clues lie in stone tool manufacture. Chimpanzees shape termite twigs with their teeth from convenient wood fragments, removing leaves so they can poke the "artifact" down a small hole. Stone toolmaking requires good hand–eye coordination, the ability to recognize acute angles in stone, and the mental processes necessary to shape one tool by using another. But the Oldowan stoneworkers were carrying out simple tasks: shaping stones so they could hold them in one hand to crack bones, and striking off sharp-edged flakes. Their artifacts defy precise classification in the way that one can subdivide later stone tools into forms such as choppers, scrapers, and knives, for example. Their lumps and flakes display continuous variability, an understanding of basic fracture mechanics, not the ability to impose standardized forms or to choose easily worked raw materials. Could chimpanzees have made such tools, as has been suggested? Nicholas Toth tried to train a bonobo named Kanzi to make Oldowan tools by demonstration. Kanzi learned by trial and error. Ten years later, his learning curve has risen sharply, to where his skills are much closer to those of Oldowan toolmakers. But there are significant differences between Kanzi's artifacts and those of the Oldowan (Schick et al., 1999). Steven Mithen (1996) argues for two possibilities: Either a more general intelligence had evolved or some specialized cognitive processes for basic stoneworking had appeared—intuitive physics in the mind of *H. habilis*.

Oldowan stone tools were mainly used to process animal carcasses: skinning, cutting joints and meat, and breaking open bones. But how did *H. habilis* interact with the natural world?

One obvious and significant difference between *H. habilis* and chimpanzees appears in the archaeological record of 2 mya: a dramatic rise in meat consumption. As we have seen, prolonged controversies have surrounded the issue of hunting as opposed to scavenging by the earliest humans, with a consensus leaning toward a major emphasis on scavenging. In practice, *H. habilis* was probably a behaviorally flexible, nonspecialized forager whose lifeway was marked by diversity: by shifts between hunting and scavenging and between food sharing and feeding on the move. As biological anthropologists Leslie Aiello and Peter Wheeler have theorized (1995), the larger brain of *H. habilis* would have required the consumption of more energy and a higher-quality diet. The stable basal metabolic rate was maintained by a reduction in the size of the gut, which could become reduced only as a result of a higher meat diet, as a high-fiber diet requires more intestinal action.

Mithen (1996) believes that this need for more meat required another cognitive ability besides that for toolmaking: being able to use one's knowledge of the environment to develop ideas about where to find predator kills and high densities of animals. He argues that the presence of toolmaking stone up to 10 km (6 miles) from its source is a sign that *H. habilis* was moving not only stone but also meat to different, ever-changing locations. Such ability suggests a relatively sophisticated interaction with the environment when compared with that of chimpanzees, which transport "tools" only to fixed locations.

H. habilis appears to have been confined to tropical Africa and to a relatively narrow range of savanna and grassland environments, in contrast with later humans, who adapted to every kind of climate imaginable. Many groups lived close to permanent water, tethered, as it were, to places like the shallow lake at Olduvai, where sites were stacked one above another over considerable periods of time. Many animal species appear in the Olduvai caches, as if our ancestors ranged widely over the surrounding landscape, but they may have transported much of their food to well-defined locations.

H. habilis shared the ability of its earlier ancestors to "map" resources over wide areas. But it may also have possessed additional cognitive abilities: to develop ideas about where food might be found and to use telltale signs such as animal droppings to find it—within a relatively narrow environmental setting. At the same time, its general intelligence was supplemented by some specialized abilities in artifact manufacture that were to be an important foundation for environmental intelligence in later millennia.

Social intelligence may have evolved significantly. Anthropologist Robin Dunbar (1992) has studied living primates and discovered evidence of larger brain size in individuals living in larger groups, developing an equation for relating brain to group size. He then estimated the brain size of *H. habilis* and applied his figures to the chimpanzee equation. Chimpanzees live in predicted group sizes of about 60 individuals. In contrast, Dunbar hypothesized, australopithecines lived in groups with a mean size of about 67 individuals, whereas *H. habilis* flourished in larger groups of about 81. Group living was an essential for *H. habilis*, who lived in an environment teeming with carnivores, often competing with them for meat with only the simplest of weaponry for protection. Large-group living has dramatic advantages for hominins living in environments where resources come in large "parcels" that are irregularly distributed across the landscape. Members of a group can search for food individually or in pairs, then share it with others, so that the group as a whole can cover a much larger area. Mithen (1996) believes that the larger brain of the first humans allowed for greater social intelligence, that is, for coping with the complexities of living in closer juxtaposition to others, where assuming that others know things is of vital importance.

The Development of Language

Cooperation, the ability to get together to solve problems of both subsistence and potential conflict, is a vital quality in human beings. We are unique in having a spoken, symbolic language that enables us to communicate our most intimate feelings to one another. One fundamental question about early prehistory surrounds this development: At what point did hominins acquire the ability to speak (Lieberman, 1991)?

Our closest living relatives, the chimpanzees, communicate with gestures and many voice sounds in the wild, whereas other apes use sounds only to convey territorial information. However, chimpanzees cannot talk to us because they do not have the vocal apparatus to do so. In the 1960s, Beatrice and Allen Gardner trained a chimpanzee named Washoe to use American Sign Language (Gardner and Gardner, 1969). Within three years, Washoe had acquired at least 85 signs and could conduct a form of conversation with humans. But can chimpanzees construct sentences? Some argue that flawed methodology has exaggerated chimpanzee linguistic abilities and that chimpanzees are incapable of sentence building.

Sue Savage-Rumbaugh and her colleagues have used a bonabo named Kanzi to suggest otherwise (Savage-Rumbaugh and Lewin, 1996). Kanzi was raised in a 22-ha (55-acre) forest (not in a laboratory), where much communication was concerned with normal chimpanzeelike activities. He was taught how to understand spoken words, and he learned the symbols for them on a computer keyboard. By age 6, he could identify 150 different symbols and also understand the meaning of sentences that consisted of several words strung together. By age 8, he had the linguistic abilities of a human 2-year-old.

Savage-Rumbaugh's team claims that Kanzi constructs sentences using some grammatical rules, but the sentences are a far cry from those used by a human 6-year-old. Almost all Kanzi's sentences are demands for things, whereas a 6-year-old human has a vocabulary of about 13,000 words and goes far beyond asking for things. In short, the ways in which humans and chimpanzees acquire language are totally different, to the point where linguist Stephen Pinker has called Kanzi and other "talking" chimpanzees "highly trained animal acts" (1994: 151)—perhaps a harsh judgment but one that recognizes that humans acquire specialized language modules after age 2 and that they possess linguistic intelligence.

Clearly, articulate speech was an important threshold in human evolution because it opened up whole new vistas of cooperative behavior and unlimited potential for the enrichment of life. When did hominins abandon grunts for speech? We cannot infer language from the simple artifacts made by *H. habilis*, but two potential lines of research are open. One uses endocasts. The endocasts of the early australopithecines are apelike. The brain cell of Skull 1470 (see Figure 2.9) is about 300 cc larger, and the frontal lobe of its endocast is more humanlike, especially in Broca's area, where speech control is located.

Endocast research is much more generalized than detailed anatomical studies of the position of the voice box (the larynx), another way to glean clues about the development of speech. Both comparative anatomy and actual fossils can be used to study differences between apes and humans. Jeffrey Laitman and others (1991) studied the position of the larynx in a wide variety of mammals, including humans. They found that all mammals except adult humans have a larynx high in the neck, a position that enables the larynx to lock into the air space at the back of the nasal cavity. Although this position allows animals like monkeys and cats to breathe and swallow at the same time, it limits the sounds they can produce. The pharynx (the air cavity part of the food pathway) can produce sounds, but animals use their mouths to modify sounds because they are anatomically incapable of producing the range of sounds needed for articulate speech.

Until they are about 18 months to 2 years old, human children's larynxes are also situated high in the neck. Then the larynx begins to descend, ending up between the fourth and seventh neck vertebrae. How and why are still a mystery, but the change completely alters the way the child breathes, speaks, and swallows. Adult humans cannot separate breathing and swallowing, so they can suffocate when food lodges in an airway. However, an enlarged pharyngeal chamber above the vocal cords enables them to modify the sounds they emit in an infinite variety of ways, which is the key to human speech.

Fortunately, the shape of the base of the skull is highly informative. Most mammals have flat-based skulls and high larynxes, but humans have an arched skull base associated with their low larynx. Using sophisticated statistical analyses, Laitman and his colleagues (1991) ran tests on as many complete fossil skulls as possible. They found that the australopithecines of 4 to 1 mya had flat skull bases and high larynxes, whereas those of *H. erectus*, dating to about 1.5 million years and later, show somewhat more curvature, suggesting that the larynx was beginning to descend to its modern position. It was only about 300,000 years ago that the skull base finally assumed a modern curvature, which allowed fully articulate speech to evolve.

Anthropologist Robin Dunbar (1998) has studied grooming, the process of picking out fleas and lice, in primate groups (Figure 2.19). This seemingly trivial activity was vital to socialization because the individual being groomed, the length of time the grooming took, and those allowed to watch it were part of a process of sending social messages. Dunbar believes that as primate group size increased, so the necessity for transferring social information increased. He believes language evolved as a means of exchanging social information within increasingly large and more complex groups, initially as a supplement to grooming and later as a replacement for it. Language, he says, is more efficient than grooming. Using computer simulations, he found that *H. habilis* spent about 28 percent of its time grooming, very close to a projected maximum time allocation for such an activity of 30 percent. But with so much time taken up with grooming, he believes that these hominins began to embed social information into their vocalizations, in ways somewhat akin to the contented purring of cats or the chattering among groups of modern gelada baboons.

FIGURE 2.19 A female chimpanzee grooms her infant daughter in her nest in the Gombe National Park, Tanzania. Like other primates, chimpanzees occupy fairly small territories, smaller than those occupied by humans.

Chimpanzees, our closest living relations, seem to have a natural talent for learning symbolic language under controlled conditions. As we have seen, the chimpanzee Washoe was trained to communicate with humans, using language gestures similar to those of American Sign Language. After more than a year, Washoe could associate particular signs with specific activities such as eating and drinking. There is no evidence that chimpanzees can combine visual symbols to create new meanings or use syntax. Sequences of signs produced by trained chimpanzees may have a superficial resemblance to the first multiword sentences produced by children, but beyond the stage of learning isolated symbols, an ape's language learning is severely restricted.

The real value of language, apart from the stimulation it gives brain development, is that with it we can convey feelings and nuances far beyond the power of gestures or grunts to communicate. We may assume that the first humans had more ways to communicate than the gestures and grunts of nonhuman primates, but it appears that modern articulate speech was a more recent stimulus to biological and cultural evolution.

Social Organization

The first phase of human evolution involved shifts in the basic patterns of subsistence and locomotion as well as new ingredients: food sharing and toolmaking. These led ultimately to enhanced communication, information exchange, and economic and social insight, as well as cunning and restraint. Hominin, then later, human, anatomy was augmented with tools. Culture became an inseparable part of humanity, and social life acquired a new, and as yet little understood, complexity.

What sort of social organization did *H. habilis* enjoy? However much we look at contemporary nonhuman primates, we cannot be sure. Most primates are intensely social and live in groups in which the mother–infant relationship forms a central bond. The period of infants' dependency on mothers found in, say, chimpanzees was probably lengthened considerably in *H. habilis*. The larger brain size would mean that infants were born with much smaller heads than adults, at an earlier stage of mental maturity. This biological reality would have had a major impact on social organization and daily habits.

Chimpanzees have flexible matriarchal social groups and may even have different cultures. They occupy a relatively small territory, one with sufficient vegetable resources to support a considerable population density; this pattern contrasts sharply with that of the average hunter-gatherer band, typically a close-knit group of about 25 people of several families (Figure 2.19). The kind of systematic hunting such people engage in requires much larger territories and permits much lower densities per square kilometer. The few sites that have been excavated suggest that *H. habilis* tended to live in bands that were somewhat like those of modern hunter-gatherers. But in all probability, their social organization resembled more closely those of chimpanzees and baboons, which are very different from that of humans.

Chimpanzees and baboons live in a world created in their brains by the integration of sight, sound, smell, and touch. The more complex the inputs and their neural processing are, the more complex is the inner world built by the brain. It may well be that this increase in complexity is what underlies the cumulative growth in brain size that is such a distinctive feature of mammalian evolution, from amphibians to reptiles and then through mammals to humans. The world of *H. habilis* was much less predictable and more demanding than that of even *Australopithecus*. What was it that was more complex? Why do we have to be so intelligent? Not for hunting animals or gathering food, but for our interactions with other people. The increased complexity of our social interactions is likely to have been a powerful force in the evolution of the human brain. For *H. habilis*, the adoption of a wider-based diet with a food-sharing social group would have placed much more acute demands on the ability to cope with the complex and the unpredictable. And the brilliant technological, artistic, and expressive skills of humankind may well be a consequence of the fact that our early ancestors had to be more and more socially adept.

The first chapter of human evolution ended about 2 mya, with the appearance of the first true humans, classified generically as *H. ergaster* and *H. erectus*, described in Chapter 3.

Summary

- The story of human evolution begins with the separation of the chimpanzee and human lines from a common, and as yet unknown, ancestor about 5 to 6 mya.
- The first hominins were tree living, with long arms and legs and broad chests, who eventually became bipedal, walking on two limbs. They adapted to more open country in Africa, which resulted from global cooling over 4 mya, by broadening their diet to include more meat and by achieving great mobility and behavioral flexibility.
- The earliest known possible hominin is *Sahelanthropus tchadensis* from Chad, which may date to between 6 and 7 mya. A small bipedal hominin named *Ardipithecus ramidus* flourished in Ethiopia 4.5 mya. A hominin, *A. afarensis*, was ancestral to later hominins and flourished 3.5 to 3.0 mya.
- By 2 mya, the hominin line had radiated into many forms, among them the robust and more gracile australopithecines and the larger-brained *H. habilis*, another hominin form. *H. habilis* was a forager who also scavenged game meat and perhaps hunted. These hominins used a simple stone technology, had some ability to communicate, and had a very rudimentary social organization.
- New definitions of the genus *Homo* make a major distinction between the more apelike hominins described in this chapter, which flourished before 2 mya, and the true humans, beginning with *H. erectus*, which evolved after 1.9 million years before the present.
- Three lines of evidence can be used to test hypotheses about human behavior: artifact scatters, manufactured artifacts, and food remains. The earliest known artifact scatters were not "central places," or camps, as was once thought. Some may have been places to which food was carried, processed, and eaten by hominins, who scavenged much of their meat from predator kills rather than hunting large animals—but this is a controversial hypothesis. Plant remains were also important.
- The earliest human technology, known as the Oldowan, was a simple, effective use of stone cobbles and sharp-edged flakes, which eventually evolved into artifacts flaked on both sides—bifaces.
- *H. habilis* shared the ability of their earlier ancestors to "map" resources over the landscape, their intelligence amplified by toolmaking.
- These hominins may have lived in larger groups, something made possible by greater social intelligence resulting from larger brain size.
- Despite these enhanced skills at communicating with others, the first humans probably had only the most rudimentary forms of speech, in addition to the grunts and gestures of other primates.

Key Terms

adaptive radiation (42)	dental ape (28)	microwear studies (48)	prosimian (26)
anthropoid (26)	hominidae (27)	monophyletic (42)	sexual dimorphism (40)
bipedal (30)	hominin (27)	Pleistocene (25)	stratigraphy (34)
carrying capacity (32)	hominoid (28)	ponginae (27)	taphonomy (48)
curation (54)	knuckle walking (32)	primate (26)	ungulate (48)

Further Reading

Johanson, Donald C., and Maitland A. Edey. 1981. *Lucy: The Beginnings of Humankind.* New York: Simon & Schuster.

Klein, Richard. 2009. *The Human Career*, 3rd ed. Chicago: University of Chicago Press.

Lewin, Roger. 1987. *Bones of Contention.* New York: Simon & Schuster.

Stringer, Chris, and Peter Andrews. 2005. *The Complete World of Human Evolution.* London and New York: Thames & Hudson.

Tattersall, Ian. 1996. *The Fossil Trail: How We Know What We Think We Know About Human Evolution.* New York: Oxford University Press.

Archaic Humans: *Homo ergaster, Homo erectus,* and *Homo heidelbergensis*

1.9 MILLION TO 150,000 YEARS AGO

Eugene Dubois was a Dutchman obsessed with the "missing link," the mythical human that was the evolutionary connection between apes and modern people. A surgeon by profession, in 1887 young Dubois wangled a posting as an army physician to distant Sumatra in Southeast Asia, where, he was convinced, the missing link would be found. He remembered the words of the great biologist Alfred Russel Wallace, who had developed a theory of evolution parallel to Darwin's. "With what interest must every naturalist look forward to the time when the caves of the tropics be thoroughly examined," Wallace wrote, theorizing that the ancestors of humankind had originated in a "warm forest-clad land." Incredible though it may seem, Dubois actually found what he claimed was such an ancestor on nearby Java in 1891. Digging into fossil-rich ash and river sediments at Trinil on the Solo River in northeastern Java, he found not only the bones of extinct animals but also a human tooth, a thick-walled skull, and a human thighbone.

Dubois was ecstatic and named his fossil *Pithecanthropus erectus*, "ape-human which stood upright." This, he claimed, was the missing link between apes and humans, a very primitive human being. On his return to Europe in 1895, he was greeted with skepticism, then scorn. Dubois's reaction was to withdraw from the scientific arena. He is said to have kept his fossils under his bed, becoming increasingly convinced that they were the bones of an ancestor of the apes rather than of human beings. Modern science has vindicated Eugene Dubois, for he was the first to discover what is now known as *Homo erectus*, a direct ancestor of modern humanity (Lewin, 1987).

A lifelike reconstruction of a Neanderthal man.

his chapter describes what little we know about the human story after the appearance of the first true humans, commonly known to scientists as *Homo ergaster.* We cover an immensely long period of time from about 2 million years ago (mya) up to the advent of the first truly modern humans, *Homo sapiens,* in tropical Africa about 200,000 years ago. During this time span, *Homo ergaster* diversified ultimately into at least three different human lineages—*Homo erectus* in eastern Asia, *Homo neanderthalis,* the celebrated Neanderthals, in Europe, and *Homo sapiens* in Africa. The first diversification came with the emergence of *Homo erectus* about a million years ago. The Neanderthals and *Homo sapiens* shared a common ancestor as late as 600,000 to 500,000 years ago, a human form named *Homo heidelbergensis,* which originated in Africa and spread from there to Europe. All of these humans shared intensely conservative behavior. Their technologies and lifeways changed remarkably little over hundreds of thousands of years. They were thin on the ground. We are merely guessing that 250,000 years ago, the world's population probably numbered no more than a few hundred thousand people. Archaic humans like these may have been adept hunters, but they were opportunistic ones, who lacked much of the cognitive abilities of planning and communication typical of modern humans. Their dwellings were at best rudimentary; the same kinds of stone tools sufficed without significant change for millennia. Apparently they made little use of antler, bone or wood, created little or no art, and at most rudimentary spiritual beliefs. Fully modern human behavior only developed with the emergence of fully modern humans with all the intellectual potential we possess well after 200,000 years ago, a development described in Chapter 4.

Homo sapiens

Homo neanderthalensis
before 100,000 to c. 30,000 years ago

Homo heidelbergensis

Pleistocene Background

The archaic world of *Homo ergaster* and its successors was one of unpredictable climatic change, which began about 2.5 mya and intensified with the beginning of the Pleistocene (the Great Ice Age) about 1.6 mya. These climatic changes were the backdrop for an accelerating pace of human biological and cultural change that culminated in the appearance of modern humans and the spread of hunter-gatherer groups to all corners of the world in the late Ice Age (see Chapter 4).

Lower Pleistocene (1.6 Million to c. 780,000 Years Ago)

The Pleistocene began about 1.6 mya, after an intensification of glaciation about 2.5 mya (Figure 3.1a, Table 3.1 on p. 63). This arbitrary boundary for the beginning of the Pleistocene coincides with a major geomagnetic reversal in the earth's magnetic field, which can be recognized on a worldwide basis. By this time, great mountain chains had formed in the Alps, the Himalayas, and elsewhere. Landmasses had been uplifted; there was a reduction in the connection between these latitudes and southern areas, lessening their heat exchange and causing greater temperature differences between them. Three million years ago, northern latitudes were still warmer than today, but they were much cooler by the beginning of the Pleistocene.

The Lower Pleistocene is distinguished by surviving Pliocene animal forms and by the appearance of horses, cattle, elephants, and camels. Deep-sea cores tell us that climatic fluctuations between warmer and colder regimens were still relatively minor during this, the first million years of the Ice Age (Kurtén, 1968). This was a critically important time, when *Homo erectus* evolved in Africa and moved out of the tropics into Asia and Europe.

Middle Pleistocene (c. 780,000 to 128,000 Years Ago)

An abrupt reversal of the earth's magnetic field, back from reversed to normal, occurred about 780,000 years ago, an event that has been identified all over the world in both deep-sea cores and terrestrial deposits. This **Matuyama-Brunhes boundary,** named after the geologists who first identified it, marks the arbitrary division between the Lower and Middle Pleistocene (Maslin, 2009b; Roberts, 2010). The seesaw pattern of deep-sea-core changes tells of constant climatic change from this point on. Consistently, the cores tell us, ice sheets formed gradually, but deglaciation took place with great rapidity during phases that geologists call **terminations.** These corresponded with major rises in sea level that flooded low-lying coastal areas. Glaciers covered a full third of the earth's surface during glacial maxima. Great ice sheets mantled Scandinavia and the Alps, as well as much of northern North America (Figure 3.1b). The recently drilled Vostok ice core from Antarctica, which reached a depth of 3,623 m (11,886 feet) in the Antarctic ice sheet, has produced a record of four transitions from cold to warm periods going back some 335,000 years, with a periodicity of about 100,000 years, the last occurring 18,000 years ago at the end of the Ice Age (Petit et al., 1999).

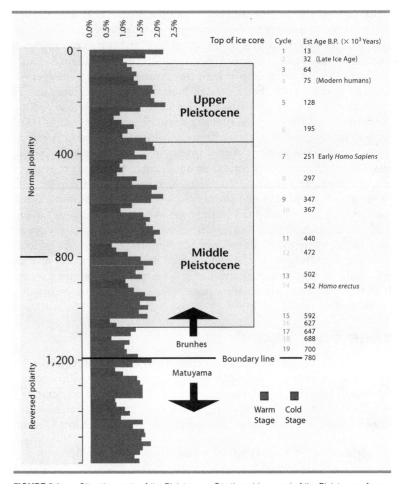

FIGURE 3.1a Climatic events of the Pleistocene. Stratigraphic record of the Pleistocene from deep-sea core V28–238, from the Solomon Plateau in the Pacific Ocean (Shackleton and Opdyke, 1973). The Matuyama-Brunhes boundary occurs at about 780,000 years ago, at a depth of 1,200 cm (39.3 feet). Above it, a sawtoothlike curve records the relative size of the world's oceans and ice caps and identifies eight complete glacial and interglacial cycles, a more complete record of the Middle and Upper Pleistocene that comes from land sediments. The Vostok ice core from Antarctica covers the past 335,000 years and documents a periodicity of about 100,000 years for transitions from cold to warm conditions.

During **interglacials,** the glaciers were about as extensive as they are today. Thus, sea levels were then within 5.5 to 6.0 m (18 to 20 feet) of present shorelines. Much less is known about changes in tropical regions. It is known that the southern fringes of the Sahara expanded dramatically during cold periods.

The outlines of Middle Pleistocene climatic change are still imperfectly known, but we know that there was a major glacial episode, called by European geologists the Elster glaciation, about 525,000 years ago. At its height, there was ice as far south as present-day Seattle, St. Louis, and New York in North America, and sea levels were about 197 m (650 feet) below modern levels. In contrast, there were periods of more temperate conditions between about 515,000 and 315,000 years ago, with colder incidents breaking up the warmer climate. It was during this interglacial that the human settlement of temperate latitudes really took hold, as small bands of hunter-gatherers exploited the rich animal and plant resources of European and Asian river valleys and woodlands.

The Middle Pleistocene ended with another intense glaciation, the Saale (known as the Illinoian in North America), which lasted from about 180,000 to 128,000 years ago. As we shall see, this colder cycle coincided in general terms with the period when anatomically modern humans (*Homo sapiens*) were evolving in tropical Africa.

Both *H. erectus* and *H. sapiens* evolved during a period of constant climatic transition between warmer and colder regimens in the northern latitudes. Experts believe that the world's climate has been in transition from one extreme to the other for over 75 percent of the past 730,000 years, with a predominance of colder climate over the entire period. These constant climatic changes played an important role in the spread of archaic humans throughout the temperate and tropical latitudes (Gamble, 1999).

The climatic events of the Upper Pleistocene are described at the beginning of Chapter 4.

TABLE 3.1
Homo erectus and early modern humans

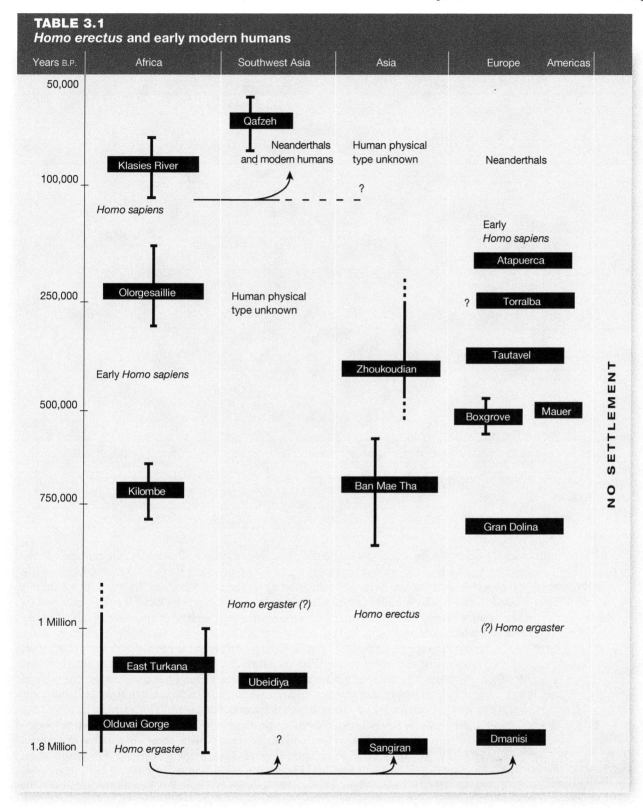

Homo ergaster in Africa

Our story begins with *Homo ergaster*, which appeared in tropical Africa at a time of increasing aridity. Significant anatomical changes and other behavioral changes as well as technological innovations, such as making larger stone flakes, allowed *ergaster* to adapt successfully to drier, more open African environments where water was often at a premium, there was marked seasonal variation in climatic conditions, and shade was often rare. *Homo ergaster* operated over much larger ranges, tamed fire, was more versatile, and soon migrated in steps and starts over long distances. These were the first humans to move out of Africa into Europe and Asia. A word of caution is in

Homo ergaster
1.9 mya

Klasies River
120,000 to 70,000 years ago

Ban Mae Tha
700,000 years ago

FIGURE 3.1b Pleistocene glaciers in the Northern Hemisphere at their maximum extent. Shorelines caused by low sea levels are not known.

order, however, for we still know very little about *Homo ergaster*. Early hominin evolution forms a complex pattern of constant diversification, to the point where there were probably about five or six species of living hominins at the beginning of the Ice Age some 1.6 mya. The numbers thinned over time. By a million years ago, the only known survivors were *Homo ergaster* and its Asian relative *Homo erectus*, both larger humans with overall skeletal proportions much more like those of modern humans.

Nariokotome
1.6 mya

Homo ergaster was a powerfully built human with massive brow ridges and a large face and with a long, low skull to accommodate a much larger brain, which flourished from about 1.8 mya to 600,000 years ago. That the new human evolved from a *H. habilis*–like hominin seems unquestionable, but we still await the discovery of larger-brained transitional forms. The earliest East African *H. ergaster* specimens come from the Lake Turkana region of northern Kenya, where current estimates place their appearance at about 2 mya or slightly later (Figure 3.2). Skull KNM-ER 3733 from East Turkana dates to between 1.6 and 1.5 mya. This fossil, with its massive brow ridges, enlarged brain size, and high forehead, is morphologically very close to examples of *H. erectus* dating to a million years ago and later. We also know that *Australopithecus boisei* survived alongside *H. erectus* until at least 1.5 mya (Suwa et al., 1997). The latest known *Homo habilis* fossil from Koobi Fora dates to about 1.44 mya, whereas a skull from a small *Homo ergaster* dates to 1.55 mya. These two hominins apparently lived alongside one another for a long time, about a half million years, which makes it unlikely that the one evolved from the other, another reason

FIGURE 3.2 Skull KNM-ER 3733, East Turkana, Kenya. This important early *Homo* fossil has a rounder skull than that of an australopithecine. The distance between the temples is less pronounced, owing to a large brain size of about 750 cc.

FIGURE 3.3 Lake Turkana, East Africa. A reconstruction of a young *Homo ergaster* boy, who died in a small lagoon on the western shores of Lake Turkana about 1.6 mya. Drawing by Ian Everard.

to reject linear views of human evolution (Spoor et al., 2007).

Richard Leakey and anatomist Alan Walker discovered the virtually complete skeleton of an 11-year-old *H. ergaster* boy at Nariokotome on the western shores of Lake Turkana dating to about 1.6 mya (Walker and Leakey, 1993) (Figure 3.3). The footprints of hippopotamuses and other animals nearby suggest that the decomposing corpse was trampled to pieces. From the neck down, the boy's bones are remarkably modern looking. The skull and jawbone are more primitive, with brow ridges and a brain capacity perhaps as much as 700 to 800 cc, about half the modern size. The skeleton shows that the boy stood about 1.6 m (5 feet 4 inches) tall, taller than many modern 12-year-olds. This Turkana find tends to confirm many scientists' view that different parts of the body evolved at different rates, the body achieving fully modern form long before the head. In particular, *Homo ergaster* may have been the first hominin to run fast, a critical ability for hunting and scavenging over long distances. These new humans had longer, more slender legs, narrower rib cages and hip bones, and a ligament, not present in *Homo habilis*, which kept the head steady as they ran (Bramble and Lieberman, 2004).

Homo ergaster's brain size was only some 130 cc larger than that of *H. habilis*, and smaller than that of modern humans. This may have allowed them to develop new tool forms, but they and their archaic descendants made few changes in their simple technology over hundreds of thousands of years. In many respects, however, the new humans were radically different—flat and receding foreheads, long skulls with thick walls, with a projecting, humanlike nose, in contrast to the ape-like noses of the australopithecines. They were chinless people with massive, projecting jaws and large teeth, adept at chewing. *Homo ergaster* had short arms and long legs, for these hominins lived entirely on the ground. They had barrel-like chests and narrower hips, which led to more efficient muscles for walking and running bipedally. The more constricted pelvis would have reduced the amount of brain growth before birth and led to a longer dependence on the mother, like modern humans. *Homo ergaster* was an African, adapted with a long, slim body to living in hot, arid environments. These may have been the first nearly hairless, naked humans, for they could not have sweated efficiently if covered with apelike body hair. The marked sexual dimorphism of the australopithecines and perhaps *H. habilis* has now vanished, perhaps creating social environments where males no longer competed for females and male–female relationships lasted longer.

At about 1.9 mya, *Homo ergaster* is older than its close relative, *Homo erectus,* known from Eugene Dubois's discoveries in Southeast Asia and from Chinese fossils (see below), meaning that the latter may have originated in Africa before migrating to Asia (Table 3.2 on p. 66). The African hominids have less massive faces, thinner skull walls, and other features that are either more primitive or less specialized than those of *H. erectus*. So they are classified separately by most experts as *H. ergaster*, although many researchers still classify them as *H. erectus*, on the grounds that we have too few specimens to work with.

One major argument for considering *Homo ergaster* a separate form comes from the larger perspective. At some point, the new humans migrated to Asia, where they evolved into specialized, long-lasting forms. In contrast, by 600,000 years ago, early forms of *Homo sapiens* had appeared in tropical Africa, as well as in Europe, in the guise of *Homo heidelbergensis*, named after a 500,000-year-old human jaw from Mauer, Germany, found in 1907. Thus, *Homo ergaster* may have been the common ancestor not only of later Africans but of Europeans as well.

The Radiation of *Homo ergaster*

We know that the earliest hominins could adapt to a variety of climates and habitats. Both the australopithecines and *Homo habilis* adjusted to plunging global temperatures during a glacial episode between about 2.7 and 2.5 mya. The colder conditions turned much of Africa's moist

TABLE 3.2
Human evolution: 3 mya to 200,000 years ago

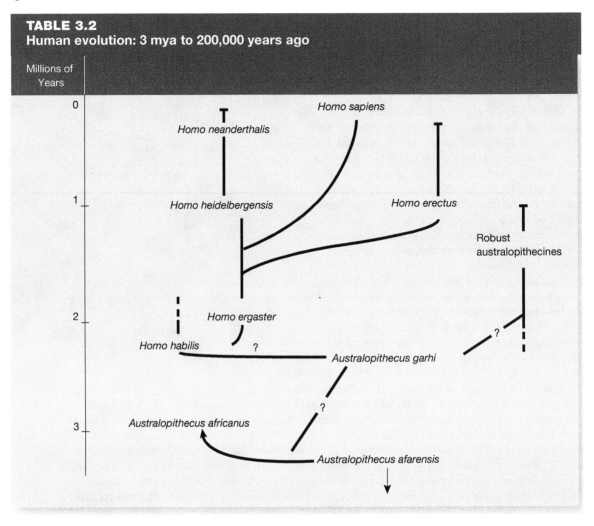

woodlands into much drier, open savanna. The hominins thrived in these conditions, as tree-dwelling primates yielded to bipedal forms better able to survive in the open. Around 2 mya, as the Ice Age began, they were adjusting to cyclic alterations among savanna, forest, and desert. They did so by migrating with changing vegetational zones, as many mammals did, or by adapting to new environments and changing their dietary emphasis from meat to plant foods. Finally, they could move out of tropical latitudes altogether into habitats that human beings had never occupied before.

Very likely, *H. ergaster* adapted to changed circumstances in all these ways, radiating out of Africa by way of the Sahara, when the desert was capable of supporting human life. Geologist Neil Roberts (2010) has likened the Sahara to a pump, sucking in population during wetter savanna phases and forcing hunter-gatherers out northward to the margins of the desert during drier cycles. In radiating out of Africa, *H. ergaster* behaved just like other mammals in its ecological community. *Homo ergaster* was an omnivore and thus was linked ecologically with other predators. There was widespread interchange of mammals between Africa and more temperate latitudes during the Pliocene and the Lower Pleistocene. For example, a major change in the mammalian populations of Europe took place about 700,000 years ago. Hippopotamuses, forest elephants, and other herbivores and carnivores, such as the lion, leopard, and spotted hyena, seem to have migrated northward from Africa at this time. Migrations by the lion, leopard, and hyena—the animals with which hominins shared many ecological characteristics—were in the same direction as that taken earlier by *H. ergaster*. That the first successful human settlement of tropical Asia and of temperate Europe coincided with radiations of mammalian communities out of Africa seems plausible (Figure 3.4 on p. 68).

The grandmother hypothesis, described in Chapter 2, has some relevance here. James O'Connell and his colleagues (1999) have developed the following scenario. By about 1.8 mya, long-term climatic trends toward cooler, drier conditions led to sharp seasonal reductions in many plant foods, especially those exploited by juveniles. In response, hominins increased their use of foods that were inaccessible to juveniles, with mothers and older kin providing shares to the young. Aging females fed their daughters' offspring, so they were weaned earlier and the mothers became pregnant again sooner. The lineages with the highest fertility rates were those with postmenopausal helpers to feed the young. Now that the limits imposed on foraging by juveniles were lifted, foraging territories grew rapidly, opening a much broader range of habitats to exploitation. Thus, longer-lived, later-maturing, larger-bodied hominins with greater brain capacity—*H. ergaster* and *H. erectus*—spread rapidly throughout the tropics and more temperate regions of the Old World.

O'Connell and his team believe that tubers were among the food resources that helped to accelerate these changes. Tubers have many advantages: They store water and carbohydrates; come in many forms, from bulbs to woody rootstocks; and are common in both dry and cold habitats. However, they often had to be dug up, using simple digging sticks—artifacts that could be fashioned with stone flakes and axes made by *H. ergaster* and *H. erectus*. Many of them also had to be boiled, leached, or otherwise processed before they could be eaten. Starch, sucrose, and fructan are the main carbohydrates in tubers, which are more easily digested if cooked—and the first use of fire seems to coincide with the appearance of *H. ergaster*. Tubers are foods that generally cannot be prepared by juveniles, as they require processing and cooking; chimpanzees, for example, never collect them.

Homo ergaster and its archaic successors ranged far wider than earlier hominins, including *Homo habilis*. Traditionally, this increase in range has been seen as the result of a greater reliance on hunting. But game is simply not abundant enough, especially in more arid environments, to feed people as reliably as tubers. Tubers were a much more reliable food supply in Old World environments as far north as 50° latitude (about the latitude of Paris). Significantly, no *H. ergaster* or *H. erectus* sites or finds have come from farther north, the same latitude also being the farthest north for tuber use by modern hunter-gatherers. It may be no coincidence that the modern form of the human digestive tract first appeared in *H. ergaster* (Aiello and Walker, 1995).

This hypothesis requires the assumption that premodern humans had longer life spans than often suggested, something not yet conclusively proven with skeletal data. Both life spans and age at maturity were probably longer in archaic people, but perhaps short of those of modern humans. There could have been important social changes, too. The advent of provisioning would have meant that daughters would remain close to their natal group throughout their lives, with males tending to move away. The benefits of grandmothers assisting daughters were far greater than helping sons, whose fitness depended on their success in competing with other males.

Almost all the archaeological evidence for the lifeways of *H. ergaster* and *H. erectus* comes from sites with only stone tools, or places where they are found in association with the bones of large animals, such as Boxgrove, Schöningen, and Torralba-Ambrona in Europe (see below). But if one assumes that tubers and other plant foods were all-important, especially when combined with provisioning, then the larger group sizes associated with such activities could allow not only better defense against predators but also much more aggressive scavenging.

Schöningen
400,000 B.P.

It may have been that the earliest humans at Olduvai and elsewhere were successful and aggressive competitors with other predators, who seized meat from large animal kills and then carried it away to eat close by. Perhaps the hominins scavenged successfully from kills at the same general locations, so much so that they would carry the meat and bones to the same place again and again, thereby creating the bone concentrations bearing both cut marks and the gnawing of predators (O'Connell, 1997). Thus, such bone concentrations may not reflect a use of central places or caches but simply a world in which fundamental changes in hominin groups and the quiet labors of grandmothers made for more aggressive scavenging—even if large prey was not necessarily acquired very frequently.

The grandmother hypothesis highlights an oft-neglected reality of early human life: the fundamental importance of plant foods and especially the humble tuber as staples for human existence.

During the long history of *H. ergaster* and its successors, humanity adapted to many different environments, from tropical savannas in East Africa to forested Indonesian valleys, temperate climates in North Africa and Europe, and the harsh winters of China and northern Europe. With such a wide distribution, it is hardly surprising that some physical variations in populations also appeared (Howell, 1999). For example, some had more robust skulls than others. Whatever the local variations, *H. ergaster* was far more "human" than *H. habilis* and was a habitual biped that had probably lost the thick hair covering that is characteristic of nonhuman primates. Unfortunately, we are unlikely to know when we lost our dense facial hair because soft parts are never preserved. But it seems possible that this loss occurred when the dramatic enlargement of hominin brains reset the developmental "clock"—perhaps with *H. habilis* (Rightmire, 1990).

Most experts believe that *H. ergaster* originated in Africa. They point to the continuous record of human evolution in that continent, from *Ardipithecus ramidus* to the australopithecines, then *H. habilis* and *H. erectus*. However bushlike the evolutionary tree—and it was much more complicated than we know today—the best and longest fossil record comes from tropical Africa. And, as we shall see in Chapter 4, the same continent may also have been the cradle of modern humans, *H. sapiens*.

FIGURE 3.4 The Archaic World

Homo ergaster, evolved in tropical Africa by 1.9 mya. These archaic humans spread rapidly out of Africa and were flourishing in Southeast Asia by 1.7 mya. They evolved into *Homo erectus* in Asia and adapted to temperate as well as tropical climates, including rain forest, a flexibility of adaptation attributable in part to the use of fire and to more effective technology. *Homo heidelbergensis* evolved from *Homo ergaster* in Africa and spread into Europe about 600,000 years ago. The European Neanderthals descended from *H. heidelbergensis* and adapted to an extremely cold late Ice Age climate.

Homo erectus had modern limbs but a bun-shaped cranium and a smaller brain capacity than modern humans.

At Boxgrove, *Homo heidelbergensis* hunted a wide range of animals, driving at least some of them over cliffs.

Atapuerca in Spain has yielded numerous remains of early *Homo sapiens*, dating to some 200,000 years ago.

A young *Homo ergaster* boy, dating to about 1.6 mya, was found at Nariokotome, Lake Turkana, in northern Kenya.

It is thought that early humanoids arrived in Europe from Africa c. 1 million years ago

Neanderthal bones show that they suffered from diseases including arthritis and blindness

Easternmost known of Neanderthals; bu with a deposit of ibe

Modern-type huma present here c. 100 ago, and seem to h coincided with Nea still present 60,000

Possible directio of human move out of Africa

The emergence ▶ of modern humans

◆ finds of **Homo habilis**
◇ finds of **Homo erectus**
◆ finds of archaic **Homo sapiens**
◇ finds of Neanderthals
◇ finds of modern **Homo sapiens**
  (over 50,000 years old)

Archaic Technology

The earliest tools were sharp flakes struck from lava cobbles. About 1.3 mya, stone hand axes appeared, used for butchering animals and other purposes. After 100,000 years ago, archaic humans shaped smaller tools, including scrapers for processing skins. Neanderthal hunters mounted points on wooden shafts—the first composite tools.

Hand ax

Flint scraper

Later hominid evolution

c. 120,000 years ago: *Neanderthals:* short-limbed, thick-bodied. Average male height, 1.65 m

c. 35,000 years ago: First fully modern humans in Europe; disappearance of Neanderthals

c. 2.5 million years ago: *Homo habilis:* large brain in relation to body size. Average male height, 1.32m

c. 1 million years ago: Earliest evidence of the use of fire

c. 900,000 years ago: Earliest evidence of hominins in Asia

2000000 B.C. — 1000000 — 170000 — present

c. 1.8 million years ago: *Homo erectus:* distinguished by long limbs. Average male height, 1.77 m

c. 850,000 years ago: Hominins reach Europe from Africa

c. 800,000 years ago: *Archaic Homo sapiens;* Average male height, 1.75 m

c. 170,000 years ago: *Homo sapiens* (anatomically modern humans): earliest evidence in Africa

Neanderthals

The Neanderthals were an archaic branch of the *Homo* genus that evolved in Europe and western Asia from *Homo heidelbergensis* at least 200,000 years ago, surviving until about 30,000 years ago. In Europe, Neanderthals adapted to extreme cold with powerful, squat bodies. Their heads had broad noses, pronounced brow ridges, and projecting jaws.

The Neanderthal burial at Kebara in Israel is about 60,000 years old. Neanderthal burials, often with items for the afterlife, refute the common view that they were brutal and primitive.

Map labels: Japan, f Homo munity 450,000 ars ago, Zhoukoudian, River, Lantian, Yangtze, China, Maba, PACIFIC OCEAN, South China Sea, Borneo, AUSTRALIA, Mekong, Yuanmou Earliest evidence of hominids in East Asia, 1.7 million years ago, Plateau of Tibet, Irrawaddy, Malay Peninsula, Trinil, Kedungbrubus, Sangiran Earliest evidence of hominids in maritime Southeast Asia, 1.8 million years ago, Java, Sumatra, alayas, Ganges, Bay of Bengal, Equator, Narmada, India, Thar Desert, Indus, Arabian Sea, an ula, INDIAN OCEAN, Madagascar, Mozambique Channel, Herto, thiopian ighlands, no, kotome na Boy' is complete a human dating to years ago, Koobi Fora, Great Rift Valley, Olduvai Gorge, Laetoli, Lake Victoria, Matupi, Great Rift Valley, Lake Nyasa, Lake Tanganyika, Zambezi, go in, Anatomically modern humans emerge in the south of continent c. 170,000 years ago, Klasies River Mouth Site of some of the earliest known of anatomically modern humans, c. 100,000 years ago, Orange, Tropic of Capricorn, Langebaan

Science   "You Are What You Eat": Taming Fire and Then . . . Cuisine

It may be no coincidence that the earliest human settlement of Europe and Asia, of more temperate latitudes, occurred after *Homo ergaster* appeared in East Africa and mastered fire a million years ago. Perhaps the conservation and taming of fire—as much as food sharing, meat eating, and new forms of sexual behavior—helped to forge close-knit family groups among hominin bands. Another important development has been a new ability to cook meat and other foods. Primatologist Richard Wrangham (2009) believes that individuals learned about cooking by picking up morsels accidently dropped in fire. Finding such food palatable, they eventually began cooking food deliberately. Cooking makes eating easier and faster and extracts more calories from food. Cooked food also freed humans from the lengthy chewing of tough root foods and allowed them to devote themselves to more productive activities such as technology and developing social networks. Consumption of a primarily cooked diet conveyed great nutritional benefits. The mouths and guts of hominids became smaller than those of other primates. At the same time, high meat intake and cooked food may have led to an increase in brain size from about 950 to 1,200 cc around 900,000 years ago, for the brain accounts for 20 percent of our metabolic requirements. *Homo ergaster* and *Homo erectus* may have been the first humans to benefit from cooked food. Thus, fire was a major factor in human evolution.

Wrangham also theorizes that fire and cooking fostered profound changes in human relationships, making home bases and family ties more important. At the same time, male/female roles may have changed profoundly, with a new distribution of labor between men and women. According to Wrangham, women now did the cooking, one of the major bases for lasting human relationships, and protected the food supplies while men developed new social and economic ties and bolstered their social standing. Wrangham argues that every human society cooks, and that we are adapted to cooking. Cooked food affects us biologically, culturally, and socially. Wrangham's provocative theory has ignited new debates about the importance of fire in early human history, a neglected topic for many years.

How was fire tamed? Fire caused by natural conflagrations was certainly part of the savanna environment in which our earlier ancestors lived (Bellomo, 1994). Great grass and brush fires swept across open and wooded country during the dry months, especially, perhaps, when markedly drier conditions were widespread in East Africa about 1.7 mya. This was a time when the faunal communities of East Africa adapted to drier, more open grassland conditions. From this point on, there are signs that human behavior changed. Archaeological sites now appear at higher East African elevations, in less densely vegetated areas, which are more intensively occupied.

We can assume the early hominins had learned to live with natural fires and were not afraid of them. Fire offers protection against predators and is an easy way of hunting game—even insects and rodents, fleeing from a line of flames. Many common vegetables can be roasted or parched in hot ashes to neutralize toxins, allowing people to use a wider range of plants in their diet (Stahl, 1984). The prevalence of such toxins may be the reason chimpanzees eat so many insects—still an important protein source for many African peoples and perhaps for early hominins, too. Perhaps *H. erectus* had the habit of conserving fire, taking advantage of long-smoldering tree stumps that had been ignited by lightning strikes and other natural causes, to kindle flames to light dry brush or simply scare off predators.

Hominin body size had increased dramatically with the appearance of *H. ergaster*. An ecological consequence of enlarged body size is extension of the home range, a fact well documented from animal behavior studies (Foley, 1984b). Larger quantities of food are needed because of higher metabolic rates. This may have been the time when hominins not only relied on smoldering tree stumps but also began to carry simple firebrands as protection against large predators. The new weapon would also allow them to move into more open country, where trees were much rarer, and to extend their home ranges into unfamiliar habitats.

Somewhere around 1.7 mya—the date is still controversial—*Homo ergaster* spread out of Africa and soon reached Asia. At about this time and thereafter, the distribution of archaeological and hominin sites reflects greatly increased home ranges and may have been the time when humans domesticated fire (see Science box).

Swartkrans
1.6 mya

The earliest traces of what may have been tamed fire come from Swartkrans in South Africa, dating to about 1.6 mya, and possibly from Chesowanya in the Kenya Rift Valley. Both examples are assumed to be the work of *H. ergaster*, but whether these are examples of the controlled use of fire is unknown. The earliest unimpeachable evidence for such use comes from a 780,000-year-old lakeside settlement at Gesher Benot Ya'aqov in Israel, where burnt clusters of stone chips may have formed around humanly constructed fireplaces (Alperson-Afil et al., 2009; Goren-Inbar et al., 2004). There is also evidence for hearths at Zhoukoudian, China, described later (pp. 71–72).

Chesowanya

Zhoukoudian
460,000 to 230,000 years ago

Out of Africa: *Homo erectus* in Asia

Quite when and why *Homo ergaster* expanded out of tropical Africa into Southwest Asia and further afield remains one of the great mysteries of archaic humanity. All we have is a scatter of paleomagnetic and potassium-argon dates to document a complex series of small-scale population movements that unfolded over hundreds of thousands of years.

Despite many years of searching, no one has yet discovered an australopithecine or *Homo habilis* in any part of Asia. Most likely the first human settler was *Homo ergaster*. The characteristic hand axes fabricated by archaic humans are commonplace in India and may date to earlier than 1.5 mya, but these artifacts come from a single location (Pappu et al., 2011). Most experts date the first settlement of Southeast Asia to about 1.7 mya, a date that hints at a relatively rapid expansion of humans out of Africa, perhaps within a time span of a mere 200,000 years or so. Wide-ranging *ergaster* occupied territories of open landscape over which food resources were scattered unevenly. Under these circumstances, even a rate of expansion of 32 to 48 km (20 to 30 miles) a year soon translates into hundreds, even thousands, of miles within a few generations. Nor should we think of one-way movements. A *H. erectus* skull and fragments of six other individuals have come from Bouri, in Ethiopia's Middle Awash, dating to between 1 million and 800,000 years ago (Asfaw et al., 2002). The cranium displays both African and Asian features, such as one might expect if there was ebb and flow of populations to and from Africa, perhaps as a result of cooling temperatures in northern latitudes. Most likely, there was constant intermingling and interbreeding between the continents over many hundreds of thousands of years. *Homo ergaster* was the first human form flexible and mobile enough to adapt to temperate, even bitterly cold, environments. It did so with the aid of more elaborate tool kits and by domesticating fire (Foley, 1987b).

Southeast Asia

The earliest dated humans in Asia are the Modjokerto and Sangiran fossils in Indonesia's Solo River valley, which are dated to about 1.66 mya (Larick et al., 2001; Swisher et al., 1994), but the dating problem is both complex and controversial. However, most scientists cautiously accept this chronology in far of a later one of about a million years ago. The first settlements took place at a time of dry, glacial conditions in the north, when lowered sea levels linked Java to the Asian mainland and forest cover gave way to more open country, to which hominins were well adapted.

Eugene Dubois's *H. erectus* finds and more recent discoveries from Indonesia are thought to date to no earlier than about 800,000 years ago (Figure 3.5). Offshore, some stone tools from Flores Island date to between 900,000 and 800,000 years ago, with others from another site dating to as early as 1.2 mya (Morwood et al., 1999).

Five *H. erectus* specimens dating to about 500,000 years ago come from Lang Trang Caves in Vietnam. They are the earliest securely dated human fossils in Southeast Asia. *Homo erectus* may have reached Southeast Asia in the very late Lower Pleistocene, perhaps via the so-called Sunda Shelf, low-lying ground that joined many of the Southeast Asian islands during cooler cycles (see Figure 4.9 on p. 107). This shelf appears to have acted as a faunal filter, preventing many tropical ungulate species from reaching the east. Southeast Asia was a tropical forest environment, with extensive patches of dense forest even during the driest periods of the Pleistocene. Bamboo and other wood resources from these forests must have been of vital importance for the highly portable tool kit used by *H. erectus* in this environment. Fire must also have been an important component in forest technology. Thus, the crude stone choppers and flakes that may have formed the simple stone technology of Asia for tens of thousands of years were only a limited part of forest material culture (Schick, 1994). Such implements are all that remain of a Stone Age lifeway that was based not on the pursuit of large savanna animals but on smaller game and forest resources, many concentrated around natural springs, sinkholes, and caves.

China

No one knows when humans first settled in what is now China, but it was probably at about the same time as they arrived in Southeast Asia, perhaps as early as 1.9 to 1.6 mya (Klein, 2009). Two other sites, Gonwangling in Lant'ien and Q'en-Xia-wo in central China, have yielded *H. erectus* specimens that date to between 800,000 and 750,000 years ago.

The most famous, and the largest Middle Pleistocene, site in China is the Zhoukoudian Cave, 46 km (28.5 miles) west of Beijing (Figure 3.6a). Zhoukoudian consists of many caverns and fissures, the most famous of which is Locality I, where both stone implements and human fossils have been found. These caverns were visited by *H. erectus* over an immensely long period of time, from about 460,000 to 230,000 years

Flores Island
800,000 years ago

Lang Trang
500,000 years ago

Bouri
1 mya to 800,000 years ago

Lant'ien
600,000 years ago

Modjokerto Sangiran
1.66 mya

FIGURE 3.5 A cast of *Homo erectus* from Zhoukoudian, China. The skull bones of *H. erectus* show that these hominins had a brain capacity between 775 and 1,300 cc, indicating much variation. Their vision was probably excellent, and it is probable that they were capable of extensive thought. The *H. erectus* skull is more rounded than that of earlier hominins; it also has conspicuous brow ridges and a sloping forehead. With a massive jaw, much thicker skull bones, and teeth with cusp patterns somewhat similar to those of *Australopithecus africanus* and modern humans, *H. erectus* also had limbs and hips fully adapted to an upright posture. It stood over 1.8 m (5 feet 6 inches) tall and had hands fully capable of precision gripping and many kinds of toolmaking.

(a)

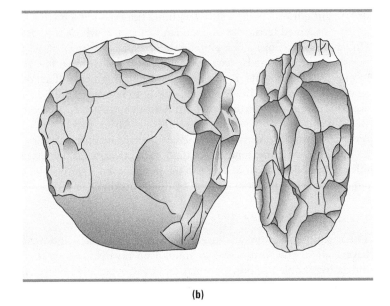

(b)

FIGURE 3.6 (a) Zhoukoudian Cave. (b) A stone chopper from Zhoukoudian.

ago. People visited the caves when the climate was perhaps a trifle warmer and moister than it is today. They hunted deer and other animals; more than 60 species are represented in the deposits.

At least 40 *H. erectus* individuals have been found at Zhoukoudian, most of whom died before they were 14 years old. Many appear to have perished from injuries.

About 100,000 stone implements come from Zhoukoudian, most of them made on flakes of rough-vein quartz. The people made choppers and scrapers, awls, crude points, and many multipurpose artifacts (Figure 3.6b). The tool kit evolved over the millennia, with the earliest artifacts tending to be larger and made with simple percussion techniques. As time went on, the toolmakers produced smaller implements, many of them made of finer raw materials.

Taken together, the Asian fossils are remarkably homogeneous. They have broad-based skulls, low, receding foreheads, and **prognathous** faces. The upper skull bones are thick and show every sign that these humans had strong chewing muscles. These people were up to 1.67 m (5 feet 6 inches) tall and had a brain capacity between 775 and 1,300 cc. One has the impression of a biologically conservative human population that changed little over enormously long periods of time.

Early Asian Technology

The early Asians took full advantage of the forest resources available to them. Instead of stone, they turned to wood, fiber, and bamboo, all of them organic materials that survive poorly in archaeological sites. In other words, our view of early Asia is biased simply because we lack evidence of the whole range of their forest cultures. Tropical forests are rich in animal and plant foods, but they are widely dispersed. Thus, human groups subsisting off forest foods must move constantly, carrying their artifacts with them. Under these circumstances, it is logical for them to use bamboo, wood, and other fibrous materials for their tool kits—the most convenient and lightweight materials at hand.

Bamboo, one of the most versatile materials known to humankind, was efficient, durable, and portable (Pope, 1989). It could be used to manufacture containers, sharp knives, spears, weapon tips, ropes, and dwellings. To this day, it is widely used in Asia as scaffolding for building skyscrapers (Figure 3.7). It is an ideal material for people subsisting not on large game but on smaller forest animals such as monkeys, rats, squirrels, lizards, and snakes, as well as plant foods. Simple stone flakes and jagged-edged choppers would be ideal for working bamboo and may indeed have been used for this purpose over many millennia (Schick, 1994). Controlled experiments have shown that bamboo knives are very effective at cutting flesh, but stone tools work best with hide.

Not that the early Chinese were incapable of expert stone toolmaking. About 803,000 years ago, a meteorite struck southern China. The impact caused huge fires, which burnt off dense forest across the Bose basin, exposing large tracts of red earth and deposits of large cobblestones. Local hunter-gatherer groups took advantage of the cleared land with its natural stone outcrops and settled along the banks of the Youjiang River. Hundreds of their stone artifacts lie in the fourth terrace above the modern river, dating to soon after the meteorite event—many of them chipped cobbles turned into simple axes and bifacial tools. The basic technology is very similar to that used by contemporary peoples in the west, except that the characteristic teardrop-shaped Acheulian hand ax (described later, p. 76) is absent. The Bose find shows that the archaic people of the region were perfectly capable of using stone technologies as sophisticated as those used in the west at the time when they settled in deforested areas (Yamei et al., 2000).

The latest known *H. erectus* fossils in East Asia date to about 300,000 years ago. Those from Southeast Asia may be as late as 100,000 years old or even later.

Moving to the North: The Settlement of Temperate Latitudes

Homo ergaster dispersed out of Africa, not only eastward, but also northward into Southwest Asia. We know that these hominins had settled over wide areas of East Africa's Great Rift Valley by 1.5 mya, when they also colonized the Ethiopian plateau, as high as 7,900 feet (2,400 m) above sea level. About a million years ago, humans lived throughout the northern and southern extremities of Africa. They crossed the arid Sahara desert during periods of higher rainfall, which transformed the desert landscape. And, inevitably, given the dynamics of hunter-gatherers, groups would have split off one from the other, expanding into uninhabited territory in search of food and water. And, at some point, some of them moved out of Africa into Southwest Asia.

The first human settlement of more temperate latitudes was also part of a broader set of ecological processes, one of them the simultaneous radiation of modern grazing animals and new vegetational communities into Europe and other northern latitudes of the Old World. Humans were part of this vast animal community. Their long-term success resulted from their ability to adapt to the cyclical changes in the Ice Age environment, from temperate to much colder, then to full glacial conditions and an abrupt deglaciation as the climate warmed up again rapidly. These early human populations may have flourished in regions where dense, abundant, and predictable resources were to be found, isolated from other regions where similar conditions existed. The climatic changes of the Ice Age sometimes brought these isolated populations together, then separated them again, ensuring gene flow and continued biological and cultural evolution over the millennia (Butzer, 1982).

The first settlement of temperate latitudes was not simply a case of an opportunistic species seizing a set of favorable environmental circumstances. Long before a million years ago, hominins had mastered the necessary hunting and foraging strategies to survive in much more diverse environments than tropical savanna. Most regions of the temperate world had the energy and resources for hominin settlement even when *H. habilis* flourished. But *H. habilis* had not evolved the long-term solutions such as clothing for coping with cyclic climatic change and all the resource changes that resulted from it.

Most evidence for Middle Pleistocene settlement, between about 500,000 and 130,000 years ago, falls in periods when the climate was colder than today but not fully glacial, as it has been for most of the past 700,000 years—times when grazing animals formed the principal food resource in cooler latitudes. Plant and marine foods were much more costly to exploit and often sparse. The successful colonists of northern latitudes were those hominins who could exploit game animals distributed unevenly, and at times very densely, over the landscape.

That is not to say, of course, that people lived by hunting alone, for, as we have discussed, tubers and other plant foods were critically important. They had to cope with long, sparse winter months, when their prey dispersed so widely that it was beyond human capacity to hunt them effectively. Perhaps people searched for frozen animal carcasses, a winter strategy that was adaptive for highly mobile predators like humans. This would have been a lower-risk strategy if a large group worked together, searching for the predictable refrigerated carcasses of large animals that died during the winter months (Gamble, 1999). During the spring and summer, the people could concentrate on hunting migratory game, eating their kills quickly and stripping them of meat before other predators

FIGURE 3.7 Bamboo scaffolding in use to build a modern high-rise. This flexible and versatile material has been used by Asians since the earliest times.

moved in. Many known sites are near lakes and streams, perhaps the places where the bands most commonly hunted, where plant foods were seasonally abundant, and also where wood might have been found for toolmaking and for the fires used to thaw frozen meat. The key to this entire adaptation was mobility; the bands could respond quickly to changes in resource distribution by moving into new areas. Clive Gamble believes that this was a primarily opportunistic adaptation based on a knowledge of resource distribution rather than on deliberate planning.

Dmanisi
1.7 mya

Judging from the Southeast Asian dates, *Homo ergaster* moved rapidly eastward out of Africa, but settling in the more northerly latitudes of Europe and Eurasia may have presented a more formidable challenge, especially during glacial cycles. There are finds of hand axes in Turkey, but definitive fossil evidence comes from Dmanisi, southwest of Tbilisi in Georgia. Here hominin skulls resembling those of *Homo ergaster* in East Africa lay in association with crudely shaped choppers and flakes. The crania came from river deposits dated by argon isotope and paleomagnetic methods to between a million and 1.7 mya, making them the earliest humans to be unearthed in Eurasia and apparently predating the earliest known western Europeans by several hundred thousand years. A scatter of humanly struck flakes in a lower level dates to as early as 1.85 mya. These finds are evidence that archaic humans foraged widely in search of game and plant foods, their movements driven perhaps as much by hunger as by superior technology (Ferring, 2011; Gabunia et al., 2000).

Ubeidiya
1.4 mya

The Dmanisi skulls are an isolated discovery, for all other signs of archaic human occupation in the region are considerably later. Human artifacts date to at least a million years ago in Morocco, whereas the Ubeidiya site in Israel has yielded both stone tools and some very fragmentary human remains dating to about 1.4 mya (Bar-Yosef, 1999).

Europe

Sima del Elefante
1.2 to 1.1 mya

First Settlement The earliest settlement of temperate Europe itself currently dates to about 1.2 to 1.1 mya on the basis of a human jaw associated with simple stone tools excavated from the Sima del Elefante at Atapuerca, near Burgos in northern Spain (Figure 3.8) (Carbonell et al., 2008). The excavators believe that western Europe was settled by hominin populations moving in from the east, Dmanisi representing an earlier stage in the process. However, settlement must have been sporadic at best, given the often harsh climatic conditions and major temperature extremes.

(a)

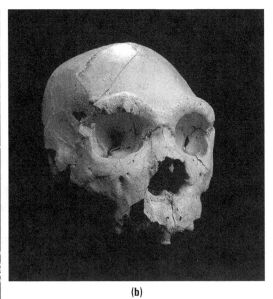

(b)

FIGURE 3.8 Two-hundred-thousand-year-old Europeans. (a) Some of the 1,600 human bones from the Sima de los Huesos (Pit of Bones), Sierra de Atapuerca, Spain. (b) The best preserved of the archaic *Homo sapiens* skulls from Atapuerca.

Europe continued to present obstacles for human settlement for hundreds of thousands of years, for there are only faint traces of visitors. Layer TD6 from the Gran Dolina site, also at Atapuerca, has yielded the remains of several people from layers immediately below a layer dated by a variety of means to around 800,000 years ago (Carbonell et al., 1999). The bones are probably from a still unidentified archaic human form, called by Spanish scientists *Homo antecessor*. Whether *antecessor* is the ancestor of later archaic Europeans is a matter of continued discussion. They might represent small numbers of *Homo ergaster*, who reached Europe, then vanished in the face of harsh glacial episodes that gripped Europe between 800,000 and 600,000 years ago. At about the same time, around 800,000 years ago, a few people visited Central and eastern England, where they dropped a few handfuls of stone tools, but finding their sites challenges even the most expert fieldworkers (Stringer, 2006).

Gran Dolina
800,000 years ago

Permanent Settlement: Homo heidelbergensis The first permanent European residents arrived in what may have been an uninhabited continent between 600,000 and 500,000 years ago. These newcomers, known as *Homo heidelbergensis* after a jaw found near Mauer, Germany, over a century ago, were originally Africans, archaic humans with large and projecting faces, chinless, massive jaws, large brow ridges and teeth, and flattened foreheads. Both *ergaster* and *erectus* shared many of these features, but *Homo heidelbergensis* had a much larger brain, which averaged over 1,200 cc, compared with the 900 cc of *Homo ergaster* (Klein, 2009). *Homo heidelbergensis* probably evolved from *Homo ergaster*, then spread out of Africa into Europe, where it became the ancestor of the Neanderthals, and in Africa, of *Homo sapiens*, anatomically modern humans.

Mauer
500,000 years ago

One could argue that permanent settlement in Europe resulted from warmer climatic conditions, but there were undoubtedly other factors in play as well. This first widespread colonization appears to coincide with the appearance of stone hand axes in Europe, part of the distinctive Acheulian technology that had originated in tropical Africa at least 1.6 mya. Several important European fossil finds date to about 500,000 years B.P. (Roebroeks and von Kolfschoten, 1994). Among them is the Mauer jaw, which was the oldest known European for almost a century. The robust thighbone of an equivalent human has come from Boxgrove in southern England, dated by highly diagnostic vole (small rodent) bones to between 524,000 and 475,000 years ago.

Boxgrove

By 400,000 years ago, human settlement was widespread throughout western and central Europe and perhaps farther east (Arsuaga et al., 1993). Fossil remains from sites like Tautavel, France, and Vértesszőlős, Hungary, display larger cranial vaults and more receding faces, foreshadowing some features of the Neanderthal anatomy of later millennia (see p. 83).

The Sima de los Huesos (Pit of Bones), in northern Spain's Sierra de Atapuerca, has yielded a mass of fossil human bones dating to about 300,000 years ago, the remains of between 32 and 50 individuals (Figure 3.8). All are archaic *H. sapiens*, a human form intermediate between *H. hiedelbergensis* and the Neanderthals. The human remains are from young adults and adolescents, their bodies apparently cast into the natural fissure without ceremony, perhaps to dispose of them—a process distinct from formal, ceremonial burial, which developed later.

Sima de los Huesos
300,000 years ago

Archaic Human Technology

Human fossils are rare finds, often discovered without the artifacts once used by their owners. So we have to fall back on stone artifacts for most of the story. Technological innovations were glacially slow. The Oldowan technology used by the earliest forms of *Homo* remained in use for as long as a million years, with its more diverse successor used by *Homo ergaster* and *Homo erectus* for nearly half as long again. There is a tendency to think of both technologies as monolithic, unchanging chronicles of human prehistory, fixed stages in human cultural evolution, partly because of the timescales involved and also because stone tools appear to have changed so little over hundreds of thousands of years. In fact, however, the technology of *H. ergaster* and its successors, like that of *H. habilis*, displays considerable variability and development (Ambrose, 2001).

These people did not rely exclusively on stone, for we can say with confidence that our remote ancestors also made use of wood, one of the most versatile raw materials. The earliest known wooden artifacts are some long spears and a throwing stick dated to 400,000 years ago, found with broken animal bones and stone tools in an open coal mine at Schöningen, Germany (Thieme, 2005) (see Site box on page 81). These artifacts are 200,000 years older than a wooden spear tip from Clacton in eastern England, dating to about 200,000 years ago (Figure 3.9), and a 150,000-year-old wooden spear from Lehringen in Germany. Most insights into the technology of archaic humans like *Homo heidelbergensis* and *Homo erectus* come from stone tools and the by-products associated with them, because wood and other organic materials are rarely preserved.

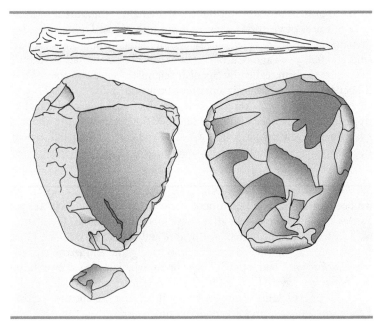

FIGURE 3.9 Top, a wooden spear tip from Clacton, England, dating to about 200,000 years ago (approximately one-eighth full size). Bottom, views of a flake from the same location. The upper surface is shown at the left, and the flake (lower) surface on the right. The striking platform is at the base (one-third actual size).

Hand Axes and Other Tools

Acheulian tradition
1.5 mya to 150,000 years ago

In Africa, Europe, and some parts of Asia, *H. ergaster* and its successors are associated with a distinctive tool kit that includes not only a variety of flake tools and sometimes choppers but also bifacially flaked hand axes. These hand-ax industries are grouped under the technological label *Acheulian*, after the town of St. Acheul in northern France, where many such artifacts have been found. Hand axes come in many sizes and shapes; they are sometimes artifacts of such great refinement and beauty that people ignore all the other tools *H. erectus* made. In fact, human stone tool technology between 1.5 million and 150,000 years ago shows considerable diversity, probably associated with local adaptations and the availability of suitable raw materials.

A big change seems to have come around 600,000 years ago, when the crude, pointed axes of earlier times gave way to much more symmetrical axes. To manufacture such regularly shaped tools required considerable mental dexterity to imagine the shape of an axe before one fashioned it out of a lump of rock. This would have been a significant cognitive advance that may have coincided with a rapid expansion in brain size that seems to have occurred at about the same time (Ruff et al., 1997; Wynn, 1995). Human brain size had remained at about 65 percent of average modern capacity from between about 1.8 million and 600,000 years ago. Now the size increased to about 90 percent, perhaps coinciding with the appearance of a more advanced human, *Homo heidelbergensis*. This is as yet just a hypothesis, for we lack both numerous fossil fragments and the associations between fossils and stone tools to nail down this tantalizing link between brain size and technological innovation. It is as if there was a sudden evolutionary punctuation event that had the same effects as those when *Homo ergaster* appeared over a million years earlier.

The hand ax occurs over a vast area of the Old World in all shapes and sizes, from crude, teardrop-shaped forms to ovals and from tongue-shaped to occasional finely pointed specimens. Unlike the crude scrapers and choppers of the Oldowan, the Acheulian hand ax was an artifact with converging edges that met at a point. The maker had to envisage the shape of the artifact, which was to be produced from a mere lump of stone, and then fashion it, not with opportunistic blows but with carefully directed hammer blows (Figure 3.10). Acheulian hand axes come in every size, from elegant oval types a few inches long to heavy axes more than 0.3 m (1 foot) long and weighing 2.3 kg (5 pounds) or more. They must have been a versatile, thoroughly practical artifact to have continued in use for so long.

What exactly were hand axes used for? Almost certainly they were held in the hand rather than being hafted on the end of a wooden shaft. They were simply too cumbersome, and in any case, hafted tools probably did not come into use until much later. Conventional wisdom has it that

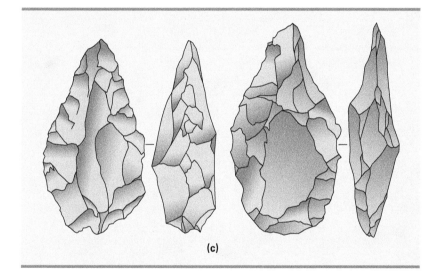

FIGURE 3.10 Acheulian technology. Hand axes were multipurpose artifacts that were shaped symmetrically around a long axis. (a) As the hand ax from Kilombe, Kenya, of 700,000 years ago shows, the stoneworker would sometimes use a minimum of blows with a simple hammerstone to achieve the desired shape. (b) Sometimes a hammer made of animal bone served to strike off the shallower flakes that adorn the margins of these tools.

Later hand axes assume many forms, among them the finely pointed shape in (c), which shows front and side views of two early hand axes from Bed II, Olduvai Gorge, Tanzania (three-quarters actual size). As time went on, the stoneworkers used carefully prepared cores to fashion large flakes that served as blanks for axes and other artifacts. They also produced flakes that were used as opportunistic artifacts, for woodworking and for many other purposes.

they were multipurpose artifacts, used for grubbing up roots, working wood, scraping skins, and, especially, skinning and butchering large and small game. There is no question that they were highly effective butchery tools. Many archaeologists have tried cutting up antelope carcasses with them and also slicing through hippopotamus and elephant hide—with great success. In some ways, the hand ax was ideal for this purpose because it could be sharpened again and again, and when it became a useless lump of stone, it could be recycled into flake tools. But effective butchery can be achieved with simple flakes as well, and a number of researchers have wondered whether the hand ax, which took longer to make, was not used for other purposes, such as for throwing or for digging up edible roots.

In addition to hand axes, the new technology resulted in scrapers and other artifacts for wood-working, skinning, and other purposes. But hand axes remain the most characteristic artifact of many archaic human populations (Figure 3.11). Fine specimens are scattered in the gravels of the Somme and Thames rivers in northern Europe, in North African quarries and ancient Saharan lake beds, and in sub-Saharan Africa from the Nile Valley to the Cape of Good Hope. Acheulian tools are common in some parts of India, in Arabia, and in Southwest Asia as far as the southern shores of the Caspian Sea and perhaps even farther north. They are rare east of the Rhine and in East Asia, where chopping tools were commonly used until comparatively recent times (Howell and Clark, 1963; Brumm and Moore, 2012). No one has been able to explain why hand axes have this distribution. Were such multipurpose tools used only in big-game hunting camps? Was their use restricted by the availability of flint and other suitable raw materials? Did environmental conditions affect the hunters' choice of tool kits? Or were they used as projectiles in areas where big game abounded? We do not know.

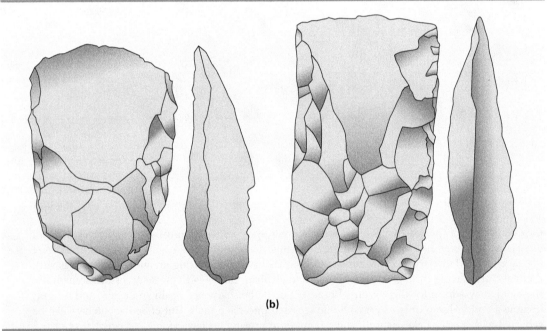

FIGURE 3.11   Hand ax technology. (a) Acheulian hand ax from Swanscombe, England (one-third actual size). (b) Two Acheulian cleavers, from Baia Farta, Angola (left), and Kalambo Falls, Zambia (right) (both one-half actual size). Cleavers are thought to have been butchering tools, artifacts with a single unfinished edge that modern experiments have proved effective in skinning and dismembering game.

Hand Axes and the Evolution of the Human Mind

Although we recognize that archaic humans made a wide variety of artifacts, the fact remains that the Acheulian hand ax is the most characteristic and one of the most widely distributed tools made between 1.5 million and 150,000 years ago. It also provides us with an opportunity to consider the relationship between an artifact and the evolution of the mind. Hand axes were the logical result of long-used stone technology, made to a degree of standardization unimaginable in earlier times. For example, the hand axes from Kilombe, Kenya, date to more than 700,000 years ago. They display a very high statistical correlation among length, breadth, and thickness, standardization within a length of 8 to 24 cm (3.14 to 9.40 inches). Such a correlation implies a well-defined mental image of the ideal end product, shared by more than one person (Figure 3.12).

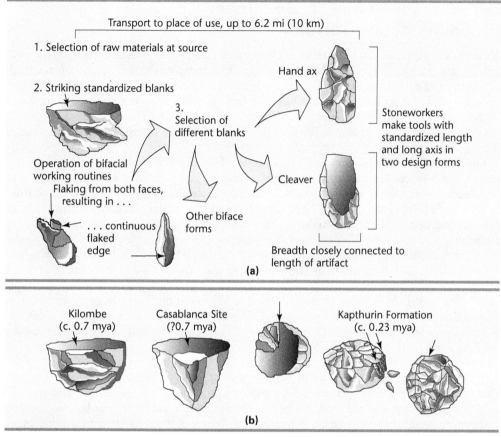

FIGURE 3.12 Making Acheulian bifaces. (a) The ax-making process used about a million years ago. (b) Early and late methods. The simple flaking process of 700,000 years ago (left), used in East and North Africa, compares with the expertise of the stoneworkers at Kapthurin, Kenya, 230,000 years ago (right). They prepared elaborately shaped cores to create flakes about 16 cm (6 inches) long as hand ax blanks.

Homo erectus had a geometrically accurate sense of proportion, which was imposed accurately on stone (Gowlett, 1978). Symmetrical hand axes resulted from careful selection of the stone cobble used as a blank, both for shape and for potential fracture dynamics. Then the stoneworker had to rough out the ax with a stone hammer and finish it off with a more delicate, softer bone or wood striker. Each hand ax required careful planning and the application of toolmaking knowledge acquired over a considerable period of time, not just mindless flaking on either side of the nodule. No mechanical set of rules led to hand axes. The maker had to "feel" the raw material and use visual clues to decide where to strike next, constantly adjusting plans as the artifact emerged from the raw material. A much higher degree of technical intelligence lay behind Acheulian hand ax manufacture than behind Oldowan technology.

For example, another East African site, Kapthurin, near Kenya's Lake Baringo, contains hundreds of late Acheulian hand axes dating to about 230,000 years ago. The stoneworkers there used elaborately **prepared cores,** fashioned with perhaps. 40 or more strokes, as the blanks for a single large flake—a dramatic contrast to the three or four flakes removed in earlier millennia (see Figure 3.12). The large flake that resulted was then bifacially flaked into an elegant, versatile hand ax in a wide variety of useful shapes (see Figure 3.11).

Yet puzzling questions remain: Why did archaic humans ignore antler, bone, and ivory, staples of later Stone Age technology? Why did they make only multipurpose tools, none of which were mounted on handles or spear shafts, as was commonplace in later millennia? And finally, why did they manufacture such a limited range of stone artifacts, despite their ability to exploit a remarkable range of natural environments?

Steven Mithen (1996) believes that the ability of archaic humans to exploit markedly seasonal environments reflects a high degree of what he calls "natural history intelligence," the ability to think one's way through a wide variety of often savage landscapes with only a simple technology. He argues that *H. erectus* lacked the ability to integrate toolmaking with its knowledge about the environment and animal behavior. This would account for the lack of specialized tools used for specialized tasks. The same compartmentalized reasoning would account for the great conservatism of archaic human technology. The making of stone tools was never integrated with subsistence activities except at the most generalized level.

Evidence for Behavior: Boxgrove, Schöningen, and Torralba

What do we know of the subsistence activities of *H. heidelbergensis*? These archaic people were far more adept hunters than earlier humans had been, who relied heavily on scavenging. Generations of archaeologists have studied large collections of hand axes and other butchering artifacts found in association with the bones of large game animals but, until now, have lacked firsthand evidence of hunting methods. A series of spectacular archaeological discoveries at a 400,000-year-old hunting camp at Schöningen, Germany, have changed our perceptions of early hunting skills (see Site box).

The Schöningen sites leave no doubt that people of the day were sophisticated, expert big-game hunters with a precise knowledge of raw materials and the mental abilities to create highly effective throwing weapons. Apparently, too, the Schöningen people also cut meat into strips and dried it for later use, a form of food storage that has been thought an attribute of later humans alone. They also mounted stone tools in wooden shafts, a technological advance once thought to have developed much later.

Further evidence of big-game hunting comes from the Boxgrove site in southern England, a series of activity areas used over tens of thousands of years about 500,000 years ago (Figure 3.13). Here, a cliff 75 to 100 m (250 to 330 feet) high overlooked a shallow lake fed by a spring (Roberts and Parfitt, 1999). At the foot of the cliff, people killed and butchered large mammals, among them rhinoceros, bison, deer, horse, and bear. One horse shoulder blade displayed a hole made by a wooden spear about 50 mm (2 inches) across. A forensic pathologist suspects the spear was spinning when it made the wound. Weapons similar to the Schöningen spears from Germany may have been used by the Boxgrove hunters. Much of the prey was butchered near a water hole where the animals gathered, as if people lay in wait for game at the same location over many generations. The meat yields from the larger animals were enormous, especially if the marrow and entrails are included. A rhinoceros would yield 700 kg (1,550 pounds) of meat alone. The butchery was thorough; much of the meat and skin was removed for later use. Most likely, considerable amounts of flesh were dried, as at Schöningen. One hand ax bears the distinctive wear patterns associated with scraping hide.

Torralba
Ambrona
400,000 or 200,000 years ago

Evidence for big-game hunting also comes from two Acheulian sites, at Torralba and Ambrona, northeast of Madrid in Spain (F. C. Howell, 1966). The Acheulians probably lived in this deep, swampy valley either 200,000 or 400,000 years ago (the date is disputed). Torralba yielded most

FIGURE 3.13 Excavations on an artifact and bone scatter at Boxgrove, England.

SiTE > A 400,000-Year-Old Hunt at Schöningen, Germany <

Since 1983, Hartmut Thieme has investigated a 6-sq-km (2.31-square-mile) area within an open cast coal mine at Schöningen, northern Germany, where mining operations cut deep into massive Pleistocene deposits (Thieme, 2005). He has uncovered important lakeshore sites at which *Homo erectus* once camped. At the location known as Schöningen 12, a campsite by a lake, the inhabitants butchered elephants and other animals, and also caught birds and fish. Here Thieme recovered four worked branches from silver fir trees, each with a diagonal groove cut into one end, perhaps to hold sharp stone flakes or flint tools. The wood was carefully selected—the hard, intact roots of the boughs of rotted fir trunks.

About 10 m (33 feet) below the modern ground surface at another location, Schöningen 13 II–4, a hunt had taken place on the shores of a shallow, elongated lake. Because the area was dry and treeless, the hunters could watch their prey. Here a hunting band stalked, intercepted, killed, and butchered a complete herd of wild horses.

Thieme and his colleagues excavated more than 3,200 sq m (3,445 square feet) of an organic mud where the artifacts lie. Pollens from the mud reveal a meadow and forest landscape that thrived in a cool, temperate climate. The inhabitants of the site butchered at least 20 wild horses, whose remains represent more than 90 percent of the 25,000 bone fragments at Schöningen 13. The hunters carried stone scrapers and points manufactured elsewhere and resharpened or reworked on-site—there is no toolmaking debris, just refinishing flakes. Three spectacular wooden spears came to light in 1995. Since then, more than a half dozen additional weapons have been found. Most of the spears are made of spruce, between 1.82 and 2.5 m (5.9 and 8.2 feet) long, each made from an individual tree that was felled, the branches and bark stripped off, with tips made from the hardest wood at the foot of the tree. The points are carefully shaped and symmetrical, the tails pointed and tapering toward the proximal end. The hunters smoothed and shaped the surfaces of their weapons with great care so that the maximum thickness and weight lay a third of the way from the tip. Thieme remarked that the spears resembled modern hunting javelins. A replica spear tested under controlled conditions displayed excellent ballistic qualities and a range of about 60 m (198 feet), with good penetrating power.

The first wooden tool from the site, found in 1994, was a spruce stick with carefully sharpened ends, 0.78 m long (2.6 feet long), made from the trunk of a small tree. Thieme believes that this was a throwing stick, its shape and size like those used by Australian Aborigines to hunt birds in flight. It would have been very effective against the geese that lived in the reeds around the lake and whose bones appear in the site.

Numerous other worked wood fragments came from this large hunting camp, among them a carefully shaped and charred stick that may have been used to cook meat over a fire. Hearths lie along the western edge of the main concentration of finds, each about a meter (3 feet) apart. The nearby finds include large bison bones whose flat surfaces show traces of repeated cut marks, as if people were slicing meat into strips for drying. Thieme points out that the hearths lay on dry ground, thus they were probably used in late summer or fall when water levels were low and rainfall sparse. Then, in late autumn, the first snow covered the bones and abandoned tools with a thick layer of decaying reeds before rising waters in spring preserved the site for posterity.

---

of the left side of a large elephant that had been cut into small pieces, and Ambrona contained the remains of 30 to 35 dismembered elephants. Concentrations of broken food bones were found all over the site, and the skulls of the elephants had been broken open to expose the brains (see Figure 3.14). Both kill sites were littered with crude hand axes, cleavers, scrapers, and cutting tools. The elephant bones at both sites were buried in clays that were once treacherous marsh. The original scenario for the sites had hunters watching the valley floors where the elephants roamed. At a strategic moment, several bands would gather quietly, set brushfires, and drive the unsuspecting beasts into the swamps, where they could be killed and butchered at leisure. Torralba and Ambrona were on important game trails between summer and winter grazing areas (Butzer, 1982). The hunters thus preyed on migrating elephants each spring and fall (Figure 3.14), dispersing into smaller groups during the other seasons. Other archaeologists believe that the hunters were actually scavenging meat from animals that had perished when enmired (Shipman and Rose, 1983).

Almost certainly, *Homo heidelbergensis* and its contemporaries were eclectic and flexible hunter-gatherers who relied on hunting, scavenging, and plant foods. They may have understood the telltale signs of the passage of seasons, the meanings of cloud formations, the timing of game and bird migrations, and the geography of their territories. For example, at the Qesem Cave in Israel people using Acheulian tools butchered large numbers of fallow

Moutain glaciers

High-altitude grassland
(Spring and autum hunting)

Steep grassland
(Summer hunting)

▲ Temporary camp

◇ Ephemeral camp

★ Seasonal camp

◯ Quarry

Grassland and parkland
(Winter hunting)

Horse and elephant
migration routes

- - - Major annual group movements

FIGURE 3.14 From Torralba, Spain. Reconstructed model for seasonal movement by Acheulian hunters at Torralba-Ambrona, Spain, involving the interception of migrating animals in spring and fall. The model was based on information recovered from excavations (Butzer, 1982).

deer between 380,000 and 200,000 years ago (Lemorini et al., 2006) But they never exploited small game, birds, fish, or sea mammals on any significant scale, as modern humans did almost at once.

These people probably lived in relatively large groups at times, both to reduce the danger from carnivores and to improve the chances of finding food, especially from larger animals. At other times, band size may have been much smaller, especially when plant foods were more abundant and easily obtained by individuals. All of this argues for considerable social flexibility and intelligence in *H. erectus*, reflected in their larger brain size. But as was true of their natural history intelligence, they may have been unable to integrate their social intelligence—their ability to share food and cooperate in the hunt—with other aspects of human intelligence.

Language

Homo erectus and Homo heidelbergensis had a large brain with a well-developed Broca's area, the zone associated with speaking ability. Their vocal tracts were more modern than those of *Homo habilis*, which suggests considerable potential for articulate speech. Anthropologists Leslie Aiello and Robin Dunbar (1993) have argued that the basis for language ability appeared in humans by at least 250,000 years ago. They believe it first evolved as a way to handle increasingly complex social information. As group sizes increased, so did a capacity for language, used primarily to talk about social relations. It was only later that humans developed the kind of general-purpose language we use today, which allows us to communicate freely, whatever the behavioral domain. So like us in many ways, archaic humans lacked the cognitive flexibility characteristic of modern humans, yet it was from this early human that *H. sapiens* ultimately evolved. Nor had the larynx shifted into a position where the range of sounds modern humans use was possible.

The Neanderthals

Much of what we know about early *Homo sapiens*, the descendant of *Homo heidelbergensis*, comes from the Neanderthals, long-term inhabitants of Europe and Eurasia, whose anatomical features appear in archaic European populations such as those from Atapuerca, Spain, at least 200,000 years ago (see Figure 3.8). The Neanderthals are still the subject of much controversy among physical anthropologists. Some people use the word *Neanderthal* to describe dim-witted, ugly people who are like apes, an insult aimed at those they consider stupid. This stereotype and that of the shambling cave people so beloved by cartoonists come from mistaken studies of Neanderthal skeletons in the early years of the twentieth century. In fact, the Neanderthals were strong, robustly built humans with some archaic features. For example, their skulls display retreating foreheads, projecting faces,

FIGURE 3.15 A classic Neanderthal cranium, showing the prominent brow ridges, prognathous faces, and massive jaw.

and sometimes eyebrow ridges. But there is every reason to believe that they were expert hunters and beings capable of considerable intellectual reasoning.

There are, of course, striking anatomical differences between Neanderthals and modern humans, both in the robust postcranial skeleton of the Neanderthal and in its more bun-shaped skull, sometimes with heavy brow ridges and a forward-projecting face (Figure 3.15). These features are the reason that this extinct hominin form is classified as *Homo neanderthalensis,* a subspecies of *Homo sapiens,* and not as *Homo sapiens,* a fully modern human.

In the century and a half since the first Neanderthal skull from the German village of that name was unearthed, substantial numbers of Neanderthal individuals have been found, mostly in western Europe but also in Southwest Asia, Africa, and Asia (Figure 3.16). Neanderthals first appeared during the Eem interglacial, well before 100,000 years ago, but they were apparently few in number

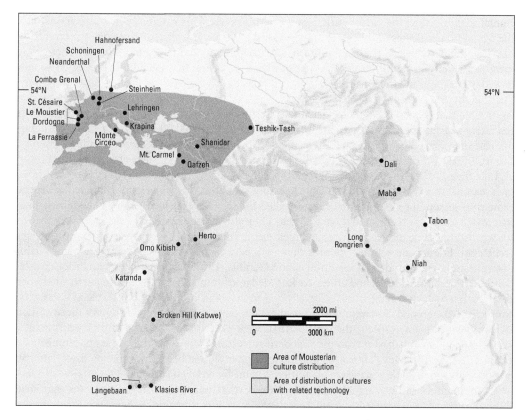

FIGURE 3.16 Distribution of the Neanderthals, their culture, and related technologies. Also shown are sites mentioned in the remainder of this chapter.

Dating the Past Radiocarbon Dating

The later Neanderthals can be dated by the most universal of all archaeological dating methods: radiocarbon (^{14}C) dating. Radiocarbon dating is based on the knowledge that living organisms build up their own organic matter by photosynthesis and by using atmospheric carbon dioxide. The percentage of radiocarbon in the organism is equal to that in the atmosphere. When the organism dies, the carbon-14 (^{14}C) atoms disintegrate at a known rate, with a half-life of 5,730 years. It is possible then to calculate the date of an organic object by measuring the amount of ^{14}C left in the sample. The initial quantity in the sample is low, so the limit of detectability is soon reached, making the oldest reliable radiocarbon dates about 40,000 years old.

Radiocarbon dates can be obtained from many types of organic material, including charcoal, shell, wood, and hair. The beta-particle decay rate is conventionally measured with a proportional counter, but the use of accelerator mass spectrometry has refined the procedure dramatically (see Chapter 8). Every radiocarbon date arrives with a statistical error, a standard deviation. For example, a date of 2,200 ± 200 years means that the date has a probable range of 200 years, with a two-out-of-three chance the date lies between the span of one standard deviation (2,400 and 2,000 years).

Unfortunately, the concentration of radiocarbon in the atmosphere has varied considerably over time as a result of alterations in solar activity and changes in the strength of the earth's magnetic field. It is possible to correct dates by calibrating them against accurate dates from radiocarbon-dated tree rings and developing a master correction curve. Dates as far back as nearly 8000 B.C. can be calibrated with tree rings, and experiments are currently under way with highly accurately dated fossil coral beds to extend the calibration back much farther into the past.

Radiocarbon dating is the most universally applied chronological method in archaeology, but unless calibrated with tree rings or coral, such dates should be recognized for what they are: statistical estimates of radiocarbon age. Nevertheless, remarkable precision and statistical treatment of large numbers of samples are producing much more accurate chronologies than ever before (see Doing Archaeology box in Chapter 8, on p. 194).

(see the Dating the Past box). Large Neanderthal sites occur in the Dordogne area of southwest France, where deep river valleys and vast limestone cliffs offered abundant shelter during the Weichsel glaciation (Muller and Shrenk, 2008; Stringer and Gamble, 1993).

The skeletons found in French caves may look like anatomical anachronisms, with massive brow ridges and squat bodies, but they walked upright and as nimbly as modern humans. They stood just over 153 cm (5 feet) tall, and their forearms were relatively short compared with those of modern people. This "classic" variety of Neanderthal is confined to western Europe and is more noticeably different from *H. sapiens* than its contemporary populations found elsewhere, especially around the shores of the Mediterranean and in Asia (Figure 3.17). We find much variability among nonclassic Neanderthals, who most often display less extreme features, particularly brow ridges and other cranial features, than the classic variety of western France. This variability is well demonstrated at the Mount Carmel sites of et-Tabun and es-Skhul in Israel, as well as at Krapina in central Europe.

The Neanderthals had the same posture, manual abilities, and range and characteristics of movement as modern people (Figure 3.18). They differed in having massive limb bones, often somewhat bowed in the thigh and the forearm, features that reflect the Neanderthals' greater muscular power. For their height, the Neanderthals were bulky and heavily muscled, and their brain capacity was slightly larger than that of modern humans. Their antecedents are chronicled by the archaic individuals from the Sierra de Atapuerca in northern Spain, dating to more than 200,000 years ago. The more complete of these specimens display anatomical features closer to those of early *H. sapiens* than to *H. erectus*, as if the evolutionary roots of the Neanderthals lie deep in earlier times (Arsuaga et al., 1993).

Like their predecessors, Neanderthal bands occupied large territories, which they probably exploited on a seasonal round, returning to the same locations year after year when game migrated or vegetables came into season. The Neanderthals were skilled hunters who pursued large game animals like the mammoth as well as reindeer and wild horses. They also caught birds and fish. It appears that many western European bands lived in caves and rock shelters during much of the year as a protection against arctic cold. During the summer months they may have fanned out over the tundra plains, living in open encampments (for details, see Stringer and Gamble, 1993). But theirs was a precarious existence, dependent on hunting skills and an expert knowledge of animal habits, which required the hunter to come within such close range that he literally had to touch his prey before being able to spear, club, or wrestle it to the ground. As a result, many of these hunters' injuries are reminiscent of those of modern rodeo riders. In many respects, the Neanderthals were predators at the apex of their ecosystem, with much less consistent behavior than their modern successors. Above all, they were opportunistic hunters, hunting a wide range of animals as the opportunity arose, and becoming more predatory after about 50,000 years ago. They also ate large quantities of plant foods when available.

Clive Gamble (1999) argues that the Neanderthal adaptation in Europe was significantly different from that of earlier human populations. He points to major changes in human settlement

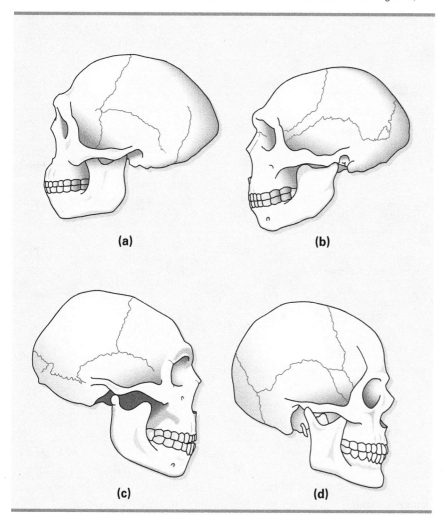

FIGURE 3.17 Comparisons of four fossil skulls and jaws. (a) The reconstructed skull has prominent brow ridges, a bun-shaped rear to the cranium, and a retreating chin. (b) A "classic" Neanderthal skull found at Monte Circeo, Italy, still has well-marked brow ridges and a bun-shaped cranium but an increased brain capacity. The skull is lower and flatter than those of modern humans, and the jaw is chinless. (c) The Shanidar Neanderthal from Iraq is a less extreme example, with a higher forehead, somewhat reduced brow ridges, and a much more rounded skull. (d) A modern skull, with well-rounded contours, no brow ridges, a high forehead, and a well-marked chin.

patterns—that is, to a greater use of rock shelters and caves, as well as the repeated use of open sites as temporary stopping places for people away from the larger main group. This may have been a time when technology became more organized, when planning assumed greater importance, to reduce the risk of starvation. People were now developing hunting and foraging strategies based on four main herd species: bison, horse, red deer, and reindeer. Gamble theorizes that storage assumed much greater importance for surviving winter shortages by maximizing the meat culled from seasonally migrating animals. There may have been higher population densities, greater population stability, and more adaptive stability, with less risk of local populations dying out in times of stress.

For the new adaptive strategies in the cold north, environmental knowledge and larger group sizes were keys to effective survival. Factors such as herd size, migration seasons, and predictability of animal movements assumed vital importance. This pattern of adaptation resulted in considerable interregional differences within the Neanderthal world. The southwestern areas of Europe, with their deep river valleys and large rock shelters, were occupied continuously, whereas more open areas to the north and east were more extensively exploited during periods of warmer climate and were largely abandoned during glacial times. No Neanderthal sites have yet come to light north of 54°N (see Figure 3.16).

A More Complex Technology

The Neanderthals' Mousterian technology (named after the Le Moustier rock shelter in southwest France) was far more complex and sophisticated than its Acheulian predecessor, with many regional variations (Mellars, 1996).

Mousterian

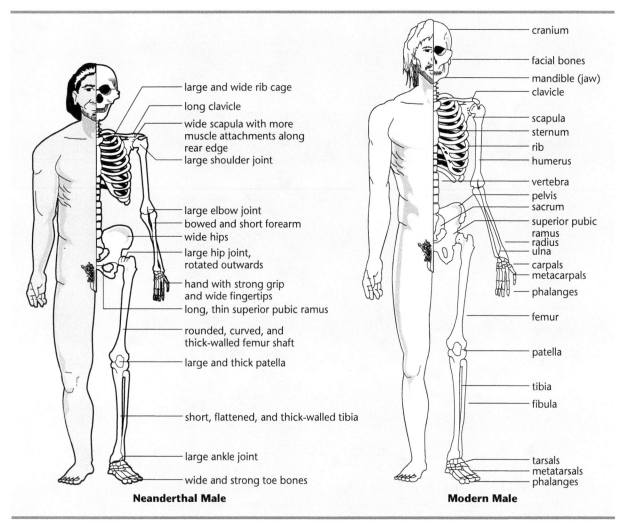

Neanderthal Male

- large and wide rib cage
- long clavicle
- wide scapula with more muscle attachments along rear edge
- large shoulder joint
- large elbow joint
- bowed and short forearm
- wide hips
- large hip joint, rotated outwards
- hand with strong grip and wide fingertips
- long, thin superior pubic ramus
- rounded, curved, and thick-walled femur shaft
- large and thick patella
- short, flattened, and thick-walled tibia
- large ankle joint
- wide and strong toe bones

Modern Male

- cranium
- facial bones
- mandible (jaw)
- clavicle
- scapula
- sternum
- rib
- humerus
- vertebra
- pelvis
- sacrum
- superior pubic ramus
- radius
- ulna
- carpals
- metacarpals
- phalanges
- femur
- patella
- tibia
- fibula
- tarsals
- metatarsals
- phalanges

FIGURE 3.18 The skeleton of a male Neanderthal (left) compared with that of a modern male. The Neanderthal is more robust and stockier than his modern counterpart. (After Stringer and Gamble, 1993.)

The stone technology used by the Neanderthals and other early *Homo sapiens* forms has often been subsumed under the label *Middle Paleolithic* (Greek: *paleos,* "old," and *lithos,* "stone") on the grounds that the techniques used were distinct from those of *H. erectus.* In fact, the basic differences are much less radical than has often been assumed. There was a basic continuum in stoneworking skills that began in the Lower Paleolithic and continued through the Middle into the Upper Paleolithic and even later in prehistory. Even the more efficient technological changes associated with the spread of *H. sapiens* after 40,000 years ago had a strong basis in much earlier, simpler technologies (Figure 3.19).

Levallois and Disk-Core-Reduction Strategies

At Kapthurin and other East African sites, Acheulian stoneworkers demonstrated a remarkable skill in preshaping cores to produce large flakes for making axes and other artifacts. With such pre-pared-core techniques, which were to assume great importance after 100,000 years ago, the core was shaped to predetermine the flake or blade that was to be removed. The **Levallois technique,** named after the Paris suburb where specimens were first found, produces broad, flat flakes, large blades, and triangular points (Figure 3.20). This is a very difficult technique to execute successfully. Probably no more than about a score of modern flintknappers can rival the Neanderthals' skill in conceiving and making Levallois flakes. The **disk core technique** was used to produce as many flakes of varying size as possible and resulted in residual cores with an approximately round shape. The size of the raw material lumps available to the stoneworker probably had a major effect on the flakes produced, for both techniques, as well as simpler flaking, were widely used in Europe, Africa, and Asia.

Tool Forms and Variability

For the most part, Mousterian and other Middle Paleolithic tools were made of flakes, the most characteristic artifacts being points and scrapers (Figure 3.21). Some of these were composite tools,

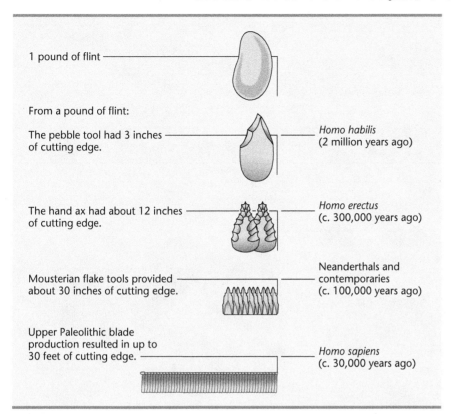

1 pound of flint

From a pound of flint:

The pebble tool had 3 inches of cutting edge. — *Homo habilis* (2 million years ago)

The hand ax had about 12 inches of cutting edge. — *Homo erectus* (c. 300,000 years ago)

Mousterian flake tools provided about 30 inches of cutting edge. — Neanderthals and contemporaries (c. 100,000 years ago)

Upper Paleolithic blade production resulted in up to 30 feet of cutting edge. — *Homo sapiens* (c. 30,000 years ago)

FIGURE 3.19   The growing efficiency of Stone Age technology is shown by the ability of ancient stoneworkers to produce ever-larger numbers of cutting edges from a pound of flint or other fine-grained rock. The Neanderthals were far more efficient stone artisans than their predecessors. By the same token, *H. sapiens* used a blade technology (see Figure 4.4) that produced up to 9.1 m (30 feet) of blades per pound of flint.

artifacts made of more than one component, for example, a point, a shaft, and the binding that secured the head to the shaft to make a spear. The edges of points and scrapers were sharpened by fine trimming, that is, the removal of small, steplike chips from the edge of the implement. These artifacts, almost universally distributed in Middle Paleolithic sites, were used in the chase, in woodworking, and in preparing skins. However, recent microwear research has revealed that many untrimmed flakes were used for cutting, scraping, and other tasks; they were convenient working edges when needed at a moment's notice (Gamble, 1999). In spite of their technical proficiency, Neanderthals made only a narrow range of artifacts compared with, say, modern Inuit of the Canadian Arctic, who use a wide variety of specialized tools made from a wide variety of raw materials, and all with specific uses.

The French sites have yielded a great diversity of Mousterian artifacts and tool kits (Mellars, 1996). Some levels include hand axes; others, notched flakes, artifacts perhaps used for stripping meat for drying or pressing fibrous plants. Subdivisions of Mousterian technology have been identified by the prevalence of specific tool types. The French archaeologist François Bordes (1968) excavated the Combe Grenal Cave in the Perigord and studied a stratified series of intermittent Mousterian occupations from between 90,000 and 40,000 years ago. Bordes identified no fewer than 60 different Mousterian tool types, made with a variety of toolmaking techniques, including the Levallois method, and with carefully prepared disk cores. He also identified four distinct tool kits in the Combe Grenal levels: one associated with small hand axes, another with thousands of heavy-duty side scrapers, a third with a high proportion of saw-edged flakes, and some that contained an even balance of different tool types.

Such wide variation in Mousterian tool kits such as scraper size is found not only at Combe Grenal but also at other Neanderthal sites throughout Europe and Southwest Asia and in North Africa, where other early *H. sapiens* made similar tools. Nicolas Rolland and Harold Dibble (1990) have studied Mousterian scraper technology on the assumption that the various shapes of these artifacts represent a "reduction continuum," that is, a continuous process of flaking the edge of flake blanks. Thus, collections with more large side scrapers represent less intensive utilization of scrapers than those with greater variability in scraper forms. They argue that neither style nor function was the overriding factor in stone tool variability. Rather, the Neanderthals were using a fundamentally very simple stone technology, with both flaking techniques and reduction processes varying considerably in response to all kinds of external factors—availability and size of raw materials,

Archaic *Homo sapiens* ? c. 250,000 years ago

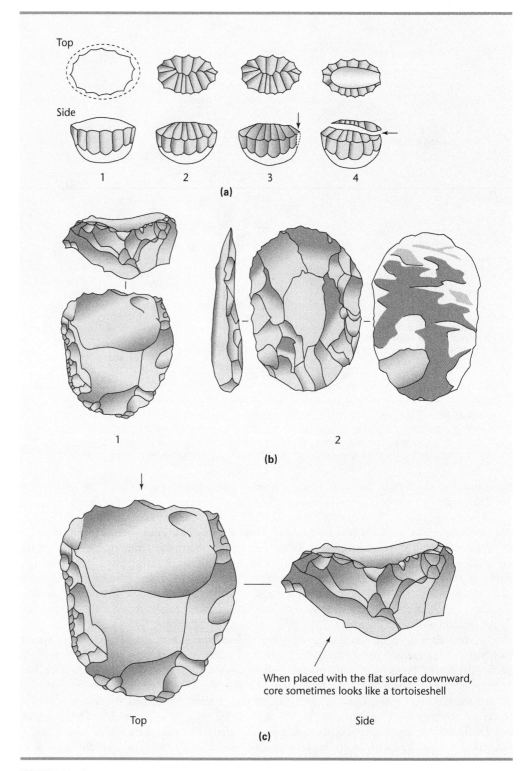

Top

Side

1   2   3   4

(a)

1   2

(b)

When placed with the flat surface downward,
core sometimes looks like a tortoiseshell

Top   Side

(c)

FIGURE 3.20 Prepared-core techniques. Prepared cores were carefully flaked to enable the toolmaker to strike off large flakes of predetermined size. The Levallois technique meant that the stoneworker would shape a lump of flint into an inverted bun-shaped core (often compared to an inverted tortoiseshell). The flat upper surface was struck at one end, the resulting flake forming the only product from the core. Another form was the disk core, a prepared core from which several flakes of predetermined size and shape were removed. The core gradually became smaller, until it resembled a flat disk. Disk cores were often used to produce points and scrapers. (a) Making a Levallois core: (1) The edges of a suitable stone are trimmed; (2) the top surface is trimmed; (3) a striking platform, the point where the flake will originate, is made by trimming to form a straight edge on the side; (4) a flake is struck from the core and removed. (b) (1) A Levallois core from the Thames Valley, England, with a view of the top of the core (top left) and the resulting flake (2). (c) When placed with the flat surface downward, the core sometimes looks like a tortoiseshell. One half actual size.

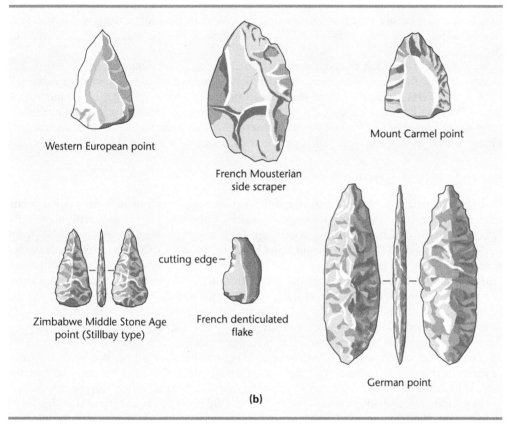

FIGURE 3.21   Middle Paleolithic tools and technology. This technology was based on simple stone techniques that were used for tens of thousands of years before the emergence of early *Homo sapiens.* By 100,000 years ago, artifacts of many types were of composite form, that is, made from several different parts. A wooden spear might have a stone tip, a flint scraper, a bone handle. Unfortunately, we know almost nothing about the bone and wood tools used. (a) Stone-tipped Mousterian spear (a hypothetical example). The spear was made from a pointed stone head attached to a wooden handle to form the projectile. The head probably fitted into a slot in the wooden shaft and was fixed to it with resin or beeswax; a binding was added to the end of the shaft. (b) Mousterian artifacts.

climate, differing activities, and subsistence needs among them. They even transported lumps of coal for fuel up to 15 km (9.4 miles) from natural outcrops in parts of France.

The Neanderthals and their contemporaries were developing tools for different activities far more quickly than ever before, perhaps at a time of growing human populations and slightly enhanced social complexity. Fundamentally, Middle Paleolithic technology was simple and highly variable and was a logical development of technologies refined over many millennia.

The Origins of Burial and Religious Belief

The Neanderthals were hunter-gatherers; and the world's population was still small, but life was gradually becoming more complex. Some experts claim that the Neanderthals regularly buried their dead, showing the first signs of religious ideology and of a preoccupation with the life here-after. Some Neanderthals were indeed buried by their companions, but all known burials have come from caves or rock shelters in Europe, Southwest Asia, and Eurasia, often found under unscientific circumstances. Christopher Stringer and Clive Gamble (1993) point out that most complete Neanderthal bodies occur in caves where predator bones are rare, as if carnivores were not using such places for their dens. Thus, the abandoned corpses have survived more or less intact, even if they were disposed of underground, for no hibernating bears dug them up and no hyenas scattered the decaying bodies lying in their dens.

Single burials are the most common, normally accompanied by flint tools, food offerings, or even cooked game meat (identified by charred bones); but many such associations are dubious, given unscientific excavation many years ago. One rock shelter, La Ferrassie, near Les Eyzies in France, yielded the remains of two adult Neanderthals and four children buried close together in a campsite. One band of Siberian mountain-goat hunters lived at Teshik-Tash in the western foothills of the Himalayas. They buried one of their children in a shallow pit, surrounding the body with six pairs of wild goat horns.

Another remarkable single burial came from the Shanidar Cave in the Zagros Mountains of Iraq. There a 30-year-old man was crushed by a rockfall from the roof of the cave. He was buried in a shallow pit. Other single graves from France and central Europe were covered with red ocher powder.

There is no question that the Neanderthals buried some of their dead, but whether such burial was mere corpse disposal or was associated with beliefs in an afterlife is a matter for debate. We can be almost certain that they were sometimes cannibals. A cave occupied by Neanderthals at Moula-Guercy in France about 100,000 years ago has yielded red deer and human bone fragments, among them human skulls broken to get at the brain, and limb fragments with clear signs of butchery and defleshing identical to that practiced on animals (Defleur et al., 1999).

Sibudu Cave
61,000 years ago

Longgupo
?? 2 mya

Howieson's Poort culture

Neanderthal Speech?

Did the Neanderthals have language and the ability to pass complex information from one generation to the next? Like music, language is intangible, which can only be studied indirectly, notably from tiny bones like the hyoid, attached to the cartilage at the larynx, which anchors the muscles needed for speech. Only one Neanderthal hyoid bone has survived, on a 63,000-year-old skeleton from Kebara Cave in Israel, but it is lower in the throat than that of *Homo sapiens*. The dimensions of the hypoglossal canal, which carries the nerves from the brain to the tongue, are equivalent in Neanderthals to those of modern humans, and the dimensions of the canal in the thoracic vertebrae, which house the nerves for controlling the diaphragm and breathing, are also similar. Thus, we know that Neanderthals had the same motor control over their tongues and breathing as we do. They also appear to have had the same sound perception qualities as people today. Despite all these anatomical features, there are very strong reasons to believe that they did not possess fluent speech.

Firstly, the Neanderthals lived in small intimate groups. They shared knowledge and experience about their environment and their tiny social world, always with a common purpose. Secondly, no one has yet found a convincing art object or artifacts modified for symbolic reasons in a Neanderthal site. However, the most powerful argument against language is the long-term stability of Neanderthal culture. The tools they made and their way of life survived virtually unchanged between about 250,000 and 30,000 years ago. Language is a force for change, for exchanging ideas, and for complex thought. Of course, their culture was extremely diverse and their behavior often complex. They had a high appreciation of good toolmaking stone and, presumably, of other raw materials. But there were no innovations, just a narrow repertoire of ancient technologies that sustained them for thousands of years. No Neanderthal ever invented a needle and thread, a harpoon, or a bow and arrow. Such inventions were the domain of language-using modern humans. Steven Mithen (2006, 2007) argues provocatively that the Neanderthals used dancing and simple hums or chants to enhance cooperation, and developed forms of much more rudimentary communication in earlier times, what he calls a "Hmmmmm" form of communication system.

The Denisovans

As the Neanderthals developed and flourished in Europe, there may have been as many as seven distinct human forms, from Africa to Europe, in Siberia, and in the Indonesian islands. Anatomically modern humans (*Homo* sapiens) are the only survivors. We know little about these various people, among them the mysterious Denisovans of Eurasia. All we have of them are a broken finger bone and a wisdom tooth of a woman, found in Denisova Cave in southern Siberia (Reich et al., 2010). The bones date to between 30,000 and 50,000 years ago. The genome sequence recovered from the bones and mitochondria from the tooth shows that its owner shared common ancestry with the Neanderthals, but was not one of them. The Denisovans are genetically distinct from the Neanderthals, but traces of their DNA survive in the genes of some modern-day Papuans and Pacific Islanders. The Denisovans had long diverged from the Neanderthals and may represent a hitherto unknown human form.

For the moment, no one is assigning the Denisovans to a known human form or proposing a taxonomic label. They are simply known as Denisovans until more discoveries flesh out what appears to be a distinct human group that lived in Eurasia while the Neanderthals flourished in Europe. How widespread they were remains a question mark. Perhaps they also dwelt in places like China where some human fossils appear to resemble neither Neanderthals nor *Homo erectus.* The Denisova bones hint that there were at least two archaic human forms in Eurasia before modern humans arrived. The Neanderthals dwelt to the west, while the Denisovans flourished to the east and perhaps further southward. But a great deal more research will be needed before we can firmly identify different hominin groups between whom gene flow occurred over long periods of time.

As the Denisovans and Neanderthals flourished in Europe and Eurasia, tiny groups of anatomically modern humans inhabited parts of sub-Saharan Africa. They, like the Neanderthals, were descendants of *Homo heidelbergensis,* but evolved into the immediate ancestors of ourselves— *Homo sapiens* equipped with the full and almost open-ended cognitive skills of humanity today. In Part II, we tell the story of their origins and trace the complex population movements that carried them to all parts of the Old World and, eventually, into the Americas. And with the spread of modern humans, the immensely long history of archaic humanity ends.

Summary

- This chapter covers a long period of time, from about 1.9 million to about 50,000 years ago. We describe the climatic events of the Great Ice Age (the Pleistocene) between about 1.6 million and 128,000 years ago. These complex fluctuations between glacial maxima and much shorter interglacial periods were the backdrop to the evolution of not only archaic humans like *Homo ergaster, Homo erectus,* and *Homo heidelbergensis,* but of modern people—*H. sapiens*—as well, the latter described in Chapter 4.

- *Homo ergaster* had evolved from *Homo habilis* or some other early *Homo* form in tropical Africa by 1.9 mya. It then radiated out of Africa into Asia, perhaps as early as 1.7 mya, where it evolved into *Homo erectus.* At about the same time, a very few humans settled, perhaps unsuccessfully, in Europe, but were defeated by harsh climatic conditions. These population movements were part of a general radiation of mammalian species soon afterward.

- Sometime after 1.8 mya, humans domesticated fire, but the date is much debated. Full control may have not come until much later. One consequence may have been a growing importance of cooked food to human life and development.

- *Homo erectus* evolved slowly in Asia, relying both on stone technology and bamboo artifacts in forested environments, surviving until after 100,000 years ago.

- *Homo heidelbergensis,* a new human form with a larger brain, evolved out of *Homo ergaster* in tropical Africa. *Homo heidelbergensis* may be associated with more sophisticated tool technology known from the distinctive, refined Acheulian hand axes that appear after about 600,000 years ago. This was the time when humans settled in Europe permanently.

- Archaic humans were adept, opportunistic hunters, who also relied on wild plant foods. They probably also scavenged predator kills, but were capable of killing large animals. However, they lacked the linguistic skills of modern humans.

- The Neanderthals of Europe, the Near East, and western Eurasia evolved from *Homo heidelbergensis* over 200,000 years ago. Neanderthals developed more sophisticated toolmaking technology than *H. erectus,* were more adept hunters and foragers, and were the first humans to bury some of their dead.

Key Terms

disk core technique (86)
interglacial (63)
Levallois technique (86)

Matuyama-Brunhes boundary (61)
prepared cores (79)

prognathous (72)
terminations (61)

Further Reading

Klein, Richard L. 2009. *The Human Career*, 3rd ed. Chicago: University of Chicago Press.

Stringer, Chris, and Peter Andrews. 2005. *The Complete World of Human Evolution*. London and New York: Thames & Hudson.

Stringer, Christopher B., and Clive Gamble. 1993. *The Search for the Neanderthals*. London: Thames & Hudson.

THE GREAT DIASPORA: THE ORIGINS AND SPREAD OF MODERN HUMANS

PART II

C. 150,000 YEARS AGO TO MODERN TIMES

"I want you to remind yourself," he said, "that you have now spent one field season of excavation, 15 years of analyses, and thousands of dollars of taxpayers' money to find out no more than this: what a family of five did during the autumn, on six different occasions, scattered over a 2,000-year period. I earnestly hope that the thought will keep you humble."
"Would you believe 'deeply depressed'?"

Kent Flannery, *Guilá Naquitz* (1986)

The curtain raises on the fourth act of the human past, sometime after 100,000 years ago, with the appearance of anatomically modern humans in Southwest Asia. By 45,000 years ago, only one human actor remained on the world stage: *Homo sapiens*, modern humans, ourselves. And by that time, too, there was a dramatic cultural florescence—new human behaviors, the use of new artifact materials, the first art—and people ventured over oceans and into hitherto uninhabited continents. Steven Mithen (1996) calls this moment the "Big Bang"—when the human mind ceased to function through multiple intelligences, and when all such intelligences functioned smoothly together, harmonizing to create the almost limitless imagination of the modern human mind.

The Great Diaspora Timeline

Period already covered

Partial coverage

Period covered in **Part II**

| 5 mya | 2.5 mya | 1 mya | 150,000 B.P. | 10000 B.C. | A.D. 1 | A.D. 1500 |

FIG. 2.2

FIG. 3.1a

FIG. 4.9

Origins and the Diaspora Begins

C. 200,000 YEARS AGO AND LATER

I
n A.D. 1772, a small band of seamen led by French explorer Marion du Fresne landed on a sandy beach in southern Tasmania far off the southern coast of Australia. As his boat grounded, a band of about 30 Aborigines carrying pointed sticks and sharp stones emerged from the trees to greet the strangers. They were exotic looking people to the French, "in color black, the hair woolly and all were naked." It was perhaps surprising that the Tasmanians recognized their visitors as fellow humans. Marion du Fresne was the first outsider to greet them in at least 8,000 years.

The Tasmanians had been isolated on their remote island home after the Ice Age by the rising waters of the Bass Strait that separated them from the Australian mainland. At the time of du Fresne's visit, some 3,000 to 5,000 Aborigines occupied Tasmania, divided into at least 80 bands of between 30 and 50 people. The Aborigines greeted the French in a language that seemed to draw words "from the bottom of the throat." Unfortunately, du Fresne's brief visit ended in violence and the Aborigines never returned to the beach. So he sailed away to New Zealand, where the intrepid explorer was "devoured by natives."

Du Fresne's experience with the Tasmanians was by no means unusual during the European Age of Discovery, when Western explorers were voyaging to every corner of the globe. But, just for a moment, an eighteenth-century European explorer came in contact with a small group of people, whose very remote ancestors had been part of the great diaspora of *Homo sapiens*, which had begun in Africa at least 80,000 years ago, and probably even before that. This chapter describes the origins of modern humans and describes the first chapter in this vast diaspora, which culminated in the settlement of Australia (Figure 4.1). Throughout Australia and especially in Tasmania, there was such a high degree of biological and cultural continuity, as if we are peering back into one of the most important chapters in human history—the spread of modern humans across the Old World. Unfortunately, the Tasmanians did not survive the onslaught of European colonists for long. Almost all of them had vanished within 80 years. ■

Eland and San hunters. A rock painting from the Draskensberg Mountains, South Africa. Rock painting from Natal, South Africa.

Origins

Except, perhaps, for human beginnings, no question surrounding remoter human history generates more controversy than that of the origins of modern humans, ourselves. When and where did the first fully modern humans, *Homo sapiens*, often called AMH (anatomically modern humans) evolve from more archaic people? When and how did our awesome cognitive abilities develop and in what part of the world? Today, the ultimate descendants of these very first modern people inhabit every continent and every kind of natural environment imaginable. This raises another important question. When, how, and why did *Homo sapiens* spread and colonize the Old World and the New? These are now the questions that we must confront, navigating cautiously through complex arguments, rapidly changing environmental conditions, and still very inadequate scientific data.

As far as we can tell, *Homo heidelbergensis* and *Homo erectus* remained remarkably stable in evolutionary terms until less than 500,000 years ago. Eventually, *Homo heidelbergensis* evolved into early *Homo sapiens* in Africa, but we do not know when the gradual transition began or how it took place.

For hundreds of thousands of years, archaic humans survived and evolved with the aid of what Steven Mithen calls multiple intelligences, separated by walls analogous to those dividing the chapels of a medieval cathedral. As Mithen says (1996), the thoughts in one chapel could barely be heard in another. Archaic humans lacked one vital component of the modern mind: cognitive flexibility, the ability to bridge the walls between their many intelligences. Such flexibility appears to have been the prerogative of modern humans, *Homo sapiens*.

Homo sapien means "wise person." What is it that separates us from earlier humans, scientists wonder. First and foremost must be our ability to speak fluently and articulately. We communicate, we tell stories, we pass on knowledge and ideas—all through the medium of language. Consciousness, cognition, self-awareness, foresight, and the ability to express oneself and one's emotions—these are direct consequences of fluent speech. They can be linked with another attribute of the fully fledged human psyche: the capacity for symbolic and spiritual thought, concerned not only with subsistence and technology but also with defining the boundaries of existence and the relationship among the individual, the group, and the universe. Fluent speech, the full flowering of human creativity expressed in art and religion, expert toolmaking—these are some of the hallmarks of anatomically modern humans. With these abilities, humankind eventually colonized not just temperate and tropical environments but the entire globe. With the appearance of fully modern *H. sapiens*, we begin the study of people biologically identical to ourselves, those with the same intellectual abilities and potential. It is hardly surprising that controversy surrounds the appearance of our remote ancestors (Klein, 2009; Lewin, 1998; Stringer and McKie, 1996).

Where Did We Originate?

Africa was the cradle of humanity after 7 million years ago (mya). But was tropical Africa also the birthplace of modern humans, who then spread to other continents? Or did AMH evolve from several hominin species in different parts of the Old World? Over generations of debate, with arguments supported by a very thin fossil record, two competing, and seemingly diametrically opposed, hypotheses emerged (Figure 4.2):

- The multiregional model (Figure 4.2a) hypothesizes that human populations throughout the Old World evolved independently, first to archaic *H. sapiens*, then to fully modern humans. This continuity model argues for multiple origins of *H. sapiens* and no migrations later than those of *H. erectus*. Thus, modern geographic populations have been separated from one another for a long time, perhaps for nearly 2 million years (Wolpoff et al., 2000). In this scenario, continuous gene flow within the group meant that highly adaptive, novel anatomical features spread rapidly, thereby keeping all human populations on the same fundamental evolutionary path toward anatomically modern people, even if some evolved into fully modern humans before others.

- The out-of-Africa model (Figure 4.2b) takes the diametrically opposite view. According to it, *H. sapiens* evolved in one place, and then spread to all other parts of the Old World. This model, which assumes population movement from a single point of origin, implies that modern geographic populations have shallow roots and were derived from a single source in relatively recent times (Stringer and McKie, 1996).

These two models represent extremes that pit advocates of anatomical continuity against those who favor the rapid replacement of primeval populations. There are intermediate models, too, that allow, for example, for some genetic hybridization between archaic and early modern populations in Africa (see the discussion in Lewin and Foley, 2004). Until fairly recently, most anthropologists strongly favored the multiregional model. The reason was that finds from western Europe and

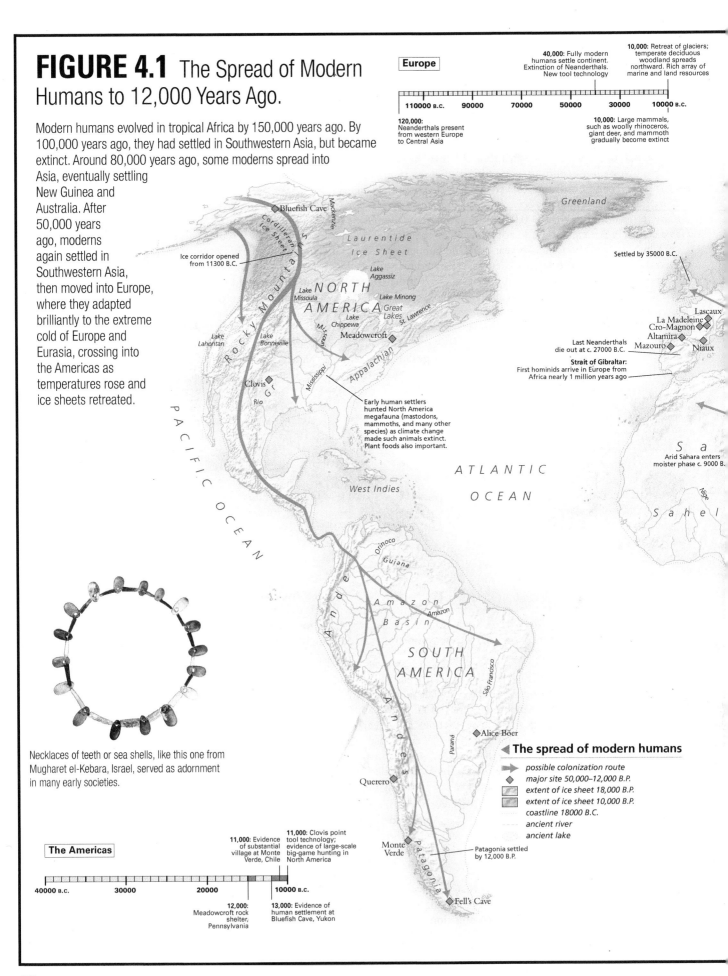

FIGURE 4.1 The Spread of Modern Humans to 12,000 Years Ago.

Modern humans evolved in tropical Africa by 150,000 years ago. By 100,000 years ago, they had settled in Southwestern Asia, but became extinct. Around 80,000 years ago, some moderns spread into Asia, eventually settling New Guinea and Australia. After 50,000 years ago, moderns again settled in Southwestern Asia, then moved into Europe, where they adapted brilliantly to the extreme cold of Europe and Eurasia, crossing into the Americas as temperatures rose and ice sheets retreated.

Europe

110000 B.C. 90000 70000 50000 30000 10000 B.C.

40,000: Fully modern humans settle continent. Extinction of Neanderthals. New tool technology

10,000: Retreat of glaciers; temperate deciduous woodland spreads northward. Rich array of marine and land resources

120,000: Neanderthals present from western Europe to Central Asia

10,000: Large mammals, such as woolly rhinoceros, giant deer, and mammoth gradually become extinct

Bluefish Cave

Ice corridor opened from 11300 B.C.

Cordilleran Ice Sheet

Mackenzie

Greenland

Laurentide Ice Sheet

Lake Agassiz

Lake Missoula

NORTH AMERICA

Lake Minong

Great Lakes

Lake Chippewa

St. Lawrence

Meadowcroft

Missouri

Appalachian

Mississippi

Clovis

Gr

Rio

Rocky Mountains

Lake Lahontan

Lake Bonneville

Settled by 35000 B.C.

Lascaux

La Madeleine
Cro-Magnon

Altamira

Mazouro

Niaux

Last Neanderthals die out at c. 27000 B.C.

Strait of Gibraltar: First hominids arrive in Europe from Africa nearly 1 million years ago

Early human settlers hunted North America megafauna (mastodons, mammoths, and many other species) as climate change made such animals extinct. Plant foods also important.

PACIFIC OCEAN

ATLANTIC OCEAN

West Indies

S a

Arid Sahara enters moister phase c. 9000 B.

Niger

S a h e l

Orinoco

Guiana

Andes

Amazon Basin

Amazon

SOUTH AMERICA

São Francisco

Alice Böer

Paraná

Querero

Necklaces of teeth or sea shells, like this one from Mugharet el-Kebara, Israel, served as adornment in many early societies.

The spread of modern humans

- → possible colonization route
- ◆ major site 50,000–12,000 B.P.
- extent of ice sheet 18,000 B.P.
- extent of ice sheet 10,000 B.P.
- coastline 18000 B.C.
- --- ancient river
- ancient lake

The Americas

40000 B.C. 30000 20000 10000 B.C.

11,000: Evidence of substantial village at Monte Verde, Chile

11,000: Clovis point tool technology; evidence of large-scale big-game hunting in North America

12,000: Meadowcroft rock shelter, Pennsylvania

13,000: Evidence of human settlement at Bluefish Cave, Yukon

Monte Verde

Patagonia

Patagonia settled by 12,000 B.P.

Fell's Cave

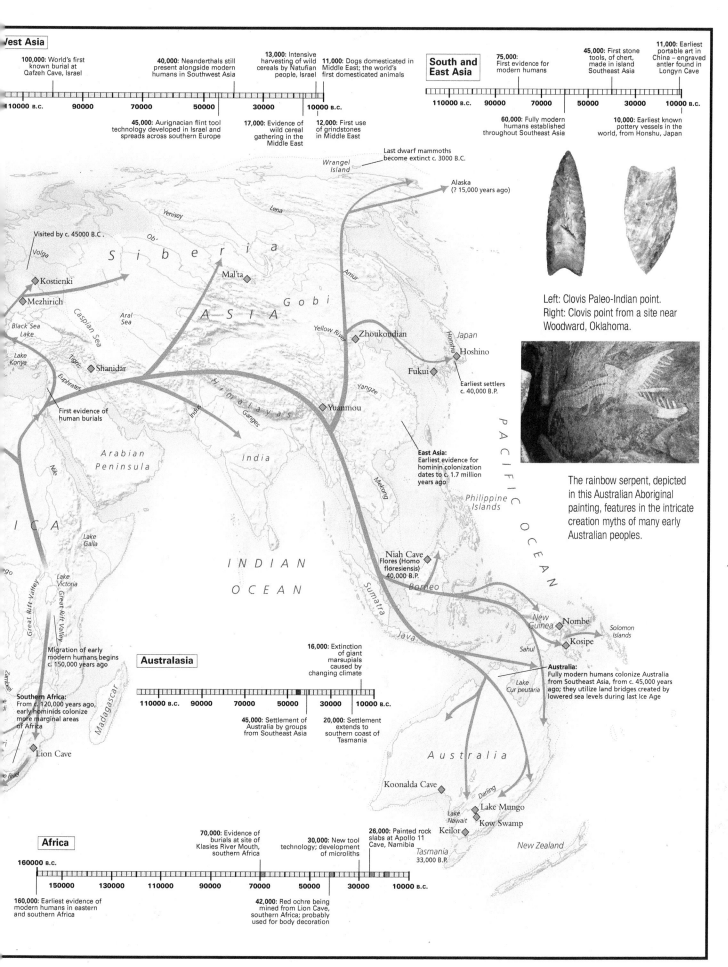

West Asia

100,000: World's first known burial at Qafzeh Cave, Israel

40,000: Neanderthals still present alongside modern humans in Southwest Asia

13,000: Intensive harvesting of wild cereals by Natufian people, Israel

11,000: Dogs domesticated in Middle East; the world's first domesticated animals

45,000: Aurignacian flint tool technology developed in Israel and spreads across southern Europe

17,000: Evidence of wild cereal gathering in the Middle East

12,000: First use of grindstones in Middle East

110000 B.C.   90000   70000   50000   30000   10000 B.C.

South and East Asia

75,000: First evidence for modern humans

45,000: First stone tools, of chert, made in island Southeast Asia

11,000: Earliest portable art in China – engraved antler found in Longyn Cave

110000 B.C.   90000   70000   50000   30000   10000 B.C.

60,000: Fully modern humans established throughout Southeast Asia

10,000: Earliest known pottery vessels in the world, from Honshu, Japan

Last dwarf mammoths become extinct c. 3000 B.C.

Wrangel Island

Alaska (? 15,000 years ago)

Visited by c. 45000 B.C.

Volga

Kostienki

Mezhirich

Caspian Sea   *Aral Sea*

Black Sea Lake

Lake Konya

Tigris   Shanidar   *Euphrates*

First evidence of human burials

Nile

Arabian Peninsula

Siberia

Yenisey   *Ob*   *Lena*

Mal'ta

ASIA   *Gobi*   *Amur*

Yellow River   Zhoukoudian   *Japan*   *Honshu*

Hoshino

Fukui

Yangze

Earliest settlers c. 40,000 B.P.

Yuanmou

Himalayas   *Indus*   *Ganges*

India

Mekong

East Asia: Earliest evidence for hominin colonization dates to c. 1.7 million years ago

Philippine Islands

PACIFIC OCEAN

Left: Clovis Paleo-Indian point.
Right: Clovis point from a site near Woodward, Oklahoma.

The rainbow serpent, depicted in this Australian Aboriginal painting, features in the intricate creation myths of many early Australian peoples.

ICA

Lake Galla

Lake Victoria

Great Rift Valley   *Great Rift Valley*

Migration of early modern humans begins c. 150,000 years ago

Southern Africa: From c. 120,000 years ago, early hominids colonize more marginal areas of Africa

Lion Cave

Madagascar

INDIAN OCEAN

Niah Cave
Flores (Homo floresiensis) 40,000 B.P.

Sumatra   *Borneo*   *Java*

New Guinea   Nombe

Kosipe

Sahul

Solomon Islands

Australasia

16,000: Extinction of giant marsupials caused by changing climate

110000 B.C.   90000   70000   50000   30000   10000 B.C.

45,000: Settlement of Australia by groups from Southeast Asia

20,000: Settlement extends to southern coast of Tasmania

Lake Cur peutaria

Australia: Fully modern humans colonize Australia from Southeast Asia, from c. 45,000 years ago; they utilize land bridges created by lowered sea levels during last Ice Age

Australia

Koonalda Cave

Darling

Lake Mungo

Lake Nawait   Kow Swamp

Keilor

Tasmania 33,000 B.P.

New Zealand

Africa

70,000: Evidence of burials at site of Klasies River Mouth, southern Africa

30,000: New tool technology; development of microliths

26,000: Painted rock slabs at Apollo 11 Cave, Namibia

160000 B.C.   150000   130000   110000   90000   70000   50000   30000   10000 B.C.

160,000: Earliest evidence of modern humans in eastern and southern Africa

42,000: Red ochre being mined from Lion Cave, southern Africa; probably used for body decoration

97

TABLE 4.1
Climate change and cultural developments in Africa, Southeast Asia, and the Pacific Islands, 50000 B.C. to A.D. 1000.

Years B.C.	Generalized Climatic Change	Western Europe	Central Europe & Asia	Northeast Asia	Americas
		Chapter 7			Chapter 5
8000	HOLOCENE	Magdalenian		Diuktai	? First settlement
15000		Solutrean			
20000			East Gravettian	Mal'ta	
25000	LATE WURM (WEICHSEL) GLACIATION	Gravettian		Afontova-Gora	
		Aurignacian			
30000					
35000					
		Mousterian			No apparent settlement
40000					
45000				Settlement unknown	
		Neanderthals	Neanderthals		
50000			Some Mousterian settlement		
	Colder Warmer		Chapter 3		

There was considerable overlap among European cultures. Climatic changes are approximate, as they are subject to considerable controversy among experts.

Southwest Asia dominated academic discussion, mainly because the largest numbers of fossils came from these areas and seemed to provide evidence for at least two points of origin. Furthermore, many deep, well-excavated caves and rock shelters appeared to document technological change from simple, relatively unsophisticated toolkits to the much more elaborate artifacts characteristic of *H. sapiens.* Now, however, the pendulum has swung toward a consensus that Africa played the

(a)

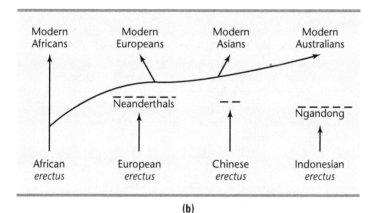

(b)

FIGURE 4.2 Theories of the origins of modern humans, each of which interprets the fossil evidence in very different ways. (a) The multiregional model, which argues for the evolution of *H. sapiens* in many regions of the world. (b) The out-of-Africa model, which has modern humanity evolving in Africa, then spreading to other parts of the world.

major role in modern human origins. Current research focuses not so much on origins as on the complex events that led to the dispersal of AMH from Africa. Were there multiple dispersals? Are these reflected in modern human genetics? How important was fluent speech to the process? Above all, when did fully modern behavior and cognitive abilities appear? Was this a gradual process or a sudden event?

Homo sapiens in Africa

The Fossils What fossils document the putative appearance of AMH in Africa? Africa may have been the cradle of humankind, but for years it was regarded as a backwater in later times, a place where modern humans arose very much later than they did in Europe. These ideas were formulated before radiocarbon chronologies and were based on a mere handful of fossil finds, among them the famous robust Kabwe (Broken Hill) skull from Zambia, an archaic-looking cranium that seemed to epitomize a backward continent (Figure 4.3) (Phillipson, 2005; Stringer and Andrews, 2005).

Today we know that *Homo heidelbergensis* was widely distributed from southern to northeast Africa before 200,000 years. A new generation of research based on radiometric dates and sophisticated cave excavation has painted a radically different picture of African life after that date. For example, in East Africa, Richard Leakey found a large, thick-boned human skull and limb bones at Omo Kibish in Ethiopia, dating to about 195,000 years ago. They came from a tall, well-built male, with a broad forehead and well-defined brow ridges that thinned at the edges (Stringer and Gamble, 1993).

FIGURE 4.3 *Homo heidelbergensis* from Kabwe, central Zambia.

Omo Kibish
195,000 years ago

FIGURE 4.4 *Homo sapiens idaltu* from Herto, Ethiopia.

Herto
160, 000 years ago

At Herto, about 225 km (140 miles) northeast of Addis Ababa, Ethiopian paleo-anthropologist Y. Haile-Selassie and his colleagues unearthed three 160,000-year-old skulls, one of them a child, as well as other human fragments, from a location where people had caught numerous fish and killed or scavenged hippopotamuses (T. White et al., 2003) (Figure 4.4). The skulls are clearly from anatomically modern people, although minor differences that mark them as more primitive are sufficient for them to be labeled *Homo sapiens idaltu* (after the local Afar name for elder). The adult male skull is long and rugged, with heavily worn teeth, and is slightly larger than modern crania. Interestingly, there are signs that the skulls were defleshed with stone tools after death, and the child's skull displays a polish resulting from repeated handling. Judging from modern-day practices in New Guinea and elsewhere, the people may have preserved heads as part of some ancestor cult—the earliest evidence of any form of death ritual from the past.

The Herto finds show that the anatomical developments that led to the emergence of *H. sapiens* were running their course in Africa as early as 160,000 years ago, far earlier than any equivalent developments in Europe or Southwest Asia. In evolutionary terms, the transition from *H. heidelbergensis* to archaic *H. sapiens* seems to have occurred not quickly but relatively slowly and continuously. It is difficult to draw a line between the two species. This is the case not only at Herto, but also with human remains from Jebel Irhoud cave in Morocco, which also show a mix of archaic and modern features, dating to between 190,000 and 90,000 years ago (Hublin, 2001).

In contrast to these earlier, still rather shadowy humans, all known human finds in Africa dating to later than 120,000 years ago are fully modern, by which time it is clear that the anatomical transition was complete.

Genetics   A long fossil record documents the changeover, but can we nail down modern human origins to Africa? Molecular biology has played a significant role in dating earlier human evolution and is now yielding important clues to the origins of *H. sapiens* (Cann, 2001; Cann et al., 1995). Researchers have zeroed in on **mitochondrial DNA (mtDNA),** a useful tool for calibrating mutation rates because it accumulates mutations much faster than nuclear DNA (Figure 4.5). mtDNA is inherited only through the maternal line; it does not mix with and become diluted by paternal DNA. Thus, it provides a potentially reliable link with ancestral populations. When genetic researchers analyzed the mtDNA of 182 women from Africa, Asia, Europe, Australia, and New Guinea, they found that the differences among them were very small. Therefore, they argued, the five populations were all of comparatively recent origin. There were some differences, sufficient to separate two groups within the sample: a set of African individuals and another comprising individuals from all groups. The biologists concluded that all modern humans derived from a 200,000-year-old African population from which populations migrated to the rest of the Old World, with little or no interbreeding with existing, more archaic human groups. Research using the Y chromosome, which makes an embryo male, produces somewhat similar results.

Today, with data from the entire mtDNA genome, there is evidence that Africans display more diverse types of mtDNA than other present-day populations elsewhere in the world, a finding that suggests they had more time to develop such mutations. The database of normal (nuclear) DNA and of its products (blood groups and enzymes) displays a hierarchy of clusters. There was a primary split between Africans and non-Africans, then a later one between Eurasians and Southeast Asians. These findings also imply that modern humans originated in Africa, then dispersed from there to split again in Asia (Cann, 2001).

A later generation of research based on the entire mtDNA genome uses new models and even more sophisticated statistical approaches. These show that the process of origin and spread was more complex than originally thought. The three deepest branches of the African tree were exclusively African. The next deepest was a mixture of Africans and non-Africans. This pattern arose from the evolution of DNA lineages in Africa for some time, followed by an out-migration by a few people. This resulted in a population bottleneck, followed by a rapid expansion. Their estimate for the start of the process is 171,500 ± 50,000 years ago. The first clade, with both African and non-African members, dates to an estimated 52,000 ± 27,500 years ago. In recent years, researchers have focused on microsatellite DNA, the short strands of DNA, which mutate so quickly that the rates can be calculated in a laboratory. A far more secure chronology for the coalescence of modern human genes gives a date of about 150,000 years ago. This means that, assuming a constant rate of genetic diversification, all human variation could have arisen in the past 150,000 years or so.

FIGURE 4.5 Alan Wilson and his research team used mitochondrial DNA from 182 women around the world to develop this family tree of modern human origins.

Molecular biology and the fossil evidence seem to be in broad agreement. The high degree of genetic variation in African populations south of the Sahara is probably a sign that this was the continent where modern humans emerged. However, to speak, as people have, of a primordial "African Eve," the grandmother of us all, is not only wrong but also masks a much more complex reality. Anatomically modern humans may have evolved in many locations south of the Sahara within highly varied and very isolated African populations.

Ecology For generations, anthropologists have tended to treat the origin of *H. sapiens* as a unique event that took place outside the processes of evolutionary biology. As Robert Foley (1984c) argues, one can understand this event only within a comparative ecological framework. Foley points out that modern humans are most likely to have originated within a single general location. The savanna woodland of Africa around 100,000 years ago was an ideal environment for promoting the speciation of modern humans, he believes. Foley has studied monkey evolution in Africa and found that the widely dispersed populations had diverged; they did not continue on a single evolutionary course. Africa experienced considerable habitat fragmentation and re-formation during the alternating cold and warmth of the Ice Age, fluctuations that enhanced the prospects of speciation among the continent's animals and plants. For example, Foley found that one monkey genus alone radiated into 16 species at about the same time that modern humans may have evolved on the continent. The tropical environments of Africa consisted of a constant mosaic of changing environmental patterns, a mosaic that tended to foster local evolution. In contrast, in higher latitudes, environmental changes were more marked, and animal distributions changed significantly and rapidly over short periods of time.

Foley's monkey studies have convinced him that modern humans evolved in such a mosaic of tropical environments, developing distinctive characteristics that separated them from their archaic predecessors. Within tropical Africa's patchy environments were areas where food supplies were both predictable and of high quality. In response to such regions, some humans may have developed wide-ranging behavior, may have lived in larger social groups with a considerable kin-based substructure, and may have been highly selective in their diet. As part of these responses, some groups may have developed exceptional hunting skills, a technology so effective that they could use projectiles to prey on animals from a distance. With more efficient technology, more advance planning, and better organization of both hunting and foraging, our ancestors could have reduced the unpredictability of the environment in dramatic ways.

Droughts and Climate Change

Africa is an enormous continent, where early human populations were always thin on the ground, even during periods of ample rainfall. Sparse numbers is one thing, extreme isolation quite another, so the only possible cause must have been a climatic one. Modern humans first appeared at a time of constant long-term climatic change, reflected in the Northern Hemisphere by long glacial periods separated by shorter, warmer intervals. The effects would have been more muted in tropical latitudes, except for prolonged droughts. The effects of droughts and other climatic shifts on tiny human populations could have played a significant part not only on human behavior, but in the initial spread of AMH out of Africa.

What sub-Saharan Africa was like between 200,000 and 100,000 years ago remains a considerable question mark, for, until recently, the only information on climate change over 150,000 years ago came from deep sea cores, not from land. Then as now, monsoon rains and El Niños played a major role in bringing ample rainfall or drought to the lands south of the Sahara where the first modern human populations thrived. Or at least they appear to have thrived until a series of megadroughts descended on East and southern Africa 135,000 years ago.

We knew nothing of these droughts until a team of researchers laboriously transported a drill rig to the waters of Lakes Malawi and Tanganyika in East Africa, two of the world's oldest and deepest lakes (Scholtz et al., 2007). They drilled a core into Lake Malawi in an area that was mainly submerged for the past million years. The core documented great climatic variability 135,000 years ago, marked by periods of extreme, prolonged drought, with shorter intervals of higher rainfall about every 11,000 years. There were periods of severe droughts between about 135,000 and 75,000 years ago, which reduced the lake's water level by at least 95 percent. The level of aridity was almost unimaginable; 75,000 years ago, 550-km (340-mile)-long Lake Malawi was no more than a couple of insignificant pools, no more than 10 km (6 miles) across and 200 m (656 feet) deep. Only about 70,000 years ago did wetter, more stable conditions return as lake levels rose dramatically. It may be no coincidence that a major population expansion took hold in Africa 60,000 years ago.

Out of Africa

If tropical Africa was the cradle of modern humans, how and why did *H. sapiens* move into Asia and Europe (Brauer, 1992)? We have a tendency to think of deliberate migrations, of linear movements of large numbers of people from A to B, perhaps because we spend much of our time driving along highways. But in fact, the process was always on a small scale, involving tiny numbers of people simply hunting and foraging on the move as they always had. Relatives might quarrel, violence might erupt between two men, a son and his family hive off into unexplored valley nearby— the possibilities for movement were endless and untidy. From an archaeologist's point of view, identifying population movements is virtually impossible, except from the occasional dated archaeological site with human remains and distinctive artifacts.

Intense controversy also surrounds another issue. Was there just one movement out of Africa, or were there several? Complex arguments based on fossils and molecular biology come into play and there is not yet a consensus. We believe that the process was complex and is still beyond our ability to fully decipher. However, a combination of archaeological and genetic evidence leads anthropologist Stephen Oppenheimer (2008) to believe that AMH first moved rapidly out of Africa along a huge arc of coastline from Africa, around the coasts of the Indian Ocean (Figure 4.6). He argues that shellfish and other marine foods may have played a decisive part in movements eastward. As he points out, we know that people were exploiting molluscs in South Africa as early as 160,000 years ago (Mareen et al., 2007). Shell middens are known from the west coast of the Red Sea dating to about 125,000 years before present (Walker et al., 2000). Far away in Southeast Asia, marine foods were important on Timor and to early Australian groups by 40,000 years ago (O'Connor, 2007). Oppenheimer argues that there was a single southern exit of modern humans during a dry period of low sea levels sometime around 83,000 years ago (the date, based on genetic data, is approximate) that resulted in a rapid movement around the Indian Ocean that eventually took AMH to the

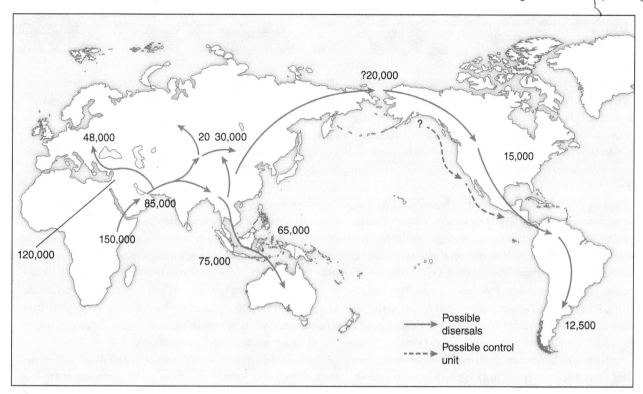

FIGURE 4.6 AMH dispersal as reconstructed by Stephen Oppenheimer and others, using archaeological and genetic data. The dates are provisional at best.

then-exposed continental shelf off Southeast Asia (see section "First AMH Settlement in East and Southeast Asia," pp. 106–107).

Unfortunately, almost no archaeological sites or human fossils document early AMH occupation of South and Southeast Asia. For a start, the numbers of people involved were tiny. Stone artifacts dating to around 70,000 years ago are known in the Lenggong Valley on the Malay peninsula (Zuraina, 1998). Despite a lack of conclusive finds, there is wide agreement that AMH were already living in Southeast Asia at about the time of a huge natural disaster that convulsed Southeast Asia 73,000 years ago. Mount Toba on Sumatra in Southeast Asia blew into space (see Science box).

Claims as to the severity of the eruptions and their effects on human populations vary considerably. There are those who consider Mount Toba an epochal disaster and others who argue that the effects were less than sometimes claimed. The jury is still out. For example, despite claims, there is still no well-documented proof that modern humans were in India and smothered by volcanic ash. If there were, surely by no means all of them would have perished. However, as we point out in the box, this was a critical time for Africans, and perhaps the moment when *Homo sapiens* south of the Sahara acquired the cognitive skills of modern humanity.

When Did Modern Cognitive Skills Appear?

Cognitive abilities like fluent speech, enhanced planning abilities, and powerful intellectual skills are intangibles, which makes it extremely difficult to establish quite when AMH acquired modern forms of human behavior. We can only search for tangible remains of such behavior in the form of distinctive artifacts and such items as ornaments or art works, which required enhanced cognitive skills. Modern human behavior appears to have developed as a kind of package long after anatomically modern people appeared, apparently about the time or after the Mount Toba catastrophe.

The clues come in various forms of ornaments and weapons (McBrearty and Brooks, 2000). Blombos Cave, on the Indian Ocean shore near the southern tip of South Africa, has yielded extensive occupation deposits dating to at least 65,000 years ago, where numerous finely bladed tools, spear points (including some flaked with pressure, a much later innovation in Europe), and some possible bone points were found. The occupants ate a broad range of foods, including deepwater and shallow-water fish, shellfish, game of different sizes, and plants. Numerous fragments of red ocher came to light. One of them has edges worn by grinding and scraping, and bears crosshatched

Blombos
65, 000 years ago

Science   Cataclysm! The Mount Toba Eruption, c. 73,000 Years Ago

Imagine a sudden deluge of choking volcanic dust. Animals and humans alike cough and wheeze in the suffocating ash and heat, then die. Only a few hunting bands survive, those lucky enough to be close to caves and natural overhangs, or who live in rare sheltered enclaves, where vagaries of topography and prevailing wind allow them to survive. That's what happened when Mount Toba, a large volcano on Sumatra in Southeast Asia, exploded 73,000 years ago in one of the greatest eruptions of all time. Around 2,800 cu km (670 cubic miles) of the mountain vanished into space (Ambrose, 2003; Rampino and Ambrose, 2000). Lava flows from the eruption covered over 20,000 sq km (7,700 sq miles). Hundreds of square kilometers of solid rock fractured into vast clouds of volcanic ash that rose over 32.5 km (20 miles) into the atmosphere. Millions of tons of sulfur gas reached the stratosphere and lingered there for years. When the eruption subsided, only a huge crater remained, which is now the world's largest volcanic crater lake—100 km (62 miles) long, 30 km (18.6 miles) wide, and up to 505 m (1,666 feet) deep.

The Toba eruption was the greatest volcanic event of the past 23 million years. To put it in perspective, another Southeast Asian volcano, Mount Tambora, erupted in 1815. Tambora's ash clouds mantled the sun over much of the world and caused the famous "Year without a Summer" throughout Europe in 1816. Tambora's temper tantrum was 40 times *smaller* than Toba's. The notorious Krakatau explosion of 1883, heard hundreds of miles away, was even smaller—and that was a monstrous catastrophe that killed more than 38,000 people.

Patient mapping and satellite observation are plotting the extent of the eruption, especially of the ash that mantled so much of Asia. Volcanic ash fell on a huge area—the northeastern Arabian Sea, much of the Indian Ocean as far south as 14° south of the Equator, northern India and Bangladesh up to 25° north, most of island and mainland Southeast Asia, and the South China Sea. The thickness of the ash layer varied from place to place, sometimes a few inches, often much deeper. Some ash deposits in Indian lakes are up to 3 m (9 feet) thick.

The ash was just the first chapter of the disaster. The sulfur gas from the eruption formed a long-lasting stratospheric haze that reflected sunlight and triggered prolonged global cooling. Almost immediately, the temperature of the South China Sea dropped by 1°C (1.8°F). One Greenland ice core displays a massive sulfur peak lasting about 6 years at 71,000 years ago. The temperature over Greenland may have dropped as much as 6°C (11°F). Some of the lowest temperatures of the late Ice Age coincided with the Toba eruption and lasted for as long as 2,000 years.

The effects were especially severe in the tropics. Tropical forests in particular are extremely vulnerable to cooling, for seed banks are often limited and aboveground plant tissues die rapidly when exposed to even a few days of low temperatures. Temperate forests can also suffer badly from summer cold, especially deciduous trees, which lose their sprouting foliage almost immediately. The sudden cold may also have coincided with significant cooling of the Southwest Pacific and weakening of the trade wind circulation. As a result, long-term El Niño–like conditions could have contributed to the megadrought conditions already prevailing over much of Africa.

Without question, the human cost was significant. Thousands of people must have perished from starvation. Geneticists theorize that a severe population bottleneck ensued among humans over a wide area about 70,000 years ago. Population bottlenecks involve substantial reductions in the size of a population that leads to the extinction of many genetic lineages within it. The lack of genetic diversity among humans results from a series of bottlenecks over the past million years or more, the last of which was about 70,000 years ago. There is more genetic diversity between individual members of chimpanzee troops in West Africa than among all living humans on earth.

The Mount Toba disaster decimated animal and plant communities over much of the tropics. South of the Sahara, the extreme aridity of the African megadroughts must already have been affecting human groups. Toba added exceptional cold and even drier conditions to the climatic equation. Some geneticists estimate that the African population declined to a total of between 4,000 and 10,000 females of reproductive age. Add to this an average of two children, a male mate, and a small number of elders beyond reproductive age, and you have a population that would not fill the average Big 10 college football stadium. This by any standards was a narrow bottleneck, when you reflect that there are about a billion reproducing females on earth today.

The survivors dwelt in refuge areas in East and southern Africa, living in complete isolation from the wider world, and usually from neighboring groups. The effects of genetic drift may have kicked in, the accumulation of random changes in gene frequencies in isolated populations that may have compounded over time. The genetic bottleneck lasted for some 20,000 years. These were some of the most critical millennia in human history, for it was during this period that *Homo sapiens* acquired its full cognitive powers. Once the bottleneck ended and rainfall improved, Africa's population grew rapidly. *Homo sapiens* once again moved out of the tropics, but this time with a difference. They possessed all the awesome mental abilities of modern humanity.

lines (Figures 4.7a and b). Other finds, from even earlier levels as much as 75,000 years old, include perforated seashells, and 41 tick shells perforated for suspension (Henshilwood et al., 2004). These are currently the earliest known, securely dated bone tools in the world.

Sibudu Cave, in South Africa, has yielded a bone projectile point, a spatulalike tool for hide working, and a needlelike object, from a layer dating to about 61,000 years ago, also traces of grass bedding dating to about 77,000 years ago. The Sibudu artifacts form part of a little-known Howieson's Poort culture dating to about 62,000 years ago, which is marked by a smaller size of stone projectile points, as if hunting technology was changing. The Sibudu point is smaller than those from Blombos, which were almost certainly spearheads. A third of the animals taken at Sibudu were duiker, a tiny, shy antelope that rarely weighs more than 5 kg (11 pounds) and thrives in forested environments. There are other signs of a more humid environment, too, in marked contrast to later times after 60,000 years ago, when the environment was drier and more open. The hunters now took zebra and medium-sized

(a)

(b)

FIGURE 4.7 (a) Excavations at Blombos Cave, South Africa. (b) A red ocher "crayon" bearing crosshatch marks. Is this the world's earliest art?

antelope such as hartebeest that prefer grassland and savanna. They used spears tipped with quite substantial stone points, which contrast sharply with earlier Howieson's Poort weapons, perhaps a weaponry that was an adaptation to closed forest environments (Backwell et al., 2007).

The Sibudu discoveries raise an interesting point. Could the Howieson's Poort people have been the first humans to develop the bow and arrow, perhaps for use against shy, small animals in forests? One fine bone point is insufficient evidence for such an innovation, but there are other clues as well. Howieson's Poort stone workers made numerous small backed tools that could have served as arrow heads or barbs for arrows that were sharp enough to penetrate animal hide. Many of the backed tools at Sibudu show distinctive fractures that are characteristic of breaks caused by a sharp impact, and wear patterns are consistent with those on artifacts used as barbs or mounted heads (Lombard and Phillipson, 2010).

It is interesting to note that bow-and-arrow technology, if that is what this is, apparently vanished after 60,000 years ago, to reappear many millennia later. This should not surprise us, for all kinds of environmental changes, such as prolonged droughts or population movements, could have led to the loss of new technologies at a time when human cognitive abilities were evolving rapidly.

Thousands of years passed before there were dramatic changes in human life, what has been described as a "cultural explosion." As Steven Mithen points out (1996), there was no one explosion but, rather, a series of "sparks." There would be rapid culture change in one area but not in others. One such spark was the development of blade technology in Southwest Asia by 50,000 years ago; another, the first appearance of art objects in Europe about 40,000 years ago; a third, the first settlement of Australia by 45,000 years before the present. Only after about 30,000 years ago, during the late Ice Age, did rapid culture change take hold in all parts of the world.

First settlement
?45,000 years ago 36000 B.C.

Many theories surround these sudden developments, among them increased economic specialization, the restructuring of social relations, a major technological revolution, and even the development of fully articulate speech. But Mithen believes that the new types of behavior associated with the cultural explosion resulted from the knocking down of the barriers between different parts of the human mind. With full cognitive fluidity, human beings developed new connections between the previously isolated domains of natural history, technical, and social intelligence.

One of the consequences was much more sophisticated social relations; another was visual symbolism, the development of art as a means of expression and communication. As the great cave paintings of western France, described in Chapter 5, show, humankind now had the ability to bring the natural and the social worlds together in a seamless synthesis that is characteristic of many human societies, whether hunter-gatherers or farmers, to this day. The evolution of cognitive fluidity gave *H. sapiens*, spreading throughout the world after 60,000 years ago and perhaps earlier, a competitive edge over resident earlier human populations. With their superior intellectual capabilities, they pushed earlier populations into extinction, perhaps occasionally interbreeding with them. Once the move toward cognitive fluidity began, there was no stopping the process.

Fully modern behavior appears to have developed over a long period in fits and starts, perhaps over 100,000 years or more. The final catalyst may have been fully articulate speech, with its syntax that enables us to string words together to communicate different meanings, both obvious and subtle. Recent research suggests that the FOXP2 gene may have been a decisive factor in the emergence of modern linguistic abilities sometime between 100,000 and 50,000 years ago. Whether this emergence was a gradual or sudden event is a matter of controversy. However, the chances are that AMH possessed sophisticated language skills identical to our own, at the very latest by 50,000 years ago.

SiTE > Exotic Islanders: *Homo floresiensis* <

The earliest known occupation of Sunda comes from the island of Flores, where *Homo erectus* fragments have been fission-track-dated to between 900,000 and 800,000 years ago, perhaps before a million years ago, but these dates remain controversial (Morwood et al., 1999).

One would reasonably expect this remote island to have been settled once efficient watercraft came into use, but this was not the case. Excavations in Liang Bua Cave on Flores yielded a remarkable series of diminutive human skeletons dating to before 38,000 and 13,000 years ago, associated with stone flakes and other artifacts, as well as the bones of a now extinct elephantlike animal known as a stegodon (Morwood et al., 2004). These people were only about a meter (3.2 feet) tall (Figure 4.8) (P. Brown et al., 2004). Their bones display a unique mixture of primitive and more advanced characteristics. Their brains are the same size as those of chimpanzees (c. 380 cc), the skull displaying prominent brow ridges and a low braincase. However, the face is small and delicate like that of modern humans, being tucked under the brain, like that of *Homo sapiens*. The teeth also are entirely modern, whereas the legs are slight and the hips like those of an australopithecine.

Michael Morwood and his colleagues have named the hominins *Homo floresiensis*, but their evolutionary status is a puzzle. Are these a remnant *H. erectus* population, or are they modern humans who crossed to Flores before 40,000 years ago, then developed their unique anatomical characteristics and small stature as

a result of isolation that led, among other things, to endemic dwarfing? Or did they descend from a much earlier, still unknown, small-brained hominin? At this early stage in research, we do not know, and the debate still rages. Certainly the artifacts, and evidence for use of fire, suggest fully human behavior.

Flores has always been an island, isolated from neighboring land even during periods of low sea level during the Ice Age. How, then, did the ancestors of *H. floresiensis* cross open water? On rafts or in canoes, or by accident, clasping driftwood? The earliest known offshore journeys, to New Guinea and the Solomons, occurred before 45,000 years ago, so a deliberate passage is not totally out of the question.

FIGURE 4.8 Artist's reconstruction of *Homo floresiensis*.

By 50,000 years ago, AMH in Africa were broad spectrum hunter-gatherers, preying off animals of every size, consuming sea foods, and exploiting a wide range of plant foods. Modern humans were firmly established throughout the continent, and flourished, albeit in small numbers, in eastern and southwestern Asia. Thereafter, a complex process of colonization and dispersal carried their descendants into every kind of natural environment imaginable—to East and Southeast Asia, to New Guinea, Australia, and the frontiers of the Pacific, to Southwest Asia, Europe, and Eurasia, and into the Americas.

This great diaspora—it was nothing less—encompassed the late Ice Age and just beyond, a time bracket from about 50,000 to 12,000 years ago. It is logical to begin by following modern humans into Asia, for genetics suggest that this was where they first journeyed some 83,000 years ago, before Mount Toba decimated their numbers. Chapter 5 will then summarize what happened in Europe and Eurasia, before describing the first settlement of the Americas in Chapter 6.

First AMH Settlement in East and Southeast Asia

No one knows when modern humans first moved into East and Southeast Asia, although, as we have seen, there are indications of a sparse AMH presence by about 70,000 years ago. The oldest dated modern skeleton in Asia comes from Liujang in southern China, a skull and few bones somewhat tenuously dated to about 68,000 years ago, or earlier (Shen et al., 2002). Zhiren Cave, in southern China, has yielded a human jaw said to date to about 10,000 years ago and to be of modern form. Unfortunately, these finds add little to the picture as they are either incomplete or poorly dated. Elsewhere, the fossil record is also meager, the best dated fossils coming from Niah Cave in Borneo, at around 42,000 years ago, and Tianyuan Cave near Zhoukoudian, China, where well-dated human bones of modern form date to 42,000 to 39,000 years ago (Barker et al., 2007; Shang et al., 2007).

Niah
42,000 years ago

With Niah and Tianyuan, we are within the range of radiocarbon dating, but the chronology of earlier AMH settlement is tenuous at best. It seems, however, that modern humans arrived in Asia before they moved northward into Europe and Eurasia, after 50,000 years ago. We can speculate that they first arrived in Southeast Asia, then moved northward into what is now China, where

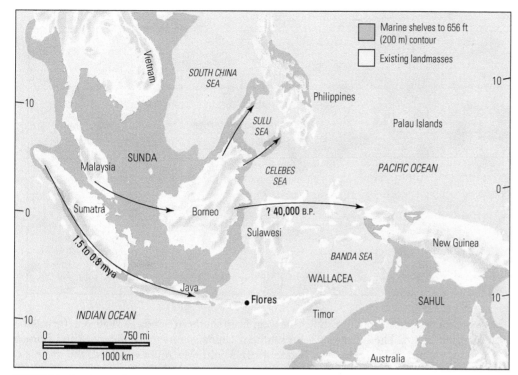

FIGURE 4.9 Late Ice Age Southeast Asia. Low sea levels exposed dry land off mainland Asia and between Australia and New Guinea during the last glaciation, creating Sahul and Sunda. The hypothetical human migration routes and dates are shown.

archaic human populations survived into the late Ice Age. Other groups settled on the huge continental shelf off Southeast Asia (see Site box).

Sunda and Sahul

At the height of the last glaciation, about 18,000 years ago, sea levels were over 100 m (300 feet) below modern levels. Dry land joined Sumatra to Borneo. Rolling plains joined many of today's islands, which were connected to the Southeast Asian mainland. Great rivers dissected the now sunken plains, known to geologists as Sunda (Figure 4.9). Farther offshore, nearly 30 km (19 miles) of open water separated Sunda from the island of Wallacea (modern Sulawesi and Timor); and 100 km (62 miles) farther offshore lay a vast landmass, Sahul, consisting of what are now Australia (including Tasmania), New Guinea, and a low-lying shelf between them that is now the Arafura Sea. These are, of course, the coastlines of the glacial maximum, and sea levels were considerably higher for most of the last glaciation. For most of the period between about 100,000 and 13,000 years ago, people would have had to cross much wider stretches of ocean than those at the glacial maximum. Even at the height of the last glaciation, the colonization of Wallacea and Sahul would have required some form of watercraft and the technology to build them. This necessity raises a fundamental and deeply interesting question: How long ago did people go offshore and cross wide tracts of ocean, perhaps paddling out of sight of land?

New Guinea and Adjacent Islands

If *Homo sapiens* had settled in mainland Southeast Asia by about 70,000 years ago, we can reasonably expect colonization of offshore landmasses to have occurred sometime after that date (O'Connell and Allen, 2004, 2012; O'Connell et al., 2008). At the time, the plains of Sunda were relatively dry. Human settlement was probably concentrated in areas such as coasts, lakeshores, and rivers, which had more diverse and predictable food resources. As in the rain forests, easily split bamboo and other woods sufficed for many tasks. Relatively benign waters lapped the coastlines that faced Wallacea and Sahul. Here people could take plenty of shallow-water fish and shellfish, especially giant clams, to supplement game and plant foods. Perhaps the people living along these shores fashioned simple rafts of bamboo and mangrove logs lashed together with forest vines. Such rafts were stable platforms for fishing in sheltered, shallow water and for reaching offshore shell beds. Perhaps it was in such craft that some people crossed to Wallacea and Sahul well before the glacial maximum of 18,000 years ago. We know, for example, that tuna fishers visited the Jerimalai Cave on East Timor at least 42,000 years ago. Nearby Lene Hara Cave contains traces of occupation dating to at least 30,000 to 35,000 years ago (O'Connor, 2007; O'Connor, Spriggs, and Veth, 2002).

Jerimalai
Lene Hara
29000 B.C.

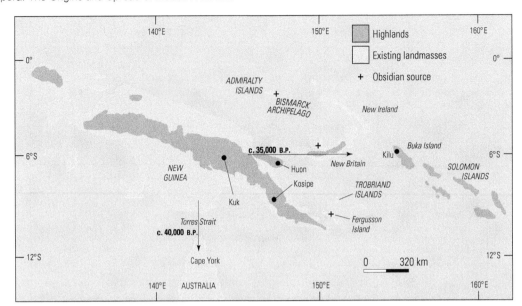

FIGURE 4.10 Map showing New Guinea and adjacent islands mentioned in Chapters 7 and 12.

Two main routes led offshore to Sahul. One went from southern Sunda to Wallacea, then across to the Australian shore. The other was from southern China, across the Philippines and Borneo, and into New Guinea via Sulawesi (see Figure 4.10). Whichever route was used, the process of colonization involved both island hopping and open-water travel, the earliest instance of regular seafaring by human beings. As is always the case with ocean crossings, scholars debate endlessly about whether the first settlement was accidental or deliberate. Computer simulations have shown that there are moderate chances of a raft drifting from Timor to Australia in about seven days in front of strong monsoon winds. However, as archaeological evidence accumulates, it is clear that deliberate voyages brought modern humans down a natural voyaging corridor marked by predictable seasonal reversals of wind and current. Many of these passages were never out of sight of land, which would have favored exploration. A network of sites and radiocarbon dates place this colonization to within a remarkably short time frame, between 44,000 and 45,000 years ago. Soon people had settled along the then 3,000-km (1,850-mile) coastline of Sahul. They were fishing on Timor between 30,000 and 45,000 years ago.

Much of Sahul was rolling, semiarid lowlands—what is now Australia, with New Guinea in the far north offering a quite different landscape of rugged mountains and highland valleys. The earliest evidence for human settlement in New Guinea comes from the highlands about 45,000 years ago.

Bobongara
?38000 B.C.

At Bobongara on the Huon Peninsula, archaeologist Les Groube found ground axes, with indented waists for mounting them, and a single stone flake sealed under volcanic ash. The ash dates to at least 38000 B.C. Groube believes that these waisted axes were used to ring trees and clear forests, perhaps to encourage the growth of plants on the forest fringes—a form of deliberate manipulation of wild plants to enhance the growth of wild plant foods such as yams, sugarcane, and perhaps taro and fruit trees (Groube et al., 1986; Hope and Golson, 1995).

The Huon Peninsula faces the Bismarck Strait, with the island of New Britain only a 50-km (30-mile) or so passage offshore. From there, it is only a short voyage to New Ireland. These two islands are visible from one another but are separated by deep water and were never joined during the last glaciation. Open-water voyages were needed to colonize them and must have been commonplace by 33000 B.C. (Pavlides and Gosden, 1994). People were catching sharks and tuna by 35,000 to 45,000 years ago at Buang Meraback on New Ireland (Leavesley and Chapell, 2004). Later New Irelanders were fisherfolk who caught shellfish and fish and hunted bats, reptiles, and birds. By 18000 B.C., their successors were regularly trading obsidian for toolmaking, across 30 km (19 miles) of open water to west New Britain.

Kilu
26000 to 18000 B.C.

Even farther offshore to the south, the inhabitants of Kilu Rock Shelter on Buka Island in the northern Solomons were catching tuna, mackerel, and other pelagic fish as early as 30,000 years ago (Figure 4.11) (Wickler, 2001). Open-water crossings of at least 130 to 180 km (81 to 112 miles) would have been required to settle on Buka, depending on the route selected. Voyaging over this distance would certainly have required some form of open-water craft, as well as foods that could be preserved for use during long voyages of days on end. Substantial water containers would also have been essential. From Buka, it would have been an easy matter to colonize the rest of the Solomon chain, for the islands are separated only by short distances.

FIGURE 4.11   Excavations at Kilu Rock Shelter, northern Solomon Islands, where evidence of human occupation dates to as early as 26000 B.C.

Farther offshore lay the limits of the late Ice Age world, for sea distances become much larger. More than 300 km (186 miles) lie between the Solomons and the environmentally impoverished Santa Cruz Islands, which were a much smaller target area even for expert navigators. The islands to the south and east of the Solomons lie within a region with no indigenous terrestrial mammals except bats, and a progressively impoverished flora and fauna. Such remote oceanic environments were insufficient to support hunter-gatherers. It was not until much later that the development of larger offshore canoes, much more sophisticated navigational skills, and easily storable food crops enabled humans to colonize islands far offshore (see Chapter 12).

Everything points to a relatively rapid spread of hunter-gatherer peoples with expert seagoing abilities throughout northern Sahul and contiguous islands at least as early as 33000 B.C. Favorable climatic conditions helped. Generally good weather and predictable winds and currents carried people in small crafts from island to island without the necessity of elaborate technology. The Sunda-Sahul area was a superb "nursery" for seafaring expertise. It is no coincidence that islanders in the western Pacific were venturing far offshore long before Westerners undertook ambitious voyages in the Mediterranean, after 12000 B.C. (Irwin, 1992).

Australia

Intense controversy surrounds the first settlement of Australia, just as it does that of the Americas (Hiscock, 2008). (For the Americas, see Chapter 6.) The earliest human occupation certainly dates to before 45,000 years ago, on the basis of skeletons from Lake Mungo in western New South Wales, said to date to about 40,000 years ago, and other possible dated occupations (Bowler et al., 2003) (Figure 4.12). Human settlement is well documented after 36,000 to 38,000 B.P., but traces of earlier occupation are very thin (Allen and Holloway, 1995). It is, of course, possible that there

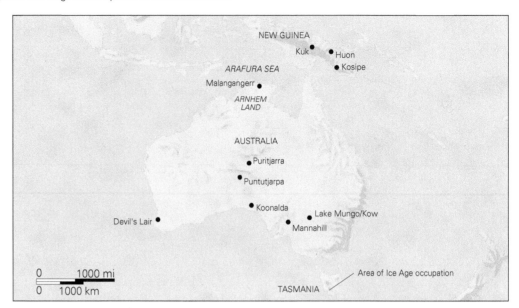

FIGURE 4.12 Archaeological sites in Australia and Tasmania.

was a long period of what archaeologist Jim Allen calls "invisible colonization" for thousands of years by peoples who are not represented in the archaeological record.

Whatever the date of initial colonization, geomorphological researches have shown that humans could have walked over dry land all the way from New Guinea into Tasmania far to the south throughout the late Ice Age (Kershaw, 1995).

Traces of human occupation immediately before and around 28000 B.C. have accumulated rapidly in recent years. Some hunter-gatherers visited Devil's Lair Cave, near Perth in the southwest part of Western Australia, as early as 30500 B.C. and used the site more regularly from 21000 B.C. to the end of the Ice Age. The Puritjarra Rock Shelter in the arid center of Australia, near the Northern Territory's Cleland Hills, was occupied from at least 25000 to about 4000 B.C. Humans were living in the arid zones of Australia, at places like Koonalda Cave on South Australia's Nullarbor Plain, by 22000 B.C. People lived there until 13000 B.C., visiting the site to quarry stone and making patterned lines or "flutings" on the cave walls during their stays. Arnhem Land in the north was certainly occupied well before 18000 B.C., with radiocarbon-dated occupations of about 20900 B.C. from Malangangerr Rock Shelter. Ocher pencils with traces of wear date to at least 17000 and perhaps. 28000 B.C. There seems little reason to doubt, however, that Aboriginal Australians were painting as early as were artists in Europe and Africa (Figures 4.13 and 4.14). Hunter-gatherers were living around the coast and on the fringes of the central Australian desert by 18000 B.C. By 8000 B.C., they were exploiting every major environmental zone.

Devil's Lair
30500 B.C.
Puritjarra
25000 to 4000 B.C.
Koonalda
22000 B.C.

FIGURE 4.13 An artist's impression of the extinct Tasmanian wolf (thylacine), which has been extinct for more than 3,000 years.

FIGURE 4.14 Australian Aboriginal painting of a mythic creature. Australian art had a deep symbolic meaning, forming part of the "Dreamtime," the spiritual world.

As for the first settlement itself, scientists are deeply divided (Hiscock, 2008). Some believe that initial colonization was a slow and gradual process along coasts and then into the interior by people forced to adapt not only to a new maritime environment but also to unfamiliar animal and plant foods (White and O'Connell, 1982). Others argue for a rapid colonization, with small groups expanding rapidly over the continent as a result of their highly mobile lifeway (J. Allen, 1994). In both cases, however, the colonists may have used fire to burn away low-lying desert brush as a way of locating game. They would have then moved on to unfired ground, as animal and plant foods were reduced. Anthropologist Joseph Birdsell (1977) hypothesized that a mere doubling of the Australian population every 20 years after the first settlement would have resulted in a natural population growth to eighteenth-century levels within only 2,000 years. Recent discoveries of evidence of late Ice Age wallaby hunters in Tasmania tend to support his hypothesis.

Ice Age Wallaby Hunters in Tasmania

Tasmania is now an island, but a land bridge connected it to mainland Australia for at least 55,000 years of the late Ice Age, so that first settlement was a matter of hunting and foraging across dry land. During much of the last glaciation, climatic conditions throughout Tasmania were quite severe, with ice sheets on higher ground in the interior and temperatures at the glacial maximum as much as 6°C (10.8°F) lower than today. Human settlement dates to about 32000 B.C. at the Parmerpar Meethaner Rock Shelter in the Forth Valley in the central southwest of the island, occupied until about 780 years ago (Cosgrove, 1995). Another site, Warreen Cave, was first visited in about 33000 B.C. (Porch and Allen, 1995). Richard Cosgrove has excavated the Bluff and ORS 7 Rock Shelters in south-central Tasmania. The Bluff site (Figure 4.15) was first occupied about 28500 B.C., whereas ORS 7 was in use by 28800 B.C. Both of these occupation levels contain emu eggs, which can be collected only during late winter and early spring, a bitterly cold time of the year (Cosgrove, Allen, and Marshall, 1990).

These sites were occupied before the glacial maximum, but people continued to live in the rugged landscape of southwestern and central Tasmania through the coldest millennia of the last glaciation. The Kutikina Cave was occupied between 18000 and 12000 B.C., when what is now dense forestland was open tundra and grassland. The inhabitants hunted red wallabies, as did the people who lived in at least 20 other occupied caves nearby. Slightly to the east, in another rugged area that is now rain forest is Bone Cave, occupied between 15000 and 11000 B.C. The groups in these areas appear to have been part of a common social system that flourished over a large area for many thousands of years. Some groups used Darwin glass, a natural glass from a meteorite crater a minimum distance of 45 km (28 miles) from Kutikina and over 100 straight-line km (62 miles) from the Bluff Rock Shelter area. Some of these people were painting hand stencils and other designs long before the end of the Ice Age.

Parmerpar Meethaner
32000 B.C.

Warreen
33000 B.C.

Bluff
28500 B.C.

Kutikina
18000 to 12000 B.C.

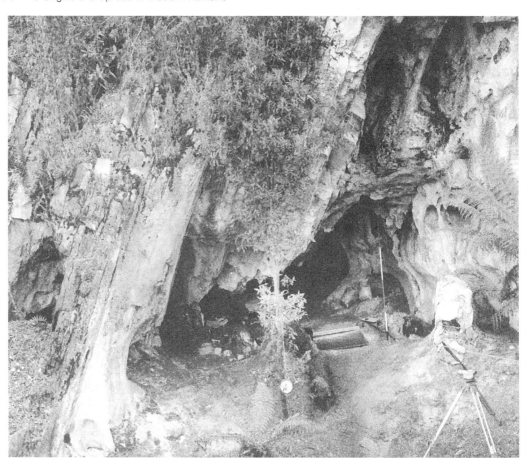

FIGURE 4.15 Excavations at the Bluff Rock Shelter, Tasmania, visited by late Ice Age wallaby hunters as early as 28500 B.C.

These were the southernmost people living on earth during the last glaciation. With the severing of the land bridge, their successors remained isolated from the outside world for thousands of years until French explorer Marion du Fresne met some Aboriginal Tasmanians face to face in A.D. 1772. The occupation levels of the Parmerpar Meethaner Rock Shelter document how the Tasmanians adapted to warmer, more forested conditions over many millennia.

Later Australian Cultures

Between 23000 and 8000 B.C., the population of Australia may have reached approximately modern levels, perhaps as many as a million people. Cultural change was gradual right into modern times, reflecting much regional diversity and the basic efficiency of ancient Australian technology. (For a summary of later archaeology, see Hiscock, 2008; Mulvaney and Kamminga, 1999.) The same traditions of stoneworking and bone technology found in early sites survived almost unchanged for thousands of years. For instance, flakes showing wear patterns characteristic of adze blades made by modern Aborigines date back as far as 18000 B.C., and the same bone points used to fasten skin clothes in historic times have been found deep in the prehistoric levels of Devil's Lair. The Australian Aborigines were famous for their artistic traditions and elaborate ceremonial life. Abundant traces of ritual belief have been found in Australian sites. The Devil's Lair site yielded stone plaques, a deep pit, and human incisor teeth that had been knocked out with a sharp blow: Such evulsion of teeth was an ancient Australian tradition.

Despite the essential conservatism of Australian stoneworking practices, some regional variations did appear over the millennia. Steep-edged scrapers, which were probably used as woodworking tools, were made over a wide area of Australia during much of the Upper Pleistocene. These and plainly crafted flake tools remained in use until recent times; in some areas, they were joined after 4000 B.C. by stone points, set on shafts, and other microliths. There is good reason to believe that Aboriginal technology developed within Australia over a long period in response to local needs and without the benefit of cultural innovation from outside (Hiscock, 2008) (Figure 4.16).

Some idea of the dynamics of early Australian life can be obtained from the saga of the Tasmanians. When the first European voyagers visited Tasmania in 1642, they found bands of hunter-gatherers living on the island. The Tasmanians lasted precisely 80 years after European settlement in 1802. They had no shafted tools (i.e., tools made of stone heads or points with wooden shafts or handles) but relied instead on scrapers and choppers somewhat like those used by early hunter-gatherers on the mainland; they lacked the boomerangs, spear-throwers, shields, axes, adzes, and lightweight stone tools the Australians of the mainland had when they first entered written history. Tasmania's isolated population, although forming part of the Australian cultural group, never received the later cultural innovations that spread throughout Australia, because of rising sea levels. Henry Lourandos (1997) and others have suggested that Tasmanian adaptations preserved a rather specialized lifeway that was typical of much of Australia from the late Ice Age into modern times.

Fortunately for archaeology, at least some investigations of Aboriginal culture have been made that have an important bearing on the interpretation of the archaeological record. Richard Gould (1977) spent many months among the Ngatatjara people of the Western Desert, carrying out ethnographic investigations that had objectives somewhat similar to those of Richard Lee among the San in Africa: He was interested in their cultural ecology and in the ways ethnographic observations could be used to interpret the archaeological record. His Aboriginal informants took him to Puntutjarpa Rock Shelter, a site that they still visited regularly. Gould excavated the occupation levels in the shelter and found that people had lived there for more than 6,800 years. The later stone implements were almost indistinguishable from modern Ngatatjara tools, to the extent that Gould was able to compare the wear patterns on both ancient and modern artifacts and decide which 5,000-year-old tools had been mounted on shafts and which had not.

The study of living Aboriginal bands shows just how conservative Australian lifeways have been. There were few major technological innovations during Australia's pre-European past. Indeed, it was possible for the Aboriginal Australians to maintain a thoroughly viable lifeway with minimal technology and only the simplest of artifacts. The Tasmanians, for instance, used only two dozen or so tools to hunt and forage (Figure 4.17) (R. Jones, 1995). The great elaboration of Australian and Tasmanian culture was in social and ritual life, neither of which can be readily recovered by archaeological investigation. That much of this activity was designed to maintain the delicate balance between the Aborigines, and the available resources in their environment was no coincidence. A belief in such balance lay at the core of Australian life.

Early Australian history chronicles a remarkable biological and cultural continuity, which extends back into the late Ice Age and survives into modern times. This continuity is a legacy of the great diaspora eastward into Asia that began in Africa perhaps as early as 80,000 years ago. And it

FIGURE 4.16 Eighteenth century rendering of an Australian Aborigines' camp site by an unknown artist.

NOUVELLE - HOLLANDE : ...ᴸᴸᴱˢ GALLES DU SUD.

NOROU - GAL - DERRI s'avançant pour combattre

De l'Imprimerie de Langlois

FIGURE 4.17 An Australian Aborigine with his portable toolkit depicted by Nicholas-Martin Petit and Bartholemy Roger, 1824.

is to Africa that we must now return to examine the stories of human societies whose genetic ancestry goes back to the very beginnings of modern humanity.

African Hunter-Gatherers

Sub-Saharan Africa supports some of the oldest surviving, but, alas, dwindling, hunter-gatherers on earth. The Hadza of Tanzania, the Pygmies of the rainforest, and the San of the Kalahari Desert have been studied intensively by anthropologists and others and there can be little doubt that their biological and cultural roots lie thousands of years in the remote past. There is good reason to believe that the genetic roots of the Hazda and the San go back to very early modern human links indeed. They are among the most ancient human biological lineages on earth.

As we have seen, tantalizing signs of modern human behavior appeared in southern Africa as early as 65,000 years ago. The changes were irregular, perhaps sporadic, but, as in Europe, AMH with a broadly based hunter-gatherer lifeway were well established throughout sub-Saharan Africa by 50,000 years ago. As the mil-

Klasies River
120,000 to 70,000 years ago

lennia passed, so Africans developed ever more efficient ways of hunting and foraging (Phillipson, 2005). Blombos, Klasies River Mouth, and Sibudu Cave record some of the slow changes over time (Backwell et al., 2007; Deacon and Deacon, 1999). Richard Klein (1979, 2009) found that the people who inhabited these caves lived not only off vegetable foods but off game and marine resources as well. Klasies River offers an interesting contrast in changing lifeways (Figure 4.18). Between about 120,000 and 70,000 years ago, inhabitants collected limpets and also pursued seals and penguins. They took few fish, preferring game on the hoof, especially such docile animals as the eland and the hartebeest. They did kill some more formidable beasts like the buffalo in smaller numbers, and some of the meat was perhaps scavenged. Interestingly, the bones of more dangerous species came from either very old or young individuals, which is the sort of age pattern found in predator kills. Only the eland and hartebeest were taken at all ages. Klein concluded that they may have been driven into traps or over cliffs.

FIGURE 4.18 Klasies River Cave, South Africa, where modern humans lived about 100,000 years ago.

Another coastal cavern, Nelson's Bay Cave, was occupied by modern *H. sapiens* populations after 13000 B.C. Again, eland and hartebeest were common and taken at all ages, perhaps by game drives. The Nelson's Bay folk took bush pigs and warthogs, much fiercer and more formidable prey. Not only that, they used nets and fishhooks to catch a wide range of ocean fish. They also lived off flying sea birds such as cormorants. One could argue, of course, that the Klasies River people simply preferred game on the hoof, but the relative abundance of wild pigs strongly suggests that the Nelson's Bay hunters were much more expert and capable of exploiting a far wider range of game. They may have used the bow and arrow. Although the eland lives in widely dispersed herds, other antelope do not and would have been much more vulnerable to efficient hunting.

Nelson's Bay
13000 B.C. 7000 B.C.

By about 7000 B.C., the world's southern oceans were warmer than today. It was not until 3,000 years later, during the so-called postglacial climatic optimum, that the northern seas achieved higher temperatures. This delay was due to different land and water distributions in the two hemispheres, Antarctica being much colder than the Arctic Ocean. Warmer, drier conditions in southern Africa led to more succulent vegetation at the expense of grassland and heath, with major changes in human subsistence. These changes are hard to document. John Parkington (1987) has chronicled one changing scenario at Eland's Bay Cave in the far south. In 11000 B.C., the inhabitants hunted large- and medium-sized antelope. But between 9000 and 7000 B.C., they turned their attention to smaller browsing animals, with estuarine and marine animals as well as limpets becoming ever more common. By 6000 B.C., the entire coastal plain was flooded, with only small browsing animals, mussels, and fish being taken. Then, Eland's Bay Cave was abandoned suddenly, never to be reoccupied.

Eland's Bay
11000 to 6000 B.C.

After 9000 B.C., the quantity of food bones increases dramatically, as does the variety of ostrich-eggshell beads, water containers, bone tools, decorated bone work, and other artifacts (Figure 4.19). Parkington believes that this intensification in domestic activity was due to environmental change, that is, to the dramatic encroachments of the postglacial ocean. Eland's Bay Cave was first visited, then lived in for long periods of time as the coastal plain shrank. Finally, the people moved into the interior or elsewhere along the shore when this stretch of coastline was no longer productive. It would be a mistake to describe the major changes in artifact inventories or subsistence as evolving culture change. Rather, they may reflect continual adaptation to rapidly altering climatic conditions, changes that were reflected by other adaptive shifts elsewhere on the coast, as at Nelson's Bay, and also in the warm interior.

The long-term trend over the past 15,000 years may have been toward hunting smaller game and increased specialization in plant collecting (Parkington, 1987). Many late Stone Age caves and rock shelters in southern Africa were used much more regularly in postglacial times, as if mountain and near-coastal locations were extremely favorable places to settle, places where smaller browsing animal herds would be concentrated. The warming trend in the earlier millennia of postglacial times may have led to increased aridity in many parts of the interior, with the densest human populations concentrated in areas of abundant water and diverse animal and plant resources. A great diversity of hunter-gatherer societies now developed throughout much of Africa.

Hilary Deacon (1979) excavated several late rock shelters and caves with exceptional care. He believes that there was a trend toward hunting smaller game

FIGURE 4.19 An ostrich-eggshell-bead necklace from a burial at Gwisho, Zambia, Central Africa (c. 1500 B.C.). The bead maker cut the beads to a roughly circular shape, then ground them against a fine, rocky surface to produce beads of even size.

0 1 2 3 cm

and especially toward the exploitation of plant foods in later times. Rabbits, tortoises, and grasses and root plants became vital components in the hunter-gatherers' diet. Just when plant foods came to be of overwhelming importance is much debated, but they were especially significant after about A.D. 1, when herding peoples settled in extreme southern Africa (see Chapter 11), perhaps when the newcomers squeezed hunter-gatherers into more limited territories, away from cattle-grazing grounds.

The same general trend toward increasingly specialized subsistence strategies may also have developed in other parts of sub-Saharan Africa, just as it did in other parts of the world (see Chapter 7). The peoples of the open savanna lived off the abundant game populations and supplemented their diet with seasonal gathering of the rich vegetable resources of the woodland. Other bands settled on the shores of lakes and on riverbanks and lived by fishing. This valuable and reliable source of protein encouraged more lasting settlement and increased specialization. The rain forest peoples of the Congo River basin in Central Africa were unable to hunt as wide a range of game as their savanna counterparts, so they relied heavily on vegetable foods and wild roots.

The later hunter-gatherers of the eastern and southern African savanna are comparatively well documented, not only from archaeological sites but also from their own rock paintings and engravings. Unfortunately, preservation conditions are usually such that only stone implements and, sometimes, animal bones are preserved, making study of cultural diversity a challenging task. Only a handful of sites offer a more complete picture.

The Gwisho hot springs in central Zambia lie on the edge of the seasonally inundated floodplain of the Kafue River and provide a picture of hunter-gatherer life along the river more than 3,000 years ago (Fagan and van Noten, 1971). At least four forager camps once nestled among the bubbling hot springs, all locations that were occupied repeatedly over many centuries. The reed-surrounded springs offered abundant water, protection from predators, and a fine view of the floodplain, which teemed with game animals, especially during the spring flood, when the river was high. Abundant plant foods were within easy reach, too.

The Gwisho sites remained waterlogged after their abandonment, so not only bone fragments but also wooden tools and all kinds of plant remains survived in excellent condition, giving an unrivaled picture of late Stone Age life in this region. The waterlogged levels contained more than 10,000 plant remains, most from only eight species, especially the edible fruit of the *Bauhinia*. The emphasis on only a few edible species suggests that food supplies were relatively abundant, to the point that the people could focus on a few plants to the exclusion of others. The deposits also yielded the remains of plants that yield vegetable poisons, known to have been used by modern-day San for arrow poison. Nearby lay some fine arrowheads and some of the wooden artifacts made by the inhabitants, including some simple digging sticks used for uprooting tubers. These tools are identical to those used by Kalahari San today. There were traces of a grass-and-stick shelter, of hearths, and of layers of grass that may have served as bedding. Thirty-five burials were deposited in the soil of the campsites. The deposits were littered with hundreds of stone arrow barbs and tiny scraping tools that lay alongside pestles and grinding stones used to process the vegetable foods that were an important part of the Gwisho diet (see Figure 7.7 on p. 176).

Gwisho
1000 B.C.

So little have gathering habits changed in the past 3,000 years that a San from the Kalahari was able to identify seeds from the excavations and tell archaeologists what they were used for. The economy and the material culture of the Gwisho people show a striking resemblance to those of modern San peoples in the Kalahari, although, of course, there are environmental differences (Lee, 1979).

The Gwisho hot springs confirm ethnographic observations made about the present-day San. Like that of their modern successors, the toolkit of the Gwisho people was highly portable, and much of it was disposable. Except for bows and arrows, modern-day Kalahari San improvise many of their tools from the bush as they need them, making snares from vegetable fibers and clubs from convenient branches. The women use digging sticks like the Gwisho artifacts for digging tubers and a softened antelope hide, or *kaross*, as a garment and carrying bag. Their only other artifacts are a pair of pounding stones for breaking up nuts. The Gwisho site contained both digging sticks and pounders. We know from cave paintings that the San used skin cloaks for thousands of years, and we can assume they were employed at Gwisho and elsewhere.

We should not, of course, assume that the 3,000-year-old Gwisho site was a prototype for historic San lifeways, but the general similarities are striking, at least at a superficial level. Comprehensive, multidisciplinary studies of Kalahari San provide us with a useful database for looking at earlier societies known only from archaeology. For example, the average present-day San camp holds approximately 10 to 30 people, just as the Gwisho camps probably did. The small population of a San territory leads to a continual turnover of the composition of camp populations. This constant change is a reality reflected in the San's highly flexible kinship system. Every member of a band has not only close family ties but also kin connections with a much wider number of people living all

FIGURE 4.20 San hunter-gatherers depicted in a rock painting from Natal, South Africa. This scene has deep symbolic meaning that defies modern interpretation, but the human figures are elongated to depict an altered state of consciousness.

over San territory. The San kinship system is based on an elaborate network of commonly possessed personal names, which are transmitted from grandparent to grandchild. People with similar names share kin ties even if they live some distance from one another. This network is such that individuals can move to a new camp and find a family with which they have kin ties to accept them. The resulting flexibility of movement prevents total social chaos and also provides a network for mutual assistance in times of food scarcity. Presumably, the ancient San had similar political and social systems to aid in survival.

Ancient San paintings and engravings depict the game hunted, the chase, and life in camp. The San drew running hunters, people fishing from boats, and scenes of gathering honey and vegetable foods (Figure 4.20). The hunters can be seen stalking game in disguise, hotly pursuing wounded quarry, and even raiding the cattle herds of their agricultural neighbors of later centuries.

David Lewis-Williams, who has studied ethnographic records of San bands, has shown convincingly (2002; Lewis-Williams and Challis, 2011) that many of the paintings depict complex metaphors that represent symbolic values in the San world. Each superimposition of paintings and each relationship between human figures and animals had profound meaning to the artists and the people. For instance, many of the paintings depict eland with dancers cavorting around them (see rock painting of San hunter-gatherers at beginning of chapter). Lewis-Williams believes that the dancers were acquiring the potency released by the death of the eland. The dancers go into trances so powerful (Figure 4.21) that they become eland themselves. This symbolism survived into the nineteenth century. When Victorian anthropologist George Stow showed some

FIGURE 4.21 A San healing dance.

rock-painting pictures to an elderly San couple, the woman began to sing and dance. The man begged her to desist because the old songs made him sad. Eventually, he joined in, and Stow watched the couple reliving the symbolism of past days. Only now, more than a century later, are archaeologists trying to probe this forgotten world. (For a contrary view, see Bahn, 2010.)

Stone Age hunter-gatherers enjoyed the savanna-woodlands of eastern and southern Africa undisturbed until approximately A.D. 1, when the first farming peoples (other African folk) settled by the banks of the Zambezi and Limpopo rivers. The San placed second in the resulting competition for land: The farmers wanted grazing grass and prime land for cultivating, so they drove off the bands of San hunter-gatherers, who had to retreat into less favored areas. Some took up the new economies and married into farming communities. White settlement in South Africa increased the isolation of the San. As the pressure on their hunting grounds grew, the San moved into mountainous areas and desert regions. Even there, they were harassed and hunted. Some of the white settlers made a sport of shooting them on Sunday afternoons. The doomed San of South Africa calmly continued to paint scenes of cattle raids and of European ships and wagons. They even depicted red-coated English soldiers on expeditions into the mountains. By the end of the nineteenth century, there was no San painting in South Africa, and the art of stone toolmaking had all but died out. The last stoneworkers used glass bottle fragments to make their sharp arrowheads. They found this unusually pure "stone" vastly preferable to their usual quartz pebbles (Barnard, 1992).

In this chapter, we've discussed the origins of modern humans in Africa and traced their long journeys eastward into Asia, to Australia, and to the edge of the Pacific. A few pages ago, we returned to sub-Saharan Africa, where it all began. Again, we've described long-surviving hunter-gatherer traditions with ties to the earliest modern humans of all. In Chapter 5, we'll start in Africa once more, for it was from south of the Sahara that the first attempts to settle in Southwest Asia began about 1,000,000 years ago. This was the first chapter in the population movements that took AMH into Europe and Eurasia at about the same time as people crossed to Australia on the other side of the world.

Summary

- Two competing theories account for the appearance of anatomically modern humans. The multiregional hypothesis for modern human origins has it that modern humans developed independently in Africa, Europe, and Asia, and that the biological diversity of contemporary humankind has very deep roots in prehistory.

- The out-of-Africa hypothesis argues that modern humans evolved in tropical Africa before 150,000 years ago, then spread into other parts of the world. The dating and nature of this spread is controversial. One school of thought believes there was a single out-movement, perhaps around 83,000 years ago. A competing hypothesis argues for two exits, one before 80,000 years ago, the other one after about 70,000 from Southwest Asia. The issue is unresolved, but it is certain that the diaspora of modern humans was a long, complex process involving small groups of people.

- The date of first settlement of China and East Asia by modern humans is unknown, but was probably at least as early as 70,000 years ago.

- During much of the last glaciation, New Guinea and Australia formed a single landmass called Sahul. Sahul was settled perhaps as early as 50,000 to 70,000 years ago. The earliest documented settlement of Sahul is about 45,000 years ago, probably as a result of deliberate voyaging.

- Diminutive hominins, named *Homo floresiensis* and displaying a mixture of archaic and modern characteristics, had settled on Flores by at least 38,000 years ago, their unique features due, perhaps, to isolation. There is also evidence for much earlier human settlement.

- People using open-water craft had settled in the Solomon Islands of the southwestern Pacific by 30000 B.C. First settlement of Australia dates to at least 45,000 years ago. The controversy over first settlement continues.

- Securely dated sites proliferate in Australia after 35,000 years ago. Late Ice Age hunters flourished in Tasmania by 29000 B.C.

- The later archaeological record shows that the Australian lifeway changed little over the millennia, except for some significant innovations in tool technology such as the boomerang.

- Modern humans flourished throughout sub-Saharan Africa by 50,000 years ago. As time went on, they turned their attention to smaller browsing animals, continually adapting to changing environmental conditions, a change well documented at Eland's Bay in South Africa. They focused heavily on edible plant foods.

- The densest populations concentrated in areas of abundant water and diverse animal and plant resources. It was from these diverse societies that modern-day African hunter-gatherer groups are descended.

- The later hunter-gatherers of southern Africa are well documented from rock paintings and archaeology. Controversy surrounds the interpretation of San art from this region, which may be connected with shamanistic rituals and altered states of consciousness.

- In both Australia and sub-Saharan Africa, there is striking evidence for long-term cultural continuity, at least some of which dates back to the earliest appearance of AMH in these regions.

Key Terms

mitochondrial DNA (mtDNA) (100)

Further Reading

Hiscock, Peter. 2008. *Archaeology of Ancient Australia.* London: Routledge.

Oppenheimer, Stephen. 2008. "The great arc of dispersal of modern humans: Africa to Australia." *Quaternary International* 202: 1–12.

Stringer, C. B., and R. McKie. 1996. *African Exodus.* New York: Henry.

5

Europe and Eurasia

C. 48,000 YEARS AGO TO 8000 B.C.

panish landowner Marcellino de Sautuola had a casual interest in archaeology. He had visited an exhibit in Paris of some of the fine stone tools from French caves. In 1875, he decided to dig for some artifacts of his own in the caverns of Altamira on his estate. Sautuola's 8-year-old daughter, Maria, begged for the chance to dig with him, so he good-naturedly agreed. Maria soon tired of the muddy work and wandered off with a flickering lantern into a low side chamber of the cave. Suddenly, he heard cries of "Toros! Toros!" ("Bulls! Bulls!"). Maria pointed excitedly at brightly painted figures of bison and a charging boar on the low ceiling. Daughter and father marveled at the well-preserved paintings, arranged so cleverly around bulges in the rock that they seemed to move in the flickering light.

Sautuola was convinced the paintings had been executed by the same people who had dropped stone tools in the cave. But the experts laughed at him and accused the marquis of smuggling an artist into Altamira to forge the bison. It was not until 1904 that the long-dead Spaniard was vindicated, when some paintings with strong stylistic links to Altamira came to light in a French cave that had been sealed since the prehistoric artists had worked there. Clearly, whoever had painted on the cave walls at Altamira was a far cry from earlier humans like the Neanderthals.

A Cro-Magnon hand outline on the wall of a French cave.

n Chapter 4, we described a scenario that had modern humans spreading from Africa into South Asia and beyond around 83,000 years ago. This hypothesis, based on still highly provisional genetic and archaeological evidence, argues that moderns did not settle permanently in Southwest Asia until after 60,000 years ago, perhaps. 10,000 years later. In fact, *Homo sapiens* had moved into the region much earlier, but become extinct there. This chapter reviews this brief stay, then describes the first permanent settlement of Southwest Asia, Europe, and Eurasia by modern humans (Table 5.1).

TABLE 5.1
Climate change and cultural developments, c. 50,000 to 8000 B.C.

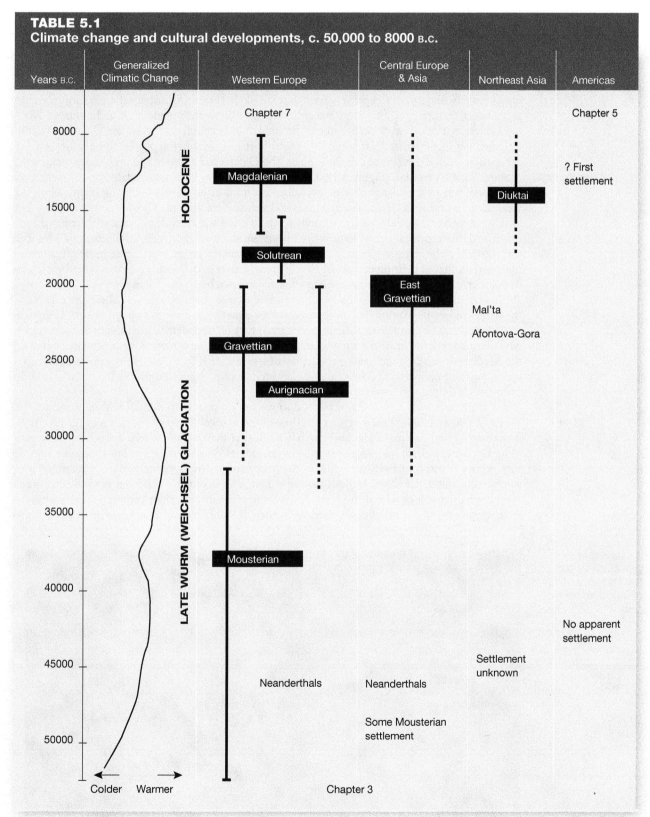

There was considerable overlap among European cultures. Climatic changes are approximate, as they are subject to considerable controversy among experts.

Unsuccessful Colonization

Imperceptibly, in small numbers and widely dispersed over inhospitable terrain, anatomically modern humans (AMH) expanded out of their tropical African homeland. These were people who were used to maintaining connections with others, often living some distance away. They ranged over long distances in search of game and plant foods. As we saw in Chapter 4, there is some support for a movement of AMH out of Africa into Asia about 83,000 years ago, although the date is tentative at best. But there are signs of an earlier movement as well, which took place about 100,000 years ago, when handfuls of modern people moved into Southwest Asia, perhaps from Northeast Africa and the Nile Valley. Unlike the Asian out-migration, this one was to fail.

Qafzeh

c. 100,000 B.P.

92,000 years ago

Before World War II, Biological anthropologist Ted McCown excavated an unprepossessing rock shelter known as es-Skhul, close to a cave known as Mugharet el-Wad on the slopes of Mt. Carmel in what is now Israel. He unearthed at least eight burials associated with tools normally found with Neanderthal occupation levels, but the skeletal remains displayed a mixture of archaic and modern features, as if they were transitional people between Neanderthals and moderns. Many years later, in 1965, French archaeologist Bernard Vandereersch excavated the Qafzeh cave, also in Israel and recovered at least seven *H. sapiens* burials from what appeared to be a Neanderthal occupation level. To everyone's astonishment, the Qafzeh burials were thermoluminescence dated to about 92,000 years ago (Figure 5.1). The es-Skhul skeletons were soon redated to about the same age. There was now evidence that modern humans lived in Southwest Asia, apparently alongside Neanderthals perhaps at least as early as 100,000 years before present.

The Qafzeh and es-Skhul people display a mix of archaic and modern traits, with reduced brow ridges and modern vocal tracts. Effectively, they were moderns, but their intellectual abilities were still those of earlier humans, even if their stone tool manufacturing was a little more efficient and flexible than that of their predecessors. Interestingly, one es-Skhul individual was buried with a red deer antler, and other at a nearby cave named Kebara with a boar jaw. There were perforated marine shells with the Kebara graves, while red ocher came from sources 30 km (19 miles) away. It is as if the small modern population had more extensive social networks than their predecessors. Otherwise there is nothing to distinguish their behavior from that of Neanderthals living in the same region. Most human settlement of the time seems to have centered on a narrow strip of woodland along the Mediterranean coast and along the flanks of the Jordan Rift Valley. Here, rich nut harvests, a variety of game animals and relatively reliable water supplies supported people in a narrow corridor of landscape dotted with caves and rock shelters.

Climatic data from two caves in Israel document a drop in both rainfall and temperatures between 75,000 and 70,000 years ago, at the time of the first cold snap of the last Ice Age glaciation. The entire region became colder and much drier, just at the time when Mt. Toba blew into space. Whether the cataclysm had adverse effects in Southwest Asia is uncertain, but it appears that the tiny groups of modern humans living in the area vanished into extinction. As conditions grew warmer and wetter, the Neanderthals reoccupied wide areas of what had been very arid landscape. Neanderthals, some of whom displayed less anatomical variation than contemporary Europeans, were apparently on an evolutionary dead end (Shea, 2003). About 20,000 years or so were to pass

FIGURE 5.1 The early modern human skull from Qafzeh 9 (cast) compared with a Neanderthal from et-Tabun at Mount Carmel (right), both from Israel.

before moderns reappeared in Southwest Asia. And when they did so, they arrived with the full cognitive abilities that define modern human behavior.

Successful Colonization

Quite when moderns returned to Southwest Asia is a matter of debate, but it appears to have been about 50,000 years ago, when a 5,000-year cooling spell caused Neanderthals to contract into much smaller territories, especially along the coastal lowlands. Nor can we be certain which way they came. The only major barrier to population movement between tropical Africa and the Mediterranean basin is the Sahara, today some of the driest territory on earth. During the early Weichsel glaciation, the Sahara went through phases of relative aridity and greater rainfall. A cooler and wetter climate prevailed in the desert from 100,000 until about 40,000 years ago and again between 32,000 and 24,000 years ago. Thus, for long periods, the country between sub-Saharan Africa and the Mediterranean was passable, especially through now dried-up river valleys supporting scattered game herds and open grassland. The Nile Valley was always habitable, even during periods of great aridity in the desert. Thus, the moderns may have hunted and foraged across the Sahara into the Nile Valley and Southwest Asia in the early Weichsel. An alternative theory based on mitochondrial DNA (mtDNA) argues that they arrived in Southwest Asia from South Asia (Oppenheimer, 2008). Much more research will be needed to provide a definitive answer.

The landscape in Southwest Asia was arid, with many fewer trees and more steppe-desert plants than tropical Africa. This does not seem to have deterred the newcomers, who were familiar with drought-plagued African environments with their patchy food and water supplies. Burials tell us that the new arrivals were tall and thin, with long legs, a biological adaptation to tropical conditions, which helped them spread widely over semiarid Southwest Asian environments. Cooperation, planning, intelligence—these were the qualities that gave the newcomers the edge. They brought with them lighter tool kits, based on finely and efficiently made stone blades, a technology that had been used sporadically in southern Africa thousands of years earlier.

For generations, experts on the Stone Age assumed that the appearance of *H. sapiens* coincided with the invention of radically new, much more advanced technologies that involved, among other things, the use of punches to produce fine, parallel-sided blades and a proliferation of specialized tools, not only in stone but in antler and bone as well (Figure 5.2). Although there is no doubt that such innovations were used by moderns, careful examination of earlier technological traditions shows that they were foreshadowed tens of thousands of years earlier. Rock shelters and caves in eastern and southern Africa have yielded large tools made of blades fabricated by skilled percussion from carefully prepared cores. The same peoples of 100,000 years ago were using composite tools and a wider range of artifacts than many of their predecessors. In Southwest Asia, great caves and rock shelters, like the Mount Carmel sites et-Tabun and Mugharet el-Wad in Israel and Shanidar in Iraq, document thousands of years of Neanderthal toolmaking. These sites were visited again and again by hunter-gatherer bands from more than 70,000 years ago right into modern times.

The Mousterian levels in these caves contain tens of thousands of carefully retouched flakes and side scrapers, as well as the bones of large deer and wild cattle. This technology was a very simple and conservative one that displayed considerable variability within fairly restricted limits. This variability included some horizons (occupation levels) in which large, bladelike blanks were made with sophisticated percussion flaking. Later occupation levels containing different tool kits covered the Mousterian horizons. The new tools gradually replaced earlier artifact forms and technologies. In these later levels, the long, parallel-sided blades that were the first stage in making stone tools came from cylindrical flint cores with a punch and a hammerstone (see Figure 5.2). Some blades were up to 15.2 cm (6 inches) long. The tools made from them varied greatly, were designed for specific tasks, and, in later millennia, were mounted in handles.

stone hammer

antler punch

flint core

blades

FIGURE 5.2 A stoneworker demonstrates blade manufacture with an antler punch. Various tools were used to strike off the blades—a hand-held punch (as here) or a longer chest-impelled punch. The punch allows intense pressure to be applied to a single point on the top of the core and channels the direction of the shock waves.

45,000 years ago

Anthony Marks (1983) studied hunter-gatherer camps in Israel's Negev Desert and found an interesting change in ancient settlement patterns. The climate was wetter and the hunting population tended to concentrate in more circumscribed areas by 45,000 years ago. As the climate dried up, the people became more mobile. Instead of camping close to convenient sources of toolmaking stone, they moved around constantly, a reality that necessitated new ways of using precious fine-grained rock. Instead of employing wasteful Levallois techniques (see Figure 3.21 on p. 88), they experimented with more economical flaking methods, which evolved into the long, parallel-sided blades favored by AMH stoneworkers. So **blade technology** was the logical result of millennia of gradual adjustment to more mobile lifeways, in which prudent curation of toolmaking stone was essential. Now blade technology and refined hunting technology came into their own, among the weaponry, perhaps, the wooden throwing stick, which allowed a hunter to propel a stone or bone-tipped spear over longer distances with lethal accuracy. This may have been the moment when modern humans finally developed their full cognitive abilities (Ervard et al., 2002; Klein, 2001). However, a major player was the constant climatic shifts of the late Ice Age.

The Upper Pleistocene (c. 126,000 Years Ago to 8000 B.C.)

The Upper Pleistocene, often called the Late Ice Age, began in about 126,000 B.P. and coincided with the last interglacial and glacial cycles of the Ice Age. The detailed picture we have of this cycle gives us important clues to the general nature of the Ice Age climate: gradual glaciation and rapid deglaciation in cycles of cold, dry weather prevailing over northern latitudes for some 60 percent of the past 730,000 years. Full interglacial conditions, when the climate was warmer than today, brought forest and woodland to Europe (Figure 5.3a on p. 125). The Upper Pleistocene began with the Eemian interglacial, which lasted only some 10,000 years. About 116,000 B.P., global temperatures started to cool gradually with the onset of the Weichsel glaciation. By 113,000 B.P., North American and European ice sheets were expanding again, and sea levels had already fallen some 70 m (230 feet). Glacial conditions were intense about 75,000 B.P., when the Neanderthals were flourishing in Europe and the Americas were still uninhabited, and again after 27,000 B.P., reaching their height about 18,000 B.P., when sea levels fell to about 130 m (425 feet) below modern levels. This drop led to the exposure of huge continental shelves in Southeast Asia and elsewhere; the Bering Strait was dry land.

At the height of the last glaciation, world temperatures fell by as much as 15.5°C (60°F) near the ice sheets. The world's vegetation was very different at the height of the Weichsel glaciation (Figure 5.3b). Treeless tundra (open scrub) vegetation extended south of the ice sheets, giving way to a wide belt of cold continental steppe (open plain) that extended from the Low Countries into China and from Siberia to the Mediterranean. The steppe was much narrower in North America, soon giving way to coniferous forest farther south. Huge zones of desert occupied more than half the earth's surface between latitudes 30° N and S, but some of today's desert areas—like the American Southwest, the northern Sahara, and the southern African deserts—were more hospitable, supporting scrub, grassland, and shallow lakes. The rain forests of tropical Africa and Asia gave way to open woodland and grassland; coral reefs and mangrove swamps contracted drastically as a result of cooler temperatures. However, despite the harsh world climate, humankind managed to survive and flourish in this very different world. Those who settled in Europe and Eurasia had to adapt constantly to short- and long-term climatic shifts from bitter cold to warmer conditions and back again.

The First Modern Europeans

H. sapiens first appeared in continental Europe during a brief spell of more temperate climate around 50,000 years ago. Even then, climatic conditions and seasonal contrasts may have been severe enough to require new artifacts and more sophisticated hunting skills to exploit northern environments to the full.

Sixty thousand years ago, Neanderthals thrived throughout Europe. They had adapted to a long period of extremely cold, fully glacial conditions, with very long, severe winters. There were, however, major climatic shifts throughout this long period, sometimes to near-temperate conditions. By 48,000 B.P., small numbers of modern humans had settled in south-central and possibly eastern Europe (Hoffecker, 2009). By 30,000 years before present, AMH occupied the entire continent and the Neanderthals were extinct in a dramatic transition from the archaic to the modern.

There are two schools of thought regarding this transition. Most scholars believe that AMH dispersed out of Africa—perhaps to the east and then northward into Eurasia, replacing indigenous Neanderthal groups. Under this argument, the Neanderthals made no significant cultural or genetic contribution to later European populations. A second "assimilation" model argues for significant

FIGURE 5.3 (a) Generalized distribution of vegetation in Europe during the height of the Holstein interglacial. The succeeding Eemian interglacial was not quite as warm and was of shorter duration, but the same general vegetational patterns prevailed (Butzer, 1974). (b) Generalized vegetation map of Europe at the height of the Weichsel glaciation, showing ice sheets (Butzer, 1974).

genetic exchange and substantial cultural influence between Neanderthals and AMH (Trinkaus, 2005). The controversy continues to unfold, with the current weight of the evidence favoring replacement.

The earliest known modern human presence in Europe dates to about 48,000 years ago, where a series of sites in Moravia and Bulgaria have yielded artifacts that are similar to stone tool assemblages found at sites of similar age in Southwest Asia. They are grouped collectively into the Bohunician industry and were occupied to the beginning of a major warm interval and were abandoned when the climate cooled rapidly. This warming may be significant, for there are few signs of technological innovation. It is as if people using somewhat old fashioned artifacts and no bone tools moved northward into new territories at a time of climatic amelioration. No modern human remains have yet come from Bohunician sites. A second tentative movement may have followed between 45,000 and 44,000 years ago, the newcomers carrying different artifacts, which also bear resemblance to contemporary tool kits from Southwest Asia certainly made by modern humans. Like the Bohunicians, the newcomers, labeled Proto-Aurignacians, moved into Europe through the Balkans. Proto-Aurignacian tool kits occur not only in Southeast Europe, but also in Italy and as far west as southwestern France and northern Spain.

These immigrants, as yet known only from scatters of stone artifacts, arrived in the north in tiny numbers, group by group, movement over large territories being an integral part of their daily lives. For thousands of years, they had foraged in landscapes that were often extremely hot during the day and intensely cold at night. Now they moved, apparently effortlessly, into very different terrain, where subzero temperatures were commonplace. The bestiary was generally larger and more diverse, and predators were especially common. They moved into a seemingly empty world, where Neanderthals were rarely encountered. Many of the newcomers may never have seen their elusive, quiet neighbors.

Soon after their arrival, there was a defining geological moment. About 39,000 years ago, a violent explosion collapsed a huge caldera spanning some 230 sq. km (89 sq. miles) in an area that now lies under Naples and the northwestern portion of the Bay of Naples. Lava flows from the eruption extended over at least 80 km (50 miles). A huge ash plume rose as much as 44 km (27 miles) into the atmosphere and descended over a large area of the eastern Mediterranean and more than 2,500 km (1,550 miles) northeast across the Balkans and into eastern Europe. A classic "volcanic winter" followed the eruption. The Campanian explosion was a dwarf by Mt. Toba standards, but far more powerful than the eruption of nearby Mt. Vesuvius, which devastated the Roman cities of Herculaneum and Pompeii in A.D. 79.

Like the Mt. Toba cataclysm, the Campanian explosion must have caused widespread disruption to hunting territories and food supplies over a wide area. Fortunately, people were thin on the ground, which meant that a significant number survived during the ensuing cold event by moving into areas where game and edible plants could be found. Fortunately for science, AMH tools and food remains occasionally appear above and below the ash (tephra) layers from the explosion, which are like the filling of a chronological layer cake, even as far away as a place named Kostenki by the Don river valley in the Russian Federation, first occupied about 40,000 years ago and for thousands of years afterward. Most Kostenki settlements lie at the mouths of large ravines cut into the west bank of the river, where springs come to the surface and game must have abounded. A few people camped at Kostenki about 40,000 years ago. Their Proto-Aurignacian artifacts lie below the ash layer and include artifacts made on blades. They took not only larger game but also foxes and hares, prey that may reflect the use of new devices such as nets and snares. More camps appear above the ash layer dating to between 30,000 and 40,000 years ago, this time with artifacts that recall well established Aurignacian technology, described below and widespread throughout Europe.

There are signs, then, of widespread but sparse AMH occupation of much of Europe before 40,000 years ago, a time when moderns first came in contact with indigenous Neanderthal groups. These **Mamontovaya Kurya** people were very thin on the ground, but they ranged widely. One short-term camp at Mamontovaya **40,000 years ago** Kurya lies on the Usa River close to the polar Ural Mountains in northern Russia dates to nearly 40,000 years ago (Pavlov et al., 2001). A mammoth tusk with human-made grooves, a few stone tools, and some animal bones are all that survive. During the Ice Age, the Mamontavaya site was on a bleak open prairie, far colder than today's spruce and pine forest environment where winter temperatures still fall below −40°F. It was not until after the Campanian explosion 39,000 years ago that AMH populations in Europe rose significantly and moderns settled throughout the continent.

The early millennia of modern settlement must have been ones of exploration and familiarization, of gaining intelligence about new landscapes, new sources of toolmaking stone and other resources. Then the eruption and a cold event changed the dynamics of human life. Food shortages and the cold may have made contacts with others of prime importance, so much so that the newcomers tended to concentrate in more circumscribed areas. Isolation broke down; intelligence and contacts between different groups intensified; technological innovations flowered. This may have been the time when technological innovation flourished. Blade technology, with its portable cores and efficient small blanks, was highly adaptive for hunter-gatherers exploiting large hunting territories in often arduous, bitterly cold terrain. This technology has been likened to the Swiss army knife with its strong hinge and many blades. The knife is a foundation for many tool forms, as was the blade core (Figure 5.4). The stoneworker knocked off numerous blade blanks, which could be fashioned into a great variety of scrapers, awls, and knives, to say nothing of fine-edged graving tools—or **burins**, as archaeologists call them. This versatile stone technology produced the fine, sharp working edges necessary for grooving bone and antler, raw materials available in abundance in the periglacial north (areas close to ice sheets). The development of blade technology may well have enabled modern humans to move north from Southwest Asia (Mellars, 2005).

In time, too, the innovation extended to social and ritual life—to art, music, and intricate beliefs that defined a harsh and ever-changing world. We can imagine the cautious first encounters between bands that rarely saw anyone else during their lifetimes—perhaps a chance sighting of people on a distant ridge, perhaps some hunters hearing of others as a result of a hunting accident. The exchanging of intelligence, a shared story, perhaps a joke, or a young man attracted to a girl: the sources of contact, then more prolonged interaction were open-ended and almost inevitable in a world where fluent speech was a catalyst, survival depended on cooperation, and symbolic meanings defined the landscape. After the Campanian explosion, a vigorous AMH culture developed, probably in eastern Europe and spread rapidly throughout much of temperate Europe. After 39,000 years ago, the same general tool kits, body ornaments, and social institutions flourished from the Don Valley in the east to the Atlantic Ocean, a cultural tradition known to archaeologists as the Aurignacian, named after the Aurignac cave in the foothills of the French Pyrenees. For some 10,000 years, Aurignacian groups flourished in a wide variety of European environments, using a simple but effective technology based on stone blades, thick scraping tools, and knives combined with a new weaponry that used lethally effective antler points (see Figure 5.5). The technology may have been a response to cold, often variable climatic conditions.

FIGURE 5.4 The Swiss army knife effect. Blade technology acted like the celebrated Swiss army knife, producing blanks for making many specialized artifacts for working bone and antler.

Neanderthals and Newcomers

The millennia between about 48,000 and 30,000 years ago witnessed one of human history's most discussed encounters, that of Neanderthals and moderns. This was far more than a contest over hunting territories. It was a confrontation, if that is the right word, between two radically different lifeways—the ancient, little-changing routine of archaic humans, personified by the Neanderthals, and the flexible, much more sophisticated trajectories of modern human existence. What happened when modern met Neanderthal? Did AMH slaughter Neanderthals on sight with their superior weaponry that could engage prey at greater range? Were there angry confrontations over hunting territories, where men died and the Neanderthals slowly gave way, retreating to the margins of their former lands or occupying hitherto uninhabited landscapes? Did the indigenous population melt into remote forests and marginal hunting territories, pushed out by the immigrants? Were there regular contacts between archaic and modern humans, perhaps some exchanges of commodities like honey and toolmaking stone, even sexual encounters and interbreeding? Or did the Neanderthals wilt in the face of people with much more powerful cognitive abilities, superior technology, and better hunting skills? The potential scenarios are intriguing, but it is, unfortunately, impossible to provide a definitive scenario (Fagan, 2010; Finlayson, 2010; van Andel and Davis, 2003).

Population replacement took over 15,000 years. It was a long process of gene flow and small-scale population movement, as well as cultural innovations—new technologies and fresh strategies for the hunt. The flow of ideas may have been accelerated in situations in which hunters exploited large hunting territories and wandered far and wide in search of game and good toolmaking stone. Under such circumstances, technological innovation may have preceded gene flow and population movement, resulting in the Neanderthals' experimenting with more sophisticated artifacts, as apparently was the case at St. Césaire in France around 34,000 years ago. Most likely, the moment *H. sapiens* spread across Europe, the Neanderthals were at a disadvantage. Both premoderns and moderns hunted much the same quarry, even if the latter's weaponry was lighter and had greater penetrating power. Neanderthals relied on ambushes; so did the moderns. Nevertheless, the main differences between the two were insurmountable. Newcomers had fully articulate speech and all

St. Césaire
34,000 years ago

the cognitive abilities of *H. sapiens*. The Neanderthals were no slouches, but their communication skills were more limited. Above all, they lacked the qualities of imagination and self-awareness found in moderns, an ability to plan far ahead, and all the complex social mechanisms found in AMH society. The moderns lived in progressively larger groups, with enhanced social interaction and longer life expectancy. Innovation was commonplace; knowledge passed effortlessly from one longer-lived generation to the next.

To the moderns, the Neanderthals were probably little more than a lesser form of themselves, something considered inferior. They may even have been repelled by their hirsute, squat appearance, even their body odor. They may also have feared their strength, especially at close quarters, as a Neanderthal would certainly have prevailed in a hand-to-hand fight to the death. However, the Neanderthals would probably have feared the razor-sharp, bone-tipped spears of the moderns, which could deliver a fatal wound from far beyond the range of a throwing stick or a heavy stone-tipped spear.

Each probably observed the other from a distance, cautiously and silently, perhaps with unspoken understanding between them. Quietly, the Neanderthals observed the more refined technology of their neighbors, sometimes picking up abandoned tools from rock shelter floors. Judging from modern-day controlled experiments at replicating their artifacts they were competent artisans, who could "read" stone as easily as you and I peruse a book, a quality learned by today's stoneworkers. So it was easy for them to copy simple tools like bone points and backed knives and to incorporate them into their daily tool kits. But their qualities of innovation, of original thought, never allowed them to elaborate the newcomer's technology and to create tools and weapons that competed with AMH weaponry.

Neadnerthals survived longest in the drier environments of Spain. A Neanderthal lower jaw from the Zafarraya site in Andalusia has been radiocarbon-dated to as late as about 30,000 B.P. and survival until as late as 27,000 years ago is likely (Mellars and Dark, 1998). However, by 30,000 years ago, AMH were *Cro-Magnons* effectively the only humans in Europe. (These modern people are sometimes called Cro-Magnons, after the rock shelter of that name near the village of Les Eyzies in southwestern France.)

Aurignacians and Their Successor (39,000 Years Ago to 8000 B.C.)

Central and Western Europe were cold and dry during much late Ice Age, with great ice sheets covering large expanses of the northern latitudes. South of the ice sheets, thousands of square kilometers of steppe-grassland, with occasional stands of trees, covered much of the unglaciated land. There were many local variations, with extensive tree growth in deep river valleys and other sheltered areas. A rich mammalian community flourished in these diverse environments. It included bison, horses, reindeer, and mountain goats in more rugged areas; large herbivores like the mammoth, the woolly rhinoceros, and the wild ox were common on the open steppe. The human inhabitants could exploit not only a rich animal biomass but also a wide variety of plant foods, including blueberries, raspberries, acorns, and hazelnuts. The climate was changing constantly, so the people had to readapt by altering their diet, their hunting-and-gathering strategies, and their technology. Much of the great variability in Upper Paleolithic culture resulted from such readaptations.

Human behavior and cultural adaptations changed constantly 39,000 years ago and for the next 25,000 years (Mellars, 2006). Over a century and a half of research have defined and redefined these cultural shifts into a bewildering array of cultural periods, each with its own technology and technological innovations (Figure 5.5; Table 5.2 on p. 130). At first, French archaeologists, who developed this cultural sequence from excavations in caves and rock shelters, thought of each period as a rigid "epoch," like a geologic layer. Today, the cultural phases are seen as changes stimulated by a variety of complex and little-understood factors. Some of them may have been responses to practical needs; others, purely dictates of fashion or small technological innovations.

As time went on, major regional differences emerged throughout Central and Western Europe (Gamble, 1999). These can be identified from stone and antler tool types of contrasting stone technologies. As Randall White (1986) remarks, it is almost as if barriers to communication were arising, as if there were regional dialects in Europe for the first time.

Diverse and Predictable Food Resources

The "Cro-Magnon" peoples of southwest France have long been thought of as one of the prehistoric models for the cave people so beloved of modern-day cartoonists. Although it is true that much of our knowledge of their cultures comes from French caves and rock shelters, these were by no means the only settlements occupied after 40,000 B.P. Southwest France is remarkable for its high density of Upper Paleolithic sites within a restricted area, which were sometimes intensively occupied over long periods of time.

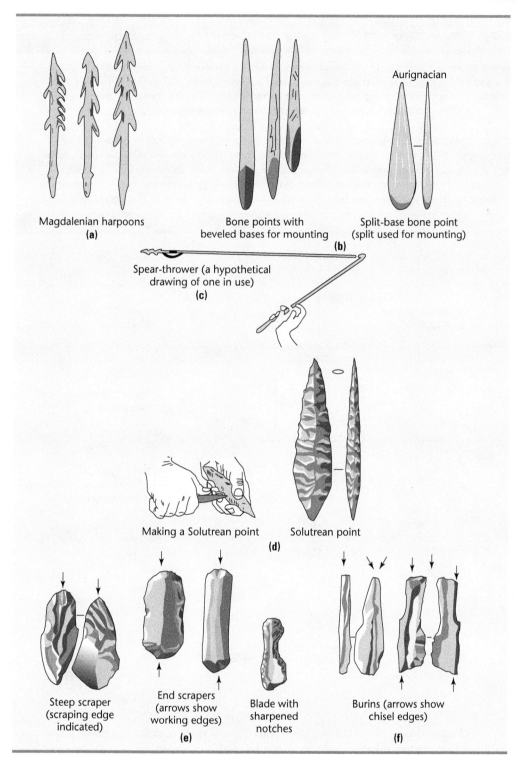

FIGURE 5.5 Characteristic artifacts used by modern human groups in Western Europe. Antler and bone artifacts were of vital importance, especially harpoons (a) and bone points (b) mounted on wooden shafts. The spear-thrower (c) was a hooked shaft, used to propel a spear a longer distance with great accuracy. Stone tools were made from blades for the most part, reaching their highest degree of sophistication about 20,000 years ago, with pressure-flaked Solutrean points (d), named after the Solutré site in southwestern France. Every group relied heavily on scrapers (e) used for processing skins, for working bone and antler, and for woodworking. The most important artifact was the chisel-ended burin (f), employed for grooving wood, bone, and especially reindeer antler.

Between 35,000 and 12,000 B.P., the climate of this region was strongly oceanic, with cool summers and mild winters by Ice Age standards. Summer temperatures may have been in the 12°C to 15°C (53.6°F to 59°F) range, with winter readings around 0°C (32°F). The plant-growing season was longer than on the open plains to the north and east, and snow cover was considerably less. Thus, the increase in food resources for large and small herbivores may have resulted in a much higher density of game animals as well as more plentiful edible plant foods. Two periods of more

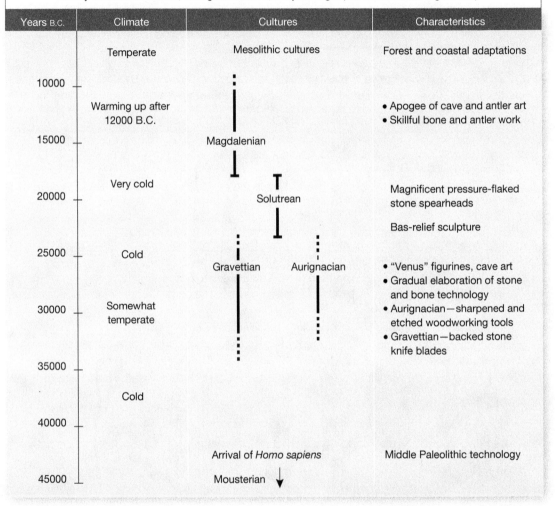

TABLE 5.2
Outline of the late Ice Age traditions of Western Europe

The most commonly accepted scheme has two parallel cultural traditions: the Gravettian, characterized by backed knives, and the Aurignacian, favoring scrapers and sharpened blades. The Gravettian, with increasingly finer backed knives, became dominant after 30,000 years ago. Thereafter, there were considerable regional variations, reflected in different tool traditions.

The Solutrean, a culture that relied on sophisticated "cooking" of large pieces of flint so that they became porcelainlike in texture, flourished in France and Spain. The stoneworker could exert pressure on the flake edge to produce magnificent leaf-shaped spear points. Many variations of the Gravettian culture are found in Central and Eastern Europe. In the west, the Magdalenian tradition, which relied heavily on antler and bone, emerged about 18,000 years ago. (For artifacts, see Figure 5.5.)

Years B.C.	Climate	Cultures	Characteristics
	Temperate	Mesolithic cultures	Forest and coastal adaptations
10000			
	Warming up after 12000 B.C.		• Apogee of cave and antler art • Skillful bone and antler work
15000		Magdalenian	
	Very cold		Magnificent pressure-flaked stone spearheads
20000		Solutrean	
			Bas-relief sculpture
25000	Cold		• "Venus" figurines, cave art
		Gravettian Aurignacian	• Gradual elaboration of stone and bone technology
30000	Somewhat temperate		• Aurignacian—sharpened and etched woodworking tools • Gravettian—backed stone knife blades
35000			
	Cold		
40000			
		Arrival of *Homo sapiens*	Middle Paleolithic technology
45000		Mousterian ↓	

moderate climate, between 29,000 and 21,000 years ago and again after the last glacial maximum of 18,000 years ago, witnessed efflorescences of late Ice Age hunter-gatherer society, times in which regional cultures developed and social networks extended over wide areas (Roebroeks et al., 2000). During the glacial maximum, more exposed, more northern latitudes were abandoned, with people concentrated in warmer refuge areas in southern Europe.

This was a region of diverse food resources, reflected not only in tree pollens in sheltered archaeological sites but also in the range of animals recovered from them. The people subsisted mainly on reindeer, but they also took wild ox, red deer, bison, ibex, chamois, woolly rhinoceros, and mammoth, as well as numerous smaller animals such as rabbits and birds. The sheer diversity of the environment gave the human inhabitants some economic security. In years when reindeer migrations were unpredictable, there were other sources of animal protein close at hand, to say nothing of plant foods.

Many of these resources were relatively predictable. There were seasonal reindeer migrations, from the higher ground of the east in summer to the deep river valleys of the west in winter, where food resources could be found even in the coldest months. The hunters could intercept animals from a broad range of species, many of them migratory, from an ecological range extending perhaps some 100 km (62 miles) on either side of their central places. Large-scale salmon fishing during seasonal runs may have been a major factor in the evolution of complex hunter-gatherer societies in this region. The concentration of settlement along riverbanks, at places where the salmon runs were most prevalent, was a logical response to predictable food resources. Unfortunately, few salmon bones have been found in the region's Upper Paleolithic sites (Mellars, 1985). Rabbits and other small game, perhaps taken with nets, were also a major food source (Adovasio et al., 1996).

Although fishhooks and harpoons, as well as fine engravings of salmon and seals, are known from many later Upper Paleolithic sites, it appears likely that hunting mammals of all kinds, large and small, was the predominant subsistence activity between 35,000 and about 10,000 years ago. Fishing does seem to have assumed much greater importance at the very end of the Ice Age, perhaps as forests encroached on open grazing grounds and rising sea levels brought more fish to French rivers. Whatever the precise makeup of late Ice Age diet in southwest France, there were direct adaptive responses to these highly favorable ecological conditions. Population densities were locally much higher than in other parts of Europe, and groups lived in the same locations for much of the year, close to seasonal concentrations of food resources. They exploited these resources with high efficiency, and some part of the population lived almost permanently in certain key locations. Smaller groups then exploited more distant resources in summer and according to need.

The people tended to choose many of their settlement sites with reference to plentiful water supplies and good views of the surrounding landscape so that they could observe game and perhaps their neighbors. More than 90 percent of all known sites are close to springs or riverbanks. The bands could live wherever they wanted to, for they had the technology to survive hard winters in the open. Some of the largest cave and rock shelter sites lay close to river fords, places, perhaps, where migrating reindeer would cross each year. One such site is Laugerie Haute, near Les Eyzies in the Dordogne, where the skeletons of several reindeer lay between the great rock shelter and the river ford. When the people occupied a rock shelter or cave, it invariably faced south so they could benefit from the sun's rays on cool days. They appear to have erected tents and hide curtains in the shelters for additional protection. Some shelters lay near places where it was possible to stampede reindeer, horses, and other herd animals over cliffs. In the open, some groups laid out pavements of river cobbles as foundations for wood, skin, or sod structures. Sometimes they heated the pebbles first, perhaps so they could lay them over frozen ground to form a secure platform.

Laugerie Haute

Social Life and Group Size

Many of the largest French sites are close to places where seasonally abundant resources like reindeer or small animals could be exploited by large numbers of people, perhaps, sometimes, with nets as opposed to spears. Other settlements were much smaller, little more than temporary camps occupied by a few families. Perhaps it is significant that the larger sites—like Laugerie Haute and Laugerie Basse, or La Madeleine, the type site of the Magdalenian—contain many more art objects. To cooperate in the food quest, the bands may have come together into larger social units at locations where abundant resources were available for a few months or weeks. Such aggregations could not have lasted year-round, partly because the environment would not have supported so many people in one place for long. If modern hunter-gatherers are any guide, the bands probably had no mechanisms for resolving disputes, except that practiced by the modern San of southern Africa: walking away. This is what anthropologist Richard Lee (1979) calls "voting with your feet."

Magdalenian culture

The days, weeks, and even months of aggregation are the high point of the year in today's hunter-gatherer societies, as they must have been in the Upper Paleolithic. This was the time of marriage and initiation ceremonies, of highly intense rituals, including chant and dance, in which the fine art objects of the people may have played important roles (Figure 5.6). This was when shamans told tales and wove spells, when the forces of the ancestors and the spirit world were invoked to ensure the continuity of life and the success of the hunt. It was also a time when men and women exchanged artifacts, ornaments, and exotic raw materials from near and far. Seashells from the English Channel and the Mediterranean, Baltic amber, and other exotica—items that were sometimes imbued with special magical, social, or

FIGURE 5.6 A 30,000-year-old mammoth ivory flute from a cave near Ulm in southern Germany. The ivory had to be split, then glued together to form an airtight seam. The flute is 20 cm (7.8 inches) long. A modern replica in elder wood produced quite harmonic sounds.

SiTE > Grotte de Chauvet, France <

Discovered in December 1994, the Grotte de Chauvet is a series of painted and engraved chambers undisturbed since the late Ice Age (Chauvet et al., 1996). Hearths on the floor looked as if they had been extinguished the day before. Flaming torches had been rubbed against the wall to remove the charcoal so they would flare anew. More than 300 paintings adorn the walls (Figure 5.7). They include a frieze of black horses, wild oxen with twisted horns, and two rhinoceroses facing one another. The horses have half-open muzzles; the eyes are depicted in detail. There are lions, stags, and engravings of an owl, animals never before seen in painted caves, covering an area of more than 10 m (30 feet). A little farther on in the chamber lies a slab that had fallen from the ceiling. A bear skull had been set atop it. The remains of a small fire lie behind it. More than 30 calcite-covered, and intentionally placed, bear skulls surround the slab. A 10-m (30-foot) frieze of black figures dominated by lions or lionesses (without manes), rhinoceros, bison, and mammoth lies in an end chamber, a human figure with a bison head standing to its right (see illustration). The discoverers wrote that it "seemed to us a sorcerer supervising this immense frieze" (Chauvet et al., 1996: 110).

The artists were masters of perspective, overlapping the heads of animals to give the effect of movement and numbers. They even scraped some of the walls before painting them to make the figures stand out better. They would spread the paint with their hands over the rock, obtaining values that showed dimension and color tonality.

Accelerator mass spectrometry (AMS) radiocarbon dates (see Dating the Past box in Chapter 8) from two rhinoceroses and a large bison point to a 1,300-year period around 32,000 B.P., making these paintings the earliest securely dated art in the world. Two more dates from torch smears on the walls are around 26,500 B.P., while two charcoal samples on the floor gave readings of about 24,500 B.P., suggesting that humans visited Chauvet on several occasions

over at least 6,000 or 7,000 years. Whether they painted over that long period is still unknown, but AMS dates will ultimately produce some answers. (Objections have been raised to this chronology; see Bahn, 2010.)

Grotte de Chauvet was a bear cave, a place where these powerful animals hibernated. Interestingly, many of the animals on the cave walls represent dangerous members of the late Ice Age bestiary: the bear and the lion, the mammoth, rhinoceros, and bison, even, occasionally, the nimble and ferocious aurochs. Perhaps human visitors to the cave, with its claw marks, hollows, prints, and scattered bones, came to the chambers to acquire the potency of the great beast, whose smell probably lingered in the darkness.

FIGURE 5.7 Panel with horses and woolly rhinoceros at Grotte de Chauvet, France. This same wall space was used repeatedly.

prestige value—were apparently exchanged from hand to hand. Many of these may have been given and received as gestures of social obligation between individuals and groups.

The late Ice Age societies of southwest France lived in relatively close juxtaposition, in a diverse environment with rich, predictable food resources. For at least part of the year, these societies may have lived a relatively sedentary existence and come together in much larger aggregations. Under these circumstances, it is reasonable to expect that their social organization would become more complex than was normal among egalitarian band societies.

Magdalenian culture was elaborate and sophisticated, to the point where we can predict that more sedentary living and larger group size may have resulted in social change, in more complex hunter-gatherer societies (Mellars, 1985). Certainly, the sometimes elaborate decoration of seashells, bracelets, and even sewn clothing associated with the dead argues for complex spiritual beliefs, many involving abstract symbolic images of the Ice Age world that we will never be able to recover.

Art and the Symbolic World

Sometime between 48,000 and 30,000 B.P., Europeans began making ornaments such as beads, pendants, and perforated animal teeth to adorn their persons. And at about the same time, they painted images of animals, signs, and anthropomorphic figures on cave walls. (Although there are some earlier scratched bones from Neanderthal sites, these hardly constitute art; Bahn, 1998). But the Europeans were by no means alone. Art was a worldwide phenomenon by 25,000 B.P., perhaps much earlier. Painted slabs dating to about 25,500 B.P. have come from the Apollo 11

25,000 B.P.

FIGURE 5.8 A lion-headed anthropomorphic statuette, carved from a small mammoth tusk, reconstructed from fragments found in the Stadel Cave, southern Germany. One of the earliest known human artworks, it dates to about 32,000 years ago.

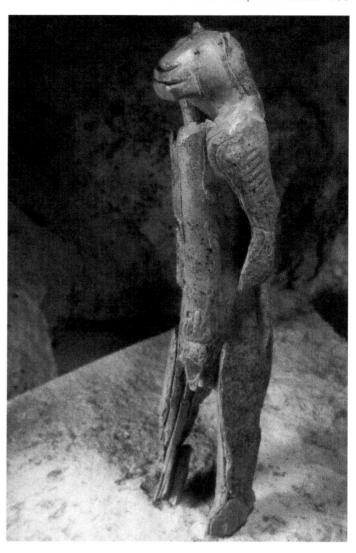

Cave in southern Africa, and wall engravings in Australia are at least as early. We know of only a few paintings and engravings this early, for art does not seem to have become commonplace anywhere until after about 18,000 B.P., the height of the last glaciation. The cave art of Western Europe is the best known and most thoroughly studied (Bahn, 2007; Bahn and Vertut, 1988).

As Steven Mithen (1996) has argued, there can be little doubt that the sudden appearance of art was connected with the development of human cognitive fluidity. But this was not art for art's sake; it was art with vital symbolic meaning, with, as it were, a "code" behind it. *H. sapiens* created visual images that had complex meanings and great emotional power—and that are beyond our ability to decode. Many of their paintings and engravings hint at anthropomorphic themes, where animals become humans, and humans, animals. This suggests that late Ice Age artists, like modern hunter-gatherers, linked the social, spiritual, and natural worlds into a single continuum, and that the environment was imbued with great potency.

Nowhere does this close connection between animal and human, the living and the spiritual worlds, appear more vividly than at the Grotte de Chauvet, deep in southeastern France's Ardèche region (see Site box on page 132).

Paintings and Engravings

Grotte de Chauvet offers dramatic evidence for the very early flowering of late Ice Age art. Until recently, most scholars thought in terms of a steady evolution of Upper Paleolithic art, from simple, unsophisticated beginnings to the magnificent polychrome paintings at Altamira in northern Spain and Lascaux in southwestern France. But both the Chauvet paintings and a lion-headed anthropomorphic figure carved in ivory from the Stadel Cave in southern Germany (Figure 5.8), as well as other animal sculptures from the same site (Hahn, 1993), suggest another scenario: one of brilliant flowerings of art in different areas at different times over a period of more than 20,000 years.

The evidence for these flowerings comes from nearly 200 caves in southwest Europe, mainly France and Spain, bearing wall paintings and engravings. Some 10,000 sculpted and engraved art objects have come from Upper Paleolithic sites across Europe and far into Siberia. Upper Paleolithic people were brilliant artists in stone, antler, bone, clay, ivory, and wood. They used paint on rock walls, sculpted in bas-relief and the round, and made musical instruments like bone flutes (see Figure 5.7) (Bahn and Vertut, 1988). The artists created thousands of naturalistic images of animals, sometimes human and humanlike forms, and dozens of enigmatic signs. All this art conveys complex, long-forgotten ideas, a symbolic world of spirit animals and spirit humans, of forces benevolent and evil. Some of the earlier art comprised "Venus" figurines: sculptures and bas-reliefs of females, sometimes with pendulous breasts, sometimes pregnant, and with exaggerated sexual characteristics (Figures 5.9a and b). They have been found from Russia in the east to the Dordogne region of France in the west, most in deposits dating to about 23000 B.C. We have no means of knowing what rituals were associated with these figurines, but they seem to have been associated with a relatively short-lived set of beliefs that was prevalent over a wide area of Europe, even, perhaps, with divination ceremonies.

Bas-reliefs in the form of friezes of animals like wild horses came into fashion in about 22,000 B.P. But 80 percent of all known art comes from the Magdalenian, beginning around 18,000 B.P. The earlier Magdalenian saw some remarkable cave painting from places like Lascaux, painted about 17,000 years ago (Aujoulat, 2005). Lascaux's walls were covered again and again with depictions of wild horses, bulls, reindeer, and many other animals. Many of the animals were painted with long, distorted necks and thick bodies, as if the artists were unaware of perspective (Figure 5.10). The

Lascaux
17,000 years ago

(a)   **(b)**

FIGURE 5.9 Paleolithic art. (a) Venus figurines from Willendorf, Austria (left). (b) Dolní Vestonice, Czech Republic (right). (Right: Neg. No. 329316, courtesy the Library, American Museum of Natural History.)

paintings also include squiggles, spaghetti-like patterns, and tentlike symbols. A Great Hall of the Bulls features four immense wild bulls, drawn in thick, black lines, with some of the body details filled in. Horses, deer, a small bear, and a strange unicornlike beast prance with the great bulls in a fantastic display of blacks, browns, reds, and yellows that truly bring the animals to life in a flickering light. It is hard to believe that the paintings are at least 17,000 years old.

Magdalenian artistry reached its height with an explosion of antler and bone work after 18,000 B.P. The people decorated their harpoons, spear points, spear-throwers, and other artifacts with naturalistic engravings, fine carvings of wild animals, and elaborate schematic patterns. Even fine eye details and hair texture were shown by delicate graving strokes. But the Magdalenians are most famous for their beautiful rock art, engravings, paintings, and even clay sculptures deep in the caves of northern Spain and southwest France (Figure 5.11). At Altamira, in northern Spain, you walk deep into the hillside to enter a low-ceilinged chamber, where the painters left fine renderings of bison in red and black (Figure 5.12) (Saura Ramos, 1999). By painting and engraving the animals around natural bulges in the rock, the artists conveyed a sense of dimension and life.

Explaining the Art

An enormous and highly speculative literature concerns the motives behind this remarkable art. Originally, Henri Breuil (1952) and other experts argued that the caves were sacred places where the hunters gathered to perform rituals and sympathetic magic that would ensure the fertility of game and the success of the hunt. Even the signs on the cave walls were interpreted as snares and traps. Today we know a great deal more about symbolic behavior and the art that goes with it and much more about how hunter-gatherer societies function.

French prehistorian André Leroi-Gourhan argued (1984) that the art was not random but part of a system of meanings, an expression of a worldview that organized Upper Paleolithic life. By counting the associations of subjects and the clusters of motifs, Leroi-Gourhan found that certain themes, among them female figures, appeared in rock shelters and better-lit locales, whereas others were in dark caverns. Leroi-Gourhan and his contemporaries lacked ways of dating individual paintings, so many of their theories were too generalized to stand up to close scrutiny.

FIGURE 5.10 The wild ox or aurochs, *Bos primigenius* on the wall of Lascaux, France.

FIGURE 5.11 Two bison sculpted in clay in the depths of Tuc d'Audoubert Cave, France. Each bison is about 62 cm (2 feet) long.

The development of AMS radiocarbon dating, which requires only tiny paint samples, has allowed the dating of individual figures in caves like Niaux in southern France. There, Jean Clottes (1995), combining AMS dating with chemical analysis of the paintings, has dated Niaux's bison to between about 13,850 and 12,890 B.P. He has also been able to show that the paintings in such accessible chambers as the famous Salon Noir (Figure 5.13) were painted much more carefully than hastily executed figures in deep, inaccessible chambers, painted, perhaps, by individuals on solitary vision quests (searches for spiritual enlightenment).

Niaux
13,850 to 12,890 B.P.

Today, we know that many hunter-gatherer groups around the world use ritual and art, creating and manipulating visual forms to structure and give meaning to their existence (Boyer, 1994). Many ethnographic studies show that symmetry and other artistic principles may underlie the designs of many art traditions and characterize every aspect of daily life, from social relationships to village planning. The people may use relatively few symbols to communicate meanings. Very often, it is the context of the symbols that reveals the meaning. For the artists of Lascaux and elsewhere, there were clearly continuities between animal and human life and with their social world. Thus, their art was a symbolic depiction of these continuities. The artists did not choose just any wall or piece of antler or bone for their drawings, nor just any animal or geometric form to depict. Their selections were deliberate, symbolic acts that provide clues to the significance of the world's earliest artistic tradition (Bahn and Vertut, 1988). Ancient San rock art from southern Africa, some from the Paleolithic, has strong shamanistic associations that have been partially reconstructed from historical records and oral traditions (Clottes, 1998; Lewis-Williams, 1981, 2002) and provide at least some general clues to the kinds of activities that may have been associated with European cave art (see Chapter 4). (This does not, of course, imply that San art can be used to interpret art traditions of 18,000 years ago.)

FIGURE 5.12 A bison in a polychrome cave painting from Altamira, Spain.

Engraved portable objects, such as the spear-throwers and harpoons found in Magdalenian caves, may have had a quite different significance, perhaps as a new form of tool for recording information. Alexander Marshack (1972) carried out detailed microphotographic studies of the portable art and argues that many of the visual forms are ecologically and seasonally related. Rather than concentrating on the naturalistic pictures of animals, he studied hundreds of nonnaturalistic pieces, with their patterns of lines, notches, dots, and groupings of marks (Figures 5.14a and b). On some pieces, the marks were made with different tools at different times. These pieces, which Marshack named "time-factorial" objects, were used, he believed, as sequential notations of events and phenomena, predecessors of calendars. The Magdalenian and earlier notations were for the engraver alone to read, even if this person explained them to others on occasion. To

FIGURE 5.13 Bison from the Salon Noir, Niaux, France, AMS radiocarbon-dated to about 13,000 B.P.

formulate such a system required thought and theoretical abstractions far more advanced than those hitherto attributed to the hunter-gatherers of this age. Another scholar, Francesco d'Errico, who uses a rigorous methodology, checking his own interpretations against replicas of engraved artifacts produced under controlled conditions, believes many engraved notations were an "artificial memory system with a complex code based on the morphology and spatial distribution of the engraved marks" (1995: 163).

About 12,000 B.P., the Magdalenians seem to have stopped painting and engraving deep caves. Most art after that appears at cave entrances and in rock shelters, always exposed to the light of day. The paintings and engravings were no longer naturalistic, and they vanished altogether about 11,000 B.P. By this time, much warmer climatic conditions had brought forest to the open plains, and the large arctic animals depicted in the earlier art were largely extinct. The brilliant efflorescence of Magdalenian culture had been replaced by new adaptations—to forests, rivers, and coasts. And cave and antler art had given way to a complex symbol system, incompletely recorded on flat pebbles (Courand, 1985).

Settling Eurasia (39,000 to 15,000 Years Ago)

The vast, undulating plains of western Russia and central Europe as far east as the Ural Mountains were a much less hospitable environment for Stone Age hunter-gatherers than the deep, well-watered valleys to the west (Hoffecker, 2002). There were no convenient caves or rock shelters. For warmth and shelter, the inhabitants of this area had to create artificial dwellings with their own tools and locally available raw materials. It may be no coincidence that few archaeological sites are found on these frigid plains, with their nine-month winters and short summers, until Upper Paleolithic times. The Neanderthals and early Upper Paleolithic populations may have ventured onto the steppe during the warmer summer months. It took some significant technological innovations, providing better cultural adaptations to bitter cold, to allow people to live there year-round. One important invention may have been the

FIGURE 5.14 (a) Engraved bone, 21 cm (8.2 inches) long, from La Marche, France, which was intensively studied by Alexander Marshack. (b) The close-up shot shows tiny marks in two groups, each engraved by a different point, with a different type of stroke. Recent research using microscopic and experimental methods has suggested that these marks were a form of early artificial memory system. (© Alexander Marshack, 1972.)

(a)   **(b)**

perforated bone needle, which enabled people to fabricate tailored layers of clothing, for layered garments provide the best protection against subzero temperatures. Advances in bone and antler technology may also have played a decisive role in arctic adaptation, for they allowed not only more efficient hunting but also the development of such important artifacts as the spear-thrower, a highly effective weapon against large, gregarious animals.

Surprisingly, AMH settled in this relatively inhospitable region as early as they did in southeast Europe. Small hunting bands were living at Kostenki in a group of open sites on the Don River by at least 40,000 years ago (Anikovich et al., 2007). Here, people were snaring birds and small animals, and also catching fish. The earliest needles in the world come from levels occupied after 40,000 years ago.

Between about 30,000 and 10,000 B.P., a series of hunting-and-gathering societies known to archaeologists as the Eastern Gravettian complex flourished on the plains and the varied terrain of Central and Eastern Europe (here the Gravettian flourished much later than in Western Europe). There were many local groups within this large complex, people adapted to life on frigid, open plains (Hoffecker, 2002; Roebroeks et al., 2000). Many of their campsites contain mammoth bones; in fact, many earlier interpretations of these societies referred to them as "mammoth hunters."

Eastern Gravettian complex
30,000 to 10,000 B.P.

Actually, the Eastern Gravettians exploited a wide range of late Ice Age mammals, ranging in size from bison to rabbits and arctic fox, the latter much prized for its soft fur. They may indeed have killed some mammoth, for such animals provided not only bones for constructing dwellings in treeless environments but also an abundance of meat and hide. But this would have been a memorable occurrence by any standards. Many of the mammoth bones may have come from animals that died of natural causes, or even from mammoth "cemeteries," places where animals perished in large numbers in spring floods, such as the ones known from Siberia. At the famous Dolní Vestonice and Pavlov sites in the Czech Republic, for example, the nearby landscape is rich in calcite and other minerals that, when licked, provide vital magnesium and calcium for elephants in late spring and summer, at a time when fresh grass is high in potassium. The most common animal bones come from rabbits and other small animals, which were clearly a staple food, as they may have been over much of late Ice Age Europe.

Dolní Vestonice and Pavlov were occupied again and again between about 27,000 and 25,000 B.P., with campsites overlooking the Dyje River valley and a nearby swamp. Perhaps between 100 and 120 people dwelled at Dolní Vestonice, sometimes in summer, at other times in oval bone-and-timber winter huts with hide roofs, dug partially into the ground (Figure 5.15a). Both sites are remarkable for their numerous burnt clay figures, which were fired in a small, oval-shaped oven inside a winter house, the earliest fired-clay objects in the world by at least 15,000 years. Burnt clay fragments also preserved traces of basketry and twined textiles made from plant fibers that are the earliest known in the world (Figure 5.16) (Adovasio et al., 1996). James Adovasio and his colleagues believe that the inhabitants of both sites used nets to capture large numbers of rabbits and other small game animals in cooperative hunts that involved men, women, and children. Such hunts yielded so much food that larger, more densely occupied settlements may have been more common than in earlier times (Soffer et al., 1998).

Dolní Vestonice
27,000 to 25,000 B.P.

Groups living in what is now the Czech Republic were highly mobile and habitually visited the Danube region of Austria, southern Poland, and northern Hungary. As the late Ice Age climate grew colder and resources grew scarcer, some of these people moved southward; others followed game herds onto the open steppe of the central Russian plains. This west-to-east population movement took at least 4,000 years, with constant abandonment and resettlement of different regions in response to climate and resource changes (Hoffecker, 2002).

Only a few rivers dissect the Russian plains, among them the Don and the Dnieper. It is no coincidence that ancient river terraces were the most common locations for Stone Age hunting settlements. These were often promontories overlooking the river, where the hunters could spy on the movements of the herds of arctic elephant (mammoth), woolly rhinoceros, and wild horse that flourished in the valleys, as well as prey on smaller mammal populations. At the height of the last glaciation, this area was a treeless periglacial landscape, a meadow steppe in warmer periods. It was a very inhospitable environment, but one where hunter-gatherer societies flourished for thousands of years.

The earliest Upper Paleolithic sites, probably settlements of anatomically modern people, date to at least 40,000 B.P. (Hoffecker, 2002). The most intensive (Eastern Gravettian) occupation dates to the period between 18,000 and 14,000 B.P., when scattered hunter-gatherer bands lived in what were often spectacular mammoth-bone structures (Soffer, 1985). The Mezhirich site overlooks the Dnieper River southeast of Kiev; it is a 15,000-year-old settlement of five houses, covering an area of some 10,219 sq. m (110,000 sq. feet). Each house was about 4 to 7 m (13 to 22 feet) across and up to 79 sq. m (850 sq. feet) in area (see Figure 5.15b). Foundation walls of

Mezhirich
15,000 years ago

(a)

(b)

FIGURE 5.15 Late Ice Age houses. (a) An artist's reconstruction of a winter house excavated at Dolní Vestonice, Czech Republic, dating to c. 25000 B.C. The timber-and-bone structure supported a hide roof. This dwelling contained an oval oven used to bake clay figurines. (b) An artist's impression of two mammoth-bone huts at Mezhirich, Ukraine.

massive mammoth bones supported an intricate framework of smaller limb bones, vertebrae, and other parts, sometimes arranged in fine herringbone patterns. Uprights stuck into holes broken through large mammoth bones supported the roof. Elephant hide or sod covered the entire structure. Hearths and work areas were inside the houses, which seem to have been occupied over long periods of time. More hearths, as well as deep storage pits that kept meat refrigerated in the permafrost, were between the houses.

The Mezhirich dwellings housed about 50 people, each dwelling taking ten men about five or six days to complete, a considerable investment of effort. Because mammoth-bone dwellings found at other locations are less elaborate, it may be that this settlement was of unusual importance. The inhabitants hunted not only mammoth but also many smaller mammals such as rabbits, as well as taking river fish and river birds. Judging by the evidence from several sites, they pursued the occasional mammoth in autumn and winter, reindeer in spring and early summer, fur-bearing animals in winter, and waterfowl in summer. So many mammoth bones were used in house construction that the people must have scavenged them from carcasses on the plains in addition to using their own kills. Russian archaeologists report that seashells from between 640 and 800 km (400 and 500 miles) away were found in the Mezhirich houses, and amber, a stone thought by many prehistoric peoples to have magic qualities, was traded from 160 km (100 miles) away.

Kostenki
24,000 B.P.
The Kostenki Gravettian sites on the Don River were occupied about 2,000 years after those to the west, between 24,000 and 23,000 B.P. They contain large hollows filled with bones and other debris. Their plans are so irregular that it is difficult to be sure whether they were dwellings or storage pits. In some cases, several circular structures up to 4.6 m (15 feet) in diameter were built together in a huge depression with a row of hearths down the middle. Bands of considerable size must have congregated in these tented areas.

To the east of the western plains stretches central Asia, a vast area of continental territory that covers not only northern Afghanistan but also the arid Turan Depression and the central Asian highlands. There are numerous Mousterian sites dating to the early part of the Weichsel glaciation, as they do in the west, displaying different tool kit variations that probably reflect different seasonal

FIGURE 5.16 An impression of a woven fragment preserved on clay: An open diagonal twining with an S twist weft, from Pavlov, Czech Republic.

activities. It is not yet known when the transition to the Upper Paleolithic took place, but one hunting camp at Malaia Suja, on the White Iyus River, west of Lake Baikal, has been radiocarbon-dated to about 34,500 B.P. Here people hunted mammoth, horse, reindeer, and other steppe animals, whose images they also engraved on bone, some of the earliest art in the world. Undoubtedly, however, the human population of this harsh country was very small.

Malaia Suja
34,500 B.P.

The Upper Paleolithic of central Asia is known from a late Ice Age culture that was widespread in caves, rock shelters, and open sites but is still not well known. The Shugnou site, southwest of the city of Samarkand, lies at an altitude of 2,000 m (6,700 feet), one of the highest Upper Paleolithic sites in the world. Russian archaeologists found five occupation layers in a site above a mountain river, yielding evidence of big-game hunting and of horses, wild oxen, wild sheep, and goats, dating to at least 20,000 to 15,000 B.P. Pollen grains suggest that weather conditions were somewhat cooler and wetter than today. The hunter-gatherer population of central Asia may have been sparse for thousands of years, perhaps because of unfavorable climate conditions, but this is pure conjecture. Population densities rose at the end of the Pleistocene, and human settlement expanded into higher elevations.

Shugnou
20,000 to 15,000 B.P.

Central Asia was subjected to cultural influences from both the flake and the blade traditions of the West and the chopper/chopping-tool traditions of the Far East. Consequently, stone tools here were frequently based on stone cobbles and were simple, highly effective artifacts that rarely achieved the sophistication or artistry of Western traditions. The same amalgam of cultural traditions filtered into Siberia in Far East Asia (Larichev et al., 1987).

Siberia (?33,000 to 13,000 Years Ago)

Remote from Atlantic and Pacific weather patterns, Siberia is dry country with harsh, dry winters and short, hot summers. Treeless plains predominate in the far north and extend to the shores of the Arctic Ocean. Rainfall was so sparse during the Weichsel glaciation that the great ice sheets of the west never formed here. Herds of gregarious mammoths grazed on the tundra and on the edges of the river valleys, where small bands of hunter-gatherers weathered the long winters. The archaeology of this enormous area and of Northeast Asia is still little known, despite long-term excavation campaigns in recent years (Dolukhanov et al., 2002; West, 1996). Nonetheless, Siberia and Northeast Asia are of vital importance, for they were the staging areas from which the first settlement of the Americas took place, across the Bering Strait.

There is no reliable evidence of human settlement in northeastern Siberia before the late Ice Age. Local archaeologists claim that sites contemporary with Malaia Suja lie east of Lake Baikal, including one at Tolbaga said to date to as early as 34,900 B.P., but few details of the site have been published (Larichev, 1988). All these settlements contain well-developed blade technology and also artifacts made by using Middle Paleolithic techniques. There is far less variation in tool forms than in later Stone Age cultures in the region.

By 22,000 B.P., two very different cultural traditions flourished in Siberia and into Northeast Asia. The Mal'ta tradition is known from clusters of sites west of Lake Baikal and the Yenesei River valley, many of them located in places sheltered from the prevailing northerly winds. The **Mal'ta** Mal'ta site itself, one of semisubterranean houses, covers more than 600 sq. m (6,458 sq. feet) **26,000 to 20,000 B.P.** and may have been reoccupied many times between 26,000 and 20,000 B.P. Mal'ta was probably a winter base camp of houses framed with large animal bones and covered with a lattice of reindeer antler to support a skin or sod covering. The hunters pursued mammoth, woolly rhinoceros, and reindeer, as well as small animals. The Mal'ta people were expert bone workers who carved female and bird figurines (Figure 5.17).

Afontova Gora-Oshurkovo The Afontova Gora-Oshurkovo tradition flourished over a much wider area not only in the **tradition** Yenesei River valley but also over an enormous area of northern Asia, perhaps all the way from **21,000 and 20,000 B.P.** the Altai Mountains to the Amur River. The oldest sites, Afontova Gora itself on the Yenesei and Mogochino on the Ob' River, date to between 21,000 and 20,000 B.P. Again, the people hunted periglacial steppe mammals, making large tools fashioned on cobbles, blade artifacts, large cobble scrapers known locally as *skreblos*, and occasionally small blade artifacts.

There are many general similarities between the Mal'ta and Afontova Gora-Oshurkovo traditions that tend to transcend the local differences between them. Together, they reflect a varied adaptation by *H. sapiens* to an enormous area of central Asia and southern Siberia from well west of Lake Baikal to the Pacific Ocean far to the east. Late Ice Age populations in this harsh area were never large and were concentrated for the most part in river valleys and near lakes. In general terms, their lifeway may have resembled that of plains big-game hunters on the steppe-tundra to the west, but it would be a mistake to argue that these Siberian groups originated in western Eurasia. They may have moved north or northeastward onto the open steppe-tundra from more temperate environments, perhaps at about the same time as Cro-Magnons moved into Europe. Although Neanderthal settlements are known in the mountainous Altai region of central Asia, there are no signs of Middle Paleolithic sites on the steppe-tundra itself. AMH may have been the first to venture north into periglacial regions.

The Settlement of Far Northeast Asia

The first human settlement of periglacial Northeast Asia appeared between 40,000 and 30,000 B.P. and was well established just before the late glacial maximum of about 18,000 B.P. The Mal'ta and Afontova Gora-Oshurkovo traditions peter out as one moves north and east into the far frontiers of Northeast Asia. The Verkhoyansk Mountains are thought to have been a major barrier to late Ice Age human settlement (Hoffecker, 2005). The western slopes of the range adjoin the Lena River basin, which we know had been settled by humans from 22,000 to 15,000 B.P. Beyond the Verkoyansk unfolds the vast landscape of extreme northeastern Siberia, which ends at the shores of the Bering Strait.

The earliest known site in northeastern Siberia is north of latitude 70° N, far above the Arctic Circle and 140 km (87 miles) from the Arctic Ocean on the Yana River. Here, the broken bones of mammoth, wild horse, reindeer, and birds lie with a variety of stone tools, including choppers, scrapers, and incomplete bifaces, as well as a bone awl. A foreshaft made of woolly rhinoceros horn came from the site some years ago, and gave the name to the site: Yana RHS (Yana Rhinoceros **Yana RHS** Horn Site) (Pitulko et al., 2004). Yana RHS has been radiocarbon-dated to 25,000 to 27,000 years **27,000 years ago** ago, which means that humans were living in extreme northeastern Siberia before the intense cold of the late Ice Age, which began after 26,000 B.P.

It is important to note that Yana dates to a time when northeastern Siberia was somewhat warmer than it was during the height of the last glaciation, around 20,000 years ago. At the height of the last Ice Age cold snap, all of the northeast was an extremely cold and windy desert environment, exceptionally forbidding for any form of human settlement until sporadic warming began after 18,000 B.P. Over enormous areas, the landscape was vegetationless, offering little for animals or humans. Such human inhabitants as there were probably moved southward into more hospitable environments, just as they did in Eurasia (Hoffecker, 2005), for arctic deserts were just like the Sahara in one sense: They pushed out populations in cold, dry times and sucked them in when it was warmer and moister.

Relatively soon after warming began, we find traces of human settlement once again. Archaeologist Yuri Mochanov (1996) has identified a late Ice Age culture that once flourished in the Middle

FIGURE 5.17 Ivory figurines from Mal'ta, Siberia.

FIGURE 5.18 Artifacts of the Diuktai tradition. Top, four views of a wedge-shaped core, used to make tiny blades. Bottom, two bifacially flaked projectile points. The wedge-shaped core is a characteristic artifact found on both sides of the Bering Strait about 11,000 to 10,000 years ago. It is, of course, a by-product of the production of fine microblades.

Aldan Valley, far north and east of Lake Baikal. He excavated Diuktai (Dyuktai) Cave, close to the river floodplain. There he found mammoth and musk-ox remains associated with large stone choppers, bifacially flaked stone points, burins, and small blade artifacts. The cave deposits had been much disturbed by freezing, thawing, and other natural phenomena, but Mochanov was able to date the occupation levels to between 18,000 and 12,000 B.P. He soon found more Diuktai-like sites on the banks of the Aldan, sites that contained not only points and choppers but also highly distinctive small blades and the characteristic wedge-shaped cores from which they had been formed (see Figure 5.18).

Diuktai (Dyuktai)
?18,000 B.P.

Bifaces, Microblades, and the First Americans

Clearly, the Diuktai tradition owes little to the well-defined big-game-hunting plains traditions of central and western Eurasia. It is marked by small blades, bifaces, and some stone spear points. This may be one of the cultural traditions from which the culture of the first Americans ultimately came. Some of the Diuktai stone points recall those made by Clovis people in the New World but without the distinctive "flute," a longitudinal thinning flake at the base of the head (see Chapter 6). However, there are no signs of small blades in the earliest human cultures of the Americas. These distinctive artifacts do appear, though, later, in Alaska, by about 11,000 years ago.

The most important artifacts used by the first Americans were stone-tipped spears and stone knives made from flakes of fine-grained stone struck off large cores, often themselves fashioned into bifaces so they could be carried around from one camp to the next. Such artifacts must also have been important on the steppe-tundra of Northeast Asia long before small blades came into use. Unfortunately, we know so little of Diuktai that we can only guess that it may represent more than one cultural tradition, one using bifaces and stone-tipped spears—a technology that spread early into the Americas—and perhaps a later version that relied more heavily on small blades, often called **microblades**.

If there is one significant trend in human stoneworking technology during the late Ice Age, about 25,000 years ago, it is a progressive elaboration and diminution of stone tools. This trend is well documented in Africa, Europe, and southern Asia, and in the Far East as well. Chinese archaeologists Tang Chun and Gai Pei (1986) believe that a primitive microblade tradition emerged in Asia quite soon after *H. sapiens* appeared in the region. In time, microblade technologies were to dominate stone technology throughout northern China, Korea, Japan, and far to the northeast in Siberia and possibly extreme northwestern America as well.

Microblades are diminutive blades that were struck in the thousands of carefully prepared conical or wedge-shaped cores (Figure 5.18). By their very size, microblades were designed to be mounted in antler, bone, or wooden handles to serve as spear barbs, arrow points, or small knife or scraper blades. Microblade technology first appeared in northern China about 30,000 B.P. and soon spread over an enormous area, even into tropical environments far to the south (Chun and Pei, 1986). They were widely used in China by 20,000 B.P., in Japan by about the same time (Reynolds and Barnes, 1984), and at the Studenoe-2 site, southeast of Lake Baikal in Siberia, by 17,800 B.P. (Goebel et al., 2000). However, no human occupation whatsoever is yet known from the Kamchatka Peninsula or extreme northeastern Siberia that dates to earlier than about 13000 B.C. (Goebel, 1999; Goebel and Slobodin, 1999; Kuzmin and Tankersley, 1996). If these areas were devoid of human settlement before that date, we should not be surprised that people did not cross into the Americas until after the Ice Age.

Studenoe-2
17,800 B.P.

We can propose a scenario for what occurred. Perhaps microblade technology first developed in temperate Asia, in areas like the Gobi Desert and Mongolia, where people hunted over enormous areas. Here, they needed a stone technology that was economical, easy to carry and manufacture and yet capable of arming spears. And perhaps, very late in the Ice Age, they needed bows and arrows with sharp, lethal points for taking game on the run in open country. In time, the same technology spread north and east into the harsh periglacial landscapes of Siberia, where small-scale and portable tool kits were highly adaptive, especially when used against such migratory animals as the reindeer. In time, small groups of microblade-using people may have carried the same technology across the dry land of the Bering Strait into Alaska, perhaps after simpler biface and spear point tool kits had spread into the Americas. But, if the present field evidence is correct, there were no such population

?15,000 years ago

movements before about 15,000 years ago, some time after post–Ice Age warming began.

This scenario receives some support from the dental research of Christy Turner (1984). He has shown that the characteristic tooth features of Native Americans include specialized attributes, such as shovel-shaped incisors, that are mirrored in northern Chinese skeletons dating to about 20,000 years ago. He calls this group of features **sinodonty**, features that are never found on European Stone Age teeth. Turner believes that the first Americans originated in northern China, reaching their new homeland through eastern Mongolia and northeastern Siberia. With that momentous development, *H. sapiens* eventually reached the Americas.

Summary

- This chapter documents the spread of *H. sapiens* into Europe and Eurasia from Africa and Southwest Asia around 48,000 years ago, during the late Ice Age.

- An unsuccessful colonization of Southwestern Asia by AMH occurred around 100,000 years ago, from Northeast Africa. The newcomers survived alongside Neanderthals for about 20,000 years before becoming extinct. It is not known whether the Mt. Toba eruption caused their demise.

- Modern humans settled permanently in Southwestern Asia by about 50,000 years ago: they possessed the full cognitive abilities of *H. sapiens*. They brought with them more refined and sophisticated hunting methods and tool technologies.

- Small numbers of moderns settled in eastern and Central Europe and apparently in the west as early as 48,000 years

ago, during a period of somewhat warmer conditions. A massive eruption in the Bay of Naples area in Italy around 39,000 years ago may have held back larger scale settlement.

- Much larger scale settlement took hold with the appearance of the Aurgnacian culture after the eruption about 39,000 years ago. Aurignacians settled in all parts of what is now temperate Europe south of the ice sheets.

- The sheer diversity of the late Ice Age environment gave moderns in western Europe great flexibility. They developed more complex societies and elaborate bone and antler technology, as well as a complex symbolic life reflected in intricate artistic traditions. These cultures reached their apogee in the Magdalenian culture, which flourished about 18,000 B.P. for about 5,000 years.

- Cro-Magnon art traditions developed before 30,000 years ago and involved engraving, painting, and sculpture, as well as the adornment of portable objects. The motives behind the art are much debated. Some of the cave art may be connected with shamanistic activity and initiation ceremonies.

- The Eastern Gravettian cultural complex of eastern Europe and Eurasia was contemporary with Cro-Magnon societies in the west and was based on the exploitation of open plains and steppe. The many groups within this complex spread slowly eastward from the Czech Republic onto the Russian plains, relying heavily on game of all kinds.

- Far to the northeast, western Siberia was settled at least as early as 30,000 years ago, but the extreme northeast was devoid of human settlement until the very late Ice Age, perhaps as late as 15,000 B.P.

- Most experts agree that northeastern Siberia was the stepping-off point for the first settlement of the Americas. From there, humans first crossed the Bering land bridge into Alaska, either during the late Ice Age or when global warming began about 16,000 years ago.

Key Terms

blade technology (124)
burin (127)

microblade (141)

sinodonty (142)

Further Reading

Bahn, Paul, and Jan Vertut. 1988. *Images of the Ice Age*. New York: Viking Press.

Fagan, Brian. 2010. *Cro-Magnon: How the Ice Age Gave Birth to the First Modern Humans*. New York: Bloomsbury Press.

Hoffecker, John. 2002. *Desolate Landscapes*. New Brunswick, NJ: Rutgers University Press.

———. 2005. *A Prehistory of the North*. New Brunswick, NJ: Rutgers University Press.

6

The First Americans

AROUND 14000 B.C. TO MODERN TIMES

O ne fine spring morning in 1908, a black cowboy named George McJunkin was riding slowly along the edge of a dry gully near Folsom, New Mexico. He was casting over the range in search of stray cattle. Suddenly, he saw some sun-bleached bones protruding from the side of the arroyo. He pried some out with his knife. As he did so, a sharp stone fragment came loose in his hands, a stone spear point like the ones he had seen lying on the surface elsewhere on the ranch. McJunkin took his finds back to the ranch house, where they lay around for 17 years.

Years later, in 1925, someone was curious enough to send the bones to Jesse Figgins, the director of the Colorado Museum of Natural History. Figgins realized they were from an extinct form of plains bison, apparently from the same level as the stone point. The following year, he dug into the arroyo, finding more stone tools and bison bones. He realized he had the proof that humans had lived in North America at the same time as long-extinct animals. Soon, experts came to Folsom and were convinced that Figgins had finally found proof of the considerable antiquity of humankind in the Americas. ■

Model of an Aleutian open water kayak or *baidarka*.

he controversies over the first Americans raged long before the Folsom excavations, and they are still among the most vigorous of all debates in archaeology (Barton et al., 2004). How long ago did humans set foot in the Americas? What manner of people were they? By what route did they reach the New World? These questions have preoccupied scientists since soon after Columbus landed in the Bahamas in 1492. This chapter discusses these controversies and describes the diverse later hunter-gatherer societies of the Americas.

The First Settlement of the Americas

Many archaeologists believe that the first inhabitants of the Americas set foot in the New World by way of the Bering land bridge, at a time when the strait of that name was dry land (Figure 6.1). However, for all the agreement about the Siberian route, intense controversies surround the beginnings of human settlement in the Americas (Adovasio, 2002; Jablonski, 2002; Meltzer, 2008) (see Table 6.1). These controversies revolve around three fundamental questions:

- How long ago did humans first settle in the Americas?
- What tool kit did they bring with them, and what was their lifeway?
- What was the ultimate ancestry of the first Native Americans?

Several competing hypotheses account for first settlement, each with passionate advocates:

- One (minority) school of thought holds that the Americas were colonized by some time during the Wisconsin glaciation, perhaps as early as 40,000 years ago, or even earlier.

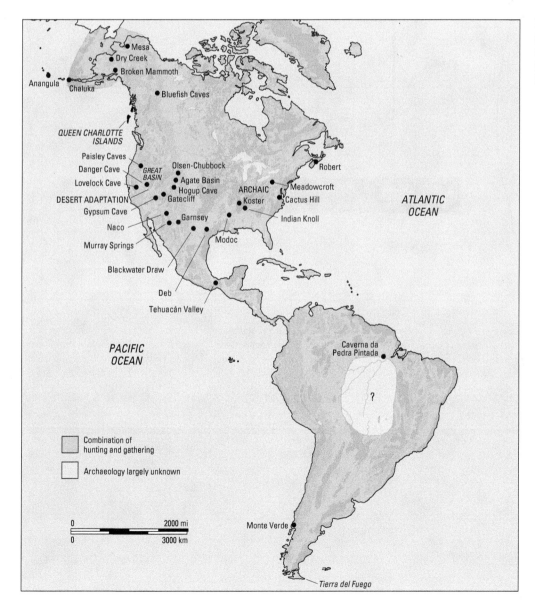

FIGURE 6.1 Ancient hunter-gatherers in the Americas. Sites mentioned in the text are indicated. (For the Bering land bridge, see Figure 6.2.)

TABLE 6.1
Major cultural developments in the Americas, c. 15000 B.C to A.D. 1500

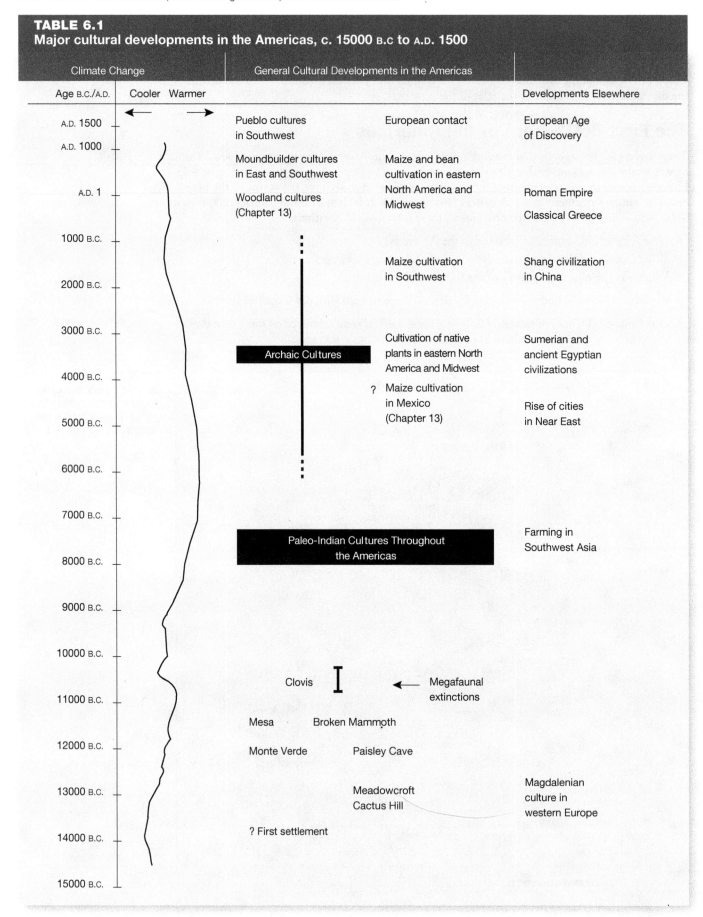

- A second hypothesis argues that the first Americans crossed into the New World considerably later, perhaps about 20,000 years ago, during the late Ice Age. Some scholars of this school suspect that settlement took hold even later than this, at the very end of the Wisconsin glaciation, perhaps as recently as about 13000 B.C. or later, and penetrated south of the Upper Pleistocene ice sheets as they retreated.

- Other theories include possible settlement by boat-using late Ice Age Solutreans across the North Atlantic, a theory based on similarities between stone artifacts in Europe and North America, but it is only fair to say that there is little convincing evidence to support this idea.

Intense controversy surrounds not only the specific archaeological evidence for the first settlement but also the criteria that can be used to establish it. However, most archaeologists agree that securely radiocarbon-dated, well-stratified cultural remains of undoubted human manufacture are the only acceptable evidence. So far, data whose quality is universally acceptable have eluded even persistent search, leaving one of the major mysteries of world prehistory still unsolved. In recent years, a flood of new genetic and linguistic information has added to the controversy.

Ice Sheets and the Bering Land Bridge

As we saw in Chapter 4, uman settlement in far northeast Asia is documented as early as 27,000 years ago, during a warmer interval of the last glaciation. During the height of the last cold snap after 26,000 years ago, the region was probably uninhabited owing to lack of vegetation and intense cold. Judging from sites in western and central Europe, the human settlement of extreme arctic environments expanded after about 16000 B.C., with the first consistent warming, so a somewhat later settlement of the harsh and unforgiving extreme northeast would be logical. If we accept the notion that *Homo sapiens* was living near the shores of the Bering Strait sometime after that date, how did people cross into Alaska, only a short distance away?

At the time we are considering, world sea levels were as much as 100 m (330 feet) lower than today—so low that a land bridge stood where the Bering Strait now separates Asia and Alaska. (Sea levels drop when quantities of ocean water are frozen into continental ice sheets.) The strait formed part of a now almost submerged landmass known to geologists as Beringia. Only parts of west and east Beringia are dry land today—in Siberia and Alaska.

Some 18,000 years ago, central Beringia was an exposed coastal plain, denuded and dissected by many rivers, which covered the floors of the Chukchi Sea and the northeast Bering Sea. This was the famous Bering land bridge, commonly believed to be the land route by which human beings first reached the Americas (Figure 6.2) (Hoffecker, 2007; Hopkins et al., 1982; Madsen,

FIGURE 6.2 The Bering land bridge at the last glacial maximum, as reconstructed by the latest research. The land bridge is thought to have been the major route by which humans first colonized Alaska and the Americas, during or immediately after the late Ice Age.

2010). The Bering land bridge has a complicated geological history, known both from land-based studies and deep-sea cores. The cores show that the last glaciation began about 100,000 years ago, with a gradual cooling trend that exposed the land bridge from about 75,000 to 45,000 years ago. A lengthy period of less cold climate ensued from about 40,000 to 25,000 years ago, when the land bridge was no more than a narrow, periodically flooded isthmus. Bitter cold returned as sea levels fell about 25,000 years ago. This time, the land bridge lasted until around 11,000 years ago, perhaps later, when rapid postglacial warming began. During this last period of intense cold, the windy land bridge stretched from Asia to Alaska and covered much of the Chukchi Sea. Its southern coastline extended from the Gulf of Anadyr in Siberia to the Alaska Peninsula in North America.

The low-lying land bridge was no landscape of gently waving grass, where half-naked hunters pursued big game from Asia into a new continent. Beringia was a treeless, arctic land, covered with a patchwork of very different types of vegetation. A 1,000-sq.-km (400-sq.-mile) patch of the Beringian landscape of 17,000 years ago has come to light under a thick volcanic ash. The plant samples include grasses, sedges, mosses, and many other varieties in a nearly continuous ground cover. But the root mat was thin, with no soil formation, meaning that the plant cover enjoyed little long-term stability (Hoffecker, 2007). The land bridge was a place of violent climatic extremes and strong winter winds, which may have kept animal and human population densities low. John Hoffecker (2005) argues that a shortage of firewood during the late Ice Age would have inhibited human settlement until warmer temperatures enabled trees to be established in Beringia; for French research has shown that animal bone, like mammoth limbs, will not burn without a "starter" of firewood to raise the temperature (Thery-Parisot, 2001).

The land bridge could have supported a diversity of large and small herbivores, provided it had sufficient variety, and quantity, of plant communities to do so (Elias, 2002). It never teemed with game animals, for they were probably scattered throughout the landscape, concentrated at dozens of special sites, in lowland meadows and near rivers. They would have succeeded one another, utilizing patches of the bare, treeless environment in an endless succession of grazing patterns that persisted as long as the continental ecosystem of the land bridge remained intact.

Hardly surprisingly, no archaeological remains have yet come from the floor of the Bering Strait, so we can only assume that there was once a sparse human population dwelling on the land bridge, preying on the large and small animals that lived there. There may have been coastal settlements on the southern shores, too, settlements now flooded by rising sea levels, where people might have taken fish and sea mammals. However, without effective canoe technology, they would have been severely limited in their ability to take maritime resources. In all likelihood, the first Beringians were terrestrial and, perhaps, sea mammal hunters, practicing a lifeway that had flourished for thousands of years on the steppe-tundra.

When human beings first set foot on the land bridge remains a complete mystery, but, given the present dates for Diuktai sites in Siberia, it may have been after 18,000 radiocarbon years ago. And at some point afterwards, some of these people foraged their way across to higher ground in the east and ultimately into the Americas. At present, it is not possible to give an even slightly precise date for this crossing. Alternatively, it may have been a response to the rapid flooding of the land bridge after 14,000 years ago, although it was at least partially in existence until around 11,000 before present.

Could the first Americans have made their way along the shores of the land bridge by boat? We know that people colonized the remote landmass of Australia before by 45,000 years ago and that they could have done so only by crossing over some 88.5 km (55 miles) of open water even at the height of the glaciation, when sea levels were much lower than today (see Chapter 5). These were more benign tropical waters, where such hazards as floating ice, strong arctic winds, and the ever-present danger of hypothermia were unknown. The risks in the far north were much greater. Even in summer, fogs and rough seas make the strait a chancy place, and to cross winter pack ice is to invite disaster.

Unfortunately, we have no means of knowing whether early northeast Asians had skin boats, or even kayaks, for their long-abandoned settlements lie under modern sea levels. We do know that the predominant dietary source for Stone Age hunters over an enormous area of Europe and Asia was land mammals of all sizes, with apparently much less concentration on seasonal vegetable foods, fish, and marine mammals. To venture onto the Bering land bridge required no new skills, merely the same foraging expertise that characterized generations of Ice Age hunters. That the first crossing into Alaska was by land rather than by boat seems likely, simply on deductive grounds. It may have been only later that arctic peoples adapted to postglacial coasts and crossed freely from Asia to Alaska, maintaining social and cultural ties on both sides of the Bering Strait.

The First Settlement of Alaska

Finding human occupation in Alaska is rather like looking for a needle in a frozen haystack. So the first Alaskans are still a very shadowy entity, known only from a few stratified locations, but they appear to date to just after 10000 B.C. (Bever, 2001).

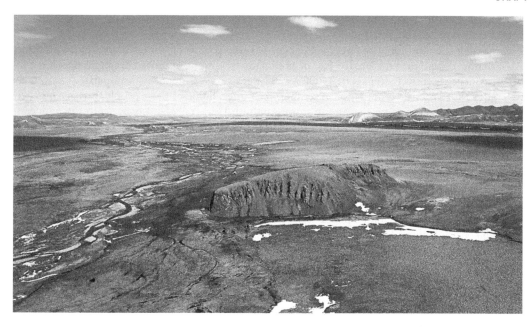

FIGURE 6.3 The Mesa site in Alaska's Brooks Range, one of the northernmost archaeological sites in the Americas, dating to before 11,000 years ago.

About 20,000 years ago, glaciers covered the Alaska Range and the Alaska Peninsula, as well as the Brooks Range, but much of the land immediately east of the Bering Strait was dry and ice free. Some archaeologists believe these ice-free areas of Alaska were uninhabitable during the late Wisconsin glacial period. Others have considered Alaska little more than a passageway, a "natural highway" to more temperate latitudes. In fact, a sparse population spread over this vast arctic landscape, adapted to it in many ways, and evolved distinctive cultures over very long periods of time indeed. Unfortunately, the archaeological potential of Alaska and the Yukon has hardly been tapped (Figure 6.3). The level of speculation about first settlement vastly exceeds the amount of archaeological data. Only a handful of sites give us clues (Hoffecker, 2007).

The Nenana Valley, 97 km (60 miles) southeast of Fairbanks, has yielded a series of temporary encampments on well-drained ridges overlooking marshy lowlands where game would have grazed in summer (see the summaries in West, 1996). The Broken Mammoth, Mead, and Swan Point sites contain stratified occupation layers with stone tools and animal bones. AMS dates from the three locations place the earliest occupation to about 11700 B.C. The Swan Point levels contain unmistakable microblades as well as swan bones, which means that some form of terrestrial flyway between the heart of North America and Alaska existed at this time—an argument for the existence of some form of ice-free corridor with ample water and marshes at the time.

Broken Mammoth
11700 B.C.

To the north, the Tenana River valley in the northern foothills of the Alaska Range contains two radiocarbon-dated levels (Hoffecker, 2001; Holmes, 2001). The earliest, Dry Creek I, dates to about 11500 B.C. and contains some cobble and flake tools, as well as broken blades, thin bifacial knives, and points. Dry Creek II dates to about 8700 B.C., and this level contains microblades and other artifacts associated with such technology.

Dry Creek I
11500 B.C.

Walker Road, about 16 km (10 miles) north of Dry Creek in the Nenana River valley, has been AMS-dated to between 11400 and 11100 B.C. Walker Road's cultural occupation, stratigraphic position, and age are similar to those of Dry Creek I. Two concentrations of stone tools, including small bifacial points and scrapers but no microblades, cluster around small hearths and represent a single Nenana occupation. Broken Mammoth, Dry Creek, and Walker Road belong within a generalized, and as yet poorly defined, "Northern Paleo-Indian traditions," which is thought of as a northern equivalent of the Paleo-Indian traditions like Clovis to the south, described later in this chapter.

Walker Road
11400 to 11100 B.C.

Alaskan archaeologists have grappled with the problem of classifying the little-known Northern Paleo-Indian cultures, although they all agree that they may form part of a highly varied cultural tradition that reflects adaptations to a complex mosaic of local environments at the end of the Ice Age. The same hunting and foraging cultures may have been the ancestors of the first human societies to flourish south of the ice sheets that mantled northern North America during the Wisconsin glaciation.

Many experts favor a relatively late settlement of the Americas, one that coincided with the general global warming between 15000 and 10000 B.C. that submerged the Bering land bridge. As far as can be established, the predominant lifeway in the northern latitudes of Eurasia and Northeast Asia during the last glacial climax was based on large- and small-game hunting. That this lifeway was pursued in Beringia seems unquestionable. Once the ice sheets retreated, however, many Ice Age game species became extinct, and human bands had to adapt to a far more diverse tundra and birch forest environment. This environmental diversity is reflected in considerable tool kit variation within early Alaskan settlements.

A possible scenario for first settlement, then, has tiny groups of hunter-gatherers crossing into Alaska either during the very late Ice Age or as climatic conditions improved dramatically—if the Siberian evidence is correct after about 14000 B.C. The crossing was not a single population movement but, rather, dozens of such migrations over many centuries. Some of these people, perhaps numbering only in the dozens, were the first to move southward either by land or sea into the temperate latitudes that lay beyond the great ice sheets covering much of Canada and the Rocky Mountains.

There remains one fundamental question: Why did humans settle in the New World at all? Was it an inner urge that caused the first Americans to endure the harsh climate of the Bering land bridge? Or was there some more prosaic reason?

Two great population dispersals occurred during prehistory, the first when archaic humans radiated from the tropics nearly 2 million years ago. The second took place after the evolution of *H. sapiens*, when the first human populations crossed from the Old World into the New and when Australia was inhabited for the first time. The exact dates of this later dispersal are still highly uncertain, but it seems to have occurred soon after modern peoples appeared. The explanation for these sudden radiations seems to lie mostly in the fact that humans tended to behave as other animals did. They spent their days tracking the game herds, and perhaps sea mammals, that formed an important part of their subsistence. When Siberian game herds moved onto the Bering land bridge toward the end of the last glaciation, their human predators followed. The higher ground to the east—Alaska—formed part of the same hunting grounds.

Biological and Linguistic Evidence for the First Americans

For more than a century, anthropologists have pointed to biological similarities between Siberians and North American Indians. Biological anthropologist Christy Turner (1984, 2002) has studied the changing physical characteristics of Native American teeth, especially their crowns and roots, and has compared them with those of Old World populations. These dental features are more stable than most evolutionary traits, with a high genetic component that minimizes the effects of environmental differences, sexual dimorphism, and age variations. After examining more than 4,000 individuals, ancient and modern, Turner has developed a series of hypotheses, based on dental morphology, about the first settlement of the Americas (Figure 6.4).

Turner points out that ancient Americans display many fewer variations in their dental morphology than do eastern Asians. He calls these characteristics *sinodonty*, a pattern of dental features that includes incisor shoveling, single-rooted upper first premolars, triple-rooted lower first molars, and other attributes. Sinodonty occurs only in northern Asia and the Americas. Turner's earliest evidence for sinodonty comes from northern China in about 18000 B.C., but he believes that it emerged much earlier, perhaps as early as 40,000 years ago. European Upper Paleolithic skeletons do not display sinodonty. Turner believes that the sinodont northern Chinese may have evolved from a primeval Southeast Asian *Homo sapiens* population, whom they resemble more closely than they do northeastern Asians and American Indians.

Using statistics to study evolutionary divergence, Turner has estimated the approximate dates at which sinodont populations split off from ancestral Chinese groups. He hypothesizes that the first settlement of the Americas resulted from a population movement through eastern Siberia and across the now submerged continental shelf around 12000 B.C. Two subsequent population movements brought the present-day Athabaskan and Eskimo-Aleut populations into the Americas a few thousand years later. Neither of these groups penetrated deep into the continent.

Turner's dental work gains support from both genetic and linguistic researches (M. H. Crawford, 2001; Pertago et al., 2009; Renfrew, 2000). As we saw in Chapter 3, mitochondrial DNA (mtDNA) has proved a useful tool for calibrating mutation rates and studying human genealogies, because it is inherited through the female line and accumulates mutation rates much faster than nuclear DNA. Mitochondria trace modern human ancestry back to tropical Africa at least 100,000 years ago, while no less than five mtDNA lineages are shared by ancient and modern Native American populations in North and South America (Merriwether, 2002). The molecular biologists believe that all Native Americans are descended ultimately from a single, somewhat diverse group of Asians, from eastern Siberia and Beringia (for a survey, see Torroni, 2000). New mtDNA studies of two rare haplogroups suggest that at least two separate groups arrived in North America at about the same time. One group (identified by the haplogroup D4h3) crossed the Bering land bridge, then moved southward along the ice-free Pacific coast some 15,000 years ago, while another traveled through

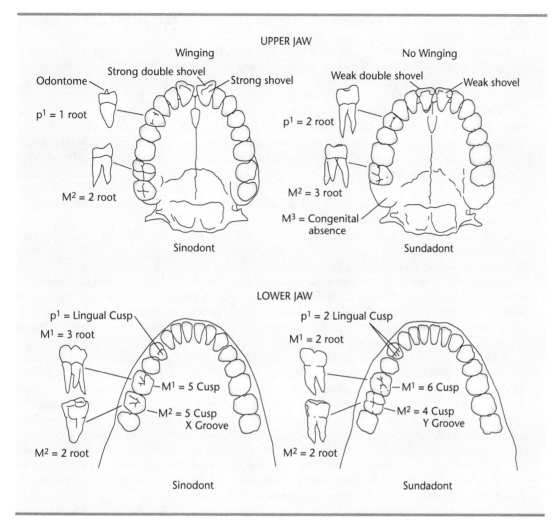

FIGURE 6.4 Dental morphology and the first Americans. Some of Christy Turner's theories about the peopling of the Americas are based on differences between the teeth of the so-called sinodonts (northern Asians and all Native Americans) and sundadonts (eastern Asians). Sinodonts display, among other features, strong incisor shoveling (scooping out on one or both surfaces of the tooth), single-rooted upper first premolars, and triple-rooted lower first molars.

the widening corridor between the Cordilleran and Laurentide ice sheets (Torroni et al., 2009). If these conclusions stand up to future scrutiny, it means that there was biological and linguistic diversity among Native Americans from the beginning.

Back in 1956, the Stanford linguist Joseph Greenberg (1987) proposed that most North American and all South American languages were part of a single, large "Amerind" family. Aleut-Eskimo and Na-Dene were quite separate linguistic groups, making a total of three for the whole of the Americas. Greenberg then spent years compiling a vast database on the vocabulary and grammar of the 140 families of American Indian languages, which confirmed his belief that there were three linguistic groups that corresponded to migrations into the Americas. Greenberg estimated that his Amerind group arrived before 9000 B.C., Na-Denes around 7000 B.C., and that Aleuts and Eskimos diverged about 2000 B.C. Greenberg's large grouping of many languages into an Amerind family has been severely criticized by other linguists (see the surveys in Golla, 2000, and Kaufman and Golla, 2000). Despite this drumbeat of criticism, some geneticists claim that the genetic evidence agrees well with Greenberg's tripartite subdivision of Native American languages. The controversy is unresolved.

Settlement Routes: Ice-Free Corridors and Sea Coasts

If tiny bands of hunter-gatherers penetrated the plains of central Beringia during the late Wisconsin glaciation, how, then, did they reach the heart of the Americas? Again, the first settlement is fraught with controversies about hypothetical routes and the boundaries of ice sheets (for routes, see Figure 6.1).

North America was very different during the Wisconsin glaciation. We know from studies of deep-sea cores that the Wisconsin began some 117,000 years ago, with an inexorable cooling of world temperatures. Great ice sheets covered much of northern North America during the early Wisconsin, until about 60,000 years ago. Between about 60,000 and 25,000 years ago, there was a prolonged period of glacial retreat, and sea levels rose. With the possible exception of a much-reduced ice sheet around Hudson Bay, most of North America was freed of glacial barriers. For these 35,000 years, any (hypothetical) human settlers would have encountered environments not very different from modern tundra and boreal forest.

The late Wisconsin glaciation, the earliest time period when human settlement seems possible, began about 23000 B.C. The Laurentide glaciers, centered on Labrador and in the Keewatin areas of Canada, expanded south, west, and east, eventually fusing into a huge frozen wilderness. At its maximum, in about 16000 B.C., the Laurentide ice sheet extended from the Atlantic seaboard across the Great Lakes region into southeast Alberta. The mountain ranges of southern Alaska and British Columbia were heavily glaciated at the time, forming the Cordilleran glacier complex in the west. The Cordilleran extended about 48 km (30 miles) south of Seattle as recently as 12500 B.C., apparently reaching its maximum extent after the Laurentide.

Clearly, these great late Wisconsin ice barriers would have inhibited travel between Beringia and the southern latitudes of the New World. Did they stop human settlement altogether? In the 1950s, Canadian geologists reported that the Cordilleran ice flowed down the eastern flanks of the Rockies but apparently did not join the Laurentide ice sheet. The idea of an ice-free corridor soon took hold of archaeologists' imaginations. "Doubtless it was a formidable place," wrote Thomas Canby of the National Geographic Society, "an ice-walled valley of frigid winds, fierce snows, and clinging fogs . . . yet grazing animals would have entered, and behind them would have come a rivulet of human hunters" (1979, p. 221). The picture is a compelling one—but was it reality?

The ice-free corridor has been mapped more thoroughly in recent years, to the point where we can be sure it was no superhighway for Stone Age hunters. In some places, the ice sheets merged. In others, especially in the far north and the south, there was a corridor, but it twisted and turned through the roughest of terrain, country restricted by chill meltwater lakes, often with biologically sterile shores. At best, the late Wisconsin ice-free corridor was a barren and impoverished landscape. Even if it were passable, there is a good chance that there was no incentive to cross it between about 23000 and 13000 B.C., for much better food resources lay in Beringia. In any case, we lack evidence that human settlers had made Beringia their homeland earlier than 13500 B.C. If an interior route was used, chances are that it was traversed during a time of glacial retreat, sometime after 13000 B.C., when the Laurentide glaciers shrank rapidly.

Despite these discouraging conditions, there are some traces of relatively early settlement along the coast to the south. Human occupation on the Queen Charlotte Islands dates back to at least 12,000 years ago, and there may have been biologically rich and diverse coastal environments in a southeast Alaska and British Columbia largely deglaciated by that time.

If the ice-free corridor was a barrier to human settlement, could people have passed down ice-free coastal areas along the Alaskan and British Columbian coasts into temperate regions (Erlandson, 2001)? Perhaps the late Wisconsin northwest coasts were relatively warmer and more productive than other areas, to the extent that they might have sustained human life. Unfortunately, however, we do not know whether these areas were accessible from mainland Beringia, or indeed whether there were late Wisconsin populations on the land bridge at all. If such people did exist, their sites are buried deep beneath modern sea levels. The earliest documented coastal settlement in south Alaska occurs around 8000 B.C., but is estimated to have begun perhaps. 2,000 years earlier (Ames and Maschner, 1999). The extensive tracts of open tundra along the continental shelf might have attracted terrestrial hunters from the interior, who then moved southward past the ice sheets and also began fishing and sea mammal hunting, major occupations of their later descendants (Fedje, 2003).

Pre-Clovis Settlement in the Americas

Decades of ardent search have produced only a handful of sites that may date to earlier than 13000 B.C. (Adovasio, 2002; Meltzer, 2008). However, a number of "Pre-Clovis" sites throughout the Americas document sparse human settlement during the late Ice Age or immediately after the ice sheets began retreating. At this stage in research we still know little about these people beyond the fact they were present, because most of the evidence for them is little more than stone tools. Some of the sites remain controversial; others are well documented to the point that there can be no doubt that first settlement took place long before the Clovis people (described in the following section) frequented North America.

North America

Meadowcroft Rock Shelter, 48 km (30 miles) southwest of Pittsburgh, Pennsylvania, lies a sheltered location close to permanent water supplies. James Adovasio meticulously excavated and dated the 11 levels of the shelter with more than 70 radiocarbon dates. They show that it was occupied from about A.D. 1300 back to at least 10000 and perhaps to 14000 B.C. (Adovasio et al., 1981, 1998). Controversy swirls around the lowest levels of the rock shelter, which were claimed to date to as early as 17600 B.C. The earliest date of human occupation at Meadowcroft has now been estimated as being between 2,000 and 3,000 years before 9500 B.C., that is, perhaps as early as 12500 B.C. (Adovasio et al., 1998).

Meadowcroft
A.D. 1300 to ?14000 B.C.

Some of the best evidence for Pre-Clovis settlement comes from the Debra L. Friedkin site north of Austin, Texas, where a large assemblage of stone artifacts including bifaces, small blades, and possible adze-like tools dated to between 11100 and 10800 B.C. lie stratified beneath a Clovis layer (Figure 6.5) (Waters et al., 2011). The nearby Gault site also documents a similar sequence.

Debra L. Friedkin site
11100 and 10800 B.C.

Another such site is Cactus Hill, a stratified Paleo-Indian and Archaic site in coastal Virginia, with both a Clovis and possible well-defined pre-Clovis occupation, the latter dated to about 13000 and 14600 B.C. The pre-Clovis artifacts are said to be unlike those made by Clovis people and to include blades and points (McAvoy and McAvoy, 1997; Wagner and McAvoy, 2004).

Cactus Hill
14600 to 13000 B.C.

A few other sites date to before 12000 B.C.; most of them are little more than artifact scatters, a reflection of highly mobile groups with portable tool kits who left little behind them. Stone tools associated with the remains of two mammoths come from the Schaefer and Hebior sites in Wisconsin and date to between 12800 and 12200 B.C. (Joyce, 2006). One small group of early settlers visited the Paisley 5 Mile Point Caves in Oregon's Cascade Range, leaving a scatter of feces behind them that date to 12,300 years ago. These yielded genetic material that associates them with Native Americans, but no artifacts or food remains came with the coprolites (Gilbert et al., 2008).

Paisley 5 Mile Point
10300 B.C.

Central and South America

The evidence for early human occupation is also sparse south of the Rio Grande (for a review, see Dillehay, 2000). The earliest well-documented site comes from Chile, but there are other possible, but usually discounted, locations (see Meltzer, Adovasio, and Dillehay, 1994). Among them is the skull of a woman about 20 years old, the so-called Luzia woman, found in the Lagoa Santa region of eastern Brazil, said to be about 11,500 years old. Unfortunately, the provenience of the found is open to doubt.

The Monte Verde site lies in a small river valley in southern Chile, a streamside settlement covered by a peat bog, so that not only stone and bone but also wooden artifacts survive. The site has been thoroughly excavated and has been radiocarbon-dated to between 11800 and 12000 B.C. (Dillehay, 1989, 1997). Thus far, only a portion of the site has been excavated, revealing two parallel rows of what are said to be rectangular houses, joined by connecting walls. The skin-covered houses were 3 to 4 m (9 to 13 feet) square, with log and crude-plank foundations and a wooden framework. Clay-lined hearths, wooden mortars, and large quantities of vegetable foods were found in the houses. A short distance away lay a wishbone-shaped structure associated with chewed bolo-plant leaves (used today to make a form of medicinal tea), mastodon bones, and other work debris. This may have been a work area.

Monte Verde
11800 to 12000 B.C.

The Monte Verde people exploited a wide range of vegetable foods, including wild potatoes; they also hunted small game and perhaps mammals such as extinct camels and mastodons (it is possible that they scavenged such meat, however) (Dillehay and Rossen, 2002). Monte Verde was in a forest, with abundant vegetable foods year-round. The site was almost certainly a long-term campsite. What is fascinating is that 90 percent of the stone artifacts are crude river cobbles. It is clear that wood was the most important raw material. It was certainly used for spears and digging sticks and for hafting stone scrapers, three of which have survived in their wooden handles. Sites yielding simple flaked stone artifacts like those from Monte Verde have been found elsewhere in South America, as far south as Patagonia, but this is the first place that anyone has been able to make more complete discoveries.

A Scenario for First Settlement

Assuming that the earliest evidence for human activity dates to well after 20,000 years ago, as most experts currently believe, we can describe a tentative scenario for first settlement, which goes as follows: Few human beings lived in frigid Beringia during the height of the last glaciation (Hoffecker, 2007). So far, there is no evidence that there were many people living in extreme northeast Siberia

FIGURE 6.5 Pre-Clovis artifacts from the Debra L. Friedkin site, Texas. (a) Preform for a lanceolate point. (b) Chopper/adze. (c) Discoidal flake core. (d) Broken flake with notch. (e) Graver (burin). (f–h) Retouched flakes. (i) Polished hematite fragment. (j) Bifacially retouched flake. (k, l) Broken flake and biface. (m–s) Broken blades and bladelets.

before 15,000 years ago. Somewhere around 12700 B.C., temperatures rose rapidly in the far north. The vast Laurentide ice sheet melted rapidly, releasing enormous amounts of freshwater into northern oceans. This may have been when the first human groups crossed the vanishing Bering land bridge and settled in Alaska. By this time, too, the ice-free corridor was already passable, even if it was not an attractive place to live. The rapidly warming climate may have drawn tiny numbers of Paleo-Indians southward into the heart of an uninhabited continent after 12700 B.C., through the widening gap between the ice sheets or along the Pacific continental shelf.

These initial forays into new lands must have involved a diversity of paths. Judging from Monte Verde and some other locations, the first settlers ranged widely and far to the south. Computer modeling offers new opportunities to examine possible paths along which first settlement occurred (Anderson and Gillam, 2000). Analyses based on the notion of "least cost" assume that people took the least arduous routes into unknown territory that gave them the best chance of finding food and stone for tool manufacture. Such analyses suggest that the Americas could have been traversed and been filled up by hunter-gatherer populations fairly quickly, perhaps in about 2,000 years from the date of first arrival. This process of settlement could have taken place linearly, with bands splitting off from one territory into another as population densities increased, along main lines of spread, with people then branching out into neighboring areas. However, the earliest known sites are scattered thinly over enormous regions, not in lines, which makes a form of "leapfrog model" more plausible, in which hunter-gatherer groups fissioned from one territory into another, often separated from the original one by long distances. This model would explain the wide separation of very early sites with uninhabited areas between them that were filled in by later generations.

The leapfrog model would explain why settlement took hold in some areas well before it occurred in others. Under this scenario, the well-known Clovis and other fluted point cultures, described later in this chapter, may well have been founder populations in hitherto unoccupied areas, while earlier groups had already leapfrogged their way through resource-rich areas to the southern extremities of the Americas.

After 11400 B.C., the world entered another near-glacial cold snap called the Younger Dryas (see Chapter 7). In most parts of the Americas, especially North America, the climate was probably relatively cold and arid. But a change in the jet stream path may have brought dry conditions to the Pacific Northwest but wetter, more favorable circumstances to the Great Plains and the Southwest, where the Clovis culture expanded over much of North America. People using fluted point technology may now have occupied many hitherto empty areas and adapted to a wide range of environments over several centuries. This process explains the increasing diversity of artifact forms as a result of what is called *stylistic drift*. Not that human populations were large or densely packed anywhere in the Americas. Most groups were isolated, with relatively few contacts with neighbors.

11400 B.C.

All this is, of course, still little more than a theoretical scenario. There is only one certainty: About 11200 B.C., the Clovis culture appears, marked by a veritable explosion in the number of archaeological sites throughout North America, from the California deserts to the Eastern Woodlands.

The Paleo-Indians: Clovis and Others

About 11200 B.C., the highly distinctive Clovis culture appeared all over eastern North America, on the Great Plains, and much farther afield. These Paleo-Indian people are the first well-documented inhabitants of the New World. Many questions still remain about their ancestry and lifeway, but what is certain, however, is that the Clovis culture was relatively short-lived. Judging from dated sites in western North America, most sites were occupied during the three centuries after 11200 B.C. We now move onto solid ground, for the archaeological record suddenly mushrooms from nothing to a well-documented scatter of locations from coast to coast in North America, with well-established, diverse Paleo-Indian occupation in Mesoamerica and Latin America as well (G. Haynes, 2002; Hofman and Graham, 1998).

Clovis
11200 to 10900 B.C.

The first Clovis sites to be discovered were big-game kills on the Great Plains, so, hardly surprisingly, they were seen as big-game hunters who lived off a diminishing number of large, now extinct Ice Age animals like the mammoth and mastodon. At Murray Springs, Arizona, for example, the people killed mammoth and bison, butchering them at separate locations, with a campsite nearby. Eleven bison died at Murray Springs, yielding enough meat to support up to 50 to 100 people, perhaps many fewer. Distinctive Clovis projectile points and other tools were found among the bones. At Naco, Arizona, no fewer than eight points lay in one mammoth carcass. Perhaps between 4 and 8 hunters, a fifth of a band of 20 to 40 people, killed or scavenged the great beast (Figure 6.7). The hunters partially dismembered their quarry, sometimes making piles of the disarticulated bones. The

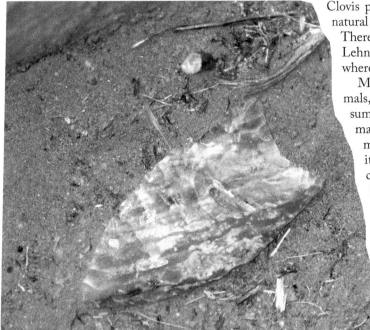

FIGURE 6.6 A Clovis point from an unknown location on the Great Plains. Length: c. 6 cm. (2.4 in.).

Clovis people who camped in Blackwater Draw, New Mexico, a natural arroyo trap, could drive large animals into swampy ground. There they took mammoth, bison, horse, camel, and deer. Lehner, also in Arizona, is another well-known waterside site, where Clovis hunters may have killed 13 mammoth in one hunt.

Many Clovis groups hunted both big game and smaller animals, besides foraging for wild vegetable foods during spring, summer, and fall (Cannon and Meltzer, 2004). But large animals may have been rare kills, sometimes of solitary mammoths. Their spear technology could not stop an elephant in its tracks—just wound it severely. They would stalk herds, concentrating on straying animals, sometimes perhaps driving them into swamps (for an extended discussion, see C. V. Haynes, 1982). The hunters would wound an animal, then take their time to kill it with thrusting spears. Like all hunter-gatherers, the Clovis people relied heavily on a broad range of animal and plant foods and adapted effortlessly to a wide variety of environments, from open plains and desert to woodland.

Like all Paleo-Indians, they were constantly on the move, using a portable tool kit that included bone, cordage, stone, and wood artifacts. The hunters traveled great distances for toolmaking stone, carrying it in core form for hundreds of kilometers. These cores were like a savings account, carried around so that flakes could be used to make finely pressure-flaked projectile points. The finished heads were mounted in wood or bone foreshafts set on the end of spear shafts. Once the spear penetrated an animal, the foreshaft would break off. The hunter could then rearm the spear with a new foreshaft in a few moments. Damaged points were resharpened and used again; some exceptionally large ones may even have been ceremonial artifacts.

The origins of Clovis technology are unknown but must lie ultimately in Upper Paleolithic big-game-hunting traditions in the Old World. Are there, then, archaeological links between Clovis artifacts and Stone Age tools made in the far north at the same time, or earlier? Distinctive Clovis points with or without fluted bases are found in all the Canadian provinces and throughout the rest of North America. In Alaska, the Broken Mammoth, Dry Creek, and Mesa artifacts include bifaces and other items that are reminiscent of early Paleo-Indian points and tools from temperate North America. There are still too few artifacts from any Alaskan site to make detailed, meaningful comparisons, but it seems increasingly likely that Clovis origins, and those of its immediate, and putative, ancestors, are among very early cultural traditions in Alaska. The Clovis point itself may have been an indigenous development, first fabricated south of the ice sheets and not in the Arctic at all (Tankersley, 1994).

People using the Clovis tool kit spread rapidly south of the ice sheets, covering enormous distances in a continent of very diverse environments. If the dates are to be trusted, then people colonized most of what is now the United States within a thousand years or so. As David Meltzer has pointed out (2008), population densities must have been low, the learning curve in unfamiliar environments very steep. Just learning the edible and medicinal properties of even some of the more than 30,000 plant varieties in North America would have required considerable trial and error.

Many of the Americas' natural environments are unpredictable, with food resources occurring in broadly separated patches. Under such circumstances, one would expect a rapid dispersal of hunter-gatherers across the landscape. Interestingly, caches of fine-grained toolmaking stone abandoned by Clovis groups have come to light in recent years. Presumably the people left the carefully dumped stone with the intention of returning to use it. But they never did, perhaps because they were constantly on the move in a landscape where there were no well-drawn territorial boundaries. By the same token, as Meltzer also argues, each group would have needed extensive, flexible social contacts, both to gain intelligence about food and water supplies and as a means of finding marriage partners. The widespread distribution of Clovis points across so much of the Americas may reflect such social networks in a world where one only encountered a few other people in the course of one's life. These circumstances did not last long. By 9000 B.C., well-defined regional projectile point forms had appeared across North America, many of them associated with distinctive cultural adaptations.

When we broaden our canvas to look at the Americas as a whole, it is clear that "Clovis," in a strict sense, is a North American phenomenon. The diverse environments of Central and South America were very different from environments to the north—wooded river basins, temperate and tropical seacoasts, tropical lowlands, rain forests, and the southern pampas. Three different regions of South America have yielded radiocarbon-dated sequences that begin at about the same time as Clovis—maritime foragers along the Pacific coast, guanaco hunters on the southern pampas, and tropical forest foragers in the eastern tropical lowlands of Brazil. All of these finds contradict a common theory of earlier decades that had the first settlers concentrated in open, temperate habitats. Under that rubric, only after about 9000 B.C. did people diversify into other environments. As for the rain forest, hunter-gatherers did not settle there until farming began in about 3000 B.C. This scenario is just plain wrong.

Few well-documented sites contemporary with Clovis are known from South America. Two sites on the southern Peruvian coast were occupied by broad-spectrum hunter-gatherers as early as 9200 to 7000 B.C., while human skeletons from late Paleo-Indian burials on the north coast date to between 8500 and 6500 B.C. Guanaco and smaller game were taken by hunters living in the Fell Cave area of southern Patagonia dating to between 19000 and 8300 B.C. At least 12 Paleo-Indian sites in southeastern and northeastern Brazil date to between 9500 and 6500 B.C., some of them with human skeletons associated with burned animal and plant foods, as well as a wide range of stone tools, among them triangular and stemmed points. There are contemporary sites from the Lower Amazon region, hitherto considered to be much later. The Caverna da Pedra Pintada lies in the Amazon basin near the town of Monte Alegre in northern Brazil (Figure 6.7). Anna Roosevelt of Chicago's Field Museum found stone projectile points, as well as charred plant and animal remains, in levels radiocarbon-dated to about 9000 B.C. Unlike other early groups, the inhabitants of this site subsisted in a humid and forested tropical environment, where plant foods such as Brazil nuts and palm seeds were all-important. According to Roosevelt (1996), the earliest inhabitants of the cave visited the site irregularly over a period of 1,200 years—evidence for a considerable diversity of human culture in the Americas from the time of first settlement onward.

Everything points to a fast radiation of people throughout the Americas sometime after 12000 B.C. Within a short time, and certainly by 8000 B.C., distinct regional cultures appeared in many parts of the hemisphere, but we still know almost nothing of the very first societies that moved south of the ice sheets by land, and perhaps by sea. Nor do we know if different cultures with distinct adaptations moved southward, or whether, as we suspect, the founder groups adapted with

Peruvian coast
9200 B.C.

Caverna da Pedra Pintada
c. 9000 B.C.

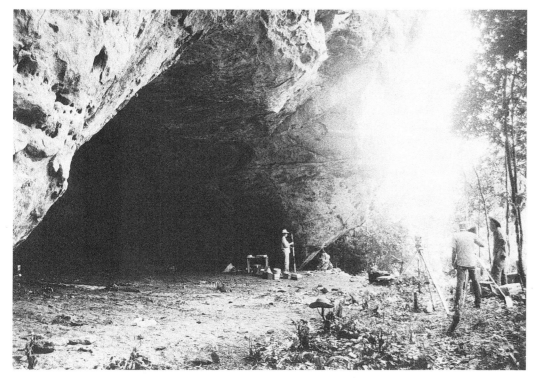

FIGURE 6.7 Excavations at Caverna da Pedra Pintada, Brazil, an early settlement in a rain forest environment. This site shatters stereotypes of the first Americans as purely big-game hunters.

rapid brilliance to an astounding diversity of changing natural environments. In many areas with relatively thin vegetable resources, the first settlers may well have concentrated on game, large and small. In others, like coastal southern California, mollusks may have served as a reliable winter food. South of the Rio Grande, it seems likely that plant foods were of fundamental importance in many different environments. Certainly the roots of the extraordinary expertise of Native Americans with wild and domesticated plant foods came from deep in the past and developed rapidly soon after first settlement.

This scenario for first settlement is almost as inadequately documented as those espousing earlier dates. However, the cumulative sum of the limited data tends to support rather than undermine it (Meltzer, 2008).

Big-Game Extinctions

c. 10900 B.C.

The Clovis people flourished for about 300 years and then, about 11000 B.C., evolved into a multitude of hunting-and-gathering cultures. This sudden change coincides with one of the great mysteries of modern science: the catastrophic extinction of Ice Age big-game animals in the Americas. Many large animals became extinct throughout the world at this time but nowhere as drastically as in the Americas. Three-quarters of the large mammalian genera there vanished abruptly at the end of the Pleistocene (Grayson and Meltzer, 2002). Speculations about this extinction have been long and lively. One long-established theory argues that the large mammals were killed off by the Paleo-Indian bands' intensive hunting, as they preyed on large herds of animals that formerly had had relatively few predators to control their populations. In fact, many Pleistocene animals disappeared before the heyday of the Paleo-Indians. Besides, the Indians existed in very small numbers, and they had other subsistence activities as well. Surely, the animals would have adapted to changed conditions and new dangers. Instead, the extinctions accelerated after the hunters had been around for a while; the modern bison, for example, never adapted to mounted hunters.

Another hypothesis argues that changing environments, spreading aridity, and shrinking habitats for big game after the Ice Age may have reduced the mammalian population drastically. This theory faces strong objections, too. The very animals that became extinct had already survived enormous fluctuations in Pleistocene climate without harm. If they had once migrated into more hospitable habitats, they could have done so again. Furthermore, the animals that became extinct were not just the browsers; they were selected from all types of habitat. This hypothesis assumes that desiccation leads to mass starvation in game populations, an idea refuted by ecological research in Africa. What actually occurs is that the smaller species and those with lower growth rates adapt to the less favorable conditions, leaving the population changed but not defunct.

A third hypothesis cites the great variation in mean temperatures at the end of the Pleistocene as a primary cause of extinction. In both the New and Old Worlds, the more pronounced seasonal temperature contrasts in temperature climates would have been harder on the young of species that are born in small litters, after long gestation periods, and at fixed times of the year. These traits are characteristic of larger mammals, precisely those that became extinct. The less equable climate at the end of the Pleistocene, then, would have been a major cause of late Pleistocene extinctions in North America (Grayson, 2007).

All three hypotheses have some validity. Complex variables must have affected the steps that led to extinction, with intricate feedback among the effects of intensive big-game hunting, changing ecology, and the intolerance of some mammalian species to seasonal contrasts in weather. It may be that the hunters, being persistent predators, were one of the final variables, causing more drastic mammalian extinctions than might otherwise have occurred.

Later Hunters and Gatherers

As the world climate warmed up rapidly at the end of the last glaciation, American environments changed drastically. The great ice sheets of the north shrank, mountain snow lines and sea levels rose, and forest vegetation established itself in hitherto glaciated regions. If one word can be used to describe these momentous changes, it is diversity, a great diversity of local environments: lush river floodplains, great deserts, grassy plains, and miles upon miles of boreal and deciduous woodland. The late Paleo-Indians and their successors adapted to this great diversity with brilliant success and ingenuity (see a summary in Fagan, 2005a, 2011).

In general, the western and southwestern United States became drier, but the East Coast and much of the Midwest became densely forested. The large Pleistocene mammals became extinct, but the bison remained a major source of food. In the Southeast, the more favorable climate brought drier conditions, which meant less standing water, markedly seasonal rainfalls, and specialization among humans in fishing or intensive gathering. Many areas had much economic diversity, as we see among the desert forager peoples of the Tehuacán Valley in Mexico. They flourished between 10000 and 7000 B.C., at the same time that hunter-gatherers in the Pacific Northwest were probably taking advantage of seasonal salmon runs in the fast-moving rivers.

North American climate and sea levels seem to have coincided with social change in many areas, which was still climaxing as European explorers and colonists arrived in the Americas. The human population of North America was still sparse, scattered in myriad isolated hunter-gatherer bands. Judging from sites in many areas, people spent most of the year living in small family groups and exploiting large hunting territories. They may have come together with their neighbors for a few weeks during the summer months at favored locations near rivers or nut groves. The bands would have held ceremonies, arranged marriages, and traded fine-grained rocks and other commodities. Then they would have gone their separate ways, following migrating game, trapping small animals, and foraging for wild vegetable foods.

At first there was plenty of vacant territory to go around, continues this hypothetical scenario. In time, natural population growth and the low carrying capacity of the land combined to restrict mobility. Several long-term adaptive trends developed.

First, the extinction of the Ice Age megafauna meant that hunters focused even more on smaller mammals, especially the white-tailed deer. Inevitably, people turned to alternative food sources, including wild vegetable foods, birds, mollusks, and fish. Wild vegetable foods were a particularly favored dietary source, especially in areas like river valley bottoms and lakeshores, where they were seasonally abundant and diverse. From the earliest times, Native Americans developed a remarkable expertise with wild plant foods, which preadapted them in later millennia to the cultivation of native grasses and tubers.

Second, there was a long-term trend toward less mobility and toward base camps that were occupied for many months of the year. These served as anchors for larger territories, which were exploited seasonally from outlying settlements. This settlement pattern was by no means universal, but it took hold in areas where there was an unusual diversity of food resources. Examples of base settlements are to be found in the desert West, in midwestern and southeastern river valleys, and in the Northeast.

Third, some areas witnessed a move toward sedentary settlement, occupation of the same settlement year-round or for most of the year. This type of settlement is different from a base camp used on a seasonal basis, even if the latter lasts for many months. It implies a permanent settlement within a highly restricted territory, a settlement lying within easy reach of sufficient game, vegetable, and aquatic resources that enables the occupants to stay through every season of the year. Sedentary settlement is hard to identify in the archaeological record, except by the presence of substantial dwellings or cemeteries. Such occupation was well established in some midwestern river valley bottoms by 2000 B.C. and perhaps in favored coastal areas, such as southern California and the Pacific Northwest, somewhat later.

These trends coincided with accelerating population growth in more favored areas after 2000 B.C. Such was the diversity of North American environments in Holocene times that only a few relatively limited areas witnessed sedentary settlement and large-scale population growth. Perhaps it is no coincidence that it was in some of these areas, notably midwestern and southeastern river valleys and the Southwest, that people turned to the cultivation of domesticated plants.

Plains Hunters

In only one region—the arid grasslands from the frontiers of Alaska to the Gulf of Mexico—did big-game hunting survive. This was the "great bison belt," which lay in the rain shadow of the western mountains. The short-grass range of the plains was an ideal environment for the bison, one of the few Ice Age big-game species to adapt to Holocene conditions. The postglacial descendants of the Ice Age steppe bison have increased digestive efficiency to cope with the high-fiber, low-nutrient dead grass of winter. They can feed in deep snow and are less selective eaters than many of the Ice Age species that died out. By 10500 B.C., bison were the dominant species in all archaeological sites in the bison belt.

Plains hunting cultures
10900 B.C. onward

At first glance, the Great Plains appear homogeneous, even monotonous. Closer examination reveals many subtle differences: stream courses and water holes where game congregated, places where longer grass and seasonal water favored larger bison herds. The late Paleo-Indians and their successors, who preyed on the herds right into historic times, could survive only by a careful, planned utilization of the plains' complex ecosystem (Wood, 1998).

After 10000 B.C., numerous variations of bison-hunting cultures appeared on the plains, all of them using portable tool kits that bear a strong resemblance to those of their Clovis ancestors. Stone-tipped

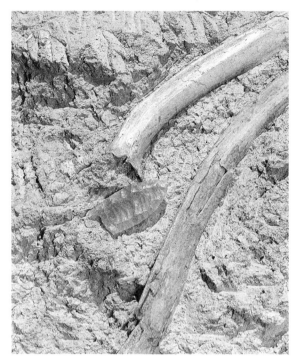

FIGURE 6.8   A Paleo-Indian Folsom point from Folsom, New Mexico, lying next to two ribs of an extinct bison. This find (c. 10500 B.C.) proved that humans were contemporary with extinct animals in North America.

projectile points with carefully thinned and ground bases made spear-throwers and spears effective weapons for bison hunting. At least seven major forms are known, with names like Eden, Folsom, Plainview, and Scottsbluff—to mention only a few (Meltzer, 2006) (Figure 6.8). Whether all these forms actually represent distinct cultural entities is a matter of controversy. The entire Paleo-Indian tool kit was highly portable and capable of being used for a wide variety of purposes, everything from woodworking to bison butchery. Many plains sites are kill locations, strategic places where mass game drives could be organized. Such drives were far from daily events, perhaps taking place every couple of years or so. To pursue bison on foot meant days of patient stalking and an intimate knowledge of the animals' habits. Perhaps several bands would cooperate in a game drive. They would encircle a few beasts or, more often, stampede a herd into a swamp or a narrow defile. In some cases, they would drive the frightened animals over a cliff or into dune areas. The archaeological evidence for such activities comes from a series of sites, among them the Agate Basin site in eastern Wyoming, where, judging from the age of the animals, the hunters apparently maneuvered 10 to 20 animals into an arroyo bottom in late February or early March (Frison, 2010). The hunters then drove them upstream until they reached a natural trap in the gully, where the confused bison could be killed with stone-tipped spears.

Olsen-Chubbuck
c. 7000 B.C.

The Olsen-Chubbuck site in Colorado is an example of a kill site, where approximately 200 bison of all ages were stampeded into a deep, narrow arroyo, probably during the summer or fall (Wheat, 1972). Because the skeletons of the ancient bison faced north, the excavators concluded that the wind was blowing from the south on the day of the hunt (Figure 6.9). The stampeding herd was driven into a gully and could not catch the scent of the people waiting for them at the arroyo. The hunters' artifacts were scattered around the carcasses of their quarry: scraping tools, stone knives, and flakes used to dismember the bison.

Garnsey
A.D. 1540

Smaller communal hunts were probably much more commonplace. John Speth's (1983) excavations at Garnsey, New Mexico, chronicle such a kill. About 400 years ago, a group of hunters visited a small gully where they knew bison would congregate in late March or early April. Instead of killing every animal on sight, they tended to concentrate on the males because, Speth believes, male bison are in better condition in the spring, when their bone marrow has a higher fat content. Fatty meat is an important source of energy and essential fatty acids, and is difficult to come by after the lean winter months. So if Garnsey hunters killed a cow, they consumed only the choice, fatty parts.

FIGURE 6.9   The Head-Smashed-In buffalo jump, Alberta, Canada, a strategic location where hunters stamped the great beasts to their deaths for thousands of years.

Bison hunting was practiced on the plains right up to the advent of the horse and the repeating rifle, but Paleo-Indian peoples flourished throughout North America. Clovis-like projectile points are known from many locations in the East. Herds of caribou may have provided sustenance in northern sites around the Great Lakes and in the Northeast at locations such as present-day Robert, Nova Scotia, where caribou hunters flourished (Meltzer, 1988). Paleo-Indian hunting-and-gathering economies may have varied a great deal from region to region, some bands specializing more heavily in big game, others in fishing or gathering, depending on the resources available in each territory. This diversity is reflected in Paleo-Indian archaeological sites, which vary from kill locations to shell middens. That hunting was important in places where large game was abundant seems unquestionable, but this activity diminished rapidly in importance as the big game became extinct.

The Desert West

Economic emphasis shifted in the arid West and Southwest. As big game became scarce, many hunting bands relied more heavily on wild vegetable foods that required much more energy to collect and process than game meat. In the Great Basin, smaller animals such as rabbits, squirrels, and deer became more common prey.

FIGURE 6.10 A hunter-gatherer group in the northern Great Basin harvesting bitterroot in early summer. Roots were an important food source for many foraging societies.

At the same time, gathering of vegetable foods grew to dominate economic life, combined with some fishing and, in maritime areas, exploitation of shellfish. We are fortunate that arid climates in Utah, Nevada, and elsewhere have preserved many plant and vegetable foods eaten by these early hunter-gatherers. By 9000 B.C., a distinctive, desertlike form of archaic culture had been developed over much of the western United States by small bands camping in caves, rock shelters, and temporary sites (Grayson, 2011; Simms, 2008).

Excavations at later sites like Danger Cave in Utah and the Gypsum and Lovelock sites in Nevada reveal that the hunters were making nets, mats, and baskets, as well as rope (Figures 6.10 and 6.11) (Beck, 1999; Jennings, 1957). Hogup Cave in Utah has yielded one of the world's most complete and longest archaeological culture sequences (Aikens, 1970). The site displays gradual adaptations at one settlement, changing it from a base camp to a short-stay camp that was associated with other base camps or with horticultural villages after people learned how to produce food. At all these sites, the inhabitants used digging sticks to uproot edible tubers, and much of their tool kit consisted of grinding stones used in preparing vegetable foods. Most Great Basin peoples were obliged to be constantly on the move, searching for different vegetable foods as they came into season and camping near scanty water supplies. For example, the deposits at Gatecliff Rock Shelter near Austin, Nevada, are 12.1 m (40 feet) deep and span more than 8,000 years of human occupation. The inhabitants lived by valley side streams in the winter, then moved up to the shelter in the summer, gathering piñon nuts on the mountain slopes and hunting game, just as Shoshone Indians did in recent times (Kelly, 2001; D. Thomas and Bettinger, 1983).

Hogup Cave

Gatecliff
6000 B.C. onward

Most western North American societies continued to live by hunting and foraging right up to European contact. It was only in the most favored areas that people could stay in one place for months on end. One such location was Lovelock Cave in Nevada, where the base camp overlooked a lake rich in fish and waterfowl. The people hunted their prey with bows and arrows, using extremely lifelike reed duck decoys. Human feces show that over 90 percent of the Lovelock

FIGURE 6.11 Deerskin moccasins C. A.D.500, found in Hogup Cave, Utah..

inhabitants' diet came from the lake area, including wetland grasses, fish such as chub, and ducks and mud hens (Grayson, 2011).

The southern California coast was another challenging area, first exploited by small bands combining fishing with marine mammal hunting as early as 11000 B.C. The coastal population remained sparse except in favored areas, where much more elaborate societies evolved (Erlandson, 1994, 2001). For example, the historic Chumash people of the Santa Barbara Channel area congregated in large, more or less permanent villages ruled by local chiefs, who maintained trading contacts between offshore islands and the mainland (Arnold, 2001). Such sedentism was possible because of exceptional resource diversity, but unpredictable rainfall made large communities a high-risk proposition and required conservative adaptations to the semiarid environment.

From November to March, the Chumash subsisted on dried meat and stored vegetable foods. They also collected shellfish and caught fish in the dense kelp beds close inshore. Come spring, they ranged far afield, collecting plants and tubers. Summer brought tuna and other warm-water fish to local waters. The people caught enormous quantities of fish from their canoes. Pine nuts and acorns were gathered in the fall and stored for the leaner months ahead. The Chumash hunted marine mammals and scavenged stranded whales whenever the opportunity arose. This maritime bounty resulted from an upwelling that replenishes the surface layers of the Santa Barbara Channel with nutrients and zooplankton. At least 125 fish species flourished in local waters, part of an incredibly diverse range of food resources that enabled not only relatively sedentary settlement but also higher population densities—as many as 15,000 people living near the shores of the channel and on the offshore islands at the time of European contact. However, periodic strong El Niños and severe droughts made life precarious, even in good years, and there is evidence of fighting between different groups, perhaps over territory and resources.

Eastern North America

Whereas the Great Plains are dominated by grasslands, eastern North America, the region from the Mississippi Valley eastward, is covered by deciduous woodlands and the Southeast by evergreen forest. Superficially, this could be considered a homogeneous natural environment with no sharp geographic barriers to interaction among different human groups, but in fact, the area includes an almost bewildering array of microenvironments. As a result, it is almost impossible to generalize about cultural developments after first settlement before 11500 B.C.

Paleo-Indian bands settled widely over the Eastern Woodlands from as far north as Nova Scotia to southern Florida (Meltzer, 2008). They combined hunting with foraging, turning to the pursuit of the white-tailed deer and other small mammals as the Ice Age megafauna van
11000 B.C. ished. By 11000 B.C., a widespread shift to more generalized hunting and gathering was underway, as the peoples of the Eastern Woodlands exploited a broad variety of foods: forest resources, like gray squirrels and annual nut harvests, and pioneer seed-bearing grasses. It seems certain that small game, fish, mollusks, and vegetable foods assumed greater importance in the eastern diet after about 10500 B.C. Inhabitants were part of the broad-spectrum hunting-and-gathering tradition known as the *Archaic*, which lasted until about 1000 B.C. in many areas (Sassaman and Anderson, 1996).

During the many millennia of the Archaic, there was a long-term trend toward increased efficiency and success in exploiting forest and river valley resources. The Archaic has been subdivided into early, middle, and late stages on the basis of stylistic changes in projectile points and the introduction of slate tools, copper artifacts, and other technological innovations (see Griffin, 1967, for details), but the basic patterns of Archaic life were established early on and are known to us from excavations and surveys in northeastern Arkansas and the Little Tennessee River valley (J. Chapman, 1994).

Dalton The Dalton Archaic tradition flourished over a wide area of the Southeast and the Midwest from
9950 to 7900 B.C. about 9950 to 7900 B.C. Dan and Phyllis Morse (1983) argue that in northeastern Arkansas, Dalton band organization allowed a network of stable local family bands of 20 to 30 people who regularly used base camps centered on watershed territories (Figure 6.12). There they exploited easily accessible shallow-water fish, vegetable foods, seasonal nut harvests, and deer; the women married into neighboring bands in nearby river valleys, thereby maintaining trading links between each area drained by a river system, contacts that ensured ample supplies of fine-grained chert over large areas (see also Anderson and Sassaman, 1996).

6000 to 4000 B.C. By about 6000 B.C., warmer and drier climates were developing in the East, culminating between 4500 and 4000 B.C. The major rivers of the Midwest and the Southeast stabilized their courses, and the population densities were still low. The highest concentrations of population were in major river valley bottoms and lakeshores, which offered the greatest diversity of aquatic, game, and vegetable

FIGURE 6.12 Artist's reconstruction of an Archaic camp on the Little Tennessee River (c. 6300 B.C.), which gives a general impression of foraging lifeways in a woodland environment after the Ice Age.

foods. In some favored areas, there was a slow trend toward living within more circumscribed territories and toward more sedentary settlement, made possible by an abundant constellation of seasonal foods. The famous Koster site in the Midwest's Illinois Valley chronicles this trend (see Site box).

A similar trend appears at other midwestern sites, among them the Modoc Rock Shelter near the Mississippi River (Brown and Phillips, 1983; Fowler, 1958). Modoc was occupied between about 8000 and 2000 B.C. As time went on, it became more and more of a base camp, where people lived for much of the year while they caught fish and exploited nut harvests. Both Koster and Modoc show that the middle Archaic adaptation was a conservative one, requiring at least a degree of careful scheduling to maximize the potential of nut harvests and to capitalize on the game that fed on the rich forest mast (undergrowth) each fall.

By about 2500 B.C., there had been a dramatic increase in the use of riverine resources over much of the Southeast and the Midwest, when stabilized river bottoms provided an abundance of oxbow lakes and swamps where fish abounded and native grasses, shellfish, and other foods were to be found. Some of the river valleys lay on seasonal waterfowl migration routes, too, providing a bounty of food in spring and fall. This enhancement of aquatic habitats increased potential food supplies over long sections of river floodplains. In response, many groups adopted more sedentary lifeways, perhaps best described as a shift toward centrally based wandering, which involved a seasonally mobile lifeway and a regular return to the same base location for much of each year, especially during the summers.

Archaic populations in the East increased sharply after 4000 B.C., especially in favored areas. Rising sea levels and warming ocean temperatures allowed a steady northward expansion of fish and shellfish habitats. Flooded estuaries allowed more upriver fish runs in spring and fall. Nut-bearing forests spread farther north, into parts of the Great Lakes region, and river valley bottoms were exceptionally diverse and rich environments for Archaic hunter-gatherers.

In all probability, Archaic population growth was a response not only to environmental change but also to technological and subsistence advances, as well as new settlement patterns that took advantage of new riverine environments. The more sedentary living that accompanied the growth in many areas allowed people to store nuts and other winter foods on a much larger scale than if they were always on the move. This storage, in turn, created larger food surpluses, the ability to support higher population densities year-round, and opportunities for kin groups and individuals to play important roles in controlling labor and the redistribution of food and luxury goods. By the same token, people lived within more restricted territories, and there was far more local cultural variation.

There were also long-term changes in the ways people interacted with one another and their neighbors. The smaller territories inhabited by more people contained a diversity of food resources and raw materials, but there was always something lacking. Such items as obsidian for toolmaking had to be sought elsewhere, by a special journey or regular economic and social contacts with groups living nearer to the sources of what was needed. Over time, these trading connections assumed ever greater importance in the year-round. They became a source not only of valued possessions and raw materials but also of social connections and prestige—a way of maintaining "diplomatic" relations with the outside world. These interactions also affected population densities, especially when the demand for prestige items, such as copper objects or seashells, soared. More and more hands would be needed to increase the output of food and trade goods. The intensification of hunting and foraging to meet these demands would lead to population increases—and to the emergence of social ranks based on prestige and social and economic power within previously egalitarian societies.

The late Archaic witnessed much greater regional variety in hunter-gatherer culture in the East (B. Smith, 1986). The so-called Central Riverine Archaic was the most developed of all eastern late

---

SiTE > Koster, Illinois <

The famous Koster site in the Illinois River valley, with its 14 stratified occupation levels separated by sterile layers, provides an extraordinary chronicle of human exploitation of a midwestern river valley from about 7500 B.C. until A.D. 1200 (Figure 6.13) (Struever and Holton, 1979). The first visitors to camp at Koster were Paleo-Indians, who visited the locality occasionally. By about 6500 B.C., an early Archaic camp at Koster covered about 0.3 ha (0.75 acre). This was a seasonal camp with temporary buildings, visited by an extended family group of about 25 people who came to the same site every few years over many centuries, perhaps to exploit rich fall nut harvests. Between 5600 and 5000 B.C., a large permanent camp with longhouses covered in hides or mats came into use; the inhabitants focused on a narrow spectrum of abundant foods throughout much of the year. The substantial dwellings were occupied for most if not all the year, the settlement covering about 0.7 ha (1.75 acres). During spring and summer, the inhabitants took thousands of fish, gathering freshwater mussels and hickory nuts in fall and migratory birds in spring. Perhaps the people moved to the nearby uplands to hunt deer. As long as this middle Archaic population remained stable, they could find most of their food resources within 5 km (3 miles) of their settlement.

Horizon 6 at Koster dates to between 3900 and 2800 B.C., a time when people lived there year-round. The village covered about 2 ha (5 acres), perhaps housing 100 to 150 people. Stuart Struever and his colleagues found six houses, built on sunken earthen floors that were cut like shallow terraces about 45 cm (18 inches) into a hill slope. The builders erected rows of stout posts along the long walls, then filled in the gaps between them with woven brush and clay. Apparently they covered the ends with skins, mats, or more brush. Each dwelling covered between 12 and 15 sq. m (96 and 140 sq. feet), sufficient space for a nuclear family.

The food remains from this settlement reveal striking contrasts with earlier Archaic diet in the Illinois Valley. Earlier fisherfolk had concentrated mainly on fish species that preferred fast-moving river water. Their Horizon 6 successors exploited the shallow backwater lakes and swamps that now abounded near Koster. They speared and netted vast numbers of sluggish, shallow-water fish like bass, buffalo fish, and catfish, species that can be eaten fresh or be dried or smoked for consumption during the winter. Dozens of fish could also be taken by poisoning the water with the chemicals in powdered hickory nut husks, or by driving fish into oxygen-starved pools where they could be scooped up with baskets. One Illinois fisheries biologist has estimated that Koster's inhabitants could have taken between 136 and 272 kg (300 and 600 pounds) of fish flesh per acre every year from backwater lakes that covered hundreds of acres. The same shallow lakes also contained rich mollusk beds that could be used as a supplementary food source.

Like their predecessors, the people relied on the fall hickory and acorn harvests, as well as black walnuts, pecans, and hazelnuts. But they now exploited many more seed plants, including marsh elder (sumpweed), a swampside grass, grinding the seeds with stone pestles and mortars. The hunters took deer and other small mammals, but they also harvested another seasonal food—waterfowl that paused to feed and rest on the shallow lakes of the Illinois Valley during spring and fall migrations. The Illinois River is on the Mississippi flyway, the narrow migration route used by millions of waterfowl flying north and south to and from their Canadian breeding grounds each year. The Koster people could take hundreds of ducks, geese, and other migrants with bows, or by trapping them with light, weighted nets cast over sleeping birds, or by using silently paddled canoes to drive them into waiting cages during stealthy dawn raids.

Koster Horizon 6 saw the exploitation of a much broader spectrum of animal, aquatic, and vegetable foods. This implies larger food surpluses used to feed more people. Enhanced food procurement abilities coincide with more commonplace sedentary occupation, perhaps resulting in part from even more restricted territorial mobility than in the middle Archaic.

The Koster excavations yielded a treasure trove of chronological information that provided a framework for studying major changes in Native American society over many thousands of years. Later cultural resource management investigations have discovered other locations occupied over long periods of time, in Ohio and elsewhere, but they remain unpublished.

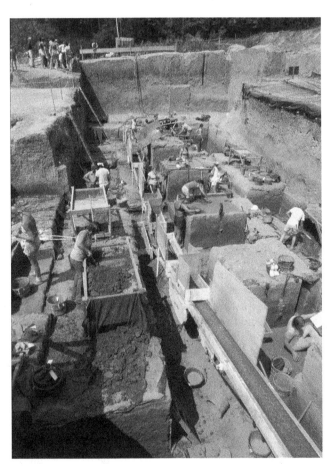

FIGURE 6.13 Excavations at Koster, Illinois.

Archaic traditions, for it was centered in midwestern and southeastern river valleys with a super-abundance of aquatic, game, and vegetable foods. This form of Archaic culture is well documented at the famous Koster site (see Site box).

Koster
7580 B.C. to A.D. 1200

Similar broad-spectrum exploitation is found at other midwestern sites, among them the celebrated Indian Knoll site in Kentucky (Webb, 1974), which has yielded more than 1,000 burials. Judging from these graves, the people still lived in fairly egalitarian societies, even if a few individuals were buried with prized possessions traded from afar, such as turtleshell ornaments or copper ornaments from Lake Superior (Figure 6.14) (for other middle and late Archaic sites, see Jeffries, 1987; Winters, 1967).

By 4000 B.C., the diverse hunter-gatherer populations of the East were living under very different social conditions from those of their remote ancestors; in territories with restricted boundaries, they cherished tenuous social and economic links that connected individual to individual, kin to kin, through valleys and entire drainages, over hundreds, even thousands of miles of North America. The long-distance exchange of materials associated with these networks first appeared about 4000 B.C. and escalated over the next 3,000 years. Lake Superior copper and hematite, Atlantic and Gulf Coast seashells, jasper from eastern Pennsylvania, chert and other fine-grained rocks—all these materials were exchanged between individuals just as obsidian was in ancient Southwest Asia (for Southwest Asian obsidian trade, see Chapter 9).

4000 B.C.

As studies of Lake Superior copper have shown, exotic artifacts and materials acquired greater prestige the farther they were traded. Within this context of regular social gatherings and exchanges, a greater degree of social differentiation based on reciprocity may have developed in late Archaic society. This may have been nothing more than a ranking between younger and older members of society or perhaps the emergence of one kin group as the "ranking" one. Judging from burial customs, both kin-based and individual social ranking took place within a context of increasingly elaborate ritual life.

More intensive exploitation of food resources (even some cultivation of native plants), greater sedentism, regular social interaction and long-distance exchange, increased ceremonialism—all these were the culminating elements in late Archaic life that were to persist into the last few centuries B.C., when new, much more elaborate burial customs appeared in the Eastern Woodlands (see Chapter 13). In some areas of the Northeast and eastern Canada, much of the Archaic hunter-gatherer tradition survived until modern times, when people came into contact with European explorers.

Specialized Foraging Societies in Central and South America

The hunter-gatherers of the central and southern portions of the New World enjoyed a wide variety of specialized adaptations after 10000 B.C. Sites of these specialized hunter-gatherer groups have been excavated from Mexico to Tierra del Fuego. One characteristic adaptation has been identified in the Andes, and another flourished on the uplands of eastern Brazil (Moseley, 2000; Rick, 1980). As in North America, intensified hunting and gathering concentrated the human population in favored localities such as lakeshores and seacoasts, where resources were unusually abundant.

Sophisticated hunting-and-gathering strategies ensured food at all seasons. Kent Flannery (1968) has shown, for instance, that the hunter-gatherers of the Tehuacán Valley in Mexico had a regular, almost scheduled, annual round of hunting-and-gathering activities that caused the population to gather in large camps during the plentiful season and scatter into small groups during the lean months. The people obtained a balanced diet by using different food-procurement systems that varied in importance with the time of year. In some areas of Mesoamerica and on the coast and the highland Andes, hunter-gatherer bands began to experiment with the deliberate planting of vegetable foods, perhaps in attempts to expand the areas in which certain favored vegetable foods were found. These experiments became one of the vehicles of dynamic culture change that resulted from the first development of agriculture in the Americas (see Chapter 13).

Along the coasts of Ecuador and Peru, hunter-gatherer societies exploited the rich inshore Pacific fisheries, gathered shellfish, and collected wild plant foods, a resource base so varied and locally abundant that many groups were able to live in semisedentary settlements as early as 8000 B.C. Shellfish collecting dates to as early as 10200 B.C. along the Peruvian coast, but most early foraging sites date to after 9500 B.C. Maritime economies expanded and flourished during the sixth millennium B.C., with the first mounds appearing in villages known mainly from their shell middens. Even as early as 9000 to 8000 B.C., anchovies were already important, assuming even greater significance with the development of netting methods when Holocene sea levels stabilized after 6000 B.C.

The southernmost extremities of South America were inhabited until recent times by scattered bands of hunters and fisherfolk. The Ona, Yaghan, and Alacaluf peoples were vividly described by early missionaries who settled among them. They lived in small bands, using only the crudest shelters of skins or grass and driftwood, with nothing but guanaco skin for body covering during the height of the Antarctic winter. Shellfish, some game, fruits, berries, and fish provided a simple diet; and for tools they had none of the more sophisticated weapons made by more northern hunters. Tierra del Fuego, however, was occupied remarkably early, and it is thought that the Fuegian tradition began as early as 4000 B.C., if not earlier. Many roots of these most southerly Native Americans lay in early foraging cultures that elsewhere had been replaced thousands of years before by more advanced farming cultures.

Aleuts and Inuit (Eskimo)

We started the story of the first Americans with Alaska, and we now end with a brief return to arctic latitudes to trace the origins of the Aleuts and the Inuit, whose remarkable hunter-gatherer cultures survived long beyond European contact and into recent times (Dumond and Bland, 1995; McGhee, 1996). The origins of both the Aleut and the Inuit go back many thousands of years into prehistory, and their ultimate ancestry may lie both in Asian roots and in local cultural evolution. The differences between the two groups are more cultural than physical and reflect varied adaptations to arctic maritime environments. It is logical to end this chapter with the Arctic, for the Inuit were the first Native Americans to come into contact with Europeans, in Greenland and in the extreme continental Northeast (Dumond, 1987).

Paleoarctic
9000 B.C. to 7000 B.C.

By 9000 B.C., a small but diverse population of tundra-dwelling hunter-gatherers flourished along the shores of the Bering Strait and throughout Alaska. Little is known of these "Paleoarctic" people, except for their diminutive stone microblades, which have some connections with contemporary cultures in Siberia. Nor is their relationship with earlier cultural traditions in Alaska understood. Paleoarctic people, culture, and language may be the ancestor of both the Inuit and the Aleut culture and language. Both peoples are the most Asian of all indigenous Americans. By 7000 B.C., these two peoples had moved south as far as the Alaska Peninsula. Only a millennium later, they had settled in the Aleutian Islands.

More cultural diversity developed in the Arctic around 4000 B.C., as specialized adaptations developed on the coast and in the interior, and some Native American groups moved northward into formerly glaciated regions in the interior. On the Pacific coast and in the eastern Aleutians, the Aleutian tradition first appeared at about this time. The Aleuts have been in their island homeland twice as long as the Inuit have been in Greenland. Their ancestors entered the archipelago at a time when the sea level was lower than it is today. Their ancestry is perhaps in the Norton tradition (explained later in this section; Dumond, 1987). The earliest occupation dates to approximately 6700 B.C. at Anangula,

Anangula
6700 B.C.

about a third of the way along the chain, at the terminus of the Bering land bridge. Anangula lies on a cliff 20 m (65.5 feet) above sea level and was probably occupied for at least 500 years by an estimated group of at least 100 (Dumond and Bland, 1995). The inhabitants lived by fishing, sea-mammal hunting, and fowling—an ideal strategy for an isolated, stable marine environment. The nearby, later site of Chaluka carries the story of Aleutian occupation up to recent times. Radiocarbon dates suggest that the eastern and western ends of the Aleutian archipelago were occupied by approximately 1000 B.C., the people expanding outward from the Anangula area as the population density grew.

Arctic Small Tool tradition
2300 to 1500 B.C.

The origins of the Inuit (Eskimo) cultural tradition of modern times may lie in the Arctic Small Tool tradition, a distinctive small-artifact technology that appeared in Alaska approximately 2300 B.C. The Arctic Small Tool people may have had strong connections with Siberia, and they are thought to have been nomadic land-mammal hunters who preyed on caribou and musk-ox. Some settled in Alaska; others had wandered as far east as Greenland by 2000 B.C., becoming the first people to settle in the eastern Arctic. The eastern Small Tool tradition eventually evolved into the long-lived Thule tradition, whose people were the first Native Americans to come into contact with Europeans (Maxwell, 1985; Schledermann, 1990).

Norton tradition
500 B.C.

The Arctic Small Tool tradition began to disappear in Alaska in about 1500 B.C., to be replaced by cultures based on the intensive hunting of both sea mammals and land animals. These cultures, called the Norton tradition, gave rise in turn to the Thule tradition, which is thought to have originated among whale hunters in the Bering Strait. Thule first emerged in the first millennium A.D. and developed into a highly distinctive sea-mammal-hunting culture with all the Inuit artifacts so well known from popular publications— among them, the kayak, the umiak (open skin boat), and toggled harpoons, as well as fine ivory work (Figure 6.15). By then, many of the Inuit, especially those who hunted whales, lived in larger settlements.

FIGURE 6.14 Hand-lining and clubbing a halibut from skin kayaks. A painting by H. Elliott, 1872, which reflects ancient fishing methods from small arctic watercraft.

In approximately A.D. 900, the Thule people started to expand to the south and then to the east. Thule whale hunters appeared in the arctic islands of the east in approximately A.D. 1000, where their open-water-hunting techniques could be used to great effect. By the time the Thule reached northwest Greenland, the Norse had been living in the southern parts of the island for some time (McGhee, 1984).

Thule expansion
A.D. 900

Inuit cultural traditions, like those of the Fuegians and other hunter-gatherer groups, continued to flourish after European contact, but within a few centuries traditional lifeways had been modified beyond recognition, and exotic diseases had decimated hunter-gatherer populations. Today, few of the Americas' hunter-gatherers still practice their millennia-old lifeways; there are no longer the resources or the territory for them to do so.

Summary

- The first humans to settle the Americas crossed from northeastern Asia, probably across the Bering land bridge (central Beringia), but the date of their arrival is highly controversial. No archaic humans ever settled in the Americas, which were colonized by *Homo sapiens* alone.

- Some scientists claim that archaeological evidence from South America proves that Native Americans were flourishing in the Americas as early as 40,000 years ago, but this is a minority view. Most experts believe that first settlement occurred much later, perhaps at the very end of the Ice Age, as early as 13500 B.C., or even earlier.

- There is evidence for widespread but sparse Pre-Clovis occupation in the Americas dating to about 12000 B.C., perhaps some thousands of years earlier.

- Their successors, the Clovis people of North America, flourished between 11200 and 10900 B.C.

- After 11000 B.C., many species of Ice Age animals, large and small, became extinct, so Native American hunter-gatherers diversified their economies to take full advantage of local resources.

- Paleo-Indian groups continued to hunt bison on the North American plains, this being the only area where any large animals survived. Big-game hunting flourished here until historic times.

- An always sparse population of hunter-gatherers adapted to the harsh desert conditions of the West and flourished there right into historic times. Most such groups "anchored" themselves to reliable water supplies such as small lakes and marshes.

- In the Eastern Woodlands, hunter-gatherers subsisted off deer and other small game as well as a wide variety of plant foods. As time passed, both fishing and birds assumed greater importance, as did fall nut harvests. The densest populations flourished in fertile river valleys, along estuaries, and by lakeshores, where more sedentary settlements developed and hunting territories became more circumscribed.
- More complex hunter-gatherer societies developed in the Pacific Northwest and in midwestern river valleys, as well as along the California coast—all cultures depending on abundant, seasonally predictable aquatic, animal, and plant resources.

- In other parts of the Americas, Archaic cultures based on hunting and foraging survived until the adoption of native plant cultivation or maize agriculture within the last 6,000 years.
- In the Arctic and southernmost South America, hunter-gatherer societies flourished until historic times. In the far north, there was regular interchange of ideas with people in Siberia and, much later, with the Norse in the east, the only contacts between ancient America and the Old World until Columbus's day.

Further Reading

Fagan, Brian. 2011. *The First North Americans*. London and New York: Thames and Hudson.

Mann, Charles C. 2006. *1491: New Revelations of the Americas Before Columbus*. New York: Vintage.

Meltzer, David. 2008. *First Peoples in a New World: Colonizing Ice Age America*. Berkeley: University of California Press.

After the Ice

BEFORE 10000 B.C. TO MODERN TIMES

n about 7000 B.C., a small group of hunters and foragers camped in a sandy clearing near Meer in northern Belgium. They built a hearth and presumably erected brush or skin shelters, but no signs of these survive. After a while, a right-handed artisan walked a short distance away from the settlement, sat down on a small boulder, and made some stone tools with prepared blanks he had brought along with him. Among them were three borers for working wood or hide. Minute abrasions on the tips reveal that he turned them clockwise, showing that he was right-handed. Later, a left-handed stoneworker came and sat down next to him, bringing a core. He proceeded to knock off some flakes, the scars from which showed clearly that he was a southpaw.

This remarkable, fine-grained research was the work of two Belgian archaeologists, David Cahen and Francis van Noten (1981). It demonstrates a high level of detail, using refitting, edge-wear analysis, and other analytical techniques that are needed to understand the new hunter-gatherer societies that developed after the Ice Age. ■

Artist's impression of crewmen lifting a Chumash *tool*, planked canoe, from the water. The bear-skin clad captain watches.

Despite the harshness of late Ice Age climates, especially in northern latitudes, *Homo sapiens* adapted successfully to a remarkable range of global environments. The last 50,000 years of the Ice Age saw human settlement of the globe reach its premodern limits, with two major exceptions. The subarctic lands and eastern arctic regions of North America were mantled by ice and were uninhabitable until long after the Ice Age (see Chapter 6). The far offshore islands of the Pacific were not to be settled until much later, after the development of outrigger and twin-hulled offshore canoes and new navigational techniques that allowed seafarers to voyage far out of sight of land during the last 5,000 years of ancient times (see Chapter 12; see also Figure 4.1).

All later cultural developments, including a new focus on both agriculture and animal domestication and the establishment of much more complex human societies, which included the first civilizations, stemmed ultimately from the progressive settlement of the globe by *Homo sapiens* during the last glaciation (Mellars et al., 2007). The immediate consequences of the end of the Ice Age affected many hunter-gatherer societies scattered across the world when the great ice sheets finally retreated.

The Holocene (After 10000 B.C.)

When the last cold episode of the Ice Age ended in about 13700 B.C., widespread global warming ensued, followed by an abrupt cold snap. Paleoclimatologists divide the earliest part of the **Holocene** into two phases:

Bølling-Allerød Interstadial (c. 12700 to c. 10950 B.C.) This 2,000-year period saw dramatic global warming, massive ice sheet retreats, sea level rises, and much higher temperatures. It conventionally marks the end of the Würm glaciation.

Younger Dryas Interval (c. 10950 to 9650 B.C.) The Younger Dryas witnessed a dramatic fall in temperatures, back to near-glacial conditions in a mere decade or so. This 1,100-year-long cold snap ended as abruptly as it began, with the renewed onset of warmer conditions. But, as we shall see, it had a lasting effect on human life (see Chapter 9).

Changes in ice distribution and sea levels were very irregular. Using core borings from coral beds off Barbados in the Caribbean, Richard Fairbanks (1989) showed that sea levels at the glacial maximum were 121 m (396 feet) below modern levels. They rose by 20 m (66 feet) between about 15000 and 10500 B.C. Then there was an abrupt rise of 24 m (79 feet) in a mere 1,000 years, a slight rise at about 9000 B.C., and another 28-m (92-foot) rise after 8500 B.C. that culminated in 7500 B.C. These new levels led to major changes in world geography. The Bering Strait was dry land as late as 13000 B.C. and ocean again by 7000 B.C. By this time, sea levels were rising rapidly, especially in areas such as Scandinavia, where the earth's crust was depressed by the massive weight of retreating ice sheets. The North Sea was flooded, and Britain was separated from the continent by approximately 6000 B.C. Enormous areas of North America and northern Europe were exposed by retreating ice sheets and were available for human settlement for the first time in nearly 100,000 years.

We have hardly begun to understand the dramatic changes in temperature, rainfall, and vegetation that occurred during the early millennia of the Holocene, between about 13000 and 5000 B.C. (Björck et al., 1996; N. Roberts, 2010) (Table 7.1). Recent ice core research shows that the Holocene's atmosphere was about a third richer in carbon dioxide than at any time during the preceding 120,000 years of the late Ice Age. This enrichment increased photosynthesis, biomass, and seed yield, so that Holocene plants were more productive and more cold- and drought-tolerant than Pleistocene plants. This greater productivity may have been an important watershed for hunter-gatherers, who were now adapting to a very different world, one that was more productive and more climatically stable than its constantly changing Pleistocene predecessor.

The most striking environmental transformations took place in northern latitudes, in areas like western and central Europe and in regions of North America contiguous to the great ice sheets. During the height of the Weichsel glaciation, for example, central Europe had been treeless periglacial tundra and the Baltic Sea did not exist. Only 5,000 years after the Scandinavian ice sheet began retreating, forests covered most of Europe and sparse human populations had settled on the shores of a newly exposed northern sea.

Throughout the world, game populations changed radically in the millennia after the Ice Age. By 10000 B.C., the familiar mammoth and woolly rhinoceros hunted by the Cro-Magnons were extinct in central and western Europe, as were steppe bison and reindeer—all replaced by forest animals like the red and roe deer. In North America, mammoths, mastodons, camellike species, and many other large animal species vanished abruptly about 9000 B.C. (Grayson and Meltzer, 2002). Even in tropical Africa, the rich and diverse savanna faunas suffered losses at the end of the Ice Age. The extent to which humans were responsible for the rapid extinction of late Ice Age animals is a matter of great controversy (see Chapter 6).

There were major and highly significant vegetational changes in warmer latitudes, too. For much of the last glacial maximum, for example, the Sahara had been as arid as it is today, but rainfall patterns

TABLE 7.1
Climatic and generalized archaeological sequence in Europe and Southeast Asia after the Ice Age

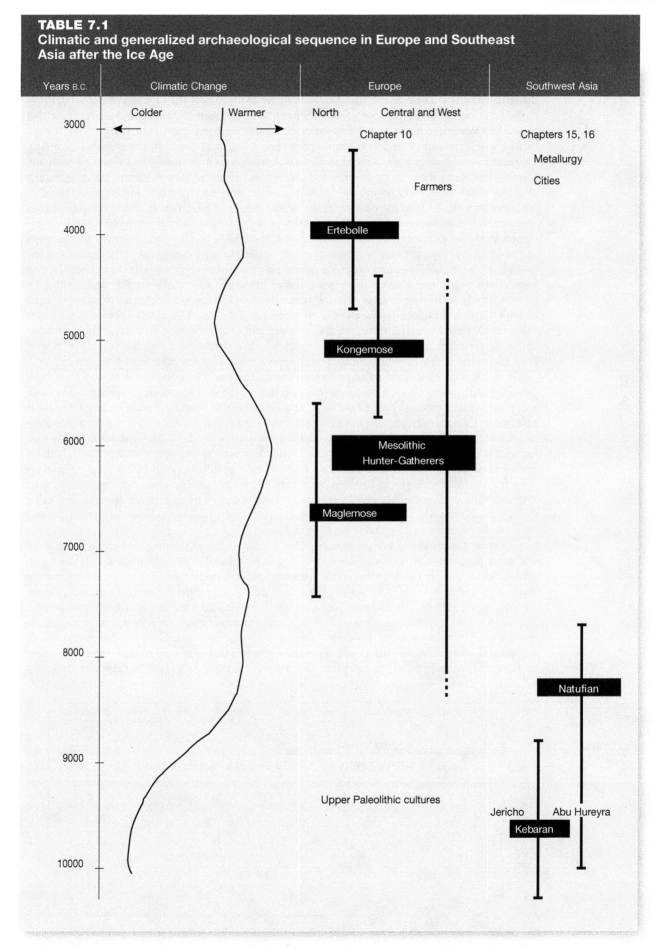

changed at the end of the Ice Age, bringing large, shallow lakes and short grasslands to the desert. As late as 6000 B.C., hunter-gatherer populations flourished in the heart of the Sahara in areas that are now arid wilderness. In Southwest Asia, the late Ice Age climate of the Taurus and Zagros mountains was so cold and dry that no trees grew in the uplands. After about 9000 B.C., new plant assemblages immigrated into the now warmer highlands, among them wild cereal grasses were to become the ancestors of domesticated crops. These cereals had long been native to the region, having survived the late Ice Age in sheltered locales. With the onset of warmer conditions, their distribution expanded greatly, so that they were accessible to many more hunter-gatherer bands distributed over a vast area.

In Mexico, the climate of 18000 B.C. was drier and colder than today. At the end of the Ice Age, temperatures rose, bringing a rich forest of cacti and legume trees to the mountain valleys of Puebla and Oaxaca. This thorn-scrub-cactus forest included many wild ancestors of domesticated plants, including maguey, squash, bean, and teosinte, and the wild grass that was the ancestor of domesticated maize.

These and other Holocene climatic changes had profound effects on hunter-gatherer societies throughout the world, especially on the intensity of the food quest and the complexity of their societies. Why had such changes not occurred earlier in prehistory? There had been climatic changes of similar, if not even greater, magnitude in early millennia, say, during the early part of the last interglacial, some 128,000 years ago. One reason may have been population density. Then, human populations were much smaller, and a great deal of the world was uninhabited. It was possible for human populations living in large hunting territories to move around freely and to adapt to rapid climatic shifts by traveling to new areas, even over large distances. This ability enabled them to develop highly flexible survival strategies that took account of the constant fluctuations in food availability. If, for example, an African band experienced two dry years in a row, it could move away or fall back on less nutritious edible foods, perhaps species that required more energy to harvest.

By 10000 B.C., circumstances were very different. The world's hunter-gatherer population was probably approaching about 8.5 million people (Hassan, 1981). The carrying capacity of the earth still exceeded that required by the human population, largely because humans were becoming more efficient in their exploitation of a broad spectrum of food resources. After 10000 B.C., the population curve approached that of carrying capacity in many areas (Figure 7.1). This development may have set off behavioral changes resulting from restricted mobility and greater competition. Notable among these changes would have been a necessity to solve problems locally rather than just moving away from them. People would have tended to exploit a wider range of local resources, both to avert starvation and to protect themselves from food shortages caused by short-term droughts and other unpredictable changes. The increased plant productivity of the Holocene meant that people became much more dependent on vegetable foods of all kinds.

In a sense, the world was fully, or at least sparsely, occupied by people who lived off its game, plant, and other food resources. *Homo sapiens* had settled in **periglacial** regions, in tropical rain forests, on offshore islands, and in the Americas. There were scattered hunter-gatherer populations throughout the world, many of them living in areas such as southern Africa and central Australia, for example, where the carrying capacities of the land were very low indeed (Figure 7.2). Human populations had increased considerably, too, especially in areas with diverse and seasonally predictable food resources. Even in sparsely inhabited environments, hunting territories were more confined. There was less room to move around and, often, more mouths to feed. Thus, new adaptive strategies were needed—strategies aimed at more efficient and productive exploitation of the environment. As a result of these new strategies,

FIGURE 7.1 Increases in world population during the Ice Age matched against the carrying capacity of the globe for humans.

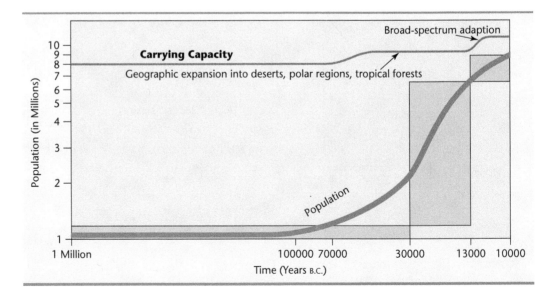

FIGURE 7.2 San hunter with weapons from Ho Khotso rock shelter, Lesotho, southern Africa, from a late Stone Age painting colored purple-red. The figure is approximately 21 cm (8 inches) high. Such paintings provide invaluable generalized information on ancient lifeways, as well as insights into ancient rituals.

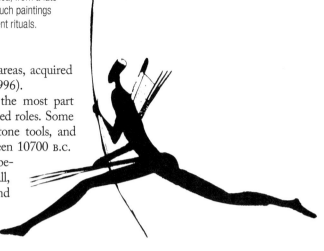

hunter-gatherer societies underwent profound changes and, in some areas, acquired much greater complexity (for a series of area surveys, see Straus et al., 1996).

The technology used by Holocene hunter-gatherer societies for the most part comprised adaptations of much earlier tool kits for new, more specialized roles. Some of these artifacts, such as microblades, baked clay objects, ground stone tools, and woodworking implements, clearly come from earlier prototypes. Between 10700 B.C. and 8800 B.C., the climate was more stable and becoming warmer, a period when many societies turned to fish, smaller game, and, above all, newly productive plant foods. The result—more specialized tool kits and a narrower focus on food resources that could be procured in large quantities. Among the innovations were bows and arrows, elaborate traps, hunting nets, fishhooks, harpoons, and fishing weirs.

Coping with Environmental Variation

Increasingly during the late Ice Age and more frequently in Holocene times, hunter-gatherer populations were confronted with new challenges, those created both by major climatic changes at the end of the Pleistocene and by local population growth. Everywhere, much more circumscribed hunter-gatherers were forced to improve their strategies for coping with local environmental variations, both in predictable seasonal resources and in unpredictable shifts in such phenomena as rainfall patterns or game migration routes (see an extended discussion in Bettinger, 2001).

This shift can be seen clearly in the Americas. As we saw in Chapter 6, the Americans of 11500 B.C. were small in numbers, highly mobile, and sparsely distributed on the ground. They subsisted in some part off Ice Age big game, which became extinct very rapidly after 11000 B.C. The archaeological record now shows a much greater diversity of local adaptations over the millennia, as thousands of isolated hunter-gatherer groups became more and more restricted in their movements. The change was especially marked in areas of exceptional resource diversity like the Pacific Northwest coast, the southern California coast, and the fertile river valleys of the southern Midwest and the southeastern United States (Figure 7.3). In all these areas, hunter-gatherer populations became more sedentary and developed often highly specialized technologies for hunting, foraging, or fishing (Figure 7.4).

Several long-term technological developments that went hand in hand marked the **intensification** of hunting and gathering.

Diminution of Tool Kits There was a gradual downsizing of stone artifacts and the perishable antler, bone, and wood tool kit that went with them. As early as 28000 B.C., and even more extensively after 13000 B.C., stone tool technologies became more and more standardized and more and more oriented toward the production of parts of composite tools, especially small arrow and knife barbs, scrapers, and awls. In Europe and Southwest Asia, this technology involved the production of thousands of small **microliths,** geometrically shaped barbs used on all manner of weapons (Figure 7.5).

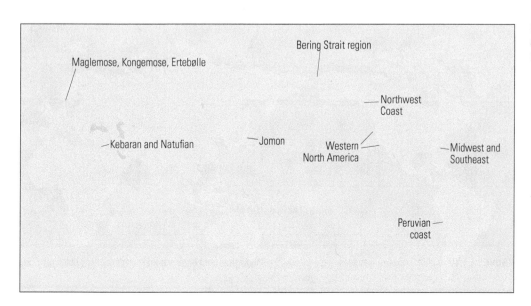

FIGURE 7.3 Map showing general areas where affluent hunter-gatherers mentioned in this book flourished.

FIGURE 7.4 Salmon fishing in the Pacific Northwest; nineteenth-century painting by Paul Kane. Harvesting salmon runs required a carefully organized "production line" to process, dry, and store the fish as they were speared and netted by the thousands.

A complete blade is notched on opposite sides or the same edge, depending on the shape of microlith required.

The blade is then snapped across the notch.

The middle segment forms the finished implement, here a parallelogram-shaped (left) or a trapezoidal (right) arrow barb.

Microliths (Actual size)

Mounted barbs (hypothetical) (Actual size)

FIGURE 7.5 Microliths. Stages in manufacturing a microlith, a small arrow barb or similar implement made by notching a blade and snapping off its base after the implement is formed.

These standardized artifacts were made by striking small bladelets off a conical core, then notching and snapping off the thicker end to form a small microlith. Microlith-tipped and barbed wooden arrows have been found intact in Danish swamps, environments where they were used to hunt forest game, rodents, and birds for many centuries.

Bows and Arrows It was sometime during the late Ice Age, too, that the bow and arrow came into use, perhaps even arriving in Europe with modern humans—the evidence is very uncertain for this, however. Bows were certainly in common use in Europe by 9000 B.C. and in Africa and Southwest Asia at about the same time. In contrast, the technology reached arctic America by 2000 B.C., then spread southward later, reaching areas as late as 200 B.C. Bows have many advantages, among them greater accuracy, enhanced portability, and the ability to fire off several missiles within a very short space of time. They were more versatile than the spear, for the hunters could carry many more lightweight lethal points with them in a small quiver, arrows that could be brought into use in a few moments. Under these circumstances, the chances of a kill were greatly enhanced (Figure 7.6). Bows allowed individual hunters to pursue quite large game alone, without the cooperation of others, a major change with obvious social implications (Bettinger, 2001).

Specialized Tool Kits The diminution of stone technology reflected a much greater emphasis on specialized but versatile tool kits that were modified to reflect local needs. The early Holocene saw a much greater localization of artifacts of all kinds, a development reflected in a proliferation of new archaeological "cultures"; these, in fact, reflected a world in which movement was more circumscribed, in which thousands of small bands, and occasionally larger population groups, adapted to constant local environmental variation. This localization is well documented in areas like Europe, Australia, Southwest Asia, and the North American Great Basin, as well as by Kent Flannery's important work on a small forager band that visited Guilá Naquitz Cave, Mexico, between about 8750 and 6670 B.C. As Flannery has eloquently pointed out, the new local tool kits were part of a process whereby humans coped not only with long-term climatic change but also with the constant uncertainties of local climates. "Humans are well suited to the working out of resilient strategies for environmental variability," Flannery writes, "since they possess multigenerational memory and have unique methods for exchanging information and establishing cooperative relationships over long periods" (1986, p. 76).

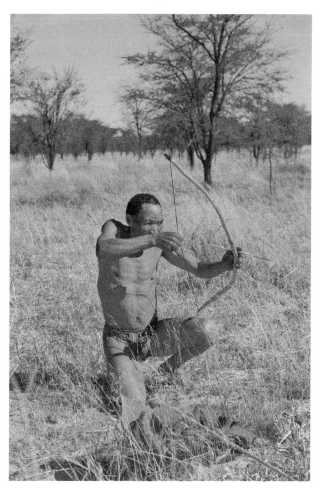

FIGURE 7.6 A San hunter in the Kalahari Desert shoots with bow and arrow.

Intensive Exploitation The new subsistence strategies often involved highly intensive exploitation of locally abundant and predictable resources such as salmon or nuts. Such intensive exploitation was adaptive in environments where seasonal phenomena such as salmon runs, caribou migrations, or hickory harvests required not only the harvesting of enormous quantities of food in a short time but also their processing and storage for later use. Storage technology now assumed a new importance; thousands of fish were dried on racks in the sun or in front of fires, and the nut and wild cereal harvests were placed in basket- or clay-lined pits for later consumption. There was nothing new in the notion of storage; much earlier, big-game hunters, for example, dried meat and pounded it up to eat on the march. What was new, however, was the notion of large-scale storage in more sedentary settlements, where mobility was no longer a viable strategy. By the use of storage and by the careful seasonal "mapping" of game, plant, and aquatic resources, early Holocene hunter-gatherers compensated for periodic food shortages caused by short-term climatic change and seasonal fluctuations. At the same time, they broadened their diet to include foods that were less nourishing, another way of ensuring fallback in the diet in the event of staple shortages.

Storage Storage went hand in hand with very specialized sets of hunting weapons or food-processing implements designed for the intensive exploitation of specific food resources, such as reindeer, sea mammals, birds, or acorns. As early as 18000 B.C., and more markedly after 10000 B.C., tool kits displayed much greater specialization and elaboration. We have already mentioned in Chapter 5 the development of the needle as a catalyst for layered, tailored clothing in periglacial environments, and both the Magdalenians and the eastern Gravettian hunters used a wide variety of

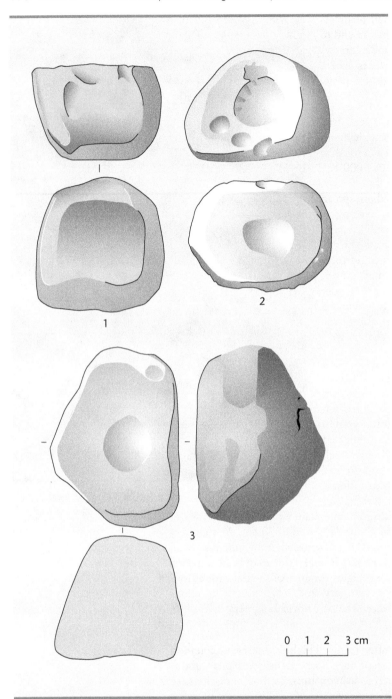

FIGURE 7.7 Pounders and grinders used for processing wild vegetable foods from the Gwisho late Stone Age campsite, Zambia, central Africa, c. 1500 B.C. The peck marks served to hold the grains in place.

specialized, and sometimes elaborate, antler and bone tools in the chase and in domestic life, as well as for nets and cordage (see Chapter 5).

Holocene hunter-gatherer societies worldwide developed even more specialized tool kits for many purposes. Many African and North American societies relied heavily on seeds and nuts. They developed many forms of grinders and pestles to process such harvests (Figure 7.7), and the rich organic deposits of such sites as the Hoko River and Ozette on the Olympic Peninsula in the Pacific Northwest document a highly effective halibut-fishing and whale-hunting technology based on wood, bone, slate, and fiber (Croes, 1996). Canoes, bone-tipped fish spears, and wooden birding arrows were part of the specialized fishing and fowling tool kit of Holocene groups in northern Europe. Perhaps the ultimate in specialized hunting technology for sea mammals comes from the Bering Sea coasts of Alaska and the Thule culture of the Canadian Arctic (see Chapter 6).

More restricted territories, less mobility, rising local population, and new strategies for dealing with seasonal and unpredictable environmental variations—all these problems were common to postglacial hunter-gatherer societies throughout the world. A few of these societies, especially those living in areas with rich and diverse food resources that included fish or sea mammals, achieved a high degree of social complexity, with signs of some social ranking.

Mesolithic Hunter-Gatherers in Europe

An excellent example of how late Ice Age hunter-gatherers adapted to global warming comes from northwestern Europe, where Mesolithic forest and coastal hunter-gatherers replaced tundra reindeer hunters after 11000 B.C. (A comprehensive summary appears in Bailey and Spikins, 2008.) The European Mesolithic spanned about 4,500 years, from about 8000 B.C. to the beginnings of farming in northwestern Europe, about 3500 B.C.

The environmental changes in Europe after 13000 B.C. were so dramatic that the Magdalenian and other late Ice Age cultures vanished relatively quickly. The traditional view held that Europe was now populated by impoverished Mesolithic hunters and gatherers who had lost much of their capacity for economic and social relations. This notion of a cultural hiatus has crumbled in the face of recent sophisticated ecological researches. Instead of impoverished environments, each change in postglacial forest composition probably brought greater ecological productivity. A range of forest ungulates such as red and roe deer replaced the migratory reindeer that were so important in the Ice Age. Plant foods such as nuts assumed much greater importance in Mesolithic life (Zvelebil, 1994).

These food sources may have contributed to an increase in Mesolithic populations. Coasts, estuaries, and lakes were highly productive, especially with such seasonal resources as salmon, water birds, and sea mammals, many of them relying on seasonal plankton production in the oceans. Many of these aquatic foods could be taken and stored, especially by people who occupied relatively permanent encampments nearby. Thus, larger populations were possible in some areas among people who relied on seasonal resources and used such nonseasonal foods as shellfish to plug the gaps. Some of these more sedentary groups enjoyed a bounty of food sources and a complexity of life that has been called *affluent foraging.*

Were all European Mesolithic groups affluent foragers? The interplay of different resources varied dramatically throughout Europe, with its seasonal climates and productive environments. This was not a hostile environment peopled by only minimally complex hunter-gatherer bands, but one where a great variety of adaptations were possible. At least two general models have been proposed for Mesolithic Europe:

- Lower latitudes supported somewhat generalized environments where highly mobile bands exploited evenly dispersed animal and plant resources, shifting camp regularly as local resources were exhausted.
- Higher-latitude environments were more uneven in productivity and resource reliability, having few species in large numbers. These were specialized environments, where human groups moved less often and frequently directed their moves toward the exploitation of a single seasonal resource such as caribou. Larger numbers of people sometimes congregated for seasonal hunts.

These are, of course, by no means the only models for Mesolithic life that could be put forward, but they serve to remind us that this was a period when European populations enjoyed a wide range of adaptations—from peoples with highly mobile lifeways to permanently settled "affluent" groups that dwelled in large villages or base camps, such as those found in northwestern Europe and by the Iron Gates area of the Danube River. Without question, the Mesolithic was a period of broad variation in economic and social life, with some intensification of the food quest where uncertain environmental conditions dictated it (see Site box).

The adaptive trends seen in the European Mesolithic are not particularly innovative; indeed, most of them had their roots in a much earlier restructuring of the organization and use of resources with the arrival of modern humans in temperate latitudes some 35,000 years ago. The Upper Paleolithic saw much greater exploitation of regional resources and an enhanced ability to adapt to extremes of both glacial and fully interglacial climates. This restructuring gave Europeans the ability to solve the problems of exploiting not just a few resources but many different ones at once. This ability became vital at the end of the Ice Age, when food management strategies had to cope with extremely varied combinations of food resources. These strategies included some elements that were of critical importance when people began to grow crops and tame animals—adaptations that were attuned to the scheduling of seasonal activities connected with growing and harvesting seasons and systems of information sharing. The Mesolithic hunters' schedule was comprehensive and flexible enough to cope with anything and could easily accommodate strategies that relied on deliberate cultivation of the soil or careful animal husbandry.

Efficient food management strategies involved more effective technology, too—more diverse tool kits for hunting forest animals and exploiting coastal resources such as sea mammals and shallow-water fish. The Mesolithic peoples who lived along the shores of the newly emerging Baltic Sea developed an astonishing range of fish spears, nets, harpoons, and traps, many of them preserved in waterlogged sites. Spears and arrows were tipped with tiny stone, bone, or antler barbs. Grounded-edged tools were used for woodworking and processing forest plants. Large canoes, some of them dugouts hollowed from tree trunks, were in evidence. We know that Stone Age people were crossing open water as early as 10000 B.C., for miners were visiting the island of Melos in the Mediterranean to collect obsidian that was traded far and wide (Torrance, 1986).

Star Carr
8700 to 8400 B.C.

In a trend toward increasing **sedentism,** many Mesolithic groups lived in larger, more permanent settlements, a number of them located on strategic bays or near lakes or rivers. Some locations were probably used year-round or certainly for many months, anchored by abundant aquatic resources nearby. There were smaller camps and specialist activity areas, too. Everything points to greater internal differentiation in society and to more intensive subsistence activities. Nuts and shellfish became far more important, and hunters took a far wider range of game than their Ice Age predecessors. It was not the dietary staples that changed, but merely the diversity of exploited food resources.

Perhaps the most profound changes were those in population densities and social organization. J. G. D. Clark (1981) identified three major "social territories" at the end of the Upper Paleolithic, between the Netherlands, Poland, and southern Sweden. Three distinct cultures (Ahrensburgian, Swiderian, and Bromme) each covered territories of about 100,000 sq. km (38,610 sq. miles). As the Holocene wore on, these territories were rapidly reduced in size. By 6000 B.C., at least

6000 B.C.

SiTE > Star Carr, England <

Star Carr, probably the most famous Mesolithic site in the world, lies in northeastern England. One of the first Stone Age locations dug with environmental experts on site, Star Carr became a classic example of ecological archaeology for generations of students; however, in recent years new fieldwork and interpretations have radically changed interpretations of the site.

Star Carr came to light in 1947, when amateur archaeologist John Moore unearthed some flint tools and broken bones at the edge of a long dried-up lake in northeastern England, only a few miles from the North Sea coast. Indefatigable Cambridge University archaeologist, Grahame Clark, recruited the services of pollen experts Harry Goodwin and Donald Walker. They spent three seasons (1949–1951) on excavations that recovered stone tools and manufacturing debris, bone and wooden artifacts, and a wealth of food remains, including bones from red deer, roe deer, elk, wild cattle, and pig (Figure 7.8). Notable among the organic artifacts were 191 barbed antler points and 21 red deer frontlets, which appeared to have been worn as headgear. Clark suggested these could have been used either by hunters stalking deer or as costumes in ritual dances. He believed Star Carr to have been a small residential base camp occupied by four or five families. Pollen samples placed Star Carr to a time when birch forests first spread into northern Britain and much of the southern North Sea was still dry land. Radiocarbon pioneer Willard Libby of the University of Chicago put the date of Star Carr to 7538 ± 350 B.C., while Clark and his experts argued from the red deer antlers that the site was occupied in winter. These were exciting brave new times for research.

In 1954, Grahame Clark published his classic monograph, *Excavations at Star Carr*. Ever since, the site has been the focus of numerous reinterpretations. Was it a base camp, hunting camp, kill site, or a place for tanning hides? All these ideas have been mooted. When was it occupied? Winter, summer, or spring, have all been suggested, depending on which seasonal indicator and scientific methods are used. Subsequent excavations have also changed our understanding of the site. So what is the latest thinking?

Small-scale excavations in 1985 and 1989 improved our understanding of the duration of occupation at the site (Mellars and Dark, 1998). A new trench 20 m (66 feet) east of Clark's original excavation produced 12 closely spaced accelerator mass spectrometry (AMS) radiocarbon dates on charcoal and minute plant remains taken from a stratigraphic column excavated for paleoecological analysis (for AMS dating, see Chapter 8).

These and more recent radiocarbon results suggest that the site was in fact occupied between 9000 and 8500 B.C.

Petra Dark examined the distribution of charcoal particles associated with the AMS dates. She showed that there was an initial period of intense charcoal deposition that lasted for about 80 years, then a century with little activity, followed by fairly continuous distribution for a further 130 years. Botanist Jon Hather identified the charcoals as those of reeds that were burnt off when they were dry, namely between autumn and spring, when new growth begins. Mellars and Dark believe the reeds were fired repeatedly by humans, with the evidence suggesting that the burning was tightly controlled. Such conflagrations, commonplace among historic foragers, would have fostered new plant growth, which in turn tends to attract feeding animals. They might also have created a better view of the lake and surrounding terrain, and provided a convenient landing place for canoes.

From 1975 excavations also took place around the lake on which Star Carr was situated (Conneller and Schadla-Hall, 2003). Here the archaeologists located further Mesolithic sites on the lake-shore and on islands in the middle of the lake. However, despite reasonably good levels of organic preservation, these are very different from Star Carr. They consist of sites focused on a range of different activities, while animal remains are small in quantity and heavily processed. In 30 years of excavations around the lake, only one further barbed point has been discovered, and no frontlets or beads were found (another artifact type common at Star Carr). Why should this matter? It may support recent ideas that Star Carr, rather being a typical domestic base camp as Clark supposed, was actually a site where certain rites also took place—potentially involving the ritual deposition of antler barbed points and frontlets into the waters of the lake.

FIGURE 7.8 Elk antler mattock from Star Carr, England (one-half actual size).

Since 2004 excavations, undertaken by Chantal Conneller, Nicky Milner and Barry Taylor, have recommenced at Star Carr. The team hopes to elucidate key aspects of the wetland archaeology and investigate the hitherto unexplored dryland settlement. Clark claimed that occupation at Star Carr took place on a platform of unworked birchwood. However, doubts have been expressed as to whether this was humanly modified or simply wood that would naturally wash up at the edge of a lake. Small-scale excavations in 1985 revealed another, quite different wooden structure east of the original trenches, this time a concentration of large aspen timbers, split into planks, laid parallel and at right angles to the lake shore. This structure was only known from a 2-m wide trench so its function was uncertain.

SiTE   Star Carr, England

The new excavations have uncovered further traces of this structure on other parts of the site. In all it stretches at least 30 m along the edge of the lake, and seems to have provided easy access to the lake waters for the inhabitants of the site. This is a significant structure and its erection would probably have required the sort of communal effort more frequently associated with the construction of Neolithic monuments.

Excavations of the dryland areas of the site have revealed dense spreads of animal bones and lithic material, while clusters of burnt flint indicate the presence of hearths. A variety of activities appear to have been undertaken here: tool manufacture, axe resharpening, the working of bone and antler, hide and wood. But most important of the finds in the dryland has been a small, circular structure, measuring about 3.5 m in diameter. This consists of a series of postholes encircling a pit filled with organic material, probably reeds or moss to create a soft floor. Given that only a small portion of the dryland area has been excavated, it seems likely that more of these structures exist.

Sixty years of new interpretations at Star Carr, which look further afield than the confines of the site, confirm that this lakeside location was enormously attractive to local foragers over several centuries. Red deer seem to have been spiritually important animals and their remains (in particular their antlers) were deposited in the waters of the lake. Recent excavations confirm the significance of the site to its inhabitants. It is clear that considerable effort was expanded in modifying the landscape through burning of the lakeside vegetation and through construction projects. Previous work has suggested that people at this time, some of the first migrants back in northern England after the last Paleolithic cold episode, were extremely mobile and generated little impact on their environment. Though people seem to have been nomadic, the evidence from Star Carr indicates that these first settlers had already generated attachments to significant places in the landscape, attachments that were strong enough to generate repeated occupation over several hundred years (Conneller and Schadla-Hall, 2003).

---

15 territories were in this same area, identified by different artifact styles or distributions of raw materials. Each of these zones was 15,000 to 20,000 sq. km (5,791 to 7,722 sq. miles) in extent. This pattern may reflect major changes in the regional distribution, density, and social organization of Mesolithic populations.

As these changes were taking place, new artifact forms and presumably other innovations were spreading across wide areas of Europe. Among them was a characteristic trapeze-shaped microlith, widely used as an arrow barb by later Mesolithic peoples, that appeared throughout the continent about 6000 B.C., perhaps somewhat earlier in southeast Europe (J. G. D. Clark, 1958). The Mesolithic ended with the rapid spread of agricultural economies into southeastern Europe about 6000 B.C. From there, they spread sporadically into central Europe by 4500 B.C. and to the northwest after 3500 B.C.

The European Mesolithic testifies to a continuity in human culture from Ice Age times, but this continuity was based on continuous adjustment to changing postglacial environments. In time, the same Mesolithic societies readapted to the warmest millennia of postglacial times, not only by shifting their hunting and foraging methods but also by taking up new subsistence practices, often within the context of their existing society.

Mesolithic Complexity in Scandinavia

This continuity is well documented from waterlogged Mesolithic sites in Britain and Scandinavia, where three broad subdivisions of the northern Mesolithic are known (Zvelebil, 2008).

The Maglemose Period (7500 to 5700 B.C.)

The Maglemose was a time of seasonal exploitation of rivers and lakes, combined with terrestrial hunting and foraging. Inland, late spring and early summer settlements are represented by the Ulkestrup site in Denmark, where the people lived in large huts with bark and wood floors, on a peat island in a swamp by a lake. One hut lay close to poles where canoes were once moored. A large wooden paddle lay nearby. The Maglemose people fished with bone- and antler-barbed points, trapped birds, and hunted red deer, wild ox, and pig. In fall, the bands foraged for hazelnuts and other edible plant foods, killing elk and other game in winter, when fishing was apparently less important.

Maglemose
7500 to 5700 B.C.

The Kongemose Period (5700 to 4600 B.C.)

Kongemose
5700 to 4600 B.C.

Kongemose sites are mainly on Baltic Sea coasts, along bays and near lagoons, where the people exploited both marine and terrestrial resources. Many Kongemose sites are somewhat larger than Maglemose ones; among the better known is the Segebro settlement, now submerged in brackish water near the southwestern Swedish coast. This settlement covered 50 m by 25 m (164 feet by 82 feet) and was occupied year-round but mainly in spring and summer. Carbon isotope analyses of human bones from Segebro show that fish and sea mammals constituted most of the diet, with no fewer than 66 species of animals found in the site. Not only freshwater and saltwater fish but also red deer, elk, boars, and seals were commonplace.

The Ertebølle Period (4600 to 3200 B.C.)

Ertebølle
4600 to 3200 B.C.

Ertebølle was the culmination of Mesolithic culture in southern Scandinavia (Price, 1987). By this time, the Scandinavians were occupying many coastal settlements year-round, subsisting off a very wide range of food resources indeed. These included forest game and waterfowl, shellfish, sea mammals, and both shallow-water and deepwater fish. There were smaller seasonal coastal sites, too, many for specific activities such as deepwater fishing, sealing, or hunting of migratory birds. The Aggersund site in Denmark was occupied for a short period in the autumn, when the inhabitants collected oysters and hunted some game, especially migratory swans. Ertebølle technology was far more elaborate than that of its Mesolithic predecessors; a wide variety of antler, bone, and wood tools for specialized purposes such as fowling and sea mammal hunting were developed, including dugout canoes up to 10 m (32.8 feet) long.

Vedbaek
5000 B.C. to 3000 B.C.

With sedentary settlement comes evidence of greater social complexity. Some Ertebølle communities buried their dead in cemeteries, placing the bodies in various positions, with dog interments alongside the human. The Vedbaek Bogebakken cemetery in Denmark dates to about 5000 B.C. and contains the graves of at least 22 people of different ages. Everyone was buried in an extended position (Figure 7.9); at least three people were buried after injury or a violent death. Men and women were deposited with different grave goods, and older people with red deer antlers. Other Ertebølle cemeteries from Denmark contain evidence of violent death; some people have projectile points in their ribs. There are also traces of cannibalism (Price, 1985).

The trend toward more sedentary settlement, the cemeteries, and the occasional social differentiation revealed by elaborate burials are all reflections of an intensification among these relatively affluent hunter-gatherers of 3000 B.C. Mesolithic societies intensified the food quest by exploiting many more marine species, making productive use of migratory waterfowl and their breeding grounds, and collecting shellfish in enormous numbers. This intensification is also reflected in a much more elaborate and diverse technology, more exchange of goods and materials between neighbors, greater variety in settlement types, and a slowly rising population throughout southern Scandinavia (Figure 7.10). These phenomena may, in part, be a reflection of rising sea levels throughout the Mesolithic, inundations that flooded many valuable territories. There are signs, too, of regional variations in artifact forms and styles, of cultural differences between people living in carefully delineated territories and competing for resources.

Mesolithic cultures are much less well defined elsewhere in Europe, partly because the climatic changes were less extreme than in southern Scandinavia and because there were fewer opportunities for coastal adaptation (Bailey and Spikins, 2008). In many areas, settlement was confined to lakeside and riverside locations, widely separated from one another by

FIGURE 7.9 Burial of a man, a woman, and, between them, a small child, from Vedbaek, Denmark, c. 5000 B.C. A bone point is embedded in the man's throat; the woman wears a ring of animal teeth, which lies on her chest. (Burial from Vedbaek, Denmark. National Museum of Denmark, Danish Collections.)

dense forests. Many Mesolithic sites were located on **ecotones,** so that the inhabitants could return to a central base location, where for much of the year they lived close to predictable resources such as lake fish. However, they would exploit both forest game and other seasonal resources from satellite camps. For example, Michael Jochim (2008) believes that in central Europe, some groups wintered in camps along the Danube, moving to summer encampments on the shores of neighboring lakes. In many areas, like Spain, there appears to have been intensified exploitation of marine and forest resources. There was a trend nearly everywhere toward greater variety in the diet, with more attention being paid to less obvious foods as well as to those, like shellfish, that require more complex processing methods than do game and other such resources.

Thus, in parts of Europe, there was a long-term trend among hunter-gatherer societies toward a more extensive exploitation of food resources, often within the context of a strategy that sought ways to minimize the impact of environmental uncertainty. In more favored areas, such as southern Scandinavia, some such societies achieved a level of nascent social complexity that was to become commonplace among later farming peoples. When farming did come to Europe, this preadaptation was an important catalyst for rapid economic and social change (Chapter 10).

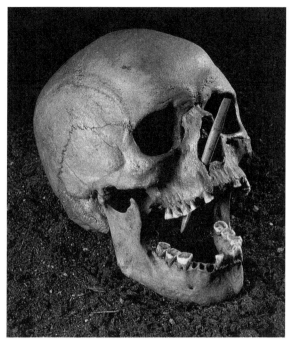

FIGURE 7.10 A 35-year-old man from Porsmose, Denmark, who died of bone arrow wounds, c. 3000 B.C. One arrow went through his nose and into his brain.

Hunter-Gatherer Complexity

"Hunter-gatherers move around a lot and live in small groups." This statement has been a universal label for hunter-gatherer societies, ancient and modern, for a generation (Lee and DeVore, 1976). It paints a picture of hunter-gatherers in prefarming times, who lived in small, temporary camps; were constantly on the move; and possessed a highly portable technology and a flexible social system. However, these models were based in large part on anthropological research among living societies like the !Kung San of the Kalahari Desert in southern Africa or the Inuit of the Canadian Arctic (Binford, 2001a). Most of them are dwindling populations living in areas of the world, like tropical rain forests, Arctic regions, or semideserts, where agriculture is an impossibility. Almost invariably, they have been in touch with farmers, and the wider world, for many centuries, which suggests they may have little to tell us about ancient foraging societies. Only a handful of hunter-gatherer societies, peoples like the Ainu of Japan or the Pacific Northwest coast Indians of North America, enjoyed complex adaptations at the time of European contact around the eighteenth century A.D. Generalizations about highly mobile, small-scale hunter-gatherer societies took little account of the great diversity among the many hunting and foraging societies that once existed on earth. This diversity, known almost entirely from archaeological research, developed during the late Ice Age and the Holocene. Above all, the archaeological record of the world of 13000 to 4000 B.C. reveals a global trend toward great complexity in hunter-gatherer societies in well-defined regions as widely separated as northern Europe, southern Africa, Japan, the North American Midwest, and coastal Peru.

Conditions for Greater Complexity

Complex hunter-gatherer societies did not appear everywhere, but they occurred in a remarkable variety of environments, from fertile river valleys to coastal deserts. Whatever the environment, however, certain general conditions were necessary. First, population movements had to be limited by either geography or the presence of neighbors. Thus, one could not move away from resource shortages; solutions had to be found on the spot. Second, resources had to be abundant and predictable in their seasonal appearance. Small, numerous organisms with high reproductive rates played an especially important role in intensifying hunting and gathering. Such organisms included fish, shellfish, nuts, and seeds, species that were available in abundance and seldom exhausted. Third, population growth might reach a point at which food shortages occurred and there was an imbalance between people and their food supply. Again, a solution was to intensify the food quest, an intensification that might result in a more complex society.

Attributes of Greater Complexity

What features distinguish a more complex hunter-gatherer society from its less elaborate neighbors? The following appear to be of fundamental importance:

- Higher than normal population, concentrated in relatively small and restricted territories, such as individual river valleys, where movement is circumscribed by either geography or neighbors.

- A more intensive, more diversified, and more specialized food quest. Selected species such as nuts and seeds become more important, and foods that were not exploited previously because they required more effort are adopted into the diet. In some cases, people deliberately sow wild plants to ensure an adequate harvest.
- A system of food storage and preservation.
- Permanent and nearly permanent settlements, often base camps of much greater size than in earlier times. Settlements are often linear, distributed along, say, riverbanks; contain different forms of structures; and are often associated with burial grounds, which may serve as territorial boundaries.
- Highly developed hunting, fishing, or plant-processing equipment.
- Division of labor not only by sex and age but also by activity, such as whale hunting, or a craft specialty like canoe building.
- Some form of simple social ranking, probably based on differences between lineages or other kin groupings, such as wealth, diet, and burial customs.
- Often, intensive exchange in exotic objects and raw materials with neighboring groups.
- More elaborate ritual beliefs and ceremonial life.

Debates about Social Complexity

We do not know when the first more complex hunter-gatherer societies appeared, but at least some late Ice Age societies may have enjoyed some level of complexity. Possible candidates include the Magdalenians of southwestern France and northern Spain as well as the eastern Gravettian plains hunters, with their mammoth-bone houses, who lived in the river valleys of Ukraine in 16000 b.c. (see Chapter 5).

Complexity among hunter-gatherer societies became widespread after the Ice Age, especially in areas where freshwater or marine fish, shellfish, or sea mammals were available in abundance. Aquatic resources have the advantage of being both relatively plentiful and predictable, so that there are strong incentives for people to adopt sedentary lifeways along rivers and at lake and ocean shores. However, the full potential of marine and freshwater resources was realized in only a relatively few areas of the world, and then within the past 10,000 years.

The debates about social complexity among hunter-gatherers revolve around two opposing viewpoints. One viewpoint sees the oceans as a kind of "Garden of Eden" (Binford, 2001b). Proponents of this theory point to the enormous abundance of shellfish in many areas of the world and to the great productivity of many estuaries and coastal waters easily exploited by shore-dwelling fisherfolk. This abundance allowed societies to become sedentary and to maintain population densities (Moseley, 1975).

In contrast, another group of archaeologists, many of them studying post–Ice Age hunter-gatherers in Europe, argue that aquatic resources were a strategy of last resort, a response to population pressure and shortages of terrestrial resources such as game and plant foods (Gamble, 1986). These authorities assume that marine and freshwater resources, no matter how productive, were more labor-intensive to harvest and were less nutritionally valuable than food sources on land.

David Yesner (1987) takes a somewhat different perspective. He argues that the shift to the exploitation of aquatic resources was the result of decisions made in periods of rapid environmental change, when population pressure was causing food shortages. The "optimal" strategy for people under these circumstances would have been to turn to a resource that did involve more work and was, perhaps, as productive as big game.

All of these viewpoints assume, however, that maritime resources played a key role in the emergence of social complexity among Stone Age hunter-gatherers. The debate is unresolved, for we do not know exactly how decisive marine or riverine resources were in allowing dense populations and sedentary living, both essential prerequisites for social complexity. Nor do we know whether we can make comparisons between the elaborate and socially complex Pacific Northwest coast Indian cultures that flourished a few centuries ago in North America and early Holocene hunter-gatherer groups living thousands of years earlier (see Bettinger, 2001).

Hunter-Gatherer Societies in Southwest Asia

Ohalo II
23000 b.c.

Southwest Asia has provided a fascinating picture of emerging social and cultural complexity among hunter-gatherers at the end of the Ice Age. As early as 23,000 years ago, people living in a cluster of wood and brush huts known as Ohalo II on the southwestern shore of the Sea of Galilee were relying on a wide range of wild plants, even grinding wild wheat and barley seeds before baking them into some form of dough (E. Weiss et al., 2004), a sign that broad spectrum foraging and food storage had begun long before people took up farming. Ohalo II is atypical of the time, for most sites of this date were temporary encampments, but it foreshadows the more sedentary settlement of Holocene times.

Between 13000 and 8000 b.c., the simple hunter-gatherer societies of the eastern Mediterranean—the coastal zone of present-day Israel and Syria—gave way to more complex hunting and gathering societies and eventually to farmers (for a site map, see Figure 9.1). For years, scientists have discussed the origins of agriculture in Southwest Asia, believing it to be a more radical transformation in human life than almost any other development in prehistory (see Chapter 8). In fact, recent research has suggested that the earlier transition to more complex hunter-gatherer societies may have been much more profound.

In 13000 b.c., small and highly mobile hunter-gatherer bands inhabited the **Levant,** subsumed under the general cultural name of Kebaran. Kebaran sites, marked by thousands of small geometric microliths, occur not only in wooded country but also in the steppe and desert of the Negev and the Sinai (Goring-Morris and Belfer-Cohen, 2011). The Kebarans are found in a wide variety of environments, which may account for the great variation in their tool kits (Figure 7.11). The Kebarans enjoyed a simple hunter-gatherer strategy, which placed a high premium on mobility (Bar-Yosef, 1987). In some areas, the people may have dispersed to the uplands in summer, moving into caves and rock shelters near lowland lakes in the winter. Apparently, plant foods were not overwhelmingly important, and the Kebaran tool kit lacks the specialized grinders and pounders found in later cultures, except at lower elevations, where some wild cereal grasses grew.

By about 13000 b.c., warming temperatures throughout Southwest Asia brought significant environmental and vegetational changes. During the late Ice Age, warmth-loving plants like wild emmer wheat and barley, oaks, almonds, and pistachio trees were restricted to refuge areas lying below modern sea level. These sandy-soil areas would have given only poor yields of wild cereals. As early Holocene temperatures rose, these plant and tree species colonized higher country, where clayey soils produced much higher yields (Henry, 1989). New, denser cereal stands were now much more resistant to short-term climatic change and were also harvestable over a longer period of time each year. Many hunter-gatherer sites on higher ground, from after 13000 b.c., contain ground stone tools: pestles and mortars, implements used to process seed harvests for storage, an essential in much more seasonal, and increasingly arid, climates.

Kebaran
13000 to 11000 b.c.

The Natufian Culture (Before 11000 to 8500 b.c.)

These abundant cereal and nut resources within the Mediterranean hill zone stimulated the development of more intensive foraging strategies, more sedentary settlement, and rapid territorial expansion until the most favored territories were filled. The emergence of these more plentiful plant resources coincided with the emergence of the Natufian culture from the earlier Kebaran in about 11000 b.c., a culture that expanded rapidly to the edges of the Mediterranean zone within about 1,500 years.

The Natufians used a more complex hunting and foraging strategy than the Kebarans. Their complex adaptation included totally mobile groups, others stayed in one place for much of the year, and communities in favorable settings who were sedentary (Goring-Morris and Belfer-Cohen, 2011). The densest populations were in areas settled by more sedentary communities.

Everywhere, Natufians intensified their hunting and foraging. They targeted migrating gazelle herds and exploited wild emmer and barley intensively, as well as acorn, almond, and pistachio, all highly productive resources that were easily stored (Bar-Yosef and Valla, 1990; Byrd, 1989). The new subsistence strategies encouraged more sedentary lifeways and the development of much larger settlements, averaging about 700 sq. m (7,500 sq. feet) in area. These villages, which contained semisubterranean houses, storage pits, and pavements, were associated with nearby small, transitory camps, where food was collected and processed (Figure 7.12). The Natufian tool kit contained all manner of specialized plant-processing tools, including querns, grinding slabs, pestles, mortars, and bone sickles with flint blades (Figure 7.13). These bear a characteristic "sickle gloss" caused by the silica in cereal grass stalks.

The larger Natufian sites were close to the boundaries between the coastal plains or grassland valleys and the hill zone. Some were placed strategically to take advantage of good toolmaking stone. Such settlements enabled the Natufians to exploit spring cereal crops, fall nut harvests, and the game that flourished on the lowlands and on the rich nut **mast** on the forest floor in the hills above. Unlike their more mobile ancestors and neighbors, the sedentary Natufians enjoyed many months of plentiful food by exploiting spring cereals and then following nut harvests up the slopes as the nuts ripened at

Natufian
11000 to 8500 b.c.

FIGURE 7.11 Geometric Kebaran microliths, full size. Such small artifacts were manufactured in large numbers and mounted on wooden shafts as arrowheads or barbs.

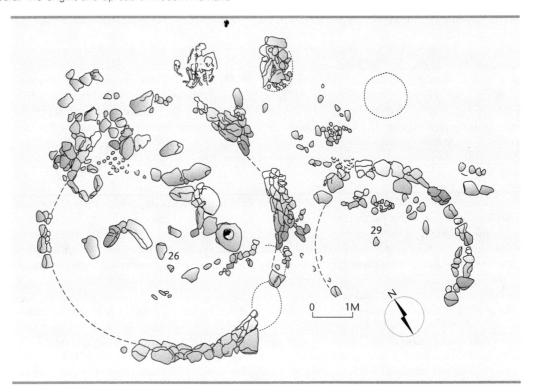

FIGURE 7.12 Natufian house foundations from Ain Mallaha, Jordan. There are mortars, pestles, and storage areas in Structure 26 (left) and a burial in a shallow pit immediately outside the north wall. Structure 29 (right) may have served as a storage area.

progressively higher elevations. Gazelle hunting assumed great importance at certain seasons of the year, with neighboring communities cooperating in game drives, ambushes, and other mass-hunting enterprises.

Natufian society offers intriguing glimpses at a new, more complex social order. In areas where community size increased, such issues as spacing between villages and territorial boundaries may have become important. The presence of a number of burials in and near settlements suggests that people felt they belonged to specific communities and locations in a way that was unknown in earlier times and that was to become very important once farming began. There are some signs of social ranking. One symbolic artifact, the *dentalium* seashell, is confined to a few burials, whereas the elaborate grave furniture, such as stone bowls found with some individuals, including children, hints strongly at some form of social differences. Perhaps this social ranking was the result of a need for the redistribution of food surpluses and to maintain order within much larger sedentary communities. Also, the stone slab grave covers and mortar markers associated with the cemeteries may have served as ritual markers of territorial boundaries, perhaps of lands vested in revered ancestors (see People of the Past box). At the same time, many settlements maintained exchange networks that transported both exotics like shell and more prosaic commodities like ground stone bowls over considerable distances, even if the activity was sporadic.

To the north, in the Euphrates Valley, hunter-gatherer settlements thrived on the margins of woodland and steppe zones. Abu Hureyra, the best known of these sites, began life as a small village settlement of a few families that lived in pit dwellings with simple reed roofs supported by wooden uprights (Moore et al., 2000). When the site was first occupied, the climate was somewhat warmer and damper than it is today. As a result, the village lay in a well-wooded steppe area where animals and wild cereals were abundant, so permanent settlement was possible. The inhabitants also had access to a reliable meat source: Persian gazelles that arrived from the south each spring. The arrivals were apparently killed en masse each year, and the meat was stored. More than 80 percent of the mammal bones in this small settlement were from gazelle. At the same time, the people exploited half a dozen staple wild plants as well as

FIGURE 7.13 Natufian bone-handled sickle and flint blades.

Sickle blades

Sickle handle

People of the Past   The Hilazon Tachtit Shaman, Israel, c. 10400 B.C.

The Grotte de Chauvet and other European art sites highlight the rich symbolic life enjoyed by many late Ice Age societies as early as 30,000 years ago. As we also saw in Chapters 4 and 5, at least some of the images painted on cave and rock shelter walls were probably associated with altered states of consciousness and perhaps shamanism. The word shaman or saman is a Siberian word, which originated with the Tungus people, in whose society shamans were individuals of unusual supernatural power. Perhaps it is best to call them "people of power," for their ability to communicate with ancestors and the powers of the supernatural realm set them apart from other members of the society. If living groups are any guide, then shamans, whether men or women alike, were both feared and respected in societies where the realm of the living passed imperceptibly into the supernatural realm—and it was shamans who passed effortless from one to the other, often with the aid of hallucinogenic substances.

Shamans may have been commonplace—they may even appear very rarely on late Ice Age cave walls—but it is only rarely that we can identify them in an archaeological site. Hilazon Tachtit is a small cave in Israel's Galilee region, which served as a burial ground for at least 28 Natufians as well as being occupied between about 10400 and 10000 B.C. (Grosman et al., 2008). Three burial pits lying alongside to circular structures built of limestone cobbles contained the remains of at least 25 people. They may have served as burial places, which were later reopened to recover skulls and limb bones that were buried elsewhere—a common Natufian practice that was also followed by later farming communities.

One burial stood out, that of a lightly built woman about 45 years old, who was in poor health. Her pathological conditions may have caused her to limp and given her an unusual appearance. She was not in the mass graves but in a single grave pit inside one of the structures. The woman lay with her legs apart, folded inward at the knee. About ten large stones were placed on her body at the time of burial as well as a series of remarkable grave goods. These included a worn basalt bowl and a complete human foot from a much larger person placed above her left legs. She was buried with about 50 complete tortoise shells, most of them deliberately snapped to extract the body, which was apparently consumed in a feast at the time of interment. Other animals also lay in the grave, among them the skulls of two stone martens, which were not disarticulated at the neck and may have been buried with the fur attached. Wing tip bones from a golden eagle may have borne the spectacular colored feathers of the bird in the grave. A male gazelle horn, known to have had spiritual associations to Natufians, and also the bones of other animals, including the tail of an aurochs, lay by the body.

More than 400 Natufian individuals have been excavated, yet the woman is unique. Her body was carefully arranged in position in her grave before being weighted with boulders. Tortoise shells lay under her pelvis and skull and at the edge of the grave. Furthermore, she was carried to the remote cave before it was occupied at a time when the nearest known village was 10 km (6 miles) away. She must have been an important person to justify such a laborious journey for the corpse of a disabled woman. The excavators believe she was a shaman, for she lay with objects such as tortoise shells, eagle wing, an aurochs tail, and fur-bearing animals that have powerful supernatural association in many societies. Most likely the woman, set apart by her disabilities, had close associations with these animal spirits. As a respected, perhaps feared, individual, perhaps a shaman who was set apart, she seems to have been buried with unusual care in a remote place with grave goods often associated with people of power in other societies. At the time of her death, Natufian society was undergoing profound change that would lead, in the end, to farming. The Hilazon Tachtit burial tells us, as do later shrines, that the symbolic and supernatural realms played an important role in increasing complex hunter-gatherer societies over 10,000 years ago.

---

more than 200 other species for a wide variety of purposes, among them hallucinogens and dyes. To this extent, they were managing and tending their environment to a significant degree. With such a favorable location, Abu Hureyra slowly increased in size to 300 to 400 people, until much more arid conditions, and perhaps deforestation due to heavy firewood consumption, caused them to leave (Moore and Hillman, 1992). In its heyday, its people may have enjoyed a higher degree of social organization than that found in nomadic hunter-gatherer societies.

By the end of Natufian times, about 10500 B.C., local populations were considerably higher than in earlier times. There are signs of stress, perhaps triggered by the more arid conditions that descended on the region with the advent of the cold and dry Younger Dryas. Increasing aridity shrank the cereal habitats in the Mediterranean zone, causing the most productive stands to be found at higher altitudes. At the same time, the Natufians were forced to remain in sedentary settlements close to permanent water supplies, a fact of life that made the cost of harvesting cereals and nuts at remote locations much higher. How, then, could people living in a complex hunter-gatherer system solve the problem of declining staples? After nearly 2,000 years of close involvement with cereal plants, they would have been well aware of what was needed to plant and grow cereal grasses deliberately. By deliberately planting cereals on a modest scale, the people tried to cope with uncertainty, to augment declining stands of wild wheat and barley with their own supplemental crops.

The Natufian scenario from the eastern Mediterranean was mirrored under different circumstances in many parts of the world, where trajectories of culture change followed many paths. In some areas, the new shape of hunter-gatherer societies preadapted people for the deliberate planting of cereal and root crops and for the domestication of animals. In other regions, such as southern California, that were marginal for subsistence farming, complex hunter-gatherer societies flourished until modern times.

Part III describes the origins of food production and early agricultural societies in all parts of the world.

Summary

- The Ice Age ended after 13000 B.C., ushering in the beginning of the Holocene period. Dramatic climatic changes marked the Holocene, including retreating ice sheets, major shifts in vegetational zones, and rises in sea level. Many large mammal species became extinct.

- Hunter-gatherer societies throughout the world developed highly localized adaptations to new, less predictable conditions, with a more intensive exploitation of food resources and, in many areas, a trend toward more permanent settlement, the use of storage technologies, and more complex societies.

- Complexity among hunter-gatherers became widespread after the Ice Age, especially in areas of exceptional resource diversity. Controversy surrounds the issue of complexity, with one school of thought arguing for a connection between resource diversity and abundant, diverse food supplies, and the other considering fishing a strategy of last resort resulting from population pressure and shortage of other foods. Alternatively, it may be due to rapid environmental change.

- This increased social complexity is well documented in the Mesolithic cultures of Scandinavia, where groups exploited maritime resources and birds extensively. Such increases in social complexity were marked by higher population densities, more intensive food exploitation, more long-distance exchange, and greater social ranking, detected in burial ornaments.

- These shifts also appear in the eastern Mediterranean region of Southwest Asia, especially among the Natufian people, who were intensive foragers of wild cereals and nuts, as well as expert gazelle hunters. Such intensification of the food quest and greater sedentism preadapted many groups for adopting agriculture and animal domestication.

Key Terms

ecotone (191)
Holocene (170)
intensification (173)

Levant (183)
mast (183)
microlith (173)

periglacial (172)
sedentism (177)

Further Reading

Bailey, Geoff, and Penny Spikins, eds. 2008. *Mesolithic Europe*. Cambridge, UK: Cambridge University Press.

Mithen, Steven. 2006. *After the Ice: A Global Human History*. Cambridge, MA: Harvard University Press.

FIRST FARMERS
C. 10000 B.C. TO MODERN TIMES

Agriculture is not to be looked on as a difficult or out-of-the-way invention, for the rudest savage, skilled as he is in the habits of the food-plants he gathers, must know well that if seeds or roots are put in a proper place in the ground they will grow.

Sir Edward Tylor, *Anthropology* (1871)

Part III tells the story of how food production began, starting with a discussion of some of the theories about the origins of agriculture and animal domestication. We then describe the archaeological evidence for the origins of food production in different parts of the world, starting in Southwest Asia.

First Farmers

Period already covered   Partial coverage

Period covered in **Part III**

5 mya   2.5 mya   1 mya   150,000 B.P.   10000 B.C.   A.D. 1   A.D. 1500

FIG. 2.2   FIG. 3.1a   FIG. 4.9   FIG. 9.5

8 Agriculture and Animal Domestication

The men climb high above the ground, lopping off small branches with their stone-bladed axes. The women and children gather up the foliage and pile it around the bare tree trunks. It is hard, backbreaking work that goes on for days on end, as the farmers watch the brazen sky for thunderclouds and signs of rain. A few spits of rain and gathering clouds bring hope of imminent showers. The people fire the tinder-dry brush, which burns fiercely. The sky fills with dense brown smoke as far as the eye can see, as the women hoe the fresh ash into the cleared soil and plant their precious seed. Then everyone waits for the life-giving rains to conjure bright green shoots from the soil (Figure 8.1).

Maasai herders driving their livestock, northern Tanzania, East Africa.

I t is sometimes hard for us to imagine, buying our food from supermarkets, that for more than 99 percent of our existence as humans we were hunters and gatherers, tied to the seasons of plant foods, the movements of game, and the ebb and flow of aquatic resources. **Food production,** the deliberate cultivation of cereal grasses and edible root plants, is a phenomenon of the last 12,000 years of human existence. This relatively new human subsistence strategy is in large part responsible for the rapidly accelerating rates of population growth and culture change in the past ten millennia. One of the major controversies in world prehistory surrounds the origins of food production: Why, when, and where did people first grow crops and domesticate wild animals? This chapter describes some of the major theories developed over more than a century of research.

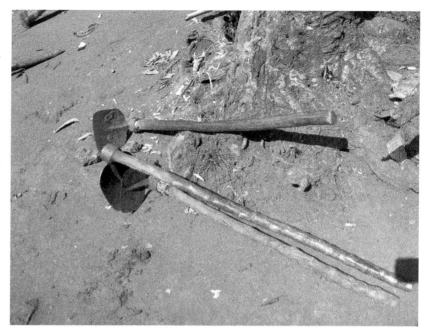

FIGURE 8.1 African hoes lying in a Ugandan village.

Theories About the Origins of Food Production

As we saw in Chapter 7, changing environmental and demographic conditions at the end of the Ice Age, after 13000 B.C., caused major long-term changes in hunter-gatherer societies. There was more localization, considerable technological innovation, and a trend toward sedentary settlement in areas with abundant and seasonally predictable food resources. And as we saw with the Natufian culture of the eastern Mediterranean, many of these societies were, in many respects, preadapted to food production and even experimenting with planting wild grasses. When and why did they choose to grow their own crops?

Early Hypotheses

Late Victorian archaeologists were the first to speculate about agricultural origins. They envisaged a solitary genius who suddenly had the brilliant idea of planting seed. Today, no one looks for a single genius or for the earliest maize cob. Rather, modern theory concentrates on the complex processes that caused gradual changes in human subsistence patterns (B. Smith, 1998).

The best-known and longest-lived of the early theories was Vere Gordon Childe's "Neolithic Revolution" (**Neolithic**). He proposed a major economic revolution in prehistory that took place in Southwest Asia during a period of severe drought, a climatic crisis that caused a symbiotic relationship between humans and animals in fertile oases. The new economies ensured a richer and more reliable food source for people on the edge of starvation after the Ice Age (Childe, 1936, 1952). Childe's simple theory was widely accepted, but it was based on inadequate archaeological and environmental data. It has long been surpassed by much more sophisticated formulations (H. Wright, 1993).

Systematic fieldwork on the origins of food production began only in the late 1940s, when Robert J. Braidwood of the University of Chicago mounted an expedition to the Kurdish foothills of Iran to test Childe's theory. He soon rejected any notion of catastrophic climatic change, arguing that economic change came from "ever increasing cultural differentiation and specialization of human communities" (Braidwood and Braidwood, 1983: 23). Thus, people were culturally receptive to innovation and experimentation with the cultivation of wild grasses. Braidwood believed that Stone Age hunters had domesticated animals and plants in "nuclear zones," areas such as the hilly flanks of the Zagros Mountains in Iraq and upland areas overlooking the Mesopotamian lowlands. He was convinced that the human capacity and enthusiasm for experimentation made it possible for people to domesticate animals. Most modern theories of food production have their beginnings in Braidwood's work, which focused on the notion that people were culturally receptive to new subsistence practices.

Multivariate Theories

Since the 1960s, theorizing about the origins of food production revolves around complex multivariate models, which combine many factors (Flannery, 1965, 1968). Graeme Barker remarks that many scholars have been tempted to put "a little bit of everything into the pot ... stir well ... and bring to the boil with a little climatic change" (Barker, 2006: 411). He is right, but all multivariate models take into account the reality that many early Holocene hunter-gatherer societies were more complex and well preadapted to food production before anyone started planting wild cereal grasses or penning animals.

For example, as recently as the eighteenth century A.D., the Kumeyaay Indians of southern California reduced the risk of starvation by "domesticating" their landscape. They lived in semiarid valleys, encouraging the growth of wild grasses by burning harvested stands, then broadcasting some of the seed over the burned ground. They created groves of oaks and pines by planting edible nuts at high elevations, and they planted agave and other desert plants in suitable habitats. In this way, they flourished by means of a complex mosaic of manipulated wild plants (B. Smith, 1998).

Population Pressure   Now that we can look at world prehistory on a far wider canvas than the pioneers in this field, we know that agriculture appeared at approximately the same time in Southwest Asia and China and somewhat later in the Americas, in **Mesoamerica** and the **Andean region**. This development has led some scholars to think in terms of worldwide population pressure that caused many hunter-gatherer societies to abandon gathering because their growing populations had reached the limit that their food resources could support (Cohen, 1977). No one denies that food production led to higher population densities and indeed ignited a population explosion (Figure 8.2). But there is no evidence for very high population densities in Southwest Asia or Mesoamerica during the millennia when agriculture was taking hold, certainly not for the kinds of density that cause chronic food shortages (Flannery, 1983).

Social Theories   Barbara Bender (1985) argues for social factors. She theorizes that some hunter-gatherer societies were becoming more socially complex, with far more elaborate hierarchical social organization. She points to the increasing abundance of trade objects and the appearance of richly decorated burials in preagricultural societies in Southwest Asia, Europe, and elsewhere. Perhaps, she hypothesizes, an expansion of trade and of political alliances between neighboring groups created new social and economic pressures to produce more and more surplus goods, not only foodstuffs but other objects as well. This development, in turn, led to more sedentary lifeways. Bender's social hypothesis tends to ignore the compelling factors of now well-documented environmental changes that were apparently one of the key elements in a move toward cultivation in areas like Southwest Asia.

Population and Resources Theories   Another category of theories is based on relationships between populations and resources. This category is an extension of a famous argument by economist Ester Boserup (1965) that points out that food production systems of any type are highly flexible. Thus, hunter-gatherers responded to favorable relationships between population densities and available resources by intensifying their hunting and gathering (see Site box). However, population growth in restricted areas with diverse resources can cause food shortages because there is less mobility and everyone has less territory to move around in, a situation that may have arisen in parts of Southwest Asia (Chapter 9), northwestern Europe (Chapter 10), and the Americas (Chapter 13).

Thus, population and resource theories tend to concentrate on interdependent factors: risk and population-resource imbalances. Apart from environmental change, all environments involve some form of risk for hunter-gatherer societies: drought cycles; long, cold winters; or unpredictable floods, to mention only a few possibilities. People respond to these risks by moving, by developing new food storage technologies, and by drying foods like powdered bison meat or salmon. A straightforward solution to rising populations, resulting food shortages, or risk factors may be to go one step farther: to cultivate familiar plants and to domesticate common prey so that people can draw on familiar "stored" resources in scarce months (B. Smith, 1998).

FIGURE 8.2 World population changes since the beginnings of food production. There has been an explosion in human population densities in the past 10,000 years.

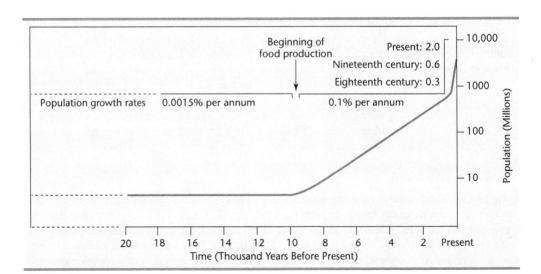

SiTE > Guilá Naquitz, Mexico <

Kent Flannery's investigations in the Valley of Oaxaca, Mexico, offer a classic example of ecological approaches to early food production. As part of a long-term archaeological project, Flannery and his research team excavated Guilá Naquitz Cave, a small shelter used about six times over a 2,000-year period between 8750 and 6670 B.C. (Flannery, 1986; Marcus and Flannery, 1996). These sporadic occupations extended from the early Archaic, soon after the extinction of big game in the region, to a period when the occupants were using domesticated plants. The early Archaic occupants spent some of the year in large bands, splitting up to exploit larger areas of territory in much smaller groups, one of which used Guilá Naquitz on occasion.

The multidisciplinary research project revealed a wealth of information about the visitors to this shelter, identifying not only subsistence strategies but also the division of labor between the women, who processed plant foods, and the men, who did the hunting, through the distribution of artifacts and features in the cave's occupation levels. The excavations also produced evidence for the domestication of the gourd *Cucurbita pepo* by 8000 B.C. (B. Smith, 1997). Most important of all, Flannery and his colleagues tried to answer two questions: What was the strategy that led to the choice of the wild plants eaten by the inhabitants? And how did this strategy change when they began planting?

Robert Reynolds (1986) developed a comprehensive and ingenious "adaptive computer simulation model" to approach these questions. He started with a hypothetical, and totally ignorant, band of five people who settle in the area. Over a long period of trial and error, they "learn" how to schedule 11 major food plants over the year, in an environment where the sequence of dry, wet, and "average" years is totally unpredictable. The collective memories of successive generations prove to be vital, for experience is the basis on which they modify their strategies in future years that prove to be the same as experienced ones. For example, a cycle of drought years may yield survival strategies that are remembered through the succeeding wet years, despite the passage of a generation or more, and are then used again during drought years. The strategies rank plants and vegetational zones in order of the size of the harvest, yielding collective decisions followed by the band. By the time the last preagricultural occupation occurs at Guilá Naquitz, the band is so efficient in all conditions that very few modifications improve the adaptation. Basically, there is a stable performance level.

The computer simulation produced a mix of plant species that matched the mix found in the occupation deposits very well. It also showed that one set of strategies was used for wet years, when plant foods were available in abundance and a wide range of them was used, and another in dry years, when the people took fewer species and those with higher yields. Reynolds's simulation is based on the assumption that the first stages of agriculture were attempts to alter the distributions of the natural densities of specific plants. The wet-year strategies were the ones that were the most flexible and the most capable of incorporating experimentation without risk. At first, deliberate planting may have been a rarity, a strategy that was successful but was employed only in wet years. It was a specialized strategy whose yields were seen eventually to have advantages, to the point where planting became more frequent, occurring not only in wet years but in dry ones as well, once the experiment had been shown to work. If the simulation is correct, the pace of experimentation was very slow, confined at first to wet years; at the same time, centuries-old foraging strategies continued.

This scenario suggests that bean cultivation near the cave itself allowed the people to collect more food and travel less, with, ultimately, a greater emphasis on foraging in the thorn forest near the site rather than farther afield. At the same time, traveling time decreased and collecting time increased; for example, acorns from the thorn forest became much more common. Less time was spent on lower-yielding, more marginal wild plants, as greater emphasis was placed on beans, squash, and maize. As the group gained experience with planting, yields rose, and the people placed ever more emphasis on cultivation as opposed to foraging.

Reynolds's simulation corresponds well with the shifts in plant species found in the six occupation levels at Guilá Naquitz. When he added climatic change and population growth to the equation, he found that two sources of uncertainty—unpredictable climate fluctuations and population shifts—were the factors that led to the most rapid increase in the density of high-yielding domesticated plants near the site. Reynolds believes that a high level of annual climatic variation—with its frequent wet years, for experimentation, and dry years, which put pressure on people to be efficient—was a major factor in the shift to food production in Oaxaca. So were short-term as opposed to long-term fluctuations in population densities, which also led to an accelerating reliance on cultivation not only on hill slopes but also on river plains in Oaxaca, the environments in which the first larger villages have been found.

This model is remarkable in that it corresponds well with the excavated data. Reynolds demonstrates that these Oaxaca people were well preadapted to food production. There was no "trigger" that started cultivation. The people simply added gourds first, then beans, and a simple form of maize to a much earlier foraging adaptation, at first as a wet-year innovation, which came into use in average and dry years once it proved reliable. As Flannery says, "Human hunting and gathering is, after all, economic behavior" (1986: 75).

Climatic Change   Climatic changes, such as sudden cold snaps or droughts lasting decades, even centuries, have been invoked as causes of food production. Although climatic change was never a prime mover, a harsh drought or some other short-term climatic shift could have a profound effect on peoples' choices of food and their ways of feeding themselves—witness the complex interplay between drought and early farming at Abu Hureyra, Syria (described in Chapter 9).

Ecological Theories Another group of theorists focuses on ecological factors such as local variability in food resources and the interactive effects of human exploitation. Proponents of these ecological models talk of "opportunities" for the introduction of agriculture, of people turning to superior local resources when the moment arrived. That is, some resources—say, wild wheat or barley or wild goats—were seen as attractive. People used them more and more, to the point where they were eventually domesticated.

Kent Flannery (1968) used this approach to examine the mechanisms by which Mesoamericans took up agriculture. The preagricultural peoples of the region adapted to a few animal genera and plants whose range cut across several environments, such as deer, rabbits, cactus fruit, and wild grasses, including the wild ancestor of maize. They scheduled their annual round so as to be in the right place at the right time to harvest, say, cactus fruit. Over the centuries, genetic changes in the ancestor of maize made it more productive and progressively more important in the diet. As time went on, people spent more and more time cultivating it and rescheduled their annual round accordingly, neglecting foods they had once exploited in favor of cultivated crops.

The crux of ecological models is trying to identify the processes that caused people to make the shift to deliberate cultivation, again a very difficult task. For example, did cultivation enable people to widen their adaptive niches? Were there new cost-benefit realities that favored farming? What about such factors as the nutritive value and the seasonal availability of foods? Did genetic changes in animals and plants play a role?

Social Competition The Canadian archaeologist Brian Hayden (2003) has argued that competition within complex hunter-gatherer societies, like the Natufian of southwestern Asia (see Chapter 9), led to agriculture. Ambitious individuals acquire prestige and social standing by throwing feasts, which creates obligations that others are unable to match, in societies where reciprocity is all-important. Hayden believes that many of the first cultivated plants, like chili peppers, were flavorings rather than basic staples. Cultivation may have been adopted to provide supplies of especially prized forms of food and drink.

Most theories about the origins of food production, like Hayden's, are far from easy to test. It is difficult to link complex models with actual field data, largely because the models do not lend themselves to easy documentation. Such documentation will come only from very meticulous excavations at single sites that will be combined, eventually, into larger regional models (H. Wright, 1993). Such research has been conducted successfully at Abu Hureyra, Syria; in the southern part of the eastern Mediterranean (Chapter 9); and at Guilá Naquitz, Mexico (see Site box). In the final analysis, however, no one theory of the origins of food production embraces all regions of the world. The shift from plant gathering to food production was much more complicated, as people adapted to very localized cultural and environmental challenges. These changes may have taken many centuries, even millennia, in some places. But everywhere the key element was human decision making in the face of various selective pressures.

The Guilá Naquitz excavation shows us that foragers make decisions about the distances to travel and the plants and territory to exploit. When they shift to agriculture, they are changing the pattern of their decision making, not in an irreversible way but probably as one of several alternatives open to them. This change "has to be understood in terms of their previous decision-making pattern, the options open to them, and that new situation" (Flannery, 1986: 76). At the same time, this culturally based explanation also emerges from circumstances arising from larger processes, among them a worldwide climatic change at the end of the Ice Age and long-term evolutionary processes. In time, for example, early farmers anywhere acquired a selective advantage by virtue of their ability to disperse seeds from "a group of plants whose genetic program they had altered, in defiance of natural selection" (p. 77).

The Guilá Naquitz research, with its sophisticated computer simulations, is an example of what much research into agricultural origins involves. In the final analysis, Flannery seems to prefer what he calls a "probabilistic ecosystem model." This model allows people to respond to changes in the ecosystem in several ways. The Guilá Naquitz people reduced their search area for wild plants, which may have led to protein deficiencies. Their solution was to grow beans, a protein-rich crop that allowed them to reduce their search area still more. In other parts of the world, like southern California and the Pacific Northwest, people intensified fishing and sea-mammal hunting, and agriculture was never adopted on any scale, even if the people were well aware of it. Agriculture was not the only option. It was one of many, and one that achieved remarkable success in the regions where it did develop.

Differing Dates for Food Production

As we shall see in Chapters 9 to 13, food production began at very different times in various parts of the world, being well established, for example, in Southwest Asia and China by 10000 B.C., in Mesoamerica by 5000 B.C., but in tropical Africa by about 1000 B.C., and then only in some locations. What were the local variations that accounted for this time lag?

We know that hunter-gatherers in subtropical zones such as Southwest Asia and highland Mesoamerica were beginning to manipulate potential domesticates among wild grasses and root species at the end of the Ice Age. Dependence on such foods probably came earlier in these regions, where there were only a few forageable species. Such dependence was essential to long-term survival. In contrast, populations in more humid tropical regions, like the African and Amazonian rain forests, probably did little more than manipulate a few wild species to minimize risk in lean years; as a corollary, many African agricultural peoples turn to hunting and gathering in lean years to this day. The archaeological record shows that agriculture was established considerably earlier in subtropical Southwest Asia, northern China, Middle and South America, Southeast Asia, and India than it was in humid, tropical zones, undoubtedly because these regions were rich in game and wild vegetable foods. Furthermore, domesticated crops and animals were more susceptible to irregular rainfall, locusts and other insect attacks, and endemic stock diseases. A strong and sustained incentive to obtain food must have been a prerequisite for a lasting shift from foraging to agriculture.

Many variables must be understood before we can reconstruct the conditions under which agriculture was first regarded as a profitable activity. We are searching for sets of conditions in which population pressure, the distribution of plants, the rate at which the environment was changing, and even the techniques of harvesting wild grasses all played their part in making agriculture work. Then there are variations among the potentially domesticable plants and animals, some of which resisted domestication because of their long life span or because parts of their lives took place outside human control. The seasonal distribution of wild vegetable foods or game may also have prevented experiments in domestication, when the seasons during which these wild foods were exploited coincided with the times of year when it was important that experimenting farmers stay near their growing crops. Under these circumstances, people would tend to pursue their traditional food-getting strategies rather than risk their lives for an uncertain outcome. We sometimes forget that the development of both farming and animal domestication stemmed not from a desire to invent a new way of life, but to perpetuate an old and familiar one—foraging.

However, the most critical factor in the emergence of food production was the same human intellect that carried to every corner of the world during the previous 50,000 to 30,000 years. As Steven Mithen (1996: 505–506) remarks, humanity "shared the same biological drives and the means to achieve them—a mix of cooperation and competition, sharing and selfishness, virtue and violence. All possessed a peculiar type of mind, one with insatiable curiosity and new-found creativity.… Without it there would have been no human history, but merely a continuous cycle of the adaptation and readaptation that had begun several million years ago."

Studying Early Food Production

Flotation methods, which pass soil samples through water and recover substantial samples of even the tiniest seeds, have revolutionized our knowledge of early plant domestication. The development of accelerator mass spectrometry (AMS) radiocarbon dating now allows the dating of individual seeds, not just the levels they come from (see Dating the Past box). This has allowed investigators to pin down with great precision the dates for domesticated wheat and barley at sites like Abu Hureyra, Syria. Maize domestication is now dated to at least 6700 B.C. in Central America (Ranere et al., 2009).

Scanning electron microscopy (SEM) is providing vital information on the micromorphology of tiny wild and domesticated seeds. SEM has allowed scientists to identify domesticated native quinoa seeds in the Peruvian Andes dating to between 3000 and 2000 B.C. (B. Smith, 1998). And by using genetic fingerprinting, botanists have been able to identify the present location of populations of wild einkorn wheat that led to domesticated einkorn in southeastern Turkey, less than 250 km (155 miles) from Abu Hureyra in Syria, one of the earliest farming villages in the world (see Chapter 9) (Heun et al., 1997).

The invention of agriculture was not, in and of itself, that important an event. What was of all-embracing significance was the transition from hunting and gathering to cultivation—the catalyst for all the elaborate cultural developments of later millennia, of which urban civilization was but one (B. Smith, 2001). In strictly archaeological terms, we will never document the moment of invention, but over many years we have been able to chronicle the rapid spread of the new economies, which soon reached all parts of the world where farming or animal herding were possible. Thanks to new and cutting-edge research, we now know that the process of spread was a very complex one, involving both long periods when people subsisted off wild foods as well as domestic crops, then moments when the new economies spread rapidly.

Twenty-first-century science is documenting new information not only about seeds but also about **phytoliths**, or vegetable tissues. For the first time, root crops are coming to the fore, a hitherto neglected aspect of early agriculture (Hather, 1994). Staggering advances in knowledge will shortly come from pioneering work on the genetic fingerprinting of modern wild grain populations, on their

Dating the Past   Accelerator Mass Spectrometry (AMS) Radiocarbon Dating

Until about 20 years ago, dating the rate of decay (beta counts) from different radiocarbon samples had a calculated ratio that gave only approximations. Using carbon-14 (^{14}C) and carbon-12 (^{12}C), scientists could detect and count individual decay events with radiocarbon. They would observe the emission of beta particles to determine the rate of radioactive breakdown and so estimate the number of ^{14}C atoms remaining in the sample. Because only a small number of ^{14}C atoms break down over the many hours of the sample count, the samples had to be large enough to provide an adequate number of beta counts.

Back in the 1960s, archaeologists collected handfuls of charcoal from hearths in plastic bags, the rule being, the larger the sample, the better. Scientists could not date small objects like maize cobs or tiny wood fragments embedded in the sockets of prehistoric bronze spearheads. Because they make up too-small samples, such objects are especially hard to date—and very difficult to pin down chronologically when the ratio can be only approximate. Minute samples such as seeds can easily move upward or downward into older or younger occupation layers, either through human agencies such as trampling or through natural phenomena such as burrowing animals. The development of a new radiocarbon method based on accelerator mass spectrometry (AMS)

radiocarbon dating in 1983 revolutionized radiocarbon chronologies and the study of early food production (Figure 8.3).

An accelerator mass spectrometer can date the age of sample material by counting the number of ^{14}C atoms present. Rather than counting decay events (beta counts), researchers estimate the remaining ^{14}C by directly counting ^{14}C atoms. By doing this, they can date samples 1,000 times smaller than the handful of charcoal used a generation ago. The development of small, high-energy mass spectrometers solved a major problem, that of background noise from ions or molecules of a similar mass to the ^{14}C masking their presence. The new instruments filter out background, as a proportion of the sample's atoms are propelled through an accelerator toward a detector (see Figure 8.3). Ionized carbon atoms from the sample are pulled in beam form toward the accelerator. A magnet bends the beam, so lighter atoms turn more sharply than heavier ones and move to the inside of the diverging beam. A filter blocks the passage of all charged particles except those of atomic mass 14. The accelerator pushes the stripped beam through a second beam-bending magnet, filtering out any last non-^{14}C particles. A magnetic lens focuses the beam as a ^{14}C detector counts the number of remaining ions, allowing the calculation of the age of the sample.

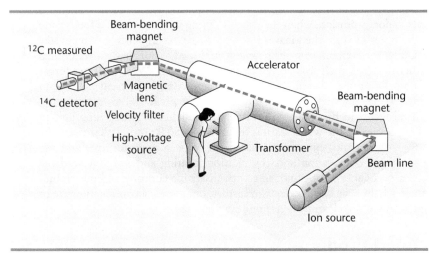

FIGURE 8.3   AMS radiocarbon dating. Modified from B. Smith (1998).

---

similarities to domesticated relatives, and on their original homelands (Jones and Brown, 2000). For example, we now know that the heartland of einkorn was in eastern Turkey (Heun et al., 1997), and that of maize, in the Rio Balsas region of Mexico (Doebley, 2004). Parallel studies on the genetic makeup of modern animal domesticates show that there were multiple origin centers for cattle, horses, sheep, goats, and pigs (Zeder et al., 2002).

DNA and other multidisciplinary research into the transition from hunting and gathering to agriculture have only just begun but are likely to revolutionize our knowledge of this all-important chapter in human history. Chapter 8 in future editions of this book is likely to be very different from this one!

Why Did Food Production Take Hold So Late?

Once successful, food production spread rapidly, partly because the resulting population growth prevented people from reverting to hunting and gathering. An interesting question remains: Why did food production not take hold much earlier? Surely, there were many previous occasions during the Ice Age when conditions were favorable for people to start cultivating plants. Here, population models for prehistory offer some clues. We know there was gradual population growth during the Stone Age. The constant, cyclic changes of the past 700,000 years must have led to conditions in some areas that presented human societies with the challenge of constant environmental change and population shifts. However, as we saw in Chapter 7, it was not until the end of the Ice Age that global populations rose sufficiently to limit mobility, and the easiest strategy for people faced with food shortages is to move. There was initially a slow and then a rapidly accelerating intensification of hunter-gatherer lifeways during and after the last glacial maximum, especially during Holocene times. This intensification preadapted many societies to food production for the first time (McCorriston and Hole, 1991). And, as we saw in Chapter 7, increased plant productivity resulted from higher carbon dioxide levels in the atmosphere after the Ice Age.

Consequences of Food Production

The new food-producing economies proved dramatically successful. In 10000 B.C., virtually everybody in the world lived by hunting and gathering. By A.D. 1, most people were farmers or herders, and only a minority were still hunter-gatherers. The spread of food production throughout the world took only about 8,000 years. The problem for archaeologists is to explain not only why people took up agriculture but also why so many populations adopted this new, and initially risky, economic transition in such a short time. Food production spread to all corners of the world except where an environment with extreme aridity, heat, or cold rendered agriculture or herding impossible, or where people chose to remain hunters and gatherers.

Food production resulted, ultimately, in much higher population densities in many locations, for the domestication of plants and animals can lead to an economic strategy that increases and stabilizes the available food supplies, although more energy is used to produce them (see Figure 8.2). Farmers use concentrated tracts of territory for agriculture and for grazing cattle and small stock if they practice mixed farming. Their territory is much smaller than that of hunter-gatherers (although **pastoralists** [animal herders] need huge areas of grazing land for seasonal pasture). Within a smaller area of farming land, property lines are carefully delineated as individual ownership and problems of inheritance arise. Shortages of land can lead to disputes and to the founding of new village settlements on previously uncultivated soil.

More enduring settlements brought other changes. Heavier tool kits and more lasting houses replaced the portable and lightweight material possessions of many hunter-gatherers (Figure 8.4a). Grindstones and ground-edged axes were even more essential to farming culture than they were to gathering societies. Hoes and other implements of tillage were vital for the planting and harvesting of crops. New social units came into being as more lasting home bases were developed; these social links reflected the ownership and inheritance of land and led to much larger settlements that brought hitherto scattered populations into closer and more regular contact.

Food production led to changed attitudes toward the environment (Butzer, 1995). Cereal crops were such that people could store their food for winter (Figure 8.4b). The hunter-gatherers exploited game, fish, and vegetable foods, but the farmers did more: They altered the environment by the very nature of their exploitation. Expansion of agriculture meant felling trees and burning vegetation to clear the ground for planting. The same fields were then abandoned after a few years to lie fallow, and more woodland was cleared. The original vegetation began to regenerate, but it may have been cleared again before reaching its original state. This shifting pattern of farming is called slash-and-burn or **swidden agriculture.** Voracious domesticated animals stripped pastures of their grass cover; then heavy rainfalls denuded the hills of valuable soil, and the pastures were never the same again. However elementary the agricultural technology, the farmer changed the environment, if only with

(a)   (b)

FIGURE 8.4   (a) Village granaries in Burkina Faso, West Africa. (b) Pounding grain in a Niger village, with thatched dwellings in the background.

fires lit to clear scrub from gardens and to fertilize the soil with wood ash. Hunter-gatherers had deliberately set fires to encourage the growth of new grass for their grazing prey. In a sense, shifting to slash-and-burn agriculture was merely an extension of the age-old use of fire to encourage the regeneration of vegetation.

Food production resulted in high population densities, but disease, the available food supplies, the water supplies, and particularly famine controlled population increases. Also, early agricultural methods depended heavily on a careful selection of the soil. The technology of the first farmers was hardly potent enough for the extensive clearing of the dense woodland under which many good soils lay, so only accessible land was cultivated. Gardens were probably scattered over a much wider territory than is necessary today. One authority estimates that today only 40 percent of the moderately fertile soil in Africa is available for cultivation (Allan, 1965). This figure must have been lower in the early days of agriculture, with their simpler stone tools and fewer crops. In regions of seasonal rainfall, such as Southwest Asia, other parts of Asia, and sub-Saharan Africa, periods of prolonged drought are common. Famine was a real possibility as population densities rose. Many early agriculturalists must have worriedly watched the sky and had frequent crop failures in times of drought. Their small stores of grain from the previous season would not have carried them through another year, especially if they had been careless with their surplus. Farmers were forced to shift their economic strategy in such times.

We know that the earliest farmers availed themselves of game and wild vegetable foods to supplement their agriculture, just as today some farmers are obliged to rely heavily on wild vegetable foods and hunting to survive in bad years (Scudder, 1962, 1971). Many hunter-gatherer bands collect intensively just a few species of edible plants in their large territories. Aware of many other edible vegetables, they fall back on these only in times of stress; the less favored foods can carry a comparatively small population through to the next rains. A larger agricultural population is not so flexible and quickly exhausts wild vegetables and game in the much smaller territory used for farming and grazing. If the drought lasts for years, famine, death, and reduced population can follow.

Nutrition and Early Food Production

Was food production a real improvement in human lifeways? For generations, archaeologists have argued that human health improved dramatically as a result of agriculture, because people worked less and lived on more reliable food supplies (Butzer, 1982). But some have argued that, in fact, agriculture brought diminishing returns in relation to the labor expended in the new systems that were adopted to feed many more people. Richard Lee's (1979) studies of the !Kung San of the Kalahari Desert tend to support these views. They show that, at the time of the studies, these hunter-gatherers, and presumably others, had abundant leisure and worked less than farmers. Some nutritionists point out that foragers may have had better-balanced diets than many farmers, who relied heavily on root or cereal crops. Further, farmers, with their sedentary settlements and higher population densities, were much more vulnerable to famine than their hunter-gatherer predecessors. They would also have been more vulnerable to gastrointestinal infections and epidemics because of crowded village populations (Cohen, 1988).

Nutrition studies based on the skeletons of early farmers suggest some incidence of anemia and slow growth resulting from malnutrition. Regional studies of prehistoric populations have suggested a decline in mean age life expectancy in agricultural populations. Taken as a whole, **paleopathological** studies suggest a general decline in the quality, and perhaps the length, of human life with the advent of food production. However, many unknowns are involved, among them changes in fertility and population growth rates, which caused the world's population to rise even if general health standards and life expectancy fell (C. Larsen, 1995). What impact these studies will have on population pressure theories about the origins of agriculture is still uncertain. Certainly, any shift to food production caused by increasing population pressure could be reflected in a decline in the overall health and nutrition displayed by prehistoric skeletons.

In the final analysis, some people probably turned to food production only when other alternatives were no longer practicable. The classic example is the Aborigines of extreme northern Australia, who were well aware that their neighbors in New Guinea were engaged in intensive agriculture. They, too, knew how to plant the top of the wild yam so that it resprouted, but they never adopted food production, simply because they had no need to become dependent on a lifeway that would reduce their leisure time and produce more food than they required.

Herding: Domestication of Animals

Potentially tamable species like the wild ox, goat, sheep, and dog were widely distributed in the Old World during the Upper Pleistocene. Dogs were probably first domesticated as hunting companions during the late Ice Age, long before 15,000 years ago. They were easily tamed from wolf ancestors in situations where humans became leaders of the wolf pack, the allegiance of the members being transferred to a person as opposed to another wolf (Pennisi, 2002). New World farmers domesticated only such animals as the llama, the guinea pig, and the turkey, and then only under special conditions and within narrow geographic limits. It is possible that the domesticated dog crossed into the New World with the first Americans before 12000 b.c., or perhaps it was domesticated elsewhere in the Americas. The evidence is uncertain.

Having one's own herds of domesticated mammals ensured a regular meat supply. The advantages to having a major source of meat under one's control are obvious. Later, domesticated animals provided byproducts such as milk, cheese, and butter, as well as skins for clothes and tent coverings and materials for leather shields and armor. In later millennia, people learned how to breed animals for specialized tasks such as plowing, transportation, and traction (Clutton-Brock, 1989).

Domestication implies a genetic selection emphasizing special features of continuing use to the domesticator. Wild sheep have no wool, wild cows produce milk only for their offspring, and undomesticated chickens do not lay surplus eggs. Changes in wool bearing, lactation, or egg production could be achieved by isolating wild populations for selective breeding under human care. Isolating species from a larger gene pool produced domestic sheep with thick, woolly coats and domestic goats providing regular supplies of milk, which formed a staple in the diet of many human populations.

No one knows exactly how the domestication of animals began. Three elements are vital to domestication: constraint on the movement of the target populations, regulation of their breeding, and control of their feeding to shape future generations. During the Upper Pleistocene, people were already beginning to concentrate heavily on some species of large mammals for their diet. The Magdalenians of southwestern France directed much of their lives toward pursuing reindeer. At the end of the Pleistocene, hunters in Southwest Asia were concentrating on gazelles and other steppe animals. Wild sheep and goats were intensively hunted on the southern shores of the Caspian Sea. Gregarious, highly social animals like goats and sheep are the most easily domesticated beasts; they follow the lead of a dominant herd member or all move together. They also tolerate feeding and breeding in a confined environment. Most likely a prolonged period of what one could call "herd management" preceded full domestication (Zeder, 2011).

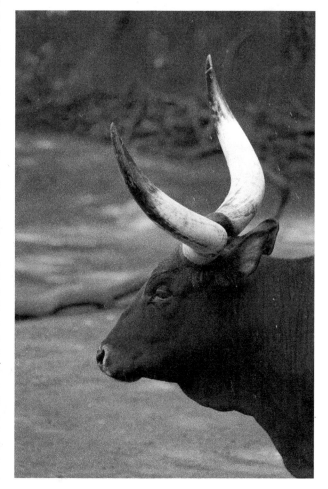

FIGURE 8.5 *Bos primigenius,* the aurochs, or wild ox. It became extinct in Europe in 1627, although modern breeding experiments have reconstructed this formidable beast.

Hunters often fed off the same herd for a long time, sometimes deliberately sparing young females and immature beasts to keep the source of food alive. Young animals captured in the chase might be taken back to the camp and might grow dependent on those who caged them, thus becoming partially tamed. A hunter could grasp the possibility of gaining control of the movements of a few key members of a herd, which would be followed by the others. Once the experience of keeping pets or of restricting game movements had suggested a new way of life, people might have experimented with different species. As part of domestication, animals and humans increased their mutual dependence.

The archaeological evidence for early domestication is so fragile that nothing survives except the bones of the animals kept by the early farmers, and the differences between wild and domestic animal bones are often so small initially that it is difficult to distinguish them unless very large collections are found. In the earliest centuries of domestication, corralled animals were nearly indistinguishable from wild species. The process of animal domestication was undoubtedly prolonged, developing in several areas of Southwest Asia at approximately the same time. Although animal bones are scarce and often unsatisfactory as evidence of early domestication, most authorities now agree that the first species to be domesticated in Southwest Asia were goats and sheep, about 8500 b.c. Goats and sheep are small herd animals whose carcasses yield much meat for their size. They can readily be penned and isolated to develop a symbiotic relationship with people. By 8500 b.c., goat bones at sites like Nevali Çori in Turkey display the characteristic mortality profile of managed herds: Surplus males were slaughtered before adulthood, with females being kept for breeding and milk purposes. Earlier hunting mortality profiles show a focus on adult males (Zeder and Hesse, 2000).

Cattle are much more formidable to domesticate, for their prototype was *Bos primigenius*, the wild ox much hunted by Stone Age people (Figure 8.5). Andrew Smith (1992) believes that the first domesticated animals came from better-disciplined wild herds in arid environments, where it was easier to control the movements of animals. Such conditions may have pertained to much of Southwest Asia and the Sahara as the climate became drier after 7000 B.C.

Some animals, such as sea mammals, resist domestication because much of their lives is spent out of the range of human influence. Most early successes with domestication took place with gregarious animals. They can be thought of as a food reserve, as "grain on the hoof."

Plant Cultivation

Many fewer wild vegetable foods were domesticated than foraged over the millennia (Zeder, 2011). In the Old World, wheat, barley, and other cereals that grow wild over much of Asia and Europe became cultivated. In the New World, a different set of crops was tamed (Harris and Hillman, 1989; Zohary and Hopf, 1988). These included Indian corn (*Zea mays*), the only important wild grass to be domesticated. Root crops such as manioc and sweet potatoes, chili peppers, tobacco, and several types of bean were grown. As Christine Hastorf (1999) remarks, very often the plants first domesticated were "flavorful, spicy, sweet, industrial, hallucinatory, or medicinal." (Common to both Old and New Worlds are gourds, cotton, and two or three other minor crops; see B. Smith, 1998.)

In the Old World, tropical regions had many potential domesticates such as the yam and gourds. In Southeast Asia and sub-Saharan Africa, a long period of intensive gathering and experimenting with the deliberate planting of wild root crops probably preceded the beginnings of formal agriculture. Perhaps, however, the transition from the gathering to the cultivation of root crops was almost unconscious, for many tubers are easy to grow deliberately. The African yam, for example, will sprout if its top is cut off and buried in the ground. The hunter-gatherer bands that were familiar with this easy means of conserving their food supplies may simply have intensified their planting efforts to supplement shortages caused by changed circumstances. As with animals, however, certain heavily exploited species tended to resist domestication; among them were long-lived trees like the oak and plants whose life spans were so long that they inhibited human selection. They also tended to cross-pollinate, a process that undoubtedly discouraged human efforts to trigger or control their genetic variation.

In the Old World, the qualities of wild wheat, barley, and similar grains are quite different from those of their domestic equivalents (Harris and Hillman, 1989). In the wild, these grains occur in dense stands. One can harvest them by tapping the stem with the hands and gathering the seeds in a basket as they fall off, or by uprooting the plant. The tapping technique is effective because the wild grain is attached to the stem by a brittle joint, or **rachis.** When the grass is tapped, the weak rachis breaks and the seed falls into the basket.

The first cultivated wheat and barley crops were of the wild, brittle-rachis type, and the resulting crops would probably have been large enough to generate domestic-type mutants in the first two to five years (Figure 8.6). Selection for the semitough rachis forms was an unconscious process during the earliest stages of domestication, perhaps accelerated by the use of sickles or the uprooting of individual plants to harvest ripe seeds rather than merely tapping them into waiting baskets. Computer

FIGURE 8.6 The features affecting seed dispersal and spikelet implantation in wild and domesticated einkorn wheat.

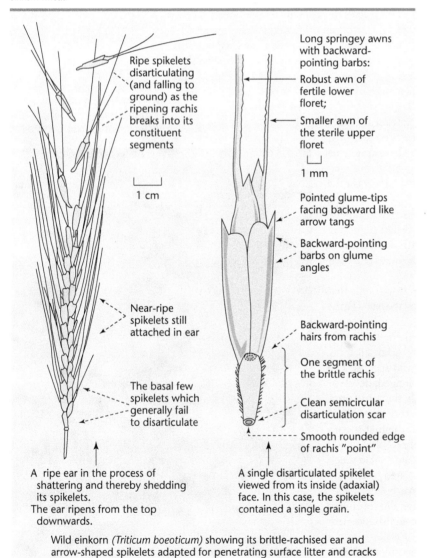

Ripe spikelets disarticulating (and falling to ground) as the ripening rachis breaks into its constituent segments

1 cm

Near-ripe spikelets still attached in ear

The basal few spikelets which generally fail to disarticulate

A ripe ear in the process of shattering and thereby shedding its spikelets.
The ear ripens from the top downwards.

Long springey awns with backward-pointing barbs:

Robust awn of fertile lower floret;

Smaller awn of the sterile upper floret

1 mm

Pointed glume-tips facing backward like arrow tangs

Backward-pointing barbs on glume angles

Backward-pointing hairs from rachis

One segment of the brittle rachis

Clean semicircular disarticulation scar

Smooth rounded edge of rachis "point"

A single disarticulated spikelet viewed from its inside (adaxial) face. In this case, the spikelets contained a single grain.

Wild einkorn (*Triticum boeoticum*) showing its brittle-rachised ear and arrow-shaped spikelets adapted for penetrating surface litter and cracks in the ground.

simulations have shown that semitough rachis domestic forms may have been rare at first, but they would have been fully domesticated within 20 to 30 generations—for these cereals, between 20 and 30 years (Figure 8.7) (Hillman and Davis, 1990). In fact, recent research suggests that the process could have taken between 1,000 and 2,000 years (Zeder, 2011).

Although the broad outlines of the process of domestication can be reconstructed through controlled experimentation and computer simulation, it is most unlikely that anyone will ever find "transitional" grains in Southwest Asian sites that will document the actual process underway. Botanists have, however, located in southeastern Turkey the wild populations of einkorn that were the source of very early domesticated wheat crops. The changeover from wild to domesticated strains involved many centuries of experimentation (see Chapter 9).

Technology and Domestication

The technological consequences of food production were, in their way, as important as the new economies. A more settled way of life and some decline in hunting and gathering slowly led to long-term residences, lasting agricultural styles, and more substantial housing. As they had done for millennia, people built their permanent homes with the raw materials most abundant in their environment. The early farmers of Southwest Asia worked dried mud into small houses with flat roofs; these were cool in summer and warm in winter. At night during the hot season,

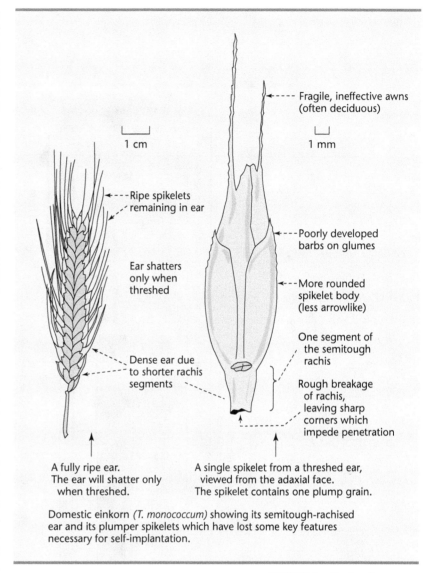

1 cm

1 mm

Fragile, ineffective awns (often deciduous)

Ripe spikelets remaining in ear

Poorly developed barbs on glumes

Ear shatters only when threshed

More rounded spikelet body (less arrowlike)

Dense ear due to shorter rachis segments

One segment of the semitough rachis

Rough breakage of rachis, leaving sharp corners which impede penetration

A fully ripe ear. The ear will shatter only when threshed.

A single spikelet from a threshed ear, viewed from the adaxial face. The spikelet contains one plump grain.

Domestic einkorn *(T. monococcum)* showing its semitough-rachised ear and its plumper spikelets which have lost some key features necessary for self-implantation.

FIGURE 8.6 *(Continued)*

people may have slept on the flat roofs. Some less substantial houses had reed roofs. In the more temperate zones of Europe, with wetter climates, timber was used to build thatched-roof houses of various shapes and sizes. Early African farmers often built huts of grass, sticks, and anthill clay. Nomadic pastoralists of the northern steppes had no concern with a permanent and durable home, yet they, too, took advantage of the related benefits of having a domestic food supply. They used animal skins to make clothing, as well as tents to shelter themselves during the icy winters.

Agriculture is a seasonal activity, with long periods of the year in which the fields are lying fallow or are supporting growing crops. Any farmer is confronted with the problem of keeping food in ways the hunter-gatherer never has to ponder. Thus, a new technology of storage came into being. Grain bins, jars, or clay-lined pits became an essential part of the agricultural economy for stockpiling food for the lean months and against periods of famine. The bins may have been made of wattle and daub, clay, or timber (see Figure 8.4b). Basket and clay-lined silos protected valuable grain against rodents.

Hunter-gatherers use skins, wood containers, gut pouches, and sometimes baskets to carry vegetable foods back to base. Farmers face far more formidable transport problems: They must carry their harvest back to the village, keep ready-for-use supplies of foods in the house as opposed to storage bins, and store water. Early farmers began to use gourds as water carriers and to make clay vessels that were both waterproof and capable of carrying and cooking food (Figure 8.8). They made pots by coiling rolls of clay or building up the walls of vessels from a lump and firing them in simple hearths. Clay vessels were much more durable than skin or leather receptacles. Some pots were used for several decades before being broken and abandoned.

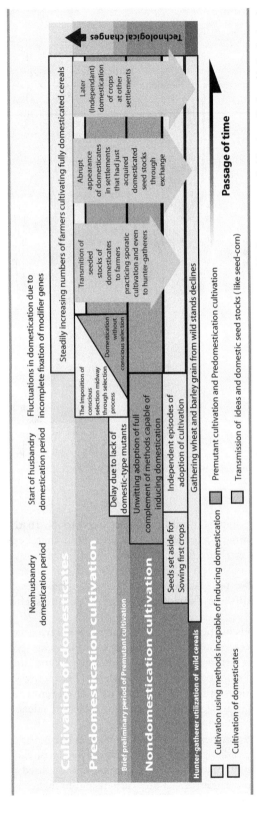

FIGURE 8.7 A summary of the principal events associated with the domestication of wheat and barley. For the sake of argument, this diagram assumes that the domestication of both wheat and barley occurred at several settlements independently. Key to the table: Nonhusbandry domestication. Husbandry (cultivation) methods are incapable of causing domestication. This process may have continued for a long time at some sites but was not universal. A possible temporary period (at some settlements) of premutant cultivation of crops in which domestication-inducing methods were now applied but domestic-type mutants were still absent, so that the start of domestication was delayed even further. Effect of imposing conscious selection midway through the selection process. The primary domestication curve—without conscious selection. Fluctuations in the completeness of domestication due to the incomplete fixation of modifier genes. Transmission of seeded stocks of domesticates to farmers practicing sporadic cultivation and even to hunter-gatherers. Also, transmission of the knowledge of domestication-inducing methods of husbandry to farmers lacking the technology. Abrupt appearance of domesticates in settlements that had just acquired domesticated seed stocks through exchange. Later (independent) domestication of crops at other settlements.

FIGURE 8.8 Pottery manufacture. An Ethiopian woman fabricates a clay bowl. She has built up the sides with clay and is now smoothing the surfaces of the vessel.

Pottery did not appear simultaneously with agriculture. It came into use at different times in many widely separated places. For example, people living along China's Yangtze River were making pottery as early as 18,300 to 13,800 years ago (Boaretto et al., 2009). Meanwhile, the Jomon hunter-gatherers of Japan fabricated simple clay pots by at least 12500 B.C., if not a couple of millennia before this. Yet their culture has few signs of domesticated animals and plants. Rather, they were predominantly fishers, gatherers, and hunters, albeit with relatively sedentary lives. Around 14,000 years ago, the Jomon began to construct large villages of well-built pit and longhouses, developing a highly complex system of what was essentially food collection and storage (Bailey et al., 2010). In Southwest Asia, however, farmers first used pottery by approximately 6000 B.C. (Mellaart, 1975).

For tens of thousands of years, people dug up wild edible roots with simple wooden sticks, sometimes made more effective with the aid of a stone weight. The first farmers continued to use the digging stick to plant crops a few inches below the surface, probably in readily cultivable soils. They also used wooden or stone-bladed hoes (and, much later, iron hoes) to break up the soft soil. These they fitted with short or long handles, depending on cultural preferences. European and Southwest Asian farmers made use of the ox-drawn plow in later millennia, at first with a blade tipped with wood, then with bronze, and later with iron (Chapter 15). The plow was an important innovation, for it enabled people to turn the soil over to a much greater depth than ever before. Every farmer has to clear wild vegetation and weeds from the fields, and it is hardly surprising to find a new emphasis on the ax and the adze. In Southwest Asia, the simple axes of pioneer farmers were replaced by more elaborate forms in metal by 2500 B.C. Present-day experiments in Denmark and New Guinea have shown that the ground and polished edges of stone axes are remarkably effective in clearing woodland and felling trees (Figure 8.9). In later millennia, the alloying of copper and bronze and, later, the development of iron cutting edges made forest clearance even easier.

New tools meant new technologies to produce tougher working edges. At first, the farmers used ground and polished stone, placing a high premium on suitable rocks, which were traded from quarry sites over enormous distances. Perhaps the most famous ax quarries are in western Europe, where ax blanks were traded the length of the British Isles. Grand Pressigny flint from France was prized over thousands of square miles. In Southwest Asia and Mexico, one valuable toolmaking material, not for axes but for knives and sickles, was **obsidian**, a volcanic rock prized for its easy working properties, sharp edges, and ornamental appearance. Early obsidian trade routes carried tools and ornaments hundreds of miles from their places of origin. By using spectrographic techniques, scientists have been able to trace obsidian over long distances to such places of origin as Lipari Island off Italy and Lake Van in Turkey (Torrance, 1986).

FIGURE 8.9 Early Food Production

After the Ice Age, many hunter-gatherer groups turned to wild plant foods for much of their diet. Communities in southeastern Turkey, the Euphrates River Valley, and Jordan planted wild seeds to supplement their diet during a savage drought dating to about 10000 B.C. Within a few centuries many of them had become permanent farming villages, dependent on domesticated animals and cereal crops. The earliest farming villages lay near carefully selected, fertile soils. Everyone remained dependent on game and wild plant foods for many centuries, even as the new economies spread rapidly.

Ways of Life

Cereal grains and root crops became the staples of early agriculture. Easily stored, they could feed many more people than hunting and gathering in good harvest years. Nevertheless, most subsistence farming communities of 5000 B.C. lived in fear of crop failure and hunger. For this reason, storage technologies were all-important.

Clay pots were used in early times for carrying water, for cooking, and storage. In late times, ceramics achieved considerable elaboration, like this finely made beaker from southern England.

Greenland

Icelan

NORTH AMERICA

Rocky Mountains

Great Plains

Great Lakes

St. Lawrence

Appalachian Mountains

Missouri

Mississippi

Rio Grande

Gulf of Mexico

ATLANTIC OCEAN

c. 4500 B.C.

Eastern North America:
sunflower
sumpweed
tepary bean

c. 4750 B.C.

Central America:
maize
sweet potato
manioc
squash
bottle gourd
tomato
avocado
cotton

PACIFIC OCEAN

Caribbean Sea

1000 B.C.

Orinoco

Guiana Highlands

c. 3000 B.C.

Andes

Amazon Basin

Amazon

São Francisco

c. 4500 B.C.

SOUTH AMERICA

South America:
manioc
potato
cotton
peanut
squash
bottle gourd
chilli pepper
lima bean

Andes

Paraná

Patagonia

ATLANTI

OCEAN

Settlement and innovation

c.10,500: Earliest pottery in the world, from southern Japan

9000: Earliest Chinese pottery

7000: First pottery in Southwest Asia
7000: Foundation of Çatalhöyük, Anatolia, the largest neolithic site in the Near East

6500: Small-scale copper smelting at Çatalhöyük

5500: World's earliest irrigation system, at Choga Mami, Mesopotamia

5000: Gold and copper metallurgy in the Balkans

| 10,000 B.C. | 9000 | 8000 | 7000 | 6000 | 5000 B.C. |

c. 8500: Saharan rock art depicts wild animals, long since extinct in the region

6500: Linen from Çatalhöyük is earliest known textile in the world

6000: Pottery produced at Mehrgarh, South Asia; first pottery in mainland Southeast Asia

5200: Bandkeramik pottery produced by farmers of central Europe

Domestication

Each farming region depended on different animals and crops: wheat and barley in southwestern and South Asia; millet and rice in China and Southeast Asia; maize and beans in the Americas. Sheep and goats were all-important in southwestern Asia, while cattle were soon prized as draft animals, hauling plows and wheeled carts.

Stone querns like this, dating to about 6,000 years ago, ground grain into flour, eaten as bread or simple porridge. They were developed out of earlier grinders used by ancient hunter-gatherers.

The spread of agriculture

- areas of early agriculture, with dates of first domestication of plants and animals
- diffusion of agricultural skills

Staple crops under cultivation by c. 4000 B.C.
- wheat
- barley
- millet
- maize
- rice

Central Asia: alfalfa, taro, carrot

Northern China: millet, broomcorn

Southeast Asia: rice, taro, sago palm

Indus Valley: cotton

Southwest Asia: wheat, barley, pea, lentil, onion, date palm

Early Farming

- **c. 9000:** Einkorn wheat grown in northern Syria: first evidence of true cultivation
- **c. 7000:** Farming in northern India; barley is main crop
- **c. 6500:** Farming spreads to Balkans from Southwest Asia
- **c. 6000:** Farming spreads to Nile Valley from Near East
- **c. 4500:** Cultivation of maize in eastern North America
- **c. 4000:** Plants domesticated in sub-Saharan Africa

9000 B.C. — 8000 — 7000 — 6000 — 5000 — 4000 B.C.

- **c. 8500:** Rice domesticated in southern China
- **c. 7750:** Broomcorn and foxtail millets domesticated on North China Plain
- **c. 6500:** Cattle domesticated in Saharan region
- **c. 4750:** First evidence of plant and animal domestication in Central America
- **c. 4500:** Evidence of agriculture in south-central Andes

FIGURE 8.10   Using a stone ax to fell a tree. A Tefalmin farmer at work in New Guinea in 1966. (Copyright The British Museum.)

All these developments in technology made people more and more dependent on exotic raw materials, many of which were unobtainable in their own territory. We see the beginnings of widespread long-distance trading networks, which were to burgeon even more rapidly with the emergence of the first urban civilizations (Figure 8.10).

We still know tantalizingly little about the ways humankind began to exercise control over food resources (see Figure 8.9). We know that in Southwest Asia there was a dramatic shift in human subsistence patterns by 9500 B.C., in northern China by 5000 B.C., and in Mesoamerica about 6500 B.C. Some fascinating clues, such as the example of southern California's Kumeyaay Indians, suggest that people were exercising some sort of control over their food supplies very much earlier. Perhaps Upper Paleolithic people who specialized in hunting reindeer or mountain goats made some attempts to manage their prey herds. Conceivably, too, hunter-gatherers living on the fringes of tropical rain forests may have engaged in deliberate opportunistic horticulture, planting yams and other food plants that could be regenerated for future use. The beginnings of the agricultural revolution took hold many thousands of years before the explosion came. After all, we should never forget that humans have always been opportunistic, and the planting of food crops and the first taming of animals may have been one simple result.

Summary

- Many late Ice Age and early Holocene hunter-gatherer societies were preadapted to food production, as they were already exploiting some food resources intensively and following more sedentary lifeways.

- Most of these societies were in regions where food resources were diverse and seasonally predictable. Higher levels of carbon dioxide in the atmosphere after the Ice Age resulted in much higher plant productivity and increased the importance of such foods in human diet.

- In contrast to early theories that food production was a revolutionary development, modern hypotheses invoke social relations, population growth, and ecological factors as multivariate causes of food production.

- The development of food production was a gradual process, one that saw increasing reliance on food crops, especially in areas with constant and unpredictable environmental change.

- Food production resulted in more sedentary human settlement, more substantial housing, elaborate storage technologies, and special implements for agricultural tasks.

- All these technological developments led to greater interdependence and to more long-distance exchange of raw materials, as well as increasing human social complexity.

Key Terms

accelerator mass spectrometry (AMS) radiocarbon dating (194)
Andean region (190)
flotation (193)
food production (189)

Mesoamerica (190)
Neolithic (189)
obsidian (201)
paleopathology (196)
pastoralist (195)

phytolith (193)
rachis (198)
scanning electron microscopy (SEM) (193)
swidden agriculture (195)

Further Reading

Barker, Graeme. 2006. *The Agricultural Revolution in Prehistory*. Oxford: Oxford University Press.

Flannery, Kent V. 1965. "The Ecology of Early Food Production in Mesopotamia." *Science* 147: 1247–1256.

Price, T. Douglas, and Ofer Bar-Yosef, eds. 2011. "The Origins of Agriculture: New Data, New Ideas." *Current Anthropology* 52: S4.

Smith, B. D. 1998. *The Emergence of Agriculture*, 2nd ed. New York: Freeman.

The Origins of Food Production in Southwest Asia

t was the final day of the 1953 excavation season at Jericho. For weeks, the top of a human skull had projected from the side of the trench dug deep into one of the earliest farming communities in the world. Excavator Kathleen Kenyon (1981) had given strict instructions that it was not to be disturbed until the stratigraphic layers in the trench wall had been drawn and photographed. Drawing completed, she somewhat unwillingly gave the site supervisor permission to remove the skull from the wall. That evening, he carried back to camp a complete cranium, carefully covered in clay, the human features modeled in, the eyes inset with shells.

The next morning, Kenyon looked closely at the small hole in the wall. She could see two more plastered skulls within. They were removed. Three more now appeared behind them, then a seventh, and final, head. It took five days to extract the nest of skulls from the wall, for the crushed bones were packed tightly with stones and hard earth. They formed the earliest portrait gallery in the world, each head modeled with individual features—nose, mouth, ears, and eyebrows molded with delicacy. Kenyon believed she had found the heads of revered ancestors who were critical intermediaries between the living and the spiritual world. They were symbols to their makers of a new spiritual order that linked people closely to the land that brought forth their crops. ▦

A human figurine from 'Ain Ghazal, Jordan.

Much of the theorizing about early food production has stemmed from archaeological research in Southwest Asia, where many early farming settlements have been found (Figure 9.1 and Table 9.1). The time when food production began is called the **Neolithic**, the "period in which a pattern of village settlement based on subsistence farming and stockbreeding became the basis of existence for communities throughout southwest Asia" (Moore, 1985: 223). The Neolithic of Southwest Asia began by at least 9500 B.C. nearly everywhere (the beginning date is blurred) and lasted until the sixth millennium B.C. in Mesopotamia and until as late as 4000 B.C. along parts of the eastern Mediterranean coast (Barker, 2006; Bellwood, 2004).

Neolithic

16,000 to 10,500 B.C.

Climate Change and Adaptation

Deep-sea cores and pollen studies tell us that the Southwest Asian climate was cool and dry from about 21000 to 16000 B.C., during the late Weichsel glaciation (Bar-Yosef, 2011). Sea levels dropped more than 100 m (300 feet); much of the interior was covered by dry steppe, with forest restricted to the eastern Mediterranean and Turkish coasts. After 16000 B.C., the climate warmed up considerably. Forests expanded rapidly at the end of the Ice Age, for the climate was still cooler than today and considerably wetter. Many areas of Southwest Asia were richer in animal and plant species than they are now, so that they were highly favorable for human occupation.

A widely accepted scenario for the first farming goes as follows: The extreme eastern Mediterranean coast lay at the junction of mediterranean, continental, and monsoon-influenced climates and nurtured a unique and ever-changing set of ecotones. In the early Holocene, the climate shifted from continental to mediterranean, with warmer temperatures, more forest cover, and increasing summer aridity. The vegetation became far more diverse, with a dramatic increase in annual cereal grasses that flowered and produced seed in spring and became dormant through the long, dry

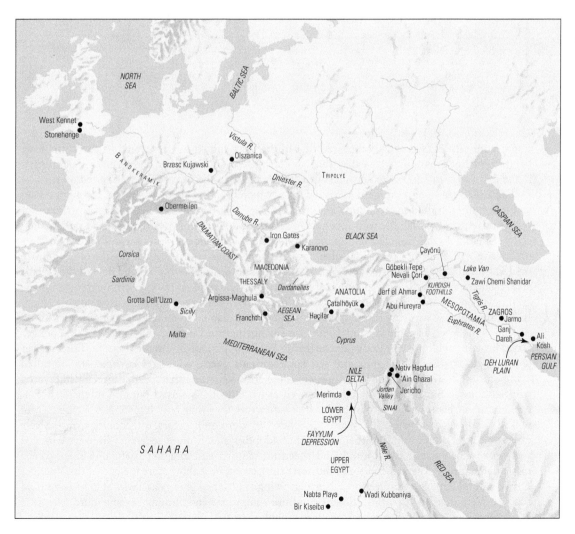

FIGURE 9.1 Early farming sites in Southwest Asia, Europe, and the Nile.

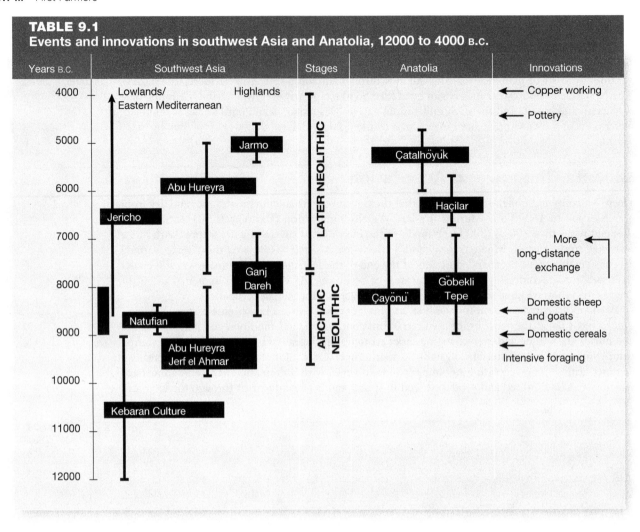

TABLE 9.1
Events and innovations in southwest Asia and Anatolia, 12000 to 4000 B.C.

summer months. These cereals appeared first in the west and spread eastward. At the same time, hunter-gatherer groups may have disturbed and unconsciously diversified the vegetation by firing it in the dry season to encourage new grass growth for the deer and other animals that fed on it.

The 1,000-year long Younger Dryas cold snap, which began in about 10800 B.C., brought cooler and much drier conditions to Southwestern Asia (see Chapter 7). This was the main trigger for people turning to growing the wild ancestors of crops like emmer wheat, barley, rye, and millet. Such shifts either led to full-time farming or to failure. When such climatic shifts occur, hunter-gatherers use a variety of strategies to handle such natural phenomena as droughts or floods—to minimize risk. They may simply move to a new area or enlarge their territories, stay put and defend their available resources against their competitors, or intensify the yield of plant resources through technological innovation, inventions, or part-time cultivation, even corralling of herd animals as pets and food. In Southwestern Asia, many communities stayed put and adapted to much drier conditions.

The climatic crisis came around 10800 B.C. in northern areas of the Levant, as the Younger Dryas brought cold, dry conditions to the region and long periods of intense drought. Forest cover declined, decimating cereal grass and nut harvest yields over a wide area occupied by Natufian communities. By this time, the landscape was more crowded than it had been, especially in favored woodland areas. Some people may have moved away, but others stayed put and intensified their exploitation of plant foods. As part of this intensification, they may have hunted and foraged lower ranked foods such as hares. They also responded by developing storage technology, intensively exploiting cereals and grinding their seeds, and adopting much more sedentary lifeways. All this was not so much a shift away from broad-spectrum hunting and foraging as an adjustment to climatic fluctuations. And somewhere in the northern Levant, probably before the end of the Younger Dryas, around 9500 B.C., some groups began growing wild cereal grasses as a way of increasing food supplies. Within a few centuries, climatic conditions improved and farming became more successful as winter rainfall increased and became more reliable.

The First Farmers

We still have only fleeting portraits of Southwest Asia's first farmers, communities where people were cultivating wild cereals as a supplement to their foraging diets. It is a major challenge to distinguish between communities that were experimenting with crops and those who were planting fully domesticated cereals. For example, a tough rachis is indeed a feature of fully domesticated cereals, but many factors affected the changeover. Beating ripened grain heads into baskets or harvesting cereals before they were fully ripe could have slowed morphological changes. So could the frequent introduction of new wild plants when cultivated crops failed. The appearance of the tough rachis is not necessarily a barometer of change, but rather a reflection of changing management and handling practices.

We know that by the closing centuries of the Younger Dryas, cultivation was well established, different sets of wild plants being cultivated in diverse regions. Rye, einkorn, emmer wheat, barley, and oats were cultivated by different groups. Figs are thought to have been grown as early as about 9700 to 9000 B.C. near the Jordan River (Kislev et al., 2006). At the same time, weeds known to flourish in cleared fields appear in village deposits, a clear sign of cultivation. Many **archaeobotanists** believe that it took between 1,000 and 2,000 years of systematic cultivation of wild cereals before most of the plants acquired the mutations of nonshattering ears and increased grain size. For full domestication to take place, there would have to have been continual sowing and harvesting, otherwise the domesticated plants would not have taken over the fields.

We do not know exactly when the first fully domesticated cereals came into regular use. The process unfolded over many generations in many different places. The earliest fully domesticated einkorn and emmer come from sites in the Upper Euphrates Valley dating to about 8500 to 8200 B.C. (Zeder, 2011). Barley came into wide use centuries later. Only small proportions of these early crops boasted of tough rachises; even smaller proportions come from earlier sites, where cultivation of wild cereals was under way. For many centuries before full domestication, many communities were actively modifying local environments to increase the availability of economically important plants. Weeds normally associated with cleared fields occur at many sites, at some sites like Abu Hureyra in Syria, described in the next section, as early as 10000 B.C. In many places, people transplanted plants like barley and einkorn from their preferred habitants to less favorable ones, even diverting water to tended plants. As agricultural activity intensified over the generations, so weeds increased as well. All of this activity, involving many cereal plants, also fruit trees, had deep roots in the broad spectrum plant exploitation strategies that had been in use since Ice Age times. Agriculture was not a dramatic invention, merely the logical culmination of risk reducing strategies that had been in use for a very long time.

Abu Hureyra
10500 to 6000 B.C.

Pre-Pottery Neolithic A

The so-called Pre-Pottery Neolithic (PPN), defining farming societies without clay vessels, began around 10000 B.C. and lasted for about 4,000 years. These four millennia are divided culturally into A and B phases, arbitrary terms that distinguish between people experimenting with crops and those using almost entirely domesticated ones.

The so-called Pre-Pottery Neolithic A (PPNA) lasted a mere 40 generations or so, between about 9750 and 8550 B.C., about 800 years. Nevertheless, it was a period of population growth and significant changes in social organization. PPNA communities had clear roots in Natufian society. In the south, many of them lay in lowland settings. Most were of small size, with only a few like Jericho or Netiv Hagdud covering about a couple of hectares and housing maybe 200 people. The inhabitants lived in semisubterranean, oval houses in villages remarkable for well-developed food storage silos. There were few communal structures, as if life was still based predominantly on the household and family.

The tiny settlement of Netiv Hagdud, 80 km (50 miles) north of Jericho in present-day Israel, flourished for about 300 years after 10000 B.C. and documents an early stage in the changeover (Bar-Yosef et al., 1991). Perhaps, 100 to 200 people, as many as 30 families, lived on a tributary of the Jordan River, hunting gazelle, taking fish and waterfowl, and collecting more than 50 species of wild plants, especially wild cereal grasses harvested with flint-bladed sickles. This small village of oval and circular mud-brick houses collected so much plant food that the grain was stored in small storage bins. The seeds included semi-tough rachis, two-row barley, a domesticated grain raised in small fields on nearby, easily tilled soils close to the alluvial plain and a small freshwater lake. Netiv Hagdud documents early efforts at farming only one cereal crop, probably as an important supplementary food.

Netiv Hagdud
10000 B.C.

FIGURE 9.2 Abu Hureyra, Syria. Left, the mound of Abu Hureyra from the southwest. The site, which overlooks the Euphrates floodplain, consists of two superimposed settlements. Right, the earlier settlement, comprising a series of interconnecting pits dug into the natural subsoil. These were roofed with poles, branches, and reeds to form huts. Part of a later rectilinear house can be seen near the top of the picture.

Jericho
10000 B.C. and later

The earliest permanent settlement at the site of the biblical city of Jericho extended over at least 4 ha (9.8 acres). A temporary Natufian camp had flourished at the bubbling Jericho spring by at least 10000 B.C. (Kenyon, 1981), but a more lasting farming settlement quickly followed. Soon these people, whose technology did not include clay vessels, were building massive walls around their settlement. A finely built stone wall complete with a tower bordered a rock-cut ditch nearly 3 m (9 feet) deep and 3.2 m (10 feet) wide (Figure 9.2). The beehive-shaped huts of Jericho were clustered within the walls. The communal labor of wall building required both political and economic resources on a scale unheard of a few thousand years earlier. Why walls were needed remains a mystery, but they may have been for defense from group competition for scarce resources. Some geomorphological research hints that the walls may have been flood-control works, but the theory is controversial.

In about 9000 B.C., a new settlement rose on the low mound at Abu Hureyra near the Euphrates, described in Chapter 7 (Moore et al., 2000). This was a new village, which grew to cover nearly 12 ha (30 acres) (Figure 9.3). At first, the inhabitants still hunted gazelle intensively. Then, about 9000 B.C., within the space of a generation or two, they switched to herding domesticated sheep and goats. Visitors to the village would have found themselves wandering through a closely knit community of rectangular one-story, mud-brick houses joined by narrow lanes and courtyards. The multiroom dwellings had polished black plaster floors, sometimes decorated with red designs. A single family occupied each house. We know the women did most of the food preparation because their knee joints bear the telltale signs of arthritis caused by kneeling (Molleson, 1994). Abu Hureyra was finally abandoned in about 6500 B.C.

The farmers of 10000 to 9000 B.C. hunted gazelles, wild cattle, pigs, goats, and other species. None of the bones shows the characteristic morphological features of domesticated animals. Judging from the proportions of immature gazelles at some sites, the people were very efficient, selective hunters. This pattern of animal exploitation had begun millennia earlier, during the Upper Paleolithic. Sheep and goats very rapidly replaced gazelle as the principal meat supply at Abu Hureyra and elsewhere after about 8000 B.C. At the same time, there are signs that cattle and pigs were subject to increasing human control. By this time, the domestication of sheep and goats had proceeded to the point where surplus males were slaughtered for meat before adulthood, a characteristic mortality profile for managed herds. By about 7500 B.C., it appears that the local gazelle herds were depleted. Sheep and goats now composed 60 percent of all meat consumed (Legge and Rowley-Conwy, 1987).

Were PPNA communities practicing farming with fully domesticated crops? They certainly practiced small-scale cultivation on the alluvial fans where they were located, but the plants they were growing were sometimes not ones that were eventually domesticated in the area. Silos were commonplace, perhaps a sign that there were significant food surpluses, even exchange of basic

FIGURE 9.3 Excavated remains of the great tower in early Jericho. Part of a massive stone wall, a passageway inside the tower contained many human skeletons deposited at a later date.

commodities between different communities. Some sites, such as Jericho, may have been centers for the exchange of such valuable raw materials as obsidian, salt, and malachite.

In the north, there was a significant population explosion, with settlements established at intervals of about 15 miles (25 km) along the Euphrates. Once again, the economy was probably based on floodplain cultivation, but hunting and foraging were still important. By this time, the relationships between different communities were assuming greater importance, both in the context of exchanges of commodities and other items, and also in terms of marriage connections between isolated settlements. For the first time, too, there are communal structures in some villages, a development that was to lead each much greater elaboration in later settlements such as Göbekli Tepe in Southeastern Turkey, described in the Site box.

Mureybet on the west bank of the Euphrates in Syria was a PPNA settlement, occupied between about 10200 and 8000 B.C. The earliest inhabitants were people with a culture akin to that of the Natufians, probably transitory occupants, who harvested barley and rye near the river, as well as hunting gazelles. By 9700 B.C., cereals had become more important in the diet and the people lived in oval, semisubterranean houses, just as their contemporaries did elsewhere. Five hundred years later, the inhabitants lived in oval dwellings but also constructed retangular buildings that probably had a communal purpose as well as acting as storage areas. Another site, Jerf el Ahmar, near the Euphrates to the north, boasts of at least 11 occupation levels dating to as early as 9200 B.C. Here again, there were some larger, rectangular houses that appeared to have a communal function. Human skulls had been laid in the foundation deposits. Some of the Jerf el Ahmar structures are up to 25 feet (7.5 m) in diameter. At first these were multifunction communal buildings, but later developed into single purpose structures with possible cult associations.

To the south of the Dead Sea, a site known as Wadi Feynan 16, located on two adjacent low hills has yielded more than 30 clay-walled, partially submerged structures, some of them flanking an elliptical structure with a mud-plaster floor, surrounded for most of its extent by a double layer of benches (Mithen et al, 2011: 350–364). Massive postholes once held wooden beams that supported a roof. The floor and structure were repeatedly rebuilt between 1078 and 8220 B.C. The effect is that of a honeycomb of oval and larger structures used for various purposes, among them burial and ritual activities, perhaps including feasting.

These structures signal the emergence of major social changes among people who were now anchored to their lands. As their ancestors had been before them. This may be why plastered skulls lay under the floors of Jericho houses and why detached crania occur elsewhere as foundation offerings (Figure 9.4). It is as if reverence, and perhaps worship, of ancestors was assuming a major role in farming societies where those who had gone before might have been seen as guardians of the land. There are signs that common religious beliefs and ritual practices were emerging over a wide area of Southwestern Asia as early as PPNA and certainly in later centuries.

Pre-Pottery Neolithic B

With the emergence of what is called Pre-Pottery Neolithic B (PPNB) around 8750 B.C., during favorable climatic conditions after the Younger Dryas, village societies developed in the northern Levant and much further afield. PPNB flourished for about 2,500 years and extended across the entire Levant, into central Anatolia and Cyprus. This was a large interaction sphere, which included large-scale permanent villages based on agriculture and

FIGURE 9.4 Plastered skull from Jericho, perhaps evidence of an early ancestor cult.

FIGURE 9.5 Plaster figurine from 'Ain Ghazal, Jordan. Found on a small platform, this may be a domestic house figure.

herding, also mobile groups. In a large region of great environmental diversity, there were inevitable, major differences in economic life. Some communities subsisted almost entirely off cereals. Others relied on lentils. At some sites, like 'Ain Ghazal in Jordan, at least half the meat supply came from game. But by 7000 B.C., over three quarters of the animal bones come from sheep and goats. Then, around 6200 B.C., a rapid climatic change with increased aridity, made worse, perhaps, by the effects of farming without manuring, and overexploitation of local food resources, and other factors, led to the demise of this once flourishing interaction sphere. Here again, there is, perhaps, evidence of respect for ancestors, in the form of remarkable human figurines, modeled in clay, once set on a house platform (Figure 9.5).

It is easy to ascribe these changes over many centuries to slowly changing cultural continuity, but reality was much more complicated. There were intricate, often small-scale population movements, constant changes in exchange and mating networks, and rapid population growth to add to the change equation. Above all, there was no clear-cut division between farmers and hunter-gatherers during the PPN. The region was a complex mosaic of agriculturalists and hunter-gatherers, of people practicing both economies. It was only toward the end of the PPN that everyone subsisted mostly on domesticated plants and animals, with a new and emerging division—between farmers and herders, the latter often living on the margins of settled lands. This distinction was to have a major impact on the history of the first civilizations.

8000 B.C.
Many larger settlements became trading centers, for the numbers of imported materials and exotic objects rose dramatically after 8000 B.C. The farmers were using obsidian from Anatolia, turquoise from Sinai, and seashells from the Mediterranean and the Red Sea (Kozlowski, 1999). The volume of trade was such that many villagers used small clay spheres, cones, and disks to keep track of the commodities traded. Some archaeologists believe these tokens to have been a simple recording system that later evolved into written script (Schmandt-Besserat, 1992).

The new, larger communities of the time required some form of mechanism for making decisions and exercising authority. With no signs of social hierarchy to be seen in excavated sites, most likely such societies operated through lineages, with seniority in them being defined by birth and seniority.

The Zagros and Mesopotamia

What about the Zagros foothills and Mesopotamia, to the east? There were sporadic contacts between these areas and the Mediterranean coast, but cultural developments in this region were parallel to, and independent of, those at Abu Hureyra, Mureybet, Jericho, and other western locations.

Thanks to the pioneering work of Robert Braidwood, who looked for agricultural origins on the hilly flanks of Mesopotamia, we know more about the highlands, where agricultural conditions were less favorable, than we do about early food production in the lowlands, the undulating northern Mesopotamian steppe, where the Assyrian civilization flourished millennia later (Kozlowski, 1999). To the south, the sandy Mesopotamian plain accumulated deep layers of silt throughout the Holocene. Early farming settlement there is probably buried under several feet of alluvium. Some small farming villages are preserved under great city mounds like those of Ur and Eridu, and they date to not much earlier than about 5800 B.C.

During the late Ice Age, human groups probably lived in the warmer lowlands. In the very early Holocene, the mountains were cool and dry, so agriculture probably began in the lowlands first, a natural habitat for wild cereals and pulses. As the climate warmed up, people moved into the mountain valleys of Zagros, open steppe country with seasonal resources spaced vertically up hill slopes. This was ideal country for herding sheep and goats, to the extent that herding may have developed earlier here than in other parts of Southwest Asia as an adaptation to territory with limited, and scattered, resources (Abdi, 2003).

Zawi Chemi Shanidar

About 10500 B.C., wild goats were a primary quarry for the hunters and gatherers exploiting the resources of the foothills. The people of a small encampment named Zawi Chemi Shanidar in the mountains of Kurdistan were hunting and gathering at this time, living in small circular huts. The inhabitants were killing large numbers of immature sheep, as if they had fenced in their grazing grounds for efficient, intensive hunting. Zawi Chemi may have been a summer encampment on the steppe. Pollen studies show an increase in cereal grasses during the occupation, perhaps evidence of sporadic cultivation.

Zawi Chemi Shanidar
10500 B.C.

Ganj Dareh

High in a mountain valley nearby lies another early farming village, named Ganj Dareh, first occupied about 10000 B.C. (P. E. L. Smith, 1978). The earliest settlement was probably a seasonal camp used by hunter-gatherers, but a later occupation, around 8000 B.C., consisted of a small village of rectangular mud-brick houses, some two stories high. The lower stories may have been used for storage because clay bins have been found there. Ganj Dareh represents the beginnings of permanent settlement in the Zagros, based on goat and cattle herding and possibly agriculture. The goat bones reveal a high proportion of subadult males and mostly older females, the characteristic mortality profile of managed herds (Zeder and Hesse, 2000).

Ganj Dareh
10000 B.C.

Jarmo

One of the best-known Zagros farming villages is Jarmo, a permanent hill village southeast of Zawi Chemi, occupied in about 7000 B.C. (Braidwood and Braidwood, 1983). Jarmo was little more than a cluster of 25 houses built of mud bricks and forming an irregular huddle separated by small alleyways and courtyards. Storage bins and clay ovens were an integral part of the structures. The Jarmo deposits yielded abundant traces of agriculture: Seeds of barley, emmer wheat, and minor crops were found with the bones of sheep and goats. Hunting had declined in importance—only a few wild animal bones testify to such activity—but the tool kit still included Stone Age–type tools with sickle blades, grinding stones, and other implements of tillage. Jarmo contains exotic materials such as obsidian, seashells, and turquoise traded into the Zagros from afar. There are also numerous clay tokens, perhaps again evidence of a recording system connected with long-distance trade. Jarmo was a fully permanent, well-established village engaged in far more intensive agriculture than its predecessors. More than 80 percent of the villagers' food came from herds or crops.

Jarmo
7000 B.C.

Ali Kosh and the Lowlands

Below, in the lowlands, farming began along the eastern edge of the flat Mesopotamian plain at least as early as along the eastern Mediterranean coast. The Ali Kosh site on the Deh Luran plain of Khuzistan, north of where the Tigris and Euphrates join waters, chronicles human occupation from about 7500 B.C. Ali Kosh began life as a small village of mud-brick rectangular houses with several rooms (Hole et al., 1969). As time went on, the houses became larger, separated from one another by lanes or courtyards. The people herded goats and sheep, which may have been driven to highland pastures in the mountains during the hot summer months. This *transhumance pattern*—the seasonal movement of herding peoples to new pastures—continues in the area to this day. Emmer, einkorn, barley, and lentils were cultivated from the earliest days of Ali Kosh. Hunting and gathering were important, as were catching fish and waterfowl from a nearby marsh. This well-excavated site documents the maturing of farming and herding on the lowlands, with the development of improved cereal strains and the first appearance of irrigation as a way of intensifying agricultural production.

Ali Kosh
7500 B.C.

Agriculture and herding were well established in the lowlands when Ali Kosh was founded in about 7500 B.C. As along the coast, cereal cultivation and animal husbandry were probably developed first by hunter-gatherer groups in the very early Holocene.

Early Farmers in Anatolia

Anatolia (Turkey) was a diverse, favorable highland and lowland environment for human settlement from early in the Holocene. Food production probably began in this region at about the same time as it did in the Levant, but archaeological research is still in its early stages (for a useful survey, see Özdogan and Basgelen, 1999). The earliest discoveries come from the southeast.

The upper reaches of the Euphrates and Tigris rivers drain the tableland of the Urfa region of southeastern Turkey. This is a place of arid, limestone hills, where the summers are hot and dry, the winters wet, and diverse soils supported natural stands of wild cereals and eventually became ideal for farming. DNA researches have pinpointed the Karacadag Mountains in this area as an original homeland of domesticated einkorn. Meanwhile, the world's oldest known domesticated einkorn has been recently identified at the (still occupied southeastern Turkish city of) Sanliurfa Yeni-Mahalle and dates to 9400 cal B.C. (Çelik, 2011).

The Urfa was an area where farming began at an early date. Here, as in the Levant, there must have been centuries of experimentation with cereal cultivation at a time of prolonged drought. Hunting, foraging, and at least some farming still relied on simple technology, notably a broad array of grinders and other grain-processing tools. However, society was changing dramatically in other ways, with a remarkable elaboration of spiritual beliefs and communal rituals reflected in ambitious communal structures. Some such buildings occur at sites like Mureybet in Syria, already described, as they do at village sites in the Urfa region.

At Çayönü Tepesi in southeastern Turkey, occupied from about 8600 to 7000 B.C., the settlement lay on a terrace above a small river, the rectangular houses standing at right angles to the river (Braidwood and Cambel, 1980; Özdogan and Basgelen, 1999). They form an arc, with a large open space at the center. Three quite distinct buildings once stood in this plaza. One of them was continually rebuilt, with three stone-built cells crammed with human bones under one end of the structure. One cell contained more than 40 human skulls. This "House of the Dead" also yielded a flat stone slab bearing traces of animal and human blood, as if some of the dead were sacrificial victims. Were the dead part of ancestor rituals, or were they sacrificed war captives? Our knowledge of religious beliefs during this early time is so incomplete that the question is unanswerable. The remains of at least 400 people lay in the cells. Another of the public buildings was virtually square, with a floor made of small stones pressed into plaster and tall, stone monoliths set into the floor. Such uprights, often decorated, may have served as roof supports, but they obviously had other functions as well.

Nowhere do such structures achieve greater elaboration than at Göbekli Tepe, justly famous for insights into the flamboyant beliefs of early farmers (see Site box).

What are we to make of these extraordinary sites, which apparently straddle the changeover from hunting and gathering to food production? They hint that elaborate rituals and more complex social organization predated agriculture in this region. Steven Mithen (2006), an expert on human cognition, believes that the religious beliefs behind these early carvings not only predated farming but may also have led to it. Likewise, Göbekli's excavator, Klaus Schmidt (2006) argues that it was the extensive, coordinated effort expended to construct the monumental, presumably ritual, buildings at Göbekli that laid the groundwork for the development of complex societies, and that this very site may in fact play a critical role in the transition from hunting to agriculture. Certainly, the elaborate construction and ritual activities at all of the aforementioned sites would have required dozens, if not hundreds, of people. Feeding them would have required large quantities of wild grain, some of which would have fallen on the ground, germinated, and been gathered again—a form of domestication. In time, some of this quality Karacadag grain would have been carried back home and, eventually, been traded, like obsidian and seashells, to communities many kilometers away, perhaps even as far as Jericho. This theory offers a speculative alternative to the common view that Younger Dryas drought was a major contributor to the changeover—the unresolved debate continues. But whatever the impetus for early food production in this region, we can be sure that it resulted in major adjustments not only to society but also to its complex relationship to the cosmos and the environment.

Çatalhöyük: "History Houses"

Nowhere so we obtain a clearer portrait of early farming life than at Çatalhöyük to the west on the Anatolian Plateau. This area was also an early center for food production, as well as a major source of obsidian for toolmaking since the end of the Ice Age. As early as 8300 B.C., villages flourished near major outcrops. (For a summary of work on obsidian sources and local sites, see Özdogan and Basgelen, 1999.)

Most Neolithic sites in central and eastern Anatolia were within easy reach of the rich obsidian sources near Lake Van and elsewhere. Villages close to the volcanic flows where the fine stone came from used it almost exclusively for artifacts, trading a great deal of obsidian to communities near and far in the form of prepared blade cores. Small quantities of Anatolian obsidian traveled hundreds of miles along the eastern Mediterranean coast and as far as the Persian Gulf. Trace element analyses of artifacts from many sites show that the patterns of exchange were exceedingly complex, as different sources came into and went out of fashion. By 7500 B.C., some of these early farming settlements had boasted of closely packed houses for a thousand years. There were many such villages in Central Anatolia by that date, but none of them as thoroughly studied as Çatalhöyük.

SITE > Ritual Buildings in Southeastern Turkey <

Göbekli Tepe lies on the summit of a hill with a fine view of the surrounding landscape (K. Schmidt, 2001). In about 9600 B.C., at least four circular structures were partially cut into the limestone bedrock—semisubterranean, almost cryptlike. Two huge stone pillars stood in the center of each crypt, with as many as eight others around the edges of each (Figure 9.6a). Rectangular, with flat cross sections, they are up to 2.4 m (8 feet) high and weigh as much as 7 tons. Stone-cut benches lie between the pillars. The pillars bore carvings of game animals like wild boar, gazelle, and aurochs, as well as snakes and birds, but no domesticated animals or

(a)   **(b)**

FIGURE 9.6   (a) The largest subterranean building at Göbekli Tepe under excavation, showing the tops of two central T-shaped monoliths and other monoliths embedded in the dry stone wall at the edge of the building, where a bench is emerging from the excavation. (b) A T-shaped monolith from the site, with low-relief sculpture.

humans (Figure 9.6b). One pillar bears a human arm, as if the columns were partially anthropomorphic. The pillars came from a quarry 91 m (300 feet) away, where at least one still in place would have been 6 m (20 feet) high and weighed 50 tons. Göbekli Tepe is contemporary with early PPN cultures to the south. The excavators believe that the inhabitants were hunter-gatherers rather than cultivators, but future excavations may reveal that they were also engaged in at least some cultivation. This would not be surprising given the extensive communal works required to construct the major structures.

We do not yet know for sure whether Göbekli Tepe was a residential settlement or purely a series of shrines. Considerable debate surrounds the shrines. Were they purely for ritual activity, or did people live in them as well, but clean out their refuse? The same issues arise at other sites like Çatalhöyük a later village (or even small town) several hundred miles to the west, where people lived

in structures surrounded by ritual art. Whether a settlement or merely a ritual center, Göbekli Tepe was certainly an important center for spiritual observances, for religious practices that originated centuries earlier and became increasingly elaborated over the generations. (If the site was purely a series of temples, then it is the earliest such location in the world by an enormous time span: the fourth millennium B.C. sanctuaries on Malta previously held that accolade). Its purpose was unknown—but it may have been a place where people reinforced beliefs, or strengthened kin or other social ties. Some of its visitors may have come from settlements as far away as Jerf el Ahmar, 100 km (62 miles) away on the west bank of the Euphrates River, where, as we have seen, there are also round structures with stone benches and carvings of animals (Figure 9.7).

Göbekli Tepe was not unique. A contemporary site, nearby Nevali Çori was excavated before a dam was built across the nearby Euphrates. The excavations yielded 29 limestone and mud houses, some of them cult buildings set slightly into a slope so that the visitor stepped down into the interior, which was surrounded by a stone bench along the walls. Monolithic stone pillars interrupted the bench, as did a niche, out of sight of the entrance. Some of the pillars were carved, reminiscent of those found at Göbekli and the same religious beliefs appear to have persisted over several rebuildings. Sculptures interred in a later cult building include an intriguing figure with a human head and the body of a bird. In others, a bird perches on the head of a human; symmetrical human figures stand back-to-back. Perhaps the connections between birds and human heads reflect the soul of a person or a link with the otherworld (Hauptmann, 1999).

FIGURE 9.7   A large subterranean structure at Jerf el Ahmar, Syria. A spread-eagled, headless human skeleton lay in the center of the floor; and a severed human head was in one of the structure's postholes. The structure was burnt after being filled in.

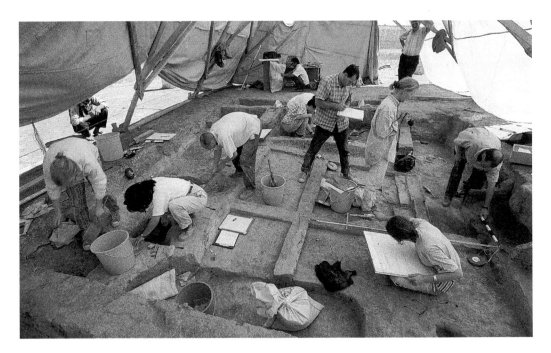

FIGURE 9.8 Excavation of a house at Çatalhöyük.

Çatalhöyük
7500 B.C.

The great Neolithic mound known as Çatalhöyük East covers 13.7 ha (34 acres). It was a large village or town of numerous small houses built of sun-dried brick that were designed to back onto one another, occasionally separated by small courtyards with midden areas between them. Roofs were flat, and the outside walls of the houses provided a convenient defense wall (Figure 9.8). The town was rebuilt at least 18 times over 1,400 years, presumably when the houses began to crumble or the population swelled, the last occupation being in about 6000 B.C. The site is currently being excavated on a large scale by an international team of researchers (Balter, 2005; Hodder, 1996, 2006, 2010; Özdogan and Basgelen, 1999). More than likely their work will change the interpretation of the site offered here (Figure 9.9).

Çatalhöyük's inhabitants never built large public buildings, ceremonial centers, or specialized production areas. Nor did they bury their dead in cemeteries. Every aspect of daily life unfolded in the houses, whether secular or concerned with ritual. So far 166 houses have been excavated, some of them grouped in small clusters bounded by middens or narrow alleyways, as if they shared ancestral burial houses and perhaps kin ties. Meticulous excavation of house sequences leaves no doubt that the same groups occupied the same, albeit rebuilt dwellings for many generations.

Many of the houses are lavishly decorated in an art style that displays elaborate symbolism. Çatalhöyük is a rich archive of information on spiritual life of the day, a time contemporary with PPNB and later farming societies elsewhere in Southwestern Asia (Hodder, 2010). There are paintings of humans and dangerous animals, burials in many of the houses, sometimes detached skulls of the dead removed after death, and installations of animal body parts such as ox horns in walls and benches. Plastered skulls of humans and bulls were circulated and deposited on important occasions such as the founding of a house. There was a strong tradition of passing skulls of ancestors down from one generation to the next. All of this speaks of a complex world of myths and meanings that were recognized over a wide area.

When Hodder and his colleagues plotted the finds and features in the houses, they found a complete blurring between the secular and the symbolic, even to the point of depositing objects that created memories of past events such as parts of figurines in hearths or foundation. Obsidian laid under floors as well as symbols painted on the walls may have been ways of interacting with ancestors. To quote Ian Hodder: "The lived-in

FIGURE 9.9 Hypothetical reconstruction of the east and south walls of what was originally called Shrine VI.14 at Çatalhöyük, Turkey, in fact a "History House," with sculpted ox heads, horns, benches, and relief models of bulls and rams. A ladder at right entered the house.

houses were religious in the sense that they were about imagining, remembering and interacting with past houses and those who had lived in them" (Hodder, 2010: 17).

A small number of Çatalhöyük houses contain the skeletons of many more people than could have lived there, in one case 62 bodies for a 40-year family occupation span, whereas the average number is 5 to 8. Clearly, people were buried in these special dwellings who never lived there. The houses themselves were rebuilt over longer periods than other ones and contained more elaborate symbolism, each carefully placed atop the previous structure. Each of these structures had a history to its inhabitants, to the point that they sometimes dug into earlier houses underneath to recover bull's skulls. Teeth from earlier burials were placed in later burials deposited in a later rebuild. The researches call them "History Houses," economically not necessarily different from other dwellings, but with a status that may have involved control of history, religion, and access to ancestors. They may also have played an important role in ceremonial feasts involving wild bulls that had mythical and spiritual associations. Çatalhöyük's History Houses may have provided and controlled and rituals for a larger kin group in a society, which was still egalitarian, even if some kin groups enjoyed more prestige than others.

We can never hope to recreate the symbolic world of Çatalhöyük in anything but the most general terms. Judging from the earlier Göbekli Tepe site and its monoliths adorned with humans and animals, and other sites, there was a suite of themes involving human skulls and birds of prey, also wild cattle, and other dangerous animals, that circulated widely through Southwest Asia during the time when people settled into large villages, even small towns and took up agriculture. Judging from the similarities in artifacts and some art styles from different sites, myths, ideas, and symbolic acts and beliefs were common, in general terms, to a huge area, where human life was changing profoundly as people became ever more tied to their land. These interconnections developed as people settled in villages where social structure was assuming ever greater importance. These were long-term relationships, with individual histories, perhaps reflected in such structures as History Houses, a tradition of house rebuilding that may go back to prefarming days. At the same time, history was created and maintained by living on and over human remains and by circulating body parts. Ancestors, human and animal, protected the dead, the house, and tits inhabitants. Associations between dangerous wild animals, headless humans, and birds, all these motifs were party of the strong option of continuity that was a central part of life in societies whose routines revolved around the endless passage of the seasons.

Much of Çatalhöyük's prosperity resulted from its monopoly on the obsidian volcanic glass trade from quarries in nearby mountains. Obsidian, however, was only one of many materials traded by Southwest Asian farmers after 9000 B.C. Marine shells, jadeite, serpentine, turquoise, and many other exotic commodities moved from village to village through myriad barter transactions. Perhaps these regular exchanges were used not only to obtain exotic materials but also to cement social relationships. This widespread exchange of raw materials accelerated the diffusion of all manner of innovations far and wide, among them sheepherding, the introduction of pottery, and eventually copper and bronze metallurgy.

Just how important the obsidian trade was in the area has been shown by spectrographic analyses of fragments of the volcanic glass in hundreds of sites between Turkey and Mesopotamia. The trace elements in obsidian are so distinctive that it is possible to identify the natural source of the glass by this analysis and to reconstruct the distribution of obsidian from dozens of localities. Thousands of obsidian samples document widespread exchange of this most desirable of tool-making stones throughout Anatolia and deep into the Levant. The percentages of obsidian fall away rapidly the farther one gets from the source, which suggests that much early farming trade was probably a form of "down-the-line" bartering that passed various commodities from one village to the next.

Two Stages of Farming Development

Until about 6000 B.C., cultural development proceeded independently in each of these three regions: the eastern Mediterranean coast, the Zagros highlands, and Anatolia. In each area, herding and agriculture emerged separately. Not that they were isolated one from another—far from it. There were regular trading contacts between each area, contacts that may have led to the spread of cereal crops, herding, pottery, religious beliefs and ideologies, and other innovations. In time, well-established barter networks helped spread both economic and technological innovations throughout ancient Southwest Asia, and that is why similar developments and intensifications of agricultural production occur at about the same time in several places. By 6000 B.C., the new economies had become **6000 B.C.** the foundations of human diet throughout Southwest Asia. Major changes in settlement patterns ensued. Sustained population growth took hold a while after farming became commonplace and agriculture sufficiently productive to feed many more people.

This was a time of profound social change, when human societies developed new mechanisms for social control, the settlement of disputes, and the regulation of the cultivation and inheritance of land. For the most part, however, the new societies were still egalitarian, their economies based on the productive abilities of the household and the nuclear family. The plastered skulls from 'Ain Ghazal, Jericho, and other Neolithic sites (see Figures 9.4 and 9.5) and their complex rituals and ancestor cults show that farmers were already defining the relationship between living people and the spiritual world, the world of soil fertility, bountiful crops, and revered ancestors.

Summary

- Southwest Asia was cool and dry immediately after the Ice Age, with dry steppe over much of the interior. Human populations were sparse and highly mobile as forests spread more widely throughout the region.
- The Younger Dryas cold snap began in about 10800 B.C. and lasted for a thousand years. Prolonged droughts and cooler conditions over Southwestern Asia caused significant drops in environmental productivity.
- Hunter-gatherer societies had three options—move elsewhere, protect their territory, or stay in place and intensify the food quest, also cultivating wild cereals. Many groups chose to experiment with agriculture.
- The PPNA saw extensive experimentation with the cultivation, an increase in trade and exchange, and the beginnings of distinctive religious beliefs.
- The PPNB saw full-fledged farming well established over a wide area, with extensive trade and interaction networks.

- Herding was well established somewhat earlier in the Zagros highlands, whereas Anatolia was inhabited by farming communities linked by long-distance exchange routes handling obsidian and other exotica by at least 9500 B.C.
- Some PPN settlements boasted of larger structures, which served both as dwellings and as shrines for rituals involving relationships with ancestors and other themes. Some like Göbekli Tepe in Southwestern Turkey had substantial subterranean structures adorned with richly decorated monoliths, perhaps symbolic representations of humans.
- Çatalhöyük, a large village on the Central Anatolian Plateau, was a crowded settlement, first occupied around 7500 B.C. Some of its dwellings have been named "History Houses," as they appear to commemorate ancestors and be associated with widely used religious beliefs common at the time over much of Southwestern Asia.

Key Terms

Archaeobotanist (209)   Neolithic (207)

Further Reading

Barker, Graeme. 2006. *The Agricultural Revolution in Prehistory*. Oxford, UK: Oxford University Press.

Hodder, Ian, ed. 2010 *Religion in the Emergence of Civilization: Çatalhöyük as a Case Study* . Cambridge, UK: Cambridge University Press.

Moore, Andrew et al. 2000. *Village on the Euphrates*. New York: Oxford University Press.

The First European Farmers

10

For many years, fishermen on the Swiss lakes had spread rumors of submerged forests that snagged their nets. Then a drought in the 1850s shrank the lakes dramatically and exposed veritable "forests" of wooden pilings set in the mud. Zurich archaeologist Ferdinand Keller dug around the piles at Obermeilen on Lake Zurich. The mud had preserved all manner of objects, large and small, not only prehistoric ax handles and weapons but fruit and ripe hazelnuts, thousands of animal bones, and all the perishable debris of a long-abandoned farming settlement of "high antiquity," as Keller (1866: 53) put it (Figure 10.1).

Keller's methods were rough and ready, for he merely dug into the mud around the pilings to recover as much as he could. He theorized that "lake dwellings" had been built on piles over the water, and that the inhabitants had dropped their artifacts, food remains, and garbage into the lake. It was not until the 1920s that more meticulous excavators showed that the villages had flourished on dry land before being flooded by rising lake levels. But Obermeilen and other Swiss sites were the first evidence for early farming in Europe, sites that are now known to be relatively late in the history of European farming (Coles and Coles, 1989). In this chapter, we examine the evidence for the spread of food production throughout temperate Europe (Barker, 1985; Milisauskas, 2002; Price, 2000). ▨

Stone alignments at Carnac, Brittany, France, c. 3300 B.C.

FIGURE 10.1 A romantic Victorian view of the Swiss Lake Dwellings based on the work of Ferdinand Keller.

Mesolithic Prelude

In Chapter 7, we described the Mesolithic hunter-gatherers of central and western Europe, the indigenous peoples of those densely forested regions concentrated by seashores, lakes, and rivers and in forest clearings (Table 10.1). Europe's Mesolithic lasted for about 4,000 years, from about 8000 B.C. until the introduction of farming in northwestern Europe, about 4000 B.C. This temperate and boreal forest adaptation displayed considerable location variation. Except in areas of abundant aquatic resources and predictable food supplies, population densities were very low. In some areas, however, such as the Danube's Iron Gates region and the Baltic shores of Scandinavia, population densities were unusually high, and there are some signs of social ranking and great complexity in some late Mesolithic groups (Bailey and Spikins, 2008).

These trends toward greater complexity, more sedentary lifeways, and more intensive hunting, foraging, and fishing took hold in Mesolithic societies throughout Europe when Southwest Asian societies were already experimenting with the deliberate cultivation and domestication of crops and animals. After about 6000 B.C., farming was well established in parts of the Aegean and in southeastern Europe. During the 2000 years that followed, European Mesolithic societies apparently embraced these new subsistence practices quite readily (Barker, 1985), abandoning the hunter-gatherer lifeways that had sustained their immediate and more remote ancestors for hundreds of thousands of years. The details of this transition are still little understood, but it can be argued that the Mesolithic population was preadapted to cultivation and animal domestication, especially in areas where short-term population shifts and local environmental change may have required conservative subsistence strategies.

The Transition to Farming in Europe

Did farming spread into Europe as a result of diffusion from Southwest Asia, or did food production develop independently in the temperate zone? There are almost as many theories about this controversial subject as there are archaeologists; the theories pit diffusionists against those who argue that Europeans developed their own farming culture in southeastern Europe before 6000 B.C. (Van Andel and Runnels, 1995).

One reason why many scholars have assumed that agriculture spread into Europe from Southwest Asia is that they have thought of Europe as one geographic entity and of Turkey and the rest of Southwest Asia just across the Dardanelles as another (Thorpe, 1996). They also assumed that rising population densities caused surplus farmers to spill over into Europe, bringing goats, sheep, and Southwest Asian cereal crops with them. There is no evidence of uncomfortably high population

TABLE 10.1
Early farming in Southwest Asia and Europe, 10000 B.C. to 2000 B.C.

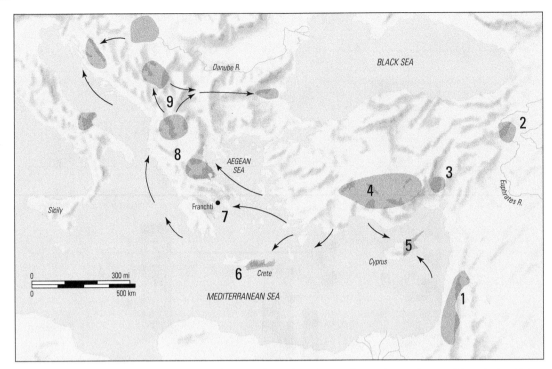

FIGURE 10.2 Map showing early farming areas in Southwest Asia and southeastern Europe. Arrows show possible routes by which the new economies spread. (1) Jordan Valley and the eastern Mediterranean; (2) Çayönü region; (3, 4) Anatolian region, including Çatalhöyük and Haçilar; (5) Cyprus; (6) Crete; (7) Franchthi Cave; (8) Macedonia; (9) Balkans region.

densities anywhere in Anatolia at this time (although our knowledge is incomplete). Furthermore, the earliest farming sites in southeastern Europe are situated in very favorable places, which could have been familiar only to people who had lived in the region for many generations. However, it is undeniable that food production began in Southwest Asia around 10000 B.C. and some 2,000 years later in southeastern Europe. Thus, it is most likely that the new economies spread into temperate lands from Southwest Asia (Figure 10.2). But how are we to account for the chronological gradient?

We begin our discussion with some hypothetical scenarios. The assumption that the natural distributions of wild cereals and of potential animal domesticates have remained unchanged since the early Holocene is at best questionable. As many authors have pointed out, human activity alone may have drastically reduced present-day ranges to the point where all we record are residual distributions. Late glacial and early Holocene pollen diagrams from northern Greece demonstrate that barley and perhaps other cereals were present in southeastern Europe long before farmers appeared, around 6000 B.C. Cereal grasses may have moved into temperate Europe ahead of woodlands in early Holocene times. Pulses may also have grown in Europe—the evidence is uncertain. As for potential animal domesticates, wild sheep are known to have flourished, although in scattered groups, in Upper Paleolithic Europe.

Robin Dennell (1983) argues that the development of food production in southeastern Europe went through three phases. First, climatic conditions in the early Holocene favored more plant growth. Grasses like einkorn and barley became more abundant, growing in dense stands that could be harvested in sufficient quantities to support a family for a year. However, most groups probably relied on shorter-term supplies, as wild plant harvests were unpredictable. So they moved on and obtained much of their diet from hunting and other foraged foods.

A second stage began when trees colonized the areas previously occupied by grasses. This change would have scattered grass stands, decreasing the amount of the grasses worth harvesting by human groups. The grasses were worth maintaining as a seasonally important food, so the people may have ringbarked tree trunks or burned the forest to clear space for wild grasses to grow. The harvested plots would gradually revert to woodland, where young shoots would attract deer, wild sheep, and other animals. Dennell believes that a simple interdependence between plant harvesting and animal exploitation developed in areas where woodlands were expanding at the expense of cereals. In such areas, human beings lived in small transitory settlements, many of them seasonal camps—just the kinds of sites found in the southern European Mesolithic (Bailey and Spikins, 2008; Zvelebil, 1986).

A third phase saw the establishment of permanent agricultural settlements. Through either local bartering or natural means, large-grained, tough-rachis cereals were introduced into southeastern Europe. These were Southwest Asian cereals like emmer and bread wheat, which were more predictable and productive than wild cereals. They required much more work to cultivate and careful sowing in specially prepared and selected fields. The farmers had to weed and protect their growing crops. All this extra effort involved creating special fields and gardens for crops, a mosaic of cultivated land based on carefully chosen soils and a rotation system that allowed exhausted soils to rest. Both domestic emmer and bread wheat take large quantities of nutrients from the soil, which could be replaced by the underplanting of nitrogen-fixing legumes and the use of animal manure. This new farming habitat involved the integration of cultivation and animal husbandry into a closely knit subsistence strategy based on individual households supplying their own food needs.

This model envisages food production in southeastern Europe as a largely indigenous development, stimulated in part by the immigration of some domestic plants and animals from across the Dardanelles, perhaps as a result of trading activity (B. Smith, 1998). It also accounts for the chronological gradient, a time lag that resulted from the gradual "drift" of new crops and domesticated animals from Southwest Asia.

Farming in Greece and Southern Europe

The earliest known evidence of food production in southern Europe comes from the Argissa-Magula village mound on the plains of Greek Thessaly (Perlès, 2001) (Figure 10.3). These once-empty plains with their many rivers and lakes provided a favorable environment for natural irrigation of easily cultivatable floodplain lands. As early as 7000 B.C., farmers settled in this region, cultivating emmer wheat and barley and herding cattle, sheep, and pigs. Van Andel and Runnels (1995) have argued convincingly for a spread of farming from Anatolia into this fertile area and into southeastern Europe (see Figure 10.2).

Within a few centuries, farmers were well established elsewhere in Greece's mountainous terrain. The Franchthi Cave in southern Greece was occupied in Mesolithic times and continued in use for many thousands of years. Farming appeared there around 6000 B.C., when the people began herding goats and sheep and extended their settlement outside the cave itself. These people had trading contacts with the Aegean islands (Jacobsen and Farrand, 1987). Because domesticated crops appeared abruptly at Franchthi, it is reasonable to suppose that cereal agriculture had been developed somewhat earlier or elsewhere. By 5500 B.C., established farming settlements were commonplace in Greece, as well as along the Adriatic Sea's Dalmatian coast.

Franchthi
6000 B.C.

FIGURE 10.3 Archaeological sites in temperate Europe and the distribution of Bandkeramik (Danubian) pottery, Cardial ware, and western Neolithic cultures.

| Danubian | Cardial | Balkan Neolithic | Western farmers |

Like Franchthi Cave in Greece, the Grotta dell'Uzzo on the northwest coast of Sicily was occupied for many millennia by hunter-gatherers. Between 6000 and 5800 B.C., the cave's inhabitants abruptly began raising einkorn, wheat, barley, and lentils. They also kept cattle and small stock, continuing, however, to hunt and to gather wild plant foods on a considerable scale. This was selective agriculture, in which indigenous hunter-gatherers adopted some Southwest Asian domesticates as supplemental foods. Sheep, for example, represent only about 2 to 20 percent of the animal bones at dell'Uzzo. But by 5000 B.C., sheepherding and sedentary agriculture were well established along the Mediterranean coast and inland.

The Spread of Agriculture into Temperate Europe

The beginnings of farming in Europe have traditionally been explained as a process of colonization from Southwest Asia (Price, 2000). According to this theory, the newcomers spread across Europe from about 6000 B.C., ending with the introduction of farming to northwestern Europe in about 3500 B.C. The new economies effectively terminated hunter-gatherer societies in Europe. In fact, the process was much more complicated, a combination of both local and intrusive developments.

The adaptive processes and population movements involved are still little understood. These temperate zones have year-round rainfall and marked contrasts between winter and summer seasons. Timber and thatch replaced the mud-brick architecture used so effectively for houses in Southwest Asian villages. Agricultural techniques had to reflect the heavier soils and perennial rainfall of European latitudes, but the first introduction of farming coincided with a warm, moist phase, when midsummer temperatures were at least 2°C (3°F) higher than today. The forest cover was mainly mixed oak, shady tree cover that reduced the grazing resources of large game animals such as deer and wild cattle. Many of the indigenous Mesolithic populations lived by coasts, lakes, and rivers on ecotones, where they could exploit several ecological zones from summer and winter camps. The first European farmers settled on the mostly **loess** soils of central Europe, which were lightly wooded, fertile, and easily tilled with simple digging sticks and hoes.

No one questions that there was a directional movement of farming from the southeast to the northwest (Dennell, 1983), but whether it was a matter of population replacement, as claimed by some geneticists, or of the adoption of the new economies by indigenous Europeans is a matter of continuing debate (Cavalli-Sforza and Cavalli-Sforza, 1995). This is a far cry, however, from thinking in terms of a wave of Southwest Asian colonists, eager for new land, pouring into Europe. In fact, the first European farming societies were sparse in numbers, and the land had the potential to support far larger numbers of cultivators. Furthermore, indigenous Mesolithic peoples were probably important players in the adoption of the new economies. Indeed, European farmers have been remarkable for the ways in which they have adapted to the challenging and varied environments of temperate Europe. Here, as in Southwest Asia, China, and the Americas, early farming was a matter of trial and error, of success and sometimes failure.

There is also the possibility that some animals and plants were actually domesticated in southeastern Europe and not introduced from Southwest Asia. The natural ranges of sheep and such plants as barley, einkorn, and some legumes may have once extended into southeastern Europe (Dennell, 1983). Only emmer and bread wheat were certainly domesticated in Southwest Asia. Thus, hunter-gatherer societies in southeastern Europe may have developed food production on their own, in response to such stresses as population pressure or environmental change. The exact stresses are still a mystery.

One potentially major stress has emerged from remarkable deep-sea core research in the Mediterranean and Black seas. In about 6200 B.C., four centuries of much cooler, drier conditions may have caused widespread drought across southeastern Europe. Under these circumstances, farming settlements would have tended to concentrate near lakes, seacoasts, and rivers. At the time, the Black Sea was an enormous freshwater lake, for the brackish Mediterranean had not risen sufficiently from its late Ice Age low to breach an earthen barrier that lay at the mouth of the Bosphorus Valley. Better

rainfall and wetter conditions returned in about 5800 B.C.; the Mediterranean continued to rise, lapping at the crest of the barrier that separated it from the Black Sea, 150 m (492 feet) below. Suddenly,

around 5500 B.C., seawater cascaded over the rim in a violent waterfall that cut deep into the underlying bedrock. The Euxine Lake rose rapidly and became part of the ocean, inundating thousands of square kilometers of low-lying coastal terrain. (Details of this event remain controversial—the rise may have been slower and less than originally claimed.) Although we have no archaeological evidence to document the now-submerged settlements, there must have been considerable population disruptions in the face of this natural catastrophe, which may have brought farmers upstream into the fertile Danube Valley, well away from the rising Black Sea (Ryan and Pitman, 1999).

Graeme Barker (1985) proposes a general scenario: In Greece, farming villages were well established by 6000 B.C. and were based on sheep husbandry and the cultivation of crops sown each fall.

North of Greece, about 5500 B.C., the expansion of farming activity appears to have coincided with a cycle of higher rainfall, warmer winters, and the rise of the Black Sea, which brought Mediterranean styles of farming viable in the southern Balkans and somewhat different forms of agriculture possible to the Danube basin.

About 5500 B.C., farming based on cattle herding combined with spring-sown crops developed during a period of wetter conditions over enormous areas of continental Europe, especially on optimum loess soils. This agricultural system was perfectly adapted to such conditions, whereas stock herding assumed much greater importance in nearby, more low-lying regions. At the same time, hunter-gatherer societies continued to flourish for at least another millennium in areas that were marginal for cultivation or herding. Eventually, distinctive local farming adaptations replaced hunting and gathering in southern Scandinavia and lowland Britain, as well as along the Atlantic coast and at higher altitudes. Hunting, foraging, and fishing remained dominant subsistence strategies only in the farthest north, in areas that were vulnerable to minor climatic change.

The Balkans

In the Balkans, the earliest farmers settled on fertile agricultural soils on floodplains and elsewhere (Tringham, 1971; Whittle, 1996). Many of them lived in compact villages of one-room dwellings built of baked mud plastered on poles and wicker (Tringham et al., 1980). These Karanovo culture settlements, named after the first site dug, were occupied over long periods. The economy was based on cultivated wheat and barley and domesticated sheep and goats. A number of culture traits, including *Spondylus* shells (a characteristic Mediterranean mussel much used for ornamentation), clay seals and figurines, and reaping knives, show continuing connections with the Mediterranean world. This is an area with great environmental variability and ranges in temperature. For example, there are fertile plains and spring areas where the soils are permanently moist. It was here that many farming communities settled in the same locations for centuries, just as Southwest Asian and Anatolian farmers had done. The largest mounds are found where good arable soils are most widespread. It was in this area that metallurgy developed in approximately 3000 B.C. (see Chapter 20).

Karanovo culture
5500 B.C.

Bandkeramik Cultures

Very complete radiocarbon chronologies characterize the spread of farming in Europe as a stop-and-start process. There were major expansions and then long pauses, not gradual waves of advance. Barker (2006) believes that the expansions coincided with climatic changes that affected local landscapes and made farming viable in new areas. In short, the spread of farming was a complex process that involved major culture change over many centuries.

The best-known early European farming culture is called the Bandkeramik (or the Danubian) complex, named after its distinctive linear-decorated pottery (Figure 10.4). Its first colonization of the Middle Danube was on a small scale about 5300 B.C. It appears that small groups of people migrated along river valleys, avoiding areas where Mesolithic folk lived. Their farming territories were widely spaced and apparently very small, perhaps on the order of about 200 ha (500 acres), of which about a tenth to a third was in cultivation at one time. The people lived in hamlets made up of individual farmsteads, separated by about 90-m (100-yard) intervals. Individual houses were rectangular, from 5.5 to 14 m (18 to 46 feet) long, made of timber and thatch, and presumably sheltering families, their grain, and their animals.

Bandkeramik complex
5300 B.C.

The Bandkeramik people cultivated barley, einkorn, emmer wheat, and minor crops such as flax. These they grew by using systems of crop rotation and fallowing, which enabled the farmers to remain in the same place for long periods of time, sometimes even growing hedges to delineate their fields and to fence in their animals. Cattle were the most important animal in Bandkeramik life; indeed, they may have been domesticated from wild strains locally. The people also kept sheep, goats, and dogs. Population estimates of between 40 and 60 people per village seem reasonable, with a new settlement being founded as the population expanded. Population growth after first settlement was slow. The founding of companion villages gradually filled in the gaps between widely spaced neighboring communities. Within four or five centuries, population densities in parts of Germany rose from 1 per 1,000 sq. km (386 sq. miles) to 1 per 120 sq. km (46 sq. miles).

By 4000 B.C., cereal crops and domesticated animals were widespread in southeastern and central Europe and perhaps also in southern France. These farming communities were surrounded by scattered hunter-gatherer societies. The Bandkeramik people had spread far west to southern Holland, where they had settled by 4800 B.C., and east to the Vistula River and the upper Dniester (Price et al., 2001). In the prime agricultural areas, the people relied heavily on their cattle, sheep, and pigs. They may have moved their herds onto the northern European plain for part of the year. The Brzesc Kujawski site in southern Poland was inhabited by summer cattle herders, who also gathered wild vegetable foods and caught perch in northern streams (Bogucki, 1993). Eventually,

4000 B.C.

FIGURE 10.4 Linear Bandkeramik pottery (linear-decorated pottery) from Sittard, Holland, with characteristic line decoration (one-fourth actual size).

farmers settled on heavier soils. We find regional variations of Danubian culture in many parts of central Europe. Some farmers had to rely more on hunting and gathering because the soils of their gardens did not yield enough food to support their families. Defensive earthworks appeared later, as if vigorous competition for land had caused intertribal stress. At Talheim, a Bandkeramik settlement in Germany dating to the sixth millennium, 34 men, women, and children died during an attack, slaughtered with stone axes or adzes, or by arrows, and their bodies thrown into a pit.

Frontiers and Transitions

The Bandkeramik expansion created a "frontier" in many parts of Europe between farming communities and Mesolithic groups. It would be a mistake to think of this as a rigid boundary between different peoples, although both hunter-gatherer and farming societies have a tendency to stay within their own territories and to continue the way of life with which they are familiar (Dennell, 1983). By the same token, however, the peoples who lived on either side of the frontier inhabited a far from closed world. They knew of one another's presence, traded with one another, and interacted through an intricate web of contacts that were beneficial to both sides. Mesolithic people were well aware of cereal crops and domesticated animals. In many cases, they saw no advantage in adopting a new way of life that involved a great deal more work for few significant changes in their diet.

More likely, they incorporated some aspects of Neolithic culture into their lives, those that gave them an immediate advantage. These may have included clay vessels for storage and cooking, perhaps status items acquired by trade that were soon copied by local artisans. Cereal crops and sheep may have been valuable simply because they solved problems of winter food supplies. Sheep have lower feeding requirements than deer, have higher reproductive and growing rates, and can be used to keep woodland open for cereal growth. Stored nuts, wild cereal grains, and dried deer meat or fish may have been Mesolithic winter staples. It would have been easy for Mesolithic people to graft sheep and domestic cereals onto their existing hunting and gathering practices. These processes of assimilation caused farming to spread over much of temperate Europe from after 6000 B.C. to as late as 3500 B.C., when many Scandinavian groups finally adopted food production.

Marek Zvelebil and Peter Rowley-Conwy (1984) take the argument a stage farther, distinguishing three transition phases from hunting and gathering to farming:

- An *availability phase*, when farming was known to Mesolithic peoples and there was some exchange of materials and information. Both farmers and hunter-gatherers were still independent units.
- A *substitution phase* that had two forms: (1) Farmers moved into and settled hunter-gatherer territory in competition with the indigenous residents, and (2) hunter-gatherers added cultivation or animal husbandry to their range of subsistence activities. During this phase, there was competition for land, food, and raw materials, and perhaps social competition as well.
- A *consolidation phase*, when food production became extensive and widespread, with hunting and gathering becoming subsistence strategies in emergencies. Farmers had now occupied the best soils and were using secondary areas with more intensive farming methods. By this time, the frontier had vanished.

The Zvelebil–Rowley-Conwy model serves as a descriptive device for analyzing the spread of food production into western and central Europe, but more data are needed to bolster it.

Social Changes, Lineages, and the Individual

Bandkeramik communities settled on very specific parts of the landscape: gravel river terraces overlooking medium-sized streams in areas of loess soils. These forest farmers deliberately selected places where damp lowland pasture coincided with tracts of light, friable upland soils. They cultivated fertile soils, land where hoe-using farmers could grow emmer wheat and other crops year after year, fertilizing their fields with cattle dung and domestic waste. Cattle were an important element in the Bandkeramik economy, pointing to a "pioneer" economy introduced from southeastern Europe rather than an indigenous farming culture that made full use of local plants and game animals.

After 4550 B.C.

The Bandkeramik people built large, permanent timber houses, investments in time and labor that would have been totally uneconomical if they had been engaged in slash-and-burn agriculture and had shifted their villages regularly. Bandkeramik sites formed clusters of settlements, separated from one another by distances of 20 to 30 km (12 to 19 miles). The houses were apparently rebuilt again and again in much the same place. Bandkeramik settlements were occupied over long periods of time so that a basic site and the social structure within it survived over many generations. There was continuity of residence location and inheritance from one generation to the next. In some areas, settlements were closely packed within small areas, each hamlet owning a territory of 15 ha (37 acres) or so—not because land was in short supply but because factors such as trade and local outcrops of flint and other materials may have played a role (Figure 10.5).

All of these characteristics point to farming societies that were producing food at the household level but with cooperation between different lineages at the settlement level—to build houses, erect enclosures, and herd cattle (J. Thomas, 1987). The first settlement in an area was, perhaps, the senior one, the place where the elders of the senior lineage lived. In burials, there were two general distinctions among grave goods: between graves of males and females and between those of young and old. Many graves of Bandkeramik women, members of families who lived in longhouses, are richly decorated. Such dwellings are commonly associated in modern societies with *matrilineage*, a kin group that traces its lineage through the maternal line. In such circumstances, women have high status, and this may have been so in Bandkeramik society. Political power and social authority, however, may have been in the hands of a group of older men who controlled cattle ownership and the exchange of cattle and other exotic commodities with other settlements. In Bandkeramik society, then, a complex network of social relations controlled productivity. Lineages within the society formed the links between people and the lands of their ancestors.

Around 4500 B.C., Bandkeramik settlements became more clustered and turned into villages. Many were protected by earthen enclosures. Divergent pottery styles hint that different settlement clusters had well-defined territories (J. Thomas, 1987). This was a time when more elaborate burial customs developed throughout Europe as ancestor cults became more complex.

FIGURE 10.5 Reconstruction of a Bandkeramik farming complex, showing longhouses and field boundaries.

In western Europe, communal tombs came into fashion, among them the celebrated megaliths, sepulchers fashioned from rough-hewn boulders and buried under earthen mounds (see "The Megaliths," pp. 230–232). Such corporate burial places may have been where revered kin leaders were buried, along with people who had genealogical ties to the ancestors and thus were of paramount, collective importance to a group of farming communities that held ancestors to be guardians of the land. In time, communal tombs may have become important power symbols among local groups that were linked with their neighbors and others by both lasting kin ties and the burgeoning exchange networks that were expanding throughout Europe at this time. Perhaps the communal burial mounds of northern Europe embody in earth and stone the notion of linearity, perhaps an ideology that came from Bandkeramik longhouses (Hodder, 1990).

2800 B.C.   Somewhat later, between about 2800 and 2400 B.C., another change in burial customs took hold in central and eastern Europe. For the first time, individual graves as well as communal sepulchers appeared. S. J. Shennan (1993) has argued that group-based ideologies were replaced by new beliefs that reinforced individual power and prestige. It would have been very hard for a single elder to preempt political and economic authority in Bandkeramik society. There were simply too many kin ties and reciprocal obligations to overcome, as well as the collective bond with the ancestors. By being buried separately, however, in a burial adorned with elaborate grave furniture, a prominent elder could take on the role of sole male ancestor, the fountain of authority over landownership, a role now assumed by his successor. Inheritance of land and wealth was now legitimized.

This is, of course, a speculative scenario, but one supported by telling clues. There are many cases in which men and women were buried together in a single grave. This practice, argue some archaeologists, indicates monogamous marriages rather than the polygamous ones of lineage-based Bandkeramik society. The dominance of male burials from this period suggests that men were of great importance in establishing descent and rights of inheritance. Many individual graves were dug into older communal monuments, perhaps to reinforce the idea that individual ancestors were more important than collective ones. The rich grave goods found in such burials reveal new emphases in society: Many weapons such as daggers and swords appear, as well as battle axes, fine copper ornaments, and drinking cups. Everything points to the emergence of individuals who thought of themselves as warriors. Personal achievement and prestige were associated with males, who were involved in expanding exchange networks that handled luxury goods such as amber, gold ornaments, and weapons. The beginnings of metallurgy in Europe may have been tied to a rising demand for shiny, prestigious ornaments. Luxury artifacts were the symbols of prestige, the means of cementing individual relationships, political links, and reciprocal obligations. There are striking differences in the people buried, too. Bandkeramik farmers lavished their finest goods on older individuals. The later individual burials are those of men in their prime, indicating that personal achievement was the avenue to power and prestige.

The Introduction of the Plow

Andrew Sherratt (1994a) believed that the introduction of plow agriculture was a seminal development in Europe. Plows are known to have been used as early as 3600 B.C., but Sherratt says they
2600 B.C.   came into far more widespread and intensive use about 2600 B.C., when a number of other innovations reached Europe from Southwest Asia. These included sheep shearing, milking, horse riding, and the use of oxen for traction. He goes so far as to argue for a "secondary products revolution," which transformed both settlement patterns and social organization throughout Europe.

Plow agriculture allows fewer people to work an acre of land; thus, more land would be cleared and an individual's fields would be more widely scattered, sometimes close to the outer limits of daily walking. The result was a much more dispersed settlement pattern, with a rapid expansion onto heavier soils and hitherto uncultivated areas around 2600 B.C. With much more acreage to clear and the technology to do it, the farmers of 2600 B.C. were less tied to ancestral lands and the realities of household production and to the kin ties these imply. Fewer people worked in the field, so that there were "unproductive" individuals in greater numbers and, therefore, compelling needs for social change. Thus, in place of the kin-based society, a new social order arose in which individual success, prestige, and inheritance of land were the norm—with momentous consequences.

Plains Farmers: Tripolye

While the Bandkeramik complex was developing in central Europe, a mosaic of different subsis-
6000 B.C.   tence patterns emerged on the Russian plains to the east between 6000 and 4500 B.C. (Zvelebil and Dolukhanov, 1991). Agricultural peoples settled the areas best suited to farming, such as intermountain basins, while hunter-gatherers continued to exploit the river basins, such as that of the Dniester River. The farmers and foragers interacted with one another, living in complementary environments where one did not threaten the other. By 4500 B.C., Bandkeramik peoples had moved

as far east as Ukraine, bringing a mixed farming economy with them. They settled on the higher terraces of major rivers, still interacting with Mesolithic folk in the valley bottoms. Both Mesolithic and Neolithic peoples maintained their own identities.

Farming reached its greatest extent in the forest-steppe regions of western Russia with the Tripolye culture in about 4000 B.C. (Zbenovich, 1996). Soon after, the farmers finally submerged the Mesolithic foragers of the valleys, perhaps because the cultivators relied extensively on cattle, whose grazing demands may have competed with hunter-gatherers' foraging needs. In about 2800 B.C., the climate deteriorated, making cultivation less viable. At this point, balanced economies emerged, relying on stock breeding on the steppe and farming in the forest-steppe—a balanced dynamic that survived into recent times—with important historical consequences.

Tripolye culture
4000 B.C.
2800 B.C.

Mediterranean and Western Europe

New artifacts, such as pottery, and food sources, such as sheep, were added to hunter-gatherer adaptations as farming took hold in central Europe and farther afield. This transitional phase lasted for centuries throughout Europe. In many areas, the new items added to existing practices, but they did little to change the fundamental structure of Mesolithic society or lifeways. The full-scale adoption of farming economies in areas such as western Russia took a long time to achieve, whereas in other areas, such as Britain, a complete changeover occurred within five centuries or so.

In the Iron Gates region of the Danube Valley, coastal Yugoslavia, central Italy, and southern France, pottery, cereal crops, and sheep appeared, but there was little immediate change in daily life. Many sites where such artifacts occur are in the same type of setting as Mesolithic settlements, where hunting continued for centuries, even millennia. The shift to farming was only partial in many areas, for game and wild plant foods continued to be important; witness the well-preserved berries and nuts in waterlogged lakeside villages in Switzerland (Coles and Coles, 1989). In the Mediterranean basin, the long-term changes were an expansion in the use of obsidian and much wider ranging trade in this material after 5000 B.C. Obsidian was found on three Mediterranean islands, including Sardinia, and was now regularly traded to neighboring islands and the mainland. This trade was part of a widespread network of contacts, linked partly by sea, which carried seashells, exotic rocks, and, later, copper ore the length and breadth of the Mediterranean.

5000 B.C.

This trade also coincided in general terms with the manufacture of distinctive pottery styles decorated with impressions of seashells, among them the shell of the cockle *Cardium* (Figure 10.6). This motif has given rise to the term *Cardial ware* to describe a range of indigenously developed pottery styles that mark the first use of clay vessels by western peoples. Like sheep and goats and perhaps cereal crops, pottery was selectively adopted by different groups, as were other elements of farming culture, long before full-time farming took hold.

Cardial ware
4000 B.C.

The decisive shift from hunting and gathering in the west took place in the sixth millennium B.C., with sheep and goats being acquired by trade, exchange, or theft considerably earlier, and cereal crops arriving somewhat later. By 4000 B.C., a series of fishing villages was thriving on the shores of the Swiss lakes (Coles and Coles, 1989). These were peopled by cattle and sheep farmers, who cultivated barley and wheat as well as many minor crops, including cider apples and flax (to make linen cloth) (Figure 10.7). Their houses stood on the damp ground between the lake reed beds and the scrub brush of the valley behind. The first dwellings were small rectangular huts, but they eventually gave way to larger two-room houses. Some villages grew to include between 24 and 75 houses clustered on the lakeshore, a density of population much the same as that of modern Swiss villages, which have approximately 30 households.

In the extreme northwest, food production was adopted comparatively late. From 6000 through 4000 B.C., the newly isolated Mesolithic peoples of Britain developed with little or no significant contact with the continent. The earliest traces of pottery and forest clearance appeared soon after

FIGURE 10.6 *Cardium*-shell–impressed pottery from southern France (one-fourth actual size). The *Cardium* shell was widely traded and used for ornamentation.

FIGURE 10.7 Simple prehistoric stone axes mounted in deer antler handles from the Swiss lake dwellings, typical of those used by early farmers in Europe. Modern experiments have shown that such implements were surprisingly effective in clearing small trees and woodland.

4000 B.C., with well-documented cereal agriculture by 4300 B.C. The same processes may have operated here as in western Europe. Robin Dennell (1983) theorizes that European farmers did not cross the Channel and settle in Britain. Rather, Mesolithic peoples in Britain experienced population pressure about 4000 B.C., perhaps as a result of forest expansion due to warmer climate and also because of population growth. Hunting became more difficult, so the people began clearing woodland to provide more animal forage and plant foods and to make hunting more predictable. The people also increased their exploitation of marine resources, and seafaring techniques developed, leading to contacts with other coastal communities in Britain and on the continent. Eventually, Mesolithic populations in Britain became aware of new food resources, like domestic cereals and sheep, and acquired them. Ample open grassland was available for herding and cultivation in southern Britain. Within five centuries or so, Mesolithic populations had transformed themselves into farmers with their own distinctive cultural traditions. Somewhat similar processes probably led to the adoption of agriculture and stock rearing among Mesolithic Scandinavians.

The Megaliths

It seems likely that early European farming societies were basically egalitarian, the family being the basic productive unit at the center of a web of intricate kin ties and reciprocal social relationships that linked communities near and far and tied people to the land of their ancestors (for the British Neolithic, see J. Thomas, 1999). There was probably equal access to resources, with sufficient food being produced to feed individual families. In a real sense, the subsistence farming economy was society. Generally, early Neolithic burials in Europe do not reflect any social differentiation between individuals.

There are signs of variation, notably in the intensity of trading activities through barter networks and in burial customs. Notable social changes are apparent throughout Europe after 4000 B.C., with a movement toward a greater emphasis on craft specialization and burial ritual and the emergence of regional trading centers that controlled exchange networks, and perhaps ritual as well. The famous megalithic tombs of the Mediterranean and western Europe are one symbol of this trend toward social change.

Megaliths
4500 B.C. and later

As early as 4500 B.C., some French farmers were building large communal stone tombs, known to archaeologists as **megaliths** (Figure 10.8). Megaliths are found as far north as Scandinavia, in Britain, Ireland, France, Spain, the western Mediterranean, Corsica, and Malta. For years, scholars thought that megaliths had originated in the eastern Mediterranean in approximately 2500 B.C. and had spread westward into Spain with colonists from the Aegean who had carried a custom of collective burial and their religion with them (Daniel, 1973; Renfrew, 1983). Megalithic tombs were believed to have been built in western Europe, witnesses to a lost faith perhaps spread by pilgrims, missionaries, or merchants.

This popular and widely accepted hypothesis was considerably weakened by carbon-14 dates from France that turned out to be earlier than others from western Europe (Renfrew, 1972). Furthermore, calibrated radiocarbon dates have placed Spanish megalithic sites and their associated culture as early as approximately 4500 B.C., much earlier than their alleged prototypes in the Aegean. Thus, megaliths were being built in western Europe at least a millennium before massive funerary architecture became fashionable in the eastern Mediterranean. This type of remarkable freestanding architecture is a unique local European creation.

What, exactly, were megaliths? Were they the surviving remains of a powerful religious cult that swept western Europe, or did they symbolize the emergence of new, more sophisticated political and social structures in the west? Colin Renfrew (1983) has argued that the tradition of communal burial

FIGURE 10.8 The megalithic tomb at New Grange, Ireland, c. 3200 B.C. The structure measures up to 85 m (280 feet) across. The rising sun shines directly into the burial chamber at the winter solstice (December 21) every year.

developed in very early western European farming societies. He believes that it is manifested by the famous long barrows of southern Britain (Figure 10.9), many of which had stone-boulder megalithic interiors. The long barrows were fairly small structures, requiring not more than about 5,000 to 10,000 worker-hours to build (a figure equivalent to 20 workers taking 50 days). Ian Hodder (1990) believes they may be a reflection of long-held ideologies surrounding longhouses that were perpetuated in tomb design, on the grounds that ideology was a vital component in early European farming societies. Between 4000 and 3500 B.C., these barrows were associated with more elaborate monuments, among them enclosed earthworks (often called *causewayed camps*), which are known to have been protected by timber palisades. Recent excavations have shown that these camps were littered with human bones, many of them skeletons from which the flesh had weathered in the open. Perhaps these camps were places where the dead were exposed for months before their bones were deposited in nearby communal burials.

Long barrows
3200 B.C.

As time went on, the argument goes, burial ceremonies revolved around even larger monuments, the so-called **henges**, stone- and wood-built circles of which Stonehenge in southern Britain is the most famous (see Figure 20.8). In this sense, megaliths of all types formed a kind of settlement hierarchy on the prehistoric landscape, a hierarchy that may have reflected profound changes in European society. (For more on Stonehenge, see the Site box in Chapter 20.)

Another ingenious theory argues that megalithic monuments appeared in western Europe at just the time when farming took hold all across Europe. This final colonization must have had a major impact on the stable Mesolithic societies that were exploiting coastal resources along the Atlantic Ocean and North Sea shores from the Bay of Biscay in France to the Baltic. Megaliths may have first appeared in the margins of Neolithic society, along the Atlantic coast, where the competition with Mesolithic groups may have been most acute. Perhaps, he says, the megaliths served as territorial markers, signs of ancestral ownership of the surrounding land. (For a closely argued assessment, see J. Thomas, 1999.) (See Site box.)

2550 B.C.

Colin Renfrew and others have called megaliths the "tombs of the living," lasting, human-made symbols of the continuity of human life, as well as symbols of the continuity of ownership of land from one generation to the next. The annual round of religious rituals at places like Stonehenge reinforced this continuity; and at a time when population densities were rising sharply, the megaliths associated with the rituals became important symbols of political and social continuity. They also reinforced the political, economic, and spiritual power of those who supervised the building and worshiped at places such as Stonehenge. That such supervision was necessary is certain, for it has been estimated that Stonehenge required at least 30,000 worker-hours to complete. So the appearance of megaliths and the hierarchy of more elaborate stone and wooden monuments associated with them may have foreshadowed profound social changes in prehistoric Europe that came with the increasing use of bronze and other metals (Chippindale, 2004).

A complex set of processes governed the emergence of food production in temperate Europe, processes only rarely involving the movement of entire populations from one region to the next. Here, as in other parts of the world, one should think of agriculture not as a miracle invention or in terms of conquest but as yet another instance of how readily hunter-gatherers adapted to new opportunities and conditions. As is so often the case in prehistory, continuity was as important as change, but this continuity was born of inherent flexibility, an ability to adapt to new circumstances.

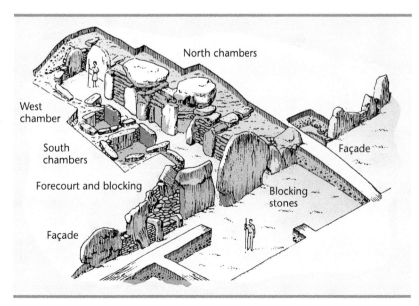

FIGURE 10.9 Interior of a megalithic chamber tomb in West Kennet, near Avebury, England, ¹⁴C-dated to approximately 3500 B.C. (after Piggott, 1965). The West Kennet sepulcher was probably a communal grave, used by a kin group over many generations.

SiTE > Easton Down and the Avebury Landscape <

The great earthworks and megalithic monuments of western Europe did not stand alone. For example, Avebury in southern England (Figure 10.10) lies at the center of a vast, long-vanished sacred landscape that was marked by burial mounds, enclosures, charnel houses, and other sites for commemorating the ancestors (Gillings and Pollard, 2002; Whittle, 1993). Avebury itself was built in around 2550 B.C., in a natural amphitheater ideal for a large stone circle. In its final form, its earthwork and ditch dug into the

FIGURE 10.10 Aerial view of Avebury stone circles in southern England.

underlying white chalk encompassed 11.5 ha (28.5 acres) and measured about 350 m (1150 feet) across. Four causewayed entrances divide the monument into four unequal arcs. Ninety-eight standing stones set up inside the ditch once adorned the interior, some of them up to 14 m (46 feet) high. Two inner circles stood within the outer circle. This staggering construction was built by farming communities with no wheeled carts and only the simplest levers, rollers, and stone, antler, and wooden tools. When new, the white earthworks with their exposed subsurface chalk must have stood out for kilometers.

Generations of archaeologists have excavated Avebury, but only recently have they paid close attention to its now-invisible landscape, very different from the rolling farmland of today. Obtaining evidence of ancient landscapes requires careful excavation and sample collection, most often of the original land surfaces under burial mounds and earthworks. When archaeologist Alisdair Whittle excavated some test trenches into a long burial mound at Easton Down in southern England, he exposed the original land surface, as well as the core of stacked turf, chalk, and topsoil under the mound. These

discoveries gave him an unusual opportunity to obtain a portrait of the local vegetation in about 3200 B.C. (Whittle et al., 1993).

First, he turned to pollen analysis. Small amounts of pollen grains from the land surface were predominantly from grasses, showing that no woodland grew close to the tumulus when it was built. A well-sealed section of the pre-mound soil yielded 11 mollusk samples, which chronicled a dramatic change from woodland to open grassland forms over a short period of time. Whittle located an ancient tree hollow under the mound, which, hardly surprisingly, contained woodland mollusks. A sudden increase in open-country mollusks followed, a change so rapid that human clearance of the land seemed the only logical explanation. Interestingly, soil scientists found signs of lateral movement of the soil below the mound, which could have resulted only from cultivation before the mound was built.

Excavations such as Easton Down can give us only snapshots of the complex mosaic of cleared and uncleared land that characterizes any agricultural landscape. For example, mollusks and soil samples under nearby Avebury itself tell us that the great temple of 2550 B.C. rose on long-established but little-grazed natural grassland close to a forest that had regenerated after being cleared for farming.

This kind of environmental archaeology is now so precise that we can fix the exact seasons when monuments were built or buildings erected. For example, soil samples from carefully cut sod laid under the original ground surface of the 40-m (130-foot) Silbury Hill, built in around 2200 B.C. and close to Easton Down, show that the builders started work in the late summer, most likely after the harvest when people had time for construction work (Figure 10.11). We know this because the well-preserved sods contain ants and anthills. The ants were beginning to grow wings and fly away from their anthills, as they do in late summer (Field et al., 2010).

As environmental and landscape studies continue, we will learn a surprising amount about the setting, and perhaps the meaning, of major religious sites like Avebury and Stonehenge.

FIGURE 10.11 Silbury Hill, near Avebury.

Summary

- The European Mesolithic lasted from about 8000 B.C. to the introduction of farming in northwestern Europe in around 4000 B.C.
- There were considerable local variations, with a trend toward more permanent settlement in more favored areas.
- By about 6000 B.C., farming was well established in parts of the Aegean area and in southeastern Europe. Agriculture and animal husbandry developed in southeastern Europe because of a local shift to the more intensive exploitation of cereals and wild sheep, and also because of a "drift" of domestic animals and cereals from Southwest Asia. This was a largely indigenous development.
- The widely distributed Bandkeramik complex documents the first settlement of southeastern European farmers in the middle Danube Valley and on the light loess soils of central Europe around 5000 B.C.
- This may be connected, at least in part, with fallout from the flooding of the Euxine Lake, which became the Black Sea.

The flooding may have caused people to move into forested lands, away from the lake.

- During the next millennium, food production spread widely throughout Europe, largely among indigenous Mesolithic peoples, who adopted sheep, pottery, and cereals, which they considered of immediate advantage to them.
- From about 4500 B.C., new religious ideologies spread widely in central and western Europe, as indicated by the building of communal burial mounds and megalithic monuments.
- Some of these new beliefs reflected centuries-old ideologies connected with the longhouses and the communal ethics of the Bandkeramik farmers. Others, derived from central and eastern Europe, were beliefs growing out of the emergence of individual power and prestige as a potent factor in local life, power reflected in the growing numbers of exotic artifacts and materials.

Key Terms

henge (231)   loess (224)   megalith (230)

Further Reading

Barker, Graeme. 2006. *The Agricultural Revolution in Prehistory.* Oxford, UK: Oxford University Press.

Dennell, Robin C. 1983. *European Economic Prehistory: A New Approach.* New York: Academic Press.

Price, T. Douglas, ed. 2000. *Europe's First Farmers.* Cambridge, UK: Cambridge University Press.

11 First Farmers in Egypt and Tropical Africa

CHAPTER OUTLINE

"Our finds caused quite a stir," recalled 80-year-old Gertrude Caton-Thompson to one of us (BF) back in 1968. "People didn't believe us when we showed them carbonized emmer and barley seeds from the baskets. They told us they were modern seeds that were mixed into the pits by accident." Caton-Thompson's memories of her late-1920s excavations in early farming settlements in Egypt's Fayum Depression were as vivid as if they had been from yesterday. She told Brian how she had worked almost alone, camping in the wilderness at the edge of a dried-up lake. It was there that she had uncovered the remains of small oval-shaped pole-and-reed dwellings and small storage pits lined with baskets still containing domestic grains.

Caton-Thompson's finds were revolutionary in the late 1920s, for they pushed the origins of agriculture back to earlier than 4000 B.C. Though she worked with almost no money and facilities, her research started a quest for the first farmers on the Nile that continues to this day (Caton-Thompson and Gardner, 1934). ■

The Nile River near Beni Hasan, Egypt.

The Nile slashes like a green arrow through the arid wastes of the eastern Sahara, rising high in the Ethiopian highlands and flowing northward more than 4,800 km (3,000 miles) to the Mediterranean. For most of its last 1,100 km (700 miles), the Nile has cut a deep gorge through the desert, which it has filled with layer after layer of fertile river silt. This was a land of bounty but also an uncertain one, dependent on rainfall far upstream. If there were good winter rains in the highlands, then the annual flood would inundate the fertile floodplain and replenish plant life. Poor rains would trigger only a meager flood, leaving the Nile Valley baking under the summer sun. Occasionally, too, record rainfall in Ethiopia would bring catastrophic floods downstream that swept everything before them. For all these uncertainties, the Nile Valley was always an isolated oasis, a strip of green, fertile land between desert bastions. The valley floor itself consisted for the most part of seasonally flooded natural basins that supported grass and brushland. People lived on higher levees along the river, where trees grew and settlements escaped the annual inundation. For tens of thousands of years, the region was a paradise for hunters and foragers (Table 11.1; for map, see Figure 9.1).

Hunter-Gatherers on the Nile

During the last millennia of the Ice Age, the Nile Valley was a rich, diverse habitat, abounding in game of all sizes and in wild vegetable foods. Fish and waterfowl added to the bounty of resources. But those who lived there had to employ both flexible and conservative ways of life to adjust to constant fluctuations in the flood levels.

We know something of their lifeways from excavations at ancient camps in Wadi Kubbaniya dating to between 17000 and 15000 B.C., northwest of Aswan in Upper Egypt (Wendorf et al., 1980). The tiny settlements, little more than scatters of stone tools, bones, and charcoal, lay atop sandy dunes about 3 km (1.9 miles) from the narrow Nile floodplain. Rising floodwaters inundated

Wadi Kubbaniya
17000 to 15000 B.C.

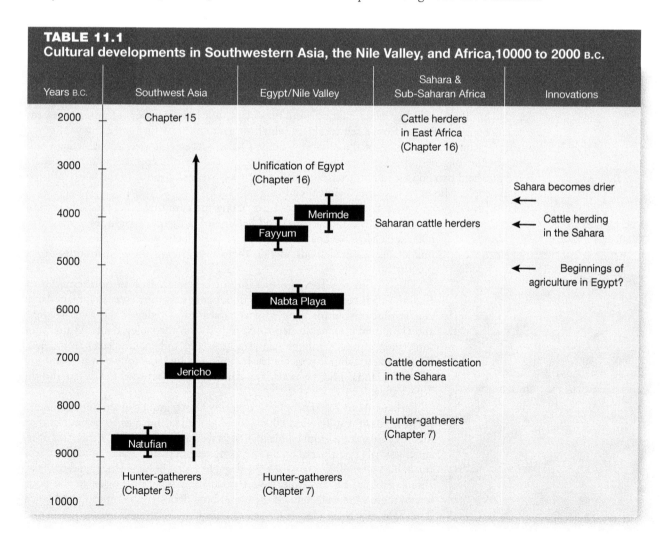

TABLE 11.1
Cultural developments in Southwestern Asia, the Nile Valley, and Africa,10000 to 2000 B.C.

Years B.C.	Southwest Asia	Egypt/Nile Valley	Sahara & Sub-Saharan Africa	Innovations
2000	Chapter 15		Cattle herders in East Africa (Chapter 16)	
3000		Unification of Egypt (Chapter 16)		
4000		Merimde / Fayyum	Saharan cattle herders	Sahara becomes drier ← / ← Cattle herding in the Sahara
5000				← Beginnings of agriculture in Egypt?
6000		Nabta Playa		
7000	Jericho		Cattle domestication in the Sahara	
8000				
9000	Natufian		Hunter-gatherers (Chapter 7)	
10000	Hunter-gatherers (Chapter 5)	Hunter-gatherers (Chapter 7)		

the dunes for some weeks each summer, but for the rest of the year the inhabitants looked out over a marshy floodplain. The annual cycle at Wadi Kubbaniya began with rising floodwaters in July, when vast numbers of catfish congregated in the shallows to spawn. After mating, they lay sluggish in the water for several hours. It was then that the inhabitants would flock to the water's edge, catching fish with their hands, impaling them with spears, or even trapping them with upturned containers. Hundreds of fish were gutted and laid out to dry in the sun during the precious few days of spawning.

When the floodwaters reached their height, flooding root plants in the wetlands, the people fished and foraged at water's edge, harvesting ripe dates and acacia seeds from trees at the edge of the desert. As the inundation receded, people would comb the shallow pools left by the retreating water for trapped catfish. Meanwhile, others, armed with wooden digging sticks, turned their attention to the ripe swards of nut grass and club-rush tubers in the newly exposed wetlands. Even today, nut grass is abundant along the Nile, yielding small, bitter-tasting tubers high in carbohydrates and fiber. But they are toxic, especially during later stages of growth, so they would be rubbed, ground, and then leached before consumption. A family armed with digging sticks could have gathered enough carbohydrates for several days within a matter of hours.

As fall and winter came, the foragers would turn to water lilies, sedges, wild millets, and other wetland plants, while the hunters would take migratory coots, ducks, and geese. Come spring, the people would eat acacia seeds and dates and cattail and other wetland plants, relying on a broad spectrum of edible plant foods that were vital when staples were in short supply.

Not that the Wadi people enjoyed a comfortable life, for the annual floods varied so much that they lived in a constant state of uncertainty. A high flood could delay plant harvests, and low waters caused the marshlands to dry up for months on end. For this reason, the people exploited a very broad range of food resources, seeking in any way possible to adapt to their demanding environment.

The same broad-based hunter-gatherer economies persisted for the remainder of the Ice Age and well into Holocene times, with, however, a trend toward more sedentary settlement and a more intensified exploitation of plants and fish. In all probability, numerous local groups lived in the valley, all the way from the Nile Delta in the north into the Sudan (Nubia) in the far south, distinguishable in the archaeological record by minor differences in their toolkits.

Qadan culture
10000 B.C.

One such group was the so-called Qadan culture from central Egypt, best known from microlithic tools found at riverside campsites near the Nile (J. D. Clark, 1971). In the earlier stages of the Qadan, fishing and big-game hunting were important, but large numbers of grindstones and grinding equipment came from a few localities, which seems to indicate that gathering wild grains was significant in at least part of the economy. Some Qadan settlements were probably large and occupied for long periods. The dead lay in cemeteries, in shallow pits covered with stone slabs. Some pits held two bodies. In six instances, small stone tools were embedded in the bones of these Qadan people, who must have met a violent end (Figure 11.1).

These war casualties are a sign that life was not easy along the bountiful Nile, probably because of the sheer unpredictability of the annual flood and because of constant drought, especially after 6000 B.C. Most groups settled close to permanent water supplies, relying on predictable seasonal foods to tide them over during the lean months of the inundation.

FIGURE 11.1 War casualties from a cemetery of c. 11000 B.C. in the Sudan.

The end of the Ice Age brought increased rainfall to northern Africa. Raging floods cut through the Nile floodplain, sweeping away rich marshlands and fertile soils, until rising Holocene sea levels reduced the river gradient and the inundation again deposited rich silt on the valley floor. At the same time, more rainfall brought semiarid grassland and shallow lakes to much of the Sahara, making it possible for hunters and foragers to live in hitherto uninhabited lands. There was also regular movement between the desert and the Nile Valley.

Perhaps about 1,000 people lived in tiny family groups in this unpredictable, harsh environment between 8000 and 3000 B.C. As much as 80 percent of their diet may have come from edible plants, as well as from gazelles, hares, and other small animals that flourished on the stony terrain. Life became much harder in the Sahara after 6000 B.C., when the drought cycles became longer and the lakes shrank rapidly. By this time, desert populations may have risen to the point where there were well-defined territorial boundaries and no unexploited lands. The Saharans responded to drier conditions by settling closer to permanent water, where they faced the same problem as the people of the Nile: seasonal food shortages and the constant threat of starvation.

Agricultural Origins Along the Nile

For years, people assumed that cereal crops and domesticated animals had been introduced into the Nile Valley from Southwest Asia sometime after 8000 B.C. (Childe, 1952). In more recent years, as part of a wider school of thought that sought to understand socio-economic developments in indigenous terms, this view has been challenged by those who believe that food production arose independently in Egypt, the Sudan, and even the Sahara (Hassan, 1986). The evidence for such a development, however, is both fragmentary and controversial, for the deep alluvium of the Nile Valley has long buried the relevant settlements near the valley. Now, prevailing expert opinion seems to favor an outside introduction. This scenario goes as follows.

In about 6000 B.C., severe drought conditions prevailed over much of Southwest Asia, decimating game populations and causing widespread crop failures among the tiny farming populations that flourished in what are now Israel and Syria. The farmers responded by moving from drier zones into the Mediterranean forest zone near the coast, one day to be the source of the famed "cedars of Lebanon" mentioned in the scriptures. During these years of dislocation and resettlement, some nomadic groups with goats and sheep may have crossed the Sinai into Lower Egypt, bringing domesticated barley, emmer wheat, and other crops with them.

6000 B.C.

The Nile Valley was also gripped by drought. Human populations moved closer to the shrinking river, where animals still grazed and plant foods were still plentiful. Inevitably, group territories shrank, too, so people responded by turning to domesticated plants and animals as part of a complex safety net that protected them against a very unpredictable environment. Not that there was any drastic change in daily life, for initially the new economies were practiced on a very small scale. Early Nile agriculture may have been a form of insurance, practiced sporadically and on the smallest of scales when circumstances merited, by people who were preadapted to the new lifeway (Hassan, 1986).

Agricultural methods were probably of the simplest. Some villagers would plant wheat, a crop timed to ripen when food was short, on damp ground at the receding floodwaters' edge. The plots were small and left to fend for themselves. Thus, farming began along the Nile when people living in an unpredictable riverine environment wanted to amplify their food supplies. Within a remarkably short time, probably only a few centuries, domesticated forms of these same cereals became important staples. These new strains were much more demanding than their wild ancestors, needing constant attention, weeding, and watering. Each village was now tied to its herds and gardens.

Archaeological evidence for early farming is virtually nonexistent. Domesticated barley is known from the Nabta Playa site in the Western Desert and dates to about 6000 B.C. These cultivators and their neighbors at Bir Kiseiba, to the west, were living in large settlements with houses set in rows or in an arc. Perhaps as many as 14 families lived in these villages, dwelling in low pit houses sunk into the ground (Wendorf et al., 1984).

Nabta Playa
6000 B.C.

Farther north, in the Fayum Depression west of the Nile, small fishing camps flourished along the water's edge at the time of Bir Kiseiba and Nabta Playa. Unlike their relatives far to the south, they did not use cereals. Then, before 5000 B.C., the lakeshores were home to people living in short-term seasonal camps that were moved as the lake level rose or fell (Figure 11.2). These people cultivated wheat and barley, locating their gardens on patches of fertile soil whose distribution changed as the lake did. They also herded cattle, goats, pigs, and sheep, but fish were overwhelmingly important in their diet. Unlike their contemporaries in Southwest Asia, the Fayum people never built permanent villages, for their environment was too unpredictable to allow complete dependence on agriculture.

Fayum Depression
Before 5000 B.C.

Considerable debate surrounds the Fayum discoveries, which have long been hailed as evidence for the earliest farming in the Nile area. In fact, this lake-filled depression may have supported groups that only partially adopted the new lifeways because of the unpredictable environment. Dozens of farming villages may have flourished in the fertile Nile Valley as early as 6000 B.C., if not earlier, settlements that are now inaccessible beneath deep alluvial deposits laid down by thousands of years of river floods.

The earliest dated farming settlements from the Nile Valley, both from Egypt and the Sudan, date to between 5000 and 3300 B.C. Hassan (1986) believes that the nomadic peoples of the desert now included the fertile river valley in their wanderings, moving in and out of the desert as conditions warranted, as they do in the Sahel region at the southern fringes of the Sahara today. These movements, he believes, were especially significant after 2500 B.C., when conditions became very arid indeed. This was also a time of exceptionally low Nile floods, so the sparse agricultural sites dating from early farming times are probably buried under many feet of later river alluvium. Hassan argues that irregular population movements into the valley, involving small numbers of people from many desert regions, continued for thousands of years. The result was considerable cultural diversity within the Nile Valley, caused by both immigration and fusion with existing populations.

5000 to 3300 B.C.

FIGURE 11.2 Excavations at an early farming site in the Fayum, Egypt.

Merimde
3900 B.C.

Many of the new floodplain settlements may have been like the village of Merimde Beni Salama near the Nile Delta. There, a cluster of oval houses and shelters was built half underground and roofed with mud and sticks (Hoffman, 1979). An occupation mound 2 m (7 feet) high was accumulated over 600 years, from approximately 3900 B.C. Farming at a subsistence level was characteristic of large areas of the Nile floodplain for thousands of years (Hassan, 1988).

Cemetery burials are our main source of information on the other farmers who flourished along the Upper Nile. Like their northern neighbors, they used bows and arrows in the chase, many tipped with finely flaked arrowheads. Emmer wheat and barley were cultivated, and cattle and small stock provided much of the meat. Settlements here were typified by mud-brick and transient architecture. The dead, however, were buried with some ceremony—in linen shrouds and covered with animal skins. The women wore ivory combs and plaited their hair. This culture, named the Badarian after a village where the first settlements were found, is thought to have been broadly contemporary with that of Merimde (Hassan, 1988). The early farming communities of the Nile continued to use the forested riverbanks for settlement (Butzer, 1976). Animals grazed on the flat grasslands of the plain for most of the year, and crops were planted on wet basin soils as the waters receded. Game was still abundant in the Nile Valley in 4000 B.C.; even so, the people ventured to the edge of the desert in search of gazelles and other small animals. They buried their dead in cemeteries overlooking the Nile, where the graves would not take up valuable agricultural land. Desert people maintained widespread contacts with other peoples. At Gebel Ramlah, near Nabta Playa in the Western Desert, a cemetery of about 4500 B.C., perhaps that of an extended family of nomads, contains elaborate grave goods, including shells and mica from the Red Sea shore, even turquoise from Sinai. Such nomads may have had a strong influence on the early formation of the Egyptian state in later centuries (Kobusiewicz et al., 2004).

3500 B.C.

By 3500 B.C., the inhabitants of the Nile Valley were living almost entirely off agriculture, with hunting playing a negligible role in daily life. The density of population was probably low enough so that the people had no need of either centralized government or government-regulated irrigation canals. They farmed without any form of large-scale irrigation. The modern Egyptian landscape bears no resemblance to the riverine environment of 3000 B.C. We know little of the narrow floodplain's original appearance. We can only draw analogies from other large rivers, like the North American Mississippi or the African Zambezi, which flood each year.

The Nile must have had a well-defined channel that meandered between natural banks. Shallow basins and swamps retained receding floodwater, capturing fertile silt. Small farming villages flourished on higher ground or on the riverbanks, in strategic locations near good soils. As the floodwaters receded, the farmers planted their crops in the fresh silt, grazing their cattle in nearby meadows and scrublands. By the time the waters rose again, the harvest was over. The villagers' herds grazed on dry lands at the margins of the flood. The Egyptian farmer of 5,500 years ago had no need of elaborate irrigation technology, just the ability to exploit flood basins and a varied environment teeming with edible plants, fish, and game animals. The first appearance of irrigation seems to have coincided with the unification of Egypt and is described in Chapter 16 (see Figure 16.8).

Saharan Pastoralists

Many people think of the Sahara as a vast sand sea, one of the most desolate places on earth. In fact, the Sahara is a highly diverse, albeit dry, region that has undergone major climatic changes since 10000 B.C. (McIntosh and McIntosh, 1988). As recently as 6000 B.C., the southern frontier of   6000 B.C. the desert was far to the north, and semiarid grassland and shallow freshwater lakes covered much of what are now arid plains. This was a landscape where antelope of all kinds abounded, as well as *Bos primigenius*, the wild ox. The areas that are now desert were, like all arid regions, very susceptible to cycles of higher and lower rainfall, resulting in major, sudden changes in distributions of plants and animals. The people who preyed on the sparse desert fauna responded to drought by managing the wild resources they hunted and gathered, especially wild oxen, which had to have regular water supplies to survive.

Even before the drought, the Sahara was never well watered. Both humans and animals were constantly on the move, in search of food and reliable water supplies. Under these circumstances, archaeologist Andrew Smith believes (1992), the small herds of *Bos primigenius* in the desert became closer-knit, smaller breeding units. The beasts were more disciplined, so that it was easier for hunters to move among them, predict their habits, and cull animals at will. At the same time, both cattle and humans were more confined in their movements, staying much closer to permanent water supplies for long periods of time. As a result, cattle and humans came into close association.

Smith believes that the hunters were well aware of the more disciplined ways in which their prey behaved. Instead of following the cattle on their annual migrations, the hunters prevented the herd from moving from one spot to another. They did this in such a way that they were no threat to the beasts, moving around and through the herd on its home range. At first, they controlled the movement of the herd while still maintaining their all-important ritual relationships with their prey and ensuring continuance of their meat diet. But soon they also gained genetic control of the animals, which led to rapid physical changes in the herd. South African farmers who maintain herds of wild eland report that the offspring soon diminish in size unless wild bulls are introduced constantly from outside. The same effects of inbreeding may have occurred in controlled cattle populations, with some additional, and perhaps unrecognized, advantages. The newly domesticated animals behaved better, were easier to control, and may have enjoyed a higher calving rate, which in turn yielded greater milk supplies. We know from rock paintings from deep in the Sahara that the herders were soon selecting for different horn shapes and hide colors (Figure 11.3).

It is still unclear whether domesticated cattle were tamed independently in northern Africa or introduced to the continent from Southwest Asia. Whatever the source of the original tamed herds, it seems entirely likely that much the same process of control and juxtaposition occurred in both Southwest Asia and northern Africa, and even in Europe, among peoples who had an intimate

FIGURE 11.3 Cattle in a Saharan rock painting from Tassili n'Ajjer. Saharan rock paintings had symbolic meaning to those who painted them. For archaeologists, they are a source of vital information on early cattle herders and trade in the desert.

knowledge of wild cattle's behavior. The experiments with domestication probably occurred in many places, as people living in ever-drier environments cast around for more predictable food supplies. Fiona Marshall and Elisabeth Hildebrand (2002) believe cattle were domesticated somewhere in the eastern Sahara by about 7000 B.C., perhaps by hunter-gatherer bands based in desert basins, where plant remains attracted plenty of game. Taming the aurochs ensured a much more predictable food supply, stored on the readily accessible hoof. We also know that wild cattle had major ritual significance long before they were tamed; burials accompanied by cattle horns became important in the region before 10000 B.C.

The cattle herders had only a few possessions: unsophisticated round-based pots and flaked and polished adzes. They also hunted with bow and arrow. The Saharan people left a remarkable record of their lives on the walls of caves deep in the desert. Wild animals, cattle, goats, humans, and scenes of daily life are preserved in a complicated jumble of artistic endeavor extending back perhaps to 5000 B.C. (Muzzolini, 1995). The widespread distribution of pastoral sites of this period suggests that the Saharans ranged their herds over widely separated summer and winter grazing grounds.

3500 B.C.   About 3500 B.C., climatic conditions again deteriorated. The Sahara slowly became drier and lakes vanished. Rainfall rose in the interior of western Africa, and the northern limit of the **tsetse fly** belt moved south. So the herders shifted south, following the major river systems into savanna regions. By this time, the Saharan people were probably using domestic crops, experimenting with such summer rainfall crops as sorghum and millet as they moved out of areas where they could grow wheat, barley, and other Mediterranean crops (McIntosh and McIntosh, 1988).

Early Food Production in Sub-Saharan Africa

At the end of the Pleistocene, the indigenous inhabitants of sub-Saharan Africa were already adapted to many kinds of specialized environments (Phillipson, 2005; Stahl, 2005). Some lived by intensive fishing and others by gathering or hunting, depending on their environment. In a simple way, the techniques of food production may already have been employed on the fringes of the rain forests of western and central Africa, where the common use of such root plants as the African yam led people to recognize the advantages of growing their own food. The yam can easily be resprouted if its top is planted. This primitive form of **vegeculture** may have been the economic tradition onto which the cultivation of summer rainfall cereal crops was grafted as it came into use south of the grassland areas on the Sahara's southern borders (Harlan et al., 1976).

3000 B.C.   As the Sahara dried up after 5000 B.C., pastoral peoples moved southward along major watercourses into the savanna belt of West Africa and the Sudan. By 3000 B.C., just as ancient Egyptian civilization was coming into being along the Nile, they had settled in the heart of the East African highlands far to the south. The East African highlands are ideal cattle country and the home of such famous cattle-herding peoples as the Masai today. Hunter-gatherers living around mountains near the plains inhabited the highlands until about 3300 B.C., when the first cattle herders appeared. These cattle people may have moved between fixed settlements during the wet and dry seasons, living off hunting in the dry months and their own livestock and agriculture during the rains (Ambrose, 1984; Bower, 1984).

As was the case elsewhere, cattle were demanding animals in Africa. They required water at least every 24 hours and large tracts of grazing grass if herds of any size were to be maintained. The secret was the careful selection of grazing land, especially in environments where seasonal rainfall led to marked differences in graze quality throughout the year. Even modest cattle herds required plenty of land and considerable mobility. To acquire such land often meant moving herds considerable distances, even from summer to winter pastures. At the same time, the cattle owners had to graze their stock in tsetse fly–free areas. The only protection against human and animal **trypanosomiasis** was to avoid settling or farming such areas—a constraint severely limiting the movements of cattle-owning farmers in eastern and central Africa. As a result, small cattle herds spread south rapidly in areas where they could be grazed. Long before cereal agriculture took hold far south of the Sahara, some hunter-gatherer groups in the savanna woodlands of eastern and southern Africa may have acquired cattle, and perhaps other domesticated animals, by gift exchange or through raids on herding neighbors.

1500 B.C.   Contrary to popular belief, there is no such phenomenon as "pure" pastoralists, a society that subsists on its herds alone. Almost certainly, the Saharan herders who moved southward to escape drought were also cultivating sorghum, millet, and other tropical rainfall crops. By 1500 B.C., cereal agriculture was widespread throughout the savanna belt south of the Sahara. Small farming communities dotted the grasslands and forest margins of eastern West Africa, all of them depending on what is called *shifting agriculture*. This form of agriculture involves clearing woodland, burning the felled brush over the cleared plot, mixing the ash into the soil, and then cultivating the prepared

FIGURE 11.4 Traditional iron smelting in central Africa. The furnace, made of sticks and anthill clay, is in the form of a woman giving birth. The goatskin bellows operate from the back. The man in the foreground with a stick is raking out the smelted iron.

fields. After a few years, the soil is exhausted, so the farmer moves on, exploiting new woodland and leaving the abandoned fields to lie fallow. Shifting agriculture, also called slash-and-burn, is highly adaptive for savanna farmers without plows, for it allows cereal farming with the minimal expenditure of energy. It is also wasteful of land.

The process of clearance and burning may have seemed haphazard to the uninformed eye, but it was not. Except in favored areas such as regularly inundated river floodplains, tropical Africa's soils are of only moderate to low fertility. One expert has estimated that only about 40 percent of such soils are cultivable, even with plows (Allan, 1965). Farmers using simple axes, digging sticks, and hoes would have been at an even greater disadvantage, especially on the heavily wooded, clayey soils so common on the African savanna. The art of farming was careful soil selection—that is, knowing which soils were light and easily cultivable, could be readily turned with small hoes, and would maintain their fertility over several years' planting (cereal crops rapidly remove nitrogen and other nutrients from the soil).

Iron technology, which appeared south of the Sahara about 700 B.C., was one catalyst for the spread of farming throughout sub-Saharan Africa (Figure 11.4) (P. Schmidt, 1996). Once it had taken hold, slash-and-burn agriculture expanded its frontiers rapidly, as village after village took up new lands, moving forward so rapidly that one expert has estimated it took a mere two centuries to cover 2,000 km (1,250 miles) from eastern to southern Africa. By A.D. 1, farming villages flourished on the banks of the Zambezi River. Other farmers and cattle herders had crossed into what is now South Africa within a few centuries (see Chapter 16).

700 B.C.

Summary

- Food production was probably introduced into the Nile Valley at a time of drought, by 6000 B.C. The hunter-gatherers of the Nile and of the then-inhabitable Sahara were preadapted to the new economies, which they may have taken up as a means of staving off food shortages in drought years.

- By 4000 B.C., agriculture was well established along the Nile, and cattle were being domesticated and herded in the depths of the Sahara. Nile Valley communities soon became dependent on agriculture and relied on natural flooding to water their gardens until about 3000 B.C.

- As the Sahara dried up after 5000 B.C., pastoralists with cereal crops moved south of the desert, introducing cattle herding as far south as the East African highlands.

- Cereal cultivation, based on shifting agriculture, did not take hold in much of sub-Saharan Africa until the introduction of ironworking south of the desert in the first millennium B.C.

Key Terms

Trypanosomiasis (240)   Tsetse fly (240)   Vegeculture (240)

Further Reading

Barker, Graeme. 2006. *The Agricultural Revolution in Prehistory*. Oxford: Oxford University Press.

Hassan, Fekri. 1988. "The Pre-Dynastic of Egypt." *Journal of World Prehistory* 2 (2): 135–186.

Hoffman, Michael A. 1979. *Egypt Before the Pharaohs*. New York: Knopf.

Asia and the Pacific

RICE, ROOTS, AND OCEAN VOYAGES

12

"In these Proes or Pahee's as they call them from all accounts we can learn, these people sail in these seas from Island to Island for several hundred leagues, the Sun serving them for a compass by day and the Moon and Stars by night. When this comes to be prov'd we Shall no longer be at a loss to know how the Islands lying in these Seas came to be people'd" (Beaglehole, 1974: 178). Captain James Cook landed on Tahiti in the heart of the South Pacific in A.D. 1769. He befriended a Polynesian navigator named Tupaia, who accompanied him southwest to New Zealand. "We may trace them from Island to Island quite to the East Indias," wrote Cook prophetically. Ever since then, scientists have been fascinated by the origin of these remarkable Polynesian seamen. This chapter explores the beginnings of food production in Asia and the developments that led to the settlement of the remotest landmasses of the Pacific Ocean (Table 12.1). ■

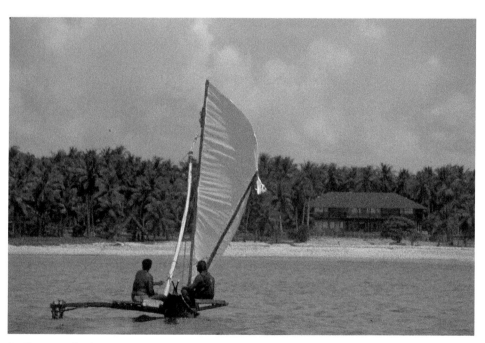

A sailing canoe, Caroline Islands, Micronesia.

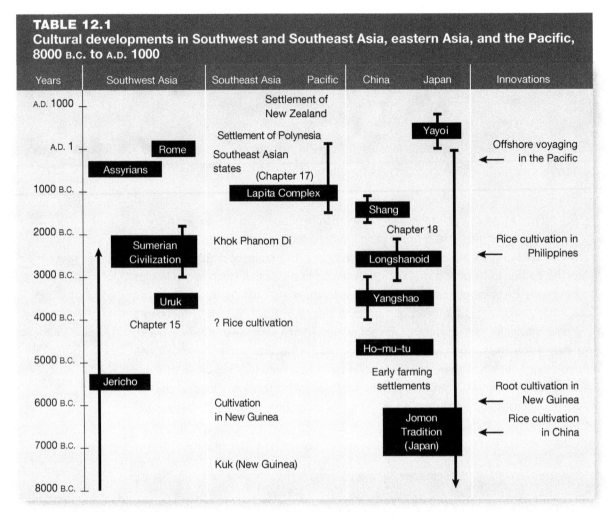

TABLE 12.1
Cultural developments in Southwest and Southeast Asia, eastern Asia, and the Pacific, 8000 B.C. to A.D. 1000

Years	Southwest Asia	Southeast Asia	Pacific	China	Japan	Innovations
A.D. 1000		Settlement of New Zealand			Yayoi	
A.D. 1	Rome	Settlement of Polynesia				Offshore voyaging in the Pacific
	Assyrians	Southeast Asian states (Chapter 17)				
1000 B.C.		Lapita Complex		Shang		
				Chapter 18		
2000 B.C.	Sumerian Civilization	Khok Phanom Di		Longshanoid		Rice cultivation in Philippines
3000 B.C.						
	Uruk			Yangshao		
4000 B.C.	Chapter 15	? Rice cultivation				
5000 B.C.				Ho–mu–tu		
	Jericho			Early farming settlements		
6000 B.C.		Cultivation in New Guinea		Jomon Tradition (Japan)		Root cultivation in New Guinea
7000 B.C.						Rice cultivation in China
		Kuk (New Guinea)				
8000 B.C.						

The Origins of Rice Cultivation

Rice was the staple of ancient agriculture over an enormous area of southern and southeastern Asia and of southern China. Today, rice accounts for half the food eaten by 1.7 billion people and 21 percent of the total calories consumed by all of humankind (B. Smith, 1998). Unfortunately, we still know almost nothing about the origins of this most important of domesticated crops. As a result of recent intensive research on the actual rice remains from prehistoric settlements in the lower Yangzi valley, we can now trace in detail the progressive stages in the domestication of this plant species (Fuller et al., 2010). This is made all the more informative because sites such as Hemudu and Tianluoshan, like the Swiss Lake Villages, have survived waterlogged and organic remains, such as house foundations, boats, paddles, and most significantly plant remains, are available for study.

Rice was the earliest plant to be domesticated in the vital Yangzi Valley, while millet was domesticated in the colder Yellow River (Huang He River) to the north. Rice is in nature a marsh grass. It flourishes in relatively warm conditions that would have existed during the post Pleistocene climatic optimum as far north as the Yangzi valley. Botanists believe that the rice and Asian millets ancestral to the present domesticated species radiated from perennial ancestors around the eastern borders of the Himalaya Mountains at the end of the Ice Age. The initial propagation of the wild progenitor is thought to have taken place in an alluvial swamp area such as the middle Yangzi Valley, where there was plenty of water to stimulate cereal growth, in a region at the northern limits of wild rice. The first form to be domesticated may have flourished in shallow water, where seasonal flooding dispersed the seed on the border zone between permanently dry and permanently inundated lands (B. Smith, 1998). Perhaps this cultivation occurred under conditions in which seasonal flooding made field preparation a far from burdensome task.

The wetland habitat encouraged not only rice, but a myriad of other edible aquatic plants, such as the water chestnuts and camellia roots. There was also an abundance of fish, wild animals such as deer and pigs, and on the drier land, acorns. Initially, rice was a minor player in the diet. As in Southwest Asia, the wild grass seeds shatter easily when mature, and individual

FIGURE 12.1 Early Chinese farming cultures, with names of some major local variants. Yangshao sites occur both within the northern shaded area and outside it. Southern sites of corded pottery are found in the Kwangtung, Fukien, and Taiwan areas.

plants tend to mature at different rates. Therefore, harvesting is not straightforward for it would naturally disperse the very seeds being sought. Over time, however, plants that underwent a genetic change in favor of non-shattering would be favored, which in turn led to a recognizable domesticated variety.

The history of rice domestication is therefore a long one, involving millennia of progressive selection, traced by the analysis of the so-called abscission scar on the base of the seed. This progress has been traced at several sites in the lower Yangzi region south of Hangzhou Bay, most famously at Hemudu, but more recently at its twin site of Tianluoshan. It may be that the first attempts to cultivate rice resulted from deliberate efforts to expand seasonally inundated habitats by constructing dams to trap runoff. The dams could then be breached so that the flooded land could be used for rice planting, creating additional stands of wild rice. From there, it was a short step to deliberate sowing and harvesting in wet fields (paddies). Most likely, a sedentary lifeway based on the gathering of rice developed at the beginning of the Holocene in low-lying, seasonally flooded areas. Systematic cultivation resulted from a response to population growth, climatic change, or some other stress (Higham and Glover, 1996).

The earliest known rice-farming sites come from the Yangzi River region of southern China, a contradiction of earlier theories which held that the first domestication took place farther south. Although the Yangzi Valley now lies outside the modern range of wild rice, warmer, more humid conditions after 8000 B.C. supported extensive wetlands where the cereal once flourished. Wild rice was gathered in this region between 10000 and 6000 B.C., activity documented at the Yuchan Cave in Hunan province, a location that overlooked swampy terrain where wild rice would have flourished.

Early Farming in China

At about the same time as farming began in southern Europe, two quite distinct agricultural lifeways developed along two great Chinese river systems: the Huang Ho, or Yellow River, in the north and the Yangzi in the south (D. Cohen, 2011; B. Smith, 1998) (Figure 12.1). Food production took over 4,000 years to become firmly established in different regions. The steps toward full agriculture were small, often taking hold after sedentary living and other changes had begun. China's interlacing river systems made the spread of farming somewhat easier. As early as 7900 B.C., people in northern and southern China were living differently than their Ice Age forebears, even if they had not adopted agriculture.

Southern and Eastern China

Southern China is a strong candidate as the region where rice cultivation first began (G. Crawford, 2011; Higham and Lu, 1998). During the early Holocene, warmer conditions may have allowed wild rice to colonize the lakes and marshes of the middle and lower Yangzi Valley, when hunter-gatherer societies throughout China were exploiting a broad spectrum of animal and plant resources. The inhabitants of Diaotonghuan cave were exploiting wild rice from nearby lowlands by 10000 B.C. By 8000 to 7000 B.C., they were growing it. This was during warmer, more humid conditions after the cold of the Younger Dryas, when wild rice would have retreated southward to warmer environments (Zhao, 1998).

Diaotonghuan Cave
10000 B.C.

With rice farming came much larger, permanent settlements. The Pengtoushan site in the middle Yangzi Valley dates to between 6500 and 5800 B.C. and provides definite evidence for rice farming. This large settlement with substantial dwellings and 19 discovered graves was a rice-farming village, occupied for seven centuries at a time when agriculture was spreading rapidly in southern China (Underhill and Habu, 2006). The nearby and contemporary Bashidang site had a defensive ditch, a village where people lived in houses raised on piles and ate a wide range of plant foods. Both settlements were part of an agricultural culture that may have begun as early as 7000 B.C. and flourished for as long as 1,500 years (see Site box). From southern China, rice farming appears to have spread into India and Southeast Asia.

Pengtoushan
6500 to 5800 B.C.

SiTE > Early Rice Cultivation at Kuahuqiao, China <

Recent excavations at the waterlogged Kuahuqiao village, some 200 km (124 miles) southwest of Shanghai, have thrown new light on the beginnings of rice agriculture in southern China. For thousands of years, hunter-gatherer groups in the middle Yangtze Basin and downstream gathered large quantities of wild aquatic rice (*Oryza rufipogon*) at a time when warm, moist conditions favored its growth. Such intensive exploitation of the wild resource preceded domestication of what was to become a staple crop. The Kuahuqiao site in the lower Yangtze region lies at a strategic point between upland valleys and coastal wetlands along Hangzhou Bay (Zong et al., 2007). Kuahuqiao is a waterlogged village with superb preservation that was occupied between about 5700 and 5550 B.C. The settlement lay amidst an estuarine environment, surrounded by swamp and marshland scrub. Kuahuqiao yielded spectacular organic finds, among them were bones from domestic dogs and pigs and wild animals, also a series of bamboo and wood tools, pig shoulder blade shovels. The excavators found numerous pilings, which they believe to be the foundations of thatched houses set on posts above the swampy, often waterlogged ground.

The first inhabitants chose lowland swamps for their rice cultivation and cleared the scrub. Rice pollen becomes common, as do the ova of a parasite worm that is associated with both humans and pigs. After about a century, the site was flooded by rising water and abandoned, before being reoccupied by new generations of farmers. Now pig bones abound, as do fungi associated with animal dung and the remains of oysters, a dietary staple. The excavators believe that the inhabitants grew rice in fields that were flooded regularly, then burnt off and manured with animal dung to enhance crop yields. Cattails grew thickly around the cultivated fields, themselves an important food source and useful raw material for a variety of purposes. This intensive human manipulation of the environment continued until about 5550 B.C., when marine flooding made cultivation impossible. Kuahuqiao gives us a scenario for the transition from intensive exploitation of wild rice to its domestication, a process encouraged by warm, wet conditions that coincided with a strengthening of the summer monsoon after about 7000 B.C. Thus, the earliest rice cultivation in eastern China took hold in slightly brackish coastal reed-swamps. From the earliest attempts at cultivation, the new farmers cleared much indigenous vegetation and managed the coastal marsh environment with fire. At the same time, they appear to have taken careful steps to control the amount of brackish tidal water that reached their fields. They would have used some artificial dikes to retain nutrient-rich fresh water, prevent catastrophic flooding, and to provide the consistent water regime that rice requires.

Rice cultivation at Kuahuqiao eventually broke down when rising sea levels inundated the farmer's fields. The farmers abandoned their fields and vibrant community. They moved to other settlements like Hemudu, where rice agriculture flourished and local societies became more complex within a relatively short time.

Kuahuqiao is by no means unique, for the same process of gradual rice domestication unfolded at other sites in wetland areas and swamp environments along the warm, humid Yangtze River valley over many centuries, and at about the same time.

Hemudu culture
c. 7000 B.C.

Other farming cultures flourished in other parts of southern China, where rice cultivation was well established by at least 7000 B.C. The best known is the Hemudu culture, south of Shanghai, dating to about the same period as Bashidang. The Hemudu site itself lies in a marshy area and was once surrounded by forests and ponds and a great diversity of natural resources. Four cultural layers have been radiocarbon-dated to between about 5000 and 4500 B.C. The lowest level of this remarkable site has yielded beautifully mortise-and-tenon-joined building planks, bone hoes, and coarse black pots decorated with impressions made with twisted cords. This is ideal rice-growing country, and it was hardly surprising to find abundant rice in the site as well as the remains of bone shovels, bottle gourds, and numerous wild vegetable foods (Figure 12.2). The Hemudu people were skilled hunters who kept water buffalo, pigs, and dogs.

Much of the earliest agricultural development may be associated with the widely distributed cord-decorated pottery traditions found in Hemudu and other mainland sites. Offshore, the

Tapenkeng culture
c. 5000 B.C.

Tapenkeng culture of Taiwan is one of the better-known early farming traditions, a culture of people who lived close to lakes and rivers. As early as 5000 B.C., perhaps a millennium earlier, the Tapenkeng people were engaged in intensive fishing and shellfish collecting, as well as hunting and foraging. There is no archaeological evidence for agriculture, but it seems certain that rice and root crops were farmed. It is likely that this is only one of many cord-decorated pottery traditions that flourished throughout southern China and its offshore islands in the millennia after the first development of agriculture.

In the lower Yangtze area, rice was a component of a broad-spectrum hunting and gathering economy during the first half of the sixth millennium B.C. Some of the rice may have been cultivated. One millennium on, data from the lacustrine site of Tianluoshan (dating from 4900 to 4600 B.C.) indicate that rice was growing in importance to other plant foods, such as acorns or water chestnuts (Higham, 2011). By 3000 B.C., much more sophisticated agricultural societies were flourishing on the Yangzi River and farther afield (Barnes, 1993). The archaeology

FIGURE 12.2 Artist's reconstruction of a Hemudu culture shovel-like agricultural implement, based on well-preserved examples of such artifacts at the site. The blade was formed from a shoulder blade of a water buffalo.

of these traditions is known primarily from cemetery excavations that show slow changes in grave goods. The earliest graves indicate few social differentiations, but later sepulchers show not only a much wider variety of artifacts—pottery, bone and stone tools, jade objects, and other ornaments—but also an increase in the number of elaborately adorned burials. Richard Pearson, who has analyzed several cemeteries, argues that they demonstrate an increase in the concentration of wealth, a trend toward ranked societies, and a shift in the relative importance of males at the expense of females (Pearson et al., 1986). This last trend may be associated with the development of more intensive agriculture, an activity in which males were valued for their major roles in the cultivation and production of food. But it was only with the Liangzhu culture (3200 to 2300 B.C.) that rice became a dominant part of the local economy. With it, population grew markedly (Higham, 2011).

Northern China

The second great center of early Chinese agriculture lies nearly 650 km (400 miles) north of the Yangzi, where the Huang Ho flows out of mountainous terrain into the low-lying plains of northern China. Northern Chinese agriculture was based on millet, whereas the southern staple was rice. However, rice was cultivated as early as 6500 to 5500 B.C. at the Jiahu site in the Huai River valley, 800 km (500 miles) south of Beijing. The southern staple arrived in the north many centuries after millet was domesticated.

Jiahu
6500 to 5500 B.C.

One of the few known early sedentary settlements in the north is Nanzhuangtou in Hubei province, which flourished during a period of warm and moist climate, around 12000 B.C., but no seed

Nanzhuangtou
c. 12000 B.C.

identifications are known (G. Crawford, 2011). Certainly, wild plant foods were of great importance in the north, especially green foxtail millet. If there was cultivation of cereal grasses this early, then there is a gap of 3,000 to 4,000 years before firm archaeological evidence of millet agriculture appears. The first well-attested northern agricultural communities lie in the central regions of the Huang Ho valley (see Figure 12.1). The area is a small basin, forming a border between the wooded western highlands and the swampy lowlands to the east. As in the south, the early Holocene saw a warming trend, followed by a cooler interval, then a more prolonged period of climatic amelioration. It was during the colder period, dating to about 6500 B.C., that the first sedentary farming villages are documented in the Huang Ho valley.

During Pleistocene glaciations, loess soils formed over a wide area of the north. The fine, soft-textured earth was both homogeneous and porous and could be tilled with simple digging sticks. Because of the concentrated summer rainfall, cereal crops, the key to agriculture in this region, could be grown successfully. The indigenous plants available for domestication included the wild ancestors of foxtail millet, broomcorn millet, sorghum, hemp, and the mulberry. Many villages lay near small streams on lower-level river terraces, along foothills and plains. Ancient Chinese farmers developed their own cultivation techniques, which persisted for thousands of years. Although irrigation gradually became the basis of the agricultural economies of Egypt, the Indus Valley, and Mesopotamia, it was not important in northern China until much later (Ho, 1984).

How, then, did northern Chinese agriculture begin? There are two possible scenarios. We can assume that the inhabitants of the Huang Ho region passed through a long phase of experimental cultivation and intensive exploitation of the indigenous flora before developing their own distinctive agricultural techniques, or we can assume that food production was developed farther south in China and adopted later in the north. Neither hypothesis can be tested with the available evidence. It is known that early farming villages were associated with the coarse, cord-marked pottery found on the banks of the Huang Ho in western Henan province. Perhaps these vessels are related to the cord-decorated pottery traditions of southern China.

FIGURE 12.3   Reconstruction of Yangshao houses from Banpo, China.

Peiligang culture
6300 to 5100 B.C.

The earliest farming villages in central and northern China date to as early as 6300 to 5100 B.C. Four groups of sites belong within a loosely defined Peiligang culture (Barnes, 1993; B. Smith, 1998). Many settlements consisted of semisubterranean houses with large storage pits. Their owners grew foxtail millet and kept dogs and pigs. Other regional cultures are slowly being identified from new research (for a discussion, see Underhill and Habu, 2006).

Yangshao culture
4800 to 3200 B.C.

By far, the best known of China's early farming cultures is the Yangshao, which flourished over much of the Huang Ho basin, an area as large as the early centers of agriculture in Egypt or Mesopotamia, from about 5200 B.C. to about 3000 B.C. Each Yangshao village was a self-contained community, usually built on a terrace overlooking fertile river valleys and situated to avoid flooding and to allow maximal use of floodplain soils (Figure 12.3). Using hoes and digging sticks, the farmers cultivated foxtail millet as a staple, mainly in riverside gardens that were flooded every spring. Hunting, foraging, and fishing were still important, and the people moved their villages when local soils became exhausted. Yangshao culture evolved over many centuries. By 3200 B.C., it boasted of a characteristic, and thoroughly Chinese, culture, with its own naturalistic art style (Figure 12.4) and expert potters who made cooking pots for steaming food, the technique that forms the basis of much Chinese cuisine to this day. The Chinese language may have its roots in Yangshao culture as well.

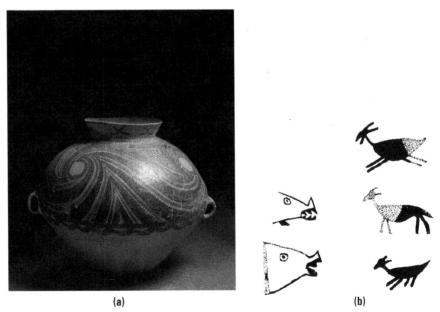

(a)   (b)

FIGURE 12.4   (a) Yangshao pottery from Gansu. (b) Fish motifs often decorate Yangshao vessels, as well as the other naturalistic designs.

Over the centuries, Yangshao culture expanded as new villages split off from older communities and brought new land under cultivation. Yangshao villages and other settlements tended to follow a pattern of river valleys as many regional variations of peasant farming culture developed throughout China (Figure 12.5). Agriculture developed over wide areas at about the same time, with people adapting their crops and farming techniques to local conditions and developing distinctive local farming cultures. In time, the success of the new economies led to local population increases, more complex cultures, and the concentration of wealth in privileged hands.

By 3000 B.C., Longshanoid farming cultures (named after the Longshan site) flourished throughout much of northern China, based on larger, more permanent, and often earthen-walled settlements. Longshanoid cultures were based in part on irrigation and rice cultivation, for the new tropical crop had been introduced from the lush water meadows of the south and had reduced dependence on dry agriculture. These much more elaborate, and wealthier, farming cultures were among the foundations of Chinese civilization (Figure 12.6). (For Korea, see Nelson, 1993, 2006.)

Longshanoid cultures
3000 B.C.

In both northern and southern China, village farming life was well established by 6500 B.C. The agricultural economies of the two regions were very different, but both supported large, stable settlements, increasingly complex ranked societies, and more advanced agricultural technologies than the simpler earlier methods. This parallel development of large, kin-based communities was to endure throughout rural China until modern times.

Jomon and Early Agriculture in Japan

By 10000 B.C., sea levels around Japan were rising, and the area of landmass available to hunter-gatherers had shrunk considerably. In postglacial times, many Asian groups settled along coastlines and lakeshores, just as they did in Europe. They began exploiting a wide range of land and maritime resources in many different climatic zones. In some areas where resources were concentrated, people began to adopt more sedentary settlement patterns and live in well-defined territories. In Japan, for example, shellfish collecting provided a relatively stable subsistence base for the Jomon people. (*Jomon* means "cord pattern," a distinctive feature of their pottery.) By 12500 B.C. (and possibly a couple of millennia before this), they were making clay vessels. Initially the pots were essentially used for food preparation, such as steaming mollusks and making vegetable foods palatable as people adapted to radically new environmental conditions and exploited an even wider resource base. As the millennia rolled by, their ceramics became ever more elaborate and decorated and were used for other purposes including for serving and storing food (Figure 12.7) (Habu, 2004). As postglacial times continued, the people turned to another logical adaptive strategy: the deliberate growing of crops and taming of animals to ensure more reliable food supplies.

Jomon culture
10500 to 300 B.C.

FIGURE 12.5 Approximate distribution of later farming cultures in China (dark shaded area).

More than 30,000 Jomon sites are known, most of them from Honshu in central Japan. All are linked by a seemingly common cultural tradition that lasted for at least 12,000 years, but there were probably different ethnic groups that perhaps spoke different languages and adapted to diverse environments. The Jomon people hunted deer and other game with bows and arrows, collected shellfish, mainly in the spring, and fished much of the year. At first, they caught all types of fish, but as time went on, they concentrated on a few carefully selected species, inshore and lake fish as well as deepwater forms such as the bonito and the tuna. Above all, their diet depended heavily on wild vegetable foods, such as acorns, nuts, and edible seeds. They lived in relatively sedentary settlements, perhaps because of carefully scheduled seasonal hunting, gathering, and fishing activities. Some researchers believe that they supplemented these activities with the cultivation of root crops and cereals or simply by the careful management of nut trees. The evidence for agriculture is sketchy, but it seems possible that the Jomon people flourished by developing an elaborate technology for processing and storing huge stocks of nuts, an activity they may have combined with the cultivation of milletlike plants (Habu, 2004).

The Jomon tradition lasted from as early as 12500 B.C. until as late as 300 B.C. During this period, the focus of settlement shifted from the coasts to central Honshu and to the northern shores of Japan. By 5000 B.C., the inhabitants of Honshu were enjoying an

FIGURE 12.6   Some typical Longshanoid vessels used for cooking and other purposes from Miao-ti-Rai, China (scale not recorded). From the earliest times, Chinese ceramics reflected the distinctive Chinese cuisine based on steaming and stir-frying.

elaborate material culture, including finely made ritual clay pots adorned with intricate decorations. The people often lived not in the caves and simple pit houses of earlier times but in large clusters of wooden houses with elaborate hearths. After 3000 B.C., the climate became cooler; overpopulation may have strained the carrying capacity of arable land, and the clearance of natural vegetation affected hunting activities. Hence, the population declined and the major centers of Jomon occupation moved toward the coasts. In the south, the inhabitants of Kyushu took up rice and barley cultivation after 1000 B.C.

Yayoi period
after 300 B.C.

The basis for what was to become traditional Japanese society was formed during the Yayoi period, which began after 300 B.C., when new crops and technologies spread throughout the islands. Japan was unified into a single state in approximately A.D. 600, by which time complex, stratified societies were commonplace throughout the archipelago.

Early Agriculture in Southeast Asia

The development of agriculture in Southeast Asia was an important element in the eventual colonization of the offshore islands of the Pacific, some of the last landmasses on earth to be settled by modern humans.

13000 B.C.

In 13000 B.C., hunter-gatherer groups inhabited much of Southeast Asia (Figure 12.8). Their stone toolkits reveal remarkable uniformity over large areas of the mainland and islands (Higham, 2002). These stone assemblages do not necessarily reflect a stagnation of cultural innovation or a simple lifeway. Rather, it seems certain that the people were exploiting a broad range of game and vegetable foods. By this time, the vast area of low-lying continental shelf off Southeast Asia, exposed during the late Ice Age, was now under water. Almost certainly, as sea levels rose higher than today

FIGURE 12.7   Old style (left) and late (right) Jomon vessels. Jomon pottery, the earliest in the world, achieved great elaboration and evolved over many centuries.

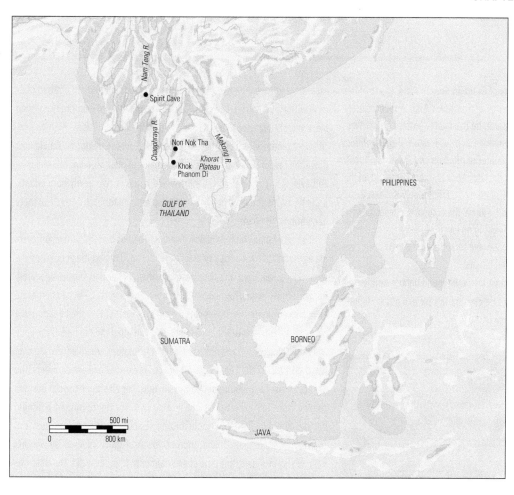

FIGURE 12.8 Southeast Asian sites mentioned in this chapter. Shaded areas show the extent of low sea levels during the last glaciation.

in about 4000 B.C., coastal communities flourished along the shore, making pottery and living off the rich maritime resources. People at sites like Khok Phanom Di were making polished axes and pottery, but apparently not farming. But there are strong hints that these people were interacting with, and even intermarrying with, rice farmers who were moving into the area and then settling in the interior.

Hunter-gatherer groups exploited a wide variety of yams and other potential domesticates in Thailand and elsewhere in Southeast Asia at the end of the Pleistocene. As we have pointed out, yam planting is very simple, and hunter-gatherers are well aware that deliberate cultivation is possible. The problem is to identify the factors that led people to deliberate experimentation with various plants. In the absence of firm archaeological evidence, we can speculate that primitive shifting agriculture, with a combination of diverse crops and some animal herding, may have had its origins in a broad spectrum of hunting and gathering, as it did in other regions of the world. In the final analysis, all that is needed for a culture to make the transition are some clearings at the edge of the forest and a simple digging stick, already used for gathering, to plant the crop. Core borings into Lake Kumphawapi in northeastern Thailand document a striking decline in forest cover in about 4500 B.C., coinciding with a sudden increase in charcoal particles in the lake mud. This may be due to human interference, or even cultivation—archaeological sites are needed to date agriculture this early (Penny, 1999).

When rice cultivation actually spread into Southeast Asia from China remains a mystery (Bellwood, 2006). Did farming immigrants from the north introduce the new crop, or did indigenous hunter-gatherers adopt new economies? We know that rice farming was well established south of the Yangzi Valley by 2800 B.C. and in Vietnam's lower Red River valley by 2500 to 2000 B.C. A date for the first arrival of rice farming in Southeast and South Asia of about 2500 B.C. is not unreasonable, with well-documented agricultural communities on Thailand's Khorat Plateau by 2200 B.C. (Higham, 2000).

Not that rice cultivation was universal, especially near low-lying coasts with saline soils. Charles Higham (1994) has excavated a large and wealthy hunter-gatherer community at Khok Phanom Di, a settlement that was close to coastal mangrove swamps between 2000 and 1400 B.C. but is now more than 19.3 km (12 miles) from the sea (see Site box on p. 252). The site covers 5 ha (12.3 acres) and is 12 m (39 feet) deep. It contains rice husks, but Higham and Thosearat (1998) believe that

2800 to 2500 B.C.

Khok Phanom Di
2000 to 1400 B.C.

SiTE > The Princess of Khok Phanom Di, Thailand <

Charles Higham, of the University of Otago in New Zealand, is one of the world's experts on the archaeology of Southeast Asia. Working closely with Thai archaeologist Rachanie Thosarat, he has made spectacular discoveries of coastal hunter-gatherer communities and well-established Neolithic, Bronze, and Iron Age settlements in the interior (Higham and Thosearat, 1998). In 1984, Higham began excavations at the large Khok Phanom Di mound on the floodplain of the Bang Pakong River (Figure 12.9). From a previous test excavation carried out by a Thai colleague, he knew the occupation deposits were nearly 9 m (30 feet) deep, the mound resting on layers of shell midden debris. In the trial pit, Higham spotted "the hollow eye sockets of some prehistoric person," so he knew he would probably find burials.

After digging through the uppermost levels, he found lighter, sandier soil about 1 m (3 feet) below the surface. He cleaned the surface of the deposit carefully and spotted the telltale outline of the dark filling of a grave. Soon the

FIGURE 12.9 Excavation at Khok Phanom Di, Thailand. This site has yielded important evidence of early rice cultivation.

excavators uncovered a row of graves close to the foundation of a raised platform with a building on it. Their trowels traced the walls of beautifully polished black vessels, many of them decorated with curvilinear designs. Higham's excitement mounted as he uncovered 14 burials. From the platform, "I could look down the row of skeletons and see the remains of men, women, and children, and even a tiny grave with the intertwined bones of two newly born infants, probably twins. It looked like a family group running through a couple or more generations" (Higham, 1994).

The excavation penetrated downward into a large burial chamber, uncovering a pyramid of circular clay cylinders once destined to become pots. When the pyramid was removed, the skeleton of a woman in her mid-thirties appeared, her wrist muscles well formed, probably from kneading clay. She had borne one or two children. Her chest was covered with a carpet of tiny shell beads and a necklace of large, white I-shaped beads. Higham lifted the top half of the body in a single block of soil and dissected it in the laboratory, where he recovered no less than 120,787 shell beads, once sewn onto two ornate upper garments. The princess must have shimmered in the sunlight, her wealth and social position coming from her expertise at pot making, witness the burnished polishing pebbles found by her feet and the broken vessels covering her legs. Just 2 m (6 feet) away, Higham found another, identical grave covered by another heap of clay cylinders, this time of an infant only 15 months old. The child was adorned with identical decoration to that of her mother and lay with a tiny pot making anvil, a smaller version of those used by adults, by her side. Higham is convinced that this was the princess's daughter.

By the time the excavation finished six months later, Higham and his colleagues had recovered another 139 burials, representing 17 to 20 generations of expert potters who traded pots to obtain exotic shell ornaments. But none of them rivaled the splendor of the Princess of Khok Phanom Di.

most of the domestic grains were imported from elsewhere because the local soils were unsuitable for growing the crop, despite a brief interlude when lowered sea levels allowed rice farming.

During the late third millennium B.C., new dry-rice-farming villages appeared far inland, but few of them are known archaeologically. There was a slow expansion in farming activity, which was to affect societies living far from the coast in coming centuries. Southeast Asia did not suffer from the drastic climatic changes of the northern latitudes, but its long dry season makes food storage essential, an important characteristic of domesticated rice. Only dramatic rises in low sea levels altered the geography and environment of Southeast Asia, creating islands from dry land and reducing the amount of coastal floodplain available to hunters and gatherers. Conceivably, these major changes in the coastline and the available land surface were among many factors that moved the inhabitants of Southeast Asia to experiment with plants and domestic animals.

Rice and Root Cultivation in Island Southeast Asia

Offshore from mainland Asia, one enters what archaeologist Peter Bellwood has called "a totally different Neolithic world" (1997: 121). He believes that the swamp cultivation of rice was introduced from the north, where it had taken hold considerably earlier. Rice agriculture dates to around 3500 B.C. on Taiwan, or perhaps earlier. It dates back to only about 1200 B.C. in the Philippines, although agriculture may have occurred as early as 2000 B.C. there and on Sulawesi (Spriggs, 1989). Root crops like taro

2000 B.C.

became the staple crop as opposed to rice outside Luzon in the Philippines and Borneo. Farmers were living on East Timor before 2100 B.C. and offshore in the Bismarck Archipelago by 1900 to 1500 B.C. The archaeology of early agriculture in this entire area is in a state of exciting, rapid change, but it is clear that the adoption of food production through this region was a complex process (Spriggs, 2003).

A relatively homogeneous early farming culture of people who settled mainly by coasts and rivers marks this first settlement. Canoes played a major role in intervillage exchange, which persisted for 2,000 years. These constant exchanges meant that such items as clay vessels, adzes, and axes were fairly standardized over large areas, and communities as far separated as Taiwan and Manus enjoyed the same general economy, material culture, and social organization (see Figure 12.10). The same exchange networks carried New Britain obsidian and occasional metal objects over hundreds of kilometers.

This culture does not appear to have penetrated highland New Guinea, where agriculture developed quite independently. Here hunter-gatherers lived in damp, often densely forested environments, where the cultivation of root crops like taro and yams and fruit trees such as bananas required less forest clearance. Agricultural systems of this type became widespread in parts of Indonesia and in island Melanesia after 2500 B.C.

For many years, scholars assumed that agriculture first developed in the New Guinea lowlands, then spread to higher ground. But we now know from AMS dates that taro cultivation was well established in the upper Wahgi Valley near Kuk in the highlands by about 4900 to 4400 B.C., and a strong case can be made for independent development of agriculture in highland New Guinea. This may have arisen from broad-spectrum plant exploitation during the late Ice Age, which allowed permanent occupation of higher ground. Existing plant practices changed as a result of climatic and environmental change during the early Holocene, when people focused more on taro and local bananas. Thus came about more intensive exploitation of wild forms that led to the domestication of both plants at an early date, probably earlier than 5000 B.C. (Denham et al., 2004). There are inconclusive signs of deliberate diversion of river water in the Kuk basin at about 7000 B.C., but whether this resulted from taro or yam cultivation is uncertain (Golson and Gardiner, 1990).

Kuk
4900 to 4400 B.C.

By 4000 to 3500 B.C., much more organized horticultural works were found in the Kuk basin. There is pollen evidence for quite extensive forest clearance in the general area. The clearance may have been done for yam and taro crops, while indigenous plants were grown on the better-drained

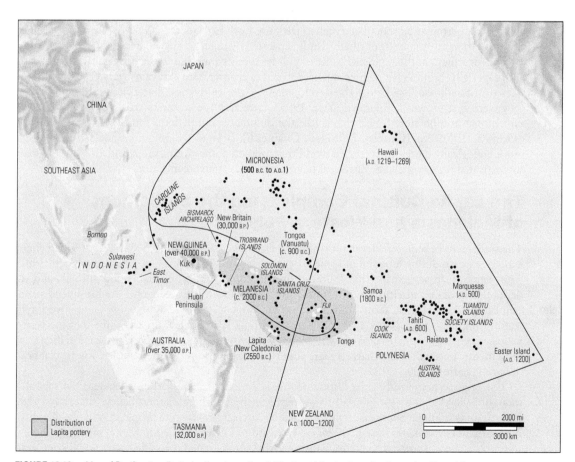

FIGURE 12.10 Map of Pacific sites. Dark shading shows the distribution of the Lapita cultural complex. Lines delineate Melanesia, Micronesia, and Polynesia. Dates are for first settlement.

2000 B.C.

soils between the channel banks. After 2000 B.C., the first highly developed drainage systems appeared in the area, a sign that people were farming much more intensively.

After 500 B.C., the people depended more and more on dry and wet agriculture, for an environment altered permanently by human activity had replaced the forest resources of earlier times. Slow population growth resulted eventually in the farming of uncleared land. After that was exhausted, the only option was to shorten the fallow periods in cleared gardens—a choice that, if taro was the crop, would have resulted in lower crop yields.

The archaeological investigations and pollen analyses by Golson and Gardiner (1990) have produced firm evidence for sedentism, forest clearance, stone agricultural tools, and water-control techniques in the New Guinea highlands by 4000 to 3000 B.C. What is uncertain, however, is the means by which food production began in New Guinea. Was it developed locally with introduced plants after the local hunter-gatherers had manipulated indigenous plants for centuries? Or did the people manipulate local plants as a result of adopting a few introduced crops first? Whatever the answer, it appears that the New Guinea highlands were an area where people created an artificial garden environment as a result of a long period of experimentation in which they raised plants native to their natural environment. By exploiting a wide range of tropical animals and plants, the people became more sedentary and later started to plant small plots of root crops; ultimately, they would have intensified their food production until they had modified their environment beyond recognition. This hypothetical model of early agriculture in New Guinea may serve as a possible model for other tropical areas in Asia as well.

Agriculture in the Pacific Islands

The origins of the peoples of the Pacific islands have fascinated scientists since the seventeenth century. Today, most authorities look to Southeast Asia for the origins of the Melanesians, Micronesians, and Polynesians (Blust, 1995). They point out that the settlement of the offshore islands depended on the successful cultivation of root crops such as taro and yam, as well as breadfruit, coconuts, and sugarcane. Chickens, dogs, and pigs were also valued as food and were domesticated in Asia before being introduced to the Pacific. Oceanic islands lack much in the way of wild food resources, so domesticated plants and animals were essential for successful colonization. Small animals such as pigs and chickens could have been carried readily from island to island in canoes, as could easily germinating root plants such as the yam. Both food sources allowed a sizable population to spread to many hundreds of small islands separated by miles of open water.

The settlement of the remoter Pacific islands is closely connected to the early cultivation of yams and, especially, taro. As we pointed out earlier in this chapter, taro and yams were probably domesticated in Southeast Asia before the development of rice cultivation, but exactly when and where they were first grown is unknown (Yen, 1995). Late Ice Age seafarers settled not only on New Guinea but also on close island chains like the Solomons and perhaps the Bismarck Archipelago as early as 35000 B.C. (Gosden, 1995) (see Chapter 6). Beyond the Solomons and farther offshore was a biologically more impoverished world that awaited domesticated crops and animals and more sophisticated seafaring and navigational techniques for human colonization.

The Lapita Cultural Complex and the Settlement of Melanesia and Western Polynesia

Lapita cultural complex
1600 to 1000 B.C. and later

The settlement of remoter Melanesia covered a distance of 5,000 km (3,100 miles) of island chains and open ocean during a period of some six centuries from about 1550 to 1000 B.C. (Kirch, 1997). This was human settlement that followed on the domestication of plants and animals and the development of new maritime technologies, presumably including oceangoing double-hulled sailing canoes. In archaeological terms, this development is associated with the highly distinctive Lapita cultural complex, named after a site on New Caledonia Island. Most experts agree that the Lapita people were Austronesian-speakers who traded widely throughout the southwestern Pacific. Their settlements are marked by characteristic stamp-decorated pottery, often adorned with elaborate designs (Figure 12.11).

The original homeland of the Lapita people is a matter of considerable debate. One school of thought believes that they originated in western Melanesia, whereas others believe that they arrived in the islands from the Southeast Asian mainland (Kirch, 1997). Lapita people moved obsidian from New Britain Island 3,700 km (2,300 miles) eastward to Fiji and 3,800 km (2,400 miles) northwestward to northern Borneo through exchange networks that carried the same toolmaking stone as far west as farming settlements on the eastern coast of Borneo (Bellwood and Koon, 1989). That is not to say, of course, that Lapita canoes traveled all the way to Borneo. Rather, by 1000 B.C., there was

1000 B.C.

FIGURE 12.11 Lapita pottery from Melanesia. The distinctive dentate- or tooth-stamped motifs used by Lapita potters can be employed to trace the extent of human settlement. This example is from the Teouma site in Vanuatu.

what Peter Bellwood (1997) calls a "linked chain" of exchange networks over more than 8,100 km (5,000 miles) throughout the Southeast Asian islands deep into the central Pacific. There was a great deal of still unstudied diversity within what we call the Lapita cultural complex (see, for example, Sand, 2000; Spriggs, 2007). Clearly, much of the agricultural tradition of the Lapita people owed at least something to New Guinea.

People living on small islands usually depend on their neighbors for many important commodities, an interdependency that was reflected in these complex exchange networks spanning many miles of open ocean. The commodities carried in canoes ranged from foodstuffs to manufactured items and may have included ceremonial objects as well. The social and economic complexities of Melanesian trading systems have long excited anthropologists, starting with Bronislaw Malinowski (1922) in his famous fieldwork on the celebrated *kula* ring of the Trobriand Islanders that circulated shell necklaces and bracelets from island to island in complex circles. The *kula* ring, with its elaborate ceremonial, was just one of many related exchange trading systems that linked all parts of coastal New Guinea and much of Melanesia. These networks were reciprocal and self-perpetuating; they had their ancestry in much earlier exchange patterns that began, although in a simpler form, among the Lapita people (J. Allen and White, 1989).

The most likely Lapita homeland was the Bismarck Archipelago area, which was inhabited during the late Ice Age (see Chapter 6) as far back as about 35000 B.C. (Gosden et al., 1989). There is clear evidence for open-water voyaging by 2900 B.C. as far as Manus Island, where obsidian is to be found, some 200 km (124 miles) straight-line, open-water away. An Australian research team has identified widespread human occupation throughout the Bismarck Archipelago before Lapita pottery appeared about 1500 B.C., and it may be that some, if not most, elements of the Lapita cultural complex came from local roots. By identifying the sources of island obsidians and pottery clays, the Australians have been able to show that local trading patterns changed constantly during pre-Lapita times and throughout the Lapita occupation of the archipelago. Clearly, Lapita cultures were dynamic, ever-changing systems.

These excavations show that there is a very long history of human occupation indeed in the Bismarck Archipelago, one that stretches far back into the Ice Age. Throughout most of this long period, obsidian was moved through the islands and far beyond them toward Southeast Asia. For instance, obsidian from Talasea in New Britain traveled more than 2,000 km (1,242 miles) southeastward to New Caledonia in early Lapita times (Sand and Sheppard, 2000). The region was never isolated from the outside world. Its inhabitants were part of a vast network of interconnections that linked the entire western Pacific and island Southeast Asia over a period of at least 1,500 years. It was not until sometime after 2,000 years ago that these broad links vanished, to be replaced by more local cultural developments.

The Lapita cultural complex was either a migration of new peoples from Southeast Asia into the islands, as was once thought, or a vast exchange system that linked island after island through reciprocal trading between kinspeople. Archaeologically, we know that Lapita pottery from the Santa Cruz Islands, decorated with stamped designs and made of clay tempered with shell, is found as far east as Vanuatu (Tongoa), Fiji, Tonga, and Samoa. We know it dates generally to the last thousand years B.C. but seems to have gone out of fashion by A.D. 200 (Kirch, 1997). To associate this pottery distribution with a migrating ethnic group is to oversimplify a very complex picture of long-distance exchange, ocean voyaging, and island settlement.

Clearly, one catalyst for this expansion was the development of the oceangoing double-hulled canoe (Finney, 1994). This canoe was the means by which efficient exchange networks were maintained from island to island over distances up to 600 km (372 miles), from Melanesia far out into the Pacific into western Polynesia. The rapid expansion from island to island that carried Lapita pottery far to the east developed among societies living in an island environment that extended from the Southeast Asian mainland far southeastward. The inhabitants of this vast archipelago lived on coasts with relatively calm weather and maintained contacts with one another that extended over hundreds of miles. That there was some standardization of artifacts and culture among them after 2000 B.C. is hardly surprising. It is only when one reaches off-lying islands such as Fiji and Tonga

FIGURE 12.12 A headless Lapita burial from a cemetery at Teouma, Efate Island.

that one can legitimately think in terms of Lapita "colonists" as the first settlers of the Pacific. Here, open-water distances are much longer, involving, for example, voyages of nearly 592 open-water km (600 miles). In Fiji, Samoa, and Tonga, the first settlers carried Lapita artifacts with them, but subsequent cultural development proceeded along local lines, such as burial customs (Figure 12.12).

Long-Distance Voyaging in the Pacific

From Melanesia, canoes voyaged through western Polynesia, taking the plants and domesticated animals of their home islands with them. As distances grew longer, so did the navigational challenges, challenges so formidable that many early scholars argued that the Polynesian islands were settled by accidental voyages (Finney, 1994). Some compelling studies of Polynesian navigation and voyaging by both anthropologists and small-boat sailors have dispelled any lingering doubts about the navigational abilities of the early Polynesians. Geoffrey Irwin (1992), himself an expert sailor, has used computer modeling and his own voyages to suggest that the exploration was rapid and deliberate, a systematic process that led to ever more improved navigational techniques. At the same time, he believes that rather than sailing randomly downwind, the early voyagers made their explorations upwind, against the prevailing winds, knowing that they could always turn downwind and return home with ease.

Nearly all the long trips attributed to the Polynesians were from north to south and therefore involved simple dead-reckoning calculations and an elementary way of measuring latitude from the stars. Several modern studies have collected navigators' lore from surviving practitioners of the art (Finney, 1994). The pilots were a respected and close-knit group. Young apprentices learned their skills over many years of making passages and from orally transmitted knowledge about the stars and the oceans accumulated by generations of navigators. The navigational techniques used the angles of rising and setting stars, the trend of ocean swells, and the myriad inconspicuous phenomena that indicate the general direction and distance of small islands. The navigators were perfectly capable of voyaging over long stretches of open water; their geographic knowledge was astonishing. They had no need for the compass or other modern aids, and their landfalls were accurate.

Indigenous Pacific Navigation

When British navigator Captain James Cook visited Tahiti in 1769, he puzzled over a question that has always fascinated scholars: How had the Tahitians colonized their remote homeland? How had humans, with only simple canoes and no metals, sailed across vast tracts of open ocean and settled on the remotest islands of the Pacific? Cook met the great Tahitian navigator Tupaia and asked him how canoe skippers made their way from island to island out of sight of land. Tupaia explained how they used the sun as a compass by day and the moon and stars by night. When Cook marveled at the Polynesians' ability to sail against the prevailing trade winds for hundreds of kilometers, Tupaia pointed out that westerlies blew from November to January, and so these were the months when canoes could make good progress to windward.

Tupaia carried a mental file of Polynesia with him. He listed islands, the number of days required to sail to them, and their direction, which Cook made up into a rough sketch map. Modern scholars believe Tupaia could define an area bounded by the Marquesas in the northeast, the Tuamotus to the east, the Australs to the south, and the Cook Islands to the southwest. Even Fiji and Samoa to the west lay within his consciousness, a mental map of an area as large as Australia or the United States.

No later explorers interviewed Tahitian navigators. Many scholars assumed the Pacific islands had been colonized by canoes blown accidentally far offshore. But, in 1965, English cruising sailor David Lewis encountered aged canoe navigators in the Caroline Islands of Micronesia. He learned how the navigators used the zenith passages of key stars to navigate far from land, as well as swell direction, waves reflected off distant land, and even the flights of sea and land birds to make landfall on island archipelagos far from the departure point. These navigators were also able to return to their homes safely, using the same signs of sea and sky. Determined to preserve a rapidly vanishing art, Lewis sailed his European-designed, oceangoing catamaran from Rarotonga in the Cook Islands to New Zealand, using only a star map and a Polynesian navigator to help him. In the 1970s, Lewis apprenticed himself to the pilots of the Caroline Islands, learning how they made passages with the aid of sun, moon, stars, cloud and swell formations, and even by passing birds.

In the late 1960s, anthropologist Ben Finney (1994) began long-term experiments with replicas of ancient Polynesian canoes. Finney's first replica was *Nalehia*, a 12-m (40-foot) copy of a Hawaiian royal canoe. Tests in Hawaii's windy waters showed that the vessel could sail across the wind, so Finney planned a voyage from Hawaii to Tahiti and back, using a replica built from a composite of known canoe designs from throughout the Pacific islands. *Hokule'a*, designed by Hawaiian Herb Kawainui Kane, is 19 m (62 feet) long, with double hulls and two crab-claw-shaped sails. Finney, Micronesian navigator Mau Piailug, and a mainly Hawaiian crew sailed *Hokule'a* from Hawaii to Tahiti and back in 1976. This journey was followed by a two-year voyage around the Pacific using only indigenous pilotage. Thanks to the successful *Hokule'a* experiments, ancient Polynesian navigational skills have been preserved for posterity.

The Settlement of Micronesia and Eastern Polynesia

The settlement of Micronesia and eastern Polynesia (sometimes called Remote Oceania) unfolded much later, long after Lapita canoes had sailed as far eastward as Samoa and Tonga. More than 1,400 radiocarbon dates, each checked meticulously for accuracy and their associations with human activity or with Pacific rats, which live only with humans, reveal a dramatic burst of ocean voyaging between A.D. 1000 and 1300. For about 1,800 years after arriving in Samoa and Tonga, the Polynesians sailed no further eastward. Then, suddenly, their canoes discovered, and usually colonized nearly every other island in the eastern Pacific within just under three centuries.

The colonization dates speak for themselves (Wilmshurst et al., 2010). A wave of canoes arrived in the Society Islands between A.D. 1025 and 1121, in the Marquesas between A.D. 1200 and 1400. Other voyagers reached New Zealand between A.D. 1230 and 1280, Rapa Nui between A.D. 1200 and 1263, and Hawai'i between A.D. 1219 and 1269 (Kirch and Sahlins, 1992). The rapid pace of colonization may account for the remarkable similarities in artifacts such as adzes and fishhooks in places as widely separated as the Societies, Marquesas, and New Zealand (Figure 12.13) (Kirch, 1985). A mere three centuries of ocean voyaging wrote the last chapter in the 100,000-year journey of *Homo sapiens* across the world.

The great voyages were long over when European explorers like Captain Cook arrived in the Society Islands in the eighteenth century A.D. However, the deeds of the great pilots linger in Polynesian oral traditions as part of common beliefs and values transmitted from one generation to the next. Great culture heroes like Maui, the fisher of lands, and Rata, an expert canoe builder, figure in historical narratives throughout much of Polynesia and may date back to Lapita times (Taonui, 2006). Maui snared the sun, fished up islands, and obtained fire, a symbol of the human struggle to harness the forces of nature. Rata, the canoe builder, perhaps himself a voyager, figures in traditions that may be at least 3,000 years old. The oral traditions preserve the names of great navigators like Hiro. He was born in the Societies and, as an adult, acquired a passion for sailing, stealing, and womanizing. He is said to have sailed to the Marquesas, Hawai'i, the Australs, and Rapa Nui in large canoes with sewn planks. Whoever the navigators were, they carried far more than sailing lore with them. Generic place names for "passage" or "reef" traveled around with them throughout Polynesia. They designated small islands at the entrances to natural harbors as places of sanctuary for visiting canoes waiting to see if it was safe to go ashore. The mosaic of oral memories provides some names, some shared cultural traditions, but does not answer

Offshore Pacific settlement
Before A.D. 1 to 900
A.D. 1000 to 1200

FIGURE 12.13 Bone fishhooks from Polynesia. Fishhook forms vary greatly from island to island and through time, allowing chronological comparisons between different island culture sequences. (The Field Museum, Neg. #100629, Chicago.)

the question of questions: Why did small numbers of people suddenly decide to sail over the horizon in search of new lands?

What prompted such deliberate voyages? Were they quests for religious enlightenment, for the realm of the ancestors, or simply a reflection of those most human of all qualities, curiosity and restlessness? (Hunt and Lipo, 2011; Kirch, 2000).

We don't know. Whatever the motivation, to sail eastward toward sunrise into unknown waters was a hazardous enterprise, given the prevailing northeasterly trades. To cover any distance would require setting sail when the trades were down, something that happened for only a few weeks a year between January and March, except when El Niños dampened the trades. It may be no coincidence that the eastern voyages occurred during a documented spike of El Niño activity during these centuries. Even with unexpected breaks from the wind, the social reasons for taking off into the unknown must have been compelling and we can only speculate about them.

Like their Lapita forebears, early Polynesian societies placed great emphasis on birth, inheritance, and kin ties. As was the case further west, older siblings outranked their younger brothers and sisters. Oral traditions are full of rivalries between older and younger brothers. Some siblings sailed away to seek new homelands, where they could find their own privileged lineage and pass land to their offspring. Such ventures were expensive, but prestigious, requiring superlative navigational skills acquired over many years.

Thus, successful voyages over the horizon acquired a mystique that passed down the generations, not necessarily because their leaders were superlative pilots, but because they became founders of descent lines firmly anchored in new lands.

The settlement of Polynesia was in the hands of people who were still, technologically speaking, in the Stone Age. They relied heavily on stone axes and adzes and on an elaborate array of bone and shell fishhooks (M. Allen, 1995) (see Figure 12.13). The crops planted varied from island to island, but breadfruit, taro, coconut, yams, and bananas were the staples. Sweet potato, a South American plant, was a staple when Europeans first arrived. No one knows how this crop reached eastern Polynesia—perhaps by (as yet unidentified) Polynesian voyaging to the South American mainland (Hather and Kirch, 1991). More evidence of early voyaging: Chicken bones from ancient Polynesian sites in Tonga and Samoa have identical DNA to that from chicken bones at El Arenal in Chile, a settlement occupied between A.D. 700 and 1390 (A. Storey, 2008). The chicken was domesticated in Southeast Asia, but it has always been a mystery as to how it reached the Americas before Europeans arrived. Perhaps Polynesian seafarers brought them, but the identity of the people, the frequency of the voyages, and cultural evidence for such contact eludes us.

The food surpluses generated on the larger islands were used as a form of wealth. New evidence for long distance voyaging between widely separated islands comes from 19 basalt adzes collected in the early twentieth century in the Tuamotu Archipelago, more than 1,609 km (1,000 miles) southeast of Tahiti. The chemical signatures of the axes, when compared to those of basalt sources across the Pacific, revealed that they came from as far afield as the Marquesas, Austral and Society Islands, and Pitcairn. One adze came from Kaho'olawe, a Hawaiian island far to the northwest, some 4,000 km (2,500 miles) across the southeast Pacific, the longest known nonstop voyage of ancient times. (For a survey of island perspectives on culture change, see Kirch and Hunt, 1996.)

When the French and British visited Tahiti in the eighteenth century, they chanced upon the center of a vigorous eastern Polynesian society (Oliver, 1977). Tahiti and the surrounding islands were ruled by a powerful hierarchy of chiefs and nobles, many of them descendants of the canoe crews that had settled in the archipelago (Kirch, 1984). The chiefs had acquired prestige by controlling and redistributing wealth and food supplies. Their formidable religious and social powers had led them to warfare and to the undertaking of elaborate agricultural projects and the erection of monumental shrines and temples of stone: The famous *maraes* (temples) of Tahiti are typical examples (Figure 12.14). On remote Rapa Nui (Easter Island), the people erected *moaes*, vast statues up to 9.8 m (32 feet) high (Figure 12.15). They are thought to be images of deified ancestors associated with different kin groups (Bahn and Flenley, 1992; Hunt and Lipo, 2011; Van Tilburg, 1994). The full diversity of Polynesian culture is still imperfectly understood, for archaeological research has hardly begun in the South Seas. Nonetheless, it is certain that the Polynesians were making ocean voyages on a large scale when the Greeks and Romans were little more than coastal navigators.

FIGURE 12.14   Tahitian *marae* at Tuputaputia on Raiatea Island, where many ancient long-distance voyages began. This *marae* has been restored and is shown decorated to commemorate its restoration.

The Settlement of New Zealand

New Zealand is the largest and among the most remote of the Pacific islands; it is actually two large islands. It has a temperate climate, not the tropical warmth enjoyed by most Polynesians. Despite this ecological difference, Polynesians voyaged southward in comparatively recent times and settled on the North Island. Maori legends tell of a migration from Polynesia in the mid-fourteenth century A.D. The first settlers—including a chief named Toi Ete'hutai, who came to New Zealand in search of two grandsons blown away from Tahiti during a canoe race—may have arrived about 400 years before. The earliest carbon-14 dates for New Zealand archaeological sites are a matter of controversy, but a careful study places first settlement between A.D. 1230 and 1280 (Wilmshurst et al., 2010; see also A. Anderson, 1991).

The temperate climate of North Island formed a southern frontier for most of the basic food plants of Polynesia. Taro, yams, and gourd could be grown only there, but the sweet potato could be cultivated in the northern part of South Island if adequate winter storage pits were used. The Polynesian coconut never grew in New Zealand. The earliest settlers relied heavily on hunting, fishing, and gathering. Even later, though some peoples specialized in food production, others did not, especially on South Island, where many settlements were close to abundant ocean resources (Davidson, 1987).

The first settlers found great flocks of moa birds, flightless creatures that were helpless in the face of systematic hunting. The settlers hunted the moa into extinction within a few centuries (A. Anderson, 1992; A. Anderson and McGlone, 1991). Fish, fern roots, and shellfish were important throughout New Zealand's short prehistory (Shawcross, 1967). The introduction of the sweet potato made a dramatic difference to the New Zealanders, for the tubers, if carefully protected from cold, could be eaten in the winter months, and some could be kept for the next year's planting. Sweet potatoes have a large crop yield and are thought to have contributed to a rapid population buildup, especially on North Island. This buildup, in turn, led to competition among groups for suitable agricultural land on which to grow the new staple (Davidson, 1987).

FIGURE 12.15   *Moae* statues at Ahu Nau Nau on the north coast of Easter Island. The ancestral figures once bore topknots of red volcanic rock.

FIGURE 12.16 A fortified Maori *pa* (right) at Sheenan 's Creek, North Island, New Zealand.

When the moa became extinct, the Maori had few meat supplies except other bird species, dogs, and rats. Their only other meat source was human flesh. The archaeological record of Maori culture from approximately A.D. 1400 onward shows not only population growth but also an increasing emphasis on warfare, marked by the appearance of numerous fortified encampments, or *pa*, protected with earthen banks (Figure 12.16). The distribution of *pa* coincides to a large extent with the best sweet-potato lands (Bellwood, 1970). In the course of a few centuries, warfare became a key element in Maori culture, to the extent that it was institutionalized and was an important factor in maintaining cohesion and leadership in Maori society. The booty of war was not only *kumara* (sweet potato) but also the flesh of captives, which became a limited part of the Maori diet.

Maori warfare, mainly confined to North Island, where more than 5,000 *pa* have been found, was seasonal and closely connected with the planting and harvesting of sweet potatoes, when everyone was busy in the gardens. Military campaigns were short and intense, very often launched from the sea in war canoes up to 24 m (78.7 feet) or more in length (Figure 12.17). These elaborately carved craft could each hold as many as 150 men on a short expedition. So formidable was the reputation of the Maori that European ships avoided New Zealand ports for years before permanent white settlement was achieved. The last Maori war ended in 1872, by which time the indigenous population had been decimated by disease, warfare, and other effects of European colonization.

FIGURE 12.17 Maori war canoe, drawn in 1769 by Captain James Cook's artist, Sidney Parkington.

Summary

- As in Southwest Asia, food production began in Asia during the early Holocene, perhaps as early as 10000 B.C., but became fully established in a cold interval that followed initial warming, around 6500 B.C.
- In southern China, some rice was cultivated perhaps as early as 8000 B.C. Widespread rice agriculture was well established by 6500 B.C.
- The staple in the Huang Ho valley of northern China was millet, cultivated at least as early as 6500 B.C., perhaps much earlier.
- The Yangshao culture flourished over much of the Huang Ho basin, a society of self-contained villages, replaced by the more elaborate Longshanoid cultures by 3000 B.C.

- In Southeast Asia, the staple crop was rice, probably first cultivated along low-lying, swampy coasts. The new economies soon spread inland during the third millennium B.C., bringing village life to much of the region.
- Island Southeast Asia was settled by hunters and foragers at least as early as 38000 B.C., and simple root horticulture had been established in highland New Guinea by 6000 B.C.
- The people of the Lapita cultural complex traded widely throughout the southwestern Pacific after 1600 B.C., but it was not until the past 2,000 years that offshore canoes settled Micronesia and Polynesia, and New Zealand was colonized just after A.D. 1200.

Further Reading

Bellwood, Peter. 1997. *The History of the Indo-Malaysian Archipelago*, 2nd ed. Honolulu: University of Hawaii Press.

Hunt, Terry, and Carl Lipo. 2011. *The Statues that Walked.* New York: Free Press.

Kirch, Patrick. 2000. *On the Road of the Winds: An Archaeological History of the Pacific Islands Before European Contact.* Berkeley: University of California Press.

Square Tower Ruin at Mesa Verde, Colorado.

When Harvard archaeologist Alfred Kidder dug into the complex layers of Pecos Pueblo, New Mexico, in 1915, he was searching for the ancient roots of Pueblo Indian culture deep in the middens of this long-occupied site. Kidder had visited archaeological sites in Egypt and Greece and had seen firsthand that careful stratigraphic observation had yielded rich chronological dividends. Over many field seasons, he sunk enormous trenches into the depths of the Pecos deposits, uncovering dozens of small occupation layers and dense concentrations of potsherds. Back in the laboratory, he pored over thousands of painted potsherds and turned them into a long cultural sequence that has been the foundation of all subsequent research in the North American Southwest. "It is safe enough to postulate the former presence in the Southwest of a more or less nomadic people, thinly scattered over the country, ignorant of agriculture and pottery making," he wrote (1927: 56) of the earliest occupants. Ever since, American archaeologists have searched for the first Native American farmers not only in the North American Southwest but also throughout the Americas. ▮

The Native Americans domesticated an impressive range of native New World plants, some of which—like maize, potatoes, and tobacco—were rapidly adopted by farmers on other continents after European contact (Table 13.1). The most important staple crop was Indian corn, properly called *maize*, the only significant wild grass in the New World to be fully domesticated (B. Smith, 1998). It remains the most important food crop in the Americas, being used in more than 150 varieties as both food and cattle fodder. Root crops were another substantial food source, especially in South America, and included manioc, sweet potatoes, and white potatoes. Chili peppers were grown as hot seasoning; amaranth, sunflowers, cacao, peanuts, and several types of bean were also significant crops. Some crops, such as cotton and gourds, are common to both the Old and New Worlds but were probably domesticated separately.

In contrast to Old World farmers, the Native Americans had few domesticated animals; they included the alpaca and the llama of the Andes, which provided wool. Dogs appeared in the Americas, and the raucous and unruly turkey and the Muscovy duck were domesticated. Most archaeologists now agree that there were at least two, perhaps three, major centers of plant domestication in the Americas: Mesoamerica for maize, beans, squash, and sweet potatoes, and the highlands of the central Andes for root crops. The lowland tropics in Panama, Colombia, Ecuador, and Peru may have been a center for cultivating squashes and other tropical plants. There were also four major areas of later cultivation activity: tropical (northern) South America, the Andean area, Mesoamerica, and eastern North America (B. Smith, 1998).

The First Plant Domestication

As long ago as 1952, cultural geographer Carl Sauer expressed the belief that agriculture first began in the Americas in humid tropical forest environments. His ideas have been largely forgotten in recent years, as researchers focused on the origins of maize, then thought to have been domesticated in more open environments. Recent investigations using pollen analysis, phytoliths, and plant remains have, however, supported Sauer's belief, with researchers now theorizing that tropical food production first began in small-scale house gardens in forest villages in Panama as early as the ninth millennium B.C. (Piperno and Pearsall, 1998). This "dooryard" horticulture of wild plants developed eventually into slash-and-burn (swidden) farming and, ultimately, into fully settled village life, a process that took as long as 5,000 years in the lowland tropics.

By 5000 to 4000 B.C., extensive forest clearance for fields appears to have been under way. In Panama, surveys show that population growth accompanied the new farming methods, which may have come into use as maize, manioc, and sweet potato became available over wider areas. Slash-and-burn agriculture may also have spread because of drier conditions at the time. Piperno and Pearsall believe that the humid tropical lowlands were an important setting for the development of early American agriculture and that the more arid highland areas of Mesoamerica, long claimed as the cradle of maize domestication, acquired domesticated crops later. New support for their theory comes from excavations at the San Andrés site on the Gulf Coast of Tabasco in Mexico, where evidence of forest clearance and maize pollen date to about 5100 B.C. (Pohl et al., 2007).

Squashes and a plant called *leren* were probably the first domesticates. Bottle gourds were invaluable containers for holding liquids both before and after domestication. Domesticated gourd remains come from Guilá Naquitz in the Valley of Oaxaca as early as 8000 B.C. This gourd may have originated in Africa, where it is widely used as a fishing-net float. Perhaps, argue some experts, it floated across the Atlantic and washed up on New World shores before European settlement. At any rate, the seeds would have provided tropical hunter-gatherers with an easy source of water containers, a preadaptation that might have led to the cultivation of wild squashes and other cucurbits. Domesticated squash was also in use in Mesoamerica as early as 8000 B.C.

As is well known, maize, beans, and squash, which can be grown in the same garden, are a classic triumvirate of food crops in the Americas. Initially, this association probably occurred in the wild, for runner beans and squashes grow naturally around the stalks and bases of teosinte, a wild grass thought to be the ancestor of maize. In the end, humans disturbed the land by clearing it, observed the association of teosinte, beans, and squash, and domesticated the three in combination. Of these three crops, by far the most complex and most debated is *Zea mays*, maize.

The Origins of Maize Agriculture

Maize was the staff of life for many Native Americans when Christopher Columbus landed in the New World. It was cultivated over an enormous area of the Americas, from Argentina and Chile northward to Canada, from sea level to high in the Andes, in low-lying swampy environments and in arid lands. Hundreds of races of domesticated maize evolved over the millennia, each a special adaptation to local environmental conditions.

Gourd
8000 B.C.

TABLE 13.1
Chronological table of major developments in the Americas, 7000 B.C. to A.D. 1500

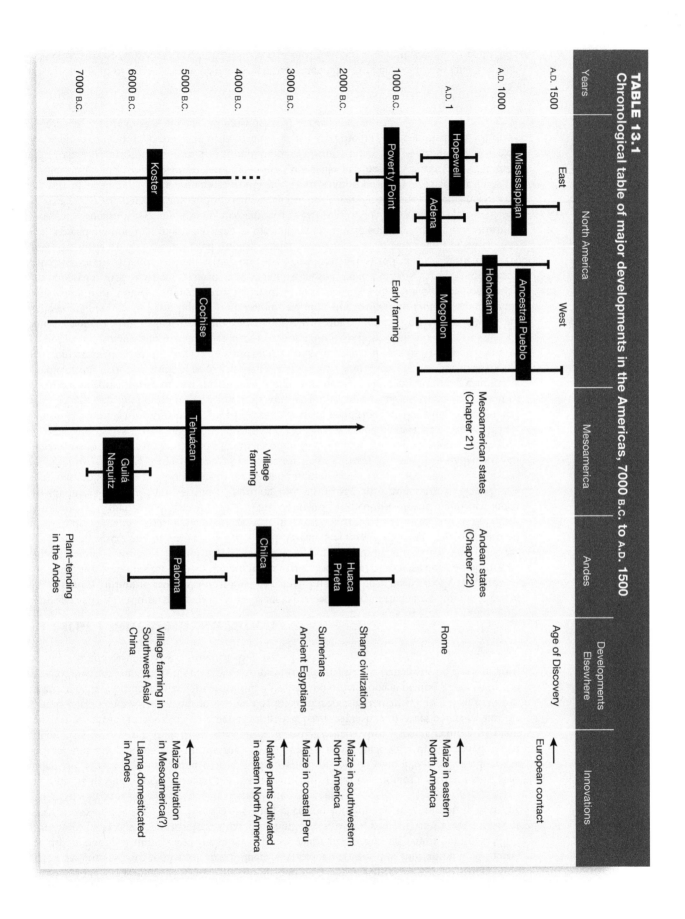

Zea mexicana, which grows over much of Mesoamerica, was the ancestor of domesticated maize.

Botanist George Beadle (1981) theorized that a teosinte of about 13000 to 6000 B.C. was the direct ancestor of modern corn and was transformed into a primitive corn through human selection. According to Beadle, there was a mutation in a gene in an ancestral form of teosinte that converted the hard fruit cases of the grass into shallow, softer cupules (cups) that carried elongated glumes (husks) enclosing and protecting the kernels. This change made wild teosinte much easier to thresh. The transformation into a domesticated form of early maize may have taken place more or less simultaneously in many areas.

Impressive grounds exist for considering the wild ancestor of domesticated maize. There are major differences between this grass and corn. Teosinte has long branches tipped with tassels, whereas maize has short branches tipped with ears. Botanist John Doebley and his colleagues have identified the gene that controls this difference and think that changes in the regulatory regions of this gene (named tb1 [teosinte branched1]) were involved in the switch from teosinte to maize. The tb1 protein suppresses production of lateral branches, and the greater the accumulation of tb1, the shorter the branches. Thus, it is a mutation that increases the amount of tb1 that controls the teosinte shape to a maize-like plant. Doebley (2004) believes this changeover took many centuries, that it occurred in southwestern Mexico, and that it came about specifically as a result of the modification of teosinte in the deciduous forests of the Balsas Valley region. The process of domestication involved selecting seeds of the preferred form and rejecting those from other, less desirable types. A perennial teosinte found in Mexico in recent years has been crossbred with maize.

Piperno and Pearsall (1998) argue for an origin in the tropical lowlands, which did not have the richness of wild plant foods found in more open areas. From its earliest introduction, maize would have been a more efficient source of calories than many wild forest plants, and thus a source of experimentation. The Guilá Naquitz Cave in Oaxaca has yielded an accelerator mass spectrometry (AMS) date for maize of 4250 B.C. (Piperno and Flannery, 2001). There is indirect evidence of even earlier maize cultivation, before 5000 B.C. at San Andrés, on the Gulf coast, and elsewhere, but we lack the cobs or kernels to firmly establish an earlier date (Pohl et al., 2007).

We still do not know exactly when wild teosinte was transformed into maize, but Bruce Smith (1998) is probably right in hypothesizing that the process took place in river valleys that flow from the highlands into the Pacific—areas where the wild teosinte most bio-chemically similar to maize still grows today (Doebley, 2004). For example, the central Balsas Valley in south-western Mexico abounds in such teosinte. Here, human populations settled around the lakes that abounded in this region during warmer and more humid conditions after the Ice Age. Phytoliths hint that maize and squash were already under cultivation by about 6000 B.C.; both pollen and phytoliths from crop weeds became common after about 4300 B.C. (Ranere et al., 2009). The long process of maize domestication may have been some-what similar to that in lowland eastern China described in Chapter 12.

One commonly accepted hypothetical scenario for maize domestication goes as follows (Figure 13.1). The process may have started as an unintentional by-product of gathering wild teosinte, for gathering would lead to selective pressure for harvestable types of the grass, with spikes shrunken into fascicles (bunches). The fascicles would have made it harder for the seeds to scatter. In time, this form of teosinte would become established by campsites and in aban-doned middens. These colonies would automatically

Guilá Naquitz
4250 B.C.

San Andrés
c. 5100 B.C.

FIGURE 13.1 The stages through which teosinte passed on its way to becoming domesticated maize, with (a) showing the earliest teosinte form. (b to d) The harvesting process increased the shrinking of the teosinte branches and led to the husks becoming the enclosures for corn ears. (e) Shows the stabilized maize phenotype. (After (Galinat) Walter C. 1985.)

diverge toward greater domestic kinds of variation, from which human beings could select the most useful types. In time, too, humans would remove weeds from these teosinte stands, then start deliberately planting the more useful types. Thus, the female teosinte spike evolved down a pathway leading toward maize. The cultivation and fertilization of semiwild grass populations were followed by attempts to sow selected seed from the most desirable types. At first, the planted teosinte was no more productive than the wild forms, but it was easier to harvest, a critical stage in the process of domestication. When people began the selective harvesting and planting of transitional forms of teosinte, the grass's reproductive strategy changed to dependency on human intervention. A genetic revolution followed, in which attributes that made harvesting easier and favored teosinte's use as a human food had a selective advantage.

Tehuacán Valley

The dry highland Tehuacán Valley in southern Mexico is an important chronicle of early maize agriculture in more arid environments (Figure 13.2). Richard MacNeish (1970) found domestic maize cobs dating back to approximately 1000 B.C., but not until he began digging in the small Coxcatlán Rock Shelter (Figure 13.3) did he find maize that even vaguely resembled what at that time was considered the hypothetical ancestor of maize. Coxcatlán contains 28 occupation levels, the earliest of which dates to approximately 10000 B.C.

Coxcatlán
10000 B.C. and later

MacNeish found that the earliest Tehuacán people lived mainly by hunting horses, deer, and other mammals and by collecting wild vegetable foods. These hunters used stone-tipped lances in the chase. They also hunted large numbers of jackrabbits, probably in organized drives. MacNeish estimates that 50 to 60 percent of the people's food came from game in 10000 B.C. After 8000 B.C.,

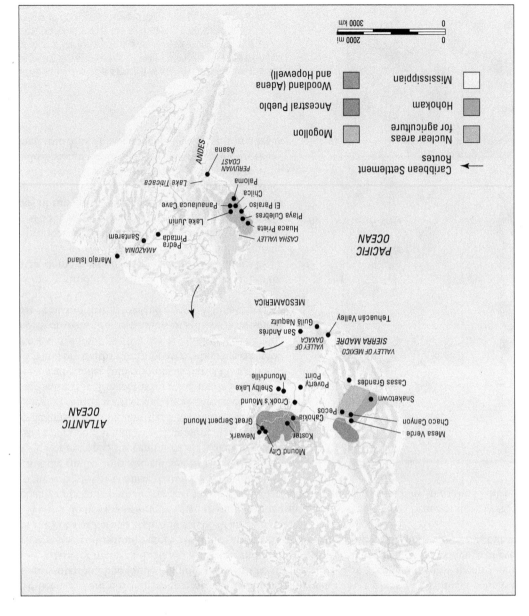

FIGURE 13.2 Archaeological sites and culture areas mentioned in this chapter.

FIGURE 13.3 Excavations at Coxcatlán Rock Shelter, Tehuacán, Mexico, where evidence for maize agriculture dating to about 2500 B.C. was found.

the game population declined, and the people turned more and more to wild plant foods. Instead of hunting year-round, the Tehuacán bands scheduled their food gathering on a seasonal basis and were able to exploit the vegetable and other foods in their environment very intensively. The dietary scenario has been reconstructed from the carbon and nitrogen isotope ratios in the bone collagen of people who lived in the Tehuacán Valley after 6000 B.C. (Farnsworth et al., 1985). By at least 4500 B.C., about 90 percent of the Tehuacáno diet consisted of tropical grasses such as *Setaria* and such plants as cacti and maguey. So much grain was necessary that some form of cultivation or domestication of native plants may have been essential by this time.

Crop yields increased after 2500 B.C. People grew foods that, when stored, would tide them over lean months: beans, amaranth, gourds, and maize. They lived in larger and more permanent settlements, grinding their maize on well-made grindstones (*metates*). The maize itself was smaller than modern strains and probably much like teosinte (see Figure 13.1). By this time, more sedentary villages had replaced the scheduled gathering and nomadic settlement patterns of earlier times. Their ample storage facilities helped the people live through the lean months.

Dry caves elsewhere in northern Mesoamerica show that other cultures paralleled the cultural events in Tehuacán. At the same time, the highland lakes of the Valley of Mexico and elsewhere may well have supported sedentary communities subsisting on fish and wild vegetable foods as well as experimenting with amaranth and other crops.

More than 24,000 maize specimens have come from the caves of the Tehuacán Valley. They document a long sequence of maize evolution, beginning with 71 small cobs from the lowest levels of the San Marcos Cave and from deep in the Coxcatlán Rock Shelter. The cobs are less than 20 mm (2 inches) long and lack the ability to disperse their kernels naturally, a clear sign of full domestication. Originally, MacNeish (1970) used conventional radiocarbon dating to date the layers where the earliest maize cobs were found to be between 5000 and 3500 B.C. New AMS dates on actual early maize cobs from San Marcos date to about 2700 to 2600 B.C., much later than originally thought. Future discoveries may, of course, push the date much farther back into the past. By 2000 B.C., Mesoamericans living in all kinds of environments relied at least partially on food production. Only a millennium later, the precursors of state-organized societies appeared in the Mexican lowlands (see Chapter 21).

San Marcos Cave
c. 3600 B.C. and earlier

Beans and Squash

The domestication of beans may have occurred at much the same time as that of maize, but there is, at present, no archaeological evidence of the first stages of cultivation of this all-important staple. If Kent Flannery's hypothesis is correct, plant domestication in Mesoamerica was not so much an invention in one small area as a shift in ecological adaptation deliberately chosen by peoples living where economic strategies necessitated the intensive exploitation of plant foods. It appears that the evidence from both Tehuacán and Guilá Naquitz bears out this hypothesis.

Earlier theories of the origins of maize assumed that it was domesticated in many areas of the Americas from six or more presumed wild races. Modern pollen studies have shown convincingly that there was never a wild *Zea* with a wide range that extended outside southern Mexico and Guatemala. Apparently, a primitive form of domesticated eight-rowed maize (*maíz de ocho*) with soft glumes, represented at Tehuacán, was the common ancestral corn that spread thousands of miles from its original homeland after 3000 B.C.

Early Food Production in the Andes

Farming began in two areas of the Andean region: in the mountain highlands and along the low-lying, arid Pacific Coast.

The Highlands

The great eighteenth-century German naturalist Alexander von Humboldt was the first European scientist to explore the high Andes. He marveled at the great variety of wild plants and animals that thrived in the harsh and varied landscape of high peaks and mountain valleys. Only a handful of these many species had been tamed by the farmers living in the foothills of the great mountains. The cultivators lived in terraced environmental zones stacked one above the other on the sides of deep valleys.

Humboldt observed how the ever-growing human populations moved upward and outward into much harsher and more marginal environments. As they did so, they tried to encourage animals and plants living in one zone to adapt to another, to extend their range into unoccupied land. By seeding beans and cereal and transplanting roots and fruit trees, they struggled constantly to maintain a foothold outside natural faunal and floral ranges. The same upward assault continues to this day in the Andes, a quiet battle waged with robust root crops and hardy cereal strains (Moseley, 2000).

Five important Andean species were of vital importance to highland economies: the llama, the alpaca, and the guinea pig, as well as the potato and a grain crop, quinoa (*Chenopodium quinoa*).

Panaulauca Cave
2500 B.C.

Llamas were perhaps domesticated alongside quinoa. Camelid bones from Panaulauca Cave, overlooking the Junin basin 150 km (93 miles) northwest of Lima, display a dramatic increase in younger animals by about 2500 B.C. (Figure 13.4). Eight hundred kilometers (500 miles) to the south, Mark Aldenderfer (1995) found a corral with animal dung dating to about 2000 B.C. at

Asana
2000 B.C.

the Asana site, outhwest of Lake Titicaca. Llama (and perhaps alpaca) herding was widespread throughout the highlands and along the north coast of Peru by 900 B.C. Guinea pigs, an important

FIGURE 13.4 Panaulauca Cave, near Lake Junin, Peru. Excavations here yielded evidence of early quinoa cultivation and llama domestication by 2500 B.C.

wild food for many thousands of years, may have been domesticated in high mountain valleys at about the same time.

According to plant biologist Hugh Wilson (1988), quinoa was first domesticated in the south-central Andes. The new crop spread rapidly in the highlands and to the coast. The earliest archaeological occurrence is at Panaulauca Cave, where quinoa seeds with a thickness identical to that of modern domesticated forms come from levels dating to about 3000 B.C. Direct AMS dates are still awaited, but there is good reason to believe that this important highland staple was already widely cultivated by 2500 B.C.

At the time of European contact in the fifteenth century A.D., Andean farmers used literally hundreds of potato varieties. Four major strains were domesticated in the highlands, of which one, *Solanum tuberosum*, is now grown all over the world. Wild potatoes were an important food for highland Andean foragers from the time of earliest settlement. Well-documented potato tubers come from midden sites dating to about 2000 B.C. at the mouth of the Casma Valley on the Peruvian coast, but earlier specimens will, undoubtedly, come to light in the south-central highlands, where other animal and plant species, including lima beans, were domesticated between 3000 and 2000 B.C.

Some form of early plant tending may have persisted in the Andes for many centuries. In the same area, gourds, potatoes, and ulluco (a root crop) were probably grown by 8000 to 7000 B.C. but, like beans, served as a supplementary food and as a means of expanding into hitherto marginal areas. Many thousands of years passed before these plants became economic staples. Quite when maize was introduced to the highlands remains uncertain, but it may have been before it arrived on the coast.

In both highlands and lowlands, the beginnings of agriculture were a gradual adjustment, food production gradually supplanting gathering as the major subsistence activity.

The Peruvian Coast

On the Ecuadorian and Peruvian coasts, people supplemented fishing and the gathering of vegetable foods with irrigation farming as early as 3000 B.C., and highland peoples were cultivating a variety of crops by the same time, crops that amplified the horizontally stacked natural resources of their mountain homeland.

The Peruvian coast forms a narrow shelf at the foot of the Andes, crossed by small river valleys descending from the mountains to the sea (Figure 13.5). These valleys are oases on the desert plain, with deep, rich soils, blooming vegetation, and plentiful water. For thousands of years, Peruvians have cultivated these valley floors, building their settlements, pyramids, and palaces at the edges of their agricultural land. Because conditions for preservation in this arid country are exceptional, the archaeological record is often quite complete. The coast itself forms a series of related microenvironments, such as rocky bars where shellfish are abundant and places where seasonal vegetable foods nourished by damp fogs are common.

FIGURE 13.5 The Peruvian coast, one of the driest environments on earth.

One would assume that a combination of these microenvironments would provide a rich and uniform constellation of food resources that could normally be exploited with ease from relatively sedentary base camps (Moseley, 1975). However, the bountiful maritime environment is occasionally disrupted by a warm countercurrent known as El Niño, which can flow for as long as 12 months. El Niño (the "Christmas Child," because the current usually appears around that time of year) occurs at highly irregular intervals, perhaps every six years, with major events every quarter century or so. It reduces marine upwelling of cold water so much that in big El Niños, the fish migrate elsewhere, and thus one of the coastal people's staple diet sources is greatly reduced, although replaced to some extent by warm-water fish species. The greatest economic disruption occurred during major El Niños, but even lesser events could cause catastrophic rains that damaged crops. The El Niño phenomenon is so unpredictable that the people could not store food against its arrival; they also could not move from the coast, and they did not have the offshore vessels needed for deepwater fishing. Their only strategy, other than moving or starving, was to limit their population densities to the lowest levels of available natural resources until such time as they developed alternative food sources, such as maize grown by intensive irrigation agriculture.

The archaeological evidence along the Peruvian coast is incomplete for the period immediately preceding early food production. During the dry winter months, the inhabitants collected shellfish and other marine resources, and game and vegetable foods were more plentiful in the summer. After 5000 B.C., however, more efficient collecting strategies came into use, with greater attention to the maximal exploitation of natural food sources. Fishing, in particular, became more important. Between approximately 4200 and 2500 B.C., Peruvian coastal peoples depended on marine resources—fish, seabirds, and mollusks—for much of their diet. During the warmest and driest period after the Pleistocene, the coastal peoples moved closer to the shore, living in larger and more stable settlements. Along with the shift to more lasting coastal dwelling came the development of sophisticated equipment for deep-sea fishing.

Paloma
Before 5500 B.C.

As early as 5500 B.C., the coastal peoples were manipulating plants for their own purposes. The Paloma site on the central coast was occupied earlier than 5500 B.C.; it was a settled community with numerous simple huts and grass-lined pits where the inhabitants stored food for the occasional lean year. The people relied heavily on fishing and gathering but also manipulated some plant species, including tuberous begonias, gourds, squashes, and peppers. They also may have kept llamas, the same species used much later by the Incas for carrying loads in the Andes (Benfer, 1982).

Chilca
3800 to 2650 B.C.

A later coastal settlement that perpetuated the same subsistence pattern flourished at Chilca, 72 km (45 miles) south of present-day Lima. Frédéric Engel excavated refuse heaps there and radiocarbon-dated the earlier Chilca occupation to between 3800 and 2650 B.C. (Engel, 1963). When the site was in use, it probably was near a reedy marsh, which provided both matting and building materials, as well as sites for small gardens (Figure 13.6). The Chilca people lived on sea mollusks, fish, and sea lions, and apparently hunted few land mammals. They cultivated jack beans and lima beans, gourds, and squashes, probably relying on river floods as well as rainfall for their simple agriculture.

The new emphasis on fish, an increased use of flour ground from wild grass seed, and the availability of cultivated squashes became new sources of nutrition for some coastal groups. This supply may ultimately have set off a sustained period of population growth. Certainly, the succeeding millennia saw many permanent settlements established near the ocean; the people combined agriculture with fishing and mollusk gathering. Domesticated cotton first appeared around 2500 B.C.

Squashes, peppers, lima beans, and other crops remained staple foods until recent times. Maize and other basic foods were either unknown or of lesser importance, if carbon isotopic analyses are any guide (Burger and van der Merwe, 1990). Agriculture remained a secondary activity much later than it did in Mesoamerica.

Huaca Prieta
2500 to 1800 B.C.

One later site is Huaca Prieta, a sedentary village that housed several hundred people on the north coast of Peru between 2500 and 1800 B.C. (Hyslop et al., 1987). The vast refuse mound there contains small one- or two-room houses built partially into the ground and roofed with timber or whalebone beams. The inhabitants were remarkably skillful cotton weavers who devised a sophisticated art style with animal, human, and geometric designs (Figure 13.7). (See also Chapter 22 for more discussion.)

Maize made its first appearance on the coast at Playa Culebras, another important and contemporary settlement south of Huaca Prieta (Moseley, 2000). The new crop was soon grown on a considerable scale in large irrigation systems in coastal river valleys. Irrigation required the efficient organization and deployment of people to dig and maintain canals, communal work on a scale that could be organized only by a system of taxation by labor, such as was commonplace in the Andes in later millennia. Much higher crop yields resulted as the focus of coastal population moved inland and local kin leaders and priests assumed much more prominent roles in society.

These social changes were reflected in more permanent housing and in large ceremonial pyramids and other public buildings. A complex of stone and mud mortar platforms lies at El Paraíso on the floodplain of the Chillón Valley, some distance from the sea (see Chapter 22). At least one mound had complexes of connected rooms built in successive stages. Settlements such as El Paraíso obviously depended more on agriculture than had earlier sites. By the time the temple complexes were built there, after 1800 B.C., loom-woven textiles and pottery had come into widespread use. All the major food plants that formed the basis of later Peruvian civilization were in use.

FIGURE 13.6 Reconstruction of a Chilca house. A circular structure, it had a domelike frame of canes bound with rope and covered with bundles of grass; the interior was braced with bones from stranded whales. Seven burials had been deposited in the house before it was intentionally collapsed on top of them. The skeletons were wrapped in mats and all buried at the same time, perhaps because of an epidemic. (Wiley, Gordon R. 1971.)

FIGURE 13.7 A double-headed snakelike figure with rock crabs appended to it, as it appears in a Preceramic twined cloth fabric from Huaca Prieta, Peru. The rock crabs are revealed by plotting the warp measurements. The original length was approximately 40 cm (16 inches). The shaded area indicates the surviving textile. Double-headed motifs persisted through more than 3,000 years of Andean art.

Early Farmers in Southwestern North America

In 10000 B.C., the Southwest of the United States was populated by hunter-gatherers whose culture was adapted to desert living (Cordell, 2009; Plog, 2008). A distinctive foraging culture, the Cochise, flourished in southeastern Arizona and southwestern New Mexico from about this time. The Cochise people gathered many plant foods, including yucca seeds, cacti, and sunflower seeds. They used small milling stones, basketry, cordage, nets, and spear-throwers. Many features of their material culture remained in use in later times, when cultivated plants were introduced into the Southwest (Matson, 1991).

Cochise Culture
10000 B.C. and later

The earliest Mesoamerican crops to cross the Rio Grande were maize, beans, and squash, which were probably cultivated for some time in northern Mexico before they reached the Southwest. The maize farmers of northern Mexico must have had sporadic contact with Archaic hunter-gatherers living in the deserts to the north, so it would have been easy for knowledge of plants, even gifts of seeds or seedlings, to pass from south to north. Probably, the opportunity for adopting crops was there long before anyone thought it worthwhile.

Between about 2500 and 100 B.C., the southwestern climate was relatively stable, perhaps somewhat wetter than it is today. However, it was an environment where hunting and gathering were high-risk occupations, mainly because rainfall patterns were always unpredictable. Despite generally low population densities, local populations may have occasionally risen to the point where there were food shortages. Domesticated plants like maize and beans had one major advantage: They might have low yields, but they were predictable. Cultivators of the new crops could control their location and their availability at different seasons by storing them carefully (Roth and Wellman, 2001).

2500 B.C.

Perhaps people living in the southern deserts of the Southwest began growing maize because it gave them food supplies to tide them over the lean months until spring. Farther north, in the uplands, growing crops would have enabled hunter-gatherer peoples to exercise more effective control over their environment. In the final analysis, it was probably a combination of rising populations and food shortages that caused the adoption of low-yielding forms of maize. Indeed, one could argue that the people accepted the new crops not because they wanted to become farmers but so they could be more effective foragers (Matson, 1991; Wills, 1989). Linda Cordell (2009) believes that southwestern groups adopted agriculture when what she calls a "situation of regional imbalance" developed between local populations and local resources. Such situations could result from either environmental degradation or population increases. She believes that climatic changes during the Archaic were not sufficient to cause local degradation. Thus, rising population densities may have been a factor.

Maize
2000 to 1500 B.C.

The hardy, low-yielding maize that first entered the Southwest was the so-called Chapalote form, a small popcorn of great genetic diversity. It may have arrived during a period of higher rainfall between 2000 and 1500 B.C. It was soon crossbred with the indigenous wild teosinte, the result being a highly varied, more productive hybrid maize with larger cobs and more kernel rows.

Maize is a demanding crop, not a cereal that one can rely on to provide all one's food if one plants it casually and simply returns to harvest the resulting stand later, as is possible with many native plants like goosefoot. Maize also lacks two of the vital amino acids needed to make protein, lysine, and tryptophan (high in squash), and it is only an effective staple when grown in combination with other crops like beans (lysine-rich) or squash (tryptophan-rich) that provide the necessary protein ingredients for a maize-based diet. Because most southwestern groups continued to enjoy a highly mobile lifeway for at least a millennium after maize first appeared north of the Rio Grande, there is good reason to believe that it first served as a casual supplement to wild plant resources. This was especially so in favorable areas where corn could be planted and then left largely untended, the process of cultivating it not being allowed to interfere with other subsistence activities.

However, a radically different maize, *maíz de ocho*, was the key to new cultural developments in the Southwest. *Maíz de ocho*, with its large, more productive, flowery kernels, may have evolved from earlier, highly variable Chapalote maize. It may have resulted from a selection for a large-kerneled corn that was easier to grind and that flowered earlier, both important attributes in the hot and arid Southwest. Here, the irregular timing and distribution of rainfall restrict growing seasons, leaving little time for kernels to fill out. These characteristics of *maíz de ocho* were highly adaptive in North America, with its short growing seasons and very diverse, temperate environments.

Once again, precise AMS dating of actual maize cobs and other domesticated seeds provides the only unimpeachable evidence of cultivation. Broad application of the new dating method has narrowed the window for the arrival of maize and squash in the Southwest to a five-century span between 2000 and 1500 B.C. Both crops spread widely through the Southwest in later centuries, as did other maize forms. Southwestern farmers experimented with the new crop at many elevations. Across the border, in northwestern Mexico, Robert Hard and John Roney (Hard and Roney, 1998) have excavated the Cerro Juanaqueña farming village with 7 km (5 miles) of stone house terraces, where maize cobs have been dated to about 1150 B.C. This was also a substantial farming settlement, equivalent to about a 135-room pit house village, where native grasses may also have been processed.

Cerro Juanaqueña
c. 1150 B.C.

Beans
500 B.C.

After 500 B.C., southwestern farmers combined maize with beans, for these legumes when underplanted with corn return vital nitrogen to the soil, nitrogen that is depleted by maize. (The earliest known beans date to about 520 B.C.) By planting the two crops together, the southwestern farmer could maintain the fertility of the soil for longer periods of time. The late arrival of beans was probably one reason why some time elapsed between the first appearance of maize and significant dependence on agriculture.

In the Southwest, as in the Andes, the farmers were working close to the limits of corn's range. Maize is intolerant of too short a growing season, weak soil conditions, and such hazards as crop disease and strong winds. Most important were adequate soil moisture and water supplies. By careful seed selection, the farmers developed higher-elevation varieties with elongated cobs, distinctive root structures, and seeds that could be planted at considerable depths and thus nourished by the retained ground moisture. The farmers became experts at soil selection, favoring soils with good moisture-retaining properties on north- and east-facing slopes that received little direct sunlight. They also favored floodplains and canyon mouths, where the soil was naturally irrigated. They would divert water from seasonal streams, springs, or rainfall runoff to irrigate their lands. As in hunting and foraging, risk management was vital, so the cultivators widely dispersed their gardens to minimize the danger of local drought or flood. Over the centuries, a great diversity of highly effective dry-climate agricultural techniques developed throughout the Southwest.

Between A.D. 300 and 500, another complex of domestic tropical plants, including pigweed, cotton, and several varieties of beans, arrived in the region. (Cotton may have arrived earlier.) These tended to require more irrigation and were confined to the hot regions of the south, where the irrigation-experienced Hohokam adopted them (see next section).

The appearance of maize did not trigger a dramatic revolution in southwestern life. The earlier corns were not very productive and could be planted fairly casually. Under these circumstances, their yields were probably less than those of good piñon nut harvests. Eventually, however, they became an important food staple for many southwestern peoples who were now living in more

FIGURE 13.8 The Hohokam settlement at Snaketown, Arizona, during 1965 excavations, showing kivas and dwellings.

permanent villages and in more restricted territories. As life became more sedentary, the people invested more time and energy in their crops, which provided protection from shortages of wild plant foods in their smaller territories (Rocek, 1995). The culture changes of the period culminated in the great southwestern archaeological traditions: Hohokam, Mogollon, and Ancestral Pueblo (Cordell, 2009).

Hohokam

The Hohokam tradition has long been thought to have originated in the Cochise culture. The tradition probably emerged from indigenous roots in the first five centuries A.D., acquiring much greater social complexity through time (Bayman, 2002; Fish and Fish, 2007). One major Hohokam settlement was the Snaketown site (so-called after the O'odham name *Skoaquik*, "place of snakes") in the Gila River valley (Figure 13.8) (Haury, 1976).

The Hohokam enjoyed complex trading and ceremonial relationships with peoples living all over the Southwest and in northern Mexico. As time went on, this trade expanded, perhaps within the context of a common ceremonial system centered on the ball courts and other ceremonial structures at Snaketown and other focal points (Whalen and Minnis, 1996).

Hohokam subsistence was based on maize, beans, cucurbits, cotton, and other crops, as well as on gathering. The people planted their crops to coincide with the semiannual rainfall and flooding patterns. Where they could, they practiced irrigation from flowing rivers; otherwise, they cultivated floodplains and caught runoff from local storms with dams, terraces, and other devices. Hohokam people occupied much of what is now southern Arizona. Their cultural heirs are the O'odham people of today.

Hohokam
A.D. 500 to 1450

Hohokam culture evolved slowly over as long as 2,000 years. In about A.D. 650 to 700, a wave of influence from Mesoamerica brought new varieties of maize, the appearance of platform mounds and ball or dance courts at Snaketown and elsewhere, and imports such as copper bells (Ericson and Baugh, 1993). There were at least five stages of the Hohokam culture, culminating in a classical period from approximately A.D. 1100 to 1450, when adobe compounds were built and canal irrigation was especially important.

Originally, anthropologists believed that the Mexican influence was transitory and weak, but this belief changed after excavations at a prehistoric town named Casas Grandes in northern Chihuahua, Mexico (Schaafsma and Riley, 1999; Whalen and Minnis, 2001). (This site should not be confused with Casa Grande, Arizona.) At the height of its prosperity, around A.D. 1,400, Casas Grandes boasted approximately 1,600 rooms and housed more than 2,400 people. The inhabitants showed exchanged turquoise and painted pottery from the Southwest for marine shells, copper bells, and exotic birds (tropical macaws) from Mexico.

Casas Grandes
A.D. 1400

Mogollon

The Mogollon tradition emerged from Archaic roots between 300 B.C. and A.D. 200 and disappeared as a separate entity between A.D. 850 and 1000 to 1150, when it became part of various local traditions (Haury, 1985). The Mogollon is well-known from dry caves in New Mexico as an agricultural tradition in which hunting and gathering in the highlands were always important. Mogollon agriculture depended on direct rainfall, with only very limited use of irrigation. The people lived in small villages of pit dwellings with timber frames and mat or brush roofs. Their material culture was utilitarian and included milling stones, digging sticks, bows and arrows, fine baskets, and characteristic red-on-brown pottery.

Mogollon
C. 300 B.C. to A.D. 1000

At least six regional variants of the Mogollon culture are known, and there were five chronological stages, the fifth ending approximately 500 years ago. Early Mogollon villages were often located on high promontories close to fertile lands. The settlement pattern varied from area to area but had a tendency toward larger sites and increased populations throughout the life of the tradition. By A.D. 1350, pueblos of several hundred rooms had developed in some areas, but by this time the

SiTE > The Chaco Phenomenon <

By 1050, an estimated 5,500 people lived in Chaco Canyon, New Mexico, maintaining contacts over an enormous area of the Southwest, as the so-called Chaco Phenomenon reached its apogee. By A.D. 1115, at least 70 communities were dispersed over more than 64,750 sq. km (25,000 sq. miles) of northwestern New Mexico, and parts of southern Colorado were linked through the socioeconomic and ritual networks centered on Chaco Canyon.

The Chaco Phenomenon was the center of a vast regional system that extended far beyond the San Juan basin and is famous for its "road system." Over 650 km (400 miles) of unpaved ancient trackways link Chaco in an intricate web with over 30 outlying settlements. The "roads" are up to 12 m (40 feet) wide and were cut a few inches into the soil or marked by low banks or stone walls. Sometimes, the road makers simply cleared the vegetation and loose soil or stones from the pathway, lining some segments with boulders. The roads run straight for long distances, in one instance 95 km (60 miles). They do not follow contours, but change direction in abrupt turns, with stairways and ramps to surmount steep obstacles. These may be little more than toeholds or elaborate stairways with wide steps cut out of bedrock or formed from masonry blocks (Figure 13.9). Each approaches the canyon, then descends via stone-cut steps down the cliffs to the valley floor. There they merge in the narrow defiles and split, each leading to a different great house.

By using aerial photographs, fieldworkers have been able to trace roads extending from Chaco almost to the Colorado–New Mexico border and Aztec Ruins, some 80 km (50 miles) away. Other roads connect Chaco to natural resource areas in modern-day Zuni country and elsewhere. The system may have extended to the San Juan Range in the Rocky Mountains to the north, the

Mogollon Mountains to the south, and from the turquoise mines near Santa Fe in the east to the Little Colorado River in the west.

Chaco road construction must have involved the deployment of large numbers of people and considerable group organization. Were they highways for transporting valuable natural resources to major pueblos? Or were they pilgrim roads? Did they have some much more profound spiritual importance? One prevalent hypothesis argues that without draft animals or wheeled carts, the Chaco people had no use for formal roads for their everyday business. Originally, perhaps, people traveled from outlying communities to Chaco to acquire turquoise objects manufactured there, to trade food for ritual paraphernalia. In time, this trade became institutionalized in regular ceremonies and festivals, where people gathered from many miles around for seasonal rituals and where leaders from widely dispersed communities gathered to cement political and economic alliances. Each member of the network would have complex obligations to fulfill, among them, presumably, the supplying of people to construct and maintain the road system, to transport wooden beams for building the great houses in Chaco (more than 200,000 were needed to build them), and for many communal tasks. In other words, the Chaco system was a mechanism for integrating a large number of communities scattered widely in a harsh and unpredictable environment.

This ingenious theory stumbles on two points. First, the focus of Ancestral Pueblo life was the household and ties of kin, which were the means by which people fed themselves and passed on accumulated expertise about making a living from one generation to the next. Second, many of the Chaco roads go nowhere, although they are linked to a great house or kiva. We Westerners tend to think of roads as traveling from A to B, which means that we have tended to join incomplete segments of Chacoan roads with straight dotted lines. The roads may not have actually been joined. While major north and south tracks radiated from Chaco, only about 250 km (155 miles) of the roads have been verified on the ground.

A more likely explanation lies in Pueblo cosmology. The so-called Great North Road travels 63 km (40 miles) north from Chaco before it disappears abruptly in Kutz Canyon. North is the primary direction among modern-day Keresan-speaking Pueblo peoples, who may have ancestry among the Chaco people. North led to the Origin, the place where the spirits of the dead traveled. Perhaps the Great North Road was an umbilical cord to the underworld and a conduit of spiritual power. The Keresan also believe in a Middle Place, a point where the four cardinal directions converged. Pueblo Bonito is laid out according to these directions and may have served as Chaco's Middle Place. Thus, Chaco and its trackways may have formed a sacred landscape that gave order to the world and linked outlying communities with a powerful Middle Place through spiritual ties that remained even as many households moved away from the canyon.

Think of a giant ideological spider's web with a lattice of obligations among its component parts, and you probably have a credible model for Chaco's role in the eleventh-century Ancestral Pueblo world. Archaeologist Gwinn Vivian calls the landscape a powerful statement, what he calls "We the Chaco." (See a summary of roads and theories in Fagan, 2005c; Lekson, 1999.)

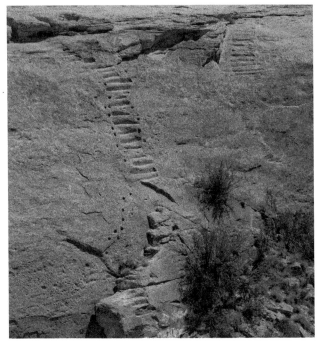

FIGURE 13.9 Jackson Stairway, Chaco Canyon. Stone-cut steps into the walls of the canyon formed part of the Chacoan road system.

Mogollon tradition had become part of the Ancestral Pueblo tradition. Much of the Mogollon area was completely abandoned by A.D. 1500.

Ancestral Pueblo

The Ancestral Pueblo (formerly called Anasazi) tradition is, in general terms, ancestral to the cultures of the modern Pueblo Indians: the Hopi, the Zuni, and others (Cordell, 2009; Plog, 2008). Its emergence is conventionally dated to A.D. 1, but this is a purely arbitrary date, for the Ancestral Pueblo tradition's roots lie in Archaic cultures that flourished for a long time before. The Ancestral Pueblo tradition is centered in the Four Corners area, where Utah, Arizona, Colorado, and New Mexico meet. The Ancestral Pueblo people made heavy use of wild vegetable foods, even after they took up maize agriculture seriously, after A.D. 400. Most of their farming depended on dry agriculture and seasonal rainfall, although they, like the Hohokam, used irrigation techniques when practicable. They made use of flood areas, where the soil would remain damp for weeks after sudden storms. Moisture in the flooded soil could be used to germinate seeds in the spring and to bring ripening crops to fruition after later rains. However, this is a very high-risk type of agriculture, and the Ancestral Pueblo relied on wild resources to carry them through lean years.

Ancestral Pueblo chronology is well established, thanks to the use of tree-ring dating on beams from abandoned pueblos. There are at least six Basketmaker and Pueblo subdivisions of the Ancestral Pueblo; each marked a gradual increase in the importance of agriculture and the emergence of some larger sites. By approximately A.D. 800, the basic Ancestral Pueblo settlement pattern had evolved and aboveground houses were being substituted for the pit dwellings of earlier centuries. The pit dwellings themselves developed into **kivas**, subterranean ceremonial structures that existed in every large village. *Pueblos*, large settlements of contiguous dwellings, became the rule after A.D. 900 to 1000, with clusters of "rooms" serving as homes for separate families or lineages. Such small towns became more common after A.D. 900.

One major center of Ancestral Pueblo culture developed in Chaco Canyon, New Mexico (Fagan, 2005c; Lekson, 1999) (see Site box). The first sedentary villages appeared there in about A.D. 490. Between the ninth and tenth centuries, summer rainfall was highly variable. Instead of dispersing in response to drought, the Chaco Ancestral Pueblo built a series of "great houses" at the junctions of major drainages. The largest of them, Pueblo Bonito was a huge D-shaped complex of at least 600 rooms rising several stories around the rim of an arc, housing at least 1,000 people (Figure 13.10). The room complexes surrounded courts, with the highest stories at the back. They formed a blank wall; a line of one-story rooms cut off the fourth side. Within the court lay the kivas, usually one great kiva and often several smaller ones. The great kivas were up to 18.2 m (60 feet) in diameter, with wide masonry benches encircling the interior. The roof was supported by four large masonry pillars or upright logs placed around a central hearth. A staircase leading from the floor of the kiva to the large room above it gave access to the sacred precinct.

Ancestral Pueblo
A.D. 1 to 1300

Chaco Canyon
A.D. 490 to 1130

FIGURE 13.10 Pueblo Bonito in Chaco Canyon. The round structures are kivas.

FIGURE 13.11 The Cliff Palace at Mesa Verde.

The Ancestral Pueblo enjoyed a relatively elaborate material culture at the height of their prosperity; at this time, they were making distinctive black-on-white pottery, well-formed baskets, and fine sandals. However, their architecture was neither very sophisticated nor particularly innovative. Rocks and mud were formed into boxlike rooms; a roof of mud rested on horizontal timbers. Room after room was added as the need arose, built from local materials and in a simple architectural style entirely appropriate to its environment.

Tree rings tell us that a great drought in A.D. 1130 endured for a half century. The Chaco population dispersed into smaller settlements as the political gravity of Ancestral Pueblo culture shifted to the Four Corners region. During the twelfth century, large pueblos developed in the Montezuma Valley and outlying regions like Mesa Verde. Some communities moved from the open to under cliff overhangs, the so-called cliff dwellings (Figure 13.11). Some of the features of these sites, such as turrets and loopholed walls, appear to have been defensive (Crown and Judge, 1991). All these larger pueblos were probably communities run for the collective good, with at least some ranking of society under a chieftain. In modern Hopi society, clan superiority and kinship lineages play an important role in the election of leaders. Thrust into close intimacy by the nature of pueblo architecture, the people developed well-integrated religious and ceremonial structures to counteract the tensions of close living. Another serious drought cycle between A.D. 1276 and 1299 saw dozens of Ancestral Pueblo settlements large and small disperse into less affected regions, where they joined groups ancestral to modern Pueblo Indian communities (Adler, 1996) (Figure 13.12).

The southwestern farmer won success by skillfully using scarce water resources and bringing together soil and water by means of dams, floodwater irrigation, and other systems for distributing runoff. Planting techniques were carefully adapted to desert conditions, and numerous tiny gardens supplied food for each family or lineage. This successful adaptation is also reflected in the architecture.

Mesa Verde
A.D. 1130

Preagricultural and Agricultural Societies in Eastern North America

The Archaic hunter-gatherer traditions of eastern North America enjoyed many regional variations in material culture; these occurred because the people concentrated on different locally abundant food sources (see Sassaman and Anderson, 1996). In general, however, the lifeway was similar among them: a seasonal one, based on a very broad spectrum of game and vegetable foods. As long as the population density was low, every band could react relatively easily to changes in local conditions. Because many of their favorite vegetable foods were subject to cycles of lean and abundant years, a flexibility in choice and movement was essential. However, as populations grew slowly throughout the Archaic, this flexibility was increasingly restricted and the people tended to specialize in local resources that were available most of the year. They developed better storage techniques and fostered closer contacts with their neighbors through exchange networks that handled foodstuffs and other commodities. The development of these types of response may have required more complex social organization than the simple band structure of earlier times, and it is no coincidence that burial patterns during the late Archaic, in about 1700 B.C., reflect greater differentiation in social status. Cemeteries may also have served as territorial markers.

Late Archaic
1700 B.C.

Under these circumstances, perhaps it was inevitable that late Archaic peoples in the Eastern Woodlands turned to the deliberate cultivation of food plants to supplement wild plant yields. They did so quite independently of other centers of plant domestication (B. Smith, 1998). The four seeds eventually taken under domestication were collected from rich wild stands along river floodplains for many centuries before they were cultivated deliberately. Bruce Smith notes that goosefoot, marsh elder, and the gourd flourished on naturally disturbed flood soils, where they produced abundant seeds in the wild. Sunflowers had numerous small seed heads, which propagated rapidly, and were valued for their oil. Smith hypothesizes that the inhabitants of large riverside settlements gathered seeds from stands of floodplain weeds. Some of the harvested seeds dropped onto disturbed soil, where they established new colonies. Within 50 to 100 years, Smith believes, the foragers would have domesticated the native plants, first by weeding their stands and then by deliberate planting.

AMS dates suggest that such planting began as early as 2500 B.C., all four seeds coming under cultivation within five centuries. This development took hold not at one location but within a number of more or less isolated hunter-gatherer societies living in small river valleys. At first, cultivated plants seem to have filled a small niche in a diverse diet, which comprised game, fish, waterfowl, and plant foods of all kinds. Several plant species were grown outside their natural ranges, but it seems likely that the domestication of these native plants first took hold in locations like the lower Mississippi River delta, where wild ancestors of these species still grow in abundance. None of the domesticates required the kind of wholesale adaptive shift in year-round routine that maize cultivation demanded of its practitioners.

FIGURE 13.12 Painted Mimbres bowls from the North American Southwest, work of another Ancestral Pueblo group.

This form of supplementary cultivation of native plants continued for more than 1,500 years. But by 200 B.C., people throughout the region had shifted to a greater reliance on local seed plants, centuries before maize was introduced into the Eastern Woodlands.

Moundbuilder Cultures

After 2000 B.C., when eastern North American societies still relied heavily on hunting and foraging, we find increasing signs of preoccupation with burial and with life after death, a new ideological foundation for local society in eastern North America. These burial cults shared many practices, among them cremation, the deposition of exotic objects with the dead, and the custom of building burial mounds (Milner, 2004).

More intensive exploitation of food resources, greater sedentism, regular social interaction and exchange, a degree of social ranking, and increased ceremonialism—these were the culminating elements in late Archaic life in eastern North America. Although most groups still lived in temporary encampments or even sizable base camps used for most, if not all, of the year, the Poverty Point culture of the lower Mississippi Valley and the adjacent Gulf Coast offers a dramatic contrast.

FIGURE 13.13 Poverty Point, Louisiana. An aerial view taken about a half century ago, showing the concentric earth ridges. The ridges and intervening swales (hollows) show up as light and dark stripes in the fields.

Poverty Point culture
2200 to 600 B.C.

The earliest Poverty Point region sites date to about 2200 B.C., forming a major component in a cultural sequence involving earthwork construction that began as early as 3000 B.C. Poverty Point itself is the nexus of the culture and stands on Macon Ridge overlooking the Mississippi floodplain, near the confluence of six rivers (Figure 13.13). This was a strategic point from which to trade upstream and downstream, to receive and exchange raw materials and finished products. Some of the exotic materials at Poverty Point came from as far away as 997 km (620 miles).

Poverty Point, with its great earthworks, is a remarkable contrast to the humble base camps elsewhere in eastern North America, although it was foreshadowed by other large Archaic earthworks. Six concentric semicircular earthen ridges are divided into segments. They average about 25 m (82 feet) wide and 3 m (10 feet) high and are set about 40 m (131 feet) apart. Their significance is a complete mystery, beyond a suspicion that they were connected with astronomical observations. To the west lies an artificial mound more than 20 m (66 feet) high and more than 200 m (660 feet) long. A person standing on this mound can sight the vernal and autumnal equinoxes directly across the center of the earthworks to the east. These are the points where the sun rises on the first days of spring and fall. Built between 1000 and 600 B.C., Poverty Point itself took more than 35,000 cu m (1,236,007 cu feet) of basket-loaded soil, a task that would have taken 1,350 adults laboring 70 days a year for 3 years to complete. Estimates of Poverty Point's population are hard to come by, but even a population of 1,000 people makes the site unique for the period. The significance of this extraordinary site and the associated culture is still little understood (Gibson, 2001). The Poverty Point culture went into decline in about 600 B.C., just as moundbuilding reached new heights in the Ohio Valley, to the northeast.

Early Woodland (Adena)

By 700 B.C., the people of eastern North America enjoyed a tradition of long-distance trading that had flourished for centuries. The trade carried not only prosaic commodities such as stone ax blades but also large quantities of prestigious imports such as conch shells and copper artifacts, most of which were deposited in the graves of their owners. These exotic objects may have been status symbols, indicating some social differentiation within groups. As far as is known, these artifacts were buried with their owners at death, and the special status associated with them was not passed on from one generation to the next.

Between 500 B.C. and about A.D. 400, Early Woodland people (sometimes called Adena) flourished in the Ohio Valley. The people lived in seasonal camps, relying not only on hunting and gathering but also on the cultivation of squash and local starchy and oily plants. Major camps lay close to ceremonial burial mounds. The construction of even the largest mounds involved relatively few people. This moundbuilding and other earthwork construction may have reflected a strengthening of group identity and the establishment of social and territorial boundaries, which were often marked by cemeteries.

Early Woodland (Adena)
500 B.C. to A.D. 400

At the same time, the Early Woodland groups developed large exchange networks that extended over enormous distances, the prototypes of even more elaborate trade routes in later centuries. Powerful loyalties to local lineages caused the people to commemorate their dead not only with imposing burial mounds but with extensive earthworks as well.

Early Woodland earthworks follow the contours of flat-topped hills and form circles, squares, and other shapes, enclosing areas perhaps as much as 105 m (350 feet) in diameter. The earth used to make the enclosures came from just inside the walls, giving a false impression of an interior moat. These were probably ceremonial compounds rather than defensive earthworks. Early Woodland people built large burial mounds, some placed inside. Important individuals lie in log-lined tombs. Their corpses are smeared with red ocher or graphite. Nearby lie ceremonial soapstone pipes and tablets engraved with curving designs or birds of prey. Some prestigious individuals were buried inside enclosures or mortuary structures, which were burned down as part of the funeral rites. Occasionally, the burial chamber was left open so that bodies could be added later. Dozens of people from miles around piled basketfuls of earth to form an imposing burial mound for a single individual (Clay, 1998). More often, the mounds were piled up gradually over the years, as layers of bodies were added. However, the vast majority of less important people were cremated; only their ashes were placed inside the burial mound.

This was not so much a culture as a ceremonial complex that flourished over an enormous area of eastern North America. *Adena* is merely a convenient archaeological term that covers dozens of local early Woodland cultures in the Eastern Woodlands, cultures that were contemporary, often close neighbors, and interacting with one another continuously.

Hopewell

For nearly 1,000 years, the Midwest experienced a dramatic flowering of artistic traditions and of long-distance trade that brought copper from the upper Great Lakes region, obsidian from Yellowstone, and mica from the southern Appalachians (Baugh and Ericson, 1994). Nowhere is this flowering better documented than in the so-called Hopewell tradition, a later elaboration of eastern North American ceremonial traditions that first appeared in Illinois in about A.D. 1 (Carr and Case, 2005; Case and Carr, 2008). The Hopewell people themselves lived in relatively small settlements and used only stone artifacts to plant, hunt game, and fish. They wore leather and woven clothes of pliable fibers. Much wealth and creative skill were lavished on a few individuals and on their life after death. At first glance, the exotic artifacts and ritual traditions of the Hopewell culture seem completely alien to the indigenous cultures, but a closer look reveals the links between the underlying traditions and the magnificent art created by Hopewell artisans. Their manufactures were traded in a vast exchange network of prestige goods, which moved between local elites and were used in status-enhancing ceremonies and in burial rituals. Such exchanges also linked kin leaders with lasting obligations to one another.

Hopewell
A.D. 1 to 400

The cult objects associated with this trade are found in dozens of Hopewell burial mounds and tell us something of the rank and social roles of the people with whom they are buried. Some of the exotic grave goods, such as pipe bowls or axes, were buried as gifts from living clan members to a dead leader. Others were personal possessions, cherished weapons, or sometimes symbols of status or wealth. Hopewell graves contain soapstone pipe bowls in the form of beavers, frogs, birds, bears, and even humans. Skilled smiths fashioned thin copper sheets into head and breast ornaments that bear elaborate animal motifs hammered in relief (Figure 13.14). There were copper axes and arrowheads, trinkets, and beads. Specialists cut mica sheets into striking and lustrous silhouettes of human figures, bird talons, and abstract designs. A few artisans produced most of these artifacts, perhaps in workshops within large earthwork complexes, themselves close to major sources of important raw materials. Some elaborate artifacts may also have been manufactured at special "mortuary camps" for use in the graves of high-status individuals. The same prestigious objects may have been distributed via the trade networks that carried foodstuffs and tools throughout Hopewell territory. Many of them show surprisingly little wear, as if they were soon buried with their owners.

(a)

(b)

FIGURE 13.14 Hopewell ceremonial artifacts found in burial mounds. (a) Raven or crow in beaten copper; (b) Raptor in beaten copper; (c) soapstone frog. Such objects were high-status possessions, often symbols of rank, perhaps acquired in ceremonial gift exchanges. ([b]) The Field Museum, Neg. #A90925, Chicago.)

(c)

By this time, burial mounds were much more elaborate than those of the Adena predecessors. A Hopewell burial mound complex in Ohio, appropriately named Mound City, contains no fewer than 24 mounds inside an enclosure covering 15.2 ha (32 acres) (Figure 13.15). The Newark, Ohio, Hopewell earthworks cover 1,040 ha (4 sq. miles). Farther afield, the Crook's Mound in Louisiana rises 12 m (40 feet) and is more than 30 m (100 feet) across. Its builders followed the established custom when they buried 168 bodies within an extensive earthen platform. Then they placed another 214 corpses on the platform before covering the entire sepulcher with a large mound.

We still know little of Hopewell society, despite the excavation of large mound and earthwork complexes like Marksville in the lower Mississippi Valley. William Dancey and Paul Pacheco (1997) believe that Hopewell communities were made up of single- or multiple-family households scattered across the landscape but were concentrated around centrally located burial mounds and ceremonial precincts. These households were stable, long-term settlements, occupied by people who not only foraged but cultivated indigenous domesticated plants. A dispersed settlement pattern was necessary to accommodate the often conflicting demands of cultivation and intensive foraging activity. Many local communities lie in areas defined by local drainage systems, with household sites, specialized camps, and ritual precincts, normally close to the center of the community and the focus of local life. Although individual households were stable units, the constant hiving off of new generations made for a dynamic settlement pattern, where different settlements were occupied for shorter or longer periods of time, with the number of settlement clusters increasing through time. Ceremonial precincts also changed continually through time, with the building of new burial mounds, fresh earthworks, and other features.

On a larger scale, neighboring communities may have formed what one might call *peer polities*, anchored by centrally located earthworks and burial mounds. Hopewell, Newark, and other earthwork groups may represent examples of such larger polities, each strategically located at the intersections of different physiographic provinces. This may reflect a basic self-sufficiency in foodstuffs during good years, but also the need for intercommunity exchange to balance out shortages during cycles of drought and other scarce times caused by short-term climatic shifts. These exchange links also extended to outlying areas where contemporary societies still retained strong Adena ties and did not adopt Hopewell beliefs.

The intricate Hopewell exchange systems endured in the Midwest until about A.D. 400. Then the networks collapsed, interregional art styles broke down, and moundbuilding by entire communities was interrupted. Three theories seek to explain the collapse. The first argues that horticulture became so successful that the ecological incentives for long-distance exchange, for reciprocal gift

FIGURE 13.15 Circular Hopewell mounds at Mound City National Monument, Ohio. Each covers a charnel house where cremated dead were deposited.

giving, were removed. There was much less variation in resource availability between local areas, so ample food was available closer to hand. By the same token, local leadership by talented individuals became less important.

The second hypothesis argues that any form of agriculture may increase the carrying capacity of the land, but it also brings serious risks with it, owing to variations in rainfall and other natural phenomena from one year to the next. The best strategies for minimizing such risks are those of developing food storage systems, diversifying the crops planted and growing them in different, considerably separated fields, and developing reciprocal ties with kin living outside the immediate local area. Much of Hopewell exchange may have been based initially on competition of individuals vying for prestige and success, rather than on the need to provide for mutual assistance in scarce times. Thus, goes the argument, long-distance exchange networks and personal prestige became less important as maize cultivation became more important, more intensive, and more successful.

William Dancey (1996) argues that specialized food production became common among dispersed, stable groups, of which Hopewell was one, during the first millennium B.C. More fixed territories resulted, which contained such permanent features as earthworks. Population growth resulting from the higher production rates of more specialized production sparked competition for good, arable land. This, Dancey argues, may have been the period when Hopewell ceremonialism flowered, with enormous expenditure of energy, perhaps even meant as a device to control growing population. Now larger settlements dominated the landscape. By this time, Hopewell ceremonialism had vanished, because the densely settled communities no longer needed to come together for religious observances at central places, as their more dispersed Hopewell predecessors had done.

None of these theories is fully supported by the scanty archaeological data, but only a few centuries later, between A.D. 800 and 1200, maize cultivation spread throughout eastern North America. Maize may have spread from the Southwest, in forms preadapted to high altitudes and lower temperatures, along riverine areas toward the Northeast. Midwestern twelve-row, or Chapalote, maize was known to southeastern populations by the late first millennium A.D., but it was some time before its dietary staple potential was realized in the late Woodland and Mississippian cultures of the Midwest (B. Smith, 1998). The lush floodplain of the lower Mississippi was ideal for cultivating high-yielding maize strains and, in later centuries, supported considerably denser populations.

Mississippian

Between A.D. 1 and about 450, two important cultural developments emerged in the Southeast. First, mortuary customs became far more elaborate. Second, there are signs that some individuals achieved greater social and political importance in what had been relatively egalitarian societies. These four and a half centuries saw the construction of hundreds of low, oval, or circular burial mounds throughout much of the Southeast. The burials within them varied considerably in their elaborations, a reflection of the increased social complexity that accompanied accelerating population growth, intercommunity exchange, and more intensive cultivation of native plants and, later, maize between A.D. 450 and 800. Beans arrived after the full potential of maize agriculture was realized. They had not only the advantage of a high protein value but also the asset of compensating for the amino acid deficiencies of corn. These developments were to culminate in a series of remarkable riverine cultures after A.D. 900, in the great Mississippian tradition of the South, the Southeast, and the southern Midwest (D. G. Anderson, 1994).

Mississippian
A.D. 900 to European contact

The underlying catalysts for the brilliant flowering of Mississippian culture after A.D. 1000 were, first, widespread political and religious changes that saw the appearance of important chieftains; second, the widespread adoption of maize cultivation throughout the Eastern Woodlands after A.D. 800; and, last, the efflorescence of sacred ceremonial complexes that led to the emergence of numerous powerful chiefdoms throughout the Southeast.

Major political changes began before widespread maize cultivation, with important thresholds that saw the abrupt appearance of complex chiefdoms at Cahokia and, later, at Moundville and elsewhere. Lesser chiefs must have emulated their more powerful peers in the regions between the major centers, but the sheer size and power of Cahokia and later large centers may have stunted the full historical potential of neighboring areas (D. G. Anderson, 1997). But what were the remarkable political and religious institutions that distinguished the Mississippian from its predecessors?

The term *Mississippian* defies precise definition. Bruce Smith (1992) used the term to define ancient populations living in the Eastern Woodlands from A.D. 1000 to 1500/1600 that "had a ranked form of social organization and had developed a specific complex adaptation to linear, environmentally circumscribed floodplain habitat zones." Smith's definition is flexible and allows for great differences in social organization. Another archaeologist, James Knight (1986), believes that distinctive social and religious institutions set the Mississippian apart from other cultural traditions. He argues convincingly that the religious institutions of Mississippian societies were highly distinctive, "a prevalent variety of socio-religious organization crosscutting other cultural and ecological boundaries, recognizable by virtue of shared classes of sacra [sacred artifacts]."

Chiefly Warfare Cult (the So-Called Southern Cult)   Knight envisages a pluralistic Mississippian institutionalized religion, with a chiefly cult of elite nobles based on warfare, which can be identified by exotic motifs and symbols and by costly raw materials such as seashells or imported copper. Such objects occur in elite burials, together with war axes, maces, and other weapons. These warrior symbols occur alongside other artifacts that bear exotic cosmic imagery, depicting animals, humans, and mythic beasts. This symbolic imagery bound together warfare, cosmology, and nobility into a coherent whole. Some of these categories of artifacts were used as markers of chiefly office, which varied from one location to another.

FIGURE 13.16 Southern Cult. A human effigy vessel with weeping eyes. Themes such as this link Mississippian art traditions to a wide area of the South and the Southeast.

Dozens of Mississippian cemeteries and mound centers contain finely made pottery and other artifacts associated with this chiefly cult, bearing elaborate decoration and distinctive artistic motifs. They include axes with head and shaft carved from a single piece of stone, copper pendants adorned with circles or weeping eyes, shell disks or gorgets showing woodpeckers, rattlesnakes, elaborately decorated clay pots and effigy vessels, copper plates, and engraved shell cups adorned with male figures in ceremonial dress (Figure 13.16) (Brain and Phillips, 1995).

The themes and motifs have many features in common over a vast area. Generations of archaeologists have grouped these artifact styles and art themes into a distinctive "Southern Cult," which appeared to link sites hundreds of kilometers apart and which originated in earlier centuries. The oldest art objects of any complexity found in the Eastern Woodlands are found in early and middle Woodland sites. These can be shown to have general connections with the basic themes of Southern Cult art. Such themes include widespread use of bird symbolism, "weeping eyes," and circles and crosses. They appear to have been common to all eastern societies, themes that were used, refined, and developed as new traditions and beliefs arose.

The term *Southern Cult* is probably somewhat outdated, for it reflects a complex, highly variable set of religious mechanisms that defy precise definition that supported the authority of local chieftains. (For a discussion of the cult, see Muller, 1989.)

Earth/Fertility   A second Mississippian cult, a communal earth/fertility cult, was associated with the earthen platform mounds, which may seem like unlikely religious artifacts. However, the act of rebuilding them, of adding additional layers of earth over burials, served as a symbol of renewal, which renewed the earthwork as much as it did human life. The earthen platform served as the earth, a symbolism that endured into historic times. There are historically documented connections between additions to platform mounds and the communal "green corn" ceremony, which celebrated the new harvest and the fertility of the earth. The quadrilateral, flat-topped design of many platform mounds may represent the southeastern Indian belief that the earth was a flat surface oriented toward four quarters of the world.

Ancestor Worship Still a third cult may have mediated between the two dominant ones, this one represented by well-preserved temple statuary representing both men and women kneeling in deathlike poses. Such figures occur in many Mississippian centers, among them Moundville and Spiro, as well as dozens of smaller sites. Knight believes that ethnohistorical data link such statues to ancestor cults, which were organized by temple priests, but archaeological finds add little to the ethnohistorical sources.

This triad of Mississippian cult institutions had distinctive features. The warfare cult was exclusive, confined to certain kin groups, and gave privileged rights to chiefly posts within these groups, and in its cosmological aspects serving to underpin and sanctify political power by means of chiefly rituals. In contrast, the platform mound cults were based on communal rituals that involved entire kin groups and communities who labored in their mound construction as part of ceremonies that drew on deeply felt religious beliefs common to all society, such as survived among southeastern Indians until historic times. Priests supervised ancestor cults. They were also responsible for maintaining temples, burial houses, sacred fires, and mortuary rituals. These ancestor rituals, supervised by individuals with special supernatural powers, must have intermeshed with both chiefly and communal cults, to the point that they may have mediated between different interests within society.

James Knight theorizes that the sudden expansion of the Mississippian tradition unfolded within the context of developing political and religious institutions. Newly emerging cults, which themselves developed from much earlier and simpler institutions, provided a framework of changing social forms, where coexisting cult institutions struggled constantly to assimilate ever-expanding spheres of influence by manipulating supernatural beliefs.

If Knight is correct, then the development of the Mississippian tradition was a complex process driven more by political and social changes than by economic considerations. The powerful Mississippian cults, which defined both chiefly and communal society, cut across the South and Southeast and all their different local cultural and ecological boundaries. They created a dynamic, constantly changing, and highly factionalized society. The archaeological record documents the tremendous variation in social complexity in the Mississippian culture area, with major centers like Cahokia in the so-called American Bottom near the modern city of St. Louis at one end of the spectrum and hundreds of small, local centers and minor chiefdoms at the other.

The Mississippian tradition's ultimate roots lay in much earlier Archaic and Woodland cultures that had flourished long before maize agriculture became widespread in the great river valleys of eastern North America (Cobb and Garrow, 1996). But it was the widespread cultivation of maize and beans that helped foster higher population densities and the more complex social and political organization of the centuries immediately before European contact in the sixteenth century. Most likely, the shift to maize agriculture was the result of stress largely precipitated by population pressure or the demands of elites. Such stress could easily have occurred even if plenty of land was available because the start-up labor needed to create maize gardens was much larger than that required for native plants. Begun initially to create more supplemental foods, the new agriculture transformed valley landscapes in such ways that hunting and foraging soon provided less food for the energy expended than maize cultivation. Within a short time, an entirely new economic pattern came into being.

Between A.D. 800 and 1000, there were significant changes in subsistence, material culture, trade, and settlement patterns over much of the South and the Southeast. The Mississippian people not only grew maize, squashes, and beans but also relied heavily on seasonal crops of nuts, fruits, berries, and seed-bearing plants. They hunted deer, raccoon, and turkey and took thousands of migratory waterfowl in spring and fall. Fish and waterfowl may have constituted up to 50 percent of the diet of the villagers living within the floodplain. Maize and bean agriculture now transformed many valley landscapes. Many of the culture changes of these centuries, including new pottery forms, platform mounds, and substantial rectangular houses, may have reflected the adoption of maize not only as a crop to be eaten at once but also as one to be stored for use throughout the year.

Settlements became more complex. Some were palisaded, perhaps for defense. More formal layouts included grouping houses around open plazas and mounds. Regional Mississippian societies developed in river valleys, large and small, over a large area at about the same time and interacted with one another for several centuries (Cobb and Garrow, 1996). Many Mississippian societies flourished on river valley soils fertilized by waterborne nutrients. It has always been assumed that this distribution occurred because of the availability of easily tilled soils. In fact, we know now that this restricted distribution was the result of the complex adaptation that the people developed in an area with well-defined bands of arable soils fertilized by spring floods just before planting season. They lived in valleys with many lakes and swamps, where fish trapped by receding floods were plentiful and migrating waterfowl paused to rest in spring and fall.

The process of volatile political change is best known from the great center at Cahokia, Illinois, one of North America's most spectacular sites. Sedentary villages existed at or near the Cahokia site after A.D. 600, but the huge mound-and-plaza complex we see today was built between the eleventh and thirteenth centuries (Figure 13.17). For these three centuries, a hitherto dispersed rural population was suddenly transformed into a much more tightly integrated society (Pauketat, 1994). Yet, Cahokia only held close sway over a small area of the American Bottom, an area in Illinois and Missouri that encompassed some 100 to 150 km (60 to 90 miles) from its core in the Bottom, although Cahokia-like artifacts and ideas spread much farther afield, far north in the Midwest.

The great center emerged as a regional capital with dramatic suddenness, not as a result of external trade or gradual cultural evolution but through a complicated and still little understood process of political and social negotiation that melded new political realities with the everyday lives of communities and households. Instead of early Mississippian villages, hamlets, and farmsteads, a new, three-tiered settlement hierarchy suddenly appears: a great capital at Cahokia, several smaller political and administrative centers, and rural homesteads in the northern part of the floodplain—a diverse and highly organized settlement pattern (Emerson, 1997).

(a)

(b)

FIGURE 13.17 Mississippian centers. (a) Cahokia, Illinois, as it may have appeared around A.D. 1150, at its peak. The reconstruction shows Monk's Mound and the central precincts, which were surrounded by a palisade. (b) Moundville, Alabama, another great Mississippian center, showing the central area.

Cahokia's population suddenly increased fivefold a few decades after A.D. 1050. Hundreds of people were resettled in small and large villages, even at some distance from Cahokia. This complex process, which involved political negotiations, the use of force, and carefully orchestrated integrative strategies, fostered a common interest between the center and the periphery, between chief and villager. Imposing public structures and shrines, sweat houses, common art traditions, and the promotion of carefully chosen community traditions—all may have been symbols that linked elite and commoner in displays of common cultural meanings and values that helped create a regional chiefdom that combined Cahokia's authority with ancient community interests. The result was a short-lived, imposing polity lasting a century and a half, where competing factions and periodic inabilities to mobilize community labor fashioned an inherently unstable chiefdom that appeared and dissipated with bewildering speed. After A.D. 1100, Cahokia's population gradually tapered off over the next century and a half, as people migrated outward from the American Bottom, and a more dispersed settlement pattern again prevailed.

Cahokia was briefly a magnificent capital. At the height of its power, between A.D. 1050 and 1250, Cahokia extended over an area of more than 13 sq. km (5 sq. miles) (Milner, 1998; Pauketat, 2004, 2010; Pauketat and Emerson, 1997). Some 800 ha (2,000 acres) of this vast area were covered with dwellings, housing perhaps as many as 16,000 people, although others argue for much smaller numbers. The inhabitants lived in pole-and-thatch houses clustered along a central east–west ridge. Several residences per hectare was the rule, the same building site being used again and again over the generations. The dwellings varied greatly in size, perhaps a reflection of different social status. They may have been grouped in clusters, each associated with mound and plaza complexes, subdivisions of the community.

The Cahokia people erected more than 100 earthen mounds over the centuries, mounds of various sizes, shapes, and functions in an apparently carefully planned layout. Most of them cluster along the central ridge of the site, the driest higher ground in the vicinity. They are grouped around a series of what must have been open plazas. The most extensive grouping is around Monk's Mound, the largest earthwork built by the ancient North Americans.

Monk's Mound was built on four levels starting before A.D. 1000 and ending some three centuries later. The mound is 30.4 m (100 feet) high, measures 316 by 240 m (1,037 by 790 feet), and covers 6.4 ha (16 acres). The builders, probably teams of villagers supervised by expert moundbuilders, heaped up more than 614,478 cu m (21,700,000 cu feet) of earth in baskets to erect this vast tumulus. The entire earthwork would have taken a theoretical 370,000 workdays to complete, with additional days for contouring and finishing the mound. The mound was built in several stages, with a large thatched structure on the summit.

Some of the largest Cahokia mounds lie in two rows on either side of Monk's Mound with a central 19-ha (47-acre) plaza area immediately to the south. Most of these were platform mounds, flat-topped earthworks where important public buildings or elite residences of pole and thatch lay. Excavators believe that charnel houses once stood on some of the Cahokia mounds, where the dead were exposed while their flesh decayed and before their bones were interred. A large log palisade with watchtowers and gates surrounded the entire 80.9 ha (200 acres) of the central area, perhaps to isolate Monk's Mound and other ceremonial structures and high-status individuals from commoners. The defensive wall was rebuilt at least four times in a similar style to those found at other centers—the result of serious factional conflict in the region.

During Cahokia's heyday, some individuals enjoyed high social status, living in large houses and being buried in great splendor. There is striking evidence for elaborate burial customs in Mound 72 at Cahokia. Melvin Fowler (1997) records a male burial laid out on a platform of 20,000 shell beads. This was an important man, for he was accompanied by three high-status men and women buried nearby. About 800 arrowheads, copper and mica sheets, and 15 polished stone disks used in a spear-throwing game lay with these skeletons, perhaps those of close relatives sacrificed at the funeral. Nearby were the bodies of four men with their heads and hands cut off. More than 50 young women aged between 18 and 23 were buried in a pit close by. Fowler suspects they were strangled to death.

Much of Cahokia's power came not only from compelling ideologies but also from a highly centralized economy, where foodstuffs and communal labor were appropriated by the elite. Most of the prestigious objects manufactured at the site were made from local materials for domestic use. Few of them were exported to distant locations. Cahokia's leaders achieved dominance by appropriating everything to themselves, including ideology, in what can be described as a "centrifugal process" (Pauketat, 2010). During the thirteenth century, this centrally controlled chiefdom fell apart. Cahokia's demise is still little understood, but it was probably as much political as economic, because other major and competing centers arose elsewhere.

At the height of their powers, Cahokia, Moundville, Etowah, Georgia, and other Mississippian centers formed large, complex chiefdoms, ruled by high-status individuals of great political, social, and religious influence. Increasing control of long-distance exchange, especially in exotic, prestigious goods, and the use of this wealth to control local labor may have been important catalysts for political change. There is every indication that Mississippian chiefs used the exotic, and highly valuable, objects they received from outside as symbols of their legitimacy, of their special relationship to supernatural powers that were theirs alone to control. This form of ideological governance is vulnerable to the uncontrollable forces of long-distance exchange, so stability was achieved by linking the exotic objects used in major ceremonies with ceremonial architecture and with landownership. Thus, the great earthworks of Cahokia, Moundville, and other centers were a way, albeit an inherently unstable way, of fostering bonds between the people and the elite, between one community and another.

Under these circumstances, Mississippian chiefdoms were fragile institutions, the end products of a constant process of balancing economic interdependence, ideology, and force. These chiefdoms were in a constant state of change; as centers of power changed, some chiefdoms collapsed, and others nearby rose in their place. Local and regional conditions changed frequently, fueled by the competitive political dynamics that are so characteristic of chiefdoms everywhere—societies with few high-status positions.

The Mississippian was no political and social monolith, with important rulers maintaining absolute authority over vast areas of the Midwest and South. Rather, hundreds of local societies, large and small, fall under the general category "Mississippian." They enjoyed an infinite variety of local subsistence patterns, which exploited a very diverse resource base, and varied greatly in their dependence on maize and bean agriculture. Long-distance exchange networks brought a degree of cultural continuity to the entire vast area, and there was some common religious tradition among many of them, reflected in widely used art styles and abiding ritual symbolism. The people lived under dozens of chiefdoms, large and small, many of them virtually egalitarian, and others, like Cahokia, highly complex, powerful political and social units. But these complex chiefdoms still depended heavily on kin ties and notions of reciprocity to function properly. With their regular feasts and elaborate ceremonies, Mississippian chiefs validated their authority in vivid, symbolic ways, well aware that their power depended on a fine line between coercion and reciprocity and on the balance of the powerful cults that underpinned human existence over wide areas.

Most great Mississippian centers were past the height of their powers by the time European traders and explorers reached the Mississippi Valley. Cahokia declined, then was abandoned by A.D. 1500, even though Moundville may still have been an important center (Knight and Steponaitis, 1998). Numerous chiefdoms still flourished in the mid-South and the Southeast right up to European contact and beyond, some of which, like the Coosa, were visited by conquistador Hernando de Soto during his journey across the Southeast in 1540 to 1542 (M. T. Smith, 1987). There are grounds to suspect, however, that smallpox and other diseases had spread among the peoples of the interior before the arrival of the Spaniards, weakening and decimating Mississippian society (Ramenofsky, 1987).

In 1720, French explorer Le Page du Pratz spent some time among the Natchez people of the Mississippi Valley. He found himself in a rigidly stratified society—divided into nobles and commoners and headed by a chieftain known as the Great Sun—whose members lived in a village of nine houses and a temple built on the summit of an earthen mound. Pratz witnessed the funeral of the Great Sun. His wives, relatives, and servants were drugged, then clubbed to accompany him in death (Swanton, 1911). Pratz was the first and only European to witness a Mississippian funeral, for epidemics of smallpox and other exotic diseases had already caused the fabric of this most complex of North American societies to fall apart. The Natchez were not the only Mississippian survivors, but within two centuries of the arrival of de Soto, the last vestiges of Mississippian society had been submerged.

Human Settlement in the Caribbean

On October 14, 1492, Christopher Columbus, Admiral of the Ocean Sea, landed on San Salvador island in the Bahamas. There he encountered small numbers of Taíno people, whom he named "Indios," Indians, in the mistaken belief that he had landed in eastern Asia, the "East Indies." Within a few generations, the Taíno were decimated by exotic diseases like smallpox and by ruthless exploitation by gold-hungry conquistadors and settlers. Today, the Caribbean is one of the most ethnically diverse regions on earth, a melting pot not only of indigenous people but also of immigrants from Europe, Africa, and all parts of the Americas (S. Wilson, 2001).

Columbus described the Taíno as gentle, good-looking people with a simple way of life. They were farmers and fishers—the inhabitants of the Bahamas being outliers of much denser, socially more complex groups in the Greater Antilles (Cuba and what the Spaniards called Hispaniola, now the Dominican Republic and Haiti, Jamaica, and Puerto Rico). By 1514, the consequences of Spanish colonization reduced a Taíno population perhaps numbering in the millions to a few thousand.

First Settlement (Preceramic Cultures)

The earliest traces of human occupation occur in Cuba, the Dominican Republic, and Haiti (the western Greater Antilles) and date to between 4000 and 3500 B.C. Small numbers of immigrants brought with them a simple stone tool technology based on a fine quality chert. They found good toolmaking stone in their new homeland, and made their living by hunting, fishing, and plant gathering, just as they had on the mainland. Most likely, the first islanders came from the Yucatán Peninsula, where similar stone artifacts are reported from sites in Belize, but their place of origin is still the subject of debate (S. Wilson et al., 1998) (Figure 13.18).

4000 to 3500 B.C.

The Greater Antilles lacked many of the animals and plants of the mainland, so the newcomers had to adjust their subsistence strategies to new environmental realities. Unfortunately, we know little about these early cultures, which are largely known from stone tool scatters. The immigrant population grew; by 2000 B.C., differences in stone tool assemblages provide indications of different regional cultures. By now, some groups had settled on Puerto Rico and in the eastern Caribbean, taking with them a technology based on both flaked and ground stone, the latter producing axes, bowls, and some carvings (Rouse, 1992).

2000 B.C.

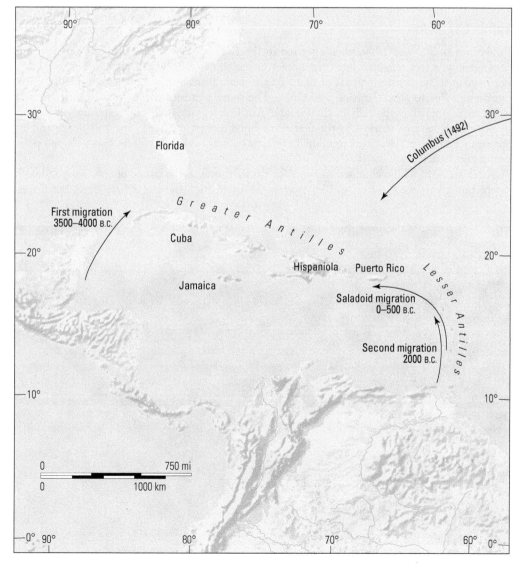

FIGURE 13.18 Human settlement in the Caribbean.

By about the same time, different immigrants from South America moved into the Lesser Antilles and as far north as Puerto Rico. They were collectors and fishers, settling mainly on island coasts and using mainly fiber and wood artifacts that no longer survive, together with axes made from stone and the thick portions of conch shells. These groups were expert seafarers who moved freely from island to island (Rouse, 1992). Over the centuries, they developed an elaborate technology based on ground stone axes and interacted with people of different cultural traditions in the Greater Antilles.

The entire Preceramic, or Archaic, period of Caribbean prehistory is still largely a blank on the historical map.

Saladoid Migrations

Saladoid migrations
500 B.C. to A.D. 100

In the last five centuries B.C., immigrants from the Orinoco Basin and adjacent parts of South America crossed into the Lesser Antilles and settled as far north as Puerto Rico. Unlike their predecessors, the Saladoid people, named after a Venezuelan site named Saladero, lived in larger, permanent settlements. They made highly distinctive white-on-red painted and incised pottery that enables us to trace what may have been a series of separate migrations from the southern mainland between 500 B.C. and A.D. 100 by people who moved from island to island, often without staying in one place for a long period of time.

After 100 B.c., more permanent Saladoid occupation took hold throughout the Lesser Antilles and on Puerto Rico. We know these people cultivated cassava and other South American crops, while relying heavily on game and fish. They dwelled in sizable villages of large pole-and-thatch huts, located some distance from one another (Siegel, 1989). In the north, Saladoid communities interacted with Preceramic groups for several centuries.

Taíno Chiefdoms

Between A.D. 500 and 1000, people settled in the Bahamas for the first time. Populations grew considerably, a fact reflected in many more archaeological sites, which appear, however, to have been occupied for shorter periods of time. At the same time, village farmers occupied the upland interiors of Puerto Rico, Jamaica, and Cuba. The same centuries witnessed a significant increase in social complexity, especially in the Greater Antilles, where larger political units now appeared by the eighth century, marked by the first stone-lined ceremonial plazas and ball courts and by the appearance of more elaborate ceremonial artifacts such as basketry, objects that reflected personal power and status.

Taíno
A.D. 500 to 1000

After A.D. 700, Taíno chiefdoms appear for the first time, as the tempo of economic and political interaction across the Greater Antilles accelerated. Interaction there may have been, but it was not

FIGURE 13.19 A Taíno ball court. Caguana Indian Ceremonial Park, Puerto Rico.

reflected in cultural homogeneity. Rather, a great diversity of cultures and languages flourished throughout the islands, among them the descendants of earlier Preceramic peoples. Both Archaic and Salodoid cultural traditions added much to the brilliantly expressive culture of the Taíno. Archaeologist Samuel Wilson (1993) has aptly described the Caribbean of the day as a cultural mosaic, with the north densely populated until European contact and the Lesser Antilles in a constant state of cultural flux, with a significant loss of population after 1200 A.D.

By the fifteenth century, the Taíno of the north lived in large villages, some of them with thousands of inhabitants, linked in larger chiefdoms of 70 or more communities. There were at least five large chiefdoms on Hispaniola and many smaller ones, ruled by chiefs of high status who were carried in litters or on the backs of servants. Elite men and women wore gold ornaments and elaborate costumes of woven cotton adorned with beads, bone, and feathers. Interestingly, women enjoyed high status, for descent was through the female line.

These elaborate chiefdoms depended on manioc and fishing, with dried fish being transported far inland. The Taíno were constantly on the move, traveling from island to island in large, oceangoing canoes, some capably transporting heavy cargoes or as many as a hundred people (S. Wilson, 1990). Chiefdoms fought with one another, or came together for elaborate ceremonies and ball games in courts and plazas that sometimes lay on the boundaries between neighboring polities (Figure 13.19).

This dramatic cultural explosion expressed itself in elaborate ceremonialism, in magnificent beadwork, ceramics, weaving, and woodworking. Taíno art reflected an ancient tradition of shamanism combined with elaborate mythology, inherited from Saladoid and Central American roots (S. Wilson, 2001). A diverse environment, constant trading and interaction, and rich ceremonial traditions came together in a dynamic political and social environment that was unique in the ancient Americas (Figure 13.20).

All of this ended dramatically with the arrival of the Spaniards, whose harsh tribute demands and labor practices disrupted the subsistence economy. Famine and exotic diseases destroyed the Taíno chiefdoms of 1492 within a decade. The islanders of the Lesser Antilles became the target of rapacious slavers, but survived the onslaught of infectious diseases more successfully. Mobile, they melted away in their canoes before European visitors in their canoes and attacked at will, effectively preventing colonial settlement for over a century. From Colombus's day, they became known as Caribs, with a reputation for fierceness, even cannibalism, playing an important role, as allies and enemies, in the colonization of the Lesser Antilles. Their descendants live in the islands to this day.

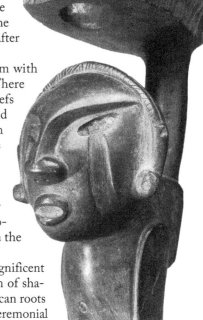

FIGURE 13.20   A wooden table made by a fifteenth-century Taíno artisan.

A.D. 1492

Summary

- Native American agriculture was based on quite different crops from those in the Old World: root crops like potatoes and sweet potatoes. Maize was the most important cereal. Because there were many fewer potential domesticates than in the Old World, domesticated animals were limited to, for example, the llama, the turkey, and the guinea fowl.

- The earliest cultivation may have begun in the humid tropical lowlands, for traces of cultivation are said to date to as early as 7000 B.C. in Panama. In drier, more open country, agriculture developed in hunter-gatherer societies that were coping with constant environmental change and unpredictable population shifts.

- At locations like Guilá Naquitz, Mexico, wet-year subsistence strategies involving deliberate planting eventually became permanent shifts in subsistence activities.

- Among the staples of Native American agriculture were beans and maize, probably domesticated from a Central American native grass called teosinte as early as 4000 B.C.

- Maize agriculture spread from southern Mexico and Guatemala thousands of miles to the north and south. The earliest domestication of maize probably occurred in the Balsas Valley area of southwestern Mexico and other tropical regions. There were farmers in the highland Andes and in coastal Peru by 3000 B.C., but maize and cotton did not become vital cultivated staples until about a thousand years later.

- Maize agriculture reached the North American Southwest by about 1500 to 2000 B.C. By 300 B.C., sedentary villages and a much greater dependence on farming were characteristic of the Southwest, leading to the emergence of the Hohokam, Mogollon, and Ancestral Pueblo cultural traditions, among which the ultimate ancestry of modern southwestern peoples lie.

- Many groups in eastern North America turned to the deliberate cultivation of native plants as food supplements after 2000 B.C., but maize and bean agriculture did not arrive from the Southwest until the first millennium B.C.

- After 1000 B.C., a series of powerful chiefdoms arose in the Southeast and the Midwest, peoples among whom elaborate burial customs and the building of burial mounds and earthworks were commonplace. The Adena tradition appeared in about 700 B.C. and was overlapped by the Hopewell in approximately A.D. 1.
- About A.D. 800, the focus of economic, religious, and political power shifted to the Mississippi Valley and the Southeast with the rise of the Mississippian tradition. This tradition, with its powerful religious and secular leaders, survived in a modified form until European contact in the sixteenth century A.D.
- The earliest traces of human settlement in the Caribbean date to between 4000 and 3500 B.C., hunter-gatherers from the Yucatán Peninsula. By 2000 B.C., people had settled throughout the Caribbean, as seafaring, Pre-ceramic immigrants, this time from South America, moved into the Lesser Antilles and as far north as Puerto Rico.
- Between 500 B.C. and A.D. 100, Saladoid people with distinctive painted pottery brought cassava and other crops to the islands. The following centuries saw the first settlement of the Bahamas and the development of Taíno chiefdoms after A.D. 700, which exhibited considerable diversity and traded widely. The arrival of the Spaniards in 1492 led to the rapid destruction of these dynamic Caribbean cultures.

Key Term

kivas (275)

Further Reading

Cordell, Linda. 2009. *Prehistory of the Southwest*, 2nd ed. Walnut Creek, CA: Left Coast Press.

Fagan, Brian. 2011. *The First North Americans*. London and New York: Thames & Hudson.

Milner, George R. 2004. *The Moundbuilders*. London and New York: Thames & Hudson.

OLD WORLD CIVILIZATIONS

C. 3000 B.C. TO MODERN TIMES

Part IV deals with the beginnings of complex states and urban civilization, not only in Southwest Asia but also in lesser-known parts of the world, such as Africa and Southeast Asia. Research in Africa and Asia has hardly begun; future excavations in these regions are likely to throw significant new light on such much-debated issues as the importance of ceremonial centers and long-distance trade in the emergence of complex societies. The reader is urged to start with the theoretical background in Chapter 14 before embarking on the narrative cultural history in subsequent chapters.

Old World Civilizations

| Period already covered | Partial coverage |
| Period covered in **Part IV** |

| 5 mya | 2.5 mya | 1 mya | 150,000 B.P. | 10000 B.C. | A.D. 1 | A.D. 1500 |

FIG. 2.2   FIG. 3.1a   FIG. 4.9   FIG. 9.5   FIG. 14.3

14 The Development of Civilization

aul Émile Botta was appointed the French consul in Mosul in northern Iraq in 1840, with one official objective: to dig the nearby mounds of biblical Nineveh. Botta had no archaeological qualifications whatsoever, except that he was an experienced traveler who spoke several western Asian languages. At first he dug fruitlessly into Nineveh, finding nothing but inscribed bricks. Then one of his workers told him of similar bricks that formed the chimney of his house at a village named Khorsabad, 23 km (14 miles) away. To get rid of the man, he sent two of his laborers to investigate. A week later, they returned with stories of richly carved walls adorned with strange animals. Botta leaped on his horse and rode to Khorsabad, where he gasped at the curious bas-reliefs in the walls of the small pit—of bearded men in long gowns, winged animals, and wild beasts. He moved his excavations to Khorsabad. Within a few weeks, he had uncovered room after room of sculpted limestone slabs, the wall decorations of a magnificent, exotic royal palace. "I believe myself to be the first who had discovered sculptures which with some reason can be referred to the period when Nineveh was flourishing," he wrote excitedly of the palace (Fagan, 2007: 102). ■

The Sphinx, with Khufu's Pyramid at Giza in the background.

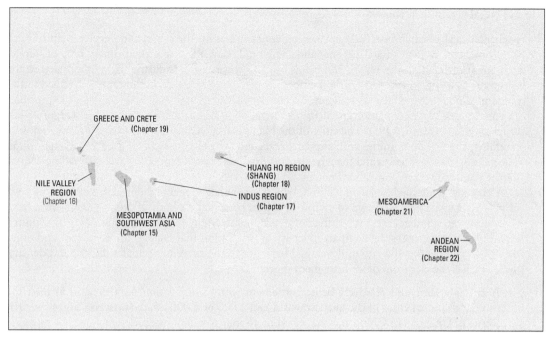

FIGURE 14.1 Locations of major preindustrial states described in this book.

We know now that Botta had uncovered not Nineveh but Assyrian King Sargon's palace, constructed at great expense in the eighth century B.C. Even so, Botta's remarkable discoveries ushered in a classical era of nineteenth-century archaeology. Archaeologists revealed to an astonished world not only the Assyrians but, in addition, the Sumerians, the Maya, the Minoans, the Mycenaeans, and other hitherto-unknown civilizations (Figure 14.1). Today, there are no more unknown civilizations to be unearthed, but archaeologists are still striving to understand the origins and workings of the world's earliest states. In this chapter, we review some of the attempts to explain their beginnings.

Civilization

Everyone who has studied the prehistory of human society agrees that the emergence of civilization in different parts of the world was a major event in human adaptation. The word *civilization* has a familiar meaning for us. It implies "civility," a measure of decency in the behavior of the individual. Such definitions inevitably reflect ethnocentrism or value judgments because what is "civilized" behavior in one civilization may be antisocial or baffling in another. This simplistic meaning is of no use to students of prehistoric civilizations seeking basic definitions and cultural processes (Scarre and Fagan, 2003).

Today, archaeologists use the term *civilization* as shorthand for urbanized, state-level societies. Those described in these pages are sometimes called preindustrial civilizations, because they relied on manual labor rather than fossil fuels such as coal. There are many variations among the preindustrial civilizations, but the following features are characteristic of them all:

- Societies based on cities, with large, very complex social organizations. The preindustrial civilization was invariably based on a larger territory, such as the Nile Valley, as opposed to smaller areas owned by individual kin groups (Schwartz and Falconer, 1994; Stein and Rothman, 1994).

- Economies based on the centralized accumulation of capital and social status through tribute and taxation. For instance, the Sumerian kings in Mesopotamia monopolized trading activity in the name of the state. This type of economy allows the support of hundreds, often thousands, of non-food producers, such as smiths and priests. Long-distance trade and a division of labor, as well as craft specialization, are often characteristics of early civilizations.

- Advances toward formal record keeping, science, and mathematics, as well as some form of written script. Such advances took many forms, from Egyptian hieroglyphs to the knotted strings used by the Inca of the Andes.

- Impressive public buildings and monumental architecture, like Khmer or Maya ceremonial centers and Roman temples.

- Some form of all-embracing state religion in which the ruler played a leading role. The Khmer of Cambodia considered their leaders living gods. Such kings lived in great palaces built as depictions of the symbolic Hindu world (Higham, 2002).

Cities

Archaeological research into early civilization concentrates on the origin and development of both state-organized societies (civilizations) and the city. Today, the city is the primary type of human settlement throughout the world, and it has become so since the Industrial Revolution altered the economic face of the globe. The earliest cities assumed many forms, from the compact, walled settlement of Mesopotamia to the Mesoamerican ceremonial center, with a core population in its precincts and a scattered rural population in villages arranged over the surrounding landscape (Figure 14.2) (Nichols and Charlton, 1995). The cities of the Harappan civilization of the Indus River region were carefully planned communities with regular streets and assigned quarters for different living groups. The palaces of the Minoans and the Mycenaeans functioned as secular economic and trading centers for the scattered village populations nearby.

A **city** can be defined by its population, which is generally larger and denser than that of a town or village. A generally used rule of thumb is a lower population limit of 5,000 people for a large city. However, numbers are not a sufficient determinant: Many people can congregate in a limited area and still not possess the compact diversity of population that enables the economic and organizational complexity of a city to develop. This complexity, as well as population size and density, distinguishes the city from other settlement types:

- A city is a large and relatively dense settlement, with a population numbered in at least the thousands. Small cities of the ancient world had 2,000 or 3,000 inhabitants; the largest, such as Rome or Changan in China, may have had more than a million people.
- Cities are also characterized by specialization and interdependence between the city and its rural hinterland and between specialist craftspeople and other groups within the city. The city is a central place in its region, providing services for the villages of the surrounding area, at the same time depending on those villages for food. Most ancient cities, for example, had a marketplace where agricultural produce could be exchanged.
- Cities also have a degree of organizational complexity well beyond that of small farming communities. There are centralized institutions to regulate internal affairs and to ensure security. These usually find expression in monumental architecture such as temples or palaces or, sometimes, a city wall. Here we must recognize an overlap between the concept of the city and the concept of the state. States, too, are characterized by centralized institutions. It may be possible to have states without cities, but it is hard to envisage a city that is not embedded within a state.

An ancient city site is usually obvious to archaeologists, both from its size and from the scale of its remains. The state is more difficult to define. It is a political unit governed by a central authority whose power crosscuts bonds of kinship. Kin groups do not disappear, of course, but their power is reduced, and a new axis of control emerges based on allegiance to a ruling elite.

FIGURE 14.2 The mud-brick ruins of the Sumerian city of Nippur, southern Iraq.

A great deal of new research using aerial photography, remote sensing, and ethnoarchaeology, as well as archaeological survey and excavation, is producing new data on population densities and early urban settlement. Recent fieldwork has also concentrated on agriculture and herding systems that fed early cities, as well as craft production and exchange (see a summary in Stein, 2001).

Six Classic Theories of the Emergence of States

As we saw in Chapter 1, explanations of human culture change have moved far beyond the ladderlike evolutionary schemes of a century ago. Today's scholars tend to stress social and political organization, to speak of "states" and "complex societies" in contrast to simpler human societies. With its emphasis on the study of culture change and with its long-time perspective, archaeology lies at the very core of the study of early civilization.

Few developments in world prehistory have generated as much theoretical debate as the origins of states. These controversies rage in the context of six early and well-established theoretical models for the rise of state-organized societies.

V. Gordon Childe and the "Urban Revolution"

The Victorians, like the Greeks and the Romans before them, assumed that civilization had originated along the Nile, in the "Land of the Pharaohs"—this in spite of the discovery, in the 1870s, of the Sumerian civilization in Mesopotamia. Eventually, early theorizing took in a broader canvas, embracing all of Southwest Asia. In the 1920s, American archaeologist James Breasted coined the enduring phrase the **Fertile Crescent**, a curve of territory encompassing the Nile and Jordan valleys and the uplands of Iran and lower Mesopotamia. The Fertile Crescent was the cradle of early civilization, of the first complex societies in the world (Scarre and Fagan, 2003).

Australian-born archaeologist V. Gordon Childe formulated the first relatively sophisticated theories about the origins of civilization. Childe (1936, 1952) claimed that an **Urban Revolution** followed on the "Neolithic Revolution," which witnessed the beginnings of farming. He theorized that this second revolution saw the development of metallurgy and the appearance of a new social class of full-time artisans and specialists who lived in much larger settlements: cities. Among the Sumerians of Mesopotamia, for example, Childe believed that the new specialists were fed by surpluses raised by peasant farmers. But the artisans' products had to be distributed, and raw materials obtained, often from long distances. Both needs reduced the self-sufficiency of peasant communities, Childe argued. Agricultural techniques became more sophisticated as a higher yield of food per capita was needed to support a growing nonagricultural population. Irrigation increased productivity, leading to the centralization of food supplies and of production and distribution. Taxation and tribute led to the accumulation of capital. Ultimately, said Childe, a new class-stratified society came into being, based on economic classes rather than traditional ties of kin. Writing was essential for keeping records and for developing exact and predictive sciences. Transportation by land and water was part of the new order. A unifying religious force dominated urban life as priest-kings and despots rose to power. Monumental architecture testified to their activities.

Childe considered technology and the development of craft specialization in the hands of full-time artisans a cornerstone of Urban Revolution. A half-century later, most archaeologists associate craft specialization with cultural complexity, to the point where they equate the appearance of specialist artisans with the formation of states. Thus, goes the argument, evidence of increased levels of craft specialization thereafter indicates even further cultural complexity. Many scholars challenge this perspective. They point out that craft specialization is a feature of many more egalitarian societies. Many chiefs, ruling over chiefdoms large and small, patronized specialists with unusual expertise, who produced prestige goods and artifacts, such as canoes. Another theory considers craft specialization the fate of peasant farmers disfranchised from their lands as states expanded and cities grew.

John Clark and William Parry (1990) tested these theories against a sample of data from societies living in widely contrasting environments and with very different cultural institutions. Craft specialization is common in both chiefdoms and states, but these researchers doubt from their studies that it was a major factor in the development of civilization, although there was a strong correlation between full-time craft specialization and civilization. They are intrigued by the possibility that craft specialization supported by the elite was crucial to the emergence of states, for it is associated with rank and may have been a major factor in the acquisition of economic power outside the confines of the kin system. They believe that patronizing artisans was one way to acquire social prestige and rank, as well as wealth, through production and exchange with other communities, as may have happened along the Nile. Craft specialization was not, in itself, a major cause of civilization, but it may have laid a foundation for more permanent investments in what eventually became inheritable wealth, a major feature of civilizations.

Childe's Urban Revolution enjoyed widespread popularity between the 1930s and 1950s. It was a logical synthesis of complex events when relatively little was known about early Southwest Asian civilizations, and even less about complex states in China, South Asia, and the Americas. But the revolution hypothesis has serious flaws. For example, craft specialization is more a sign than a cause of state formation, and it is not unique to civilizations. Furthermore, predicating state and city formation on surplus production does not explain why surpluses came about in the first place.

Robert Adams and other Mesopotamian archaeologists argued in the 1960s that the term *Urban Revolution* implies undue emphasis on the city at the expense of social change, that is, the development of social classes and political institutions. Adams (1966) pointed out that both early Mesopotamian and early American civilizations followed a basically similar course of development in which the communal control of land by kin groups gave way to the growth of private estates owned by noble families. The eventual result was a stratified form of social organization rigidly divided along class lines.

Ecology and Irrigation

Most scholars now agree that three elements of Childe's Urban Revolution were of great importance in the development of all the world's early civilizations: large food surpluses, diversified farming economies, and irrigation agriculture. Early ecological theories revolved around three broad themes:

The Ecological Potential of River Floodplains   Floodplains have rich, fertile soils. James Breasted's Fertile Crescent hypothesis assumed that the exceptional fertility of the Mesopotamian floodplain and the Nile Valley was the primary cause for the appearance of cities and states in these regions. Larger grain surpluses, as well as social and culture changes, resulted from increased agricultural efficiency and abundant fish (Figure 14.3). The extra food supported nonfood producers, such as artisans, priests, and traders, new classes of society that were the backbone of state-organized societies.

Some scholars, among them economist Ester Boserup (1965), took the opposite tack. They believed that population growth, not food surplus, was the incentive for intensified agriculture and eventually more complex societies. Following Boserup, others have argued that more lasting field agriculture, like that in early Mesopotamia or along the banks of the Nile River, where annual floods inundated the fields, tended to be more intensive and to exploit the environment in a more ordered and systematic way (Spooner, 1972). It created conditions in which more settlements per square mile could exist on foods whose annual yields were at least roughly predictable. The more specialized ecosystems created by these efforts supported more concentrated, rapidly growing populations and, thus, civilization. But though important, dense populations did not characterize all state-organized societies, as the Mycenaean and Inca civilizations illustrate.

The Ecological Diversity of Local Environments   Differences in altitude, access to food and other resources, and soil fertility varied greatly from one area to another. Diversified agricultural economies tended to focus on fewer, more productive crops, but the ultimate subsistence base remained wide.

FIGURE 14.3 Ancient Egyptian workers busy at a variety of tasks.

The Egyptians farmed wheat and barley on a large scale, but also raised large herds of cattle and goats, for example. The earliest civilizations in the Old World and the New World were certainly based on complex subsistence patterns that integrated several ecological zones. For instance, the highland Andean states relied heavily on their lowland neighbors for fish meal, cotton, and other resources. The Harappans of the Indus Valley may have exchanged cotton for semiprecious stones, while highland and lowland Mesoamerican civilizations depended on one another for all manner of commodities, foodstuffs, and artifacts. The resulting diversity of food resources protected the people against famine and stimulated trade and exchange for food and other products, as well as the growth of distributive organizations that encouraged centralized authority. Under these circumstances, a local center might control products from several nearby ecological zones, giving it a vital hedge for managing and controlling food surpluses against crop failure and famine.

The Adoption of Irrigation Agriculture Irrigation agriculture was a major factor in the rise of civilizations because it supported far higher population densities. Early ecological theories were closely tied to the apparently widespread use of irrigation agriculture by early states to enhance agricultural output. The intensification of agriculture implies a major modification of the environment, which usually means irrigation: the development of canals and other works for storing water and irrigating fields during dry months. Irrigation theories were popular half a century ago, when anthropologist Julian Steward and historian Karl Wittfogel argued during the 1950s that irrigation lay behind the development of socially stratified societies in Egypt, Mesopotamia, and elsewhere, which Wittfogel famously called "hydraulic civilizations" (Figure 14.4) (Steward et al., 1955; Wittfogel, 1957). In areas where irrigation was practiced, both scholars argued, the relationship between the environment, food production, and social institutions was identical.

Wittfogel, a Chinese specialist, argued that early Asian civilizations became mighty "hydraulic bureaucracies," which owed their despotic control over densely populated areas like China, Egypt, and India to the technological and environmental demands required by large-scale water-control projects in areas of scant rainfall. The state bureaucracy controlled the labor forces that built hydraulic works and maintained them. Thus, the social requirements of irrigation led to the development of states and urban societies in several parts of the Old World. And the same requirements led to remarkable similarities in their economic and social structure.

FIGURE 14.4 Irrigated fields in modern-day southern Iraq.

Wittfogel's arguments were originally formulated in the 1920s and were refined over more than 30 years, during which a mass of new data, including large-scale landscape surveys, sharpened our perceptions of early irrigation. For example, archaeologist Robert Adams carried out major field surveys of ancient irrigation works in Mesopotamia in the 1960s. Adams found that early Mesopotamian irrigation consisted of cleaning natural river channels and building only a few smaller feeder canals (R. Adams, 1981; R. Adams and Nissen, 1972). Most settlements lay near major rivers and made the most of the natural hydrology of the waterways. Each community controlled its own small-scale irrigation works (T. J. Wilkinson, 2003). Only centuries later did a highly centralized state government organize irrigation schemes on a massive scale. The same was true in Egypt, where the greatest irrigation works were undertaken during the New Kingdom, using thousands of laborers fulfilling tax obligations to the state (Butzer, 1976). In contrast, early Egyptian agriculture had relied on natural basins to hold back the Nile water—a village-level, small-scale operation requiring no official supervision. Large-scale irrigation requires constant maintenance and supervision, to say nothing of political stability and the control of water sources (Scarborough, 2003). For example, the Chimor state on the Peruvian coast was overthrown by the expanding Inca Empire, partly through the latter's acquiring control of the watersheds that fed coastal irrigation schemes (Moseley, 2000) (see Chapter 22).

Although some form of irrigation was a necessary precondition for the settlement of the southern Mesopotamian plains, where the world's first cities arose, large-scale irrigation does not everywhere appear to have been a factor in the rise of early civilization. By the same token, modern research has shown that ecology was only one component in a mosaic of many changes that led to state-organized societies. But climate may have been of particular significance in some areas, in view of the major environmental changes, especially shifts in rainfall patterns and rising sea levels, which affected the world during post–Ice Age global warming.

Technology and Trade

The origins and evolution of complex societies have long been linked to technological innovation and to growing trade in raw materials like obsidian (volcanic glass used for stone tools, mirrors, and ornaments) and copper and in luxuries of all kinds. Gordon Childe considered metallurgy an important component in his Urban Revolution, but in fact, copper and other exotic materials were at first used in Southwest Asia for the small-scale production of cult objects and jewelry. In many cases, the technological innovations that did appear, like the wheel in Mesopotamia and the sailing ship in Egypt, were of more benefit in transportation than in production. Not until several centuries after civilization started were copper and bronze more abundant, as demands for transportation and military needs burgeoned. Technology did evolve, but only in response to developing markets, new demands, and the expanded needs of a tiny segment of the population: the elite. Trade developed as local communities exchanged basic commodities on an increasingly large scale. The exchange of luxury goods also played an important part. It is important to note that the nature of trade changed constantly, for elites often used prestigious trade goods as a means to maintain their status and power. In other words, they redefined prestige goods for their own ends (see a summary and references in Stein, 2001).

Any form of trade involves two elements: the goods and commodities being exchanged and the people doing the exchanging. People make trade connections when they need to acquire goods and services that are not available to them within their local area. This trade (more conventionally called an **exchange system**) may be gift giving, the exchange of gifts that reinforces a social relationship between both individuals and groups as a whole. The gifts serve as gestures that place obligations on both parties and are often a preliminary to bartering for all manner of commodities. This kind of preliminary **gift exchange** is still commonplace in New Guinea and the Pacific and was widespread in Africa during the past 2,000 years.

Bartering, the exchange of commodities or goods, was another basic trading mechanism for many thousands of years, often sporadic, and usually based on notions of **reciprocity**: the mutual exchange of commodities or objects between individuals or groups. The **redistribution** of these goods through society lay in the hands of chiefs, religious leaders, or kin groups. As we have seen, such redistribution was a basic element in chiefdoms. The change from redistribution to an impersonal market economy trade, often based on regulated commerce and involving, perhaps, fixed prices and even currency, was a change closely tied to growing political and social complexity and, hence, to the development of the state (Figure 14.5).

FIGURE 14.5 A medieval market in Europe epitomizes the market economy of many early states.

In the 1970s, a number of archaeologists gave trade a primary role in the rise of states. In the Aegean area, British archaeologist Colin Renfrew (1972) attributed the dramatic flowering of the Minoan civilization on Crete and throughout the Aegean to intensified trading contacts and to the impact of olive and vine cultivation on local communities. As agricultural economies became more diversified and local food supplies could be purchased both locally and over longer distances, a far-reaching economic interdependence resulted. Eventually, this led to redistribution systems for luxuries and basic commodities, systems that were organized and controlled by Minoan palaces and elsewhere in the Aegean where there were major centers of olive production. As time went on, the self-sufficiency of communities was replaced by mutual dependence. Interest in long-distance trade brought about some cultural homogeneity from trade, gift exchange, and, perhaps, piracy. Thus, intensified trade and interaction, and the flowering of specialist crafts, in a complex process of positive feedback, led to much more complex societies based on palaces, which were the economic hubs of a new Minoan civilization.

Renfrew's model made some assumptions that are now discounted (see Chapter 19). For example, he argued that the introduction of domesticated vines and olives allowed a substantial expansion in the amounts of land under cultivation and helped to power the emergence of complex society. Many archaeologists and paleobotanists now question this view, pointing out that the available evidence for cultivated vines and olives suggests that they were present only in the later Bronze Age. Trade, nevertheless, was probably one of many variables that led to the emergence of palace economies in Minoan Crete.

American archaeologist William Rathje (1971) developed a hypothesis that considered an explosion in long-distance exchange a fundamental cause of Maya civilization. He suggested that the lowland Maya environment was deficient in many vital resources, among them obsidian, salt, stone for grinding maize, and many luxury materials. All these could be obtained from the nearby highlands, from the Valley of Mexico, and from other regions, if the necessary trading networks came into being. Such connections, and the trading expeditions to maintain them, could not be organized by individual villages alone. The Maya lived in a relatively uniform environment, where every community suffered from the same resource deficiencies. Thus, argued Rathje, long-distance trade networks were organized through local ceremonial centers and their leaders. In time, this organization became a state, and knowledge of its functioning was exportable, as were pottery, tropical bird feathers, specialized stone materials, and other local commodities.

Rathje's hypothesis probably explains part of the complex process of Maya state formation, but it suffers from the objection that suitable alternative raw materials can be found in the lowlands. It could be, too, that warfare became a competitive response to population growth and to the increasing scarcity of prime agricultural land, and that it played an important role in the emergence of the Maya states.

Now that we know much more about ancient exchange and commerce, we know that trade can never be looked upon as a unifying factor or as a primary cause of ancient civilization, simply because no one aspect of it was an overriding cause of culture change or evolution in trading practices (Kohl, 1978). Many ever-changing variables affected ancient trade, among them the demand for goods. This demand prompted a search for supplies, themselves a product of production above local needs. Then there were the logistics of transportation, the extent of the trading network, and also the social and political environment. Intricate market networks channeled supplies along well-defined routes. Authorities at both ends might regulate the profits fed back to the source, providing the incentive for further transactions. There may or may not have been a market organization. Extensive long-distance trade, like large-scale irrigation, was a consequence rather than a cause of civilization.

Warfare

Robert Carneiro (1970) used the archaeology of coastal valleys in Peru to argue that warfare played a key role in state formation. His "coercive theory" of state origins argued that the amount of agricultural land in these valleys was limited and surrounded by desert. So a series of predictable events led to the development of states. At first, autonomous farming villages flourished in the valley landscape. But as the population grew and more land was taken up, the communities started fighting over land and raided each other's fields as they competed for limited acreage. Some of the village leaders emerged as successful warlords, became chieftains, and presided over large tribal polities. The valley population continued to grow, and warfare intensified until the entire region fell under the sway of a single, successful warrior, who presided over a single state centered on the valley. Then, this ambitious ruler and his successors started raiding neighboring valleys. Eventually a multivalley state developed, creating a much larger civilization.

Carneiro's theory is hard to test in the field, but an attempt to do so in Peru's Santa Valley showed no sign of autonomous villages. Rather, it depicted a much more complex, evolving settlement pattern over many centuries. Archaeologist David Wilson (1983) points out that the only "coercive" processes came about in about A.D. 400, when the Moche people carved out a multivalley state by their military conquest of neighboring valleys (see Chapter 22). The conquest took place long after complex irrigation-based societies flourished in the Santa Valley. As with irrigation hypotheses, reality is more complex than the straightforward Carneiro scenario. Some of Carneiro's ideas on state formation have formed a basis for more sophisticated theories of the 1990s (see next section).

Cultural Systems and Civilization

Most archaeologists agree that urban life and preindustrial civilization came into existence gradually, during a period of major social and economic change. Everyone also agrees that linear explanations rooted in irrigation, trade, or warfare are inadequate. Recent theories of the rise of states invoke multiple, and often intricate, causes and are frequently based on systems models.

In the 1960s, Robert Adams, an expert on ancient Mesopotamia, introduced a new generation of complex theories when he argued (1966) that irrigation agriculture, increased warfare, and "local resource variability" were three factors vital in the newly appearing urban civilizations. Each affected society and the other factors with positive feedback, helping to reinforce each other. The creation of food surpluses and the emergence of a stratified society were critical developments. Irrigation agriculture could feed a bigger population. Larger populations, an increase in permanent settlement, and trade with regular centers for redistributing goods were all pressures for greater production and increased surpluses, actively fostered by the dominant groups in society. The greatly enlarged surpluses enabled those who controlled them to employ larger numbers of artisans and other specialists, who did not themselves grow crops.

Adams argued that some societies were better able to transform themselves into states because of the variety of resources on which they could draw. Higher populations led to monopolies over strategic resources. These communities eventually became more powerful than their neighbors, expanding their territories by military campaigns and efficiently exploiting their advantages over other peoples. Such cities also became early centers of major religious activities, of technological and artistic innovations, and of writing. Literacy, a skill confined to a few people, became an important source of power (Robinson, 2007).

Archaeologists like Kent Flannery (1972), who was working in Mesoamerica, now saw the state as a very complicated "living" system, the complexity of which could be measured by the internal differentiation and intricacy of its subsystems, such as those for agriculture, technology, or religious beliefs (Figure 14.6). The way these subsystems were linked and the controls that society imposed on the system were vital. This model seemed to work well with Mesoamerican states, where pervasive religious beliefs formed close links between public architecture, the economy, and other subsystems of civilization.

The management of a state is far more elaborate and central an undertaking than that of a small chiefdom (R. Adams, 2001). Indeed, the most striking difference between states and less complicated societies is the degree of complexity in civilizations' ways of reaching decisions and their hierarchical organization, not necessarily in their subsistence activities. Systems models of early states are bound to be complex, for they have to distinguish between the mechanisms and processes of culture change and the socioenvironmental pressures by which we have sought to explain the origins of civilization (Redman, 1978). Religion and control of information now appear to be key elements in the regulation of environmental and economic variables in early civilizations and, indeed, in any human society.

Environmental Change

Ecologically based theories, which also rely heavily on systems approaches, have enjoyed a relatively long life compared with many other hypotheses. For example, in a classic study of

FIGURE 14.6 Hypothetical model of the state's beginnings. (Compiled from R. M. Adams, 1966.)

the Valley of Mexico, William Sanders and a group of archaeologists showed how the Aztec state created and organized huge agricultural systems that spread over the shallow waters of the lakes that once filled the valley (Sanders, Parsons, and Santley, 1979). The variability of the local environment meant that the Aztecs had to exploit every environmental opportunity afforded them. Thus, Sanders argues, the state organized large-scale agriculture to support a population of up to 250,000 just in and close around the Aztec capital, Tenochtitlán. Environmental factors were decisive in each area where civilization began, he believes. Another important factor was centralized leadership.

Some support for this perspective comes from Mesopotamia, where recent studies of rising sea levels have thrown new light on the changing geography of the low-lying Mesopotamian Delta between the Tigris and Euphrates rivers. During the late Ice Age, world sea levels were about 91 m (300 feet) below modern shorelines. The Persian Gulf was dry land 20,000 years ago, with rising seawaters entering the basin in only about 10000 B.C. At the time, the Tigris and Euphrates river system flowed through the deepest part of the gulf, down a deep canyon caused by the rivers' cutting down to the low sea level of the Indian Ocean. Today's Mesopotamian Delta did not exist, and the entire region was very arid. Between 10000 and 4000 B.C., shorelines rose rapidly in the Persian Gulf, sometimes at a rate of 11 m (36 feet) a year, at a time when rainfall increased slightly throughout Southwest Asia. By 6500 B.C., the sea had flooded the old river system and had reached the northern shore of the gulf. Sea-level rise slowed in about 5000 B.C., as river estuaries reached their northern limits, extending as far inland as the ancient city of Ur. The vast estuaries filled with windblown sand from the Arabian Desert, but the water table remained high, creating large swampy areas in the silt-choked river mouths.

Unfortunately, the archaeological record of these millennia lies buried under deep layers of silt and today's high sea levels. After 7000 B.C., and for about 1,500 years, southern Mesopotamia enjoyed an unusually favorable climate, with greater and more reliable rainfall. This may have been a period when people hunted and gathered along the rapidly changing seacoast, using temporary settlements now buried under gulf waters. Some of these communities may have begun cereal farming. To what extent low-lying, marshy environments played a role in the emergence of cities and civilization remains a matter of debate.

As the climate became drier and the floodplain expanded, some groups may have turned to simple irrigation farming, which provided higher crop yields. Population densities rose proportionately with the yields, increasing competition for agricultural land and other food resources, just when the rising gulf was moving inland as much as 1 km (0.6 mile) a decade. Under such circumstances, communities living near the water's edge may have moved at regular intervals, eventually coalescing into larger villages. At first, small communities dug their own watercourses, diverting river meanders and side streams. Kin leaders, men and women believed to possess unusual supernatural powers, may have been those who organized canal digging, perhaps even allocating land, as they still do in many village communities. In time, these individuals became the spiritual and political leaders of a farming village in transition, on its way to becoming a settlement and society of far greater complexity. Small villages became towns, then bustling cities, central places with political and economic tentacles extending into settlements near and far. Thus was born the city and, ultimately, Mesopotamian civilization.

This scenario is based on new and highly sophisticated climatic data, but it remains entirely hypothetical in archaeological terms. It contrasts with the traditional view that farming spread into southern Mesopotamia from the north and east. But it does highlight the great importance of local environmental change to the origins of all preindustrial civilizations. Declining Nile floods may have been a factor in the formation of the Egyptian state, for example. The scenario also suggests that centralized organization was of significant importance. A powerful leader has at his or her disposal the information about state-held resources necessary to make decisions, along with the ability to command people's labor and to collect and redistribute the results of that labor. Thus, goes the argument, states arise in social and environmental contexts in which centralized management solves problems effectively.

The ecological approach has serious problems. How, for example, does one tell which environments would foster state formation? Fertile floodplains like those in Mesopotamia and Egypt? Coastal river valleys like those in Peru? Highland plateaus like those of Mesoamerica? Or areas where land is in short supply (also coastal Peru)? States arose in regions where there were few geographic constraints, like the Maya lowlands of Mesoamerica. Further, preindustrial civilizations developed, without any sign of rapid population growth, in Iran and other parts of Southwest Asia. But there can be no doubt that environmental factors were major players in a very complex process of culture change and response (Feinman and Manzanilla, 2002).

Social Theories

In recent years, archaeology has shifted away from systems-ecological approaches toward a greater concern with individuals and groups, also with what one might call "state dynamics"—how early states functioned (Stein, 2001). The former theories have often been somewhat impersonal, treating states as rather complex, even mechanical, entities that operated according to complex processes of culture change. A new generation of researchers is carrying social approaches in new directions, arguing that all human societies consist, ultimately, of individuals and groups interacting with one another, and all pursuing their own agendas. The new hypotheses revolve around such phenomena as power, ideology, factionalism, and the role of the individual.

Power in Three Domains

Archaeologically, one can look at power in three domains: economic power, social and ideological power, and political power. The combination of economic control over the sources and distribution of food and wealth, the development and maintenance of the stratified social system and its ideology, and the ability to maintain control by force was vital in early states. Each of these domains was closely linked to the others, but they can be studied separately in the archaeological record (Bowman and Woolf, 1994; Yoffee, 1995).

Economic power depends on the ability to organize more specialized production and the diverse tasks of food storage and food distribution. In time, stored wealth in food and goods develops into relationships of dependency between those who produce or acquire the wealth and those who control and distribute it. A state comprises elites (the noble class), officials (the managers), and dependents (the commoners). In ancient civilizations, the landowning class and the privately owned estate—whether owned by a temple, the ruler, or a private individual—provided security for the estate's dependents. All early states developed where agricultural production became more intensified and diverse. At the same time, early states moved away from purely kin-based organization into centralized structures that crosscut or overrode kinship ties (Figure 14.7).

Economic power also rested in trade and long-distance exchange networks, which provided access to commodities not available locally. Sumer obtained its metal from Anatolia, Iran, and the Persian Gulf. Egypt acquired gold and ivory from Nubia, and highland Andean civilizations imported fish meal from the Pacific Coast. The acquisition of exotic commodities or goods on any scale required organization, record keeping, and supervision. The archaeological record shows that the extent of state supervision of trade and traders varied considerably from civilization to civilization.

Social power means ideological power, and it comes from the creation or modification of certain symbols of cultural and political commonality (Brumfiel, 1983, 1992). This common ideology, expressed in public and private ceremonials, in art and architecture, and in literature, served to link individuals and communities with common ties that transcend those of kin. Those who create and perpetuate ideologies are held in high honor and enjoy considerable prestige, for they are often perceived as interceding with the spiritual world and the deities and sometimes even seen as flesh-and-blood divines themselves. The guardians of ideology are privileged individuals, for their spiritual

FIGURE 14.7 A Minoan city ringed by mountains and rivers. People watch departing ships, and a lion hunts deer. A wall painting from Akrotiri, Santorini island, Aegean Sea, sixteenth century B.C.

SiTE > The Lord of Sicán at Huaca Loro, Peru <

During 1990–1992, archaeologist Izumu Shimada and a team of researchers excavated the Huaco Loro pyramid in the Lambayeque Valley area of Peru's north coast, to investigate the little-known Sicán culture, successor to the flamboyant Moche state in the region. The archaeologists unearthed a tomb at the north base of the pyramid that comprised a 3-m (10-foot) square burial chamber at the base of a 10-m (33-foot) vertical shaft sunk into the clay of the river floodplain. They are now excavating a second tomb (Figure 14.8).

In the first (East) tomb, a man of 40 to 50 years of age lay in an inverted position in the chamber, surrounded by his full ceremonial regalia. This included a large textile shawl with almost 2,000 small gold foils sewn to the now-vanished cloth. The owner would have glittered and shimmered in the sun when he wore the mantle. A pair of ceremonial gloves were fashioned of gold, silver, and copper, one holding a golden cup, the other a wooden staff ornamented with gold and gold-silver-copper alloy. The man owned several golden headdresses, a semicircular bladed ceremonial knife with silver working edge, and a formal standard. He wore a gold mask, symbolic of his role as a shaman and a living personification of the Sicán deity, who is depicted in similar regalia (see Figure 22.15, p. 468).

The burial chamber included the skeletons of two young women and two juveniles, who were sacrificial victims; a disassembled litter, which had once carried the lord to his grave; imported seashells; clusters of beads; and bundles of copper, metal scrap, and thousands of copper sheet fragments, thought to have been a simple form of currency.

The Sicán lord's grave shows the extraordinary skills of Peruvian metalsmiths centuries before the Spanish Conquest. They were well aware of alloying, developed ways of joining metal sheets without solder, and made ornaments by cutting out metal and by hammering decoration into sheets for a repoussé effect. Like other Andean metalworkers, they used depletion gilding, a technique that used acids to deplete baser metals from the surface of alloyed metal objects, leaving them high in gold concentration and with a golden appearance.

FIGURE 14.8 Excavations in the West Tomb of a Lord of Sicán at Huaca Loro, Peru.

---

powers give them special social status and allow them to perpetuate social inequality. So important was ideology in the ancient world that one can speak of the Mesopotamian or Maya areas not in a political sense, for they were made up of patchworks of city-states, but in an ideological sense. Many great cities of the past, like Teotihuacán in the Valley of Mexico or Angkor Thom in Cambodia, were a combination of the spiritual and the secular. They all boasted powerful priesthoods and religious institutions, which owed their wealth to their ability to manage the spiritual affairs of the state and to legitimize rulers as upholders of the cosmic order (see Site box). The temples and public buildings they erected formed imposing settings for elaborate public ceremonies, which ensured the continuity of human life and the universe.

Political power rested in the ruler's ability to impose authority throughout society by both administrative and military means. Those who held positions of authority in either the bureaucracy or the army did not come from within the kin system but were recruited from outside it (Figure 14.9). This political power lay in foreign relations and in defense and making war. It also operated on a statewide level, dealing with the resolution of major disputes between different factions. But a great deal of power lay outside the political estate, in the hands of community and kin leaders, who handled many legal matters revolving around such issues as landownership and family law.

Norman Yoffee (1995) believes that the interplay between these three sources of power led to the development of new, societywide institutions: supreme rulers and the state. There was, he says, no one moment when civilization came into being, for social evolution did not end with the rise

FIGURE 14.9 An eagle knight, a class of elite warriors that formed an important part of the Aztec power structure in pre-Hispanic Mexico.

of the state. Preindustrial states functioned in an atmosphere of continual change and constant disputation. Some collapsed; others survived for many centuries.

This theory argues not for neoevolutionary ladders but, rather, for many trajectories for the development of social complexity (Yoffee, 2005). Many societies operated under significant constraints; they may have lacked, say, dependable crops or domesticated animals or the ability to store large amounts of food. Constraints like these took human societies along very different evolutionary paths from those of the state. That some societies did not become civilizations does not mean that they were stuck in a backward "stage" but simply that constraints on growth prevented the interplay of the major factors that led to state formation elsewhere. Thus, the chiefdom is an alternative trajectory to the state. In the chiefdom, social inequality came from within the kin system; in the state, inequality was based on access to resources and the power this access provided. It is no coincidence that the latest theories on state formation begin with the chiefdom.

Chiefly Cycling: Processes and Agents

The world's first states, politically centralized and socially stratified societies, developed in only a few locations—in Egypt and Mesopotamia by 3000 B.C. and in Mexico and the Andean region by 200 B.C. Invariably, they developed in a distinctive political environment, in what Kent Flannery calls "the dynamic crucible of cycling chiefdoms" (1999: 5). He and others believe that states arise in situations where a group of chiefdoms are competing with one another, as they did along the Nile River in the fourth millennium B.C., for example. Eventually, one of the competitors succeeds in achieving political dominance over its neighbors, so that they become provinces of a larger political unit. This competition can arise from many causes: rivalry between chiefly families, factionalism, endemic warfare and raiding, dramatic differences in population densities from one area to the next, crop failure, or just plain weak leadership or outright conquest.

Henry Wright (1984) described this process among chiefdoms as "cycling," a constant fluctuation between simple and more complex chiefdoms. Each chief presides over a single village and some lesser hamlets nearby. Then one leader usurps the power of his once egalitarian neighbors and forms a much larger political unit, where the former village chiefs become subchiefs. The newly powerful kingdom expands, then breaks down into smaller chiefdoms again, or simply collapses in a recurrent process of emergence, expansion, and fragmentation.

Ancient chiefdoms had the hereditary inequality and hierarchical social structure from which a state could arise, but this rarely happened. Robert Carneiro (1994), an expert on chiefdoms, has suggested no less than six processes for creating one. You defeat neighboring communities in war, then incorporate them into a larger political unit. At the same time, you take prisoners and force them to work for you as slaves. Once you have established control, you appoint close supporters to administer the conquered areas, unless the defeated chiefs are cooperative. Your subjects pay you tribute at regular intervals and are expected to provide fighting men in times of war. States were much larger and more centralized than chiefdoms, as well as being much more stratified socially and politically. Invariably, however, they shared the processes that Carneiro lays out.

Under this argument, then, state formation began with Carneiro's six processes, with the addition of chiefly cycling. Centuries might pass with the usual cycles of simplicity and complexity without any quantum jump in social and political complexity. Then, suddenly, three processes come together (Wright, 1984):

- A standoff of some kind between neighboring and constantly warring chiefdoms develops, reflected in the dispersal of population of the development of "buffer zones" between neighbors.
- One center rapidly acquires additional population, perhaps at the expense of its neighbors. Sometimes highly organized warfare comes into play, as campaigns of conquest replace the constant raiding of earlier times. Conquered areas are incorporated into the new, much larger kingdom.

- A large capital settlement, usually a city, develops as the ultimate level in a four-level settlement hierarchy: city, regional centers, subcenters, and villages.

Carneiro and Wright believe that the formation of states required some form of territorial expansion. But there are limits to the amount of resources that chiefs and their elites can extract from their followers. When that moment comes, they have several options: increase their demands on their subjects, which raises the specter of rebellion; intensify agricultural production with technological innovation; or expand their territory by subjugating their neighbors. If the third alternative is chosen, the kingdom rapidly comes to a point where it becomes larger than the chief himself can administer, so he has to restructure the way he administers his domains and probably make ideological changes to reflect the new political system—a state. This process is reasonably well documented in Mesopotamia and Egypt, as well as in Mesoamerica and the Andes.

These are, however, generalized, anonymous processes, like those criticized by post-processualists. As scholars of the latter school have often pointed out, it is people, individuals and groups, who are responsible for political and other cultural change. They are the "agents," as opposed to the "processes" (Flannery, 1999). To study ancient agents requires very rich historical records, which enable us to identify individuals and their deeds. In some cases, like Egypt, we know the names of seminal rulers like the early Egyptian pharaoh Menes (Narmer), but they are little more than shadowy personages on the stage of history. There is no question, however, that people of great ability and charisma were responsible

FIGURE 14.10 One of the Zulu ruler Shaka's warriors.

for the rise of many powerful states known from historical times. Flannery (1999) describes the remarkable King Shaka, who set up the Zulu state in South Africa in the early nineteenth century (Figure 14.10), King Kamehameha of Hawaii, and others. All were individuals who were products of their times, whose personal abilities made the most of unusual circumstances, accidental situations, and other moments where they could further their political and military goals. The result was, invariably, a process of historical change.

Flannery goes on to list several qualities that marked Shaka and other agents and argues that they were shared by the chiefs of unusual ability who created the first civilizations. They were members of an elite, people with aggressive and authoritarian personalities, with outstanding military abilities that gave them upward social mobility. They usurped the position of chief by fair means or foul, then conquered their immediate neighbors while seeking a competitive advantage over more distant rivals (this could be technological, a matter of military strategy, and so on). They used this advantage to expand into more distant lands while using forced labor to intensify agricultural production as a means of keeping one's subjects content and of provisioning armies. If they could not intensify their food production, they acquired additional resources by raiding. Finally, they solidified their position by power sharing, even if it was nothing more than a nominal gesture. This was definitely not democracy. Strong, able rulers headed the earliest states. They governed autocratically, even if they had nominal councils of advisers.

Much depends on ideology, too, for invariably the preindustrial states were held together by a powerful and distinctive ideology. The famous *Epic of Gilgamesh* gives us a flavor of Mesopotamian ideology. The pharaohs ruled as the living personification of the sun god. Maya lords were shamans and intermediaries between the people and the ancestors. These ideologies were reflected in sacred places, where lavish ceremonies and public appearances by the ruler were important symbols of continuity and stability, where the ruler's subjects directed their loyalty to the central figure at the pinnacle of the state. Ideology never caused states to come into being but was an invariable and important part of their fabric once they had come into being.

Both processes and individual agents played vital roles in the formation of states (Figure 14.11). Aggressive individuals of great ambition have been members of human societies since the beginning, but, until about 6,000 years ago, they never lived at a time when conditions of social inequality and chiefly competition were endemic in areas like Mesopotamia and the Nile Valley, or later in Mesoamerica and the Andes. Then these circumstances, competitive advantage, military prowess, and other factors turned a very few of them from powerful chiefs into authoritarian kings, soon supported by compelling new ideologies developed from earlier and less complex worldviews.

FIGURE 14.11 Old World Civilizations

The world's first state-organized societies, or civilizations, developed along the Nile and in Mesopotamia, more or less simultaneously, in 3100 B.C. Subsequently, preindustrial civilizations developed in the Indus Valley, in China, and, later, in Greece and the Aegean, and Southeast Asia. Distinctive civilizations flourished at Meroe and Aksum in the Ethiopian highlands 2,000 years ago. The chapters that follow describe the different trajectories of preindustrial civilizations throughout the Old World.

The Hittites came into prominence in what is now Turkey c. 1500 B.C. A warlike people who were expert traders, they were among the first societies to use iron tools and weapons.

Mycenaean civilization, a civilization of Bronze Age traders and warriors, flourished on the Greek mainland c. 1400 B.C.

The Minoans of Crete in the Aegean Sea were consummate traders who sent ships as far as Egypt, c. 2000 to 1450 B.C.

Ancient Egyptian civilization, one of the earliest in the world, endured despite vicissitudes for 3,000 years until Egypt became a province of the Roman Empire in A.D. 30.

Aksum, an important state on the Ethiopian highlands in northeast Africa, was remarkable for its fine palaces and royal tombs. The Aksumites traded with India and Red Sea ports. Aksum collapsed in the face of Islam, c. A.D. 1000.

Sumerian civilization flourished in what is now southern Iraq after 3100 B.C., a mosaic of city-states only unified briefly by the Third Dynasty of Ur kings.

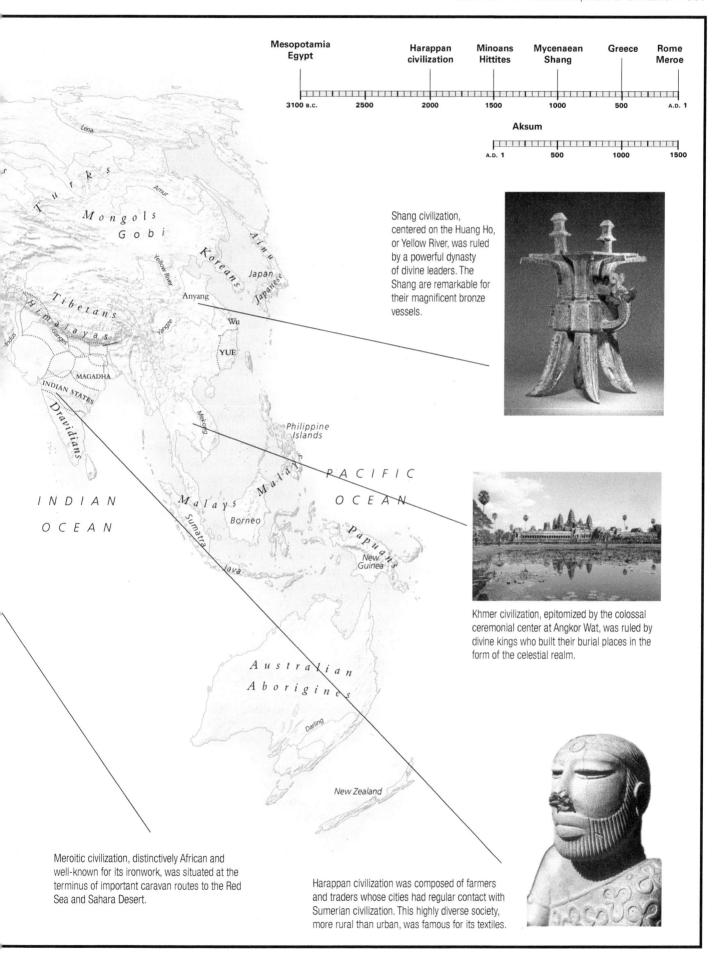

Mesopotamia Egypt		Harappan civilization	Minoans Hittites	Mycenaean Shang	Greece	Rome Meroe

3100 B.C.   2500   2000   1500   1000   500   A.D. 1

Aksum

A.D. 1   500   1000   1500

Shang civilization, centered on the Huang Ho, or Yellow River, was ruled by a powerful dynasty of divine leaders. The Shang are remarkable for their magnificent bronze vessels.

Khmer civilization, epitomized by the colossal ceremonial center at Angkor Wat, was ruled by divine kings who built their burial places in the form of the celestial realm.

Meroitic civilization, distinctively African and well-known for its ironwork, was situated at the terminus of important caravan routes to the Red Sea and Sahara Desert.

Harappan civilization was composed of farmers and traders whose cities had regular contact with Sumerian civilization. This highly diverse society, more rural than urban, was famous for its textiles.

Imploding Civilizations

Many scholars, among them Jared Diamond (2005) and Paul Kennedy (1987), have written about cycles of history, the rise of civilizations, their brilliant apogees, and their sudden declines. Eventually one civilization falls and another rises to take its place; this replacement in turn goes through the same cycle of rise and fall. The record of early civilizations could easily be written in cyclical terms, for states have risen and then imploded with bewildering rapidity in all parts of the world within the past 5,000 years. In the Mexican highlands, for example, the great city of Teotihuacán flourished between about 200 B.C. and A.D. 700. In A.D. 600, it had a population of more than 125,000 people. For 600 of these years, more than 85 percent of the population of the Valley of Mexico lived in or close to Teotihuacán. Then the city declined rapidly in the eighth century A.D. Within half a century, the population shrank to a quarter of its former size. A series of lesser states competed to fill the political vacuum left by the great city's fall, until the Toltecs, and later the Aztecs, rose to supremacy (see Chapter 21).

To us the word *collapse* is perhaps misleading, for the record of the past shows that human societies are resilient to sudden, even catastrophic, change. Population densities may fall; trade and economic activity dry up; information flow declines, and the known world shrinks, but the people themselves survive. What do not vanish are long-held beliefs and values, the very core of a cultural tradition, even if rulers' ideologies vanish with their overthrow. The boundaries of a state or an empire shift all the time, and, with a seeming inevitability, the center of gravity of political and economic power may move elsewhere, but the people, their kin ties and most basic social institutions survive, perhaps in a modified form as they move into villages across the once urbanized countryside to move to new homelands in the face of drought or flood. Human societies are resilient in the face of major change, even if they become smaller, simpler, and much more egalitarian (McAnany and Yoffee, 2010).

Joseph Tainter (1988) points out that an initial investment by a society in growing complexity is a rational way of trying to solve the needs of the moment. At first, the strategy works. Agricultural production increases through more intensive farming methods; an emerging bureaucracy works well; and expanding trade networks bring wealth to a new elite who use their authority and economic clout to undertake great public works, such as pyramids and temples, that validate their spiritual authority and divine associations. Maya civilization is an excellent example of these processes in action. It prospered greatly for centuries in the Mesoamerican lowlands until a point of diminishing returns was reached.

As the most costly solutions to a society's needs are exhausted, it becomes imperative to find new organizational and economic answers, which may have much lower yields and may cost a great deal more. As these stresses develop, argues Tainter, a complex society such as that of the Maya is increasingly vulnerable. There are few reserves to carry the society through droughts, famines, floods, and other natural disasters. Eventually, civilizations change in major ways, especially when important segments of society perceive that centralization and social complexity simply do not work any more and that they are better off on their own. The trend toward decentralization becomes compelling. Tainter calls such implosions not a catastrophe but a rational process that occurs when increasing stress requires some organizational change. The population decline and other catastrophic effects that just preceded, accompanied, or followed collapse may have been traumatic at the time, but they can be looked at as part of what one might call an economizing process.

There is, of course, more to a society's collapse than merely an economizing process. Complete collapse can occur only where there is a power vacuum. In many cases, a powerful neighbor may be waiting in the wings. In early times, numerous city-states traded and competed with one another within a small area. Sumerian cities, Minoan and Mycenaean palace kingdoms in Greece and the Aegean, the Maya centers in Mesoamerica—all existed in close interdependence within their cultural areas, in a state of constant **peer–polity interaction**. They traded, fought, and engaged in constant diplomacy. Under these circumstances, to collapse is an invitation to be dominated by one's competitors. There is loss of complexity only when every polity in the interacting cluster collapses at the same time (Yoffee and Cowgill, 1988).

The implosion of early civilizations, then, may be closely connected to declining returns from social complexity and to the normal political processes of factionalism, social unrest, succession disputes, and even civil war, as well as to ecological degradation or climate change (Brumfiel and Fox, 1994; Diamond, 2005).

Summary

- This chapter contrasts the historical and anthropological approaches to the origins of states and summarizes the six main theories developed by archaeologists.

- Gordon Childe's Urban Revolution theory centered on the development of the city. Another group of theories involved the intensification of agriculture and irrigation. Exchange networks and warfare have also been espoused as potential causes of civilization.

- Many modern theories revolve around systems-evolutionary hypotheses and explanations involving environmental change.

- A new generation of social approaches, on the other hand, argues that religious and informational factors, epitomized by centralized authority, have been key elements in the regulation of environmental and economic variables in early civilization.

- Such theories also stress that the social structure of a society ultimately determines its transformation, so the search for the causes of civilization focuses on ecological variables and the opportunities they present to individuals pursuing political goals in different societies. In other words, how is ecological opportunity or necessity translated into political change?

- Recent research is now focusing on the dynamics of how ancient civilizations functioned—on factionalism, ideology, and gender as promising areas of inquiry.

- The record of early civilizations can be written in cyclical terms. Their collapse may be closely connected to diminishing returns from social complexity, as well as normal political processes, such as succession disputes. However, human societies are resilient and many basic values, beliefs, and institutions can survive the implosion of a complex society.

Key Terms

bartering (298)	Fertile Crescent (295)	reciprocity (298)
city (294)	gift exchange (298)	redistribution (298)
exchange system (298)	peer–polity interaction (308)	Urban Revolution (295)

Further Reading

Redman, Charles L. 1978. *The Rise of Civilization: From Early Farmers to Urban Society in the Ancient Near East.* San Francisco: Freeman.

McAnany, Patricia, and Norman Yoffee, eds. 2010 *Questioning Collapse: Human Resilience, Ecological Vulnerability,* *and the Aftermath of Empire.* Cambridge, UK: Cambridge University Press.

Scarre, Chris, and Brian Fagan. 2003. *Ancient Civilizations,* 2nd ed. Upper Saddle River, NJ: Prentice Hall.

15 Early Civilizations in Southwest Asia

n 1872, an earnest banknote engraver turned clay-tablet expert named George Smith was sorting through the dusty fragments of Assyrian king Assurbanipal's royal library in the British Museum. Suddenly, he came across a tablet bearing a reference to a large ship grounded on a mountain. Immediately, he realized he had found an account of a flood that bore a remarkable resemblance to the biblical story of the Flood in Genesis. A prophet named Hasisadra is warned of the gods' intention to destroy all of sinful humankind. He builds a large ship and loads it with his family and "the beast of the field, the animal of the field." The flood destroys "all [other] life from the face of the earth." The ship goes aground on a mountain. Hasisadra sends out a dove, which returns. Eventually, a raven is dispatched and never returns. Hasisadra releases the animals, becomes a god, and lives happily ever after.

George Smith's discovery caused a public sensation at a time when people believed in the literal historical truth of the Scriptures. Seventeen lines of the story were missing, so the London *Daily Telegraph* paid Smith's way to Nineveh to find the missing fragments. Incredible though it may seem, Smith found them within five days. The tablets can be seen on display in the British Museum, duly labeled "DT," for *Daily Telegraph*. ▪

Figure in the Sumerian style from Mari, Syria, c. 2500 B.C.

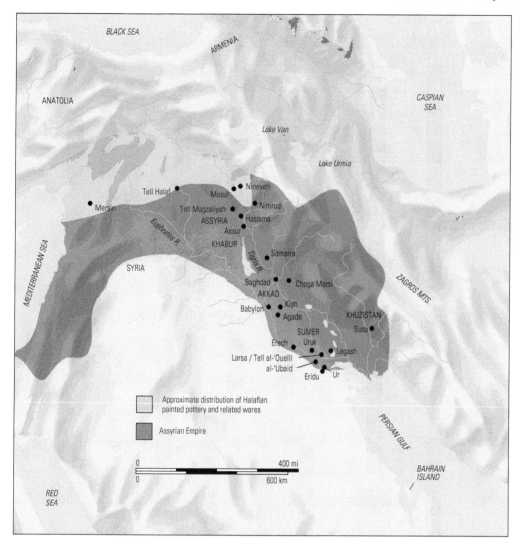

FIGURE 15.1 Sites and cultural distributions mentioned in this chapter. (Tepe Yahya and Shari-i-Shokhta lie to the east of the map.)

The Victorians thought of Mesopotamia (Greek for "land between the rivers") as the location of the biblical Garden of Eden. Today, it is a far from paradisal place, for the delta regions and floodplain (Figure 15.1) between the Tigris and Euphrates rivers form a hot, low-lying environment, much of it inhospitable sand, swamp, and dry mudflats. Yet this now inhospitable region was the cradle of the world's earliest urban civilizations (Table 15.1) (Matthews, 2003; Pollock, 1999; Postgate, 1992). From north to south, Mesopotamia is approximately 965 km (600 miles) long and 400 km (250 miles) wide, extending from the uplands of Iran to the east to the Arabian and Syrian deserts in the west. The plains are subject to long, intensely hot summers and harsh, cold winters, and would be desert but for the Euphrates and Tigris. There are few permanent water supplies other than these great rivers and their tributaries. Rainfall is slight, undependable, and insufficient for the growing of crops. But with irrigation, the alluvial soils of the lower plain can be farmed and their natural fertility unlocked. Farmers can obtain high crop yields from relatively limited areas of land, sufficient to feed relatively dense populations. By 6000 B.C., and perhaps earlier, village farmers were diverting the waters of the rivers. Within 2,000 years, the urban civilization of the Sumerians was flourishing in Mesopotamia (Maisels, 1993, 2001).

Upland Villages

With continued improvement in agricultural methods and the development of such technological innovations as pottery, the village communities of the Zagros foothills, east of Mesopotamia, achieved a more efficient subsistence base that fed a gradually increasing farming population. These technological and economic changes were far from spectacular: By at least 7000 B.C., farmers were living on the Assyrian plains, at first in areas where they could rely on seasonal rainfall to water their crops; later, they settled by the rivers, with animals and crops that could tolerate the climate of the lowlands. There they developed simple irrigation methods to bring water to their fields (Zeder, 1994).

TABLE 15.1
Major early civilizations of Southwest Asia and thier interconnectedness

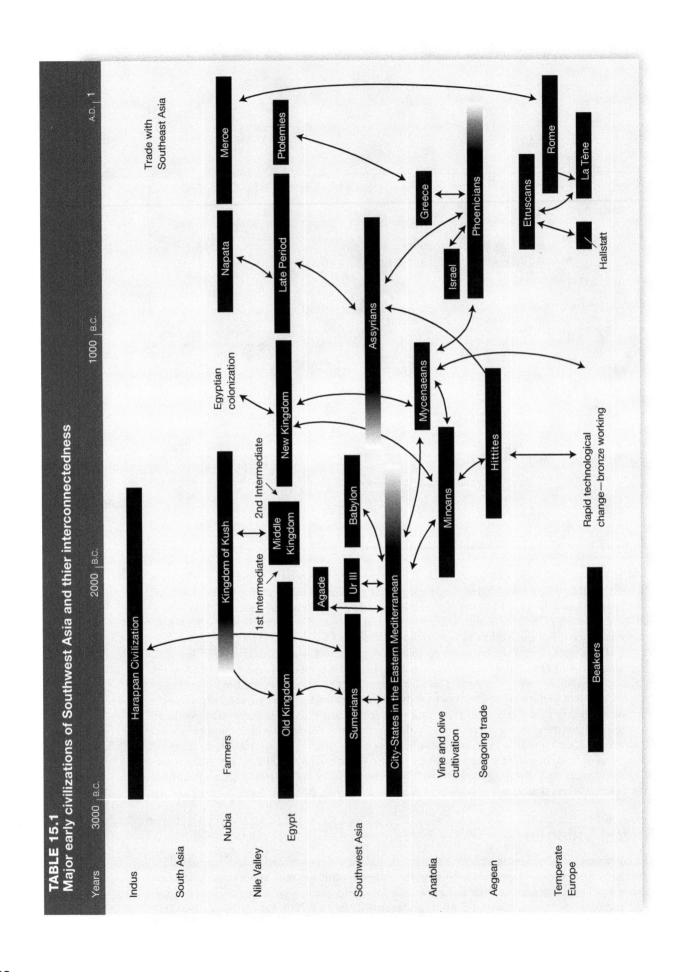

The first farmers to settle in Assyria were scattered over the undulating plains in compact village settlements like Tell Magzaliyah. The successive occupation layers of these sites are filled with handmade pottery of coarse clay painted or incised with dots, circles, and other designs (Figure 15.2a). Such wares—named Hassunan pottery, after Hassuna, the first excavated village of this type—are found over a wide area of the north, from the upper Tigris Valley to the plains west of the modern city of Mosul.

Hassuna
6000 B.C.

Irrigation farmers inhabited the regions between Mosul in the north and Baghdad in the south by at least 6000 B.C., and probably many centuries earlier. We know this from discoveries of villages in the region of Samarra, on the fringes of the Mesopotamian Delta. Samarran painted pottery (Figure 15.2b), which comes from such sites as Choga Mami, reveals early farming villages in areas where irrigation agriculture was the only viable means of food production (Oates, 1973; T. J. Wilkinson, 2003). The Samarran sites near Choga Mami are situated along low ridges parallel

Choga Mami

(a)

(b)

FIGURE 15.2 Early Mesopotamian painted pottery: (a) vessels from Hassuna; (b) Samarra-type vessels from Hassuna. (All one-eighth full size.)

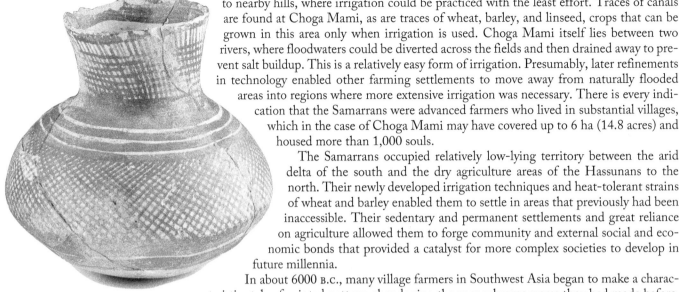

FIGURE 15.3 Halafian painted pot from northern Iraq.

Halafian
6000 B.C.

to nearby hills, where irrigation could be practiced with the least effort. Traces of canals are found at Choga Mami, as are traces of wheat, barley, and linseed, crops that can be grown in this area only when irrigation is used. Choga Mami itself lies between two rivers, where floodwaters could be diverted across the fields and then drained away to prevent salt buildup. This is a relatively easy form of irrigation. Presumably, later refinements in technology enabled other farming settlements to move away from naturally flooded areas into regions where more extensive irrigation was necessary. There is every indication that the Samarrans were advanced farmers who lived in substantial villages, which in the case of Choga Mami may have covered up to 6 ha (14.8 acres) and housed more than 1,000 souls.

The Samarrans occupied relatively low-lying territory between the arid delta of the south and the dry agriculture areas of the Hassunans to the north. Their newly developed irrigation techniques and heat-tolerant strains of wheat and barley enabled them to settle in areas that previously had been inaccessible. Their sedentary and permanent settlements and great reliance on agriculture allowed them to forge community and external social and economic bonds that provided a catalyst for more complex societies to develop in future millennia.

In about 6000 B.C., many village farmers in Southwest Asia began to make a characteristic style of painted pottery, abandoning the monochrome wares they had made before. The new fashion spread from southwest Turkey around the shores of Lake Van, famous for its obsidian, and as far east as the Zagros Mountains. The most brilliantly painted pottery was made in northern Iraq by the inhabitants of Tell Halaf, whose enormous kilns produced bowls, dishes, and flasks adorned with elaborate, stylized patterns and representations of people and animals (Figure 15.3). The Halafian cultural tradition flourished in what had once been Hassunan territory, and the people maintained regular contact with the Samarrans in the south.

The Halafians still lived in much the same ways as did their predecessors, and they made no startling agricultural or technological innovations. They developed new contacts between villages hundreds of miles apart, trading such commodities as obsidian, semiprecious stone, and other luxury items, including painted pots with motifs that were standardized over large distances. Neutron activation and other chemical studies of pottery clays have shown that Halafian painted pots, made at a so-far unidentified location, were traded to settlements like Mersin and Choga Mami, about 960 km (600 miles) apart. In some areas, the main settlement produced most of the fine pottery found in the villages of the surrounding area. It is as if the production and distribution of some items favored by elite members of society were concentrated at key trade centers along water routes. In the Khabur area, the same clay studies hint that both major and minor Halafian settlements produced the goods consumed in their own hinterlands, while restricting the access of nearby subordinate villages to this higher-level trade. This may be a sign that chiefdoms had evolved among Halafian communities in the region. As with the Hopewell in North America, these new elite groups required greater communication and the sharing of status goods, such as painted pottery, to reinforce their authority (Redman, 1978).

Settlement of the Lowlands

Human settlement along the Persian Gulf shifted as sea levels rose at the end of the Ice Age. The complicated climatic changes in this region since 15,000 years ago form the environmental backdrop to the rise of civilization in Mesopotamia.

Environmental Change

In about 15000 B.C., during the late Ice Age, the Persian Gulf was dry land, so the Tigris and Euphrates rivers flowed into the Gulf of Oman 800 km (500 miles) south of their present mouths. After 12000 B.C., sea levels rose rapidly, as they did in other parts of the world, from about −20 m (−66 feet) in 6000 B.C. to 2 m (7 feet) above modern levels between 4000 and 3000 B.C. As sea levels rose, riverborne alluvium filled the Persian Gulf, building a vast delta that advanced gradually to the south and leaving freshwater lakes and marshes in its wake. These thick layers of alluvium mask the archaeological record of any late Ice Age or early Holocene occupation of the lowlands. Almost certainly, however, both hunter-gatherers and farmers lived off fish and other resources in these low-lying areas for many thousands of years.

The dramatic environmental changes at the end of the Ice Age were significant factors in the development of city-states in southern Mesopotamia. Frank Hole (1994) has developed a hypothetical scenario. Two environmental factors played a vital role: drastic changes in sea level at the end of the Ice Age and intense climatic variability, especially during the fifth millennium B.C., when the so-called climatic optimum after the Ice Age finally ended (Chapter 7). Summer temperatures were considerably higher, with more rainfall, which lasted for a long period, allowing longer growing seasons for crops planted during the winter. The water table may have been higher, so that dry agriculture was possible in areas that a few centuries later could be cultivated only with irrigation.

Before 6000 B.C., villages—each of them self-sufficient and egalitarian—supported populations of between 50 and 200 people. In about 6000B.C., a population decline began; people now lived in much larger towns, and much of the landscape was devoid of settlement. In other words, the gradual expansion of farming communities that had begun 2,000 years earlier now ceased. At the same time, contacts between neighboring communities intensified, perhaps in part to make up for shortages of grain and other commodities in different areas during a time of climatic change. By about 4600 B.C., settlements were linked by canals, once handmade pottery was now wheel produced, and the building of temples became more prevalent.

6000 B.C.

Within a millennium, there were large cities in Mesopotamia. These changes took place as the Mesopotamian landscape changed dramatically. Rising sea levels caused settlements to change locations frequently, rainfall became more irregular, the environment became drier, and agricultural populations were dislocated. Some areas were abandoned altogether, as many groups dispersed into nomadic lifeways and others gathered in favored locations on the Mesopotamian floodplain.

By the mid-fourth millennium B.C., the climate and land had stabilized, so that the development of more extensive irrigation systems and the support of much larger communities were possible. The people who had abandoned dispersed villages and moved to favored areas provided the labor forces that could be organized to develop large-scale irrigation systems and a new economic infrastructure. Within a short time, a new demographic and social order developed that culminated in the appearance of the world's first literate urban civilization. Hole believes it was no coincidence that the first cities in southern Mesopotamia formed between 3500 and 3000 B.C., soon after local sea levels stabilized. Hole's scenario is somewhat hypothetical. What, then, do we know from archaeology?

Archaeological Evidence

The first known lowland farming communities date to around 5800 B.C., small communities located in clusters along the Euphrates channels. The largest of these clusters consisted of small rural communities located around a larger town that covered about 10 ha (28 acres) and housed perhaps between 2,500 and 4,000 people. Small canals up to 5 km (3 miles) long watered the fields around these settlements. The farmers grew barley and dates and herded cattle, sheep, and goats. These clusters of settlements are subsumed under the term *'Ubaid*, after a small site (al-'Ubaid) near Ur.

'Ubaid
5800 B.C.

We do not know anything about how the first inhabitants of the Mesopotamian floodplain acquired or developed the skills needed to survive in their harsh environment. Communal effort was essential because raw materials suitable for building houses had to be improvised from the plentiful sand, clay, palm trees, and reeds between the rivers. Digging even the smallest canal required at least a little political and social leadership. The backbreaking annual task of clearing silt from clogged river courses and canals could have been achieved only by communal effort. As both Robert Adams (1966) and Kent Flannery (1972) point out, the relationship between developing a stratified society and creating food surpluses is close. Distinctive social changes came from the more efficient systems for producing food that were essential in the delta. As food surpluses grew and the specialized agricultural economies of these 'Ubaid villages became successful, the trend toward sedentary settlement and higher population densities increased (Stein, 1994). Expanded trade networks, many of them facilitated by waterways, and the redistribution of surpluses and trade goods also affected society, with dominant groups of 'Ubaid people becoming more active in producing surpluses, which eventually supported more and more people who were not farmers (Algaze, 2008).

'Ubaid sites display considerable variation. The earliest known community is Tell al 'Ouelli, near Larsa, which dates to as early as 5800 B.C. (Forest, 1986). Within a few centuries, some of the larger settlements had substantial buildings, alleyways, and courtyards, but rural settlements like al-'Ubaid itself consisted of mud-brick and reed huts with roofs formed of bent sticks (Adams and Nissen, 1972). Al-'Ubaid and similar small clusters of hamlets shared ceremonial centers and were linked by kin and clan ties, one clan authority overseeing the villagers' affairs and, probably, the irrigation schemes that connected them. In time, the small village ceremonial centers grew, as did the one at Eridu (first settled around 4750 B.C., when the Tell Halaf peoples were still making their painted pottery in the north). 'Ubaid people traded, too; their distinctive pottery has been found as far afield as Iran, Syria, and Saudi Arabia. Excavations at Tell Zeidan far to the north near the Euphrates in modern-day Syria are revealing important new information about far-flung 'Ubaid trading activities between about 5000 and 4400 B.C.

Tell al 'Ouelli
5800 B.C.

Eridu
4750 B.C.

SiTE > The Temple at Eridu, Iraq <

Sumerian legends called Eridu the earliest city of all, the dwelling place of Enki, God of the Abyss, the fountain of human wisdom. "All lands were the sea, then Eridu was made," proclaims a much later Mesopotamian creation legend. Sumerians considered Enki's word to have created order from the chaos of the primordial waters. Eridu itself once lay in the heart of a fertile riverside landscape. Today, harsh desert surrounds the ancient city. Its ruined temple platform stands at one end of the great city mounds, a low, flat mass of clay and sand with a dune forming downwind of the crumbling mound. For generations, the desolate site defied some of the best archaeologists in the world, who lacked the expertise to distinguish sun-dried mudbrick from the surrounding soil. British archaeologist Richard Campbell-Thompson dug into Eridu in 1918 and complained that he found nothing but loose sand.

Thirty years later, Iraqi archaeologist Fuad Safar and his British colleague Seton Lloyd returned to the city with a large labor force and a small mining railroad, which enabled them to move enormous amounts of sand. They also had an expertise with mud-brick structures, using methods developed by German archaeologists at the great city of Babylon just before World War I, which used picks to "feel" different soil textures. To this simple technique, they added brushes and compressed air, which proved an excellent way to clear mudbrick. The two excavators removed enough sand to expose a small complex of mud-brick public buildings, still standing, about 2.4 m (8 feet) high. Then they embarked on a long-term project to decipher the history of the great shrine that had once stood at the heart of the city.

Safar and Lloyd soon found a solid brickwork platform extending from the base of the much later-dated ruined ziggurat (temple). They spent two weeks piecing together scattered brick and reconstructed the foundations of a small, rectangular building surrounded by concentric brickwork triangles. After days of puzzlement, they realized they were looking at a temple platform that had been extended again and again by the simple expedient of adding another layer of brickwork around the shrine to build ever-larger, brilliantly decorated

FIGURE 15.4 Artist's reconstruction of an Uruk culture temple at Eridu. Notice the great platform supporting the temple and the drainage pipes in the walls.

shrines, culminating in the great ziggurat that adorned the city before it was abandoned. At least five temples had stood atop the one exposed by Safar and Lloyd (Figure 15.4). They dismantled the rectangular structure and penetrated deep toward bedrock, uncovering no less than ten earlier shrines, each built atop its predecessor. Temple XVI, dated to c. 4500 B.C., lay on clean sand, a small mud-brick shrine 14 m (46 feet) square, with one entrance, an altar, and an offering table. Hundreds of fish bones, including the complete skeleton of a sea perch, still lay on the offering table. Sea perch live in brackish water, like the shallow estuaries that were once close to Eridu.

Five hundred years later, Eridu's temple platform lay inside a sacred enclosure at least 180 m (197 yards) square. A magnificent stepped ziggurat now rose in the center of the city, its façade adorned with brightly colored fired bricks. Crowded residential quarters and markets crowded on the sacred enclosure, and the ziggurat was visible for kilometers around. Thanks to months of sophisticated and painstaking mud-brick excavation, we know that this imposing shrine was the descendant of much humbler temples that had commemorated the same sacred place.

Eridu, a rapidly growing town, consisted of a mud-brick temple with fairly substantial mud-brick houses around it, often with a rectangular floor plan (see Site box). The craftsworkers lived a short distance from the elite, who were clustered around the temple, and still farther away were the dwellings of the farmers, who grew the crops that supported everyone. By 4500 B.C., the Eridu temple had grown large, containing altars and offering places and a central room bounded by rows of smaller compartments. The population of Eridu was as high as 5,000 at this time, but exact computations are impossible. 'Ubaid may have been the cultural precursor of later Mesopotamian civilization, both in the northern region of Assyria and in the south (Algaze, 2008).

Uruk: The Mesopotamian City

As Mesopotamian society grew in complexity, so did the need for social, political, and religious institutions that would provide an integrative function for everyone (H. Crawford, 2004). The ancient city of Uruk epitomizes cultural developments just before and during the early stages of Sumerian civilization (H. Crawford, 2004; Pollock, 1992; Yoffee, 1995). Archaeologically, we know most about the later stages of the city. At about 2800 B.C., the city core covered an estimated 250 ha (617 acres), with more people living in the hinterland. Built with an enormous expenditure of work as a community project, the ziggurat complex and its satellite temples were the center of Uruk life. The temples were not only storehouses and places of worship but also redistribution centers for surplus food. Hundreds of craftsworkers labored for the temple as stonemasons, copper workers, and weavers and in dozens of other specialized tasks. None of these people tilled the ground or worked on irrigation; they formed a distinctive class in a well-stratified society. In its earliest manifestations, between 4600 and 3800 B.C., Uruk was a nascent city on a much smaller scale but a settlement that was growing rapidly, many surrounding villages becoming part of the dense urban landscape. An earlier and smaller ziggurat towered over the city, which, just like Eridu, formed the core for the later monumental structure of Sumerian civilization.

Uruk
Before 4600 B.C.

Even as early as 3500 B.C., the entire life of Uruk and its connections with cities, towns, merchants, and mines hundreds of miles away revolved around the temple. The ruler of Uruk and the keeper of the temple was the *en*, both the secular and the religious leader. In its heyday, Uruk was far more than a city. Satellite villages extended out at least 10 km (6 miles), each with its own irrigation system, but population densities around the city were lower than they had been in earlier times. All provided food for those in the city, whether grain, fish, or meat. Each settlement depended on the others for survival, at first because each provided things essential for a well-balanced existence; later, because the settlements needed protection from outsiders, who would have plundered their goods (Schwartz and Falconer, 1994). The Mesopotamian city had developed an elaborate system of management with a well-defined hierarchy of rulers and priests, landowners and bureaucrats, traders and peasants. This system organized and regulated society, meted out reward and punishment, and made policy decisions for the thousands of people who lived under it. The countryside became the hinterland of the city and, later, the city-state.

The city was a hallmark of early Mesopotamian civilization, but each urban center had different settlement characteristics and histories. Archaeological surveys record the remarkable fact that more than 80 percent of the Sumerian population lived in settlements covering at least 10 ha (25 acres), in a form of "hyperurbanism" in the third millennium B.C., a figure that had declined steadily by just under 50 percent by 2000 B.C. (R. Adams, 1981).

FIGURE 15.5 A cuneiform tablet showing 14 lines of a mathematical text.

As far back as 8000 B.C., the ancient Mesopotamians used clay tokens to record commercial dealings between people living at some distance from one another (Schmandt-Besserat, 1996). One possible explanation for the invention of tokens is that as Mesopotamian transactions became increasingly complex and exceeded the power of memory, they suffered from accounting errors, disputes and dishonest practices. The tokens could be carried around on strings, transported across long distances and even enclosed in clay envelopes, which were sealed by the sender of the goods and unsealed by their recipient. A few of these sealed clay envelopes still exist, with loose tokens inside them, and token impressions in the clay surface of the envelope to provide a record of the contents of the envelope without having to break the seal.

Such tokens were nevertheless very limited in their application, and could not be used for representing spoken language. But by around 3300 B.C., the Sumerians had invented the world's earliest-known form of writing—that is a graphic system to express spoken language and thought. By this time there is evidence of a system. At any rate, the earliest economic texts deal with internal administrative matters, usually small numbers and inventories, not with external trade. The new script was also commonly used for compiling lists of all kinds— occupations, places, things in the world, and so on—a common application of writing systems all over the globe—for example, that of the Mycenaeans of Greece (see Chapter 19).

At first, specially trained scribes used **cuneiform** to record inventories and administrative and commercial transactions (Nissen et al., 1993). Over more than 1,000 years, the scribes gradually began to explore the limitless opportunities afforded by the ability to express oneself in writing (Figures 15.5 and

	Fish	Head of an Ass	Bird	Ear of Barley	Head and Body of a Man	Head with Mouth Indicated	Mouth and Food	Mouth and Water	Bowl of Food	Stream of Water
Earliest Pictographs (3000 B.C.)										
Cuneiform Signs (1900 B.C.)										
Basic Logographic Value Reading	KUA	ANŠE	MUŠEN	ŠE	LÚ	KA	KÚ	NAG	NINDA	A
Basic Logographic Value Meaning	FISH	ASS	BIRD	BARLEY	MAN	MOUTH	TO EAT	TO DRINK	FOOD, BREAD	WATER

FIGURE 15.6 Development of Sumerian writing, from a pictographic script to a cuneiform script and then to a phonetic system. The word *cuneiform* is derived from the Latin *cuneus*, meaning "a wedge," after the characteristic impression of the script.

15.6). Kings used tablets to trumpet their victories and political triumphs. Fathers chided errant sons, and lawyers recorded complicated land transactions. Sumerian poetry includes love stories, great epics, hymns to the gods, and tragic laments bemoaning the destruction of city after city (Kramer, 1963). Temple records and accounts tell us much not only of economic and social organization but also of Mesopotamian folklore and religion.

Meanwhile, on the plateau to the north, other developments had been underway: the use of metal—in the form of copper tools and ornaments—first occurred as early as the fifth or sixth millennium B.C. (Moorey, 1994).

Although many peasant societies were aware of the properties of native copper, and both early Egyptians and Native Americans made hammered ornaments from it, the softness of the metal limits its uses. Eventually, though, people familiar with the kiln firing of pottery developed techniques for smelting copper ore. Copper is fine and lustrous and makes admirable ornaments. At first, it was a high-status metal, valued for its prestige. Copper was in widespread use for ornamentation in Iran during the fourth millennium and was imported into southern Mesopotamia as early as 3500 B.C., perhaps earlier. It enjoyed high status, for utilitarian implements like stone-bladed sickles remained in use throughout the third millennium B.C. Eventually, during the early second millennium, alloying with lead or tin came into widespread use, as metalsmiths learned how to produce bronze and other forms of tougher metal. Once alloying was understood, copper assumed a more central place in agriculture and warfare.

The later development of bronze weapons can be linked to the rise of warfare as a method of attaining political ends, for cities like Eridu and Uruk were not isolated from other centers. Indeed, they were only too aware of their neighbors. The city-states of Lagash and Umma were uneasy neighbors and engaged in a tendentious border dispute that dragged on for three or four centuries. Cities soon had walls, a sure sign that they needed protection against marauders. Earlier cylinder seals (inscribed clay cylinders used as seals) bear scenes with prisoners of war.

By this time, too, there were southern Mesopotamian "colonies" in what is now northern Iraq, at Susa across the Tigris, in the Zagros, and elsewhere on the northern and northeastern peripheries of the lowlands. Some of these colonies were entire transplanted communities; others were small enclaves of traders in foreign towns, identified by their characteristic Uruk-style artifacts. Artifacts and artistic styles typical of Uruk and also Susa have come from the Nile Delta during the centuries when long-distance caravan trade was expanding rapidly in Egypt and across the Sinai.

Sumerian Civilization

Sumerian civilization c. 3000 to 2334 B.C.

With the appearance of the Sumerian civilization in about 3000 B.C., we enter a new era in human experience, one in which the economic, political, and social mechanisms created by humans began to affect the lives of cities, towns, and villages located hundreds, if not thousands, of miles apart. No human society created by *Homo sapiens* has ever flourished in complete isolation, and, as we saw in Chapter 7, regular interaction and exchange between neighboring hunter-gatherer groups assumed ever-greater importance in the late Ice Age and the early Holocene. In Southwest

Asia, after 9000 B.C., long-distance exchanges in such vital commodities as obsidian, to say nothing of luxury goods like seashells, reached considerable proportions and extended over much of Anatolia, the coastal eastern Mediterranean, and even farther afield (Algaze, 1993, 2008). The real launching point in long-distance exchange and organized trade took place during the fourth millennium B.C., the first millennium in prehistory when the history of an individual society can be understood only against a background of much broader regional developments. In a real sense, a rapidly evolving "world system" linked, with ever-changing cultural tentacles, hundreds of Southwest Asian societies all the way from eastern Iran and the Indus Valley in Pakistan to Mesopotamia, the eastern Mediterranean, Anatolia, and the Nile Valley. In the third millennium B.C., this system not only embraced Southwest Asia but also extended to Cyprus, the Aegean, and mainland Greece.

This nascent world system developed as a result of insatiable demands for nonlocal raw materials in different ecological regions where societies were developing along very similar general evolutionary tracks toward greater complexity. The broad, and apparently linear, cultural sequence in southern Mesopotamia just described can be matched by equivalent developments in northern Mesopotamia and east of the Tigris.

In each area, these developments and many technological innovations were triggered not only by basic economic needs but also by the competitive instincts of newly urbanized elites, who used lavish display and exotic luxuries to reaffirm their social prestige and authority.

Sumerian civilization is a mirror of this developing regional interdependence. The Sumerians lived in a treeless lowland environment with fertile soils but no metal, little timber, and no semiprecious stones. They obtained these commodities by trading with areas where such items were abundant, perhaps initially on a village-by-village basis and later in a far more organized fashion. Much of this trade was in the hands of temple organizations, for the temples served as centralized storehouses, and many luxury goods were used to embellish public buildings (Figure 15.7). Trade was an integral part of Sumerian life, a multifaceted activity absorbing the energies of many people. Food and many basic commodities were redistributed by different institutions for specific purposes. For example, temples would distribute food rations to those who labored for them. Petty officials were allocated land for their services. Raw materials were obtained from the highlands and the Iranian Plateau to the east for the manufacture of weapons, ornaments, and prestigious luxuries.

Increased wealth in archaeological sites both within Sumer and outside its boundaries reflects a quickened tempo of international trade. Metal tools became much more common, and domestic tools as well as weapons proliferated (Postgate, 1992). Metallurgy benefited from technological innovations carried along trade routes, among them the development of alloying copper with tin

FIGURE 15.7 The ruins of Sumerian Ur. The ziggurat is in the background, c. 2300 B.C.

to make bronze. This produced tougher-edged, more durable artifacts that could be used for more arduous, day-to-day tasks. One resulting innovation was the metal- and wood-tipped plow, an implement dragged by oxen that was capable of digging a far deeper furrow than the simple hoes and digging sticks of earlier times. The plow, which, incidentally, was never developed in the Americas, evolved as irrigation agriculture assumed greater importance in Sumer, and the combined innovations increased agricultural yields dramatically. These yields not only supported larger urban and rural populations but also provided a means for the rulers of city-states both in Sumer and farther afield to exercise more control over food surpluses and over the wealth obtained by long-distance exchange. Eventually, Sumerian rulers became more despotic, controlling their subjects by military strength, religious power, and economic incentive (Yoffee, 1995).

Lowland Mesopotamia lacked the mineral and stone resources that were plentiful in distant, more highland environments in Anatolia to the northwest and on the Iranian Plateau to the east. At the same time, the Sumerians controlled not only large surpluses of grain that could be moved in ships but also a flourishing industry in textiles and other luxuries (Algaze, 2008). Demand rose steadily for raw materials, which arrived in Sumerian cities along southern Mesopotamian waterways, especially up the placid Euphrates, easily navigable for long distances. This great river transmitted raw materials from the north and trade goods from the Persian Gulf to the Mediterranean. From the rivers and cities, intricate, centuries-old exchange networks and sometimes formal caravan routes carried metals, timber, skins, ivory, and precious stones over enormous distances and often rugged terrain. Even as early as Sumerian times, caravans of pack animals (in later times, often black asses) joined Anatolia to the Euphrates, the eastern Mediterranean coastal region to Mesopotamia, and Mesopotamia to isolated towns on the Iranian Plateau.

An intricate and ever-changing system of political alliances and individual obligations of friendship linked community with community and city-state with city-state. In time, financial and logistical checks and balances were maintained by an administrative system based in the temples to bring order to what had begun as informal bartering. Specialized merchants began to handle such commodities as copper and lapis lazuli. There was wholesaling and contracting, loans were floated, and individual profit was a prime motivation. Increasingly, every city-state, and indeed entire civilizations, came to depend on what we have called a nascent world system, not so much for political stability but for survival. Reliable, long-term interdependence had become a vital factor in the history of Southwest Asian states by 3000 B.C. (Algaze, 1993, 2008).

Exchange on the Iranian Plateau

The rise of urbanization in Sumer was by no means a unique phenomenon, for by 3500 B.C., cities had come into being upstream of the lowlands in areas where only dry farming was possible (Weiss, 1986). Cultural developments remarkably parallel to those in Sumer unfolded in the area between the Zagros foothills and the Tigris and Euphrates (Lamberg-Karlovsky, 1978). These developments did not occur in isolation, for even as early as 3000 B.C., there was regular interaction between the two regions.

During the sixth and early fifth millennia B.C., small farming villages flourished in the heart of Khuzistan. The people were irrigation farmers who herded goats, sheep, and cattle as well. So many of their sites are known that it seems certain that areas such as the Deh Luran plain had been intensively settled by this time. During the next thousand years or so, Khuzistan was still densely populated, and village settlements grew larger and larger. About this time, the city of Susa began to achieve special prominence.

Susa
Before 3200 B.C.

The earliest occupation levels at Susa are broadly contemporary with the late 'Ubaid occupation of Mesopotamia. The first village on the site was 25 to 30 ha (62 to 74 acres) in area and was inhabited by metal-using farmers. Strong Mesopotamian influence can be detected in slightly later levels at Susa, as if there was at least some colonization of Khuzistan by Uruk people from the delta toward the end of the fourth millennium B.C.

By 3200 B.C., a distinctive cultural tradition known as the Proto-Elamite (Elamite is a language) appeared at Susa and elsewhere in Khuzistan (D. Potts, 1999). The Proto-Elamite state seems to have evolved in what is now southwestern Iran, but within a short time its distinctive tablets, seals, and ceramic types came to be found in widely scattered sites in the Iranian highlands (Carter and Stolper, 1984). Proto-Elamite clay tablets have turned up in settlements in every corner of the Iranian Plateau, in central Iran, and on the borders of Afghanistan. Susa, where the trade routes between Mesopotamia and the east converged, itself grew into a great city. The Elamite state

Elamite state
3000 to 2000 B.C.

emerged in all its complexity after 3000 B.C. and came under the rule of Akkadian kings from central Mesopotamia for a while, but by 2000 B.C., the Elamites were strong enough to attack and destroy Ur in Sumer. The Elamites' power and importance depended on their geographic position at the center of a network of trade routes that led to the Iranian Plateau, the Persian Gulf, and most city-states in the lowlands.

From as early as 6000 B.C., raw materials from the Iranian Plateau arrived in the lowlands. As the volume of the plateau trade increased, Susa was in an increasingly strategic position to control access routes (Figure 15.8). Proto-Elamite developments at Susa followed on the Uruk episode at the site and can be seen as a local reaction to the Uruk domination of lowland Khuzistan, even if the same administrative devices, such as writing and cylinder seals, were retained in local forms.

On the resource-rich Iranian Plateau, long-distance exchange joined widely separated communities in what has been called an interaction sphere, which linked most of the southern part of the region for many centuries. These long-lived networks may have connected major centers near key sources of such commodities as lapis lazuli, turquoise, chlorite, and other materials. Each center became a locus for the manufacture and exchange of prestigious objects made of these commodities, and each center maintained contacts with remote areas such as Sumer and Elam, east of the Tigris River.

One such center was Tepe Yahya, which was a prosperous rural community between 3400 and 3200 B.C. (Lamberg-Karlovsky and Beale, 1986). The inhabitants exploited local sources of chlorite (steatite). After 3200 B.C., Tepe Yahya grew and was engaged in much more intensive trading activities. Eventually, it became a political and administrative center that manufactured and traded carved chlorite bowls. The bowls produced at Tepe Yahya and elsewhere were definitely luxury items, so highly prized in Mesopotamia that they may have caused keen competition among those rich enough to afford them (Kohl, 1978). Chlorite tools and ornaments were so popular that they have been found over a very wide area of the Iranian Plateau, as well as on islands in the Persian Gulf and at Mohenjodaro, one of the major cities of the Harappan civilization of the Indus Valley (see Chapter 17).

Tepe Yahya
3400 B.C. and later

The plateau trading networks also extended to the settlement of Shari-i-Sokhta, which stood by the shores of Lake Helmand, south of the Hindu Kush in eastern Iran. An extensive trade in turquoise and lapis lazuli flourished there after 2800 B.C. The lapis was embedded in limestone in the distant Hindu Kush. Shari-i-Sokhta's artisans chipped away the limestone and turned the semiprecious stone into beads. The beads and lumps of raw lapis were then traded across the desert to Mesopotamia and also north into central Asia, probably in exchange for textiles (Tosi, 1983).

Shari-i-Shokhta
2800 B.C.

The plateau trade handled the work of local artisans but was ultimately founded on the movement of a number of vital, staple commodities, among them textiles and timber (Possehl, 1986). This trade is the subject of some controversy. Some scholars believe that the commerce was based on markets in, and was in the hands of traders controlled by, Sumer and Elam, who could affect the trade by a simple application of the laws of supply and demand (Kohl, 1978). Or perhaps the trade itself may have been controlled by entrepreneurs, but the areas of high demand for its products were both local and at a distance in Sumer and Elam. Although some of the commodities found on the Iranian Plateau may have been transported in large quantities, much exchange proceeded in more informal ways, through occasional purchases, gift exchanges, tribute, booty taking, and individual initiative. It was not until the third millennium B.C. that much larger-scale, highly organized trade became the rule rather than the exception. The Iranian Plateau trade may

FIGURE 15.8 The artisan's quarter at Susa, Iran.

have developed as an indigenous exchange system, which later spilled over to the west in response to demands from the lowlands. However, this latter trade was a question of people's getting what they could get rather than of a high degree of organization. In other words, supplies were irregular, in sharp contrast to the much more highly organized regional trade organizations that evolved after 2000 B.C. (Possehl, 1986).

Whatever the mechanisms of the Iranian trade, it is clear that an extensive network of interdependence was linking widely separated city-states and polities all over Southwest Asia by 2500 B.C. This network of interaction was highly flexible and continued to develop over many centuries, as different city-states and larger states vied with one another to control and administer ever-larger kingdoms.

The Widening of Political Authority

By 2800 B.C., Mesopotamia held several city-states, each headed by a ruler who vied with the others for status and prestige. The Sumerians were in contact with other states and urban centers in northern Mesopotamia and across the rivers in Elam and farther afield to the east. They maintained regular contacts with Anatolia, with the eastern Mediterranean coast, and sporadically with the Nile Valley. Political authority was still most effective at the city level, with temple priests as the primary controllers of trade, economic life, and political matters. Inevitably, as the societies became more complex, so the city rulers became more secular. At the same time, the volume of long-distance trade rose dramatically, to the point, some experts believe, where Sumerian rulers made a conscious decision to develop a formal maritime trade, through the Persian Gulf, with areas to the east such as the Indus Valley (see Chapter 17).

The population shifts of the third millennium B.C. may also reflect a much greater concern with defense, for both Sumerian tablets and the archaeological record tell of warfare and constant bickering between neighbors. Competition over natural resources intensified as each city-state raised an army to defend its water rights, trade routes, and city walls. As the wealth and power of the two dozen or so Sumerian cities increased, so did internecine strife. Such city-states as Erech, Kish, and Ur had periods of political strength and prosperity when they dominated their neighbors. Then, just as swiftly, the tide of their fortunes would change and they would sink into obscurity. There was a constant threat from nomadic peoples of the surrounding mountains and deserts, who encroached constantly on settled Sumerian lands. At times they disrupted city life so completely that any form of travel became an impossibility. In a real sense, the city-states were the settings for economic and social strife in early Mesopotamia (Yoffee, 1995).

Some Sumerian cities nurtured powerful leaders. When Sir Leonard Woolley (1934) excavated the Royal Cemetery in Ur (Figure 15.9), he found a series of wealthy individuals who had been buried in huge graves with their entire retinue of followers. One tomb contained the remains of 59 people who had been poisoned to accompany the deceased—courtiers and soldiers as well as serving women. Each wore his or her official dress and insignia and, having taken the poison, lay down to die in the correct order of precedence. Unfortunately, Woolley's records are too incomplete for present-day archaeologists to check his funerary scenario.

Inevitably, the ambitions of some of these powerful and proud Sumerian rulers led them to entertain bolder visions than merely the control of a few city-states in the lowlands (Postgate, 1992). They were well aware that they lived in a wider world of prosperous and not-so-prosperous neighbors, in a world in which the control of lucrative sources of raw materials and trade routes was the secret of vast political power. The first recorded success in such an endeavor was that of Lugalzagesi (c. 2360 to 2335 B.C.). Not content with the control of Uruk, Ur, Lagash, and several other cities, he boasted of overseeing the entire area from the Persian Gulf to the Mediterranean. The god Enlil, king of the lands, "made the people lie down in peaceful pastures like cattle and supplied Sumer with water bringing joyful abundance" (Kramer, 1963: 212). Lugalzagesi's boasts must be taken with a large pinch of historical salt and must be judged not in terms of conquering armies but in the context of a nascent world system of interaction and trading, which carried Sumerian political and religious ideas as far as the shores of the Mediterranean.

The tenuous and sometimes more regular contacts maintained by Mesopotamia with dozens of city-states in Anatolia and along the eastern Mediterranean coast foreshadow the constant political and economic rivalry that was to dominate Southwest Asian history during the second

FIGURE 15.9   A famous ornament from the Royal Cemetery at Ur, titled Ram in the Thicket. The wood figure of a goat was covered with gold leaf and lapis lazuli, the belly in silver leaf, and the fleece in shell. ("Ram in the Thicket." Accession #30-12-702. University of Pennsylvania Museum Neg. #T4-1000.)

millennium B.C.—rivalry over the control of Mediterranean coastal ports. Here two oceans and three continents meet. The eastern Mediterranean coast had no natural harbors, so the control of its overland routes was the key to dominating a vast area of the known world, including resource-rich Anatolia and grain-rich Egypt. There were also important copper deposits in the region.

Copper production exploded, especially in the copper-rich Jordan region. Recent excavations at Khirbat Hamra Ifdan, in the Faynan district of southern Jordan, have uncovered the largest known early Bronze Age metal workshop in southwestern Asia, dating to between 2700 and 2200 B.C. (Levy et al., 2002). This was a time of major political upheaval and social change throughout the region, yet the Khirbat workshops produced copper implements on a large scale, larger than that of major copper sources in Cyprus to the northeast. Using GIS (Geographic Information Systems) maps, Thomas Levy and his colleagues have been able to reconstruct all the stages of metal processing at the site, which operated like a production line, from mining to finished artifacts. The smelting and casting of metal took place on the south side of the site. Then the metal objects were moved into rooms on the north side of the site, where grinding and other specialized processes took place.

Khirbat Hamra Ifdan
2700 to 2200 B.C.

Khirbat Hamra Ifdan documents a quantum leap in metal production at a time when urban centers in the Levant were growing and Old Kingdom Egypt was achieving much greater complexity. The copper from the site passed along ancient trade routes to the north and even to the southwest, to the Nile Valley.

As we shall see in Chapter 19, the history of this region was bound inextricably to the fortunes of the larger powers that surrounded it.

The Akkadians

While Sumerian civilization prospered, urban centers waxed and waned in neighboring areas. In these regions, too, lived rulers with wider ambitions, who had a vision of a larger role (Sinapoli, 2001). By 2500 B.C., Akkadian cities to the north of Sumer were competing with lowland cities for trade and prestige. In approximately 2334 B.C., a Semitic-speaking leader, Sargon, founded a ruling dynasty at the town of Agade, south of Babylon. By skillful commercial ventures and judicious military campaigns, his northern dynasty soon established its rule over a much larger kingdom that included both Sumer and northern Mesopotamia (Liverani, 1993).

Akkadian state
c. 2334 to 2112 B.C.

After a short period of economic prosperity, northern Mesopotamia went through a catastrophic drought that lasted some 300 years (Weiss, 2000). Starving farmers thronged to the rich southern cities. Violent clashes ensued, and the Akkadian kingdom collapsed. Fifty years of political instability followed before King Ur-Nammu of Ur took control of Sumer and Akkad in 2112 B.C. and created an empire that extended far to the north. Sargon had forged an empire by military conquest but had never followed up his victories with proper administrative governance. Ur-Nammu and his successors of III Dynasty of Ur were a new breed of rulers who placed great emphasis on consolidating their new empire into a powerful and well-organized bureaucracy. We know much of this kingdom from thousands of administrative tablets from III Dynasty levels at Ur (Steinkeller, 1989). With the Akkadian and Ur empires was forged a persistent tradition of Mesopotamian civilization: the combination of trade, conquest, ruthless administration, and tribute to create large, poorly integrated, and highly volatile empires that sought to rule an enormous territory between the Mediterranean and the Persian Gulf.

III Dynasty of Ur
2112 to 1990 B.C.

Babylon

Ur in turn gave way to Babylon and its Semitic rulers by 1990 B.C. Babylon's early greatness culminated in the reign of the great king Hammurabi in 1792 B.C. He integrated the smaller kingdoms of Mesopotamia for a short period, but his empire declined after his death, as Babylonian trade to the Persian Gulf collapsed and trade ties to Assur in the north and for Mediterranean copper in the west were strengthened.

The Assyrians

By this time, the various masters of Mesopotamia had become major players in a much wider eastern Mediterranean world (see Chapter 19). They vied with the Hittites of Anatolia, with the city of Mitanni on the Euphrates, and with the Egyptians for control of the eastern Mediterranean coast. Perhaps the most successful of these Mesopotamian masters were the Assyrians, who rose to prominence in the mid-fourteenth century B.C. as Babylon declined.

Assyrian Empire
c. 1000 to 612 B.C.

Assur on the Tigris had been a major force in Southwest Asian trade since Sumerian times (M. Larsen, 1995; Postgate, 1992). The merchants of Assur traded far to the east and west and controlled the trade down the Tigris to Babylon and beyond. The city came into great prominence during the reign of King Assuruballit (1365 to 1330 B.C.). He created a great state through ruthless and efficient conquest and political maneuvering that maintained diplomatic relations with the pharaohs of Egypt, with the Hittite and Mitanni kingdoms of Anatolia (see Chapter 19) and with Babylon. His power was based on control of trade routes and of the rich cereal-growing lands of northern Iraq, as well as on military prowess. His armies swept everything before them and occupied Babylon for a while. The empire collapsed soon after the king's death.

A second imperial expansion occurred in the ninth century B.C. under Assyrian monarchs based in northern Iraq, who expanded their domains with annual campaigns of military conquest. These were absolute despots, vain and grandiloquent men, who boasted of their conquests on their palace walls (Figure 15.10) (Russell, 1991). When King Assurnasirpal completed his palace at Nimrud, he threw a party for the 16,000 inhabitants of the city, 1,500 royal officials, "47,074 men and women from the length of my country," and 5,000 foreign envoys (Postgate, 1992). The king fed this throng of more than 69,000 people for 10 days, during which time his guests ate 14,000 sheep and consumed more than 10,000 skins of wine. Following a succession crisis, the Assyrian Empire collapsed but was revived in a more bureaucratically efficient form by King Tiglath-pileser III.

The last of the great Assyrian kings was Assurbanipal, who died in approximately 630 B.C. When he died, the Assyrian Empire entered a period of political chaos. The Babylonians achieved inde-

Babylonian Empire
612 to 556 B.C.

pendence, and Assyrian power was finally broken in 612 B.C., when the Persians and Babylonians sacked the capital at Nineveh. For 43 years, the mighty King Nebuchadnezzar of Babylon ruled over Mesopotamia and turned his capital into one of the showpieces of the ancient world (Wiseman, 1985). Imposing mud-brick palaces with elaborate hanging gardens, a great processional way, and a huge ziggurat adorned his double-walled city. It was to Babylon that a large contingent of Jews were taken as captives after Nebuchadnezzar's armies sacked Jerusalem, an exile immortalized by the lament "By the waters of Babylon we sat down and wept" (Psalms 137:1).

The Babylonian Empire did not long survive the death of Nebuchadnezzar, in 556 B.C. His successors were weak men who were unable to resist the external forces that now pressed on Meso-

539 B.C.

potamia. The armies of Cyrus, the Great of Persia, took Babylon virtually without resistance in 539 B.C., and Mesopotamia became part of an empire even larger than that of the Assyrians. By this time, the effects of constant political instability and bad agricultural management were beginning to make themselves felt. The Mesopotamian Delta was a totally artificial environment by 2000 B.C., and poor drainage and badly maintained irrigation works in later centuries led to inexorable rises in the salt content of the soil and to drastic falls in crop yields in some areas. Nothing could be done to reverse this trend until modern soil science and irrigation techniques could be imported to the delta at vast expense.

FIGURE 15.10 Assyrian King Assurbanipal kills lions released from cages in his park and driven toward him, c. 645 B.C.

Summary

- By 7000 B.C., highland peoples had settled in northern Mesopotamia in areas where agriculture was possible through the use of seasonal rainfall. These Hassuna people lived in close contact with other societies downstream that developed irrigation agriculture.

- In about 6500 B.C., Halafian painted wares appeared over a wide area of upland northern Mesopotamia and Anatolia; they are thought to have coincided with the emergence of chiefdoms in this area.

- The delta lowlands may have supported farmers before 6500 B.C., but the first traces of them appear in the 'Ubaid culture of the sixth millennium. They practiced small-scale irrigation and lived in groups of communities linked by trade networks.

- In time, some villages, like Eridu, became ceremonial centers and towns. A rapid evolution to urban life ensued, marked by fast population growth, the congregation of people in small cities, and the development of long-distance trade. This new urban society was organized in distinctive stratified social classes. Copper metallurgy developed at about the same time in the highlands and soon came into widespread use.

- By 2900 B.C., Sumerian civilization was in full swing and was part of what we call a nascent world system, which linked polities as far afield as the Iranian Plateau and the Indus in the east and the Mediterranean and the Nile Valley in the west.

- Mesopotamia never achieved political unification under the Sumerians. Rather, dozens of city-states vied for political and economic supremacy and competed with other societies in northern Mesopotamia and close to the Zagros Mountains.

- Sumerian civilization flourished until about 2000 B.C., when it was eclipsed by Akkadian and then Babylonian power.

- In the late second millennium B.C., the city of Assur in the north nurtured the Assyrian Empire, which was extended by vigorous and despotic kings during the first half of the succeeding millennium. At one time, the Assyrian Empire stretched from the Mediterranean to the Persian Gulf.

- The Assyrian Empire fell in 612 B.C., and the power vacuum was filled by the Babylonians under the rule of Nebuchadnezzar. Babylon fell to Cyrus the Great of Persia in 539 B.C., and Mesopotamia became part of the Persian Empire.

Key Term

cuneiform (317)

Further Reading

Crawford, Harriett. 2004. *Sumer and the Sumerians*, 2nd ed. Cambridge, UK: Cambridge University Press.

Kramer, Samuel. 1963. *The Sumerians.* Chicago: University of Chicago Press.

Postgate, Nicholas. 1992. *Early Mesopotamia: Economy and Society at the Dawn of History.* London: Kegan Paul.

16 Egypt, Nubia, and Tropical Africa

"Nearly overcome, I . . . contrived to sit; but when my weight bore on the body of an Egyptian, it crushed it like a band-box. . . . I sank altogether among the broken mummies, with a crash of bones, rags, and wooden cases, which raised such a dust as kept me motionless for a quarter of an hour, waiting till it subsided again." Thus did the notorious Giovanni Belzoni, circus performer turned tomb robber, explore ancient Egypt in 1817. Belzoni and his ilk thought nothing of using gunpowder, even of going after rivals with a gun, for everyone was out for spectacular finds and all the loot they could gather. Yet the modern science of Egyptology sprang from these adventurous roots. A gentler breed of patient scientists and hieroglyph experts followed Belzoni. They have spent more than a century piecing together the portrait of ancient Egyptian civilization we enjoy today (Fagan, 2004b). ■

Bas-relief of the goddess Ma'at.
Painted stone relief. Egypt, Nineteenth Dynasty. Museo Archeologico, Florence, Italy.
Copyright Scala/Art Resource, NY.

The Origins of the Egyptian State

Archaeological evidence tells us that by 5000 B.C. simple farming based on cattle herding and cereal agriculture had replaced a combination of foraging and cultivation along the Nile as far south as what is now the Sudan, ushering in the pre-Dynastic period of Egyptian history (Bard, 1994; see relevant articles in Shaw, 2000). Two thousand years later, a patchwork of small kingdoms and villages had become a unified state with a distinctive, common ideology (Figure 16.1; Table 16.1).

From the earliest centuries of farming, Egypt formed two broad regions. Lower Egypt encompassed the Nile Delta and Mediterranean coast and the Nile River as far upstream as modern Cairo. Upper Egypt extended upstream as far south as the First Cataract, just above the modern town of Aswân. The process of unification brought these two regions under a single government.

FIGURE 16.1 Ancient Egypt, Ethiopia, and Nubia.

Ancient Monopoly?

Most explanations of the origin of the state focus on population growth and competition for land and natural resources. In Egypt's case, state formation took place where population densities were still relatively low and there was plenty of vacant land, so neither of these factors played a significant role. Egyptologist Barry Kemp (2005) believes that the village farmers of 4000 B.C. had strong ties to their ancestral lands, expressed in deeply symbolic terms. At first, dozens of small communities, each with its own patchwork of farming land, competed and traded with their neighbors.

Kemp likens the behavior and long-term effects to those in a game of Monopoly. In Monopoly, each player maximizes the opportunities presented by a throw of the dice. In Egypt, both individuals and entire villages took full advantage of favorable locations; of their access to desirable resources, like potting clay; and of chance breaks that came their way. At first the communities, like Monopoly players, were basically equal, but inevitably someone, or some hamlet, gained an unforeseen advantage, perhaps from trading expertise or unusually high crop yields. Equilibrium gave way to a seemingly inevitable momentum in which some communities acquired more wealth and more power than their neighbors—the prehistoric equivalent of building Monopoly hotels on Park Avenue. Their victory was inevitable, as they established a monopoly over local trade, food surpluses, and so on, which overrode any threat posed by other political or economic players.

In pre-Dynastic times, there were probably hundreds of such "games" in progress. As time went on, the number of players decreased, but the stakes were higher as increasingly large chiefdoms vied for economic power and political dominance. Just as in Monopoly, the players changed over time, some acquiring great power, then losing it as charismatic individuals died or trading opportunities changed. Kemp points out that Egypt had more than enough fertile land and resources to enable such games to play out over many generations. Surplus resources like grain or toolmaking stone were the foundation of power. But he believes that the Egyptians also had a genius for weaving a distinctive ideology that connected leadership and authority with elaborate symbols and rituals. These ideologies became a powerful factor in promoting unification.

The elaborate processes of state formation leave few signals in the archaeological record. In Egypt, such changes triggered the formation of larger settlements, small towns with all their potential for intensive interaction among individuals. Their leaders were buried with elaborate grave goods and with symbols denoting an emerging ideology of power.

Naqada, Nekhen, and Maadi

At least three pre-Dynastic chiefdoms flourished in Upper Egypt in about 3500 B.C.: Naqada, Nekhen, and This, near Abydos (little known and not discussed here), the ancestors of a larger "proto-kingdom" that eventually formed the nucleus of a unified Egypt (Figure 16.2). Another chiefdom, centered on Maadi, ruled part of the delta.

Naqada Major changes in human settlement can be seen at Naqada in Upper Egypt, 25 km (15.5 miles) south of Thebes (the ancient Egyptian Waset), where small hamlets were spaced about 1 km (0.6 mile) apart in 4000 B.C. (Midant-Reynes, 2000). Demographic archaeologist Fekri

Naqada
c. 4000 B.C.

TABLE 16.1
The web of relationships between Asia, Africa, and other regions after 500 B.C.

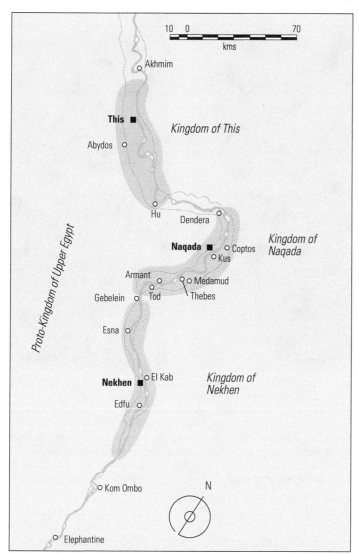

FIGURE 16.2 The spread of the Upper Egyptian proto-kingdom through the Nile Valley, c. 3300 B.C. This is a gross simplification of a very complex, and ever-changing, political situation.

Hassan (1988) calculated that these small settlements grew enough grain on land at the edge of the floodplain to support 76 to 114 persons per sq. km (0.36 sq. mile). By clearing trees and removing dense grass growth, and by building dikes and digging drainage canals to clear still-inundated acreage, the farmers opened up much larger tracts of agricultural land. By the time the farmers had taken four, or even eight, times more ground under cultivation, they could support as many as 760 to 1,520 people per square kilometer, many of them nonfarmers: officials, traders, and artisans living in permanent towns. A walled town with cemeteries stood in the heart of the Naqada area by 3600 B.C. The housing form was new: rectangular mud-brick dwellings that were typical of later Egyptian villages. In some settlements, larger, more palatial residences housed a prosperous elite who enjoyed contacts with other communities up- and downstream. Naqada may have been the capital of a major chiefdom.

Nekhen Nekhen (the Greek name is Hierankopolis) flourished upstream, the "City of the Falcon" in Upper Egypt (R. Friedman et al., 1999; M. Hoffman et al., 1982). In 3800 B.C., Nekhen was still a small, insignificant community inhabited by a few hundred people. During the next three centuries, the population mushroomed to as many as 10,500 townsfolk. People lived in closely clustered mud-brick and plaster dwellings, the wealthier artisans and traders in larger houses with separate compounds. For the first time, there were signs of social differentiation in Egyptian society. The Abu Suffian cemetery near Nekhen housed prominent citizens, many of them prosperous traders who had profited from locally made, fine-quality Plum Red pottery, which was used to adorn tombs up and down the river. These people became powerful members of the community, having widespread contacts with settlements near and far. One "royal" tomb was adorned with wall paintings depicting a ruler smiting his enemies and sitting under an awning. Both motifs survived into later pharaonic times.

Nekhen
3800 to 3000 B.C.

FIGURE 16.3 The Narmer palette, a slab of slate carved on both sides with scenes commemorating King Narmer of Nekhen. Narmer lived just before the First Dynasty. On this side, he wears the white crown of Upper Egypt. He carries a pear-shaped macehead in his right hand and is about to smite a captive, perhaps from the delta in Lower Egypt. Above the victim, a falcon head (the southern Horus) emerges from papyrus reeds carrying a human head. A sandal bearer follows the king, who stands on two dead enemies. The other side shows the ruler wearing the red crown of Lower Egypt as he inspects decapitated enemies from the town of Buto in the delta. A central design of two mythical beasts with intertwined necks symbolizes harmony. The palette symbolizes not only Narmer's military victories but also the complex process of unification, which took several centuries, much fighting, and complex diplomatic maneuvering. Palette height: 63 cm (29 inches).

About 3500 B.C., the fragile ecological balance of desert and grassland collapsed, perhaps as a result of overgrazing by goats and sheep and of intensive pottery firing by local artisans, both of which stripped local tree cover. Hoffman believes that some of the local leaders profited from the disaster by using their wealth to foster irrigation agriculture and settlement closer to the Nile. Their venture was successful and yielded large grain surpluses under the control of the new elite. They used their wealth to increase trade, erect public buildings like temples, and invest in imposing sepulchers. The ambitious leaders of Nekhen were buried in the same Abu Suffian cemetery, which straddled a dry gulch, their graves laid out on either side of the wadi (gully) in what Hoffman believes is a symbolic map of a unified Upper and Lower Egypt.

Nekhen yielded the celebrated Narmer palette (Figure 16.3), which commemorates King Narmer's victory over a northern ruler in about 3000 B.C. Narmer wears the crowns of Upper and Lower Egypt. He is faced on one side by the god Horus. The palette displays the full artistic canon of pharaonic Egypt and is a powerful symbol of unification.

Maadi There were certainly other polities downstream in Lower Egypt, but their capitals lie under thousands of years of accumulated silt. A poorly defined Maadi culture flourished over much of the delta, made up of small towns and farming villages. The Maadi site itself, on the outskirts of modern Cairo, was a major trading center in about 3650 B.C., a place with large, roofed oval or rectangular cellars up to 4 m (13 feet) long and 1 to 2 m (3 to 7 feet) deep. They contained jars, grains, animal and fish bones, stone vases, beads, and lumps of imported asphalt. Rows of large clay storage pots held grain, cooked meat, dried fish, flint tools, spindle whorls, and other objects. Maadi was a key link in a major trade network that brought commodities from the eastern Mediterranean coastal region and perhaps even from Mesopotamia to the Nile, probably by donkey caravan (Caneva et al., 1987).

The delta's archaeological record also reflects major political and social change in other places. At the El-Omari sites, one location contains more than 100 dwellings, as well as the burial of a chief or ruler holding a well-made wooden staff or scepter. This remarkable object, pointed at one end and flat at the other, foreshadows the ceremonial staffs carried by later Egyptian pharaohs and

Maadi
3650 B.C.

gods. Many imports have been found in the El-Omari settlements, among them seashells, ostrich eggshells, mother of pearl, and necklaces and pendants fabricated from Red Sea gastropods.

In contrast to the simpler burials of earlier centuries, the El-Omari dead were buried in cemeteries outside the settlement, the body wrapped in a mat or coarse fabric and placed on its left side, facing south. One cemetery associated with a small village contained the burials of higher-status individuals, graves covered with stone mounds. Interestingly, the village contained many cellarlike storage areas that held large numbers of stone tools and roughed-out blanks for such implements as knife blades and arrowheads. The settlement may have belonged to traders, who apparently maintained contacts with the eastern Mediterranean coast (Rizkana and Seeher, 1984).

Expanded trading activity helped fill in rural populations along the floodplain. Contacts between people living both within and outside the Nile Valley intensified dramatically. But distances along the Nile were so large that significant regional differences emerged, with a boundary between Upper and Lower Egypt somewhere near modern Cairo. The increased volume of trade during late pre-Dynastic times is reflected in the importation of not only copper but also other exotic items that occur in profusion in sites of about 3500 B.C. Some of these objects are of unmistakable west Asian or Mesopotamian origin. The Naqada site, for example, yielded a cylinder seal of Mesopotamian form. Some pots bear depictions of Mesopotamian boat designs and of fabulous animals and creatures with intertwined necks and other motifs that derive from Asia.

Writing

The same trade brought another innovation: the art of writing, which became fully developed in Egypt in about 3100 B.C. **Hieroglyphs** (Greek for "sacred carving") are commonly thought to be a form of picture writing. In fact they constitute a script that combines pictographs (pictures) and phonetics (vocal sounds), and they were not only written on papyrus but also carved on public buildings or painted on clay or wood. Writing was probably first developed in Mesopotamia, and Egyptian priests developed their own script, which was easier to produce with papyrus-reed paper and ink than on clay. Doubtless, early hieroglyphs played a significant role in trade and record keeping, but they also may have evolved as a way of conveying the meanings of funerary rituals on painted pots deposited with the dead (Hassan, 1988).

3100 B.C.

Ultimately, Egyptian scribes developed a cursive (running-on) hieroglyphic script that was a form of handwriting and was much easier to use on documents and other, less formal communications. Only the consonants were written in all forms of hieroglyphs; the vowel sounds were omitted, although both were pronounced. With practice, reading this form of script is easy enough, and a sample test of this script should show this quite well (Figure 16.4) (Robinson, 2007).

The acquisition of writing, with all its organizational possibilities, was one of the catalysts for the unification of all Egypt into a single political entity.

A Scenario for Unification

Archaeology and myth combine for a hypothetical scenario of unification: By 3500 B.C., the kingdoms of Upper Egypt may have had direct contact with southern Arabia and Southwest Asia, bypassing Lower Egypt. Mesopotamian cylinder seals have come from Upper Egyptian sites, and gold was obtained from mines in the desert east of the Nile. Conflict ensued, with the politically most developed center, Nekhen, emerging victorious. The rulers of Nekhen finally embarked on a campaign of military conquest, which eventually engulfed all of Egypt between the Mediterranean and Aswân. By 3100 B.C., a semblance of political unity, commemorated by the Narmer palette, joined Upper and Lower Egypt in the symbolic linking of the gods Horus and Seth depicted in later Egyptian art. As these events unfolded, a new state came into being, founded not only on physical but also

Unification
c. 3100 B.C.

FIGURE 16.4 Egyptian writing is referred to as hieroglyphs, the familiar symbols that appear in formal inscriptions and on tomb walls. In fact, Egyptian scribes also developed cursive hands used for everyday purposes. These examples show formal hieroglyphic script (top line) and below it both the cursive script and the scribe's shorthand, which was used for rapid writing.

Hieroglyphs				
Cursive hand (hieratic script)				
Shorthand				
Translation	Amun	ròemt humankind	per-'o Pharaoh	hru day

on a symbolic geography, a harmony achieved by balanced opposites, of which Horus and Seth are only one manifestation. For thousands of years, the Egyptians were concerned with the potential of a world torn between potential chaos and order. They believed that disorder—disequilibrium—could be contained by the rule of kings and by the benign force of the power of the sun. Thus, the Egyptians' intellectual view of the universe coincided with the structure of political power.

Unification was the culmination of local social and political developments that resulted from centuries of gradual change in economic and social life. Pre-Dynastic villages were autonomous units, each with its local deities. During the fourth millennium B.C., the larger villages became the focal points of different territories, which in Dynastic times became the *nomes*, or provinces, through which the pharaohs administered Egypt. The *nomarchs* (provincial leaders) were responsible for the gradual coalescence of Egypt into larger political and social units. Their deeds are recorded on ceremonial palettes that were used for moistening eye powder. Some of these palettes show alliances of local leaders dismantling conquered villages. Others commemorate the administrative skills of leaders who had brought their villages through drought years by skillful management.

The unification of Egypt was a gradual process of both voluntary and involuntary amalgamation. Voluntary unification resulted from common needs and economic advantage. Perhaps it was only in the final stages of unification that military force came into play to bring larger and larger political units under single rulers (Bard, 2000).

Intensification of Agriculture and Irrigation

Unification may have involved some intensification of agriculture as population densities rose; but as Karl Butzer (1976) pointed out, the Egyptian technology for lifting water was so rudimentary that the early rulers were unable to organize any elaborate forms of irrigation. In all probability, most ancient Egyptian agriculture involved irrigation schemes on a modest scale that merely extended the distribution of seasonal floodwaters from natural flood basins. Still, even these efforts must have required a considerable degree of administrative organization. Also, with a centralized form of administration, the divine leader, the pharaoh himself, was responsible for the success of the harvest. Since the Nile flood fluctuated considerably in cycles of abundant and lean years, and the pharaohs could do little to control the success or failure of irrigation without much more elaborate technology than they possessed, their political position could, theoretically, be threatened by famine years: If the divine leader could not provide, who could? Perhaps a different leader would provide. Small wonder that some periods of political instability, which may have coincided with poor flood years, saw rapid successions of ineffective pharaohs, as was the case at the end of the Old Kingdom, c. 2180 B.C.

Butzer (1976) pointed out that civilizations can be regarded as ecosystems that emerge in response to sets of ecological opportunities. Over time, a variety of social and environmental adjustments are inevitable, some of them successful, leading to population growth, and others unsuccessful, so that the population shrinks. These demographic adjustments are commonly associated with ups and downs of political power. The political structures of, say, ancient Egyptian civilization were not nearly as durable as the basic adaptive system they purported to control or the cultural identity of which they had once been a part. Butzer draws an analogy with the ecological concept of trophic levels among biotic communities, in which organisms such as herbivores and carnivores define successive tiers interlinked in a vertical chain. Likewise, he hypothesizes, an efficient social hierarchy comprises several levels arranged in what he calls a "low-angle pyramid, supported by a broad base of farmers and linked to the peak of the pyramid by a middle-level bureaucracy. The vertical structures channel food and information through the system, and an efficient energy flow allows each trophic level to flourish in a steady state" (p. 22). In this model, a flatter pyramid with little vertical structure would provide less information flow and would limit the potential productivity of the lower levels. Butzer's pyramid would allow growth at the lower levels, with new technologies or organizational devices favoring expanded energy generation. A steep, top-heavy pyramid laden with nobles and bureaucrats, however, places so much burden on the lowest levels that external and internal forces can undermine the stability of the society.

This model, when applied to the long history of ancient Egyptian civilization, shows how the Egyptians persisted in adjusting to a floodplain environment for thousands of years. They overcame external and internal crises by reorganizing their state and economic structure. The key variables were the fluctuations of the Nile itself, occasional foreign intervention, the character of the pharaohs' leadership, and a progressively more out-of-touch society of elite nonproducers who persisted in exploiting the common farmer, a process that led to eventual social collapse. However, through all these variables, the essential components of the sociopolitical system survived more or less intact, right up to the nineteenth century B.C. Indeed, the visitor to rural Egypt can still see farming villages functioning much as they did in ancient Egyptian times.

Archaic Egypt and the Creation of the Great Culture (2920 to 2575 B.C.)

Egyptologists conventionally divide ancient Egyptian civilization into four broad periods: Archaic Egypt and the Old Kingdom, the Middle Kingdom, the New Kingdom, and the Late period. The first three were separated by two intermediate periods that were intervals of political change and instability (Table 16.2) (Aldred, 2004; Kemp. 2005; T. Wilkinson, 2011).

The Archaic period, comprising the first four and a half centuries of Egyptian civilization, was a long and complex period of consolidation, of subordinating powerful local chiefdoms into a unified whole (T. Wilkinson, 2001). Narmer and his successors assumed awesome responsibilities. They inherited all the powers of village shamans, or curers, and were thought to have complete authority over the Nile, its life-giving inundation and the fertility of the soil. Contending with the forces of evil, they were depicted smiting nomads from the desert east of the Nile and hostile Nubians from upstream. The pharaohs wore the regalia of pastoral chiefs, carrying the crook and the incense-gum-collecting flail of a shepherd. They developed the centralized bureaucracy that directed labor and collected taxes. Above all, they "invented" Egypt's pharaonic tradition, converting its ideology into architectural and artistic styles that survived for centuries. Royal tombs became statements on kingship. The early pharaohs and their high officials developed a mechanism of symbolic geography, a national framework of myth, which accommodated regional diversity, reflected in art and architecture. Just like the Mesoamerican rulers (Chapter 21), the pharaohs made a great play of their rare public appearances, developing spectacular settings for major ritual events and festivals.

At the center of the state lay the concept of a great king, a terrestrial ruler, who symbolized the triumph of order over universal chaos. The ideas and ideals that legitimized the rule of the pharaohs over their subjects survived the ups and downs of political history for 3,000 years. In Egypt, the terms *father*, *king*, and *god* were metaphors for one another and for a form of political power based on the inequality considered part of a natural order established by the gods at the time of creation.

Archaic period
2920 to 2575 B.C.

TABLE 16.2
Major subdivisions and developments of ancient Egyptain civilizations

Years B.C.	Period	Characteristics
30	Roman occupation	Egypt becomes an imperial province of Rome.
332 to 30	Ptolemaic period	The Ptolemies bring Greek influence to Egypt, beginning with the conquest of Egypt by Alexander the Great in 332 B.C.
1070 to 332	Late period	Gradual decline in pharaonic authority, culminating in Persian rule (525 to 404 and 343 to 332 B.C.).
1530 to 1070	New Kingdom	Great imperial period of Egyptian history, with pharaohs buried in the Valley of Kings; pharaohs include Rameses II, Seti I, and Tutankhamun, as well as Akhenaten, the heretic ruler.
1640 to 1530	Second Intermediate period	Hyksos rulers in the delta.
2040 to 1640	Middle Kingdom	Thebes achieves prominence, also the priesthood of Amun.
2180 to 2040	First Intermediate period	Political chaos and disunity.
2575 to 2180	Old Kingdom	Despotic pharaohs build the pyramids and favor conspicuous funerary monuments; institutions, economic strategies, and artistic traditions of ancient Egypt established.
3100 to 2575	Archaic period	Consolidation of the state (treated as part of the Old Kingdom in this book).
c. 3150	Unification of Egypt under Narmer (Menes)	

The early civilizations depended on the skillful administration of resources of all kinds. Power came not so much from landownership as from the control of agricultural surpluses and labor, also from draconian force (T. Wilkinson, 2011). The manipulation of these resources was for the benefit of a tiny elite, but the benefits spread to a significant sector of the general population. Rulers everywhere in the ancient world relied on a classic resource cycle: taxation, which brought in resources, and redistribution, which distributed them to large numbers of people working for the benefit of the state. Such resource cycles require precise record keeping and an army of officials to monitor every transaction. Two words sum up the passions of early bureaucracies: system and detail. In a preindustrial society like Egypt, where money was unknown, people bartered food and other commodities. The entire Egyptian government functioned on a system of rations and bartering. At the core of this nonmoney society, as in other early civilizations, was writing.

Most people in modern industrial societies can read and write. But in Egyptian society, those who could read and write were among the elite. To be a scribe ("writing man") was an honored calling. "Be a scribe. Your limbs will be sleek, your hands will grow soft. You will go forth in white clothes, honored, with courtiers saluting you," a young man is advised. The title of scribe was an essential part of a high Egyptian official's qualifications, writing being the accomplishment valued above all other crafts, even highly skilled ones. Writing was power, the key to controlling the labor of hundreds, if not thousands, of people.

Bureaucracy is sometimes a pejorative word in our society, but it was a valued institution in Egypt, where everything depended on the equitable and prompt distribution of food rations instead of wages. Scribes supervised every moment of the food cycle. They measured grain yields at the threshing floor, monitored the grain in transit to curb pilfering, and inventoried granaries—even the loaves turned out by bakers. They also collected taxation, in kind and in labor. Officialdom was essential to Egypt's long-term survival. High officials could raise armies and build temples. They were the instruments of cooperation, conservative, long-term planners who tried to mitigate the impact of an unpredictable river. Egyptian civilization survived because of this conservatism and the cohesion wrought by strongly centralized economic control and the use of a mailed fist when deemed necessary.

This new administrative mechanism was put to an early test. Between 3000 and 2800 B.C., average Nile floods dropped 1 to 2 m (3 to 5 feet), to about 30 percent below normal. Judging from the historically documented inundation of A.D. 1877, which was 2.1 m (6.5 feet) below average, about a third of the valley would have remained dry. Simple irrigation and flood basin agriculture would have been no protection against such a disaster. During these two centuries, we know that desert nomads encroached on settled valley lands and that the pharaohs barely survived armed insurrection and civil unrest. But the state endured, probably because of decisive administration and the increasing government control of food surpluses.

Abydos
3150 B.C.

We know little of the earliest pharaohs except from their tombs in the Umm el-Qa'ab cemetery at Abydos, believed to be the sacred gateway to the mythic realm of the underworld. The First and Second Dynasty kings lay in mud-brick chambers built in large pits. Such sepulchers were a direct development from earlier graves, marked with a pair of freestanding columns carved with the king's name. A separate funerary palace closer to the Nile floodplain consisted of a double enclosure with a freestanding building inside. Both the enclosure walls and the building were adorned with niches decorated with paintings and brightly colored matting. The entire structure was a formal setting for the receipt of tribute and other major ceremonial occasions when the king appeared in public. The royal tomb had already become a key symbol of kingship. Such symbols were magnified tenfold a generation later with the appearance of the first pyramids.

These were the centuries when the "Great Culture" of Egypt was born, a culture that originated in royal courts from large-scale public works and carefully organized patronage of the arts and crafts. The Great Culture was a tradition that became part of the instruments of authority, a distinctive ideology that systematized religion and other cultural expressions over wide areas at the expense of local traditions. As the Great Culture expanded, so the "little culture" of provincial towns and villages shrank, even if local gods made their appearances at state ceremonies as symbols of unification.

The Old Kingdom and the Pyramids (c. 2575 to 2180 B.C.)

Old Kingdom
2575 to 2180 B.C.

The Old Kingdom saw four dynasties of pharaohs governing Egypt from a royal capital at Memphis, near Cairo. By this time, Egyptian society had been shaped in the image of a state where the well-being of the common people depended on their ruler, who was supported by their labors. Some of the pharaohs had reputations as cruel despots, notably Khufu and Khafre, who built the pyramid-tombs of Giza, stretching the state's economic resources to the limit and using force to achieve their goals and keep the populace in check.

The Archaic and Old Kingdom pharaohs used dramatic settings for their public appearances. A large open space, an elevated place shaded with a canopy where the king would be glimpsed, and a small palace for donning formal attire and resting—these were the ingredients of a setting for the pageantry accompanying the eternity of death, and for the vital Sed festival, the jubilee celebration of 30 years of royal rule. The first, and one of the most spectacular, setting for such a ceremony was the famous Step Pyramid of Djoser at Saqqara (see Site box).

Saqqara
2650 B.C.

Djoser and his predecessors were terrestrial monarchs, supreme rulers epitomizing the triumph of order over chaos. But a new image of kingship emerged some time after his death in 2649 B.C. The ruler was now absorbed into the mystic symbol of the sun. An increasingly powerful priesthood fused sun worship with the cult of the pharaoh. The sun god became a heavenly monarch, the pharaoh no longer a territorial conqueror but the deity's representative on earth. After death, the king assumed the identity of Osiris, the Lord of the Dead. According to Egyptian beliefs, the stars were divine beings and the ruler was destined to take his place among them. "The king goes to his double. . . a ladder is set up for him that he may ascend on it," says a spell in a royal Pyramid Text (Edwards, 1985: 12). (Pyramid Texts are texts inscribed in pyramid chambers.) Thus it was that the Old Kingdom pharaohs lavished enormous resources on the building of their sepulchers—at first, earthen mounds, then pyramids that became symbolic ladders to heaven.

Egyptologist I. E. S. Edwards believes that the growing influence of the sun cult led to new conceptions of the afterlife that had the deceased ruler following the sun god across the sky. Thus, he needed a new way to climb to heaven, on the rays of the sun itself. "I have laid down for myself those rays of yours as a stairway under my feet on which I will ascend," the king tells the sun god Ra in one Fifth Dynasty Pyramid Text (Edwards, 1985). The pyramids were symbolic depictions in stone of the sun's rays bursting through the clouds, a permanent stone stairway with the king's mortuary temple on the east side, the side of the rising sun (Lehner, 1997) (Figure 16.5).

The court cemeteries and pyramid complexes of the Old Kingdom pharaohs extend over a 35-km (22-mile) stretch of the western desert edge, most of it slightly north of Memphis. In about 2528 B.C., Khufu built the Great Pyramid of Giza, one of the spectacular wonders of ancient Africa and one of the Seven Wonders of the Ancient World. It covers 5.3 ha (13.1 acres) and is 146 m (481 feet) high. Well over 2 million limestone blocks, some weighing 15 tons each, went into its construction. A long causeway linked each pyramid in the Giza complex to a royal mortuary temple. These were austere buildings that housed statues of the king, best shown in the complex of Khafra, who built the second pyramid of Giza. Khafra's temple was crafted in limestone and granite. Ceiling-height louvers let in a diffused glow that shone on the royal figures within. Khafra himself sat on a royal throne, protected by the god Horus, who wraps his wings around the nape of the pharaoh's neck. The nearby sepulchers vested these temples with great authority, for they associated the ruler with what was, in effect, a powerful ancestor cult that linked them to their predecessors and to the gods.

Giza
2528 B.C.

We do not know why the pharaohs suddenly embarked on this orgy of pyramid construction, with all the accompanying demands that it made on the fledgling state. Their construction, like other major Egyptian public works, was a triumph of bureaucratic organization, of organizing and transporting food and building materials. Officials marshaled skilled artisans and village laborers to quarry, dig, and drag stone into place. What is staggering is the efficient management overview, achieved without computers, deploying and supporting thousands of villagers for short periods of time, as they fulfilled their annual tax-by-labor obligations to the state.

Perhaps, as Kurt Mendelssohn (1974) argued, the pyramids were built as a means of linking the people to their guardian, the king, and to the sun god, the source of human life and of bountiful harvests. The relationship between the king and his subjects was both one of mutual obligation and of spiritual fellowship. The pharaoh was a divine king, whose person was served by annual labor. In short, pyramid building created public works that helped to define the authority of the ruler and to make his subjects dependent on him. Every flood season, when agriculture was at a standstill, the pharaohs organized thousands of peasants into construction teams. The permanent (year-round) labor force comprised relatively few, mainly skilled artisans, the fruit of whose work was placed in position on the main

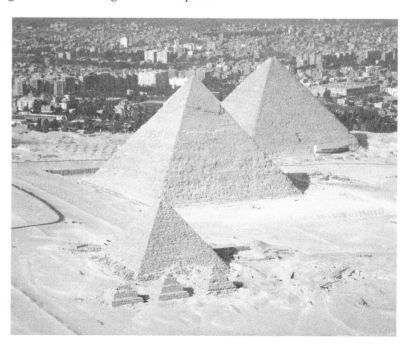

FIGURE 16.5 The pyramids of Giza. The culmination of royal pyramid building, these stupendous tombs formed part of a much larger mortuary complex of causeways, temples, and elite cemeteries.

SiTE > The Step Pyramid at Saqqara, Egypt <

Like other early Old Kingdom kings, Third Dynasty pharaoh Djoser (2668 to 2649 B.C.) grappled with internal political problems. He managed to extend his rule as far upstream as Aswân and put great emphasis on his role as king and supreme territorial claimant—a role he celebrated within a large enclosure dominated by a unique structure, the Step Pyramid at Saqqara opposite the royal capital at Memphis.

Djoser's vizier Imhotep devised the architecture of the Step Pyramid (Figure 16.6). The great architect drew his inspiration from earlier royal tombs, rectangular structures like those at Abydos, which were eternal mansions for dead monarchs. Such *tumuli* (mounds) had associations with the primordial earthen mound that formed an integral part of the Egyptian legend of the creation. Imhotep erected a stepped pyramid instead of a mound. It rose in six diminishing steps to over 60 m (372 feet) above the desert, the faces oriented to the cardinal points. The effect is like a giant double staircase rising toward heaven. A wall with a palacelike façade over 1.6 km (1 mile) in perimeter surrounded the entire mortuary complex. The court before the pyramid was a setting for royal appearances, complete with ceremonial territorial markers, a throne platform, and a token palace. On occasion, the pharaoh laid claim to his kingdom by striding around the limits of the court and its markers. The entire complex was an arena for the eternal pageantry of kingship on earth (Kemp, 2005).

The Step Pyramid was an area for the king's spirit, comprising six platforms, one atop the other. Each formed a bench, or *mastaba*, resembling earlier royal tombs, here built into a stepped pyramid. The substructure is a honeycomb of shafts and tunnels, many dug by tomb robbers, others containing large numbers of often exquisite stone vases. Some of them bear the names of earlier kings, as if Djoser incorporated them into his pyramid as an act of piety to his predecessors. Only a mummified left foot remains of the king himself. Other members of the royal family were buried in some of the shafts and tunnels.

As the pyramid grew, so these burial chambers were sealed off. Finally, the builders dug a new entrance for Djoser's burial chamber on the north side. They sealed it with a 3-ton granite plug.

A thick stone wall surrounded the pyramid, forming a huge courtyard, 108 by 187 m (354 by 613 feet), with a main gateway at the southeastern corner. An entrance hall decorated with columns opened into a vestibule. The king's internal organs were buried in the so-called South Tomb facing the main pyramid on the south side of the enclosure. Thus, there were two sepulchers, one for the Two Lands, Upper and Lower Egypt.

The Step Pyramid was an elaborate formal setting for the display of kingship—and of the ruler himself—either to his courtiers or the populace at large. Here the ruler could be seen by a large number of people, adorned in his ceremonial robes. The "appearance of the king" was an important occasion throughout Egyptian history.

FIGURE 16.6 The Step Pyramid of Djoser I at Saqqara. The stepped pyramid was part of an elaborate setting for public ceremonies, symbolizing the king's role as supreme territorial ruler and claimant.

structure once a year. As far as is known, the peasants were paid volunteers, whose loyalty to the divine pharaoh provided the motivation for the work.

Mendelssohn believes that the construction of the pyramids was a practical administrative device designed to organize and institutionalize the state by trading redistributed food for labor. As construction proceeded from one generation to the next, the villagers became dependent on the central administration for food for three months a year, food obtained from surpluses contributed by the villagers themselves in the form of taxation. After a while, the pyramids had fulfilled their purpose, and the state-directed labor forces could be diverted to other, less conspicuous state works. A new form of state organization had been created, one that both fostered and exploited the interdependence of Egyptian villages.

The Egyptian State

Egypt was the first state of its size in history (Kemp, 2005; T. Wilkinson, 2011). The pharaohs ruled by their own word, following no written laws, unlike the legislators of Mesopotamian city-states. The pharaoh had power over the Nile flood, rainfall, and all people, including foreigners. He was a god, respected by all people as a tangible divinity whose being was the personification of *Ma'at*, or "rightness." *Ma'at* was far more than just rightness; it was a "right order" and stood for order and justice. *Ma'at* was pharaonic status and eternity itself—the very embodiment of the Egyptian state.

FIGURE 16.7 Officials carefully monitored each harvest. Below, two boys quarrel over stubble. New Kingdom, tomb of Menna, scribe of the fields and estate inspector under Pharaoh Tutmosis of the Eighteenth Dynasty, Deir el-Medina, Thebes.

As the embodiment of *Ma'at*, the pharaoh pronounced the law, regulated by a massive background of precedent set by earlier rulers.

A massive hereditary bureaucracy effectively ruled the kingdom, with rows of officials forming veritable dynasties. Their records tell us that much official energy was devoted to tax collection, the supervision of harvests, and the administration of irrigation (Figure 16.7). An army of 20,000 men, many of them mercenaries, was maintained at the height of Egypt's prosperity. The Egyptian Empire was a literate one; that is, trained scribes were an integral part of the state government. Special schools trained writers for careers in the army, the palace, the treasury, and numerous other callings (Aldred, 2004; Kemp, 2005).

A vast gulf separated the person who could read and write from the uneducated peasant worker. The life of an Egyptian peasant, given good harvests, was easier than that of a Greek or a Syrian farmer, but still one of brutal hard work, with discipline maintained by force. The state was a demanding master, which required occasional bouts of forced labor to clear irrigation canals or to haul stone, both tasks being essential to maintain Egyptian agriculture. Minor craftsworkers and unskilled laborers lived more regimented lives, working on temples and pharaohs' tombs. Many were organized in shifts under foremen. There were strikes, and absenteeism was common. A scale of rations and daily work was imposed. Like many early states, however, Egypt depended on slave labor for some public works and much domestic service, but foreign serfs and war prisoners could wield much influence in public affairs. They were allowed to rent and cultivate land.

The Old Kingdom in Egypt was a time of powerful, confident rulers, of a virile state governed by a privileged class of royal relatives and high officials. Their talents created a civilization, maintained in part by force that was for the benefit of a tiny minority. It was for this privileged elite, headed by a divine king, that Egyptian merchants traded for the famed cedars of Lebanon, mined turquoise and copper in Sinai, and sought ivory, semiprecious stones, and mercenaries for Egypt's armies from Nubia.

The First Intermediate Period and the Middle Kingdom (2180 to 1640 B.C.)

But the prosperity did not last long. The last great Old Kingdom pharaoh was Pepi II (2278 to 2184 B.C.), who reigned for a staggering 94 years, having ascended the throne as a 6-year-old. His successors never matched his authority. As the central power of the state declined, so local leaders

First Intermediate period
2180 to 2134 B.C.

(*nomarchs*) became more or less independent rulers within their own provinces. This decline in the monarchy coincided with a prolonged drought cycle that settled over northern Africa after 2180 B.C. The droughts of early dynastic times had taught the pharaohs the importance of centrally controlled agriculture. They had responded to new economic realities by expanding irrigation works, canals, and the agricultural development of the delta. In the short term, they were so successful that Egypt's population had risen to more than a million by 2250 B.C. But the intensification of agriculture made the Egyptians even more vulnerable, for when another lean cycle struck in that year, there were many more mouths to feed. There were repeated famines for more than 300 years. Contemporary writers refer to widespread plundering and anarchy, to drinking-water shortages, and corpses rotting in the fields. "The Nile was empty and men crossed over on foot," laments a chronicler of the day, as the magical powers of short-lived pharaohs fell into disrepute (Kemp, 2005: 16). Egypt became a competing mosaic of small kingdoms, whose rulers ignored the steady procession of short-lived pharaohs in Memphis.

In about 2134 B.C., the city of Thebes in Upper Egypt became the center of rebel movements that eventually took over the country under Pharaoh Mentuhotep II in 2040 B.C. The Middle Kingdom pharaohs who followed were mostly energetic rulers who extended trading contacts throughout Southwest Asia and conquered the desert lands of Nubia south of the First Cataract (see Figure 16.1). The pharaohs became somewhat less despotic, considered themselves more like shepherds of the people, and had some concern for the common welfare. The Middle Kingdom has

Middle Kingdom
2134 to 1640 B.C.

been described as the classic period of Egyptian civilization, centuries when the pharaohs became more human and more approachable than their Old Kingdom predecessors, who had cast themselves in the role of gods. During these centuries, Egypt's rulers strove to create a kingdom in the image of a bureaucratic utopia, a realm where there were logical, often mathematical, solutions to every economic problem. The experiment was successful for a while, but it faltered when Egypt's human and natural resources proved unequal to the task.

At the same time, trade relations with the eastern Mediterranean expanded dramatically. The pharaohs mined copper and gold in the Sinai and imported cedar from Lebanon. Objects bearing their inscriptions have been found as far afield as Byblos and the port of Ugarit on the northern Syrian coast. It was from such centers that objects from the Aegean islands and the Minoan towns on Crete reached the Nile (see Chapter 19). The government also tried to increase agricultural production. At the height of the Middle Kingdom, the pharaoh Senusret II began the development of the Fayyum Oasis about 80 km (50 miles) southwest of Memphis. He and his successors turned the marshy oasis into a vast network of fields and irrigation canals protected by large dikes, an unprecedented agricultural project that provided high crop yields for the state, even in drought years. This kind of organized irrigation was very different from the informal, village-based canals and drainage ditches that marked most of the earlier Egyptian agriculture. The Fayyum project was only one manifestation of a state concerned with remodeling a society with strong local roots into a closely regimented and centralized society and planted planned towns even in sparsely populated areas. The pharaohs strove for an organized oasis.

Kahun
c. 1890 B.C.

Enormous public works and royal mortuaries required small armies of workers, sometimes housed in special communities some distance from their place of work. The Middle Kingdom town at Kahun (known to the Egyptians as Hetep-Senusret (meaning "King Senusret is at peace") stood close to the entrance to the Fayyum, near the pyramid of Senusret II. Here lived the priests and workers responsible for the king's mortuary cult, as well as people engaged in other construction work and agriculture (Kemp, 2005). Kahun lay inside mud-brick walls, the interior laid out on a strict grid pattern of small houses and streets. Egyptologist Flinders Petrie (1890) uncovered intricately designed, fairly large houses with substantial granaries in which household activities revolved around an inner court and walled garden. Much smaller houses outnumbered these residences by about 20 to 1, and an estimated 3,000 people lived within the tightly packed community. The town plan indicates a society with well-defined social classes, reflected in house design as well as occupation.

Papyri found during Petrie's excavations reveal the existence of a mayor, legal offices, and a prison. They also contain census data, including the household of a mortuary priest with only one son and daughter but many "serfs," some of them attached to his office, others domestic servants, field laborers, cooks, tutors, and women who were clothmakers and gardeners. These groups of workers depended on the granaries of the larger houses for their rations, thus forming the economic teams that were so much a part of Egyptian society. Kahun's population also included scribes and soldiers, as well as numerous small households of half a dozen people or more, many of them relatives and widows with dependent children.

Kahun represents the ultimate in Egyptian bureaucracy, a town laid out by noble officials with little conception of the realities of society. The pharaohs organized Kahun at two levels: top officials and others. In fact, the papyri reveal a more complex reality, of individuals and households wrestling with the realities of debt and children, of sudden inheritances and caring for the elderly. These realities meant that, after the Middle Kingdom, the state gave up planning any form of community other than small workers' camps.

The Second Intermediate Period (1640 to 1530 B.C.)

The Middle Kingdom lasted until approximately 1640 B.C., when another period of political instability and economic disorder began. Disputes over the royal succession at Thebes led to a series of pharaohs who reigned for short periods. Pharaonic control of the Nile Valley as a whole weakened. By this time, large numbers of Asians lived in Egypt. They were cooks and brewers, seamstresses and merchants. Many of the finest Egyptian winemakers came from Syria. Others were nomadic herders from neighboring regions, who had moved into the delta to seek sanctuary from drought or to buy corn. Their chiefs were called *Hikau khasut*, "Princes of Desert Uplands," known as the *Hyksos*, a term referring not only to the chiefs but to all their people. By the seventeenth century B.C., the delta had come under the political control of a line of Hyksos kings, who had taken advantage of the weakness of the Thirteenth Dynasty pharaohs to seize power over Lower Egypt, ruling it from the town of Avaris. They assumed the titles, traditions, and religious beliefs of the pharaohs, acquiring such prestige that the rulers of Thebes paid them tribute, perhaps linking the royal houses through intermarriage.

The Second Intermediate period was a turning point in Egyptian history. The Hyksos brought new ideas to a conservative civilization that was slowly stagnating away from the mainstream of the Southwest Asian world. They introduced more sophisticated bronze technology and traded silver from Asian mines. Friezes in the palace at Avaris in the delta are painted in the Minoan style, as if Cretan merchants and artisans lived in the Hyksos capital (Chapter 19). In their battles with the Thebans, the Hyksos brought new weaponry to the Nile: stronger bows, new forms of swords and daggers, and the horse-drawn chariot.

All these innovations kept Egypt up to date and ensured that subsequent pharaohs would play a leading role in the wider eastern Mediterranean world.

Second Intermediate period
1640 to 1530 B.C.

The New Kingdom (1530 to 1070 B.C.)

The New Kingdom began when a series of Theban rulers fought and won a war of independence from the Hyksos. It was Ahmose the Liberator who finally overcame the foreigners and established a firm hold on Egypt from the delta to Nubia. At the same time, Ahmose turned Egypt into an efficiently run military state, tolerating no rivals and rewarding his soldiers and mercenaries with grants of land, but retaining economic power and wealth in his own hands. Like Mentuhotep in the Middle Kingdom, Ahmose set the tone for an entire era, the greatest in Egyptian history. Now the pharaoh became a national hero, a military leader who sat on a throne midway between the Asian world in the north and the black Nubian kingdoms of the south. He was an imperial ruler, a skilled general, the leader of a great power. Egypt became a major player in the shifting sands of Southwest Asian politics, competing with two great states: Mitanni, to the east of the Euphrates, and Hatti, the kingdom of the Hittites in Anatolia (see Chapter 19). Each wanted to control the lucrative gold, copper, and pottery trade of the eastern Mediterranean for itself.

The pharaohs financed their state and their empire with Nubian gold, turning the lands upstream of the First Cataract into a lucrative colony. At the same time, the Egyptians expanded their trade routes down the Red Sea to the mysterious and bountiful "Land of Punt." Its original location has been the subject of much heated debate, perhaps precisely because it was a slightly mythical (and thus moveable) land of plenty. However, most now agree that it probably lay between the Red Sea and the Middle Nile, on the north and northwest flanks of the Ethiopian highlands (with Somalia, to the south, as an alternative). A Punt expedition was a major undertaking, involving an overland journey from Koptos on the Nile to the Red Sea coast, then by ship southward through windy, often treacherous waters. In 1472 B.C., Queen Hatshepsut, the only female pharaoh, sent a royal trading party to Punt. Spectacular reliefs on her mortuary temple chronicle the successful voyage (Figure 16.8). Separate scenes depict the ships under sail, the arrival at Punt, the exchange of gifts with the lord of the land, and the loading of the ships "very heavily with the marvels of the land of Punt: with . . ., good herbs of God's Land and heaps of nodules of myrrh" (Kemp, 2005: 213). The story ends with the triumphant return to the sun god Amun's sacred city: Thebes.

New Kingdom
1530 to 1070 B.C.

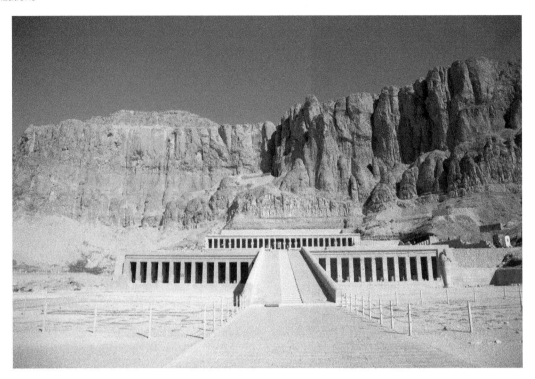

FIGURE 16.8 The mortuary temple of Queen Hatshepsut near the Valley of Kings.

The "Estate of Amun"

Thebes, the home of Amun, was known to the Egyptians as the "City," or the "Estate of Amun." The Temples of Amun at Karnak and Luxor, built mostly during the Eighteenth Dynasty (1550 to 1307 B.C.), were the heart of the sacred capital (R. Wilkinson, 2000). The temples lay on the old city mound, surrounded by the buildings of the New Kingdom city. Karnak represented a major shift in public architecture. Earlier kings had built their most imposing monuments on the edges of the western desert. Local temples were usually modest mud-brick structures in the heart of a community. Karnak and its lesser equivalents were settings for public ceremonies and processions (Figure 16.9), as when the boatlike shrine of Amun was carried along carefully prepared parade routes. Religion now became public spectacle, a psychological way of influencing public opinion, more subtle and probably more effective than the bureaucratic regulation of earlier times.

Karnak and its equivalents were surrounded by white, painted mud-brick walls modeled like turreted battlements, which kept out most of the Theban populace. The great pylons marking the entrance bore brightly colored scenes of the king conquering his enemies in the presence of the gods. Karnak was a statement of raw imperial power but was also the place where the gods found shelter and were nurtured by food offerings. Amun's temples owned cattle and mineral rights and maintained enormous grain stores. In short, as Barry Kemp (2005) points out, the gods were landed gentry, fed from vast temple estates cultivated by small-scale farmers who paid their rent in produce. The mortuary temple of Rameses II near Thebes had storerooms capable (theoretically) of feeding as many as 20,000 people. The wealth of the large temples and the authority of their gods were such that the temples were not only a major element in the New Kingdom economy but also a significant factor in the affairs of state.

Amun-Ra was the "king of the gods," a solar deity portrayed in human form and the source of fecundity. He was the divine father figure who conceived the kings, then protected them in life and death. The great pageants at Thebes, the processions between the temples at Karnak and Luxor during the annual Opet festival, proclaimed to the populace that the king had renewed his divine *ka*, or spiritual essence, in the innermost shrine of Amun himself. The myths, rituals, and great temples all served to guarantee the continuity of proper rule, a concept absolutely central to Egyptian thinking. At the same time, the priesthood had little political power, for the ultimate authority lay in the hands of the king and his host of carefully trained scribes.

The "Estate of Amun" extended across the Nile to the western bank. Here, the pharaohs erected an elaborate city of the dead. At the beginning of the Eighteenth Dynasty, in about 1505 B.C., Pharaoh Amenhotep and his illustrious successors elected to be buried in secret rock-cut tombs in the arid Valley of Kings on the west bank of the river opposite Thebes. The underground tombs evolved over the centuries to become models of the caverns of the underworld traversed by the night-sun. The royal mortuary temples lay on the plain nearby, surrounded by the tombs of queens, princes, and court officials (see the Science box).

FIGURE 16.9 The Temple of Amun at Karnak. Two rows of sphinxes line the central processional way through the great pylons that form the entry. Like all major temples, Karnak was rebuilt, and rebuilt again, by successive pharaohs anxious to honor the sun god.

Amarna and Akhenaten

Amun's power came through the age-old cult of Ra Herakhty, the primordial sun god of Heliopolis. His Great Disk, Aten, illuminated the worlds of the living and the dead. Amun was all-powerful until the pharaoh Akhenaten came to the throne in 1353 B.C. (Reeves, 2001; Van Dijk, 2000). The new ruler departed from religious orthodoxy in placing a greater emphasis on Aten and Aten alone, excluding all the old gods of the pantheon from their association with the sun. In effect, Akhenaten made Aten a divine pharaoh, the equivalent in heaven of the living king on earth. We do not know why Akhenaten altered the sacred canon, but the art of his day suggests he regarded himself and his family as the sole intermediaries between the people and the sun god. Akhenaten expected to be adored like a god and perhaps considered himself a living personification of one.

In the fifth year of his reign, the heretic pharaoh founded a brand-new capital at El-Amarna, on land associated with no established deity. El-Amarna was occupied for little more than a quarter century before being abandoned, leaving an Egyptian city of more than 20,000 inhabitants for archaeologists to investigate. The ceremonial precincts of El-Amarna centered on a processional way that linked the north (royal) city to the central city. The fortified royal palace at the north end was isolated from the rest of El-Amarna. Here, Akhenaten and his court resided in a self-sufficient, well-guarded community with its own warehouses. The pharaoh rode down the processional way on festival days, protected by his bodyguard as his subjects adulated him. The road ended at the Great Palace, a huge structure by the waterfront with a central courtyard where the king received emissaries and conducted many ceremonies, including the rewarding of high officials who were dependent on his largesse. The administrative functions of state were performed in offices attached to the palace. It was here that the "Bureau for the Correspondence of the Pharaoh" lay. The bureau was the archive that housed the now famous El-Amarna diplomatic tablets, which tell us much of diplomatic relations between Egypt and other powers like the Hittites. The Great Temple of Aten stood nearby.

But El-Amarna's greatest significance lies in its unique archaeological evidence concerning New Kingdom Egyptian society. Most El-Amarna residents lived on two large housing tracts north and south of the central city, huddled in small houses along streets parallel to the river, intersected by smaller alleys. The larger flat-roofed dwellings stood in a small, walled compound among a maze of alleyways and garbage heaps. Each had a central living room with a low brick dais for receiving guests. Around the central space were reception rooms, bedrooms, and storage rooms. We know the names of only a few individual owners, among them Ra-nefer, a chief charioteer, who lived in a modest house, and Thutmose, a sculptor who carried out his work in small courtyards by his house, in an area of the town devoted to sculptors.

El-Amarna
1350 B.C.

Science   Mummies and Mummification

Mummies: They have become lasting symbols of ancient Egyptian civilization and the subject of innumerable Hollywood movies. Who can forget actor Boris Karloff as a hyperactive Egyptian mummy come back to life?

The practice of mummification dates back to the early third millennium B.C. or even earlier (Ikram and Dodson, 1998). Hitherto, Egyptians had been buried in shallow pits in the desert sand. But when walled graves came into use, bodies soon rotted away because they were no longer in contact with desiccating sand. The first attempts at mummification involved little more than bandaging the body with cloth stiffened with resin. About 2575 B.C., the embalmers began to remove the abdominal organs, putting them in special canopic jars. They also discovered the properties of natron, a compound of sodium carbonate and sodium chloride, which dehydrated human and animal tissue.

By New Kingdom times, the process was highly sophisticated (Figure 16.10). Two or three days after a person died, the embalmers extracted the internal organs through a slit below the left ribs. They removed the liver, stomach, intestines, and lungs, leaving the heart, which was thought to be the center of human feelings, in place. Next, the embalmers took a bronze rod, inserted it into the left nostril and removed the brain through an enlarged opening made by smashing the fragile ethmoid bone. Resin, sawdust, or cloth was then poured or packed into the skull cavity. The body was sewn up, cleaned, and covered with natron to dehydrate it completely. Once completely dried out, the corpse was washed in Nile water and anointed with unguents to make it smooth and sweet-smelling. Laying the body on a lion-shaped funerary bed, the embalmers now bandaged it, using a strict protocol, which began with the fingers and limbs, the head being last. Numerous small amulets were placed between the layers of bandages, which were soaked with resin and other unguents. Finally, the fully bandaged and mummified body was placed in a coffin and returned to the family.

This elaborate procedure was extremely expensive and was reserved for royalty, high officials, and the very wealthy. Simpler techniques involved simply desiccating the body with natron and bandaging it with recycled household linens. The poorer Egyptians were often just stacked in remote caves without any formal grave goods or elaborate funerary rituals.

Through the process of mummification, the preserved body became identified with the body of the god Osiris, ruler of the underworld. At burial, the mummy began a second life, which began with a ritual known as the "Opening of the Mouth" ceremony, performed just before the body was laid in its tomb. Anubis, the keeper of the kingdom of the dead, would receive the deceased, who was now judged in the presence of Osiris. His or her heart was weighed on a balance against a feather, the symbol of *Ma'at* ("goodness"). If "justified," the dead person could now undertake the journey through the underworld. If the heart was too heavy, it was gobbled up by the waiting goddess Ammit, and the guilty person was consigned to lasting death.

FIGURE 16.10   The mummy of pharaoh Rameses II.

Papyri tell us how some prominent officials struggled to maintain a prosperous lifestyle, using income from their small country estates and donations from the king. Minor officials, domestic servants, merchants, fisherfolk, sailors, and farmers huddled in the crowded smaller houses. The inhabitants all had close ties to the countryside, to their home villages, often many kilometers away. Few Egyptians were true city dwellers. Egyptian cities were little more than large agglomerations of villages. Their inhabitants lived their lives in another world from that of the pharaoh, who dwelled in splendid isolation from the common people, surrounded by his relatives and bodyguards and appearing at regular intervals to receive the adoration of his subjects.

The Restoration of Amun

Religious fanatic, indolent madman, benevolent pacifist, or heretic—history's judgments on Akhenaten have rarely been favorable. He died in the seventeenth year of his reign, leaving a corrupt and chaotic kingdom behind him. His successor, Smenkhkare, a son of Amenhotep III, reigned for a mere three years and was succeeded in turn by 8-year-old Tutankhamun (1333 to 1323 B.C.), who achieved in death an immortality that transcends that of all other pharaohs, simply because Howard Carter and Lord Carnarvon discovered his intact tomb in the Valley of Kings (Figure 16.11) (Reeves, 1990).

(a)

(b)

FIGURE 16.11 Tutankhamun's tomb. Tutankhamun's jumbled possessions were so opulent that it has taken generations for us to appreciate their wealth and significance. The dead pharaoh traveled through the heavens in the sun god's bark. His many gold-leaf and inlaid figures and amulets ensured his well-being during the eternal journey. At the same time, his tomb provided for his material needs: clothing, perfume and cosmetics, personal jewelry, and chests to keep them in. There are chairs, stools, beds, and headrests, as well as weapons and hunting gear. Baskets and vases contained food and wine. Even the pharaoh's chariots lay in pieces inside the tomb. The tomb provides a fleeting portrait of the fabulous wealth of Egypt's court. (a) The antechamber with its jumble of furnishings. (b) The golden sarcophagus of the king. ([a] Egyptian Dynasty XVIII, Thebes: Valley of the Kings, Tomb of Tut-ankh-amun: Antechamber south end. [a, b] Photography by Egyptian Expedition, The Metropolitan Museum of Art.)

Tutankhamun presided over a troubled country, abandoned to chaos by the alienated gods. The young king's powerful and experienced advisers took the course obvious to someone reared in the deeply religious Egyptian world. They propitiated the gods by restoring the old spiritual order, rebuilding temples, and reverting to the dynastic traditions of the early pharaohs. The cult of Amun was revived at Thebes; Amarna was abandoned. An able general named Horemhab campaigned in Syria, while Tutankhamun himself may have led a raiding party into Nubia in 1323 B.C. His unexpected death caught the court by surprise. An MRI has failed to establish the cause of death; Tutankhamun was certainly not murdered but had suffered a broken leg. Conceivably the break became infected and he died—we simply do not know. It was not until Horemhab assumed the throne in 1319 B.C. that the old ways were fully restored.

The Rameside pharaohs of the Nineteenth Dynasty (1307 to 1196 B.C.) who followed labored hard to elevate the kingdom to its former glory as an imperial power. Their wealth came from Nubian gold and far-flung trade, for Nubia was now an Egyptian dependency. Rameses II (1290 to 1224 B.C.) campaigned far into Syria until he met his match at the Battle of Kadesh, where the Hittites fought his army to a standstill. From then on, Egypt lost political influence in Southwest Asia and began a slow, at first barely perceptible, decline.

The Late Period (1070 to 332 B.C.)

With the death of Rameses III in 1070 B.C., Egypt entered a period of political weakness, when local rulers exercised varying control over the Nile. Nubian rulers threatened the pharaohs and actually ruled over Egypt for a short time in the eighth century B.C. The Assyrians were a constant hazard after 725 B.C. Their army occupied parts of the country and looted Thebes in 665 B.C. After the eclipse of Assyria, the Egyptians enjoyed a few centuries of independence before being conquered by the Persians in 343 B.C. and by Alexander the Great in 332 B.C. The Ptolemies, pharaohs of Greek ancestry, succeeded Alexander and ruled Egypt until Roman times. It was the Ptolemies who brought much of Egyptian lore and learning into the mainstream of emerging Greek civilization and ensured that the Land of the Pharaohs would make a critical contribution to Western civilization.

Late Period
1070 to 332 B.C.

Egypt and Africa

The ancient Greeks and Romans believed that Egypt was the fountain of all civilization. While archaeological discoveries have shown that urban civilization developed in both Egypt and Mesopotamia at much the same time, scholars still argue over the contribution of the ancient Egyptians to the roots of Western civilization. Most Egyptologists argue that civilization developed in isolation along the Nile, in a fertile, if unpredictable, river valley that was a world unto its own. They believe it became an integral part of a cosmopolitan eastern Mediterranean world, especially during the New Kingdom, when Egypt vied with Assyria and the Hittite kings for control of the eastern Mediterranean trade routes.

Some African-American historians of the so-called Afrocentrism school disagree, for they believe that the institutions of urban Western civilization were born in tropical Africa and that ancient Egypt was a black African civilization. It was from the Nile, they argue, that the institutions of Western civilization were derived. These arguments, which first surfaced in the 1950s, have reached a high level of complexity in Martin Bernal's so-called Black Athena theory (1987), in which he presents historical, linguistic, and even archaeological evidence to place ancient Egypt at the core of Western civilization. Bernal's research has been severely criticized by Egyptologists, who have effectively demolished his arguments on the basis that they do not stand against scientific data. For example, Afrocentrists claim that the ancient Egyptians were black-skinned tropical Africans. In fact, both tomb paintings and biological data point to a generally Mediterranean population (remember that the Mediterranean Sea stretches across the whole of north Africa and washes the Levant to the east). However, it was also one that became increasingly cosmopolitan in later centuries as Egypt enjoyed closer contacts with other lands, including tropical Africa (Lefkowitz, 1996).

Nubia: The Land of Kush

If ancient Egypt was indeed a civilization unto itself, what connections did it enjoy with the people of the Nile Valley living south of the First Cataract at Aswân? The arid country that lay upstream was Nubia, sometimes called the Land of Kush, famous to the ancient Egyptians for its gold, ivory, and slaves. As Nubian expert William Adams (1977) remarked, "For millennia Egypt treated [Nubia] as a kind of private game reserve for human and animal game" (p. 3). Nubia straddled the Middle Nile on a narrow strip of fertile land that extended far upstream into modern-day Sudan as far as the borders of highland Ethiopia. The most fertile valley lands lie along the Dongola Reach between the Third and Fourth Cataracts. It was here that some of the earliest complex Nubian **4000 B.C.** societies developed, among groups that had been herders and farmers since before 4000 B.C. Even as early as 3500 B.C., what Adams calls the "shadow of Egypt" was falling across Nubia, whose raw materials attracted a civilization where wealth and divine kingship went together.

Old Kingdom pharaohs sent their armies to subdue Nubia and boasted of lucrative cattle raids. Egyptian prospectors journeyed far into the desert in search of fine rocks and semiprecious stones. **1900 B.C.** The Middle Kingdom kings were more ambitious, for they discovered Nubian gold. In 1900 B.C., pharaoh Amenemhet fortified strategic reaches with ten strongholds, most of them at points where trade routes intersected with the river. This trade lay in the hands of the Nubian chieftains of **Kerma** Kerma, in the heart of the Dongola Reach, a small town with palaces and temples, fortified with elaborate defenses and four gates. Kerma's rulers enjoyed great wealth and were buried under large burial mounds surrounded by as many as 400 sacrificial victims (Figure 16.12). All this wealth came from trade connections with people living in the desert and farther upstream and with the Egyptians far downstream. But the New Kingdom pharaohs wanted this wealth for themselves; they **Kush** marched on Kerma and the state of Kush in 1500 B.C. and made it a colony. Nubia now changed **1500 B.C.** from a country of village farmers and chiefdoms into something resembling a vast plantation state, worked for the benefit of absentee landlords to provide commodities of all types at the cheapest possible cost (S. Smith, 1995).

The economic and political shock waves that rolled over the eastern Mediterranean after **1200 B.C.** 1200 B.C. (see Chapter 19) not only overthrew the Hittites and weakened Egypt but also loosened the pharaohs' hold on Nubia. After four centuries of confusion, Nubian civilization achieved new heights. The rulers of the new Kush espoused ancient Egyptian religious beliefs and assumed the powers and ideology of the pharaohs. Their wealth came from the Egyptian export trade, from gold, ivory, and many other commodities. They were buried under royal pyramids in large cemeteries, not **806 B.C.** only in Kush but, later, far upstream at Meroe. The list of Nubian kings begins in about 806 B.C. and ends in A.D. 320, a thousand years later.

Nubian pharaohs Between 730 and 663 B.C. Nubian monarchs ruled not only over Kush but also over Egypt itself. **730 to 663 B.C.** King Piye marched north in 730 B.C., honored the sun god Amun at Thebes, and then subdued rebellious rulers in the delta far downstream. Piye was content to rule Egypt from Kush, but his

FIGURE 16.12 A royal tomb at Kerma—people rush to complete the mound as the burial takes place.

successors transferred their court to Thebes, as the servant became the master, the conquered the conquerors. The Nubian pharaohs did much to restore art and religion, but they were inexperienced in foreign affairs, and this inexperience led to their downfall. In 663 B.C., King Assurbanipal of Assyria sacked Thebes, and the ruler of the day fled to the safety of Kush. In 591 B.C., an Egyptian army marched upstream and "waded in Kushite blood." Nubian king Aspelta fled some 500 km (300 miles) upstream to Meroe, where Nubian monarchs ruled in peace for more than 800 years.

591 B.C.

Meroe and Aksum

The move to Meroe came when the focus of Nubian trade was shifting away from the eastern Mediterranean to the Red Sea and the Indian Ocean. This new commercial world linked the Red Sea, the Persian Gulf states, India, and ultimately Southeast Asia and China into a vast web (see Table 16.1). India, for example, had an insatiable demand for African ivory, favored over that of Indian elephants for making bridal ornaments. Cotton cloth, porcelain and china vessels, silk, and glass items came from India and farther east. Gold, spices, and even mangrove poles—all were staples of a trade that flowed along overland caravan routes and on the wings of the monsoon winds of the Indian Ocean. These predictable winds allowed sailing vessels to voyage from India to the Red Sea and East Africa and back in the course of a year.

Meroe
593 B.C. to A.D. 350

The island of Socotra off the Horn of Africa (south of Egypt) (see the map in Figure 16.15), South West Arabia (Yemen), dubbed Arabia Felix—Happy Arabia—by the Romans; and the mysterious Land of Punt, probably located in the northern Ethiopian highlands, were spice- and incense-rich lands where Africans rubbed shoulders with Arabians, Indians with Egyptians. Well-traveled trade routes linked Red Sea coasts with the Nile and the eastern Mediterranean coastline, traversed by laden asses and increasingly by camels, aptly named the "ships of the desert" by the Arabians, who first domesticated them as early as 2500 B.C. Centuries passed before desert nomads developed fighting saddles for their beasts, turning them from mere beasts of burden into a potent military weapon. By the third century B.C., camel breeders dominated the overland caravan trade and brought prosperity to Meroe.

Meroe lies on the east bank of the White Nile, some 200 km (124 miles) north of Khartoum, Sudan (Robertson, 1992; Shinnie, 1967). Its rulers administered a string of villages and towns along the river from lower Nubia to Sennar on the Blue Nile, controlling the gold, ivory, and slave trade with Egypt. The city also lay astride bustling caravan routes that linked the river with the Red Sea and extended far to the west, along the southern margins of the Sahara. Today, Meroe lies in a desert landscape, but in ancient times large herds of cattle, goats, and sheep grazed nearby (Figure 16.13). Centuries of overgrazing, combined with voracious charcoal burning to fuel iron-smelting furnaces, helped chronic drought turn the environment into an arid wilderness.

FIGURE 16.13 Royal pyramids at Meroe, Sudan.

Some 24 kings and queens ruled over Meroe between 593 and 220 B.C. These black-skinned rulers were the descendants of the great pharaoh Piye and his successors. They preserved many of the conservative standards of ancient Egyptian civilization, but with a distinctive black African slant. For centuries, they administered a complex, exploitative economic enterprise for their own benefit, controlling trade through a network of carefully policed trade routes and by force. Most people lived at the subsistence level, for the international trade benefited only a minority. Ironworking was big business at Meroe, since iron ore was plentiful nearby.

Huge slag heaps overlook the temples and palaces of the city, accumulated over centuries of manufacture that began as early as the seventh century B.C. Iron-tipped tools and weapons gave Meroe's armies strategic advantages over their desert neighbors. Early scholars believed that Meroe's ironsmiths introduced the new technology to tropical Africa, but we now know that iron was introduced into the central Sahara and West Africa at about the same time as it was to Meroe itself. Meroe reached the height of its prosperity during the first century B.C., when it maintained regular trading contacts with the Roman Empire. A century later, the city was in decline and, between A.D. 325 and 350, was finally overthrown by the armies of King Ezana of Aksum in the nearby Ethiopian highlands.

Almost a thousand years before the rise of Aksum, archaeologists have identified the presence of a relatively poorly understood "pre-Aksumite" culture. It too was ruled by kings. In the first half of the first millennium B.C., these kings appear to have been somehow linked with those of South West Arabia (modern Yemen) for both areas possess the same elite architectural and artistic styles, and even the same monumental script that mentions the same gods indicating shared religious beliefs (Durrani, 2005).

It is hardly surprising that great civilizations flourished on the Ethiopian highlands for they were both fertile and rich with natural resources. Though few early archaeo-botanical remains survive, other strands of evidence indicate that the pre-Aksumite people were probably irrigating cereal crops, including the (possibly) indigenous crop of sorghum, and a native grass called *teff*. Both are very nutritious and would feasibly have provided large surpluses in the good years. By the first century A.D., the Kingdom of Aksum—with loose connections to the pre-Aksumite era—had established itself as a powerful kingdom in regular contact with Rome, handling all manner of exotic luxuries and commodities through its port at Adulis on the Red Sea (Connah, 2001). An eight-day journey took one inland to the town of Aksum, while another caravan route reached Aswân in Egypt in 30 days. Adulis became so important that Aksum soon overshadowed Meroe as the Nile trade declined. By the third century A.D., the Persian Gnostic Mani is reported by his followers to have described Aksum as one of the four most important kingdoms in the world.

Aksum's rulers lived in imposing multistory palaces and were buried in association with tall columns, or stelae, intricately carved to represent multistory buildings (Figure 16.14). Some were veritable sky-scrapers, measuring up to 33 m (108 feet) high and weighing several tons (Phillipson, 2001).

In the fourth century A.D., at about the time he overthrew Meroe, King Ezana abandoned the religion of his forefathers and adopted Christianity, which had reached his domains through Aksum's widespread trading connections. Thus, though unbeknown to many modern Christians, Ethiopia was in fact one of the greatest and earliest Christian Kingdoms in the world.

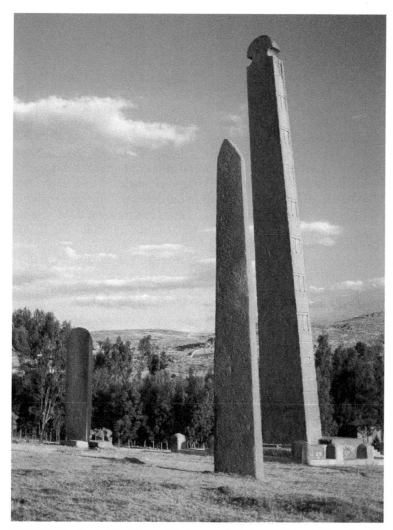

FIGURE 16.14 Royal stela at Aksum, Ethiopia, carved to depict a multistory building. (Copyright Werner Forman/Art Resource, NY.)

Christianity flourishes in Ethiopia to this day, but Aksum faltered, retreating from its world stage by the seventh century A.D. Why this happened remains unclear. Perhaps, as Islam acquired increasing influence over the Red Sea trade and all the countries bordering it from the seventh century A.D. onwards, the resolutely Christian kingdom of Aksum became increasingly isolated. Certainly, it is an isolation that persists to this day. Of all the world's important ancient civilizations, it is fair to say that Aksum remains the least well-known. Yet, at the height of its powers, Aksum was a potent symbol of a new, much more international world that sprang from the ruins of the Roman Empire and linked Asia and Africa with lasting ties.

Aksum was an African kingdom whose rulers adopted many ideas from southern Arabia in the five centuries B.C. (Connah, 2001; Phillipson, 2001). Its highland homeland was fertile, although it had an unpredictable environment, and irrigated cereal crops, among them a native grass called *teff*, flourished, providing large food surpluses in good years. By the first century A.D., Aksum was a powerful kingdom in regular contact with Rome, handling all manner of exotic luxuries and commodities through its port at Adulis on the Red Sea. An eight-day journey took one inland to the town of Aksum, while another caravan route reached Aswân in Egypt in 30 days. Adulis became so important that Aksum soon overshadowed Meroe as the Nile trade declined.

Aksum
A.D. 100 to 650

Aksum's rulers lived in imposing multistory palaces and were buried under tall columns up to 33 m (108 feet) high, carved to represent multistory buildings (Phillipson, 2001) (Figure 16.14). At about the time he overthrew Meroe, King Ezana abandoned the religion of his forefathers and adopted Christianity, which had reached his domains through Aksum's widespread trading connections.

Christianity flourishes in Ethiopia to this day, but Aksum faltered as Islam acquired increasing influence over the Red Sea trade in the seventh century A.D. At the height of its powers, Aksum was a potent symbol of a new, much more international world that sprang from the ruins of the Roman Empire and linked Asia and Africa with lasting ties.

North Africa

The North African coast had long been a staging post for maritime traders from the eastern Mediterranean. During the first millennium B.C., the Phoenicians (see Chapter 19) set up port colonies (Aubet, 1993), among them was the great city of Carthage. Carthage had become a domi-

400 B.C. nant power by 400 B.C., but a series of devastating wars led to its destruction at the hands of Rome. The Romans realized the agricultural potential of the North African hinterland and turned their new colony into a vast grain combine. It was said that North African granaries fed Rome's masses for nine months a year, Egypt's for four.

The Romans had little interest in the desert, although there were some indirect contacts with peoples living deep in the Sahara. It was the camel that opened up the desert, once camel breeders had developed a saddle for load carrying and riding over long distances. Soon after A.D. 1, camel routes linked the Nile with the central highlands of the desert and the same mountains with North Africa. There, the Romans used the camel for agriculture and for some cavalry operations. The real expansion of the Saharan caravan trade came in later centuries, especially after Islamic armies swept

A.D. 700 across North Africa in the seventh century A.D.

Gold and salt—these were the commodities that fueled the Saharan caravan trade (Connah, 2001). Salt deposits were plentiful in parts of the desert. Salt was easily mined and carried on camelback to farmers south of the Sahara, who lacked this vital substance in their homeland. They craved salt and had gold dust to offer in exchange. So eager were some West Africans for salt that they would trade it for its equivalent weight in gold. The Saharan gold and salt trade soon grew into an elaborate network of local and long-distance connections that linked North Africa with the West African savanna and forest regions far to the south (Figure 16.15). Tropical foodstuffs and

FIGURE 16.15 Map showing the extent of Bantu Africa and the indigenous states mentioned in the text.

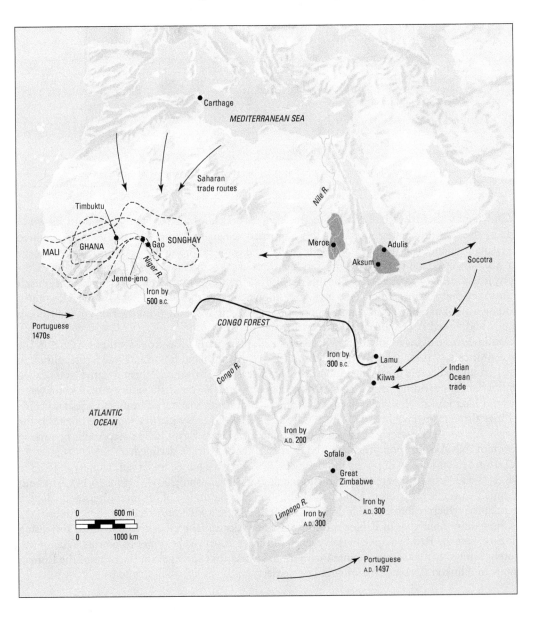

stimulants like the kola nut were in constant demand, as were woollen garments and leather goods from the north, as well as copper, slaves, and glassware. By the time Christopher Columbus landed in the Bahamas in A.D. 1492, two-thirds of Europe's gold was coming from West African sources.

Jenne-jeno and the Rise of West African States

By 1000 B.C., small farming communities flourished throughout the West African savanna and in the forest regions of the south. Iron technology had arrived at some of these villages by the sixth century B.C., at about the same time it arrived at distant Meroe in Northeast Africa (Phillipson, 2005). Iron axes and adzes improved the efficiency of forest clearance and agriculture, but it was the long-distance trade that offered new opportunities for ambitious African leaders. For example, Jenne-jeno in Mali's inland Niger Delta began as a small village of mixed farmers in the third century B.C. (McIntosh and McIntosh, 1980). Initially, the settlement was no more than a few acres in extent, but even at this early date, the inhabitants were obtaining iron ore, grindstones, and stone beads from outside their delta homeland. Most likely, they were bartering surplus grain, fish, and animal products in exchange.

During the next five centuries, Jenne-jeno grew rapidly, covering 25 ha (62 acres) by A.D. 300 and becoming a prosperous farming and fishing community of brush and mud houses (Figure 16.16). Soon, Jenne-jeno's trading contacts expanded considerably. Copper from Saharan sources appeared by A.D. 400, and savanna or forest gold between A.D. 600 and 800, by which time the town covered 33 ha (82 acres) and boasted of a mud fortification wall 2 km (1.2 miles) in circumference and 3.6 m (11.8 feet) wide. Ten centuries after its founding, Jenne-jeno was a mature town, with numerous round houses up to 3.9 m (13 feet) in diameter, constructed of cylindrical bricks. This growth to maturity coincided with a gradual buildup in local and long-distance trade. Lying as it did at the extreme southwestern end of the Niger Delta, Jenne-jeno was ideally placed to barter savanna gold, iron, and agricultural produce. It also became a leading exchange point for trading these commodities against Saharan copper and salt (a dietary supplement in poor supply in West Africa). In addition, it is highly likely that Jenne-jeno's growth over this period was linked to increased cross-Saharan trade, West African gold being traded on by Saharan merchants to the North African coast, and North African luxury products in turn arriving in West Africa. Judging from the hierarchy of lesser contemporary settlements found nearby, the rulers of Jenne-jeno presided over a considerable area of the floodplain, a territory that may have extended at least 100 km (60 miles) downstream of the town. Their government provided a stable environment for a growing volume of trade with the Sahara.

Jenne-jeno was only one of many such growing communities and states south of the desert (Connah, 2001; Phillipson, 2005). With the Islamic trade there was an increased demand for West African gold and an increasingly organized network of traders and cross-Saharan trading towns—including

1000 B.C.

Jenne-jeno
200 B.C. to A.D. 800 and later

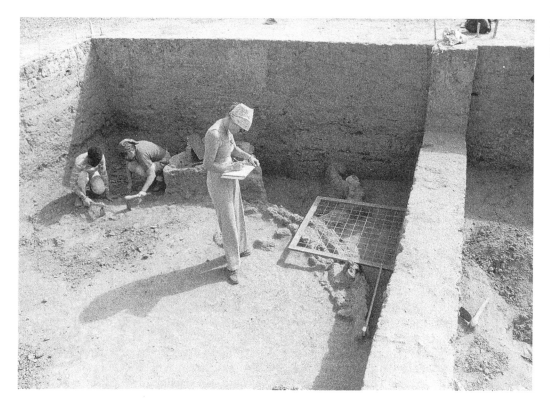

FIGURE 16.16 Excavations at Jenne-jeno, Mali, showing early house foundations.

Audaghust, Tadmekka, and then later Timbuktu—developed to supply this. The increased demand for gold in the Islamic period enabled the West African states to further augment their wealth and power. The geographer al-Bakri drew a vivid picture of the most famous of these early kingdoms, Ghana, whose gold was well-known in northern latitudes by the eleventh century. "It is said," he wrote, "that the king owns a nugget as large as a big stone" (Levetzion, 1973: 186).

Ghana

Ghana
c. A.D. 700 to 1100

The kingdom of Ghana straddled the northern borders of the gold-bearing river valleys of the upper Niger and Senegal (Levetzion, 1973). No one knows when it first came into being, but the kingdom was described by Arab writers in the eighth century A.D. The Ghanians' prosperity depended on the gold trade and also the constant demand for ivory in the north. Other products such as kola nuts and slaves also crossed the desert, but trade in old, ivory, and salt were the foundations of their power. Islam was brought to Ghana sometime in the late first millennium A.D. and linked the kingdom more closely to the desert trade. The king of Ghana was a powerful ruler, who, wrote al-Bakri, "can put 200,000 men in the field, more than 40,000 of whom were bowmen" (Levetzion, 1973: 189).

Ghana was a prime target for Islamic reform movements, whose desert leaders longingly eyed the power and wealth of their southern neighbor. One such group, the Almoravids, attacked Ghana in approximately A.D. 1062, laying siege to it for 14 years. Whether through the Almoravid attack, or other internal processes, Ghana was fatally weakened. The kingdom disintegrated into a series of minor chiefdoms, somewhat, perhaps, as many early Egyptian polities had done in the centuries preceding unification in 3100 B.C.

Mali

Mali
c. A.D. 1230 to 1460

The kingdom of Mali appeared two centuries later. A group of Kangaba people under the leadership of Sundiata came into prominence in about A.D. 1230 and annexed their neighbors' lands. The fame of the Mali kings spread throughout the Muslim world. Timbuktu, whose very name evokes dreams of gold and far-flung fortunes, developed at the edge of the desert and was taken into Mali's power. It became a widely known center of Islamic scholarship. Malian gold was valued everywhere. When the king of Mali went on a pilgrimage to Mecca in A.D. 1324, the price of gold in Egypt was reduced sharply by the king's liberal spending. Mali appeared on the earliest European maps of West Africa as the outside frontier of the literate world. It provided most of Europe's gold reserves and royal wealth.

The key to Mali's prosperity and political stability was the unifying effect of Islam, which overcame much factionalism and many tribal rivalries. Mali's Islamic rulers governed with supreme powers granted by Allah and ruled their conquered provinces with carefully selected religious appointees, or even with astute slaves chosen for their loyalty and political acumen. Islam provided a reservoir of thoroughly trained, literate administrators who believed that political stability resulted from efficient governance and sound trading practices.

Songhay

In approximately A.D. 1325, the most famous of the kings of Mali, Mansa Musa, brought the key trading center of Gao on the Niger under his sway. Gao was the capital of the Dia kings, who shook off Mali's yoke in about A.D. 1340 and founded the kingdom of Songhay. Their state prospered increasingly as Mali's power weakened and then expired in A.D. 1460. The great chieftain Sonni Ali led the Songhay to new conquests between A.D. 1464 and 1492, expanding the frontiers of his empire deep into Mali country and far north into the Sahara. He monopolized much of the Saharan trade, seeking to impose law and order with his vast armies to increase the volume of trade that passed through Songhay hands. Sonni Ali was followed by other competent rulers who further expanded Songhay. Its collapse came in the sixteenth century. Powerful kingdoms arose in the rain forest to the south after A.D. 1600 (Figure 16.17).

Songhay
1340 to 1460

Farmers and Traders in Eastern and Southern Africa

2000 B.C.

While cattle herders had settled in the East African highlands as early as 3000 B.C. (Chapter 11), the great savannas of eastern and southern Africa were still home to Stone Age hunter-gatherer groups. The spread of farming economies into the savanna coincided in part with the spread of iron technology and perhaps with the dispersal of Bantu languages over much of eastern, central, and southern Africa from a homeland in eastern West Africa (Robertson and Bradley, 2000). This complex series of local population movements is still little understood, but we know that iron-using farmers had settled in the East African lakes region (now Uganda and Tanzania) by 300 B.C. and

300 B.C.

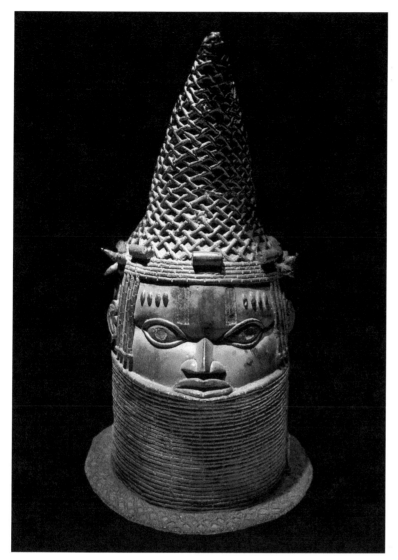

FIGURE 16.17 Brass head of a Benin oba, a ruler of the heavily urbanized kingdom of Benin in modern-day Nigeria. The head was cast to adorn an ancestral altar in the royal palace.

that they lived in the Zambezi Valley soon after A.D. 1, moving across the Limpopo River into South Africa soon afterward. These savanna farmers used shifting agriculture and careful soil selection to produce a diet of sorghum, millet, and other cereal crops. They kept cattle and small stock, relying on hunting and foraging for much of their diet. Their architectural styles and pottery have a clear but indirect relationship to those of many present-day African groups (Phillipson, 2005).

Towns and Trade on the East African Coast

The same monsoon winds that linked the Red Sea with India also linked the East African coast between Somalia and Mozambique with a much wider commercial world. According to a sailors' manual, the *Periplus of the Erythraean Sea*, dated to around the first century A.D., traders from Arabia were coasting southward in search of gold, ivory, and other commodities, trading with small farming communities near the Red Sea shore (though in all likelihood people from both sides of the Red Sea had probably learnt to work the monsoon winds for millennia before this). By the end of the first millennium A.D., the coastal trade was under Islamic control, centered on small towns and strategic bays. Lamu in northern Kenya was one such port. So was Kilwa Island off the Tanzanian coast, a strategic transshipment point, where oceangoing dhows (sailing ships) loaded gold dust and ivory obtained from Sofala in southeast Africa (Figure 16.18). Meanwhile, on the Arabian side of the Red Sea, further ports and towns also began to thrive—among them the southern Yemeni port of Mocha (al-Mukhā in Arabic), which by the seventeenth century A.D. was world famous for its trade in luxury "Mocha" coffee.

As for the East African coast, for more than 1,000 years, a distinctive coastal civilization flourished along the shore, represented by a cosmopolitan blend of African and Islamic culture based

A.D. 500 to 1500

FIGURE 16.18 Architect Peter Garlake's reconstruction of the Sultan's Palace at Kilwa, on the East African coast.

on "stone towns," compact trading settlements of rock and coral houses controlled by prominent merchant families.

Until the early nineteenth century, most contacts between the coast and the far interior were indirect, through local intermediaries. But the volume of gold, ivory, and copper that flowed to the coast was impressive. These commodities, in high demand overseas, were bartered for cheap baubles like glass beads and cotton cloth. Another popular item was Indian Ocean seashells, worn as ornaments, which assumed great prestige in the interior. When explorer David Livingstone passed through western Zambia in 1855, the going price for one circular *Conus* shell was a slave; for five, a tusk of elephant ivory. They could be picked up by the dozen on coastal reefs. Just as in West Africa, a series of powerful African states took advantage of the coastal trade.

Great Zimbabwe

Great Zimbabwe
c. A.D. 950 to 1450

Trading states first appear to the south of the Congo Forest in central Africa as early as the ninth century A.D., and especially south of the Zambezi River, where Shona-speaking peoples had settled at about the same time. The Shona were cattle-herding people living in a highland environment, where political power was measured by wealth on the hoof. Both agriculture and herding were high-risk enterprises in a landscape where rainfall was unpredictable, so Shona chiefs were quick to realize the potential of long-distance trade with the coast. They mined gold and hunted elephants, using their exports to acquire "exotic" commodities like cloth and glass beads, which they then used to acquire more grain and cattle.

By A.D. 1200, Shona society was acquiring some complexity, perhaps a mosaic of small chiefdoms, each having its own territory with sufficient range to graze cattle not only through the rainy season but through the dry months as well. One of them, Great Zimbabwe on the southern plateau, rose to prominence. Its rulers were able to maintain and raise armies and to intervene in the politics of their neighbors. For many generations, they exacted tribute not only from their own "core" area but also from surrounding chiefdoms. The size of the state fluctuated constantly, for vassal chiefs often acted with remarkable independence.

The gold trade with the Indian Ocean coast flourished because the Shona encouraged it. From the region known as Sofala, the tentacles of the gold and ivory trade extended far inland, up the Limpopo, Sabi, and Zambezi rivers to the plateau country of the interior. For centuries, this trade was at best sporadic and on a small scale. It was a long-distance trade that merged imperceptibly with the myriad bush paths that carried essential commodities and luxuries from one village to the next. The change came after the tenth century A.D. on the coast, and sometime later in the interior, when the international demand for gold and ivory skyrocketed. It can be no coincidence that the trade with Sofala picked up dramatically as the East African coastal towns enjoyed their greatest prosperity. The chiefs of Great Zimbabwe managed to dominate the trade between the southwestern goldfields and the coast.

FIGURE 16.19 The Great Enclosure or Elliptical Building at Great Zimbabwe with valley ruins in the foreground. A solid masonry Conical Tower dominates the interior and is thought to be a symbolic grain bin, an expression of chiefly power.

The word *Zimbabwe* is either a contraction of the Shona words *dzimba dza mabwe*, "houses of stone," or, more likely, of *dzimba hoye*, "venerated houses," an expression used to describe chiefs' houses or graves. Judging from archaeological data, Great Zimbabwe served both these roles (Garlake, 1973; Huffman, 1987; Pikirayi, 2001). In about A.D. 1000, Shona groups, probably direct ancestors of the present-day inhabitants of the area, settled near Great Zimbabwe (Beach, 1993). One village lay on the western end of the low hill that now dominates the site, its cattle enclosures and millet gardens spread out over the valley below. These people and their neighbors lived in good farming and cattle country, where they were able to maintain large grain surpluses and to develop great wealth on the hoof, but theirs was not a vital gold-producing area.

At first, only a few families farmed and grazed their herds at the site. They built circular mud-and-stick thatched huts both on the hill and in the valley below. As time went on, they erected stone cattle enclosures, then more and more walls. They reinforced the walls of the larger huts and joined the large boulders atop the hill to form small enclosures, creating the first stages of a complex known to archaeologists as the Acropolis or Hill Ruin. By 1250, like their neighbors, the Great Zimbabwe chiefs presided over a sizable territory and measured their wealth in large herds. Perhaps it was the uncertainty of cereal agriculture and cattle herding that made trading with foreigners an attractive risk-management strategy—a way of cushioning themselves against the depredations of cattle disease, of drought, and even of marauding neighbors. Within a few generations, Great Zimbabwe became a sizable town, perhaps with as many as 18,000 people living in it and nearby. Great Zimbabwe was in part a military state, capable of raising armies from its herding population that could enforce tribute assessments and toll collections. At the same time, the chiefs could manipulate their cattle as a means of acquiring wives and, eventually, relatives and supporters. Great Zimbabwe's stone buildings, built of easily quarried granite slabs, sprawl over about 8 sq. km (3 sq. miles).

The Hill Ruin overlooks the valley, the summit a mass of weathered granite boulders linked by freestanding stone walls. These form a maze of large and small enclosures, accessible by a narrow stepped entrance on the north side or via a secretive defile that squeezes between large boulders on its way up to the western enclosure on the summit.

The Hill Ruin looks down on the celebrated "Elliptical Building" or "Great Enclosure" that dominates the valley (Figure 16.19). Its oval-shaped freestanding outer wall is more than 244 m (800 feet) long and rises 9.7 m (32 feet) at its highest point. The Elliptical Building is a secluded place, divided by low stone walls into several enclosures. Substantially built mud huts once stood within them, for this was the residence of the chief. The valley between the Hill Ruin and the Elliptical Building is a jumble of stone-walled enclosures and large occupation sites; it was in some of these that the chief's many wives may have resided.

By the fifteenth century, Great Zimbabwe was the most powerful of some ten chiefdoms that flourished on the plateau. Each controlled a territory about 160 km (100 miles) across, sufficient land to allow not only shifting cultivation but also large-scale seasonal grazing of sizable cattle herds. Eventually, overgrazing, exhausted soils, and denuded woodland may have caused much of the population to move elsewhere. Great Zimbabwe was abandoned in about 1,500 A.D., as the center of political power shifted northward, closer to the Zambezi River, a major trade route to the coast.

Europe and Africa

Even as Christopher Columbus landed in the Bahamas, Portuguese ships were coasting southward, seeking to outflank Islam by reaching the West African gold mines from the sea (R. Oliver, 2000). By 1470, they had rounded the bulge of Africa. In 1488, Bartholomeu Dias rounded the Cape of Good Hope. Nine years later, Vasco da Gama sailed up the East African coast and used the monsoon route to reach India. During the next four centuries, Africans were drawn increasingly into a much wider economic world fueled by insatiable demands for raw materials and, above all,

A.D. 1488

slaves to work the sugar and cotton plantations of the New World. During these years, Africans were aggressive in seizing new opportunities and in acquiring wealth and political prestige. It was they who controlled the sources of slaves, who mined for gold, and who organized the hunting of elephants. Increasingly, the destiny of Africa became intertwined with the unfolding economic and political fortunes of a wider and ever more international and industrialized world.

Summary

- Ancient Egyptian civilization arose out of complex processes of forced and voluntary integration along the Nile Valley. This process was accelerated by increasing trade contacts with Southwest Asia, culminating in the emergence of the ancient Egyptian state in about 3100 B.C.
- Egyptologists conventionally subdivide ancient Egyptian civilization into four main periods: the Archaic and Old Kingdom, Middle Kingdom, New Kingdom, and the Late period, the first three of which were separated by brief intermediate periods of political chaos.
- The Old Kingdom was notable for its despotic pharaohs and its frenzy of pyramid construction, an activity that may be connected with pragmatic notions of fostering national unity.
- The Middle Kingdom saw a shift of political and religious power to Thebes and Upper Egypt.
- New Kingdom pharaohs made Egypt an imperial power with strong interests in Asia and Nubia. Ancient Egyptian civilization began to decline after 1000 B.C., and Egypt fell under Roman rule in 30 B.C.

- Nubia, upstream of the First Cataract, was exploited by the Egyptians for centuries, but it came into its own as the pharaohs' power declined. Nubian kings from Kush actually ruled over Egypt in the eighth century B.C., but they were forced to retreat to Meroe, far upstream, two centuries later.
- Meroe became a center for the Red Sea and Indian Ocean trade, ruled by kings and queens who preserved Egyptian customs. It prospered until the fourth century A.D., when it was conquered and finally eclipsed by the kingdom of Aksum centered on the Ethiopian highlands.
- The camel opened up the Sahara to regular gold and salt trade, fostering the development of powerful West African states such as Ghana, Mali, and Songhay.
- At the same time, expanding Indian Ocean trade nurtured a network of trading towns on the East African coast. During the fourteenth and fifteenth centuries A.D., Great Zimbabwe in southern Africa controlled much of the gold and ivory trade in southeastern Africa.

Key Term

hieroglyph (331)

Further Reading

Aldred, Cyril. 2004. *The Egyptians*, 4th ed., updated by Aidan Dodson. New York: Thames & Hudson.

Kemp, Barry. 2005. *Ancient Egypt: The Anatomy of a Civilization*, 2nd ed. London: Routledge.

Wilkinson Toby, A.H. 2011. *The Rise and Fall of Ancient Egypt*. New York: Random House.

Early States in South and Southeast Asia

17

I n 1950, the famed excavator Sir Mortimer Wheeler assembled a team of young archaeologists, students, and local laborers to work on a confusion of mud bricks that projected out of a weathered citadel mound at Mohenjodaro on the banks of the Indus River, in Pakistan. The laborers removed foot after foot of sand, the few bricks grew into many, "until the stark walls of a huge platform began to emerge from the hillside. The aspect was of a fortress, towering grim and forbidding above the plain" (Wheeler, 1968: 317).

Wheeler puzzled over the mass of brickwork. A grid of narrow passages, signs of a timber superstructure, a carefully designed platform with an approach way: The enormous structure looked less and less like a fortress, but what was it? Suddenly a light went on in his brain. The narrow passages were ducts for air to dry the floor of the timber barn that once housed the city's grain, accessible only from the site, away from the teeming streets. The "fortress" was the municipal granary. More recent excavations have thrown Wheeler's bold interpretation into doubt, but many details of the Harappan civilization of South Asia, one of the world's least known (see Table 15.1), have come from his classic investigations of a half century ago.

Thai solders, allies of the Khmer, march into battle, Angkor Wat, Cambodia.

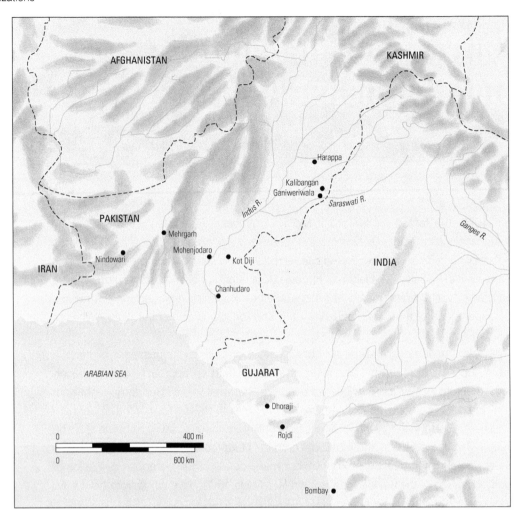

FIGURE 17.1 The Harappan civilization, showing sites mentioned in this chapter.

South Asia lies within vast geographic barriers (Figure 17.1). To the north lie the Himalayas, a vast mountain chain extending more than 2,000 km (1,200 miles) from the Hindu Kush in the west to Assam in the east. High passes traverse the mountains into Afghanistan, central Asia, and Tibet, but the most accessible routes are the northwestern defiles into western Afghanistan, Iran, and Baluchistan. The Arabian Sea, the Indian Ocean, and the Bay of Bengal surround the Indian subcontinent, and tropical rain forests restrict access to the east.

A rim of mountainous terrain rings the north and northwest of South Asia, giving way in the west to the alluvial plains of the Indus River, which merge with the Thar Desert in the east, 150 m (500 feet) above the floodplain. The desert, in turn, yields to the central tableland, the Deccan Plateau, more fertile than the lowlands and once densely forested. North and east of the central tableland lies the Ganges basin, which extends into Bihar, Bengal, and Bangladesh. This vast alluvial corridor enjoys greater rainfall as one moves east, and it gives way to the dense tropical forests that continue into Southeast Asia. The Deccan Peninsula lies south of the higher terrain of the central tableland, higher on the west than in the east, which means rivers flow eastward and the coastal plain is wider on the Bay of Bengal side.

Hemmed in by mountains, oceans, and tropical rain forest, South Asia developed its own distinctive civilizations, marked by the ability to assimilate ideas from outside. The subcontinent itself always had, and still has, a distinctive cultural identity along with great local diversity created by the isolation caused by east–west flowing rivers, different ethnic origins, and linguistic differences (Allchin and Allchin, 1983).

The Roots of South Asian Civilization

The Indus River, on the banks of which South Asian civilization began, rises in southern Tibet and then descends 1,600 km (1,000 miles) through Kashmir before flowing through the semiarid Indus plains. Here, deep silt deposits provide soft, easily turned soils that can be cultivated on a large scale without metal tools. The Indus plains border on Baluchistan and eastern Afghanistan, forming a region with some environmental resemblances to the southern Mesopotamian plains and the neighboring Iranian Plateau. Like Mesopotamia, this is an area of climatic extremes: searingly hot summers and sometimes very cold winters. Farmers living in this harsh region obtain their water supplies from rivers and streams that rise in the mountains.

Twelve thousand years ago, both borderland and plains were home to Stone Age hunter-gatherer groups that continued to flourish for many thousands of years. Despite now-refuted claims to the contrary, there is little evidence for agricultural communities in South Asia before the third millennium B.C., except in the northwest, where farming was probably introduced from the west. And even when agriculture took hold, as it did over wide areas between the fifth and third millennium B.C., hunting and gathering remained a viable lifeway for many South Asians, as it did into modern times. Most authorities on South Asian archaeology agree that humped cattle, buffalo, and pig were domesticated there from local wild populations. Evidence from Mehrgarh (see the following paragraph) suggests that goats and sheep were domesticated in the aceramic period, so by at least 5300 B.C. The farmers eventually domesticated not only indigenous Indian including various forms of millet, gram, jujube and sesame, but also peas, barley, lentils, and other west Asian species; the dates of this early domestication are still unknown.

The best-known early farming settlement is the aforementioned site of Mehrgarh, 200 km (125 miles) west of the Indus River, occupied by village farmers as early as 7000 B.C. (Jarrige, 1993). They grew west Asian wheat and used domesticated goats from the same region, as if the new economies had been introduced from the west, for Mehrgarh had cultural links with western and central Asia (Turkmenia). A thousand years later, the local people lived in sizable, permanent mud-brick houses. Their village lay astride a centuries-old trade route from the Indus Valley to the Iranian highlands. The Mehrgarh deposits contain copper artifacts and imported turquoise from Iran and shells from the distant Arabian coast.

In the centuries before the emergence of urban civilization in India, dozens of regional variations of farming culture flourished in parts of India and Pakistan; these peasant cultures are still little understood (Allchin and Allchin, 1983; Possehl, 1993). Food production may even have begun independently in South India (Korisettar et al., 2001), but, thanks to its unique ecology, the Indus Valley was the main focus of early civilization.

The Indus River flows over a vast alluvial plain, its waters carrying enormous quantities of fine silt (Fuller and Madella, 2000). During the flood season, between June and September, the inundation rises above the banks and covers large areas, leaving the river suspended, as it were, above the plain. Much of the floodwater also flows through well-defined channels, which in turn spill their banks. The alluvial plain comprises ridges along the riverbeds and ancillary channels, with shallow valleys in between. The drainage pattern varies greatly from one area to the next, so the farmers planted their fields where water was available. The plain floods during the late summer inundation, so each community planted its wheat and barley, the winter cereals, along the flood spillage areas and along river ridges as the waters receded in October and November. No further watering was necessary, especially if there was some winter rainfall.

Indus agriculture required minimal labor and the simplest of technology, and certainly no elaborate irrigation canals or construction works, as was once assumed. These same agricultural methods were still in use as late as the nineteenth century A.D. The Indus people also planted some summer crops like cotton and oilseed in fields near the river or old flood canals, surrounding them with earthen embankments with an opening to allow floodwaters to enter the enclosure. The farmers would then block the gap, allow the water to soak in, then cultivate and sow. This was a risky form of agriculture, with the danger that floodwaters would overwhelm the field at a critical stage. Throughout the Indus Valley, it appears that villages, towns, and, later, great cities like Mohenjodaro were situated not close to major irrigation schemes but to natural flood channels, thereby making large-scale agricultural labor unnecessary. These simple agricultural systems produced the large food surpluses needed to support cities and towns, but the crops varied considerably from area to area.

The alluvial Indus plains were settled as early as the fourth millennium B.C. Scattered across a vast area of the plains are dozens of pre-Harappan settlements, many of them boasting fortifications, metallurgy, and planned streets, often grouped under the label Early Harappan.

Typical of these settlements is Kot Diji, on the left bank of the Indus, approximately 33 km (20 miles) from the river (Possehl, 1993). In the early third millennium B.C., the inhabitants were forced to pile up boulders to protect themselves against the inundation. They finally erected a massive defensive wall that served as both a flood dike and a fortress. The stone and mud-brick houses of the village were clustered inside the wall. At the end of the Early Harappan period, the site underwent a massive burning. Such deliberate destruction prior to complete rebuilding is a feature

10000 B.C.

Mehrgarh
7000 B.C.

4000 B.C.

Kot Diji
3000 B.C.

of a number of settlements. Though some researchers have suggested this was wrought by attackers, current thinking suggests it was most likely undertaken by its inhabitants. Though we must remain open to the possibility of intercommunity competition and violence, there is no secure evidence for or reasonable arguments against this. By the mature Harappan period, massive platforms and other flood defenses under and around the major settlements emerged. Indeed, at this time, settlement was probably not sufficiently dense to have brought about any raging competition. Rather, regional resource diversity would have promoted interregional cooperation and interdependence—of the sort that is very clear within the mature Harappan civilization.

During early times, forests covered much of the Indus Valley, but we still know little about the highly varied environmental conditions across the basin, or about the climate changes that descended on the region after the Holocene (Schuldenrein et al., 2004). There are signs that the larger floodplains of the Indus stabilized after the Ice Age, and there may also have been a long-term trend toward a drier climatic regimen. But it is near impossible to establish any links between climate change and the rise and fall of the Harappan civilization. We do know that Indus populations increased over the centuries. As numbers climbed, so must have pressure on agricultural land. The farmers must have cleared and burned off more and more riverine forest and grazed ever-growing herds of goats and sheep on watershed lands. Deprived of natural controls, the rising floodwaters had the potential in high inundation years to sweep over the plains, carrying everything with them. Confronted with what may have seemed like the wrath of the gods, the people had only one defense: cooperative floodworks that provided at least a degree of security from the vagaries of the elements.

Until the early second millennium B.C., another river, the Saraswati, ran parallel to and south of the Indus River. The Saraswati dried up during the second millennium as a result of tectonic upheavals in the Himalayas that diverted the course of several of the rivers that merged to become the Saraswati (Possehl, 2000). Archaeological surveys along the dried-up riverbed show that settlement along the river and its tributaries was very dense. Many unexcavated sites, including the major Harappan city of Ganweriwala, lie along its banks. Survival in these harsh environments required intense cooperation at the community level. The obvious leaders of these new communal efforts were the chieftains, priests, and kin leaders, who acted as intermediaries between the people and the gods. By 2700 B.C., the most successful leaders of larger settlements presided over hierarchies of other settlements.

Highlands and Lowlands: The Kulli Complex

This scenario fits the few archaeological facts available from the lowlands. The early stages of the Harappan civilization date to between 3200 and 2600 B.C. The people lived in small villages covering only a few acres, and there are no signs of social ranking (Kenoyer, 1997). Their environment was like that of Mesopotamia, low-lying and hot, with fertile soils but no metals. Thus, its inhabitants could not flourish in isolation. Long before the rise of Harappan civilization in the valley, the peoples of the lowlands interacted constantly with their neighbors to the north and the west, especially in the highlands of southern Baluchistan, in western Pakistan. Metals, semiprecious stones, and timber came from the highlands, where people depended for their subsistence on dry agriculture and sheepherding. Over the millennia, the relationship between lowlands and highlands was fostered not only by regular exchanges of foods and other commodities but also by seasonal population movements that brought enormous herds of goats and sheep down from mountain summer pastures in Baluchistan to the lowlands during the harsh winters in the west. In a real sense, economic and social development in both regions occurred along parallel if somewhat diverse tracks, every region being dependent on its neighbors.

Kulli complex

Nindowari

2600 to 2200 B.C.

In Baluchistan, a complex of large and small centers, subsumed under the Kulli complex, evolved during the third millennium B.C. The largest of these settlements was Nindowari, a major center dominated by a sizable monumental structure and massive public buildings. Nindowari was occupied between about 2600 and 2200 B.C. and was contemporary with mature Harappan civilization in the Indus lowlands. Harappan seals and other artifacts are found at Nindowari, and there are signs that Kulli communities were heavily involved in regular exchange with the lowlands to the east (Figure 17.2). Kulli also lay on the borders of eastern Iran, with its intricate exchange networks that reached far to the west toward Mesopotamia (see Chapter 15), but it is uncertain how many of its products flowed to the east. For centuries, the Kulli communities of the highlands were specialized partners of the Harappan civilization of the lowlands. One major commodity was cotton cloth. Cotton, a South Asian–domesticated crop, was probably first used as a fodder crop for cattle before people discovered that its fluffy white flower could be woven into fine cloth both for domestic use in a hot climate and for a hard-wearing fabric ideal for export. A thread inside a copper bracelet at

FIGURE 17.2 Mohenjodaro. Steatite seals bearing impressions of a humped ox, and elephant, and a mythical beast.

Mehrgarh, dating from the end of Period I, is the world's earliest cotton fiber suggesting the use of cotton by the mid-sixth millennium B.C., while an incredibly rarely preserved piece of fabric, perhaps the world's earliest example, comes from the Harappan city of Mohenjodaro in the third millennium B.C.

This symbiosis between Baluchistan and the Indus, among other regions, may have been a major catalyst in the rise of complex societies in both areas, a symbiosis that was vital not only in the Indus Valley but in distant Mesopotamia as well.

A Rapid Transition

Early Harappan society contrasted sharply with the complex, sometimes urban society that developed in the lowlands after about 2600 B.C. The transition from egalitarian to ranked society was an indigenous one that took place with what Gregory Possehl calls "a veritable paroxysm of change" (1986: 27). There was a short period of explosive growth over one or two centuries, ending about 2500 B.C. This span contrasts dramatically with the long period of increasing social, political, and economic complexity in Egypt and Mesopotamia.

2600 B.C.

Possehl (1999) believes that this growth may have coincided with a major shift in Sumerian trade patterns. As we saw in Chapter 15, the Sumerians obtained many exotic objects and basic raw materials from the Iranian Plateau before 2600 B.C. Judging from historical records, they experienced considerable frustration in their transactions with these exchange networks. After 2600 B.C., they reorganized their trade in luxuries and raw materials and then obtained many of their needs by sea from three foreign entities: Dilmun, Magan, and Meluha states. Dilmun, equated with the island of Bahrain in the Persian Gulf, was a prosperous, somewhat urbanized, but small-scale society. Magan, lying further to the east, was represented by a large group of communities practicing fishing, agriculture, mining, and metallurgy, but with little settlement hierarchy and no central control. And finally there was Meluha, even farther away, where ivory, oils, furniture, gold, silver, and carnelian, among other commodities, were to be obtained (Rice, 1993). But where was Meluha? Owing to such evidence as the presence of Indus Valley seals in Mesopotamia, it is now generally accepted to have been the Indus Valley region. The Sumerians exported wool, cloth, leather, oil, cereals, in exchange for these foreign items. But since the Harappans would have had no need for many, if any, of these items, it is not clear which, if any, of these, was being sent to the Indus, although the most likely items would be leather, wool, and woolen cloth (however, as with many exotic or luxury goods, "need" does not always come into it—our modern lust for Manolo Blahnik shoes being a case in point).

In about 2350 B.C., King Sargon of Agade boasted that ships from all these locations were moored at his city. There are even records of villages of Meluhans near Lagash and elsewhere in Mesopotamia. This was a highly organized mercantile trade conducted by specialized merchants, a trade quite different than that of the exchange networks in the highlands far inland. The sea trade increased the volume of Sumerian imports and exports dramatically. One shipment of 5,900 kg (13,000 pounds) of copper is recorded, and the entire enterprise was very different from the basically noncommercial exchange systems of the Iranian Plateau. It has long been assumed that this trade was under Mesopotamian control, much of it conducted through Dilmun, and in Possehl's (1986) view, it had a major impact on the growth of Harappan civilization. Interestingly, its beginnings coincide with the growth of urban centers in both Mesopotamia and the Indus Valley (Edens, 1993).

However, this model is now being revisited. Since the Mesopotamians do not seem to have sailed beyond the west coast of the Oman Peninsula, and since it was the Harappan merchants who were active in Mesopotamia (and not the other way around), a good case could be made for the Harappans controlling this trade. Though Dilmun was involved, its main period of trade prominence came later—after the decline of both southern Mesopotamia and the Indus, in the early second millennium B.C. (McIntosh, 2007). A dramatic increase in long-distance trade may well have been the context in which Harappan civilization developed, trade that amplified the centuries-old symbiosis between highlands and lowlands to the northwest (Kenoyer, 1997). With the development of these coastal trading routes between the Persian Gulf and the South Asian peninsula, South Asia became part of what some archaeologists call an early world system, linking the eastern Mediterranean, parts of Eurasia, and western and southern Asia with loose and ever-changing economic ties. However, many scholars believe overseas trade was less important than is sometimes claimed and that Harappan civilization was an entirely indigenous development. Alternatively, we might consider both perspectives and see a society built on indigenous developments but that fed into a world system.

Mature Harappan Civilization

Harappan civilization
2600 to 1700 B.C.

By 2600 B.C., the Indus people had mastered the basic problems of irrigation and flood control, partly by using millions of fired bricks made of river alluvium and baked with firewood cut from riverine forests. (For a general synthesis of the Harappan civilization, see J. McIntosh, 2007.) Mature Harappan civilization developed and flourished over a vast area of just under 1,294,900 sq. km (just under 500,000 sq. miles), a region considerably larger than modern Pakistan. The Indus and Saraswati valleys were the cultural focus of the Harappan civilization, but they were only one part of a much larger, quite varied civilization, whose influences and ties extended over the lowlands of Punjab and Sind, from the highlands and maritime sites of Baluchistan to the deserts of Rajasthan, and from the Himalayan foothills to Gujarat, the outlet to the overseas world and a major source of raw material and pastureland, and almost to Mumbai. The age-old relationship between highland Baluchistan and the Indus plains placed the Harappans within a larger cultural system, as did their maritime links with the Persian Gulf. But Possehl calls the Harappan civilization an "experiment in sociocultural organization which failed" (1993: 111). It was a large system, he says, but one that did not fully mature, with many settlements more villagelike than citylike in the Western sense. Many communities were like large 'Ubaid settlements in southern Mesopotamia before urban civilization began.

The Harappan civilization was different from that of the predominantly urban Sumerians in Mesopotamia, covering a core area of more than 777,000 sq. km (300,000 sq. miles) (Kenoyer, 1998). Possehl makes an analogy with Egypt, where the Upper and Lower Nile were part of the same civilization, but there were always administrative, cultural, and social differences between the two regions. The same may have been true of the Harappan, with Mohenjodaro in Sind and Harappa in Punjab, Ganweriwala on the Saraswati, and other sites in Gujarat, notably the immense and important site of Dholavira (discussed later), and Sawashtra. These were major regional subdivisions of the Harappan civilization, linked by common symbolism and religious beliefs, the foundations of a cultural tradition that endured, although in modified form, for many centuries.

Harappa

Like the Sumerians, the Harappans adopted the city as a means of organizing and controlling their civilization. We know of at least five major Harappan cities: Harappa, after which the civilization is known; Mohenjodaro; Ganweriwela (though this is open to question since it remains unexcavated); Rakhigarhi; and the aforementioned Dholavirai. There is also likely a sixth domain, covering the Kacchi Plain, probably with its city at Pathani Damb (J. McIntosh, 2007). Harappa and Mohenjodaro were built on artificial mounds above the floods, at Herculean effort.

Mohenjodaro

With an area of more than 250 ha (618 acres), Mohenjodaro is by far the largest of the Harappan cities, and though it depends on how much of each site one considers, it appears to have been almost double the size of Harappa, which covered an estimated 150 ha (371 acres) (Kenoyer 1998). It was rebuilt at least nine times, sometimes because of disastrous inundations. Widely accepted population estimates, based on the densities of modern, somewhat similar settlements, place some 35,000 to 40,000 people at Mohenjodaro, 23,500 at Harappa. A high citadel lies at the west end of each city, dominating the streets below. However, once the suburbs are included (revealed in riverbank sections and by archaeological test pits) the estimates leap to 100,000 for Mohenjodaro and a possible 60,000 for Harappa.

While Harappa grew organically over many centuries and is in lots of parts; Mohenjodaro may have been conceived and constructed as a planned city on virgin soil. Despite this difference, in both these cities and at other Indus settlements, there is a recurring "ideal" layout: a raised area (the "citadel") on the west, with public and (probable) religious buildings; the cardinally orientated street plan; the use of uniformly sized bricks; the emphasis on water provision and drainage; walls around the whole and/or individual parts of the center (plus unwalled suburbs). One attractive hypothesis to explain this is that after 2600 B.C., there was some religiously motivated template that informed the layout of the settlements.

Turning to the well preserved site of Mohenjodaro, its towering citadel rises 12 m (40 feet) above the plain and is protected by massive flood embankments and a vast perimeter wall with towers. The public buildings on the summit include a pillared hall almost 27 m (90 feet) square, perhaps the precinct where the rulers gave audience to petitioners and visiting officials. There are no spectacular temples or richly adorned shrines. Religious life was centered on a great lustral bath made of bitumen-sealed brickwork and fed by a well (Figure 17.3). An imposing colonnade surrounded the pool, which was approached by sets of steps at both ends. We cannot be sure of the exact use of the great bath, but *lustration* (ceremonial bathing) was an important part of later Indian religions. Perhaps the great bath was where the devotees carried out their ceremonial bathing rituals.

The rulers of each city looked down on a complex network of at least partially planned streets (Figure 17.4). The more spacious dwellings, perhaps those of the nobility and the merchants, were laid out around a central courtyard where guests may have been received, food prepared, and servants probably worked. Staircases and thick ground walls indicate that some houses had two or even three stories. The larger residences had a well and contained rooms for bathing and toilets that were usually joined to an elaborate system of public drains. At both Harappa and Mohenjodaro, there were also groups of single-row tenements. At Mohenjodaro, the single-row tenement has been interpreted as a hotel for high-class travellers; while those at Harappa are understood to have been nonresidential artisan's workshops. Drawing together many strands of evidence, Possehl (2003) argues that the population of Mohenjodaro were largely the well-to-do.

On the basis of architectural form, some areas of Harappa and Mohenjodaro have been interpreted as bazaars, complete with shops. However, there is no evidence of an economy that included buying and selling. Rather, the strongly bureaucratic nature of the Indus civilization suggests that goods probably moved through official means rather than commerce. That said, these were productive cities. Archaeologists have inventoried the finds from artisans' quarters where bead makers, coppersmiths, cotton weavers, and other specialists manufactured their wares. The potters' workshops were filled with painted pots decorated with animal figures, as well as plain, ordinary wheel-made vessels that were manufactured not only in the cities but also in villages for hundreds of miles around. There were water jars and cooking bowls, storage pots, and drinking vessels. Metalworkers cast simple axes in open molds and manufactured chisels, knives, razors, spears, and fish-hooks. Only a few expert artisans made more elaborate objects, such as small figurines (Figure 17.5), or a piece as complicated as a canopied cart. They would make a wax model of the cart and encase it in clay, which was fired to melt the wax. Then molten copper or bronze was poured into the mold. This "lost-wax" process is still used by Indian artists.

FIGURE 17.3 The great bath on the citadel at Mohenjodaro, Pakistan. Pedestals from now vanished rooms surround the pool.

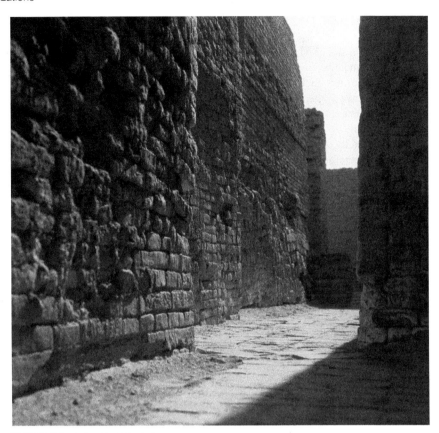

FIGURE 17.4 A street in Mohenjodaro.

The technologies used in Harappan cities had been developed centuries earlier in small villages and transferred to the cities without change. One of the most developed manufactures was the seal, made from steatite and other soft rocks. Excavations of seal workshops have yielded not only finished specimens, hardened in a furnace, but also the blocks of steatite from which square seals were cut as intaglios. For hours, the seal makers would crouch over the tiny squares, expertly cutting representations of animals in profile. They reserved some of their best efforts for religious scenes. Indian archaeologists working at the Harappan town of Chanhudaro, south of Mohenjodaro, found a complete bead maker's shop that gave some idea of the labor needed to produce small ornaments. The bead makers prepared bars of agate and carnelian approximately 7.6 cm (3 inches) long that were then ground and polished into shorter perforated cylinders and strung in necklaces. To experience the bead-making process, the archaeologists took a Harappan stone-tipped drill and some abrasive powder from the workshop and attempted to drill through one of the bead blanks. It took them 20 minutes to drill a small pit in the end of the bead. At that rate, it would have taken 24 hours to drill a single bead!

Who Were the Harappans?

Three-quarters of a century of excavations have revealed a highly varied society that archaeologists have named the Harappan simply because they do not know what the Harappans called themselves. Because no one has yet "cracked" the Indus Valley code, we do not even know the names of the rulers who controlled the major cities, like Harappa and Mohenjodaro, nor do we have insights into the intricate ties that linked city with town and major centers with minor hamlets.

There was constant interaction throughout this vast area, with abundant evidence that contemporary, relatively complex societies were developing elsewhere at the same time, developments known from sites like Kulli in Baluchistan (Possehl, 1993). The relationships between highland areas like Baluchistan, with their cold winters, and the lowlands led to complicated seasonal population shifts that brought highlanders and their herds to the Indus lowlands. This classic *transhumance* (seasonal movement) pattern may have placed the Harappans and their highland neighbors within the same larger cultural system. Moreover, this was a pattern that predated the Harappan civilization by many millennia and was probably responsible for the first (fourth millennium B.C.) settlement of the Indus region by people from Baluchistan in the fourth millennium who entered a region already populated by local hunter-gatherers and fisherfolk.

FIGURE 17.5 Bronze figurine of a dancing girl from Mohenjodaro, Pakistan, 11 cm (4.3 inches) high.

FIGURE 17.6 Limestone sculpture of a bearded, thick-lipped man, perhaps a priest or ruler, from Mohenjodaro. Height: 19 cm (7.4 inches). He stares at the world through slitted eyes, as if withdrawn in meditation, perhaps detached from worldly affairs. He wears an embroidered robe that was once inlaid with metal. One shoulder is uncovered, a sign of reverence during the Buddha's lifetime more than 1,000 years later. Perhaps the man was a priest or a priest-king.

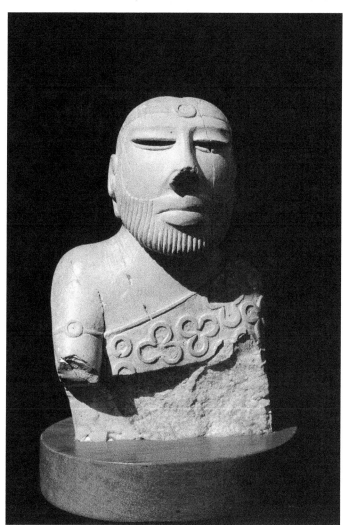

The Harappan civilization was part of a vast network of regional interactions that functioned through trade routes that extended along the Arabian coast, into northern Afghanistan and Turkmenia, and onto the Iranian Plateau, through thousands of square miles of mountainous terrain rich in minerals and other natural resources. Regular caravan routes linked lowlands and highlands. These routes carried grain and textiles, carnelian beads, pearls, and sweet-smelling rosewood—luxuries exchanged for minerals and other raw materials. Deep-sea trading vessels cruised the shores of the Indian Ocean into the Persian Gulf (Edens, 1993). During the 1950s and 1960s, archaeologists uncovered a Harappan coastal town known as Lothal, on the Gulf of Cambay. This settlement may have served as a river port, perhaps one of several Indian, as well as Pakistani coasts. The anonymity of the Harappan leaders extends even to their appearance (Figure 17.6). These were no bombastic rulers boasting of their achievements on grandiose palace walls. Thus far, the evidence of archaeology reveals leadership by rulers, perhaps merchants, ritual specialists, or people who controlled key resources or large areas of land. They seem to have led unostentatious lives marked by a complete lack of priestly pomp or lavish public display. There is nothing of the ardent militarism of the Assyrian kings or of the slavish glorification of the pharaohs.

One reason we know so little about Harappan leaders is that their script has still not been deciphered (Parpola, 1994; Possehl, 1996). Between 350 and 700 different signs have been identified from their seals. Linguists do not even agree on the language in the script, or even if it is a script in the traditional sense of the word, let alone the ultimate identity of the Harappans. However, enough of the Indus script has been deciphered to show how many of the short seal inscriptions designate the names of individuals and their ranks. It seems, too, that some describe major figures of the Harappan cosmos and name the chiefs, as well as identifying scribes and leading artisans.

The Harappan authorities developed a standard weight that was close to one half of a modern ounce. Later, Indian societies used a unit known as the *karsa* for the same purpose. This weighed the equivalent of 32 rattis, seeds of the gunja creeper, a measure that could fluctuate slightly from year to year. Four karsas weighed almost exactly the same as the basic Harappan unit of half a modern ounce. Similar devices could be found in nineteenth-century bazaars.

Everything points to some form of centralized government and a stratified society, with the focus of the civilization on agriculture and trade. Farming practices were regionally specific since the Indus realm embraced great diversity of different terrains, unlike the relative uniformity of the Euphrates and Nile Valleys of their contemporaries.

Cotton and dates were also important crops in a society where the state may have controlled many acres of land. The entire agricultural enterprise was a much larger-scale version of the communal village farming that had originally made colonization of the Indus Valley possible, but one that supported a hierarchical society.

Both Harappa and Mohenjodaro housed a comfortable and unpretentious middle class of merchants and petty officials who lived in stolid and standardized brick houses along the city streets. They wore finely woven, decorated cotton robes. Judging from clay figurines, the women wore short skirts and headdresses and perhaps longer robes. Others donned wire neck bangles, necklaces, and pendants. Unfortunately, organic materials survive badly, but we can assume the Harappans made abundant use of wood and textiles.

The artisans—metalsmiths, potters, weavers, bead makers, seal carvers, and shell bangle makers—formed another class of Harappan society, as did the minor bureaucrats and priests needed to administer the state. However, such people were a tiny minority compared with the vast mass of the populace: farmers, laborers, seafarers, and menial workers of every type. The commoners lived in small urban dwellings or, more often, in the countryside and wore the simplest cotton loincloths or robes. Perhaps, as is the case today, they might have had an extended family of several generations that provided a network of kinship ties and other benefits such as the communal ownership of property. Perhaps, too, the Harappan people were organized in a hierarchy of castes that restricted upward mobility and provided a wider identity outside the confines of the family.

Harappan Beliefs

Like the Sumerians, the Harappans lived in an environment that they modified for their own protection, one in which the annual floods meant a renewal of life and food for the coming year. Like the Mesopotamians, they seem to have believed that they lived in the valley to serve the gods, who caused crops to grow and soils to be fertile. We can speculate that the primeval roots of Indian religion may have been age-old fertility cults that served the same function as Inanna among the Sumerians and the mother goddess in many other Southwest Asian civilizations—an assurance that life would continue. The only clues we have to the origins of Indian religion come from minute seal impressions and small clay figurines from Harappan villages and cities that depict a female deity with conspicuous breasts and sexual organs. We do not know her name, but she probably embodied earth and life-giving nature for the Indus people.

A seal from Mohenjodaro bears a three-headed figure who sits in the yogic posture and wears a horned headdress. A tiger, an elephant, a rhinoceros, a water buffalo, and a deer surround him. Some Harappan experts think that the seal represents a forerunner of the great god Siva in his role of Lord of the Beasts. Many Harappan seals depict cattle, which may be symbols of Siva, who was worshiped in several forms. To judge from later beliefs, he may have had a dual role, serving as a fertility god as well as a tamer or destroyer of wild beasts (D. Miller, 1985). Siva gave life by planting the seed but could also destroy any creature, including a human being, at a flick of the finger. In part, he may have symbolized the unpredictable dangers of flood and famine that could threaten a village or a city. Harappa and Mohenjodaro have yielded dozens of carved phallic symbols and circular stones with round holes, which represent Siva's consort Devi's teeming womb. Perhaps these are simple prototypes of the Hindu *lingam* and *yoni* symbols that are found in the temples of Siva and Devi to this day. The iconography also shows a strong association of this goddess with a tiger, as found in later Hinduism. Indeed, if the evidence of figurines and seals is to be believed, the symbolism of early Indus religion bears remarkable similarities to that of modern Hinduism. Many other elements of more modern South Asian religion may have flourished in Harappan society, among them the use of fire altars in homes, worship with fruit and flowers, meditation, the use of water for ritual bathing, and well-developed astronomical knowledge. These similarities highlight the deeply ingrained conservatism of South Asian society from the earliest moments of Harappan civilization and even farther back in the past.

South Asia After the Harappans

The Harappan civilization reached its peak in about 2000 B.C. Three centuries later, Harappa and Mohenjodaro were in decline and soon abandoned. Their populations dispersed into smaller settlements over an enormous area as the volume of long-distance trade declined dramatically, except perhaps in metals (Figure 17.7). The reasons for this change are still little understood, but it may have been due to a variety of factors, among them possible flooding along the Indus, shifts in patterns of Mesopotamian trade, and changes in subsistence farming (Ghosh, 1993). One fundamental cause may have been major geological disturbances near the source of the all-important Saraswati River, which caused it to dry up and some tributaries to divert to new courses, thereby catastrophically disrupting farming life along its banks (Possehl, 2000).

1500 B.C.

Other changes followed soon afterward. By 1500 B.C., following several centuries of gradual movement into the Ganges Valley from the eastern Indus region, rice cultivation had taken hold in the Ganges basin. This opened up a new environment for farming where conditions were unsuitable for wheat and barley cultivation. At the same time, millets became important in the Gujarat region, some of them of African origin, crops that were especially suited to the more humid parts of southern India. The effect of these new crops may have been to widen the area where agriculture was practiced, thereby reducing the environmental circumscription that may have been one of the bases of Harappan civilization.

The rural components of Harappan culture continued to flourish in Gujarat and other areas for two centuries or more. After the Aryan nomads arrived in the Indus Valley and the lowlands, a hybrid culture developed. Though the Aryan nomads did not bring an end to Late Harappan culture, they did introduce new features such as horses, increased pastoralism, warfare, and the Sanskrit language (Possehl and Raval , 1989). As for the Harappans, they passed on a priceless legacy of

FIGURE 17.7 Rojdi, Gujarat, India, a Harappan town dating to the period immediately following the abandonment of cities. Left, excavation of house walls. Right, artist's reconstruction of the same dwellings.

beliefs and philosophies that formed one of the mainstreams of all subsequent Indian history. No cities developed in South Asia east of the Indus region until long after the Harappan civilization went into decline (Allchin, 1995). As the highly developed socioeconomic system of the Indus broke down, urban life vanished, to emerge once again far to the east in the Ganges Valley many centuries later. At the same time, many well-developed, but still little-known, regional farming cultures flourished both inside the Indus region and beyond.

But the second millennium B.C. was a period of vital importance in South Asian history, for it was during these centuries, sometimes called the Vedic period, that Indo-Aryan–speaking people spread into the subcontinent, an event described in the *Samhita*, a compilation of the hymns (*vedas*) of the *Rigveda*. Many of the hymns were composed centuries earlier, then passed from generation to generation by word of mouth. Many scholars argue that Indo-European–speaking peoples spread across the Iranian Plateau into South Asia during the second millennium B.C., where they intermarried with indigenous groups. Thus were born the Indo-Aryan, Sanskritic languages spoken throughout South Asia today. But another school of thought believes that there was no invasion, that Indo-Aryan developed indigenously in South Asia and was present there from a much earlier period (Mallory, 1988; Shaffer and Lichtenstein, 1995).

The process of conquest, assimilation, and acculturation may have begun in the northwest in the closing era of the Indus civilization and continued for as long as a thousand years. By 800 B.C., an indigenous iron technology was in full use throughout the subcontinent. Iron tools accelerated rice cultivation on the Ganges plain. Two centuries later 16 major kingdoms were concentrated around urban centers on the Ganges plain.

City life in the Ganges Valley marked the beginning of the classic period of South Asian civilization (Allchin, 1995). The new cities became economic powerhouses and centers of great intellectual and religious ferment. Brahmanism, a form of Hinduism that places great emphasis on ritual and sacrifice, was the dominant religion during the early first millennium. But philosophers of the sixth century B.C., like Buddha and Makhali Gosala, challenged Brahmanism with revolutionary doctrines that militated against sacrifice. Buddhism, with its teachings of personal spiritual development, spread rapidly, becoming the dominant religion in the north within five centuries.

Meanwhile, outside powers eyed the fabled riches of the subcontinent. King Darius of Persia invaded the northwest in 516 B.C. and incorporated the Indus Valley into the Persian Empire. Two centuries later, Alexander the Great ventured to the Indus River and brought Greek culture to the area. The great ruler Chandragupta Maurya of Magadha benefited from the power vacuum following Alexander's conquests and carved out the Mauryan Empire, which extended from Nepal and the northwest deep into the Deccan (Figure 17.8). His grandson Asoka presided over the empire at

Mauryan Empire
269 to 232 B.C.

FIGURE 17.8 Map of the extent of the Mauryan Empire.

its height between 269 and 232 B.C., seeking to unify its diverse people by a well-defined moral and ethical code based on Buddhist principles.

Magadha and other northern cities in Asoka's empire prospered greatly from overland trade routes leading northwest to Charsada, Taxila, and other frontier cities. Far to the east, the port of Tamluk at the mouth of the Ganges gave access to new and expanding marine trade routes to Southeast Asia. And, as the Mauryan Empire came to an end in 185 B.C., the monsoon winds of the Indian Ocean linked the South Asian coast with the Roman world and its insatiable demands for ivory, spices, and fine textiles from South Asian markets. Roman coins have come from ancient ports in the south, as well as from Arikamedu, a trading station on the east coast of the Deccan.

By Roman times, South Asia was part of a vast trading network that linked the Mediterranean world to all parts of the Indian Ocean and, indirectly, to new sources of raw materials many sea kilometers to the east.

Southeast Asian States

Ten thousand years ago, the Southeast Asian mainland extended far offshore, most of it low-lying marshland intersected by several major river systems. The three major river systems of Southeast Asia are much reduced versions of earlier rivers, each with its own fertile delta (Figure 17.9). The Middle Thailand and Chao Phraya Delta forms one such system; the lower Mekong and Tonle Sap plains, the major concern of this discussion, a second; and the Red, Ma, and Ca rivers of Vietnam, a third. The rivers flood seasonally, inundating large areas of farmland with shallow water where long-stalked, fast-growing rice can be grown. These three river valleys have been the homelands of complex societies for many centuries, fertile enclaves surrounded by higher ground where deciduous, drought-resistant forest and moist tropical forest flourish. Watered by monsoon cycles and marked by considerable local variations in climate and topography, parts of Southeast Asia supported high population densities only within the past 2,000 years.

The staple crop in ancient Southeast Asia was rice, domesticated in China's Yangtze River valley before 6500 B.C. (see Chapter 12). It was from the Yangtze Valley that rice farming communities progressively expanded to the south by riverine and coastal routes, reaching Southeast Asia from about 2000 B.C. This initial Neolithic settlement saw the establishment of farming communities in the broad lowlands of Southeast Asia. They cultivated rice and millet, and maintained domestic cattle and pigs, but also took advantage of the natural abundance of fish, shellfish and wide range of wild animals. From the eleventh century B.C., they became familiar with the bronze casting through their exchange contacts with the powerful trading states of China. At the site of Ban Non Wat, there was an immediate surge in the wealth associated with the burial of high status individuals as they controlled the ownership of not only copper-base axes and ornaments, but also marine shell and exotic stone jewelry.

Rice farming was well established in Southeast Asia by 2000 B.C., but agricultural populations were never large. Between 1500 and 500 B.C., Southeast Asia's farming communities adopted bronze metallurgy and traded widely with one another. Both mining and smelting were important activities, probably during the agriculturally quiet dry season (Higham, 2000, 2002). Thanks to recent excavations, we now know that social ranking developed for the first time.

Ban Non Wat mound is 300 km (186 miles) northeast of Bangkok, in a once forested environment that abounded in wildlife. It was first exploited by farmers in about 2200 B.C. Here, Charles Higham and Rachanie Thosarat have dug a large cutting, probing the depths of a site occupied from Neolithic through the Iron Age times (Higham, 2005). At the base lie Neolithic burials, including one of a man seated in a huge clay pot, holding a smaller vessel in his hands. The Bronze Age levels include a cemetery of 1050 to 500 B.C. The first three phases involved burials of great wealth, and high status, but during the last three most of the dead were accompanied by a handful of pots and some shell ornaments laid out in rows. The final Bronze Age cemetery contained men and women accompanied by spindle whorls—a group of weavers.

Four groups of spectacular Bronze Age graves from the earlier layers of the cemetery are much larger than was necessary to contain the body. Four individuals had been partially disinterred, then the limb bones carefully replaced to support the skull (Figure 17.10). Up to 80 clay vessels of unusual size and quality accompanied the dead, also shell and marble ornaments. A later phase of the cemetery yielded rows of commoners' graves, also a set of extremely rich graves, the heads oriented to the east rather than the usual north. The arms of their owners were swathed in marble and shell bangles, while numerous clay vessels lay beyond their heads and feet. Three graves contained bronze axes, and one person wore a bronze anklet adorned with bells.

8000 B.C.

6500 B.C.

1500 to 500 B.C.

Ban Non Wat
2200 to 500 B.C.

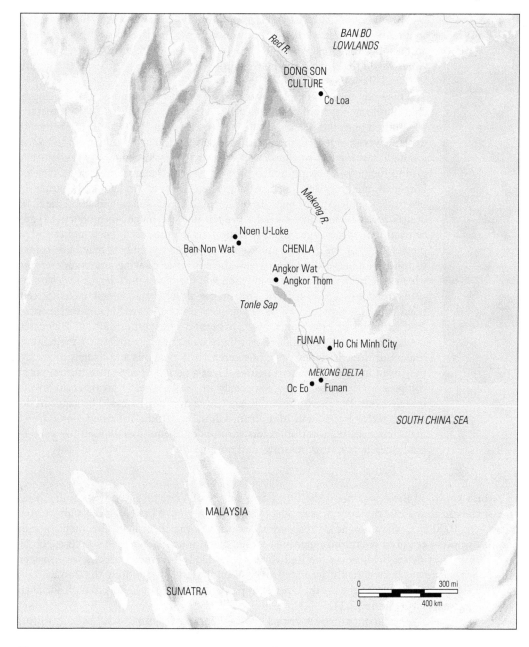

FIGURE 17.9 Southeast Asia, showing sites mentioned in the chapter.

For many years, everyone assumed that Bronze Age societies in Southeast Asia were egalitarian, with few signs of social ranking. The spectacular burials from the Ban Non Wat excavations reveal a remarkable surge in social complexity that coincides with the widespread adoption of bronze technology.

By 500 B.C., iron technology was in use as local populations rose and settlements grew much larger, some of them with as many as 25,000 inhabitants. These were the centuries when Southeast Asians began to participate in maritime trade routes that linked the mainland and offshore islands, New Guinea and the Philippines, as well as India and China. As early as the fourth century B.C., carnelian beads and a carving of a lion found at Ban Don Ta Phet in central Thailand reveal trade links with India. Bronze bowls found at the site are also Indian imports.

A portrait of society at the time comes from the Noen U-Loke site in the Mun Valley near Ban Non Wat, where a sample of 126 graves dating from 400 B.C. to about A.D. 300 shows a dramatic increase in the amount of effort expended on burying the dead. Some of the deceased were laid in graves filled with burnt rice; other graves were lined and capped with clay, like coffins. The graves lay in clusters of men, women, and children, presumably family groups. The contents of one cluster were almost all carnelian jewelry and rice, another was associated with spindle whorls, and a third with most of the clay-lined caskets. Three of them featured exceptionally wealthy men and women, adorned with bronze belts, bangles, ear disks, and other elaborate ornaments. These were not peaceful times, but a period when people competed for territory. One man lay prone with an iron arrowhead buried in his spine (Higham and Thosarat, 1998).

Noen U-Loke
400 B.C. to A.D. 300

FIGURE 17.10 Two disarticulated Bronze Age burials from Ban Non Wat, Thailand.

Throughout Southeast Asia, population densities and social complexity increased as rich and warlike chiefdoms appeared at the end of the first millennium B.C. Expert seafarers and traders, they were active participants in a much larger world that linked the Han Empire of China with India and the mainland to islands far offshore.

This trend toward complexity and competition was an indigenous development, even if innovations from outside fueled political and social change. Iron metallurgy was grafted onto the existing bronze technology, but it is uncertain whether iron-working was an independent invention or perhaps an introduction from India, where forging (smelting in a small furnace) was used, or from China, where sophisticated casting methods involving molten iron at very high temperatures were developed. Larger communities developed, usually centers for craft production. In earlier times, rice cultivation had been concentrated in small stream valleys and along the margins of major river floodplains. Such dry rice farming was much less productive than wet cultivation in waterlogged fields (paddies), which produced much higher and more predictable crop yields. The appearance of larger settlements may have coincided with both intensive wet farming and the advent of plowing and double-cropping, which greatly increased food production and produced much larger crop surpluses.

A trend toward centralized governance developed, focused on large centers ruled by highly ranked lineages. Their power was underwritten by their control of food surpluses and rice lands, by their support of expert artisans, and by carefully managed exchange monopolies over high-status imports and exotic materials. The leaders of these societies wore fine ceremonial weapons and badges of rank, and they lived in finely decorated houses. Over a period of several centuries, far more complex societies developed, especially in fertile riverine areas, societies whose leaders controlled maritime and inland trade over large areas. The exposure to artifacts, technologies, and ideas from China and India increased alongside these major changes as powerful leaders surrounded themselves with all the panoply of public ceremony, ritual feasting, and ostentation.

Dong Son

Dong Son culture
1000 B.C. to A.D. 43

The best known of these societies is the Dong Son culture of Vietnam's Red River valley, where a moist climate allows two rice crops a year. The indigenous origins of the Dong Son culture go back to at least 1000 B.C., when bronze smiths were already at work in the valley. The intensification of bronze working required enormous quantities of metal and much larger food surpluses, obtained by extensive wet rice agriculture on the Red River Delta. Dong Son metalworkers were masters of their craft, casting elaborate, richly decorated artifacts and eventually adopting the iron technology of their Chinese neighbors to the north. Drums, in particular, became symbols of high social status in Dong Son society (Figure 17.11).

Co Loa
Third century B.C.

The Lac Lords, paramount chiefs, warriors, and keepers of the drums, ruled over this prosperous society. One of them ruled from Co Loa, founded by the third century B.C. Co Loa boasted of three sets of ramparts, their moats supplied with water from a tributary of the Red River. The fortifications enclosed an area of 600 ha (1,482 acres). The Chinese Han knew of the Lac Lords as the most distant of "southern barbarians," and traded and fought with them for centuries. Finally, in A.D. 43, the warrior nobles of Dong Son succumbed to their powerful neighbors. Their domains became a Chinese protectorate, but Han records tell us they retained their traditional rights over land (Wheatley, 1979).

Trade and Kingdoms

By about A.D. 1, the sea-trading networks of Southeast Asia were part of a much larger commercial universe. Finds of sewn-plank boats dating to the third to fifth centuries A.D. testify to a long tradition of seafaring. Chinese records tell us that some oceangoing vessels were up to 50 m (164 feet) long and weighed as much as 500 tons. Striking evidence of the monsoon trade comes from the Sembiran site in Bali, where archaeologist A. W. Ardika has found Indian trade pottery from the southern Indian coast 4,350 km (2,700 miles) westward as the crow flies (Bellwood, 1997).

The traders themselves were an entirely maritime people of no particular nationality, called Mwani, or "barbarians," by the Chinese of the time. They spoke polyglot tongues and were of many lands—some Malays, some Indians—true wanderers who ventured as far east as the South China Sea. The Gulf of Tonkin and south China were served by Jiwet, Chinese mariners who brought luxuries to the coast, whence the goods were transported overland to the imperial capital (see Table 16.1).

FIGURE 17.11 A Dong Son boat that formed part of the decoration on a bronze drum. A war prisoner and well-armed warriors ride in the craft, which carries a drum stored in a cabin with an archer perched on the roof.

That India had a profound influence on the development of Southeast Asian civilization is unquestionable (Chandler, 1983). During the late third century B.C., Indian emperor Asoka's edicts spread the teachings of Buddhism throughout the territory of the Mauryan Empire in South Asia. His inscriptions make it clear that the prosperity of Buddhism was closely connected to the dealings of prosperous merchants. The older religion, Brahmanism, had placed severe and authoritarian restraints on foreign voyages, but Buddhism and Jainism (a form of Hinduism) rejected the racist teachings espoused by the predecessor religion. Travel was encouraged, which was a catalyst for expanded trade. In another political development, the Roman emperor Vespasian had prohibited exporting metals from the Roman Empire in approximately A.D. 70, a move that turned Indian merchants' eyes to the southeast. Nomadic raids on Asian caravans had also closed the Siberian gold mines to them. Metals were not the only attraction, for spices could also be obtained in abundance. Trade was expanded entirely for commercial profit.

Southeast Asia was a vital part in the chain of trading ports that linked China to India and Asia to the Roman Empire. The maritime trade brought a vigorous exchange of ideas and new cultural influences. Inevitably, argues Sinologist Paul Wheatley (1975, 1983), Southeast Asian chieftains learned a new way of seeing society and the world, perhaps by assembling commodities for trade and acquiring organizational skills. The authority and powers needed to expand and maintain the commerce were not part of the kin-linked society in which the chieftains had lived all their lives. In time, they became familiar with the Brahman and Buddhist conceptions of divine kingship. There was even a brahmanic rite by which chieftains could be inducted into the ruling class, a group whose authority was vested in an assumption of divine kingship.

Toward the end of the first millennium B.C., some Southeast Asian societies had become highly ranked, centralized kingdoms, presided over by an aristocratic class to whom formal display, feasting, and ritual were of paramount importance. They ruled by virtue of their close relationships with their ancestors. As in Maya society in Mesoamerica (see Chapter 21), rank and ancestry were closely connected. The growing complexity of such societies came in part from the ability of their overlords to attract loyal followers and to organize people. In time, many such rulers aspired to even greater status. They tried to preside over far larger kingdoms carved out by force. When they prevailed, they ruled by sheer charisma, cementing their authority with the creation of magnificent palaces and temples that served as the focus for elaborate public ceremonials and prestigious displays.

These Southeast Asian kingdoms were in a constant state of political flux and without fixed boundaries. The currency of political life was external but always fluid. Alliances developed between neighboring rulers. Everything revolved around the principal overlord, whose ability to cement alliances and deal with potential enemies dictated his relationships with his rivals. Some experts use a Sanskrit word, *mandala*, an Indian political doctrine, to describe the relationships between these rulers, whose territories are thought of as circles. It is as if they were concertinas, which expanded and contracted as different polities interacted with one another. Each society focused on its own center and on its own religious ruler and his retinue. The personal and spiritual qualities of each leader were important variables in a complex, ever-changing political equation.

Divine kingship revolutionized social and political organization in Southeast Asia. Kingdoms flourished in riverine and lowland areas, along the lower Mekong, and in the middle Mekong Valley, including the celebrated Tonle Sap plains, the homeland of Khmer-speaking peoples. (Khmer is an Austroasiatic language of considerable antiquity.) There were also kingdoms on the Khorat Plateau, along the central Vietnamese coastal plain, and in the Red River area, the latter under Chinese control. The Chinese called the lower Mekong region Funan, which means "the port of a thousand rivers," but the term has little real historical meaning. According to Chinese records, the ports of the delta handled bronze, silver, gold, spices, and even horses brought by sea from central Asia. One such port was Oc Eo, linked to the coast by a canal, a large town excavated by French archaeologists. Another was Angkor Borei. Canals linked the two communities, drained water, and also carried trade goods. Populations were densely concentrated, land was acquired through territorial conquest, and marshes were drained for more farmland. Whether there was a single kingdom or a series of competing chiefdoms is a matter of debate. Chinese accounts of Funan extol its rich trade. They tell of a drainage and transport system that rapidly transformed much of the delta from barren swamps into rich agricultural land. The development of these fields took the communal efforts of hundreds of people living off the fish that teemed in the bayous of the delta. Most Funanese lived in large lake cities fortified with great earthworks and moats swarming with crocodiles. Each major settlement was a port connected to the ocean and its neighbors by a canal network.

Oc Eo
A.D. 300 to 600

The coastal region prospered greatly from the third to the sixth centuries A.D., thanks to its long traditions of indigenous metallurgy and other crafts and trading expertise. In the sixth century A.D., many more Indian Brahmans arrived in the region. They brought the cult of the god Siva. He appeared in the temples in the form of a *linga*, a phallic emblem of masculine creative power. Where rulers were worshipers of Siva, the royal *linga* stood in a temple that symbolized the center of the capital.

The political situation along the lower Mekong was always volatile, especially because the kingdoms upstream had only indirect contact with foreign traders. Leaders inland responded by carving out new routes to the coast, bypassing the delta. In this, they were successful. By the sixth century A.D., the center of economic and political gravity had shifted to the middle Mekong and the Tonle Sap, an area the Chinese called Chenla. Numerous rivers fed the Tonle Sap, the central basin of Cambodia, its fluctuating water levels supporting many acres of fertile soil. Most of the year, the basin is a shallow series of muddy pools some 66 km (40 miles) long, drained by the Tonle Sap River, which runs into the Mekong. However, so much water floods into the Mekong Delta between August and October that the Tonle Sap's course is reversed and the pools become a vast lake, 133 to 167 km (80 to 100 miles) long, 25 to 50 km (15 to 30 miles) wide, and up to 16 m (50 feet) deep. Late in October, the water starts receding, trapping millions of fish in the muddy bayous.

In the twelfth century A.D., the environment was so bountiful that it supported dense urban populations and generated large food surpluses, sufficient to support a glittering, wealthy civilization. At A.D. 1, the farmers of this favored region lived under local chiefs who controlled local reservoirs, water control being critically important for successful agriculture. Over the next few centuries, small kingdoms developed that maintained their independence or coalesced, depending on the abilities of individual overlords to assert their authority. Constant warfare and political maneuvering eventually led to the emergence of hereditary rulers and small states.

The Rise of the God-Kings

Competing Chenla rulers acquired sufficient food surpluses to embark on ambitious conquests and, eventually, to develop a new political concept of divine kingship that united their far-flung domains in a common purpose: the glorification of the god-king on earth. Devotion to the Hindu creator Siva became a mechanism that provided divine justification for kingship, as well as a focus for the loyalty and devotion of a ruler's retinue, who would endow temples in return for royal favors.

Between A.D. 1 and the end of the eighth century A.D., centralization and high status were so unstable that they could fluctuate considerably within an individual's lifetime. Ambitious men would try and try again to raise themselves above others and their kingdoms to supreme rule. Throughout the centuries, these were never states in the Western sense of the word. Rather, the "concertina" effect of kingdom politics was constantly at work, with competing polities asserting independence at times, becoming tribute givers and vassals at others.

The Angkor State (A.D. 802 to 1430)

Angkor state
A.D. 802 to 1430

The overlords of the Tonle Sap all shared one ambition: to establish hegemony over as large an area as possible (Coe, 2005; Higham, 2000). The earlier kings were unable to hold the kingdom together until a dynamic Khmer monarch named Jayavarman II came to power in A.D. 802. He conquered his competitors and set up his new territories as tribute kingdoms, giving his loyal generals land grants. Jayavarman II is said to have merged the cult of the ancestors with that of Siva in the form of a *linga* to consolidate his new kingdom. A much later inscription tells us he called himself Supreme King. His subjects were taught to worship him as a god. All resources of an increasingly centralized government were devoted to the preservation of the cult of the god-king. Everyone, whether noble, high priest, or commoner, was expected to subordinate his or her ambitions to the need to perpetuate the existence of the king on earth and his identity with the god in this life and the next. This remarkable leader reigned for 45 years, the first of at least three dynasties of Khmer rulers, who often came to power after vicious fighting and presided over an ever-changing state that reached the height of its prosperity between A.D. 900 and 1200 (Coe, 2005; Higham, 2000).

Previous monarchs had encouraged the worship of Siva in the form of the phallic image, but now Jayavarman II presented himself as the reincarnation of Siva on earth. He was the *varman*, the protector, and his priests were the instruments of practical political power. The high priests were invariably energetic, imposing nobles who presided over a highly disciplined hierarchy of religious functionaries. The ruler himself headed a bureaucracy of high-status families, which included generals and administrators who settled land disputes. The bureaucracy supervised every aspect of Khmer life, from agriculture to warfare, tax collection, and the rituals of the state religion.

As always with preindustrial civilizations, there was a close link between food surpluses and the control of the enormous labor forces needed to construct temples, reservoirs, and other public works. Most building activity probably took place during the dry months. The custom of building a new majestic and holy temple to house the royal *linga* of each king was the most important of all the religious rituals. As a result, many of the 30 monarchs who followed Jayavarman II left massive religious edifices to commemorate their reigns. These they built on artificial mounds in the center of their capitals, the hub of the Khmer universe, an area known today as Angkor. The Khmer's unique form of kingship produced, instead of an austere civilization like that of the Indus, a society that carried the cult of wealth, luxury, and divine monarchy to amazing lengths (Higham, 2000). This cult reached its apogee in the reign of Suryavarman II, who built the temple of Angkor Wat in the twelfth century A.D. (see Site box).

Angkor Wat
A.D. 1117

Angkor Wat taxed the resources of the kingdom severely at a time of increased strife with neighboring powers. In 1181, another ruler, Jayavarman VII, who was a Buddhist, started building a huge new capital at Angkor Thom nearby. A dark and forbidding 12.8-km (8-mile) wall surrounds the capital. When visitors walked inside, they entered a symbolic Hindu world with the king's funerary temple, the Bayon, at the center (Figure 17.14). The Grand Plaza of Angkor Thom was the scene of ceremonies and contests, of vast military reviews and massed bands.

Angkor Thom
A.D. 1181

It is said that a million people once lived in or near Angkor Thom. One temple dedicated to the king's father contained no fewer than 430 images, with more than 20,000 in gold, silver, bronze, and stone in the wider precincts. An inscription in the Ta Prohm temple nearby, dedicated to the king's mother in the image of the Buddha's mother, records that 306,372 people from 13,500 villages worked for the shrine, consuming 38,000 tons of rice a year. An inscription in the nearby temple of Ta Prohm inventories a staff of 18 senior priests, 2,740 minor functionaries, 615 female dancers, and a total of 66,625 "men and women who perform the service of the gods." All this royal construction was designed to make merit for the king and his followers. He also built fully staffed hospitals and pilgrims' shelters to gain further credit. The result of Jayavarman's building projects was a totally centripetal religious utopia in which every product, every person's labor, and every thought were directed toward embellishing the hub of the universe and the kings who enjoyed it (Wheatley, 1983). The impression of prosperity and stability was illusory in a society where the ruler's power depended on the granting of favors, on his successful patronizing of the major aristocratic families. There was no stable bureaucracy with appointed officials to run the state. The king mediated with the gods for rain, settled disputes, and used the rich resources of the land to redistribute wealth among his subjects. He sat at the center of the circle represented by the *mandala*, its boundaries defined only by the loyalties of the aristocrats who ruled the outlying provinces. A Khmer king's hold on the reins of power depended on the control of the center, the Angkor. Thus, when the central administration was weak, the kingdom tended to break up into regional units.

By Jayavarman VII's death, Buddhism had gained a strong foothold, but religious dissension became common until Theravada, a form of low Buddhism preaching equality, became popular. Theravada did not deal with traditional ideas of kingship, so building activity slowed at a time when frequent monsoon failures, triggered by El Niños affected Southeast Asia. The resulting droughts may have had a serious effect on the water supplies of Angkor Wat and other major centers. The great state finally dissolved in about A.D. 1431, perhaps because of a combination of monsoon failures and endemic warfare.

A.D. 1430–1431

Late in the thirteenth century, the strategic trade routes through the Malay Straits came under Islamic control in a new chapter of international trade. Melaka became an important port and

SiTE > Angkor Wat, Cambodia <

For four years after his succession in A.D. 1113, King Suryavarman II commenced building his masterpiece, an extraordinary shrine that is a spectacle of beauty, wonder, and magnificence—the largest religious building in the world. Angkor Wat (Figure 17.12) is 1,500 m (5,000 feet) by 1,200 m (4,000 feet) across. The central block measures 215 m by 186 m (717 feet by 620 feet) and rises more than 60 m (200 feet) above the forest. It dwarfs even the largest Sumerian ziggurat and makes Mohenjodaro's citadel look like a village shrine (Mannika, 1996).

Every detail of this extraordinary building reproduces part of the heavenly world in a terrestrial mode (Figure 17.13). The Khmer believed that the world consisted of a central continent known as Jambudvipa, with the cosmic mountain, Meru, rising from its center. The gods lived at the summit of Meru, represented at Angkor Wat by the highest tower. The remaining four towers depict Meru's lesser peaks; the enclosure wall depicts the mountain at the edge of the world, and the surrounding moat depicts the ocean beyond. Angkor Wat was the culminating attempt of the Khmer to reproduce a monument to the Hindu god Vishnu, the preserver of the universe.

Angkor Wat's bas-reliefs show Suryavarman seated on a wooden throne wearing an elaborate crown and pectoral. He receives his high officials as they declare their loyalty. Next, the king progresses down a hillside on an elephant accompanied by the high priest and his generals. The court rides with him through a forest, with noble ladies in litters, everyone protected by heavily armed soldiers. Scattered throughout Angkor Wat are scenes of battles and bas-reliefs of celestial maidens (Figure 17.14). Naked to the waist, slender and sensuous, the dancers wear skirts of rich fabric. Their flowered background, the subtle rhythm of their gestures, their jeweled necklaces and diadems bring to light the delights of paradise promised to the king after his death. Inscriptions also spell out the terrible punishments that awaited ill-doers.

Angkor Wat was constructed using a measurement of 0.435 m (1.43 feet), a Khmer unit of measurement known as a *hat*. The length and breadth of the central structure of the temple corresponded to 365.37 *hat*, while the axial

FIGURE 17.13 The paved causeway at Angkor Wat approaches the temple through an entrance gallery with a tower. The causeway is 150 m (500 feet) long, flanked with balustrades adorned with mythical, multiheaded snakes. The gallery opens onto a cruciform terrace in front of a rectangular temple that rises in three imposing tiers to a central cluster of five towers. Each tower bears a lofty pinnacle that from afar looks like a giant lotus bud. The causeway leads across a huge moat, 180 m (600 feet) wide and enclosed by masonry walks 6.4 km (4 miles) in circumference. The engineers built the walls with a total error of less than 2 cm (an inch)! The moat is still a beautiful sight, with floating water lilies, wild orchids, and other shimmering blooms.

distances of the great causeway correspond with the four great eras of Hindu time. Someone standing in front of the western entrance on the spring equinox was able to see the sun rising directly over the central lotus tower. During his lifetime, Suryavarman used Angkor Wat as the place where he, as a divine monarch, communicated with the gods. When he died, his remains were placed in the central tower, so that his soul entered his divine image and made contact with the royal ancestors. Here the immortal ruler became as one with Vishnu, master of the universe.

FIGURE 17.12 Angkor Wat from the air on a hazy day, a representation of the Hindu universe.

FIGURE 17.14 Four *aspara*, celestial nymphs, dance on the wall of Angkor Wat.

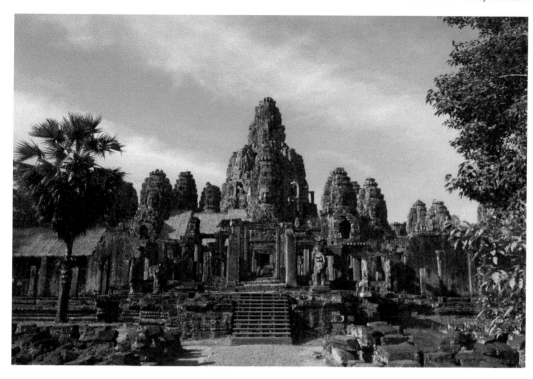

FIGURE 17.15 The East Entrance of the Bayon, Angkor Thom, Cambodia.

stronghold on the northern shore of the straits. The rest of the kingdoms and ports of the islands soon adopted the new religion, which preached a message of religious egalitarianism in the face of centuries of Indian statecraft based on notions of divine kingship. Within three centuries, the rulers of inland Java had adopted Islam, perhaps to maintain control over their subjects, who were welcoming the new beliefs with open arms. Islam and trade went hand in hand in island Southeast Asia, until the arrival of Portuguese gun-bearing sailing ships at Melaka in 1519 A.D.

A.D. 1519

The Khmer state is a classic example of how a combination of cultural processes and able individuals can lead to the appearance of powerful, yet volatile states. Yet these same states face constantly the problem of controlling not only the center but also the periphery, especially in times of weak rule and menacing competition from outside.

Summary

- State-organized societies on the Indian subcontinent developed from indigenous roots in about 2600 B.C.
- The Harappan civilization of the lowland Indus Valley developed possibly as the result of a major shift in Sumerian long-distance trade patterns and long-term interactions between the Harappan culture of the lowlands and the Kulli complex of the Baluchistan highlands.
- Harappan civilization flourished along the Indus for about a thousand years. It was an urban society with many smaller satellite settlements, carefully planned and ruled by priest-kings who controlled both religious and economic life.
- After 1700 B.C., the major cities went into decline, but Harappan society flourished in rural settings for a considerable time. The center of economic and political gravity moved eastward to the Ganges River valley, culminating in the Mauryan Empire of the first millennium B.C.

- Southeast Asian peoples had developed bronze working by at least 1500 B.C. The process of forming local states (*mandalas*) began around the same time, but the first historical records of complex states date to the third century A.D.
- Many such states developed in and around the central Mekong Valley and, later, in the central Cambodian basin. There, after A.D. 802, flourished the flamboyant Khmer civilization, a society based on divine kingship and strong notions of conformity.
- After six centuries of spectacular development, the Khmer civilization came in contact with expanding Islamic trade networks and new religious doctrines, which caused its partial demise.

Further Reading

Coe, Michael D. 2005. *Angkor and the Khmer Civilization.* London and New York: Thames & Hudson.

Higham, Charles. 2000. *The Civilization of Angkor.* Berkeley: University of California Press.

McIntosh, Jane R. 2008. *The Ancient Indus Valley: New Perspectives.* Santa Barbara: ABC-CLIO.

Early Chinese Civilization

18

The inscribed bone came from a curio shop—part of an ox shoulder blade that seemed out of place among precious jade and porcelain bowls. Archaeologist Tung Tso-pin was intrigued and wondered if the weathered bone was connected to the ancient, legendary Shang civilization. The Shang people had lived on the banks of the Huang Ho, their capital said to be near the town of Anyang. Even as early as the eleventh century, local scholars had collected exotic bronze vessels from the flat farmland where Shang kings once lived. Tung Tso-pin had visited Anyang in the late 1920s, just after the river had changed course nearby, exposing rich cultural debris—including more ox shoulder blades—in the banks. He dug several deep pits that contained carefully packed "archives" of oracle bones—ox shinbones and scapulae—and tortoiseshells, marked with inscriptions that gave historians a list of the Shang kings until their capital was destroyed by catastrophic floods. Excavations at Shang capitals have continued sporadically ever since, revealing a civilization known hitherto only from ancient legend. This chapter discusses the origins of ancient Chinese civilization, as we know it from archaeological and historical research (Table 18.1).

The Great Wall of China.

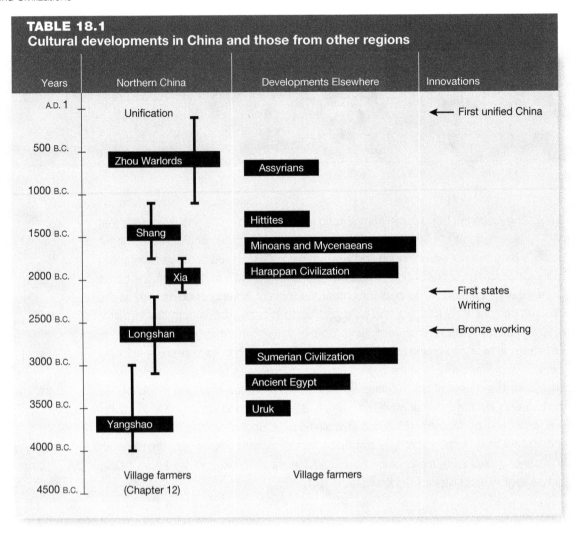

TABLE 18.1
Cultural developments in China and those from other regions

Years	Northern China	Developments Elsewhere	Innovations
A.D. 1	Unification		← First unified China
500 B.C.	Zhou Warlords	Assyrians	
1000 B.C.			
1500 B.C.	Shang	Hittites Minoans and Mycenaeans	
2000 B.C.	Xia	Harappan Civilization	← First states Writing
2500 B.C.	Longshan		← Bronze working
3000 B.C.		Sumerian Civilization	
3500 B.C.		Ancient Egypt Uruk	
4000 B.C.	Yangshao		
4500 B.C.	Village farmers (Chapter 12)	Village farmers	

The Origins of Chinese Civilization

4000 B.C. By 4000 B.C., agriculture had taken such hold in China that population densities rose throughout the country (Liu, 2004; Stark, 2006). The farmers took more and more land into cultivation until there was little new acreage available for planting. Some pollen analyses from northern villages show how the trees that once surrounded many settlements were felled as the fields lapped right up to the houses. This population growth also coincided with an expansion of wet rice farming in lowland areas, on moist floodplains, and in lush water meadows where irrigation was easy (Figure 18.1). Those villages fortunate enough to possess lands that could be irrigated, especially in the Huang Ho and Yangtze valleys, soon turned into much more permanent settlements, often protected with earthen walls to guard against floods and marauding neighbors. Even these larger communities were part of a self-regulating folk society in which kinship loyalties and the extended family were all-important and old age was deeply revered. The family ancestors were the conduit to the gods who controlled the harmony of the world.

However, there are signs that a new order existed, for some settlements of the time contain elaborate burials adorned with jade ornaments and ceremonial weapons (Underhill and Habu, 2006). Village artisans created fine clay vessels exclusively for the use of these privileged people. These were important leaders who are known to have raided their neighbors, for the corpses of their enemies have been found deposited in village wells. In both the north and the south, a few peasant villages became important centers ruled by new generations of kin leaders who became the nobles of more sophisticated societies. They were probably expert warriors and were certainly people of great spiritual authority, experts in predicting the future and communicating with the ancestors.

These developments would never have been possible without the unswerving conservatism of the country farmer. The village crops might change from cereals to rice, the fertility of the soils depend on radically different rainfall patterns, and building materials alter from brick and tile to bamboo, but what never varied was the peasants' unquestioning acceptance of an emerging social order that imposed an almost alien, wealthy, privileged society. The viability of this aristocratic civilization

FIGURE 18.1   (a) Distribution of farming cultures that immediately preceded Shang civilization in northern China. Each shaded area represents a different regional culture (not described in detail in the text). (b) The approximate distribution of Shang civilization in about 1400 B.C. (Xiao-tun and other royal sites are close to Anyang).

depended on simple loyalties that persisted from the earliest centuries of farming life into modern times. Every Chinese noble, however unimportant, cashed in on this loyalty.

Longshan and Liangzhu

After about 4000 B.C., the several regional Longshan farming cultures of north and south China became interlinked by complex exchange networks, trading raw materials, luxury goods, and other commodities over long distances. (The generic, and inaccurate, term *Longshan* is often used to label these cultures.) This interdependence spurred similar developments in more complex social organization, as well as technological changes that spilled over from narrow territorial boundaries to affect much of China (Liu and Chen, 2006, 2010). These innovations included copper metallurgy, the construction of rammed-earth town walls, and the first widespread use of earthen fortifications. Powerful new rituals and beliefs emerged, among them a doctrine based on animals and birds and the use of divination to communicate with the ancestors (Nelson, 1995). Ancestor worship became part of political institutions and reinforced the increasingly stratified political system, a trend that had begun as early as Yangshao times (see Chapter 12).

> **Longshan cultures**
> 4000 B.C.

On the east coast, the Liangzhu culture of the Shanghai Delta region had developed by 3250 B.C., a society known largely from its prestigious burials. Liangzhu's expert potters were specialist artisans, some of the first in East Asia. Many of their finely made black polished wares were made not by hand but on a potter's wheel. The wealthiest members of society were buried in special burial precincts, their graves adorned with finely made jade ornaments (Huang, 1992). The bodies of sacrificial victims surround some of the elite. Liangzhu was a highly stratified society, one of the earliest in China where extreme wealth and an enormous social distance separated the rulers from the ruled. These many changes were the result of constant interaction among many different farming societies, a kind of relationship among complex chiefdoms that inevitably drew them into a larger system. This interaction and constant warfare developed after 4000 B.C., culminating in the emergence of Chinese civilization in about 2000 B.C. (Liu and Chen, 2006).

> **Liangzhu culture**
> 3250 B.C.

Perhaps the most significant of all Longshan innovations were the rectangular defensive enclosures. The walls are of a special Chinese construction known as *hang tu*, or "rammed earth," and are the earliest examples of this technique. Regular layers of loose earth, some 10 to 15 cm (4 to 6 inches) thick, were poured between parallel lines of timber shuttering—rather in the way that concrete is poured today—then the workers compacted the layers by pounding them with long wooden poles, some 3 to 4 cm (1 to 1.5 inches) in diameter. Once that layer was finished, another would be poured on top and the process repeated until the desired height was reached. Longshan walls made in this way were up to 10 m (35 feet) thick and sometimes have survived to a height of several feet, the horizontal marks left by the timber shuttering clearly visible on their sides.

These appear to have been violent times with frequent conflict. At one Longshan site a number of people had been thrown into two dry wells, some decapitated, others showing signs of struggle. If these people suffered a violent fate, there is evidence that they themselves inflicted similar suffering on others. Six skulls had been placed as a foundation deposit beneath one of the houses, all with signs of wounds or scalping. The archaeology of the Longshan culture suggests a pattern of warring elites, struggling to maintain their position or gain greater ascendancy over their neighbors. It also indicates that ritual vessels (first, high-quality pottery; later, copper or bronze) were the all-important mark of elite status. In this as in so many other respects, Longshan directly anticipated the full civilization of the Shang Bronze Age.

Shoulder Blades and Oracles

When archaeologists dug into a walled site named Chengziya by the Huang Ho in Shandong province in 1930–1931, they found not only the remains of a farming village but also dozens of cracked ox shoulder blades that they identified as oracle bones used in divination ceremonies (Figure 18.2) (Keightley, 2006). The cracks were made by applying hot metal to the bone and then were interpreted as messages from the ancestors. None of the Longshan bones bear written inscriptions, but the hundreds of shoulder blades found in pits near Anyang farther upstream are a mine of information about the origins of Chinese civilization, a unique written archive of official deliberations by the very first kings of northern China. One scholar has suggested that Chinese writing may have originated from the need to interpret the cracks on the bones, with the new writing symbols resembling persistent crack patterns. However, there are incised potsherds in Longshan and Liangzhu cultures that may represent earlier writing traditions (Demattè, 2010).

Clearly, some Chinese ideographs originated as pictograms, such as that for "hill," originally shown with three humps and now written as a horizontal line with three vertical strokes. Perhaps as early as 2500 B.C., divination rituals were a vital part of village government. All official divinations were addressed to the royal ancestors, who acted as intermediaries between the living and the ultimate ancestor and supreme being, the ruler of heaven and the creator, Shang Di. This deity served as the ancestor not only of the royal line but also of the "multitude of the people." The ruler was the head of all family lines, which radiated from his person to the nobility and then to the common people. These actual and imputed kinship ties were the core of early Chinese civilization, for they obligated the peasants to provide food and labor for their rulers.

In addition to shoulder blades from oxen and water buffalo, the diviners used tortoiseshells for their ceremonies. The term *scapulimancy*, meaning "shoulder blade divination," refers to the bones used most frequently in the ceremonies. The bones and shells were smoothed and cleaned and perhaps soaked in liquid to be softened. Rows of hollows were then produced on the underside to make the substance thinner and the surface more susceptible to being cracked. When a question was posed, the diviner would apply a metal point to the base of the hollow, causing the surface to crack. The response of the ancestors was "read" from the fissures. A skillful diviner could control the extent and direction of the cracks. Thus, divination provided an authoritative priest with a useful and highly effective way of giving advice. A leader could regard disagreement as treason.

Erlitou: Xia and Shang

Intense controversy surrounds the origins of Chinese civilization, which emerged in a volatile political environment of highly competitive kingdoms, some ruled from a single center, others comprising a network of smaller towns (Liu and Chen, 2010). Elaborate, ever-changing, political alliances and exchange networks linked one polity to another, with rulers, who controlled

FIGURE 18.2 Shang oracle bones. Priests read cracks in the surface of the ox bone caused by applying heat to the shoulder blade and thereby interpreted messages from the ancestors as sacred divinations.

such critical resources as copper ore, gaining considerable power. These many societies flourished at a time of environmental instability around 2000 B.C., when rising sea levels and cold, dry conditions appear to have contributed to political instability. Competition between rulers may have intensified, worship of natural deities intensified, as rulers developed ideological responses to environmental instability. Military activity intensified at a time when communal projects such as flood defenses became more commonplace as responses to ecological problems.

2000 B.C.

Then the city of Erlitou in the Yilou Basin south of the Huang Ho became an important player from 1900 to 1500 B.C., at 300 ha (741 acres) the largest city in China at the time. Erlitou was the center of a strongly centralized kingdom, although many authorities question whether it was a state (Liu and Chen, 2006). In the city itself, there was a huge chasm between the rich and the poor, with a large palace complex and a densely populated urban area, whose inhabitants engaged in agriculture and specialized crafts that included highly skilled bronze working. The latter was an innovation at Erlitou, although bronze had been used for ornaments for centuries. By 1700 B.C., Erlitou artisans were using multipiece mold castings to fabricate elaborate ritual vessels. The foundry for these vessels lies close to the royal palace, reflecting their importance as symbols of economic, political, and religious power. Erlitou's rulers maintained tight control over a bronze culture that became a central part of later Shang civilization and required both highly skilled practitioners and control of reliable sources for the ore.

Erlitou
1900 to 1500 B.C.

Erlitou lay amidst fertile agricultural land but had to obtain all its major timber, toolmaking stone, kaolin clay for the white pottery used by the elite, also copper and tin, as well as salt from the kingdom's periphery. As a result, Erlitou's rulers expanded their domains and founded outposts as far as 200 km (125 miles) away in efforts to ensure reliable supplies of critical raw materials, especially copper, lead, tin, and salt. This territorial expansion came at a time of population increase, at least partly from immigration, as the kingdom became an elaborate hierarchy, where personal status, the acquisition of wealth, and control of production and trading of prestige artifacts were symbols of political power. Erlitou became the founding polity behind later Shang civilization through its rulers' control of both the core and the economically important periphery. They created what some call a form of "world system," sustained by a common ideology based on ancestor cults that practiced ritual feasts, where ritual bronze vessels were used. These rituals may have helped forge the common cultural tradition that underlay later Chinese civilization.

Can one connect Erlitou with legends surrounding the origins of Chinese civilization? Although most Chinese scholars link the city with China's first dynasty, the Xia, Western experts still regard the link as inconclusive. The legends tell us that a ruler named Huang Di founded civilization in the north in 2698 B.C. This great legendary warlord set the tone for centuries of the repressive harsh government that was the hallmark of early Chinese civilization. About 2200 B.C., a Xia ruler named Yu the Great gained power through his military prowess and his knowledge of flood control, by which he could protect the valley people from catastrophic inundations. His capital is said to have been recently located near Dengfeng in Henan province, a walled settlement with a large moat. Erlitou is also said to have been a Xia city. At present, we simply do not know.

Xia dynasty
2200 B.C.

Who, then, were the Xia and the Shang? In all probability, they were dynasties of local rulers who achieved lasting prominence among their many neighbors after generations of bitter strife. Every chieftain lived in a walled town and enjoyed much the same level of material prosperity, but each ruler came from a different lineage and was related to his competitors by intricate and closely woven allegiances and kin ties. Each dynasty assumed political dominance in the north in turn, but for all these political changes, Shang civilization itself continued more or less untouched, a loosely unified confederacy of competing small kingdoms that quarreled and warred incessantly.

The archaeological record reveals that Shang-type remains are stratified on top of Longshan occupation levels at many places in northern China, and they represent a dramatic increase in the complexity of material culture and social organization (Liu and Chen, 2006). The same trends toward increasing complexity are thought to have occurred elsewhere in China at approximately the same time, for literate states may have emerged from a Longshan base in the south and the east as well. In form, they probably resembled the Shang closely, but few details of the others are known. It seems likely that the Shang dynasty was dominant from 1766 to 1122 B.C. but that other states continued to grow at the same time. The larger area of Chinese civilization ultimately extended from the north into the middle and lower courses of the Huang Ho and Yangtze. In this account, we concentrate on northern Chinese civilization simply because more is known about the archaeology of the Shang than about that of any other early Chinese state.

Shang civilization
1766 to 1122 B.C.

Capitals and Sepulchers

The oracle bones and other historical sources provide only a sketchy outline of the early dynasties and the ways the Shang kings went about their business. The bones inform us that the rulers lived in at least seven capitals, situated near the middle reaches of the Huang Ho in the modern provinces of

Ao
1557 B.C.
Henan, Shandong, and Anhui (Keightley, 1999). The sites of all these towns are still uncertain, but in 1557 B.C., the Shang kings moved their capital to a place named Ao, which archaeologists have found under the modern industrial city of Zhengzhou, some 153 km (95 miles) south of Anyang, close to the Huang Ho (Wheatley, 1971).

Unfortunately, the royal compound lies underneath the modern downtown area, so only limited excavations have been possible. However, diggers have found traces of a vast precinct surrounded by an earthen wall more than 10 m (33 feet) high, enclosing an area of 5 sq. km (2 sq. miles). It would have taken 10,000 workers laboring 330 days a year for no fewer than 18 years to erect the fortifications alone. This walled compound housed the rulers, the temples, and the nobles. Some foundations of their large houses and ancestral altars have come from excavations inside the compound. The residential quarters and craft workshops lay outside the Shang walls. These included two bronze factories, one of them covering more than an acre. The metalworkers lived in substantial houses near their furnaces. There were bone workshops, too, where animal and human bones were fashioned into arrowheads, pins, and awls. Zhengzhou's potters lived in a satellite village close to the kilns, where they fired hundreds of fine vessels. The excavations revealed dozens of unfired and incomplete vessels.

Anyang
1400 B.C.
The capital moved to the Anyang area in approximately 1400 B.C., where it remained until the fall of the Shang more than 250 years later. This new royal domain was known as Yin and may have encompassed a network of compounds, palaces, villages, and cemeteries extending over an area some 310 sq. km (120 sq. miles) on the northern bank of the Huang Ho. The core of this "capital" was near the hamlet of Xiaotun, 2.4 km (1.5 miles) northwest of the modern city of Anyang. Years of excavations at Xiao-tun have revealed 53 rectangular foundations of rammed earth up to 36 m (120 feet) long, 19.5 m (65 feet) wide, and as much as 1.5 m (5 feet) high, many of them of buildings associated with sacrificial burials of both animals and humans (Chang, 1980, 1986). One group of 15 foundations on the north side of the excavated area supported timber houses with mud and stick walls, devoid of sacrificial victims. These are believed to have been the royal residences that housed the extended noble families living in large halls and smaller rooms closed off with doors (Figure 18.3). Twenty-one massive foundations on an elevated area in the center of the excavations formed two rows of temples associated with a series of five ceremonial gates. The builders buried animals, humans, and even chariots in this vicinity, perhaps to dedicate the temples. Nearby were semisubterranean houses where the royal servants and artisans lived. The service areas included bronze foundries, workshops, and pottery kilns.

The Shang Royal Burials

The Shang rulers at first buried their dead in a cemetery just under 2 km (1.24 miles) northeast of Anyang. Eleven royal graves from this cemetery were excavated during the 1930s (Chang, 1986). Furnished on a lavish scale, they date to between 1500 and 1200 B.C. The best-known grave is in the shape of a crosslike pit approximately 9.9 m (33 feet) deep, with slightly sloping walls. Four ramps lead from the surface to each side of the pit. The coffin of the ruler, which was placed inside a wooden chamber erected in the burial pit, was accompanied by superb bronze vessels and shell, bone, and stone ornaments. One ceremonial halberd has an engraved jade blade set in a bronze shaft adorned with dragons and inlaid with malachite. Slaves and sacrificial victims lay both in the chamber itself and on the approach ramps. Many had been decapitated: Their bodies were found in one place and their heads in another.

The Shang kings surrounded their sepulchers with hundreds of lesser burials. No fewer than 1,221 small graves have been dug up nearby, many of them burials of between 2 and 11 people in a single tomb. Some of the skeletons are associated with pottery, weapons, or bronze vessels, but most are devoid of all adornment. In 1976, archaeologists uncovered nearly 200 of these graves. Most of them contained decapitated, dismembered, or mutilated bodies. Some of the victims had been bound before death. These can only have been sacrificial offerings consecrated when the kings and their relatives died.

FIGURE 18.3 Reconstruction of a structure from the ceremonial area at Xiao-tun, Anyang, in Henan province. Throughout Chinese history, the nobility lived apart from commoners.

FIGURE 18.4 Shang bronze vessel, a ritual wind container from approximately 1300 B.C. Such cast-bronze artifacts were highly prized by the nobility and accompanied them in death.

The Bronze Smiths

The Shang people are justly famous for their bronze work, best known to us from ceremonial artifacts found in royal tombs. Their prestigious metal was not gold, which was in short supply, but bronze. Most Shang bronzes are food or drinking vessels; some are weapons, a few are musical instruments, and many are chariot and horse fittings. Bronze working was the guarded monopoly of the rulers, a complex art that the Chinese developed quite independently of the West, before 2000 B.C. Their smiths produced some of the most sophisticated and elegant bronze objects ever crafted (Figure 18.4).

The Shang people discovered bronze working on their own, perhaps as a result of their long experience with kiln-fired pottery baked at high temperatures. They made the smaller objects, such as spearheads, arrowheads, and ax blades, by pouring a mixture of copper and tin into a one- or two-piece mold. Much more complex procedures had to be employed to manufacture large ceremonial vessels. These elaborate display pieces were copies of clay prototypes carefully sculpted around a baked-clay core and encased in a segmented mold. Once the clay version had been completed, the baked outer mold was removed, the model was broken away from the core, and, in the case of the two-piece mold, the two parts were reassembled to receive the molten bronze. This complex technique remained in use for at least five centuries. An alternative would have been the lost-wax process, in which a one-piece mold encases a wax mold that is heated and then the wax poured out, to be replaced with metal.

The Warlords

Every early Chinese ruler stayed in power by virtue of a strong army. Shang society was organized on what might be called military lines so that the royal standing army could be supplemented with thousands of conscripts on very short notice. The kings were frequently at war, protecting their frontiers, suppressing rebellious rivals, or raiding for as many as 30,000 sacrificial victims at one time. In a sense, every early Chinese state was an armed garrison that could call on armies of more than 10,000 men. The secret was a sophisticated permanent military establishment and a kin organization through which people were obligated to serve the king when called upon. The same basic organization persisted long after the fall of the Shang dynasty in 1122 B.C.

The Anyang graves reveal that every foot soldier carried a set of weapons: a bow and arrows, halberd, shield, small knife, and sharpening stone. The bows were made of horn and ox sinew and were approximately a man's height. They propelled stone-, bone-, or bronze-tipped arrows equipped with feathers. The Shang soldiers used a small leather or basketry shield for chariot warfare and a longer one when they were on foot, both painted with tiger designs.

Most surviving Shang weapons come from sacrificial chariot burials, such as the one excavated near Anyang in 1973. The archaeologists uncovered not the wooden chariot itself but a cast of the wooden parts preserved in the soil (Figure 18.5). They brushed away the surrounding soil with great care until they reached the hardened particles of fine sand that had replaced the wooden structure of the buried chariot. They were able to photograph not only the "ghost" of the chariot but also the skeletons of the two horses. The charioteer had been killed at the funeral and his body placed behind the vehicle. The yokes of the chariot rested on the horses' necks. Lines of bronze roundels in the grave even marked the decayed reins. The charioteer had ridden on a wicker and leather car measuring between 0.9 and 1.2 m (3 and 4 feet) across and borne on a stout axle and two spoked wheels with large hubs adorned with bronze caps. In all probability, the nailless chariot had been held together with sinew lashings, adorned with bronze and turquoise ornaments, and perhaps painted in bright colors.

Shang civilization was by no means unique, for major, and still little known, states developed in the rice-growing areas to the south, where large cities also flourished in Sichuan province and elsewhere.

SiTE > The Burial Mound of Emperor Shihuangdi, China <

King Zheng, the "Tiger of Qin," was the first sovereign emperor (Shihuangdi) of China. He became ruler of Qin at the age of 13 in 246 B.C., unifying China after a series of ruthless military campaigns in 221 B.C. Work may have begun on the emperor's tomb as early as 246 B.C., but it intensified with unification. The emperor considered himself unique, so his sepulcher was to be the largest ever built. Later court histories write of more than 700,000 conscripts, many of them convicts, who worked on the tomb, the capital, and the royal palace.

The great burial mound measures more than 335 m (1,100 feet) on each side and rises 43 m (140 feet) above the surrounding countryside, 40 km (25 miles) east of Xianyang on the banks of the Wei River. Inside lies what is said to be a replica of the royal domains, with China's great rivers re-created in mercury flowing, by some mechanical device, into the ocean. The constellations of the heavens appear on the ceiling of the burial chamber, the earth's geography beneath. Scale models of palaces and pavilions contain the emperor's personal possessions, and models of courtiers attend him in death. Many concubines, as well as laborers who worked on the tomb, were sacrificed and buried inside the tumulus. Although Han dynasty historians state that the mound was looted after the fall of the Qin line, Chinese archaeologists have detected unusually high concentrations of mercury in the soil chemistry of the mound

and suspect that Shihuangdi's grave goods may be intact. Chinese archaeologists decline to excavate the tomb, as they say they lack the resources and skills to dig it properly and conserve the contents. The mound once lay in the middle of a large funerary park surrounded by a 6.4-km (4-mile) outer wall.

In the 1970s, Chinese archaeologists excavated a regiment of terra-cotta soldiers to the side of the funerary mound—armed cavalrymen, kneeling archers, and their officers, perhaps a ceremonial guard assigned to protect the eastern side of the tomb (Figure 18.6). The molded figures were finished with individual hairstyles, mustaches, and other features and were fully armed. Other finds near the tumulus include two half-scale bronze chariots and their horses, as well as underground stables, some with mangers containing horses that were buried alive.

(a)

(b)

FIGURE 18.6 (a) Shihuangdi's terra-cotta regiment, guarding their master's tomb. (b) An archer.

Zhou dynasty
1122 B.C.

Unification
221 B.C.

Everywhere, the political situation was volatile. The Shang dynasty fell about 1122 B.C. at the hands of the neighboring Zhou. The conquerors did not create a new civilization; rather, they took over the existing network of towns and officials and incorporated them into their own state organization. In this way they shifted the focus of political and economic power to the south and west, away from Anyang into the fertile Wei Valley near the modern city of S'ian. By this time, the influence of what may loosely be called Shang civilization extended far beyond the north, into the rice-growing areas of the south and along the eastern coasts. The Zhou divided their domains into various, almost independent provinces, which warred with one another for centuries. It was not until 221 B.C. that the great emperor Zheng (Shihuangdi) unified China into a single empire (see Site box).

FIGURE 18.5 Museum display of one of the chariots from the royal Shang tombs near Anyang preserved by the surrounding soil.

By Roman times, Chinese civilization had been flourishing for more than 2,000 years—a distinctive and highly nationalistic culture that differed sharply from its Western contemporaries in its ability to assimilate conquerors and the conquered into its own traditions (Shaugnessy, 2000). In contrast, the Roman Empire was built on the groaning backs of slaves and collapsed into the Dark Ages when attacked by barbarian nomads. The ability of the Chinese people simply to assimilate these same nomadic conquerors explains why the essential fabric of their civilization survives to this day.

Summary

- Early Chinese civilization emerged independently of state-organized societies in the West.
- By 4000 B.C., population densities were rising in farming communities throughout China, and there are signs of social differentiation in village cemeteries.
- Exchange networks already linked thousands of small communities by 4000 B.C., spurring social and technological changes that included copper metallurgy and the widespread use of earthen fortifications. A new cosmology based on animals and the use of divination to communicate with the dead came into widespread use.

- The Shang civilization of the Huang Ho is the best-known early Chinese state, flourishing from 1766 to 1122 B.C. It was probably the dominant state among several throughout northern China. Shang society was organized along class lines, with the rulers and nobles living in segregated precincts and the mass of the people scattered in townships and villages in the surrounding countryside.
- Shang civilization ended with the overthrow of its ruling dynasty by Zhou rulers, who reigned over a wide area of northern China from 1122 to 221 B.C.
- China was unified under the Emperor Zheng (Shihuangdi) in 221 B.C.

Further Reading

Barnes, Gina L. 1993. *China, Korea, and Japan.* London and New York: Thames & Hudson.

Liu, Li, and Xingcan Chen. 2010. *State Formation in Early China.* London: Duckworth.

Thorp, Robert L. 2005. *China in the Early Bronze Age: Shang Civilization.* Philadelphia: University of Pennsylvania Press.

Hittites, Minoans, and Mycenaeans

19

"I have found the graves which, according to tradition, are those of Agamemnon, Cassandra, Eurymedon, and their companions." With this dramatic telegram to the king of Greece, archaeologist Heinrich Schliemann announced the discovery of the gold-smothered graves of Mycenae to an astounded world in 1876. Fresh from his triumphs at Troy, Schliemann had descended on Mycenae like a whirlwind, excavating in a circular area inside the main gate of what he thought was the Homeric hero Agamemnon's fortress. Within a few weeks, he and his wife uncovered 15 skeletons lying in five graves, a spectacular discovery that prompted his royal telegram. One of the bodies was so well preserved that some of the nonskeletal parts still remained, the gold ornaments in perfect condition. Schliemann commissioned an oil painting of the grave while a local druggist mixed alcohol and gum arabic in a frantic effort to preserve the burial. So much gold came from the excavations that Schliemann lit great watch fires to prevent looting. It was the first watch fire, he said, to shine out at Mycenae since Agamemnon's time. ▨

Two boys boxing. Akrotiri, Santorini Island, Greece, c. 1800 B.C.

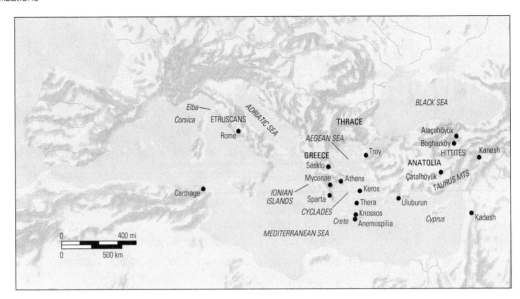

FIGURE 19.1 Sites and cultures mentioned in this chapter.

ater research has shown that Schliemann was wrong in attributing the Mycenaean graves to Agamemnon and his family; nonetheless, they are eloquent testimony to the riches and power of the earliest mainland Greek civilization. We now explore the developments that led to Mycenae and its predecessors. This chapter covers an enormous area of the ancient world. It is concerned not only with the humble beginnings of the formation of states and complex societies in areas like Anatolia but also with the rapid growth of what we have called a nascent world system over the mainland of Southwest Asia and the entire eastern Mediterranean after about 2000 B.C. (Figure 19.1). (See Table 15.1.) The societies described in this chapter all played a part in a much larger development: the growth of a truly international economic system that extended from Spain in the west to the distant Indus Valley in the east and lasted in various forms into historical times.

Early Towns in Anatolia

8000 B.C.

Anatolia, with its rich obsidian and copper outcrops, was an early player in the great regional exchange networks that developed in Southwest Asia as early as 8000 B.C. (see Chapter 9). At first, there were few large communities, but those that did flourish controlled trade over a large area around them. Çatalhöyük in central Anatolia was one such community (Balter, 2005; Hodder, 1996; Mellaart, 1967). This complex settlement was organized by the creation of ritual and other mechanisms that attempted to retain the close kinship ties of village life while adapting to the new complexities of long-distance trading and growing population. Unlike the system in Mesopotamia, where new mechanisms and organizations evolved to handle social change, the system at Çatalhöyük broke down: Anatolia's first and largest town was abandoned, and people went back to living in small villages.

3000 B.C.

The entire plateau of Anatolia seems to have experienced a subsequent gradual population increase after 3000 B.C., as long-distance trading with Mesopotamia in minerals and other materials increased. The evidence for the concentration of power and wealth in major Anatolian settlements is found after 3000 B.C. in the walled fortresses of Hisarlik (Troy) and Kültepe (ancient Kanesh) (M. Larsen, 1976).

Hissarlik
3500 B.C. and later

Hisarlik was first occupied in about 3500 B.C., when a small fortress was built on bedrock. Its foundations show that it contained a rectangular hall of a basic design that had been in use for centuries. The structure was to become the standard palace design of later centuries and perhaps a prototype for the classical Greek temple. In about 2300 B.C., a new settlement known to archaeologists as Troy II flourished at Hisarlik. This fortified town boasted more elaborate buildings and yielded valuable hoards of gold and bronze ornaments—a clear sign that the rulers of the settlement were supporting skilled craftspeople who designed and executed fine ornaments of rank.

Alaçahöyök
2000 B.C.

Thirteen royal tombs were found at the site of the town of Alacahöyük in central Anatolia, dating to about 2000 B.C. The tombs contained the bodies of men and their wives, accompanied by domestic vessels, weapons, and many metal items (Roaf, 1991). The ornaments included copper figurines with gold breasts and finely wrought cast-bronze stags inlaid with silver, which were perhaps mounted on the ends of poles (Figure 19.2).

Both the Alacahöyük and the Hisarlik finds testify to the far-flung exchange networks that crisscrossed Anatolia by 2000 B.C. They were an emerging component in the nascent world system that brought copper, tin, and other raw materials from the highlands to the lowlands of Mesopotamia and textiles and other lowland products back in return. The coastal eastern Mediterranean and the island of Cyprus now emerged as major players in the new trade networks. Maritime trade, using simple coastal vessels, was assuming considerable importance along the Turkish coast and among the Aegean islands, where a trade in obsidian, timber, pottery, wine, and olive oil had begun centuries earlier.

Toward the end of the third millennium B.C., Indo-European–speaking peoples seem to have infiltrated Anatolia from the northwest, causing considerable political unrest. Despite such upheaval, the volume of trade between Anatolia and Mesopotamia reached new heights as the two areas were becoming part of an ever more closely meshed economic system (N. K. Sanders, 1985). By 1900 B.C., for example, there was a sizable Assyrian merchant colony outside the city of Kanesh, one of several trading centers (*karums*) that were staging posts for long-distance commerce in minerals and other commodities. The *karums* served as marketplaces and caravan termini, natural entrepôts where prices for goods were carefully regulated. Local rulers levied taxes on the caravans, which brought Assyrian ideas to Anatolia and reinforced the economic and political power of the elite at both ends of the trade routes (M. Larsen, 1976).

FIGURE 19.2 Bronze stag from Alacahöyük, Anatolia, inlaid with silver. (Copyright The British Museum.)

Balance of Power: The Hittites

All these developments came from ever-closer economic ties between different regions of Southwest Asia (M. Larsen, 1987). These ties were a sign of an economic interdependency that persisted regardless of political change or war. The desert caravans of black asses and the ships that plied Mediterranean waters resulted from a more durable international economic network system that transcended the boundaries of local societies and even entire civilizations. At the center of this economic system lay the strategic eastern Mediterranean coast, a coastline with few natural harbors but with trade routes to Mesopotamia, Anatolia, and the Nile.

During the second millennium B.C., the eastern Mediterranean coastlands formed a network of small and prosperous states. These kingdoms lived in the shadow of the great kingdoms that lay inland: Egypt to the south, Mitanni to the east of the Euphrates, and Hatti (the kingdom of the Hittites in Anatolia). Each of these three kingdoms controlled a large area of territory surrounded by a hinterland that lay more or less under their influence (Figure 19.3). The three states competed directly in the coastal zone, and they had complex dealings on all frontiers. Mitanni, for example, tried to prevent the city-state of Assur in northern Mesopotamia from going its own way, and the famous El-Amarna tablets, an archive of Egyptian diplomatic correspondence, tell of shifting allegiances among the city-states of the coast. By this time, the eastern Mediterranean shore was a land of many cities, a regular military and diplomatic battlefield for its powerful neighbors.

Hittite civilization
1650–1200 B.C.

The Hittites were the newest, and perhaps the most able, diplomatic players. Originally the rulers of Kanesh, they expanded their domains and seized control of the rest of Anatolia just before 1650 B.C. (Gurney, 2007; MacQueen, 1996). A foreign minority, the Hittites rose to political power by judiciously melding conquest and astute political maneuvering, quickly becoming acculturated into their new milieu while preserving their traditional values and outlook on life. The Hittite state was a parliamentary monarchy, the first of its type. The king was not deified until after his death, if then. His duties were well defined: to ensure the state's welfare, wage war, and act

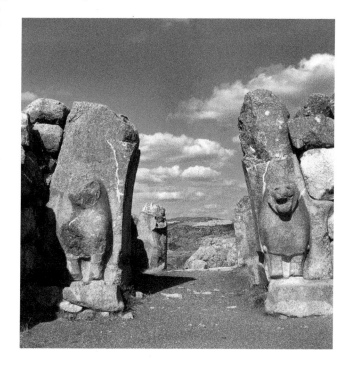

FIGURE 19.3 The Royal Gate, flanked by lions, at Boghazkoy (Hattusas), the Hittite royal capital.

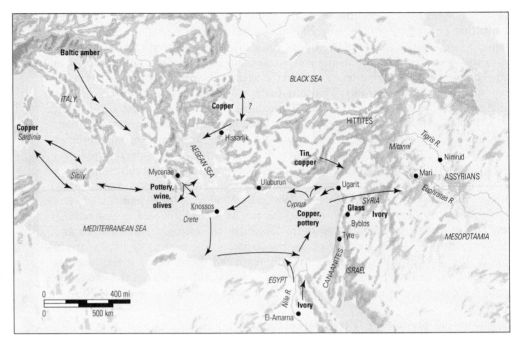

FIGURE 19.4 The balance of power in Southwest Asia in the second millennium B.C.: Egypt, Mitanni, and the Hittite Empire, showing major trade routes.

as high priest under clearly defined circumstances. A hierarchy of officials supported the king, ruling an empire based on a rigid feudal system of landownership and governance. Hittite kings

Boghazkoy   exercised enormous political influence in Southwest Asia from their capital at Boghazkoy, with its 6.5 km (4 miles) of city walls (Figure 19.4).

In the fifteenth century B.C., Syria had been a province of the Egyptian Empire. The Hittites pressed the Egyptians hard on both diplomatic and military fronts until the Great King of Hatti, Suppiluliumas I (1375 to 1335 B.C.), could claim Lebanon as his frontier. In 1286 B.C., the conflict culminated in the indecisive Battle of Kadesh between the forces of Pharaoh Rameses II and the Hittite ruler Muwatallis. Egypt was exhausted by this effort, and diplomatic archives in Akkadian cuneiform contain records of the peace treaty of about 1269 B.C. between the Hittite and Egyptian kings, which confined Egyptian interests to southern Palestine. The Kadesh Peace Treaty, the world's oldest peace treaty, is also recorded on the walls of the temple of Karnak at Thebes (and indeed a copy of it is on the walls of the United Nations building in New York). The grandiose public architecture of the period commonly depicted Egyptians and Hittites locked in battle with state-of-the-art weaponry. This included light two-wheeled chariots manned by archers and new siege machinery for use against the many walled cities in the disputed areas.

All of this diplomatic and military activity on the part of the great kingdoms was aimed at control of the lucrative gold, copper, and pottery trade of the eastern Mediterranean. This trade, in the hands of eastern Mediterranean and Mycenaean traders, has been vividly illustrated by investigations of a Bronze Age shipwreck off the southern Turkish coast. The advantage of shipwrecks from the archaeological point of view is that they provide sealed capsules of maritime trade frozen at a moment in time.

Uluburun   The Uluburun ship, excavated by Çemal Pulak from the waters near Kas off southern Turkey,
1305 B.C.   was shipwrecked in the fourteenth century B.C. The ship carried more than 350 copper ingots, each weighing about 27 kg (60 pounds), a load of 10 tons, enough to equip a small army with weapons and armor (Figure 19.5). A ton of resin traveled in two-handled jars made by people living in the Syria region; it was used, so Egyptian records tell us, as incense for Egyptian rituals. There were dozens of blue glass disks, ingots being sent to Egypt from Tyre. The cargo also included hardwood, Baltic amber, tortoiseshells, elephant tusks and hippopotamus teeth, ostrich eggs, jars of olives, and even large jars holding stacked Canaanite and Mycenaean pottery. Judging from a gold scarab found on board, at least one of the crew members was Egyptian. The Uluburun ship's cargo contained items from Africa, Egypt, the eastern Mediterranean coast, the Greek mainland and the Aegean, and Cyprus, and even copper from Sardinia (see a general description in Fagan, 1996).

The cargo is a dramatic reflection of the truly international nature of eastern Mediterranean trade in the second millennium B.C., when the Hittites were at the height of their power. The great powers of the day competed savagely for control of the eastern Mediterranean shore, for it lay at the very center of an interlocking maze of trade routes.

This maritime trade was still expanding in Hittite times. It played a major role in the diffusion of iron tools and weapons over the eastern Mediterranean. Iron was first smelted in the middle of the first millennium B.C., perhaps in the highlands immediately south of the Black Sea. The new metal had many advantages, for its tough, sharp edges were invaluable for military purposes and in farming and carpentry as well. Iron was plentiful, unlike the tin used to alloy bronze. Iron tools soon became commonplace over a wide area of Europe and Southwest Asia, although it was some time before domestic artifacts such as axes and hoes were made with the new technology (Wertime and Muhly, 1980).

By 1200 B.C., Hatti was in trouble. The Hittites had prospered by virtue of their well-organized professional army, a stabilizing influence in the eastern Mediterranean. They were expert diplomats who controlled what is now northern Syria through their rule over two great cities: Carchemish on the Euphrates and Alalakh of Mukish in the west. There were also treaty relationships with other powerful neighbors, including Ugarit (Ras Shamra) on the northern coast of the eastern Mediterranean. Ugarit was a cosmopolitan city ruled by a monarch who was almost like a merchant prince. He controlled vast supplies of gold and a fleet of more than 150 ships, some of considerable size. These ventured as far afield as Cyprus and the Nile, the former being a center of exchange with the Aegean. Ugarit was vital to the Hittites, for they depended on its ships and never became a maritime power.

FIGURE 19.5 Excavations on the Bronze Age shipwreck at Uluburun, near Kas, southern Turkey. Note copper ingots in the foreground.

Both the lack of maritime power and a rigid feudal system contributed to Hatti's undoing. A major drought around 1300 B.C. may also have caused widespread suffering and population movements in the entire eastern Mediterranean region (Butzer, 1995). About 1200 B.C., repeated migrations of foreigners flowed into Anatolia from the northwest, whence the Hittites had come only four centuries earlier (Drews, 1993). These population movements came to a head when the Phrygian peoples from Thrace ravaged the plateau as far south as the Taurus Mountains. The central Hittite government collapsed, partly because of attacks from outside but also because powerful vassals threw off their allegiance to the king. The rulers appealed to Ugarit and other maritime neighbors for assistance, but none was forthcoming. Anatolia dissolved into dozens of small city-states, each striving to maintain its independence. Only a few Hittite communities survived in small states in northern Syria until they were engulfed in the vast Persian Empire of the first millennium B.C.

The Sea Peoples and the Rise of Israel

The situation in the eastern Mediterranean was explosive, for the withdrawal of the great powers left a political vacuum that could not be filled by local rulers, who depended heavily on mercenary armies. With the collapse of the Mycenaean trade at about the same time, there was a general weakening of authority (Drews, 1993). Highly centralized palace bureaucracies ruled the imperial powers and petty kingships that made up the eastern Mediterranean world of 1200 B.C. The systems they controlled were very specialized, allowing for significant economies of operation and dense population concentrations. This very specialization made the entire system vulnerable to the effects of local upheavals, for a collapse in one area—say, the Hittite Empire—reverberated throughout the entire system. The exact causes of the almost domino-like collapse of Hittite and Mycenaean civilization, and of the weakening of the Egyptian empire, are still a mystery. But they may be connected to severe droughts, among other factors. The abrupt collapse of trade weakened the urban elites and the foundations of their power (Whitelaw and Coote, 1987).

1200 B.C.

The same interdependencies also affected the nomads and peasants who lived in the hinterlands of eastern Mediterranean cities, both on the coast and inland. The cuneiform tablets from the city of Mari, at the head of a powerful state on the Euphrates centuries earlier, provide compelling evidence of the intricate relationships between the cities and those who herded their flocks on the outskirts (Dalley, 1984). These groups were also dependent on the international trade, but as the trade declined, they became increasingly politically independent during the period of destruction, a "dark age" that lasted more than 300 years. This was a time of piracy and widespread suffering, much of it at the hands of warlike bands known to archaeologists as the Sea Peoples (N. K. Sanders, 1985).

In the eastern Mediterranean, many rural groups moved to the highlands inland during these centuries, relying more heavily on pastoralism and agriculture as their dependence on the trading centers diminished. Village communities, nomadic herders, and even bandits lived in proximity outside the reach of state power. In this milieu, a loose federation of highland villages, small towns, pastoral nomad groups, and former bandits formed to preserve and defend their sovereignty from outside states. This federation became the state of Israel, which acquired its own monarchy after 1000 B.C. and protected itself with a network of walled cities (Silberman, 1992; Whitelaw and Coote, 1987). By this time, eastern Mediterranean trade was recovering. The hillside federation expanded into lowland territory, circumscribed by the sea and the desert and by the still powerful Egyptian and Mesopotamian civilizations on either side.

Israel
c. 1000 B.C.

The Phoenicians

Phoenicians
c. 1100 to 800 B.C.

The general economic recovery of the first millennium B.C. was in large part attributable to the Phoenicians. They had first come into prominence in the eastern Mediterranean by acting as middlemen in the growing trade in raw materials and manufactured goods (Aubet, 1993; Moscati, 1988). Their ships were soon carrying Lebanese cedarwood to Cyprus and the Nile. North of Israel, powerful Phoenician cities like Tyre, Sidon, and Byblos now expanded this trade. Their ships took over the copper and iron ore trade of the Mediterranean. Their trading networks later extended as far as Carthage in North Africa and to the copper and tin mines of Spain; and Phoenician merchants made enormous profits from purple dye extracted from seashells and much used for expensive fabrics.

By 800 B.C., Phoenician merchants were everywhere in the Mediterranean, witness the recent discovery of two Phoenician cargo ships of 750 B.C. in depths of over 300 m (1000 feet) on the seabed between Phoenicia and Carthage in 2000. The vessels were heavily laden with cargos of wine amphorae. A century later, the great Phoenician cities were forced to acknowledge Assyrian rule and to pay tribute to foreign masters. Magnificent Phoenician ivories came from the royal palaces at Nimrud on the Tigris, perhaps tribute or plunder from military campaigns. Israel, too, was absorbed into the Assyrian Empire in the eighth century B.C. as the eastern Mediterranean coast came under the sway of alien empires for many centuries, right into modern times.

The Aegean and Greece

10000 B.C.
4000 B.C.

Even as early as 10000 B.C., seagoing ships were plying the waters of the Aegean, trading obsidian from the islands to mainland Greece. Seagoing trade got under way in earnest after 4000 B.C., as long-distance exchange networks expanded rapidly. In a real sense, the history of early Aegean and Greek civilizations is the story of the growth of international trade in eastern Mediterranean waters (Sansome, 2009).

Farming settlements had developed in parts of mainland Greece and the Aegean as early as 7000 B.C. More intensive settlement of western Greece, the islands, and Crete did not occur until much later. The Sesklo village in Thessaly was occupied by about 5500 B.C. and is typical of northern Greek sites of the time (Dickinson, 1994). The people lived in stone and mud houses connected by courtyards and passages. Their mixed farming economy depended heavily on cereal cultivation. Somewhat similar villages are found on Crete, where farming settlement dates back to at least 6000 B.C.

There were radical changes in the settlement pattern after 2500 B.C., when villages were established in the Cyclades, throughout Crete, and on the Ionian islands of the west. In contrast, northern Greece seems to have lagged behind. The reason may have been agriculture, for southern Greece and the islands are ideal environments for the cultivation of olives and vines, with cereal crops interspersed between them (Broodbank, 2001; Renfrew, 1972). There was a veritable explosion in village crafts as well, in the manufacture of fine painted pottery, marble vessels, and magnificent stone figures (Figure 19.6). Stone vases and fine seals were made by Cretan workers; the seals were used to mark the ownership of prized possessions or pots full of oil or other commodities. By 2500 B.C., the peoples of the Aegean and Greece were smelting copper and making bronze artifacts as well as ornaments in gold and silver. These included exquisite gold and silver drinking cups and the elaborate ornaments found at Troy II, which included more than 8700 gold beads, wire ornaments, chain links, and objects of fine gold sheet. The achievements of the Aegean metallurgists resulted in part from the rapid expansion of trading throughout the Aegean, far into Anatolia, and to Cyprus, with its rich copper outcrops (Dickinson, 1994; Manning, 1995).

2500 B.C.

The Aegean is well endowed with comfortable ports and alternative trading routes that provide easy communication from island to island for most of the year. Even relatively primitive vessels could coast from one end of the Aegean to the other in easy stages. Sailing vessels appear on Cretan seals dating to approximately 2000 B.C. The Aegean trade flourished on olive oil and wine, metal tools and ores, marble vessels and figurines, and pottery. The success of the trade led to a constant infusion of new products and ideas into Greece and the Aegean. By 2500 B.C., numerous small towns housed farmers, traders, and skilled craftsworkers on the mainland and the islands (Renfrew, 1991).

The beginnings of town life created considerable cultural diversity in the Aegean, a diversity fostered by constant trading connections and an increased complexity in social and political organization. Nowhere is this diversity better documented than on Crete, where a brilliant civilization flourished in towns and palaces throughout the island. In contrast, mainland Greece lagged somewhat behind, its many small towns having only occasional contact with the Aegean islands and Crete.

The Minoans

The development of the Minoan civilization of Crete was almost certainly the result of many local factors, among them the intensive cultivation of the olive and the grapevine. Minoan development is best documented at Knossos in northern Crete (Figure 19.7) (Cadogan, 1976; Isaakidou and Tomkins, 2008). The first prehistoric inhabitants of Knossos settled there in about 6100 B.C. No fewer than 7 m (23 feet) of early farming occupation underlie the Minoan civilization. The first Knossos settlement was founded at approximately the same time that Çatalhöyük was first occupied in Anatolia. The Knossos farmers lived in sun-dried mud-brick huts of a rectangular ground plan that provided for storage bins and sleeping platforms. By 3730 B.C., signs of long-distance trading increase in the form of exotic imports such as stone bowls. The first palace at Knossos was built by about 1930 B.C.; it is a large building with many rooms grouped around a rectangular central court.

At least nine periods of Minoan civilization have been distinguished by pottery styles found at the later levels of the Knossos site. Even during the earlier periods of the civilization, the Minoans

FIGURE 19.6   Harper in marble, executed by an artisan on the island of Keros in the Aegean.

Minoan civilization
2000–1450 B.C.

Knossos
1930–1450 B.C.

FIGURE 19.7   General view of the Palace of Knossos, Crete.

FIGURE 19.8 The throne room of the Palace of Knossos, Crete.

traded regularly with Egypt, for their pottery and metal objects have been found in burials there. About 1700 B.C., an earthquake destroyed the earlier palaces.

The high point of Minoan civilization followed that destruction, occurring between 1700 and 1450 B.C., when the Palace of Knossos reached its greatest size. This remarkable structure, said to be the home of the legendary Cretan King Minos, was made mainly of mud brick and timber beams, with occasional limestone blocks and wood columns. Some buildings had two stories; the plaster walls and floors were decorated initially with geometric designs and, after 1700 B.C., with vivid scenes or individual pictures of varying size. Sometimes the decorations were executed in relief; in other cases, colors were applied to the damp plaster. Artistic themes included formal landscapes, dolphins and other sea creatures, and scenes of Minoan life (Figure 19.8). The most remarkable art depicted dances and religious ceremonies, including acrobats leaping vigorously along the backs of bulls. Figurines of priestesses also survive (Figure 19.9). Writer Mary Renault (1963) has vividly reconstructed Cretan society at Knossos in novels that bring Minoan culture to life.

At the height of its prosperity, Crete was self-supporting in food and basic raw materials, exporting foodstuffs, cloth, and painted pottery all over the eastern Mediterranean. The Cretans were renowned mariners. Their large ships transported gold, silver, obsidian, ivory, and ornaments from central Europe, the Aegean, and Southwest Asia; and ostrich eggs were probably traded from North Africa.

Minoan religious practices differed from those of Egypt and other Southwest Asian civilizations in that they were centered on palaces, caves, and shrines, where, apparently, people offered sacrifices to individuals who metamorphosed themselves into deities. Greek archaeologist Nanno Marinatos (1993) believes that the ruling class had an investment in portraying themselves in divine forms, to the point where the imagery of gods and rulers fused into one. She argues, however, that there were no supreme Minoan rulers or divine kings in the sense of an Egyptian pharaoh or an Assyrian despot, all-conquering in war, and that the palaces were the backbone of religious life. Secular prestige may have been gained through religious office.

At times, the Minoans resorted to human sacrifice and, perhaps, cannibalism. A house on the north side of Knossos collapsed in the great earthquake of 1450 B.C. The first-floor ceiling fell into the basement, taking a magnificent set of ritual vessels with it. The basement fill also contained the scattered bones of two children in perfect health. A microscopic examination of the limb bones showed that knives had been used to remove flesh from the bone. Perhaps this find is evidence not only of human sacrifice but of ritual cannibalism as well, possibly related to a fertility rite associated with the Cretan Zeus and the Earth Mother. In another spectacular and controversial find, Greek archaeologists Yanni Sakellarakis and Efi Sapouna-Sakellarakis (1981) uncovered a shrine at Anemospilia, in the mountains south of Knossos, where, they claim, an earthquake interrupted a human sacrifice, the collapsed roof killing the priest and his attendant and leaving the crouched body of the young male victim lying on a sacrificial table.

A major event during the later stages of the Minoan civilization was the massive volcanic explosion on the island of Santorini (Thera), a Minoan outpost 113 km (70 miles) from Crete, probably during the late seventeenth century B.C. (Manning, 1988). The eruption probably caused destruction on the north coast of the Minoan kingdom, but Knossos continued to flourish long afterward. The Thera eruption is equated by some people with the eternal legend of Atlantis, the mysterious continent said to have sunk to the ocean bottom after a holocaust thousands of years ago (Doumas, 1983).

Santorini eruption
?1688 B.C.

The Thera eruption may have accelerated the decline of Minoan civilization, which was already showing signs of weakness. In about 1400 B.C., many Minoan sites were destroyed and abandoned. Warrior farmers, perhaps from mainland Greece, established sway over the empire and decorated the walls of Knossos with military scenes. Seventy-five years later, the palace was finally destroyed by fire, thought to have been the work of Mycenaeans who razed it. By this time, the center of the Aegean world had shifted to the Greek mainland, where Mycenae reached the height of its power.

A generation ago, British archaeologist Colin Renfrew (1972) emphasized an interlinked series of factors to explain the rise of the Minoan palaces. These included intensification of agriculture, growth of foreign trade, and increased craft specialization. Renfrew argued that these factors interacted with each other by the process of "positive feedback" to magnify and accelerate the scale of change (what he called the "multiplier effect") and resulted in the formation of palace-based states. Some parts of Renfrew's model, however, are now generally discounted. It implies, for instance, a steady evolution of complex society on Crete during the early Minoan period, which the available evidence does not support.

Renfrew also ascribed an important role to grapevines and olives. These are not grown on the same land as cereals and therefore do not compete with them. Renfrew proposed that the introduction of domesticated vines and olives in the early Bronze Age allowed a substantial expansion in the amount of land under cultivation and helped to power the emergence of a complex society. Some archaeologists and paleobotanists have recently questioned this view, pointing out that the available evidence for cultivated vines and olives does not show their presence much before the late Bronze Age. It is difficult to date their introduction with confidence from the scanty preserved remains, however, and some element of agricultural change would have been essential to support the larger population of palace-period Crete. Furthermore, elaborate drinking vessels appeared in Crete during the early Bronze Age and may indicate that the Cretans were already drinking wine at that period. But there is no firm evidence of extensive agricultural expansion on Crete during the early Bronze Age. Agricultural change, rather than being the driving force of Cretan state formation, was probably just one of several associated factors, along with social and ideological developments.

FIGURE 19.9 A Minoan priestess with flounced dress, holding snakes.

As agricultural economies became more diversified and goods and commodities could be exchanged both locally and over longer distances, a far-reaching economic interdependence resulted. Eventually, it led to redistribution systems that were organized and controlled by the inhabitants of Minoan palaces and elsewhere in the Aegean where there were major centers of olive production. The redistribution networks carried metal objects and other luxury products the length and breadth of the Aegean. Interest in long-distance trading brought about some cultural homogeneity from trade, gift exchange, and perhaps piracy. The skills of craftsworkers were highly valued in village and palace alike. Specialized artisans practiced their crafts in the major palaces; they lived well, in stone buildings with well-designed drainage systems, and had wooden furniture.Renfrew (1972) describes both the Minoan society and that of its successors, the Mycenaeans of the Greek mainland, as civilizations. He points to their sophisticated art and metalwork, to the complex palaces organized around specialized craftsworkers, and to their development of redistribution networks for foods. The Minoans and the Mycenaeans did not build vast temples like those in Guatemala or in Egypt. They also did not live in cities. Palaces and elaborate tombs were the major monuments. Renfrew looks for the origins of Minoan

FIGURE 19.10 Mycenae from the air. The Lion Gate is at right.

and Mycenaean civilizations within Greece and the Aegean and considers them the result of local social change and material progress.

The Mycenaeans

The landscape of mainland Greece makes it ideal territory for the development of autonomous small-scale kingdoms. Mountains break the terrain into fertile coastal plains, each of which could naturally form the focus of a separate state. These kingdoms first become visible at the beginning of the late Bronze Age, when the elites who governed them began to engage in long-distance trade with the hinterland of Europe and to proclaim their wealth and power through the richness of their grave goods (Burns, 2010).

Mycenaean civilization
1600 to 1150 B.C.

The Mycenaean civilization, centered on the fertile plain of Argos on the Greek mainland, began to flourish about 1600 B.C. (Taylour, 2004). The chieftains who ruled over the walled fortress of Mycenae (Figure 19.10) were buried in spectacular graves that contained weapons adorned with copper and gold as well as fine gold face masks modeled in the likeness of their owners (Figure 19.11). Their wealth and economic power came from their trading contacts and from their warrior skills (Figure 19.12). The kings were skilled charioteers and horsemen whose material culture and lifeway are immortalized in the Homeric epics. These epics, however, were written many centuries after the Mycenaeans themselves had become folk memories (Fagles, 1990).

Mycenaean commerce took over where the Minoans left off, although many Greek cargos were carried in ships of other nations (Burns, 2010). Much of the rulers' prestige was based on their contacts in the metal trade. As the Uluburun ship shows, minerals were in constant demand in the central and eastern Mediterranean, especially tin for alloying copper to make bronze. Both copper and tin were abundant in central Cyprus and Anatolia, and the Mycenaeans developed the necessary contacts to obtain regular supplies.

The Mycenaeans also prized Baltic amber, a yellow-brown fossil resin that, when rubbed, seems to be "electric." Occasional pieces of this precious substance reached Mycenae, and amber has been found in the royal graves there. Just how extensive the Mycenaeans' trading activities in Europe were has been much debated. They may well have been minimal (Harding, 1984).

So complex did their trading transactions become that the Mycenaeans found it necessary to establish a writing system. They refined one that had been developed by the Minoans. The Mycenaeans used a form of script written in the Greek language, known now as Linear B (Robinson, 2007). Eighty-nine characters make up Linear B, 48 of which can be traced back to Minoan writing, Linear A. Linear A probably originated in the simple pictographic script of the earliest Minoans (Figure 19.13). The terms *Linear A* and *Linear B* were coined by Sir Arthur Evans (1921) when he first studied Minoan

FIGURE 19.11 Gold mask of a bearded man, from Shaft Grave V at Mycenae, 1600 B.C.

FIGURE 19.12 Mycenaean soldiers on the march in full uniform.

writing in the early twentieth century. Linear B was in more widespread use than A, partly because the Mycenaeans exerted greater political and economic power than the Cretans (Chadwick, 1976).

Mycenae was a major partner in eastern Mediterranean trade until about 1150 B.C., when a combination of internal bickering and decline in agricultural yields led to its collapse (see Site box). In the same century, the Phrygians of the northeast overthrew the Hittite kingdom in Anatolia. This incursion into the Mediterranean world was caused by unsettled political conditions in Europe, at least partly the result of population pressures and tribal warfare (see Chapter 20).

Greek City-States After Mycenae

After Mycenae fell in 1150 B.C., small-town merchants on the Greek mainland continued to trade, monopolizing commerce in the Aegean and Black seas. By the eighth and seventh centuries B.C., trade had revived. Small colonies of Greek settlers lived on the northern and western shores of the Black Sea and along the north coast of Anatolia and developed trade in gold, copper, iron, salt, and other commodities (Bonzek, 1985). Other Greeks voyaged westward and settled in southern France; they soon had a brisk trade in wine and other goods with central Europe (Ridgeway, 1992).

In Greece, mountain ranges separate many fertile agricultural areas. Traders and seafarers of the Aegean islands and the Greek mainland therefore formed a network of small city-states that competed with one another for trade and political power (I. Morris, 1994). The concept of the *city-state* was the major organizing principle in the Greek world. Typically, it consisted of the city itself (usually fortified because the city-states were often at war with each other) and the surrounding rural hinterland, dotted with farmsteads and villages. Many such city-states were small both in extent and in population; some could field only a few hundred men of military age. On the other hand, there were those that could afford to build grandiose temples and public buildings—not palaces for the wealthy but monuments to the prestige of their own city. This is a trend seen most obviously in fifth-century Athens, when the resources of the Athenian empire were poured into the reconstruction of the Acropolis and above all the Parthenon with its gold and ivory statue of the patron goddess of the city-state, Athena.

Greek states unified only in times of grave political stress, as when Persian kings sought to add Greece to their possessions. Darius's defeat at Marathon (490 B.C.) and Xerxes' ten years later in a naval battle at Salamis ensured the security of Greece and made classical Greek civilization possible. Athens was foremost among the Greek states, becoming head of a league of

490 B.C.

dipae   mezoe   tiriowee   **2**

(larger-sized goblet with three handles)

FIGURE 19.13 Mycenaean script. Above, a tablet from the Palace of Nestor at Pylos in western Greece, bearing an inventory of goblets and cauldrons. Below, a specimen listing: "Larger sized goblet with three handles."

maritime cities that was soon turned into an empire (Bury and Meiggs, 1978; I. Morris, 1987). This was the Athens that attracted wealthy immigrants, built the Parthenon, and boasted of Aeschylus, Sophocles, and other mighty playwrights. Classical Greek civilization flourished for 50 glorious years.

However, throughout the brilliant decades of Athenian supremacy, bickering with Sparta in the Peloponnesus never abated. A deep animosity between the two cities had its roots in radically different social systems. Sparta's government was based on military discipline and a rigid class structure. Athenians enjoyed a more mobile society and a democratic government.

431 to 404 B.C.

The long rivalry culminated in the disastrous Peloponnesian War, 431 to 404 B.C., which left Sparta a dominant political force on the mainland. Political chaos ensued. Greece soon fell under

FIGURE 19.14 The Parthenon, Athens, one of the glories of classical Greece.

SiTE > The Mycenaean Shrine at Phylakopi, Melos Island, Greece <

The small Mycenaean town of Phylakopi on the island of Melos in the Aegean Sea was home to an estimated 1400 to 2100 people between 1390 and 1090 B.C. The settlement was a maze of small stone houses, narrow alleyways, and courtyards. Colin Renfrew (1985) excavated the site using a 10-m (33-foot) grid that allowed him to record architectural changes and stratigraphy with great precision. This excavation method, combined with meticulous studies of the Mycenaean pottery, provided very precise contexts for the finds and enabled Renfrew to identify an important shrine in the town.

He first suspected a shrine when he recovered broken animal and human figurines in his trenches. Slow-moving excavation over the floors of the putative shrine rooms revealed stone platforms and exotic objects like seal stones. But the evidence for religious activity was modest at best until the excavators uncovered a side chamber and a wall niche in the westernmost shrine room. This contained a pedestaled vase, the fragments of an ox-like figure, other figurines, and a remarkable female figurine, which stood upright in the room. "The

Lady of Phylakopi," as Renfrew named her, had a conical stem painted like a long skirt, a bulbous body with small breasts, a painted brown chin, staring eyes, and eyebrows and hair outlined in brown. Another complete female figurine stood to one side.

The figurines could have come from a storeroom, so Renfrew studied the design of the chambers. He found that the builders had laid them out in such a way that the symmetrically placed platforms were the focus of attention. The objects displayed on them would have caught attention at once. Furthermore, the "shrines" yielded conch-shell trumpets identical to those blown by priestesses on seals from Crete. Perforated tortoiseshell fragments were the remains of lyre bodies. The fine pottery found inside the two shrines was of much better quality than that from elsewhere on the site.

The precise contexts of these finds allowed Renfrew to conclude that he had found the town shrine, which is duplicated, at least superficially, at other sites on Crete and the Greek mainland.

the sway of Philip of Macedon, whose rule between 359 and 336 B.C. began to develop political unity. His son, Alexander the Great, then embarked on a campaign of imperial conquest that took him from Macedon into Persia and then to Mesopotamia. Alexander was welcomed as a hero and a god in Egypt, where he paused long enough to sacrifice to the local deities and have himself proclaimed pharaoh. His continued quests took him as far east as the Indus Valley and back to Babylon, where he died of fever in 323 B.C. By the time of his death, Alexander had united an enormous area of the ancient world under at least nominal Macedonian rule. His extraordinary empire fell apart within a generation, but his conquests paved the way for the uniform government of Imperial Rome.

323 B.C.

The Etruscans and the Romans

During the first millennium B.C., the Mediterranean world was linked from one end to the other by highly intricate mercantile ties. Phoenicians and Greeks controlled much of this trade in metals and other essentials, as well as exotic luxuries. The trade extended into temperate Europe and throughout the Italian peninsula, helping set the stage for large-scale Etruscan and Roman urban civilization in later centuries.

The Etruscans

By approximately 1000 B.C., some Urnfield people (named after their habit of burying cremated ashes in clay urns) from central Europe (see Chapter 20) had settled south of the Alps in the Po Valley (Wells, 1981). They developed a skilled bronze-working tradition in which products were traded far into central Europe and throughout Italy. This people evolved into the Villanovan culture, which appeared in the ninth century B.C. and was soon in touch with Greek colonies in southern Italy and perhaps with the Phoenicians (Barker and Rasmussen, 2000; S. Haynes, 2005). Ironworking was introduced to the Villanovans in approximately the ninth century B.C. Iron tools and extensive trading contacts won the Villanovans political control over much of northern and western Italy. They established colonies on the islands of Elba and Corsica. Several centuries of trade and other contacts culminated in the literate Etruscan civilization.

Villanovan culture
850 B.C.

Like classical Greece, Etruscan civilization, with its city-states, was more a unity of cultural tradition and trade than a political reality (Figure 19.15). The Etruscans traded widely in the central Mediterranean and with warrior peoples in central Europe. Etruscan culture was derived from

Etruscan civilization
450 B.C.

FIGURE 19.15 Detail of an Etruscan wall painting. A judge and a spectator at an athletic competition. Tomb of the Augurs, Tarquinia, Italy.

the Villanovan culture, but it owed much to eastern immigrants and trading contacts that brought Southwest Asian influence to Italian towns. The political units of Etruscan territory were city-states with much independence, each with substantial public buildings and fortifications. Their decentralized political organization made them vulnerable to foreign raiders. Warrior bands from central Europe overran some Etruscan city-states in the centuries after 450 B.C., at which time Etruscan prosperity began to crumble.

By the time of Etruscan decline, however, the Mediterranean was a civilized lake. Phoenician colonists had founded Carthage and other cities in North Africa and Spain and controlled the western Mediterranean. The rulers of Greece and Egypt, and later Philip of Macedon, controlled the east, and the Etruscans were in control of most of Italy and many central European trade routes.

The Romans

Rome
753 B.C.

The Etruscans had been the first people to fortify the seven famed hills of Rome. In 509 B.C., the native Romans evicted this foreign dynasty of rulers and began to develop their own distinctive city-state. The next few centuries saw the emergence of Rome from a cluster of simple villages by the Tiber River to the leadership of the Mediterranean and far beyond. The Romans inherited the mantle of classical Greece and added their own distinctive culture to this foundation. They then carried Greco-Roman civilization to many parts of the world that were still inhabited by preliterate peasant societies. Roman legions campaigned not only in Egypt, Mesopotamia, and southern Arabia but also in central and western Europe and in Britain. But for the Romans, the administrative and linguistic face of Europe would be very different today (Cornell, 1995; Holloway, 1994).

295 B.C.

By 295 B.C., the power of Rome dominated the whole of Italy. At this time, Rome was a form of democracy, governed by a delicate balance of aristocratic and popular authority. This type of governance was appropriate for a large city-state but was hopelessly inadequate for the complexities of a huge empire. Eventually, civil strife led to autocratic rule of the empire under the emperors, the first of whom was Julius Caesar, familiar to every student of Roman history for his epic conquest of Gaul (France). (His great-nephew, Augustus, was the first ruler actually to claim the title of emperor.)

200 to 50 B.C.

After two vicious wars with their rich rival Carthage, the Romans achieved mastery over the western Mediterranean by 200 B.C., and by 50 B.C. much of Asia was under uneasy Roman domination. The Romans lacked the mechanisms to administer their empire successfully until Emperor Augustus reorganized the civil service and established the *Pax Romana* ("Roman peace") over his vast domains. There ensued a period of great material prosperity and political stability, at the price of political freedom of speech.

The stresses that led to the collapse of the Roman Empire first began to appear on the European frontiers in the second and third centuries A.D. Roman power began to decline as ambition and sophistication grew among the Iron Age tribes living on the edges of Roman territory. The "barbarians" on the fringes of the empire were mainly peasant farmers who had obtained iron by trading and intermarriage with La Tène peoples (see Chapter 20). Many served as mercenaries in the Roman armies, acquiring wealth and sophistication and, perhaps most important of all, an insight into Roman military tactics.

Shortage of farmland and increasing disrespect for Rome caused many Germanic tribes to raid Rome's European provinces. The raids were so successful that the imperial armies were constantly A.D. 395 campaigning in the north. In A.D. 395, after Emperor Theodosius died, the Roman Empire was split into eastern and western divisions. Large invasions from northern Europe ensued. Fifteen years later, Germanic tribes from central Europe sacked Rome itself; then the European provinces were completely overrun by warrior peoples. Other Germanic groups disturbed North Africa and crossed much of Asia Minor but left little lasting mark on history there.

What was the legacy of Rome? Its material legacy can be seen in the road system, which still provides a basis for many of Europe's and Southwest Asia's communications, and in the towns, like London, which are still flourishing modern cities. In cultural terms, its principal legacy was the legal system, which lies at the core of most Western law codes. Roman literature and art dominated European culture for centuries after the Renaissance. Their spoken and written language, Latin, survived for centuries as the language of the educated person and as the principal means of business communication between nations. Latin lies at the base of many modern European languages and was only recently abandoned as the liturgical language of the Roman Catholic Church. The Romans and their culture are the foundation of Western civilization.

Summary

- Small towns became growing economic centers in parts of Anatolia as early as 3600 B.C.
- Communities like Çatalhöyük failed to develop the necessary administrative and social mechanisms to cope with the increased complexity of the settlement and its trading activities. The town failed, and Anatolians of the fifth millennium B.C. reverted to village life.
- Small fortified villages flourished in the fourth millennium B.C. One of them, Troy I, dates to just after 3000 B.C. Troy II, founded in about 2300 B.C., was a fortified town with more elaborate architecture and fine gold and bronze metallurgy. By this time, the Anatolians were trading widely over the highlands and into the Aegean, and chieftaincies were scattered over mineral-rich areas. About 1900 B.C., the Assyrians set up a trading colony at Kanesh in central Anatolia.
- The Hittites assumed power in Anatolia in about 1650 B.C. They held a vital place in the history of their time, for they played the Assyrians off against the Egyptians.
- Hittite power was based on diplomatic and trading skills until about 1200 B.C., when international trade in the eastern Mediterranean collapsed and a period of confusion, partly the work of the Sea Peoples, ensued.
- The state of Israel was born during this interregnum, among agricultural and herding peoples in the highlands behind the eastern Mediterranean coast.
- Farming settlements developed in Greece and the Aegean islands before 5000 B.C. There were radical changes in the late second millennium B.C., when the cultivation of the olive and the grapevine became widespread and the trading of minerals, stoneware, and other products expanded rapidly.
- Numerous small towns flourished throughout the Aegean and eastern Greece by 2500 B.C., linked by regular trading routes. The Minoan civilization of Crete developed in about 2000 B.C. and lasted until approximately 1450 B.C. The great volcanic explosion of its satellite island, Thera, in the seventeenth century B.C. may have weakened Minoan power for a while.
- After 1400 B.C., the center of civilization passed to the mainland, where the Mycenaeans flourished until 1150 B.C. Mycenaean civilization collapsed as a result of internal dissension and possibly the exhaustion of agricultural land.
- Trading activities continued to expand in the Aegean after the decline of Mycenae. Small city-states flourished, unifying only in the face of a common danger, such as the Persian invasions of the fifth century B.C.
- The Athenians enjoyed a long period of supremacy among city-states, the period of classical Greek civilization in the fifth century B.C.
- Alexander the Great built an enormous empire across Southwest Asia, of which Greece was part, in the late fourth century B.C.
- The Roman Empire, which followed, marks the entry of the entire Mediterranean area into historic times. Developed from Villanovan and Etruscan roots in Italy, Imperial Roman power was based on the ruins of Alexander's empire.

Further Reading

Broodbank, Cyprian. 2001. *An Island Archaeology of the Early Cyclades*. Cambridge, UK: Cambridge University Press.

Sanders, N. K. 1985. *The Sea People*, 2nd ed. London: Thames & Hudson.

Sansome, David. 2009. *Ancient Greek Civilization*, 2nd ed. New York: Wiley-Blackwell.

Taylour, Lord William. 2004. *The Mycenaeans*, 3rd ed. London: Thames & Hudson.

Europe Before the Romans

20

n 1667, a country squire named John Aubrey galloped into the village of Avebury in southern England during a fox hunt. He was "wonderfully surprized" to find it surrounded by a large ditch and bank and with circles of massive stones. Aubrey had visited the mysterious stone circles at Stonehenge when he was 8 years old and had long been a casual antiquary. None other than King Charles II encouraged him to survey the ancient earthworks and circles, a task that took Aubrey many years. His great work, *Monumenta Britannica*, which included his survey maps, was unfinished at the time of his death in 1697 and was not published until 1980. But archaeologists have long known what he thought of the people who built these ancient shrines: "The inhabitants were almost as savage as the Beasts, whose skins were their only rayment. They were two or three degrees I suppose less savage than the Americans. The Romans subdued and civilized them." ▪

An Iron Age salt miner's pick and wooden shovel, from Hallstatt, Austria.

FIGURE 20.1 Europe, 3500 to 2500 B.C. While extreme western and northwestern Europe remained the territory of stone-using farmers, copper working spread in central Europe and bronze came into use in Southwest Asia and peripheral regions. The building of communal tombs was widespread in the west, but more mobile lifeways developed in central Europe and on the eastern steppes. This new pattern expanded into surrounding areas.

No modern-day archaeologist would agree with Aubrey's characterization, for science has shown that both the Native Americans and the late prehistoric Europeans were much more sophisticated than Julius Caesar and other Roman authors would have us believe. By the time Roman legions campaigned north of the Alps, the society of temperate Europe enjoyed a level of complexity that has fascinated archaeologists for generations (Cunliffe, 2004, 2011) (Figure 20.1). How, then, did such complexity arise? Did it develop as a result of indigenous cultural evolution or because of a diffusion of people and ideas from Southwest Asia (see Table 15.1)?

For years, V. Gordon Childe (1952) and others argued that the constant demands by Southwest Asian societies for copper, tin, and other metals led to cultural development in the backwater that was temperate Europe. However, this traditional viewpoint has been challenged by calibrated radiocarbon chronologies that place the appearance of copper working in the Balkans earlier than in Greece or the Aegean. Many people now believe that Europeans were just as innovative as their eastern neighbors (Cunliffe, 1994).

Early Copper Working

Colin Renfrew (1978) and Ruth Tringham (1971) have argued that the farmers of southeastern Europe developed copper smelting independently, partly because they already used improved pottery-firing techniques that were very suitable for copper smelting. Witness the finds at the Varna Cemetery near the Black Sea in Bulgaria.

Varna
4600 to 4200 B.C.

At the Varna Cemetery, some richly furnished graves yielded dozens of fine copper and gold tools and ornaments (Figure 20.2). One man, 50 to 60 years old, owned more than 1,000 gold ornaments, among them beads, pendants, and a penis sheath, as well as copper artifacts. Colin Renfrew has described the Varna finds as "the earliest major assemblage of gold artifacts to be unearthed anywhere in the world" (1978:212), for they date to approximately 4600 to 4200 B.C. Both the copper and the gold are of Balkan origin; indeed, both metals were being worked there earlier than they were in Southwest Asia. (Such a statement reflects findings thus far; it does not preclude future discoveries of earlier metals in Southwest Asia.) The Balkan copper industry was quite sophisticated and was organized to serve trading networks over a wide area. In places, fissures mark the places where early miners followed ore veins deep into the ground. One mine

FIGURE 20.2 Goldwork from Varna, Bulgaria.

in Bulgaria has ancient shafts more than 10 m (33 feet) deep. These copper mines are the earliest so far discovered and show that metallurgy developed rapidly into a considerable industry in the Balkans during the fifth millennium B.C.

The Varna burials provide striking evidence for differential wealth; some of the graves are richly decorated with gold ornaments, whereas others contain few artifacts. Unfortunately, the settlement associated with the Varna Cemetery has yet to be found, but Renfrew believes that the users of the burial ground were part of a chiefdom in which the leaders used gold and copper ornaments to fulfill the social need for conspicuous display. As he points out, the problem with explaining the rise of metallurgy is not a technical but a social one—that is, defining the social conditions under which metal objects first came into widespread use. The earliest copper axes had few practical advantages over stone axes (Figure 20.3). Both copper and gold were used mainly for ornamental purposes. Perhaps it was no coincidence that the first metallurgists in temperate Europe developed a wide range of ornaments and luxury items traded through exchange networks that accelerated the spread of copper working to other parts of temperate Europe.

FIGURE 20.3 Simple copper ax heads from the Czech Republic (one-third actual size).

Battle Axes and Beakers

Copper
4000 B.C.

The technology of copper working is really an outgrowth of that used for pottery manufacture and probably arose after many experiments with fire, clay, and stone. The beginnings of copper metallurgy in temperate Europe were probably almost imperceptible, because only a handful of simple hammered copper artifacts date to as early as 4000 B.C. At least two possible areas of indigenous copper working have been identified in southern Europe, both near copper outcrops: one is in southern Spain (Iberia) and the other in northern Italy. In both regions, the copper workers started smelting by about

3000 B.C.

3000 B.C. Britain is also rich in copper ores, and the metal was exploited early there, too. Wherever it developed, coppersmithing was probably a seasonal or at best a part-time occupation, and it was not until much later that tougher bronze artifacts came into daily use in the field and the chase.

The archaeological record of the period between 3500 and 2000 B.C. is incredibly complicated, but we can discern two broad groupings of societies, the so-called Battle Ax and Beaker peoples, who ultimately mingled.

In eastern Europe, settled farming societies had lived on the edge of the huge Russian steppe for hundreds of years. Like the peoples of Anatolia and Greece, they had sporadic contacts with the nomads who roamed the plains to the east; about these dealings we know little. In the southern Russian region, a widespread population of copper-using agriculturalists lived in rectangular thatched huts, cultivated many crops, and also tamed domestic animals, possibly including the horse.

Kurgan culture
3000 B.C.

This loosely defined Kurgan culture, which was part of the Battle Ax culture, was remarkable for its burial customs, each corpse being deposited under a small mound. The Kurgans used wheeled vehicles and made the copper or stone battle ax a very important part of their armory. The wheeled cart and the battle ax had spread widely over central and parts of northern Europe by 3000 B.C. (Piggott, 1992). The globular pots associated with these artifacts, many of them bearing characteristic cord-impressed decorations, have been found at hundreds of sites. The same artifacts have often been found in megalithic tombs. These new cultural traits were absorbed into the millennia-old European cultural tradition, and many experts feel that the Indo-European language spread into Europe at about this time. (Indo-European speech is thought to have originated in the region between the Carpathian and Caucasus mountains. The entire Indo-European controversy is complex and outside the scope of this book. Interested readers should consult Mallory, 1988; Renfrew, 1987.)

It was at about this time that new house forms appeared in the European temperate zones. Smaller timber dwellings, just large enough to house a single family, replaced the Bandkeramik longhouse (see Chapter 10). With their battle axes, warriors were buried under small mounds, a reflection of new cultural traditions that were to persist in Europe for thousands of years. The warrior leaders who descended from Bronze Age chieftains were the German tribespeople whom the Romans encountered on the frontiers of their European empire.

2700 to 2000 B.C.

Between 2700 and 2000 B.C., a series of highly characteristic artifacts came into fashion over a large region of Europe: coastal Spain, southern France, Sardinia, northern Italy, east and central Europe, the Low Countries, and Britain (R. Harrison, 1980). These included finely made bell-shaped beakers found in hundreds of graves and burial mounds (Figure 20.4). Archaeologists such as V. Gordon

FIGURE 20.4 Bell beaker from a grave at Radley, Barrow Hills.

Childe (1936) thought in terms of tribes of "Beaker Folk" who spread the length and breadth of Europe, bringing a new culture and copper working with them. It seems more likely that these vessels spread widely not as a result of itinerant merchants or great population movements but simply because beakers, as well as other trinkets such as metal brooches, became prized status symbols throughout Europe. They may also have been traded for what they contained—perhaps beer or mead—and may have become valued heirlooms, priceless grave furniture, or artifacts exchanged as bride wealth (goods given by the bridegroom's family to the bride's father) or displayed at tribal gatherings. One Beaker burial from near Amesbury in southern England is that of an archer between 35 and 45 years old, buried with his bow and arrows. Oxygen isotope analysis of his teeth reveals that the "Amesbury archer" spent his childhood in central Europe (see Chapter 1, p. 5).

Beakers

Beakers were only one of several innovations that were changing the face of European society. Another was the plow, which came into widespread use about 2200 B.C., opening the way for the cultivation of heavier soils and much larger acreages.

Plow
2200 B.C.

We know something of the appearance of Bronze Age people from the remarkable discovery of the "Iceman" in the Italian Alps (see Page 406).

The European Bronze Age

In the Aegean, there was steady development from this early threshold of metalworking toward complex state organizations, but Europe remained settled by small village societies. The temperate zones were densely occupied and exploited, and vast acreages of forest had been cleared and brought under cultivation by 2000 B.C. The villagers managed woodland carefully, engaged in hunting to supplement their diet, and mined both hard ax stone and soft copper ore. They also panned for gold. Every community used basic metal technologies and had access to boats or wheeled transport. European village society was stable and self-sufficient, with thousands of communities connected by ties of kin and family and by long-established paths that led from valley to valley along the hill ridges. Above all, European society enjoyed reliable food supplies that helped bind the communities together.

The European Bronze Age began neither as a result of dramatic events and military conquest nor because of some startling invention (Coles, 1982; Coles and Harding, 1979). It was merely a gradual and inevitable quickening of responses to a number of new opportunities (Harding, 2000). Many of these changes were in material culture and settlement patterns. A series of landscape surveys in southern Britain, for example, has revealed vast networks of fields and land boundaries joining river valleys, ridges, and watersheds into a managed landscape in which different communities owned closely defined agricultural land. One Dorsetshire, England, Bronze Age agricultural system encompassed 200 ha (494 acres), with settlements of four to five huts linked to enclosures with narrow herd paths. There were fields, hoe plots, stock corrals, and homesteads, all joined in single managed agricultural units. By 900 B.C., Bronze Age food production was sophisticated. It relied heavily on plow agriculture and field fallowing as well as manuring, and it was based on the rotation of many different cereal and root crops.

From about 2000 B.C., metallurgy was a growth industry throughout temperate Europe. A series of local bronze industries developed in different parts of Europe, bringing with them a whole range of related activities: the trading of ores and finished artifacts from major mining centers and the barter of both prosaic and prestigious artifacts and ornaments over considerable distances. For the first time, a major European industry was practiced in areas where supplies of raw materials were scarce. For instance, Bronze Age communities in Scandinavia, which had no metals, went to considerable trouble to acquire metal ore and finished tools both from tribes in Britain and from central European sources. European smiths produced some of the finest bronze artifacts made in the ancient world: axes and adzes, battle axes, daggers, swords, spearheads, shields, and an enormous variety of brooches and pins. They also made delicate, prestigious gold ornaments that were highly prized and buried with important chieftains.

For all of these metallurgical innovations, the basic tenor of agricultural life remained unchanged, except for a gradual evolution in the structure of European society: the emergence of social ranking. Just what form this ranking took is a matter of lively controversy because it is reflected only in a differentiation of grave goods between a few individuals and the rest of society. In Denmark, for example, excavations on the island of Fyn have revealed rich Bronze Age burials and a nearby settlement with a wealth of gold and bronze. These are clear evidence that a powerful community was located there, having extensive trading connections with metal-rich regions to the south. The evidence from Bronze Age graves across Europe shows that rich and poor were buried side by side, the former with substantial quantities of valuable metal artifacts that were thus lost to the people

SiTE > Ötzi the Iceman, Similaun Glacier, Italian Alps <

A combination of high winds and extreme cold dried out and preserved the body of a prehistoric European found in 1991 high on the Similaun glacier in the Italian Alps (Spindler, 1996). The Similaun corpse has been radiocarbon-dated to between 3350 and 3300 B.C.

The man's body lay in a crouched position, as if he had taken shelter in bad weather when lost. Experts believe the man was in his early 40s and was either hunting or looking for minerals like copper, which are plentiful in the Alps. Others believe he was a shepherd on his way to summer pastures. The controversies continue to unfold.

His corpse and possessions are yielding a mine of information to modern-day archaeological detectives. Judging from an ember for starting a fire that he carried with him, which was from a tree species that grows to the south of the mountains, he came from that direction, perhaps from the fertile Venosta Valley in northern Italy. A single grain of wheat adhering to his clothing suggests that he was in contact with the valley within a few days of his death. The man carried a copper ax with a wooden shaft, a leather quiver with 14 bone- and wood-pointed arrows, and replacement heads and a puttylike substance for mounting them. He wore leather boots lined with hay for warmth, a stone necklace, and leather and fur garments, as well as a grass cloak of a type still worn by some peasants in the Alps a century ago (Figure 20.5). His knee and back bore small tattoos.

The latest techniques of medical science have established that his stomach contained the partly digested remains of ibex (mountain goat) meat, and some wheat grains, suggesting he had eaten less than two hours before his death. The Iceman had not been in perfect health. His lungs were black with soot, perhaps from living in smoke-filled huts. His bones carry 17 Harris lines, layers of bony material that form at times of stunted growth due to malnutrition. Experts estimate he suffered such episodes in his ninth, fifteenth, and sixteenth years, perhaps as a result of winter hunger. The dead man's hair yielded large amounts of copper dust, and there are high arsenic concentrations in his system, as if he had been involved in processing malachite, a copper carbonate commonplace in the Alps.

The Iceman seems to have been in a fight before his death. An arrowhead is buried deep in his left shoulder, and there is a dagger wound in one of his hands as if he parried an attack (Gostner and Vigl, 2002). Maybe he was killed where he fell, or perhaps he ran away wounded, then collapsed, helpless, and died of hyperthermia. We will probably never know.

FIGURE 20.5 Reconstruction of the appearance of the Iceman from Similaun, Italy. He wears a fur cap, an outer cape with coat underneath, leggings, and shoes. Two birch-bark containers and a backpack lay at his feet. He carries a stringless bow.

burying them. This can only mean that some members of society, perhaps important traders and more influential kin leaders, aggrandized wealth and power at the expense of others and became a new elite in European society (Gilman, 1995; Sherratt, 1994b).

2500 B.C.   Although one day the first occurrence of bronze may be shown to date to about 4000 B.C. in southeastern Europe, the earliest widespread use of tin-copper alloys occurred in approximately 2500 B.C., in what is now the Czech Republic (Coles and Harding, 1979). The new bronze implements, with their tougher working edges (Figure 20.6), were initially in short supply, but their use spread gradually as new trade routes were opened across central and western Europe. The

Unetice   earliest bronze working was centered in Unetice (see Figure 20.7), where there was an industry manufacturing axes, knife blades, halberds, and many types of ornaments (Piggott, 1965). The bronze workers themselves obviously belonged to cultural traditions long established in the area, for their burial customs were identical to those of earlier centuries. Some believe that the art of alloying

FIGURE 20.6 Copper and bronze implements from Britain. Top, socketed, flat and flanged axes. Left and center, swords and a dagger. Center right, a socketed lance head. A ceremonial 'lur', a bronze trumpet is at center/bottom. Beakers and other Bronze Age vessels appear at bottom right. Drawn to differing scales.

tin with copper, as well as casting techniques, came to Europe from Syria. Most people now argue, however, that bronze working developed independently in Europe, in that the calibrated carbon-14 dates from the Unetice industry are earlier than those for the Southwest Asian prototypes from which the other school of thought assumes the Unetice industry to have evolved.

Bronze working soon appeared in southern Germany and Switzerland as well, where deposits of copper and tin were to be found. Other places with copper outcrops were also soon using the new methods, including Brittany, the British Isles, and northern Italy, all more remote from the initial centers of bronze working. The period between approximately 1700 and 1300 B.C. was one of rapid technological progress and considerable social change, generated in large part by the reinforcing effects on the local bronze-working centers of the persistent demand for critical raw materials and finished tools.

1700 to 1300 B.C.

By this time, European trading networks carried far more than bronze artifacts and metal ores. The amber trade went from the shores of the Baltic to the Mediterranean, following well-established routes (Figure 20.7) (Harding, 1984). Seashells, perhaps faience (glass) beads, and other exotic luxuries were dispersed northward into the temperate zones in exchange for raw materials. Some centers of bronze production became major places for redistributing other goods as well. The salt miners of Austria were also very active in the long-distance trade.

During the second millennium B.C., even societies remote from metal outcrops were engaged in metallurgy. Many more copper and bronze artifacts became available for domestic consumption. Central European smiths introduced some new tool forms, including socketed axes and varied woodworking tools. More farmers were using the ard (a scraping plow drawn by oxen), which had been in use since at least 2500 B.C. The ard was a significant innovation, for it allowed deeper plowing, more advanced agricultural methods, and higher crop productivity. More intensive farming techniques were vital to feed the many new mouths, and prime farmland was harder to find than ever before. The surplus food and energy from improved agriculture were not devoted to generating additional surpluses and extra production but in some societies were channeled into erecting majestic religious monuments, of which Stonehenge in southern Britain is probably the most celebrated (see Page 409).

Stonehenge
2950 to 1500 B.C.

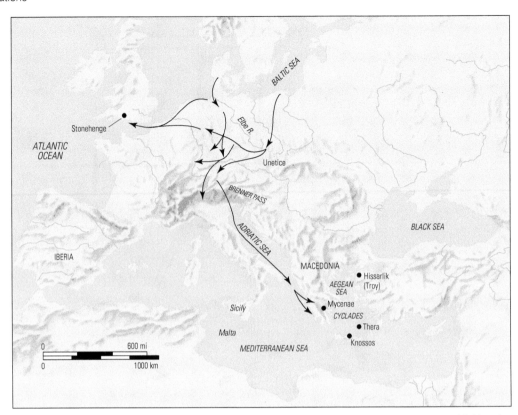

FIGURE 20.7 Amber trade routes in Europe and to Mycenae. The northern coastlines were the primary sources of Baltic amber. Amber was being passed southward to the Mediterranean by the time the Mycenaeans came to power.

Bronze Age Warriors

European societies eventually became more socially ranked. As trade intensified, local monopolies over salt and other supplies came to be concentrated in the hands of comparatively few individuals. Population growth and perhaps some climatic deterioration put new pressure on agricultural land (Figure 20.9). All of this may have led to considerable political instability in Europe and to alliances of small tribes under the rule of powerful and ambitious chieftains, themselves once minor village leaders. Some warrior groups even began to strike at the edge of the Mediterranean world, raiding Mycenae and the Hittite Empire.

Urnfield people
1800 to 1200 B.C.

One powerful group of warrior peoples in western Hungary is known to archaeologists as the Urnfield people because of their burial customs: Their dead were cremated and their ashes deposited in urns; huge cemeteries of urn burials are associated with fortified villages, sometimes built near lakes. Urnfield people began to make full use of horse-drawn vehicles and new weaponry. Skilled bronze smiths produced sheet-metal helmets, shields, and bronze body armor for a warrior elite. These fighters used the slashing sword, a devastating weapon far more effective than the cutting swords of earlier times.

The emergence of warrior elites was accompanied by a quickening of trade, reflected in a remarkable standardization of weapons and burial customs throughout much of central and western Europe (Figure 20.10). Within a couple of centuries, characteristic slashing swords and other central European tools had been deposited in cemeteries in Italy, the Balkans, and the Aegean. The exploitation of copper mines such as those in Austria's Tyrol was intensified. There, bands of miners used bronze-tipped picks to dig deep into the ground for copper ore. Their efforts increased the supplies of copper and tin available to central Europe (Coles and Harding, 1979). Urnfield weaponry and burial rites spread from Hungary throughout central and parts of western Europe. Some of the bronze and gold work was used in spectacular cult objects, often with profound symbolic meaning (Figure 20.11).

Between 1800 and 1200 B.C., the population movements associated with central European peoples introduced a more consolidated system of agriculture to much of Europe, which allowed the exploitation of much heavier soils as well as stockbreeding (Sherratt, 1994a). For the first time, stock were fully integrated into the food-producing economy and cattle were used for meat, milk, and draft work; sheep were bred as much for wool as for their flesh. At the same time, improved technology in new implements of tillage was fully exploited to achieve a truly effective

SiTE > Stonehenge, England <

Shrouded in fantasy and speculation, and associated by many people with the ancient Druids' cult, Stonehenge is in fact a fantastically old religious temple (Chippindale, 2004). It began as a simple circle of ritual pits in about 2950 B.C. and went through vigorous reconstructions, reaching the zenith of its expansion in about 2900 B.C. (Figure 20.8). That Stonehenge was associated with some form of astronomical activity seems unquestionable, although the details are much debated. Doubtless, special priests were needed to maintain this and other major shrines and to perform the rituals in their precincts. Religious activity was supported by the food surplus, not by the increased productivity in agriculture, trade, and craft specialization that generated spectacular social evolution in Southwest Asia. Thus, during the third and part of the second millennium B.C., little social evolution went on in Europe; political power and wealth belonged to chieftains and warriors rather than to divine kings and a hierarchical society.

Hardly surprisingly, the early investigations at Stonehenge focused on the stones themselves, with their uprights and lintels secured with tenons clearly derived from earlier timber prototypes. Sometime around 2500 B.C., the builders imported bluestones by hauling and floating them from a sacred location in Wales's Preseli Mountains, over 402 km (250 miles) away. Preseli's rocky outcrops may have been perceived as having healing qualities. The 80 or so bluestones transported to Stonehenge may have had magical associations, and weighed up to 7,257 kg (8 tons) each. They remained in use for the entire life of the monument, along with glacial sarsen stones from the local landscape. The labor of dragging the various uprights into position was enormous and must have involved collaboration between groups living considerable distances from one another—a powerful indication of the compelling ritual power of Stonehenge.

The stone circles are oriented outward at the summer and winter solstices, for the solstices were important signposts in the agricultural cycle that governed local life. Stonehenge also served as a major burial place. More than 240 people were interred there, most of them cremated, some as early as 3000 B.C., a remarkable continuity of burial customs that apparently lasted for much of the life of the monument, which went out of use in about 1500 B.C. No one knows who was buried there, but they may have been individuals with important spiritual powers or significant kin ties.

However, Stonehenge was far more than a monument; it was part of a much larger ancient landscape of an avenue, burial mounds, and other features. To understand more about this ritual landscape, a team led by (UK) Birmingham University's Vincent Gaffney is currently undertaking a major multimillion-dollar survey of the area using cutting edge technology. In the course of this innovative research, they have already identified previously unknown buried elements, including a "hengelike monument" lying just 900 m (984 yards) northwest of the site's iconic stone circle. By rigorously investigating the wider landscape, their work is certainly shedding new light on the site and how it might have been used in antiquity.

In recent years, other investigations, part of a long-term excavation project, have concentrated on a massive earthen circle and ditch complex known as Durrington Mills, 3.2 km (2 miles) northeast of Stonehenge. Two circles of wooden uprights lie inside Durrington Mills; a third, known as Woodhenge, is outside. These were clearly sacred places of limited access, perhaps shielded by temporary screens. Inside Durrington, the excavators found the remains of two large cult houses, places where ritual leaders dwelt. Outside the bank and ditch, the diggers found at least seven houses dating to between 2600 and 2500 B.C., aligned with a flint-paved avenue leading to the nearby Avon River. There are strong hints from test excavations that as many as 300 houses may await discovery, making this the largest village of the time in Britain.

Mike Parker Pearson theorizes that the Stonehenge landscape encompasses two symbolic realms: One is at Stonehenge itself with its cold, stone uprights—representing a permanent monument to the dead, to the ancestors. The other, made up of perishable timber structures and circles at Durrington Mills, was the domain of the living, of transitory human existence. There are many animal bones at Durrington, as if feasting was commonplace. In contrast, Stonehenge is more austere, the two sites linked by ceremonial avenues, which could have served as processional ways at the solstices. Parker Pearson's bold hypothesis is based, albeit loosely, on ethnographic observations of ancestor rituals in Madagascar and on careful observation of the Stonehenge landscape. It offers as plausible an explanation of the significance of these remarkable sites as any other one offered over the centuries, and one based on meticulous archaeological excavations (Alexander, 2008).

FIGURE 20.8 Stonehenge, England, from the air, with the surrounding ditch clearly visible.

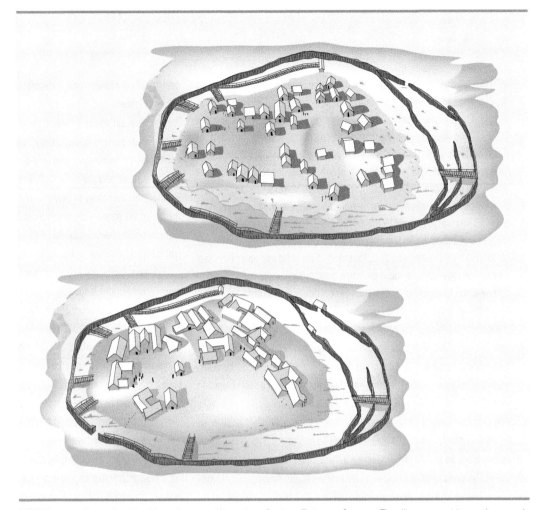

FIGURE 20.9 Bronze Age lakeside settlement at Wasserburg-Buchau, Federsee, Germany. The village was set in marshy ground and first occupied in about 1100 B.C., at a time when climatic change may have put pressure on good agricultural land. Fortified settlements may have been a response to territorial disputes. Top, the village was oval, and was surrounded by a wooden palisade, with 38 log-cabin-like structures inside. Bottom, somewhat later, the village was rebuilt with large rectangular buildings, some joined to make H-shaped or L-shaped houses. The settlement was eventually destroyed by fire.

economic symbiosis between flora and fauna, carefully balancing forest clearance with cultivation and pasturage.

The Scythians and Other Steppe Peoples

The vast rolling grasslands and steppes from China to Ukraine were not settled by farming peoples until they had a culture enabling them to survive in an environment with extreme contrasts of climate and relatively infertile soils. The carrying capacity of the land is such that only a vast territory can support herds of domestic stock. The prehistory of this huge area is obscure until the first millennium B.C., when the Scythians (from an area in southeast Europe) and other steppe peoples first appeared in the historical record. No one should doubt, however, the importance of nomads in the prehistory of Europe in earlier millennia (Phillips, 1972). The Kurgan people and other possible Indo-European speakers were familiar with the vast open spaces of the steppes.

Dereivka
4000 B.C.

As early as 4000 B.C., people living at the Dereivka site on Ukraine's Dnieper River were riding horses with rope bits. Their successors roamed the steppes for centuries before the Scythians came out of history's shadows, living in stout felt tents and subsisting mostly on horse's milk and cheese as well as on food from hunting and fishing. The nomadic life, though, leaves few traces in the archaeological record, except when permafrost has preserved burials in a refrigerated state.

Pazyryk
400 B.C.

We are fortunate in having extensive data about the vigorous society of nomad peoples from the spectacular frozen tombs of Siberia. Russian archaeologist Sergei Rudenko (1970) excavated several nomad burial mounds erected in 400 B.C. at Pazyryk in northeastern Siberia. The chiefs of Pazyryk were elaborately tattooed, wore woollen and leather clothes, and employed skillful artists to adorn

ATLANTIC
OCEAN

FRANCE

TYROL

HUNGARY

BLACK SEA

BALKANS

IBERIA

ITALY

MEDITERRANEAN SEA

0   600 mi
0   1000 km

☐ Thirteenth century B.C.   ▨ Twelfth to tenth centuries B.C.   ☐ Tenth to eighth centuries B.C.

FIGURE 20.10 Approximate distribution of Urnfield cultures in Europe.

their horse trappings and harnesses with exuberant and elaborate stylized animal art. A powerful chief was accompanied to the next world by his wife and servants, horses and chariots, and many of his smaller possessions. The Pazyryk burials contain fragments of woven rugs, the earliest examples of such art in the world.

The steppe peoples lived to the north of the well-traveled trade routes of Greek merchants, but their territory was constantly being explored and sometimes colonized by farmers whose lands were becoming overpopulated or overgrazed. Enormous areas of steppe were needed to support even a small band of horse riders, for just a slight increase in population could drastically affect the food supplies of the original inhabitants. The result was constant displacement of populations as the nomads sought to expand their shrinking territory to accommodate their own population pressures. The nomads menaced the northern frontiers of the Mediterranean world throughout classical and more recent times.

The First Ironworking

Late Bronze Age Europeans were effective farmers, traders, and metallurgists, capable of exploiting Europe's forested environment far more efficiently than their predecessors could. They lived amid a complicated network of trade that carried not only metals but also salt, grain, gold, pottery, and many other commodities. Their economic organization probably included community smiths, specialists supported by the village, but still no centralized state system of the Southwest Asian type.

FIGURE 20.11 The Nebra sky-disk, a bronze orb with the sun and moon attached in gold sheet, with 32 stars and originally three curving edge bands. The cluster of seven stars may represent the Pleiades. (Juraj Lipták/Landesamt für Denkmalpflege und Archäeologie Sachsen-Anhalt.)

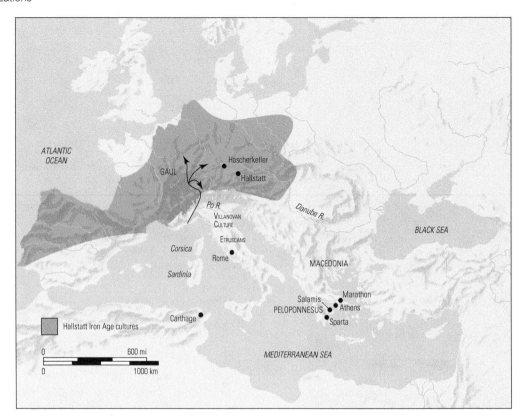

FIGURE 20.12 Distribution of the Hallstatt Iron Age cultures (shaded area) in Europe during the eighth to fifth centuries B.C.

Iron
1000 B.C.

These exchange networks facilitated the spread of ironworking techniques across Europe with considerable rapidity after 1000 B.C. In widespread use for both weapons and utilitarian objects by 700 B.C., ironworking is much more difficult than bronze working, for the technology is harder to acquire and takes much longer; however, once it is learned, the advantages of the new metal are obvious. Because the ore is found more widely, the metal is much cheaper and can be used for weapons and utilitarian artifacts as well. These would include axes, hoes, and plowshares, all of which contributed much to agricultural efficiency, higher crop yields, and greater food surpluses. The population increases and intensified trading activities of the centuries immediately preceding the Roman Empire are partly attributed to the success of iron technology in changing European agriculture and craftsmanship (Collis, 1997).

As iron technology spread across of the Alps, new societies arose whose leaders exploited the metal's artistic and economic potentials. The tribal chieftaincy was the structure of government; the most coherent broader political unit was a loose confederacy of tribes formed in time of war or temporarily under the aegis of a charismatic chieftain. Despite the onslaught of Roman colonization and exploitation, culture beyond the frontiers retained its essentially central European cast, an indigenous slant toward cultural traditions that began when farming did (Wells, 1981).

Hascherkeller
1000 to 800 B.C.

For all the technological changes, farming life continued much as before. Peter Wells (1984) has excavated an Iron Age farming community near Hascherkeller in lower Bavaria, Germany (Figure 20.12), where he found three enclosed farmsteads. The farmstead complexes included dwellings, barns, sheds, and workshops; between 15 and 30 people lived in each settlement. Occupied between 1000 and 800 B.C., these farmsteads were self-sufficient communities without iron tools. They traded foodstuffs for such items as imported bronze scraps, beads, and graphite, the latter used for pottery decoration. Hascherkeller was apparently without iron, which was still a new metal.

The Hallstatt Culture

Hallstatt culture
c. 750 B.C.

One strong culture was the Hallstatt, named after a site near Salzburg, Austria (see Figure 20.11) (James, 1992; Wells, 1981). Hallstatt culture began in the eighth and seventh centuries B.C. and owed much to Urnfield practices. The skillful bronze working of earlier times was still practiced, and bronze was still the dominant metal for horse trappings, weapons, and ornaments. Chiefs were buried, some in wagons, in large mounds within wooden chambers (Figure 20.13).

The Hallstatt people and their culture spread throughout former Urnfield territories as far north as Belgium and the Netherlands and into France and parts of Spain. Many Hallstatt sites are notable for their fortifications. The Hallstatt people traded with the Mediterranean along well-traveled routes up the Rhone River and through the Alps into central Europe. A significant import was the

FIGURE 20.13   Bronze ritual cart from a Hallstatt grave in Austria, approximately 0.3 m (1 foot) long. Copper and bronze were still important ornamental metals.

serving vessel for wine; containers of Mediterranean wine were carried far into central Europe as Hallstatt chieftains discovered wine drinking.

La Tène Culture

By the last quarter of the fifth century B.C., a new and highly distinctive technology, La Tène, had developed in the Rhine and Danube valleys (Cunliffe, 2000; James, 1992; Megaw and Megaw, 1989). An aristocratic clique of chieftains in the Danube Valley enjoyed implements and weapons elaborately worked in bronze and gold. Much of their sophisticated art had roots in the classical Greek and Mediterranean traditions, for La Tène craftsworkers were quick to adopt new motifs and ideas from the centers of higher civilization to the south. La Tène people spoke Celtic, a language that spread widely throughout Europe from perhaps as early as the ninth century B.C. Greek and Roman writers referred to these people as *Celts*, a term that has survived in their linguistic label.

La Tène technology was a specific adaptation of ironworking to woodland Europe. The cul ture extended north into the Low Countries and Britain in the fourth century B.C. (Figure 20.14). La Tène art is deservedly famous, and the hill forts and defensive settlements of this Iron Age cul ture are widespread in western Europe. The superior military tactics of La Tène people introduced the Romans to the short sword, for Celts sacked Rome in about 390 B.C. The last three centuries B.C. saw considerable change in Europe, with the appearance of coinage, the development of small autonomous states, and the foundation of large settlements known to archaeologists and historians as oppida, the Latin word for "towns." Many were fortified and somewhat similar to later towns in medieval Europe. La Tène peoples survived long after France and southern Britain had been con quered by Rome in 55 B.C. (Cunliffe, 1974).

Much territory in the temperate zones came under the domination of Rome, an uneasy fron tier province that eventually crumbled before the inexorable pressure of the warlike tribes on its boundaries. The illiterate peoples who eventually sacked Rome and ravaged its provinces were the descendants of prehistoric Europeans whose cultural traditions had been evolving ever since the first farming cultures had developed north of the Mediterranean basin.

La Tène culture
late fifth century B.C. and later

390 B.C.

55 B.C.

FIGURE 20.14 Iron Age (Celtic) helmet from the bed of the Thames River in London, 20.5 cm (8.07 inches) at the base. La Tène artistry and bronze and iron technology reached a high state of development in Britain.

Summary

- Copper working developed in southeastern Europe by about 4600 B.C., and soon afterward in Spain and northern Italy. The new technology flourished because of a demand for fine metal ornaments. It was a logical outgrowth of earlier stone and ceramic technologies.

- Copper's more widespread use coincides with the spread of Beaker and Battle Ax artifacts throughout much of Europe.

- Bronze working began at an unknown date but was widespread in what is now the Czech Republic by 2000 B.C., as part of the Unetice culture. The trading networks of earlier times expanded to meet the increased indigenous demand for metal artifacts during a period of rapid technological change after 1700 B.C. Some wealthy chieftaincies developed in the temperate zones.

- About 1800 B.C., new Urnfield burial customs and more advanced bronze-working techniques spread over much of central and western Europe. These were associated with an intensification of trading activity and greater social ranking, which resulted in an elite warrior class.

- After 1000 B.C., ironworking techniques spread into temperate Europe and diffused through the Hallstatt and La Tène cultural traditions during the first millennium B.C.

Further Reading

Cunliffe, Barry. 2004. *Facing the Ocean: The Atlantic and Its Peoples 8000 BC–AD 1500*. Oxford: Oxford University Press.

Cunliffe, Barry. 2011. *Europe Between the Oceans: 9000 BC–AD 1000*. New Haven and London: Yale University Press.

Spindler, Konrad. 1996. *The Man in the Ice*. New York: Crown.

NATIVE AMERICAN CIVILIZATIONS

BEFORE 2000 B.C. TO A.D. 1534

When yet all was in darkness, when yet no sun had shone and no dawn had broken—it is said—the gods gathered themselves together and took counsel among themselves there in Teotihuacán. They spoke, they said among themselves: "Come hither, O gods! Who will carry the burden? Who will take it upon himself to be the sun, to bring the dawn?"

From an Aztec legend of the Creation, quoted from Anderson and Dibble, *The Florentine Codex* (1978)

One of the remarkable phenomena of the human past is the way in which cultural developments unfolded along broadly parallel lines in many parts of the world. Part V describes the brilliant diversity of state-organized societies that flourished in the Americas over a period of more than 3,500 years and ends with the arrival of the Spanish conquistadors in Mexico and Peru in the early sixteenth century A.D.

The theoretical literature surrounding the development of states and civilizations in the Americas is as voluminous as that for the Old World. Interested readers are referred to Chapter 14 for general theoretical background relevant to state origins throughout the world.

Native American Civilizations Timeline

Period already covered

Partial coverage

Period covered in **Part V**

| 5 mya | 2.5 mya | 1 mya | 150,000 B.P. | 10000 B.C. | A.D. 1 | A.D. 1500 |

FIG. 2.2   FIG. 3.1a   FIG. 4.9   FIG. 9.5   FIG. 14.3   FIG. 21.6

21 Mesoamerican Civilizations

By any standards, New York lawyer turned traveler John Lloyd Stephens was a remarkable man. In 1839, he and Scottish artist Frederick Catherwood journeyed deep into the Mesoamerican rain forest, following rumors of vanished civilizations and great ruins masked by primordial jungle. They came first to the tiny modern village of Copán, where "around them lay the dark outlines of ruins shrouded by the brooding forest. The only sound that disturbed the quiet of this buried city was the noise of monkeys moving around among the tops of the trees" (Stephens, 1841: 48). While Catherwood drew the intricate hieroglyphs he had found on the Mayan stelae, Stephens tried to buy the ancient city of Copán for 50 dollars so that he could transport it block by block to New York. The deal fell through when he found he could not float the antiquities downstream. Stephens and Catherwood visited Palenque, Uxmal, Chichén Itzá, and other sites. They were the first to recognize the Maya as the builders of these great sites: "These cities . . . are not the works of people who have passed away . . . but of the same great race . . . which still clings around their ruins," Stephens wrote (p. 222). All subsequent research into the Maya and into ancient Mesoamerican civilization has been based on his premises (Figure 21.1). Today, Maya civilization, with its intricate, recently deciphered glyphs and spectacular cities, ranks among the most fascinating in the world. As we shall see in this chapter (Table 21.1), its origins lie deep in the remote past. ■

A reconstruction of a Maya ball game, Copán, Honduras.

Village Farming

Like other tropical cultivators, the Maya used ancient slash-and-burn farming methods to grow maize and beans (Coe and Koontz, 2008; S. Evans, 2008). Come late spring, the farmer would cut down a patch of forest on well-drained land during the last of the dry season, then burn off the wood and brush. This was a critical time in the farming year, when the air was thick with wood smoke and dust. Great clouds of gray smoke billowed into the washed-out blue sky as the afternoon wind blew fine ash and soot over everything. As the burn subsided, the ash and charcoal fell on the soil. The farmers and their families worked the natural fertilizer into the earth, then planted maize seed in holes poked into the soft ground with a stick. Timing was everything, for planting had to coincide with the first rain showers. Such cleared gardens, called *milpa*, remain fertile for only about two years. The farmer must then move on to a new plot and begin again, leaving the original milpa to lie fallow for between four and seven years. When the Maya were purely village farmers, their settlements lay amidst patchwork quilts of newly cleared plots and regenerating land, surrounded by thick forest that separated them from their neighbors. But as the farming population rose, expanding communities gradually ate up virgin land.

Slash-and-burn cultivation worked well enough when the Maya farming population was small, but the crop yields were never sufficient to support large settlements. Nor could the stocks of surplus grain feed more than a handful of nonfarmers, such as stone ax makers or priests. However, until the last few centuries B.C., this simple farming system was the staple of an increasingly complex village society that flourished in a hot, low-lying environment with poor, shallow soils.

In 1972, geographer Albert Siemans and archaeologist Dennis Puleston used aerial photographs to study extensive tracts of wetlands in Mexico's southern Campeche (Fedick, 1996; Flannery, 1982). They identified irregular grids of gray lines in ladder, lattice, and curvilinear patterns, which turned out to be long-forgotten raised field systems. Most of them were narrow, rectangular plots elevated above the low-lying seasonally inundated land bordering rivers. The Siemans and Puleston research seemed to explain how village farmers had managed to build flourishing cities. The Maya started draining and canalizing swamps at least 2,000 years ago, turning agriculturally useless land into highly productive acreage as long as there was ample groundwater. They also began cultivating steep hillsides. The stone-walled terraces rise in serried rows, thereby trapping silt that would otherwise cascade down dry hillsides during torrential rainstorms. Like the heavily cultivated wetlands, the terrace systems were a sign of intensive farming that made use of every patch of fertile land. Some estimates placed the Maya population at between 8 and 10 million people in A.D. 800, a staggeringly high density for a tropical environment with such low natural carrying capacity.

There are no easy answers to how the Maya managed to support so many nonfarmers in a lowland tropical environment with only moderately fertile soils. Almost certainly, their agricultural systems were under severe stress as urban and rural populations rose during the first millennium A.D.

The Mesoamerican highlands (Figure 21.2) are highly diverse agricultural environments, as we have seen in the Tehuacán Valley (see Chapter 13). The earliest farming villages in the Valley of Oaxaca were concentrated in the valley floors, where water is within easy reach of the surface. Modern farmers choose similar villages for simple "pot" irrigation, where they plant their maize and other crops near small shallow wells. They simply dip pots into the wells and pour water from the shallow water table on the surrounding plants (Flannery, 1976). Flannery has argued that the Oaxacans used the same technique in prehistoric times, for it does not require large numbers of people. In time, as population densities rose, the Oaxacans were able to build on their simple and highly effective farming techniques, expanding onto slopes and into more arid lands with great success. Eventually, the economic power generated by these rising populations gave highland areas like this a decided edge.

A similar diversity of agricultural techniques is found in the Valley of Mexico, where a variety of slash-and-burn methods and irrigation agriculture were all in use. The farmers used both floodwaters and canals to bring water to dry gardens. The most famous of all raised-field techniques, however, is the *chinampa*, or "floating garden," method, a highly intensive and productive agricultural system based on the reclaiming of swamps. The farmers piled up natural vegetation and lake mud to form huge grids of naturally irrigated gardens. The *chinampas* were used very systematically to grow a variety of crops, so timed that different crops came into harvest throughout the year. This system is amazingly productive and is estimated to have supported approximately 100,000 people from 10,117 ha (25,000 acres) in 1519, the date of Spanish contact. Each *chinampa* produced large food surpluses that could be used to feed thousands of nonagricultural workers and specialists.

FIGURE 21.1 Native American Civilizations

Native American civilizations emerged in the Andes and Mesoamerica at more or less the same time. Mesoamerican civilization developed rapidly after 1200 B.C., culminating in the Maya civilization of the lowlands, and Teotihuacán, the Toltec, and the Aztec in the highlands. More complex societies appeared in coastal Peru after 3000 B.C. During the past 2,000 years, two poles of civilization flourished, one on the north coast of Peru, the other in the highlands around Lake Titicaca. The Inca unified them into a single vast empire, Tawantinsuyu, "the Land of the Four Quarters."

Andean civilization was renowned for its textiles, well-known from the Paracas cemetery on the coast. Many textiles depicted anthropomorphic beings and other aspects of religious iconography.

1000 km
1000 miles

intensive hunting and gathering

Teotihuacán developed rapidly from a series of small villages in 200 B.C. to the largest city in the Americas, with some 200,000 inhabitants, by A.D. 450. The city was an important religious center and prospered from the obsidian trade.

Mesoamerican civilization developed in both the lowlands and highlands, with the Maya achieving prominence in the Yucatán during the first millennium B.C. Although some Maya centers collapsed in the ninth century A.D., others flourished until the Spaniards arrived in 1519. On the highlands, the Toltec civilization briefly filled the political vacuum left by the collapse of Teotihuacán. The Aztecs dominated the Mesoamerican world only to decline rapidly in the face of Hernán Cortés and his conquistadors.

Andean civilization developed out of a period of experimentation and religious innovation that began on the Peruvian coast around 3000 B.C. A thousand years later, major religious centers flourished in coastal river valleys and new religious beliefs were developing at Chavín de Huantár in the Andes foothills. By 2,000 years ago, two poles of civilization had developed at opposite ends of the Andean world—on Peru's north coast and around Lake Titicaca. During the fourteenth and fifteenth centuries A.D., the Inca forged a vast empire out of the coastal and highland states that survived until the arrival of Spanish conquistadors and Francisco Pizarro in 1531.

TABLE 21.1
Mesoamerican civilizations and cultural developments elsewhere

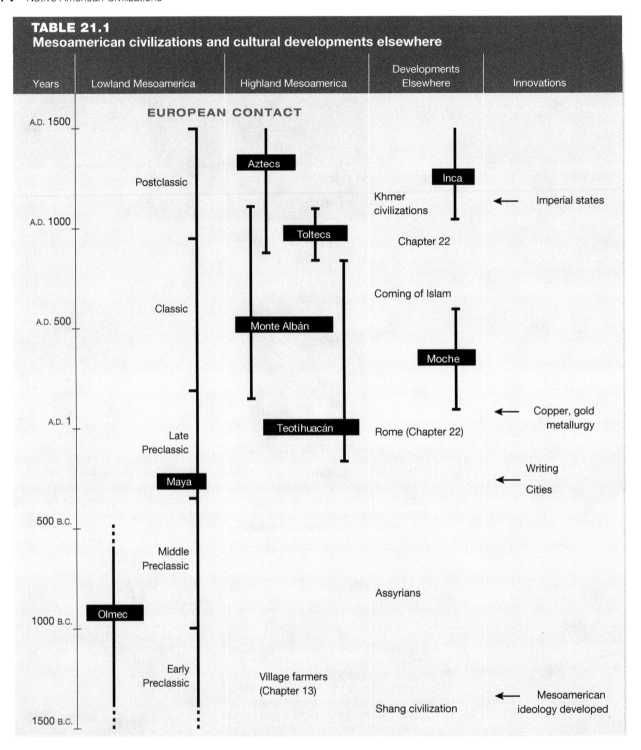

William Sanders and his colleagues (1970) argued that these *chinampas* could actually have supported approximately 180,000 people. That this highly effective agricultural system was the basis of early civilization and urban life in the Valley of Mexico is beyond question.

The agricultural system of the Valley of Mexico may seem complicated, but it supported and was part of a far more elaborate system of food marketing that provided not only tribute for taxes but also opportunities for the trading of special foodstuffs from one area of the highlands to another. The highland peoples relied on elaborate markets that were strictly regulated by the state and conducted on a barter system. The Valley of Mexico was an economic unit before Teotihuacán made it a political one as well. It was the great agricultural productivity of the valley and the sophisticated market economy of the emerging city that made the prodigious social and religious as well as material developments of later centuries possible. This economic system fostered the development of specialist crafts that were sold in the city markets and exported over wide areas.

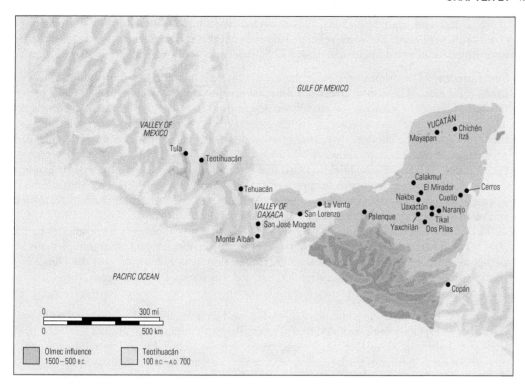

FIGURE 21.2 Mesoamerican archaeological sites mentioned in this chapter. Approximate distributions of two cultural traditions are shown.

Preclassic Peoples in Mesoamerica

Early Preclassic

Many centuries elapsed between the beginnings of village life and that of Mesoamerican civilization. By 2000 B.C., sedentary farming villages were common in most of Mesoamerica (S. Evans, 2008). The first signs of political and social complexity appear in many regions of Mesoamerica between about 1500 and 1000 B.C., during the early part of an era named the Preclassic or Formative by archaeologists, a period that lasted to as late as A.D. 250 in some areas. In many regions, small but often powerful chiefdoms appeared, headed by a chief and an elite. The elite dominated economic, political, and religious life and ruled over large general populations. A similar pattern of emerging social and political complexity has been documented in Mesopotamia, Egypt, China, and other areas where early state-organized societies evolved.

In Mesoamerica, as elsewhere, the new chiefdoms can be identified by differences in house designs, by the appearance of small shrines, by social rankings detectable through grave goods, and by prestigious as opposed to more utilitarian artifacts. This process is well documented at Cuello, in lowland northern Belize, which is radiocarbon-dated to between about 1200 B.C. and A.D. 400 (Hammond, 1991). The inhabitants of this site were maize farmers, who also relied heavily on wild plant foods; their meat came from wild deer and turtles and domestic dogs, killed and eaten after their first year of growth.

There was no one region where this emerging sociopolitical complexity occurred first. Rather, it was a development that took place more or less simultaneously in many regions of Mesoamerica, each region interacting with others (Pool, 2007). The most famous of these societies is that of the Olmec.

Middle Preclassic: The Olmec

The Olmec people ("rubber people," a name given them by the Aztecs because of the tribute they paid in this substance) lived on the Mexican southern Gulf Coast from about 1500 to 500 B.C. (Coe and Diehl, 1980; Diehl, 2005; Pool, 2007). The debate over their importance continues to unfold. There can be no question, however, that many Olmec ideas, artistic and architectural traditions, and religious beliefs were an integral part of later civilizations, which often remembered the Olmec with reverence.

The Olmec homeland is low-lying, tropical, and humid, with fertile soils. The swamps, lakes, and rivers are rich in fish, birds, and other animals. It was in this region that the Olmec created a highly distinctive art style, executed in sculpture and in relief. The artists concentrated on natural and supernatural beings, the dominant motif being the "were-jaguar," or humanlike jaguar. Many jaguars were given infantile faces, drooping lips, and large, swollen eyes, a style also applied to human figures, some

Early Preclassic
1500 to 1000 B.C.

Cuello
1200 B.C. to A.D. 400

Middle Preclassic
1000 to 400 B.C.
Olmec
1500 to 500 B.C.

of which resemble snarling demons. Olmec contributions to Mesoamerican art and religion were enormously significant. For years, scholars have believed that elements of their art style and imagery were diffused southward to Guatemala and El Salvador and northward into the Valley of Mexico.

San Lorenzo   The origins of the Olmec are a complete mystery, but the culture probably had strong local roots. The earliest traces of Olmec occupation are best documented at San Lorenzo in the Mexican state of Veracruz, where Olmec people lived on a platform in the midst of frequently inundated woodland plains. Around their platform, they erected ridges and mounds, on which they built groups of elaborate platforms, altars, and possibly ball courts (Figure 21.3). The earliest occupation of San Lorenzo shows few Olmec features, but by 1250 B.C., the inhabitants were beginning to build some raised fields, a task that required organized labor forces. By that time, too, distinctive Olmec sculpture began to appear. A century later, vast monumental carvings adorned San Lorenzo, human heads with bearing expressions of contempt and savagery (Figure 21.4), distinctive and often mutilated by the Olmec themselves, perhaps when rulers died.

San Lorenzo
1250 to 900 B.C.

The population of San Lorenzo may have numbered many thousands of people (J. E. Clark, 2007). The inhabitants enjoyed extensive trade, especially in obsidian and other semiprecious materials obtained from many parts of Mesoamerica; their pottery is widespread over the Olmec homeland. San Lorenzo fell into decline after 900 B.C. and was surpassed by La Venta, the most famous Olmec site, near the Gulf of Mexico.

La Venta
800 to 400 B.C.

La Venta   The La Venta ceremonial center was built on a small island in the middle of a swamp (Drucker, 1959; González Lauck, 1996). A rectangular earth mound, 120 m (393 feet) long by 70 m (229 feet) wide and 32 m (105 feet) high, dominates the island. Long, low mounds surround a rectangular plaza in front of the large mound, faced by walls and terraced mounds at the other end of the plaza. Vast monumental stone sculptures and altars litter the site, including some Olmec heads. Caches of jade objects, figurines, and a dull green rock (serpentine) are common, too. Every stone for sculptures and temples had to be brought from at least 96 km (60 miles) away, a vast undertaking, for some sculptured blocks weigh more than 40 tons. The people traded ceremonial jade and serpentine from as far away as Costa Rica. La Venta flourished for approximately 400 years from 800 B.C. After approximately 400 B.C., the site was probably destroyed; we deduce this occurrence from signs that many of its finest monuments were intentionally defaced.

San Lorenzo and La Venta, with their relatively small populations, are manifestations of a much more complex social and political order, not in the fashion of a state-organized society, as earlier scholars suggested, but a series of chiefdoms with powerful leaders who maintained contacts with other such societies in the lowlands and perhaps farther afield. For years, scholars thought of the Olmec as the "mother culture" of Mesoamerican civilization. Increasingly, however, this theory is being questioned.

FIGURE 21.3   Monumental Olmec head from San Lorenzo.

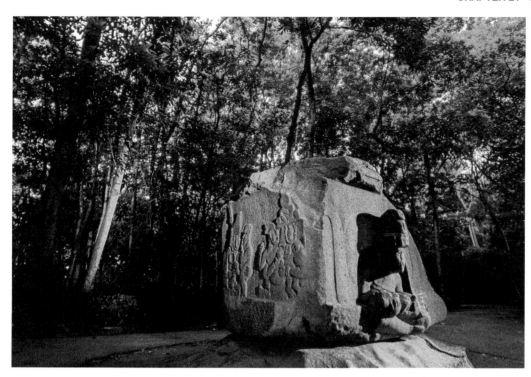

FIGURE 21.4 Olmec altar from La Venta, Mexico. A sculpted ruler emerges from a symbolic cave, a portal to the underworld.

Arthur Demarest (1989) points out that Olmec society changed over the centuries. At first, during the early Preclassic, it was a set of chiefdoms along the Gulf Coast of Veracruz and Tabasco that may have exercised some influence over adjacent areas of Chiapas and central Mexico. Later, during the middle Preclassic, Olmec society flourished during a period when art motifs, religious symbols, and ritual beliefs were shared by developing chiefdoms in many regions through the regular contacts between elites and day-to-day trade from region to region (for ancient Mexican religion, see M. Miller and Taube, 1993). It was what Demarest calls a "lattice of Middle Formative interaction" over many centuries that produced the complex and sophisticated traditions of Mesoamerican civilization that were to follow. Another archaeologist, Kent Reilly (1991) believes that Olmec kingship was antecedent to, and basically similar to, that of the lowland Maya.

Late Preclassic

The trajectory of rapid culture change continued in many regions during the late Preclassic (300 B.C. to A.D. 250). This was the period when a common religious system and ideology began to unify large areas of Mesoamerica. The leaders of the new orders validated their rule with elaborate public ceremonies in spectacular ceremonial centers, dedicated to potent and widely recognized deities. Distinctive art and architecture went with the new religion, the practice of which required precise measurements of calendar years and of longer cycles of time. Writing and mathematical calculations were developed to affirm religious practices, a unifying political force in the sense that they welded scattered village communities into larger political units. By the time the Classic Mesoamerican civilizations arose, dynasties of elites had been ruling parts of Mesoamerica along well-established lines for nearly 1,000 years (Sabloff, 1989).

The Rise of Complex Society in Oaxaca

The Preclassic cultures of the Valley of Oaxaca have been studied intensively by Kent Flannery, Joyce Marcus, and their students, using highly sophisticated systems approaches to document changing settlement patterns and economic and demographic trends (Marcus and Flannery, 1996). Something like 90 percent of the Preclassic Oaxaca villages were little more than hamlets of 50 to 60 people, and the remainder were much larger settlements of 1,000 to 1,200, with populations of priests and craftspeople.

The evolution of larger settlements in Oaxaca and elsewhere was closely connected with the development of long-distance trade in obsidian and other luxuries such as seashells and stingray spines from the Gulf of Mexico. The simple barter networks for obsidian of earlier times evolved into sophisticated regional trading organizations in which village leaders controlled monopolies over sources of obsidian and its distribution. Magnetite mirrors, seashells, feathers, and ceramics were all traded in the highlands, and from the highlands to the lowlands as well. Olmec pottery and other ritual objects began to appear in highland settlements between 1150 and 650 B.C., many of them bearing the distinctive were-jaguar motif of the lowlands, which had an important place in Olmec cosmology.

San José Mogote
1200 to 1150 B.C.

To Marcus and Flannery (1996), the defining moment in the Valley of Oaxaca was between 1200 and 1150 B.C., during the so-called San José phase, named after a large site, San José Mogote. They draw analogies between what happened in Oaxaca and a model for the emergence of ranked societies in Southeast Asian villages developed by anthropologist Jonathan Friedman (1979).

Friedman describes egalitarian villages composed of lineages of equal prestige, each community associated with a *nat*, or village spirit, the remote ancestor of all lineages who owns the village land. Originally, according to this model, all lineages share equal responsibility in sponsoring feasts and other community activities, but in time, one harder-working lineage acquires enough resources to become the permanent sponsor. Public opinion supports this move, for this particular lineage is seen as having an especially close association with the *nat*—indeed, as being directly descended from it. The leader of this lineage eventually becomes a hereditary ruler, who serves as a mediator between the community and the supernatural. Eventually, individual villages lose autonomy and become part of larger regional entities as the new rulers enter into alliances with neighbors and become associated with the highest ranks of celestial spirits, who control much larger areas.

Marcus and Flannery (1996) point out that what appear to be images of celestial ancestors of human lineages were carved on pottery from San José Mogote and contemporary villages (Figure 21.5, left). They believe that these images reflect an ancient belief in the power of Earth and Sky, which could express anger in the forms of earthquakes and lightning. Judging from male burials, Earth and Sky appear to be associated with male descent groups in some villages of the San José phase, some even with infant graves, as if such association and status were inherited. In burials and middens at San José Mogote itself, different residential areas appear to be associated with Earth and Sky. Finds of *nat* motifs on San José pottery, as well as on models of four-footed stools, later to become symbols of rulership, appear to confirm the appearance of social ranking and status by 1150 B.C.

Public buildings now appear in villages such as San José Mogote. Many of them were oriented 8° west of north; they were built on adobe and earth platforms. Conch shell trumpets and turtle shell drums from the Gulf of Mexico are associated with these buildings, as are clay figurines of dancers wearing costumes and masks (Figure 21.5, right). There were marine fish spines, too, probably used in personal bloodletting ceremonies that were still practiced even in Aztec times. The Spanish described how Aztec nobles would gash themselves with knives or with the spines of fish or stingrays in acts of mutilation before the gods, penances required of the devout (Saunders, 1989). The diffusion of common art styles throughout Mesoamerica may have resulted both because of an increased need for religious rituals to bring the various elements of society together and because a new Oaxacan elite, aspiring to the status of their chiefly neighbors, took to the new beliefs in slavish conformity.

Monte Albán

Monte Albán
400 B.C. to A.D. 700

By 400 B.C., at least seven small polities were in the Valley of Oaxaca, of which the one centered at the growing city of Monte Albán soon became dominant. Although massive population growth and increased economic power were among the interacting factors that aided in the rise of Monte Albán, its special terrain may have been vital in its ascendancy (Blanton et al., 1999; Marcus and Flannery, 1996).

Richard Blanton (1978) has surveyed more than 2,000 terraces on the slopes of Monte Albán, terraces used for agriculture and housing areas. Monte Albán commanded the best terrain in the valley, sloping land that was organized for agriculture and dense settlement by a population of several thousand people, far larger than that of most major settlements in Mesoamerica at the time. Even as early as 400 B.C., some of the terraces were in use by a highly organized population whose leaders resided in a ceremonial and civic center built on the summit of the Monte Albán ridge. Although the large-scale buildings of later times have contoured the summit beyond recognition, it is clear that the first leaders undertook major public works, many of them wood and thatch buildings that had incised sculptures of what may be dead and tortured enemies set into the walls.

Monte Albán went on to develop into a vast ceremonial center, with splendid public architecture, public buildings, terraces, and housing zones that extended over approximately 40 sq. km

FIGURE 21.5 Social ranking appears in the Valley of Oaxaca. Left, evolution of stylized lightning and earthquake motifs in pottery of the San José phase: Panels (a) to (c) show lightning as a realistic "fire serpent" and its stylization into a symbol found on a carved vessel; panels (d) to (f) show earthquake as a realistic "cleft-head" mask and a similar stylistic progression to a carved and incised vessel. Right, ritual scene composed of four clay figurines from San José Mogote, which may represent the burial of a high-status individual with three retainers; buried under an early Preclassic house at San José Mogote. Height of largest figurine: 16 cm (6 inches).

(15 sq. miles) (Figure 21.6). The more than 2,000 terraces each held one or two houses, and small ravines were dammed to pond valuable water supplies. Perhaps. 16,500 people lived at Monte Albán between A.D. 200 and 700. Many large villages and hamlets lay close to the city; the entire Valley of Oaxaca had about 115,000 inhabitants living in dispersed settlements (Marcus and Flannery, 1996). The enormous platforms on the ridge of Monte Albán supported complex layouts of temples and pyramid-temples, palaces, patios, and tombs. A hereditary elite seems to have ruled Monte Albán, the leaders of a state that had emerged in the Valley of Oaxaca by A.D. 200. Their religious power was based on ancestor worship, also a pantheon of at least 39 gods, grouped around major themes of ritual life. The rain god and lightning were associated with the jaguar motif; another group of deities was linked with the maize god, Pitao Cozabi. Nearly all these gods were still worshiped at the time of Spanish contact.

Monte Albán itself was abandoned after A.D. 700, even if many villages continued to flourish in the Valley of Oaxaca at about the same time as another great ceremonial center, Teotihuacán in the Valley of Mexico, began to decline.

Teotihuacán

We have already referred to the Valley of Mexico as an economic unit, a network of markets that probably flourished long before large states came into being in the highlands. Perhaps the sequence of events that led to the founding of such polities, especially Teotihuacán, began with the buildup of agricultural populations in diverse environments such as the Valley of Oaxaca in the first and second millennia B.C. This population growth led to the development of more intensive agricultural methods, including both irrigation and *chinampa* systems. At the same time, different areas were

Teotihuacán
200 B.C. to A.D. 700

FIGURE 21.6 Monte Albán, Valley of Oaxaca, a major Mesoamerican city that was a rival to Teotihuacán in the middle of the first millennium A.D.

linked by increasingly sophisticated trading networks and by an emerging market economy, perhaps with some specialized merchants.

The introduction of beliefs and sacred objects from the lowlands stimulated religious activity. Trade in exotic luxuries increased as ceremonial centers and stratified societies were founded. By 200 B.C., the effects of increased religious doings, intensified trading, and the production of huge food surpluses from the diverse environment had led to the founding of at least two major cities in the Valley of Mexico. One of these, Teotihuacán, reached an enormous size and enjoyed vast political, economic, and religious power in the centuries that followed. In the Valley of Oaxaca, Monte Albán achieved a similar dominance. The two great states probably maintained an uneasy alliance through regular diplomatic exchanges.

Teotihuacán lies northeast of Mexico City and is now one of the great archaeological tourist attractions of the world. It was one of the dominant political and cultural centers of all Mesoamerica in approximately A.D. 500, the culmination of centuries of vigorous cultural development in the Valley of Mexico (Berrin and Pasztory, 1994; Millon, Drewitt, and Cowgill, 1974; Pasztory, 1997; Storey, 1992). The first buildings appeared at Teotihuacán in approximately 200 B.C., making up a handful of villages, at least one of which may have specialized in obsidian manufacture. By 100 B.C., Teotihuacán had begun to expand rapidly, and the scattered villages became a settlement covering more than 9 sq. km (3.5 sq. miles). Much of this early settlement is overlain by the vast structures of later times. It is estimated that several thousand people inhabited this early town. There were several public buildings.

René Millon (1996), who carried out a systematic survey of Teotihuacán, found that by A.D. 150, the city extended over 13 sq. km (5 sq. miles) and housed more than 20,000 people. Obsidian trade and manufacture were expanding fast. There were two major religious complexes for which, among other structures, the Pyramids of the Sun and of the Moon were first built at this time.

Between A.D. 150 and 600, Teotihuacán exploded in size. Anyone traversing the Valley of Mexico had to pass through the city, with its diverse population of priests, merchants, craftspeople, and other specialists. The rulers of the city erected hundreds of standardized apartment complexes and continued a master plan that laid out the city on a north–south axis, centered on the Street of the Dead (Figure 21.7), with another great avenue oriented east–west. The city consisted of avenues and plazas, markets, temples, palaces, apartment buildings, and complex drainage and agricultural works. The entire city was dominated by the Pyramid of the Sun, a vast structure of earth, adobe, and piled rubble. The pyramid, faced with stone, is 64 m (210 feet) high and 1098 m (650 feet) square. A wooden temple probably sat on the summit of the terraced pyramid. The long Street of the Dead passes the west face of the pyramid, leading to the Pyramid of the Moon, the second largest structure at the site. The avenue is lined with civic, palace, and religious buildings, and the side streets lead to residential areas. A large palace and temple complex dedicated to the Plumed Serpent (Quetzalcoatl), with platform and stairways around the central court, lies south of the middle of Teotihuacán, across from a central marketplace. More than 200 burials of sacrificial victims wearing warrior's apparel lie inside (Sugiyama, 2005) (Figure 21.8a and b).

The Street of the Dead and the pyramids lie amid a sprawling mass of small houses. Priests and craftsworkers lived in dwellings around small courtyards; the less privileged lived in large compounds of rooms connected by narrow alleyways and patios. By any standard, Teotihuacán was a city, and it once housed up to 120,000 people. Although some farmers probably lived within the city, we know that rural villages flourished nearby. These were compact, expertly planned, and administered by city rulers. In contrast to Monte Albán, much of the population lived in humble dwellings or apartments within the city limits.

The comprehensive settlement-pattern data from the Millon survey enable us to say something about the structure of Teotihuacán society. Farmers living in the city and in satellite villages produced the food surpluses that supported the city. Tribute from neighboring states also helped feed the city, and control of large areas of the plateau ensured that adequate food supplies would come to Teotihuacán's huge market. It is not known how significant *chinampa* agriculture was for Teotihuacán, but irrigation farming was a key element in subsistence. Craftspeople accounted for perhaps 25 percent of the urban population; they lived in compounds of apartments near the more than 500 workshops, which produced everything from obsidian tools to clay vessels.

Merchants were probably a major class in the city, as were civil servants, who carried out the routine administration of Teotihuacán. There were even foreign quarters, one of which housed Oaxacans and another, people from Veracruz in the lowlands (Paddock, 1983; Price, Manzanilla, and Middleton, 2000). The elite included priests, warriors, and secular leaders, who controlled the vast city and its many dealings through a strict class society. Religious beliefs continued the rituals of earlier times, but it appears that human sacrifice became increasingly prominent in later centuries as the leaders of the city became more and more militaristic, a trend that was to continue into Aztec times.

Teotihuacán ruled the Valley of Mexico and parts of Puebla, but its influence through alliance, tribute, and warfare, as well as trading, extended over a far larger area of Mesoamerica. As in later times, the rulers of Teotihuacán probably controlled some highly strategic and economically significant zones, but there were large areas where their influence was minimal. In the final

FIGURE 21.7 Teotihuacán, looking down from the Pyramid of the Moon along the Street of the Dead.

(a)

(b)

FIGURE 21.8   (a) Plan of the major public buildings at Teotihuacán. (b) Façade of the Temple of Quetzalcoatl at Teotihuacán, Mexico, showing the head of the rain god Tlaloc.

analysis, Teotihuacán was probably a huge city-state bound to other city-states by uneasy alliances and tribute exchanges.

By A.D. 500, a secular ruler probably governed Teotihuacán, probably a divine king of some kind. A class of nobles controlled the kinship groups that organized the bulk of the city's huge population. In approximately A.D. 500–550, Teotihuacán was deliberately burned down, perhaps as a result of internal revolt and outside intervention (Millon, 1988). The very success of Teotihuacán may have accelerated its downfall. The new orders of society and politics spawned by the city may have been copied by other leaders, perhaps more aggressive and less tradition-bound than those of the mother city. No one knows exactly why this great city collapsed so suddenly. Its rapid development may have resulted in serious internal weaknesses that made Teotihuacán vulnerable to easy overthrow. A drought may also have weakened the city and provided an opportunity for jealous rivals to attempt an attack. Whatever the precise cause, by A.D. 700, the city's population had dropped sharply, although as many as 30,000 to 40,000 people lived around the old ceremonial precincts. Even as late as the sixteenth century, Teotihuacán was a city-state with a ruler and had as many as 10,000 subjects. The city remained a place of pilgrimage and sacred association right into Aztec times more than 600 years later. Indeed, the Aztecs believed that their world was created there, atop the Pyramid of the Sun.

Regardless of why Teotihuacán collapsed, its heyday marks the moment when one can begin to think of the Mesoamerican world in more than purely local, or even regional, terms. Teotihuacán's political and social influence was considerable, and its traders ventured to many parts of the highlands and lowlands. For example, the ways in which Maya kings went to war were greatly influenced by the military practices and war-making rituals of Teotihuacán. The greatest legacy of Teotihuacán was not merely its cosmology, ideology, and trade networks, but a new interconnectedness among the many societies of prehistoric Mesoamerica.

Joyce Marcus (1976) points to the remarkable similarity in the ways in which Mesoamerican states rose, reached their peak, and then collapsed. She notes a consistent scenario in both the lowlands and the highlands, not only in Maya civilization but at Monte Albán and Teotihuacán and in the Toltec and Aztec civilizations in the highlands: First, a new city-state—say, Maya Tikal or Teotihuacán—expanded its territory through diplomacy, political marriages, and military conquest. This new city-state reached its maximum territorial limits early in its history. Then, once some provinces had reached a significant level of cultural complexity and development, they broke away from their nominal master and became independent polities. Far from being weakened, the core city-state still prospered, investing its energy and resources in its own local area rather than in expansion. But sometimes the old provinces, now independent states, would ally themselves against their former overlord and conquer it, so that it then became a subordinate center. This cycle of rise, expansion on the margins, fissioning, and then decline repeated itself again and again, to the point where it can be considered a consistent pattern of Mesoamerican civilization.

Maya Civilization

The Maya civilization is the best known of all early American civilizations, one that has excited the imagination of scholars for more than a century. It took shape in lowland rain forest areas that provided a highly varied environment in which people grew maize and other crops and harvested trees, such as the ramon.

Maya civilization
Before 300 B.C. to A.D. 1519

Maya Origins

Although the ultimate roots of Maya culture go back far into the Preclassic period, considerable debate surrounds the origins of Maya civilization, partly because until recently virtually nothing was known about Maya subsistence patterns (Coe, 2011; S. Evans, 2008). Perhaps the initial Maya settlement was dispersed, with villages scattered throughout the rain forest, in situations that seemed to militate against political or economic unity. The people thrived in a fundamentally empty landscape where there was plenty of room for slash-and-burn agriculture and little incentive for cooperation. Their predecessors were hunter-gatherers, small groups occupying tiny campsites, who made no pottery. One such Archaic camp is known from the Colha site in Belize, in a level overlaid by farming occupation that dates to later than 900 B.C. (Hester et al., 1982). Early farming settlement at Cuello dates to the late second millennium B.C. (Hammond, 1991). It is not known whether the Colha and Cuello sites represent the changeover from hunting and gathering to farming in this part of the lowlands, but a date of around 1500 to 1200 B.C. would not be unexpected.

The earliest certain Maya communities come from the middle Preclassic (1000 to 400 B.C.). During this period, large numbers of farmers moved into the lowlands, bringing with them settled village life, the use of fine clay vessels, and domesticated plants. The Maya were well established in the Yucatán by 800 B.C., and they were constructing massive pyramids at several sites in the central Petén by 600 B.C. No one has yet accounted for this rapid buildup, but there are reasons to suspect that it was connected with a growing demand for such lowland products as honey and salt by elites elsewhere. A growing volume of long-distance exchange contributed, then, to an efflorescence of indigenous lowland civilization within a few centuries.

At the same time, ancestral burial within platforms and the cores of other structures took hold as a persistent pattern of internment, as opposed to merely burying people under their houses. This changeover represented the sanctification of an ancestral place, where ancestors were venerated, as a basis for reckoning genealogy and claiming ownership of places. In other words, ancestor veneration was a way of structuring the inheritance of property and resources from one generation to the next (see a discussion in McAnany, 1995).

Between 600 and 400 B.C., the middle Preclassic inhabitants of Nakbe were constructing elaborate complexes of finely finished stone buildings that stood on huge platforms (Coe, 2011). Within

Nakbe
600 to 400 B.C.

a few centuries, they began erecting carved stelae (stone uprights) that are thought to depict the center's rulers. Certainly by late Preclassic times, the lords of Nakbe were commissioning for their pyramids beautiful masonry and plaster masks of the gods and ancestors. These façades seem to relate directly to the emerging notion of divine kingship, *Ch'ul Ahau*, in Maya civilization—a form of kingship that between 600 and 100 B.C. developed rapidly out of some earlier form of central authority (Freidel and Schele, 1988). Another site of the same general antiquity, Uaxactún, has yielded images of kings with deity masks wearing the Jester God crown of kingship.

El Mirador
150 B.C. to A.D. 50

By far the largest Preclassic Maya center was El Mirador, which was built between about 150 B.C. and A.D. 50. El Mirador covered about 16 sq. km (6 sq. miles), lying on low, undulating land; parts of the area were flooded during the rainy season. The scale of El Mirador is vast, and it bears all the complicated iconography associated with Maya kingship. Archaeologists from Brigham Young University have uncovered more than 200 structures; among them are great complexes of pyramids, plazas, causeways, and buildings (Estrada-Belli, 2010; Sabloff, 1990).

The Danta Pyramid at the east end of the site dominates El Mirador. It rises from a natural hill more than 70 m (210 feet) high. The western face of the hill is sculpted into large platforms that are surmounted by buildings and temples. A little over 2 km (1 mile) west rises the Tigre complex, a pyramid 55 m (182 feet) high surrounded by a plaza, a small temple, and several smaller buildings (Figure 21.9). The Tigre complex covers about 58,000 sq. m (624,000 sq. feet), an area a little larger than the base of Teotihuacán's Pyramid of the Sun. Three buildings, the largest in the center, are on a truncated landing on the pyramid. This "triad" theme is also found at later sites, such as Tikal.

(a)

(b)

FIGURE 21.9 The difficulties of Maya archaeology. (a) El Mirador is mantled in thick forest cover. (b) A temple complex exposed during excavations.

El Mirador is unique because it was not altered in any significant way after the Preclassic period. As excavations proceed, it should be possible to compare Preclassic with Classic occupation and to study the evolution of Maya architecture, city planning, and social and political organization. El Mirador is yielding some of the earliest examples of Maya writing. They appear on an inscribed pot fragment, and some symbols are inscribed on the Tigre sculpture.

El Mirador itself was an elaborate city and was probably controlled by a highly organized elite. They used artisans, priests, architects, and engineers, as well as traders and thousands of unskilled villagers. The Preclassic was the time when the Maya began modifying the landscape on a massive scale. They moved millions of cubic meters of soil to create reservoirs and canals. El Mirador lay in a depressed zone, where water could be trapped for later use during the dry season. By this time, reservoirs and other water storage systems were in common use in a society that was well aware of the need to plan for drought years. All these public works, and the construction of increasingly elaborate temples and palaces, led to an increasingly stratified society, where the elite distanced themselves from the commoners and competed with one another through diplomatic exchanges, gift giving, and long-distance exchange. Conspicuous consumption, the need to justify one's rule, and good, old-fashioned one-upmanship all played their parts in elaborating Maya society.

The great Preclassic city flourished successfully for centuries before it suddenly collapsed in the early Christian era. By A.D. 250, the cities in the Mirador Basin had suffered through a traumatic decline, fully as disastrous as that which decimated the southern Maya centers centuries later. The volatility of many centers may have been connected to endemic warfare, but despite this constant change, many centers, among them Tikal and Uaxactún, developed continuously into Classic times.

In 50 B.C., the small late Preclassic town of Cerros, on the eastern coast of the Yucatán, housed fisherfolk and traders. Within two generations, this tiny community transformed itself into a large center. The village disappeared under plazas and temples, deliberately abandoned in favor of houses erected around the new sacred center. The unknown leaders of Cerros built their new temple according to pyramid designs that had developed among earlier peoples like the Olmec, designs that invoked a symbolic landscape in which religious activity took place (Schele and Freidel, 1990). The ruler, the *ajaw*, ascended the pyramid, passing between stucco sculptures of the Sun and the planet Venus and of the mythic Hero Twins, who battled unfriendly gods in the underworld and rescued their father the Maize God, the source of human life.

Cerros
50 B.C.

The *ajaw* was the intermediary to the spiritual world, supported by the commoners, while everyone in the community shared in the communal labor of building the sacred mountain, a gateway to the Otherworld that was very important in Maya religion. It was a symbolic act that acknowledged the arrival of kingship in the community. The first temple at Cerros was followed by later shrines, the settings for the ritual bloodlettings and sacrifices that served to legitimize the roles of the emerging nobility and of the leader. Kingship flourished at Cerros for a short time and then collapsed for reasons that are still a mystery. Perhaps there were problems in transferring power from one generation to the next, or perhaps the experiment simply failed, as it did in other Maya communities of the day. In any event, the great temples fell into disuse, but people still lived around the ruined structures, living off fishing and trade.

Water Management

The Classic centuries of Maya civilization saw new adaptations to the challenging lowland environment. Many communities now lay at the summits of hillocks and ridges so that the quarries at their base, used to build pyramids and other structures, became large reservoirs surrounded by artificial hills and plazas that were catchment pavements to funnel water into them. With brilliant ingenuity, Maya architects built gravity canals that released water from the elevated central reservoir system into tanks and surrounding irrigation systems.

These elaborate water management systems developed over many centuries, based on what Vernon Scarborough (2000) calls "microwatersheds" to make up for rainfall deficiencies. But there were severe constraints. Such systems could only serve small areas; rainfall fluctuated from year to year, making controlled release of water difficult to achieve.

Over centuries, Maya farmers slowly created a highly engineered infrastructure that became increasingly productive over time. Everything was slow and deliberate, set in a social and political context that accommodated the realities of a fragile tropical environment. The Maya were successful because they spent many centuries learning how to farm this environment. They worked successfully within environmental limitations they had learned the hard way, kept their villages dispersed, and developed a level of interdependency that reflected the uneven distribution of soils and food resources across the landscape. As long as this system worked well, they were relatively immune to climatic stress. It was no coincidence that Maya civilization developed as a mosaic of much smaller city-states, each centered on microwatersheds, which gave it a flexibility and resilience to short-term climatic events that endured for many centuries.

As populations rose, especially on the outskirts of cities, the Maya expanded the scope of their agriculture. As early as the first century A.D., they began draining and canalizing swamps, turning hitherto unfarmable lands into grids of raised field systems elevated above low-lying, seasonally inundated land that bordered rivers. As populations climbed even further, the Maya began terracing steep hillsides to trap silt that cascaded downslope during heavy rainstorms.

By A.D. 800, perhaps 8 million to 10 million Maya lived in the lowlands, a staggeringly high density for a tropical environment with low natural carrying capacity.

Kingship: Sacred Space and Time

The leaders of Cerros and other Preclassic Maya communities are now anonymous. They left no record of their names or personal histories. Their only legacy to their successors was a distinctive architectural heritage that stressed social ranking and the use of large-scale structures to perpetuate royal dynasties. The rituals performed by these shaman-lords took place on the pyramids and in the plazas of the great Maya centers, which were symbolic replicas of the sacred landscape created by the gods at the beginning of the world. The architecture of the great ritual structures replicated forests, mountains, and caves as stelae, pyramids, and temple openings. The rituals were powerful, so powerful that the places where they were conducted became more and more sacred as successive rulers built new temples on the same spots. Generations of rulers replicated the iconography and sculpture of earlier buildings, elaborating on them to produce the sacred settings within which the strategies of political competition between neighbors were carried out (Miller and Taube, 1993). A solitary painted mural from San Bartolo, a small site in the Petén 42 km (25 miles) northeast of Tikal, shows how the cosmic view and legends of later times were already in being. The mural depicts the Maize God being offered tamales and water after his resurrection.

Maya civilization was also embedded in a matrix of unfolding cyclic time. Maya priests used the movements of planets and stars to mark the passage of time. They tried to understand the cycles of the cosmos, deciding which days were propitious for ritual, trade, royal marriages, war, and so on. Religious events were regulated according to a sacred year (*tzolkin*) with 13 months of 20 days each (see Figure 21.10a and b). The 260 days of the sacred year were unrelated to any astronomical phenomenon, being closely tied to ritual and divination. The length of this year was arbitrary and had probably been established by long tradition. *Tzolkins* were, however, closely intermeshed with a secular year (*haab*) of 365 days, an astronomical calendar based on the solar cycle. The *haab* was used to regulate state affairs, but the connections between sacred and secular years were of great significance in Maya life. Every 52 years, a complete cycle of all the variations of the day and month names of the two calendars occurred, an occasion for intense religious activity.

| (a) | (b) |

FIGURE 21.10 The Maya calendar. (a) A Venus calendar depicted on stone tablets with glyphs, mythological figures, warriors, and gods. (b) The Maya calendar comprised two interlocking cycles. The left wheel is the 260-day *tzolkin*, the sacred calendar with 13 numbers (inner wheel) and 20 day names (outer wheel). The right-hand wheel is the *haab*, or secular cycle, with 20 months of 18 days each.

FIGURE 21.11 Maya glyphs. Left, the Leiden Plate, a jade plaque that shows a Maya lord trampling a captive underfoot. Right, the reverse side shows the Long Count (the Maya count of years) date in glyphs: 8.14.3.1.12, a day in the year A.D. 320. Height: 21.6 cm (8.5 inches).

The calendar was vital to Maya life, for the complex geography of sacred time helped determine political strategies and social moves. The records kept by Maya scribes in hieroglyphic codices (books) were incredibly intricate records of divine actions on each day of the cyclic calendar (Figure 21.10a). Each day had a character, a distinctive identity in the *tzolkin* and *haab*, and a position in all the permutations of cyclic time (Figure 21.10b). Each Maya king developed a relationship to this constantly moving time scale. Some events, like planting and harvest, were regular events on the calendar. Others, like dates of accession, important victories, and royal deaths and births, left their marks on the calendar, sometimes as days that assumed great significance in the history of an individual dynasty. Maya rulers linked their actions to those of the gods and the ancestors, sometimes legitimizing their descent by claiming that it reenacted mythical events. Maya history was linked to the present and the Otherworld, to the legendary Olmec civilization of the past. Society was embedded in a matrix of sacred place and time (Schele and Freidel, 1990; Schele, Freidel, and Parker, 1993).

The Maya developed a hieroglyphic script for calculating calendars and regulating religious observances (Coe, 1999). The script was also much used to record genealogies, king lists, conquests, and dynastic histories. The symbols are fantastically grotesque, consisting mostly of humans, monsters, or gods' heads (Figure 21.11). After more than a decade of intensive research, over 80 percent of the extant Classic inscriptions have been deciphered. In its emphasis on religious and cosmological matters, Maya writing is closest to ancient Egyptian script in terms of its role in society.

These hieroglyphic records were of cardinal importance in Maya life, for the institution of kingship was based on the principle that the royal crown passed from father to son, or brother to brother to son, in a line that led back to a founding ancestor. From there, families and clans were carefully ranked by their distance from the central royal descent line. This system of family ranking and allegiance was the basis of political power, a system that worked well but that depended on a careful documentation of genealogies.

The Maya prized social status above almost everything else, as we can see at the great center of Copán, a major frontier capital of the Maya world at the edge of the Central American chiefdoms. Its pyramids, temples, and stelae are a remarkable record of Maya kings exercising political and social power. Although cosmology was a feature of Copán's building designs, the main function of the civic structures there, as elsewhere, was to commemorate major events in the lives of kings and the political histories of kingdoms. Each building was dedicated by the king who built it in the context of a specific event, everything from a royal accession to an important victory or a new alliance. Among its many buildings, Copán features a ball court, a stadium used for an elaborate ceremonial contest in which sacrificial victims and kings descended through a symbolic "abyss" into the Otherworld. The players wore protective padding and used a rubber ball, which perhaps they aimed at markers—sometimes stone rings or macaw heads high on the side walls. We do not know the rules of this ball game, but the games were associated with human sacrifice and much pomp and circumstance (see chapter opening illustration, "A reconstruction of a Maya ball game, Copán, Honduras").

By combining archaeological excavation at Copán with historical art interpretation and text translations, scholars have been able to trace a lineage of nobles who specialized in hieroglyphic writing, a skill that gave them special prestige (Fash, 1991). Members of another noble rank, the *sahalob* (vassals), served as expert administrators and received many privileges for their skill. Status was inherited and was one way in which the legitimacy of society as a whole was maintained.

Copán is just one of many sites where archaeologists have documented the complicated political and social history of Maya civilization. The public monuments erected by the Classic Maya emphasize not only the king's role as shaman, as the intermediary with the Otherworld, but also his position as family patriarch. Genealogical texts on stelae legitimized his descent, his close relationship to his often long-deceased parents. Maya kings used both the awesome regalia of their office and elaborate rituals to stress their close identity with mythical ancestral gods. This was a way in which the kings asserted their kin relationship to and political authority over subordinate leaders and every member of society.

The king believed himself to have a divine covenant with the gods and ancestors, a covenant that was reinforced again and again in elaborate private and public rituals. The ruler was often depicted as the World Tree, the conduit by which humans communicated with the Otherworld. Trees were the living environment of Maya life and a metaphor for human power. So the kings of the Maya were a forest of symbolic human World Trees within a natural forested landscape.

The Maya calendar ensured a constant round of ceremonies and rituals at the great ceremonial centers erected by the labor of hundreds of people, farmers who also fed the kings, priests, and artisans. Yet the Maya worldview created serious and binding obligations among the king and his nobility and all the people, reflected in the king's responsibilities in gathering and redistributing commodities of all kinds and in implementing agricultural schemes that turned swamps into organized, productive landscapes. The lives of Maya rulers and all their subjects were interconnected in vital, dynamic ways. The king was state shaman, the individual who enriched everyone's life in spiritual and ceremonial ways. His success in organizing trade and agriculture gave all levels of society access to goods and commodities. The great ceremonial centers built by Maya leaders created a setting in which elaborate rituals and ceremonies took on intense significance. The "histories written and pictured by the kings on the tree stones standing before human-made mountains gave form to time and space in both the material and spiritual worlds" (Schele and Freidel, 1990: 319).

Political Organization

Maya civilization was far from uniform. It appears to have been a mosaic of political units, large and small, and it is difficult to be specific about the political relationships among Maya settlements, divided as the people were into many small and multicenter polities (Martin and Grube, 2000). One possible approach is through the identification of "emblem glyphs," titles that were carried by kings and their highest nobility in the major kingdoms. The emblem glyph of Palenque was *Ch'ul Bac Ahaw* ("Holy Bone Lord"), and that of Tikal was *Mutul* ("tied bundle" or "tied flower"), depicting a man's hair topknot seen from the rear. The emblem glyphs can be taken as statements of political affiliation with particular kingdoms, for subordinate centers would sometimes use their overlord's glyph. They would identify political control over a territory by stating that events occurred *u cab* ("in the land of") (Culbert, 1991).

Many Mayanists have thought of Maya civilization in terms of small competing kingdoms. But Joyce Marcus (1993) has studied Maya political territoriality using a combination of epigraphy (the study of inscriptions), iconography, and settlement patterns, assuming that site emblem glyphs and their distributions would reflect the structure and ranking of ceremonial centers. She has developed a general scenario for Maya political history and organization that envisages four major city-states during the Classic period, rather than dozens of smaller polities, as follows: Between

A.D. 292 to 434   A.D. 292 and 434, there were no regional capitals, no well-defined hierarchy of settlement, and different monument styles in the various regions of the Maya homeland. Most centers were, on average, about 27 km (18 miles) apart, apparently autonomous and competitive and of roughly equal rank. Tikal and Uaxactún appear to have been the earliest dominant centers. By A.D. 514 to 534, a standardized symbolic system was being used at monuments at even the most dispersed Maya centers. There were now four regional capitals, each with its own emblem glyph and each ruling over a well-defined hierarchy of lesser settlements, an arrangement suggesting a form of pyramidical state dominated by a few ruling dynasties. A hieroglyphic text of A.D. 731 from Copán, perhaps a biased source, lists these four capitals: Tikal, Palenque, Calakmul, and Copán.

Marcus believes that the Maya capitals enjoyed some form of military alliance between A.D. 672 and 751. The ruler of each communicated with his neighbors of equal rank, a situation reflected by the adoption of a uniform lunar calendar and a homogeneous style and iconography of monuments. Within each region, the ruler achieved integration by strategic marriage alliances with ruling families from lesser, dependent centers—between, for example, Palenque and nearby Yaxchilán. But these arrangements did not last long. After A.D. 830 to 909, over 60 percent of all monuments were erected at what had previously been lesser centers, as if the authority of the original capitals had been replaced by more appropriate mechanisms for governing smaller, more dispersed populations. This changeover coincides with the so-called Maya collapse (see next section).

The Marcus scenario was developed at a time when Maya glyphs were less well understood than they are today and may not reflect true political reality. There were other major centers than the

Caracol
900 B.C. to A.D. 800   great four, some of which have only been excavated in recent years. Caracol in Belize is a case in point. Another important Maya center, Caracol started as a few hamlets in 900 B.C., but became a

growing city by the first century A.D. (Chase and Chase, 1996). Caracol's rulers engaged in widespread trading in jadeite and other materials. During the sixth century, Caracol embarked on military campaigns throughout the southern lowlands. Lord *Yahaw Te K'inich* ("Lord Water") defeated Tikal in A.D. 562. The city was now a major political player. Its rulers developed strategic alliances with other states, among them Calakmul to the north. Caracol's population swelled from about 19,000 to more than 120,000, larger than either Calakmul or Tikal, the people fed by elaborate complexes of terraced fields and reservoirs. This was a period of major building activity, including roads that connected the city to outlying settlements and allowed rapid deployment of the army. Caracol was a prosperous state, apparently marked by much closer social integration than other polities such as Tikal. There is clear evidence of a flourishing middle class who enjoyed many luxury goods, found in their burials (Chase, 1996). The city began to lose population after A.D. 800. Much of Caracol was burned a century later as the fabric of the state collapsed.

There were many elements common to all Maya polities, among them the calendar and the hieroglyphic script, essential to the regulation of religious life and the worship of the gods. Architectural and artistic styles in ceramics and small artifacts varied from center to center as each developed its own characteristics and cultural traditions (Coe, 2011). Religion unified the Maya more than political or economic interests, in much the same way, perhaps, as the spread of Islam unified diverse cultures.

The political mechanisms used by the Maya included warfare, which had strong ritual overtones and was probably very destructive. It may have been aimed more at economic hegemony than territorial expansion. Much art and many inscriptions concentrate on the ceremonial and ideological aspects of war—the capture and sacrifice of prisoners as a way of validating political authority (Schele and Miller, 1992). Whether this was the primary purpose of going to war is uncertain. However, judging from emblem glyphs, most wars were between immediate neighbors, the capture and sacrifice of a ruler sometimes leading to the dominance of one capital by another for generations but at other times apparently having little effect. The inscriptions tell us that visits by rulers or their representatives to other capitals were important occurrences, usually to commemorate significant political events, such as an accession or when a ruler designated his heir (Schele and Mathews, 1991). At the core of all these diplomatic and military maneuvers were ongoing rivalries between powerful noble families, which endured over many centuries. For example, the Jaguar Claw clan seems to have risen to prominence at Preclassic El Mirador, then spread its influence to Tikal, Caracol, and ultimately to Dos Pilas. Much of Maya warfare was more between factions of powerful clans than between different clans.

Classic and Late Classic Maya Political History

With this general scenario in mind, one can lay out the beginnings of a narrative of Maya political history from as early as the third century A.D. (Coe, 2011; Sabloff and Henderson, 1993; Schele and Freidel, 1990). With constant new discoveries and decipherments, the snapshots given here, based on individual site histories, give, necessarily, an incomplete picture.

Tikal and Uaxactún Cerros and El Mirador were major centers during the late Preclassic, but even as they prospered, new centers were emerging a short distance away. Tikal and Uaxactún were growing during the late Preclassic and stepped into the political vacuum left by the decline of El Mirador. The two centers were less than 20 km (12 miles) apart, too close for bitter rivals to coexist. Tikal rose in a strategic position atop some low hills, where extensive chert deposits occur. Nearby seasonal swamps may have provided a basis for intensive agriculture and some protection against sudden attack. The growing settlement also sat astride a critical river portage between water systems that carried trade goods from east to west across the Maya lowlands. Important trade routes to highland cities like Teotihuacán also passed through Tikal. At the same time, Tikal had powerful supernatural associations as the current seat of one of the oldest royal dynasties in the region.

Tikal
first century A.D. to A.D. 800

Tikal had expanded greatly during the first century as large public buildings rose on the foundations of earlier, more humble structures (P. Harrison, 1999). Clearly, the intent was to rival, and outdo, El Mirador's splendor. During this century an elite emerged at Tikal, people represented by the burial of a noblewoman under a shrine and tomb paintings of richly decorated nobles. One burial contained a headless and thighless corpse tied up in a bundle, with a green fucsite portrait head that had once been the chest pectoral of the deceased. The human face on the pectoral wears the Jester God headdress that kings wore for centuries afterward. Uaxactún, just to the north, underwent a similar transition during the same century. Here, Preclassic temples bear stucco masks and façades that depict the Maya world and the king who built the structures. At both Tikal and Uaxactún, Maya kings memorialized themselves on their temples, but the two centers were political and economic equals during this century (Figure 21.12).

The earliest recorded monarch is Yax Ehb Xook ("First Scaffold Shark"), who is thought to have reigned around A.D. 200, although the city had a long and much earlier history. On January 14,

FIGURE 21.12 The central precincts of Tikal.

378, militaristic strangers "from the west" arrived at Tikal, just as the city's then-ruler Chak Tok Ich'aak I ("Jaguar Paw") "entered the water" [the watery Underworld]. Most likely, they fought the city and conquered it. A year later a new ruler, Yak Nuun Ahiin ("First Crocodile"), became king, under the sponsorship of the leader of the strangers, Sihyaj K'ahk' ("Fire Is Born"). This new *ajaw*, but 13 years old when he ascended to the throne, was of Teotihuacán descent, perhaps even the son of the lord of that great city. During his reign, strong influences from Teotihuacán on the highlands appear—architectural style and highland pottery styles and green obsidian from the city's closely controlled sources. Eventually, these distinctive features were swamped by the indigenous culture, but the militarism remained (Stuart, 2001). A tradition of Teotihuacano overlordship flourished in the Tikal–Uaxactún region until the sixth century. But throughout later Maya history, the glories of Teotihuacán remained in the minds of the lowland's great lords as they fought military campaigns and went to battle attired like warriors from the great city (Coe, 2011).

Uaxactún
first century A.D. to A.D. 800

Tikal's hieroglyphic texts identify 31 rulers (18 known by name) after the founder, the earliest dating to A.D. 292, the last known one to A.D. 869, making for 669 years of recorded history. Uaxactún also fostered a powerful royal dynasty, whose monuments, like those of the Tikal kings, soon depicted rulers with sacrificial victims cowering at their feet, noble victims taken in hand-to-hand combat for later sacrifice in public rituals. These portraits signal a crucial development in Maya history: the increasing role of warfare and campaigns of deliberate conquest. Tikal attacked and subdued nearby Uaxactún (see a discussion, including unpublished primary references, in P. Harrison, 1999). The war was associated with new rituals first developed at Teotihuacán in the highlands that linked the rain god Tlaloc and the planet Venus. Tikal's military expansion took place during a period of regular trading contacts between the great highland city and many Maya centers, marked by many finds of the distinctive green obsidian mined in the Basin of Mexico. The same contacts may have brought new philosophies of war and conquest and the rituals associated with them. These rituals were to become part of the Mesoamerican religious tradition for centuries (Figure 21.13).

Tikal's royal dynasty prospered in the coming centuries. It eventually headed a multicenter polity, extending its influence by conquest and long-distance trade and by judicious political marriages that gave neighboring rulers maternal kin ties to the center. At the height of its powers, Tikal's territory may have supported an estimated population of as many as 300,000 people, the city and its immediate hinterland perhaps 200,000; however, these are perhaps high estimates.

In about A.D. 557, Tikal went into decline after its defeat by the lord of a new rising state, Caracol, then prospered anew during the late Classic.

Calakmul
first century A.D. to A.D. 820

Calakmul and Caracol Caracol, which lies in south-central Belize, 70 km (43 miles) southeast of Tikal, controlled important crystalline rock supplies and was an important rival. Its imposing ceremonial core covered at least 2.25 sq. km (0.9 sq. mile) during the seventh century, when between 30,000 and 50,000 people lived there, and as many as 100,000 in the surrounding countryside (see the summary in

FIGURE 21.13 Lord Stormy Sky of Tikal is depicted on Stela 31 at Tikal, together with his parentage. The lord died on February 19, 456.

Shaffer and Lichtenstein, 1995). Caracol commenced hostilities against Tikal in A.D. 557, soon after Tikal had captured and executed a prominent lord. The Caracol ruler, Lord Water, defeated Tikal, apparently capturing the city's then-ruler, Double Bird. Tikal now became a tribute dependency of Caracol, which grew in size and prestige as its vassal declined. Lord Water's successors dominated Tikal for at least 150 years and embarked on ambitious conquests against neighboring Calakmul and Naranjo. But eventually Caracol paid the price for its military adventures, only to rise again during the late Classic.

The ever-shifting diplomatic and military landscape in the lowlands involved dozens of city-states and cities, large and small, whose relationships with the major centers and lesser kingdoms are a tangle of claims, counterclaims, and archaeological data. In addition to Caracol, both Tikal and Calakmul, also in the southern lowlands, were rival regional capitals during the early Classic. At its height in the seventh century, Calakmul had a ceremonial precinct covering about 2 sq. km (0.7 sq. mile) and a surrounding residential area over 20 sq. km (7.7 sq. miles) in extent. At least 50,000 people lived in the urban core of a great city and important rival of Tikal between at least A.D. 514 and 814 (Folan, Marcus, and Miller, 1995).

Like Tikal, Calakmul sat astride an important overland trade route. The rivalry between the two cities may have been both a power play and a struggle for dominance of long-distance exchange. There may have been family ties between the two cities. The rivalry was intense, culminating in warfare and constant shifts in allegiance between Tikal, Calakmul, and Caracol, which are virtually impossible to decipher today. Tikal defeated Calakmul in 695; the latter never recovered its earlier importance.

Tikal had few allies in its immediate vicinity but maintained friendlier relations with two more distant city-states—Palenque and Copán.

Palenque The city of Palenque, another Maya capital but in the western lowlands, is remarkable not only for its fine buildings but also for its rulers' obsession with their ancestry (Figure 21.14). Two Palenque rulers, Pacal (or Pakal) the Great ("Shield") and his oldest son, Chan-Bahlum ("Snake-Jaguar"), who ruled in the seventh century A.D., stand out for their vision and wisdom. Palenque's dynastic history began on March 11, 431, when Bahlum-Kuk ("Jaguar-Quetzal") became ruler, and lasted until sometime after 799. The experts have used the rich inscriptions left by Pacal and others to reconstruct a dynasty of no fewer than 12 kings, with, however, what Schele and Mathews (1990) call some "minor sidesteps." These sidesteps accounted for the obsession with history that was so remarkable in Pacal and Chan-Bahlum's day.

Succession was through the male line, yet Pacal inherited the throne from his mother, Lady Zac-Kuk, who served for a time as ruler. She must have been a remarkable woman, although we know nothing of her. Pacal claimed the throne as her son and, in so doing, had to change the genealogical rules so that he could override the age-old rule of descent through the father and claim succession.

Palenque
Before A.D. 431 to 800

FIGURE 21.14 Palenque, with the Temple of the Inscriptions at left, the palace at right.

In short, he and, later, his son orchestrated orthodox belief with clever fictions. First, they declared Lady Zac-Kuk to be equivalent to the first mother of gods and kings at the beginning of the present creation. This mother deity was the mother of the three major gods of Maya religion. Next, Pacal and Chan-Bahlum claimed that Pacal had been born on the very day of the calendar that coincided with that of the goddess's birth. Thus, both Pacal and the goddess were of the same divine substance. Pacal inherited the throne from his mother because this was what had happened at the beginning of creation: Authority had been transmitted through both males and females (Figure 21.15).

It may have helped that Pacal ascended to the throne at the age of 12 while his mother was still alive, and that she lived for another 25 years. The real power may have been in her hands all that time, for it was only after her death, in 640, that Pacal commissioned major inscriptions that justified his own rule.

Toward the end of his long reign, which lasted 67 years, Pacal built the Temple of the Inscriptions, a masterpiece of Maya architecture under which his tomb lies. His artists carved the images of his direct ancestors around his coffin deep under the temple, and on the sarcophagus his strategy of dynastic legitimization was recorded (Schele and Freidel, 1990). Chan-Bahlum continued his father's preoccupation with dynastic succession.

Both rulers made Palenque a major power that dominated the southwestern lowlands during their lifetimes, between A.D. 603 and 702, but the dynasty survived for only another century or so after Chan-Bahlum's death (Figure 21.16).

Copán
A.D. 435 to 800

Copán Copán, in Honduras, is adorned with pyramids and plazas covering 12 ha (30 acres), rising from the vast open spaces of the Great and Middle Plazas to an elaborate complex of raised enclosed courtyards, pyramids, and temples known to archaeologists as the Acropolis (Figure 21.17). Here successive rulers built their

FIGURE 21.15 A Maya plate depicts Hunahpu, the father of the mythical Hero Twins, as a scribe. In his left hand, he supports a folded book covered in jaguar skin, in which he is writing.

FIGURE 21.16 A Maya frieze from Bonampak, showing a lord and executed prisoners.

architectural statements atop those of their predecessors in an archaeological jigsaw puzzle of the first magnitude.

The earliest inscription at the site dates to December 11, 435, and was the work of ruler K'inich Yax Ku'k Mo' ("Great Sun Quetzal Macaw"), although there may have been earlier rulers. For four centuries, Great Sun Quetzal Macaw's successors formed a powerful dynasty at Copán and became a major force in the Maya world. At one point, Copán ruled over neighboring Quirigua. More than 10,000 people lived in the surrounding valley. However, on May 3, 738, the subordinate ruler of Quirigua turned on his master and captured and sacrificed him. But Copán seems to have maintained a measure of independence and survived. In 749, a new ruler, Smoke Shell, ascended to the throne of the once-great city. He embarked on an ambitious campaign of rehabilitation, even marrying a princess from distant Palenque. He also embarked on a building frenzy, which culminated in the Temple of the Hieroglyphic Stairway, built in 755 and one of the oldest and most sacred of Copán's precincts (see Site box). Smoke Shell's son from his Palenque marriage, Yax-Pac ("First Dawn"), ruled during troubled times, with internal factionalism on the rise. Collapse was imminent (See Site Box).

FIGURE 21.17 Artist Tatiana Proskouriakoff's reconstruction of the central precincts at Copán.

SiTE **>** Architecture as a Political Statement: The Hieroglyphic Stairway at Copán, Honduras **<**

Today's Maya archaeologist works closely with epigraphers, using carefully deciphered glyphs and inscriptions to reconstruct complex architectural events, as well as the ritual or political motives behind them. William and Barbara Fash (1991) combined both lines of evidence to reconstruct the Hieroglyphic Stairway at Copán, erected by the ruler Smoke Shell in A.D. 755 on one of the city's most sacred precincts.

In the 1930s, archaeologists of the Carnegie Institution restored much of the ruined stairway, replacing the glyph blocks in approximate order. They were unable to read the inscriptions, which made the task difficult. In 1986, a team of archaeologists and epigraphers headed by the Fashes set out to restore and conserve the building and to establish the true meaning of the stairway. Using meticulous excavation, the archaeologists recovered thousands of tenoned mosaic fragments from the structure, which were drawn and photographed, then pieced together in a precise reconstruction of the building. They recovered a powerful political statement (Figure 21.18).

More than 2200 glyphs ascend the sides of the stairway and provide an elegant statement of the Maya kings' supernatural path. William Fash believes the building was an attempt by Smoke Shell to relegitimize the conquered dynasty of earlier times. Portraits on the stairs depict Copán's lords as warriors carrying shields, with inscriptions recounting their deeds. A figure, perhaps Smoke Shell himself, stands where an altar forms the base of the stairway, in the form of an inverted head of the rain god Tlaloc. Tlaloc seems to be belching forth the inscriptions, his lower jaw forming the top of the stairs. Inside his head lay an offering of decorated flints in the form of portraits and artifacts perhaps used by Smoke Shell himself in the sacrificial and bloodletting ceremonies that dedicated

the stairway. Unfortunately, the stairway was shoddily, and hastily, built. It soon collapsed, at a time when Copán was rapidly losing its political authority.

FIGURE 21.18   Artist Tatiana Proskouriakoff's reconstruction of the Hieroglyphic Stairway at Copán.

The diplomatic and military landscape was constantly changing, as alliances were formed and just as rapidly collapsed again. During the very late Classic, after A.D. 771, a new political pattern emerged, indicative of changed conditions and stressful times. Carved inscriptions began to appear in the houses of local nobles at Copán and other sites, as if the rulers were now granting the privilege of using inscriptions to important individuals, perhaps as a way of gaining their continued support in times of trouble. This proliferation of inscriptions in the Petén and elsewhere may also reflect minor nobles' taking advantage of confused times and a disintegrating political authority to claim their own, brief independence. The confusion accelerated. By A.D. 800, Maya populations were declining sharply, and both monument carving and major construction soon came to an end.

The central institution of Maya civilization was kingship, for it was the concept that unified society as a whole. Maya kings lived and carried out their deeds in the context of a history they recorded in building projects at Copán, Palenque, Tikal, and elsewhere. Maya elites lived out their lives in the context of the kings who ruled them, and in turn, thousands of commoners lived their lives with respect to the nobility (see Figure 21.13 on p. 437). We are only beginning to understand the tapestry of their history.

The Ninth-Century Collapse

Maya civilization reached its peak after A.D. 600 (see Figure 21.19). Then, at the end of the eighth century A.D., the great ceremonial centers of the Petén and the southern lowlands were abandoned, the Long Court calendar was discontinued, and the structure of religious life and the state decayed. Within a century, huge sections of the southern lowlands were abandoned, never to be reoccupied (Webster, 2002). At Tikal, perhaps the greatest Maya center, the elite vanished and the population declined to a third of its earlier level. The nonelite survivors clustered in the remains of great masonry structures and tried to retain a semblance of their earlier life. Within a century, even they were gone. As Michael Coe puts it: "One by one the lights of Classic urban civilization had winked out" (2011: 162). All this is not to say that Maya civilization vanished completely, for new centers may have emerged in neighboring areas, taking in some of the displaced population. Maya civilization continued to flourish in the northern Yucatán (Sabloff and Freidel, 1984).

Scholars studying this ninth-century decline agree that a multiplicity of factors—some ecological, some political and social—led to catastrophe in the southern lowlands. The theories of a generation ago argued that the collapse of Teotihuacán gave the Maya a chance to enlarge their managerial functions in Mesoamerican trade. According to these theories, the elite became increasingly involved in warfare and competition between regions. The late Classic saw a frenzy of public building and increased pressure on the people, the source of both food and labor for prestige projects. Agricultural productivity fell, disease may have reached epidemic proportions, and population densities plummeted, so that recovery was impossible. There is some evidence of disease, stature decline, and malnutrition, but the data are incomplete (Wright and White, 1996).

More recently, endemic warfare has been invoked as a powerful factor in the collapse. At Dos Pilas, in northern Guatemala, 105 km (65 miles) from Tikal, and founded by a renegade noble from Tikal in A.D. 645, Arthur Demarest (2004) uncovered evidence of civil war and prolonged conflict. Dos Pilas's later rulers embarked on campaigns of expansion that enlarged their territory to more than 3884 sq. km (1500 sq. miles) by the mid-eighth century. Dos Pilas now controlled major jade and obsidian routes. Its lords lavished wealth on ornate palaces and a pyramid topped by three temples. Demarest and Juan Antonio Valdés dug deep under a small temple behind a stela that commemorated "Ruler 2," who reigned between A.D. 698 and 726, and uncovered the ruler's burial chamber. He wore a shell mosaic headdress adorned with monster faces, a heavy jade necklace, and jade bracelets. At his waist hung a stingray spine, once used for genital bloodletting. Hieroglyphs associated with the grave tell of the lord's carefully contrived diplomatic marriages with neighbors and of his delicate political marriages and his military campaigns.

Dos Pilas
A.D. 645 to 761

Dos Pilas flourished until A.D. 761. By then, its rulers had overextended themselves, despite frantic efforts to maintain their domains. In that year, nearby Tamarindo attacked its former sovereign and killed "Ruler 4," despite desperate resistance by the Dos Pilas inhabitants. The invaders tore down the royal palace and robbed temple façades to build rough defensive walls with wooden palisades to surround the central precinct. Here, the people huddled in a small village of crude huts while the nobles fled and built a new center at Aguateca. The new center lay atop a steep cliff above a deep chasm, protected on three sides by natural features, as well as by massive defense walls. The Aguatecans held out for another half century, despite repeated attacks. In the early ninth century A.D., Demarest believes, intensive warfare drove these survivors of Dos Pilas into fortified towns and villages, where they erected defensive walls even around large tracts of agricultural land. Local conditions may have become so insecure that farmers were limited to defended acreage, so that crop

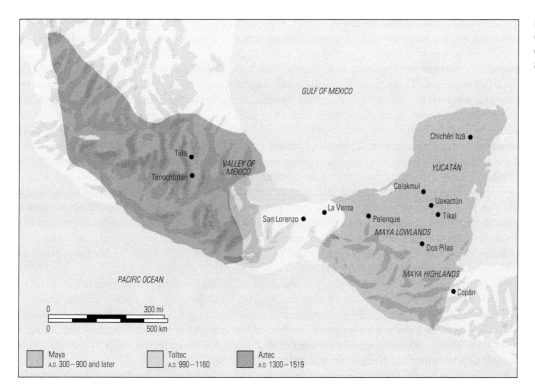

FIGURE 21.19 Distribution of Classic Maya, Toltec, and Aztec civilizations. (The Toltec and Aztec areas overlap.)

yields may have been affected dramatically. In a last desperate stand, the remaining Aguatecans dug three moats, one 140.2 m (460 feet) long, across a peninsula in Lake Petexbatun, creating an island fortress. The bedrock from the canals became defensive walls and a walled wharf for a canoe landing. The outpost did not last long, for the inhabitants abandoned it in the 800s (Demarest, 2004).

The various collapse theories have been subjected to exhaustive analysis by research that involves both simulation studies and examinations of trading patterns and demographic and ecological stresses that could have affected population densities. Patrick Culbert and Don Rice (1990) have examined population densities and the potential for agricultural production in the southern lowlands. They have shown that population densities rose to as many as 200 persons per sq. km (518 per sq. mile) during the late Classic over an area so large that it was impossible for people to adapt to bad times by moving to new land or emigrating. They believe that the magnitude of the population loss during the two centuries after 800 was such that social malfunction alone cannot account for it. Failure of the agricultural base must have been an important component in the collapse equation at the local level.

Maya agriculture became increasingly intense as populations rose, and both terrace and raised-field systems covered large areas in many parts of the lowlands. At some of the larger sites, like Tikal, the people may have been transporting great quantities of foodstuffs from distances of between 50 and 100 km (31 and 62 miles) away. In the short term, the intensification strategies worked, but they carried the seeds of collapse. The risks of climatic change, plant disease, erosion, and long-term declines in soil fertility are always present in such enterprises. To continue functioning efficiently, the newly intensified systems would have had to be managed constantly. Just the repair of field systems after floods and rains would have required watchful effort on a large scale. There are no signs that the Maya made any social changes that enabled them to achieve such a level of management, especially when so many people were engaged in public construction projects and apparently in military activity (perhaps the Maya were under pressure from the north).

Long-term environmental degradation was an important element in the scenario, where short-term gains in productivity were followed by catastrophic declines. For example, as populations rose, fallow cycles may have been shortened, so that there was increased competition between crop plants and weeds; this is a problem that can be solved only by constant weeding, a very labor-intensive activity. Shortened fallow cycles also lead to lower levels of plant nutrients and declining crop yields, and we do not know whether the Maya tried to counteract these trends by systematic mulching or by planting soil-restoring crops. The problem of erosion may have been even more acute. There are signs that the people lost much soil to runoff in the lowlands, for they did not build the terraces needed in time to retain the soil. Some of this erosion may have resulted from extensive deforestation. At the same time, severe drought cycles played havoc with subsistence agriculture in an environment with only moderately fertile soils and already overly dense populations, phenomena now well documented in Mesoamerican lake sediments (Gill, 2000; Gill et al., 2007; Haug et al., 2003; Hodell et al., 1995, 2001). Such droughts may, indeed, have been the trigger that brought about the collapse in the southern lowlands.

Long-term field surveys of Copán and its hinterland have documented dramatic population changes during the collapse period (Freter, 1994). Between A.D. 550 and 700 the Copán city-state expanded rapidly, with most of the population concentrated in the core and the immediate periphery. There was only a small, scattered rural population. Between 700 and 850, the Copán Valley reached its greatest sociopolitical complexity, with a rapid population increase to between 18,000 and 20,000 people. These figures, calculated from site size, suggest that the local population was doubling every 80 to 100 years, with about 80 percent of the people living within the core and the immediate periphery. Rural settlement expanded outward along the valley floor, but it was still relatively scattered. But now people were farming foothill areas, as the population density of the urban core reached more several thousand people per sq. km (0.3 sq. mile) and the periphery housing about 500 people per sq. km. Eighty-two percent of the population lived in relatively humble dwellings, an indication of the extreme stratification of Copán society.

Copán's ruling dynasty ended in 810, just as serious urban depopulation began. The urban core and the periphery zones lost about half their population after 850, while the rural population increased by almost 20 percent. Small regional settlements replaced the scattered villages of earlier times, in response to cumulative deforestation, the overexploitation of even marginal agricultural soils, and uncontrolled soil erosion near the capital. By 1150, the Copán Valley population had fallen to between 5,000 and 8,000 people.

The expanding Maya population was dependent on an agricultural system that made no allowance for long-term problems. Eventually, the system could produce no further riches, could not expand, and could only decline—with catastrophic results. But it would be a mistake to think of the Maya "collapse" as a universal phenomenon. Rather, the collapse of the ninth century was a marked episode in a long series of periodic flowerings and collapses characteristic of Maya civilization—indeed, of Mesoamerican civilization generally.

The Toltecs

Although by A.D. 900 the Classic period had ended, Maya religious and social orders continued in northern Yucatán. The continuity of the ancient Mesoamerican tradition survived unscathed. Basic economic patterns and technological traditions were retained, although religious and ideological patterns and priorities were disarranged. New ceremonial centers were built, but war and violence became primary as militaristic rulers achieved dominance in Mesoamerica (Davies, 1977, 1980; S. Evans, 2008).

We have mentioned the unsettled Postclassic political conditions caused by population movements and tribal warfare. Many groups of invaders vied for political power in central Mexico until the Toltecs achieved dominance in the tenth century A.D. The oral legends of the Aztec rulers, who followed them, describe how the Toltecs came into Mesoamerica from the northwest frontiers beyond the civilized world. They settled at Tula, 57 km (37 miles) south of the Valley of Mexico, where they built a ceremonial center dedicated to their serpent god, Quetzalcoatl (Figure 21.20) (Diehl, 1984; Healan, 1989). Tula is notable for its animal sculpture and pottery styles, but it did not have a long life, for in approximately A.D. 1160, some newcomers with a less developed religious organization arrived from the north and destroyed the temples.

Chichén Itzá in northern Yucatán was an important Maya ceremonial center in Postclassic times (Figure 21.21). In the ninth century A.D., Chichén Itzá came under Toltec influence (S. Evans, 2008). The extent of this influence is much debated, but it probably represented a fresh political order, a complex mixing of Mexican and Maya factions among the elite. The new leaders developed new artistic and political styles that separated political functions from the personality of an individual ruler. The Chichén Toltecs developed a flexibility and a resilience that enabled them to be far more adaptive to changing political conditions than their southern neighbors had been.

The leaders of Chichén Itzá developed a truly regional state. They controlled the two great resources of the northern Yucatán: a well-organized population and massive salt fields along the coast. The site was abandoned after about A.D. 1150, but the city of Mayapán, a walled settlement clustered around a ceremonial center, rose to prominence elsewhere in northern Yucatán. At least 12,000 people lived in this Maya city, which was ruled by the Cocom family. Maya civilization enjoyed a resurgence in this area, although Mayapán declined during the civil wars of the fifteenth century. A century later, the Spanish found Yucatán ruled by numerous petty chiefs.

The militaristic Toltecs were the leading military and political force in Mesoamerica for such a short time that their influence evaporated rapidly when Tula was destroyed. Another period of political chaos in the Valley of Mexico ensued as more nomadic groups from the north (Chichimecs) maneuvered for political power (Davies, 1980).

Aztec Civilization and the Spanish Conquest

When the first Spanish conquistadors arrived in highland Mexico in 1519, they were astounded by the rich civilization they found. The capital city of Tenochtitlán was the headquarters of a series of militaristic Aztec kings who ruled over a wide area by religious decree, constant human sacrifice, and bloodthirsty campaigning. Within a few years of Spanish contact, Aztec civilization literally ceased to exist. Tenochtitlán was reduced to rubble after a siege that lasted 91 days (Clendinnen, 1991).

The Aztecs were one of several nomadic, semicivilized Chichimeca groups who settled in the Valley of Mexico after the fall of Tula (M. Smith, 2002; Townsend, 2009). They arrived during the early twelfth century, a politically weak but aggressive group that barely retained its own identity. After years of military harassment, the Aztecs fled into the swamps of Lake Texcoco in about 1325. There they founded a small hamlet named Tenochtitlán (now under Mexico City). Less than two centuries later, this village had become the largest city in pre-Columbian America (Conrad and Demarest, 1984).

Toltec civilization
A.D. 900 to 1200

Chichén Itzá
A.D. 1100

Aztec civilization
twelfth century A.D. to 1521

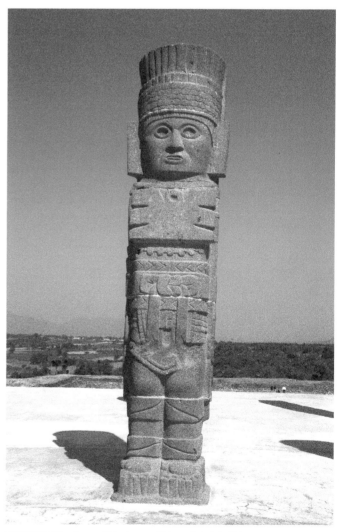

FIGURE 21.20 A monolithic statue at Tula, capital of the Toltecs.

At first, the Aztecs lived peaceably with their neighbors, and Tenochtitlán flourished as an important market center. By judicious diplomacy, discreet military alliance, and well-timed royal marriages, the Aztecs quietly advanced their cause until they were a force to be reckoned with in local politics. Then, in the early fifteenth century, they abruptly changed their foreign policy and embarked on a ruthless campaign of long-term military and economic conquest. Soon they controlled a loosely connected network of minor states and cities that extended across Mesoamerica. The real leader behind this change was a general named Tlacaelel, who was adviser to a series of aggressive Aztec rulers. It was he who encouraged the use of terror and human sacrifice as a means of controlling conquered territory. The rich tribute from conquered states and cities made Tenochtitlán the center of the Mesoamerican world, the hub of a political and economic confederacy that extended from near the Pacific Ocean to the Gulf of Mexico and from northern Mexico as far south as Guatemala.

The Aztec Empire was far from a monolithic and highly centralized state, like that of Imperial Rome (M. Smith, 2002). It was a mosaic of ever-changing alliances, cemented by an elaborate tribute-gathering machine. A tiny group of rulers controlled the state, the lord of Tenochtitlán being principal among them. Everything was run for the benefit of a growing elite, who maintained their power by ruthless and efficient taxation campaigns, political marriages, and the constant threat of military force. Tribute was assessed on conquered cities and taken in many forms, as raw materials like gold dust or tropical bird feathers for ceremonial mantles and headdresses (Figure 21.22). Fine ornaments, even capes, were assessed from communities specializing in such products. Twenty-six cities did nothing but provide firewood for one royal palace alone. Metal artifacts were major tribute items, for they played a telling role in the Aztec and the earlier Mesoamerican states. Expert smiths made musical instruments like bells, and they alloyed copper to bring out shimmering gold and silver hues. Both color and sound were central parts of Mesoamerican ideology, commemorating the sun and the moon, the sounds of rain, thunder, and rattlesnakes, helping to bring symbolic order to the world.

Both settlement data and other archaeological data suggest that the Aztec Empire was less centralized, both as a society and as an economy, than its great predecessor, Teotihuacán (Berdan et al., 1996). To what extent it had originated through decision making at the top, as opposed to market dynamics such as supply and demand, is still unknown. For example, pottery distributions show that political considerations such as alliances were more important than proximity to major markets in determining access to certain types of clay serving vessels. And both archaeology and ethnohistorical studies of market locations hint that imperial rulers located markets and decided the craft specializations within them to the advantage of their own cities and at the expense of subordinate communities. There is clear evidence of major changes in standards of living under imperial Aztec rule. For example, in the western Morelos area of central Mexico, agricultural and textile production increased under Aztec rule while living standards declined.

Under the highly visible and much touted imperial veneer lay a complex foundation of small kingdoms, towns, and villages, all integrated into local economies. Many of them had existed before the Aztec, or even earlier, civilizations came into being, and they continued after the Spanish

(a)   (b)

FIGURE 21.21 Chichén Itzá. (a) The center at its height, looking south from the Sacred Cenote. Painting by Tatiana Proskouriakoff. (b) The Castillo, the largest building at the site.

FIGURE 21.22 A tribute list from the Codex Mendoza, one of the few surviving Aztec codices. The list records tributes owed by the conquered province of Tochtepec, including feathered masks, warriors' regalia, and dried fish.

Conquest. At the same time, the economic and political patterns of the empire were highly variable, both regionally and socially, in everything from land tenure to craft specialization, from patterns of urbanization to merchants and markets. This intricate social mosaic, only now being revealed by a new generation of archaeological research, lay behind a façade of seeming political and economic uniformity and centralization (M. Smith, 2002).

Tenochtitlán, a city of more than 200,000 people, was a spectacular sight in the sixteenth century, with markets where more than 60,000 people are said to have assembled every day (Figure 21.23) (Diaz, 1963; J. B. Morris, 1962). The market sold every form of foodstuff and provided every luxury and service. The principal streets of Tenochtitlán were of beaten earth, and there were at least 40 pyramids adorned with fine decorated stonework (Moctezuma, 1988) (Figure 21.23). Tenochtitlán was certainly larger, and probably cleaner, than many European cities of the time.

Large residential areas surrounded the central precincts, and houses with *chinampa* gardens lay on the outskirts of the city. Six major canals ran through Tenochtitlán, and three causeways connected the city with the shore. At least 200,000 canoes provided convenient transport for the people of the city, which was divided into 60 or 70 well-organized wards. Tenochtitlán was a magnificent city set in a green swath of country in the middle of a clear lake, with a superb backdrop of snow-capped volcanoes.

Aztec society was moving closer and closer to a rigid, highly stratified class system at the time of Spanish contact. No ordinary person was allowed to enter a waiting room in the palace used by nobles. The king was revered as a semigod and had virtually despotic powers. He was elected from a limited class group of *pipiltin*, or nobles. There were full-time professional merchants, called *pochteca*, and also a class of warriors whose ranks were determined by the number of people they

Tenochtitlán
A.D. 1325 to 1521

FIGURE 21.23 A reconstruction drawing of the central precincts at Tenochtitlán, with the Temple of Huitzilopochtli and Tlaloc at the left.

had killed in battle. Groups of lineages called *calpulli* ("big house") were the most significant factor in most people's religious, social, and political life. Many of these groups coincided with the wards in the city. The great mass of the people were free people, or *macehualtin*; serfs, landless peasants, and slaves made up the bottom strata of society. (For a discussion of women in Aztec society, see Brumfiel, 1991.)

Much of Aztec society's efforts went toward placating the formidable war and rain gods, Huitzilopochtli and Tlaloc, whose benevolence was ensured by constant human sacrifices. These sacrifices reached their peak at the end of each 52-year cycle, like those of the Maya, when blood-thirsty rites ensured the continuity of the world (Figure 21.24).

A.D. 1519 By the time of the Spanish Conquest in 1519, Aztec society seems to have been in a state of fre-netic and bloody terrorism that flourished at the behest of arrogant imperial rulers. The Aztecs had learned the fine art of terror as a political instrument and regularly staged elaborate public displays in Tenochtitlán to which subject leaders were invited. The Spaniards estimated that at least 20,000 people were sacrificed to the gods throughout the Aztec Empire each year. This figure may be an exaggeration, but there is no doubt that a considerable number of prisoners of war and slaves per-ished by having their hearts ripped out in the presence of the gods. Indeed, the finest death for an Aztec warrior was to perish under the sacrificial knife after honorable capture in battle. Such a fate was known as the "flowery death."

The Aztecs have acquired a formidable reputation from historians—and, it must be confessed, from some archaeologists—because of their penchant for human sacrifice and cannibalism. That they were addicted to human sacrifice is certain; the cannibalism is less well documented. Some believe that the Aztec nobles ate human flesh to compensate for a lack of meat in their diet, but the beans they ate as a staple were more than sufficient as a source of protein. It seems more likely that the Aztec nobles and priests engaged in occasional ritual cannibalism as part of their intensely sym-bolic religious beliefs (Townsend, 2009). Human sacrifice was also an instrument for social control and intimidation, especially of prospective conquests.

By the time the Spaniards arrived in the Mexican lowlands, Aztec civilization was in danger of being torn apart. The society was becoming top-heavy with nobles because they were allowed to marry commoners and their children automatically became aristocrats. The demands for tribute both from subject states and from the free people of the city became ever larger and more exacting. There may well have been intense philosophical disagreements between the militant priests and warriors, who increasingly encouraged conquest and human sacrifice, and those more sophisticated and educated Aztecs who believed in a gentler, less aggressive world. It is fascinating to speculate what would have happened had Hernán Cortés not landed in Mexico. Given the past history of Mexico, it seems likely that Aztec civilization would have collapsed suddenly, to be replaced in due time by another society much like it. In truth, Aztec civilization had reached a point of complexity that was beyond the capacity of its rulers to control and administer, a complexity that Old World civilizations had brought under control. We can be certain that the Aztecs' successors would have eventually done so as well.

The Aztecs were the most important political entity in Mesoamerica when the Spaniards first explored the Americas. From coastal villagers in the lowlands, the explorers heard stories of the fabled rich kingdoms in the high interior. Soon the conquistadors pressed inland. Hernán Cortés

FIGURE 21.24 Aztec human sacrifice. Priests ripped out the still-beating hearts of sacrificial victims and rolled their corpses down the temple steps.

was the first Spaniard to come into contact with the Aztecs, now ruled by Moctezuma II, a despotic ruler who had assassinated most of his predecessor's counselors and had had himself deified. Moctezuma's reign was disturbed by constant omens of impending doom and predictions that the god Quetzalcoatl would reclaim his homeland (Anderson and Dibble, 1978). The king was deeply alarmed by the reports of Spanish ships on the coast. There were, then, considerable psychological stresses on Moctezuma and his followers before the Spaniards arrived (Clendinnen, 1991).

Cortés spent two tough years reducing the Aztecs to slaves and their marvelous capital to rubble. A handful of explorers on imported horses, armed with a few muskets and cannons, were able to overthrow one of the most powerful tribute states in the history of America. Without question, Cortés's task was made easier by both rebellious subjects of the Aztecs and the extraordinary tensions the Aztecs had placed on themselves. Cortés also unwittingly introduced smallpox, which decimated his adversaries.

By A.D. 1680, the Indian population of the Aztec heartland had been reduced from approxi-   A.D. 1680
mately 1.2 million to some 70,000—a decimation resulting from war, slavery, disease, overwork and exploitation, famine, and malnutrition. Mesoamerica as a whole lost between 85 and 95 percent of its indigenous population during that 160-year period. Only a few fragments of the fabulous Mesoamerican cultural tradition survived into modern times, and the Native American population faced a new and uncertain chapter in its long history.

Summary

- The Preclassic period of Mesoamerican prehistory lasted from approximately 2000 B.C. to A.D. 250, a time of major culture change in both lowlands and highlands.

- Sedentary villages traded with each other in raw materials and exotic objects. These exchange networks became increasingly complex and eventually came under the monopolistic control of larger villages.

- Increasing social complexity went hand in hand with the appearance of the first public buildings and the evidence of social stratification.

- These developments are well chronicled in the Valley of Oaxaca and in the Olmec culture of the lowlands, which flourished from approximately 1500 to 500 B.C. Olmec art styles and religious beliefs were among those that spread widely over lowlands and highlands during the late Preclassic period.

- Preclassic cultural developments culminated in the highlands in a number of great cities, among them Monte Albán and Teotihuacán. Teotihuacán had collapsed by approximately A.D. 700, probably as a result of warfare with other rival states in the highlands. Drought may also have played a role in its demise.

- Religious ideologies, ritual organization, and extensive trading networks were key factors in the development of Maya society in the lowlands after 1000 B.C.
- Classic Maya civilization flourished from A.D. 250 to 900 and consisted of an ever-changing patchwork of competing states. Maya glyphs show that Maya civilization was far from uniform. Religious beliefs rather than political or economic interests unified the Maya. Until about A.D. 600, the largest states were in northeast Petén, now in Guatemala, with a multicenter polity headed by the "Sky" rulers of Tikal.

- Maya civilization reached its height in the southern lowlands after the seventh century A.D., collapsing suddenly in the Yucatán after A.D. 900. The reasons for the collapse are still uncertain, but droughts, environmental degradation, pressure on the labor force, and food shortages were doubtless among them.
- Teotihuacán's collapse in the highlands resulted in a political vacuum for some centuries, which was eventually filled by the Toltecs and then the Aztecs, whose civilization was dominant in the Valley of Mexico at the time of the Spanish Conquest in A.D. 1519.

Further Reading

Coe, M.D. 2011. *The Maya*, 8th ed. London and New York: Thames & Hudson.

Evans, Susan Toby. 2008. *Ancient Mexico and Central America*, 2nd ed. London and New York: Thames & Hudson.

Townsend, Richard F. 2009. *The Aztecs*, 3rd ed. London and New York: Thames & Hudson.

Andean Civilizations

The year was 1911. American explorer Hiram Bingham was high in the Andes, struggling along precipitous, densely forested paths, slipping ankle-deep in mud at every step. He and his men climbed in places on all fours, high above the tumbling Urubamba River. Suddenly he emerged into the open, high atop a mountain ridge. Bingham climbed a granite stairway leading to a plaza with two temples. He wandered through "a maze of beautiful granite houses . . . covered with trees and moss and the growth of centuries." He wandered for hours among "walls of white granite . . . carefully cut and exquisitely fitted together" (Bingham, 1963: 267). This was Machu Picchu, an Inca settlement in such a remote, inaccessible setting that Bingham claimed it was the "lost city of the Incas." For three years, Bingham worked at Machu Picchu, clearing, excavating, and mapping houses and temples (see Figure 22.20, p. 473).

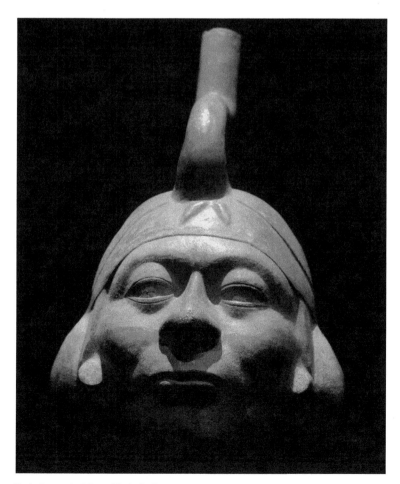

Portrait vase depicting a Moche lord.

Machu Picchu is one of the most spectacular archaeological sites in the world; but it was never a lost city, for the local farmers were well aware of its existence. What makes it so dramatic is its mountain setting, its testimony to the incredible skill of the Andeans in mastering climatic extremes.

In its late-fifteenth-century heyday, the vast Inca Empire, known as *Tawantinsuyu* ("The Land of the Four Quarters"), extended from high-altitude mountain valleys in the Andes, through dry highland plains, to foothills, tropical rain forests, and coastal deserts, some of the driest landscape on earth (Figure 22.1). (For the chronology of later Andean archaeology, see Table 22.1.)

Over many centuries, two "poles" of Andean civilization developed: one along the north coast of what is now Peru, the other in the south-central Andes (Silverman, 2004). Only the Inca succeeded in joining the two into one vast empire.

The northern pole was centered on the bleak and effectively rainless Peruvian desert plain, which extends south nearly 550 km (350 miles) along the coast as far as Collasuyu, reaching a width of up to 100 km (62 miles) in the area of the Lambayeque River. Some 40 rivers and streams fueled by mountain runoff flow across the plain, but they can be used for irrigation only in areas where the surrounding desert is low enough. Four such locations were the most densely settled in ancient times. The two largest were centered on the north coast, in the Chicama-Moche area and in the Motupe-Lambayeque-Jequetepeque region. Local topography allowed farmers to link their field systems to canals, which brought water from several rivers, permitting far higher population densities.

The southern pole embraced the altiplano (high-altitude grasslands) and the Lake Titicaca basin, highland Bolivia, and parts of Argentina and northern Chile in the south-central Andes. Much of the altiplano was too dry and cold to sustain dense human populations. The northern end of the Lake Titicaca basin was somewhat warmer and better watered, so that both alpaca and llama

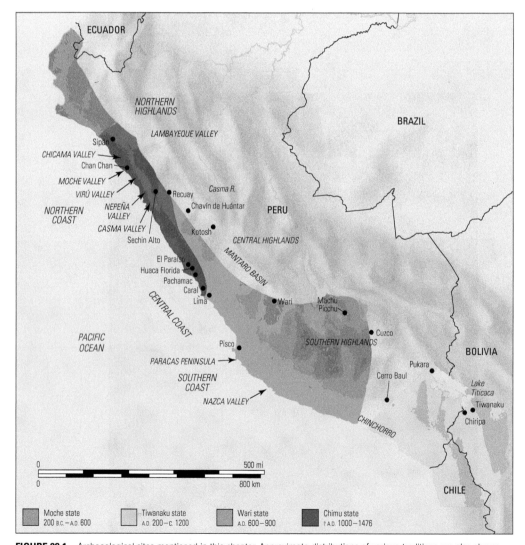

FIGURE 22.1 Archaeological sites mentioned in this chapter. Approximate distributions of various traditions are also shown. Some sites in coastal river valleys are omitted from the map, but their general location is clear from the text.

TABLE 22.1

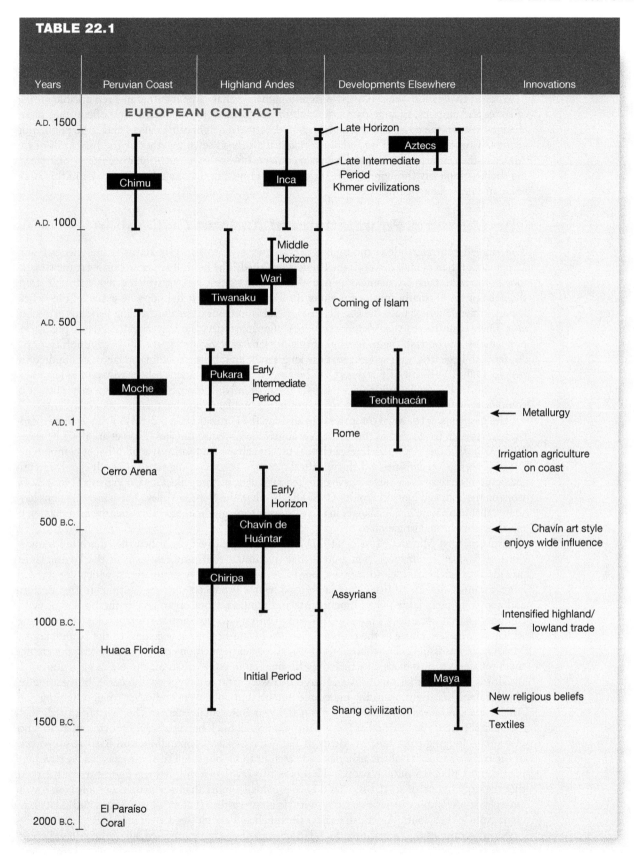

Years	Peruvian Coast	Highland Andes	Developments Elsewhere	Innovations

EUROPEAN CONTACT

A.D. 1500 — Late Horizon

Chimu

Aztecs

Inca — Late Intermediate Period

Khmer civilizations

A.D. 1000

Middle Horizon

Wari

Tiwanaku — Coming of Islam

A.D. 500

Pukara — Early Intermediate Period

Moche

Teotihuacán

A.D. 1 — Rome ← Metallurgy

Cerro Arena

← Irrigation agriculture on coast

Early Horizon

500 B.C.

Chavín de Huántar ← Chavín art style enjoys wide influence

Chiripa

Assyrians

1000 B.C.

Huaca Florida ← Intensified highland/ lowland trade

Initial Period

Maya

Shang civilization ← New religious beliefs

1500 B.C.

Textiles

El Paraíso

2000 B.C. Coral

herding and potato and quinoa agriculture were possible. This was where the powerful Tiwanaku state flourished in the first millennium A.D. The puna grasslands of the higher altiplano were used to graze alpaca and llama, the economic exploitation of the plains varying with the altitude. The civilizations of the southern highlands traded regularly with the southern coast, bounded in the north by the Ica River and in the south by the Moquegua Valley.

Andean civilization pursued many different pathways that came together in a remarkable mosaic of states and empires, in large part as a result of widely held spiritual beliefs and of constant interchange between the coast and the highlands and between neighboring valleys and large population centers. Tawantinsuyu itself was a unique political synthesis sewn together by the Inca lords of the Andes in the centuries just before European contact. It was the culmination of centuries of increasing social complexity throughout the Andean area. How did such complex states arise in this landscape of extraordinary contrasts?

The Maritime Foundations of Andean Civilization

The rugged central Andean mountains are second only to the Himalayas in height, but only 10 percent of their rainfall descends the Pacific watershed. The foothill slopes and plains at the western foot of the mountains are mantled by one of the world's driest deserts, which extends virtually from the equator to 30° south, much of it along the Peruvian coast. At the opposite extreme, the richest fishery in the Americas hugs the Pacific shore, yielding millions of small schooling fish such as anchovies. These easily netted shoals support millions of people today, and they supported dense prehistoric populations. In contrast, the cultivation of this dry landscape requires controlling the runoff from the Andes with large irrigation systems that use long canals built by the coordinated labors of hundreds of people. Only 10 percent of this desert can be farmed, so its inhabitants rely heavily on the incredible bounty of the Pacific. Surprisingly, perhaps, this apparently inhospitable desert was a major center of complex early states that traded with neighbors in the highlands and built large ceremonial centers.

The mechanisms by which complex states arose on the Peruvian coast are still little understood, partly because research has tended to concentrate on larger, more spectacular sites (Haas et al., 1987; Moseley, 1975; D. J. Wilson, 1983). Such research tells us little about the relative size of different communities or about population densities, which are critical measures of an evolving state society. It is only recently that large-scale river valley surveys have collected such data, research like Gordon Willey's (1963) classic work on the Virú and Donald Proulx's (1985) fieldwork in the Nepeña Valley. These investigations have shown that there were major changes in site clustering through time, especially after the introduction of maize agriculture and irrigation to the coast after 2500 B.C.

Archaeologist Michael Moseley (1975) proposed a hypothesis he called the "maritime foundations of Andean civilization." He argued that the unique maritime resources of the Pacific Coast provided sufficient calories to support rapidly growing sedentary populations, which clustered in large communities. In addition, the same food source produced sufficient surplus to free up time and people to erect large public monuments and temples, work organized by the leaders of newly complex coastal societies. This scenario runs contrary to conventional archaeological thinking, which regards agriculture as the economic basis for state-organized societies. In the Andes, argued Moseley, it was fishing. For thousands of years, coastal populations rose, and their rise preadapted them to later circumstances, in which they adopted large-scale irrigation and maize agriculture.

Moseley implies that mollusks and large fish were vital resources on the coast, but marine biologists drew his attention to the incredible potential of anchoveta and other small schooling fish. Anchoveta can be easily netted throughout the year from small canoes. The fish offer predictable food supplies that can be dried or ground into fine meal. Such harvests would provide an abundance of protein. Judging from modern yields, if prehistoric coastal populations had lived at 60 percent of the carrying capacity of the fisheries and eaten nothing but small fish, the coast could have supported more than 6.5 million people. That is not to say that it did, but the figures make the point that the exploitation of small fish would have provided a more than adequate economic base for the emergence of complex societies on the coast. It is interesting that small mesh nets and floats have come from earlier South American coastal sites such as Paloma (see Chapter 13).

Several critiques of the maritime foundations hypothesis have appeared, all of them based on the assumption that large coastal settlements could not have been supported by maritime resources alone (see, for example, Raymond, 1981; D. J. Wilson, 1981, 1983). Most of these critiques have tended to ignore the potential of anchovetas. Another argument revolves around the famous El Niño phenomenon, the periodic changes in Pacific currents that reduce the fisheries to a shadow of their normal selves for several years at a time. In fact, as Moseley (1985) points out, El Niño brings unfamiliar, but edible, fish species to the coast as well as torrential rainfall that has the potential to disrupt irrigation systems with catastrophic results, some of which are now being identified in the archaeological record. Overall, the maritime foundations hypothesis has stood the test of time well, provided it is seen as a component in a much broader evolutionary process that also took place inland, in the highlands, and in areas where the width of the coastal shelf precluded extensive anchoveta fishing.

Richard Burger (1985) argues that changing dietary patterns in the highlands, where agriculture became increasingly important, would have created a demand among farmers for lowland products: salt, fish, and seaweed. Seaweed is rich in marine iodine and may have been an important medicine in the highlands, used to combat endemic goiter and other conditions. By the same token, carbohydrate foods like oca, ullucu, and white potatoes that could not be grown on the coast have been found in preceramic sites in the Ancón-Chillón area of the Pacific lowlands. Thus, the formation of states in both lowlands and highlands may have been fostered by continuous, often highly localized interchange between coast and interior.

Michael Moseley (1985) believes that this reliance on maritime resources led to the formation of large, densely concentrated populations whose leaders were able to organize the labor forces needed not only for building large ceremonial centers but also for transforming river valleys with sizable irrigation schemes. In this scenario, irrigation farming was in the hands of a well-defined group of authority figures who took advantage of the existing simple technology and local populations to create new economies. This transformation, based as it was on trade, maize agriculture, and a maritime diet, acted as a "kick" for radical changes in Andean society. But the transformation was based on ancient fishing traditions, which can be documented thousands of years earlier at early coastal villages. Most coastal populations drew more than 90 percent of their subsistence from the ocean.

Moseley's key point is that Andean civilization evolved in many ways, in many ecological zones, from highland, tropical rain forest, and lowland strategies of great antiquity, some dating to the earliest millennia of human settlement. Thus, the maritime foundations hypothesis may help explain the development of states on the Peruvian coast, but it cannot account for parallel developments elsewhere in South America.

Coastal Foundations: The Initial Period

Until comparatively recently, agriculture remained a secondary activity in the lowlands. Nevertheless, sedentary villages of several hundred people flourished along the north coast between 2500 and 1800 B.C., among them Huaca Prieta, whose inhabitants were remarkably skillful cotton weavers. This "Initial Period" of Andean civilization was a critical millennium because new concerns both with the cosmos and with religion permeated the Andes. For centuries, communities large and small grappled with problems of political authority, with emerging social inequality, and with new definitions of the cosmos that were not to crystallize for a long time. This was a time of experimentation, of accelerating change, and, probably, intense rivalries triggered by ambitious, newly emergent rulers. The new beliefs manifested themselves in a wave of monumental construction in both lowlands and highlands. The Initial Period saw the development of distinctive coastal and highland societies at either end of the Andean world: on the north coast and on the shores of Lake Titicaca far to the south. At the same time, textiles, like those found in the Paracas cemeteries (see pp. 458–460), assumed great importance in Andean life.

Huaca Prieta
2500 to 1800 B.C.

Caral

We do not know when this experimentation began, when the first, more complex societies developed along the coast, but it was at least 5,000 years ago. At Aspero, near the mouth of the Rio Supe, a sprawling coastal community covered at least 15 ha (37 acres), including platform mounds with buildings on top of them. One, Huaca de los Idolos, has been radiocarbon dated to 3055 B.C. By 2600 B.C., a large kingdom ruled by a center named Caral developed in the hot Supe Valley, about 193 km (120 miles) north of modern-day Lima and 20 km (12.4 miles) from the Pacific (Shady Solís, 1997; Shady Solís, Haas, and Creamer, 2001). There were as many as 17 centers in the Supe region, supported by cultivating guavas, beans, peppers, and fruit grown with skilled irrigation agriculture. The farmers also grew cotton, but not maize and potatoes, the two later staples of Andean life. The kingdom may have prospered by growing and trading industrial crops like cotton and gourds for floats and for net manufacture. Certainly, much of its subsistence came from anchovies, which were found in desiccated feces from the site.

Caral
3055 to c. 2000 B.C.

Caral is dominated by six large stone platforms with structures atop them built of quarried stone and filled in with cobbles from the nearby river (Figure 22.2). The largest is 152 m by 137 m (500 feet by 450 feet) and 18 m (60 feet) high. There are three sunken plazas and eight sectors containing different types of dwellings—apartment complexes, modest houses, and grand, stone-walled residences. Fortunately for science, the platform builders had carried their loads of cobbles in bags

FIGURE 22.2 A terraced Caral pyramid in the Supe Valley, 207 km (128 miles) north of Lima, Peru.

woven from reeds, which were added to the fill, carriers, and so on. Radiocarbon dates from the netting date the construction to about 2627 B.C., a task carried out in two efficiently organized stages.

Clearly, a small and authoritative elite governed this important kingdom, but we still know almost nothing about them or about the ways in which they commanded the loyalty of the hundreds, if not thousands, of people who built their imposing centers. Caral was abandoned for unknown reasons between 2000 and 1500 B.C., just as other kingdoms came into prominence along the coast to the north. This remarkable site, called by some a city, was the largest settlement in the Americas in its day, a full millennium and a half before Teotihuacán in Mexico. It rose in the Supe Valley at the time when the Egyptian pharaohs were building pyramids on the other side of the world—the earliest preindustrial state in the Americas.

El Paraíso and Huaca Florida

A set of interacting chiefdoms emerged along the northern and central parts of the coast after 1800 B.C. Political units centered on the Moche, Casma, Chillón, and other river valleys where irrigation agriculture developed. Centuries before, when pottery was unknown on the coast but cotton had already been widely cultivated, communication networks had arisen that linked not only neighboring coastal river valleys but lowlands and highlands as well. These trade routes, which straddled all manner of environmental zones, helped spread technology, ideology, pottery making, and architectural styles over large areas, creating a superficial sense of unity that was reflected in the widespread use of common art motifs.

El Paraíso
1800 B.C.

During the Initial Period, coastal ceremonial buildings were greatly elaborated and new architectural devices were adopted (Haas, 2001; Haas et al., 1987). Among them was a distinctive U-shaped platform often associated with elaborate adobe friezes. El Paraíso, built close to the mouth of the Chillón River near an area of arable food plain in about 1800 B.C., is the oldest of these U-shaped ceremonial complexes and the closest one to the Pacific (Figure 22.3) (Quilter, 1985). This vast site, covering some 58 ha (143 acres), consists of at least six huge square buildings constructed of roughly shaped stone blocks cemented with unfired clay. The people painted the polished clay-faced outer walls in brilliant hues. Each complex consisted of a square building surrounded by tiers of platforms reached by stone and clay staircases. The largest is more than 250 m (830 feet) long and 50 m (166 feet) wide, standing more than 10 m (30 feet) above the plain. The rooms were apparently covered with matting roofs supported by willow posts. Perhaps as many as 100,000 tons of rock excavated from the nearby hills were needed to build the El Paraíso buildings. There are few signs of occupation around them, however, as if they were shrines and public precincts rather than residential quarters. Most people probably lived close to the Pacific and only visited this major ritual center. The two largest mounds of collapsed masonry lie parallel to one another, defining a vast, elongated patio, presumably for public ceremonies, covering more than 2.5 ha (6 acres). The same arrangement is found in the great Río Rímac complex of Huaca Florida, built in about 1700 B.C.

Huaca Florida
1700 B.C.

Huaca Florida is an imposing mound of boulders and adobe lying approximately 13 km (8 miles) inland of El Paraíso (Patterson, 1985). Built somewhat later, in about 1700 B.C., and on an even larger scale, the great platform is more than 252 m (840 feet) long and 54 m (180 feet) wide and towers 30 m (100 feet) above the valley. A rectangular court lies close to the north side of the platform, but here the landscape is revealing, for Huaca Florida lies in the midst of an artificial environment created by irrigation. The focus of human settlement had moved inland, and the subsistence base had changed from fishing to large-scale irrigation agriculture.

What is most surprising about these huge structures is that people from dozens of scattered villages erected them. For reasons not yet understood, these people united in a building project that channeled most of their surplus energies into a vast monumental center, a place where few people lived but where everyone apparently congregated for major public ceremonies. The people themselves lived lives of seeming simplicity. They owned only simple stone and wooden artifacts and wore cotton clothing decorated with basic geometric patterns and stylized animal-like motifs. They buried their dead in several layers of garments, nets, or looped sacks. Why should such a village society build such enormous structures, and who were the leaders who organized these massive public works?

FIGURE 22.3 El Paraíso, a major ceremonial center on the coast dating to about 1800 B.C. This was one of the first U-shaped sacred buildings constructed in the Andean region.

People who subsisted on a fish-meal diet from the incredibly rich fisheries close offshore and who traded extensively with communities inland built El Paraíso. Its U-shaped layout coincides with the florescence of similarly shaped ceremonial centers in the interior at a time when coastal people began to consume much larger amounts of root crops, make pottery, and shift their settlements inland to river valleys. Some scholars believe that this move coincided with the introduction of large-scale canal irrigation (Moseley, 1985). Perhaps the spread of U-shaped ceremonial centers reflects a radical restructuring of society that coincided with a major economic change. Moseley argues that the introduction of irrigation technology required a major reorganization of labor that coincided with the appearance of new artistic traditions and architectural devices.

In many parts of the Americas, the ritual manipulation of smoke and water served as a way of bridging stratified layers of air, earth, and bodies of water (Sullivan, 1989). Thus, it is argued, the early ceremonial centers of the coast and the highlands reflect an ancient tradition of using these substances to maintain communication with the cosmos. Burnt offerings are found at some Andean sites, among them Kotosh in the mountain foothills. Water flowed through masonry channels at many highland sites and also at the famous ritual center at Chavín de Huántar. There, galleries and ritual waterways flowed through the ceremonial platform and beneath a circular sunken court, connections that allowed the water to resonate under the ground so that the temple "roared." The vast, open courts of coastal U-shaped ceremonial complexes may have housed sacred orchards and gardens irrigated with specially manipulated water supplies. These ritual waterways were to reach their greatest elaboration thousands of years later in the coastal state of Chimu and the great imperial Inca capital at Cuzco (Donnan, 1985).

Water and irrigation assumed major roles in Andean civilization. Irrigation dates back far earlier than Huaca Florida, for the first farmers had probably made some limited use of canals to water their riverside gardens. However, the new works were on a far larger scale, spurred by the availability of an army of workers fed by abundant Pacific fish; by the presence of gentle, cultivable slopes inland; and by the expertise of the local people in farming cotton, gourds, and many lesser crops such as squashes and beans. Huaca Florida's leaders organized the reclamation of the desert by building canals along the steeper areas of the coastal valleys, where the gradients made the diversion of river water an easy task.

At first, the members of each individual family may have worked together to irrigate the family's own sloping gardens, but gradually each community grew so much that essential irrigation works could be handled only by cooperative effort. Perhaps organized irrigation began as many minor cooperative works between individual families and neighboring villages. These simple projects eventually evolved over many centuries into elaborate public works that embraced entire inland valleys and were controlled by a corporate authority that held a monopoly over both the water and the land it irrigated. The process of organization was the result of many complex factors, among them population growth and the emergence of increasing numbers of nonfarming society members, such as priests and artisans, whose food needs had to be met by other people.

By 1400 B.C., the inhabitants of the Casma Valley on the coast were building the huge stone-faced 40-m (130-foot) high platform of Sechin Alto. This mound, nearly 300 m (1,000 feet) long and more than 250 m (800 feet) wide, formed the base of a huge U-shaped ceremonial center

Sechin Alto

1400 B.C.

FIGURE 22.4 Figure from Cerro Sechin.

Early Horizon
900 B.C.

Chavín de Huántar
1500 to 600 B.C.

with sunken courts, plazas, and flanking mounds. A vast sprawl of houses and platforms lies around this largest of all early ceremonial structures on the coast. Only parts of the site have been excavated, including a small building, erected in about 1300 B.C., surrounded by a mosaic of carved monoliths depicting a procession of armed men with dismembered human remains (Figure 22.4). The shrines at Sechin employ one of the persistent themes of ceremonial architecture in the Andes and on the coast: that of artificially raising or lowering sacred spaces relative to one another (Moseley, 1985).

On the coast, early ceremonial sites feature rectangular platform mounds fronting on a circular sunken court that is usually housed in a rectangular forecourt (Donnan, 1985). This form of architecture had appeared by at least 2000 B.C. People entered the forecourt of the sacred complex at ground level, descended into the sunken court, and then climbed the temple platform.

In social and political terms, the Initial Period remains somewhat of a mystery. There are few signs in burial rituals of any social ranking or personal wealth. Leadership and the power of making decisions were probably not inherited and may have been regularly rotated from one person to the next. The many ceremonial centers suggest that different kin groups commemorated their identities by erecting their own shrines, perhaps competitively. There were probably some larger polities extending over several river valleys, one centered in the Casma Valley and three others along nearby parts of the coast, but no one knows who held sway over each of these political units (Pozorski and Pozorski, 1987).

Chavín de Huántar

In 1943, archaeologist Julio Tello identified a distinctive art style in stone, ceramics, and precious metals over a wide area of highland Peru, a style he named Chavín, after a famous prehistoric ceremonial center at Chavín de Huántar in central Peru. Tello's research led to a long-held belief among Peruvianists that the widespread Chavín art style was a "mother culture" for all later Andean civilizations, somewhat equivalent to the Olmec phenomenon in Mesoamerican prehistory (Pozorski and Pozorski, 1987). This became a distinctive "Early Horizon" in Peruvian prehistory, dating to about 900 B.C., when there was a great expansion of indigenous religious belief by conquest, trade, and colonization—when civilization began.

Like many great shrines, Chavín de Huántar has a long and complex history that is only now being unraveled, perhaps starting as early as 1200 B.C. (Kembel, 2005; Rick, 2005). (There was also much earlier occupation dating to as early as 10,000 years ago.) From small-scale beginnings, the builders expanded the center, adapting the local geology and topography by diverting the nearby Mosna River, using massive landfills to raise land surfaces, and erecting heavy foundations to stabilize plazas on swampy ground. At the same time, they used precisely cut and engraved stone plaques to adorn plaza walls, lintels, and terrace fronts. All of this culminated in the world-famous ceremonial buildings of Chavín after 900 B.C., a maze of plazas, stairways, and galleries, associated with a well-established and highly distinctive iconography that was to exercise influence across the Andes (Conklin and Quilter, 2008).

The temple area is terraced, with an impressive truncated pyramid on the uppermost level (Figure 22.5a) (Burger, 1992a). The 10-m (32-foot) high pyramid appears solid but is in fact hollow, a honeycomb of stone passages and rooms. Special rectangular tubes ventilate the galleries. The temple housed a remarkable carving of a jaguarlike human with hair in the form of serpents, the famous "Lanzón," which may have served as an axis joining the heavens, the earth, and the underworld (Figure 22.5b). The deity seems to be acting as an arbiter of balance and order (Burger, 1992b). The entire center was a place of mediation with the heavens and the underworld. Chavín's priests and religious functionaries served as intermediaries between the living and the supernatural. In this shamanlike role, they transformed themselves into supernatural jaguars and crested eagles.

Chavín art reflects these transformations. Jaguar motifs predominate; humans, gods, and animals have jaguarlike fangs or limbs; snakes flow from the bodies of many figures (Figure 22.5c). The art is both grotesque and slightly sinister. Many figures were carved in stone, others in clay or bone, their nostrils dripping with mucus from ingesting hallucinogenic substances. The rituals at Chavín de Huántar included shamanistic transformations and involved both music and elaborate costumes

(a)

(b)   **(c)**

FIGURE 22.5 *Chavín de Huántar. (a) Plan of the ceremonial center showing major architectural features. (b) The "Lanzón" god carved on a pillar set in the midst of the temple interior. (c) A Chavín wall insert approximately 20 cm (7.8 inches) high, showing feline features. Stone inserts such as these are common on the walls of the ceremonial buildings.*

as priests in jaguar and other animal costumes proceeded up the stairway leading to the summit of the temple. The principal god may have been a nature deity associated with thunder and other powerful meteorological phenomena of the nearby high mountains.

Conceivably, theorizes Burger, Chavín de Huántar was a four-stage artificial mountain where rituals surrounded the circulation of water. In these beliefs, the earth floated on a vast ocean. From there, water circulated through mountains to the Milky Way in the heavens, where it became rain to water crops before flowing back into the ocean. Peruvian archaeologist Luis Lumbreras has replicated the deep roaring sound of water flowing through the elaborate stone-lined tunnels and canals of the great shrine. The priests may have used commonly found anthracite mirrors to reflect light down ventilator shafts into the darkest of galleries. Lumbreras believes that the roar of the water would have echoed through the temple during the rainy season and created a symbolic link between the rain-giving mountains, the temple, and the layers of the cosmos (Burger, 1992b).

With its tangled animal and human motifs, Chavín art has all the flamboyance and exotic touches of the tropical forest. The animals depicted—cayman, jaguar, and snake—are all forest animals. The art may have originated in the tropical forests to the east of the Andes, but the Early Horizon Chavín temple has a U-shape with a sunken central plaza, an architectural design documented centuries earlier at other coastal and highland sites (Burger, 1985; Pozorski and Pozorski, 1987).

Chavín de Huántar was a place where a small number of people orchestrated a combination of architecture, decoration, light, sound, and drugs to promote a vision of the world that was different from that of earlier times (see "People of the Past" box). This vision may have promoted the notion that there were new rules, fresh notions of authority that now governed local society. In the event, these new beliefs seem to have attracted considerable numbers of people to Chavín's public rituals, and led to the spread not only of a distinctive art tradition but also of new religious beliefs and practices that were to crystallize even further in the coming centuries. The entire Initial Period in the Andes was one of experimentation, of jostling for authority and preeminence, a time when the Andeans first legitimized social inequality and the institutions of power that concentrated political and religious authority in the hands of a few—the classic ingredients of preindustrial civilization.

By 600 B.C., Chavín de Huántar's great shrine was in decline. A century later, squatters lived in the heart of its central plaza. Chavín was never a great city—only 2,000 to 3,000 people lived there in its heyday. As the shrine was abandoned, it became a modest village of squatters living in the shadow of once sacred precincts. Chavín de Huántar was certainly a large center, probably an influential place within its local area, and one of the largest settlements in Peru at the time of its occupation. It failed to expand into a fully developed urban center, however, and the nascent civilization that worshiped there collapsed, leaving nothing more than a village and a persistent art style and iconography.

The Chavín style may have influenced artistic traditions over a wide area of Peru. Perhaps the religious beliefs behind the motifs were more significant than the art itself. Settlements like Chavín de Huántar were important ceremonial centers that unified surrounding farming villages in a common religious belief, but Chavín de Huántar was not unique. There were many other, often much earlier, centers with the same general architectural and iconographic style. For example, from about **Huaricoto** 2000 to 200 B.C., the small ceremonial center at Huaricoto in the highlands, only 55 km (34 miles) **2000 to 200 B.C.** from Chavín de Huántar, was the home of a religious ideology (Burger and Salazar-Burger, 1985). **Kotosh religious tradition** The "Kotosh religious tradition" practiced here is known to us by sacrificial hearths on which ceremonial offerings were burned. These included animal bones and grain. The ritual hearth was sunk into the floor with a ventilator leading to the outside. Once the sacrifice was complete, the hearth was filled in. At first, the rituals were performed in the open, but larger superstructures surrounded the hearths by the late Initial Period. The rituals may have been performed sporadically at certain times of the year, with the audience watching in the open. The Kotosh religious tradition appears to have flourished over an area of at least 250 km (155 miles) north to south in the highlands in the region where the Chavín cult, with its wild and extravagant animal motifs, was to gain strength.

Many scholars have assumed that the so-called Early Horizon associated with Chavín was a period of the unification and coalescence of early Peruvian culture under a single theology, but in reality the situation was more complicated than that. Chavín itself was a late manifestation of a primeval Andean architectural style, a coalescence of traits and ideas from both the coast and the forest that formed a flamboyant culture in a local area of the highlands. The centuries of its efflorescence, rather than being a catalytic time of unification, may well have been a long period of disruption of age-old communication networks and well-established small polities on the coast. For instance, foreigners from the highlands invaded the coastal Casma. The newcomers forged the coastal valley and neighboring highlands into a single political unit for the first time in prehistory. This development was the precursor of far larger states, a culmination of a prolonged time of culture change and political adjustment.

Paracas: Textiles and Coastal Prehistory

Initial Period and Early Horizon sites are remarkable for their fine textiles. Few ancient societies rivaled the textile artistry of the coastal Peruvians. They lived in an environment in which both animal and plant (especially cotton) fibers were plentiful, and they were able to create fine, complex

People of the Past

"And the Trumpet Shall Sound"
—Chavín de Huantar, Peru, A.D. 800

Chavín de Huantar, the Andes foothills, Peru, 800 B.C., steady rain mingles with wood smoke and incense above the plazas and terraces of the ancient shrine. Hidden passages inside the Old Temple sound and thunder with fast-flowing water in the calm morning air. A watching crowd stands in silence, oblivious to the damp. Suddenly a conch trumpet sounds and sounds again. A dancing, masked shaman appears, deep in a hallucinogenic trance. He chants, sings, utters the pronouncements of the revered oracle, and then vanishes into clouds of smoke and into the depths of the shrine as suddenly as he appeared. Thanks to the discovery of 20 conch trumpets at Chavín, Andean scholars have gained new understandings of ancient rituals.

Strombus, the conch, forms a natural trumpet, easily fashioned by cutting off the spine and grinding out a mouthpiece. Conch trumpets are part of humanity's musical history (Glowacki, 2004). The Greek fish-tailed sea god Triton was said to control the waves by blowing his conch trumpet. An ancient Hindu text, the *Bhagavad Gita*, a Song of God, describes how the Lord Krishna and the Prince Arjuna blew conch shell horns as they rode into battle seated in a giant chariot pulled by white horses. The ancient Maya considered conches sacred. The U.S. Coast Guard even lists conch horns as a legitimate sound making device in its official *Navigation Rules*.

The Maya considered conches sacred, for they symbolized the Moon Goddess, night, darkness, and connections with the Underworld, the place where the Moon died and was reborn. When conch trumpets sounded, they symbolized rebirth, also timeless wisdom. Conch trumpets sounded at great public ceremonies, announced approaching visitors, played important roles in the hunt and in war. These versatile instruments had many symbolic voices, which were pregnant with numerous associations.

Strombus was valued throughout much of the ancient American world, far beyond the confines of lowland kingdoms. The conch thrives in shallow water, which makes the shells easy to collect. In the Andes, artisans scraped away the spines and white nacre (mother of pearl) from *spondylus* shells to expose the brilliant red-orange interior colors that linked the shells symbolically to sacred figures associated with origin myths, also with gods and ancestors. Andeans used its shell as inlay for fine jewelry and other ornaments. There were links between *Spondylus* and water, too. We know that in later times Andean lords offered *spondylus* shell dust to the gods to avert drought. In Mesoamerica,

Spondylus and jade were symbolic of earth and water; the same association, this time with greenstone, was true in the Andes. The red colors inside the shell linked it to blood, females, and sacrifice. It may also have symbolized spiritual transformation, the ability to move from the realm of the living to that of the ancestors, an important, and ancient, practice in Andean shamanism.

Spondylus flesh is seasonally toxic, so much so that the Quechua Indians of the highlands called it the "Food of the Gods," for their myths proclaimed that only deities could consume it safely. When toxic, the meat has hallucinogenic qualities that could induce shamanistic trances. The precious flesh could have been smoked or dried on the coast before being transported inland by llama caravans. Thus, *Spondylus* served as a conduit between the human and supernatural worlds. The "Food of the Gods" was one way of feeding the appetites of the ancestors who controlled water sources and the future of human existence. *Spondylus* was far more than a valued possession; it was a symbolic bridge to life itself in both Andean and Maya society. For over 3,000 years, *Strombus* shells, and probably their dried flesh passed from the Pacific coast in what is now Ecuador southward along the arid Peruvian coast and high into the Andes.

Thanks to the fortunate discovery of the 20 conch trumpets at Chavín de Huantar, experts have been able to expand our understanding how conch trumpets played an important part in rituals at this revered and ancient shrine. Chavín's temple is a maze of subterranean tunnels, where water resonates through hidden defiles. While an expert conch trumpet player blew, researchers recorded him with tiny microphones inside his mouth, the shell's mouthpiece, and in the main body and opening. The effect was like a French horn, the pitch changing when the player put his hand inside the bell. By placing microphones inside the temple's ceremonial chamber, they found that the drone of the trumpet sounded as if it came from several directions simultaneously. The effect was a sense of droning confusion, which must have added to the sense of awe and supernatural fear.

We forget that many of the great monuments of the past were settings for public ceremonies, where sound and acoustic effects were part of the public theater. We also fail to remember that places like the Parthenon, the Temple of Amun at Karnak, Egypt, Maya Tikal, and Chavín de Huántar were not only ablaze with bright, symbolic colors, but resonated with powerful sounds as well. We're finding that the past had powerful voices that are just much part of the archaeological record as stone ruins.

---

fabrics adorned with colorful, intricate patterns (Figure 22.6). The textiles have survived remarkably well in the dry coastal environment, in cemeteries where the dead were wrapped in fabric burial shrouds. The most spectacular textile finds come from very large cemeteries of mummified individuals on the sandy, desolate Paracas Peninsula south of the modern town of Pisco, and also from the Chinchorro culture of southern Peru and northern Chile. (For south coast sites and cultures, see Silverman, 1996.)

Paracas

The Paracas bodies lie in bottle-shaped chambers or stone-lined subterranean vaults with wooden roofs, approximately 5 m (16 feet) high and 4 m (13 feet) across, and cut through sand into soft rock. The sepulchers were divided into small chambers where dozens of mummy bundles were placed. The Andeans did not practice mummification in the formal ancient Egyptian sense; they simply took advantage of the exceptionally dry climate. Each corpse was disemboweled and then allowed to dry out in the hot sand in a fetal position, with the knees at the chin. Eventually, the bodies were wrapped in brightly colored cotton, wool, or both. Sometimes the dead wore decorated mantles, shirts, turbans, or loincloths tailored to the size of the mummy bundle rather than the

FIGURE 22.6   A Paracas woolen mantle showing anthropomorphic shamans.

FIGURE 22.7   Andean backstrap loom.

living person. Occasionally, the mourners attached small ornaments to the mummies or buried tools, food, or even pet monkeys or parrots with the deceased.

From these mummies, we learn the most minute details of Peruvian textiles, for the wrapping cloths are often almost perfectly preserved. The earliest textiles preserved on the coast date to approximately 4500 B.C., soon after cotton was first cultivated. The weavers were expert dyers and used more than 190 hues from plant dyes. The earliest dye in common use was blue, followed by red, and then a multitude of bright colors. Decorative motifs included simple checkerboards, filled squares, and stylized depictions of birds, felines, and other animals. The oldest textiles had rather coarse and uneven yarns produced by the twisting of untreated yarn. After 2000 B.C., however, the weavers began to use delicate wood-and-thorn spindles mounted in a special pottery, gourd, or wooden cup that minimized vibration. Thus they could produce much finer cloth.

Most of the textiles found in coastal tombs were made on backstrap looms just like those still in use in Peru today (Figure 22.7). Two sticks carry the lengthwise threads, the upper one suspended from a post and the lower tied to a belt around the weaver's back. As the work proceeds, the fabric is unrolled from the upper bar and the finished cloth is rolled onto the lower stick. The yarn is wound with a figure-eight motion between the two stakes and is laced fast to the loom sticks so that the edges of the fabric are uniformly finished off. The disadvantage of this type of loom is that the width of the cloth is limited by the span of the weaver's arms. The weavers sometimes combine several backstrap looms to create wider cloths.

Complex Society in the Southern Highlands: Chiripa and Pukara

As Chavín de Huántar rose to prominence in the northern highlands, a separate Early Horizon tradition of complex society developed around Lake Titicaca far to the south (Stanish, 2002, 2011). The plains landscape of the basin was gradually transformed by ever more intensive agriculture and herding.

Chiripa (1400 to 100 B.C.) Chiripa, on the southern shore of Lake Titicaca, was a fishing and fowling settlement where farming and herding were integrated into much earlier hunter-gatherer traditions. Chiripa itself remained a small village until about 1000 B.C., when a platform mound was built in the community, then modified many times over the centuries. The platform itself was stone-faced, with a sunken square court surrounded by rectangular buildings on the platform summit.

Between 600 and 100 B.C., the Chiripa platform was enlarged until it measured 55 m (180 feet) square and 6 m (20 feet) high. The stone-faced sunken court was now 23 m (75 feet) square and 1.5 m (5 feet) deep. Carved stone plaques set into the walls depicted serpents, animals, and humans in the earliest appearance of a stone-carving tradition that persisted along the shores of the lake for many centuries. Sixteen rectangular buildings surrounded the court. Many features of the Chiripa shrine—especially the stepped doorways, sunken courts, and nichelike windows—are ancestral to the later Tiwanaku architectural tradition, which used the same devices for its ceremonial architecture. The religious beliefs associated with this architecture have been grouped under the "Yaya-Mama religious tradition," which flourished for many centuries.

Pukara (400 B.C. to A.D. 100) Pukara, 75 km (47 miles) northwest of Lake Titicaca, was a major center, with a large residential area and an imposing ceremonial complex on a stone-faced terrace, complete with rectangular sunken court and one-room structures on three sides. Pukara's elite lived on nearby terraces, the entire settlement being large enough to be classified as a protocity. Such a dense population could be achieved only by a major investment in agriculture, including many acres of raised fields and large shallow ponds, known as *cochas*, which filled seasonally and where crops were planted at water's edge as the pond dried up.

Judging from the distribution of Pukara pottery styles, the kingdom's power was confined to the northern Titicaca basin, but ceramics and other artifacts from as far afield as the northern coast reflect widespread trade connections. Tiwanaku, then a smaller center than in later centuries, presided over the southern shores of the lake between 400 B.C. and A.D. 100. There is no evidence that Pukara incorporated its southern neighbor.

By 1200 B.C., ceramics, woven textiles, and irrigation agriculture had spread from the Titicaca region to the southern coast, where human population was much smaller.

From the Initial Period onward, the Andean region witnessed an extraordinary array of state-organized societies that displayed a remarkable diversity of culture, art, organization, and religious belief. At the same time, there were broad similarities in cosmology and culture that distinguished these societies from states elsewhere in the prehistoric world.

The Early Intermediate Period

A series of brilliant states flourished on the coast and in the highlands during the Early Intermediate Period: Moche on the northern coast, Nasca in the south, and Recuay and Pukara in the highlands, to mention only a few.

By 200 B.C., some settlements, such as Cerro Arena in the Moche Valley, covered more than a square kilometer. Excavations there during the 1970s revealed more than 2000 separate structures, some with as many as 20 rooms. A small group of 25 finely finished houses may have formed the administrative and residential quarters of Cerro Arena. There were considerable variations between these quarters and the humbler dwellings that surrounded them, as if Cerro Arena society was more complex than that of earlier settlements. This and other large settlements were supported by irrigation systems that required much labor to construct and maintain, as well as strict water controls.

Most of the cultivated land lay along the terraced edges of the valley, where the soils were better drained and easily planted with simple wooden digging sticks, just as they are to this day. Even today the local people divert the seasonal river water into side canals by building dams of stakes and boulders in the streams. There is no reason to suppose that the same simple but effective technique was not used in antiquity. The ancient irrigation canals wound along the sides of the valley, a series of narrow channels approximately 1.2 m (4 feet) wide, set in loops and S-shaped curves, watering plots approximately 21 m (70 feet) square. The surplus flowed off into the Pacific.

The Moche State

By 200 B.C., the Moche state had begun in northern coastal Peru; it flourished for 800 years. Its origins lay in the Chicama and Moche valleys, with great ceremonial centers and huge irrigation works (Donnan and McClelland, 1979; Quilter, 2002). Information about the Moche people of 2000 years ago comes not only from irrigation systems and spectacular monuments but also from hundreds of finely modeled clay pots and human burials preserved in the dry desert sand of the

Chiripa
1400 to 100 B.C.

Pukara
400 B.C. to A.D. 100

Cerro Arena
200 B.C.

Moche state
200 B.C. to A.D. 700

Moche cemeteries. Unfortunately, these burials are a prime target of commercial grave robbers. Many Moche cemeteries look like battlefields after heavy bombardment, for their pots fetch astronomical prices in the international art market.

Sipán
A.D. 400

The spectacular discovery of undisturbed Moche tombs near the village of Sipán, about 680 km (420 miles) northwest of Lima, has revolutionized our knowledge of Moche's elite (Alva and Donnan, 1989) (see Site box). Peruvian archaeologist Walter Alva excavated three unlooted royal burials. The first contained a plank coffin that held the extended skeleton of a man in his late 30s or early 40s lying on his back with his arms along his sides. He wore gold nose and ear ornaments, gold and turquoise bead bracelets, and copper sandals. A ceremonial rattle, crescent-shaped knives, scepters, spears, and exotic seashells surrounded the body (Figure 22.8).

SiTE The Lords of Sipán, Peru

The discovery of the undisturbed Moche burials at Sipán, on Peru's northern coast, ranks as one of the greatest archaeological discoveries of all time (Alva and Donnan, 1989). Peruvian archaeologist Walter Alva spent months painstakingly excavating the royal tombs, using conservation laboratories in Peru and Europe. The result is a triumph of scientific archaeology.

Tomb I held the body of a warrior-priest in his late 30s or early 40s. The mourners had built a brick burial chamber deep in the pyramid (see Figure 22.8), building the sepulcher like a room with solid mud-brick benches along the sides and at the head end. They set hundreds of clay pots in small niches in the benches. Priests dressed the dead lord in his full regalia, including a golden mask, and wrapped his corpse and regalia in textile shrouds. Then they placed him in a plank coffin and set it in the center of the burial chamber, the lid secured with copper straps. They laid out more ceramics, mainly fine spouted bottles, at the foot and head of the coffin. Next, someone sacrificed two llamas and placed them on either side of the foot of the coffin. At some point, the priests also sat the body of a 9- or 10-year-old child in poor health at the head of the warrior-priest.

Five cane coffins were then lowered into the grave, each containing the body of an adult. The two male dead, perhaps bodyguards or members of the lord's entourage, were each laid on top of one of the llamas. One was a strongly built male, more than 35 years old, adorned with copper ornaments and laid out with a war club. The other bore a beaded pectoral and was between 35 and 45 years old. Two of the three women's coffins lay at the head of the royal casket; in the third, at the foot of the coffin, the woman had been turned on her side. Interestingly, the women's disarticulated and jumbled bones suggest they were not sacrificial victims, for they had died long before the lord and were partly decomposed at the time of their burial. Perhaps they had been wives, concubines, or servants. Once the coffins had been positioned, a low beam roof was set in place, too low for someone to stand inside the chamber. Then the tomb was covered, a footless male victim being laid out in the fill. Finally, a seated body with crossed legs watched over the burial chamber from a small niche in the south wall, about 1 m (3 feet) above the roof.

FIGURE 22.8 Burial chamber of a lord of Sipán.

FIGURE 22.9   Using a rotating stand, photographers have "unrolled" both Maya and Moche pots, allowing researchers to view complete scenes painted on them as friezes. This scene from an unrolled Moche pot is an excellent example. Prisoners of war arrive at a ceremonial center for arraignment and sacrifice.

Comparing the objects found in the Sipán tombs with people depicted in Moche art, Christopher Donnan (Alva and Donnan, 1989) has identified the man as a warrior-priest. Such individuals are depicted on Moche pots presiding over sacrifices of prisoners of war (Figure 22.9). Apparently, Moche warriors went to war specifically to take captives. They would strip them of their armor and weapons and lead them in front of the warrior-priest. Then the prisoner's throat was cut, the warrior-priest and others drinking the blood of the slain victim while the corpse was dismembered. On pot after pot, the warrior-priest wears a crescent-shaped headdress atop a conical helmet, exactly the regalia found in the Sipán tombs. Such men were a priesthood of nobles, living in different parts of the kingdom, who enacted the sacrifice ceremony at prescribed times.

When warrior-priests died, they were buried where they had performed the ritual, wearing the formal regalia and the objects they had used in the ceremony. Their successors assumed their roles, wearing new sets of the same costumes and artifacts not only perpetuating the official religion but also ensuring work for the dozens of skilled artisans who manufactured precious artifacts for the nobility. Alva has unearthed two earlier burials, one of them an older man with a gold funerary mask, a magnificent necklace of golden spiders atop their webs, and a gilded copper crab effigy of a deity more than 0.6 m (2 feet) tall that had once been mounted on a fabric banner.

What little we know about the Moche state comes mainly from undisturbed burials and from museum studies of looted pots (Quilter, 2002). They show that Moche society consisted of farmers and fisherfolk as well as skilled artisans and priests, who are depicted on pots with felinelike fangs set in their mouths and wearing puma skin headdresses. A few expert craft potters created superb modeled vessels with striking portraits of handsome, arrogant men who can only have been the leaders of Moche society (see Figure 1.6). The potters modeled warriors, too, complete with shields and war clubs, well-padded helmets, and colorful cotton uniforms. Moche burials show that some members of society were much richer than others, lying in graves filled with as many as 50 vessels or with weapons or staffs of rank. We do not know exactly how Moche society was organized, but we can assume that the ruler wielded authority over a hierarchical state of warrior-priests, doctors, artisans, and the mass of the agricultural population. For instance, there was at least one Moche-style settlement in each subordinate valley.

Fortunately, the Moche artists and artisans gave us some more intimate glances at their society than did those of many civilizations. Their paintings show the ruler with a fine feather headdress seated on a pyramid as a line of naked prisoners parades before him. A decapitated sacrifice at the base of one painting reminds us that human sacrifice may have been the fate of some prisoners of war. We see Moche soldiers in battle, charging their opponents with raised clubs. The defenders raise their feather-decked shields in defiance as the battle is fought to the death. The potters modeled maize beer–befuddled drunks being supported by their solicitous friends, women with owl features, women giving birth with the midwife in attendance, and wives carrying babies on their backs in shawls and in wooden cradles suspended by nets. The women carried out all domestic activities, and the men were warriors, farmers, and fishers. We see the men on a seal hunt, clubbing young seals on the rocky coast as their prey scurry in every direction. A clay llama carries a heavy load, and a mouse eats a maize cob (Figure 22.10).

FIGURE 22.10 A Moche fisher-man paddles a reed canoe.

The pots also depict vividly what the Moche people wore. The men worked in short loincloths or cotton breeches and short, sleeveless shirts underneath tunics that ended above the knee and were fastened around the waist with colorful woven belts. More socially prominent people wore large mantles and headdresses made from puma heads or feathers from highland jungles. Nearly everyone donned some form of headgear. Brightly decorated cotton turbans wound around small caps and held in place with fabric chinstraps were in common use. A small cloth protected the back of the neck from the burning sun. Moche women dressed in loose tunics that reached the knee, and they went bareheaded or draped a piece of cloth around their heads. Many men painted their lower legs and feet in bright colors and tattooed or daubed their faces with lines and other motifs. They often wore disk or crescent nose ornaments and cylindrical bar earrings, sometimes modeled in gold. Their necks bore large collars of stone beads or precious metal, and bracelets covered their arms and legs. Many people wore fiber sandals to protect their feet from the hot sand.

By this time, the coastal people were expert metalworkers (Benson, 1979). They had discovered the properties of gold ore, and they extracted it by panning in streambeds rather than by mining. Soon they had developed ways of hammering it into fine sheets and had learned how to emboss it to make raised designs (Figure 22.11). They had also worked out the technique of annealing, making it possible to soften the metal, hammer it into more elaborate forms, and then join sheets with fine solder. The smiths used gold as a setting for turquoise and shell ornaments and as crafted crowns, circlets, necklaces, pins, and tweezers. Gold was in such short supply in prehistoric times that the metalworkers became expert at depletion gilding, an annealing technique that oxidizes the metal in an alloy of copper and gold to give the finished product a goldlike appearance even when the gold content is as low as 12 percent by weight. Many of the large gold objects, such as animals and plate decorations seized from the Inca by Francisco Pizarro's soldiers, were made of an elaborate alloy of gold, silver, and copper.

The greatest efforts of the Moche people were devoted not to irrigation systems or elaborate burials but to the erection of vast monumental platforms and temples on the southern edge of the cultivated land in the Moche Valley, approximately 6.45 km (4 miles) southeast of the modern city of Trujillo. They used tax labor to build a huge adobe temple platform rising 23 m (76 feet) above **Cerro Blanco** the plain at the foot of a conical hill named Cerro Blanco. The Spaniards called this complex Huaca **A.D. 600** de la Luna, the Temple of the Moon. Huaca del Sol (the Temple of the Sun), standing close by to

FIGURE 22.11 A golden ear ornament worn by a lord of Sipán, inlaid with turquoise. The warrior at center wears a ceremonial headdress and an owl's head necklace. He is accompanied by two attendants. (Courtesy of UCLA Fowler Museum of Cultural History.)

the west, is a confused mass of mud brick that once consisted of a ramp that gave access to five temple platforms, the highest, to the south, towering 41 m (135 feet) above the ground (Figure 22.12). The sides of the pyramid were steeply terraced and have been badly damaged by erosion and looters. Both platforms once supported courts, corridors, and room complexes, perhaps roofed with matting. Huaca del Sol may have been a palace, for there are deep rubbish heaps on the summit of the platform. In contrast, Huaca de la Luna is spotlessly clean, its temple buildings painted with brightly colored murals.

The Moche kingdom was a multivalley state that may have consisted of a series of satellite centers that ruled over individual valleys but owed allegiance to the great centers of the Moche Valley. At one time, the Moche presided over the coast as far south as the Nepeña Valley. Where possible, the Moche extended their ambitious irrigation systems to link several neighboring river valleys and then constructed lesser copies of their capital as a basis for the secure administration of their new domains. Their traders were in contact with the north and with the Nasca people on the southern coast as well (Proulx, 1985).

Like all Andean coastal societies, the Moche lived at the mercy of droughts and El Niños. Michael Moseley (2000) believes that a series of natural disasters struck Moche domains in the late sixth century A.D. The first may have been a devastating drought cycle between A.D. 564 and 594, identified from the growth lines deep in mountain glaciers between Cuzco and Lake Titicaca. Crop yields in some valleys may have fallen as much as 20 percent.

Moche lords were, apparently, well aware of the potential devastation caused by major El Niño events. They integrated such disasters into their religion and ideology. The pectorals, bracelets, and other ornaments worn by the Sipán lords, and from other looted tombs, prominently depict exotic animals like the Peruvian eagle ray and swimming crabs that only arrived off the North Coast when the El Niño countercurrent was flowing. The elite also wore depictions of local species affected by El Niño events such as octopuses, catfish, seabirds, and sea lions. The temple walls of Huaca de la Luna and other shrines also bear painted reliefs of animals associated with El Niños. Archaeologist Steve Bourget theorizes that Moche rulers responded to the threat of El Niños by associating

FIGURE 22.12 Huaca del Sol.

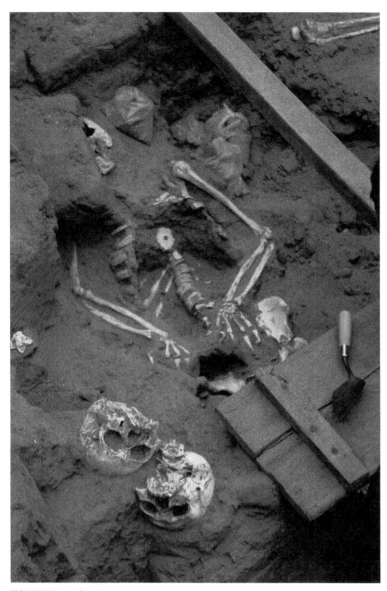

FIGURE 22.13 Sacrificial victims at Huaca de la Luna.

their authority with the awesome power of such events, which could transform the marine environment. When an El Niño brought torrential rains that washed away entire irrigation systems and decimated the anchovy fisheries, the rulers used the occasion to reinforce their authority at times of crisis. They already wore the iconography of such events on their bodies, and caused it to be displayed on temples and on ritual vessels. Their authority came from their unique relationship with the powers of the supernatural, reinforced by human sacrifice (Figure 22.13).

Sometime between A.D. 650 and 700, a great earthquake struck the Andes, choking rivers with debris from landslides. Silt-laden floodwaters may have blocked irrigation canals, preventing water from reaching the nearby fields. The silt flowed into the ocean and was washed ashore, then blown inland by the prevailing winds to form huge sand dunes. Dense sandstorms may have blanketed entire villages and many acres of irrigated land.

An El Niño flooded the imperial capital itself just before A.D. 600. The city was repaired, and then was overwhelmed by coastal dunes that buried most of it, except the great huacas, under fine sand. The same El Niño devastated the coastal fisheries. Anchovies vanished from the inshore waters and torrential rains flooded the arid coastal plains, turning them into swamps and sweeping away entire villages and carefully maintained irrigation schemes. At this point, the southern Moche domains broke off from the state. The great lords abandoned Huaca del Sol and moved northward to Pampa Grande in the Lambayeque Valley, more than 50 km (30 miles) from the Pacific and close to where the rivers debouched from the mountain foothills and intensive irrigation maximized water supplies. But only half a century later, another El Niño descended on the coast with catastrophic effects, and Moche civilization collapsed (Chapdelaine, 2000).

The Middle Horizon: Tiwanaku and Wari

Middle Horizon
A.D. 600 to 1000

The Middle Horizon flourished between A.D. 600 and 1000 in the southern highlands. This period saw the beginnings of monumental building at a highland site—Tiwanaku—that would influence much of the Peruvian world (Kolata, 1993, 2002).

Tiwanaku

Tiwanaku
C. A.D. 450 to 1200

Between A.D. 600 and 1000, the wealthiest highland districts lay at the southern end of the central Andes, in the high, flat country surrounding Lake Titicaca. This was fine llama country. The local people maintained enormous herds of these beasts of burden and were also expert irrigation farmers. The altiplano supported the densest population in the highlands, and almost inevitably, the Titicaca region became an economic and demographic pole of the prosperous northern coast. By A.D. 450, Tiwanaku, on the southern side of the lake, was becoming a major population center as well as an economic and religious focus for the region (Janusek, 2008; Kolata, 2002). The arid lands on which the site lies were irrigated and supported a population of perhap. 20,000 around the monumental structures near the center of the site. By A.D. 600, Tiwanaku was acquiring much of its prosperity from trade around the lake's southern shores. Copper working probably developed independently of the well-established copper technology on the northern coast.

Tiwanaku was not only an economic force but a religious force as well. The great sunken court of Kalasasaya is dominated by a large earth platform faced with stones (Figure 22.14a). Nearby, a rectangular enclosure is bounded with a row of upright stones, and there is a gateway carved with an anthropomorphic god, sometimes called Viracocha (Figure 22.14b). Smaller buildings, enclosures,

(a)   (b)

FIGURE 22.14   Tiwanaku. (a) The great sunken court. (b) Gateway of the Sun, made from one block of lava. The central figure is known as the Gateway God; notice its jaguar mouth and serpent-ray headdress. The running figures flanking the god often are called messengers.

and huge statues are also near the ceremonial structures. One recently excavated temple contained the skeleton of a young warrior, perhaps a captive, sacrificed in A.D. 600.

The striking Tiwanaku art style is related to earlier iconography found at Pukara. Like the Chavín tradition, this tradition probably represents a powerful iconography. Tiwanaku's art motifs include pumas and condors, as well as anthropomorphic gods attended by lesser deities or messengers. They occur over much of southern Peru, as well as in Bolivia, the southern Andes, and perhaps as far afield as northwest Argentina. So powerful was the iconography of—and presumably the political and economic forces behind—Tiwanaku that there was a serious political vacuum in the south after A.D. 1200, when the state inexplicably collapsed into obscurity.

Tiwanaku obtained much of its food from large community-based raised-field systems developed on the low-lying pampas (plains) and surrounded with irrigation canals. The water in the canals provided excellent protection for potatoes and other growing plants against harsh winter frosts, which decimated crops on higher ground. The same fields were highly fertile, the soils enriched by muck from the surrounding canals. In recent years, archaeologists have worked closely with development agencies to reintroduce the ancient agricultural expertise to local villages, with marked success (Erickson, 1992; Kolata, 1993).

Wari

Wari, in the Ayacucho Valley, is a highland urban and ceremonial center that stands on a hill (Isbell and Schreiber, 1978). It is associated with huge stone walls and many dwellings that cover several square miles. The Wari art styles also show some Pukara influence, especially in anthropomorphic feline, eagle, and serpent beings depicted on ceramic vessels. Like their southern neighbors, the Wari people seem to have revered a Viracocha-like being. By A.D. 800, their domains extended from Moche country in the Lambayeque Valley on the northern coast to south of Nasca territory, down the Moquequa Valley of the south-central Andes and into the highlands south of Cuzco. They were expert traders, who probably expanded their domain through conquest, commercial enterprise, and perhaps religious conversion. Storehouses and roads were probably maintained by the state. As with the Inca of later centuries, the state controlled food supplies and labor (Schreiber, 1987).

Wari
A.D. 600

The Cerro Baul site in the Moquequa Valley was a fortified settlement placed by the Wari on an impregnable mesa, with only a single, heavily defended trail giving access to the flat summit, where the inhabitants constructed complexes of rectangular structures, courts, patios, and occasional D-shaped buildings. Cerro Baul is a powerful Wari presence in a foreign valley, perhaps sited there to exploit local sources of copper, lapis lazuli, or obsidian (Moseley et al., 1991).

Wari itself was abandoned in the ninth century A.D., but its art styles persisted on the coast for at least two more centuries. Both Wari and Tiwanaku were a turning point in Peruvian prehistory, a stage when small regional states became integrated into much larger political units. This unification may have been achieved by conquest and other coercive means, but the iconography shared by many coastal and highland Peruvians at the time must have been a powerful catalyst for closer political unity. There was constant and often intensive interaction between two poles of Andean civilization in the highlands and the lowlands, each with quite different food resources and products. This interaction, long a feature of Andean life, was to intensify in the centuries that lay ahead.

These two great polities collapsed toward the end of the first millennium, leaving a vast political vacuum of small competing states that was filled by the Inca after a period of conflict and warfare.

The Late Intermediate Period: Sicán and Chimor

Sicán culture
A.D. 900 to 1100

The highland states traded regularly with several emerging polities on the coast, each of them founded on extensive irrigation systems. The decline of Moche in the Lambayeque Valley had left somewhat of a vacuum, filled by the Sicán culture after A.D. 700. Sicán reached its peak between A.D. 900 and 1100, centered in the Lambayeque Valley and remarkable for its magnificent gold work. In Sicán society, metals of all kinds served as markers of social status and wealth and as a prestigious medium of political, social, and religious expression, because people's access to artifacts and ornaments in different ores was carefully limited according to rank. The so-called East Tomb at the Middle Sicán capital in the La Leche Valley yielded the burial of a great lord aged between 40 and 50, who had been mummified, then dressed in his full regalia (Figure 22.15). His head had been detached and lay in front of the inverted body facing west. Sacrificial victims and elaborate grave ornaments in gold, gold and silver alloy, and bronze accompanied him, including a pair of golden gloves. The West Tomb nearby contained the remains of another personage, 30 to 40 years old. Twenty women and other victims lay in the grave; DNA, health state, and dental traits divides them into two groups, the one close kin of the deceased who perhaps practiced endogamy, the others diverse, perhaps victims from various parts of the Sicán domains. These two spectacular burials are part of an elite cemetery that remains unexcavated (Shimada et al., 2004).

Tucumé
A.D. 1000

Sicán lords encouraged intensive metal production, as well as seagoing trade in copper and other metals far to the north along the Ecuadorian coast. At the same time, they supervised massive irrigation works from major centers like Tucumé in the Leche Valley (Heyerdahl, 1996). Intervalley canals, requiring constant cooperation between lords in neighboring centers, sometimes linked these various cities. If oral traditions are to be believed, many of these lords were related to one another and had common ancestors.

Chimu state (Chimor)
A.D. 1375 to 1475

Between A.D. 1050 and 1100, an El Niño caused widespread flooding and disruption. The royal precincts at Sicán itself were burned as political power shifted west to the El Purgatorio region. In A.D. 1375, an expanding Chimu state overthrew Sicán and absorbed its domains into a new empire.

The Moche Valley had long been densely cultivated, but the Chimu people now embarked on much more ambitious irrigation schemes. They built large storage reservoirs and terraced hundreds of miles of hillside to control the flow of water down steep slopes. One channel extended nearly 32 km (20 miles), from the Chicama Valley to the capital, Chan Chan, and was designed to supplement the relatively limited water supplies that came from the nearby Moche Valley (Figure 22.16). Even in periods of extreme drought these canals carried water from the deep-cut riverbed to terraces long distances away. Thus, the Chimu created thousands of hectares of new fields and used water from great distances to harvest two or three crops a year from plots where only one crop had been possible before, and that at the time of the annual flood. So effective were these irrigation techniques that the Chimu controlled more than 12 river valleys with at least 50,590 cultivable ha (125,000 acres), all of them farmed with hoes or digging sticks. Today, the local farmers water their maize crops approximately every 10 days, and this probably was the practice in Chimu times as well.

According to seventeenth-century Spanish chroniclers, the Chimu always maintained that their domains had originally been ruled over by petty chiefs, but when the Inca conquered them between A.D. 1462 and 1470, they were led by a ruler named Michancamán, who governed through a network of hereditary local nobility. His courtiers held specific ranks, such as "Blower of the Shell Trumpet"; "Master of the Litter and Thrones"; and "Preparer of the Way," the official who scattered powdered shell dust wherever the ruler was about to walk. An archaeologist working at Chan Chan in 1969–1970 found a layer of powdered shell dust on a bench in a forecourt, perhaps evidence that the Preparer of the Way had been at work. Loyal local leaders ruled the various

FIGURE 22.15   Reconstructed gold mask of a Lord of Sicán. The mask has eyes of emeralds and amber beads. The forehead ornament is adorned with a modeled bat head; a cylindrical crown, which is hidden; and a large head ornament. 100 cm (39 inches) high.

(a)

(b)

FIGURE 22.16   Chan Chan. (a) General view. (b) Restored enclosure wall.

Chan Chan
A.D. 1400

provinces of the kingdom. They enjoyed not only tribute privileges but also rights to crops and land and to agricultural labor by commoners. Perhaps the most privileged members of society were the Oquetlupec, herb curers paid by the state to look after the sick. This was a hierarchical, highly organized society with strict social classes of nobles and commoners. Perhaps to enforce the social hierarchy, the legal system was very strict (Rowe, 1948).

The focus of the Chimu state was Chan Chan, a huge complex of walled compounds lying near the Pacific at the mouth of the Moche Valley. Chan Chan covers nearly 10 sq. km (4 sq. miles), the central part consisting of nine large enclosures laid out in a sort of broken rectangle. Each enclosure probably functioned as the palace of the current ruler of Chan Chan, who probably built himself a new headquarters near those of his predecessors (Moseley and Day, 1982). The adobe walls of these compounds once stood as high as 9.9 m (33 feet) and covered areas as large as 200 by 600 m (670 by 2000 feet). The walls were constructed not to defend the rulers but to provide physical and ritual isolation as well as privacy and some shelter from the ocean winds. Each enclosure had its own water supply, a burial platform, and lavishly decorated residential rooms roofed with cane frames covered with earth and grass. The same enclosure that served as a palace during life became the ruler's burial place in death. The common people lived in tracts of small adobe and reed-mat houses on the western side of the city. Similar dwellings can be seen on the coast to this day.

Oral traditions tell us that the Chimu rulers practiced the institution of split inheritance, whereby each ruler inherited no material possessions to finance his reign. Split inheritance, described on p. 470, was to play a major role in Inca civilization. Chimu rulers had access to and control of a huge labor pool. To expand and maintain irrigation works, they employed laborers who also served in military levies to acquire new lands and expand the tax base (Pozorski, 1987).

These rulers soon learned the value of officially maintained roadways that enabled them to move their armies from one place to the next with rapid dispatch. They constructed roads that connected each valley in their domain with the capital. The rural routes were little more than tracks between low adobe walls or widely spaced posts, mostly following centuries-old paths through the fields. In the densely populated valleys, Chimu roads were between 4.5 and 7.5 m (15 and 25 feet) across. In some places, the roadway widened dramatically to 24 m (80 feet) or more. These were the roads that carried gold ornaments and fine hammered vessels to Chan Chan and textiles and fine black-painted vessels throughout the empire. The traveler would occasionally encounter heavily laden llamas carrying goods to market, but most loads were carried on people's backs, for the Chimu never developed the wheeled cart. All revenues and tribute passed along the official roadways, as did newly conquered peoples being resettled in some area far from their original homeland. This draconian resettlement tactic was so successful that the Inca adopted it. The ruler would then install his own appointee in the new lands, in a compound palace that was a smaller version of Chan Chan itself.

The Chimu empire extended far south, at least to the Casma Valley and perhaps reaching to the vicinity of modern Lima, for the main focus of civilization lay on the northern Peruvian shore, where the soils were fertile and large-scale irrigation was a practical reality. Chimu armies fought with powerful neighbors to the south, among them the chief of Pachacamac, who controlled some narrow valleys south of Lima. Pachacamac had long been a venerated shrine and already boasted a terraced temple covering 0.3 ha (0.6 acre). Pachacamac has been a grave robbers' paradise for centuries. Later, the Inca built a vast Temple of the Sun at Pachacamac, an irregular trapezoid in a commanding position on a rocky hill.

For all its wide-ranging military activities and material wealth, the Chimu empire was vulnerable to attack from outside. The massive irrigation works of the northern river valleys were easily disrupted by an aggressive conqueror, for no leader, however powerful, could hope to fortify the entire frontier of the empire. We know little of the defenses, except for Paramonga in the Fortaleza Valley, a massive terraced structure built of rectangular adobes that overlooks the probable southern limits of Chimu territory. The Chimu were also vulnerable to prolonged drought, for the storage capacity of their great irrigation works was sufficient to carry them over only one or two lean seasons. Perhaps, too, the irrigated desert soils became too saline for agriculture, so that crop yields fell drastically when population densities were rising sharply. Because the Chimu depended on a highly specialized agricultural system, once that system was disrupted—whether naturally or artificially—military conquest and control of the irrigation network were easy, especially for aggressive and skillful conquerors such as the Inca, who conquered the Chimu in the 1460s.

The Late Horizon: The Inca State

Late Horizon
A.D. 1476 to 1534

The Late Horizon of Peruvian archaeology was also the shortest, dating from A.D. 1476 to 1534. It is the period of the Inca Empire, when those mighty Andean rulers held sway over an enormous area of highland and lowland country (D'Altroy, 2003; C. Morris and von Hagen, 2011; Rowe, 1946).

The Inca were born into an intensely competitive world, their homeland lying to the northwest of the Titicaca basin in the area around Cuzco (Conrad and Demarest, 1984). They were a small-scale farming society living in small villages and organized in kin groups known as **ayllu**, groups claiming a common ancestry and also owning land in common (Hastorf, 1992). The Inca were a self-sufficient people, and their *ayllu* leaders contributed labor to one another as a means of organizing and distributing labor reciprocally. The ancestors protected the *ayllu* and legitimized its land-ownership. It was small wonder that the Inca always took good care of their ancestral mummies. The bodies of the dead, their tombs, and their fetishes, as well as numerous other sacred places and phenomena, were known as *huaca*.

The later Inca rulers clothed their origins in a glorious panoply of heroic deeds. It is likely, however, that the Inca had originally been a fractious, constantly quarreling petty chiefdom. The chronicles of early conquest reflect the constant bickering of village headmen, and the earliest Inca rulers were probably petty war leaders (*sinchi*), elected officials whose success was measured by their victories and booty. To stay in office, they had to be politically and militarily adept so that they could both defeat and appease their many potential rivals. The official Inca histories speak of at least eight Inca rulers between A.D. 1200 and 1438, but these genealogies are hardly reliable (Rowe, 1946). They probably depict little more than legendary figures. During the fourteenth century, a number of small tribal groups in the southern highlands began to develop a more powerful military confederacy, but the Inca flourished in this competitive atmosphere because their leaders were expert politicians as well as warriors. A leader named Viracocha Inca rose to power at the beginning of the fifteenth century. Unlike his raiding predecessors, however, he turned to permanent conquest and soon presided over a small kingdom centered in Cuzco. Viracocha Inca became the living god in the first of a series of constant religious changes that kept the new kingdom under tight control. At about the same time, a new religious cult emerged, that of Inti, a celestial divine ancestor who was part of the Sky god. (We say "part" because Inti was more a cluster of solar aspects than the Sun god.)

Inca civilization
A.D. 1476 to 1534

Around 1438, a brilliant warrior named Cusi Inca Yupanqui was crowned Inca (the term *Inca* can refer to both the ruler and the people) after a memorable victory over the neighboring Chanca tribe. He immediately took the name Pachakuti ("He Who Remakes the World") and set about transforming the Inca state. In particular, he and his henchmen developed a form of royal ancestor cult. This in itself was not especially significant because Pachakuti was simply reworking an age-old Andean tradition, but the law of split inheritance that went along with it had a lasting and profound significance. A dead ruler was mummified. His palace, servants, and possessions were still considered his property and were maintained by all his male descendants except his successor, normally one of his sons. The deceased was not considered dead, however. His mummy attended great ceremonies and would even visit the houses of the living (Figure 22.17). Those entrusted to look after the king ate and talked with him, just as if he were still alive. This element of continuity made the royal mummies some of the holiest artifacts in the empire. Dead rulers were living sons of Inti, visible links with the gods, the very embodiment of the Inca state and of the fertility of nature.

Meanwhile, the ascending ruler was rich in prestige but poor in possessions. The new king had to acquire wealth so he could both live in royal splendor and provide for his mummy in the future—and the only wealth in the highland kingdom was taxable labor. Therefore, every adult male in Inca country had to render a certain amount of labor to the state each year after providing for the basic subsistence needs of his own *ayllu*. This **mit'a** system repaired bridges and roads, cultivated state-owned lands, manned the armies, and carried out public works. It was a reciprocal system. The state, or those benefiting from the work, had to feed and entertain those doing it. Because the Inca rulers needed land to provide food for those who worked for them, and the earlier kings owned most of the land near Cuzco, the only way a new ruler could obtain his own royal estates was by expansion into new territory. This expansion could not take the form of temporary raids. The conquest had to be permanent, the conquered territory had to be controlled and taxed, and the ruler's subjects had to be convinced of the value of a policy of long-term conquest.

A highly complicated set of benefits, economic incentives, rewards, and justifications fueled and nourished the Inca conquests. Inca rulers turned into brilliant propagandists, reminding everyone that they were gods and that the welfare of all depended on the prosperity of all rulers, past and present, and on constant military conquest. There were initial economic advantages, too, in the form of better protection against famine. Also, the rulers were careful to reward prowess in battle. Nobles were promoted to new posts and awarded insignia that brought their lifestyle ever closer to that of the king, and even a brave regular warrior could become a member of the secondary nobility.

The successful ideology of the Inca provided them with a crucial advantage over their neighbors, and within a decade of Pachakuti's accession they were masters of the southern highlands. Their army had become an invincible juggernaut, and in less than a century the tiny kingdom taken over by Pachakuti had become a vast empire. Topa Inca (1471–1493) extended the Inca Empire into Ecuador, northern Argentina, parts of Bolivia, and Chile. His armies also conquered the Chimu state, whose water supplies Topa Inca already controlled. The best Chimu craftsworkers were carried off to work for the court of the Inca. Another king, Wayna Capac, ruled for 32 years after Topa Inca and pushed the empire deeper into Ecuador (for a different view of Inca development; see Bauer, 1992).

The Inca rulers developed an efficient administrative system to run their empire, one based firmly on the precedents of earlier societies. Tawantinsuyu ("The Land of the Four Quarters") was divided into four large provinces known as *suyu* (quarters), each subdivided into smaller provinces and some of them coinciding with older conquered kingdoms (D'Altroy, 2003; Hyslop. 1990; Patterson, 1992). A leading member of a local family, known as a *curaca*, usually ruled conquered peoples in the Inca Empire. These hereditary chiefs were a form of secondary non-Inca nobility who governed a taxpaying population of 100 people or more, but Inca nobles held all the really important government posts. The Inca rulers realized, however, that the essence of efficient government in such varied topography was efficient communications, so the road builders commandeered a vast network of age-old highways from the states they conquered. They linked them in a coordinated system with regular rest houses so that they could move armies, trade goods, and send messengers from one end of the kingdom to the other in short order (Hyslop. 1984).

The Inca passion for organization impinged on everyone's life (Figure 22.18). Their society was organized into 12 age divisions for the purposes of census and tax assessment, divisions based on both physical changes like puberty and major social events like marriage. The most important stage was adulthood, which lasted as long as one could do a day's work. All the census and other data of the empire were recorded not on tablets but on knotted strings. These *quipu* were a complex and sophisticated record-keeping system that seems to have been so efficient that it more than made up for the lack of writing (Ascher and Ascher, 1981). They also were a powerful instrument for codifying laws and providing data for the inspectors, who regularly visited each household to check that everyone was engaged in productive work and living in sanitary conditions. Ongoing efforts to decipher the *quipu* have established that there were ways of transferring

FIGURE 22.17 An Inca royal mummy as depicted by seventeenth-century native chronicler Felipe Guaman Poma de Ayala.

(a)

(b)

FIGURE 22.18 (a) Inca terracing in the Urubama River valley. (b) Masterly Inca agricultural terracing at Moray near Cuzco, Peru.

data between different *quipus*, also suggested that some knot arrangements may have identified their makers (Urton, 2003) (Figure 22.19).

At the time of the Spanish Conquest, the Inca controlled the lives of as many as 6 million people, most of them living in small villages dispersed around religious and political centers (D'Altroy, 2003). It was here that Inca artisans labored, producing major works of art in gold and silver. Brightly painted Inca pottery occurs throughout the empire; it is decorated with black, white, and red geometric designs. Despite the widespread distribution of Inca pots and

FIGURE 22.19 A quipu from the Nazca River Valley, in southern Peru. Museum of World Cultures, Göteborg, Sweden. Photo by G. Urton.

artifacts, however, regional pottery styles flourished because the village potters, many of whom were conquered subjects, continued the cultural traditions of earlier centuries. Inca political and religious power was based on major ritual centers like Cuzco in the Andes, where the ceremonial precincts were built of carefully fitted stones (Figure 22.20) (Bauer, 2004; Gasparini and Margolies, 1980).

The Inca ruler held court in Cuzco, surrounded by plotting factions and ever-changing political tides. One villain was the very institution of split inheritance that fueled Inca military conquest. Every ruler faced increasingly complex governance problems as a result. The need for more and more conquests caused great military, economic, and administrative stress. The logistics of long-distance military campaigns were horrendous, and the soldiers had to be fed from state-owned land, not royal estates. Moreover, although their tactics were well adapted to open country, where they were invincible, the rulers eventually had to start fighting in forested country, where their armies fared badly. Meanwhile, the empire had grown so large that communication became an increasingly

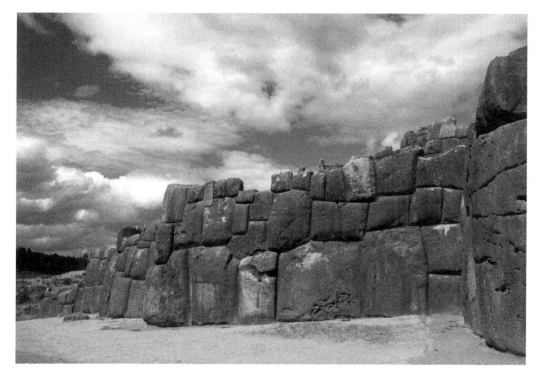

FIGURE 22.20 Inca masonry at the fortress of Sacsahuaman near Cuzco, Peru.

lengthy process, compounded by the great diversity of the people living within the Inca domain. Also, the increasing number of high-ranking nobles devoted to the interests of dead rulers led to chronic factionalism in Cuzco. Under its glittering façade, Tawantinsuyu was becoming politically unstable. In the end, the Inca Empire was overthrown not by Peruvians but by a tiny band of foreigners with firearms who could exploit the inherent vulnerability of such a conforming hierarchical society.

Amazonia

While the Inca ruled a vast area of the Andes, different cultural developments had unfolded east of the Andes. Amazonia is the largest ecological zone in South America, covered mostly with tropical rain forest and other types of forest. Seemingly environmentally homogeneous, this huge area offers all kinds of habitats for human settlement. Traditionally, archaeologists have tended to ignore the rain forest, assuming that it had but impoverished resources and small populations. In fact, the region, although far from a paradise, supported extensive farming settlements and flourishing trade networks.

8500 B.C.   Hunter-gatherers settled in Amazonia as early as 8500 B.C., perhaps earlier—witness the occupation at Caverna de Pedra Pintada (see Chapter 5). Nomadic hunter-gatherer populations grew considerably after 6000 B.C., with heavy reliance on fish and shellfish and, by at least 3500 B.C., by cultivation.

3500 B.C.   ably after 6000 B.C., with heavy reliance on fish and shellfish and, by at least 3500 B.C., by cultivation. In more open environments, people living inland relied on small game.

By 1000 B.C., as Chavín was rising to importance in the Andes, Arawk-speaking Saladoid peoples and others (who spread north into the Caribbean's Lesser Antilles after 500 B.C.; see Chapter 13) lived on the floodplain of the middle Orinoco River. They settled in quite large villages, the huts surrounding a circular plaza. At about this time, Arawak and Tupiguarani speakers spread across the Amazonian lowlands in one of the great linguistic diasporas of ancient times, perhaps connected with the spread of slash-and-burn cultivation. These peoples were organized in small chiefdoms and settled in large fortified villages as more complex societies developed slowly—in contrast with the

A.D. 500 to 1000   Andean region, where change was faster and more volatile. By A.D. 500 to 1000, local kingdoms with dense populations were well established along the major Amazonian rivers. They interacted with one another regularly, to the point that there was basic cultural homogeneity over large areas, reflected in remarkably standardized polychrome pottery.

Marajó   This Polychrome Tradition is best known from the Marajó site in the Amazon estuary, occupied
A.D. 400 to 1400   from about A.D. 400 to 1400. Here artificial mounds rose as much as 10 m (33 feet) above the river, important ceremonial structures that remained in use for nearly a millennium (Roosevelt, 1991). The mounds were occupied and also served as cemeteries, the dead being buried in anthropomorphic, carefully modeled burial urns. The most elaborate occur in the larger mounds, as if the privilege of being buried there was reserved for the elite. Some 500 km (310 miles) upstream, the Santarem

Santarem culture   culture flourished, based on an extensive capital on a bluff above the Tapajós River. Unlike its neighbor downstream, Santorem survived into historical times, thriving off a widespread trade in beautiful pottery. Signs of dense human settlement cover an area of about 25 sq. km (10 sq. miles), as if the capital rivaled places like Chan Chan and Teotihuacán in extent.

Açutuba   In the central Amazon, the Açutuba settlement near the modern city of Manaus covers more than 30 ha (75 acres), with a huge sunken amphitheater surrounded by carefully shaped slopes on three sides. Other extensive settlements lay nearby. Trade in pottery and a wide range of perishable commodities, as well as shamanistic knowledge, continued into historic times. The southern Amazon region supported densely populated chiefdoms, which, once again, developed gradually from simpler farming societies. Many of their plaza villages were carefully planned, with an elaborate ceremonial life where religious beliefs formed the basis for many lasting alliances. These polities subsisted off manioc cultivation, intensive fishing, and fruits of many kinds.

The upper Amazon enjoyed a complicated relationship with the Inca and other Andean societies on the other side of the mountains, but here again we find small-scale tropical farming societies developing gradually into small chiefdoms where shamanism was an important element of political power.

Amazonia supported numerous powerful chiefdoms, all of them developed from deep cultural roots in the linguistic diasporas of earlier times. Here, as elsewhere in South America, kinship and descent were all-important in societies where relationships to powerful ancestors and special creators were paramount (Heckenberger, 2002).

The Spanish Conquest (1532 to 1534)

In South America, as elsewhere, the arrival of Europeans disrupted millennia of cultural development. The process of disruption took many years but can be measured by the experience of the Inca.
A.D. 1532   In 1532, a small party of rapacious Spanish conquistadors landed in northern Peru (Hemming,

FIGURE 22.21 Machu Picchu. Forgotten for nearly 400 years after the Spanish Conquest, Machu Picchu was rediscovered by the American explorer Hiram Bingham in 1911.

1970). When Francisco Pizarro arrived, the Inca state was in some political chaos, its people already decimated by smallpox and other diseases introduced by the first conquistadors. Inca Wayna Capac had died in an epidemic in A.D. 1525. The empire was plunged into a civil war between his son Huascar and another son, Atahuallpa, half brother to Huascar. Atahuallpa eventually prevailed, but as he moved south from Ecuador to consolidate his territory, he learned that the Spanish adventurer Francisco Pizarro had landed in Peru.

The Spaniards had vowed to make Peru part of Spain and were bent on plunder and conquest. Pizarro arrived in the guise of a diplomat, captured Atahuallpa by treachery, collected a huge quantity of gold in ransom, and then brutally murdered him. A year later, the Spaniards captured the Inca capital with a tiny army. They took over the state bureaucracy and appointed a puppet ruler, Manco Inca, but many Inca groups continued their traditional lifeways in isolated locations like Machu Picchu high in the Andes (Burger and SalazarBurger, 2004) (Figure 22.21). Three years later, Manco Inca turned on his masters in a bloody revolt. Its suppression finally destroyed the greatest of the Peruvian empires (Figure 22.22).

The Spanish conquest of Mexico and Peru saw the last major confrontation between the forces of an expanding Europe that was emerging from centuries of feudalism and complex non-Western societies that were still living with the full legacy of earlier times.

The four and a half centuries since the Spanish conquests of Mexico and Peru have seen European settlement in all corners of the globe, the emergence of the industrial state, and the acting out of the last, tragic chapter of human prehistory: the clash between the Western and non-Western worlds (Wolf, 1984).

FIGURE 22.22 Silver Inca llamas and a female figure; these works epitomize late Andean artistry in sheet metal. Tragically, few such objects survived the depredations of the Spanish Conquest.

Summary

- The earliest complex societies of coastal Peru may have developed as a result of the intensive exploitation of maritime resources, especially small fish easily netted from canoes. In time, abundant food surpluses, growing population densities, and larger settlements may have preadapted coastal people to intensive irrigation agriculture. These societies were organized in increasingly complex ways.

- During the so-called Initial Period of Peruvian prehistory, large monumental structures appeared, many of them U-shaped, just before and during the transition toward greater dependence on maize agriculture. This was also a period of continuous interaction and extensive trade between the coast and the highlands.

- This florescence of social complexity, new art traditions, and monumental architecture coincided with the emergence of several small polities in river valleys on the coast.

- The culmination of this trend is seen in various local traditions, among them the famous Chavín style. Chavín de Huántar, once thought to have been the source of Peruvian civilization, is now known to be a late manifestation of cultural trends that began as early as 2000 B.C.

- After about 200 B.C., a series of coastal kingdoms of the so-called Middle Horizon developed between 200 B.C. and A.D. 600 and lasted until about A.D. 1000, the political and economic influence of which spread beyond their immediate valley homelands. These states included Moche and Nasca, remarkable for their fine pottery styles and expert alloy and gold metallurgy. They flourished in the first millennium A.D.

- About A.D. 1375, Chimu, with its great capital at Chan Chan on the northern coast, dominated a wide area of the lowlands. Its compounds reflect a stratified state with many expert craftspeople and a complex material culture.

- During the Late Horizon of Peruvian prehistory (A.D. 1400 to 1534), there was unification of the highlands and the lowlands under the Inca Empire, which may have emerged as early as A.D. 1200 and lasted until the Spanish Conquest in A.D. 1532–1534. The Inca rulers were masters of bureaucracy and military organization. They governed a highly structured state—one, however, that was so weakened by civil war and disease that it fell easily to the conquistador Francisco Pizarro and his small army of adventurers.

- The Amazon Basin was settled by hunter-gatherers as early as 8500 B.C., with cultivation beginning around 3500 B.C. By 1000 B.C., Awarak and Tupiguarani speakers had spread across the Amazonian lowlands, organized in small chiefdoms, which interacted with one another and with the Inca and other societies on the other side of the Andes.

Key Terms

ayllu (470)
mit'a (471)

Further Reading

Alva, Walter, and Christopher Donnan. 1989. *Royal Tombs of Sipán*. Los Angeles: Fowler Museum of Cultural History, UCLA.

Morris, Craig and Adriana von Hagen. 2011. *The Incas*. London and New York: Thames & Hudson.

Moseley, Michael. 2000. *The Incas and Their Ancestors*, 2nd ed. London and New York: Thames & Hudson.

Glossary of Technical Terms

This Glossary of Technical Terms covers both method and theory in archaeology and prehistory. It includes both key terms in bold highlighted in the text as well as various other technical methods and words commonly used in archaeology, as a general reference for the reader.

accelerator mass spectrometry (AMS) radiocarbon dating   A method of radiocarbon dating that counts actual ^{14}C atoms. Requires very small samples and can be used to date items as small as individual seeds.

adaptive radiation   A burst of evolution, when a single species fills a number of ecological niches, the result being several new forms.

agricultural revolution   A term coined by V. Gordon Childe to refer to the beginnings of food production, caused by drought and close associations between animals, humans, and plants.

analogy   A process of reasoning whereby two entities that share some similarities are assumed to share many others.

analysis   The process of classifying and describing archaeological finds.

Andes (Andean)   Term used by archaeologists to refer to those areas of Peru and adjacent countries where state-organized societies developed.

anthropoid   The taxonomic suborder of apes, humans, and monkeys.

anthropology   The study of humankind in the widest possible sense.

arboreal   Tree-living.

archaeobotanist   A specialist in the study of ancient plants.

archaeological data   The natural materials recognized by the archaeologist as significant evidence, all of which are collected and recorded as part of the research.

archaeological record   Artifacts, sites, and other humanly manufactured features or results of ancient human behavior and their matrices.

archaeological theory   A body of theoretical concepts providing both a framework and a means for archaeologists to look beyond the facts and material objects for explanations of events that took place in prehistory.

archaeological type   A grouping of artifacts created for comparison with other groups. This grouping may or may not coincide with the tool types as they would have been intended by their original makers.

archaeology   The study of the human past using the surviving material remains of human behavior.

artifact   A human-manufactured or modified object.

artifact assemblage   All the artifacts found at a site.

association   The relationship between an artifact and other archaeological finds and a site level, or another artifact, structure, or feature in the site.

attribute   Individual features of artifacts.

attritional age profile   The distribution of ages at death of animals in a population that were killed by selective hunting or predation.

ayllu   Andean kin group claiming descent from a common ancestor.

band   Egalitarian associations of families knit together by close social ties.

bartering   The exchange, from hand-to-hand, of goods or services for equivalent value.

bipedal   Walking upright on two feet.

blade technology   A stone tool technology involving the use of preshaped cores and long, parallel-sided blades produced with the aid of a punch. Characteristic of many Upper Paleolithic peoples.

Bølling-Allerød interstadial   A 2000-year period of global warming after the Ice Age, which began c. 12,400 B.C.

burin   A chisel-like stone tool made on a blade used for grooving stone, antler, bone, and wood, as well as for making rock engravings.

carbon isotope analysis   The analysis of the isotopic ratios in human bones to discern ancient diet.

carrying capacity   The ability of an environment to sustain a certain density of population per square kilometer.

ceramic analysis   The study of pottery. *See* **ceramics**.

ceramics   Clay vessels and other objects made of this substance.

chiefdom   A form of social organization, more complex than a tribal society, that has evolved some form of leadership structure and some mechanisms for distributing goods and services throughout the society. The chief of such a society and the specialists who work for the chief are supported by the voluntary contributions of the people.

chronological type   Types defined by forms that cover well-defined periods of time.

chronometric dating   Dating in calendar years before the present; absolute dating.

city Complex, relatively dense settlements with a degree of organizational complexity well beyond that of a village or town. Ancient cities had several thousand inhabitants, the lower limit being between 2,000 and 5,000 people.

civilization *See* **State-organized society**.

cladistics A method of analyzing evolutionary relationships that stresses diversity.

clan A unilineal descent group whose members do not trace their genealogical ancestry back to a historical founder, but recognize a mythic ancestor, often an animal.

classical archaeology The study of classical Greek and Roman civilizations.

codex A document, either on bark or deer skin, prepared by ancient Maya scribes.

cognitive archaeology The "archaeology of mind," using archaeological methods to study human motives, ideologies, and intangibles.

cognitive-processual archaeology An approach to archaeology that combines the methods of processual and post-processual researchers.

component An association of all the artifacts from one occupation level at a site.

composite tool An artifact made up of more than one component, such as a stone spear point and the shaft.

conchoidal fracture A property of stone fracture found in igneous rocks that allows the manufacture of flakes, blades, and, hence, stone artifacts.

context In archaeology, the exact location of a site, artifact, or other archaeological find in time and space.

contingency model In optimal foraging strategy, exploitation of foods as opportunity arises, independent of their abundance.

core In archaeology, a lump of stone from which struck flakes have been removed.

cultural ecology The study of the dynamic interactions between human societies and their environments. Under this approach, culture is the primary adaptive mechanism used by human societies.

cultural landscape A landscape as defined by a culture that dwells in it.

cultural process A deductive approach to archaeological research that is designed to study the changes and interactions in cultural systems and the processes by which human cultures change throughout time. Processual archaeologists use both descriptive and explanatory models.

cultural resource management (CRM) The conservation and management of archaeological sites and artifacts as a means of protecting the past.

cultural selection The process that leads to the acceptance of some culture traits and innovations that make a culture more adaptive to its environment; somewhat akin to natural selection in biological evolution.

cultural system The adaptive mechanism, made up of many parts, that humans use to adapt to their physical and social environments.

culture A set of designs for living that help mold human responses to different situations. Culture is our primary means of adapting to our environment. In archaeology, culture is an arbitrary unit applied to similar assemblages of artifacts found at several sites, defined in a precise context of time and space.

culture area An arbitrary geographic or research area in which general cultural homogeneity is found.

culture as adaptation approach An approach to human prehistory that uses cultural systems and ecology to study culture change over time.

culture history Descriptions of human cultures derived from archaeological evidence.

cuneiform From the Greek *cuneus*, "wedge." Mesopotamian script made by stamping clay tablets with a wedge-shaped stylus. Long used as an international diplomatic script in the ancient eastern Mediterranean world.

curation Careful use of toolmaking stone and other special materials that are in short supply.

debitage Waste by-products produced while stoneworking.

debitage analysis The study of debitage as a way of examining ancient stone technologies.

deductive reasoning The formulation of specific implications from a generalized hypothesis.

dendrochronology Tree-ring dating, from the Greek *dendros*, "tree," and *chronos*, "time."

dental apes Early apes with humanlike molar teeth but monkeylike postcranial skeletons.

descriptive types Types based on the physical or external properties of an artifact.

diffusion The spread of ideas over short or long distances.

disk core technique A stone technology based on disk-shaped cores, shaped so as to produce several relatively similarly sized flakes for manufacture into different tool forms.

ecofact Archaeological finds that are of cultural significance but were not made by humans, such as bones and vegetal remains. Not a commonly used term.

ecotone A transitional zone between different environments.

elite In archaeology, a class of nobility or relatives of a chief or ruler.

epigrapher A scholar who studies ancient inscriptions.

epiphysis The articular end of a limb bone, which fuses at adulthood in animals and humans.

ethnicity In archaeology, the study of different ethnic groups within a society.

ethnoarchaeology The study of living societies to aid in the interpretation of ancient ones.

ethnographic analogy *See* Analogy.

ethnohistory The study of history using oral and other traditional sources.

evolutionary ecology An approach to prehistory that is based on natural selection as a way of predicting variations in human behavior.

exchange system   A system for exchanging goods and services between individuals and communities.

experimental archaeology   Controlled experiment with ancient technologies and other methods to provide a basis for interpreting ancient human behavior.

faunal analysis   In archaeology, the study of animal bones.

feature   An artifact such as a storage pit or a posthole that cannot be removed from a site; normally it is only recorded.

feces   Body waste.

Fertile Crescent   Term coined by Egyptologist Henry Breasted in the 1920s; a broad semicircle of land in southwestern Asia that encompasses the areas of the earliest civilizations.

flake   In archaeology, stone fragments removed from cores, often used as blanks for finished artifacts.

flotation   A method of recovering plant remains by passing them through screens and water.

food production   Agriculture and animal domestication.

foraging   Commonly used to refer to plant gathering; also generically (in this book) to hunting and plant gathering.

foreshaft   A short staff upon which a projectile point or harpoon was mounted. The foreshaft was then hafted to a long stave. When the weapon hit its quarry, the foreshaft would break off in the wound, allowing the hunter to rearm his weapon, as well as causing a more serious injury to the quarry.

form   The physical characteristics—size and shape or composition—of any archaeological find. Form is an essential part of attribute analysis.

fowling   Bird hunting.

function   The way in which an artifact was used in the past.

functionalism   The notion that a social institution within a society has a function in fulfilling all the needs of a social organism.

functional types   A type based on cultural use or function rather than on outward form or chronological position.

general systems theory   The notion that any organism or organization can be studied as a system broken down into many interacting subsystems or parts; sometimes called cybernetics.

geographic information systems (GIS)   A system for mapping archaeological and other data in digitized form, thereby allowing the data to be manipulated for research purposes.

gift exchange   Exchange of goods and commodities between two parties marked by the ceremonial giving of gifts, which signifies a special relationship between the individuals involved.

groove-and-splinter technique   Longitudinal grooving of antler and bone to produce long, parallel-sided grooves for making spear points, harpoons, and other artifacts. Used by Upper Paleolithic and Mesolithic peoples.

ground stone   Artifacts manufactured by pecking the surface and edges with a stone, then grinding them smooth, to form sharp working edges. A technique used for axes and adzes employed for felling trees and woodworking.

henge   A British term for a wooden or stone circle—whence Stonehenge.

hieroglyph   Ancient writing featuring pictographic or ideographic symbols; used in Egypt, Mesoamerica, and elsewhere.

historical archaeology   The study of the past combining archaeology with historical records.

history   The study of the past using written records.

Holocene   From the Greek word for *recent*. Refers to the millennia since the end of the Pleistocene (Ice Age), about 10,000 B.C.

hominidae   A family of primates that includes modern humans, Asian great apes, and earlier human subspecies.

hominin/homininae   Primates of the family Homininae, which includes modern humans, earlier human subspecies, and their direct ancestors.

Hominoidea   A primate superfamily that includes apes and hominins.

hominoids   Members of the primate superfamily that includes apes and hominins.

horizon   A widely distributed set of culture traits and artifact assemblages whose distribution and chronology allow researchers to assume that they spread rapidly. Often, horizons are composed of artifacts that were associated with widespread, distinctive religious beliefs.

horizontal (area) excavation   Excavation of a large horizontal area, designed to uncover large areas of a site, especially houses and settlement layouts.

ideology   The knowledge or beliefs developed by human societies as part of their cultural adaptation.

ideology of domination   An overarching philosophy or religious belief used by rulers, or entire civilizations, to focus their power and ensure conformity among their subjects.

inductive (research methods)   Reasoning by which one proceeds from specific observations to general conclusions.

inevitable variation   Cumulative culture change due to minor differences in learned behavior over time.

intensification   In archaeology, a more focused exploitation of food resources.

interglacial   A warm period between major Ice Age glaciations.

interpretation   Conclusions drawn from data collected in the context of an original theoretical model, developed, then modified as a project proceeds.

invention   New ideas that originate in a human culture by accident or design.

kiva   Sacred ceremonial room built by prehistoric peoples in the American Southwest.

knuckle walking   Specialized way of getting around on four limbs that uses the backs of the hands for supporting body weight.

kula **ring**   A ceremonial shell ornament exchange system in the southwestern Pacific, involving gifts of shell necklaces between important individuals.

Levallois technique   A stone technology based on a core prepared to produce one large flake of predictable shape.

Levant   A somewhat old-fashioned but useful label that describes the region of the eastern Mediterranean and its immediate hinterland.

lithic analysis   Analysis of ancient stone technologies.

loess   Glacial windblown dust from Ice Age glaciers that formed light soils.

mandala   A Hindu conception of the state used in Southeast Asian archaeology.

market   A permanent place where trading or exchange takes place; usually centered on a larger village, town, or city.

mast (ma-aast)   The rich fruit droppings of oaks and other forest trees.

Matuyama–Brunhes boundary   A moment of reversal of the earth's magnetic field, c. 730,000 years ago.

megalith   From the Greek *megos lithos*, "large stone." Term applied to communal stone-built tombs, widespread throughout western Europe, generally in the fifth millenniumB.C.

Mesoamerica   That part of Central America where state-organized societies developed.

microblade   From the Greek *micros*, "small." A diminutive version of the blade used for manufacturing small spear barbs and scraping tools. Especially common in late Ice Age and early Holocene Siberia and early Holocene Alaska.

microlith   From the Greek *micros*, "small," and *lithos*, "stone": a stone artifact of diminutive size, usually employed for arrow and spear barbs.

microwear studies   Microscopic examination of tool-working surfaces to establish their use.

midden   An accumulation of domestic garbage, shells, or other occupation debris. *Compare* **shell midden**.

migration   The movement of people from one area to another.

mit'a   Taxation in labor imposed by Andean states, especially the Chimu and Inca.

mitochondrial DNA (mtDNA)   DNA inherited through the female line.

monophyletic   Descended from a single ancestor.

multilinear cultural evolution   Cultural evolution along many diverse tracks.

Neolithic   A widely used general label in Old World archaeology that refers to Stone Age farmers who did not have the use of metals.

nonintrusive archaeology   Archaeological field research conducted without excavation; it does not disturb the archaeological record.

normative view of culture   A view of human culture arguing that one can identify the abstract rules regulating a particular culture; a commonly used basis for studying archaeological cultures through time.

obsidian   Volcanic glass.

optimal foraging strategy   An approach to studying hunter-gatherer societies that is based in the assumption that people will use the most efficient foraging strategies relative to considerations of energy and time expended.

oral tradition   Historical data transmitted from one generation to the next by word of mouth.

paleoanthropology   The study of the behavior, culture, and evolution of the earliest humans by scientists from many disciplines.

paleoethnobotany   The study of ancient botanical remains.

paleopathology   The study of ancient disease.

pastoralist   An animal herder, someone who lives predominantly off domesticated animals. Usually refers to cattle herders.

peer-polity interaction   A state of interdependence between neighboring political units such as city-states that are equals.

periglacial   Around or near glaciers.

petrological analysis   The study of the mineral contents of stone or stone tools.

petrology   The study of rocks. In archaeology, analysis of trace elements and other characteristics of rocks used to make such artifacts as ax blades, which were traded over long distances.

phytolith   Minute particles of silica from plant cells produced throughout the life of the plant and used to identify plant species in archaeological sites.

pit house   A dwelling built partially into the subsoil, typically oval shaped. Common in the American Southwest, where the design provides good insulation.

Pleistocene   The last geological epoch, sometimes called the Ice Age or Quaternary.

pollen analysis (palynology)   The study of ancient vegetation by using minute pollens from said vegetation preserved in organic deposits.

ponginae   The family of nonhuman primates closest to humans.

post-processual archaeology   Approaches to the past that examine ideology, motives, and nonenvironmental aspects of culture change.

potassium-argon dating   A radiometric method that dates geological strata and early archaeological sites from volcanic rocks. Used to date prehistory from the earliest times up to about 100,000 years ago.

potsherd   A fragment of a broken clay vessel.

prehistorian   An individual who studies prehistory.

prehistoric archaeology   The study of nonliterate ancient societies.

prehistory   Human history before the advent of written records.

preindustrial civilization   A civilization organized without the use of fossil fuels. *See* **State-organized societies.**

prepared core   A stone core preshaped to produce flakes of a predictable shape.

prestate society   A small-scale egalitarian society without stratified social classes or centralized government.

prey model   In optimal foraging strategy theory, an assumption that people will maximize their exploitation of highest-ranked prey.

primary context An undisturbed association, matrix, and provenance.

primate A mammal order that includes tree-living placental mammals.

process In archaeology, the culture change that takes place as a result of interactions between a cultural system's elements and the system's environment.

processual archaeology An approach to archaeology that studies the process of culture change, usually through a systems, environmental approach.

prognathous Applied to human faces—a prognathous face juts out, whence prognathous jaw characteristic of many Neanderthals.

prosimian The taxonomic suborder that includes femurs, tarsiers, and other so-called premonkeys.

provenance The position of an archaeological find in time and space, recorded three-dimensionally.

Quaternary *See* Pleistocene.

rachis A hinge that joins a seed to a plant.

radiocarbon (¹⁴C) dating A radiometric dating method based on the decay rates of radiocarbon isotopes. It is highly effective for dating developments over the past 40,000 years.

reciprocity Obligations between individuals or fellow kin members/groups that involve the expectation that the other party will respond when called upon.

redistribution The passing out of foodstuffs, goods, or commodities by a central authority such as a chief, thereby ensuring even distribution through a community or wider group. Often used to refer to the redistribution of exotic goods traded from afar.

reductive (subtractive) technology A stoneworking technique in which stone is acquired, then shaped by removing flakes until a desired form is reached.

refitting (retrofitting) The reconstruction of ancient stone technologies by refitting flakes/blades to cores.

region An area defined by natural geographic boundaries that displays some cultural homogeneity.

relative chronology A time scale developed by the law of superposition or artifact ordering.

remote sensing Reconnaissance and site survey methods using such devices as aerial photography and satellite imagery to detect subsurface features and archaeological sites.

research design A carefully formulated and systematic plan for conducting archaeological research.

scanning electron microscopy (SEM) A method using electron microscopes for studying the micromorphology of seeds.

scientific method A method of inquiry that is based on the formal testing of hypotheses, cumulative research, and replicable experiments.

secondary context A context of an archaeological find that has been disturbed by subsequent human activity or natural phenomena. Often applies to burials.

sedentism Permanent settlement at one location for all, or sometimes most, of the year, and over more than one year.

sexual dimorphism Size difference resulting from one's sex.

shell midden An accumulation of freshwater or marine shells piled up by humans as a by-product of shellfish collection and consumption.

sinodonty A distinctive cluster of tooth features associated with Siberian and Native American populations.

site Any place where ecofacts, features, or objects manufactured or modified by humans are found. A site can range from a living site to a quarry location. It can be defined in functional and other ways.

slip A fine, wet finish applied to a clay vessel before it is decorated and fired.

social ranking In ancient human societies, evidence of differences in social status, usually detected in burial ornamentation.

social stratification In archaeology, evidence of different social classes, usually arranged hierarchically.

sourcing The study of the sources of traded commodities such as obsidian using spectrographic analysis and other scientific approaches.

spear-thrower (atlatl) A hooked and sometimes weighted stick or equivalent device used for hurling spears.

state-organized society A large-scale society with strongly centralized government and marked social stratification. Synonymous with **preindustrial civilizations**.

stela (pl. **stelae**) A commemorative column or upright. In the context of this book, a stone column, sometimes stucco-faced, erected by Maya lords to commemorate their reigns, genealogies, and deeds.

stratigraphy Observation of the superimposed layers in an archaeological site.

subsistence Ways in which humans feed themselves.

subsurface radar Radar used to detect subsurface features such as houses and pits without, or in advance of, excavation.

sundadont Teeth characteristics shared by ancient Eurasian and European populations.

superposition The relationship between two objects, structures, or layers in the vertical plane.

swidden agriculture Sometimes called slash-and-burn agriculture, swidden farming involves burning off of natural vegetation, planting of crops, and then allowing the land to regenerate before reuse.

taphonomy The study of how bones decompose after being discarded or after an animal dies.

temper Coarse material such as sand or shell added to fine potting clay to make it bond during firing.

termination A period of rapid deglaciation.

test pit Cuttings of limited size sunk into archaeological sites for sampling purposes, to establish stratigraphy or to define the limits of a site.

text-aided archaeology The study of the past using both archaeology and historical documents.

tomol Planked canoe used by the Chumash people of southern California.

tradition   A persistent technological or cultural pattern identified by characteristic artifact forms. These persistent forms outlast a single phase and can occur over a wide area.

transformation processes   Processes that change an abandoned settlement into an archaeological site through the passage of time. These processes can outlast a single phase and can occur over a wide area.

tribe   A group of bands unified by sodalities (age sets or secret societies) and governed by a council of representatives from the bands, kin groups, or sodalities within it.

trypanosomiasis   Sleeping sickness, a disease carried by the tsetse fly in Africa, which is fatal to cattle.

tsetse fly   An African insect that carries trypanosomiasis. Tsetse is endemic to much of Africa, which affects the distribution of cattle throughout the continent.

tuff   Hardened volcanic ash.

typology   The classification of archaeological types.

underwater archaeology   The study of archaeological sites underwater using special excavation methods; the objectives of the research are similar to those for sites on land.

ungulate   A hoof-footed animal.

uniformitarianism   A geological principle, which states that the earth's layers formed by natural deposition forces.

unilinear cultural evolution   A late-nineteenth-century evolutionary theory envisaging all human societies as evolving, or being capable of evolving, along one track of cultural evolution from simple hunting and gathering to literate civilization.

Urban Revolution   A concept of V. Gordon Childe based on the assumption that metallurgy, specialists, and food surpluses caused a revolution in human life and urban civilization.

use-wear (edge-wear) analysis   Microscopic analysis of artifacts to detect signs of wear through use on their working edges.

vegeculture   A simple method of growing wild root crops like yams by cutting off the tops and planting them.

vertical excavation   Excavation undertaken to establish a chronological sequence, normally covering a limited area.

world prehistory   The study of human prehistory from a global perspective.

Younger Dryas interval   A millennium-long period of sharply colder conditions around the world, which began c. 10,950 B.C.

ziggurat   A Mesopotamian temple mound.

Bibliography of World Prehistory

The literature of world prehistory proliferates more and more every year, to the point that it is now beyond the ability of any one scholar to keep abreast of it. This bibliography is not intended as a comprehensive reference guide to the subject. Rather, it is a compilation of many of the sources used to write this book and a cross section of the most important monographs and papers relating to all parts of the world. Readers interested in probing more deeply into the literature should pursue the references given in the publications listed here or consult a specialist.

Abdi, Kamyar. 2003. "Early Development of Pastoralism in the Central Zagros Mountains." *Journal of World Prehistory* 17(4): 395–448.

Adams, Robert M. 1966. *The Evolution of Urban Society.* Chicago: Aldine.

———. 1981. *Heartland of Cities.* Chicago: University of Chicago Press.

———. 2001. "Complexity in Archaic States." *Journal of Anthropological Archaeology* 20(3): 345–360.

———, and Hans J. Nissen. 1972. *The Uruk Landscape.* Chicago: University of Chicago Press.

Adams, William Y. 1977. *Nubia: Corridor to Africa.* London: Allen Lane.

Adler, Michael A., eds. 1996. *The Prehistoric Pueblo World,* A.D. *1150–1350.* Tucson: University of Arizona Press.

Adovasio, J. M. 2002. *The First Americans.* New York: Random House.

———, et al. 1981. *Meadowcroft Rockshelter and the Archaeology of the Cross Creek Drainage.* Pittsburgh: University of Pittsburgh Press.

Adovasio, J. M., et al. 1996. "Upper Palaeolithic Fibre Technology: Interlaced Woven Finds from Pavlov I, Czech Republic, c. 26,000 Years Ago." *Antiquity* 70: 526–534.

Adovasio, J. M., et al. 1998. "Two Decades of Debate on Meadowcroft Rockshelter." *North American Archaeologist* 19(4): 317–341.

Aiello, L. C., and M. C. Dean. 1990. *An Introduction to Human Evolutionary Anatomy.* London: Academic Press.

Aiello, L. C., and Robin Dunbar. 1993. "Neocortex Size, Group Size, and Cognition." *Current Anthropology* 36: 199–221.

Aiello, L. C., and P. Wheeler. 1995. "The Expensive-Tissue Hypothesis: The Brain and the Digestive System in Human and Primate Evolution." *Current Anthropology* 36(2): 199–221.

Aiello, Leslie C., and Susan C. Anton, eds. 2011. *Human Biology and the Origins of Homo. Current Anthropology* Supplement 6.

Aikens, C. Melvin. 1970. *Hogup Cave.* Salt Lake City: University of Utah Press.

Aldenderfer, Mark. 1995. *Montane Foragers: Asana and the South-Central Andean Archaic.* Iowa City: University of Iowa Press.

Aldred, Cyril. 2004. *The Egyptians,* 4th ed., updated by Aidan Dodson. New York: Thames and Hudson.

Alexander, Caroline. 2008. "If the Stones Could Speak." *National Geographic* 6: 23–36.

Algaze, Guillermo. 1993. *The Uruk World System: The Dynamics of Expansion of Early Mesopotamian Civilization.* Chicago: University of Chicago Press.

———. 2008. *Ancient Mesopotamia at the Dawn of Civilization.* Chicago: University of Chicago Press.

Allan, William. 1965. *The African Husbandman.* Edinburgh: Oliver & Boyd.

Allchin, Bridget, and Raymond Allchin. 1983. *The Rise of Civilization in India and Pakistan.* Cambridge: Cambridge University Press.

Allchin, Raymond. 1995. *The Archaeology of Early Historic South Asia.* Cambridge: Cambridge University Press.

Allen, J. 1994. "Radiocarbon Determinations, Luminescence Dating, and Australian Archaeology." *Antiquity* 68: 339–343.

———, and J. S. Holloway. 1995. "The Continuity of Pleistocene Radiocarbon Determinations in Australia." *Antiquity* 69: 101–112.

Allen, J., and J. P. White. 1989. "The Lapita Homeland: Some New Data and an Interpretation." *Journal of the Polynesian Society* 93: 129–146.

Allen, Melinda. 1995. "Style and Function in East Polynesian Fishhooks." *Antiquity* 70: 97–111.

Alperson-Afil, Nira, et al. 2009. "Spatial Organization Activities at Gesher Benot Ya'aqov, Israel." *Science* 326(5960): 1677. DOI: 10: 1126/science.1180695.

Alva, Walter, and Christopher Donnan. 1989. *Royal Tombs of Sipán.* Los Angeles: Fowler Museum of Cultural History, UCLA.

Ambrose, Stanley H. 1984. "The Introduction of Pastoral Adaptations to the High Lands of East Africa." In *From Hunters to Farmers.* J. Desmond Clark and Steven A. Brandt, eds. pp. 212–239. Berkeley: University of California Press.

———. 2001. "Paleolithic Technology and Human Evolution." *Science* 291: 1748–1753.

———. 2003. "Did the Super-Eruption of Toba Cause a Human Population Bottleneck? Reply to Gathorne-Hardy and Harcourt-Smith." *Journal of Human Evolution* 45: 231–237.

Ames, K. M., and Herbert D. Maschner. 1999. *Peoples of the Northwest Coast: Their Archaeology and Prehistory.* London and New York: Thames & Hudson.

Anawak, J. 1994. "Inuit Perceptions of the past." In *Who Needs the past?* 2nd ed. R. Layton, ed. pp. 45–50. London: Routledge.

Anderson, Arthur O., and Charles Dibble., eds. 1978. *The Florentine Codex.* Salt Lake City: University of Utah Press.

Anderson, Atholl. 1991. "The Chronology of Colonization in New Zealand." *Antiquity* 65: 767–795.

———. 1992. *Prodigious Birds: Moas and Moa-Hunting in Prehistoric New Zealand.* Cambridge: Cambridge University Press.

———, and M. McGlone. 1991. "Living on the Edge: Prehistoric Land and People in New Zealand." In *The Native Lands: Prehistory and Environmental Change in Australia and the Southwest Pacific.* J. Dodson, ed. pp. 199–241. Sydney, Australia: Longman Cheshire.

Anderson, D. G. 1994. *The Savannah River Chiefdoms: Political Change in the Late Prehistoric Southeast.* Tuscaloosa: University of Alabama Press.

———. 1997. "The Role of Cahokia in the Evolution of Southeastern Mississippian Society." In *Cahokia: Domination and Ideology in the Mississippian World.* Timothy R. Pauketat and Thomas E. Emerson, eds. pp. 248–268. Lincoln: University of Nebraska Press.

———, and J. Christopher Gillam. 2000. "Paleoindian Colonization of the Americas: Implications from an Examination of Physiography, Demography, and Artifact Distribution." *American Antiquity* 65(1): 43–66.

Anderson, D. G., and Kenneth E. Sassaman, eds. 1996. *The Paleoindian and Early Archaic Southeast.* Tuscaloosa: University of Alabama Press.

Anderson, Douglas. 1990. *Long Rongrien.* Philadelphia: University of Pennsylvania Museum.

Arnold, Jeanne, eds. 2001. *The Origins of the Pacific Coast Chiefdom.* Salt Lake City: University of Utah Press.

Anikovich, M. V., et al. 2007. "Early Upper Paleolithic in Eastern Europe and Implications for the Dispersal of Modern Humans." *Science* 315: 223–226.

Arsuaga, Juan-Luis, et al. 1993. "Three New Human Skulls from the Sima de los Huesos Middle Pleistocene Site in Sierra de Atapuerca, Spain." *Nature* 362: 534–539.

Ascher, Marcia, and Robert Ascher. 1981. *The Code of the Quipu.* Ann Arbor: University of Michigan Press.

Asfaw, Berhane, et al. 1999. "Australopithecus garhi: A New Species of Early Hominid from Ethiopia." *Science* 284: 629–634.

———, et al. 2002. "Remains of *Homo erectus* from Bouri, Middle Awash, Ethiopia." *Nature* 416: 173–320.

Aubet, Maria Eugenia. 1993. *The Phoenicians and the West: Politics, Colonies and Trade.* Cambridge: Cambridge University Press.

Aujoulat, Norbert. 2005. *The Glory of Lascaux: Rediscovering the Greatest Treasure of Prehistoric Art.* London: Thames & Hudson.

Backwell, Lucinda, et al. 2007. "Middle Stone Age Bone Tools from the Howiesons Poort Layers, Sibudu Cave, South Africa." *Journal of Archaeological Science* 35(6): 1566–1580.

Bahn, Paul, ed. 1996. *The Cambridge Illustrated History of Archaeology.* Cambridge: Cambridge University Press.

———, ed. 1998. *The Cambridge Illustrated History of Prehistoric Art.* Cambridge: Cambridge University Press.

———. 2007. *Cave Art: A Guide to the Decorated Ice Age Caves of Europe.* London: Frances Lincoln.

———. 2010. *Prehistoric Rock Art: Polemics and Progress.* Cambridge: Cambridge University Press.

———, and J. R. Flenley. 1992. *Easter Island, Earth Island.* London and New York: Thames & Hudson.

Bahn, Paul, and Jan Vertut. 1988. *Images of the Ice Age.* New York: Viking Press.

Bailey, Douglas, et al. 2010. *Unearthed: A Comparative Study of Jomon dog and Neolithic Figurines.* Norwich: SCVA.

Bailey, Geoff, and Penny Spikins, eds. 2008. *Mesolithic Europe.* Cambridge: Cambridge University Press.

Balter, Michael. 2005. *The Goddess and the Bull.* New York: Free Press.

———. 2010. "Candidate Human Ancestor from South Africa Draws Praise and Debate." *Science* 328(5975): 153.

Banning, E. B. 2011. "So Fair a House: Göbekli Tepe and the Identification of Temples in the Pre-Pottery Neolithic of the Near East." *Current Anthropology* 52(5): 619–660.

Bard, Kathryn A. 1994. "The Egyptian Predynastic: A Review of the Evidence." *Journal of World Prehistory* 21(3): 265–288.

———. 2000. "The Emergence of the Egyptian State (c. 3200–2686 b.c.)." In *The Oxford History of Ancient Egypt.* Ian Shaw, ed. pp. 61–88. Oxford: Oxford University Press.

Barker, Graeme. 1985. *Prehistoric Farming in Europe.* Cambridge: Cambridge University Press.

———. 2006. *The Agricultural Revolution in Prehistory.* Oxford: Oxford University Press.

Barker, Graeme, et al. 2007. "The 'human revolution' in lowland tropical Southeast Asia: The antiquity and behavior of anatomically modern humans at Niah Cave (Sarawak, Borneo)." *Journal of Human Evolution* 52: 243–261.

———, and Tom Rasmussen. 2000. *The Etruscans.* New York: Wiley Blackwell.

Barnard, Alan. 1992. *Hunters and Herders of Southern Africa.* Cambridge: Cambridge University Press.

Barnes, Gina L. 1993. *China, Korea, and Japan.* London and New York: Thames & Hudson.

Barton, C. Michael., et al., eds. 2004. *The Settlement of the American Continents: A Multidisciplinary Approach to Human Biogeography.* Tucson: University of Arizona Press.

Bar-Yosef, O. 1987. "Late Pleistocene Adaptations in the Levant." In *The Pleistocene Old World: Regional Perspectives.* Olga Soffer, ed. pp. 219–236. New York: Plenum Press.

———. 1999. "Lower Palaeolithic Sites in South Western Asia." *L'Anthropologie* 37: 51–69.

——— 2011. "Climatic Fluctuations and Early Farming in West and East Asia." *Current Anthropology* 52(S4):S175–S193.

———, and A. Belfer-Cohen. 1989. "The Origins of Sedentism and Farming Communities in the Levant." *Journal of World Prehistory* 3(4): 447–498.

Bar-Yosef, O., and F. Valla. 1990. "The Natufian Culture and the Origin of the Neolithic in the Levant." *Current Anthropology* 31(4): 433–436.

Bar-Yosef, Ofer, et al. 1991. "Netiv Hagdud: An Early Neolithic Village Site in the Jordan Valley." *Journal of Field Archaeology* 18: 405–424.

Basgall, Mark. 1987. "Resource Intensification Among Hunter-Gatherers: Acorn Economies in Prehistoric California." *Research in Economic Anthropology* 9: 21–52.

Bauer, Brian S. 1992. *The Development of the Inca State*. Norman: University of Oklahoma Press.

———. 2004. *Ancient Cuzco: Heartland of the Inca*. Austin: University of Texas Press.

Baugh. T.G. and J.E. Ericson, eds. 1994. *Prehistoric Exchange Systems in North America*. New York: Plenum Press.

Bayman, James. 2002. "The Hohokam of Southwest North America." *Journal of World Prehistory* 15(3): 257–311.

Beach, David. 1993. *The Shona*. Oxford: Blackwell.

Beadle, George. 1981. "The Ancestor of Corn." *Scientific American* 242(1): 96–103.

Beaglehole, J. C. 1974. *Captain James Cook: A Life*. Palo Alto, CA: Stanford University Press.

Beck, Charlotte, ed. 1999. *Models for the Millennium: Great Basin Anthropology Today*. Salt Lake City: University of Utah Press.

Bellomo, R. V. 1994. "Methods of Determining Early Hominid Behavioral Activities Associated with the Controlled Use of Fire at FxJj 20 Main, Koobi Fora." *Journal of Human Evolution* 27: 173–195.

Bellwood, Peter. 1970. "Fortifications and Economy in Prehistoric New Zealand." *Proceedings of the Prehistoric Society* 37(1): 56–95.

———. 2004. *The First Farmers: The Origins of Agricultural Societies*. Oxford: Blackwell.

———. 1997. *The History of the Indo-Malaysian Archipelago*, 2nd ed. Honolulu: University of Hawaii Press.

———. 2006. "Asian Farming Diasporas: Agriculture, Languages, and Genes in China and Southeast Asia." In *Archaeology of Asia*. Miriam T Stark, ed. pp. 96–118. Malden, MA: Blackwell.

———, and J. Koon. 1989. "Lapita Colonists Leave Boats Unburned." *Antiquity* 63(240): 613–622.

Ben-Amos, P. 1980. *The Art of Benin*. London: Thames & Hudson.

Bender, Barbara. 1985. "Emergent Tribal Formations in the American Midcontinent." *American Antiquity* 50(1): 52–62.

Benefit, B. R., and M. L. McCrossin. 1995. "Miocene Hominoids and Human Origins." *Annual Review of Anthropology* 24: 68–78.

Benfer, Robert. 1982. "The Lomas Site of Paloma (5000 to 7500 b.p.), Chilca Valley, Peru." In *Andean Archaeology*. Ramerio Matos, ed. pp. 27–54. New York: Academic Press.

Benson, Elizabeth. 1979. *Pre-Columbian Metallurgy of South America*. Washington, DC: Dumbarton Oaks.

Berdan, Francis, et al. 1996. *Aztec Imperial Strategies*. Washington, DC: Dumbarton Oaks.

Bernal, Martin. 1987. *The Afroasiatic Roots of Classical Civilization*. New Brunswick, NJ: Rutgers University Press.

Berger, Lee, et al. 2010. "Australopithecus Sediba: A New Species of *Homo*-Like Australopith from South Africa." *Science* 328(5975): 185–186.

Berrin, Kathleen, and R. Pasztory, eds. 1994. *Teotihuacán*. London: Thames & Hudson.

Bever, Michael RS. 2001. "An Overview of Alaskan Late Pleistocene Archaeology: Historical Themes and Current Perspectives." *Journal of World Prehistory* 15(2): 125–191.

Bettinger, Robert L. 2001. "Holocene Hunter-Gatherers." In *Archaeology at the Millennium*. Gary M. Feinman and T. Douglas Price, eds. pp. 137–198. New York: Kluwer Academic.

Bever, Michael R.S. 2001. "An Overview of Alaskan Late Pleistocene Archaeology: Historical Themes and Current Perspectives." *Journal of World Prehistory* 15(2): 125–191.

Binford, Lewis R. 2001a. *Constructing Frames and Reference: An Analytical Method for Archaeological Theory Building Using Ethnographic and Environmental Data Sets*. Berkeley: University of California Press.

———. 2001b. *In Pursuit of the past*, 2nd ed. Berkeley: University of California Press.

Bingham, Hiram. 1963. *Lost City of the Incas*. Reprint ed. New York: Atheneum.

Birdsell, J. 1977. "The Recalibration of a Paradigm for the First Peopling of Greater Australia." In *Sunda and Sahul: Prehistoric Studies in Southeast Asia, Melanesia, and Australia*. J. Allen, J. Golson, and R. Jones, eds., pp. 113–167. London: Academic Press.

Birley, Robin. 2009. *Vindolanda*. Stroud, UK: Amberley Publishing.

Björck, S., et al. 1996. "Synchronized Territorial-Atmospheric Deglacial Records Around the North Atlantic." *Science* 274: 1155–1160.

Blanton, Richard E. 1978. *Monte Albán: Settlement Patterns at the Ancient Zapotec Capital*. New York: Academic Press.

———, et al. 1999. *Ancient Oaxaca*. Cambridge: Cambridge University Press.

Blumenschine, Robert, and John Cavallo. 1992. "Scavenging and Human Evolution." *Scientific American* 257(10): 90–96.

Blust, Robert. 1995. "The Prehistory of the Austronesian-Speaking Peoples: A View from Language." *Journal of World Prehistory* 9(4): 453–510.

Boaretto, Elizabeth, et al. 2009. "Radiocarbon dating of chacoal and bone collagen associated with early pottery at Yuchanyan Cave, Hunan Province, China." *Proceedings of the National Academy of Sciences* 106(24): 9595–9600.

Boesch, Christophe, and Michael Tomasello. 1998. "Chimpanzee and Human Cultures." *Current Anthropology* 39(5): 591–614.

Bogucki, Peter, eds. 1993. *Case Studies in European Prehistory*. Boca Raton, FL: CRC Press.

Bonzek, Jan, ed. 1985. *The Aegean, Anatolia, and Europe in the 2nd Millennium* b.c. New York: Academic Press.

Bordes, François. 1968. *The Old Stone Age*. New York: McGraw-Hill.

Boserup, Ester. 1965. *The Conditions of Agricultural Growth: The Economics of Agrarian Change under Population Pressure*. Chicago: Aldine.

Bower, John R. F. 1984. "Settlement Behavior of Pastoral Cultures in East Africa." In *From Hunters to Farmers*. J. Desmond Clark and Steven A Brandt, eds. pp. 252–259. Berkeley: University of California Press.

Bowler, J. M., et al. 2003. "New Ages for Human Occupation and Climatic Change at Lake Mungo, Australia." *Nature* 421: 837–840.

Bowman, A. K., and G. Woolf., eds. 1994. *Literacy and Power in the Ancient World*. Cambridge: Cambridge University Press.

Boyer, Pascal. 1994. *The Naturalness of Religious Ideas: A Cognitive Theory of Religion*. Berkeley: University of California Press.

Braidwood, R. J., and L. S. Braidwood, eds. 1983. *Prehistoric Archaeology along the Zagros Flanks*. Chicago: Oriental Institute.

Braidwood, R. J., and H. Cambel. 1980. *Prehistoric Research in Southeastern Anatolia*. Istanbul: Edebiyat Facultesi Basimevi.

Brain, Jeffrey P., and Philip Phillips. 1995. *Shell Gorgets: Styles of the Late Prehistoric and Protohistoric Southeast*. Cambridge, MA: Peabody Museum, Harvard University.

Bramble, Dennis M., and Daniel E. Lieberman. 2004. "Endurance Running and the Evolution of Homo." *Nature* 432: 345–352.

Brauer, Günter. 1992. "Africa's Place in the Evolution of Homo Sapiens." In *Continuity or Replacement: Controversies in Homo Sapiens Evolution.* Günter Brauer and F. H. Smith, eds. pp. 83–98. Rotterdam: Balkema.

Breuil, Henri. 1952. *Four Hundred Centuries of Cave Art.* Montignac, France: Centred'Études et de Documentation.

Broodbank, Cyprian. 2001. *An Island Archaeology of the Early Cyclades.* Cambridge: Cambridge University Press.

Broughton, Jack M., and James O'Connell. 1999. "On Evolutionary Ecology: Selectionist Archaeology and Behavioral Archaeology." *American Antiquity* 64(1): 153–165.

Brown, J., and J. Phillips, eds. 1983. *Late Archaic Hunter-Gatherers in the Midwest.* New York: Academic Press.

Brown, P., et al. (2004). "A New Small-Bodied Hominin from the Late Pleistocene of Flores, Indonesia." *Nature* 431: 1055–1061.

Brumfiel, Elizabeth. 1983. "Aztec State Making: Ecology, Structure, and the Origin of the State." *American Anthropologist* 85(2): 261–284.

———. 1991. "Weaving and Cooking: Women's Production in Aztec Mexico." In *Engendering Archaeology.* Margaret Conkey and Joan Gero, eds. pp. 224–247. Oxford: Blackwell.

———. 1992. "Distinguished Lecture in Archaeology: Breaking and Entering the Ecosystem." *American Anthropologist* 94(3): 551–567.

———, and John Fox., eds. 1994. *Factional Competition and Political Development in the New World.* Cambridge: Cambridge University Press.

Brumm, Adam, and Mark W. Moore. 2012. "Biface Distributions and the Movius Line: A Southeast Asian perspective." *Australian Archaeology* 74: 32–46.

Brunet, Michel, et al. 2002. "A New Hominid from the Upper Miocene of Chad, Central Africa." *Nature* 418: 145–151.

———, et al. 1995. "The First Australopithecine 2500 Km West of the Rift Valley, Chad." *Nature* 378: 273–275.

Bunn, Henry. 1994. "Early Pleistocene Hominid Foraging Strategies Along the Ancestral Omo River at Koobi Fora, Kenya." *Journal of Human Evolution* 27: 247–266.

———, and J. Kroll. 1986. "Systematic Butchery by Plio/pleistocene Hominids at Olduvai Gorge, Tanzania." *Current Anthropology* 27(5): 431–451.

Burger, Richard L. 1985. "Prehistoric Stylistic Change and Cultural Development at Huaricoto, Peru." *National Geographic Research* 1(4): 505–534.

———. 1992a. *Chavín and the Origins of Andean Civilization.* London and New York: Thames & Hudson.

———. 1992b. "The Sacred Center of Chavín De Huántar." In *The Ancient Americas: Art from Sacred Landscapes.* Richard F Townsend, ed. pp. 265–277. Chicago: Art Institute of Chicago.

———, and Lucy Salazar-Burger. 1985. "The Early Ceremonial Center of Huaricoto." In *Early Ceremonial Architecture in the Andes.* Christopher Donnan, ed. pp. 111–138. Washington, DC: Dumbarton Oaks.

———, eds. 2004. *Machu Picchu: Unveiling the Mystery of the Incas.* New Haven, CT: Yale University Press.

Burger, Richard L., and Nikolaas van der Merwe. 1990. "Maize and the Origin of Highland Chavín Civilization." *American Anthropologist* 92(1): 85–92.

Burns, Bryan E. 2010. *Mycenaean Greece, Mediterranean Commerce, and the Formation of Identity.* Cambridge: Cambridge University Press.

Bury, J. B., and Russell Meiggs. 1978. *A History of Greece.* 4th ed. London: Macmillan.

Butzer, Karl. 1974. *Environment and Archaeology.* Chicago: Aldine.

———. 1976. *Early Hydraulic Civilization in Egypt.* Chicago: University of Chicago Press.

———. 1982. *Archaeology as Human Ecology.* Cambridge: Cambridge University Press.

———. 1995. "Environmental Change in the Near East and Human Impact on the Land." In *Civilizations of the Ancient Near East.* J. M. Sasson, ed. pp. 123–151. New York: Scribners.

Byrd, B. F. 1989. "The Natufian: Settlement Variability and Economic Adaptation in the Levant at the End of the Pleistocene." *Journal of World Prehistory* 3(2): 159–198.

Cadogan, Gerald. 1976. *Palaces of Minoan Crete.* London: Barrie & Jenkins.

Cahen, David, and Francis van Noten. 1981. *The Hunter-Gatherers of Meer.* Tervuren, Belgium: Musée Royal de L'Afrique Centrale.

Canby, Thomas. 1979. "The Search for the First Americans." *National Geographic* 156(3): 330–363.

Caneva, I., Marcella Frangipane, and Alba Palmieri. 1987. "Predynastic Egypt: New Data from Maadi." *African Archaeological Review* 5: 105–114.

Cann, Rebecca L. 2001. "Genetic Clues to Dispersal in Human Populations: Retracing the Past from the Present." *Science* 291: 1742–1748.

———, O. Rickards, and J. K. Lum. 1995. "Mitochondrial DNA and Human Evolution: Our One Lucky Mother." In *Origins of Anatomically Modern Humans.* M. H. Nitecki and V. Nitecki, eds. pp. 135–148. New York: Plenum Press.

Cannon, Michael D., and David J. Meltzer. 2004. "Early Paleoindian Foraging: Examining the Faunal Evidence for Large Mammal Specialization and Regional Variability in Prey Choice." *Quaternary Science Review* 23: 1955–1987.

Carbonell, Eudaid, et al. 1999. "The TD6 Level Lithic Industry from Gran Dolina, Atapuerca (Burgos, Spain): Production and use." *Journal of Human Evolution* 37: 655–693.

———, et al. 2008. "The First Hominin of Europe." *Nature* 452: 465–469.

Carneiro, Robert L. 1970. "A Theory of the Origin of the State." *Science* 169: 733–738.

———. 1994. "War and Peace: Alternating Realities in Human History." In *Studying War: Anthropological Perspective.* S. P. Reyna and R. E. Downs, eds. pp. 3–28. Amsterdam: Gordon and Breach.

Carr, Christopher, and D. Troy Case, Eds. 2005. *Gathering Hopewell: Society, Ritual and Ritual Interaction.* New York: Springer.

Carter, Elizabeth F., and Mathew Stolper. 1984. *Elam: Surveys of Political History and Archaeology.* Berkeley: University of California Press.

Case, D. Troy, and Christopher Carr. 2008. *The Scioto Hopewell and Their Neighbors.* New York: Springer.

Caton-Thompson, G., and E. W. Gardner. 1934. *The Desert Fayum.* 2 vols. London: Royal Anthropological Institute.

Cavalli-Sforza, L. L., and F. Cavalli-Sforza. 1995. *The Great Human Diasporas.* Reading, MA: Helix Books.

Chadwick, John. 1976. *The Mycenaean World.* Cambridge: Cambridge University Press.

Chandler, David. 1983. *A History of Cambodia*. Boulder, CO: Westview Press.

———. 1986. *The Archaeology of Ancient China*. 4th ed. New Haven, CT: Yale University Press.

Chapdelaine, Claude. 2000. "Struggling for Survival: The Urban Class of the Moche Site, North Coast of Peru." In *Environmental Disaster and the Archaeology of Human Response*. Garth Bawden and Richard Martin Reycraft, eds. pp. 121–142. Albuquerque: Maxwell Museum of Anthropology.

Chapman, Christopher K. 2004. *The Hunt for the Dawn Monkeys: Unearthing the Origins of Monkeys, Apes, and Humans*. Berkeley: University of California Press.

Chapman, Jefferson. 1994. *Tellico Archaeology*. 2nd ed. Knoxville: University of Tennessee Press.

Chase, Arlen F. 1996. "More than Kin and King." *Current Anthropology* 37(5): 803–829.

———, and Diane Z. Chase. 1996. "A Mighty Maya Nation." *Archaeology* 49(5): 67–72.

Chang, Kwang Chih. 1980. *Shang Civilization*. New Haven, CT: Yale University Press.

———. 1986. *The Archaeology of Ancient China*. New Haven, CT: Yale University Press.

Chauvet, Jean-Marie, et al. 1996. *Dawn of Art: The Chauvet Cave*. New York: Abrams.

Childe, V. G. 1936. *Man Makes Himself*. London: Watts.

———. 1952. *New Light on the Most Ancient East*. London: Routledge & Kegan Paul.

Chippindale, Christopher. 2004. *Stonehenge Complete*. 3rd ed. London: Thames & Hudson.

Chun, Tang, and Gai Pei. 1986. "Upper Palaeolithic Cultural Traditions in North China." *Advances in World Archaeology* 5: 339–364.

Clark, J., and W. Parry. 1990. "Craft Specialization and Cultural Complexity." *Research in Economic Anthropology* 12: 289–346.

Clark, J. D. 1971. "A Re-examination of the Evidence for Agricultural Origins in the Nile Valley." *Proceedings of the Prehistoric Society* 37(2): 34–79.

Clark, John E. 2007. "Mesoamerica's First State." In *The Political Economy of Ancient Mesoamerica*. V. L. Scarborough and John E. Clark, eds. pp. 11–46. Albuquerque: University of New Mexico Press.

Clark, J. G. D. 1954. *Star Carr*. Cambridge: Cambridge University Press.

———. 1958. "Blade and Trapeze Industries of the European Stone Age." *Proceedings of the Prehistoric Society* 24: 24–42.

———. 1981. *World Prehistory: A New Outline*. 3rd ed. Cambridge: Cambridge University Press.

Clay, R. Berle. 1998. "The Essential Features of Adena Ritual and Their Implications." *Southeastern Archaeology* 17(1): 1–21.

Clendinnen, Inga. 1991. *The Aztecs: An Interpretation*. Cambridge: Cambridge University Press.

Clottes, Jean. 1995. *Les Cavernes de Niaux: Art Préhistorique en Ariège*. Paris: Seuil.

———. 1998. *The Shamans of Prehistory: Trance and Magic in the Painted Caves*. New York: Abrams.

Clutton-Brock, Juliet. 1989. *The Walking Larder*. London: Unwin Hyman.

Cobb, C. R., and P. H. Garrow. 1996. "Woodstock Culture and the Question of Mississippian Emergence." *American Antiquity* 61: 21–37.

Coe, M. D. 1999. *Breaking the Maya Code*. London and New York: Thames & Hudson.

———. 2005. *Angkor and the Khmer Civilization*. London and New York: Thames and Hudson.

———. 2011. *The Maya*. 8th ed. London and New York: Thames & Hudson.

———, and Richard Diehl. 1980. *In the Land of the Olmec*. 2 vols. Austin: University of Texas Press.

———, and Rex Koontz. 2008. *Mexico*. 6th ed. London and New York: Thames & Hudson.

Cohen, Mark. 1977. *The Food Crisis in Prehistory*. New Haven, CT: Yale University Press.

———. 1988. *Health and the Rise of Civilization*. New Haven, CT: Yale University Press.

Coles, B., and J. M. Coles. 1989. *People of the Wetlands*. London and New York: Thames & Hudson.

Coles, J. M. 1982. "The Bronze Age in North West Europe: Problems and Advances." *Advances in World Archaeology* 1: 266–321.

———, and A. F. Harding. 1979. *The Bronze Age in Europe*. London: Methuen.

Cohen, David Joel. 2011. "The Beginnings of Agriculture in China: A Multiregional View." *Current Anthropology* 52, S4:S273-S293.

Collis, John. 1997. *The European Iron Age*. London: Routledge.

Coningham, R. A. E. 2000. "Deciphering the Indus Script." In *Indian Archaeology in Retrospect. Vol. II. Protohistory: Archaeology of the Harappan Civilization*. S. Setter and Ravi Korisettar, eds. pp. 81–104. Delhi: MANOHAR and Indian Council of Historical Research.

Conkey, Margaret., and Joan Gero, eds. 1991. *Engendering Archaeology*. Oxford: Blackwell.

Conklin, William J., and Jeffrey Quilter, eds. 2008. *Chavín: Art, Architecture, and Culture*. Los Angeles: Cotsen Institute of Archaeology.

Connah, Graham. 2001. *African Civilizations*. 2nd ed. Cambridge: Cambridge University Press.

Conneller, C. J., and T. Schadla-Hall. 2003. "Beyond Star Carr: The Vale of Pickering in the Tenth Millennium BP." *Proceedings of the Prehistoric Society* 69: 85–105.

Conrad, Geoffrey W., and Arthur A. Demarest. 1984. *Religion and Empire: The Dynamics of Aztec and Inca Expansionism*. Cambridge: Cambridge University Press.

Cordell, Linda. 2009. *Prehistory of the Southwest*. 2nd ed. Walnut Creek, CA: Left Coast Press.

Cornell, T. J. 1995. *The Beginnings of Rome*. London: Routledge.

Cosgrove, R. 1995. "Late Pleistocene Behavioral Variation and Time Trends: The Case from Tasmania." *Archaeology in Oceania* 30(3): 83–104.

———, J. Allen, and B. Marshall. 1990. "Pleistocene Occupation of Tasmania." *Antiquity* 64(242): 59–78.

Courand, Claude. 1985. *L'Art Azilien*. Paris: Gallia Préhistoire.

Crawford, Harriett. 2004. *Sumer and the Sumerians*. 2nd ed. Cambridge: Cambridge University Press.

Crawford, Michael H. 2001. *The Origins of Native Americans: Evidence from Anthropological Genetics*. Cambridge: Cambridge University Press.

Crawford, Gary. 2011. "Advances in understanding early agriculture in Japan." *Current Anthropology* 52. S4: S331–S345.

Croes, Dale R. 1996. *The Hoko River Archaeological Site Complex: The Wet/Dry Site (45ca213)*. Pullman: Washington State University.

Crown, Patricia, and W. James Judge, eds. 1991. *Chaco and Hohokam: Regional Studies in the American Southwest*. Santa Fe, NM: School of American Research Press.

Culbert, T. Patrick, ed. 1991. *Classic Maya Political History*. Cambridge and Santa Fe, NM: Cambridge University Press and School of American Research.

———, and Don S. Rice, eds. 1990. *Precolumbian Population History in the Maya Lowlands*. Albuquerque: University of New Mexico Press.

Cunliffe, Barry. 1974. *Iron Age Communities in Britain*. London: Routledge & Kegan Paul.

——— ed. 1994. *The Oxford Illustrated Prehistory of Europe*. Oxford: Oxford University Press.

———. 2000. *The Ancient Celts*. New York: Penguin.

———. 2004. *Facing the Ocean: The Atlantic and Its Peoples 8000 BC-AD 1500*. Oxford: Oxford University Press.

———. 2011. *Europe Between the Oceans: 9000 BC-AD 1000*. New Haven and London: Yale University Press.

Dalley, Stephanie. 1984. *Mari and Karana: Two Old Babylonian Cities*. London: Longmans.

D'Altroy, B. 2003. *The Incas*. New York: Wiley Black well.

Dancey, W. S. 1996. "Putting an End to Ohio Hopewell." In *A View from the Core: A Synthesis of Ohio Hopewell Archaeology*. Paul Pacheco, ed. pp. 395–405. Columbus: Ohio Archaeological Council.

———, and Paul J. Pacheco, eds. 1997. *Ohio Hopewell Community Organization*. Kent, OH: Kent State University Press.

Daniel, Glyn E. 1973. *Megaliths in History*. London: Thames & Hudson.

Dart, Raymond A. 1925. "Australopithecus Africanus: The Man-Ape of Southern Africa." *Nature* 115: 195.

Davidson, Janet. 1987. *The Prehistory of New Zealand*. Auckland: Longman Paul.

Davies, Nigel. 1977. *The Toltecs: Until the Fall of Tula*. Norman: University of Oklahoma Press.

———. 1980. *The Toltec Heritage*. Norman: University of Oklahoma Press.

Deacon, Hilary. 1979. "Excavations at Boomplas Cave: A Sequence Through the Upper Pleistocene and Holocene in South Africa." *World Archaeology* 10: 241–257.

———. 1992. "Southern Africa and Modern Human Origins." *Philosophical Transactions of the Royal Society, Series B*, 337: 177–183.

———, and Jeanette Deacon. 1999. *Human Beginnings in South Africa: Uncovering the Secrets of the Stone Age*. Walnut Creek, CA: Altamira Press.

———, and V. B. Geleijinse. 1988. "The Stratigraphy and Sedimentology of the Main Site Sequence, Klasies River, South Africa." *South African Archaeological Bulletin* 43: 5–14.

Defleur, A., et al. 1999. "Neanderthal Cannibalism at Moula-Guercy, Ardèche, France." *Science* 286: 128–131.

De Heinzelin, Jean, et al. 1999. "Environment and Behavior of 2.5-Million-Year-Old Bouri Hominids." *Science* 284: 625–629.

Demarest, Arthur. 1989. "The Olmec and the Rise of Civilization in Eastern Mesoamerica." In *Regional Perspectives on the Olmec*. Robert Sharer and David Grove, eds. pp. 303–344. Cambridge: Cambridge University Press.

———. 2004. *Ancient Maya: Rise and Fall of a Rainforest Civilization*. Cambridge: Cambridge University Press.

Demattè, Paola. 2010. "The Origins of Chinese Writing: The Neolithic Evidence." *Cambridge Archaeological Journal* 20(2): 211–228.

deMenocal, P. B., and J. Bloemendal. 1995. "Plio-Pleistocene Climatic Variability in Subtropical Africa and the Paleoenvironment of Hominid Evolution: A Combined Data-Model Approach. In *Paleoclimate and Evolution, with Emphasis on Human Origins*. E. S. Vrba et al., eds. pp. 262–288. New Haven, CT: Yale University Press.

Denham, Tim, et al. 2004. "New Evidence and Revised Interpretations of Early Agriculture in Highland New Guinea." *Antiquity* 78(302): 339–357.

Dennell, Robin C. 1983. *European Economic Prehistory: A New Approach*. New York: Academic Press.

d'Errico, Francesco. 1995. "A New Model and Its Implications for the Origin of Writing: La Marche Antler Revised." *Cambridge Archaeological Journal* 5(2): 163–206.

Diamond, Jared. 2005. *Collapse: How Societies Choose to Succeed or Fail*. New York: Viking Press.

Diaz, Bernal. 1963. *The Conquest of New Spain*. Trans by J.M.Cohen. Baltimore: Penguin Books.

Dickinson, Oliver. 1994. *The Aegean Bronze Age*. Cambridge: Cambridge University Press.

Diehl, Richard. 1984. *Tula*. London: Thames & Hudson.

———. 2005. *The Olmecs: America's First Civilization*. London and New York: Thames & Hudson.

Dillehay, Tom. 1989, 1997. *Monte Verde: A Late Pleistocene Settlement in Chile*. 2 vols. Blue Ridge Summit, PA: Smithsonian Institution Press.

———. 2000. *First Settlement of America: A New Prehistory*. New York: Basic Books.

———, and Jack Rossen. 2002. "Plant Food and Its Implications for the Peopling of the New World." In *The First Americans*. Nina Jablonski, ed. pp. 237–254. San Francisco: California Academy of Sciences.

Doebley, John F. 2004. "The Genetics of Maize Evolution." *Annual Review of Genetics* 38: 37–59.

Dolukhanov, P. M., et al. 2002. "Colonization of Northern Eurasia by Modern Humans: Radiocarbon Chronology and Environment." *Journal of Archaeological Science* 29(6): 593–606.

Dominguez-Rodrigo, Manuel, et al. 2007. *Deconstructing Olduvai: A Taphonomic Study of the Bed I Sites*. New York: Springer.

Donnan, Christopher B., ed. 1985. *Early Ceremonial Architecture in the Andes*. Washington, DC: Dumbarton Oaks.

———, and Donna McClelland. 1979. *The Burial Theme in Moche Iconography*. Washington, DC: Dumbarton Oaks.

Doumas, Christos. 1983. *Thera: Pompeii of the Aegean*. London: Thames & Hudson.

Drews, R. 1993. *The End of the Bronze Age: Changes in Warfare and the Catastropheca. 1200* B.C. Princeton, NJ: Princeton University Press.

Drucker, Phillip. 1959. *La Venta, Tabasco: A Study of Olmec Ceramics and Art.* Washington, DC: Smithsonian Institution Press.

Dumond, Don. 1987. *The Eskimos and Aleuts.* 2nd ed. London and New York: Thames and Hudson.

———, and Richard I. Bland. 1995. "Holocene Prehistory of the Northernmost North Pacific." *Journal of World Prehistory* 9(4): 401–452.

Dunbar, R. I. M. 1992. "Neocortex Size as a Constraint on Group Size in Primates." *Journal of Human Evolution* 20: 469–493.

———. 1998. *Grooming, Gossip, and the Evolution of Language.* Cambridge, MA: Harvard University Press.

Durrani, N. 2005. *The Tihamah Coastal Plain of South-West Arabia in Its Regional Context C. 6000 BC—AD 600.* Oxford: British Archaeological Reports.

Edens, Christopher. 1993. "Indus-Arabian Interaction during the Bronze Age: A Review of Evidence." In *Harappan Civilization*, Gregory Possehl, ed. 2nd ed. pp. 335–363. New Delhi: Oxford and IBH.

Edwards, I. E. S. 1985. *The Pyramids of Egypt.* Baltimore: Pelican.

Elias, Scott. 2002. "Setting the Environmental Conditions in Beringia as People Entered the New World." In *The First Americans.* Nina Jablonski, ed. pp. 9–26. San Francisco: California Academy of Sciences.

Emerson, T. E. 1997. *Cahokia and the Ideology of Power.* Tuscaloosa: University of Alabama Press.

Engel, Frederick. 1963. *A Preceramic Settlement on the Central Coast of Peru: Asia. Unit 1.* Philadelphia: American Philosophical Society.

Erickson, Clark L. 1992. "Applied Archaeology and Rural Development: Archaeology's Potential Contribution to the Future." *Journal of the Steward Anthropological Society* 20(1–2): 1–16.

Ericson, J. E., and T. G. Baugh., eds. 1993. *The American Southwest and Mesoamerica.* New York: Plenum Press.

Erlandson, John. 1994. *The Early Hunter-Gatherers of the California Coast.* New York: Plenum Press.

———. 2001. "The Archaeology of Aquatic Adaptations: Paradigms for a New Millennium." *Journal of Archaeological Research* 9(4): 281–350.

Ervard, Wolfgang, et al. 2002. "Molecular Evolution of FOXP2: Speech and Language." *Nature* 418: 869–872.

Estrada-Belli, Francisco. 2010. *The First Maya Civilization: Ritual, and Power Before the Classic Period.* Rev. ed. London: Routledge.

Evans, Arthur J. 1921. *The Palace of Minos at Knossos.* 4 vols. Oxford: Clarendon.

Evans, Susan Toby. 2008. *Ancient Mexico and Central America.* 2nd ed. London and New York: Thames & Hudson.

Fagan, Brian M. 1985. *The Adventure of Archaeology.* Washington, DC: National Geographic Society.

———. 1996. *Time Detectives.* New York: Touchstone Books.

———. 2004a. *The Long Summer.* New York: Basic Books.

———. 2004b. *The Rape of the Nile.* 3rd ed. Boulder, CO: Westview Press.

———. 2005a. *Ancient North America.* 4th ed. New York: Thames & Hudson.

———. 2005b. *A Brief History of Archaeology.* Upper Saddle River, NJ: Prentice Hall.

———. 2005c. *Chaco Canyon: Archaeologists Explore the Lives of an Ancient Society.* New York: Oxford University Press.

———. 2007. *Return to Babylon.* Rev. Ed. Boulder: University of Colorado Press.

———. 2009. *Floods, Famines, and Emperors: El Niño and the Fate of Civilizations.* Rev. ed. New York: Basic Books.

———. 2010. *Cro-Magnon: How the Ice Age Gave Birth to the First Modern Humans.* New York: Bloomsbury Press.

———. 2011. *The First North Americans.* London and New York: Thames and Hudson.

———, and N. Durrani. 2014. *In the Beginning.* 13th ed. Upper Saddle River, NJ: Pearson.

———, and F. Van Noten. 1971. *The Hunter-Gatherers of Gwisho.* Tervuren, Belgium: Musée Royal de l'Afrique Centrale.

Fagles, Robert. 1990. *The Iliad.* New York: Viking Press.

Fairbanks, Richard G. 1989. "A 17,000-Year Glacio-Eustatic Sea Level Record: Influence of Glacial Melting Rates on the Younger Dryas Event and Deep Sea Circulation." *Nature* 342: 637–642.

Farmer, Steve, et al. 2004. "The Collapse of the Indus-Script Thesis: The Myth of a Literate Harappan Civilization." *Electronic Journal of Vedic Studies* 11(2): 19–57.

Farnsworth, Paul, et al. 1985. "A Re-evaluation of the Isotopic and Archaeological Reconstruction of Diet in the Tehuacán Valley." *American Antiquity* 50(1): 102–116.

Fash, William. 1991. *Scribes, Warriors, and Kings.* London and New York: Thames & Hudson.

Feddon, Robin. 1975. *Egypt: Land of the Valley.* London: Faber & Faber.

Fedick, Scott, eds. 1996. *The Managed Mosaic.* Salt Lake City: University of Utah Press.

Fedje, Daryl. 2003. "Ancient Landscapes and Archaeology in Haida Gwaii and Hecate Strait." In *Archaeology of Coastal British Columbia.* Roy L. Carlson, ed. pp. 29–38. Burnaby, BC: Archaeology Press.

Feinman, Gary, and Linda Manzanilla, eds. 2002. *Cultural Evolution: Contemporary Viewpoints.* New York: Kluwer Plenum.

Ferring, Reid, et al. 2011. "Earliest Human Occupations at Dmanisi (Georgian Caucasus) Dated to 1.85-1.78 Ma." *Proceedings of the National Academy of Sciences, 10.*

Field, David, et al. 2010. *The Story of Silbury Hill.* Swindon, UK: English Heritage.

Finlayson, Clive. 2010. *The Humans Who Went Extinct: Why Neanderthals Died out and We Survived.* New York: Oxford University Press.

Finney, Ben R. 1994. *Voyage of Rediscovery.* Berkeley: University of California Press.

Fish, Suzanne K., and Paul R. Fish., eds. 2007. *Hohokam Millennium.* Santa Fe, NM: School of Advanced Research.

Flannery, Kent V. 1965. "The Ecology of Early Food Production in Mesopotamia." *Science* 147: 1247–1256.

———. 1968. "Archaeological Systems Theory and Early Mesoamerica." In *Anthropological Archaeology in the Americas.* Betty Meggers, ed. pp. 67–87. Washington, DC: Anthropological Society of Washington.

———. 1972. "The Cultural Evolution of Civilizations." *Annual Review of Ecology and Systematics* 4: 399–426.

———, eds. 1976. *The Early Mesoamerican Village*. New York: Academic Press.

———, eds. 1982. *Maya Subsistence*. New York: Academic Press.

———. 1983. "Settlement, Subsistence, and Social Organization of the Proto-Otomangans." In *The Cloud People*. Kent V. Flannery and Joyce Marcus, eds. pp. 32–36. New York: Academic Press.

———. 1986. *Guilá Naquitz*. Orlando, FL: Academic Press.

———. 1999. "Process and Agency in Early State Formation." *Cambridge Archaeological Journal* 9: 3–21.

Fleagle, J. 1988. *Primate Evolution and Adaptation*. London: Academic Press.

Folan, William J., Joyce Marcus, and W. Frank Miller. 1995. "Verification of a Maya Settlement Model through Remote Sensing." *Cambridge Archaeological Journal* 5(2): 277–281.

Foley, Robert. 1984a. "Early Man and the Red Queen." In *Hominid Evolution and Community Ecology*. Robert Foley, ed., pp. 85–110. London: Academic Press.

———, eds. 1984b. *Hominid Evolution and Community Ecology: Prehistoric Human Adaptation in Biological Perspective*. London: Academic Press.

———. 1984c. "Putting People into Perspective." In *Hominid Evolution and Community Ecology*. Robert Foley, ed. pp. 1–24. London: Academic Press.

———. 1987a. *Another Unique Species: Patterns in Human Evolutionary Ecology*. London: Longmans.

———. 1987b. "Hominid Species and Stone-Tool Assemblages: How Are They Related?" *Antiquity* 61: 380–392.

———. 1995. *Humans Before Humanity*. Oxford: Blackwell.

Forest, J. D. 1986. "Tell el-Ouelli: Preliminary Report on the 4th Season." *Iraq* 44(1–2): 55–60.

Fowler, Melvin L. 1958. *Modoc Rockshelter*. Springfield: Illinois State Museum.

———. 1997. *The Cahokia Atlas: A Historical Atlas of Cahokia Archaeology*. Rev. ed. Urbana: Illinois Transportation Archaeology Research Program.

Freidel, David, and Linda Schele. 1988. "Symbol and Power: A History of the Lowland Maya Cosmogram." In *Maya Iconography*. Elizabeth Benson and Gillett Griffin, eds. Princeton, NJ: Princeton University Press.

Freter, AnnCorinne. 1994. "The Classic Maya Collapse at Copán, Honduras: An Analysis of." S. E. Falconer, eds. pp. 160–176. Washington, DC: Smithsonian Institution Press.

Friedman, Jonathan. 1979. *System, Structure, and Contradiction: The Evolution of "Asiatic" Social Formations*. Cambridge: Cambridge University Press.

Friedman, Renee, et al. 1999. "Preliminary Report on Field Work at Hierakonpolis: 1996–1998." *Journal of the American Research Center in Egypt* 26: 1–35.

Frison, George C. 2010. *Prehistoric Hunters of the High Plains*. 3rd ed. Walnut Creek, CA: Left Coast Press.

Fuller, Dorian Q., and Marco Madella. 2000. "Issues in Harappan Archaeobotany: Retrospect and Prospect." In *Indian Archaeology in Retrospect. Vol. 1. Prehistory: Archaeology of South Asia*. S. Setter and Ravi Korisettar, eds. pp. 317–90. New Delhi: MANOHAR and Indian Council of Historical Research.

Fuller, Dorian Q., et al. 2010. "Consilience of genetics and archaeobotany in the entangled history of rice." *Archaelological and Anthropological Science* 2: 115–131.

Gabunia, Leo, et al. 2000. "Earliest Pleistocene Hominid Cranial Remains from Dmanisi, Republic of Georgia: Taxonomy, Geological Setting and Age." *Science* 283(5468): 1019–1025.

Gamble, Clive. 1986. "The Mesolithic Sandwich." In *Hunters in Transition*. pp. 33–42. Marek Zvelebil, ed. Cambridge: Cambridge University Press.

———. 1999. *The Palaeolithic Societies of Europe*. Cambridge: Cambridge University Press.

Gardner, R. Allen, and Beatrice A. Gardner. 1969. "Teaching Sign Language to a Chimpanzee." *Science* 165(3894): 664–672.

Glowacki, Mary. 2004. "Food of the Gods or mere mortals? Hallucinogenic *Spondylus* and its interpretive implications for early andean society." *Antiquity* 79(1): 257–268. Retrieved from http://www.wired.com/wiredscience/2010/11/conch-trumpets-Peru/

Goren-Inbar, N., et al. 2004. "Evidence of hominin control of fire at Gesher-Benot Ya'aqov, Israel." *Science* 30(4): 725–727.

Garlake, Peter. 1973. *Great Zimbabwe*. New York: McGraw-Hill.

Garrod, D. A. E., and Dorothea Bate. 1937. *The Stone Age of Mount Carmel*. Vol. 1. Cambridge: Cambridge University Press.

Gasparini, Graziano, and Luise Margolies. 1980. *Inca Architecture*. Bloomington: Indiana University Press.

Ghosh, A. 1993. "Deurbanization of the Harappan Civilization." In *Harappan Civilization*, 2nd ed. Gregory Possehl, ed. pp. 381–3. New Delhi: Oxford and IBH.

Gibson, J. L. 2001. *The Ancient Mounds of Poverty Point: Place of Rings*. Gainesville: University Presses of Florida.

Gilbert, M. Thomas P., et al. 2008. "DNA from Pre-Clovis Human Coprolites in Oregon, North America." *Sciencexpress*, April 3.

Gill, Richardson Benedict. 2000. *The Great Maya Droughts: Water, Life, and Death*. Albuquerque: University of New Mexico Press.

———, et al. 2007. "Drought and the Maya Collapse." *Ancient Mesoamerica* 18: 283–302.

Gillings, Mark, and Joshua Pollard. 2002. *Avebury*. London: Duckworth.

Gilman, A. 1995. "Prehistoric European Chiefdoms: Rethinking 'Germanic' Societies." In *Foundations of Social Inequality*. T. D. Price and G. M. Feinman, eds. pp. 235–251. New York: Plenum Press.

Goebel, T. 1999. "Pleistocene Colonization of Siberia and Peopling of the Americas: An Ecological Approach." *Evolutionary Anthropology* 8(6): 208–227.

———, and S. Slobodin. 1999. "The Colonization of Western Beringia: Technology, Ecology, and Adaptations." In *Ice Age Humans of North America*. R. Bonnichsen and K. L. Turnmier, eds. pp. 104–155. Corvallis: Oregon State University Press.

Goebel, T., et al. 2000. "Sciencexpress in Transbakal Siberia." *Antiquity* 74: 567–575.

Golla, Victor. 2000. "Language Families of North America." In *America past, America Present: Genes and Languages in the Americas and Beyond*. Colin Renfrew, ed. pp. 59–72. Cambridge: McDonald Institute for Archaeological Research.

Golson, Jack, and D. S. Gardiner. 1990. "Agriculture and Sociopolitical Organization in New Guinea Highlands Prehistory." *Annual Review of Anthropology* 19: 393–417.

González Lauck, Rebecca. 1996. "La Venta: An Olmec Capital." In *Olmec Art of Ancient Mexico*. Elizabeth P. Benson and Beatriz de la Fuente, eds. pp. 72–81. Washington, DC: National Gallery of Art.

Goodall, Jane. 1986. *The Chimpanzees of Gombe*. Cambridge, MA: Harvard University Press.

Goodman, Maurice. 1999. "The Genomic Record of Humankind's Evolutionary Roots." *American Journal of Human Genetics* 64: 31–39.

Goring-Morris, A. Nigel, and Anna Belfer-Cohen. 1911. "Neolithization Processes in the Levant: The Outer Envelope." *Current Anthropology* 52(S4): 195–208.

Gosden, C. 1995. "Arboriculture and Agriculture in Coastal Papua New Guinea." *Antiquity* 69: 807–817.

———, et al. 1989. "Lapita Sites of the Bismarck Archipelago." *Antiquity* 63(240): 561–586.

Gostner, P., and Egarter Vigl. 2002. "Insight: Report of Radiological-Forensic Findings on the Ice Man." *Journal of Archaeological Science* 29: 323–326.

Gould, Richard A. 1977. *Puntutjarpa Rockshelter and Australian Desert Culture.* New York: American Museum of Natural History.

Gowlett, John. 1978. "Culture and Conceptualization: The Oldowan-Acheulian Gradient." In *Stone Age Prehistory.* G. N. Bailey and P. Callow, eds. pp. 243–260. Cambridge: Cambridge University Press.

Grayson, Donald K. 1983. *The Establishment of Human Antiquity.* Orlando, FL: Academic Press.

———. 2007. "Deciphering North American Pleistocene Extinctions." *Journal of Anthropological Research* 63(2): 185–214.

———. 2011. *The Great Basin: A Natural Prehistory.* Rev ed. Berkeley: University of California Press.

———, and D. J. Meltzer. 2002. "Clovis Hunting and Large Mammal Extinction: A Critical Review of the Evidence." *Journal of World Prehistory* 16(4): 313–359.

Greenberg, Joseph. 1987. *Language in the Americas.* Palo Alto, CA: Stanford University Press.

Griffin, J. B. 1967. "Eastern North American Prehistory: A Summary." *Science* 156: 175–191.

Grosman, Leore, et al. 2008. "A 12,000-Year-old Shaman Burial from the Southern Levant (Israel)." *Proceedings of the National Academy of Sciences* 107(35): 1123–1128.

Groube, L., et al. 1986. "40,000-Year-Old Human Occupation Site at Huon Peninsula, Papua, New Guinea." *Nature* 324: 453–455.

Gurney, O. R. 2007. *The Hittites.* London: The Folio Society.

Haas, Jonathan., eds. 2001. *From Leaders to Rulers.* New York: Plenum/Kluwer.

———, et al., eds. 1987. *The Origins and Development of the Andean State.* Cambridge: Cambridge University Press.

Habu, Junko. 2004. *Ancient Jomon of Japan.* Cambridge: Cambridge University Press.

Hahn, J. 1993. "Aurignacian Art in Central Europe." In *Before Lascaux: The Complex Record of the Upper Palaeolithic.* H. Knecht, A. Pike-Tay, and R. White, eds. pp. 229–241. Boca Raton, FL: CRC Press.

Haile-Selassie, Y., B. Asfar, and T. D. White. 2004. "Hominid Cranial Remains from Upper Pleistocene Deposits at Aduma, Middle Awash, Ethiopia." *American Journal of Physical Anthropology* 123: 1–10.

Haile-Selassie, Yohannes, and Giday WoldeGabriel, eds. 2009. *Ardipithecus kadabba: Late Miocene Evidence from the Middle Awash, Ethiopia.* Berkeley: University of California Press.

Haldorsen, Sylvi, Hasan Akan, Bahattin Çelik, and Manfred Heun. 2011. "The Climate of the Younger Dryas as a Boundary for Einkorn Domestication." *Vegetation History and Archaeobotany* 20(4): 305–318.

Hammond, Norman, eds. 1991. *Cuello: An Early Maya Community in Belize.* Cambridge: Cambridge University Press.

Hard, Robert J., and John R. Roney. 1998. "A Massive Terraced Village Complex in Chihuahua, Mexico, 3000 Years before Present." *Science* 279: 1661–1664.

Harding, A. F. 1984. *The Mycenaeans and Europe.* New York: Academic Press.

———. 2000. *European Society in the Bronze Age.* Cambridge: Cambridge University Press.

Harlan, J. R., et al., eds. 1976. *Origins of African Plant Domestication.* The Hague: Mouton.

Harris, D., and G. Hillman., eds. 1989. *Foraging and Farming.* London: Unwin Hyman.

Harrison, Peter D. 1999. *The Lords of Tikal: Rulers of an Ancient Maya City.* London and New York: Thames & Hudson.

Harrison, Richard J. 1980. *The Beaker Folk.* London: Thames & Hudson.

Hart, Donna L., and Robert W. Sussman. 2008. *Man the Hunted: Primates, Predators, and Human Evolution.* Rev. ed. New York: Westview Press.

Hassan, Fekri. 1981. *Demographic Archaeology.* Orlando, FL: Academic Press.

———. 1986. "Desert Environment and Origins of Agriculture in Egypt." *Norwegian Archaeological Review* 19(2): 63–76.

———. 1988. "The Pre-Dynastic of Egypt." *Journal of World Prehistory* 2(2): 135–186.

Hastorf, Christine A. 1992. *Agriculture and the Onset of Political Inequality Before the Inka.* Cambridge: Cambridge University Press.

———. 1999. "The Cultural Life of Early Domestic Plant Use." *Antiquity* 72: 773–782.

Hather, J. G. 1994. *Tropical Archaeobotany.* London: Routledge.

———, and P. V. Kirch. 1991. "Prehistoric Sweet Potato (*Ipomoea Batatas*) from Mangaia Island, Central Polynesia." *Antiquity* 65: 887–893.

Haug, Gerald, et al. 2003. "Climate and the Collapse of Maya Civilization." *Science* 299: 1367–1370.

Hauptmann, H. 1999. "The Urfa Region." In *Neolithic in Turkey, Cradle of Civilization: New Discoveries.* M. Özdogan and N. Basgelen, eds. pp. 65–86. Istanbul: Arkeoloji ve Sanat Yayinlari.

Haury, Emil. 1976. *Hohokam, Desert Farmers and Craftsmen: Excavations at Snaketown.* Tucson: University of Arizona Press.

———. 1985. *Mogollon Culture in the Forestdale Valley, East-Central Arizona.* Tucson: University of Arizona Press.

Hawkes, K., et al. 1989. "Hardworking Hadza Grandmothers." In *Comparative Socioecology of Mammals and Man.* V. Standen and R. Foley, eds. pp. 341–366. London: Black well.

Hayden, Brian. 2003. "A New Overview of Domestication." In *Last Hunters–first Farmers.* T. D. Price and A. B. Gebauer, eds. pp. 273–299. Santa Fe, NM: School of American Research.

Haynes, C. Vance. 1982. "Were Clovis Progenitors in Beringia?" In *Paleoecology of Beringia.* David M. Hopkins et al., eds. pp. 383–398. New York: Academic Press.

Haynes, Gary. 2002. *The Early Settlement of North America: The Clovis Era.* Cambridge: Cambridge University Press.

Haynes, Sibylle. 2005. *Etruscan Civilization: A Cultural History.* Los Angeles: J. Paul Getty Museum.

Healan, Dan. 1989. *Tula of the Toltecs.* Iowa City: University of Iowa Press.

Heckenberger, M. J. 2002. "Rethinking the Arawakian Diaspora: Hierarchy, Regionality, and the Amazonian Formative." In *Comparative Arawakian Histories: Rethinking Culture Area and Language Group in Amazonia*. J. Hill and F. Santos-Granero, eds. pp. 27–36. Urbana: University of Illinois Press.

Hemming, John. 1970. *The Conquest of the Incas*. New York: Harcourt Brace Jovanovich.

Henry, Donald O. 1989. *From Foraging to Agriculture*. Philadelphia: University of Pennsylvania Press.

Henshilwood, C. S., et al. 2004. "Middle Stone Age Shell Beads from South Africa." *Science* 304: 404.

Hester, T. R., et al. 1982. *Archaeology at Colha, Belize: The 1981 Interim Report*. San Antonio, TX: Center for Archaeological Research.

Heun, M. R., et al. 1997. "Site of Einkorn Wheat Domestication Identified by DNA Fingerprinting." *Science* 278: 1312–1314.

Heyerdahl, Thor. 1996. *Tucumé*. London and New York: Thames & Hudson.

Higham, Charles F. W. 1994. *Khok Phanom Di: Prehistoric Adaptation to the World's Richest Habitat*. New York: Harcourt.

———. 2000. *The Civilization of Angkor*. London: Cassel.

———. 2002. *Early Cultures of Mainland Southeast Asia*. London and New York: Thames & Hudson.

———. 2005. "Ban Non Wat." *Current World Archaeology* 9: 32–39.

———, and Ian Glover. 1996. "New Evidence for Early Rice Cultivation in South, Southeast, and East Asia." In *The Origins and Spread of agriculture and Pastoralism in Eurasia*. D. R. Harris, ed. pp. 413–441. London: University College London Press.

———. 2011. "The Long and Winding Road that leads to Angkor." *Cambridge Archaeological Journal* 22(2): 265–289.

Higham, Charles F. W., and Tracey, L.-D. Lu. 1998. "The Origins and Dispersal of Rice Cultivation." *Antiquity* 72(278): 867–877.

Higham, Charles F. W., and Rachanie Thoserat. 1998. *Prehistoric Thailand*. Bangkok: River Books.

Hillman, G. C., and M. S. Davis. 1990. "Measured Domestication Rates in Wild Wheats and Barley under Primitive Cultivation, and Their Archaeological Implications." *Journal of World Prehistory* 4(2): 157–222.

Hiscock, Peter. 2008. *Archaeology of Ancient Australia*. London: Routledge.

Ho, Ping-Ti. 1984. "The Paleoenvironment of North China—A Review Article." *Journal of Asian Studies* 43(4): 723–733.

Hodder, Ian., eds. 1990. *The Domestication of Europe*. Oxford: Blackwell.

———. 1996. *On the Surface: Çatalhöyük 1993–95*. Cambridge: McDonald Institute for Archaeological Research.

———. 1999. *The Archaeological Process: An Introduction*. Oxford: Blackwell.

———. 2006. *The Leopard's Tale*. London and New York: Thames and Hudson.

Hodder, Ian, ed. 2010 *Religion in the Emergence of Civilization: Çatalhöyük as a Case Study* . Cambridge, UK: Cambridge University Press.

Hodell, David A., et al. 1995. "Possible Role of Climate in the Collapse of Classic Maya Civilization." *Nature* 375: 391–394.

———, et al. 2001. "Solar Forcing of Drought Frequency in the Maya Lowlands." *Science* 292: 1367–1370.

Hoffecker, John F. 2001. "Late Pleistocene and Early Holocene Sites in the Nenana River Valley, Central Alaska." *Arctic Anthropology* 38(2): 139–153.

———. 2002. *Desolate Landscapes*. New Brunswick, NJ: Rutgers University Press.

———. 2005. *A Prehistory of the North*. New Brunswick, NJ: Rutgers University Press.

———. 2007. *Human Ecology of Beringia*. New York: Columbia University Press.

———. 2009. "The Spread of modern humans in Europe." *Proceedings of the National Academy of Sciences*. Retrieved from http://www.pnas.org/cgi/doi/10.1073/pnas

Hoffman, Michael A. 1979. *Egypt before the Pharaohs*. New York: Knopf.

———, et al. 1982. *The Predynastic of Hierakonpolis*. Cairo: Egyptian Studies Association.

Hofman, Jack L., and Russell W. Graham. 1998. "The Paleo-Indian Cultures of the Great Plains." In *Archaeology on the Great Plains*. W. Raymond Wood, ed. pp. 87–139. Lawrence: University Press of Kansas.

Hole, Frank. 1994. "Environmental Instabilities and Urban Origins." In *Chiefdoms and Early States in the Near East: The Organizational Dynamics of Complexity*. G. Stein and M. S. Rothman, eds. pp. 121–143. Madison, WI: Prehistory Press.

———, et al. 1969. *The Prehistory and Human Ecology of the Deh Luran Plain*. Ann Arbor: University of Michigan Museum of Anthropology.

Holloway, R. Ross. 1994. *The Archaeology of Early Rome and Latium*. London: Routledge.

Holmes, Charles E. 2001. "Tenena River Valley Archaeology circa 14,000 to 9000 b.p." *Arctic Anthropology* 38(2): 154–170.

Hope, Geoff, and Jack Golson. 1995. "Late Quaternary Change in the Mountains of New Guinea." *Antiquity* 69: 818–830.

Hopkins, David M., et al., eds. 1982. *Paleoecology of Beringia*. New York: Academic Press.

Howell, F. Clark. 1966. "Observations on the Earlier Phases of the European Lower Palaeolithic." *American Anthropologist* 68(2): 111–140.

———. 1999. "Paleo-Demes, Species Clades, and Extinctions in the Pleistocene Hominin Record." *Journal of Anthropological Research* 55: 191–243.

———, and J. Desmond Clark. 1963. "Acheulian Hunter-Gatherers of Sub-Saharan Africa." *Viking Fund Publications in Anthropology* 36: 458–533.

Huang, Tsui-mei. 1992. "Liangzhu—A Late Neolithic Jade-Yielding Culture in Southeastern Coastal China." *Antiquity* 66: 75–83.

Hublin, J. -J. 2001. "Northwestern African Middle Pleistocene hominids and their bearing on the emergence of *Homo sapiens*. Comparison of Middle Pleistocene hominids from Africa and Asia." In *Human Roots: Africa and Asia in the Middle Pleistocene*. Barham, L., and K. Robson-Brown, eds. pp. 99–121. Bristol, UK: Western Academic and Specialist Press.

Huffman, Thomas N. 1987. *Symbols in Stone: Unraveling the Mystery of Great Zimbabwe*. Johannesburg: University of Witwatersrand Press.

Hunt, Terry, and Carl Lipo. 2011. *The Statues that Walked*. New York: Free Press.

Hyslop, John. 1984. *The Inca Road System*. New York: Academic Press.

———. 1990. *Inka Settlement Patterns*. Austin: University of Texas Press.

———, et al. 1987. *Huaca Prieta*. New York: American Museum of Natural History.

Ikram, Salima, and Aidan Dodson. 1998. *The Mummy in Ancient Egypt*. London and New York: Thames & Hudson.

Irwin, G. 1992. *The Prehistoric Exploration and Colonisation of the Pacific*. Cambridge: Cambridge University Press.

Isaac, Glynn. 1984. "The Archaeology of Human Origins: Studies of the Lower Palaeolithic in East Africa, 1971–1981." *Advances in World Archaeology* 3: 1–89.

———, and J. W. K. Harris. 1978. "Archaeology." In *The Fossil Hominids and an Introduction to Their Context, 1968–1974, Vol. 1: Koobi Fora Research Project*. M. D. Leakey and Richard E. Leakey, eds. pp. 47–76. Oxford: Clarendon.

Isaakidou, V., and P. Tomkins, eds. 2008. *Escaping the Labyrinth: The Cretan Neolithic in Context*. Oxford: Oxbow Books.

Isbell, William, and Katharina J. Schreiber. 1978. "Was Huari a State?" *American Antiquity* 43: 372–389.

Jablonski, Nina G., eds. 2002. *The First Americans: The Pleistocene Colonization of the New World*. San Francisco: California Academy of Sciences.

Jacobsen, Thomas W., and W. R. Farrand. 1987. *Franchthi Cave and Paralia*. Bloomington: Indiana University Press.

James, Simon. 1992. *The World of the Celts*. London and New York: Thames & Hudson.

Janusek, John Wayne. 2008. *Ancient Tiwanaku*. Cambridge: Cambridge University Press.

Jarrige, Jean-François. 1993. "Excavations at Mehrgarh: Their Significance for Understanding the Background of the Harappan Civilization." In *Harappan Civilization*, Gregory Possehl, ed. 2nd ed., pp. 79–84. New Delhi: Oxford and IBH.

Jeffries, R. W. 1987. *The Archaeology of Carrier Mills*. Carbondale: Southern Illinois University Press.

Jennings, Jesse D. 1957. *Danger Cave*. Salt Lake City: University of Utah Press.

Jochim, Michael. 2008. "The Mesolithic of the Upper Danube and Upper Rhine." In *Mesolithic Europe*. Geoff Bailey and Penny Spikins, eds. pp. 203–220. Cambridge: Cambridge University Press.

Johanson, Donald C., and Maitland A. Edey. 1981. *Lucy: The Beginnings of Humankind*. New York: Simon & Schuster.

Johnson, Allen W., and Timothy Earle., eds. 2000. *The Evolution of Human Societies: From Foraging Group to Agrarian State*. Stanford: Stanford University Press.

Johnson, Matthew. 2010. *Archaeological Theory*. 2nd ed. New York: Willey/Blackwell.

Jones, M., and T. Brown. 2000. "Agricultural Origins: The Evidence of Modern and Ancient DNA." *Holocene* 10(6): 775–792.

Jones, Rhys. 1995. "Tasmanian Archaeology: Establishing the Sequences." *Annual Review of Anthropology* 24: 423–446.

Joyce, D. J. 2006. "Chronology and new research on the Schaefer mammoth (Mammuthus primigenius) site, Kenosha County, Wisconsin, USA." *Quaternary International* 44: 142–143.

Joyce, Rosemary. 2008. *Ancient Bodies, Ancient Lives: Sex, Gender, and Archaeology*. London: Thames and Hudson.

Kaufman, Terrence, and Victor Golla. 2000. "Language Groupings in the New World: Their Reliability and Usability in Cross-Disciplinary Studies." In *America past, America Present: Genes and Languages in the Americas and Beyond*. Colin Renfrew, ed. pp. 57–67. Cambridge: McDonald Institute for Archaeological Research.

Keightley, David N. 2006. "Marks and Labels: Early Writing in Neolithic and Shang China." In *Archaeology of Asia*. Miriam T. Stark, ed. pp. 177–201. London: Routledge.

———. 1999. "The Shang." In *The Cambridge History of Ancient China*. Michael Lowe, ed. pp. 123–164. Cambridge: Cambridge University Press.

Keller, Ferdinand. 1866. *The Lake Dwellings of Switzerland and Other Parts of Europe*. London: Longmans Green.

Kelly, Robert L. 2001. *Prehistory of the Carson Desert and Stillwater Mountains: Environment, Mobility, and Subsistence in a Great Basin Wetland*. Anthropological Papers No. 23. Salt Lake City: University of Utah Press.

Kembel, Silvia. 2005. *The Architecture at the Monumental Center of Chavín de Huántar: Sequence, Transformation, and Chronology*. Washington, DC: Dumbarton Oaks.

Kemp, Barry. 2005. *Ancient Egypt: The Anatomy of a Civilization*. 2nd ed. London: Routledge.

Kennedy, Paul. 1987. *Rise and Fall of the Great Powers*. New York: Vintage Books.

Kenoyer, J. M. 1997. "Trade and Technology of the Indus Valley: New Insights from Harappa, Pakistan." *World Archaeology* 29(2): 262–280.

———. 1998. *Ancient Cities of the Indus Valley*. Karachi: Oxford University Press.

Kenyon, Kathleen. 1981. *Excavations at Jericho*. Vol. 3. Jerusalem: British School of Archaeology.

Kershaw, Peter. 1995. "Environmental Change in Greater Australia." *Antiquity* 69: 656–675.

Kidder, Alfred V. 1927. *An Introduction to the Study of Southwestern Archaeology*. New Haven, CT: Yale University Press.

Kimball, William H., et al. 1994. "The First Skull and Other New Discoveries of Australopithecus afarensis at Hadar, Ethiopia." *Nature* 368: 449–451.

Kirch, Patrick V. 1984. *The Evolution of the Polynesian Chiefdoms*. Cambridge: Cambridge University Press.

———. 1985. *Feathered Gods and Fishhooks*. Honolulu: University of Hawaii Press.

———. 1997. *The Lapita Peoples: Ancestors of the Oceanic World*. Oxford: Blackwell.

———. 2000. *On the Road of the Winds: An Archaeological History of the Pacific Islands before European Contact*. Berkeley: University of California Press.

———, and T. L. Hunt, eds. 1996. *Historical Ecology in the Pacific Islands: Prehistoric Environmental and Landscape Change*. New Haven, CT: Yale University Press.

Kirch, Patrick V., and Marshall Sahlins. 1992. *Anahulu: The Anthropology of History in the Kingdom of Hawaii*. Chicago: University of Chicago Press.

Kislev, Mordechai, et al. 2006. "Early Domesticated Fig in the Jordan Valley." *Science* 312(5778): 1372–1374.

Klein, Richard G. 1979. "Stone Age Exploitation of Animals in Southern Africa." *American Scientist* 67: 23–32.

———. 2009. *The Human Career*. 3rd ed. Chicago: University of Chicago Press.

———. 2001. "Fully Modern Humans." In *Archaeology at the Millennium: A Sourcebook*. Gary M Feinman and T. Douglas Price, eds. pp. 109–136. New York: Kluwer Academic/Plenum.

Knight, V. J. 1986. "The Institutional Organization of Mississippian Religion." *American Antiquity* 61: 675–687.

———, and Vincas Steponaitis., eds. 1998. *Archaeology of the Moundville Chiefdom*. Washington, DC: Smithsonian Institution Press.

Kobusiewicz, Michel, et al. 2004. "First Neolithic Cemetery in Egypt's Western Desert." *Antiquity* 78(301): 566–578.

Kohl, P. 1978. "The Balance of Trade in Southwestern Asia in the Mid-Third Millennium b.c." *Current Anthropology* 19: 463–492.

Kolata, Alan L. 1993. *Tiwanaku*. Oxford: Blackwell.

———. 2002. *Tiwanaku and Its Hinterland, Archaeology and Paleoecology of an Andean Civilization: Urban and Rural Archaeology*. Washington, DC: Smithsonian Institution Press.

Korisettar, Ravi, et al. 2001. "Brahmagiri and beyond: The Archaeology of the Southern Neolithic." In *Indian Archaeology in Retrospect, Vol. 1: Prehistory: Archaeology of South Asia*. S. Setter and Ravi Korisettar, eds. pp. 151–237. New Delhi: MANOHAR and Indian Council of Historical Research.

Kozlowski, S. 1999. *The Eastern Wing of the Fertile Crescent*. Oxford: British Archaeological Reports International Series 760.

Kramer, Samuel. 1963. *The Sumerians*. Chicago: University of Chicago Press.

Kuzmin, Yaroslav V., and Kenneth B. Tankersley. 1996. "The Colonization of Eastern Siberia: An Evaluation of the Paleolithic Age Radiocarbon Dates." *Journal of Archaeological Science* 32: 577–585.

Laitman, Jeffrey T., J. S. Reidenberg, D. R. Freidland, and P. J. Gannon. 1991. "What Sayeth Thou Neanderthal? A Look at the Evolution of Their Vocal Tract and Speech." *American Journal of Physical Anthropology* 12: 109.

Lamberg-Karlovsky, C. C. 1978. "The Proto-Elamites and the Iranian Plateau." *Antiquity* 52: 114–120.

Lamberg-Karlovsky, C. C., and T. Beale., eds. 1986. *Excavations at Tepe Yahya, Iran: The Early Periods*. Cambridge, MA: Harvard University Press.

Larichev, Vitaliy. 1988. "The Upper Paleolithic of Northern Asia." *Journal of World Prehistory* 2(4): 359–396.

———, et al. 1987. "Lower and Middle Paleolithic of Northern Asia: Achievements, Problems, and Perspectives." *Journal of World Prehistory* 1(4): 415–464.

Larick, R., et al. 2001. "Early Pleistocene 40Ar/39Ar dates for Bapang Formation hominins, Central Java, Indonesia." *Proceedings of the National Academy of Sciences* 98: 4866–4871.

Larsen, Clark Spencer. 1995. "Biological Changes in Human Populations with Agriculture." *Annual Review of Anthropology* 24: 185–213.

Larsen, Mogens. 1976. *The Old Assyrian City-State and Its Colonies*. Copenhagen: Akademisk Forlag.

———. 1987. "Commercial Networks in the Ancient Near East." In *Center and Periphery in the Ancient World*. Michael Rowlands et al., eds. pp. 47–56. Cambridge: Cambridge University Press.

———. 1995. *The Conquest of Assyria*. London: Routledge.

Layton, R. 1994. *Who Needs the Past?* 2nd ed. London: Routledge.

Leakey, L. S. B. 1951. *Olduvai Gorge, 1931–1951*. Cambridge: Cambridge University Press.

Leakey, M. D. 1971. *Olduvai Gorge*. Vol. 3. Cambridge: Cambridge University Press.

———, and J. D. Harris. 1990. *Laetoli: A Pliocene Site in Northern Tanzania*. Oxford: Oxford University Press.

Leakey, M. G., et al. 1995. "New Four-Million-Year-Old Hominid Species from Kanapooi and Allia Bay, Kenya." *Nature* 376: 565–571.

Leavesley, M. G., and J. Chappell. 2004. "Buang Merabak: Additional Early Radiocarbon Evidence of the Colonization of the Bismarck Archipelago." *Antiquity* 78: 301.

Lee, Richard B. 1979. *The !Kung San*. Cambridge: Cambridge University Press.

———, and Irven DeVore, eds. 1976. *Kalahari Hunter-Gatherers*. Cambridge: Cambridge University Press.

Lefkowitz, Mary. 1996. *Not out of Africa*. New York: Basic Books.

Legge, A. J., and Peter Rowley-Conwy. 1987. "Gazelle Hunting in Stone Age Syria." *Scientific American* 238(8): 88–95.

Lehner, Mark. 1997. *The Complete Pyramids*. London and New York: Thames & Hudson.

Lekson, Stephen H. 1999. *The Chaco Meridian: Centers of Political Power in the Ancient Southwest*. Walnut Creek, CA: AltaMira Press.

Lemorini, C., et al. 2006. "Use-Wear analysis of Amudian laminar assemblage from the Acheulo-Yabrudian of Qesem Cave, Israel." *Journal of Archaeological Science* 33: 921–934.

Leroi-Gourhan, André. 1984. *The Dawn of European Art: An Introduction to Palaeolithic Cave Painting*. Cambridge: Cambridge University Press.

Levetzion, Nehemiah. 1973. *Ancient Ghana and Mali*. London: Methuen.

Levy, Thomas E., et al. 2002. "Early Bronze Age Metallurgy: A Newly Discovered Copper Manufactory in Southern Jordan." *Antiquity* 76: 425–437.

Lewin, Roger. 1987. *Bones of Contention*. New York: Simon & Schuster.

———. 1998. *The Origins of Modern Humans*. New York: Scientific American Library.

———, and Robert A. Foley. 2004. *Principles of Human Evolution*. 2nd ed. Malden, MA: Black well.

Lewis-Williams, David. 1981. *Seeing and Believing: Symbolic Meaning in Southern San Rock Art*. New York: Academic Press.

Lewis-Williams, David. 2002. *The Mind in the Cave: Consciousness and the Origins of Art*. London and New York: Thames & Hudson.

———, and Sam Challis. 2010. *Deciphering Ancient Minds*. London and New York: Thames ad Hudson.

Lieberman, Philip. 1991. *Uniquely Human: The Evolution of Speech, Thought, and Selfless Behavior*. Cambridge, MA: Harvard University Press.

Liu, Li. 2004. *The Chinese Neolithic*. Cambridge: Cambridge University Press.

———, and Xingean Chen. 2006. "Sociopolitical Change from Neolithic to Bronze Age China." In *Archaeology of Asia*. Miriam T. Stark, ed. pp. 149–178. London: Routledge.

———. 2010. *State Formation in Early China*. London: Duckworth.

Liverani, M., eds. 1993. *Akkad: The First World Empire*. Padua, Italy: Sargon.

Lombard, M., and L. Phillipson. 2010. "Indications of bow and stone-tipped arrow use 64 000-years ago in Kwazulu-Natal, South Africa." *Antiquity* 84(3): 635–648.

Lourandos, Henry., eds. 1997. *Continent of Hunter-Gatherers: New Perspectives in Australian Prehistory*. Cambridge: Cambridge University Press.

MacDougall, J. D. 2004. *Frozen Earth: The Once and Future Story of Ice Ages*. Berkeley: University of California Press.

MacLatchy, L., et al. 2000. "Postcranial Functional Morphology of Morotopithecus Bishopi, with Implications for the Evolution of Modern Ape Locomotion." *Journal of Human Evolution* 39: 159–183.

MacNeish, Richard., eds. 1970. *The Prehistory of the Tehuacán Valley*. Austin: University of Texas Press.

MacQueen, J. G. 1996. *The Hittites*. 3rd ed. London: Thames & Hudson.

Madsen, David B. 2010. *Entering America: Northeast Asia and Beringia Before the Last Glacial Maximum*. Salt Lake City: University of Utah Press.

Maisels, Charles. 1993. *The Emergence of Civilization: From Hunting and Gathering to Agriculture, Cities and the State in the Near East*. London: Routledge.

———. 2001. *Early Civilizations of the Old World: The Formative Histories of Egypt, the Levant, Mesopotamia, India, and China*. London: Routledge.

Malinowski, Bronislaw. 1922. *Argonauts of the Western Pacific*. London: Routledge & Kegan Paul.

Mallory, J. P. 1988. *In Search of the Indo-Europeans*. New York: Thames & Hudson.

Mann, Charles C. 2006. *1491: New Revelations of the Americas Before Columbus*. New York: New York: Vintage.

Mannika, E. 1996. *Angkor Wat: Time, Space, Kingship*. Honolulu, HI: University of Hawaii Press.

Manning, Stuart. 1988. "The Bronze Age Eruption of Thera." *Journal of Mediterranean Archaeology* 1(1): 17–82.

———. 1995. *Absolute Chronology of the Aegean Early Bronze Age*. Sheffield, England: Sheffield Academic Press.

Marcus, Joyce. 1976. *Emblem and State in the Classic Maya Lowlands*. Washington, DC: Dumbarton Oaks.

———. 1993. *Mesoamerican Writing Systems: Propaganda, Myth, and History in Four Ancient Civilizations*. Princeton, NJ: Princeton University Press.

———, and Kent V. Flannery. 1996. *The Zapotec Civilization*. London and New York: Thames & Hudson.

Marinatos, Nanno. 1993. *Minoan Religion*. Columbia: University of South Carolina Press.

Marks, Anthony E. 1983. "The Middle to Upper Palaeolithic Transition in the Levant." *Advances in World Prehistory* 2: 51–98.

Marshack, Alexander. 1972. *The Roots of Civilization*. New York: McGraw-Hill.

Marshall, Fiona, and Elizabeth Hildebrand. 2002. "Cattle Before Crops: The Beginnings of Food Production in Africa." *Journal of World Prehistory* 16(2): 99–143.

Martin, Simon, and N. Grube. 2000. *Chronicle of the Maya Kings and Queens*. London and New York: Thames & Hudson.

Maslin, Mark. 2009a. "How the Age of Ice Began." In *The Complete Ice Age*. Brian Fagan, Ed. pp. 48–61. London: Thames and Hudson.

———. 2009b. "The Climatic Rollercoaster." In *The Complete Ice Age*. Brian Fagan, Ed. pp. 62–91. London: Thames and Hudson.

Matson, R. G. 1991. *The Origins of Southwestern Agriculture*. Tucson: University of Arizona Press.

Matthews, R. 2003. *The Archaeology of Mesopotamia: Theories and Approaches*. London: Routledge.

Maxwell, Moreau S. 1985. *Prehistory of the Eastern Arctic*. New York: Academic Press.

McAnany, Patricia. 1995. *Living with the Ancestors: Kinship and Kingship in Ancient Maya Society*. Austin: University of Texas Press.

———, and Norman Yoffee, eds. *Questioning Collapse: Human Resilience, Ecological Vulnerability, and the Aftermath of Empire*. Cambridge: Cambridge University Press.

McAvoy, Joseph M., and Lynn D. McAvoy. 1997. *Archaeological Investigations of Site 44SX202, Cactus Hill, Sussex County, Virginia*. Richmond, VA: Division of Historical Resources.

McBrearty, Sally, and Alison Brooks. 2000. "The Revolution Wasn't New: A New Interpretation of the Origin of Modern Human Behavior." *Journal of Human Evolution* 39: 453–563.

McCollum, Melissa A. 1999. "The Robust Australopithecine Face: A Morphogenetic Perspective." *Science* 284: 301–305.

McCorriston, Joy, and Hole Frank. 1991. "The Ecology of Seasonal Stress and the Origins of Agriculture in the Near East." *American Anthropologist* 93: 46–69.

McGhee, Robert. . "Contact between Native North Americans and the Medieval Norse: A Review of Evidence." *American Antiquity* 49(2): 4–26.

———. 1996. *Ancient People of the Arctic*. Vancouver: University of British Columbia Press and the Canadian Museum of Civilization.

McIntosh, Jane R. 2002. *A Peaceful Realm*. Boulder, CO: Westview Press.

———, eds. 2007. *The Ancient Indus Valley: New Perspectives*. Santa Barbara, CA: ABC-CLIO.

McIntosh, Susan K., and R. J. McIntosh. 1980. *Prehistoric Investigations at Jenne-Jeno, Mali*. Oxford: British Archaeological Reports.

———. 1988. "From Stone to Metal: New Perspectives on the Later Prehistory of West Africa." *Journal of World Prehistory* 2(1): 89–131.

Marean, C. W., et al. 2007. "Early human use of marine resources and pigment in South Africa during the Middle Pleistocene." *Nature* 433: 733–736.

Meadow, Richard H., eds. 1991. *Harappa Excavations 1986–1990*. Madison, WI: Prehistory Press.

Megaw, R., and J. V. S. Megaw. 1989. *Celtic Art from Its Beginnings to the Book of Kells*. London and New York: Thames & Hudson.

Mellaart, James. 1967. *Çatal Hüyük*. New York: McGraw-Hill.

———. 1975. *The Neolithic of the Near East*. London: Thames & Hudson.

Mellars, Paul. 1985. "The Ecological Basis of Social Complexity in the Upper Palaeolithic of Southwestern France." In *Prehistoric Hunter-Gatherers: The Emergence of Cultural Complexity*. T. Douglas Price and James Brown, eds. pp. 271–297. Orlando, FL: Academic Press.

———. 1996. *The Neanderthal Legacy*. Princeton, NJ: Princeton University Press.

———. 2005. "The Impossible Coincidence. A Single-Species Model for the Origins of Modern Human Behavior in Europe." *Evolutionary Anthropology* 14: 12–27.

———. 2006. "Archaeology and the Dispersal of Modern Humans in Europe: Deconstructing the 'aurignacian.'" *Evolutionary Anthropology* 15: 167–182.

———, and Petra Dark. 1998. *Star Carr in Context*. Cambridge: McDonald Institute for Archaeological Research.

Mellars, Paul, et al., eds. 2007. *Rethinking the Human Revolution.* Cambridge: Cambridge University Press.

Meltzer, David. 1988. "Late Pleistocene Adaptations in Eastern North America." *Journal of World Prehistory* 2(1): 1–52.

Meltzer, David. 2006. *Folsom: New Archaeological Investigations of a Classic Paleoindian Bison Kill.* Berkeley: University of California Press.

———. 2008. *First Peoples in a New World: Colonizing Ice Age America.* Berkeley: University of California Press.

———, James Adovasio, and Tom Dillehay. 1994. "On a Pleistocene Human Occupation at Pedra Furada, Brazil." *Antiquity* 68(261): 695–714.

Mendelssohn, Kurt. 1974. *The Riddle of the Pyramids.* New York: Praeger.

Mercader, Julio, Melissa Panger, and Christophe Boesch. 2002. "Excavation of a Chimpanzee Stone Tool Site in the African Rainforest." *Science* 296: 1452–1455.

Merriwether, D. Andrew. 2002. "A Mitochondrial Perspective on the Peopling of the New World." In *The First Americans.* Nina Jablonski, ed. pp. 295–310. San Francisco: California Academy of Sciences.

Midant-Reynes, Béatrice. 2000. "The Naqada Period (c. 4000 to 3200 b.c.)." In *The Oxford History of Ancient Egypt.* Ian Shaw, ed. pp. 44–60. Oxford: Oxford University Press.

Milisauskas, Samnas., eds. 2002. *European Prehistory.* New York: Kluwer Academic/Plenum.

Miller, Daniel. 1985. "Ideology and the Harappan Civilization." *Journal of Anthropological Archaeology* 4: 1–38.

Miller, Mary, and Karl Taube. 1993. *The Gods and Symbols of ancient Mexico and the Maya.* London and New York: Thames & Hudson.

Millon, R. 1988. "The Last Days of Teotihuacán." In *The Collapse of Ancient States and Civilizations.* Norman Yoffee and George Cowgill, eds. pp. 102–164. Tucson: University of Arizona Press.

———. 1996. "State and Society at Teotihuacán, Mexico." *Annual Review of Anthropology* 26: 129–161.

———, R. Bruce Drewitt, and George Cowgill. 1974. *Urbanization at Teotihuacán, Mexico.* Austin: University of Texas Press.

Milner, George R. 1998. *The Cahokia Chiefdom.* Washington, DC: Smithsonian Institution Press.

———. 2004. *The Moundbuilders.* London and New York: Thames & Hudson.

Mithen, Steven. 1996. *The Prehistory of the Mind.* London: Thames & Hudson.

———. 2006. *After the Ice: A Global Human History.* Cambridge: Harvard University Press.

———. 2007. *The Singing Neanderthals.* Cambridge, MA: Harvard University Press.

Mithen, Steven J., et al. 2011. "An 11 600 year-old communal structure from the Neolithic of Southern Jordan." *Antiquity* 85(2): 350–364.

Mochanov, Yuri A. 1996. "Dyuktai Cave." In *American Beginnings.* Richard West, ed. pp. 164–174. Chicago: University of Chicago Press.

Moctezuma, Eduardo Matos. 1988. *The Great Temple of the aztecs.* New York: Thames & Hudson.

Molleson, Theya. 1994. "The Eloquent Bones of Abu Hureyra." *Scientific American* 271(2): 70–75.

Moore, Andrew T. 1985. "The Development of Neolithic Societies in the Near East." *Advances in World Archaeology* 4: 1–70.

———, et al. 2000. *Village on the Euphrates.* New York: Oxford University Press.

Moore, A. M. T., and Gordon Hillman. 1992. "The Pleistocene to Holocene Transition and Human Economy in Southwest Asia: The Impact of the Younger Dryas." *American Antiquity* 57(3): 482–494.

Moorey, P. R. S. 1994. *Ancient Mesopotamian Materials and Industries: The Archaeological Evidence.* Oxford: Clarendon.

Morris, Craig, and Adriana von Hagen. 2011. *The Incas.* London and New York: Thames and Hudson.

Morris, I., eds. 1987. *Burial and Ancient Society. The Rise of the Greek City-State.* Cambridge: Cambridge University Press.

———. 1994. *Classical Greece: Ancient Histories and Modern Archaeologies.* Cambridge: Cambridge University Press.

Morris, J. Bayard., eds. 1962. *Five Letters of Cortés to the Emperor, 1519–1526.* New York: Norton.

Morse, Dan, and P. A. Morse. 1983. *Archaeology of the Central Mississippi Valley.* New York: Academic Press.

Morwood, M. J., et al. 1999. "Fission Track Age of Stone Tools and Fossils on the East Indonesian Island of Flores." *Nature* 392: 173–176.

Morwood, M. J., et al. 2004. "Archaeology and Age of a New Hominin from Flores in Eastern Indonesia." *Nature* 431: 1087–1091.

Moscati, Sabatino. 1988. *The Phoenicians.* Milan: Bompiani.

Moseley, Michael. 1975. *The Maritime Foundations of Andean Civilization.* Menlo Park, CA: Cummings.

———. 1985. "The Exploration and Explanation of Early Monumental Architecture in the Andes." In *Early Ceremonial Architecture in the Andes.* Christopher Donnan, ed. pp. 28–58. Washington, DC: Dumbarton Oaks.

———. 2000. *The Incas and Their Ancestors.* 2nd ed. London and New York: Thames & Hudson.

———, and Kent C. Day., eds. 1982. *Chan Chan: Andean Desert City.* Albuquerque: University of New Mexico Press.

Moseley, Michael, et al. 1991. "Colonies and Conquest: Tiahuanaco and Huari in Moquequa." In *Huari Administrative Structure.* William H. Isbell and Gordon F. McEwen, eds. pp. 121–146. Washington, DC: Dumbarton Oaks.

Muller, Jon D. 1989. "The Southern Cult." In *The Southeastern Ceremonial Complex: Artifacts and Analysis.* Patricia Galloway, ed. pp. 11–26. Lincoln: University of Nebraska Press.

Muller, Stephanie, and Friedemann Shrenk. 2008. *The Neanderthals.* London: Routledge.

Mulvaney, John, and Johan Kamminga. 1999. *The Prehistory of Australia.* Washington, DC: Smithsonian Institution Press.

Muzzolini, Alfred. 1995. *Les Images Rupestres du Sahara.* Toulouse: Author.

Nelson, Sarah. 1993. *The Archaeology of Korea.* Cambridge: Cambridge University Press.

———. 1995. *The Archaeology of Northeast China: Beyond the Great Wall.* London: Routledge.

———. 2006. "Archaeology in the Two Koreas." In *Archaeology of Asia.* Miriam T. Stark, ed. pp. 37–54. Malden, MA: Black well.

Nichols, D. L., and T. H. Charlton., eds. 1995. *The Archaeology of City-States: Cross Cultural Approaches.* Washington, DC: Smithsonian Institution Press.

Nissen, Hans J., et al. 1993. *Archaic Bookkeeping. Early Writing and Techniques of Economic Administration in the Ancient near East.* Chicago: University of Chicago Press.

Oates, Joan. 1973. "The Background and Development of Early Farming Communities in Mesopotamia and the Zagros." *Proceedings of the Prehistoric Society* 39: 147–181.

O'Connell, J. F. 1997. "On Plio-Pleistocene Archaeological Sites and Central Places." *Current Anthropology* 38: 86–88.

———, and J. Allen. 2004. "Pre-LGM Sahul (pleistocene Australia-New Giuinea) and the Archaeology of Early Modern Humans." In *Rethinking the Human Revolution.* Paul Mellars et al., eds. pp. 395–410. Cambridge: MacDonald Institute for Archaeological Research.

O'Connell, J. F., et al. 1999. "Grandmothering and the Evolution of *Homo erectus.*" *Journal of Human Evolution* 36: 461–485.

O'Connell, J. F., et al. 2008. "Getting from Sunda to Sahul." In *Islands of Inquiry: Colonization, seafaring and the archaeology of maritime landscapes.* G. Clark, F. Leach, and S. O'Connor, eds. pp. 31–46. Canberra: ANU E Press, Australian National University.

O'Connor, Sue. 2007. "New Evidence from East Timor contributes to our understanding of earliest modern human occupation east of the Sunda Shelf." *Antiquity* 81(3): 523–535.

O'Connell, James F., and Jim Allen. 2012. "The Restaurant at the end of the Universe." *Australian Archaeology* 74: 5-31.

O'Connor, Sue, Matthew Spriggs, and Peter Veth. 2002. "Excavation at Lene Hara Cave Establishes Occupation in East Timor at Least 30,000 to 35,000 Years Ago." *Antiquity* 76: 45–50.

Oliver, Douglas. 1977. *Ancient Tahitian Society.* Honolulu: University of Hawaii Press.

Oliver, Roland. 2000. *The African Experience.* London: Weidenfeld and Nicholson.

Oppenheimer, Stephen. 2008. "The great arc of dispersal of modern humans: Africa to Australia." *Quaternary International* XX: 1–12.

O'Regan, Hannah. 2009. "The Ice Age Bestiary." In *The Complete Ice Age.* Brian Fagan, Ed. pp. 142–185. London: Thames and Hudson.

Özdogan, M., and N. Basgelen., eds. 1999. *Neolithic in Turkey: New Discoveries.* Istanbul: Arkeoloji ve Sanat Yayinlari.

Paddock, John. 1983. "The Oaxaca Barrio at Teotihuacán." In *The Cloud People.* Kent Flannery and Joyce Marcus, eds. pp. 170–175. New York: Academic Press.

Pappu, Shanti, et al. 2011. "Early Pleistocene Presence of Acheulian Hominins in South India." *Science* 331(6024): 1596–1599.

Parkington, John. 1987. "Prehistory and Paleoenvironments at the Pleistocene-Holocene Boundary in the Western Cape." In *The Pleistocene Old World: Regional Perspectives.* Olga Soffer, ed. pp. 349–364. New York: Plenum Press.

Parpola, Asko. 1994. *Deciphering the Indus Script.* Cambridge: Cambridge University Press.

Pasztory, Esther. 1997. *Teotihuacán: An Experiment in Living.* Norman: University of Oklahoma Press.

Patterson, Thomas C. 1985. "The Huaca La Florida, Rímac Valley, Peru." In *Early Ceremonial Architecture in the Andes.* Christopher Donnan, ed. pp. 59–70. Washington, DC: Dumbarton Oaks.

———. 1992. *The Inca Empire.* London: Berg.

Pauketat, T. R. 1994. *The Ascent of Chiefs: Cahokia and Mississippian Politics in Native North America.* Tuscaloosa: University of Alabama Press.

———. 2004. *Ancient Cahokia and the Mississippians.* Cambridge: Cambridge University. Press.

———. 2010. *Cahokia: Ancient America's Great City on the Mississippi.* New York: Penguin.

———, and Thomas E. Emerson. 1997. *Cahokia: Domination and Ideology in the Mississippian World.* Lincoln: University of Nebraska Press.

Pavlides, C., and C. Gosden. 1994. "35,000-Year-Old Sites in the Rainforests of West New Britain, Papua New Guinea." *Antiquity* 68: 604–610.

Pavlov, Pavel, John Inge Svendsen, and Svein Indrelid. 2001. "Human Presence in the European Arctic Nearly 40,000 Years Ago." *Nature* 413: 67.

Pearson, Richard J., et al. 1986. *Windows on the Japanese past: Studies in Archaeology and Prehistory.* Ann Arbor: Center for Japanese Studies, University of Michigan.

Pennisi, E. 2002. "A Shaggy Dog History." *Science* 298: 1540–1542.

Penny, Dan. 1999. "Pollen Grains in Sands of Time: Lake Sediments Contribute to the Archaeology of Thailand." *Expedition* 41(3): 332–336.

Perlès, Catherine. 2001. *The Early Neolithic in Greece.* Cambridge: Cambridge University Press.

Pertago, U. A., et al. 2009. "Distinctive but Concomitent Paleo-Indian Migration Routes from Beringia Marked by Two Rare MtDNA Haplogroups." *Current Biology* 19: 1–8.

Petit, J. R., et al. 1999. "Climate and Atmospheric History of the Past 420,000 Years from the Vostok Ice Core, Antarctica." *Nature* 399: 429–436.

Petrie, W. M. Flinders. 1890. *Kahun, Gurob, and Hawara.* London: Egypt Exploration Society.

Phillips, E. D. 1972. "The Scythian Domination in Western Asia." *World Archaeology* 4: 129–138.

Phillipson, D. W., eds. 2001. *Archaeology at Aksum, Ethiopia, 1993–97.* London: Society of Antiquaries.

———. 2005. *African Prehistory.* 3rd ed. Cambridge: Cambridge University Press.

Piggott, Stuart. 1965. *Ancient Europe.* Chicago: Aldine.

———. 1992. *Wagon, Chariot, and Carriage.* London and New York: Thames & Hudson.

Pilbeam, David. 1986. "Distinguished Lecture: Hominoid Evolution and Hominoid origins." *American Anthropologist* 88(2): 295–312.

Pikirayi, Innocent. 2001. *The Zimbabwe Culture: Origins and Decline of Southern Zambezian States.* Walnut Creek, CA: AltaMira Press.

Pinker, Stephen. 1994. *The Language Instinct.* Cambridge, MA: MIT Press.

Piperno, Dolores R., and Kent Flannery. 2001. "The Earliest Archaeological Maize (Zea Mays L.) from Highland Mexico: New Accelerator Mass Spectrometry Dates and Their Implications." *Proceedings of the National Academy of Sciences* 98: 2101–2103.

Piperno, Dolores R., and Deborah M. Pearsall. 1998. *The Origins of Agriculture in the Lowland Neotropics.* San Diego, CA: Academic Press.

Pitulko, V. V., et al. 2004. "The Yana RHS Site: Humans in the Arctic before the Last Glacial Maximum." *Science* 330: 52–56.

Plog, Fred. 2008. *Ancient Peoples of the American Southwest.* 2 nd ed. London and New York: Thames & Hudson.

Pohl, Mary, et al. 2007. "Microfossil Evidence for Pre-Columbian Maize Dispersals in the Neotropics from San Andrés, Tabasco, Mexico." *Proceedings of the National Academy of Sciences* 104(16): 6870–6875.

Pollock, Susan. 1992. "Bureaucrats and Managers, Peasants and Pastoralists, Imperialists and Traders: Research on the Uruk and Jemdet Nasr Periods in Mesopotamia." *Journal of World Prehistory* 6: 297–336.

———. 1999. *Ancient Mesopotamia*. Cambridge: Cambridge University Press.

Pool, Christopher A. 2007. *Olmec and Early Mesoamerica*. Cambridge: Cambridge University Press.

Pope, Geoffrey G. 1989. "Bamboo and Human Evolution." *Natural History* 10(89): 49–56.

———, et al. 1986. "Earliest Radiometrically Dated Artifacts from Southeast Asia." *Current Anthropology* 27(3): 275–279.

Porch, Nick, and Jim Allen. 1995. "Tasmania: Archaeological and Palaeoecological Perspectives." *Antiquity* 69: 714–732.

Possehl, Gregory L. 1986. *Kulli*. Durham: University of North Carolina Press.

Possehl, Gregory L. 1993. *Harappan Civilization*. 2nd ed. New Delhi: Oxford University Press and IBH.

———. 1996. "Meluhha." In *The Indian Ocean in Antiquity*. Julian Reade, ed. pp. 133–208. London: Kegan Paul International.

———. 1999. *Indus Age: The Beginnings*. Delhi: Oxford University Press.

———. 2000. "The Drying up of the Sarasvati: Environmental Disruption in South Asian Prehistory." In *Environmental Disaster and the Archaeology of Human Response*. Garth Bawden and Richard Martin Reycraft, eds. pp. 63–74. Albuquerque: Maxwell Museum of Anthropology.

———. 2003. *Indus Civilization: A Contemporary Perspective*. Walnut Creek, CA: AltaMira Press.

———, and M. H. Raval. 1989. *Harappan Civilization and Rojdi*. New Delhi: Oxford and IBH.

Postgate, Nicholas. 1992. *Early Mesopotamia: Economy and Society at the Dawn of History*. London: Kegan Paul.

Potts, D. T. 1999. *The Archaeology of Elam*. Cambridge: Cambridge University Press.

Potts, Richard. 1984. "Hominid Hunters? Problems of Identifying the Earliest Hunter-Gatherers." In *Hominid Evolution and Community Ecology*. Robert Foley, ed. pp. 129–166. London: Academic Press.

———. 1996. *Humanity's Descent: The Consequences of Ecological Instability*. New York: William Morrow.

Pozorski, Thomas. 1987. "Changing Priorities within the Chimu State: The Role of Irrigation Agriculture." In *The Origins and Development of the Andean State*. Jonathan Haas et al., eds. pp. 111–120. Cambridge: Cambridge University Press.

———, and Sheila Pozorski. 1987. "Chavín, the Early Horizon, and the Initial Period." In *The Origins and Development of the Andean State*. Jonathan Haas et al., eds. pp. 36–46. Cambridge: Cambridge University Press.

Price, T. Douglas. 1985. "Foragers of Southern Scandinavia." In *Prehistoric Hunter-Gatherers: The Emergence of Cultural Complexity*. T. Douglas Price and James Brown, eds. pp. 212–236. New York: Academic Press.

———. 1987. "The Mesolithic of Western Europe." *Journal of World Prehistory* 1(3): 225–305.

———, eds. 2000. *Europe's First Farmers*. Cambridge: Cambridge University Press.

———, Linda Manzanilla, and William D. Middleton. 2000. "Immigration and the Ancient City of Teotihuacán in Mexico: A Study Using Strontium Isotope Ratios in Human Bone and Teeth." *Journal of Archaeological Science* 27(10): 903–913.

Price, T., R. Douglas, et al. 2001. "Prehistoric Human Migration in the *Linearbandkeramik* of Central Europe." *Antiquity* 75: 593–603.

Price, T. Douglas, and Ofer Bar-Yosef. 2011. "The Origins of Agriculture: New Data, New Ideas." *Current Anthropology* 52.

Proulx, Donald. 1985. "An Analysis of the Early Cultural Sequence in the Nepeña Valley, Peru." *Research Report of Department of Anthropology, University of Massachusetts, Amherst, No. 25*.

Quilter, Jeffrey. 1985. "Architecture and Chronology at El Paraíso, Peru." *Journal of Field Archaeology* 12(3): 274–298.

———. 2002. "Moche Politics, Religion, and Warfare." *Journal of World Prehistory* 16(2): 145–195.

Ramenofsky, Ann. 1987. *Vectors of Death*. Albuquerque: University of New Mexico Press.

Rampino, Michael R., and Stanley Ambrose. 2000. "Volcanic Winter in the Garden of Eden: The Toba Supereruption and the Late Pleistocene Human Population Crash." *Geological Society of American Special Paper*: 345.

Ranere, A. J., et al. 2009. "The Cultural and Chronological Context of Early Holocene Maize and Squash Domestication in the Central Balsas River Valley, Mexico." *Proceedings of the National Academy of Sciences* 106(13): 5014–5018.

Rathje, William. 1971. "The Origin and Development of Classic Maya Civilization." *American Antiquity* 36: 249–270.

Raymond, J. Scott. 1981. "The Maritime Foundations of Andean Civilization: A Reconsideration of the Evidence." *American Antiquity* 46: 806–820.

Redman, Charles L. 1978. *The Rise of Civilization: From Early Farmers to Urban Society in the Ancient near East*. San Francisco: Freeman.

Reeves, Nicholas. 1990. *The Complete Tutankhamun*. New York: Thames & Hudson.

———. 2001. *Akhenaten: Egypt's False Prophet*. London and New York: Thames & Hudson.

Reich, David, et al. 2010. "Genetic History of an Archaic Hominin Group from Denisova Cave, Siberia." *Nature* 468: 1053–1060.

Reilly, Kent. 1991. "Olmec Iconographic Influences on the Symbols of Maya Rulership: An Examination of Possible Sources." In *Sixth Palenque Round Table, 1986*. Virginia M Fields, ed. pp. 151–174. Norman: University of Oklahoma Press.

Renault, Mary. 1963. *The King Must Die*. New York: Random House.

Renfrew, Colin. 1972. *The Emergence of Civilization*. London: Methuen.

———. 1978. "Varna and the Social Context of Early Metallurgy." *Antiquity* 52: 199–203.

———. 1983. "The Social Archaeology of Megaliths." *Scientific American* 249: 152–163.

———. 1985. *The Archaeology of Cult: The Sanctuary at Phylakopi*. London: British School of Archaeology in Athens and Thames & Hudson.

———. 1987. *The Archaeology of Language*. London: Cape.

———. 1991. *The Cycladic Spirit*. Cambridge: Cambridge University Press.

———, eds. 2000. *America past, America Present: Genes and Languages in the Americas and beyond*. Cambridge: McDonald Institute for Archaeological Research.

———, and Paul Bahn. 2008. *Archaeology: A Handbook of Ideas and Methods*. 5th ed. New York: Thames & Hudson.

Reynolds, Robert. 1986. "Computer Simulation." In *Guilá Naquitz*. Kent Flannery, ed. pp. 263–289. Orlando, FL: Academic Press.

Reynolds, T. E. G., and G. L. Barnes. 1984. "The Japanese Palaeolithic: A Review." *Proceedings of the Prehistoric Society* 50: 49–62.

Rice, Michael. 1993. *The Archaeology of the Arabian Gulf*. London: Routledge.

Rick, John. 1980. *Prehistoric Hunters of the High Andes*. New York: Academic Press.

———. 2005. "The Evolution of Authority and Power at Chavín de Huántar, Peru." *Archaeological Papers of the American Anthropological Association* 14: 71–89.

Ridgeway, David. 1992. *The First Western Greeks*. Cambridge: Cambridge University Press.

Rightmire, Philip. 1990. *The Evolution of Homo Erectus*. Cambridge: Cambridge University Press.

Rizkana, I., and J. Seeher. 1984. "New Light on the Relation of Maadi to the Upper Egyptian Cultural Sequence." *Mitteilungen des Deutschen Archaologischen Instituts Abteilung Kairo* 40: 237–252.

Roaf, M. 1991. *Cultural Atlas of Mesopotamia and the Ancient near East*. Oxford: Equinox.

Roberts, Mark, and Parfitt Simon. 1999. *A Middle Pleistocene Hominid Site at Eartham Quarry, Boxgrove, West Sussex*. London: English Heritage.

Roberts, Neil. 2010. *The Holocene: An Environmental History*. 3rd ed. Oxford: Black well.

Robertson, John H. 1992. "History and Archaeology at Meroe." In *An African Commitment: Papers in Honour of Peter Lewis Shinnie*. Judy Sterner and Nicholas David, eds. pp. 35–50. Calgary, Alberta: University of Calgary Press.

———, and Rebecca Bradley. 2000. "A New Paradigm: The African Early Iron Age without Bantu Migration." *History in Africa* 27: 287–323.

Robinson, Andrew. 1995. *The Story of Writing*. London and New York: Thames and Hudson.

Robinson, Andrew. 2007. *The Story of Writing*. Rev. Ed. London and New York: Thames & Hudson.

Rocek, Thomas R. 1995. "Sedentarization and Agricultural Dependence: Perspectives from the Pithouse-to-Pueblo Transition in the American Southwest." *American Antiquity* 60(2): 218–239.

Roche, H., et al. 1999. "Early Hominid Stone Tool Production and Technical Skill 2.34 Myr Ago in West Turkana, Kenya." *Nature* 399: 57–60.

Roebroeks, W., and T. Van Kolfschoten. 1994. "The Earliest Occupation of Europe: A Short Chronology." *Antiquity* 68: 489–503.

Roebroeks, W., et al., eds. 2000. *Hunters of the Golden Age*. Leiden: University of Leiden Press.

Rolland, Nicholas, and Harold L. Dibble. 1990. "A New Synthesis of Middle Paleolithic Variability." *American Antiquity* 55(3): 480–499.

Roosevelt, Anna. 1991. *Moundbuilders of the Amazon: Geophysical Archaeology on Marajó Island, Brazil*. New York: Academic Press.

———. 1996. "Paleo-Indian Cave Dwellers in the Amazon: The Peopling of the Americas." *Science* 275: 373–374.

Roth, Barbara, and Kevin Wellman. 2001. "New Insights into the Early Agricultural Period in the Tucson Basin: Excavations at the Valley Farms Site (AZ AA: 12: 736)." *Kiva* 67(1): 59–80.

Rouse, Irving. 1992. *The Taínos; Rise and Decline of the People Who Greeted Cloumbus*. New Haven, CT: Yale University Press.

Rowe, John H. 1946. *Inca Culture at the Time of the Spanish Conquest. Vol. 2. Handbook of South American Indians*. Washington, DC: Smithsonian Institution.

———. 1948. "The Kingdom of Chimor." *Acta Americana* 6: 26–59.

Rudenko, Sergei. 1970. *The Frozen Tombs of Siberia: The Pazyryk Burials of Iron Age Horsemen*. Trans. M. W. Thompson. Berkeley: University of California Press.

Ruff, C. B., et al. 1997. "Body Mass and Encephalization in Pleistocene Homo." *Nature* 387: 173–176.

Russell, John Malcolm. 1991. *Sennacherib's Palace without Rival at Nineveh*. Chicago: University of Chicago Press.

Ryan, William, and Walter Pitman. 1999. *Noah's Flood: The New Scientific Discoveries about the Event That Changed History*. New York: Simon & Schuster.

Sabloff, Jeremy A. 1989. *The Cities of Ancient Mexico*. New York: Thames & Hudson.

———. 1990. *The New Archaeology and the Ancient Maya*. New York: Scientific American Library.

———, and David A. Freidel. 1984. *Cozumel: Late Maya Settlement Patterns*. New York: Academic Press.

Sabloff, Jeremy A., and John S. Henderson., eds. 1993. *Lowland Maya Civilization in the Eighth Century* A.D. Washington, DC: Dumbarton Oaks.

Sakellarakis, Y., and Efi Sapouna-Sakellarakis. 1981. "Drama of Death in a Minoan Temple." *National Geographic* (May): 205–223.

Sand, Christophe. 2000. "The Specificities of the 'Southern Lapita Province': The New Caledonian Case." *Archaeology in Oceania* 35: 20–33.

———, and Peter J. Sheppard. 2000. "Long Distance Prehistoric Obsidian Imports in New Caledonia: Characteristics and Meaning." *Comptes Rendus Academie des Science Paris, Science de la Terre et des planètes* 331: 235–243.

Sanders, N. K. 1985. *The Sea People*. 2nd ed. London: Thames and Hudson.

Sanders, William T., Jeffrey R. Parsons, and Robert S. Santley. 1979. *The Basin of Mexico: Ecological Processes in the Evolution of a Civilization*. New York: Academic Press.

Sanders, William T., et al. 1970. *The Natural Environment: Contemporary Occupation and Sixteenth Century Population of the Valley: Teotihuacán Valley Project Final Report*. University Park: Pennsylvania State University Press.

Sansome, David. 2009. *Ancient Greek Civilization*. 2 nd ed. New York: Wiley-Blackwell.

Sarich, Vincent. 1983. "Retrospective on Hominoid Macromolecular Systematics." In *New Interpretations of Ape and Human Ancestry*. R. L. Ciochon and R. S. Corruccini, eds. pp. 137–150. New York: Plenum Press.

Sassaman, Kenneth E., and David G. Anderson, eds. 1996. *Archaeology of the Mid-Holocene Southeast*. pp. 259–287. Gainesville: University Presses of Florida.

Saunders, Nicholas. 1989. *People of the Jaguar*. London: Souvenir Press.

Saura Ramos, Pedro A. 1999. *Cave of Altamira*. New York: Abrams.

Savage-Rumbaugh, Sue, and Roger Lewin. 1996. *Kanzi: The Ape at the Brink of the Human Mind*. New York: John Wiley.

Scarborough, Vernon L. 2000. "Resilience, Resource Use, and Socio-economic Organization: A Mesoamerican Pathway." In *Environmental Disaster and the Archaeology of Human Response*. Garth Bawdon and Richard Martin Reycraft, eds. pp. 195–212. Albuquerque: Maxwell Museum of Anthropology.

———. 2003. *The Flow of Power: Ancient Water Systems and Landscapes*. Santa Fe, NM: School of American Research Press.

Scarre, Chris, and Brian Fagan. 2003. *Ancient Civilizations*. 2nd ed. Upper Saddle River, NJ: Prentice Hall.

Schaafsma, Curtis F., and Carroll L. Riley., eds. 1999. *The Casas Grandes World*. Salt Lake City: University of Utah Press.

Schele, Linda, and David Freidel. 1990. *A Forest of Kings*. New York: William Morrow.

Schele, Linda, David Freidel, and Joy Parker. 1993. *Maya Cosmos*. New York: William Morrow.

Schele, Linda, and Peter Mathews. 1991. "Royal Visits and Other Intersite Relationships among the Classic Maya." In *Classic Maya Political History*. Patrick Culbert, ed. pp. 226–252. Cambridge: Cambridge University Press.

Schele, Linda, and E. Miller. 1992. *The Blood of Kings*. London and New York: Thames & Hudson.

Schick, Kathy D. 1994. "The Movius Line Reconsidered: Perspectives on the Earlier Paleolithic of Eastern Asia." In *Integrative Paths to the past: Paleoanthropological Advances in Honor of F. Clark Howell* ed., Vol, ed. Robert S. Corruccini and Russel L. Ciochon, . Englewood Cliffs, NJ: Prentice Hall.

———, and Nicholas Toth. 2001. "Palaeoanthropology at the Millennium." In *Archaeology at the Millennium: A Sourcebook*. Gary M Feinman and T. Douglas Price, eds. pp. 39–108. New York: Plenum/Kluwer.

Schick, Kathy D., et al. 1999. "Continuing Investigations into the Stone Tool-Making and Tool-Using Capabilities of a Bonobo (*Pan Paniscus*)." *Journal of Archaeological Science* 26: 821–832.

Shimada, I., et al. 2004. "An Integrated Analysis of Pre-Hispanic Mortuary Practices: A Middle Sicán Case Study." *Current Anthropology* 45(3): 369–402.

Schledermann, Peter. 1990. *Crossroads to Greenland*. Calgary, Alberta: Arctic Institute of North America.

Schmandt-Besserat, D. 1992. *Before Writing*. 2 vols. Austin: University of Texas Press.

———. 1996. *How Writing Came about*. Texas: University of Texas Press.

Schmidt, K. 2001. "Göbekli Tepe, Southeastern Turkey: A Preliminary Report on the 1995–1999 Excavations." *Paléorient* 26: 45–54.

———. 2006. *Sie Bauten Die Ersten Tempel*. Beck: München.

Schmidt, Peter., eds. 1996. *The Culture and Technology of African Iron Production*. Gainesville: University Presses of Florida.

Schreiber, Katharina J. 1987. "Conquest and Consolidation: A Comparison of the Wari and Inka Occupation of a Highland Peruvian Valley." *American Antiquity* 52(2): 266–284.

Scholtz, Christopher A., et al. 2007. "East African Megadroughts between 135 and 75 Thousand Years Ago and Their Bearing on Early Modern Human Origins." *Proceedings of the National Academy of Sciences* 104: 16416–16421.

Schuldenrein, Joseph, et al. 2004. "Landscapes, Soils, and Mound Histories of the Upper Indus Valley, Pakistan: New Insights on the Holocene Environments near Ancient Harappa." *Journal of Archaeological Science* 31: 777–797.

Schwartz, G. M., and S. E. Falconer., eds. 1994. *Archaeological Views from the Countryside*. Washington, DC: Smithsonian Institution Press.

Scudder, Thayer. 1962. *The Ecology of the Gwembe Tonga*. Manchester, England: Manchester University Press.

———. 1971. *Gathering among African Woodland Savannah Cultivators*. Lusaka: University of Zambia.

Semaw, S., et al. 1997. "2.5-Million-Year-Old Stone Tools from Gona, Ethiopia." *Nature* 385: 333–336.

Semaw, S., et al. 2005. "Early Pliocene Hominids from Gona, Ethiopia." *Nature* 433: 301–305.

Sept, J. M. 1994. "Beyond Bones: Archaeological Sites, Early Hominid Subsistence, and the Costs and Benefits of Exploiting Wild Plant Foods in East African Riverine Landscapes." *Journal of Human Evolution* 27: 295–320.

Service, Elman. 1962. *Primitive Social Organization*. New York: Random House.

Shackleton, N. J., and N. D. Opdyke. 1973. "Oxygen Isotope and Paleomagnetic Stratigraphy of Equatorial Pacific Ocean Core V28–238." *Quaternary Research* 3: 38–55.

Shady, Ruth. 1997. *La Ciudad Sagrada de Caral-Sue en los abrores de la civilizacion en el Peru*. Lima: UNMSM.

Shady Solis, Ruth, Jonathan Haas, and Winifred Creamer. 2001. "Dating Caral, a Prehispanic Site in the Supe Valley on the Central Coast of Peru." *Science* 292: 723–726.

Shaffer, Jim G., and Diane A. Lichtenstein. 1995. "The Concepts of 'cultural Tradition' and 'paleoethnicity' in South Asian Archaeology." In *The Indo-Aryans of Ancient South Asia*. George Erdosy, ed. pp. 126–154. Berlin and New York: De Gruyter.

Shang, H., et al. 2007. "An Early Modern Human from Tianyuan Cave, Zhoukoudian, China." *Proceedings of the National Academy of Sciences* 104(16): 6573–6578.

Sharer, Robert J., and Wendy Ashmore. 2009. *Archaeology: Discovering Our past*. 5th ed. New York: McGraw-Hill.

Shaw, Ian., eds. 2000. *The Oxford History of Ancient Egypt*. Oxford: Oxford University Press.

Shaugnessy, E. C., eds. 2000. *China: Empire and Civilization*. Oxford: Oxford University Press.

Shawcross, Kathleen. 1967. "Fern Root and Eighteenth-Century Maori Food Production in Agricultural Areas." *Journal of the Polynesian Society* 76: 330–352.

Shea, John J. 2003. "The Middle Paleolithic of the East Mediterranean Levant." *Journal of World Prehistory* 14(4): 313–394.

Shen, G., et al. 2002. "U-series Dating of Liujang Hominid Site in Guanxi, Southern China." *Journal of Human Evolution* 43: 817–829.

Shennan, Stephen J. 1993. "Settlement and Social Change in Central Europe." *Journal of World Prehistory* 7(2): 121–162.

Sherratt, Andrew G. 1994a. "The Transformation of Early Agrarian Europe: The Later Neolithic and Copper Ages." In *The Oxford*

Illustrated Prehistory of Europe. Barry Cunliffe, ed. pp. 244–276. Oxford: Oxford University Press.

———. 1994b. The Emergence of Elites: Earlier Bronze Age Europe. In *The OXFord Illustrated Prehistory of Europe.* Barry Cunliffe, ed. pp. 244–276. Oxford: Oxford University Press.

Shimada, Izumi, et al. 2004. "An Integrated Analysis of Pre-Hispanic Mortuary Practices: A Middle Sicán Case Study." *Current Anthropology* 45(3): 369–402.

Shinnie, Peter. 1967. *Meroe.* London: Thames & Hudson.

Shipman, Pat. 1984. "Scavenger Hunt." *Natural History* 93(4): 20–28.

———, and J. Rose. 1983. "Evidence of Butchery and Hominid Activities at Torralba and Ambrona." *Journal of Archaeological Science* 10(5): 475–482.

Siegel, Peter E., eds. 1989. *Early Ceramic Population: Lifeways and Adaptive Strategies in the Caribbean.* Oxford: British Archaeological Reports.

Silberman, N. A. 1992. "Who Were the Israelites?" *Archaeology* 45(2): 22–30.

Silverman, Helene. 1996. "The Formative Period on the South Coast of Peru: A Critical Review." *Journal of World Prehistory* 10(2): 95–146.

———, eds. 2004. *Andean Archaeology.* Oxford: Black well.

Simms, Steven. 2008. *Ancient Peoples of the Great Basin and Colorado Plateau.* Walnut Creek, CA: Left Coast Press.

Simons, Elwyn. 1992. "The Fossil History of Primates." In *The Cambridge Encyclopedia of Human Evolution.* J. S. Jones, R. Martin, and D. Pilbeam, eds. pp. 124–128. Cambridge: Cambridge University Press.

Sinapoli, Carla. 2001. "Empires." In *Archaeology at the Millennium: A Sourcebook.* Gary M. Feinman and T. Douglas Price, eds. pp. 439–474. New York: Kluwer/Plenum.

Smith, Andrew B. 1992. *Pastoralism in Africa.* Johannesburg: Witwatersrand University Press.

Smith, Bruce D. 1986. "The Archaeology of the Southeastern United States: From Dalton to De Soto, 10,500–500 b.p." *Advances in World Archaeology* 5: 1–92.

———. 1992. *Rivers of Change.* Washington, DC: Smithsonian Institution Press.

———. 1997. "The Initial Domestication of *Cucurbita Pepo* in the Americas as of 10,000 Years Ago." *Science* 276: 930–934.

———. 1998. *The Emergence of Agriculture.* 2nd ed. New York: Freeman.

———. 2001. "The Transition to Food Production." In *Archaeology at the Millennium: A Sourcebook.* Gary M. Feinman and T. Douglas Price, eds. pp. 199–229. New York: Kluwer/Plenum.

Smith, M. T. 1987. *Archaeology of Aboriginal Culture Change in the Interior Southeast.* Gainesville: University of Florida Presses.

Smith, Michael. 2002. *The Aztecs.* 2nd ed. Oxford: Blackwell.

Smith, P. E. L. 1978. "An Interim Report on Ganj Dareh Tepe, Iran." *American Journal of Archaeology* 82: 538–540.

Smith, Stuart T. 1995. *Askut in Nubia.* London: Routledge.

Soffer, Olga. 1985. *The Upper Palaeolithic of the Central Russian Plains.* New York: Academic Press.

———, et al. 1998. "Perishable Technologies and the Genesis of the Eastern Gravettian." *Anthropologie* 36(1): 43–68.

Sparkes, Brian. 1994. "Classical Greek Attitudes to the past." In *Who Needs the past?*, 2nd ed. R. Layton, ed. pp. 119–130. London: Routledge.

Speth, John. 1983. *Bone Kills and Bison Counts: Decision Making by Ancient Hunters.* Chicago: University of Chicago Press.

Spindler, Konrad. 1996. *The Man in the Ice.* New York: Crown.

Spooner, Brian., eds. 1972. *Population Growth: An Anthropological Perspective.* Cambridge, MA: MIT Press.

Spoor, Fred, et al. 2007. "Implications of New Homo Fossils from Ileret, East of Lake Turkana, Kenya." *Nature* 448(7154): 688.

Spriggs, Matthew. 1989. "Dating the Island Southeast Asian Neolithic." *Antiquity* 63(240): 587–613.

———. 2003. "Chronology of the Neolithic Transition in Southeast Asia and the Western Pacific: A View from 2003." *Review of Archaeology* 24(2): 57–80.

———. 2007. "The Neolithic and Austronesian Expansion within Island Southeast Asia and into the Pacific." In *From Southeast Asia to the Pacific. Archaeological Perspectives on the Austronesian Expansion and the Lapita Cultural Complex.* S. Chiu and C. Sand, eds. pp. 104–140. Taipei: Academia Sinica.

Stahl, Ann Bower. 1984. "Hominid Dietary Selection before Fire." *Current Anthropology* 25(2): 151–168.

———, eds. 2005. *African Archaeology.* Oxford: Black well.

Stanford, Craig B. 1998. "The Social Behavior of Chimpanzees and Bonobos." *Current Anthropology* 39(4): 399–420.

Stanish, Charles. 2002. *Ancient Titicaca.* Berkeley: University of California Press.

———. 2011. *Ancient Andean Political Economy.* Austin: University of Texas Press.

Stark, Miriam T., eds. 2006. *Archaeology of Asia.* Malden, MA: Blackwell.

Stein, Gil. 1994. "Economy, Ritual, and Power in 'Ubaid Mesopotamia." In *Chiefdoms and Early States in the near East.* G. Stein and M. Rothman, eds. pp. 35–46. Madison, WI: Prehistory Press.

———. 2001. "Ancient State Societies in the Old World." In *Archaeology at the Millennium: A Sourcebook.* Gary M. Feinman and T. Douglas Price, eds. pp. 353–379. New York: Kluwer Academic/Plenum.

———, and M. S. Rothman., eds. 1994. *Chiefdoms and Early States in the near East.* Madison, WI: Prehistory Press.

Steinkeller, P. 1989. *Sales Documents of the Ur III Period.* Stuttgart: Steiner Verlag.

Stephens, John Lloyd. 1841. *Incidents of Travel in Central Ametica, Chiapas, and Yucatan.* New York: Harpers.

Steward, Julian. 1970. *A Theory of Culture Change.* Urbana: University of Illinois Press.

———, et al. 1955. *Irrigation Civilizations: A Comparative Study.* Washington, DC: Pan American Union.

Storey, A. A., et al. 2008. "Pre-Columbian Chickens, Dates, Isotopes and MtDNA." *Proceedings of the National Academy of Sciences of the United States of America* 105(E99).

Storey, Rebecca. 1992. *Life and Death in the Ancient City of Teotihuacán.* Birmingham: University of Alabama Press.

Straus, L. G., et al., eds. 1996. *Humans at the End of the Ice Age.* New York: Plenum Press.

Stringer, Chris. 2006. *Homo Britannicus: The Incredible Story of Human Life in Britain.* London: Penguin Books.

Stringer, Chris, and Peter Andrews. 2011. *The Complete World of Human Evolution*. Rev. Ed. London and New York: Thames & Hudson.

Stringer, C. B., and Clive Gamble. 1993. *The Search for the Neanderthals*. London: Thames & Hudson.

Stringer, C. B., and R. McKie. 1996. *African Exodus*. New York: Henry Holt.

Stuart, David. 2001. "The Arrival of Strangers': Teotihuacán and Tollan in Classic Maya History." In *Mesoamerica's Classic Heritage: From Teotihu a Can to the Aztecs*. David Carrasco et al., eds. pp. 465–513. Boulder: University of Colorado Press.

Struever, Stuart, and Felicia Antonelli Holton. 1979. *Koster: Americans in Search of Their past*. New York: Anchor Press/Doubleday.

Sugiyama, Saburo. 2005. *Human Sacrifice, Militarism, and Rulership: Materialization of State Ideology at the Feathered Serpent Pyramid, Teotihuacán*. Cambridge University Press.

Sullivan, Lawrence. 1989. *Icanchu's Drum*. New York: Free Press.

Suwa, Gene, et al. 1997. "The First Skull of *Australopithecus boisei*." *Nature* 378: 489–492.

Swanton, John R. 1911. *Indian Tribes of the Lower Mississippi and Adjacent Coast of the Gulf of Mexico*. Washington, DC: Bureau of American Ethnology Bulletin 43.

Swisher, Carl, et al. 1994. "Age of the Earliest Known Hominids in Java, Indonesia." *Science* 263: 1118–1121.

Tainter, Joseph. 1988. *The Collapse of Civilizations*. Cambridge: Cambridge University Press.

Tankersley, K. B. 1994. "Was Clovis a Colonizing Population in Eastern North America?" In *The First Discovery of America*. W. S. Dancey, ed. pp. 95–116. Columbus: Ohio Archaeological Council.

Taonui, Rawiri. 2006. "Polynesian Oral Traditions." In *Vaka Moana: The Discovery and Settlement of the Pacific*. K. R. Howe, ed. pp. 22–53. Honolulu: University of Hawai'i Press.

Tattersall, Ian. 1996. *The Fossil Trail: How We Know What We Think We Know about Human Evolution*. New York: Oxford University Press.

Taylour, Lord William. 2004. *The Mycenaeans*. 3rd ed. London: Thames & Hudson.

Tedlock, Dennis. 1996. *Popul Vuh*. New York: Simon & Schuster.

Thery-Parisot, Isabelle. 2001. *Economie Des Combustibles Au Paleolithique*. Paris: CRNS Publications.

Thieme, H. 2005. "The Lower Palaeolithic Art of Hunting: The Case of Schöningen." In *The Hominid Individual in Context*. Clive Gamble and Marin Porr, eds. pp. 115–132. London: Routledge.

Thomas, David Hurst, and Robert L. Kelly. 2009. *Archaeology: Down to Earth*. 5th ed. Belmont, CA: Wadsworth.

———, and Robert Bettinger. 1983. *The Archaeology of the Monitor Valley*. New York: American Museum of Natural History.

Thomas, Julian. 1987. "Relations of Production and Social Change in the Neolithic of Northwestern Europe." *Man* 22(3): 405–430.

———. 1999. *Understanding the Neolithic*. 2nd ed. London: Routledge.

Thorp, Robert L. 2005. *China in the Early Bronze Age: Shang Civilization*.B.C. Philadelphia: University of Pennsylvania Press.

Thorpe, I. J. 1996. *The Origins of Agriculture in Europe*. London: Routledge.

Tobias, P. V. 1991. *Olduvai Gorge. Vol. 4. Homo Habilis*. Cambridge: Cambridge University Press.

Torrance, Robin. 1986. *Production and Exchange*. Cambridge: Cambridge University Press.

Torroni, Antonio. 2000. "Mitochondrial DNA and the Origin of Native Americans." In *America Past and Present: Genes and Languages in the Americas and beyond*. Colin Renfrew, ed. pp. 77–87. Cambridge: McDonald Institute for Archaeological Research.

———, et al. 2009. "Distinctive Paleo-Indian Migration routes from beringia marked by two rare mtDNA haplogroups." *Current Biology* 19: 1–8.

Tosi, Maurizo., eds. 1983. *Prehistoric Sistan I*. Rome: ISMEO.

Toth, Nicholas, and Kathy Schick. 2006. *The Oldowan: Case Studies into the Earliest Stone Age*. Gosport, IN: Stone Age Institute Press.

Townsend, Richard F. 2009. *The Aztecs*. 3 rd ed. London and New York: Thames & Hudson.

Traill, David A. 1995. *Schliemann of Troy*. New York: St. Martin's Press.

Trigger, Bruce G. 1991. "Distinguished Lecture in Archaeology: Constraint and Freedom." *American Anthropologist* 93(3): 551–569.

———. 2006. *A History of Archaeological Thought*. 2nd ed. Cambridge: Cambridge University Press.

Tringham, Ruth. 1971. *Hunters, Fishers, and Farmers of Eastern Europe: 6000–3000* B.C. London: Hutchinson University Library.

———, et al. 1980. "The Early Agricultural Site of Selevac, Yugoslavia." *Archaeology* 33(2): 24–32.

Trinkaus, Erik. 2005. "Early Modern Humans." *Annual Review of Anthropology* 34: 207–230.

Turner, Christy. 1984. "Advances in the Dental Search for Native American Origins." *Acta Anthropogenetica* 8: 23–78.

———. 2002. "Teeth, Needles, Dogs, and Siberia: Bioarchaeological Evidence for the Colonization of the New World." In *The First Americans*. Nina Jablonski, ed. pp. 123–158. San Francisco: California Academy of Sciences.

Underhill, Anne P., and Junko Habu. 2006. "Early Communities in East Asia: Economic and Sociopolitical Organization at the Local and Regional Levels." In *Archaeology of Asia*. Miriam T Stark, ed. pp. 121–148. Malden, MA: Blackwell.

Urton, Garry. 2003. *Signs of the Inka Khipu: Binary Coding in the Andean Knotted-String Records*. Austin, TX: University of Texas Press.

Van Andel, H. Tjeerd, and Curtis Runnels. 1995. "The Earliest Farmers in Europe." *Antiquity* 69: 481–500.

Van Andel, H. Tjeerd., and William Davies., eds. 2003. *Neanderthals and Modern Humans in the European Landscape during the Last Glaciation*. Cambridge: McDonald Institute for Archaeological Research.

Van Dijk, Jacobus. 2000. "The Amarna Period and the Later New Kingdom." In *The Oxford History of Ancient Egypt*. Ian Shaw, ed. pp. 272–313. Oxford: Oxford University Press.

Van Tilburg, J. A. 1994. *Easter Island: Archaeology, Ecology and Culture*. London: British Museum.

Vrba, Elizabeth S., et al., eds. 1995. *Paleoclimate and Evolution, with Emphasis on Human Evolution*. New Haven, CT: Yale University Press.

Wagner, Daniel P., and Joseph M. McAvoy. 2004. "Pedoarchaeology of Cactus Hill, a Sandy Paleoindian Site in Southeastern Virginia, U.S.A." *Geoarchaeology* 19(4): 297–322.

Walker, Alan. 1981. "Dietary Hypotheses and Human Evolution." *Philosophical Transactions of the Royal Society of London* 292: 56–64.

———, and R. E. Leakey. 1993. *The Nariokotome Homo Erectus Skeleton*. Cambridge: Cambridge University Press.

Ward, C. V., et al. 2011. "Complete Fourth Metatarsal and Arches in the Foot of *Australopithecus afarensis*." *Science* 331(6018): 750.

Washburn, Dorothy K., et al. 2011. "The Prehistoric Drug Trade: Widespread Consumption of Cacao in Ancestral Pueblo and Hohokam Communities in the American Southwest." *Journal of Archaeological Science* 38(7): 1634–1640.

Waters, Michael R., et al. 2011. "The Buttermilk Complex and the Origins of Clovis at the Debra L. Friedkin Site, Texas." *Science* 331(6024): 1599–1603.

Webb, W. S. 1974. *Indian Knoll*. Rev. Ed. Knoxville: University of Tennessee Press.

Webster, David. 2002. *The Fall of the Ancient Maya*. London and New York: Thames & Hudson.

Weiss, Ehud, et al. 2004. "The Broad Spectrum Revisited: Evidence from Plant Remains." *Proceedings of the National Academy of Sciences* 101(26): 9551–9555.

Weiss, Harvey. 1986. *The Origins of Cities in Dry-Farming Syria and Mesopotamia in the Third Millennium* B.C. Guilford, CT: Four Quarters.

———. 2000. "Beyond the Younger Dryas: Collapse as Adaptation to Abrupt Climate Change in Ancient West Asia and the Eastern Mediterranean." In *Environmental Disaster and the Archaeology of Human Response*. Garth Bawden and Richard Martin Reycraft, eds. pp. 75–98. Albuquerque: Maxwell Museum of Anthropology.

Wells, Peter. 1981. *Culture Contact and Culture Change*. Cambridge: Cambridge University Press.

———. 1984. "Early Iron Age Community in Central Europe." *Scientific American* 249(6): 68–93.

Wendorf, Fred, et al. 1980. *Loaves and Fishes: The Prehistory of Wadi Kubbaniya*. Dallas, TX: Department of Anthropology, Southern Methodist University.

Wendorf, Fred., et al., eds. 1984. *Cattle Keepers of the Eastern Sahara: The Neolithic of Bir Kiseiba*. Dallas: Southern Methodist University Press.

Wertime, Theodore A., and James D. Muhly., eds. 1980. *The Coming of the Age of Iron*. New Haven, CT: Yale University Press.

West, Richard H., ed. 1996. *American Beginnings*. Chicago: University of Chicago Press.

Whalen, Michael, and Paul Minnis. 1996. "Ball Courts and Political Centralization in the Casas Grandes Region." *American Antiquity* 61(4): 732–746.

———, eds. 2001. *Casas Grandes and Its Hinterland: Prehistoric Regional Organization in Northwest Mexico*. Tucson: University of Arizona Press.

Wheat, Joe Ben. 1972. *The Olsen-Chubbock Site*. Washington, DC: Society for American Archaeology.

Wheatley, Paul. 1971. *The Pivot of the Four Quarters*. Chicago: Aldine.

———. 1975. "Satyarta in Suvarnadvípa: From Reciprocity to Redistribution in ancient Southeast Asia." In *Ancient Civilization and Trade*. Jeremy A. Sabloff and C. C. Lamberg-Karlovsky, eds. pp. 227–284. Albuquerque: University of New Mexico Press.

———. 1979. "Urban Genesis in Mainland Southeast Asia." In *Early Southeast Asia*. R. B. Smith and W. Watson, eds. pp. 288–303. Oxford: Oxford University Press.

———. 1983. *Nagara and Commandery*. Chicago: University of Chicago, Department of Geography Research Unit.

Wheeler, Mortimer. 1968. *The Indus Civilization*. 3rd ed. Cambridge: Cambridge University Press.

White, J. Peter, and James O'Connell. 1982. *A Prehistory of Australia, New Guinea, and Sahul*. Sydney: Academic Press.

White, Randall. 1986. *Dark Caves and Bright Visions*. New York: American Museum of Natural History.

White, T. D. 2002. "The Earliest Hominids." In *The Primate Fossil Record*. Walter Carl-Hartwig, ed. pp. 407–417. Cambridge: Cambridge University Press.

———. 2003. "Early Hominids—diversity or Distortion?" *Science* 299: 1994–1997.

White, T. D., et al. 2003. "Pleistocene *Homo Sapiens* from Middle Awash, Ethiopia." *Nature* 423: 742–747.

White, T. D., et al. 2009. "*Ardipithecus Ramidus* and the Paleobiology of Early Hominids." *Science* 326(5949): 75–86.

Whitelaw, K. W., and R. B. Coote. 1987. *The Emergence of Israel in Historical Perspective*. Sheffield, England: Almond Press.

Whittle, Alisdair. 1993. "The Neolithic of the Avebury Area: Sequence, Environment, Settlement, and Monuments." *Oxford Journal of Archaeology* 12(1): 29–53.

———. 1996. *Europe in the Neolithic: The Creation of New Worlds*. Cambridge: Cambridge University Press.

———, et al. 1993. "A Neolithic Downland Monument in Its Environment: Excavations at the Easton Down Long Barrow, Bishops Canning, North Wiltshire." *Proceedings of the Prehistoric Society* 59: 197–239.

Wickler, Stephen. 2001. *The Prehistory of Buka: A Stepping Stone Island in the Northern Solomons*. Canberra: Research School of Pacific and Asian Studies, Australian National University.

Wilkinson, R. D., et al. 1010. "Dating Primate Divergences through an Integrated Analysis of Palaeontological and Molecular Data." *Systematic Biology*.

Wilkinson, Richard H. 2000. *The Complete Temples of Ancient Egypt*. London and New York: Thames & Hudson.

Wilkinson, Toby A. H. 2001. *Early Dynastic Egypt*. London: Routledge.

———. 2011. *The Rise and Fall of Ancient Egypt*. New York: Random House.

Wilkinson, T. J. 2003. *Archaeological Landscapes of the Near East*. Tucson: University of Arizona Press.

Willey, Gordon R. 1963. *The Archaeology of the Virú Valley, Peru*. Cambridge, MA: Peabody Museum.

Williams, Nancy M., and Daymbalipu Mununggurr. 1994. "Understanding Yolngu Signs of the past." In *Who Needs the Past?* 2nd ed. R. Layton, ed. pp. 74–83. London: Routledge.

Wills, S. H. 1989. *Early Prehistoric Agriculture in the American Southwest*. Santa Fe, NM: School of American Research.

Wilmshurst, Janet, et al. 2010. "High Precision Radiocarbon Dating Shows Recent and Rapid Initial Human Colonization of East Polynesia." *Proceedings of the National Academy of Sciences* 108(5): 1815–1820.

Wilson, David J. 1981. "Of Maize and Men: A Critique of the Maritime Hypothesis of State Origins on the Coast of Peru." *American Anthropologist* 83: 931–940.

———. 1983. "The Origins and Development of Complex Prehispanic Society in the Lower Santa Valley, Peru: Implications for Theories of State Origins." *Journal of Anthropological Archaeology* 2: 209–276.

Wilson, Hugh. 1988. "Quinoa Biosystematics. I. Domesticated Populations." *Economic Botany* 42: 461–477.

Wilson, Samuel T. 1990. *Hispaniola: Caribbean Chiefdoms in the Age of Coumbus*. Tuscaloosa: University of Alabama Press.

———. 1993. "The Cultural Mosaic of the Indigenous Caribbean." *Proceedings of the British Academy* 81: 37–66.

———. 2001. "The Prehistory and Early History of the Caribbean." In *Biogeography of the West Indies: Patterns and Perspectives.* Charles A. Woods and Florence E. Sergile, eds. pp. 519–527. Baton Rouge, FL: CRC Press.

———, et al. 1998. "Preceramic Connections between Yucatan and the Caribbean." *Latin American Antiquity* 9(4): 342–352.

Winters, Howard. 1967. *The Riverton Culture.* Springfield: Illinois State Museum.

Wiseman, David J. 1985. *Nebuchadnezzar and Babylon.* Oxford: Oxford University Press.

Wittfogel, Karl W. 1957. *Oriental Despotism: A Comparative Study of Total Power.* New Haven, CT: Yale University Press.

Wolf, Eric. 1984. *Europe and the People Without History.* Berkeley: University of California Press.

Wolpoff, M. H., et al. 2000. "Multiregional, Not Multiple Origins." *American Journal of Physical Anthropology* 112: 129–136.

Wood, Bernard, and Mark Collard. 1999. "The Human Genus." *Science* 284: 65–71.

Wood, W. Raymond. 1998. *Archaeology on the Great Plains.* Lawrence: University Press of Kansas.

Woolley, Leonard. 1934. *Ur Excavations. Vol. 2. The Royal Cemetery.* London: British Museum.

Wrangham, Richard. 2009. *Catching Fire: How Cooking Made Us Human.* New York: Basic Books.

Wright, Henry T. 1984. "Prestate Political Formations." In *On the Evolution of Complex Societies: Essays in Honor of Harry Hoijer.* W. Sanders et al., eds. pp. 41–77. Malibu, CA: Undena Press.

———. 1993. "Environmental Determinism in Near Eastern Prehistory." *Current Anthropology* 34: 458–469.

Wright, Lori E., and Christine D. White. 1996. "Human Biology in the Classic Maya Collapse: Evidence from Paleopathology and Paleodiet." *Journal of World Prehistory* 10(2): 147–199.

Wynn, T. 1991. "Tools, Grammar, and the Archaeology of Cognition." *Cambridge Archaeological Journal* 1: 191–206.

———. 1995. "Handaxe Enigmas." *Journal of World Prehistory* 27: 10–24.

Yamei, Hon, et al. 2000. "Mid-Pleistocene Acheulian-Like Stone Technology of the Bose Basin, South China." *Science* 287: 1622–1626.

Yen, D. E. 1995. "The Development of Sahul Agriculture with Australia as a Bystander." *Antiquity* 69: 831–847.

Yesner, David K. 1987. "Life in the Garden of Eden: Causes and Consequence of the Adoption of Marine Diets by Human Societies." In *Food and Evolution.* Marvin Harris and Eric B. Ross, eds. pp. 111–131. Philadelphia: Temple University Press.

Yoffee, Norman. 1995. "Political Economy in Early Mesopotamian States." *Annual Review of Anthropology* 24: 281–311.

———. 2005. *Myths of the Archaic State: Evolution of the Earliest Cities, States, and Civilizations.* Cambridge: Cambridge University Press.

———, and George Cowgill., eds. 1988. *The Collapse of Ancient States and Civilizations.* Tucson: University of Arizona Press.

Zbenovich, Vladimir G. 1996. "The Tripolye Culture: Centenary of Research." *Journal of World Prehistory* 10(2): 199–241.

Zeder, Melinda A. 1994. "After the Revolution: Post-Neolithic Subsistence in Northern Mesopotamia." *American Anthropologist* 96(1): 97–126.

———. 2011. "The Origins of Agriculture in the Near East." *Current Anthropology* 54(S4):S221–235.

Zeder, Melinda A., and Brian Hesse. 2000. "The Initial Domestication of Goats (Capra Hircus) in the Zagros Mountains 10,000 Years Ago." *Science* 287: 2254–2257.

Zeder, Melinda A., et al. 2002. *Documenting Domestication: New Genetic and Archaeological Paradigms.* Washington, DC: Smithsonian Institution Press.

Zhao, Z. 1998. "The Middle Yangtze Region in China Is One Place Where Rice Was Domesticated: Phytolith Evidence from Diaotonghuan Cave, Northern Yiangxi." *Antiquity* 72: 885–897.

Zohary, D., and Marie Hopf. 1988. *Domestication of Plants in the Old World.* Oxford: Clarendon.

Zollikofer, Christophe P. E., et al. 2005. "Virtual Cranial Reconstruction of Sahelanthropus Tchadensis." *Nature* 434: 755–759.

Zong, Y., et al. 2007. "Fire and Flood Management of Coastal Swamp Enabled First Rice Paddy Cultivation in East CHiona." *Nature* 449: 459–462.

Zuraina, M. 1998. "Radiocarbon Dates and Culture Sequence in the Lenggong Valley and beyond." *Malaysia Museums Journal* 34: 241–249.

Zvelebil, Marek. 1986. *Hunters in Transition.* Cambridge: Cambridge University Press.

———. 2008. "Innovating Hunter-Gatherers: The Mesolithic in the Baltic." In *Mesolithic Europe.* Geoff Bailey and Penny Spikins, eds. pp. 18–59. Cambridge: Cambridge University Press.

———, ed. 1994. "Plant Use in the Mesolithic and the Transition to Farming." *Proceedings of the Prehistoric Society* 60: 35–74.

———, and Paul M. Dolukhanov. 1991. "The Transition to Farming in Eastern and Northern Europe." *Journal of World Prehistory* 5(3): 233–278.

Zvelebil, Marek, and Peter Rowley-Conwy. 1984. "Transition to Farming in Northern Europe: A Hunter-Gatherer Perspective." *Norwegian Archaeological Records* 17: 104–128.

Credits

Photo Credits

Chapter 1. © imageBROKER/Alamy: *1.* © Everent Collection Historical/Alamy: *2* (top). The Print Collector/Alamy: *2* (bottom). Realimage/Alamy: *3.* Courtesy of Jane Brayne and Wessex Archaeology: *4.* B.O'Kane/Alamy: *6.* Mark Titterton/Alamy: *8.* The Trustees of the British Museum/Art Resource, NY: *9.* Pim Smit/Alamy: *10.* Image Asset Management Ltd./Alamy: *19.*

Chapter 2. Image #4936(7) American Museum of Natural History: *24.* Bettmann/Corbis: *25.* Raul Martin/Science Photo Library/Science Source: *36.* Raul Martin/MSF/SPL/Science Source: *37.* John Reader/Science Photo Library/Photo Researchers, Inc.: *38.* John Reader/Science Photo Library/Photo Researchers, Inc.: *39.* David L. Brill Photography: *40.* Mauricio Anton/Science Source: *41.* Sabena Jane Blackbird/Alamy: *44* (Left). Arizona St. Univ. Institute of Human Origins: *45* (Top left). Raul Martin/Science Photo Library/Science Source: *45* (Top right). William Kimbel, Institute of Human Origins, Arizona State University: *45* (Second left). Bettmann/Corbis: *45* (Second right). John Reader/Science Photo Library/Photo Researchers, Inc.: *45* (Third). John Reader/Science Photo Library/Photo Researchers, Inc.: (Bottom left). Mauricio Anton/Science Source: *45* (Bottom middle). John Reader/Science Photo Library/Photo Researchers, Inc.: *45* (Bottom right). David Keith Jones/Images of Africa Photobank/Alamy: *46.* Marion Kaplan/Alamy: *47.* Steve Bloom Images/Alamy: *52.* Kennan Ward/Corbis: *58.*

Chapter 3. Jochen Tack/Alamy: *60.* David L. Brill Photography: *64.* Ian Everard: *65.* Image # 315446, American Museum of Natural History, Library: *68* (Top). © Boxgrave excavation site/Natural History Museum, London, UK / Bridgeman Image: *68* (Second). Madrid Scientific Films: *68* (Third). Ian Everard: *68* (Bottom). Harry Taylor © Dorling Kindersley, Courtesy of the Natural History Museum, London: *69* (Top). Victor Abbott/Alamy: *69* (Center). Harry Taylor © Dorling Kindersley, Courtesy of the Natural History Museum, London: *69* (Bottom). The Natural History Museum/Alamy: *71.* View Stock/Alamy: *72.* Tony Kwan/Alamy: *73.* Madrid Scientific Films: *74* (Left). Javier Trueba/Madrid Scientific Films: *74* (Right). Kenneth Garrett/Danita Delimont/Alamy: *80.* Hartmut Thieme: *81.* Kolvenbach/Alamy: *83.*

Chapter 4. Prisma/Heeb Christian/Prisma Bildagentur AG/Alamy: *94.* Lynton Gardiner/Dorling Kindersley, Ltd.: *96* (Top). Prehistoric Necklace, found in caves in Palestine (shell and bone), Prehistoric/Ashmolean Museum, University of Oxford, UK/The Bridgeman Art Library: *96* (Bottom). underb/Fotolia: *97* (Top left). AP Images/The Daily Oklahoman/Chad Love: *97* (Top right). Pascal Goetgheluck/Science Source: *99.* David L. Brill Photography: *100.* John Reader/Science Source: *105* (Left). University of Bergen: *105* (Right). Mauricio Anton/Science Source: *106.* Dr. Stephen Wickler: *109.* Markku Murto/art/Alamy: *110.* Prof. Paul S.C. Tacon: *114.* Richard Cosgrove: *112.* Stapleton

Collection/Corbis: *113.* Philip de Bay/Historical Picture Archive/Corbis: *114* (Top). Kenneth Garrett/National Geographic Stock: *114* (Bottom). Reproduced with permission from the Rock Art Research Institute, University of the Witwatersrand, South Africa. WWW.SARADA.CO.ZA: *117* (Top). Neil Harris/Alamy: *117* (Bottom).

Chapter 5. RMN-Grand Palais/Art Resource, NY: *120.* National History Museum, London: *122.* Nationalmuseet Danske Afdeling: *123.* Institut fuer Ur-und Fruegeschichte Floete3 aus: *131.* Science Photo Library/Science Source: *132.* INTERFOTO/Alamy: *133.* American Museum of Natural History: *134* (Top). Dozier Marc/Hemis/Alamy: *134* (Bottom). Sisse Brimberg/National Geographic Creative: *135* (Top). Melba Photo Agency/Alamy: *135* (Bottom). Forget Patrick/Sagaphoto.Com/Alamy: *136* (Top). Peabody Museum of Archaeology and Ethnology: *136* (Bottom). Sisse Brimberg/National Geographic Stock: *140.*

Chapter 6. Smithsonian Institution/Corbis: *144.* Nigel Bean/Nature Picture Library: *150.* Dr. Michael Waters: *154.* AP Images/Chad Love: *156.* Anna C. Roosevelt: *157.* Denver Museum of Nature & Science: *160* (Top). University of Colorado Museum: *160* (Bottom). Professor Steven Simms: *161* (Top). Werner Forman/Werner Forman/Corbis: *161* (Bottom). Courtesy McClung Museum of Natural History and Culture, The University of Tennessee, Knoxville: *163.* Center for American Archeology: *164.* National Anthropological Archives, Smithsonian Institution [NAA INV 08594700]: *167.*

Chapter 7. National Geographic Image Collection/Alamy: *169.* Paul Kane/Science Source: *174.* Christian Handl/imagebroker/Alamy: *175.* National Museum of Denmark: *181.* National Museum of Denmark: *182.*

Chapter 8. Nigel Pavitt/John Warburton/Lee Photography/Alamy: *188.* Barbara Gonget/G&B Images/Alamy: *189.* Parasola.net/Alamy: *195* (Left). Jack Jackson/Robert Harding Picture Library Ltd/Alamy: *195* (Right). Oliver Brandt/Image Broker/Robert Harding World Imagery: *197.* Amos Gal/PhotoStock-Israel/Alamy: *201.* Dave King/DK Images: *202.* Science & Society Picture Library: *203.* The Trustees of the British Museum: *204.*

Chapter 9. Werner Forman Archive/Louvre Museum/Glow Images: *206.* Andrew M.T. Moore, D. Phil.: *210.* Hanan Isachar/Alamy: *211* (Top). Vanni/Art Resource, NY: *211* (Bottom). Zev Radovan/www.BibleLandPictures.com/Alamy: *212.* Deutsches Archaeologisches: *215* (Top left). Deutsches Archaeologisches Institut—Orientabteilung: *215* (Top right). Mission française El kowm-Mureybet (Ministère des Affaires étrangères France). Dir. D. Stordeur: *215.* Images & Stories/Alamy: *216.*

Chapter 10. Bensliman Hassan/Shutterstock: *219.* World History Archive/Alamy: *220.* Image # 411259, American Museum of Natural History, Library: *230.* iStockphoto/Thinkstock: *231.* English Heritage/National Monuments

Record: *232*(Top). Phil Arnold/Alamy: *232* (Bottom).

Chapter 11. Tor Eigeland/Alamy: *234*. The Trustees of the British Museum/Art Resource, NY: *236*. Excavations at the Neolithic site of Kom K in the Fayum. Photograph by Willeke Wendrich/URU Fayum Project: *238*. Chris Scarre: *239*. Brian M. Fagan: *241*.

Chapter 12. Danita Delimont/Alamy: *243*. Photo by DEA / A: DE GREGORIO / De Agostini / Getty Images: *248*. Sakamoto Photo Research Laboratory/Corbis: *250*. Charles Higham: *252* Stuart Bedford: *255*. Australian National University: *256*. © Cindy Hopkins / Alamy: *258*. Roberto Soncin Gerometta/Alamy: *259* (Top). Shin/Shutterstock: *259* (Bottom). © Rafael Ben-Ari/Alamy:*260* (Top). Library of Congress: *260* (Bottom).

Chapter 13. Dean Pennala/Fotolia: *262*. Robert S. Peabody Museum of Archaeology: *267*. John W. Rick: *268*. Cpiehl/Shutterstock: *269*. Arizona State Museum Photographic Collections: *273.* DeepEarth Photography/Alamy: *274*. Craig MacDonnell/Shutterstock: *275*. Zack Frank/Shutterstock: *276*. Richard A. Cooke/Corbis: *277*. Image # 329206, American Museum of Natural History, Library: *278*. © Tom Uhlman /Alamay: *280* (Top left). © Heritage Image Partnership Ltd/Alamy *280* (Top right). Werner Forman Archive/Ohio State Museum (c): HIP /Art Resource, NY: *280* (Bottom). VanD. Bucher/Science Source/ Photo Researchers, Inc.:*281*. Werner Forman/Art Resource, NY:*282* Richard Schlecht/National:*284*(Top). Jeff Greenberg/Alamy:*284* (Bottom). George Oze/Alamy: *288*. Werner Forman/Werner Forman/Corbis: *289*.

Chapter 14. Miroslav Beneda/Fotolia: *291*. Georg Gerster/Science Source: *294*. Everett Collection Inc./Alamy: *296*. Science Source: *297*. Ivan Vdovin/Alamy: *298*. Erich Lessing/Art Resource, NY: *302*. Izumi Shimada: *303*. Peter M. Wilson/Alamy: *304*. Brian M. Fagan: *305*. Nimatallah/Art Resource, NY: *306* (Top). Nimatallah/ Art Resource, NY: *306* (Middle left). Will & Deni McIntyre/ Science Source: *306* (Middle right). Werner Forman/Art Resource, NY: *306* (Bottom left). Head of Gudea © 2011 Museum of Fine Arts, Boston: *306* (Bottom right). Robert Harding World Imagery: *307* (Top). Tim Hall/Photodisc/Getty Images: *307* (Middle). Richard Lambert/RMN-Grand: *307* (Bottom).

Chapter 15. Michael Jenner/Alamy: *310*. Picture Desk, Inc./Kobal Collection: *314*. © www.BibleLandPicture.com / Alamy: *317*. Nik Wheeler/Alamy: *320*. © Imagestate Media Partners Limited —Impact Photos/Alamy: *321*. University of Pennsylvania Museum of Archaeology and Anthropology: *322*. Zev Radovan/www. BibleLandPictures.com/Alamy: *324*.

Chapter 16. Scala/Art Resource, NY: *326*. Ivy Close Images/ Alamy: *330*. Will & Deni McIntyre/Science Source: *335*. Naipung/ Shutterstock: *336*. Erich Lessing/Art Resource, NY: *337*. Lucarelli Temistocle/Shutterstock: *340*. J.D.Dallet/Age fotostock/Robert Harding World Imagery: *341*. O. Louis Mazzatenta/National Geographic Stock: *342.* The Stapleton Collection/Art Resource, NY: *343* (Left).©Robert Harding Picture Liberty Ltd/Alamy: *343* (Right). Urosr/Shutterstock: *346*. Julia Bayne/Robert Harding World Imagery:*347*. Roderick J. McIntosh:*349*. Peter Horree/Alamy:*351*. Nick Greaves/Images of Africa Photobank/Alamy:*353*.

Chapter 17. Luca Tettoni/Robert Harding Picture Library Ltd./Alamy: *355*. Robert Harding Picture Library Ltd./Alamy: *359*. Ursula Gahwiler/ Robert Harding Picture Library Ltd./Alamy: *361*. Richard Ashworth/ Robert Harding Picture Library Ltd./Alamy: *362* (Top). Getty Images: *362* (Bottom). Robert Harding Picture Library Ltd./Alamy: *363*. Courtesy of the Penn Museum: *365*. Charles Higham: *368*. Paul Norman/Fotolia: *372* (Top). Paul Norman/Fotolia: *372* (Bottom left). Chris Deeney/Alamy: *372* (Bottom right). Somchaij/Shutterstock: *373*.

Chapter 18. margaretwallace/Fotolia: *375*. Courtesy of the Peabody Museum of Archaeology and Ethnology, Harvard University, 35-79-60/5241: *378*. B. Christopher/Alamy: *381*. mary416/Fotolia: *382* (Left). Timur Kulgarin/Shutterstock: *382*(Right). Melvyn Longhurst China/Alamy: *383* (Right).

Chapter 19. Gavin Hellier/Robert Harding World Imagery: *385*. Universal History Archive/Getty Images: *387* (Top). Pecold/Shutterstock: *387* (Bottom). Institute of Nautical Archaeology: *389*. Gianni Dagli Orti/National Archaeological Museum Athens/The Art Archive at Art Resource, NY: *391* (Top). Shapencolour/Alamy: *391* (Bottom). Quintanilla/Shutterstock: *392*. © PRISMA ARCHIVO / Alamy: *393*. Reprinted with Permission, Photo by Raymond V. Schader © 1987 by Bolchazy-Carducci Publishers, Inc.: *394* (Top). Nick Pavlakis/Shutterstock: *394* (Bottom). Prisma Archivo/Alamy: *395*. S.Borisov/Shutterstock: *396* (Bottom). Scala/Art Resource, NY: *398*.

Chapter 20. Erich Lessing/Art Resource, NY: *401*. V. Vitanov/Ancient Art & Architecture Collection: *403* (Top). © Ashmolean Museum, University of Oxford, UK/Bridgeman Images: *404*. Marco Albonico/ Marka/Alamy: *406*. Classic Image / Alamy: *407*. Last Refuge/Robert Harding World Imagery: *409*. Pepper/Prisma Bildagentur AG/Alamy: *411* (Bottom). Brian M. Fagan: *413*. Werner Forman/Art Resource, NY: *414*.

Chapter 21. H. Tom Hall/National Geographic Stock: *416*. Charles & Josette Lenars/Corbis: *418*. Angelo Hornak/Corbis: *419* (Top). Boltin Picture Library/ The Bridgeman Art Library: *419* (Middle left). Justin Kerr: (Middle right). ©De Agostini Picture Library/G. Dagli Orti/ Bridgeman Images *419* (Bottom left). Image # 5004(1), American Museum of Natural History, Library: *419* (Bottom right). Courtesy of Kent V. Flannery and Joyce Marcus, University of Michigan: *425* (Right). F9photo/Shutterstock: *426.* CatchaSnap/Shutterstock: *427* Ragne Kabanove/Shutterstock:*428* (Bottom). Tim Draper/Rough Guides/ DK Images: *430* (Top). Tim Draper/Rough Guides/DK Images: *430* (Bottom). bpk, Berlin/Ethnologisches Museum, Staatliche Museen, Berlin, Germany/Waltraudt Schneider-Schütz/Art Resource, NY: *432* (Left). Vladimir Korostyshevskiy/Shutterstock: *436*. Suzanne Long/Shutterstock: *438* (Top). Justin Kerr: *438* (Bottom). J. Enrique Molina/Alamy: *439* (Top). Courtesy of the Peabody Museum of Archaeology and Ethnology, Harvard University, 50-63-20/18487 N31762: *439* (Bottom). Courtesy of the Peabody Museum of Archaeology and Ethnology, Harvard University, 50-63-20/18489 N28088A: *440*. Colman Lerner Gerardo/Shutterstock: *443*. Peabody Museum of Archaeology and Ethnology: *444* (Left). Nickolay Stanev/Shutterstock: *444* (Right). The Bodleian Library, University of Oxford: *445*. Image #326597 American Museum of Natural History: *446*. Mireille Vautier/Alamy: *447*.

Chapter 22. Mark Titterton/Alamy: *449*. J.Enrique Molina/Alamy: *454*. Jeffrey Quilter: *455*. Anthro-Photo File: *456*. Bert de Ruiter/ Alamy: *457*(Bottom right). © The Art Archive / Alamy:*460* (Top). Alamy Limited: *460*(Bottom). Ned Seidler/National Geographic Stock:*462*. ©Werner Forman Archive/Bridgeman Images:*464*. Courtesys of UCLA Fowler Museum of Cultural History: *465*. (Top). J. Marshall/ Tribaleye Images/Alamy: *465* (Bottom). David Evans/National Geographic Image Collection/Alamy:*466.* Daniel Wiedemann/ Shutterstock:*467*(Left). Fredy Thuerig/Shutterstock: *467* (Right).© Corey Wise/Alamy: *468*. Thomas Cockrem/Alamy:*469* (Left). Thomas Cockrem/Alamy: *469* (Right). Dave Porter/Alamy: *472* (Top). Yolka/Shutterstock: *472* (Bottom). Gary Urton: *473* (Top). Kevin Lang/Alamy: *473* (Bottom). Jarno Gonzalez Zarraonandia/ Shutterstock: *475* (Top). © American Museum of Natural History, New York, USA / Getty Images. *475* (Top).

Text Credits

Chapter 1. Copyright © Pearson Education, Inc.: *14*.

Chapter 2. Copyright © Pearson Education, Inc.: *23*. Copyright © Pearson Education, Inc.: *30*. Copyright © Pearson Education, Inc.: *31*.

Chapter 3. Lewin, Roger. Bones of Contention, 1987: *60*. Copyright © Pearson Education, Inc.: *77*. Copyright © Pearson Education, Inc.: *78*. Copyright © Pearson Education, Inc.: *85*. Copyright © Pearson Education, Inc.: *86*. Copyright © Pearson Education, Inc.: *88*.

Chapter 4. Guilá Naquitz. Kent Flannery, ed. pp. *263–289*. Orlando, FL: Academic Press: *93*.

Chapter 5. Figure 6 from C. B. M. McBurney, 'Early Man in the Soviet Union' Proceedings of the British Academy, Volume LXI, 1975, London: Oxford University Press. © The British Academy 1976, p. 210.: *125*. Reconstruction of a hut at Dolni Vestonice. Reused by kind permission of Thames and Hudson: *138* (Top). Image reproduced courtesy of Antiquity Publications, Ltd.: *139*. Figure 6 from C. B. M. McBurney, 'Early Man in the Soviet Union' Proceedings of the British Academy, Volume LXI, 1975, London: Oxford University Press. © The British Academy 1976, p. 210: *141*.

Chapter 6. Copyright © Pearson Education, Inc.: *151*.

Chapter 7. Flannery, Kent V. , 1986. Guilá Naquitz. Orlando, FL: Academic Press: *175*. Copyright © Pearson Education, Inc.: *183*. Copyright © Pearson Education, Inc.: *184* (Top). Copyright © Pearson Education, Inc.: *184* (Bottom).

Chapter 8. Anthropology, Sir Edward Tylor, 1871: *187*. Braidwood, R. J., and L. S. Braidwood, eds. 1983. Prehistoric Archaeology Along the Zagros Flanks. Chicago: Oriental Institute: *189*. Barker, Grahame. 2006. The Agricultural Revolution in Prehistory. Oxford: Oxford University Press: *189*. Flannery, Kent V. 1986. Guilá Naquitz. Orlando, FL: Academic Press: *191*. Mithen, Steven. 1996. The Prehistory of the Mind. London: Thames & Hudson: *193*. From Bruce Smith, The Emergence of Agriculture. © Bruce D. Smith. Reprinted by permission of the author. The Emergence of Agriculture, 2nd ed. New York: Freeman: *194*. Hastorf, Christine A., 1999. "The Cultural Life of Early Domestic Plant Use." Antiquity 72:773–782: *198*. Copyright © Pearson Education, Inc.: *198–199*.

Chapter 9. Moore, Andrew T. 1985. "The Development of Neolithic Societies in the Near East." Advances in World Archaeology, p.*223*, Academic Press: *207*. Copyright © Pearson Education, Inc.: *216* (Bottom). Hodder, Ian. Ed. 2010 Religion in the Emergence of Civilization: Çatalhöyük as a Case Study (Cambridge: Cambridge University Press): *217*.

Chapter 10. Copyright © Pearson Education, Inc.: *226*. Copyright © Pearson Education, Inc.: *229*.

Chapter 12. Beaglehole, J. C. 1974. Captain James Cook: A Life. Palo Alto, CA: Stanford University Press: *243*. Copyright © Pearson Education, Inc.: *247*. The Archaeology of Ancient China, Chang, 1977 Yale University Press: *248* (Top). The Archaeology of Ancient China, Chang, 1977 Yale University Press: *248* (Bottom right). The Archaeology of Ancient China, Chang, 1977 Yale University Press: *250* (Top).

Chapter 13. Kidder, Alfred V. 1927. An Introduction to the Study of Southwestern Archaeolo-gy. New Haven, CT: Yale University Press: *262*. Ford, ed. Prehistoric Food Production in North America. University of Michigan Museum of Anthropology, Ann Arber, pp. *245-278*, Figure 3: *265*. Copyright © Pearson Education, Inc.: *270*.

Chapter 14. Reprinted from The Rape of The Nile by Brian Fagan. Available from Westview Press, an imprint of the Perseus Books Group. Copyright 2004: *326* Fagan, Brian. Return to Babylon: Travelers, Archaeologists, and Monuments in Mesopotamia. University Press of Colorado, 2007: *292*.

Chapter 15. Copyright © Pearson Education, Inc.: *316*. Kramer, Sumarians. "The Sumerians: Their History, Culture, and Character". Reprinted by permission of University of Chicago Press: *318*.

Chapter 16. Copyright © Pearson Education, Inc.: *352*.

Chapter 17. Wheeler, Mortimer. 1968. The Indus Civilization, 3rd ed. Cambridge: Cambridge University Press: *355*.

Chapter 20. Copyright © Pearson Education, Inc.: *403* (Bottom). Copyright © Pearson Education, Inc.: *410*.

Chapter 21. Anderson, Arthur O., and Charles Dibble, eds. 1978. The Florentine Codex. Salt Lake City: University of Utah Press: *415*. Courtesy of Joyce Marcus and Kent Flannery: *425* (Left). Copyright © Pearson Education, Inc.: *428* (Top). Copyright © Pearson Education, Inc.: *433*. Courtesy of the Penn Museum, image #69-5-175.:4: *437*.

Chapter 22. Bingham, Hiram. 1963. Lost City of the Incas. (Reprint edition.) New York: Atheneum: *449*. Copyright © Pearson Education, Inc.: *457* (Top). Copyright © Pearson Education, Inc.: *457* (Bottom left). Copyright © Pearson Education, Inc.: *463*.

Index

Page numbers followed by *f* indicate figure; and those followed by *t* indicate table.